CASES AND MATERIALS ON FAMILY LAW

LEGAL CONCEPTS AND CHANGING HUMAN RELATIONSHIPS

Walter O. Weyrauch
University of Florida
College of Law

Sanford N. Katz
Boston College Law School

Frances Olsen
University of California at Los Angeles
School of Law

AMERICAN CASEBOOK SERIES®

WEST PUBLISHING COMPANY
ST. PAUL, MINNESOTA
1994

First Printing, 1994

Printed in the United States of America

ISBN 0-314-04200-8

TEXT IS PRINTED ON 10% POST CONSUMER RECYCLED PAPER

PRINTED WITH SOY INK

Design and electronic production by Michael Kitchen, PixelAntics, An Electronic Design & Publication Studio, Newton, Massachusetts.

We dedicate this book to Mary Joe Frug, who expected a lot from casebooks and contributed to this one.

Preface

This book attempts to bridge theory and practice in family law. It approaches the issue from two directions. First, it uses legal practice as a basis from which to develop a theory of family law. The facts of a case, as they present themselves to the practicing lawyer, tend to be diffuse and complex. For example, in a particular case whether there was a marriage or not may be obscure. A judge is expected to come to a clear result, perhaps by attaching a fictitious intent to the parties or applying a presumption. It may be difficult, however, for the lawyer to say whether a set of facts constitutes an engagement, nonmarital cohabitation, marriage, business partnership, cotenancy, employment, or something else. Traditional legal theory provides little guidance to the practicing lawyer in determining which characterization to adopt because it is too often limited to artificially tidy classifications. Moreover, legal theory tends to focus upon pairs of conceptual opposites — such as marriage or no-marriage — to the exclusion of other possibilities. The skilled lawyer selects from an open-ended checklist of multiple choices those that are strategically most advantageous to the client. What may appear later in court as fact is only a reflection of reality as seen and presented by the lawyer for judicial decision.

Second, the book places family law within legal theory more broadly. Family law is often assumed to be separate from other areas of law, especially commercial law and fields where discretion is thought to play a less prominent role. The organization of the text and the presentation is intended to facilitate an understanding of the significance of family law to legal theory in general.

Too often students are not exposed to the conflicts that have occurred, but only to the outcome of those conflicts, which takes the form of legal doctrine. This book shows not only the eventual outcome of the struggles that have taken place, but also the struggles themselves.

We draw upon feminist legal theory, critical legal studies, and other strands in contemporary jurisprudence to relate the changes taking place in families, broadly defined, to underlying principles and tensions within family law. Rather than emphasizing detailed coverage of substantive law, frozen at a moment in time, we introduce basic themes and dilemmas. An encyclopedic coverage reflects and implicitly accentuates the past. This is a useful and necessary exercise, but it would have impeded a theory of process. It also assumes a closed intellectual system. Instead of primarily surveying the present substantive rules of family law, our goal is to present engaging cases and interesting commentary designed to get discussions started.

We are concerned with a theory of practice. The intellectual tasks of the practicing lawyers are in a sense more complex than those faced by trial and appellate judges. By a process of reduction, aided by lawyers, judicial tasks have been simplified. Legal practice is in flux, and many of the recent changes have come about less through the legislatures and courts than through the creative imagination of practitioners acting on behalf of clients. Broad social changes have furthered these legal developments, just as the legal developments contributed to the social changes.

We would like to thank our families, our law schools, friends and colleagues, and the deans of our respective schools. We also thank Professor Paul Schwartz for the detailed suggestions he made while teaching from a draft version of the book in the fall of 1993. Finally, we thank Michael Kitchen for his tireless efforts formatting the book.

Walter O. Weyrauch
Sanford N. Katz
Frances Olsen

April 1994

SUMMARY OF CONTENTS

TABLE OF CONTENTS

Chapter 1

Marriage and the Relationship Between Family Law and Commercial Law

SHARP DISAGREEMENTS EXIST over who shall be considered to constitute a family. It is thus to be expected that disagreements will also exist regarding what the field of family law should encompass. We engage the question who may be considered members of a family, but do not attempt any determinative answer. We use the term "family law" broadly to include statutes, regulations and court decisions involving the formation of families, the rights and duties of family members to each other, the relationship of outsiders to family members, and the effects of dissolving a family or family-like arrangement.

Family law is often considered to be a field quite unlike the rest of law. It affects people's personal lives much more directly than most other areas of law, many decisions involve considerable judicial discretion, and interdisciplinary approaches are frequently employed in teaching family law. While it is a course that students like to study, many consider it less difficult and less serious than courses in commercial law, constitutional law, or taxation. Some consider family law a "marginal" course rather than part of the "core" curriculum.

Often this marginalization is embraced by teachers and by students. Family law is a nice break from the rest of law school and a course in which we can argue about things we care deeply about, even if (or perhaps especially because) they do not seem to be just about law. Sometimes family law will be the course in which clinical teaching is merged with academic training or where informal dispute resolution is taught.

Occasionally family law teachers react against this marginalization and try to make their family law class hard, usually by injecting a strong dose of constitutional law or taxation or by focusing attention on difficult conflicts of law issues. They may dispute the assumption that family law is marginal and emphasize the limitations that are placed upon the discretion of judges deciding family law issues. In a sense, they try to bring family law into the "core."

Rather than bringing family law into the "core" of law, this book invites the reader to challenge the imagery of core and periphery. Family law does involve considerable discretion, but that does not really distinguish family law from any of the rest of law. Many fields may disguise the discretion they involve, but they involve it nonetheless.

We would encourage our readers to reconsider assumptions that underlie much of our thinking about law and about life. One such assumption is that there is and must be a radical separation between the public world of the market, which structures our productive lives, and the private world of the family, which structures our affective lives. In fact, our ideas about the market are deeply influenced by our ideas about the family, and commercial law can be understood adequately and practiced effectively only by understanding the interrelationships between it and family law.

REFERENCE

Frances Olsen, *The Family and the Market: A Study of Ideology and Legal Reform*, 96 HARV. L. REV. 1497 (1983).

A: RELATIONSHIPS BETWEEN MARRIAGE AND BUSINESS PARTNERSHIP, MARITAL CONTRACTS AND COMMERCIAL CONTRACTS

Functional Relation Between Engagement, Formal Marriage, Cohabitation Contract, Informal Marriage, and Business Partnership

STANARD v. BOLIN
Supreme Court of Washington, En Banc.
88 Wash.2d 614, 565 P.2d 94 (1977)

HAMILTON, Associate Justice.

This appeal presents the question of whether the common-law action for breach of promise to marry should be abolished. The trial court concluded that the action was contrary to public policy and dismissed the plaintiff's (appellant's) complaint with prejudice under CR 12(b)(6) for failure to state a claim upon which relief can be granted. We accepted review and conclude that the action is not contrary to public policy.

...

In October, 1974, plaintiff and defendant (respondent) were introduced to each other by mutual friends, and their courtship developed soon thereafter. During the course of their courtship, defendant assured plaintiff that he was worth in excess of $2 million, was planning to retire in 2 years, and that the two of them would then travel. Defendant also promised plaintiff that she would never have to work again and that he would see to the support of her two teen-age boys. He also promised to see that the plaintiff's mother would never be in need.

On September 22, 1975, plaintiff accepted defendant's proposal of marriage. Thereafter, defendant took her to a jewelry store and purchased an engagement ring and matching wedding rings. The parties found a suitable home for their residence and signed the purchase agreement as husband and wife. At the insistence of defendant, plaintiff placed her home on the market for sale and sold most of her furniture at a public auction. The parties set December 13, 1975, as their wedding date, reserved a church, and engaged a minister to perform the service. Dresses for plaintiff, her mother, and the matron of honor were ordered, and a reception was arranged at a local establishment. The parties began informally announcing their plans to a wide circle of friends. After the wedding date was set, plaintiff's employer hired another person and requested plaintiff to assist in teaching the new employee the duties of her job.

On November 13, 1975, defendant informed plaintiff that he would not marry her. This came as a great shock to plaintiff and caused her to become ill and lose sleep and weight. Plaintiff sought medical advice and was treated by her physician. Plaintiff also had to take her home off the market and repurchase furniture at a cost in excess of that which she received for her older furniture. In addition, plaintiff was forced to cancel all wedding plans and reservations, and to explain to her matron of honor, her mother, and her children, that she was not marrying. Plaintiff was also obliged to return wedding gifts and to face her friends and neighbors, each of whom felt entitled to an explanation.

In her first claim for relief, plaintiff sought damages to compensate her for her pain, impairment to health, humiliation, and embarrassment. Plaintiff's second claim sought damages to compensate her for her loss of expected financial security.

The breach-of-marriage-promise action has its origins in the common law. Professor Clark, a well-known authority on family law, has posited that 17th Century English conceptions of marriage as largely a property transaction caused the English common-law courts to intervene in a subject matter which, up until the 17th Century, had been almost exclusively under the jurisdiction of the ecclesiastical courts. See H. Clark, *The Law of Domestic Relations in the United States* 2 (1968)(hereafter cited as Clark). In any event, the action was carried forward into the common law of Washington (see RCW 4.04.010) and was recognized by this court as early as 1905. See *Heasley v. Nichols*, 38 Wash. 485, 80 P. 769 (1905). Because the action has its origins in the common law and has not been acted upon by the legislature, it is proper for us to reexamine it and determine its continued viability in light of present-day society....

The breach-of-promise-to-marry action is one not easy to classify. Although the action is treated as arising from the breach of a contract (the contract being the mutual promises to marry), the damages allowable more closely resemble a tort action. Thus, the plaintiff may recover for loss to reputation, mental anguish, and injury to health, in addition to recovering for expenditures made in preparation for the marriage and loss of the pecuniary and social advantages which the promised marriage offered. In addition, some states allow aggravated damages for seduction under promise to marry and for attacks by the defendant on the plaintiff's character. Furthermore, some states allow punitive damages when the defendant's acts were malicious or fraudulent. For a comprehensive discussion of the damages allowable under a breach-of-promise-to-marry action and a collection of cases, see Annot., *Measure and elements of damages for breach of contract to marry*, 73 A.L.R.2d 553 (1960), and C. McCormick, *Handbook on the Law of Damages* 397–406 (1935).

The action in its present form is subject to almost uniform criticism by the commentators, although our research has not disclosed any cases in which a court has abolished the action.[1] In essence, these criticism are: (1) the action is used as an instrument of oppression and blackmail; (2) engaged persons should be

1. The action has been abolished or modified by statute in some states. See Ala. Code tit. 7, §114; Cal. Civ. Code Ann. §43.5 (West); Colo. Rev. Stat. §13-20-202; Conn. Gen. Stat. Ann. §52-572b (west Supp. 1977); Fla. Stat. Ann §771.01 (West); Ind. Code Ann. §34-4-4-1 (Burns Supp. 1976): Me. Rev. Stat. Ann. tit. 14, §854 (West); Md. Cts. & Jud. Proc. Code Ann. §5-301 (1974); Mass. Gen. Laws Ann. ch. 207, S47A (West); Mich. Stat. Ann. §25.191; Nev. Rev. Stat. §41.380; N.H. Rev. Stat. Ann. § 508:11; N.J. Stat. Ann. §2A:23-1 (West); N.Y. Civ. Rights Law §8080-a et seq. (McKinney); Pa. Stat. Ann. tit. 48, §171 (Purdon); W. Va. Code §56-3-2a (Supp. 1976); Wis. Stat. Ann. §248.01 (West Supp. 1976); Wyo. Stat. §1-728.

allowed to correct their mistakes without fear of publicity and legal compulsion; (3) the action is subject to great abuse at the hands of gullible and sympathetic juries; (4) it is wrong to allow under the guise of contract an action that is essentially tortious and penal in nature; and, (5) the measure of damages is unjust because damages are allowed for loss of social and economic position, whereas most persons marry for reasons of mutual love and affection.... Although some of these criticisms are not without merit, we do not believe they justify an outright abolishment of the action.

When two persons agree to marry, they should realize that certain actions will be taken during the engagement period in reliance on the mutual promises to marry. Rings will be purchased, wedding dresses and other formal attire will be ordered or reserved, and honeymoon plans with their attendant expenses will be made. Wedding plans such as the rental of a church, the engagement of a minister, the printing of wedding invitations, and so on, will commence. It is also likely that the parties will make plans for their future residence, such as purchasing a house, buying furniture, and the like. Further at the time the parties decide to marry, they should realize that their plans and visions of future happiness will be communicated to friends and relatives and that wedding gifts soon will be arriving. When the plans to marry are abruptly ended, it is certainly foreseeable that the party who was unaware that the future marriage would not take place will have expended some sums of money and will suffer some forms of mental anguish, loss to reputation, and injury to health. We do not feel these injuries should go unanswered merely because the breach-of-promise-to-marry action may be subject to abuses; rather, an attempt should be made to eradicate the abuses from the action.

One major abuse of the action is allowing the plaintiff to bring in evidence of the defendant's wealth and social position. This evidence is admissible under the theory that the plaintiff should be compensated for what she or he has lost by not marrying the defendant....

Although damages for loss of expected financial and social position more closely resemble the contract theory of recovery than the other elements of damages for breach of promise to marry, we do not believe these damages are justified in light of modern society's concept of marriage. Although it may have been that marriages were contracted for material reasons in 17th Century England, marriages today generally are not considered property transactions, but are, in the words of Professor Clark, "the result of that complex experience called being in love." Clark, *supra* at 2. A person generally does not choose a marriage partner on the basis of financial and social gain; hence, the plaintiff should not be compensated for losing an expectation which he or she did not have in the first place. Further, the breach-of-promise-to-marry action is based on injuries to the plaintiff, and evidence of the defendant's wealth tends to misdirect the jury's attention when assessing the plaintiff's damages towards an examination of the defendant's wealth rather than the plaintiff's injuries.

Professor McCormick has concluded that evidence of the defendant's wealth has a more potent effect upon the size of the verdict than any instruction on damages. See C. McCormick, *Handbook on the Law of Damages* 399, n. 36 (1935). If this is so, then it presents a very strong reason for disallowing any evidence of the defendant's wealth and social position. We conclude that damages for loss of expected financial and social position should no longer be recoverable under the breach-of-promise-to-marry actions. This means that evidence of the defendant's wealth and social position becomes immaterial in assessing the plaintiff's damages.

Other damages subject to criticism are those damages given for mental anguish, loss to reputation, and injury to health. It is argued that these injuries are "so vague and so little capable of measurement in dollars that they give free rein to the jury's passions, prejudices and sympathies." See Clark, *supra* at 12. This argument has little merit, for it places no faith in the jury's ability to evaluate objectively the evidence regarding plaintiff's injuries and render a just verdict. If a jury's verdict is tainted by passion or prejudice, or is otherwise excessive, the trial court and the appellate court have the power to reduce the award or order a new trial.... Lack of ability to quantify damages in exact dollar amounts does not justify abolishing the breach-of-promise-to-marry action. In her complaint plaintiff alleged that she had suffered pain, impairment to health, humiliation, and embarrassment as a result of the defendant's breach of his promise to marry. If this is true, and we must assume it is for purposes of review, then she is entitled to compensation for these injuries.

...

We also do not believe the action should be abolished so that engaged persons are free from compulsion to choose whether to end an engagement. Although the policy of the state should not be to encourage a person to marry when he or she has begun to have second thoughts about a prospective mate, it is also the policy of the state to afford an avenue of redress for injuries suffered due to the actions of another. Allowing recovery for injuries, which are foreseeable at the time of entering into the relationship, should not be denied on the presumption the defendant would rather enter into the marriage than pay damages for the injuries caused. Furthermore, it is hard to conceive of a plaintiff suing a defendant in order to coerce the defendant into a marriage which would be unstable at best. It is possible that there may be such a plaintiff, but that is no reason for abolishing the action for all plaintiffs, for that would cause most plaintiffs to go uncompensated for their injuries at the expense of a few unworthy plaintiffs.

In conclusion, we have decided that the breach-of-promise-to-marry action should be retained as a quasi-contract, quasi-tort action for the recovery of the foreseeable special and general damages which are caused by a defendant's breach of promise to marry. However, the action is modified to the extent that a plaintiff cannot recover for loss of expected financial and social position, because marriage is no longer considered to be a property transaction.

The judgment of the trial court is reversed on plaintiff's first claim for relief, and remanded for further proceedings consistent with this opinion. The judgment is affirmed on plaintiff's second claim for relief, which sought damages for loss of prospective economical and social advantage.

UTTER, Associate Justice (dissenting).

The majority, in a well-written opinion, has set forth the historical background of the action for breach of promise to marry. It states the policy reasons for abolishing the action, but chooses to retain its major underpinnings. The sole change is to modify the doctrine to the extent that a plaintiff can no longer recover for loss of expected financial and social position, but may still recover foreseeable special and general damages caused by breach of a defendant's promise to marry.

I believe the change advocated does not go far enough. Motive of the defendant may still, apparently, be considered in assessing damages. *Warner v. Benham*, 126

Wash. 393, 218 P. 260 (1923). Where the breach of promise to marry is wanton or deliberate, the effect is to allow exemplary damages, contrary to the public policy of our state. *Wyman v. Wallace*, 15 Wash. App. 395, 549 P.2d 71 (1976). In *Wyman*, at page 398, 549 P.2d at page 73, the Court of Appeals abolished the action for alienation of affections of a spouse by an unrelated third person on the ground, among others, that "the element of punishment is so inextricably interwoven into any award of damages for alienation of the affections of a spouse that the true nature of the award is punitive." This is no less true in this case than it was in *Wyman*. In addition, in 1973 our state adopted a new dissolution of marriage act. RCW 26.09. The establishment of the fact that a marriage is "irretrievably broken" is now a sufficient ground for dissolution, with no finding of fault necessary. The trial judge observed in his memorandum decision on motion to dismiss:

> The current public policy expressed in the 1973 Dissolution Act is to disregard fault in the judicial determination of property rights at the dissolution of a marriage. Fault is not to be considered in determining which party shall have the decree. There are no damages as such in a dissolution. Is it not obvious, however, that one of the parties to a dissolution suffers at least as much humiliation, embarrassment, mental suffering and loss of financial expectation and security as does a party to the breakup of an engagement?
>
> It is significant that there was no divorce by judicial decree at common law when the breach of promise action came into being. *Tupper v. Tupper*, 63 Wash.2d 585 (388 P.2d 225). Should not the public policy declared in the divorce statutes be applicable to engagements? I believe it is.

The majority lists the almost uniform criticisms of the action by commentators: "(1) the action is used as an instrument of oppression and blackmail; (2) engaged persons should be allowed to correct their mistakes without fear of publicity and legal compulsion; (3) the action is subject to great abuse at the hands of gullible and sympathetic juries; (4) it is wrong to allow under the guise of contract an action that is essentially tortious and penal in nature...."

I believe these criticisms are sufficient grounds, given the recently enunciated policy of the state in the dissolution of marriage act, to justify our abolition of this now obsolete, judicially created, cause of action.

CHAACHOU v. CHAACHOU

Supreme Court of Florida
135 So.2d 206 (Fla. 1961)

PER CURIAM.

On this appeal we are confronted with the culmination of one of the most protracted and bitterly contested divorce proceedings in the annals of Florida jurisprudence.

We quote in full the findings of facts, the conclusions of law and the final decree of the chancellor which is under attack herein:

"By her Complaint filed July 11, 1952 alleging a common law marriage with the defendant, Khudourie Chaachou, plaintiff, Fredericka Phillips Chaachou, seeks divorce on the ground of extreme cruelty, an award of alimony, suit money, counsel fees, and a decree for special equities in certain properties mentioned in the Complaint, which consists of four Miami Beach hotels and a residence at 5041 Collins Avenue, Miami Beach.

"The defendant...filed [his] Answer to the Complaint denying generally all its allegations including the alleged marriage, and admitted only that the defendant, Khudourie Chaachou, was born in Bagdad, Iraq, had become a naturalized American citizen, that he was engaged in the wholesale rug business in New York City, and that he was involved in the automobile accident which plaintiff alleged initiated her coming to Miami Beach and becoming both the defendant's wife and his business partner.

"On July 16, 1952, the cause was referred to a Special Master...'for the purpose of taking testimony...and for the purpose of filing his recommendations to the Court both on the facts and the law with all convenient speed.'... [T]he parties produced forty-seven witnesses whose testimony appears on more than 2,000 legal size pages, and submitted to him eight written depositions and over 150 exhibits, more than 100 of which were received in evidence.

...

"In *Chaachou v. Chaachou* (Fla.Sup.Ct., *Rehearing denied* June 21, 1954) 73 So.2d 830, the Supreme Court of Florida found the Master to be in error (as was...this Court confirming his report) when he recommended against the existence of a common law marriage between the parties. The Supreme Court held (73 So.2d 830, at p. 837):

> The summary of the evidence heretofore given as to the actual marriage, the corroborating evidence with reference thereto, cohabitation and repute, shows beyond question, *prima facie*, a common law marriage, which shifted the burden to the respondent. He has not met the burden placed upon him by law.

...

"At the final hearing beginning on August 29, 1960, this Chancellor saw and heard the testimony of twenty witnesses, whose testimony covers 861 legal size pages; and in addition received and read nineteen exhibits, one of which (Plaintiff's Exhibit 3-8) consisted of twenty-one letters, all except two being written by the defendant, Khudourie Chaachou, to plaintiff's counsel. At the conclusion of the final hearing the parties filed extensive briefs advocating their positions. Midway during the final hearing of this cause Mr. John Carruthers II, who filed defendants' counterclaim of adultery, and who had represented the defendants in the last appellate proceeding in this cause, asked leave to be relieved of his representation, which was granted.

"During the course of this litigation, including interlocutory and final hearing, this Chancellor has seen and heard a total of forty-nine witnesses, whose testimony covers 3,161 legal size pages, and has received in evidence and read fifty exhibits, including five depositions. In order to properly evaluate the equities of this cause, the record made before the Master on the original reference, which record was initially before the Supreme Court of Florida in *Chaachou v. Chaachou* (*Rehearing denied* June 24, 1954) 73 So.2d 830, has been reviewed. This record consists of an excess of 2,000 pages of testimony, 100 filed exhibits, and eight depositions.

"From this massive record it appears, and is so found, that the equities of this cause are with the plaintiff, and she is entitled to the relief prayed for in her Complaint.

"Plaintiff bases her claim for divorce on the ground of the defendant Chaachou's extreme cruelty, and there is ample evidence to sustain this ground. The plaintiff and the defendant Chaachou are both naturalized citizens, becoming such in 1950 and 1942 respectively. The plaintiff was born in Turkey of Armenian parents, and the defendant Chaachou was born in Bagdad, Iraq, of Jewish parents. The early history of their business acquaintanceship is recorded in *Chaachou v. Chaachou*, 73 So.2d 830, 832. It is apparent that plaintiff came to Miami Beach from Atlanta at defendant Chaachou's request in the Fall of 1942, and assumed the management of the Savoy Plaza Hotel which he had recently purchased for $165,000.00. Defendant Chaachou owned the Imperial Persian and Chinese Rug Company of New York City, which his counsel represented to the Court in this cause on September 12, 1952, was 'probably the largest rug importing business in the United States.' On plaintiff's advice, after she began operating the Savoy Plaza Hotel, defendant Chaachou bought the Coral Reef, the Somerset, and the Astor hotels, also located in Miami Beach. Shortly after their purchase, these hotels were released by the military forces, which had been occupying them during the war, and the plaintiff took over their active management and operation also. According to the appraisal report of Adrian McCune, M.A.I., Plaintiff's Exhibit 3-1, these hotels are located near the southerly end of Miami Beach. They are not in the class with those more recently constructed further north along the ocean. But when they were acquired and for almost ten years thereafter, these hotels, because of plaintiff's good management and the scarcity of hotel accommodations at Miami Beach, enjoyed an extraordinary patronage and produced a large amount of revenue.

"That the plaintiff worked hard and effective in the operation and management of these hotels for almost ten years after they were acquired is beyond dispute. Defendant Chaachou testified:

> A. Well, Fredericka was really my right hand. She was behind the desk; she was watching every hotel; she was a hostess, entertainer. She was on every occasion — really, she took my place. She had a free hand. Whatever she do or whatever she spend or whatever else she do — I think I was approximately more than busy man with four hotels on my hand and my importation and exportation in New York. I was hundred per cent practically depending on her, whatever she said goes...she was really equipped for that business at that time.

"When asked at the Master's hearing in what capacity plaintiff worked at the Savoy Plaza Hotel, which was the first one he bought, defendant Chaachou testified:

> Capacity of everything — as a hostess, housekeeper, manager, taking care of everything — entertainer.

"When questioned on his deposition, which was received in evidence before the Master, if he had used the plaintiff as intermediary in the transfer of funds, he testified:

> A. I used the plaintiff as everything — in business and socially, as a hostess and so forth.

"The plaintiff had been an interior decorator in Atlanta before she came to Miami Beach. Her description of what she did when she took over the management of the Savoy Plaza Hotel appears in her testimony, which is undisputed. She testified:

> I did everything that the hotel can be operated. I used to decorate; I used to be on the desk; I used to rent rooms; I looked at them, and many other things I did. I ripped the hotel, put a new bar downstairs, opened a door from the beach, all of this operation, and redecorate the hotel.
>
> When I came that hotel used to take $25 a month a room. I put everybody out. I redecorated the hotel. When I was operating, the hotel was getting $25, $18 a day.
>
> ...

"While she was at their summer residence in Tannersville, New York in November, 1951, defendant Chaachou telephoned her to fly to Miami Beach and redecorate three of the four hotels in order to get them ready for the coming season. She did this, replacing the tile, repairing the furniture, hiring the carpenters, and doing whatever was necessary to get them ready.

"On cross-examination she testified:

> Q. As a matter of fact during the last several years since Avak came to Miami Beach, you have been less and less active in the operation of the Savoy Plaza Hotel and other business owned by Mr. Chaachou, isn't that true?
>
> A. Sir, I was very active all the time.
>
> Q. Even in the past few years?
>
> A. I worked so hard until this last month ago, sir, if you don't believe me, ask thousands of people.
>
> ...
>
> A. I used to go to the bank. I used to rent rooms during the season. I used to be as hostess. I used to redecorate. Every hotel needs redecorating, and put everything. And this year I was every day in the kitchen. I was in the dining room. Sometimes they need help in the dining room. Even 3:00 o'clock in the morning, A.M., I used to work sometimes with the help. I worked very hard.
>
> Q. What hotel did you rent rooms in?
>
> A. Every hotel I have rent rooms, sir. I have rent rooms this year at Somerset. I have rent rooms in Savoy Plaza this year.
>
> ...
>
> ...When everybody comes, they want room, they want Mr. Chaachou. I'm eating, or whatever, I go.
>
> ...
>
> Sir, whatever my husband ask, I do, any time. It doesn't matter if midnight or nothing. It is our hotels, and for our profit.... If he orders me anything, I'm in it. I never say no. I'm right ready to go whether midnight, morning, or any time.

"She summarized in her testimony her work in connection with these hotels when she said:

> ...I used to work in my business 14, 15, 16 hours, doesn't matter when. He is in the office. Everything I used to control, no time, no hours. Every

morning I used to get up, go to my business. Every night, sometimes until 1:00 o'clock. We used to go home together, and I come back until 1:00, 2:00 o'clock I have to be in the hotel.

Q. You were the one?

A. Sure, it is mine. I work with my heart and soul, sir....

"The comprehensive appraisal reports of McCune Company and Bishop & Company show that the Savoy Plaza, Somerset, Astor, and the Coral Reef hotels have a total of 343 rentable rooms. The Savoy Plaza is valued at $160,000.00, the Somerset at $230,000.00, the Astor at $160,000.00 and the Coral Reef at $525,000.00, and these values are equal to or in excess of the purchase price which the defendant, Khudourie Chaachou, paid for them. That they were good revenue producers during the ten year period from 1942 to 1952 is plainly evident. The defendant, Khudourie Chaachou, testified that the profit from them was $250,000.00 a season. The plaintiff persuaded the defendant, Chaachou, to buy the Coral Reef Hotel for $250,000.00 while the Army was still in possession, and even against his lawyer's advice to buy up the outstanding lease for $225,000.00 which lease had an unexpired term of six years. When the Army released this hotel in 1945, the plaintiff redecorated the same in time for occupancy for the 1945 Christmas Season....

...

"That the defendant, Chaachou, led the plaintiff to believe, and that she did believe during this period, that she was his partner in these hotel operations, can hardly be doubted. A large part of this ten year period when she acted as such, the defendant, Chaachou, was engaged in the operation of his extensive rug business in New York, and left the actual running and management of the hotels to the plaintiff.

"The defendant, Chaachou, deliberately kept the plaintiff in ignorance of all financial matters, and she followed his wishes in this regard. He kept exclusive possession and control of all financial records. He handled them to suit himself and instructed her not to ask questions about them. All checks purporting to represent her share of her partnership income, which he gave her from time to time, she endorsed and delivered back to him on his pretext that he was 'investing' the same for her. At one time he told the plaintiff that he had $55,000.00 of her money invested, and on another occasion said it was $75,000.00 but neglected to tell her and she did not know of what the investment consisted. Whenever it was necessary for her to sign documents or papers she obeyed his instructions without question and signed at the place he indicated for her signature. This was true of all of her income tax returns which he caused his accountant to prepare for her signature. When a copy of her 1946 income tax return was produced upon her counsel's demand at trial, which defendant, Chaachou, had kept in his possession and which had been prepared by his accountant, it reflected partnership returns from the four hotels of $26,000.00 which she testified she never received. This return reflected a deduction of $1,200.00 for 'Entertaining prospects and guests at taxpayer's home in capacity as manager and partner re: Coral Reef, Somerset, Astor and Savoy Plaza Hotels, Miami Beach, Fla. including special parties of Professional Women's Club of Miami, Fla.'

"Time after time in the record of this cause the plaintiff testified that she trusted the defendant, Chaachou, and it is evident that she did not only in her finances but in her personal relationship with him. She testified:

> ...I have trusted in him, and he took everything, of the books and everything else, and I took care of everything that goes into hotel, sir.

She also testified:

> A. Armenian girls, when they are married to a man — they obey the husband no matter what he says.
>
> Q. Is that the reason you signed this way?
>
> A. Yes sir; whatever he told me, I do exactly like he wants me to do.
>
> ...
>
> Q. Did you ever read your income tax returns before you signed them?
>
> A. No, sir.
>
> Q. Why didn't you?
>
> A. Because my husband used to tell me, "You don't have to read. Don't ask any questions to the accountant. Just do what I am saying." So I just think, well, he knows, and I just signed whatever he wants me to do.
>
> Q. Don't you think it was rather foolish for a person just to sign, and not know what he was signing?
>
> A. No, sir; because I trusted him.
>
> Q. Why did you trust him?
>
> A. Well, he is my husband.
>
> Q. Is that reason enough for you?
>
> A. Well, that is enough reason. I have been obedient, because he has a violent temper. When I did not do something, he gets very upset. Sometimes he hits me.

"She testified that the only checking account that she had was one in which defendant, Chaachou, put enough money for her to issue a check for the payment of her income tax, and that he had control of all the money. That when they got married, he gave her $100.00 a week allowance, which he later reduced to $75.00 a week, and finally to $50.00 just before they separated.

"She described her last meeting with the defendant, Chaachou, in the business office of the Savoy Plaza Hotel, on June 18, 1952, as follows:

> ...I was very tired, and I went to his office to talk to him after the season, I presented the bill that Dr. Minoyian sent, to write a check, and he says, "I am not paying any more of your bills," and he threw the bill at me. Then I said "When are we going to vacation, because I am exhausted, and tired, and I want to go to the summer home to rest. You look tired too. We will go." He said. "You are not going this year to the summer home." I asked him why, and he says, "Because I am selling the house."
>
> That time I said, "Well, then I need some money. I want to get my allowance, so I can go and shop for a few things," and he says, "I am not giving you any more allowance either. I am sick and tired of you. I want you to get out of my life, and stay out."
>
> I said, "What do you mean, I should get out of your life?" He says, "I told you I want you to get out of this building too. If not, I will throw you out with the law," and I said, "What are you saying? Why are you talking like

that? Are you sick, or you are not feeling good?" He says, "No. I mean it, what I am saying. You have to get out of my life."

I says, "Well, if I have to get out, all right. Let us come to an understanding of my share. I have worked with you all these years, and I don't know what I have, what I don't have, and if you don't want, we will go to court." He says, "Go to court. Go to court, and if the court decides a million dollars, I am going to give it to you. I told you, you have no share. You spent everything. You have no more allowance coming."

I said, "Khudourie, please honey, I don't want you to act like this. I don't want no lawyers. You know I never had lawyer, or anything like that together." "No," he says, "You got to go to court to finish this." I said, "Do you know any lawyer I can go to?" He laughed. He says, "Any lawyer I know?"

I said, "Didn't you promise me that you are going to love me, honor me, keep me forever?" He says, "Man can promise and take it back." I said, "What do you mean? This is no Bagdad or Russia. If you want to take your promise, we have to go to court to let the judge decide, and you give me my share. We will leave each other, divorce each other." "Oh," he says, "Divorce — don't you know that legally you are not married to me. I have affidavits to that." I said, "Put the false affidavits one side. You get them to sign affidavits. I know the kind people. Please, Khudourie, don't let Satan destroy you. We have done everything together. The Lord gave all this money to be used for His glory. I don't want you to mistreat me." He says, "Get out of my life. You have to go, and take your — " I said, "Where am I going?" "Take the jewelry I bought you, sell it, buy a home. Get out of my life."

Then I was so shocked — I was so shocked that I can't tell you.

...

"Following this episode the defendant, Chaachou, wrote the plaintiff two letters which were introduced in evidence in this cause, the first dated July 1, 1952, and the second July 7, 1952. In the former letter defendant, Chaachou, advised the plaintiff:

> Since you have neglected and not performed your duties for the past seven or eight days, and inasmuch as we were unable to contact you several times each day during the above mentioned period, we hereby notify you that your services are no longer required.
>
> ...
>
> Due to the termination of your services, the rent of your apartment will be $15.00 per day and is payable weekly in advance. Otherwise your apartment will have to be vacated by July 5th or before....

"In the latter letter he told her that:

> Inasmuch as your rent started from Saturday July 5th and has not been paid in advance to date, we hereby give you three days notice to vacate your apartment or pay your rent of $15.00 daily or $105.00 per week, in advance, according to the Florida State Law.

"Throughout this entire record on the four occasions that plaintiff has been extensively examined by counsel for both sides, she has steadfastly maintained that she was defendant Chaachou's partner in his hotel business. That she worked with defendant, Chaachou, under that belief and that he encouraged her in her thinking is evidenced from the record. Indeed corroboration of her testimony was furnished by the defendant's admission that 'she had a partnership' and by two documents which he offered in evidence purporting to constitute her a partner in the net profits derived from the operation of the Savoy Plaza and the Astor hotels, which were dated prior to the marriage of the parties and which the plaintiff testified she read for the first time from the witness stand. The plaintiff testified that the defendant, Chaachou, advised her that she was a partner, not only in 20% of the net profits of the Savoy Plaza Hotel but of its ownership as well, and that as he acquired each of the remaining three hotels, he repeated a similar statement to her, with reference to them. The defendant denied this and attempted to reduce her to the status of an employee to avoid his obligation to her, not only financially but as her husband. Whatever partnership existed between the parties became merged in their larger partnership of marriage and its terms are now too indistinct to be specifically enforced as such. To allow him, however, to enjoy the fruits of his wife's labor from which he benefitted so substantially, as shown by this record, without any compensation to her for her contribution to the wealth he derived from these hotels, would constitute a gross inequity and result in his unjust enrichment, which should not be permitted under the rule announced by the Florida Supreme Court in the cases of *Windham v. Windham*, 144 Fla. 563, 198 So. 202; *Strauss v. Strauss*, 148 Fla. 23, 3 So.2d 727; *Engebretsen v. Engebretsen*, 151 Fla. 372, 11 So.2d 322; *Giachetti v. Giachetti*, 157 Fla. 259, 25 So.2d 658.

...

"Considering the fact that the value of all the hotels is equal to or in excess of defendant, Chaachou's original purchase price, and the large revenue which he derived from them through his wife's assistance and efforts, it is equitable that she should be, and she is hereby, awarded a special equity of three-twentieths (3/20ths) value of each of said four hotels, including its furniture, furnishings and fixtures, as shown by the appraisal report of Adrian McCune, M.A.I., filed in this cause, and that she be, and she is hereby, granted an equitable lien on each of said hotels, its furniture, furnishings and fixtures, as security for this value award.

"With reference to the residence at 5041 Collins Avenue, Miami Beach, the plaintiff testified it was a present to her on the occasion of her marriage to the defendant, Chaachou. In this she is corroborated by two witnesses who assert that they heard the plaintiff say in the defendant, Chaachou's presence, on the occasion of the wedding reception, that the defendant had given her the home. (John Kulhanjian, 27–28; Mary Kulhanjian, 2859.) The plaintiff selected the residence and spent five months, with defendant's consent, in furnishing and redecorating it so that she and the defendant could get married and move into this residence when he returned from New York in December of 1944. After their marriage the plaintiff and the defendant, Khudourie Chaachou, lived in this home for almost six years until he ordered her to leave her home and take up residence at the Savoy Plaza Hotel for no apparent reason, except that at about this time he testified 'he was more inclined to get rid of her anyway.'

"Counsel takes the position that this being an oral contract was within the statute of frauds, but the cases do not so hold. *Exchange National Bank of Tampa, etc. v. Bryan*, (1936) 122 Fla. 479, 165 So. 685; *McDowell v. Ritter* (1943) 153 Fla. 50, 13 So.2d 612. In the last mentioned case the Supreme Court, speaking through Mr. Justice Terrell, said:

> The law is settled that the statute of frauds applies only to executory contracts and has no application to agreements fully performed on both sides.

"That rule seems to be applicable to the instant case, and, therefore, the residence at 5041 Collins Avenue, Miami Beach, Florida, will be awarded to the plaintiff.

"On the question of divorce little need be said. Mrs. Chaachou testified that for no apparent reason her husband put her out of the house just before Christmas in 1949, and insisted that because of her pressing duties at the Savoy Plaza Hotel she should take up her residence there. In obedience to his command, she did move into the Savoy Plaza Hotel, but left her personal things at her home, and went back to her home each morning to have breakfast with him and returned each evening, until she found that defendant, Chaachou, was keeping company with one of his secretaries.

"If denying the fact of marriage, putting her out of the house, vigorously contesting the marriage, withholding from her support, when she was destitute, charging her with adultery after she had proven her marriage, and maligning her character by sending numerous letters to her attorneys (introduced collectively as Plaintiff's Exhibit 3-8) does not constitute extreme cruelty, it is difficult to think what would.

"On the question of adultery the defendant, Chaachou, undertook to prove same by (1) various acts of the plaintiff and one Avak Hagopian, and (2) testimony of John Durgin.

"Incidentally, it appears from the record that Mrs. Chaachou was born on March 3, 1906, and is therefore 54 years of age. She was 46 at the time the Complaint was filed. Avak is 34 years of age and was 26 at the time the Complaint was filed. Mrs. Chaachou has a son older than Avak.

> The rule has commonly been abbreviated into the statement that proof of inclination and opportunity is sufficient to prove adultery; but this statement is correct only when it is understood that inclination means more than ordinary human tendencies, and must extend to proof of conduct reasonably suggesting specific libidinous tendency of each of the parties toward the other, and opportunity must be understood as meaning more than mere chance and must include the elements which would prove guilt beyond a reasonable doubt. However, according to some authority, whatever the disposition of the parties, the mere fact that the parties may have been in each other's company, under such circumstances that the act might have occurred, will not justify the conclusion that it actually did occur. There must be some circumstances, in addition to the disposition and opportunity, tending to rebut the presumption of innocence, although proof of circumstances which lead a reasonable man to believe that the offense has been committed, in addition to an adulterous inclination and an opportunity to commit the crime, will justify a conviction, Adultery, 2 C.J.S. *Adultery* §24, p. 492.

"Of Avak, Mrs. Chaachou said:

Q. What place, if any does Avak Hagopian have in your life?

A. Avak Hagopian is like my own son. I have done more to (sic) him that I have to (sic) my own son. The reason is that he is a man of God, lives according to the Lord's Will and he was helpless when he was here. He didn't know language (sic). It was a different country, strange. I have to interpret for him. I have to write letters for him. And they were writing letters from all over, and without me he couldn't do all this work, and I drove him wherever he wanted, because of motherly love I have towards him, like I to my own son.

Q. What association, if any, has Avak had with your family?

A. He is just like one of our family.

Q. Is he presently related to you in any way?

A. Yes. He is married to my sister's daughter.

Q. Did you ever sit on Avak's lap in the same chair with him?

A. Never, never.

Q. Were you ever in Avak's room either you or Avak or both of you were in your sleeping garments?

A. Never. Mr. Miles, I haven't lost my self-respect yet. I am a Christian. I love my God.

"The plaintiff introduced in evidence at the final hearing of this cause a letter (Exhibit 3-11) over the signature of K. Chaachou, dated November 17, 1959, addressed to Mr. and Mrs. A. Balian of Auburn, New York, the body of which reads:

> Reverend Avak and his foster mother, Fredericka, will be in Rochester Friday, November 25th, Saturday, the 26th, and Sunday, the 27th of November.
>
> If you wish them to visit the Syracuse Church at your city, kindly communicate with them at that time — so that they can make a definite date in preparation.

"The defendant attempted through various witnesses to show that the plaintiff had the *opportunity* to commit adultery with Avak. Avak stayed at the defendant's hotels at the defendant's suggestion. The defendant had full knowledge of his being there, his whereabouts at all times and the opportunities that were afforded him to commit adultery with the plaintiff. There is not one word in the testimony that either the plaintiff or Avak had the *inclination* to commit adultery with each other. He not only stayed at the hotels operated by the defendant in Miami Beach, but he went to the defendant's place at Tannersville in the Catskill Mountains of New York at the defendant's suggestion. He did not appear at the trial as a witness. The proof falls far short of that required to establish that the plaintiff committed adultery with Avak. Mrs. Chaachou testified positively that she had never had sexual intercourse with any man other than Khudourie Chaachou since she married him in December, 1944.

. . .

"Honi soit qui mal y pense.

"The only other bit of evidence regarding the plaintiff's alleged adultery was from the witness John Durgin who testified that on an occasion he visited the plaintiff at her residence on Collins Avenue and went to bed with her.

"As to that Mrs. Chaachou said:

Q. Now, you heard the testimony of Mr. John Durgin?

A. Yes, sir.

Q. Tell the court whether or not the incident about which he testified to in which he said you went to bed together ever took place.

A. Mr. Niles, such a ridiculous, horrible lie I have never heard in my life.

Q. Answer the question yes or no.

A. Of course not, Mr. Niles.

Q. Did you ever pick him up and take him to your house?

A. Never in my life.

Q. Were you ever alone with him under the same roof?

A. I never had any association with that man until I saw last year he came to the house with the sheriff.

Q. I ask you, Mrs. Chaachou, did you ever have any conversation?

A. No.

Q. Please let me finish my question, Ma'am. Did you ever have any conversations with Mr. Durgin about Mr. Chaachou?

A. No.

"This Chancellor saw and heard Mr. Durgin. Apart and aside from the inherent improbability of his testimony, his manner on the witness stand was not at all convincing. He may have been influenced by Chaachou's newspaper advertisements offering $100,000.00 to any one who would furnish testimony in his behalf. This Chancellor believes him to be a liar and a perjurer and so brands him.

...

"Wherefore, the premises considered, it is

"Considered, Ordered, Adjudged and Decreed as follows:

"1. That the equities of this cause are with the plaintiff, and she is entitled to the relief for which she prays in accordance with this opinion.

"2. That the plaintiff, Fredericka Phillips Chaachou, and the defendant, Khudourie Chaachou, be, and they are hereby, divorced each from the other *a vinculo matrimonii.*

"3. That the temporary alimony heretofore ordered for the plaintiff in the amount of $750.00 each and every month be made permanent, and that the defendant, Khudourie Chaachou, pay her on the first of each and every month the sum of $750.00, and that he send the same to her at her residence.

"4. That the defendant, Khudourie Chaachou, post with the clerk of this Court a good and sufficient bond in the sum of One Hundred Eighty Thousand ($180,000.00) Dollars, to be approved by this Court, conditioned to pay the plaintiff the permanent alimony herein awarded as and when the same becomes due. That when said bond is posted and approved, the injunctive order of this Court dated the 10th day of April, 1959, and duly recorded in Chancery Order Book 1387 at Page 96, shall stand canceled and vacated without further order of this Court.

"5. That the plaintiff be, and she is hereby, awarded a special equity equal to three-twentieths (3/20ths) of the value, as shown by the appraisal report of Adrian McCune, M.A.I., in each of the following described hotel properties:

"(a) The Savoy Plaza Hotel, located at 425 Ocean Drive, Miami Beach, Florida, the legal description of which is: Lot 6, Block 116, Ocean Beach No. 4, according to the plat thereof as recorded in Plat Book 3 at Page 151 of the Public Records of Dade County, Florida.

"(b) The Astor Hotel, located at 956 Washington Avenue, Miami Beach, Florida, the legal description of which is: Lots 1 and 2 less the west 135 feet, Block 35, Ocean Beach Number 3, as recorded in Plat Book 2 at Page 81 of the Public Records of Dade County, Florida.

"(c) The Coral Reef Hotel, located at 3601 Collins Avenue, Miami Beach, Florida, the legal description of which is: Lots 1, 2, 7, and 8, Block 25, Ocean Front Amended, according to the plat thereof as recorded in Plat Book 5 at Pages 7 and 8 of the Public Records of Dade County, Florida.

"(d) The Somerset Hotel, located at 335 Ocean Drive, Miami Beach, Florida, the legal description of which is: Lot 4, Block 115, Ocean Beach No. 4, according to the plat thereof as recorded in Plat Book 3 at Page 151 of the Public Records of Dade County, Florida.

"6. That three-twentieths (3/20ths) of the value of said hotel properties, according to the appraisal report of Adrian McCune, M. A. I., equals the sum of One Hundred sixty-one thousand, Two Hundred fifth ($161,250.00) Dollars, and there is hereby created and established upon said described hotel properties a first lien in plaintiff's favor in the said amount. That in the event the defendant, Khudourie Chaachou, shall not deposit with the Clerk of this Court within thirty (30) days from the date of this decree, for the use and benefit of the plaintiff, said sum of One Hundred sixty-one thousand, Two Hundred Fifty ($161,250.00) Dollars, then the Special Master appointed in this cause shall thereafter sell said hotel properties for cash to satisfy said lien of the plaintiff at public auction of the South front door of the Dade County Court House, at Miami, Florida, after first giving thirty (30) days public notice of the time, place and manner of said sale in some newspaper of general circulation in Dade County, Florida, four (4) insertions of such notice in such newspaper at least seven (7) days apart shall be taken and deemed sufficient public notice, and said hotel properties shall be sold on the first Monday succeeding the last advertisement of said hotel properties between the hours of eleven A.M., and two P.M., on that day; that upon the said sale of said hotel properties by said Special Master, the lien of the plaintiff shall thereupon be reduced to the proceeds of said sale.

...

...[T]he order of the chancellor...is hereby affirmed.
It is so ordered.

COMMENTS

Stanard v. Bolin and *Chaachou v. Chaachou* should be read together, although they are seemingly unrelated. *Stanard* involves damages for noncohabitation, while *Chaachou* can be viewed as "damages" for cohabitation. The factual situations in the two cases may seem to be in sharp contrast with one another, the first case dealing with a mere promise to marry, while the second supposedly involves an already consummated marriage, albeit in the form of common law marriage. Obviously the level of execution of the contract is considerably higher in *Chaachou* than in *Stanard*, but this is a matter of degree. Since the conduct of the parties is more determinative of legal consequences than any of their express statements, we are dealing basically with implied contract. *Chaachou* could have been argued under a theory of engagement to marry, which would have benefitted the defendant. His point would have been that the plaintiff must fail because of the statutory abolition of actions based on breach of promise to marry in Florida. There was also some appearance of marriage in *Stanard*: The parties purchased real estate and signed as husband and wife. Whether a theory of engagement or marriage is applied in either case traditionally depends on the intent of the parties and the circumstances.

The reality of litigation is, however, more complex. What appears to be the intent of the parties may be an application of public policy by way of legal fiction. Since the judge, in finding the supposed intent, has to rely on the circumstances as pleaded by the lawyers, the representation of reality and the application of legal theories may be remote from or even opposite to what actually took place and what the parties wanted.

The pleadings of the facts in *Chaachou*, for example, determined to some extent the choices of facts presented and the theories available to the court. Other possible facts and theories are incidentally mentioned in the opinion, for example, that the case could have been based on a theory of a business partnership or a personal service contract. Even a landlord-tenant relationship is mentioned. It is conceivable that Fredricka Chaachou would have fared better under a theory of partnership than under a theory of marriage. It is also conceivable that the case could have been settled, even after a divorce action had been filed, under a theory of business partnership, which incidentally would have had tax benefits for the plaintiff, who would have had to pay income tax on any alimony she received. Of course, the defense could also have proceeded, and in fact did alternatively proceed, under theories other than marriage — for instance, that the plaintiff, according to the intention of the parties, was merely in an employment relationship and could be fired for cause.

Another aspect of *Chaachou*, generally overlooked, is that the case can be viewed as an early precedent for a cohabitation contract, comparable to *Marvin v. Marvin* (p. 214), decided fifteen years later by the California Supreme Court. The court in *Chaachou* mentioned that "whatever partnership existed between the parties became merged in their larger partnership of marriage." This theory of merger appears to be unsound, since husband and wife can have business contracts with each other. More important, especially in states that do not allow common law marriage and after the abolition of common law marriage in Florida, is the inference that the plaintiff would have recovered under contract if common law marriage had not been available (because no merger would have taken place).

Both *Stanard* and *Chaachou* can be viewed in the light of policies that led to anti-heart-balm legislation in many states, namely, that actions of this kind can be used for blackmail purposes. The same can be argued of cohabitation contracts as in *Marvin v. Marvin* (see p. 214). Yet it should not be overlooked that these policies are possibly dated. Whether or not claims of women are viewed as being in the nature of extortion depends on the climate of the times. Perhaps more acute is the question raised in *Stanard* in the dissenting opinion: how actions for breach of promise can be reconciled with the availability of no-fault divorce. In the State of Washington a man who breaks an engagement may be in a worse position than if he had married and sought an immediate divorce; in the case of a short marriage his wife may receive very little, if anything. Yet a newlywed who is summarily divorced by her husband surely suffers as much as or more than a woman rejected by her fiance before the wedding. The dissenting opinion of Mr. Justice Clark in *Marvin* raises a similar issue regarding cohabitation contracts: a woman who does not marry may be in a better legal position than a wife and be able to introduce evidence of misbehavior by her cohabitant that would be treated as irrelevant in no-fault divorce. That fault is involved in *Stanard*, even though punitive damages were not assessed, can hardly be doubted. It is no accident that the pleadings of the plaintiff fiancee were couched in a form and style identical to a request for a divorce based on extreme cruelty when she stated through her lawyer that she was in great shock, became ill and lost sleep and weight, and had to consult a physician. Here, too, the styles of action for breach of promise and divorce based on fault are very similar.

The attorneys in *Stanard* and *Chaachou* may not have been sufficiently aware that they could have used the amorphous mass of information they had in several different ways. For example, in *Chaachou* — which took almost ten years of litigation — greater efforts should have been made at an early phase to persuade the parties to settle — perhaps by abandoning the claim of common-law marriage and dissolving not marriage, but partnership, conveying straight title in one or two of the hotels to the plaintiff. As is so often the case with court-ordered alimony, Mrs. Chaachou never actually received anything at all.

It appears that many of Mr. Chaachou's financial dealings were influenced by a desire to reduce his income tax liability. Would women as a group stand to benefit from income tax laws that gave high-income taxpayers a stronger incentive to place property in their spouse's name?

REFERENCE

Lenore J. Weitzman, THE MARRIAGE CONTRACT — SPOUSES, LOVERS, AND THE LAW (1981).

EGGLESTON v. EGGLESTON

Supreme Court of North Carolina
228 N.C. 668, 47 S.E.2d 243 (1948)

SEAWELL, J.

The plaintiff brought this suit against her husband for alimony without divorce under G.S. §50-16, joining with this cause of action (b) a cause of action to have herself declared a business partner with her husband and to have her rights under the partnership adjudicated and an account taken...

...

...The case then proceeded to trial, the issues being answered as to both causes of action unfavorably to the plaintiff, who, having taken exceptions hereinafter noted, along with numerous others, preserved them for review by moving to set aside the verdict of the jury for errors committed during the trial, and this motion having been declined, objected and excepted to the judgment, and appealed.

...

THE QUESTION OF BUSINESS PARTNERSHIP

The plaintiff sought to show the existence and nature of the alleged partnership between herself and her husband by evidence of dealings inter partes for a long period of years and her contributions to the joint undertaking; and by introducing the joint partnership income tax returns for the year 1945 made by herself and husband to the Federal and State taxing authorities, respectively, with other evidence pertinent to this transaction.

More particular reference to these returns will be made further on. For clarity we may say here that in both of the returns it is declared that a partnership existed between the plaintiff and the defendant for the calendar year 1945, manifesting partnership on equal shares as to the net income. After this suit was brought the defendant filed "amended" or "corrected" returns, in point of fact *individual* returns, eliminating the partnership feature.

The evidence by which plaintiff sought to show the alleged partnership may be summarized as tending to show the following facts and conditions:

When they first moved into the filling station on the Draper road and started business she helped display the stock; while defendant went out into the "territory" plaintiff was in charge of the filling station, worked there with no assistance except casual help from little boys to whom plaintiff paid small sums; plaintiff had access to the funds, taking in the money and keeping it in the cash drawer; she put her "inheritance money," about $125, in the business at this early stage; she sometimes bought, but buying was mostly done by defendant. As more filling stations were added, plaintiff went and put up signs in the windows, displayed stock and helped them get set up in the business. She worked regularly during this period, living in the service station for 15 years, and except for a short period of time and vacations in the summer, was there continually, often being compelled to let her housework go. She had often gone without food all day except what she could pick up at the filling station. She sold things out of stock, serviced cars, putting in gas and oil; carried water from the pump in tubs, as there was, for a long time, no running water; washed cars, often making $5 a day in this way. Plaintiff handled the paid and unpaid bills, made out statements and sent them out. Later plaintiff took a bookkeeping course and learned to type, and thereafter kept books for the business. After plaintiff and defendant moved into the new home in 1940 until 1946, while plaintiff did not go to the filling station every day because of her illness, the help came to her to inquire about the business and for direction in matters with which she was familiar, and she continued in charge during Mr. Eggleston's absence. Between 1940 and 1946, when they separated, she went down and did book work. During 1945 plaintiff and her brother, Pickett Parker, did the book work together. Plaintiff took part in the conduct of the tire business, sold tires, entertained presidents of tire companies in her home; sold and delivered tires in the service station and in the territory, took orders and saw that they were delivered; delivered tires in the territory; met people on the highways with tires, delivering and taking orders.

All this proffered evidence was rejected upon objection made seriatim by defendant, and in the same manner plaintiff excepted.

The plaintiff then testified that during the year 1945, she was not certain of the date, defendant came into the kitchen where she was cooking supper, put his arm around her, started kissing her and told her she was his business partner.

> I asked him what he meant and I said I had been his business partner for twenty years. He said I had always been worried about losing a great deal of the business at his death, and he had fixed it so I would not even have to pay inheritance tax on my part of the partnership. He talked to me about it and ten days or two weeks later he signed — he said of course I would have to pay income since I was a partner in the business and he brought some papers in for me to sign. I signed three different sheets, I think, income papers and different papers, and a blank check.

After identification, plaintiff then introduced in evidence copies of the joint partnership income tax returns made by herself and husband for the calendar year 1945 to the Federal and State taxing authorities, respectively. These returns manifest a taxable net income for that year of $20,801.29 and indicated that Mattie P. Eggleston, the plaintiff, and Frank Eggleston, the defendant, were partners upon equal shares in the business, entitling each to one-half of said net income. The partnership appears as "Eggleston Brothers Filling Station." Accompanying these returns there was a partnership return of estimated tax for the year 1946.

Thereupon plaintiff sought to testify that she signed the documents above mentioned in good faith and upon objection by the defendant the evidence was excluded.

At the same time she offered to testify that she believed the defendant when he told her she was his partner and this also was excluded.

On review the rights of the plaintiff and the validity of the trial which purports to deal with them, must be made to depend on the whole evidence, both competent evidence excluded and the evidence which ran the gamut. So, before examining the instructions given the jury on the 4th issue relating to the partnership, it is necessary to turn to the evidence of the plaintiff as above noted — principally her own testimony — of the dealings between herself and husband with relation to the business in which she claims partnership.

This evidence was excluded apparently upon the theory that her complaint setting up the creation of the partnership restricts her to the transactions involved in the filing of the income tax returns, and especially to its organization on January 1, 1945. We are of the opinion that such a restriction does not necessarily follow from the allegations in her complaint, as a whole, liberally construed. However this may be, the evidence as to her contributions to the business and the circumstances under which the services were rendered are of such a nature as to support her further contentions as to the creation of the partnership, strengthening the plausibility and credibility of that claim both as a moral and legal consideration for the formation of the partnership, however and whenever it occurred. Its exclusion was error. But we do not mean by this to limit its effect to the function of supporting evidence for a partnership subsequently created. In our view of the case the whole evidence directed to the existence of the partnership must be taken together, and so taken was competent to be submitted to the jury for their consideration and evaluation.

Under the common law as a consequence of the fictional merger of husband and wife into one person, and other disabilities of the wife incident to coverture, there could be no contract and, therefore, no business partnership between husband and wife.... That incapacity has been removed in many states by the enactment of "Married Women's Acts" — statutes directly or impliedly giving them the power or the right to contract. The broad general powers of contract given under most of these statutes has in many instances been extended by judicial interpretation to authorize the formation of partnerships with the husband. In this State the "Martin Act," Chapter 109, Laws 1911, G.S. §52-2, has been held to vest the wife with the power to contract with the husband so as to create a business partnership....

"A contract, express or implied, is essential to the formation of a partnership." 40 Am.Jur., *Partnership*, p. 135, sec. 20, see notes 14, 15. But we see no reason why a course of dealings between the parties of sufficient significance and duration may not, along with other proof of the fact, be admitted as evidence tending to establish the fact of partnership provided it has sufficient substance and definiteness to evince the essentials of the legal concept, including, of course, the necessary intent....

Not only may a partnership be formed orally, but "[it] may be created by the agreement or conduct of the parties, either express or implied." *Sterman v. Ziem*, 17 Cal.App.2d 414, 62 P.2d 160, 162. As stated in *Niroad v. Farnall*, 11 Cal.App. 767, 106 P. 252, "A voluntary association of partners may be shown without proving an express agreement to form a partnership; and a finding of its existence may be based upon a rational consideration of the acts and declarations of the parties, warranting the inference that the parties understood that they were partners, and acted as such." Of significance on this issue is the statement of the plaintiff, "We divided the profits," and that when they came to a temporary separation the defendant agreed to keep her interest intact....

Where the fact at issue is the existence of partnership the admissions against interest of the person denying the partnership are significant in establishing it. The use and the function of the partnership tax returns as evidence was not per se to create the partnership but, together with other evidence directed to the fact, to establish its existence. They must be considered within the light of the circumstances, their purpose and the deliberation required in their composition. While a mere casual remark made on the streets might not be sufficient as evidence of the existence of a partnership, the tax returns in evidence are of greater significance on account of the solemnity of the oath under which they are made and the deliberate and comprehensive statement of the relation of the parties they contain. While we doubt the propriety of admitting the evidence of the amended or corrected returns, because of their self-serving nature, the hasty effort of the defendant to regain his lost status did not cancel out the evidence afforded by the original returns or such legitimate inferences as the jury under proper instructions might have drawn from them as evidence of the existence of the contract or such inferences as they might legitimately draw from the entire transaction as to the credibility of the defendant. The facts presented in the evidence of the plaintiff make out a case sufficient to "hold water taxwise" as creating a partnership. See "Husband and Wife, or 'Family' Partnerships," Indiana Law Journal, Vol. 20, p. 65, containing copious citations of authority applicable to the case at bar.

It is proper to say here that the services rendered by the wife to her husband are presumed to be gratuitous.... The presumption is not conclusive;...and may be overcome by evidence tending to show that the services were not gratuitous. *Stewart v. Wyrick*, 228 N.C. 429, 45 S.E.2d 764. That was a matter for the jury.

The court excluded evidence of the plaintiff that she had acted in good faith in signing the papers, including the partnership returns of income tax, and believed what the defendant had stated to her concerning the partnership to be true. This was error. It had a substantive bearing on the existence of the partnership; and the plaintiff had the right to say that she acted in good faith and not as a participant in a fraudulent attempt to deprive the Government or the State of its taxes.

...

...First, it is not necessary to a partnership that property or capital involved in it should belong in common to the parties to the contract. On the contrary, a familiar type of partnership, as indicated by the evidence in this case, occurs where the services of the one party is balanced against the capital furnished by the other; and the statement that the property must be held in common before plaintiff can recover is error; second, the partnership sought to be established did not necessarily involve a gift of property by the husband, and it was error to make her rights depend upon the laws respecting gifts inter vivos; third, while in partnership, as in any other kind of contract, there must be an intent, it was error to instruct the jury that before they could find for the plaintiff they must be satisfied by the greater weight of the evidence that the defendant, by the making and filing of the partnership income tax returns in evidence, intended to make his wife a partner. The instruction to that effect has a further infirmity that the plaintiff has not contended and could not contend that the partnership was created by these documents, but only introduced them as evidence of its existence.

A further instruction to the jury to the effect that they were not concerned with the question whether the defendant made and filed the partnership income tax returns for the purpose of defrauding the Government, as that was a matter between defendant and the Government, was calculated to impress the jury that such a thing, if true, need not reflect upon his credibility, and to relieve him from the most damaging situation he had to confront on this issue.

The Case for Alimony

The trial of the cause of action for enforcing partnership rights with that for alimony led to considerable embarrassment in the admission and rejection of evidence, and placing the admitted evidence in the proper cubicle for consideration. Thus, it is apparent that much of the evidence rejected by the court as not competent on the partnership issue was competent in the proceeding for alimony, and, therefore, was erroneously excluded in its relation to that subject. However, we need only refer briefly to certain salient features of the evidence and pertinent instructions to the jury to make our conclusion understood.

The evidence of the plaintiff tends to show that within a year after the marriage her husband beat her violently with his fists, leaving her bruised and bleeding about the face and mouth, and that he was convicted of the assault; that he was of a violent disposition, quick tempered, addicted to drink, and insanely jealous. She testified that on numerous occasions during the subsequent years she was the victim of brutal and unprovoked assaults, specifying that on one occasion he beat her severely with a shoe, until her body was covered with bruises; again that he threatened her life, locked her in the bathroom and kept her there for hours; that on another occasion, when she questioned the size of the dose of medicine he had been requested to give her, he grew furious and took her by the hair, choked her, and forced her to take it, and another dose of like size that had not been prescribed; that he questioned her fidelity because he saw a sailor going to the house in his absence — the sailor proved to be her brother, just returning from the service — and furiously upbraided her. She further testified that she had frequently been compelled to leave home because of his cruel treatment, and in many instances he persuaded her to return, promising to reform. That he threatened her life, and because of this mistreatment, and others she detailed, and because of fear for her life she was compelled to seek final refuge in the home of her parents. The incidents, she testified, ran through the whole twenty years of their married life.

The defendant denied all the charges except one. He admitted slapping her during the first year of the marriage, but testified that she had first assaulted him with a fire poker. His testimony represented his wife as morose, moody, capricious, and wanting to engage in fanciful enterprises beyond their means, and attributed her dissatisfaction to that state of mind. He testified that he had always contributed adequately to her support, or attempted to do so.

...

Because of the errors noted the plaintiff is entitled to a trial de novo, and it is so ordered.

McGEHEE v. McGEHEE

Supreme Court of Mississippi

227 Miss.170, 85 So.2d 799 (1956)

ARRINGTON, J.

Mrs. Tina Van Zandt, McGehee, complainant in the court below and appellant here, filed bill of complaint against Leo R. McGehee, her husband, defendant below and appellee here, for appointment of a receiver and for dissolution of partnership business. The defendant answered the bill and denied the existence of a partnership and other material allegations of the bill. From a decree dismissing the bill, the complainant appeals.

The evidence shows that the appellant and the appellee were married in March 1937; that in December 1937 they entered into business for themselves; that they borrowed $300 from the bank, with both of them signing the note and appellant's sister endorsed it. With the $300 they bought a truck and rented an office and went into the moving business. The appellant ran the office and the appellee drove the truck. Both of them devoted practically all of their time to the business; neither drew a salary for their work, but funds for living expenses were taken from the business and all profits were put back into the business; that as a result thereof, from this beginning, the business has grown to the extent that it is now worth in excess of $200,000. The various businesses are Leo Van Lines, Mississippi Moving and Storage Company, and Mississippi Storage Company, all located in Jackson, Mississippi, with branch offices at Gulfport and Greenville, Mississippi and Shreveport, Louisiana.

The evidence further shows that all bank accounts have been joint, and that all notes for money borrowed for operating expenses of the business were signed by both parties. There was no oral or written agreement evidencing the partnership at the beginning of their operations, however, according to testimony of their counsel, who had represented them since 1946, the appellant and appellee came to see him with reference to the appellee transferring one-half interest of certain real estate which was used in the business to the appellant. After this conference, the attorney wrote to the Collector of Internal Revenue requesting an opinion as to whether a gift tax would be due if the transfer were made. This letter is as follows:

June 24, 1952

Collector of Internal Revenue
Jackson, Mississippi
Attention: Mr. W. C. Eastland

Dear Sir:

Pursuant to our telephone conversation, I am taking this opportunity of writing and explaining the situation concerning two of my clients. It is the express purpose of this letter to give you these facts and to request from your department a ruling, based on the facts set out in this letter.

The clients, which we will call Mr. A and Mrs. A, were married on March 24, 1937. Three months prior to that time they jointly purchased an automobile for approximately $300.00, he paying one-half and she paying one-half. At that time they were both employed. In December of 1937, they decided to go into business for themselves, and they borrowed $300.00 from the Jackson-State National Bank of Jackson, Mississippi. Both Mr. and Mrs. A signed the note and Mrs. A's sister endorsed the note. With this $300.00 they bought a truck. They then rented a van and rented office space in Jackson and started in business. There was no written lease covering the space rented for the office; however, the rent was only $6.00 per month. Mrs. A was in complete charge of the office and Mr. A drove the truck. In the latter part of 1938, a certificate of public convenience and necessity was issued to Mr. A; however, Mrs. A was still in complete charge of running the office, Mr. A being in charge of the outside operation.

In 1944, commercial property in the city was purchased by Mr. and Mrs. A, with the title being taken in Mr. A. The down payment on this property was $1,500.00, which was paid out of the funds which they had earned in their business, and the balance of the purchase price was paid in regular monthly installments out of the income from the business.

Since that time, additional real property has been purchased and additional certificates have been obtained, all being taken in the name of Mr. A. All of the real property has been paid for out of the funds earned in the business, as well as all payments on certificates and expenses involved in obtaining certificates.

Prior to 1945, the income tax returns were prepared and filed by Mr. A himself and he is not sure whether or not separate returns were filed for himself and his wife. In 1945, a C.P.A. was employed to file his return, and the C.P.A. promptly divided the business operations into two separate businesses and filed one return in Mrs. A's name and the other return in Mr. A.'s name. This procedure was followed until the joint property law was made available to people in Mississippi, and since that time a joint return has been filed.

Mrs. A is generally recognized as the office manager for the business. She has at all times been in complete charge of the office and Mr. A has

> been in charge of the outside operation. Mrs. A spends the full working day every day in or about the office, and, as previously stated, she is recognized by the general public as being in complete charge of the office, having under her supervision and control some 25 or 30 employees at the present time.
>
> In building up this business all bank accounts have always been joint, Mr. and Mrs. A, and all loans have been signed by both Mr. and Mrs. A. No salary has been drawn by either Mr. or Mrs. A from the business, such funds as are needed for their expenses being drawn by either of them.
>
> *It seems to us that Mr. and Mrs. A have been partners in this business from the very beginning. Certainly, there could be no facts in any other partnership* that are not present here except that formal partnership papers have not been drawn by them. Mrs. A takes the position that all of the real property and other assets of the business were put in her husband's name simply for convenience, and that she is the true equitable owner of one-half of all the assets. Mr. A agrees with this and is entirely agreeable to putting the record title to one-half of these assets in Mrs. A's name. Upon advice of the writer, this has not actually been done, since there is some question concerning a gift in the event such an instrument is executed. It is submitted that the execution of such an instrument would constitute solely placing the record title in Mrs. A's name, whereas she has at all times owned the equitable title. (Emphasis ours.)
>
> We would appreciate it if your department would give us a ruling as to the ownership of this property as it now stands, under the facts as above outlined. The parties are desirous of putting the record title exactly where the equitable title now stands and has always stood, and it is our opinion that no gift tax would be due and no gift tax return should be filed.

The Collector of Internal Revenue advised the attorney that no gift tax would be due, and deeds were executed accordingly and delivered to the appellant. Although the evidence in this case is voluminous, we are of the opinion, after a careful examination of the record, that this letter by their attorney, who had represented them since 1946 and was thoroughly familiar with the business, gives a fair and accurate history of the business.

Later, according to the record, the appellant and appellee did not agree as to the operation of the business and dissension and confusion prevailed, and in June 1954 the appellant and appellee went to their attorney's office to discuss their problem. According to the testimony of counsel, the appellant wanted the appellee to "put in her name a one-half interest in all of their assets and upon his failure to do so by 12 noon, then she would immediately have a bolt and lock put on the business and close it up and file suit for divorce on Monday morning." The appellee was not agreeable to this and the matter was discussed between them and their attorney for several hours without reaching an agreement; that later, the attorney's partner was called in to relieve him, and the discussion was continued with the appellee. A tentative agreement was reached between the appellant and appellee, and this agreement was later drafted and executed by the parties on June 8, 1954, as follows:

Partnership Agreement

This Agreement In Writing, this day entered into by and between Leo R. McGehee and Tina Van Zandt McGehee, husband and wife,

Witnesseth:

Whereas, the parties have engaged in the operation of the moving and storage and furniture businesses hereinafter mentioned, for a long period of years; and

Whereas, certain of said businesses have been conducted in the name of Leo R. McGehee, individually, and certain in the name of Tina Van Zandt McGehee, individually; and

Whereas, certain of the properties used in the operation of said businesses are not now owned by the parties hereto on an equal basis; and

Whereas, it is the desire and intention of the parties to recognize the equal ownership of all of said properties, and the equal responsibility and authority for the management of said businesses; and

Whereas, it is the desire and intention of the parties to enter into this agreement, whereby said equal ownership, responsibility and authority shall be maintained by the parties on a permanent basis;

Now, Therefore, it is mutually understood and agreed between the parties hereto as follows, to-wit:

The parties hereto shall be equal partners in the ownership and operation of the local and long distance household goods moving business conducted under the trade name of Leo Van Lines and Mississippi Moving and Storage Company, and in the local moving and storage business conducted under the name of Mississippi Storage Company, and in the retail furniture business conducted under the name of Mississippi Moving and Storage Company, all of which businesses are now being conducted by the parties in the City of Jackson, Mississippi and elsewhere with general offices located at 410 South Gallatin Street, Jackson, Mississippi.

The assets of the partnership, to be equally owned by the parties, shall include the following:

All operating rights, franchises, permits, and certificates of public convenience and necessity heretofore issued to Leo R. McGehee, d/b/a Leo Van Lines and/or Mississippi Moving and Storage Company by the Mississippi Public Service Commission, the Interstate Commerce Commission, and the regulatory agencies of the other states in which operations have been conducted.

All office equipment, motor vehicles, supplies, and miscellaneous equipment of all kinds used in the operation of said businesses.

All accounts receivable of said businesses and all cash on hand and in banks.

All inventories of furniture and other merchandise on hand at the company offices in Jackson, Mississippi and elsewhere.

All real estate owned by the undersigned, including the buildings and lands located at 410 South Gallatin Street, 140 North Gallatin Street, and 1058 Arbor Vista Boulevard, in the City of Jackson, Mississippi.

It is agreed that appropriate applications will be filed with the Mississippi Public Service Commission, the Interstate Commerce Commission, and other necessary and appropriate regulatory agencies for the transfer of said franchises, certificates and permits, and that this agreement is subject to the approval of said transfer by said agencies.

Appropriate deeds of conveyance shall be executed to effect the equal ownership of said real properties.

The parties shall, from time to time by mutual consent, divide the duties and responsibilities of management of the affairs of said partnership.

The parties shall have an equal interest in the assets of said partnership, and shall share equally in the profits and losses of the businesses now conducted or hereafter to be conducted by said partnership. It is recognized and agreed that this division of ownership and this division of responsibility and authority embodied in this agreement is entered into by the parties for the purpose of insuring the stability of the operation of said businesses and the personal and business affairs of the parties. In order to accomplish this purpose it is understood and agreed that this agreement shall of necessity be permanent, and that it shall not be altered or terminated as long as the undersigned shall remain husband and wife, and that if the parties shall at any time be legally separated or divorced that this agreement shall thereupon be terminated, and the assets of the partnership divided equally between the parties, and that such division shall constitute a final and complete division of the property and property rights of the undersigned, and shall be in lieu of all other claims between the parties for separate maintenance, alimony or otherwise.

In the event of dissolution of said partnership during the lifetime of the parties, and one party desires to continue the operation of said businesses, such partner shall have the right to purchase the interest of the retiring partner in the assets of the partnership, and to defer the payment of the purchase price therefor over a period of five years from the date of such dissolution.

Witness Our Signatures, in duplicate, on this the 8 day of June, 1954.

/s/ Leo R. McGehee
/s/ Tina Van Zandt McGehee

(Duly acknowledged by both parties, and filed and recorded in the office of the Chancery Clerk of Hinds County, Mississippi on September 2, 1954.)

A few weeks after this agreement had been executed, the parties were unable to work in the business as they formerly had because of disagreement, and as a result, the appellant left the business and filed the bill now before the Court.

The chancellor held the partnership agreement invalid on three grounds: (1) That there was no consideration; (2) duress of the appellant in threatening to close the business and apply for a receivership and to file suit for divorce; and (3) that certain provisions of the agreement were never carried out. We deal with these questions in the order stated.

Forbearance to sue is a sufficient consideration for a promise, and the forbearance of appellant to sue appellee for her claimed half interest in the businesses was a sufficient consideration to support the partnership contract. We need not consider whether appellant would have prevailed in the suit with which she threatened the appellee. Appellant had reasonable grounds to believe she had a valid claim to one-half the property involved, and if it be conceded that the claim had elements of doubt as to its validity, it is nevertheless sufficient consideration for the contract....

We are of the opinion that appellee failed to prove duress. The substance of the proof on the question of duress was that appellant threatened to file suit against appellee to enforce her alleged rights to one-half of the property.

. . .

Appellee is in no position to complain that the partnership was not carried out by the parties. The franchises standing in the name of the appellee could not be transferred to appellant by her act alone, and appellee did nothing to comply with the terms of the contract in that regard. The fact that appellant did not convey one-half of the home property to appellee does not invalidate the contract, especially since appellee failed to do that required of him in reference to the franchises which were far more valuable than the home.

Appellee contends that the consideration for the contract was founded on the work and labor of appellant in the businesses, and that Section 454, Code of 1942, providing that husband and wife shall not contract with each other so as to entitle one to claim or receive any compensation from the other for work and labor, renders the contract invalid. We are of the opinion that Section 454 has no application to this case. This court has held that a married woman may lawfully enter into a partnership with her husband. *Jones v. Jones*, 99 Miss. 600, 55 So. 361.

If we should hold that the partnership contract was void either because of failure of consideration or duress, it would necessarily follow that appellee perpetrated a fraud on the United States when he caused his attorneys to urge on the Collector of Internal Revenue Department by the 1952 letter that a partnership then existed in order to save gift taxes. In such a situation, there is a presumption against fraud, bad motives and dishonesty. The partnership agreement expressly recognized prior equal ownership of the property involved, as well as equal responsibility and authority in the operation of the business, and is in full accord with the previous operation of the businesses and not inconsistent therewith.

We hold that the partnership agreement was valid. The case is reversed and remanded for further proceedings not inconsistent herewith.

The attorneys referred to in the foregoing opinion are not the attorneys now representing the parties in this suit.

Reversed and remanded.

STEINHAUER v. STEINHAUER

District Court of Appeal of Florida

252 So.2d 825 (Fla. Dist. Ct. App. 1971)

MAGER, Judge.

This is an appeal by Jerome Steinhauer, appellant-defendant, from a final judgment of divorce entered in favor of Lossie S. Steinhauer, appellee-plaintiff. The final judgment of divorce awarded plaintiff custody of their only child and awarded plaintiff lump sum alimony, property rights and child support. This appeal is concerned with that portion of the trial court's order awarding the entire marital home to the plaintiff "on account of her special equity therein and as for lump sum alimony"; and that portion of the order wherein the trial court specifically reserved jurisdiction for the award of alimony in the future if the circumstances justify such an award.

There is little if any factual dispute in this case; there is, however, an obvious conflict between the respective parties' interpretation of such facts as they relate to the final judgment. Plaintiff and defendant were married for approximately twenty-five years before divorce proceedings were instituted. The plaintiff-wife is 57 years old and the defendant-husband is 49 years old. For the last twenty years of their marriage both parties worked together in a drapery business known as Steinhauer Interiors. The wife entered into the interior design business shortly after the marriage of both parties in 1945. The husband worked with the wife in the interior design business for over twenty years. The parties maintained two checking accounts. One account was designated as "Jerome Steinhauer and Lossie Steinhauer" and the other account was designated as "Steinhauer Interiors." The record reflects that both parties had access to both accounts and that both parties wrote checks against both accounts. The evidence is not clear as to when the "Jerome Steinhauer and Lossie Steinhauer" account was opened; it appears however that the "Steinhauer Interiors" account was opened some time in 1964 or 1965. The record reflects that while both parties worked side by side in the interior design business, each party apparently had separate jobs and customers in their interior design business. The husband's earnings from his customers went into the joint account and the wife's earnings from her customers went into the "Steinhauer Interiors" account. The record reflects that the wife actually ran the business and that the husband worked with her performing such tasks as the measuring and the installing of fabrics, picking up of furniture, delivering of furniture, upholstering of furniture, picking up and delivering of fabrics.

We are given some indication from the husband's uncontroverted testimony as to the purpose of having these separate accounts and as to some of the functions the husband performed in connection with his wife's jobs or customers:

Q. (By Mr. Maloney) All right, sir. The purpose, again, you say was to keep your earnings pretty much in this account Jerome and Lossie Steinhauer, and Lossie Steinhauer's earnings in her account, Steinhauer Interiors; is that correct?

A. What was the purpose of it?

Q. Yes.

A. So that there wouldn't be confusion between her jobs and my jobs.

Q. All right. Well, did you feel that she had any separate funds of her own at all, or did you feel that you had equal right to any proceeds that were put into the Steinhauer Interiors account?

A. Well, I had as much right in the Steinhauer Interiors account as she had because I had done work for her on her jobs. I done all different kinds of work for her on her jobs.

Q. So you felt that that money was —

A. As much mine as it was hers.

Q. Okay.

A. Just like the money in my account was as much mine as it was hers. But she did help me on my jobs, too.

Q. Tell the Court, please, about your participation in your wife's jobs. What did you do?

A. Well, from its inception, if it was a drapery job I sometimes went and picked up fabrics for her, depending on who was making the draperies. I sometimes took the materials to the place to make the draperies. I hung all of them. I hung traverse rods. I picked up furniture, delivered furniture, done the upholstery work, just about everything that I could do to expedite her jobs.

Q. Now, when you did this work did you ever submit a bill to your wife?

A. No, sir.

Q. Were you ever paid for the work you did on your wife's jobs?

A. No, sir. I assumed it was a partnership and that when I worked for her she would work for me, and it would be evenly divided.

Q. Now, will you explain to the Court, please, how one account rather than another account was used for the purpose of paying regular bills?

A. It depended on which one had the most money, as to what bills would be paid.

Q. Does this explain why some bills were paid by you and some were paid by your wife?

A. That's correct.

Q. Out of different accounts?

A. Out of different accounts.

With particular regard to how the business was characterized the uncontroverted testimony of the husband indicated:

Q. (By Mr. Maloney) Now, sir, Steinhauer Interiors, is that a partnership?

A. Well, when a husband and wife are in business from 1947 on up to a few months ago, they both work in the business, there was never any record of anything made as a partnership or a corporation. We just worked with each other, for each other.

Q. Would you call that a partnership?

A. I would say so.

Q. The answer is yes?

A. Yes.

Q. Okay. Now, what was the division, or was there any division as to the profits of the partnership?

A. There was no division.

Q. How about for income tax purposes?

A. We both filed together, jointly.

With respect to the filing of a joint return the partnership return filed for the year 1968 indicated that the husband worked in the business only 20 per cent of the time. The uncontroverted testimony of the husband in explaining why the tax return showed his participation only 20 per cent of the time was:

Q. (By the Court) According to the partnership return, your wife devotes 100 percent of her time to Steinhauer Interiors and you devote 20 percent of your time?

A. I beg your pardon, sir? Who said that?

Q. That is what the tax return says. I want to know what you do with the other 80 percent of your time.

A. There's a misunderstanding then, sir. There's no truth in that at all. Now the tax return may say that that is supposedly 20 percent, but the reason for my putting on the tax return that amount toward her was because of her retirement for social security purposes, so that she would get her social security first, which she does because of her age. But we both devoted full time to the business. There's no such thing as 80/20. It was 50/50, or 100 and 100.

Again, under questioning from the court with respect to the husband's role in the business and the characterization of such business as a partnership, the following uncontroverted testimony of the husband reflects:

Q. (By the Court) Well, you had your jobs and she had her jobs?

A. That's correct.

Q. Under the name Steinhauer Interiors?

A. Yes, sir. It got so that we couldn't work together on the same job, planning it. There were differences of opinion, so we had to separate our customers where she had her customers and I had mine. And then I would go on her installations and pick-ups and deliveries to help her.

So I was devoting a lot of my time to her jobs, and then whatever time I could devote to my job, I would do.

Q. And you lumped these together under the partnership return; is that correct?

A. Yes, sir. It was a partnership. There was no difference of anything at all. This has not come up until I've left the house, that there was any difference at all. There's a witness outside, Mrs. Dilullo. She's a customer. She's an old customer. We've done about three houses for her and I've worked on every one of them, on every one of the jobs, put labor in it. My wife — it's her customer. And my wife planned the job and I done all the installation on the job.

The foregoing testimony demonstrates that both marital partners participated together during their twenty-five year marriage in a joint effort to develop a source of income to sustain the parties and their child during their lifetime together. The trial court, however, found that the wife possessed a special equity in the marital dwelling. This finding appears to have been based upon contributions made by the wife towards the purchase of their current (Tyler Street) home in early 1966. The record reflects that the husband and wife owned together by the entireties a home located at 1810 N.W. 94th Street (1810), and the wife owned, in her separate name, a home located at 1800 N.W. 94th Street (1800). The 1800 dwelling was rented out by the wife and the proceeds were used to pay the mortgage payments on the 1810 dwelling. Although the wife owned the 1800 dwelling, the record indicates that the husband helped in the actual construction of the 1800 dwelling. In 1966 both dwellings were sold. The wife realized a net gain of $8,184.95 from the 1800 dwelling and these proceeds were deposited in the "Steinhauer Interiors" account. The net proceeds of the sale of the 1810 dwelling were $10,178.39, and this was deposited in the "Jerome and Lossie Steinhauer" account. In February 1966 the parties purchased the Tyler Street home for $25,000.00. Approximately $2,500 was the down payment with $4,184.00 paid at the time of closing. Of this total cash payment of $6,684.00, some $4,600.00 came from the "Steinhauer Interiors" account and presumably the remaining $2,000.00 was drawn against the "Jerome and Lossie Steinhauer" account. All checks, however, were signed by the husband. In addition, the husband made a $9,000.00 payment from the "Jerome and Lossie Steinhauer" account in order to reduce the mortgage on the Tyler Street home. At the time of trial the mortgage balance was approximately $6,968.00, leaving an approximate equity of just over $18,000.00. The mortgage payments were made out of the "Steinhauer Interiors" account with the bulk of the checks being signed by the husband during 1966, 1967 and 1968; the wife apparently began signing the checks sometime in 1968 and during 1969. It was during this latter period that the marital difficulties seemingly intensified. The record is not clear as to when the parties actually separated, although there is an indication that the husband ceased doing any more work in the interior design business in January of 1969.

Upon divorce the wife ordinarily becomes the owner of an undivided one-half interest as a tenant in common with the husband in land formerly owned by the spouses as an estate by the entirety.... However, upon proper pleadings and sufficient and proper proof, the husband's interest in the estate by the entireties can be awarded to the wife as lump sum alimony or to the extent that she establishes a special equity therein....

In determining whether or not the award in question should be considered as lump sum alimony and deemed to have been properly made, the divorced wife's ability to be employed and earn a living, the needs of the wife and the children and the husband's capacity to meet such needs are all relevant material factors in determining the wife's need for alimony....

In the case *sub judice*, the court specifically found that the wife's income and assets presently exceeded those of the husband. It would appear therefore that the award of the entire one-half of the husband's interest in the marital domicile to the wife as "lump sum alimony" would not be consistent with the wife's financial situation.

With respect to whether the wife's contributions were of such a nature as to create a special equity in the marital dwelling, it is our opinion that the circumstances do not support such a determination. We are cognizant of the fact that the wife ran the business and perhaps through her ability and ingenuity the business thrived; we are not unmindful of the contributions made from the sale of her separately owned property towards the jointly owned dwelling. But we are equally not unmindful of the fact that the husband worked side by side with his wife over twenty years in building up the business; both parties seemingly considered their business relationship as a 'partnership'; there was a continuous use of the funds of both accounts by the husband with the approval of the wife.

From the foregoing we are not convinced that the wife has established the burden of proof necessary to acquire a legal or equitable interest in the husband's property. *Zuidhof v. Zuidhof*, Fla.App.1971, 242 So.2d 739. As Justice Adkins observed, "The unity concept of marriage has given way to the partner concept whereby a married woman stands as an equal to her husband in the eyes of the law." *Gates v. Foley*, Fla.1971, 247 So.2d 40. In *Gates*, the Supreme Court of Florida determined that based upon recent changes in the legal and societal status of women in our society the wife would now be permitted to recover for the loss of her husband's companionship, affection, and sexual relationship (consortium).

As observed earlier, by operation of law each party is entitled to one-half interest in property held by the entireties, *i.e.*, the marital dwelling, joint bank account, etc. This division is consistent with the partnership concept and gives true meaning to the equality of the status of women. As our Constitution states, "There shall be no distinction between married women and married men in the holding, control, disposition, or encumbering of their property, real or personal." Art. X, Sec. 5, Const. of Fla., F.S.A. In direct contrast to the foregoing is the general proposition that a transfer of property from a husband to a wife (as joint tenants) is presumed to be a gift; whereas, a transfer from a wife to a husband (as joint tenants) of her separate property is not presumed to be a gift, the burden being on the husband to establish that fact. *Olsen v. Olsen*, Fla.App.1967, 195 So.2d 864. This presumption is seemingly premised upon the inequality of the marital partners and the subservient status of the wife. We cannot accept the concept that a wife is anything less than an equal partner with the husband in the marital relationship. Our own Constitution and statutes place the woman on a status equal (not inferior) to the man....

We do nothing but give lip service to the concept of unity and equality of the marital partners when at the outset we balance the scale in favor of one of the partners. *Property or assets held by the entireties should be presumed to have been acquired by the joint efforts of both parties.* The partners are deemed equal and are entitled to equality in treatment; but the facts of each marital situation are not the same and therefore we should seek to formulate a general rule that has as its cornerstone the equality of the parties and a presumption of an equal partnership; any unequal distribution ought to be made dependent upon a preponderance of the special fact circumstances of each case with the burden resting upon the person asserting a disproportionate distribution.

A jointly held domicile therefore ought to be divided equally between each partner with the wife's and husband's financial contributions to the acquisition of such property to be considered as gifts to each other. To establish a special equity, the wife's contributions must be shown to have been "above and beyond the performance of ordinary marital duties." See *Eakin v. Eakin*, Fla.1958, 99 So.2d 854. A financial contribution by the wife should be interpreted as being within the realm of "ordinary marital duties" or a *prima facie* presumption of a gift. Such presumption must be considered to be a reciprocal presumption — each partner should be presumed to have made a gift to the other based upon the marital relationship.

The dissolution of the marital relationship is rarely without difficulty; it invariably has its share of physical, mental, parental and financial implications. We do little to minimize and mitigate these difficulties when we, without regard to the reciprocal relationship, "reward" one marital partner a greater interest in jointly held assets because that marital partner may have been a better bookkeeper and can better account for every dollar expended on behalf of the other partner....

We are most reluctant to disturb a chancellor's determination on questions of alimony or special equity. We are, however, of the opinion that the evidence below does not support the award of the husband's interest in the marital domicile on the basis of a special equity or lump sum alimony. The rationale for the decision which we reach herein is well stated in the *Gates* case:

> The law is not static. It must keep pace with changes in our society, for the doctrine of stare decisis is not an iron mold which can never be changed.

Holmes, in his *The Common Law* (1881), p. 5, recognizes this in the following language:

> The customs, beliefs, or needs of a primitive time establish a rule or a formula. In the course of centuries the customs, belief, or necessity disappear, but the rule remains. The reason which gave rise to the rule has been forgotten, and ingenious minds set themselves to inquire how it is to be accounted for. Some ground of policy is thought of, which seems to explain it and to reconcile it with the present state of things; and then the rule adapts itself to the new reasons which have been found for it, and [enters] on a new career. The old form receives a new content, and in time even the form modifies itself to fit the meaning which it has received.

It may be argued that any change in this rule should come from the Legislature. No recitation of authority is needed to indicate that this Court has not been backward in overturning unsound precedent in the area of tort law. Legislative action could, of course, be taken, but we abdicate our own function, in a field peculiarly nonstatutory, when we refuse to reconsider an old and unsatisfactory court-made rule.

...We therefore reject a rule that would create a presumption of gift for one partner but not for the other in property held by the entireties. The partners are equal — the presumptions are equivalent. This conclusion should not be interpreted as precluding the establishment of a special equity where facts, circumstances and the application of equitable principles so require. In determining whether a special equity exists we hold that each party is entitled to the same presumptions with respect to their contributions to each other; and in particular regard to the facts of this case we find that the wife's contributions were not shown to have been "above and beyond the performance of ordinary marital duties."

It should be pointed out that the wife has retained and still continues to run the drapery business, the husband apparently having made no claim to it.[2] For that reason as well as the husband's current financial capabilities the trial court properly reserved jurisdiction for the award of alimony in the future should the circumstances justify such an award....

Accordingly, the judgment of the trial court is affirmed in part and reversed in part, and the cause is remanded for further proceedings not inconsistent with this opinion. Nothing contained herein shall preclude the trial court from reviewing and revising the awards heretofore made to the wife inasmuch as such awards may have been gauged or influenced by the award of the entire marital dwelling to the wife.

OWENS v. OWENS

Supreme Court of Delaware
38 Del.Ch.220, 149 A.2d 320 (1959)

WOLCOTT, J.

This is an appeal from a judgment of the Chancellor denying at the suit of a wife the eviction of her husband from premises owned by the wife formerly occu-

2. The record indicates that the husband is currently employed as a salesman for another business earning an average gross income of $160.00 per week. Part of this earning is based upon commissions.

pied as the marital domicile of the parties, and ordering the entry of a money judgment upon the husband's counterclaim.

The facts are briefly summarized. In the spring of 1953 the plaintiff, at that time a widow, was the owner of certain real estate in Dewey Beach, Sussex County. At that time she decided to erect on a vacant portion of her real estate a three-unit apartment house. She, at that time, made the acquaintance of the defendant, a general contractor, and entered into a contract with him for such construction. In August of 1953, she borrowed sufficient money secured by a mortgage on her property to pay the cost of construction, and upon completion of the construction in May, 1954 paid the defendant in full.

Meanwhile, the acquaintance between the plaintiff and defendant ripened about the middle of November, 1953 into an engagement to be married. Their marriage finally took place in August, 1954 and they established their marital domicile in one of the apartments owned by the plaintiff.

Commencing in the spring of 1954, prior to the marriage of the parties, the defendant began to improve the plaintiff's property, including an additional piece of real estate purchased by her. Thus, the defendant improved the grade of the premises, and erected a garage building with two apartment units on the second floor. Part of the improvements to the premises were paid for by the proceeds of a loan secured by a mortgage on the plaintiff's real estate. The balance was paid by the defendant. The Chancellor found as a fact that the defendant put into the improvements approximately one-third of his estate, or the sum of approximately $23,000.

The plaintiff and defendant lived together as man and wife in apparent harmony until the fall of 1956, at which time incidents took place as a result of which, on October 15, 1956, the plaintiff left the marital domicile. The defendant remained living in the former marital domicile.

The plaintiff sought to prove that she left her husband because of his physical violence to her and because of her fear of future physical violence. The defendant categorically denied any physical violence. He, in fact, claimed that his wife had left him without lawful cause. The Chancellor found as a fact that the plaintiff had no lawful cause to leave her husband.

After final hearing, the Chancellor held that since the plaintiff had left her husband without cause, she could not evict him from the apartment which had been their marital domicile, but could operate her other rental properties for her own profit, and directed the imposition of a lien on the plaintiff's property in favor of the defendant in the amount of $19,616.32, which amount he held represented the extent of his own assets used to improve the plaintiff's property not intended as a gift from him to her.

From this judgment the plaintiff appeals.

First, the plaintiff argues that the Chancellor's finding, that she left her husband without lawful cause, is erroneous.... Second, the plaintiff argues that the Chancellor's finding that the defendant did not intend to make a gift to her of the amounts of his own assets used to improve her property is erroneous and should be reversed for the reason that, under such circumstances, a husband presumptively intends a gift to his wife, and that this presumption may be rebutted only by clear and convincing proof, which, it is argued, is lacking in the case at bar.

Thirdly, the plaintiff argues that the Chancellor committed error in holding that a wife, leaving her husband in possession of the former marital domicile owned by her, may not thereafter dispossess him unless her leaving was with lawful cause.

The first two matters argued by the plaintiff are fundamentally questions of fact to be resolved by the trier of fact. Ordinarily, on appeal a finding of fact if supported by the evidence will not be overturned by this court. *S & S Builders, Inc. v. Di Mondi*, 11 Terry 223, 126 A.2d 826.

With respect to the Chancellor's finding that the plaintiff left the defendant without lawful cause, the argument is made that since the evidence in support of the defendant's position consisted of his testimony alone, and since the plaintiff's witnesses — who, incidentally, were connected by relationship or marriage — testified to the contrary, this Court should make its own finding of fact to the effect that the leaving was lawful. We disagree. It seems clear to us from the record that the issue of fact of necessity had to be resolved by considerations of credibility. The Chancellor heard the testimony from the stand and, it is obvious, accepted the defendant's version of the circumstances as the more credible. He apparently believed the defendant and did not believe the plaintiff. We accept his finding.

With respect to the Chancellor's finding that the defendant had sufficiently rebutted the presumption of gift arising from the improvement of his wife's property, we think the same observation is applicable. The Chancellor heard the witnesses and, under the circumstances, we think his finding must be accepted.

With respect to the third question, a different situation presents itself. It is fundamentally a question of law. The question for our decision is the right of a wife, who owns in her sole right the property in which the marital domicile had been established, and who, without lawful cause, leaves her husband, to sue to repossess her property and to evict her husband from the former marital domicile.

Initially, we observe that under the law of this state a wife may not sue her husband in the Superior Court for any purpose, *Plotkin v. Plotkin*, 2 W.W.Harr. 455, 125 A. 455, although it is well established that a wife, because of her inability to sue her husband at law, may bring suit in equity against him for the enforcement of certain rights, *e.g.* the specific performance of a separation agreement, *Peters v. Peters*, 20 Del.Ch. 28, 169 A. 298, and for separate maintenance, *DuPont v. DuPont*, 32 Del.Ch. 413, 85 A.2d 724. The Chancellor's holding denies to a deserting wife the aid of the processes of equity to recover her sole property in his possession if that property had formerly been the marital domicile.

There is no reported decision in Delaware specifically governing the case at bar. It is a case of first instance. The courts of our sister states which have had this problem before them have divided upon it....

It is sufficient to state that one of the two lines of decision takes the view that a wife whose sole and separate property is secured to her by statute is entitled to be protected in her property even against the retention of possession by her husband, whom she has deserted, of the former marital domicile owned by her. These courts take the view that if by statute the common law inability of a wife to control her separate property has been removed, the courts are bound to protect her statutory rights irrespective of the effect upon the marital relationship.

Those courts which follow the opposing line of authority do so on the ground that a court should not lend its process in aid of a deserting wife since to do so would be a disruption of the marriage relationship which has always been sought to be preserved by the courts.

We are faced with the necessity of choosing between these two divergent lines of cases. We think our choice must be governed by two statutes enacted by our

General Assembly. The first of these is 13 Del.C. §311, the so-called Married Woman's Property Act. This act provides that the property of a married woman, together with "all the income, rents and profits thereof, shall be deemed to be her sole and separate property." The act further authorizes a married woman to sell or otherwise dispose of her separate property as though she were unmarried, but preserves the husband's common law right of curtesy in her real estate. This latter provision would, of course, be a possible deterrent to a sale of the property by the wife, but has no bearing at all on her right to possession and to the rents and profits.

It is difficult to see how the act could have conferred much broader powers on a wife in the management of her separate property. It excepts no property of the wife from the embrace of its provisions, but for the proviso continuing the husband's right of curtesy. Therefore, to follow the line of authorities holding that a wife may not evict her deserted husband from her property formerly used as the marital domicile would be to write into our act a judicially created exception to its terms. If we write the exception into the act, the anomalous situation would result that a deserting wife may evict her husband from only that part of her separate property which had not been used as the joint residence of the parties, despite the clear language of the act which in terms applies to all her property. This, it seems, would be to penalize a generous wife who has relieved her husband of his legal duty to provide a home.

Furthermore, the wisdom of engrafting such an exception on the Married Woman's Separate Property Law is doubtful. Since the reason given for the exception is the desire of courts to preserve the marital status, it should follow that the enforcement of the exception would restore the status and effect a reconciliation. It would hardly seem, however, even if the economic coercion of an inability to obtain possession of her own property led to the errant wife's return to cohabitation, that her return would in fact be a reconciliation based upon love and affection and thus a real preservation of the marital relationship. The preservation would be forced at best.

Furthermore, it is now apparently the policy of the State of Delaware not to compel the continuance of a marital relationship between unwilling parties, even though the conduct of neither the husband nor wife has been such as heretofore would have justified the entry of a divorce decree. In 1957 the General Assembly amended 13 Del.C. §1522 by the addition of a further ground for divorce consisting of living separate and apart for three consecutive years without any reasonable expectation of reconciliation. The referred-to addition to the grounds for divorce, obviously, makes divorce upon such ground available to either husband or wife at their sole option and without the fact of the other party to the marriage having given cause for the separation.

Under these circumstances, therefore, and because of our reluctance to write into an otherwise clear statute an exception to its provisions by judicial fiat, we hold in accordance with the line of authorities of other states — which is certainly the numerical majority of such states and is stated by the commentator in 21 A.L.R. 745 to be also the weight of authority — that a wife who leaves her husband without him having given her lawful cause to do so may evict him from possession of all real estate owned by her as her sole property.

One further point remains to be considered and that is, since this plaintiff is a deserting wife at whose door the fault of this controversy may be laid, whether or not the Chancellor, in his discretion, may deny her relief. We think not.... We have held that she has a legal right to possession of her property and, such being the case, the Chancellor has no discretion to deny her enforcement of that legal right.

By reason of the foregoing, we affirm that portion of the judgment of the court below imposing a lien upon the plaintiff's property and we reverse that portion of the judgment which continues the defendant in possession of the wife's premises. A mandate will be issued providing for the above, and with the direction to award such appropriate relief as may be required to put the plaintiff back into possession of her separate property.

COMMENTS

Eggleston, McGehee, Steinhauer, and *Owens* illustrate that ordinary business law practice can require a full mastery of family law. The idea that a business lawyer can avoid divorce litigation is mistaken. Of course, these cases seem to deal primarily with relatively small businesses, but they involve bread-and-butter legal practice in small and medium-sized American towns. And big business and family law matters are also sometimes closely interwoven, as evidenced by the Ford and Rockefeller empires or by the business affairs of the Onassis, Niarchos and Trump families. Marriage breakup in such situations inevitably involves liquidation of business relations. The liquidation of partnership and distribution of assets, in many instances, is not only a functional parallel to dissolution of marriage, but indistinguishable from it.

Chaachou v. Chaachou (p. 6) is an example of a complete merger of business law and family law. It demonstrates that lawyers must acquire the capability of thinking simultaneously on both levels in making their legal analysis. There is some indication that the lawyers in *Eggleston, McGehee,* and *Steinhauer* considered the tax aspects — the possibility of tax savings — in isolation when they should also have considered the impact of partnership concepts on the marriage. At least in *Eggleston,* the legal contract of partnership seemed to have hastened the breakup of the marriage (perhaps socially desirable under the circumstances) by providing to the wife the more protected financial position of business partner. Ironically, it is likely that the lawyers who handled the tax matters in *Eggleston* and *McGehee* felt themselves to be primarily representing the husbands and would not have intended to put the wives into a better financial condition at divorce. At the time of the transactions in *Eggleston,* a widow would have to pay inheritance taxes that would not be charged to a surviving business partner. Subsequently, inheritance tax law has been changed to exempt surviving spouses, and thus husbands no longer have the same tax incentives Mr. Eggleston had to make his wife into a business partner.

McGehee and *Owens* foreshadow the possibility of increased litigation between husband and wife during an ongoing marriage. Both cases were litigated in a commercial context, although they were likely preludes to divorce. The appointment of a receiver in an action for dissolution of partnership, and the successful eviction of the husband from property owned by the wife during an existing marriage, suggest the range of possibilities. Actions for accounting are also likely to increase. More often than not, as here, the wife may appear as plaintiff. *Steinhauer* reminds us, however, that the wife may have the dominant economic role in a marriage. In such instances, it is the husband who likely benefits from the conceptions of partnership.

Owens is based on extraordinary facts. The husband began as an independent contractor, doing construction work on income-producing property for his future wife. Marriage may have, in effect, lowered the cost of construction for the wife. For the husband it turned out to be a speculative business investment that did not pay off, although his rights were somewhat protected by the imposition of a lien on his wife's property. A partnership agreement could also have been argued in this case, but is was apparently not thought of or made part of the pleadings.

Any of these cases poses underlying questions as to the nature of the relationship between husband and wife within the business context. That relationship could be master-servant, principal-agent, employer-employee, employer-independent contractor, or partnership. It could also have mixed elements of these relationships. In *Steinhauer* the husband could have been a partner for tax purposes and perhaps also for purposes of external liability, yet in terms of his internal business interaction with his wife have acted merely as an employee. Whether the classification in the construction of the agreement is a matter of fact or of law may vary from jurisdiction to jurisdiction; it also depends on the nature of the proceedings. In divorce litigation, judges often act as chancellors in equity and decide both the facts and the law; thus, unless clearly unreasonable, their findings may be difficult to reverse on appeal

These cases show the tenacity of concepts of law that originated in bygone days. The presumption of gift in marriage was mentioned in *Steinhauer* and *Owens.* While modern notions of equality in marriage will require courts to treat identically transfers from husbands to wives and from wives to husbands, it is less obvious exactly what that treatment should be. Courts may choose either to abandon the presumption that a husband intends a transfer to his wife to be a gift or to extend the gift presumption to cover transfers from a wife to her husband.

The *Owens* case also talked about the husband's legal duty to provide a home for his wife. Notice that the court used this legal point in a reverse fashion: Since the wife had no legal duty to provide a home for her husband, she could evict him from property she owns. It seems clear that the traditional duties of support have to be revised under a partnership concept of marriage. The duties to support might become mutual or be supplanted by mutual rights in marital property. Once again, courts could end formal discrimination by abolishing the husband's obligation to support his wife, but they are much less likely to "even down" than to "even up" — to impose mutual obligations of support.

Although these four cases spanned almost thirty years, in all of them the lower courts took a more traditional view of the relations between husband and wife than the appellate courts. In *Eggleston, McGehee,* and *Owens,* this resulted in lower court decisions favoring the husband, which had to be reversed on appeal. Since fewer than one percent of family law cases are appealed, actual court practice may in fact be considerably more conservative than appellate cases indicate. In other words, the law generally moves faster in the appellate courts than on the trial court level in family law matters. The legal practitioner must continue to be familiar with conceptions that may have been changed in the appellate courts and by the legislature.

Antenuptial Agreements: Safeguard to Deliberation, Recognition of Party Autonomy, or Inappropriate Intrusion into Marital Ethics?

Ante-Nuptial Agreement From Transcript in the Case of Ball v. Ball*

THIS AGREEMENT, Made and entered into in duplicate this 15th day of June, A.D. 1933, by and between RUTH L. PRICE, now living in the City of Washington, D. C., and EDWARD BALL, of Duval County, State of Florida,

WITNESSETH:

That Whereas, a marriage is contemplated by and between the parties hereto; and, whereas, said parties propose to enter into and solemnize such marriage at an early date; and, whereas, the parties hereto know that marriage is a most serious and solemn relationship, and is not to be entered into lightly;

And, Whereas, many marriages are wrecked by constant bickering and dissension over various matters, oftentimes trifling and insignificant, we herewith make and declare, for our future guidance, a set of rules, by which we will and shall be governed during our married life, to wit:

First: It is agreed by and between the parties hereto to be faithful and loyal, each to the other, in thought, speech and action, at all times and under all circumstances.

Second: It is agreed by and between the parties hereto that each will maintain and exhibit toward the other a courteous and considerate attitude in all relationships and under all circumstances.

Third: It is agreed by and between the parties hereto that if for any reason either of the parties hereto should find a person that the other party is acquainted with to be objectionable, then, and in that event, the other party hereto shall not cultivate or retain an acquaintance or friendship with such person, nor shall either party show that person any favorable attention;

(a) Neither of the parties hereto shall cultivate or retain a friendship with any person who, after a short period of time, shall not prove to be mutually agreeable and satisfactory to both parties.

(b) Neither of the parties hereto shall at any time develop or cultivate a close friendship with a person of the opposite sex.

*From the case *Ball v. Ball,* 160 Fla. 601, 36 So.2d 172 (1948), found in J. Carson, A PRACTICAL TREATISE ON THE LAW OF THE FAMILY, MARRIAGE AND DIVORCE IN FLORIDA 100–104 (1950).

Fourth: It is agreed by and between the parties hereto that no kins person of either of the parties hereto shall be entertained or remain as a guest in the home of the parties hereto for a period longer than one week, unless both parties hereto are mutually agreeable to the prolongation of such visit or entertainment.

(a) No other guest shall be entertained for any period of time, except upon the mutual invitation willingly and freely extended by both parties hereto.

Fifth: It is agreed by and between the parties hereto that when both of the parties hereto enjoy good health, we shall set aside three nights a week to entertain our friends and acquaintances, or to call on our friends and acquaintances, or to seek such other recreation as may be desirable. On the other four nights of each week we shall remain quietly at home, seeking such recreation and genuine happiness as is only to be found outside of the frivolities and ostentations of our present day social life.

Sixth: It is agreed by and between the parties hereto that the property owned by the respective parties to this Agreement at the time of their marriage shall continue and remain their several separate, individual and respective properties, and each party hereto shall be at liberty to make such sale, transfer or other disposition of such party's separate and individual property as that party may desire, without objection or interference from the other party.

(a) That the earnings, increase and/or profits from such respective, individual and separate properties of the parties hereto shall become and remain a part of such separate, individual property.

(b) That the income and earnings (except that from the separate, individual properties heretofore mentioned) of the parties hereto after their marriage shall become and remain community property and that each party hereto shall at all times have an equal right and ownership in this property, except as in hereinafter in Section Seven (7) provided.

(c) Other than incidental and current household expenses, neither of the parties hereto shall disburse, invest, loan, or make any other disposition of the community property until the same shall have been fully discussed and mutually agreed to by and between the parties hereto.

Seventh: It is agreed by and between the parties hereto that in the event either party hereto violates this Agreement to the extent that such party hereto shall become involved in an affair with a person of the opposite sex, that such offending party, shall thereby immediately forfeit to the other party hereto all interest and rights of every kind and nature in the community property and shall thereupon forthwith convey and deliver the same to the other party, and that involvement in such an affair shall automatically terminate this Agreement, other than the provisions of this Section, which shall remain in full force and effect;

(a) Conclusive proof of the involvement in such an affair shall be cause for an immediate separation of the parties hereto, and, in the event there is such an offending party, such offending party shall have no claim against the other party hereto of any kind or nature whatsoever.

Eighth: It is agreed by and between the parties hereto that each of them shall take a proper pride in their personal appearance and that each of the parties hereto shall at all times be neat and orderly, both in their personal attire and personal habits.

Ninth: It is agreed by and between the parties hereto that each will welcome from the other a suggestion or constructive criticism looking towards the improvement of the happy and cordial relations of the parties hereto.

(a) Such suggestions or constructive criticisms are to be made only when there is no third person present, and such suggestions and criticisms shall not be made with a frequency to constitute fault-finding or nagging, as these two latter qualities are at all times to be most studiously avoided.

Tenth: It is agreed by and between the parties hereto that each shall make a confidant of the other and that neither party hereto shall have any other confidant, and that on all occasions and under all circumstances each party hereto shall reveal in the frankest and fullest detail any and all matters affecting either of the parties hereto.

Eleventh: It is agreed by and between the parties hereto that neither of the parties hereto shall ever speak of the other party hereto to a third person except in such a way as will reflect credit on the party so spoken of.

(a) Neither of the parties hereto shall under any circumstances discuss with a third person anything relating to the purely personal relations of the parties hereto.

Twelfth: It is agreed by and between the parties hereto that in the event the parties hereto have any child or children, that when one of the parties hereto shall have reprimanded, admonished or punished such child or children that even though the other party hereto may not have felt that such reprimand, admonishment or punishment was justified, no objection shall be raised to such reprimand, admonishment or punishment in the presence of the child or children, as the parties hereto realize that discipline is necessary and must be mutually enforced for the welfare and successful training and raising of a child or children.

Thirteenth: It is mutually agreed by and between the parties hereto that in the event the parties hereto have a child or children, that such child or children shall have the benefit of a public school education up to and including the high school and that thereafter the parties hereto shall mutually decide whether it is desirable for such child or children to have any additional educational facilities.

Fourteenth: It is agreed by and between the parties hereto that additional rules or regulations, properly executed and attested, may be added from time to time, if the parties hereto shall mutually decide that such additional rules or regulations are desirable.

Fifteenth: It is agreed by and between the parties hereto that neither party will indulge in or take up any form of recreation or sport unless both parties hereto shall simultaneously take up such form of recreation or sport, except such as may be engaged in within the home of the parties hereto.

Sixteenth: It is agreed by and between the parties hereto that a vacation or pleasure trip will be taken only when it is possible and convenient for both parties to take such vacation or pleasure trip.

Seventeenth: It is agreed by and between the parties hereto that when either of the parties are preparing to leave their place of abode or home, that such party, prior to leaving, will advise the other party where he or she proposes to go and the length of time expected to be away from the place of abode or home, so that the other party will not be caused any uneasiness or worry by the absence of such party.

Eighteenth: It is agreed by and between the parties hereto that the violation of any one of the hereinbefore mentioned rules (except Rule No. Seven, for violation of which rule penalty is hereinbefore specifically provided and set forth in said Rule No. Seven) shall cause the party violating such rule or rules to forfeit to the other party an amount which shall equal one percent (1%) of such party's portion of the monthly community earnings or income for each such violation of each rule or rules so violated in any one month, and it is further agreed by and between the parties hereto that the habitual and continued violation of any of the rules herein set forth (except Rule No. Seven, for violation of which rule penalty is hereinbefore specifically provided and set forth in said Rule No. Seven) shall be cause for a separation of the parties hereto and that in such an event the parties hereto shall equally divide and apportion between themselves any and all community property and thereafter each shall go their separate and individual way, without claims of any kind or nature whatsoever against each other.

Nineteenth: The parties hereto hereby covenant and agree, each with the other, to fully and faithfully keep, perform and abide by all rules, matters and things hereinbefore agreed to and set forth; and do hereby further covenant and agree to devote themselves to the purpose of promoting a successful marriage, with harmony, contentment and happiness as the sole objective.

IN WITNESS WHEREOF, the parties hereto have hereunto set their hands and seals the day and year first hereinbefore written.

Signed: RUTH L. PRICE (SEAL)
Signed: EDWARD BALL (SEAL)

BALL v. BALL

Supreme Court of Florida
160 Fla. 601, 36 So.2d 172 (1948)

CHAPMAN, J.

The record in this case discloses that Edward Ball and Ruth Latham were married in Washington, D.C., on June 17, 1933, and shortly thereafter established a home on the St. Johns River on the outskirts of the City of Jacksonville, where they lived together as husband and wife until the month of January, 1943. During the month of May, 1943, Mrs. Ball left the home and instituted a suit for divorce in the Circuit Court of Duval County, Florida, on the ground of mental cruelty and in her bill of complaint prayed for a divorce and other relief.

On December 6, 1943, the defendant and cross-plaintiff, Edward Ball, filed an answer to the bill of complaint and a counterclaim in which he prayed for affirmative relief. On May 30, 1944, the court below, on motion of counsel for Mrs. Ball, entered an order dismissing her bill of complaint with prejudice to her right to again maintain a suit for divorce upon the facts alleged in the bill of complaint. In the same order the defendant, Edward Ball, was permitted to prosecute his counterclaim seeking or praying for an annulment of the marriage contract and antenuptial contract of the parties entered into shortly prior to their marriage....

On February 1, 1946, by leave of the Court, the cross-plaintiff filed an amended counterclaim and, in part, alleged that the cross-defendant and the cross-plaintiff in early 1933 became engaged to marry and frequently exchanged ideas as to the responsibilities and obligations of marriage and the rearing and education of children which might be born to them as a result of their contemplated marriage, and their views on this point were set out in Sections Twelve and Thirteen of their antenuptial agreement signed by them on June 15, 1933, and are viz.:

> **Twelfth:** It is agreed by and between the parties hereto that in the event the parties hereto have any child or children, that when one of the parties hereto shall have reprimanded, admonished or punished such child or children that even though the other party hereto may not have felt that such reprimand, admonishment or punishment was justified, no objection shall be raised to such reprimand, admonishment or punishment in the presence of the child or children; as the parties hereto realize that discipline is necessary and must be mutually enforced for the welfare and successful training and raising of child or children.
>
> **Thirteenth:** It is mutually agreed by and between the parties hereto that in the event the parties hereto have a child or children that such child or children shall have the benefit of a public school education up to and including the high school and that thereafter the parties hereto shall mutually decide whether it is desirable for such a child or children to have any additional educational facilities.

No child was born to the marriage.

The amended counterclaim alleges that the antenuptial contract and the marriage between the parties are invalid and should be annulled because of fraud practiced on the cross-plaintiff by the cross-defendant. Some weeks prior to June 19, 1928, the cross-defendant consulted Dr. George B. Norberg, of Kansas City, Missouri, and was advised to undergo a surgical operation, which was performed at the Trinity Lutheran Hospital on June 19, 1928, by Dr. Norberg. The cross-defendant's right ovary and the right Fallopian tube were removed. The left ovary was not removed but cysts found thereon were punctured. The left Fallopian tube was either removed or some effort or steps taken by the surgeon to make the same patent. The cross-defendant was sterile on June 17, 1933, and for some time prior thereto, and cross-defendant knew it or had good reason to believe that she was sterile.

The amended counterclaim further alleged that it was the duty of the cross-defendant, before the marriage ceremony was performed, to make known to the cross-plaintiff the fact that in the year 1928 she had a surgical operation involving her genital organs. It was her lawful duty to give to the cross-plaintiff all the information in connection with such matters, things and conditions as were known to her and also all of the knowledge and information that she could have obtained by the exercise of ordinary diligence. The defendant failed and neglected to give the plaintiff any information whatever regarding the surgical operation and the cross-plaintiff did not know that the cross-defendant had ever had an operation involving her genital organs or that her genital organs had been diseased. He did not know prior to marriage or prior to the filing of her suit on the 24th of May, 1943, of the diseased condition of her genital organs and he learned for the first time of the surgical operation and the diseased genital organs after she had instituted suit against him for divorce.

The amended counterclaim also alleges that the cross-plaintiff performed his full duties as the husband of the cross-defendant, administered to her needs and wants in sickness and in health and transferred to her stocks and bonds and caused the title to described interests in real estate to be placed in her name. A bank account in the joint names of the parties was opened and the husband deposited therein income and earnings as provided for by the terms and provisions of the antenuptial contract and that the cross-defendant now holds this property, because of her fraud and deception, in trust for the cross-plaintiff as his trustee.

The counterclaim prays for a decree declaring the antenuptial contract and the marriage contract void ab initio and that all property transferred by the cross-plaintiff to the cross-defendant in contemplation of marriage be transferred or conveyed to him.

The cross-defendant, Ruth Latham Ball, in answering the amended counterclaim, admitted her marriage to Edward Ball; that she had been previously married at the age of 24 and lived with her former husband about seven years and she had no children; she married the cross-plaintiff in good faith at the age of 33 and he was 45, and prior to the marriage ceremony she signed the antenuptial agreement referred to; and she lived with the cross-plaintiff as his wife for approximately ten years, and no children were born to the marriage.

The cross-defendant in her answer admitted that prior to June 19, 1928, she consulted Dr. Norberg, a surgeon at Kansas City, Missouri, and, after an examination, he learned that she had a cystic ovary and a diseased appendix and advised her to undergo a surgical operation. For a short period of time prior to the operation until several hours afterward she was unconscious from the effect of an anaesthetic and of her own knowledge does not know and has never known whether her right ovary was cystic and greatly enlarged or whether her right Fallopian tube adhered around the cyst and stretched from its normal length of 2½ or 3 inches to about 8 inches, or whether her left ovary was cystic and degenerated or whether her left Fallopian tube was diseased and the fimbriated end closed as alleged; she was advised by Dr. Norberg, shortly after the operation, that he had removed her appendix and one ovary. She had no further knowledge or information about the operation than as conveyed to her supra by Dr. Norberg, excepting the information appearing in a pleading to the contrary filed December 6, 1943.

Since the filing of the original counterclaim on December 6, 1943, by investigation and inquiry, she learned and believes that in said operation her appendix, right ovary and right Fallopian tube were removed and her left ovary was treated but not removed, and also that her left Fallopian tube was treated but not removed. She denied that on June 17, 1933, at the time of her marriage to the cross-plaintiff she was sterile. She denied that on said date, or any time prior thereto, she knew or had good reason to believe that she was sterile, but, on the contrary, she alleged that she was not sterile.

Answering further she admitted the operation was performed by Dr. Norberg at the Trinity Lutheran Hospital and a record of the operation was kept by the hospital, but she failed or omitted to inspect the hospital record as kept during her operation. She inquired of Dr. Norberg, after the operation and prior to her discharge on July 3, 1928, whether she could have a child and that he told her he saw no reason why she could not have a child and that he thought the best thing she could do would be to go home and have a baby. She alleged that all that was known to her of said operation at the time of the marriage was the removal of her appendix and one ovary.

The answer of the cross-defendant admits that she did not inform cross-plaintiff that one of her ovaries had been removed in the surgical operation but prior to marriage she did inform him that she had previously had a major operation and after marriage he knew or should have known that a major operation involved her genital organs. That the cross-plaintiff did not know that she was sterile because in fact she was not and is not sterile. After informing the cross-plaintiff of the major operation prior to marriage, his lack of information as to the diseased condition of the genital organs was due solely to his failure to make inquiry after being advised and informed of the major operation by the cross-defendant.

Cross-defendant's further reply to said amended counterclaim says:

> that notwithstanding the averments thereof, which the cross-defendant has hereinbefore and here again denies, said marriage is nevertheless valid by virtue of its ratification by the cross-plaintiff in this: That in the early years of their married life together she repeatedly discussed with the cross-plaintiff her failure to become pregnant and manifested to him her distress that she had not done so; that the cross-plaintiff never at any such discussion, or at any other time, voiced or otherwise disclosed any concern or interest in, or questioned her concerning, her failure to become pregnant; that he never at any time complained to her or expressed any disappointment concerning her failure to become pregnant; that in the early part of the year 1938, of her own volition, she consulted a competent physician as to why she had not become pregnant; that said physician, after a physical examination and an investigation from which he learned that in said surgical operation her right ovary and right Fallopian tube had been removed, and that her left ovary had been treated by puncturing cysts contained therein, and that her left Fallopian tube had been treated by cutting off the thickened sacculated end and bringing the mucosa and serosa together, advised her that a slight operation would probably fix her so she could have children; that she promptly told the cross-plaintiff what the physician had said; that the cross-plaintiff then advised her to wait and never thereafter referred to said conversation or the subject thereof; that notwithstanding said next hereinabove alleged facts and circumstances the cross-plaintiff continued to live and cohabit sexually with her as his wife until on or about January 1, 1943, and thereby the cross-plaintiff ratified said marriage.

The Chancellor appointed Herbert Lamson as Special Master, with instructions to take the testimony of the parties and report the same, with his findings of law and fact. Many hearings were had before the Special Master and several hundred pages of testimony taken. The Special Master reported to the Chancellor that the equities of the cause were with the cross-plaintiff and a decree granting the relief prayed for should be entered. Exceptions were made to the report of the Special Master and, after argument before the Chancellor, the exceptions were sustained and the cross-plaintiff's amended counterclaim by an appropriate order was dismissed, and he appealed.

...

We have on many occasions ruled that to constitute fraud a misrepresentation must be of a specific material fact that it is untrue and known to be so and stated for the purpose of inducing another to act, upon which statement the other relies in acting to his injury.... There is involved in the matter of false representation as a basis for the rescission of contract the element of resulting injury to the person seeking relief which is not supplied by the bare allegation of such injury. There must appear such facts as show a connection between the representation as made and the value as affected by it. This material element of the alleged fraud must not be left to conjecture and averment. *Stokes v. Victory Land Co.*, 99 Fla. 795, 128 So. 408.

On the question of the ratification of fraud by a litigant, Pomeroy's Equity Jurisdiction, 5th Ed., says, if the plaintiff is a party to the fraud to such an extent that he is in pari delicto with the defendant, he cannot obtain relief as equity generally does not relieve a person from the consequences of his own fraud. If he is not in pari delicto, and is comparatively the more innocent of the two, he may obtain relief by doing full equity to those parties, if any, who have sustained an injury by his partial wrong. (Par. 916, pp. 595, 596.)

> Ratification. — While the party entitled to relief may either avoid the transaction or confirm it, he cannot do both; if he adopts a part, he adopts all; he must reject it entirely if he desires to obtain relief. Any material act done by him, with knowledge of the facts constituting the fraud, or under such circumstances that knowledge must be imputed, which assumes that the transaction valid, will be a ratification. (As said by the American Law Institute, "The power of avoidance for fraud or misrepresentation is lost if the injured party after acquiring knowledge of the fraud or misrepresentation manifests to the other party to the transaction an intention to affirm it, or exercises dominion over things restoration of which is a condition of his power of avoidance...." ("The victim of the fraud cannot both affirm and disaffirm, he cannot claim under and against the fraudulent transaction.")
>
> 917. — Promptness — Delay Through Ignorance of the Fraud. — The most important practical consequence of the two principles above mentioned is the requisite of promptness. The injured party must assert his remedial rights with diligence and without delay, upon becoming aware of the fraud. After he has obtained knowledge of the fraud, or has been informed of facts and circumstances from which such knowledge would be imputed to him, a delay in instituting judicial proceedings for relief, although for a less period than that prescribed by the statute of limitations, may be, and generally will be, regarded as an acquiescence, and this may be, and generally will be, a bar to any equitable remedy.
>
> To this rule there is one limitation: it applies only when the fraud is known or ought to have been known. No lapse of time, no delay in bringing a suit,

> however long, will defeat the remedy, provided the injured party was, during all this interval, ignorant of the fraud. The duty to commence proceedings can arise only upon his discovery of the fraud; and the possible effect of his laches will begin to operate only from that time.
>
> ...

A pertinent question presented on this record is, Did the appellee know or have good reason to believe that she was sterile on June 17, 1933? It is not disputed that the appellee advised the appellant that she had, during June, 1928, submitted to a major operation. The parties apparently were content to let the matter rest, as they married and lived together for a period of approximately ten years. The appellant had the opportunity prior to marriage to explore the extent of the major operation by ascertaining whether or not the operation involved her genital organs, the hospital where the operation was performed, the names of the attending nurses, and the name and address of the operating surgeon, and the information was then available as was shown to have been some ten or twelve years later. It is suggested that the law made it the duty of the appellee to voluntarily disclose to her intended husband the several details of the major operation and if it involved her reproduction organs, which operation it is contended rendered the appellee sterile. Her answer in effect was that she told him of the major operation but did not express a view or make a statement about her possible sterility.

Our study of the evidence leads to the conclusion that the appellee at the time of the marriage did not know nor did she have good reasons to believe that she was sterile. The appellant simply failed, which is clearly established when considering all the evidence, to carry the burden of proof as required by law by proving as alleged that the appellee was sterile or had good reasons to believe that she was sterile. We do not overlook the hospital records, the explanation thereof by the appellee, Dr. Mumford's testimony, the opinions of expert witnesses, and the many disputes and conflicts in the testimony. It is the writer's view that knowledge and information of her sterility became positively known to her, if at all, for the first time in January, 1944, as a result of the Rubin's test as given by Dr. Te Linde.

The comments of the Chancellor below on this point are significant and are viz.:

> ...Mrs. Ball's action in having the (Rubin's) test performed is of great significance to the issues in this case, in a way overlooked by counsel, that is, her motive. Regardless of the result of the test, she could have had but one thing in mind when she had it performed; To prove that she possessed the organs necessary to conception. Here is a woman charged with knowledge of her absolute sterility for more than fifteen years and fraudulent concealment thereof for more than ten years. What did she do when that charge was made in defendant's counterclaim? Her lawyer leaves to examine a hospital record on which the charge is based and she sets out on her own to seek irrefutable evidence that the charge is untrue. To me, it is unimportant that the result of the test disappointed her. What is important is that in January, 1944, she still did not know that she was physically incapable of bearing children. Certainly then, she had no such knowledge in June, 1933. An obvious objection can be made: She very guilefully stated that she had had the test made in order to induce the conclusion here reached. The

answer to that proposition lies in (1) her obvious reluctance to testify that the test was made and (2) the fact that neither she nor her counsel up to this time have sought to give her action the significance here attributed to it.

...

Affirmed.

POSNER v. POSNER
Supreme Court of Florida
233 So.2d 381 (Fla. 1970)

ROBERTS, Justice.

This cause is before the court on rehearing granted on petition for certiorari to review the decision of the Third District Court of Appeal in *Posner v. Posner*, Fla.App.1968, 206 So.2d 416. Both parties had appealed to the appellate court for reversal of the decree of the Chancellor entered in a divorce suit — the wife having appealed from those portions of the decree awarding a divorce to the husband and the sum of $600 per month as alimony to the wife pursuant to the terms of an antenuptial agreement between the parties, and the husband having attacked, by cross-appeal, the award of $600 per month support money for each of the two minor children of the parties.

The three appellate judges who considered the appeals agreed upon the affirmance of the decree of divorce to the husband and the award for child support of $1,200 per month. However, each took a different position respecting the antenuptial agreement concerning alimony. Their respective views were (1) that the parties may validly agree upon alimony in an antenuptial agreement but that the trial court is not bound by their agreement; (2) that such an agreement is void as against public policy; and (3) that an antenuptial agreement respecting alimony is entitled to the same consideration and should be just as binding as an antenuptial agreement settling the property rights of the wife in her husband's estate upon his death. They have certified to this court, as one of great public interest, the question of the validity and binding effect of an antenuptial agreement respecting alimony in the event of the divorce or separation of the parties. We have concluded that jurisdiction should be accepted, as authorized by Section 4(2), Article V, Florida Constitution, F.S.A.

At the outset we must recognize that there is a vast difference between a contract made in the market place and one relating to the institution of marriage.

It has long been the rule in a majority of the courts of this country and in this State that contracts intended to facilitate or promote the procurement of a divorce will be declared illegal as contrary to public policy. See *Gallemore v. Gallemore*, 1927, 94 Fla. 516, 114 So. 371; *Allen v. Allen*, 1933, 111 Fla. 733, 150 So. 237. The reason for the rule lies in the nature of the marriage contract and the interest of the State therein.

At common law, the so-called "matrimonial causes", including divorce, were cognizable only in the Ecclesiastical Courts. Because of the Church's view of the sanctity of the nuptial tie, a marriage valid in its inception would not be dissolved by an absolute divorce *a vinculo matrimonii*, even for adultery — although such divorces could be granted by an Act of Parliament. Therefore, the divorce was only from bed and board, with an appropriate allowance for sustenance of the wife out of the husband's estate. See *Ponder v. Graham*, 1851, 4 Fla. 23; Chitty's Blackstone, Vol. I, Ch. XV, 432, 441. We have, of course, changed by statute the common-law rule respecting the indissolubility of a marriage valid in its inception; but the concept of marriage as a social institution that is the foundation of the family and of society remains unchanged. See 38 Am.Jur., Marriage, Sec. 8, p. 185. Since marriage is of vital interest to society and the state, it has frequently been said that in every divorce suit the state is a third party whose interests take precedence over the private interests of the spouses....

The state's interest in the preservation of the marriage is the basis for the rule that a divorce cannot be awarded by consent of the parties, see *Underwood v. Underwood, supra*, 12 Fla. 434, as well as the doctrine of corroboration applicable in divorce suits, see *Pickston v. Dougherty*, Fla.App. 1959, 109 So.2d 577. In the *Underwood* case this court said that it "would be aiming a deadly blow at public morals to decree a dissolution of the marriage contract merely because the parties requested it;" and in the *Pickston* case it was noted that the "prime object of the corroboration doctrine is to prevent collusion and to forestall any attempt which might otherwise be made to destroy the marital relationship falsely."

And it is this same public policy that is the basis for the rule that an antenuptial agreement by which a prospective wife waives or limits her right to alimony or to the property of her husband in the event of a divorce or separation, regardless of who is at fault, has been in some states held to be invalid.... The reason that such an agreement is said to "facilitate or promote the procurement of a divorce" was stated in *Crouch v. Crouch, supra*, as follows:

> Such contract could induce a mercenary husband to inflict on his wife any wrong he might desire with the knowledge his pecuniary liability would be limited. In other words, a husband could through abuse and ill treatment of his wife force her to bring an action for divorce and thereby buy a divorce for a small fee less than he would otherwise have to pay.

Antenuptial or so-called "marriage settlement" contracts by which the parties agree upon and fix the property rights which either spouse will have in the estate of the other upon his or her death have, however, long been recognized as being conducive to marital tranquility and thus in harmony with public policy. See *Del Vecchio v. Del Vecchio*, Fla.1962, 143 So.2d 17, in which we prescribed the rules by which the validity of such antenuptial or postnuptial property settlement agreements should be tested. Such an agreement has been upheld after the death of the spouse even though it contained also a provision settling their property rights in the event of divorce or separation — the court concluding that it could not be said this provision "facilitated or tended to induce a separation or divorce." See *In re Muxlow's Estate*, 1962, 367 Mich. 133, 116 N.W.2d 43.

In this view of an antenuptial agreement that settles the right of the parties in the event of divorce as well as upon death, it is not inconceivable that a dissatisfied wife — secure in the knowledge that the provisions for alimony contained in the antenuptial agreement could not be enforced against her, but that she would be bound by the provisions limiting or waiving her property rights in the estate of her husband — might provoke her husband into divorcing her in order to collect a large alimony check every month, or a lump-sum award (since, in this State, a wife is entitled to alimony, if needed, even though the divorce is awarded to the husband) rather than take her chances on being remembered generously in her husband's will. In this situation, a valid antenuptial agreement limiting property rights upon death would have the same meretricious effect, insofar as the public policy in question is concerned, as would an antenuptial divorce provision in the circumstances hypothesized in *Crouch v. Crouch, supra*, 385 S.W.2d 288.

There can be no doubt that the institution of marriage is the foundation of the familial and social structure of our Nation and, as such, continues to be of vital interest to the State; but we cannot blind ourselves to the fact that the concept of the "sanctity" of a marriage — as being practically indissoluble, once entered into — held by our ancestors only a few generations ago, has been greatly eroded in the last several decades. This court can take judicial notice of the fact that the ratio of marriages to divorces has reached a disturbing rate in many states; and that a new concept of divorce — in which there is no "guilty" party — is being advocated by many groups and has been adopted by the State of California in a recent revision of its divorce laws providing for dissolution of a marriage upon pleading and proof of "irreconcilable differences" between the parties, without assessing the fault for the failure of the marriage against either party.

With divorce such a commonplace fact of life, it is fair to assume that many prospective marriage partners whose property and familial situation is such as to generate a valid antenuptial agreement settling their property rights upon the death of either, might want to consider and discuss also — and agree upon, if possible — the disposition of their property and the alimony rights of the wife in the event their marriage, despite their best efforts, should fail. In *Allen v. Allen, supra*, 150 So. at page 238, this court said that the agreements relating to divorce that are held to be illegal as contrary to public policy are those "withdrawing opposition to the divorce or not to contest it or to conceal the true cause thereof by alleging another" and that they "have no reference to bona fide agreements relating to alimony or the adjustment of property rights between husband and wife, though in contemplation of divorce, if they are not directly conducive to the procurement of it."

We know of no community or society in which the public policy that condemned a husband and wife to a lifetime of misery as an alternative to the opprobrium of divorce still exists. And a tendency to recognize this change in public policy and to give effect to the antenuptial agreements of the parties relating to divorce is clearly discernible. Thus, in *Hudson v. Hudson*, Okl. 1960, 350 P.2d 596, the court simply applied to an antenuptial contract respecting alimony the rule applicable to antenuptial contracts settling property rights upon the death of a spouse and thus tacitly, if not expressly, discarded the contrary-to-public-policy rule.

...

The trend of recent cases involving postnuptial agreements is well summarized by the court in *Schulz v. Fox*, 1959, 136 Mont. 152, 345 P.2d 1045, 1050, as follows:

> The conclusion to be drawn from these cases is that any agreement the purpose of which is to facilitate the granting of a divorce without proper grounds existing, is void, but that where proper grounds do exist, an agreement with respect to a property settlement, when not brought about by duress or coercion, cannot be said to perpetrate a fraud upon the court and will not be held void.... All of the well reasoned cases we have read look to the collusive intent, that is, as to whether the divorce was on proper grounds and as to whether the Court's interest in the continuity of the marriage status or support of spouse and children has been protected.

We have given careful consideration to the question of whether the change in public policy towards divorce requires a change in the rule respecting antenuptial agreements settling alimony and property rights of the parties upon divorce and have concluded that such agreements should no longer be held to be *void ab initio* as "contrary to public policy." If such an agreement is valid when tested by the stringent rules prescribed in *Del Vecchio v. Del Vecchio, supra,* 143 So.2d 17, for ante- and post-nuptial agreements settling the property rights of the spouses in the estate of the other upon death, and if, in addition, it is made to appear that the divorce was prosecuted in good faith, on proper grounds, so that, under the rules applicable to postnuptial alimony and property settlement agreements referred to above, it could not be said to facilitate or promote the procurement of a divorce, then it should be held valid as to conditions existing at the time the agreement was made.

The question of the future binding effect of such antenuptial agreements when presented to the Chancellor for approval and incorporation in the final decree, and the question of the modification thereof upon a showing of a change in circumstances after the entry of the decree of divorce, should be decided under applicable statutory law and judicial decisions relating to postnuptial contracts settling the alimony and/or property rights of the parties.

Section 61.14, Florida Statutes, F.S.A. (Ch. 16780, 1935) among other things, provides:

> (1) When a husband and wife have entered or hereafter enter into an agreement for payments for, or instead of, support, maintenance or alimony, whether in connection with an action for divorce or separate maintenance or with any voluntary property settlement or when a husband is required by court order to make any payments to his wife, and the circumstances of the parties or the financial ability of the husband has changed since the execution of such agreement or the rendition of the order, either party may apply to the circuit court of the circuit in which the parties, or either of them, resided at the date of the execution of the agreement or reside at the date of the application or in which the agreement was executed or in which the order was rendered, for a judgment decreasing or increasing the amount of support, maintenance or alimony, and the court has jurisdiction to make orders as equity requires with due regard to the changed circumstances and the financial ability of the husband, decreasing or increasing or confirming the amount of separate support, maintenance or alimony provided for in the agreement or order.

We must assume that the parties to this litigation knew of the existence of §61.14, Florida Statutes, F.S.A., when they made their agreement in 1960 and that their capacity to make the agreement was and is limited by same.

In summary, we hold that the antenuptial agreement, if entered into under the conditions outlined in *Del Vecchio v. Del Vecchio, supra,* 143 So.2d 17, was a valid and binding agreement between the parties at the time and under the conditions it was made, but subject to be increased or decreased under changed conditions as provided in §61.14, Florida Statutes, F.S.A.

Accordingly, the decision under review is quashed with instructions to the District Court of Appeal, Third District, to vacate that portion of the final decree of the trial court relating to alimony and support money and remand same for further proceedings in the trial court not inconsistent with this opinion.

It is so ordered.

...

SPECTOR, District Court Judge (concurring specially):

...

A review of the cases which have considered the court's statutory power to modify agreed or awarded alimony makes it clear that such power should be exercised only in the face of the strongest and most compelling reasons. See for example *Ohmes v. Ohmes*, 200 So.2d 849 (Fla.App.1967), and cases cited therein. Mere ability on the part of the husband to pay more than the amount awarded or agreed upon is not a proper basis for relief under the subject statute. The husband's ability is to be considered only after the wife has convincingly demonstrated an increased need on her part because of her changed circumstances. Only upon the making of such a showing can the court inquire into his ability to pay more.

The question of alimony in the case sub judice is one which was agreed upon by the parties prior to marriage in an agreement which we here hold to be valid in view of the Del Vecchio case, supra. In arriving at that conclusion, the court is unconcerned with whether the husband was initially able to pay more alimony than the amount agreed to in the antenuptial agreement since the very purpose of such an agreement is to provide a mutually satisfactory substitute for such determination of ability. If events have since transpired which have changed the wife's circumstances so as to warrant invoking the relief provided by Section 61.14, Florida Statutes, F.S.A., the trial court is empowered to grant such relief. We are not unmindful that the nation is experiencing an inflationary trend or condition, and this circumstance too may well be the basis of a finding by the chancellor that circumstances have so changed as to require equitable adjustment under the subject statute....

OSBORNE v. OSBORNE

Supreme Judicial Court of Massachusetts
384 Mass. 591, 428 N.E.2d 810 (1981)

HENNESSEY, Chief Justice.

This is an appeal from Probate Court judgments entered in connection with reciprocal divorce actions by husband and wife, and in connection with an equity action brought by the husband to establish an ownership interest in certain real estate and personal property. The husband also seeks an award of alimony and a division of property pursuant to G.L. c. 208, §34. The alimony and property claims were referred to a master, who, after a hearing, filed a report concluding that the husband should receive neither alimony nor an equitable division of property, and that ownership of the property claimed in the equity complaint belonged solely to the wife. Subsequently, upon motion of the husband, the probate judge submitted the case to a second master for additional subsidiary findings of fact on the needs of the parties and the contribution of the parties as homemakers. After the second master's report was filed, the probate judge struck the second master's report in its entirety, and adopted the first master's report, with the exception of the first master's findings relating to the husband's claim of joint ownership in three parcels of real property, which the court found to be jointly held. Both parties appealed, and we granted the wife's application for direct appellate review. The evidence has been reported.

The husband claims that the probate judge erred in adopting the first master's report because (1) the master failed to apply properly the factors enumerated in G.L. c. 208, §34, relating to the needs of the parties and their station in life, (2) the master's findings relating to the husband's ownership interest in the personal property were against the weight of the evidence, and (3) the master improperly admitted certain prejudicial evidence relating to the postseparation conduct of the husband. On cross-appeal, the wife contends that the probate judge erred in (1) failing to give full effect to an antenuptial contract entered into by the parties in which both parties waived their rights to alimony or to any portion of the other's estate, and (2) striking so much of the first master's report that found the wife to be the sole owner of the three parcels of real estate.

We think that the judge erred in striking the master's findings regarding ownership of the real property. We also conclude that the judge was correct in denying the husband's claim for alimony or for assignment of any portion of his wife's estate; however, we do so on reasoning substantially different from that of the probate judge. It is apparent that neither the first master nor the probate judge was clear on what effect should be given the antenuptial contract. The court found that the husband was not in need of any alimony or assignment of property from the wife's estate, see G.L. c. 208, §34, and thereby avoided the issue whether the antenuptial contract was effective to preclude the husband's claim. We conclude that the antenuptial contract is controlling on all claims of the husband, and, therefore, we do not reach the questions relating to the proper application of G.L. c. 208, §34.

The relevant facts as found by the master are summarized. The parties, Barbara E. Mallinckrodt (Barbara) and David P. Osborne, Jr. (David), met and became engaged while they were both attending medical school. They were married on August 19, 1967. Barbara is an heiress to a large family fortune amounting to nearly $17,000,000, most of which is held in trust. Barbara's income from these funds was approximately $540,000 in 1976. At the time of their engagement, David had no assets of significant value. A few hours before their wedding they executed an antenuptial agreement containing, among others, the following pertinent provisions: "Barbara now has sufficient property to provide adequate means for her own support and David, by reason of his becoming a member of the medical profession, contemplates that he will have adequate earning power for his own support"; "Barbara and David intend this agreement to be in full discharge of all...statutory marital property rights under the statutes or law of any state in which they are now or may hereafter be domiciled"; "neither, upon or subsequent to said marriage, shall acquire any interest, right or claim in or to the property, real and personal, of whatever kind or wherever situated, which the other now owns, possesses or is entitled to, or which the other may own, possess or become entitled to hereafter"; that if their "marriage is legally terminated in accordance with the laws of any jurisdiction in which they or either of them may be domiciled, then...neither shall be entitled to any alimony, support money, costs, attorneys fees, or to any other money by virtue thereof. This provision may be cited by either party by any court of competent jurisdiction, as a waiver and release of any money payment as aforesaid, by one to the other." Attached to the agreement was a schedule accurately showing Barbara's wealth and expectation of inheritance. David read the agreement before he signed it.

Two children were born of the marriage. During the marriage the parties maintained a high standard of living which was financed completely by the income from Barbara's trust accounts. Barbara maintained joint checking accounts upon which either party could draw funds. These accounts were funded with monies from her separate trust accounts. During the marriage the parties acquired furniture and fixtures worth approximately $15,000, jewelry valued at approximately $225,000, art valued at approximately $428,545, a wine collection worth $60,000, and three parcels of real estate valued at $100,000, $60,000, and $40,000. The husband claims an ownership interest in all these items of property. Both parties are now practicing physicians and earn respectable salaries....

VALIDITY OF THE ANTENUPTIAL AGREEMENT

We must first determine the validity of the antenuptial agreement. This court has not previously passed on the validity of an antenuptial agreement that attempts to regulate the rights of the parties in the event of their subsequent divorce. The majority of Massachusetts cases dealing with the validity of antenuptial contracts concern the rights of the parties to modify those property rights that would otherwise arise during the marriage or upon the death of one of the parties. See, *e.g., Rosenberg v. Lipnick*, 377 Mass. 666, 389 N.E.2d 385 (1979)(abandoning the rule of *Wellington v. Rugg*, 243 Mass. 30, 136 N.E. 831 (1922), that common law fraud must be proved in order to invalidate an antenuptial contract); *French v. McAnarney*, 290 Mass. 544, 195 N.E. 714 (1935). These contracts have generally been upheld where there has been no fraudulent conduct on the part of either party, or, more recently, where the parties have acted honestly and fairly and have fully disclosed their assets one to the other. *Rosenberg v. Lipnick, supra.* Antenuptial contracts are recognized by statute and at common law. G. L. c. 209, §§25, 26. *Freeland v. Freeland*, 128 Mass. 509 (1880). *Jenkins v. Holt*, 109 Mass. 261 (1872).

In many jurisdictions it has been held that an antenuptial contract made in contemplation of divorce is void as against public policy. See generally 2 A. Lindey, Separation Agreements and Ante-Nuptial Contracts §90, at 90-33 (1979 & Supp.1981). The reasons most frequently given for invalidating such contracts are (1) they are not compatible with and denigrate the status of marriage, (2) they tend to facilitate divorce by providing inducements to end the marriage, and (3) a contract waiving or minimizing alimony may turn a spouse into a ward of the State....

In *Fox v. Davis*, 113 Mass. 255, 257–258 (1873), this court stated: "The great weight of authority sustains the validity of such contracts, where the separation has taken place, or is to take place immediately. But where the agreement is made in contemplation of future separation, the current of authority is against its validity." Had the issue come before this court several decades ago, the law as stated in *Fox* might well have been held to be controlling. In *French v. McAnarney*, 290 Mass. 544 (1935), it was held that an antenuptial contract wherein the wife agreed not to make any claim for support against the husband was void as against public policy. The facts of the case are distinguishable in that there the parties were not divorced; yet the rationale is applicable. The court in *French* concluded that certain rights and duties incident to the marital relation, including the duty of the husband to support his wife, could not be avoided by an antenuptial contract. Under the case law of the time, this same reasoning would have applied to the rights of the parties upon divorce, since the obligation of the husband to pay alimony was also based on the husband's legal duty to support his wife....

...

In 1970 the Florida Supreme Court took the lead in departing from this approach. In *Posner v. Posner*, 233 So.2d 381 (Fla. 1970), the court held that antenuptial agreements settling alimony and property rights upon divorce are not void *ab initio* as contrary to public policy. The court disagreed with the traditional assumption that such agreements tended to facilitate divorce, suggesting that such contracts are no more likely to encourage divorce than antenuptial contracts in contemplation of death. *Id.* at 383–384. With respect to public policy, the court stated: "We know of no community or society in which the public policy that condemned a husband and wife to a lifetime of misery as an alternative to the opprobrium of divorce still exists. And a tendency to recognize this change in public policy and to give effect to the antenuptial agreements of the parties relating to divorce is clearly discernible." *Id.* at 384. A number of jurisdictions have followed the approach of the *Posner* case....

We conclude that we shall follow the reasoning of the *Posner* case and its progeny and uphold the contract. While the matter is not free from dispute, it is apparent that the significant changes in public policy during the last decade in the area of domestic relations warrant a tolerant approach to the use of antenuptial contracts as vehicles for settling the property rights of the parties in the event of divorce. In recent years the Legislature has abolished the doctrine of recrimination and recognized irretrievable breakdown as a ground for divorce. G.L. c. 208, §1, as appearing in St. 1975, c. 698, §1. The Legislature itself has thus removed significant obstacles to unhappy couples wishing to obtain a divorce. There is no reason not to allow persons about to enter into a marriage the freedom to settle their rights in the event their marriage should prove unsuccessful, and thus remove a potential obstacle to their divorce. We therefore hold that an antenuptial contract settling the alimony or property rights of the parties upon divorce is not *per se* against public policy and may be specifically enforced. We express no opinion on the validity of antenuptial contracts that purport to limit the duty of each spouse to support the other during the marriage.

Legal Limitations upon Antenuptial Agreements

We note that the freedom of the parties to limit or waive their legal rights in the event of a divorce is not appropriately left unrestricted. We therefore set forth some guidelines to be used in determining the extent to which such agreements should be enforced, observing at the same time that none of these comments are relevant or applicable to the decision in the case before us. At the outset, the validity of such agreements should be judged by the same "fair disclosure" rules set forth by this court in *Rosenberg v. Lipnick*, 377 Mass. 666, 389 N.E.2d 385 (1979). Consistent with our holding in *Rosenberg*, those rules should be applied prospectively from the date of our decision in that case. In addition, antenuptial agreements that settle the alimony and property rights of the parties in the event of a divorce should be binding on the courts to the same extent as postnuptial separation agreements. The public policies that underlie the laws regulating separation agreements are equally applicable whether the agreement is entered into before the marriage or after the marriage and in expectation of separation or divorce.

Accordingly, the agreement must be fair and reasonable at the time of entry of the judgment nisi, and it may be modified by the courts in certain situations, for example, where it is determined that one spouse is or will become a public charge, or where a provision affecting the right of custody of a minor child is not in the best interests of the child. See generally *Knox v. Remick*, 371 Mass. 433, 358 N.E.2d 432 (1976). See also Restatement (Second) of Contracts §191 (1981). In any case where the issue is whether payment shall be ordered in excess of that provided in the agreement, the agreement can be raised as a potential bar in the same proceeding. *Knox v. Remick, supra* at 436, 358 N.E.2d 432. Finally, we recognize that certain contracts may so unreasonably encourage divorce as to be unenforceable on grounds of public policy. See Restatement (Second) of Contracts §190 (1981).

...

The judgments of the Probate Court are reversed in so far as they entitle the husband to any ownership interest or share of the three parcels of real property. All other aspects of the judgments are affirmed. The cases are remanded to the Probate Court for entry of judgments in accordance with this opinion.

So ordered.

DAWLEY v. DAWLEY

Supreme Court of California

17 Cal. 3d 342, 551 P.2d 323, 131 Cal. Rptr. 3 (1976)

TOBRINER, Justice

The present case involves the validity of an antenuptial contract in which the parties agreed that their earnings and other property acquired during the marriage would be held as separate property. At the time they entered the agreement, the parties anticipated the early dissolution of their marriage. Relying on *In re Marriage of Higgason* (1973) 10 Cal.3d 476 [110 Cal.Rptr. 897, 516 P.2d 289], which stated in dictum that an antenuptial agreement "must be made in contemplation that the marriage relation will continue until the parties are separated by death" (p. 485), the wife contends that the agreement violates public policy.

We shall point out that the quoted language from *Higgason* does not accurately state California law. Our decisions, including *Higgason* itself, do not hold an agreement void if the parties contemplated dissolution; they hold it void only insofar as the terms of the agreement itself promote the dissolution of the marriage. The test of the validity of the contract thus does not turn on the subjective contemplation of the parties — a standard which would make it impossible to rely on any antenuptial agreement — but upon the objective language of the contract itself. Applying that test, we conclude that the agreement at bar, which provides that the parties will hold their earnings as separate property, does not offend public policy.

We reject also the wife's other contentions. We shall explain that substantial evidence supports the trial court's implied finding that the agreement was not procured by undue influence [and] that the conduct of the parties negates her claim that they rescinded the antenuptial agreement....

1. SUMMARY OF FACTS

Betty Johnson, a tenured elementary school teacher, and James Dawley, an engineer, met in 1961 and maintained an intimate relationship until March of 1964. On May 11, 1964, Betty went to James' residence to pick up her belongings, but following a long and emotional discussion they agreed to resume their relationship. Two weeks later Betty discovered that she was pregnant.

Betty told James that she feared a nonmarital pregnancy would result in her losing her teaching job. An acrimonious exchange ensued, during which Betty claims James refused to help her, and James claims she threatened him with a paternity suit accompanied by publicity intended to imperil James' employment. Finally, both agreed to a temporary marriage as a solution to their dilemma.

James insisted on an antenuptial agreement to protect his property and earnings from Betty's claims; she insisted that he agree to support Carolyn, her daughter from a previous relationship, and herself for the period of her pregnancy and thereafter until she could resume teaching duties. James and Betty agreed to ask Michael diLeonardo, James' attorney, to draft the agreement. Betty reviewed the contract with her attorney, and accepted its provisions. They signed the agreement on June 11, 1964, and married two days later.

The antenuptial agreement, the complete text of which appears in footnote,[1]

---

1. The antenuptial agreement reads as follows:

THIS AGREEMENT is entered into on the 11 day of June, 1964, by and between JAMES R. DAWLEY and BETTY JEAN CALVERT JOHNSON.

This agreement is made with reference to the following facts:

I. JAMES R. DAWLEY and BETTY JEAN CALVERT JOHNSON are contemplating marriage.

II. JAMES R. DAWLEY is the owner of real and personal property set forth and described in Exhibit "A" attached to this agreement and by this reference thereto made a part hereof as though fully set forth.

III. BETTY JEAN CALVERT JOHNSON is the owner of real and personal property set forth and described in Exhibit "B" attached this agreement and by this reference thereto made a part hereof as though fully set forth.

IV. JAMES R. DAWLEY has two children of a former marriage, whose names are: Katherine June Dawley and James R. Dawley.

V. The parties desire to define the respective rights of each in the property of the other after marriage, and the parties desire that all property owned by either of them at the time of the marriage and property purchased by either of them from their own earnings during the marriage, shall be their respective separate property.

VI. (a) BETTY JEAN CALVERT JOHNSON agrees that all property of any nature or in any place, including but not being limited to the earnings and income resulting from his personal services, skill, effort, and work, belonging to JAMES R. DAWLEY at the commencement of the marriage or acquired by or coming to JAMES R. DAWLEY by purchase, gift or inheritance during the marriage, shall be his separate property, and shall be enjoyed by him and shall be subject to his disposition as his separate property in the same manner as though the proposed marriage had never been entered into. BETTY JEAN CALVERT JOHNSON acknowledges that she understands that, except for this agreement, the earnings and income resulting from the personal services, skill, effort, and work of JAMES R. DAWLEY after the marriage would be community property, but that by this agreement such earnings and income are made his separate property.

(b) JAMES R. DAWLEY agrees that all property of any nature or in any place, including but not being limited to the earnings and income resulting from her personal services, skill, effort, and work, belonging to BETTY JEAN CALVERT JOHNSON at the commencement of the marriage or acquired by or coming to BETTY JEAN CALVERT JOHNSON by purchase, gifts or inheritance during the marriage, shall be her separate property and shall be enjoyed by her and shall be subject to her disposition as her separate property in the same manner as though the proposed marriage had never been entered into. JAMES R. DAWLEY acknowledges that he understands that, except for this agreement, the earnings and income resulting from the personal services, skill, effort, and work of BETTY JEAN CALVERT JOHNSON after the marriage would be community property, but that by this agreement such earnings and income are made her separate property.

VII. (a) BETTY JEAN CALVERT JOHNSON hereby relinquishes, disclaims, releases, and forever gives up any and all right, claim, or interest in or to the property of JAMES R. DAWLEY including but without being limited to community property rights, rights as an heir or widow, rights to family allowance, rights in case of death, or right to act as administratrix of the estate of JAMES R. DAWLEY.

(b) JAMES R. DAWLEY hereby relinquishes, disclaims, releases, and forever gives up any and all right, claim, or interest in or to the property of BETTY JEAN CALVERT JOHNSON including but without being limited to community property rights, rights as an heir or widower, rights of family allowance, rights in case of death, or right to act as administrator of the estate of BETTY JEAN CALVERT JOHNSON.

provided in paragraphs V and VI that all property, including earnings, belonging to either spouse at the commencement of marriage or acquired by him through purchase, gift or inheritance during marriage would be owned by that spouse as his separate property. Each spouse disclaimed all rights, including community property rights, in the property of the other spouse. James agreed in paragraph VIII to support Betty and Carolyn "for the minimum period of fourteen calendar months following said marriage, in order that [Betty] may take a leave of absence from the teaching profession for said period"; in paragraph IX he agreed to support any child born to Betty in the next ten months until the child reached majority.[2]

Lisa Dawley, the parties' daughter, was born in January of 1965. The 14-month period mentioned in the agreement expired in September of 1965 when Betty resumed her teaching duties. The parties, however, did not separate at that time, but continued to live together until July of 1972.[3]

In April of 1973, James filed for dissolution of the marriage. The trial court granted the dissolution, and awarded Betty spousal support of $1 per year, custody of Lisa with support of $300 per month, and $1,000 in attorney's fees. Relying on the antenuptial agreement, the court found no community property subject to division in the dissolution action, and awarded James all property purchased with his separate income. Betty appeals from the court's failure to find the existence of and to divide community property.[4]

2. THE ANTENUPTIAL AGREEMENT DOES NOT OFFEND THE POLICY AGAINST CONTRACTS WHICH ENCOURAGE OR PROMOTE THE DISSOLUTION OF A MARRIAGE.

Pursuant to Civil Code sections 5133 through 5137, "[p]arties contemplating marriage may validly contract as to their property rights, both as to property then owned by them and as to property, including earnings, which may be acquired by them after marriage." (*In re Marriage of Higgason, supra,* 10 Cal.3d 476, 486, quoting *Barker v. Barker* (1956) 139 Cal.App.2d 206, 212 [293 P.2d 85].) Betty concedes that the agreement between James and herself conforms to the statutory requirements governing antenuptial agreements.

---

1. *Continued*

VIII. JAMES R. DAWLEY agrees, that at all events, if he and BETTY JEAN CALVERT JOHNSON are married, he will support BETTY JEAN CALVERT JOHNSON and her daughter, Carolyn Kaye, in the same manner to which they are now accustomed, for the minimum period of fourteen calendar months following said marriage, in order that BETTY JEAN CALVERT JOHNSON may take a leave of absence from the teaching profession for said period.

IX. JAMES R. DAWLEY further agrees that in the event that a child or children is or are born to BETTY JEAN CALVERT JOHNSON during the next ten calendar months, he will pay to said BETTY JEAN CALVERT JOHNSON or to a legally appointed guardian or trustee for such child or children, a reasonable amount each month during the minority of said child or children for the support and education thereof. It is understood that except for the fourteen months above described JAMES R. DAWLEY has no legal or financial responsibility for Carolyn Kaye Johnson unless he so chooses.

X. It is expressly agreed by and between the parties hereto that the various provisions contained in this agreement are severable. If any provision of this agreement is held to be invalid or unenforceable all other provisions shall nevertheless continue in full force and effect.

2. diLeonardo testified that he did not recall drafting paragraphs VIII and IX of the agreement. These paragraphs may have been drafted by Betty or her attorney, but the record is not clear on the matter.

3. We discuss the financial transactions of the parties during their marriage in connection with parts 3, 4, and 5 of this opinion.

4. The notice of appeal states that Betty appeals from that portion of the interlocutory judgment adverse to her. Her briefs on appeal, however, only discuss the subject of division of property; we infer that she does not view the court's orders respecting dissolution, child support, or alimony as adverse to her interests.

Betty contends, however, that the agreement is entirely invalid because uncontradicted evidence shows that it was not entered into in contemplation of a marriage to last until death. She relies for this proposition upon a sentence taken from our opinion in *Marriage of Higgason, supra,* in which we stated that an antenuptial agreement "must be made in contemplation that the marriage relation will continue until the parties are separated by death." (10 Cal.3d 476, 485.) We shall explain, however, that the quoted language from *Higgason* does not accurately reflect California law. Enforcement of the state policy to foster and protect marriage (see *Hill v. Hill* (1943) 23 Cal.2d 82, 93 [142 P.2d 417]) does not require the invalidation of entire agreements based upon the subjective contemplation of the parties; it requires only that the courts refuse to enforce specific contractual provisions which by their terms seek to promote the dissolution of a marriage.

From *Loveren v. Loveren* (1895) 106 Cal. 509 [39 P. 801] to the most recent decision of this court on the matter, *Glickman v. Collins* (1975) 13 Cal.3d 852 [120 Cal.Rptr. 76, 533 P.2d 204], California courts have uniformly held that contracts offend the state policy favoring marriage only insofar as the terms of the contract "facilitate," "encourage," or "promote" divorce or dissolution.

Apart from *Higgason,* no case has distinguished, in terms of the policy favoring marriage, between antenuptial agreements and those executed during a viable marriage, and none have asserted that only agreements made in contemplation of a lifelong marriage are valid. The cases have uniformly directed their inquiry not to the subjective contemplation of the parties, but to the objective terms of the contract, and the effect of those terms in promoting the dissolution of the marriage.

Indeed *Higgason* itself exemplifies this objective approach to ascertaining the validity of agreements. In *Higgason* a wealthy 73-year-old woman married a man, age 48, without financial resources. Prior to the marriage they executed an agreement under which each waived all interest in the property of the other and all right to support. In the subsequent dissolution action the husband challenged the validity of the agreement.

Although our opinion in *Higgason* asserted that a valid antenuptial agreement must be made in contemplation of a marriage lasting until death, we did not attempt to determine what the parties actually contemplated at the time of the execution of the agreement....

Our disagreement with *Higgason's* dictum that parties to an antenuptial agreement must contemplate a lifelong marriage, however, is not merely a matter of adherence to precedent. A rule measuring the validity of antenuptial agreements by the subjective contemplation of the parties hazards the validity of all antenuptial agreements. No agreement would be safe against the risk that a spouse might later testify that he or she anticipated a marriage of short duration when he or she executed the agreement. Disputes concerning the validity of the agreement may arise, moreover, many years after its execution, perhaps even after the death of the parties, thus rendering any attempt to reconstruct the subjective anticipation of the parties fruitless. In consequence, under a test based upon the subjective contemplation of the parties, neither persons dealing with the parties nor even the parties themselves could rely on the terms of an antenuptial agreement.

Further uncertainties arise from the inherent vagueness of any test based on the subjective contemplation of the parties. A man and woman entering into marriage may pledge their faith "til death do us part," but the unromantic statistics show that many marriages end in separation or dissolution. Spouses who enter into an antenuptial agreement cannot forecast the future; they must, as a realistic matter, take into account both the possibility of lifelong marriage and the possibility of dissolution. In consequence a dichotomous test which insists that the contracting parties must contemplate either a marriage until death or an earlier termination is utterly unworkable. Such a test might invalidate virtually all antenuptial agreements on the ground that the parties contemplated dissolution, or it might uphold all on the ground that the parties also contemplated the possibility of a lifelong relationship, but it provides no principled basis for determining which antenuptial agreements offend public policy and which do not.

We conclude that an antenuptial agreement violates the state policy favoring marriage only insofar as its terms encourage or promote dissolution. The dictum in *Higgason* that such agreements are invalid unless the parties contemplated a marriage lasting until death is hereby disapproved.

...

In times past antenuptial agreements were most often used by wealthy men and women who feared that less wealthy fiancees might be marrying for money. In recent years, however, an increasing number of couples have executed antenuptial agreements in order to structure their legal relationship in a manner more suited to their needs and values.... Neither the reordering of property rights to fit the needs and desires of the couple, nor realistic planning that takes account of the possibility of dissolution, offends the public policy favoring and protecting marriage. It is only when the terms of an agreement go further — when they promote and encourage dissolution, and thereby threaten to induce the destruction of a marriage that might otherwise endure — that such terms offend public policy.

...

The judgment is affirmed.

SIMEONE v. SIMEONE

Supreme Court of Pennsylvania
525 Pa. 392, 581 A.2d 162 (1990)

FLAHERTY, Justice.

At issue in this appeal is the validity of a prenuptial agreement executed between the appellant, Catherine E. Walsh Simeone, and the appellee, Frederick A. Simeone. At the time of their marriage, in 1975, appellant was a twenty-three year old nurse and appellee was a thirty-nine year old neurosurgeon. Appellee had an income of approximately $90,000 per year, and appellant was unemployed. Appellee also had assets worth approximately $300,000. On the eve of the parties' wedding, appellee's attorney presented appellant with a prenuptial agreement to be signed. Appellant, without the benefit of counsel, signed the agreement. Appellee's attorney had not advised appellant regarding any legal rights that the agreement surrendered. The parties are in disagreement as to whether appellant knew in advance of that date that such an agreement would be presented for signature. Appellant denies having had such knowledge and claims to have signed under adverse circumstances, which, she contends, provide a basis for declaring it void.

The agreement limited appellant to support payments of $200 per week in the event of separation or divorce, subject to a maximum total payment of $25,000.

The parties separated in 1982, and, in 1984, divorce proceedings were commenced. Between 1982 and 1984 appellee made payments which satisfied the $25,000 limit. In 1985, appellant filed a claim for alimony *pendente lite.* A master's report upheld the validity of the prenuptial agreement and denied this claim. Exceptions to the master's report were dismissed by the Court of Common Pleas of Philadelphia County. The Superior Court affirmed. *Simeone v. Simeone*, 380 Pa.Super. 37, 551 A.2d 219 (1988).

We granted allowance of appeal because uncertainty was expressed by the Superior Court regarding the meaning of our plurality decision in *Estate of Geyer*, 516 Pa. 492, 533 A.2d 423 (1987)(Opinion Announcing Judgment of the Court). The Superior Court viewed *Geyer* as permitting a prenuptial agreement to be upheld if it either made a reasonable provision for the spouse or was entered after a full and fair disclosure of the general financial positions of the parties and the statutory rights being relinquished. Appellant contends that this interpretation of *Geyer* is in error insofar as it requires disclosure of statutory rights only in cases where there has not been made a reasonable provision for the spouse. Inasmuch as the courts below held that the provision made for appellant was a reasonable one, appellant's efforts to overturn the agreement have focused upon an assertion that there was an inadequate disclosure of statutory rights. Appellant continues to assert, however, that the payments provided in the agreement were less than reasonable.

...

While the decision of the Superior Court reflects, perhaps, a reasonable interpretation of *Geyer,* we do not view this case as a vehicle to affirm that interpretation. Rather, there is need for a reexamination of the foundations upon which *Geyer* and earlier decisions rested, and a need for clarification of the standards by which the validity of prenuptial agreements will be judged.

There is no longer validity in the implicit presumption that supplied the basis for *Geyer* and similar earlier decisions. Such decisions rested upon a belief that spouses are of unequal status and that women are not knowledgeable enough to understand the nature of contracts that they enter. Society has advanced, however, to the point where women are no longer regarded as the "weaker" party in marriage, or in society generally. Indeed, the stereotype that women serve as homemakers while men work as breadwinners is no longer viable. Quite often today both spouses are income earners. Nor is there viability in the presumption that women are uninformed, uneducated, and readily subjected to unfair advantage in marital agreements. Indeed, women nowadays quite often have substantial education, financial awareness, income, and assets.

Accordingly, the law has advanced to recognize the equal status of men and women in our society. See, *e.g.*, Pa. Const. art. 1, §28 (constitutional prohibition of sex discrimination in laws of the Commonwealth). Paternalistic presumptions and protections that arose to shelter women from the inferiorities and incapacities which they were perceived as having in earlier times have, appropriately, been discarded. See *Geyer*, 516 Pa. at 509–14, 533 A.2d at 431–33 (dissenting opinion of Mr. Chief Justice Nix setting forth detailed history of case law evidencing a shift away from the former paternalistic approach of protecting women towards a newer approach of equal treatment). It would be inconsistent, therefore, to perpetuate the standards governing prenuptial agreements that were described in *Geyer* and similar decisions, as these reflected a paternalistic approach that is now insupportable.

Further, *Geyer* and its predecessors embodied substantial departures from traditional rules of contract law, to the extent that they allowed consideration of the knowledge of the contracting parties and reasonableness of their bargain as factors governing whether to uphold an agreement. Traditional principles of contract law provide perfectly adequate remedies where contracts are procured through fraud, misrepresentation, or duress. Consideration of other factors, such as the knowledge of the parties and the reasonableness of their bargain, is inappropriate. See *Geyer*, 516 Pa. at 516–17, 533 A.2d at 434–35 (Flaherty, J. dissenting). Prenuptial agreements are contracts, and, as such, should be evaluated under the same criteria as are applicable to other types of contracts. See *Geyer*, 516 Pa. at 508, 533 A.2d at 431 ("These agreements are nothing more than contracts and should be treated as such." (Nix, C.J. dissenting)). Absent fraud, misrepresentation, or duress, spouses should be bound by the terms of their agreements.

Contracting parties are normally bound by their agreements, without regard to whether the terms thereof were read and fully understood and irrespective of whether the agreements embodied reasonable or good bargains.... *Ignorantia non excusat.*

...

...[T]he reasonableness of a prenuptial bargain is not a proper subject for judicial review. *Geyer* and earlier decisions required that, at least where there had been an inadequate disclosure made by the parties, the bargain must have been reasonable at its inception. See *Geyer*, 516 Pa. at 503, 533 A.2d at 428. Some have even suggested that prenuptial agreements should be examined with regard to whether their terms remain reasonable at the time of dissolution of the parties' marriage.

By invoking inquiries into reasonableness, however, the functioning and reliability of prenuptial agreements is severely undermined. Parties would not have entered such agreements, and, indeed, might not have entered their marriages, if they did not expect their agreements to be strictly enforced. If parties viewed an agreement as reasonable at the time of its inception, as evidenced by their having signed the agreement, they should be foreclosed from later trying to evade its terms by asserting that it was not in fact reasonable. Pertinently, the present agreement contained a clause reciting that "each of the parties considers this agreement fair, just and reasonable...."

Further, everyone who enters a long-term agreement knows that circumstances can change during its term, so that what initially appeared desirable might prove to be an unfavorable bargain. Such are the risks that contracting parties routinely assume. Certainly, the possibilities of illness, birth of children, reliance upon a spouse, career change, financial gain or loss, and numerous other events that can occur in the course of a marriage cannot be regarded as unforeseeable. If parties choose not to address such matters in their prenuptial agreements, they must be regarded as having contracted to bear the risk of events that alter the value of their bargains.

We are reluctant to interfere with the power of persons contemplating marriage to agree upon, and to act in reliance upon, what *they* regard as an acceptable distribution scheme for their property. A court should not ignore the parties' expressed intent by proceeding to determine whether a prenuptial agreement was, in the court's view, reasonable at the time of its inception or the time of divorce. These are exactly the sorts of judicial determinations that such agreements are designed to avoid. Rare indeed is the agreement that is beyond possible challenge when reasonableness is placed at issue. Parties can routinely assert some lack of fairness relating to the inception of the agreement, thereby placing the validity of the agreement at risk. And if reasonableness at the time of divorce were to be taken into account an additional problem would arise. Virtually nonexistent is the marriage in which there has been absolutely no change in the circumstances of either spouse during the course of the marriage. Every change in circumstance, foreseeable or not, and substantial or not, might be asserted as a basis for finding that an agreement is no longer reasonable.

In discarding the approach of *Geyer* that permitted examination of the reasonableness of prenuptial agreements and allowed inquiries into whether parties had attained informed understandings of the rights they were surrendering, we do not depart from the longstanding principle that a full and fair disclosure of the financial positions of the parties is required. Absent this disclosure, a material misrepresentation in the inducement for entering a prenuptial agreement may be asserted. *Hillegass*, 431 Pa. at 152–53, 244 A.2d at 676–77. Parties to these agreements do not quite deal at arm's length, but rather at the time the contract is entered into stand in a relation of mutual confidence and trust that calls for disclosure of their financial resources. Id. at 149, 244 A.2d at 675; *Gelb Estate*, 425 Pa. 117, 120, 228 A.2d 367, 369 (1967). It is well settled that this disclosure need not be exact, so long as it is "full and fair." *Kaufmann Estate*, 404 Pa. 131, 136 n. 8, 171 A.2d 48, 51 n. 8 (1961). In essence therefore, the duty of disclosure under these circumstances is consistent with traditional principles of contract law.

If an agreement provides that full disclosure has been made, a presumption of full disclosure arises. If a spouse attempts to rebut this presumption through an assertion of fraud or misrepresentation then this presumption can be rebutted if it is proven by clear and convincing evidence. *Hillegass*, 431 Pa. at 152–53, 244 A.2d at 676–77.

The present agreement recited that full disclosure had been made, and included a list of appellee's assets totalling approximately $300,000. Appellant contends that this list understated by roughly $183,000 the value of a classic car collection which appellee had included at a value of $200,000. The master, reviewing the parties' conflicting testimony regarding the value of the car collection, found that appellant failed to prove by clear and convincing evidence that the value of the collection had been understated. The courts below affirmed that finding. We have examined the record and find ample basis for concluding that the value of the car collection was fully disclosed. Appellee offered expert witnesses who testified to a value of approximately $200,000. Further, appellee's disclosure included numerous cars that appellee did not even own but which he merely hoped to inherit from his mother at some time in the future. Appellant's contention is plainly without merit.

Appellant's final contention is that the agreement was executed under conditions of duress in that it was presented to her at 5 p.m. on the eve of her wedding, a time when she could not seek counsel without the trauma, expense, and embarrassment of postponing the wedding. The master found this claim not credible. The courts below affirmed that finding, upon an ample evidentiary basis.

Although appellant testified that she did not discover until the eve of her wedding that there was going to be a prenuptial agreement, testimony from a number of other witnesses was to the contrary. Appellee testified that, although the final version of the agreement was indeed presented to appellant on the eve of the wedding, he had engaged in several discussions with appellant regarding the contents of the agreement during the six month period preceding that date. Another witness testified that appellant mentioned, approximately two or three weeks before the wedding, that she was going to enter a prenuptial agreement. Yet another witness confirmed that, during the months preceding the wedding, appellant participated in several discussions of prenuptial agreements. And the legal counsel who prepared the agreement for appellee testified that, prior to the eve of the wedding, changes were made in the agreement to increase the sums payable to appellant in the event of separation or divorce. He also stated that he was present when the agreement was signed and that appellant expressed absolutely no reluctance about signing. It should be noted, too, that during the months when the agreement was being discussed appellant had more than sufficient time to consult with independent legal counsel if she had so desired. See generally *Carrier v. William Penn Broadcasting Corp.*, 426 Pa. 427, 431, 233 A.2d 519, 521 (1967)(concept of duress as applied to contracting parties). Under these circumstances, there was plainly no error in finding that appellant failed to prove duress.

Hence, the courts below properly held that the present agreement is valid and enforceable. Appellant is barred, therefore, from receiving alimony *pendente lite.*

Order affirmed.

[Concurring opinion omitted.]

McDERMOTT, Justice, dissenting.

I dissent. I would reverse and remand to the trial court for further consideration of the validity of the prenuptial agreement executed by the appellee, Dr. Frederick Simeone, and Catherine Simeone, on the eve of their wedding.

...

...I believe that the door should remain open for a spouse to avoid the application of a pre-nuptial agreement where clear and convincing proof establishes that the result will be inequity and unfairness under the circumstances of the particular case and the public policy of this state. Some pre-nuptial agreements will be unfair and inequitable from their beginning....

...

It is...apparent that, although a pre-nuptial agreement is quite valid when drafted, the passage of time accompanied by the intervening events of a marriage, may render the terms of the agreement completely unfair and inequitable. While parties to a pre-nuptial agreement may indeed foresee, generally, the events which may come to pass during their marriage, one spouse should not be made to suffer for failing to foresee all of the surrounding circumstances which may attend the dissolution of the marriage. Although it should not be the role of the courts to void pre-nuptial agreements merely because one spouse may receive a better result in an action under the Divorce Code to recover alimony or equitable distribution, it should be the role of the courts to guard against the enforcement of pre-nuptial agreements where such enforcement will bring about only inequity and hardship. It borders on cruelty to accept that after years of living together, yielding their separate opportunities in life to each other, that two individuals emerge the same as the day they began their marriage.

At the time of the dissolution of marriage, what are the circumstances which would serve to invalidate a pre-nuptial agreement? This is a question that should only be answered on a case-by-case basis. However, it is not unrealistic to imagine that in a given situation, one spouse, although trained in the workforce at the time of marriage, may, over many years, have become economically dependent upon the other spouse. In reliance upon the permanence of marriage and in order to provide a stable home for a family, a spouse may choose, even at the suggestion of the other spouse, not to work during the marriage. As a result, at the point of dissolution of the marriage, the spouse's employability has diminished to such an extent that to enforce the support provisions of the pre-nuptial agreement will cause the spouse to become a public charge, or will provide a standard of living far below that which was enjoyed before and during marriage. In such a situation, a court may properly decide to render void all or some of the provisions of the pre-nuptial agreement.

...

MARTIN v. FARBER
Court of Special Appeals of Maryland
68 Md. App. 137, 510 A.2d 608 (1986)

GILBERT, Chief Judge.

We are asked to determine 1) whether an antenuptial agreement entered into by Morris W. Farber and Nettie Sue Farber in 1939 is still valid and enforceable; and 2) whether the imposition of a constructive trust on the estate of Nettie Sue Farber was proper.

Three days prior to their marriage on June 22, 1939, Nettie Sue Farber, then Nettie Sue Goldberg, and Morris W. Farber entered into an antenuptial agreement. The agreement provided, in essence, that Mrs. Farber would retain sole control of the property she acquired either prior to or during the marriage. Mr. Farber relinquished all rights in the property and estate of Mrs. Farber.

At the time of the execution of the agreement, Mrs. Farber was 39 years old, a widow, and the mother of two boys. Her first husband, Dr. Chester Goldberg, died in 1936. Mrs. Farber inherited property from him which included real estate located in Baltimore City. She also received from insurance proceeds more than $20,000.

Mr. Farber, although steadily employed as an electrician, had no accumulated wealth at the time of his marriage to Mrs. Farber. He did, however, continue to work until his retirement in 1967. During his forty-four year marriage to Mrs. Farber, Mr. Farber turned his paychecks over to his wife. Mrs. Farber, meanwhile, remained at home and managed the couple's household and financial affairs.

When Mrs. Farber died intestate in August, 1983, she had accumulated in her own name assets valued at approximately $275,000. The Orphan's Court for Baltimore County appointed Mr. Farber as personal representative of his deceased wife's estate. Mrs. Farber's grandchildren[1] filed a petition in the Circuit Court for Baltimore County to remove Mr. Farber from that position. They asserted that he had signed a valid antenuptial agreement in which he renounced any claim to Mrs. Farber's estate. In response, Mr. Farber filed a petition for declaratory relief alleging that the antenuptial agreement was invalid, and that under Maryland's intestacy laws he was entitled to his share of the estate.

Following a trial in the Circuit Court for Baltimore County, the judge concluded that while "[i]t is...true that many, many years ago Morris released any

1. Although Mrs. Farber was survived by three grandchildren, the youngest of those grandchildren, Harold M. Jones, was adopted outside of the family. Upon being told that he was no longer entitled to share in his grandmother's estate, Mr. Jones withdrew from the suit.

claim that he might have to Nettie's property or estate...after some forty-four years of a seemingly happy marriage, in which Morris turned everything he earned over to Nettie without question, and also upon her assurances that she would take care of Morris, it would not only be unjust, but unconscionable for the court to enforce...[the agreement]." The trial judge determined that a constructive trust should be imposed upon Mrs. Farber's estate for the benefit of Mr. Farber during his life; the remainder to be distributed equally to Mrs. Farber's heirs. Dissatisfied with the decision of the trial court, both sides appealed.

The grandchildren claim that the antenuptial agreement is "valid and enforceable" and that Mr. Farber is precluded from obtaining any interest in Mrs. Farber's estate. Mr. Farber contends, however, that the trial judge's decision not to enforce the agreement was "a correct one." He, nevertheless, maintains that since "the agreement is not to be enforced...the proper action of the lower court should have been to pass an order that the intestacy law would determine the distribution of assets of the estate." Proceeding from that premise, Mr. Farber further asserts that he is entitled to "the first $15,000 plus ½ of the residue" of his wife's estate. Md.Est. & Trusts Code Ann. §3-102.

THE ANTENUPTIAL AGREEMENT

...

In determining the validity of an antenuptial agreement, a court must consider: 1) was there a fair and reasonable provision for the spouse's relinquishing his or her rights; or 2) in the absence of such provision, was there "[f]rank, full and truthful disclosure of what is being relinquished (or in lieu thereof actual knowledge otherwise available or obtained)...." *Hartz*, 248 Md. at 57, 234 A.2d at 871. Equally important is the question of whether the agreement was entered into freely and voluntarily. *DelVecchio v. DelVecchio*, 143 So.2d 17, 20 (Fla.1962).

...

The element of "reasonableness must be weighed as of the time of the execution of the agreement." Lindey, *Separation Agreements and Antenuptial Contracts*, §90-53 (1985).

Some courts, for public policy reasons, have imposed another test — one of conscionability — in order to determine the validity of antenuptial agreements, at least with regard to provisions relating to maintenance and sustenance on dissolution of marriage. Under that particular test, "such provisions may lose their legal vitality by reason of changing circumstances which render the antenuptial provisions for maintenance to be unconscionable at the time of the marriage dissolution." *Newman v. Newman*, 653 P.2d 728, 734 (Colo.Sup.Ct.1982)....

...

Notwithstanding the apparent willingness of some courts to subject maintenance and sustenance provisions to conscionability review, there appears to be little support for extending that review to provisions respecting the devolution of property at the time of death of one of the spouses. See *Gross*, 11 Ohio St.3d 99, 464 N.E.2d 500; *Newman*, 653 P.2d 728.

...

...Historically, an agreement has been held to be unconscionable if it is "such as no man in his senses and not under delusion would make on the one hand, and as no honest and fair man would accept on the other." *Hume v. United States*, 132 U.S. 406, 10 S.Ct. 134, 33 L.Ed. 393 (1889), quoting *Earl of Chesterfield v. Janssen*,

2 Ves.Sen. 125, 155, 28 Engl.Rep. 82, 100 (Ch. 1750). Even though the doctrine of unconscionability permits the courts to exercise considerable leeway in avoiding inequitable results, that permissiveness is not without bounds.

> [W]hen determining whether an entire contract or any of its parts is so unconscionable as to justify its judicial rescission or cancellation, the matter will not be judged by hindsight but by the situation as it existed at the time the bargain was struck. &

Gladding v. Langrall, Muir & Noppinger, 285 Md. 210, 213, 401 A.2d 662, 664 (1979).

Phrased differently, the fairness of an agreement is to be determined as of the time it was made, not on the basis of conditions occurring subsequently. *Gladding*, 285 Md. at 214, 401 A.2d at 665. Courts are not possessed of unbridled discretion to undo that which the parties fairly and voluntarily assumed, even if the agreement might be deemed imprudent.

With that precept firmly in mind, we hold that the trial judge erred in ruling that the agreement was unconscionable. It was not. Nothing in the Farbers' antenuptial agreement or in the circumstances surrounding its execution renders it unconscionable or otherwise legally objectionable. The trial judge palpably relied on circumstances arising after the execution of the agreement. He was particularly concerned by the fact that Mr. Farber turned everything he earned over to Mrs. Farber, and that she repeatedly assured her husband that she would take care of him. No matter how disturbing those facts may be, they do not afford an adequate base for the court's ruling. The court, as we have said, was bound to decide the validity of the agreement and the process by which it was reached as of the time the agreement was made, and not by any post-agreement occurrences.

Constructive Trust

The decision with regard to the validity and enforceability of the agreement does not, however, end our inquiry. Yet to be determined is whether, under the circumstances of the instant case, a constructive trust was properly imposed.

A constructive trust has been defined as:

> A...remedy employed by a court...to convert the holder of the legal title to property into a trustee for one who in good conscience should reap the benefits of the possession of said property. The remedy is applied by operation of law where property has been acquired by fraud, misrepresentation, or other improper method, or where the circumstances render it inequitable for the party holding the title to retain it.

Wimmer v. Wimmer, 287 Md. 663, 668, 414 A.2d 1254, 1258 (1980); *see also Siemiesz v. Amend*, 237 Md. 438, 206 A.2d 723 (1964).

Ordinarily, before a constructive trust can be impressed by a court, there must be "clear and convincing evidence of wrongdoing" coupled with "circumstances which would render it inequitable for the holder of legal title to retain the beneficial interest." *Wimmer*, 287 Md. at 668, 414 A.2d at 1258; *Peninsula Methodist Homes and Hospitals, Inc. v. Cropper*, 256 Md. 728, 261 A.2d 787 (1970). When a confidential relationship exists, different rules are applicable. *Wimmer*, 287 Md. at 668, 414 A.2d at 1258; *Fant v. Duffy*, 232 Md. 481, 194 A.2d 293 (1963).

In order to establish the existence of a confidential relationship, it must be shown that "one party is under the domination of another, or...[that] the circumstances [are such that]...[one] party is justified in assuming that the other will not act in a manner inconsistent with his or her welfare." *Bass v. Smith*, 189 Md. 461, 469, 56 A.2d 800, 804 (1948). Once it is demonstrated that a confidential relationship exists, "a presumption arises that confidence was placed in the dominant party [by the subservient party] and that the transaction complained of resulted from fraud or undue influence and superiority or abuse of the confidential relationship by which the dominant party profited." *Wimmer*, 287 Md. at 669, 414 A.2d at 1258; *Wenger v. Rosinsky*, 232 Md. 43, 192 A.2d 82 (1963). The presumption shifts the burden to the dominant party to show, by clear and convincing evidence, that the transactions entered into were fair and reasonable. *Wimmer*, 287 Md. at 669, 414 A.2d at 1258.

The record before us reveals that throughout the Farbers' forty-four year marriage, Mrs. Farber stayed at home attending to the domestic chores as well as the couple's financial matters. Mr. Farber continued to work outside the home. He regularly earned wages which he diligently turned over to his wife. Those facts, when viewed in light of Mrs. Farber's repeated assurances to her husband that she would take care of him, lead us to the conclusion that a confidential relationship existed between the Farbers and that Mrs. Farber was the dominant of the two.

Based on the evidence presented to support Mr. Farber's assertion that his wife abused that confidential relationship by using his earnings to acquire assets which she titled or placed solely in her own name, we agree that the imposition of a constructive trust was proper. We think, however, that the trust should only be imposed to the extent that Mr. Farber's funds were used to acquire assets which were not a part of or attributable to the assets in Mrs. Farber's estate prior to the marriage of the couple. In limiting the scope of the constructive trust imposed in the case *sub judice*, we are mindful of a primary purpose of that form of trust — to prevent unjust enrichment. Therefore, the constructive trust should be limited to the extent Mr. Farber is able to trace his funds into his late wife's estate. The imposition by the trial court of a constructive trust over the entire estate, without regard to the amounts actually contributed by Mr. Farber, was error.

...

[Affirmed in part, reversed in part, and case remanded.]

COMMENTS

These materials on antenuptial agreements should be viewed from two different perspectives. One perspective focuses on the conflict between couples, who wish to order their private lives to suit their interests, and the state, which has traditionally interfered with many such efforts. The second perspective focuses on the conflict between the two contracting parties and recognizes that the state must decide under what circumstances it will allow one or the other of the parties to enlist the coercive power of the state on his or her own behalf.

(1)

While formal engagement, as traditionally understood, has declined, it has been revived in other forms. One example is cohabitation as a form of "trial marriage," which, as discussed in Chapter 2, often becomes a substitute for marriage. Another example is the increased importance and recognition of antenuptial agreements. In the past such agreements were a rare practice confined to the elderly and rich who wished to preserve their assets, but they are now also entered into by young couples attempting to articulate their mutual expectations. Reversing earlier patterns, the courts tend to accept their validity even if they contemplate and regulate the possibility of future divorce or dissolution of a marriage not yet in existence.

Antenuptial contracts herald changed attitudes on marriage. In the past, the nature and terms of marriage were to a considerable extent imposed on the parties by a formal pronouncement of policy through the state. Although, unlike most commercial contracts, marriage was not based on a printed form, the duties imposed by law had elements of a contract of adhesion. Today, although the state continues to play an important role, the nature and terms of marriage are increasingly left by the courts to the parties themselves. In other words, marriage is less of a "take-it-or-leave-it" proposition than it used to be. Parties may be allowed to vary the terms of the marriage contract, and the state's role becomes less heavy-handed and more a matter of providing the background conditions or the base from which the parties may choose to depart. Thus marriage itself, not merely the antenuptial agreement, is subject to substantial freedom of contract, with religion and the state assuming a less apparent and active role than in the past.

Marriage today is often perceived as neither a sacrament nor a status necessarily assumed for life. The relationship contemplated by parties in some modern antenuptial agreements is not dissimilar from that of other long-term contracts, such as partnerships, cotenancy, and sometimes employment.

Antenuptial agreements are related not only to engagement, marriage, and divorce, but also to cohabitation contracts. During the past thirty years they have undergone considerable change in form and content. *Posner* is a leading case, widely cited throughout the country in support of the theory that parties should also be able to regulate incidents of marriage breakup. According to the older viewpoint alluded to in the case, such regulation was against public policy. Perhaps the conception of marriage as a personal relation entered for life made any contemplation of divorce seem an impairment to the marital intent. There was also the traditional notion of the state as a third party to the marriage contract which also restricted party autonomy. These considerations had fictitious elements because they were never meant to correspond fully to reality. Marriage was treated "as if" it were intended, necessarily and without reservation, for life; participation of the state was meant further to protect this assumption.

The defendant in *Ball v. Ball*, Ed Ball, who died in 1981 at the age of ninety-three, was a multimillionaire and an extremely powerful figure in Florida politics for over half a century. He was an iron-willed trustee of nearly $2 billion in assets of the estate of Alfred I. du Pont. These facts are vital, although not referred to in the antenuptial agreement reproduced on page 41 and the following divorce and annulment action on page 44. The agreement is startlingly modern in many ways, for instance, in the details of attempting to regulate the life style of the marital parties. Today, young people without means may enter in to these kinds of agreements in an effort to be honest with each other. It should be noted, however, that the Price-Ball agreement does not provide for a disclosure of assets. Disclosure of assets is highly recommended to demonstrate fairness.

Today parties occasionally go even beyond what was attempted in *Ball* by trying to regulate sexual expectations and other intimate details of personal life. Whether these agreements are legally enforceable appears to be secondary; their main function, at least today, is to safeguard deliberation. Nevertheless, they may have legal significance insofar as they regulate what exactly is meant to be "the essence" of this particular marriage. Thus, again as in *Ball*, they may be used later as evidence in possible annulment actions. In fact it is arguable that the increased importance of antenuptial agreements may bring about a revived importance of annulment. If courts maintain the rule that the validity of an antenuptial agreement depends upon the validity of the marriage, parties may seek to annul their marriage to avoid the terms of an antenuptial agreement. This may counter arguments that in a time when dissolution of marriage is possible without fault of the parties, there is no real need for annulment as a legal institution.

It should be noted that all the gynecological detail in *Ball* came about because it was pleaded by the attorney for the defendant husband. We may mention in passing that Mr. Roberts, the defendant's attorney in *Ball*, wrote the opinion in Posner twenty-two years later as Justice of the Florida Supreme Court.

(2)

Martin v. Farber is a good example of a case that the lawyers should have settled quickly out-of-court, probably by giving the husband a life interest in all or some portion of the wife's estate. It seems implausible that either of the parties to the antenuptial contract intended for the husband to live the last years of his life in poverty (or in litigation!) so that the wife's relatives could inherit the family wealth a couple years earlier. The *Simeone* majority states the classic laissez-faire argument in favor of courts carrying out the intent of the parties. But we know from *Dawley* that courts do not mean the actual (subjective) intent of the parties. Yet once we abandon the true intent of the parties and for policy reasons focus on the objective manifestations of intent, the justification for enforcing the contract weakens. It is not clear why the policy in favor of certainty should take precedence over policies in favor of financial sharing in marriage.

Suppose the *Dawley* marriage had lasted some twenty years longer than it did, that the couple had three more children, and that the wife gave up her teaching career to raise the children and help build the engineering career of her husband. For example, the family might have moved frequently to facilitate the husband's repeated promotions within his company, but still never have changed the antenuptial contract. Should a court then allow the high-income husband to take all the accumulated property and provide no support to the unemployed, late-middle-aged wife? It would be harder for the court in such a situation than it was for the *Martin v. Farber* court to impose a constructive trust, since the wife's contribution to obtaining the property would not be in the form of money that could be traced. If the children were over 18 by the time of the divorce, the court could not use child support payments to provide any de facto compensation for the wife.

Simeone applies laissez-faire with a vengeance. Although the majority might like to think of its opinion as modern, much of its style of reasoning actually comes straight out of the end of the nineteenth and the beginning of the twentieth century. Back then, courts made the same kind of assumption that specifics of the law of contract could be logically deduced from more abstract notions of equality. For example, during the period of American constitutional law history known as the *Lochner* era, after the case of *Lochner v. New York*, 198 U.S. 45 (1905), courts invalidated protective labor legislation on the basis that political equality logically implied freedom of contract — that derogation from the principles of freedom of contract involved improper paternalistic assumptions about the inferiority of workingmen. (Interestingly, the United States Supreme Court allowed certain protective labor legislation limited to women workers, *Muller v. Oregon*, 208 U.S. 412 (1908).)

Notice that the *Simeone* court seems unconcerned about actual unequal bargaining power and appears to limit its inquiry into duress simply to whether the 23-year-old unemployed nurse did or did not know that some form of prenuptial contract would be produced by the 39-year-old neurosurgeon prior to the wedding and whether, in the opinion of the attorney who drafted the agreement, she seemed reluctant to sign or not. Back in *Stanard v. Bolin*, (p. 2) could the defendant have gotten out of his engagement without liability by presenting the plaintiff with an antenuptial agreement so unreasonable that she would refuse to sign it? The notion that men and women should be equal, or even the (counter-factual) assertion that men and women are equal in our society, says little about whether marriage should or should not entail mutual support and financial sharing or how far courts should facilitate one party's efforts to perpetuate his or her economic superiority over the other party. Pennsylvania is unusual in that up until 1980 its statutes provided for no spousal support, beyond attorneys fees and alimony pendente lite.

The *Osborne* case may seem a good example of the appropriate use of antenuptial contracts. As long as the husband in fact fairly and knowingly agreed, it might seem that the wife should be able to keep her inheritance separate from the marriage and that the state would have no interest opposing it. Yet, with children the situation may be not quite so easy, even in a case such as *Osborne* where both parties are medical doctors and financially comfortable. It is one thing to say that a divorced spouse must cut back on an extravagant standard of living, but it is usual for courts to assert that children should to the extent possible be able to maintain their pre-divorce standard of living. The awkwardness of children living at a higher standard than one of their parents becomes even more acute when children live with the less wealthy parent. Suppose Mr. Osborne rather than Mrs. Osborne had taken primary care of the children during the marriage and were to have custody upon divorce. In such a case, should the non-custodial parent not be expected to pay child support to maintain the children's standard of living? Or should the children have to live with the richer parent or else cut their standard of living as a result of their parents' divorce? The more common situation is that the ex-husband is wealthier after divorce and that the children live with their mother. Even in cases without a prenuptial agreement purporting to limit support for the ex-wife, the children and mother often live in or near poverty, even when the ex-husband is well-off financially.

Once courts abandoned the policy of keeping unhappy couples in the bonds of marriage, the issue of whether an antenuptial agreement encourages divorce changes its nature in subtle but important ways. Instead of the couple's agreement frustrating the state's effort to limit divorce, the agreement makes the financial outcome of divorce better for one party and worse for the other. A court can say that this agreement encourages divorce only by supposing that the favored party is the one who would be initiating the divorce proceedings. The "favorable out" that is said to encourage one party to seek divorce would discourage the other party from seeking it. Thus for example, when the court in *Dawley* asserted that the provisions for ten months support discouraged divorce, it was supposing that the husband would be the one seeking divorce. The term would equally encourage the wife to seek divorce, confident that she would receive ten months support anyway.

Of course few of us organize our whole lives, perhaps especially our family lives, around financial matters. Yet, money and power are closely interrelated. The financial treatment of divorce surely does have at least some marginal effect on a couple's behavior during marriage, especially on the issue of which of them is likely to call it quits on the marriage faster. It seems probable that Mr. Osborne would have found divorce a bit easier to take had he not been barred by the antenuptial agreement from sharing his wife's estate. Similarly, we can assume that Mrs. Simeone might have hesitated less to get a divorce had she not been left relatively impoverished as a result.

In law school we often forget that legal cases involve actual human beings. You will notice that in some family law cases the parties' names have been replaced by initials. Should courts make wider use of this practice? How would you expect Lisa Dawley to feel about the issue if she went to law school and found herself in a family law class?

"The Movement of the Progressive Societies Has Hitherto Been a Movement from Status to Contract"

PONDER v. GRAHAM

Supreme Court of Florida
4 Fla. 23 (1851)

Appeal from judgment of the Circuit Court of the county of Leon, rendered at the Spring term, 1850, the Honorable THOMAS BALTZELL, Judge, presiding.

Mary Graham filed her petition in the Circuit Court of the County of Leon, representing that her husband, Archibald Graham, died on or about the 2d January, 1848, after having in his life time made and executed his last will and testament — that said will and testament bears date 16th November, 1847, and that one John R. Cannon, and the defendant, William G. Ponder, were therein named and appointed executors — that defendant alone qualified and took out letters testamentary — that the provision made in the said will is not satisfactory to petitioner, and that she, in due form, and in proper manner, signified her dissent thereto, within the time limited by law. The petitioner further states, that her deceased husband died seized and possessed of a large estate, real, personal, and mixed — out of which, petitioner prays that dower may be allotted to her, under the law in such case made and provided.

The defendant for answer, or plea to said petition, alleged that the said Mary Graham ought not to have her dower, as in her petition she claimed and prayed, because the said Mary never was *accoupled* to the said Archibald Graham, deceased, in lawful matrimony. To this plea, there was a replication, affirming that petitioner was *accoupled* in lawful matrimony with the said Archibald Graham, and issue thereon. The jury found for the petitioner; and thereupon it was adjudged and ordered, that said petitioner is entitled to an assignment of dower, and a writ of dower issued as prayed for, commanding the sheriff to summon five discreet free holders as commissioners, to allot and set off, by metes and bounds, to Mary Graham, widow of Archibald Graham, one-third part, according to quantity and quality of the real estate of which the said Archibald died seized, whereof the said Mary had not relinquished her right of dower, and at the same time to allot and set off to the said widow her portion, or one-half of the personal estate of the deceased.

...

The facts of the case are succinctly these: The respondent, then Mary Buccles, about the year 1820, in South Carolina, intermarried with one Solomon Canady. Some time afterwards, they removed to, and resided in, Georgia, but soon, in consequence of domestic dissensions, separated. Mary went to reside with Graham, a bachelor, and continued to live with him, under circumstances from which an adulterous cohabitation might be inferred.

In 1832, and while the said cohabitation continued, a bill was passed by the Legislative Council of the then Territory of Florida, entitled "An act for the relief of Mary Canady."

By this act, the Legislative Council, for the cause expressed in the preamble, assumed to judge and declare that the said Mary Graham was thereby divorced from her said husband, Solomon, and that the bonds of matrimony subsisting between them, were thereby to be entirely and absolutely dissolved, as if the same had never been solemnized. (See pamphlet acts of 1833, page 123.) There does not appear to have been any petition, affidavit, or proofs — a reference to a committee to ascertain the facts, or any notice to the absent husband. In 1834, the cohabitation between Mary and the testator still subsisting, the ceremony of marriage is celebrated between them, and from this time up to the period of the testator's death, which occurred in 1848, he lived with her, and acknowledged her as his wife, and in his will he provides for her by that name, and in that relation.

...

SEMMES, Justice, delivered the opinion of the court.

...

The main question raised in this case, as to the power of a Legislative body, *as such*, to grant divorces, is not altogether a new one. It has been investigated by some of the American Courts, and grave constitutional questions have been necessarily involved in the discussion; and yet the question still remains an open one — opinions clashing — nothing settled. It is to be regretted that amid this conflict of opinion, upon a question of such deep interest, we are unable to avail ourselves of the investigation of any one of the great jurists of our country, to relieve the subject from embarrassment and difficulty, and that while almost every other legal question of importance has had light and authority imparted to it, this, one of the most important of all, has been allowed to slumber on in doubt and uncertainty.

The Legislatures of some of the States of the Union exercise exclusive jurisdiction over this subject; one or more of them by reason, as is contended for by their Courts, of the absence of any constitutional inhibition — while others claim this authority by reason, it is said, of an inherent power, analogous to that of the Parliament of Great Britain. Some exercise the power as a constitutional right, while others claim it as an original right, and without the sanction of constitutional authority.

No one doubts the right of the people by their constitution, to invest this power in the Legislature, or any where else; but the question is, when the constitution is silent on the subject, in what department of government does this authority rest? I believe that much, if not the whole difficulty, has arisen from overlooking some of the great principles which enter into the constitutional government of the States, and from not preserving the obvious distinction between legislative and judicial functions — by confounding the *right* which a legislative body has to pass *general laws* on the subject of divorce, with the *power* of dissolving the marriage *contract.*

...

The act of the Council undertakes to determine questions of fact and law exclusively within the province of the Courts. If, as is contended with much reason, there were no existing causes of divorce, as set forth in the preamble to this act, then the dissolution of the marriage contract was a mere assumption of power, exercised in the most arbitrary manner.

An act declaring that to be a crime which, by the laws of the land, was no crime, and punishing an innocent party, by depriving him of important legal rights without a hearing, without notice, and who had not, in any mode, made himself amenable to our laws, such proceeding could not be justified, on any principle of natural right, or common justice. But assuming the fact to be so — that the grounds on which the legislature acted were recognized by our law as causes for divorce — then the legislature, assuming the high prerogatives and character of a judicial tribunal, proceeds to determine the facts and administer the law — upon *ex parte* showing, pronounces judgment against an absent defendant, and declares a forfeiture of his marital rights, for causes happening in a foreign jurisdiction, and to whose laws he was alone amenable. Is there no distinction between making a law and expounding and administering a law? Between declaring that certain acts may work a forfeiture, and passing judgment of forfeiture? Between enacting a law affecting the remedy, and pronouncing a judgment dissolving a contract? Had any Court dissolved this marriage contract, with the facts before it disclosed in this record, it would have been but a poor compliment to its own sense of justice, or the high and solemn trust with which the law had clothed it.

...

It is said, and the doctrine is broadly intimated in several of the authorities, that a legislature in this country can grant divorces, in analogy to the Parliament of England. I can see no parallel in the two cases. Political writers in England claim for their Parliament omnipotent power. It is said that in that country "there is no written constitution, no fundamental law, nothing visible, nothing tangible, nothing real, nothing certain, by which a statute of Parliament can be tested." See 3 Dallas's Reports, 308; and yet, with all this acknowledged and untrammelled power, it does not assert or exercise the right of dissolving the marriage contract; to the extent and in the summary mode adopted by the Legislatures of some of the States.

Parliament never decrees a divorce, *a mensa et thoro* — that power belongs exclusively to the Courts. Parliament never even decrees a divorce *a vinculo*, but for adultery, and that upon a judgment *a mensa et thoro*, first pronounced by the Ecclesiastical Courts, and unless sufficient cause is shown, a verdict for damages in a Court of Common Law is requisite, before Parliament will take jurisdiction. The whole proceedings, from the libel filed in the Ecclesiastical Court, up to the final decree by Parliament, are, in every essential requisite, *judicial*. The formal petition to the House of Lords, with an office copy of the judgment and proceeding in the Court, notice to the defendant, the examination of witnesses, the hearing of counsel, and the judgment pronounced, all clothe it with a judicial character, of which it is impossible to divest it — done, it is true, by Parliament, but by virtue of its omnipotent power.

...

...There is another point presented by the record in this case, which I think it my duty briefly to consider — it is, whether this act of the legislature is not unconstitutional, on the ground that it impairs the obligation of a contract.

It is insisted that marriage is but a *civil relation*, and not embraced within the definition of a *contract*, as used in the constitution. In England, as well as in this country, all legal writers consider it *as purely a civil contract*. It is true it is a civil relation, but *non constat*, it is not a contract in the strict legal definition of the term. Every contract creates a legal relation between the parties. Blackstone says that "the law of England considers marriage in *no other* light than as a civil contract, and viewing it in this civil light, the law *treats* it as it does all other contracts." 1 Blackstone's Commentaries, 448. Rutherford says the contract of marriage creates important legal rights in the person and property of the other. 1 Institutes, 314. See, also, Bacon, 476, 488. The contract creates mutual rights, duties and obligations, deeply interesting to society, it is true, but none the less important and valuable to the contracting parties. It is municipal, as it affects the public — it is a contract, as it affects the rights of the person and the rights of property — it has all the attributes of a pure contract, whether we consider the capacity of the parties to contract, the subject matter or the consideration; and the rights growing out of it can be asserted and enforced in a court of justice. A man has as good a right to the property acquired by marriage, as that acquired under any other contract. Mr. Justice Story says, "As to the case of the contract of marriage, which the argument supposes not be within the prohibitory clause, (of the constitution,) because it is a manner of civil institution, I profess *not to feel the weight of the reason assigned for the exception.* In a legal sense, all contracts, recognized as valid in any country, may be properly said to be matters of civil institution, since they obtain their obligation and construction *jure loci contractus.*" 4 Condensed Supreme Court Reports, 520. I know of no reason why the word contract, as used in the Constitution, should be restricted to those of a pecuniary nature, and not embrace that of marriage, involving, as it does, considerations of the most interesting character and vital importance to society; to government, and the contracting parties. It is comprehended by the words of the Constitution, and there is no rule of construction that would exclude it, in the absence of any thing to show that it is not within its spirit.... And what was the *obligations* of the contract, but the rights and duties which grow out of it? A legislative act which discharges the duties and destroys the rights acquired under any contract, must, of necessity, impair its obligation. A law affecting the remedy, does not impair the obligation, but an act of the legislature, dissolving the contract, *destroys* the obligation.

In every respect in which I have been able to see this case, I can find no reason to sustain the act of the legislature. It appears by the record, that the parties were domiciled in the State of Georgia, where, it is alleged, the desertion and ill treatment occurred. The wife, living with the testator, Graham, removed to Florida — while the husband returned to Carolina, his former residence. The bill was introduced into the legislature one day, and passed the next. It is very clear that this divorce would not be recognized by the Courts of Georgia or Carolina, were any rights asserted under it in those States. There was an utter want of jurisdiction over the person, as well as the subject matter, and an act thus passed in defiance of the maxim, *audi alteram partem,* has no merit to recommend it to this court. The husband, in this case, in the language of Chief Justice Story, "had as good a right to his wife as his property acquired under the marriage contract — he had a legal right to her society and fortune, and to divest him of these rights, without his default, and against his will, was as flagrant a violation of the principles of justice, as the confiscation of his estate." 4 Condensed Supreme Courts Reports.

I am, therefore, of opinion that the act of the Legislative Council of February 11th, 1832, was in conflict with the organic law of Florida and the Constitution of the United States, and is, therefore, void.

Per Curiam — Let the judgment of the Court below be reversed.

MAYNARD v. HILL

United States Supreme Court
125 U.S. 190 (1888)

Appeal from the Supreme Court of the Territory of Washington.

This is a suit in equity to charge the defendants, as trustees of certain lands in King county, Washington Territory, and compel a conveyance thereof to the plaintiffs. The lands are described as lots 9, 10, 13, and 14, of section 4, and lots 6, 7, 8, and 9, of section 5, in township 24 north, range 4 east, Willamette meridian. The case comes here on appeal from a judgment of the supreme court of the territory, sustaining the defendants' demurrer, and dismissing the complaint. The material facts, as disclosed by the complaint, are briefly these: In 1828, David S. Maynard and Lydia A. Maynard intermarried in the state of Vermont, and lived there together as husband and wife until 1850, when they removed to Ohio. The plaintiffs, Henry C. Maynard and Frances J. Patterson, are their children, and the only issue of the marriage. David S. Maynard died intestate in the year 1873, and Lydia A. Maynard in the year 1879. In 1850 the husband left his family in Ohio and started overland for California, under a promise to his wife that he would either return or send for her and the children within two years, and that the mean time he would send her the means of support. He left her without such means, and never afterwards contributed anything for her support or that of the children. On the 16th of September following he took up his residence in the territory of Oregon, in that part which is now Washington Territory, and continued ever afterwards to reside there. On the 3d of April, 1852, he settled upon and claimed, as a married man, a tract of land of 640 acres, described in the bill, under the act of congress of September 27, 1850, "creating the office of surveyor general of public lands in Oregon, and to provide for the survey, and to make donations to settlers of the said public lands," and resided thereon until his death. On the 22d day of December, 1852, an act was passed by the legislative assembly of the territory, purporting to dissolve the bonds of matrimony between him and his wife. The act is in these words:

> An act to provide for the dissolution of the bonds of matrimony heretofore existing between D. S. Maynard and Lydia A. Maynard, his wife.
>
> SEC. 1 Be it enacted by the legislative assembly of the territory of Oregon, that the bonds of matrimony heretofore existing between D. S. Maynard and Lydia A. Maynard be, and the same are hereby, dissolved.
>
> Passed the house of representatives, December 22, 1852.
>
> B. F. HARDING, *Speaker of the House of Representatives.*
>
> Passed the council, December 22, 1852.
>
> M. P. DEADY, *President Council.*

The complaint alleges that no cause existed at any time for this divorce; that no notice was given to the wife of any application by the husband for a divorce, or of the introduction or pendency of the bill for that act in the legislative assembly; that she had no knowledge of the passage of the act until July, 1853; that at the time she was not within the limits or an inhabitant of Oregon; that she never became a resident of either the territory of state of Oregon; and that she never in any manner acquiesced in or consented to the act; and the plaintiffs insisted that the legislative assembly had no authority to pass the act; that the same is absolutely void; and that the parties were never lawfully divorced. On or about the 15th of January, 1853, the husband, thus divorced, intermarried with one Catherine T. Brashears, and thereafter they lived together as husband and wife until his death. On the 7th of November, 1853, he filed with the surveyor general of Oregon the certificate required under the donation act of September 27, 1850, as amended by the act of the 14th of February, 1853, accompanied with an affidavit of his residence in Oregon from the 16th of September, 1850, and on the land claimed from April 3, 1852, and that he was married to Lydia A. Maynard until the 24th of December, 1852, having been married to her in Vermont in August, 1828. The notification was also accompanied with corroborative affidavits of two other parties that he had, within their knowledge, resided upon and cultivated the land from the 3d of April, 1852.

...

Mr. Justice FIELD...

As seen by the statement of the case, two questions are presented for our consideration: first, was the act of the legislative assembly of the territory of Oregon of the 22d of December, 1852, declaring the bonds of matrimony between David S. Maynard and his wife dissolved, valid and effectual to divorce the parties? and, second, if valid and effectual for that purpose, did such divorce defeat any rights of the wife to a portion of the donation claim?

The act of congress creating the territory of Oregon...declared that the legislative power of the territory should "extend to all rightful subjects of legislation not inconsistent with the constitution and laws of the United States."...

...

Marriage, as creating the most important relation in life, as having more to do with the morals and civilization of a people than any other institution, has always been subject to the control of the legislature. That body prescribes the age at which parties may contract to marry, the procedure or form essential to constitute marriage, the duties and obligations it creates, its effects upon the property rights of both, present and prospective, and the acts which may constitute grounds for its dissolution.

...

When this country was settled, the power to grant a divorce from the bonds of matrimony was exercised by the parliament of England. The ecclesiastical courts of that country were limited to the granting of divorces from bed and board. Naturally, the legislative assemblies of the colonies followed the example of parliament and treated the subject as one within their province. And, until a recent period, legislative divorces have been granted, with few exceptions, in all the states. Says Bishop, in his *Treatise on Marriage and Divorce*: "The fact that at the time of the settlement of this country legislative divorces were common, competent, and valid in England, whence our jurisprudence was derived, makes them conclusively so here, except where an invalidity is directly or indirectly created by a written constitution binding the legislative power." Section 664. Says Cooley, in his *Treatise on Constitutional Limitations*: "The granting of divorces from the bonds of matrimony was not confided to the courts in England, and, from the earliest days, the colonial and state legislatures in this country have assumed to possess the same power over the subject which was possessed by the parliament, and from time to time they have passed special laws declaring a dissolution of the bonds of matrimony in special cases." Page 110. Says Kent, in his *Commentaries*: "During the period of our colonial government, for more than a hundred years preceding the revolution, no divorce took place in the colony of New York, and for many years after New York became an independent state there was not any lawful mode of dissolving a marriage in the life-time of the parties but by a special act of the legislature." Volume 2, p. 97. The same fact is stated in numerous decisions of the highest courts of the states. Thus, in *Cronise v. Cronise*, 54 Pa. St. 260, the supreme court of Pennsylvania said: "Special divorce laws are legislative acts. This power has been exercised from the earliest period by the legislature of the province, and by that of the state, under the constitutions of 1776 and 1790. The continual exercise of the power, after the adoption of the constitution of 1790, cannot be accounted for except on the ground that all men, learned and unlearned, believed it to be a legitimate exercise of legislative power...."

...

The facts alleged in the bill of complaint, that no cause existed for the divorce, and that it was obtained without the knowledge of the wife, cannot affect the validity of the act. Knowledge or ignorance of parties of intended legislation does not affect its validity, if within the competency of the legislature. The facts mentioned as to the neglect of the husband to send to his wife, whom he left in Ohio, any means for her support or that of her children, in disregard of his promise, shows conduct meriting the strongest reprobation, and, if the facts stated had been brought to the attention of congress, that body might and probably would have annulled the act. Be that as it may, the loose morals and shameless conduct of the husband can have no bearing upon the question of the existence or absence of power in the assembly to pass the act. The organic act extends the legislative power of the territory to all rightful subjects of legislation "not inconsistent with the constitution and laws of the United States." The only inconsistency suggested is that it impairs the obligation of the contract of marriage. Assuming that the prohibition of the federal constitution against the impairment of contracts by state legislation applies equally, as would seem to be the opinion of the supreme court of the territory, to legislation by territorial legislatures, we are clear that marriage is not a contract within the meaning of the prohibition. As was said by Chief Justice Marshall in the *Dartmouth College Case*, not by way of judgment, but in answer to objections urged to positions taken: "The provision of the constitution never has been understood to embrace other contracts than those which respect property or some object of value, and confer rights which may be asserted in a court of justice. It never has been understood to restrict the general right of the legislature to legislate on the subject of divorces."...

It is also to be observed that, whilst marriage is often termed by text writers and in decisions of courts as a civil contract, generally to indicate that it must be founded upon the agreement of the parties, and does not require any religious ceremony for its solemnization, it is something more than a mere contract. The consent of the parties is of course essential to its existence, but when the contract to marry is executed by the marriage, a relation between the parties is created which they cannot change. Other contracts may be modified, restricted, or enlarged, or entirely released upon the consent of the parties. Not so with marriage. The relation once formed, the law steps in and holds the parties to various obligations and liabilities. It is an institution, in the maintenance of which in its purity the public is deeply interested, for it is the foundation of the family and of society, without which there would be neither civilization nor progress. This view is well expressed by the supreme court of Maine in *Adams v. Palmer*, 51 Me. 481, 483. Said that court, speaking by Chief Justice Appleton:

> When the contracting parties have entered into the married state, they have not so much entered into a contract as into a new relation, the rights, duties, and obligations of which rest not upon their agreement, but upon the general law of the state, statutory or common, which defines and prescribes those rights, duties, and obligations. They are of law, not of contract. It was a contract that the relation should be established, but, being established, the power of the parties as to its extent or duration is at an end. Their rights under it are determined by the will of the sovereign, as evidenced by law. They can neither be modified nor changed by any agreement of parties. It is a relation for life, and the parties cannot terminate it at any shorter period by virtue of any contract they may make. The reciprocal rights arising from this relation, so long as it continues, are such as the law determines from time to time, and none other.

And again:

> It is not then a contract within the meaning of the clause of the constitution which prohibits the impairing the obligation of contracts. It is rather a social relation like that of parent and child, the obligations of which arise not from the consent of concurring minds, but are the creation of the law itself, a relation the most important, as affecting the happiness of individuals, the first step from barbarism to incipient civilization, the purest tie of social life, and the true basis of human progress....

...

In *Noel v. Ewing*, 9 Ind. 37, the question was before the supreme court of Indiana as to the competency of the legislature of the state to change the relative rights of husband and wife after marriage, which led to a consideration of the nature of marriage; and the court said:

> Some confusion has arisen from confounding the contract to marry with the marriage relation itself. And still more is engendered by regarding husband and wife as strictly parties to a subsisting contract. At common law, marriage as a *status* had few elements of contract about it. For instance, no other contract merged the legal existence of the parties into one. Other distinctive elements will readily suggest themselves, which rob it of most of its characteristics as a contract, and leave it simply as a *status* or institution. As such, it is not so much the result of private agreement as of public ordination. In every enlightened government it is pre-eminently the basis of civil institutions, and thus an object of the deepest public concern. In this light, marriage is more than a contract. It is not a mere matter of pecuniary consideration. It is a great public institution, giving character to our whole civil polity. pp. 49–50.

In accordance with these views was the judgment of Mr. Justice Story. In a note to the chapter on marriage in his work on the *Conflict of Laws*, after stating that he had treated marriage as a contract in the common sense of the word, because this was the light in which it was ordinarily viewed by jurists, domestic as well as foreign, he adds: "But it appears to me to be something more than a mere contract. It is rather to be deemed an institution of society founded upon consent and contract of the parties, and in this view it has some peculiarities in its nature, character, operation, and extent of obligation different from what belong to ordinary contracts." §108*n*.

...

When, therefore, the act was passed divorcing the husband and wife, he had no vested interest in the land, and she could have no interest greater than his. Nothing had then been acquired by his residence and cultivation, which gave him anything more than a mere possessory right to remain on the land so as to enable him to comply with the conditions, upon which the title was to pass to him. After the divorce she had no such relation to him as to confer upon her any interest in the title subsequently acquired by him. A divorce ends all rights not previously vested. Interests which might vest in time, upon a continuance of the marriage relation, were gone. A wife divorced has no right of dower in his property; a husband divorced has no right by the courtesy in her lands, unless the statute authorizing the divorce specially confers such right.

It follows that the wife was not entitled to the east half of the donation claim. To entitle her to that half she must have continued his wife during his residence and cultivation of the land. The judgment of the Supreme Court of the Territory must therefore be affirmed; and it is so ordered.

RYAN v. RYAN
Supreme Court of Florida
277 So.2d 266 (Fla. 1973)

DEKLE, J.

We have for consideration three certified questions of law submitted by the Circuit Court of the Eleventh Judicial Circuit concerning the constitutionality of Florida's new dissolution of marriage law....

The three questions certified to us are as follows:

1. Whether Florida Statutes Chapter 61 which abolished former grounds for divorce and provided as sole ground for divorce that:

   (1) the marriage is irretrievably broken, and/or

   (2) insanity or mental incompetence

   is constitutional in that it does not *impair* the *obligation* of the *marriage contract* nor *adversely affect property rights* of the parties?

2. Whether Florida Statute Chapter 61 which provides for the granting of a dissolution of marriage upon the court's finding that the marriage is irretrievably broken is unconstitutional in that it is *vague, uncertain and indefinite*?

3. Whether Florida Statute Chapter 61 is unconstitutional because it *applies retroactively* to marriages entered into prior to July 1, 1971? (emphasis added)

These questions seek our constitutional interpretation of the new "no-fault" divorce law. The first question has two parts: Does the new dissolution law "impair the obligation of the marriage contract" in violation of Fla. Const. art. I, §10, F.S.A.; does it "adversely affect property rights of the parties." We shall examine and decide these related issues together.

PROPERTY RIGHTS

Fla. Const. §10 of the Declaration of Rights (Art. I) states that: "No...law impairing the obligation of contracts shall be passed." The respective parties argue at length with regard to whether or not marriage is a contract thus protected, citing various cases on the point.

This Court said as early as *Ponder v. Graham*, 4 Fla. 23, in 1851, that marriage is a contract. We have consistently since that time referred to "marriage contracts" for over 120 years of Florida Jurisprudence. As recently as *Belcher v. Belcher*, 271 So.2d 7 (Fla.1972), we referred to the obligation of the husband to support his wife during continuation of the marriage contract, thus still holding our view of marriage to be a "contract" rather than a mere "relationship" as suggested in *Gleason v. Gleason*, 26 N.Y.2d 28, 308 N.Y.S.2d 347, 256 N.E.2d 513 (N.Y.Ct.App.1970), and in an 1888 U.S. Supreme Court case cited by appellee, *Maynard v. Hill*, 125 U.S. 190, 8 S.Ct. 723, 31 L.Ed. 654. In that U.S. Supreme Court holding, however, and in others it is pointed out that the contracts which were designed to be protected under the constitutional provision are those contracts providing certain, definite and fixed private rights of property which are vested in the contract.

The query arises then whether dower or curtesy is a "property right" of a spouse thus protected. The inchoate right of dower is statutory and not a matter of contract, even though such right does indeed grow out of the marriage by virtue of the parties having "contracted" for that marriage. See also 52 Am.Jur.2d, *Marriage*, §5.

Dower is not a vested right. We have said that because of its defeasible nature dower is not to be given consideration in divorce or dissolution of marriage proceedings. *Bowler v. Bowler*, 159 Fla. 447, 31 So.2d 751 (1947).

...

Next we inquire: Is *potential alimony* such a "property right" under the contract of marriage as to be "impaired" contrary to Fla.Const. §10 Decl. of Rights? Under the foregoing analysis of dower we must hold likewise that this contingent interest does not fall within the constitutional prohibition. The same result is true as to equitable interests claimed in the property of a spouse by virtue of contributions of services or other considerations within the marriage, other than interests which have already vested. (Actual transfers and independent interests not inherent in the marriage stand independently.) Such a potential equitable interest as alimony is not yet vested but arises upon subsequent judicial determination (or settlement). True, an ultimate award of such an interest upon a termination of the marriage contract (or a legal separation) stems from the marriage. Without it, such an interest would not have arisen. But these potential interests are not those property rights contemplated by the constitutional prohibition.

VAGUE AND INDEFINITE CHALLENGE

The next question of law concerns that part of F.S., Section 61.052, F.S.A., reading:

> (1) No judgment of dissolution of marriage shall be granted unless one of the following facts appears, which shall be pleaded generally:
>
> (a) The marriage is irretrievably broken....

The quoted language read in context with the remainder of the statute expresses the purpose and intent of the Legislature with sufficient clarity to render it invulnerable to attack that it is unconstitutionally vague and indefinite.

The word "irretrievably" is defined: "impossible to recoup, repair or overcome." Webster's Third International Dictionary (1966), page 1196.

When compared with the fourth statutory ground for divorce, "extreme cruelty," in the former statute (§61.041(4), F.S. 1969, F.S.A.), the new language for dissolution of marriage, "irretrievably broken," appears to us to be no more susceptible to the charge of vagueness than were the words, "extreme cruelty." "Extreme cruelty" in the former divorce law was held in case after case to envision a great variety of faults and wrongdoings that were deemed sufficient for the granting of divorce, but the phrase was never invalidated for vagueness or overbreadth. For example, in *Diem v. Diem*, 141 Fla. 260, 193 So. 65, 66, this Court held the phrase, "extreme cruelty," as a ground for divorce to be "relative." The Court added:

> What constitutes it may be determined by the degree of one's culture, his emotions, nervous reaction or moral sense.

. . .

It is the duty of a court to recognize a reasonable construction of a statute which supports its constitutionality. The Legislature does not have to give a detailed and carefully outlined plan of each and every step to be followed in each and every circumstance which could arise.... Under the principles enunciated above, the statute meets the challenge of constitutional vagueness.

PLEADINGS

It is sufficient in the petition simply to allege as an ultimate fact that the marriage is "irretrievably broken"; however, the chancellor must determine from the particular facts of each case whether a marriage is "irretrievably broken," subject, of course, to appellate review. Just as "extreme cruelty" was held in divorce cases to cover a wide range of factual predicates for divorce, so the phrase "irretrievably broken" embraces numerous factual bases for dissolution of marriages. However, by the express language of the new statute now, dissolution of marriage is no longer granted because of the fault or wrongdoing or misconduct of one or both parties, as was the case under the grounds for divorce under former Section 61.041, F.S. 1969, F.S.A. The new statutory test for determining if a marriage is irretrievably broken is simply whether for whatever reason or cause (no matter whose "fault") the marriage relationship is for all intents and purposes ended, no longer viable, a hollow sham beyond hope of reconciliation or repair.

PROOF

It is suggested that a circuit judge would hesitate to adjudicate that a marriage is not "irretrievably broken" under the present statute when the petitioner simply says that is the fact; that the judge becomes nothing more than a ministerial officer receiving the "irretrievably broken" message and having so received it, being thus compelled to drop this legislative guillotine upon the marriage, thus excising the troublesome mate from the petitioner because the petitioner has subjectively and unilaterally determined that his marriage is irretrievably broken.

We do not view the matter of dissolution as being such a simple, unilateral matter of one mate simply saying "I want out." All of the surrounding facts and circumstances are to be inquired into to arrive at the conclusion as to whether or not indeed the marriage has reached the terminal stage based upon facts which must be shown. Even in uncontested dissolutions, the court would properly make inquiry to determine this fact, for the statute itself in §61.052 provides in subsection (2) the basic predicate: "Based on the evidence at the hearing...[and even] (a)...if the respondent does not...deny that the marriage is irretrievably broken, the court shall enter a judgment of dissolution of the marriage, *if the court finds that the marriage is irretrievably broken*." (emphasis added)

It is argued that the provision in the statute for continuing the proceedings for a period not exceeding 90 days to allow the parties to effect a reconciliation, is inconsistent with the objective of determining if in fact there is no further chance for the marriage to succeed. Actually, this further test of the marriage supports the requirement that the court must make a determination, beyond a petitioner's bare assertion, that in truth and in fact the marriage is "irretrievably broken."

And so it is that in every instance the court should make that determination by proper inquiry. It is never a simple matter of "Is your marriage 'irretrievably broken'?" "Yes, your honor, I believe it is." And that ends it, like the oriental ritual of the husband severing his marriage by tossing three stones in the sand one by one and in sequence saying, "I divorce thee; I divorce thee; I divorce thee." There must be appropriate *evidence* (albeit uncorroborated as the statute allows) that in truth and in *fact* the marriage is irretrievably broken.

In *Posner I*, 233 So.2d 381 (Fla.1970), quoting from *Underwood v. Underwood*, 12 Fla. 434, we stated the law still to be as follows: (233 So.2d p. 383) "...it 'would be aiming a deadly blow at public morals to decree a dissolution of the marriage contract merely because the parties requested it....'"

FORMER DEFENSES ELIMINATED

The new Act includes a provision, §61.044, entitled "Certain Existing Defenses Abolished" and provides:

> The defenses to divorce and legal separation, of condonation, collusion, recrimination, and laches are abolished.

The heretofore well-known defenses of condonation and recrimination found their genesis in the equitable "clean hands" doctrine but even prior to this new legislative enactment, we had to some degree modified strict recrimination as a defense in the case of *Stewart v. Stewart*, 158 Fla. 326, 29 So.2d 247 (1947). There the Court found both pairs of hands so unclean that it was hardpressed to apply the doctrine against both parties and therefore proceeded to call it "a qualifying doctrine" and frankly stated that if the doctrine were applied strictly it would in such circumstances result in "great inequity" in that neither party to the suit had been free from fault. That opinion in *Stewart* did however reiterate that the application of the doctrine of clean hands still existed as a matter of judicial discretion and public policy.

FRAUD

Now we find, however, that by virtue of the new legislative action that the clean hands principle has been eliminated in marriage dissolution except for fraud and deceit which are always available in our courts. A contrived, false or fraudulent creation of the ground upon which dissolution is sought, for the very purpose of terminating the marriage through what amounts to a misuse and, in effect, a fraud upon the courts could no more be tolerated in this than in any other litigation. The courts will not knowingly become a party to contrivance or fraud, even in the simplified basis for divorce which has now been created by the new statute. This is inherent in the judicial process. It is not limited to a future discovery of the fraud but may become apparent in the proceedings for dissolution, in which event the court should deal directly with it in such proceedings. In this there may be a direct fraud perpetrated upon the other spouse by misrepresentations, concealments or untruths, manifesting itself either in the course of the proceeding or at a later time. The courts will not indulge or reward falsehood and when such a purposeful inducement or fraud upon the other spouse or the court is made to appear by the evidence, then there would be a failure of proof that the marriage was irretrievably broken. The proof having failed in such instance, there would accordingly not be sufficient evidence upon which to grant the relief sought. This is not based upon a continuation of "fault" as a basis for relief which was required under the former divorce law but as a matter of fraud and deceit. This recognition of such a fundamental concept of equity is necessary in order to preserve the integrity of the judiciary, lest it become a party to a fraud or allow a misuse of the judicial machinery. Not even under statutory imposition can an independent judiciary which is the ultimate protector of right and justice, be subjugated and undermined.

We recognize that the new "no fault" concept was a principle basis of the new legislation for a desired simplification of the procedure aimed at reducing the trauma of the dissolution experience. That is a legislative judgment. The foregoing remaining intolerance of fraud or deceit is a judicial prerogative, to protect against fraud by a party and misuse of the courts and which we view as legally consistent with the new law.

NOT RETROACTIVE

The third question is directed to the constitutionality of the Act as allegedly applying *retroactively* to marriages prior to the Act, that is, prior to July 1, 1971, and thus void under Fla. Const. art. I, §10, and the federal constitution. We have heretofore held that the authority to regulate marriages and correspondingly to provide for their dissolutions is vested in the Legislature. It is inherent in the state's police power to do so in the regulation of society and its relationships, including the very essential and important family relationship within marriage. The marriage contract perhaps more than any other has a vital and essential effect on the very life and society of the State and therefore is a very proper subject of the State's police power; the subject of marriage (and correspondingly the dissolution thereof) has a very definite bearing upon the public interest with which the Legislature is concerned and charged with its regulation.

The Legislature as representative of the people should regulate marriage and the family relationship, and those matters affecting the members of the family in that affinity, in such manner and from time to time as the wisdom of the people may be reflected in the actions of their elected representatives. You might say: "For better, for worse." It must be remembered that the State has always been considered a "third party" or "third interest" in divorce and the family tie.

Petitioner challenges the authority of the Legislature to extend the law to "grant" dissolutions upon a new, simplified test of whether the tie is "irretrievably broken." It is urged as unconstitutional to apply the new law to existing contracts of marriage entered into under the prior law which, it is claimed, was a part of that marriage contract — now being "broken" by legislative action without due process of judicial considerations of notice and hearing. The only trouble with this contention is that the "remedy" (the procedure provided in the new law for dissolution) is the ongoing prerogative of the Legislature which also legislates the marriage in its creation. "...the Lord gave, and the Lord hath taken away."

There is, as we have said, no impairment of contract here. Neither is there denial of due process in the manner in which the machinery is set up for judicial determination regarding termination of the marriage. The law provides that consideration be given to support provisions and to any interest of the wife in property of the husband by way of special equity or otherwise. Due process basically is met upon a provision for notice and opportunity to be heard. Of course these are included in the new law, as such requirements were also included in the law in existence when past marriages were entered into. Accordingly, it cannot be maintained with validity that the new provision regarding the same subject matter is void because it affects "retroactively" those earlier marriage "contracts" and the applicable procedures and remedies, which are subject to proper change from time to time.

LEGISLATIVE PREROGATIVE

An additional argument is that the new dissolution of marriage law constitutes an encroachment upon the judiciary. In all candor we must recognize that the matter of divorce is a legislative prerogative. We do not have ecclesiastical courts. In the language of the poet, it might be said as to the role of the courts upon such legislative action: "Theirs not to make reply; Theirs not to reason why...." The change in philosophy, a different approach to the dissolution of marriage (a legislative prerogative) may add to today's moral erosion of contemporary standards in reflecting an unprecedented disregard, even scorn, for law and basic morality. It may also be that the family relationship and provisions for support are no longer protected by the laws of this state by requiring proof of misconduct before such rights can be taken away, but these matters of individual rights, social mores and of state policy are to be settled in the caldron of the people's representative government, the Legislature, by such representatives as the people choose to elect, upon whatever they may have represented to the people that their standards are. If the electorate finds it has been misled in such standards, or wishes to change them, the polls will open again.

...

Better we weep over questioned legislation, or judicial decisions for that matter, and strive within the proper channels for desired change, than destroy the system, for whatever well intended purpose. Such is the reasoning behind the oft-mentioned reference to our legal system as one "of laws, not of men." Sometimes it is not easy, but it is imperative to the survival of the democratic process.

...

Appellant urges *Ponder, supra,* as a basis for voiding the legislative provision for "no fault divorce." The dissolution of marriage provided in the new law is not, however, "a legislative divorce" which was granted in the early day of *Ponder, supra,* by the Legislative Council of Florida without reference to the courts. *Ponder* is not then precedent for a prohibition of the Legislature to regulate and provide grounds and procedures for dissolution of marriage.

Ponder involved an 1832 act of the Legislative Council of the Territory of Florida entitled "An Act For the Relief of Mary Canady" wherein that body proceeded ipso facto to dissolve or annul outright the bonds of matrimony of the said Mary and one Solomon Canady. That, of course, is quite different from a *judicial* consideration of the dissolution of marriage for which the present Legislature has provided in the proceeding in the courts. In *Ponder,* Mary, being then married to Mr. Canady, came to Florida where she proceeded to cohabit with one Mr. Graham and thereafter that early Legislative Council of the Territory saw fit to "dissolve" her previous marriage. This was of course an invasion of the judiciary and recognized as such by the holding in *Ponder* that such individual act was unconstitutional. It does not, however, stand as precedent here. The decision in *Ponder* in rejecting such "legislative divorce" actually reflects a healthy respect for the judiciary's role and also a repugnance for legislation which has solely such a private limited purpose....

ROBERTS, Justice (dissenting).

Section 61.011, Florida Statutes, F.S.A., entitled, "Dissolution in Chancery", provides that proceedings under this act relating to dissolution of marriage are to be in chancery (equity).

One of the most elementary and fundamental concepts of equity jurisprudence and a universal rule which affects the entire system of equity jurisprudence is the maxim that "He who comes into equity must come with clean hands." This principle is founded upon conscience and good faith.

. . .

Under the majority view a wrongdoing husband can come home every Saturday night for five years, drunk and penniless because of skirt-chasing, gambling, or some other misdeeds; then, he may beat, bruise and abuse his wife because he is unhappy with himself, and then he will be permitted to go down and get a divorce on printed forms purchased at a department store and tell the trial judge that the marriage is "irretrievably broken." Or, the offending wife, after jumping from bed to bed with her new found paramours, chronically drunk, and when at home nagging, brawling and quarreling, all against the wishes of a faithful husband who remains at home nurturing the children, is permitted to divorce her husband who does not desire a divorce, but rather, has one forced upon him, not because of anything he has done, but because the offending wife tells the trial court that her marriage is "irretrievably broken."

In my opinion, the offending spouse should not have standing to obtain a divorce if the innocent one invokes the doctrine that,

> He who comes into equity must come with clean hands.

It is the duty of this Court to seek a construction of a statute which would support its constitutionality.

By merely retaining the "clean hands" doctrine, I could agree that the "no-fault" divorce statute is constitutional, but absent this,

I must respectfully dissent.

COMMENTS

Ponder, *Maynard*, and *Ryan* relate to the nature of marriage as contractual with terms set by the parties, or as a status set by law. Although most state courts that considered the legality of legislative divorces in the mid-nineteenth century rejected the conclusion of *Ponder* and justified legislative divorces as relief to the non-breaching party when the marriage contract had been breached by marital misconduct, *Ponder* is typical of cases of its time in its assertion that marriage is a contract. What is often lost to our understanding today, however, is the significance in 1851 of that assertion. To call marriage a contract in 1851 did not in any sense imply that the parties should be free to set the particular terms of the contract or that notions of laissez-faire should govern the marriage relation. Courts regularly found implied terms in marriage and other contracts without distinguishing between terms implied-in-fact, thus representing agreement of the parties, and terms implied-in-law by courts to promote the courts' view of justice and fair dealing.

Later in the nineteenth century, as courts began to develop laissez-faire contract law, courts and commentators concluded marriage was not a contract but a status. This conclusion facilitated the strict, formal enforcement of commercial contracts by isolating cases involving marriage as irrelevant to basic contract law.

Sir Henry Sumner Maine's famous generalization "that the movement of the progressive societies has been a movement *from Status to Contract*" has often been understood to be an argument in favor of freely allowing the parties to set the terms of the marriage contract. Yet Maine was not intending to offer support for laissez-faire contract law in marriage or other contracts. What he was referring to as progressive was the decreasing role of the kind of status relations that left women and other dependents subject to, in Maine's words, "the despotic commands of the heads of households." Maine praised the decrease in paternal power — changes such as the expanding legal capacity of women and other family dependents, the abolition of slavery, and the reduction of guardianship to a protective rather than proprietary institution.

Relational and contractual aspects of marriage have lived side by side relatively undisturbed. These cases illustrate that legal practice can live with and accommodate apparent contradictions with ease. *Maynard* stands today for the proposition that marriage is something more than a mere contract, that it is a status or a relationship and, as such, subject to regulation by the government. The case is frequently cited in the context of constitutional attacks on legislation having an impact on marriage. *Ryan* is an illustration citing *Maynard* in upholding the Florida no-fault divorce statute.

Ponder, decided thirty-seven years earlier than *Maynard*, continues to be relied on in Florida and elsewhere for the seemingly opposite proposition that marriage is contractual rather than a mere status relationship, and that legislation regulating marriage could conceivably impair the obligation of contract if it affects vested rights. *Ponder* is primarily cited in support of the theory that marriage is a contract, notwithstanding the contrary characterization by the United States Supreme Court in *Maynard.*

This illustrates how the significance of landmark cases is often entirely removed from the facts and the holdings. The cases introduce key words and phrases that are subsequently cited regardless of whether or not such reference is historically defensible or logically consistent. In actual practice, consequently, *Maynard* can be cited whenever an argument in support of the police power of the state to regulate marriage is made, while *Ponder* can be cited in support of the contractual autonomy of marital parties to regulate their own affairs. In an extreme case this may be done within the same case, and Ryan demonstrates this capacity to draw from contradictory sources for support.

The facts in *Maynard* and *Ponder* have almost nothing to do with modern reality. They arose out of frontier conditions. David S. Maynard was a powerful figure of American history. Initially trained as a doctor, he founded a medical school in Ohio and later, after his move across the country, became one of the founders of the State of Washington and the city of Seattle. The same legislature of the Territory of Oregon, having jurisdiction over what later was to become the State of Washington, granted *Maynard* his divorce from his first wife, created King County upon his suggestion, declared him to be notary for King County, and established the county seat on his land claim. He was apparently a man who could demand

and receive almost anything he wanted from the legislature. That Archibald Graham was a man of substantial means is mentioned in *Ponder.* That he too was politically influential with the legislature can be inferred from the circumstances and the tone of the special legislation that was enacted by the territorial legislature of Florida in his interest and presumably upon his instigation. Tallahassee, the seat of the legislature and his place of domicile, had been founded as a city and the capital of the new territorial government less than ten years when the Legislative Council passed the act for the relief of Mary Canady. Graham appears to have been one of the first prominent settlers in the area. By neglecting these facts and emphasizing certain fundamental considerations relating to marriage, to the power of the courts and legislatures, and to the United States Constitution, the courts facilitated a process that has led to the conceptually ambivalent, but eminently practical, solution that the current legal situation reflects.

Ponder established Florida as a leading jurisdiction for a theory of marriage as contract, modified by later Florida cases to a theory of marriage as partnership. The materials in this book attest to the increased national importance of this view, and numerous Florida cases have confirmed the pattern, for example, *Chaachou v. Chaachou* (p. 6), *Ryan v. Ryan* (p. 83), *Brown v. Brown* (p. 124), and especially *Gates v. Foley* (p. 478).

Ryan is important for another reason. It demonstrates an early split within no-fault divorce jurisdictions, namely, into those that genuinely try to avoid fault and those that have judicially encouraged its reinstitution. Florida has taken an early lead in the latter direction. Not only is the majority opinion "weeping" over the questioned legislation, it also establishes that the judge is not merely a ministerial officer who must uncritically accept a request for dissolution. Judges should have the power and indeed the duty to inquire about the reasons why the marriage is "irretrievably broken." The answer to this question, as we shall see, reestablishes the possibility of fault, both in the courts and, more importantly, in the negotiations in lawyer's offices where the vast majority of divorce cases are settled before they reach the courtroom.

REFERENCES

Duncan Kennedy, *The Rise and Fall of Classical Legal Thought* (Chapter IV)(Unpublished Manuscript, 1975).

Henry S. Maine, ANCIENT LAW (1861).

Gerhard O.W. Mueller, *Inquiry Into the State of a Divorceless Society: Domestic Relations, Law and Morals in England From 1660 to 1857,* 18 U. PITT. L. REV. 545 (1957).

Frances Olsen, *From False Paternalism to False Equality: Judicial Assaults on Feminist Community, Illinois 1869–1895,* 84 MICH. L. REV. 1518 (1986).

T. Prosch, DAVID S. MAYNARD AND CATHERINE T. MAYNARD: BIOGRAPHIES OF TWO OF THE OREGON IMMIGRANTS OF 1850 (1906).

Sybil Wolfram, *Divorce in England 1700–1857,* 5 OXFORD J. LEGAL STUD. 155 (1985).

B: MARITAL FAILURE AND THE DISTRIBUTION OF LOSSES

Despite statistics that suggest one out of every two marriages in the United States can now be expected to end in divorce, very few people, especially those marrying for the first time, believe that their marriage will fail. This is not to say that most married people are oblivious to the possibility of divorce, but to a great extent they conduct the economics of their marriage on the assumption and with the expectation that the conjugal and financial partnership will continue. Most happily married couples plan their financial futures with permanency in mind. Thus, they enter into economic and financial arrangements that seem objectively foolish, given the high incidence of actual marital breakdown.

For example, when a wife defers or abandons her own education in order that her husband can complete his, both spouses generally expect that the economic benefits of the schooling will inure to the family unit. If a married couple makes sacrifices to advance the career of one of them, they both expect voluntarily to share the benefits — economic and often social. When husband and wife have struggled to advance the husband's career, neither party expects that the marriage will fail and that the wife will suddenly be forced to live solely on her individual earnings, or that the husband will be forced to pay a significant portion of his income to an ex-wife he no longer loves. Few if any homemakers, full- or part-time, think of themselves as employees at will; yet, the high incidence of divorce has made homemaking an occupation with remarkably little job security. Successful professionals who increase their income and earning power with the loyal support of a spouse rarely if ever think of themselves as mortgaging their future earnings to a future ex-spouse. When a couple chooses to organize married life in such a way that one spouse (usually but not necessarily the husband) increases his or her earning potential, while the other spouse (almost always the wife) decreases hers (or, rarely, his), they are engaging in risky behavior, given that so many marriages end in divorce. Nevertheless, in our society there are a great many incentives built into the employment structure and the culture that encourage married couples to engage in this risky behavior. For example, to be successful and advance quickly in many jobs, a worker must be free to go on business trips out of town on short notice or must be willing to move from one city to another, options available usually to only one spouse, and most often exercised by the husband. Income tax laws indirectly reward couples with a large gap between their incomes, and no tax deduction is allowed for household help or other expenses that may be required when both spouses devote long hours to their paid employment.

There is considerable disagreement about how the risk should be shared. When a marriage dissolves, the hopes and expectations of both spouses are generally disappointed. Voluntary sharing of income ceases; the question becomes whether substantial sharing will be required by law, forcing the higher-income party to bear a share of the risk, or whether it will not be, forcing the other party to bear virtually the entire risk. In the absence of substantial transfer payments, whether in the form of "property" division or long term alimony, the spouse without the earning power (usually the wife) risks much more than the other partner.

A number of people have argued that alimony should be eliminated as outmoded and that no one should be considered to have any ownership interest in the education, profession or earning capacity of an ex-spouse. In England, this is touted as a "clean break." Proponents often acknowledge that in our society, their policies would tend to hurt women, especially women who have devoted themselves to homemaking or child care. They argue, however, that such women have only themselves to blame for choosing to become economically dependent upon their husbands. If they did not want to take the risk, then they should have developed their own careers or else protected themselves with an antenuptial (or midnuptial) agreement. Moreover, some argue, the "clean break" theory reinforces women's equality in marriage by discouraging women from falling into the outmoded unequal role allocation of traditional marriages.

While it may well be true, at least to some extent, that limiting alimony gives women a disincentive to accept an organization of married life that would leave them impoverished upon divorce, it leaves men with every incentive to promote such an organization. If, as seems likely, men are generally at least as responsible as their wives for any unequal role allocation in marriage, there is no reason that men should not bear at least half the risk. The notion of a "clean break" (or clean get-away, a critic might say) is a refusal to accept a fair share of the loss suffered when a marriage relationship breaks down. The "free choice" or contract argument made by proponents of a "clean break" is just as convincing in reverse: men saddled with alimony payments or some other form of income sharing have only themselves to blame for having encouraged their ex-wives to be economically dependent upon them; if husbands did not want to take the risk, then they should have protected themselves with an antenuptial (or midnuptial) agreement. Moreover, it can be argued that alimony or other substantial transfer payments in the case of economically unequal marriages will more effectively promote women's equality in marriage by encouraging men to eschew the outmoded unequal role allocation of traditional marriages. Whatever incentive denying alimony may place on women to form equal relationships, granting substantial alimony when economically unequal relationships dissolve may place as great an incentive on men to promote equal relationships.

Couples who increase the earning capacity of one spouse at the expense of the earning capacity of the other might be taking a risk. First, their behavior is based on the presupposition that the marriage will continue, and statistically half of American marriages fail. In addition, the role allocation may itself undermine the relationship and destabilize the marriage. We all know that attending law school, for example, puts a strain on relationships and often brings about important changes in the spouse who attends. Devoting oneself to child care also changes one, and for one parent to do a disproportionate share of child care can put a strain on a relationship. Second, a divorce law that unduly limits alimony and property division may put an additional strain on such marriages. Most people recognize that it would have some destabilizing tendency on a marriage if an outside third party were to offer the husband a seventy percent increase in his standard of living if he leaves his wife; a contract to make such a payment, for example, would probably be ruled unenforceable as a violation of public policy. Yet, studies have suggested that present divorce law, which restricts alimony (restricts it as a practical matter if not also as a matter of legal doctrine) and property division, has precisely this effect. In the average divorce, the husband's post-divorce income increases seventy percent, while the wife's decreases by some fifty percent. Under these circumstances, a growing number of feminists have argued that divorce law must be changed to provide for post-divorce support payments or for a property division that takes into account the very different earning capacities the parties take out of the marriage. Divorced husbands who have already benefitted economically from the marriage should be required to compensate for the input their wife made in reliance upon the marriage.

Most people concerned with improving the role and status of women have opposed old concepts of alimony under which post-divorce support would be ordered (though collection has always been a significant problem) to be paid to women on the basis of their gender and only if they were not "at fault" for the breakup of the marriage. The gradual abolition of these old concepts is usually seen as a step toward sex equality. Formal equality between husband and wife does not, however, eliminate the economic interaction during marriage that so often leaves wives with a much lower earning capacity than husbands. An important question is whether it is now possible to proceed further in the direction of substantive equality and to reduce the actual dependency of women upon their husbands. Pretending that equality already exists when it really does not, and thus refusing to order a fair post-divorce economic readjustment, contributes to the wife actually being dependent upon the continuation of the marriage, once she has participated in a family organization that promotes the husband's earning capacity at the expense of hers.

Some conservatives attribute the economic disparity between men and women to the biological fact that women give birth and lactate. Most proponents of women's equality have rejected this explanation, focusing instead on the social pressures that reinforce the sexual division of labor. More sophisticated "biological" analyses acknowledge the role of social pressure, but trace this social pressure also to biology. In any event, the argument for post-divorce payments does not depend upon any biological explanation. Nor would post-divorce payments be necessarily from husband to wife, rather than from wife to husband. The question in each case would be what kind of post-divorce payments would be necessary to equalize post-divorce opportunities or standards of living and to compensate the lower-income spouse for her or his reliance on the continuation of the marriage. The overall effect of such changes would be significantly to improve the economic condition of divorced women and their children, one of the major poverty groups in America at this time.

It remains a question, however, how much economic equality between men and women can be brought about through changes in divorce law. First, the law has not yet devised an effective method for collecting alimony payments (or even child support payments). Reneging on support obligations is considered by many to be as acceptable as drunk driving used to be. It is too early to say whether the establishment of child support enforcement offices and their efforts to change public attitudes may be successful. In 1992, the Republican Party was mildly embarrassed when it was discovered and widely publicized that one of their major contributors had reneged on thousands of dollars in child support.

Moreover, there is a question how much of the economic disparity between men and women can be blamed on marriage. Inequality between men and women is caused by many factors, and divorce law is only one factor. The serious disparity generally present in the post-divorce standard of living of ex-husbands and ex-wives mirrors, albeit in an exaggerated fashion, the general inequality in income between men as a group and women as a group. It could be argued that if we were to institute a system of alimony payments that would remove the economic incentives regarding divorce (the incentive to most men to divorce and the incentive to most women to stay married), this reform would simply mitigate in some cases the general effects of gender inequality. On the other hand, some, such as Professor Paul Weiler, have argued that virtually all the income disparity between men and women can be traced to marriage and the unequal organization of family responsibilities, especially child care.

REFERENCES

Bea A. Smith, *The Partnership Theory of Marriage: A Borrowed Solution Fails*, 68 TEX. L. REV. 689, 690–94, 739–43 (1990).

Paul Weiler, *The Wages of Sex: The Uses and Limits of Comparable Worth*, 99 HARV. L. REV., 1728, 1785–88 (1986).

Lenore J. Weitzman, *The Economics of Divorce: Social and Economic Consequences of Property, Alimony and Child Support Awards*, 28 U.C.L.A. L. REV. 1181 (1981).

Joint Investment in Education

MORGAN v. MORGAN [I]

Supreme Court, Trial Term, New York County
81 Misc.2d 616, 366 N.Y.S.2d 977 (1975)

BENTLEY KASSAL, J.

...

The parties were married on January 27, 1967 when the husband was in his third year pre-law course at the University of North Carolina and the wife, a sophomore, studying biology, at the Florida State University. Recognizing that both could not simultaneously continue their education and be self-supporting, they agreed it would be preferable for him to finish his undergraduate and law school education while she worked. She commenced working full-time, earning a monthly salary of $328.00 until the day before she gave birth to a son, on August 9, 1967. She resumed working a few months later, in January 1968, on a part-time basis, took care of her own and other children, on an exchange basis, and did typing at home for students, as well as her husband's theses. This continued until she and her husband separated in October 1972.

In the interim, Mrs. Morgan has become very proficient at short-hand and typing and also worked as a data analyst. I am satisfied that she is very skilled and, as an executive secretary or technician, could probably command an annual salary of at least $10,000 in normal economy and, very possibly, even in the present employment market.

In February 1973, she returned to the campus to pursue a full time educational career by undertaking a pre-medical course at Hunter College and her grades have been exceptional — a 3.83 general average (out of a 4.0 maximum) and an A score in the organic chemistry course, ranking 5th in a class of 70.

For his part, the husband has progressed well in his profession, having graduated from Columbia Law School after being selected for its Law Journal. His career started, as planned, with a one year stint as a law clerk to a Federal Circuit Judge and he immediately thereafter became an associate at a prominent Wall Street law firm. His starting salary, in August 1972 was $18,000 per annum with $500 increases on November 1, 1972, March 1, 1973, April 1, 1973, a $3,500 increase on November 1, 1973, a $1,500 increase on May 1, 1974 with the most recent increase of $3,000 on November 1, 1974, to a present salary level of $27,500. In all, he has done well and his future appears very promising.

...

At a time when some call for treating the marriage contract as any other contract, it is particularly appropriate to speak of the wife's duty to mitigate the damages to the husband upon breach. I agree that "when she can, she should also be required to mitigate the husband's burden either by her own financial means or earning potential or both." *Doyle v. Doyle*, 5 Misc.2d 4, 158 N.Y.S.2d 909. But it is a corollary to the rule of mitigation that the injured party may also recover for the expenses reasonably incurred in an effort to avoid or reduce the damages. *Norske Ameriekalinje v. Sun Printing & Pub. Ass'n*, 226 N.Y. 1, 8, 122 N.E. 463, 465. In this case, any possible short-term economic benefit which would result from the wife's returning to a position similar to the one she held over two years ago, is far outweighed by the potential benefit, economic, emotional and otherwise, of her pursuing her education.

In coming to the conclusion I do, I am seeking to effect a balancing of many factors — the parties' financial status, their obligations, age, station in life and opportunities for development and self-fulfillment. As noted in *Phillips v. Phillips*, 1 A.D.2d 393, 395, 150 N.Y.S.2d 646, 649, affd. 2 N.Y.2d 742, 157 N.Y.S.2d 378, 138 N.E.2d 738, times have changed, owing not alone to the co-equal status which a married woman shares with her husband, but also to the increase in the number of married women working in gainful occupations....

Further, I would like to cite a study by the Special Committee on Divorce of the National Conference of Commissioners on Uniform State Laws, entitled "Uniform Marriage and Divorce Legislation: a Preliminary Analysis," which, in setting forth some of the factors to be considered in determining whether alimony is indicated and the quantum thereof, lists the following, among others:

(b) The time necessary to acquire sufficient education or training to enable the party seeking maintenance to find *suitable* employment. (Emphasis added.)

Two of Webster's Dictionary's synonyms for "suitable" are "appropriate" and "fitting." True, plaintiff could spend her life working at what she has been doing for the past seven years, after she, of necessity, agreed to help provide her husband with education for his "suitable employment" but that would not in my judgment be appropriate for the wife, a person with the capabilities of becoming a doctor.

The provisions of Section 236 of the Domestic Relations Law direct, *inter alia*, that the Court consider the "ability of the wife to be self-supporting," as well as "the circumstances of the case and of the respective parties." "Self-supporting," in my judgment, does not imply that the wife shall be compelled to take any position that will be available when her obvious potential in life, in terms of "self-support," will be greatly inhibited.

Cognizance must also be taken of other language in the very same section, namely, "...the court *may* direct the husband to *provide suitably* for the support of the wife *as, in the court's discretion, justice requires...*" (emphasis added). This has been interpreted to vest broad discretion in the court, "unfettered by" literal readings of the law.... Obviously two households cannot be maintained as cheaply as one and we therefore encounter the threshold issue of whether the wife — a very capable woman, probably able to earn at least $10,000 annually as a secretary or office worker — shall be compelled to contribute this sum, or a fair share thereof, to her own support, at this time, or shall she have an opportunity to achieve a professional education based upon her potential, which will be comparable to the one her husband received as a result of her assistance by working during their marriage.

In my opinion, the answer to this issue is that under these circumstances, the wife is also entitled to equal treatment and a "break" and should not be automatically relegated to a life of being a well-paid, skilled technician laboring with a lifelong frustration as to what her future might have been as a doctor, but for her marriage and motherhood.

I am impressed by the fact that the plaintiff does not assume the posture that she wants to be an alimony drone or seek permanent alimony. Rather she had indicated that she only wants support for herself until she finishes medical school in 5½ years (1½ years more in college and 4 years in medical school) and will try to work when possible.

In this regard, she merely seeks for herself the same opportunity which she helped give to the defendant.

Accordingly, I am directing that the defendant shall pay a total sum of $200 weekly for alimony and child support, so long as she does not remarry and continues to be a full-time student, undertaking a pre-medical or medical course. (I am taking into consideration plaintiff's agreement to work during her vacation periods when not prohibited by school work.) Completion of her medical school training and the awarding of an M.D. degree shall be deemed a sufficient change of circumstances and I am granting leave to the defendant to apply at such time for an appropriate modification to delete the alimony feature of this award.

MORGAN v. MORGAN [II]
Supreme Court of New York, Appellate Division
52 A.D. 2d 804, 383 N.Y.S.2d 343 (1976)

MEMORANDUM DECISION.

Judgment, Supreme Court, New York County, entered June 23, 1975, unanimously modified, on the law and the facts and in the exercise of discretion to reduce alimony to the sum of $75 weekly, and otherwise affirmed, without costs and without disbursements....

The alimony of $100 per week awarded below was predicated upon plaintiff's ambition to obtain entrance to medical school and receive an M.D. degree. It is not disputed that the plaintiff has present earning ability, which the court below believed might be at least $10,000 per year. A wife's ability to be self-supporting is relevant when determining the amount of support a husband is to provide....

Absent a compelling showing that the wife cannot contribute to her own support, courts have "imputed" or deducted a wife's potential earnings from the amount which would otherwise be found payable as alimony by her ex-husband.... While this Court recognizes plaintiff's goal in medicine, this pursuit was never in the contemplation of the parties during marriage and appears to be of recent origin. The law requires that the alimony award should be predicated upon the present circumstances of the parties. Although the wife's ambition is most commendable, the court below was in error in including in the alimony award monies for the achievement of that goal.

...

O'BRIEN v. O'BRIEN
Court of Appeals of New York
66 N.Y. 2d 576, 489 N.E.2d 712 (1985)

SIMONS, J.,

In this divorce action, the parties' only asset of any consequence is the husband's newly acquired license to practice medicine. The principal issue presented is whether that license, acquired during their marriage, is marital property subject to equitable distribution under Domestic Relations Law §236 (B)(5)....

We now hold that plaintiff's medical license constitutes "marital property" within the meaning of Domestic Relations Law §236(B)(1)(c) and...is therefore subject to equitable distribution....

I

Plaintiff and defendant married on April 3, 1971. At the time both were employed as teachers at the same private school. Defendant had a bachelor's degree and a temporary teaching certificate but required 18 months of postgraduate classes at an approximate cost of $3,000, excluding living expenses, to obtain permanent certification in New York. She claimed, and the trial court found, that she had relinquished the opportunity to obtain permanent certification while plaintiff pursued his education. At the time of the marriage, plaintiff had completed only three and one-half years of college but shortly afterward he returned to school at night to earn his bachelor's degree and to complete sufficient pre-medical courses to enter medical school. In September 1973 the parties moved to

Guadalajara, Mexico, where plaintiff became a full-time medical student. While he pursued his studies defendant held several teaching and tutorial positions and contributed her earnings to their joint expenses. The parties returned to New York in December 1976 so that plaintiff could complete the last two semesters of medical school and internship training here. After they returned, defendant resumed her former teaching position and she remained in it at the time this action was commenced. Plaintiff was licensed to practice medicine in October 1980. He commenced this action for divorce two months later. At the time of trial, he was a resident in general surgery.

During the marriage both parties contributed to paying the living and educational expenses and they received additional help from both of their families. They disagreed on the amounts of their respective contributions but it is undisputed that in addition to performing household work and managing the family finances defendant was gainfully employed throughout the marriage, that she contributed all of her earnings to their living and educational expenses and that her financial contributions exceeded those of plaintiff. The trial court found that she had contributed 76% of the parties' income exclusive of a $10,000 student loan obtained by defendant. Finding that plaintiff's medical degree and license are marital property, the court received evidence of its value and ordered a distributive award to defendant.

Defendant presented expert testimony that the present value of plaintiff's medical license was $472,000. Her expert testified that he arrived at this figure by comparing the average income of a college graduate and that of a general surgeon between 1985, when plaintiff's residency would end, and 2012, when he would reach age 65. After considering Federal income taxes, an inflation rate of 10% and a real interest rate of 3% he capitalized the difference in average earnings and reduced the amount to present value. He also gave his opinion that the present value of defendant's contribution to plaintiff's medical education was $103,390. Plaintiff offered no expert testimony on the subject.

The court, after considering the life-style that plaintiff would enjoy from the enhanced earning potential his medical license would bring and defendant's contributions and efforts toward attainment of it, made a distributive award to her of $188,800, representing 40% of the value of the license, and ordered it paid in 11 annual installments of various amounts beginning November 1, 1982 and ending November 1, 1992. The court also directed plaintiff to maintain a life insurance policy on his life for defendant's benefit for the unpaid balance of the award and it ordered plaintiff to pay defendant's counsel fees of $7,000 and her expert witness fee of $1,000. It did not award defendant maintenance.

A divided Appellate Division...concluded that a professional license acquired during marriage is not marital property subject to distribution....

...

II

The Equitable Distribution Law contemplates only two classes of property: marital property and separate property.... The former, which is subject to equitable distribution, is defined broadly as "*all* property acquired by either or both spouses during the marriage and before the execution of a separation agreement or the commencement of a matrimonial action, *regardless of the form in which title is held*" (Domestic Relations Law §236[B][1][c] [emphasis added]; *see* §236[B][5][b], [c]). Plaintiff does not contend that his license is excluded from distribution because it is separate property; rather, he claims that it is not property at all but represents a personal attainment in acquiring knowledge. He rests his argument on decisions in similar cases from other jurisdictions and on his view that a license does not satisfy common-law concepts of property. Neither contention is controlling because decisions in other States rely principally on their own statutes, and the legislative history underlying them, and because the New York Legislature deliberately went beyond traditional property concepts when it formulated the Equitable Distribution Law.... Instead, our statute recognizes that spouses have an equitable claim to things of value arising out of the marital relationship and classifies them as subject to distribution by focusing on the marital status of the parties at the time of acquisition. Those things acquired during marriage and subject to distribution have been classified as "marital property" although, as one commentator has observed, they hardly fall within the traditional property concepts because there is no common-law property interest remotely resembling marital property. "It is a statutory creature, is of no meaning whatsoever during the normal course of a marriage and arises full-grown, like Athena, upon the signing of a separation agreement or the commencement of a matrimonial action. [Thus] [i]t is hardly surprising, and not at all relevant, that traditional common law property concepts do not fit in parsing the meaning of 'marital property'" (Florescue, *"Market Value", Professional Licenses and Marital Property: A Dilemma in Search of a Horn*, 1982 N.Y. St. Bar Assn. Fam. L. Rev. 13 [Dec.]). Having classified the "property" subject to distribution, the Legislature did not attempt to go further and define it but left it to the courts to determine what interests come within the terms of section 236(B)(1)(c).

...

Section 236 provides that in making an equitable distribution of marital property, "the court shall consider: ...(6) any equitable claim to, interest in, or direct or indirect contribution made to the acquisition of such marital property by the party not having title, including joint efforts or expenditures and contributions and services as a spouse, parent, wage earner and homemaker, and *to the career or career potential* of the other party [and]...(9) the impossibility or difficulty of evaluating any component asset or any interest in a business, corporation or *profession*" (Domestic Relations Law §236[B][5][d][6], [9][emphasis added]). Where equitable distribution of marital property is appropriate but "the distribution of an interest in a business, corporation or *profession* would be contrary to law" the court shall make a distributive award in lieu of an actual distribution of the property (Domestic Relations Law §236[B][5][e][emphasis added]). The words mean exactly what they say: that an interest in a profession or professional career potential is marital property which may be represented by direct or indirect contributions of the non-title-holding spouse, including financial contributions and nonfinancial contributions made by caring for the home and family.

The history which preceded enactment of the statute confirms this interpretation. Reform...was advocated because experience had proven that application of the traditional common-law title theory of property had caused inequities upon dissolution of a marriage. The Legislature replaced the existing system with equitable distribution of marital property, an entirely new theory which considered all the circumstances of the case and of the respective parties to the marriage.... Equitable distribution was based on the premise that a marriage is, among other things, an economic partnership to which both parties contribute as spouse, parent, wage earner or homemaker.... Consistent with this purpose, and implicit in the statutory scheme as a whole, is the view that upon dissolution of the marriage there should be a winding up of the parties' economic affairs and a severance of their economic ties by an equitable distribution of the marital assets. Thus, the concept of alimony, which often served as a means of lifetime support and dependence for one spouse upon the other long after the marriage was over, was replaced with the concept of maintenance which seeks to allow "the recipient spouse an opportunity to achieve [economic] independence"....

The determination that a professional license is marital property is also consistent with the conceptual base upon which the statute rests. As this case demonstrates, few undertakings during a marriage better qualify as the type of joint effort that the statute's economic partnership theory is intended to address than contributions toward one spouse's acquisition of a professional license. Working spouses are often required to contribute substantial income as wage earners, sacrifice their own educational or career goals and opportunities for child rearing, perform the bulk of household duties and responsibility and forego the acquisition of marital assets that could have been accumulated if the professional spouse had been employed rather than occupied with the study and training necessary to acquire a professional license. In this case, nearly all of the parties' nine-year marriage was devoted to the acquisition of plaintiff's medical license and defendant played a major role in that project. She worked continuously during the marriage and contributed all of her earnings to their joint effort, she sacrificed her own educational and career opportunities, and she traveled with plaintiff to Mexico for three and one-half years while he attended medical school there. The Legislature has decided, by its explicit reference in the statute to the contributions of one spouse to the other's profession or career...that these contributions represent investments in the economic partnership of the marriage and that the product of the parties' joint efforts, the professional license, should be considered marital property.

...

Plaintiff's principal argument...is that a professional license is not marital property because it does not fit within the traditional view of property as something which has an exchange value on the open market and is capable of sale, assignment or transfer. The position does not withstand analysis for at least two reasons. First...it ignores the fact that whether a professional license constitutes marital property is to be judged by the language of the statute which created this new species of property previously unknown at common law or under prior statutes. Thus, whether the license fits within traditional property concepts is of no consequence. Second, it is an overstatement to assert that a professional license could not be considered property even outside the context of section 236(B). A professional license is a valuable property right, reflected in the money, effort and lost opportunity for employment expended in its acquisition, and also in the enhanced earning capacity it affords its holder, which may not be revoked without due process of law.... That a professional license has no market value is irrelevant. Obviously, a license may not be alienated as may other property and for that reason the working spouse's interest in it is limited. The Legislature has recognized that limitation, however, and has provided for an award in lieu of its actual distribution....

Plaintiff also contends that alternative remedies should be employed, such as an award of rehabilitative maintenance or reimbursement for direct financial contributions.... The statute does not expressly authorize retrospective maintenance or rehabilitative awards and we have no occasion to decide in this case whether the authority to do so may ever be implied from its provisions.... It is sufficient to observe that normally a working spouse should not be restricted to that relief because to do so frustrates the purposes underlying the Equitable Distribution Law. Limiting a working spouse to a maintenance award, either general or rehabilitative, not only is contrary to the economic partnership concept underlying the statute but also retains the uncertain and inequitable economic ties of dependence that the Legislature sought to extinguish by equitable distribution. Maintenance is subject to termination upon the recipient's remarriage and a working spouse may never receive adequate consideration for his or her contribution and may even be penalized for the decision to remarry if that is the only method of compensating the contribution. As one court said so well, "[t]he function of equitable distribution is to recognize that when a marriage ends, each of the spouses, based on the totality of the contributions made to it, has a stake in and right to a share of the marital assets accumulated while it endured, not because that share is needed, but because those assets represent the capital product of what was essentially a partnership entity" (*Wood v. Wood*, 119 Misc.2d 1076, 1079). The Legislature stated its intention to eliminate such inequities by providing that a supporting spouse's "direct or indirect contribution" be recognized, considered and rewarded (Domestic Relations Law § 236[B][5][d][6]).

...[I]t has been suggested that even if a professional license is considered marital property, the working spouse is entitled only to reimbursement of his or her direct financial contributions.... By parity of reasoning, a spouse's down payment on real estate or contribution to the purchase of securities would be limited to the money contributed, without any remuneration for any incremental value in the asset because of price appreciation. Such a result is completely at odds with the statute's requirement that the court give full consideration to both direct and indirect contributions "made to the acquisition of such marital property by the party not having title, including joint *efforts* or expenditures and *contributions and services as a spouse, parent,* wage earner *and homemaker*"...[emphasis added]). If the license is marital property, then the working spouse is entitled to an equitable portion of it, not a return of funds advanced. Its value is the enhanced earning capacity it affords the holder and although fixing the present value of that enhanced earning capacity may present problems, the problems are not insurmountable. Certainly they are no more difficult than computing tort damages for wrongful death or diminished earning capacity resulting from injury and they differ only in degree from the problems presented when valuing a professional practice for purposes of a distributive award, something the courts have not hesitated to do.... The trial court retains the flexibility and discretion to structure the distributive award equitably, taking into consideration factors such as the working spouse's need for immediate payment, the licensed spouse's current ability to pay and the income tax consequences of prolonging the period of payment....

...

MEYER, J. (concurring).

I...write separately to point up for consideration by the Legislature the potential for unfairness involved in distributive awards based upon a license of a professional still in training.

An equity court normally has power to "change its decrees where there has been a change of circumstances".... [H]owever,...a distributive award...is not subject to change. Yet a professional in training who is not finally committed to a career choice when the distributive award is made may be locked into a particular kind of practice simply because the monetary obligations imposed by the distributive award made on the basis of the trial judge's conclusion (prophecy may be a better word) as to what the career choice will be leaves him or her no alternative.

The present case points up the problem. A medical license is but a step toward the practice ultimately engaged in by its holder, which follows after internship, residency and, for particular specialties, board certification. Here it is undisputed that plaintiff was in a residency for general surgery at the time of the trial, but had the previous year done a residency in internal medicine. Defendant's expert based his opinion on the difference between the average income of a general surgeon and that of a college graduate of plaintiff's age and life expectancy, which the trial judge utilized, impliedly finding that plaintiff would engage in a surgical practice despite plaintiff's testimony that he was dissatisfied with the general surgery program he was in and was attempting to return to the internal medicine training he had been in the previous year. The trial judge had the right, of course, to discredit that testimony, but the point is that equitable distribution was not intended to permit a judge to make a career decision for a licensed spouse still in training. Yet the degree of speculation involved in the award made is emphasized by the testimony of the expert on which it was based. Asked whether his assumptions and calculations were in any way speculative, he replied: "Yes. They're speculative to the extent of, will Dr. O'Brien practice medicine? Will Dr. O'Brien earn more or less than the average surgeon earns? Will Dr. O'Brien live to age sixty-five? Will Dr. O'Brien have a heart attack or will he be injured in an automobile accident? Will he be disabled? I mean, there is a degree of speculation. That speculative aspect is no more to be taken into account, cannot be taken into account, and it's a question, again, Mr. Emanuelli, not for the expert but for the courts to decide. It's not my function nor could it be."

The equitable distribution provisions of the Domestic Relations Law were intended to provide flexibility so that equity could be done. But if the assumption as to career choice on which a distributive award payable over a number of years is based turns out not to be the fact (as, for example, should a general surgery trainee accidentally lose the use of his hand), it should be possible for the court to revise the distributive award to conform to the fact....

...

MAHONEY v. MAHONEY

Supreme Court of New Jersey

91 N.J. 488, 453 A.2d 527 (1982)

PASHMAN, J.

Once again the Court must interpret this state's law regarding the distribution of marital property upon divorce. The question here is whether the defendant has the right to share the value of a professional business (M.B.A.) degree earned by her former husband during their marriage. The Court must decide whether the plaintiff's degree is "property" for purposes of N.J.S.A. 2A:34–23, which requires equitable distribution of "the property, both real and personal, which was legally and beneficially acquired...during the marriage." If the M.B.A. degree is not property, we must still decide whether the defendant can nonetheless recover the money she contributed to her husband's support while he pursued his professional education. For the reasons stated below, we hold that the plaintiff's professional degree is not property and therefore reject the defendant's claim that the degree is subject to equitable distribution. To this extent, we concur in the reasoning of the Appellate Division. Notwithstanding this concurrence, we reverse the judgment of the Appellate Division, which had the effect of denying the defendant any remedial relief for her contributions toward her husband's professional education and remand for further proceedings.

I

When the parties married in Indiana in 1971, plaintiff, Melvin Mahoney, had an engineering degree and defendant, June Lee Mahoney, had a bachelor of science degree. From that time until the parties separated in October 1978 they generally shared all household expenses. The sole exception was the period between September 1975 and January 1977, when the plaintiff attended the Wharton School of the University of Pennsylvania and received an M.B.A. degree.

During the 16-month period in which the plaintiff attended school, June Lee Mahoney contributed about $24,000 to the household. Her husband made no financial contribution while he was a student. Melvin's educational expenses of about $6,500 were paid for by a combination of veterans' benefits and a payment from the Air Force. After receiving his degree, the plaintiff went to work as a commercial lending officer for Chase Manhattan Bank.

Meanwhile, in 1976 the defendant began a part-time graduate program at Rutgers University, paid for by her employer, that led to a master's degree in microbiology one year after the parties had separated. June Lee worked full-time throughout the course of her graduate schooling.

In March 1979, Melvin Mahoney sued for divorce; his wife filed a counterclaim also seeking a divorce. In May 1980, the trial court granted dual judgments of divorce on the ground of 18 months continuous separation.

At the time of trial, plaintiff's annual income was $25,600 and defendant's income was $21,000. No claim for alimony was made. The parties owned no real property and divided the small amount of their personal property by agreement.

The only issue at trial was the defendant's claim for reimbursement of the amount of support she gave her husband while he obtained his M.B.A. degree. Defendant sought 50% of the $24,000 she had contributed to the household during that time, plus one-half of the $6,500 cost of her husband's tuition.

The trial court decided that defendant should be reimbursed, 175 N.J.Super. 443, 419 A.2d 1149 (Ch.Div.1980), holding that "the education and degree obtained by plaintiff, under the circumstances of this case, constitute a property right...." *Id.* at 447, 419 A.2d 1149. However, the court did not attempt to determine the value of plaintiff's M.B.A. degree. Instead, finding that in this case "[t]o ignore the contributions of the sacrificing spouse would be...an unjust enrichment of the educated spouse," *Id.* at 446, 419 A.2d 1149, the court ordered the award of a "reasonable sum as a credit [for]...the maintenance of the household and the support of plaintiff during the educational period." *Id.* at 447, 419 A.2d 1149. Plaintiff was ordered to reimburse his wife in the amount of $5,000, to be paid at the rate of $100 per month. The court did not explain why it chose this amount.

Plaintiff appealed to the Appellate Division, which reversed the award. 182 N.J.Super. 598, 442 A.2d 1062 (1982). It not only rejected defendant's claim for reimbursement but also held that neither a professional license nor an educational degree is "property" for the purposes of the equitable distribution statute, N.J.S.A. 2A:34-23. In so holding, the Appellate Division stated that it was bound by *Stern v. Stern*, 66 N.J. 340, 345, 331 A.2d 257 (1975), where the Court held that "a person's earning capacity...should not be recognized as a separate, particular item of property within the meaning of N.J.S.A. 2A:34–23." (footnote omitted). The Appellate Division noted that if enhanced earning capacity is not property, then "neither is the license or degree, which is merely the memorialization of the attainment of the skill, qualification and educational background which is the prerequisite of the enhanced earning capacity...." 182 N.J.Super. at 605, 442 A.2d 1062. The court noted that degrees and licenses lack many of the attributes of most property rights, *Id.* at 605, 442 A.2d 1062, and that their value is not only speculative, *Id.* at 609, 442 A.2d 1062, but also may be fully accounted for by way of alimony and equitable division of the other assets. *Id.* at 607, 442 A.2d 1062.

In rejecting defendant's claim for reimbursement, the Appellate Division disapproved of the attempt to measure the contributions of the parties to one another or to their marriage.... The Appellate Division saw no need to distinguish contributions made toward a spouse's attainment of a license or degree from other contributions, calling such special treatment "a kind of elitism which inappropriately depreciates the value of all the other types of contributions made to each other by other spouses...." 182 N.J.Super. at 613, 442 A.2d 1062. Finally, the court noted that in this case each spouse left the marriage "with comparable earning capacity and comparable educational achievements." *Id.* at 615, 442 A.2d 1062. The court did not order a remand.

We granted certification, 91 N.J. 191, 450 A.2d 526 (1982).

II

This case first involves a question of statutory interpretation. The Court must decide whether the Legislature intended an M.B.A. degree to be "property" so that, if acquired by either spouse during a marriage, its value must be equitably distributed upon divorce. In determining whether the Legislature intended to treat an M.B.A. degree as property under N.J.S.A. 2A:34–23, the Court gains little guidance from traditional rules of statutory construction. There is no legislative history on the meaning of the word "property" in the equitable distribution statute, L.1971, c. 212, N.J.S.A. 2A:34–23, and the statute itself offers no guidance.[1] Therefore, statutory construction in this case means little more than an inquiry into the extent to which professional degrees and licenses share the qualities of other things that the Legislature and courts have treated as property.

Regarding equitable distribution, this Court has frequently held that an "expansive interpretation [is] to be given to the word 'property,'" *Gauger v. Gauger*, 73 N.J. 538, 544, 376 A.2d 523 (1977). *Accord Kruger v. Kruger*, 73 N.J. 464, 468, 375 A.2d 659 (1977); *Painter v. Painter*, 65 N.J. 196, 217, 320 A.2d 484 (1974)....

This Court, however, has never subjected to equitable distribution an asset whose future monetary value is as uncertain and unquantifiable as a professional degree or license....

---

1. The 1980 amendments to the law, L.1980, c. 181, which excluded from equitable distribution property acquired after the marriage by way of gift, devise or bequest, had no bearing on the issue of what types of chattels or interests should be treated as property.

A professional license or degree is a personal achievement of the holder. It cannot be sold and its value cannot readily be determined. A professional license or degree represents the opportunity to obtain an amount of money only upon the occurrence of highly uncertain future events....

The value of a professional degree for purposes of property distribution is nothing more than the possibility of enhanced earnings that the particular academic credential will provide.... Equitable distribution of a professional degree would similarly require distribution of "earning capacity" — income that the degree holder might never acquire. The amount of future earnings would be entirely speculative. Moreover, any assets resulting from income for professional services would be property acquired after the marriage; the statute restricts equitable distribution to property acquired during the marriage. N.J.S.A. 2A:34–23. *Accord In re Marriage of Aufmuth*, 89 Cal.App.3d 446, 152 Cal.Rptr. 668, 678 (1979).

Valuing a professional degree in the hands of any particular individual at the start of his or her career would involve a gamut of calculations that reduces to little more than guesswork. As the Appellate Division noted, courts would be required to determine far more than what the degree holder could earn in the new career. The admittedly speculative dollar amount of

> earnings in the "enhanced" career [must] be reduced by the...income the spouse should be assumed to have been able to earn if otherwise employed. In our view [this] is ordinarily nothing but speculation, particularly when it is fair to assume that a person with the ability and motivation to complete professional training or higher education would probably utilize those attributes in concomitantly productive alternative endeavors. [182 N.J.Super. at 609, 442 A.2d 1062]

Even if such estimates could be made, however, there would remain a world of unforeseen events that could affect the earning potential — not to mention the actual earnings — of any particular degree holder.

> A person qualified by education for a given profession may choose not to practice it, may fail at it, or may practice in a specialty, location or manner which generates less than the average income enjoyed by fellow professionals. The potential worth of the education may never be realized for these or many other reasons. An award based upon the prediction of the degree holder's success at the chosen field may bear no relationship to the reality he or she faces after the divorce. [*DeWitt v. DeWitt*, 98 Wis.2d 44, 296 N.W.2d 761, 768 (Ct.App.1980)(footnote omitted)]

Moreover, the likelihood that an equitable distribution will prove to be unfair is increased in those cases where the court miscalculates the value of the license or degree.

> The potential for inequity to the failed professional or one who changes careers is at once apparent; his or her spouse will have been awarded a share of something which never existed in any real sense. [*Id.*]

The finality of property distribution precludes any remedy for such unfairness. "Unlike an award of alimony, which can be adjusted after divorce to reflect unanticipated changes in the parties' circumstances, a property division may not [be adjusted]." *Id.* (footnote omitted).

Because of these problems, most courts that have faced the issue have declined to treat professional degrees and licenses as marital property subject to distribution upon divorce. See, *e.g., Wisner, supra* (medical license); *Frausto v. Frausto,* 611 S.W.2d 656 (Tex.Civ.App.1981)(medical license); *DeWitt, supra* (law degree); *Aufmuth, supra* (law degree); *Graham, supra* (M.B.A.); *Wilcox v. Wilcox,* 173 Ind.App. 661, 365 N.E.2d 792 (1977)(Ph.D. degree); *Todd v. Todd,* 272 Cal.App.2d 786, 78 Cal.Rptr. 131 (1969)(law degree). Several courts, while not treating educational degrees as property, have awarded the supporting spouse an amount based on the cost to the supporting spouse of obtaining the degree. In effect, the supporting spouse was reimbursed for her financial contributions used by the supported spouse in obtaining a degree. See, *e.g., DeLa Rosa v. DeLa Rosa,* 309 N.W.2d 755, 759 (Minn.1981)(medical degree); *Hubbard v. Hubbard,* 603 P.2d 747, 751 (Okl.1979)(medical degree); *In re Marriage of Horstmann,* 263 N.W.2d 885, 891 (Iowa Ct.1978)(law degree). *Cf. Inman v. Inman,* 578 S.W.2d 266, 269 (Ky.Ct.App. 1979)(dental license held to be property but measure of wife's interest was amount of investment in husband's education).

Even if it were marital property, valuing educational assets in terms of their cost would be an erroneous application of equitable distribution law. As the Appellate Division explained, the cost of a professional degree "has little to do with any real value of the degree and fails to consider at all the nonfinancial efforts made by the degree holder in completing his course of study." 182 N.J.Super. at 610, 442 A.2d 1062. *See also DeWitt, supra,* 296 N.W.2d at 767. Once a degree candidate has earned his or her degree, the amount that a spouse — or anyone else — paid towards its attainment has no bearing whatever on its value. The cost of a spouse's financial contributions has no logical connection to the value of that degree.

As the Appellate Division correctly noted, "the cost approach [to equitable distribution] is plainly not conceptually predicated on a property theory at all but rather represents a general notion of how to do equity in this one special situation." 182 N.J.Super. at 610, 442 A.2d 1062. Equitable distribution in these cases derives from the proposition that the supporting spouse should be reimbursed for contributions to the marital unit that, because of the divorce, did not bear its expected fruit for the supporting spouse.

The trial court recognized that the theoretical basis for the amount of its award was not equitable distribution, but rather reimbursement. It held that "the education and degree obtained by plaintiff, under the circumstances of this case, constitute a property right *subject to equitable offset* upon the dissolution of the marriage." 175 N.J.Super. at 447, 419 A.2d 1149 (emphasis added). The court allowed a "reasonable sum as a credit...on behalf of the maintenance of the household and the support of the plaintiff during the educational period." *Id.* Although the court found that the degree was distributable property, it actually reimbursed the defendant without attempting to give her part of the *value* of the degree.

This Court does not support reimbursement between former spouses in alimony proceedings as a general principle. Marriage is not a business arrangement in which the parties keep track of debits and credits, their accounts to be settled upon divorce. Rather, as we have said, "marriage is a shared enterprise, a joint undertaking...in many ways it is akin to a partnership." *Rothman v. Rothman,* 65 N.J. 219, 229, 320 A.2d 496 (1974); see also *Jersey Shore Medical Center-Fitkin Hospital v. Estate of Baum,* 84 N.J. 137, 141, 417 A.2d 1003 (1980). But every joint undertaking has its bounds of fairness. Where a partner to marriage takes the benefits of his spouse's support in obtaining a professional degree or license with the understanding that future benefits will accrue and inure to both of them, and the marriage is then terminated without the supported spouse giving anything in return, an unfairness has occurred that calls for a remedy.

In this case, the supporting spouse made financial contributions towards her husband's professional education with the expectation that both parties would enjoy material benefits flowing from the professional license or degree. It is therefore patently unfair that the supporting spouse be denied the mutually anticipated benefit while the supported spouse keeps not only the degree, but also all of the financial and material rewards flowing from it.

Furthermore, it is realistic to recognize that in this case, a supporting spouse has contributed more than mere earnings to her husband with the mutual expectation that both of them — she as well as he — will realize and enjoy material improvements in their marriage as a result of his increased earning capacity. Also, the wife has presumably made personal financial sacrifices, resulting in a reduced or lowered standard of living. Additionally, her husband, by pursuing preparations for a future career, has foregone gainful employment and financial contributions to the marriage that would have been forthcoming had he been employed. He thereby has further reduced the level of support his wife might otherwise have received, as well as the standard of living both of them would have otherwise enjoyed. In effect, through her contributions, the supporting spouse has consented to live at a lower material level while her husband has prepared for another career. She has postponed, as it were, present consumption and a higher standard of living, for the future prospect of greater support and material benefits. The supporting spouse's sacrifices would have been rewarded had the marriage endured and the mutual expectations of both of them been fulfilled. The unredressed sacrifices — loss of support and reduction of the standard of living — coupled with the unfairness attendant upon the defeat of the supporting spouse's shared expectation of future advantages, further justify a remedial reward. In this sense, an award that is referable to the spouse's monetary contributions to her partner's education significantly implicates basic considerations of marital support and standard of living — factors that are clearly relevant in the determination and award of conventional alimony.

To provide a fair and effective means of compensating a supporting spouse who has suffered a loss or reduction of support, or has incurred a lower standard of living, or has been deprived of a better standard of living in the future, the Court now introduces the concept of reimbursement alimony into divorce proceedings. The concept properly accords with the Court's belief that regardless of the appropriateness of permanent alimony or the presence or absence of marital property to be equitably distributed, there will be circumstances where a supporting spouse should be reimbursed for the financial contributions he or she made to the spouse's successful professional training. Such reimbursement alimony should cover all financial contributions towards the former spouse's education, including household expenses, educational costs, school travel expenses and any other contributions used by the supported spouse in obtaining his or her degree or license.

This result is consistent with the remedial provisions of the matrimonial statute. N.J.S.A. 2A:34–23. A basic purpose of alimony relates to the quality of economic life to which one spouse is entitled and that becomes the obligation of the other. Alimony has to do with support and standard of living. See *Khalaf v. Khalaf*, 58 N.J. 63, 69, 275 A.2d 132 (1971)....

...

The Court does not hold that every spouse who contributes toward his or her partner's education or professional training is entitled to reimbursement alimony. Only monetary contributions made with the mutual and shared expectation that both parties to the marriage will derive increased income and material benefits should be a basis for such an award. For example, it is unlikely that a financially successful executive's spouse who, after many years of homemaking, returns to school would upon divorce be required to reimburse her husband for his contributions toward her degree. Reimbursement alimony should not subvert the basic goals of traditional alimony and equitable distribution.

In proper circumstances, however, courts should not hesitate to award reimbursement alimony. Marriage should not be a free ticket to professional education and training without subsequent obligations. This Court should not ignore the scenario of the young professional who after being supported through graduate school leaves his mate for supposedly greener pastures. One spouse ought not to receive a divorce complaint when the other receives a diploma.[4] Those spouses supported through professional school should recognize that they may be called upon to reimburse the supporting spouses for the financial contributions they received in pursuit of their professional training. And they cannot deny the basic fairness of this result.[5]

...

...Even though the enhanced earning potential provided by a degree or license is not "property" for purposes of N.J.S.A. 2A:34–23, it clearly should be a factor considered by the trial judge in determining a proper amount of alimony. If the degree holder's actual earnings turn out to diverge greatly from the court's estimate, making the amount of alimony unfair to either party, the alimony award can be adjusted accordingly.

...

In the present case, the defendant's financial support helped her husband to obtain his M.B.A. degree, which assistance was undertaken with the expectation of deriving material benefits for both spouses. Although the trial court awarded the defendant a sum as "equitable offset" for her contributions, the trial court's approach was not consistent with the guidelines we have announced in this opinion. Therefore, we are remanding the case so the trial court can determine whether reimbursement alimony should be awarded in this case and, if so, what amount is appropriate.

The judgment of the Appellate Division is reversed and the cause remanded for further proceedings not inconsistent with this opinion.

---

4. *New York Times*, Nov. 21, 1982, at p. 72, col. 2.

5. This decision recognizes the fairness of an award of reimbursement alimony for past contributions to a spouse's professional education that were made with the expectation of mutual economic benefit. We need not in the present posture of this case determine the degree of finality or permanency that should be accorded an award of reimbursement alimony as compared to conventional alimony. As noted, an award of reimbursement alimony combines elements relating to the support, standard of living and financial expectations of the parties with notions of marital fairness and avoidance of unjust enrichment. We must also recognize that, while these cases frequently illustrate common patterns of human behavior and experience among married couples, circumstances vary among cases. Consequently, it would be unwise to attempt to anticipate all of the ramifications that flow from our present recognition of a right to reimbursement alimony. We therefore leave for future cases questions as to whether and under what changed circumstances such awards may be modified or adjusted.

DOWNS v. DOWNS

Supreme Court of Vermont
154 Vt. 161, 574 A.2d 156 (1990)

GIBSON, Justice.

Plaintiff and defendant both appeal from a provision in their divorce decree that sought to compensate defendant Susan Downs for funds contributed during the marriage toward plaintiff Kevin Downs' attainment of a medical degree. We reverse and remand the case for further proceedings consistent with the views expressed herein.

I

Kevin and Susan were married in August of 1976. At that time, Kevin, who had just graduated from college, and Susan, who had completed three years of university study, agreed that she would leave school and work while he attended medical school. Susan worked as a clerk at a department store from the fall of 1976 until March of 1980, a month before the birth of the parties' first child. Most of her salary was used to pay for living expenses while Kevin attended school; Kevin borrowed money through various loans to pay for his school expenses. Susan did not work outside the home after the birth of the parties' first child, and a second child was born in 1982, at which time Kevin was in the midst of a four-year medical residency at the Medical Center Hospital of Vermont. In August of 1983, Kevin moved out of the family home, and later that year, moved in with another woman and her two children. Shortly thereafter, he filed for divorce. After finishing his residency in 1984, he began working as an obstetrician and gynecologist in practice with another doctor at an initial salary of approximately $60,000 a year, with an expectation of earning up to $200,000 a year in the near future.

After a hearing in July of 1984, the court granted Kevin a divorce and awarded custody of the children to Susan. The court also awarded her $1000 worth of home furnishings and a partially paid family car, and ordered that Kevin pay (1) $500 a month to Susan in rehabilitative maintenance for five years, (2) $500 a month per child in child support, (3) the children's health insurance, plus all reasonable medical, dental and hospital expenses not covered by insurance, (4) all reasonable expenses for higher education for the children, and (5) $50,590 to Susan within five years, a sum representing the total salary earned by her during the years she worked while Kevin attended medical school, plus interest at the rate of ten percent compounded annually.

In reaching the $50,590 figure, the court reasoned that an educational degree is not property, but that "the increased earning potential made possible by the degree is an asset to be distributed by the court." The court then proceeded to make its disposition of Kevin's enhanced earning potential under the property settlement statute, 15 V.S.A. §751. The court considered itself unable, however, to award Susan any portion of the increase in Kevin's earning potential resulting from his medical degree because, while there was expert testimony that he could expect future earnings with a discounted present value of three million dollars, there was no testimony regarding the differential in earning capacity between a person with a four-year college degree and a person with a medical degree. Because of this, the court felt confined to making an award based on restitution, which it determined to be $50,590.

Following Susan's motion to alter or amend the order and for a partial new trial, the court held a second hearing and issued a revised order, awarding her $125,000 for Kevin's enhanced earning capacity and $77,281 for her nonmonetary contributions to the marriage. Kevin appealed the revised order, and we reversed the judgment, reinstating the original order because the revised order had not been issued until after the expiration of the nisi period. *Downs v. Downs*, 150 Vt. 647, 549 A.2d 1382 (1988)(mem.). Susan now appeals the original order, seeking a property division or maintenance award that reflects Kevin's increased earning potential resulting from his degree and her nonmonetary contributions to the marriage. In his cross-appeal, Kevin claims that the court erred in making its property disposition, arguing that, since he did not have the ability to pay the restitution amount at the time of the divorce, the order amounted to an improper award of property not acquired during the marriage.

II

In a case of first impression in Vermont, we consider the "diploma dilemma." The issue is what remuneration is available to a spouse who sacrifices career opportunities in order to further the other spouse's attainment of a professional degree, only to see his or her expectations of future financial security undermined when the student spouse, upon receiving the degree, shortly thereafter seeks a divorce. Although the trial court retains wide discretion in fashioning property and maintenance awards, *Buttura v. Buttura*, 143 Vt. 95, 99, 463 A.2d 229, 231 (1983), any award must fall within the flexible confines of Vermont's statutory guidelines. See 15 V.S.A. §§751, 752.

Before addressing Vermont's relevant statutory provisions, we review how other jurisdictions have handled this issue. A few courts have held that a professional degree or the enhanced earning potential that it represents is a marital asset subject to distribution upon divorce of the parties. See, e.g., *In re Marriage of Horstmann*, 263 N.W.2d 885, 891 (Iowa 1978); *Woodworth v. Woodworth*, 126 Mich.App. 258, 261, 337 N.W.2d 332, 334 (1983); *O'Brien v. O'Brien*, 66 N.Y.2d 576, 586–88, 489 N.E.2d 712, 717–18, 498 N.Y.S.2d 743, 748–49 (1985)....

Some courts have held that a professional degree is not an asset to be divided, but that the supporting spouse is entitled to compensation for the amount of his or her investment in the student spouse's education. See, e.g., *DeLa Rosa v. DeLa Rosa*, 309 N.W.2d 755, 759 (Minn.1981)(supporting spouse awarded lump sum equalling monies she spent toward student spouse's living and educational expenses); *Hubbard v. Hubbard*, 603 P.2d 747, 751–52 (Okla.1979)(supporting spouse entitled to lump-sum award in lieu of property to prevent unjust enrichment). Under certain circumstances, for instance where there is insufficient property to divide, other courts have provided "reimbursement alimony" or "rehabilitative alimony" awards rather than lump-sum awards. See, e.g., *Saint-Pierre v. Saint-Pierre*, 357 N.W.2d 250, 253 (S.D.1984)(court should award reimbursement alimony in proper case); cf. *Mahoney v. Mahoney*, 91 N.J. 488, 501–05, 453 A.2d 527, 534–36 (1982)(only issue at trial was reimbursement claim, but degree holder's earning capacity was held to be a factor in determining permanent alimony, which could be adjusted in future if actual earnings diverged greatly from court's estimate). These courts point out that a professional degree, unlike a vested pension whose value can be readily computed, provides nothing more than the possibility of enhanced earnings that may never be realized. See *id.* at 496–97, 453 A.2d at 531–32.

The majority of courts have found fertile, neutral ground between the approaches described above. These courts hold that a professional degree is not an asset subject to property distribution upon divorce, but, in the interest of justice and equity, fashion a maintenance award using the increased earning potential of the spouse with the degree as a relevant factor in determining an appropriate award. See, e.g., *In re Marriage of Olar*, 747 P.2d 676, 680–81 (Colo.1987)(en banc); *Drapek v. Drapek*, 399 Mass. 240, 246, 503 N.E.2d 946, 950 (1987); *Stevens v. Stevens*, 23 Ohio St.3d 115, 120, 492 N.E.2d 131, 135 (1986); *DeWitt v. DeWitt*, 98 Wis.2d 44, 60–61, 296 N.W.2d 761, 769 (1980); cf. *Washburn v. Washburn*, 101 Wash.2d 168, 176–79, 677 P.2d 152, 157–58 (1984)(en banc)(increased earning potential is a relevant factor in making maintenance award; no need to address "metaphysical" question of whether professional degree is property). According to these courts, an award of a lump sum would be based on speculative future earnings of the degree holder and amount to an improper attempt to apportion after-acquired property. See, e.g., *DeWitt*, 98 Wis.2d at 58–59, 296 N.W.2d at 768. Further, because a maintenance award is subject to later modification, in contrast to a property award, which may not be modified, such an award could be adjusted as a result of the effect of future events on the earning capacity of the spouse holding the degree. See, e.g., *Drapek*, 399 Mass. at 244, 503 N.E.2d at 949. This approach accords with existing Vermont law. 15 V.S.A. §758; *Ellis v. Ellis*, 135 Vt. 83, 85, 370 A.2d 200, 201–02 (1977).

We agree with the majority reasoning and hold that increased earning capacity is not property subject to distribution under 15 V.S.A. §751. Thus, the trial court erred in treating Kevin's increased earning potential as an asset to be disposed of under the property settlement statute. Indeed, under §751 "the contribution by one spouse to the education, training, or increased earning power of the other" is one of the factors to be considered in making a property settlement, 15 V.S.A. §751(b)(5); hence, it is logical to conclude that increased earning power itself is not marital property. See *Hodge v. Hodge*, 337 Pa.Super. 151, 156, 486 A.2d 951, 953 (1984)(court reached similar conclusion under similar statute). Of course, as provided in §751(b)(5) and depending upon the circumstances, contributions to increased earning power could be a significant factor in determining a fair distribution of marital property. See *Mahoney*, 91 N.J. at 504, 453 A.2d at 535–36.

In situations as in the instant case, however, where there is not enough property to fairly compensate the supporting spouse for contributions toward the other spouse's attainment of a degree, Vermont's maintenance statute, 15 V.S.A. §752, is sufficiently flexible to permit the court's consideration of the future earning prospects of the student spouse. Under §752(a), a court may order permanent or rehabilitative maintenance payments if it finds that the spouse seeking maintenance (1) lacks sufficient income, property, or both, "to provide for his or her reasonable needs," and (2) cannot support himself or herself "through appropriate employment at the standard of living established during the marriage or is the custodian of a child of the parties."...

Once the threshold criteria of §752(a) have been met, the court shall award maintenance "in such amounts and for such periods of time *as the court deems just*, after considering *all relevant factors including, but not limited to*" such components as the financial resources of the party seeking maintenance, the property settlement awarded to that party, the party's ability to meet his or her needs independently, and the time and expense necessary for the party seeking maintenance to acquire an education so that he or she can find appropriate employment. §752(b)(1) and (2)(emphasis added).

The scope of the statute is clearly broad enough to permit courts to consider the increased earning capacity engendered by a professional degree in determining an award of maintenance. Accordingly, we hold that, when one spouse obtains a professional degree during the marriage, but the marriage ends before the benefits of the degree can be realized, the future value of the professional degree is a relevant factor to be considered in reaching a just and equitable maintenance award. The trial court retains broad discretion in determining the amount and duration of any maintenance award, *McCrea v. McCrea,* 150 Vt. 204, 207, 552 A.2d 392, 394 (1988); appropriate factors for the court to consider in making such an award are set forth in 15 V.S.A. §752(b), and would include the future earning prospects of the student spouse. Further, upon remand, the parties in the instant case may provide any current, relevant information in order that the court can arrive at a just maintenance award. See *Klein v. Klein,* 153 Vt. 551, 556–57, 572 A.2d 900, 904 (1990).

. . .

The provisions of the February 19, 1985 order dividing the parties' property and requiring that plaintiff pay defendant $500 per month maintenance and the sum of $50,590 within five years are vacated; in all other respects, the decree is affirmed. The matter is remanded for further proceedings consistent with this opinion. [Italics deleted.]

COMMENTS

Student marriages pose special legal problems which are frequently overlooked in legal practice. These often relatively short-term marriages among young people are treated, especially in view of the possibility of no-fault divorce in most jurisdictions, as if they involve no serious property and alimony considerations. Since the parties have lived on a minimum subsistence level, they are not yet accustomed to any particular "station in life" for purposes of support. Unless children were born from the relationship, the only issue may appear to be who gets the car. Actually the problem is much more serious. These marriages involve a pooling of resources for purposes of long-term financial security, a goal the couple expects to achieve through education. Since parents decreasingly pay for the higher education of their children beyond the age of majority, now eighteen years, and in most jurisdictions have no legal obligation to do so (see pp. 671–672, 917–924), young persons are left to their own devices. Usually it is the young woman who forgoes her own educational or career opportunities in order to earn a living for herself and her husband. A variety of reasons, for example, the birth of a child, may make it difficult or impossible for the wife to reenter education after the husband is established. Not infrequently the marriage breaks up immediately upon the husband's graduation, or even prior to graduation. The growing case law from various jurisdictions deals primarily with instances in which a man's prospect for professional status and high income have made wives willing to invest their time and efforts.

Morgan was a rare instance of a lower court proving to be more progressive than an appellate court. The widely publicized trial court opinion talks in terms of equal opportunity for the wife, who had financed her husband's law study with her earnings from clerical work and who now had a chance for a medical education. The husband, upon divorce, was ordered to help finance her education as long as she continued as a full-time premedical or medical student (and did not remarry). The appellate court reversed the decision — seemingly under legal theories of alimony, but in reality because of a fundamental difference in values.* Since the wife had the capacity to earn $10,000 per year, this amount accordingly was to be imputed to whatever the husband had to pay. That she had acquired the capacity by deferring her own studies in order to help her husband is "irrelevant" under this viewpoint.

Neither opinion is persuasive in itself, unless one injects fundamental feelings about the nature of marriage. The trial court opinion may represent the law of the future; the appellate opinion is rooted in the past. Another impressive aspect of the lower court opinion is that it recognized the contractual aspect of marriage that may impose a duty to mitigate the damages upon breach. Thus the earnings or earning potential of the wife might have to be considered upon divorce. This concept of mitigation of damages, a judicial invention of the nineteenth century to ease the financial burdens of entrepreneurs, has found an unexpected revival in modern conceptions of alimony, especially if it is viewed as fundamentally rehabilitative in nature. From this perspective, the lower court and appellate court in *Morgan* disagree on the meaning and function of "rehabilitation" of a spouse after divorce.

Morgan, O'Brien, Mahoney and *Downs* represent several different efforts by the courts to deal with the problems created by the couple's misplaced reliance on the continuation of their marriage. Each has advantages and disadvantages. Property division cannot be modified in the case of changed circumstances, which may be appealing because of its certainty and predictability, but leaves the parties less able to adjust to major financial changes. Alimony has flexibility, but in many states by caselaw, statutes (including the Uniform Marriage and Divorce Act §316) or through private agreements, it ceases upon the payee's remarriage, which would be undesirable in some cases. The tax consequences and the results if either party should declare bankruptcy also differ between property and alimony. A property award is dischargeable in bankruptcy whereas an obligation to pay alimony is not. The idea of giving the trial court flexibility to deal with the wide range of possibilities is appealing until one thinks about the variety of ways in which trial court discretion can cover over the judges' imposition of very traditional (or idiosyn-

*The wife went on to medical school and received her medical degree in 1980. She invited the trial judge to her graduation ceremony. The judge, in an interview, stated that what impressed him the most about Mrs. Morgan at the time of the trial was the fact that she received an "A" in biochemistry. (Georgia Dullea, *Controversial Alimony Case Ends Happily With a Degree,* N.Y. TIMES, June 6, 1980, §B, at 4, cols. 5 & 6.) The happy ending was due entirely to Ms. Morgan's own capabilities and resources. It appears that despite repeated efforts and numerous contempt citations, she actually received no alimony from her ex-husband. Whatever theory of property sharing courts or the parties devise can be circumvented unless adequate enforcement procedures exist.

cratic) personal values. Yet efforts to control this discretion may also result in decisions that are unfair because of their rigidity. Who should receive a larger award, a wife such as Mrs. Morgan, who struggled with raising a child, typing her husband's thesis and living on rather little money, or a wife such as Mrs. Mahoney, who contributed $24,000 she earned in sixteen months with her B.S. degree?

A possible contractual solution for young student wives would be an antenuptial agreement, in which the wife would agree to finance her husband's education upon his promise to pay for hers thereafter. A woman's bargaining power may be sufficiently great to facilitate such an agreement prior to marriage. Note, however, that in *Morgan* the woman was apparently pregnant prior to marriage, a factor that probably affected her bargaining power severely. Nevertheless, the husband might well have been sufficiently ambitious to have agreed, at that stage, to anything that would finance his law studies. These are unpleasant realities of life that tend to be overlooked by young persons in love. Love can, for instance, be invoked by the person who is in an inherently advantageous position, in order to extract services and other benefits from the weaker party that ordinarily could only be obtained at greater cost. If a question were asked by the weaker person, why such services should be rendered, the answer could be, "But don't you love me?" The social definition of love may turn out to be a set-up to exploit women. A lawyer whose counsel is sought early enough might be able to prevent exploitation.

REFERENCE

Deborah A. Batts, *Remedy Refocus: In Search of Equity in "Enhanced Spouse/Other Spouse" Divorces*, 63 N.Y.U. L. REV. 751 (1988).

Career Building — Individual Gain or Shared?

THOMPSON v. THOMPSON
Supreme Court of Florida
576 So.2d 267 (Fla. 1991)

MCDONALD, Justice.

We review *Thompson v. Thompson*, 546 So.2d 99, 100 (Fla. 4th DCA 1989), in which the district court certified the following question as one of great public importance:

> In marriage dissolution proceedings to which an owner of a professional association is a party, may the value of the professional association's goodwill be factored in in determining the professional association's value?

We have jurisdiction. Art. V, §3(b)(4), Fla. Const. We answer the certified question with a qualified affirmative.

After twenty-three years of marriage, the Thompsons received a divorce in April 1987. The wife supported the husband while he finished college and attended law school and, subsequently, maintained their home and raised their children. The husband is currently a plaintiff's attorney specializing in personal injury and medical malpractice and is the sole shareholder of a professional association. The trial court awarded the wife permanent periodic alimony, lump sum alimony to be paid over ten years, child support, and other real and personal property. The district court, concluding "that a reasonable person could have created the economic scheme employed by the trial court in this case" and that the trial court correctly applied the principles of *Canakaris v. Canakaris*, 382 So.2d 1197 (Fla.1980), affirmed the entire award. 546 So.2d at 100.

On appeal the husband argued that the trial court improperly included professional goodwill in the distribution. The district court stated: "There is no compelling reason to conclude that the trial court factored in the value of the husband's professional association's goodwill in making the property distribution." *Id.* Because the issue had been raised, however, the court certified the above-stated question regarding professional goodwill.

Marital property should be divided in an equitable manner. See *Canakaris.* Typically, a nonprofessional spouse's efforts increase the professional spouse's earning capacity. Equity justifies higher alimony in such circumstances. If marriage is viewed as an economic partnership, and assets are created or obtained during the marriage, it is only equitable to distribute them fairly. The results of paid efforts in the workplace and unpaid efforts at home should be pooled because both economic and noneconomic contributions to a marriage have value. In theory, therefore, if it exists and if it was developed during the marriage, professional goodwill is a marital asset which should be included in the marital estate upon dissolution.

This Court has defined goodwill as the advantage or benefit a business has beyond the value of its property and capital. *Swann v. Mitchell*, 435 So.2d 797 (Fla.1983). In discussing goodwill in *Swann* we noted that it has been held that although a law firm could not be sued for ethical reasons, its goodwill is "subject to evaluation as a valuable asset of the firm for other purposes."[1] *Id.* at 800. Moreover, we recognized that "goodwill of a professional practice has been held to be community property subject to division in a marriage dissolution proceeding." *Id.* Thus, the instant certified question squarely presents an issue which we have addressed only in dicta.

Numerous other jurisdictions, however, have already considered this question. Several have held that professional goodwill is not a marital asset to be considered in dissolution proceedings....

On the other hand, the courts of at least twenty states have held that professional goodwill is a marital asset that, if it exists in a particular case, should be distributed upon dissolution....

The cases that hold professional goodwill to be a marital asset are noteworthy for their diversity. There is no specific consensus as to a definition of professional goodwill, whether a sole practitioner of any profession can have goodwill, or what method or methods should be used to value professional goodwill.

Despite this, we agree with the observation of the Supreme Court of Missouri when it stated:

> Irrespective of the setting in which it is found, the meaning of goodwill does not change. It is property which attaches to and is dependant upon an

1. We find no direct prohibition against an attorney's selling his law practice in the present Rules Regulating The Florida Bar, but we do not rule on that issue in this opinion. For the purpose of dividing goodwill it must be assumed that such a sale is permissible.

> existing business entity; the reputation and skill of an individual entrepreneur — be he a professional or a traditional businessman — is not a component of the intangible asset we identify generally as goodwill.

Hanson v. Hanson, 738 S.W.2d 429, 434 (Mo.1987). That court then defined goodwill within a professional setting to mean the value of the practice which exceeds its tangible assets and which is the tendency of clients/patients to return to and recommend the practice irrespective of the reputation of the individual practitioner. Goodwill is property of an intangible nature commonly defined as the expectation of continued public patronage. *In re Marriage of Lukens*, 16 Wash.App. 481, 483, 558 P.2d 279, 280 (1976).

For those courts and commentators that articulate that the consideration of goodwill in dividing marital assets is appropriate, a common denominator to be equitable appears. If professional goodwill exists and if it was developed during a marriage, it is marital property. Denying a spouse's interest in marital property would be both unfair and unjust....

It should be emphasized that such goodwill, to be a marital asset, must exist separate and apart from the reputation or continued presence of the marital litigant....Therefore, "for professional goodwill to be marital property it must be a business asset having a value independent of the continued presence or reputation of any particular individual."...

Generally, clients come to an individual professional to receive services from that specific person. Even so, if a party can produce evidence demonstrating goodwill as an asset separate and distinct from the other party's reputation, it should be considered in distributing marital property. Several other courts have reached the same conclusion.

We therefore answer the certified question with a qualified affirmative: If a law practice has monetary value over and above its tangible assets and cases in progress which is separate and distinct from the presence and reputation of the individual attorney, then a court should consider the goodwill accumulated during the marriage as a marital asset.[3] The determination of the existence and value of goodwill is a question of fact and should be made on a case-by-case basis with the assistance of expert testimony.

...

We answer the certified question in the affirmative with the qualifications set forth herein and remand for proceedings consistent herewith.

It is so ordered.

ELKUS v. ELKUS

New York Supreme Court, Appellate Division
169 A.D.2d 134, 572 N.Y.S.2d 901 (1991)

ROSENBERGER, Justice.

In this matrimonial action, the plaintiff, Frederica von Stade Elkus, moved for an order determining, prior to trial, whether her career and/or celebrity status

3. In reaching this decision we disapprove *Moebus v. Moebus*, 529 So.2d 1163 (Fla. 3d DCA 1988), review denied, 539 So.2d 475 (Fla.1989), and *Harper v. Harper*, 546 So.2d 438 (Fla. 2d DCA), review denied, 553 So.2d 1165 (Fla.1989), insofar as they hold that goodwill can never be considered in the valuation of a professional practice.

constituted marital property subject to equitable distribution. The parties have already stipulated to mutual judgments of divorce terminating their seventeen year marriage and to joint custody of their two minor children. The trial on the remaining economic issues has been stayed pending the outcome of this appeal from the order of the Supreme Court, which had determined that the enhanced value of the plaintiff's career and/or celebrity status was not marital property subject to equitable distribution. Contrary to the conclusion reached by the Supreme Court, we find that to the extent the defendant's contributions and efforts led to an increase in the value of the plaintiff's career, this appreciation was a product of the marital partnership, and, therefore, marital property subject to equitable distribution.

At the time of her marriage to the defendant on February 9, 1973, the plaintiff had just embarked on her career, performing minor roles with the Metropolitan Opera Company. During the course of the marriage, the plaintiff's career succeeded dramatically and her income rose accordingly. In the first year of the marriage, she earned $2,250. In 1989, she earned $621,878. She is now a celebrated artist with the Metropolitan Opera, as well as an international recording artist, concert and television performer. She has garnered numerous awards, and has performed for the President of the United States.

During the marriage, the defendant travelled with the plaintiff throughout the world, attending and critiquing her performances and rehearsals, and photographed her for album covers and magazine articles. The defendant was also the plaintiff's voice coach and teacher for ten years of the marriage. He states that he sacrificed his own career as a singer and teacher to devote himself to the plaintiff's career and to the lives of their young children, and that his efforts enabled the plaintiff to become one of the most celebrated opera singers in the world. Since the plaintiff's career and/or celebrity status increased in value during the marriage due in part to his contributions, the defendant contends that he is entitled to equitable distribution of this marital property.

The Supreme Court disagreed, refusing to extend the holding in *O'Brien v. O'Brien*, 66 N.Y.2d 576, 498 N.Y.S.2d 743, 489 N.E.2d 712, in which the Court of Appeals determined that a medical license constituted marital property subject to equitable distribution, to the plaintiff's career as an opera singer. The court found that since the defendant enjoyed a substantial life style during the marriage and since he would be sufficiently compensated through distribution of the parties' other assets, the plaintiff's career was not marital property.

There is a paucity of case law and no appellate authority in New York governing the issue of whether a career as a performing artist, and its accompanying celebrity status, constitute marital property subject to equitable distribution. The plaintiff maintains that since her career and celebrity status are not licensed, are not entities which are owned like a business, nor are protected interests which are subject to due process of law, they are not marital property. In our view, neither the Domestic Relations Law, nor relevant case law, allows for such a limited interpretation of the term marital property.

Domestic Relations Law §236[B][1][c] broadly defines marital property as property acquired during the marriage "regardless of the form in which title is held." In enacting the Equitable Distribution Law (L.1980, ch. 281, §9), the Legislature created a radical change in the traditional method of distributing property upon the dissolution of a marriage (*Price v. Price*, 69 N.Y.2d 8, 14, 511

N.Y.S.2d 219, 503 N.E.2d 684). By broadly defining the term "marital property", it intended to give effect to the "economic partnership" concept of the marriage relationship (*Id.* at 15, 511 N.Y.S.2d 219, 503 N.E.2d 684; *Majauskas v. Majauskas*, 61 N.Y.2d 481, 474 N.Y.S.2d 699, 463 N.E.2d 15). It then left it to the courts to determine what interests constitute marital property.

Things of value acquired during marriage are marital property even though they may fall outside the scope of traditional property concepts.... The statutory definition of marital property does not mandate that it be an asset with an exchange value or be salable, assignable or transferable.

...

Medical licenses have been held to enhance the earning capacity of their holders, so as to enable the other spouse who made direct or indirect contributions to their acquisition, to share their value as part of equitable distribution....

Although the plaintiff's career, unlike that of the husband in *O'Brien*, is not licensed, the *O'Brien* court did not restrict its holding to professions requiring a license or degree. In reaching its conclusion that a medical license constitutes marital property, the *O'Brien* court referred to the language contained in Domestic Relations Law §236 which provides that in making an equitable distribution of marital property, "the court shall consider: ...(6) any equitable claim to, interest in, or direct or indirect contribution made to the acquisition of such marital property by the party not having title, including joint efforts or expenditures and contributions and services as a spouse, parent, wage earner and homemaker, and *to the career or career potential* of the other party [and]...(9) the impossibility or difficulty of evaluating any component asset or any interest in a business, corporation or profession" (Domestic Relations Law §236[B][5][d][6], [9](emphasis added). The court also cited §236[B][5][e] which provides that where, equitable distribution of marital property is appropriate, but "the distribution of an interest in a business, corporation or profession would be contrary to law", the court shall make a distributive award in lieu of an actual distribution of the property (*O'Brien v. O'Brien, supra*, 66 N.Y.2d at 584, 498 N.Y.S.2d 743, 489 N.E.2d 712).

The Court of Appeals' analysis of the statute is equally applicable here. "The words mean exactly what they say: that an interest in a profession or professional career potential is marital property which may be represented by direct or indirect contributions of the non-title-holding spouse, including financial contributions and nonfinancial contributions made by caring for the home and family" (*O'Brien v. O'Brien, supra* at 584, 498 N.Y.S.2d 743, 489 N.E.2d 712). Nothing in the statute or the *O'Brien* decision supports the plaintiff's contention that her career and/or celebrity status are not marital property. The purpose behind the enactment of the legislation was to prevent inequities which previously occurred upon the dissolution of a marriage. Any attempt to limit marital property to professions which are licensed would only serve to discriminate against the spouses of those engaged in other areas of employment. Such a distinction would fail to carry out the premise upon which equitable distribution is based, *i.e.*, that a marriage is an economic partnership to which both parties contribute, as spouse, parent, wage earner or homemaker....

...

...[T]here is tremendous potential for financial gain from the commercial exploitation of famous personalities. While the plaintiff insists that she will never be asked to endorse a product, this is simply speculation. More and more opportunities have presented themselves to her as her fame increased. They will continue to present themselves to her as she continues to advance in her career. The career of the plaintiff is unique, in that she has risen to the top in a field where success is rarely achieved.

Like the parties here, after Joe Piscopo and his wife married in 1973, they focused on one goal — the facilitation of his rise to stardom (*Piscopo v. Piscopo*, 231 N.J.Super. 576, 555 A.2d 1190, *aff'd.*, 232 N.J.Super. 559, 557 A.2d 1040, certification denied, 117 N.J. 156, 564 A.2d 875). The defendant wife claimed that her husband's celebrity goodwill was a distributable asset and that she was entitled to a share in his excess earning capacity to which she contributed as homemaker, caretaker of their child, and sounding board for his artistic ideas.

Rejecting Mr. Piscopo's argument that celebrity goodwill is distinguishable from professional goodwill since professional goodwill has educational and regulatory requirements while celebrity goodwill requires ineffable talent, the court held that "it is the person with particular and uncommon aptitude for some specialized discipline whether law, medicine or entertainment that transforms the average professional or entertainer into one with measurable goodwill" (*Piscopo v. Piscopo, supra*, 231 N.J.Super., at 580–581, 555 A.2d, at 1191). We agree with the courts that have considered the issue, that the enhanced skills of an artist such as the plaintiff, albeit growing from an innate talent, which have enabled her to become an exceptional earner, may be valued as marital property subject to equitable distribution.

The plaintiff additionally contends that her career is not marital property because she had already become successful prior to her marriage to the defendant. As noted, *supra*, during the first year of marriage, the plaintiff earned $2,250. By 1989, her earnings had increased more than 275 fold. Further, in *Price v. Price, supra*, 69 N.Y.2d at 11, 511 N.Y.S.2d 219, 503 N.E.2d 684, the Court of Appeals held that "under the Equitable Distribution Law an increase in the value of separate property of one spouse, occurring during the marriage and prior to the commencement of matrimonial proceedings, which is due in part to the indirect contributions or efforts of the other spouse as homemaker and parent, should be considered marital property (Domestic Relations Law §236[B][1][d][3])"; *and see*, *Capasso v. Capasso*, 119 A.D.2d 268, 506 N.Y.S.2d 686; *Clerk v. Clerk*, 132 A.D.2d 456, 517 N.Y.S.2d 512, *app. denied*, 70 N.Y.2d 611, 523 N.Y.S.2d 495, 518 N.E.2d 6). In this case, it cannot be overlooked that the defendant's contributions to plaintiff's career were direct and concrete, going far beyond child care and the like, which he also provided.

While it is true that the plaintiff was born with talent, and, while she had already been hired by the Metropolitan Opera at the time of her marriage to the defendant, her career, at this time, was only in the initial stages of development. During the course of the marriage, the defendant's active involvement in the plaintiff's career, in teaching, coaching, and critiquing her, as well as in caring for their children, clearly contributed to the increase in its value. Accordingly, to the extent the appreciation in the plaintiff's career was due to the defendant's efforts and contributions, this appreciation constitutes marital property.

In sum, we find that it is the nature and extent of the contribution by the spouse seeking equitable distribution, rather than the nature of the career, whether licensed or otherwise, that should determine the status of the enterprise as marital property.

...

Accordingly, the order of the Supreme Court, New York County (Walter M. Schackman, J.), entered September 26, 1990, which determined that the plaintiff's career and/or celebrity status was not "marital property" subject to equitable distribution, should be reversed, on the law, without costs, and the matter should be remitted to the Supreme Court for further proceedings.

...

All concur.

COMMENTS

Thompson and *Elkus* present two different approaches to the problems of distributing assets on marital breakup. While the court asserts that "[t]ypically, a nonprofessional spouse's efforts increase the professional spouse's earning capacity," *Thompson* endorses the distinction made in *Hanson v. Hanson*, 738 S.W.2d 429 (Mo. 1987), between the "reputation and skill of an individual entrepreneur," which is not subject to division as marital property, and "the tendency of clients/patients to return to and recommend the practice irrespective of the reputation of the individual practitioner," which is marital property. Thus, it is clear that the business goodwill the court divides as a marital asset is the intangible value above and beyond any professional reputation or personal goodwill of the individual professional spouse. Of course, even this limited holding allows the court to give the nonprofessional spouse some reward for her efforts and throws the professional spouse into some uncertainty.

Elkus seems to go considerably further, holding that one spouse's "enhanced skills...albeit growing from an innate talent...may be valued as marital property subject to equitable distribution." Even if the party's career was underway and thus separate property prior to the marriage, the court quotes with approval that "an increase in the value of separate property of one spouse, occurring during the marriage and...which is due in part to the indirect contributions or efforts of the other spouse as homemaker and parent, should be considered marital property." Yet the court's opinion can be read as less supportive of the homemaker and parent when it emphasizes the husband's active involvement in his wife's career in teaching, coaching and critiquing her, and that "the defendant's contributions to the plaintiff's career were direct and concrete, going far beyond child care and the like, which he also provided." Near the beginning of the opinion the court characterizes its holding as "to the extent the defendant's contributions and efforts led to an increase in the value of the plaintiff's career, this appreciation was a product of the marital partnership, and, therefore, marital property subject to equitable division."

If, as the *Elkus* court says, the nature and extent of the one spouse's contribution, not the nature of the other spouse's career, determines the character of the enterprise as marital property or not, how is the court to examine the nature and extent of the spouse's contribution? In a case like *Elkus* should the wife be allowed to show that the husband was worthless as a teacher and coach, that he was really a millstone around her neck? There may be an unresolvable tension between some efforts to value the contributions of a spouse and the impulse behind no-fault divorce. What if Mr. Elkus were a philanderer and his philandering impeded his wife's career? If a case like *Thompson* arose in New York, should the husband be allowed to argue that his wife drove him crazy and actually reduced his ability to build a law practice? What if her marital misconduct caused the problems? Should the courts be able to listen to all the ways one spouse harmed the other's efforts to build a career except by marital misconduct? An important factor may be whether entry into this inquiry will increase or decrease bitterness. When minor children are involved, some degree of parental cooperation is nearly essential, and one parent has many ways of making the life of the other parent difficult. We get another glimpse into the post-divorce lives of the Elkuses in Chapter 3.

Homemaker — A Risky Occupation?

LACEY v. LACEY
Supreme Court of Wisconsin
45 Wis.2d 378, 173 N.W.2d 142 (1970)

ROBERT W. HANSEN, JUSTICE.

In objecting to the division of property in this divorce case, the husband cites the 1914 case in which this court suggested:...a clear third of the whole is a liberal allowance to the wife....[1]

This statement has been repeated so often in subsequent decisions that one well respected law text concludes that Wisconsin, alone among all states, has adopted one-third of the marital estate to the wife as the standard to start from, to be increased or decreased only by special circumstances.

However, the varying percentages for distribution reached or upheld in these same subsequent decisions vary so often and so greatly that another well respected law text lists Wisconsin with what appears to be a majority of other states in having no formula or standard, with the facts and circumstances of the individual case to determine the proper ratio or percentage for apportionment of assets in divorce actions.[3]

When leading text authorities disagree as to whether the formula to be used derives from the facts in a given case, or whether special circumstances merely justify deviation from a general standard, the time has come to clarify the situation. That endeavor best begins with setting forth in full the statement, now fifty-five years old, in which the dower-type allowance to the wife was termed "liberal." The statement then made reads:

> The nearest approach thereto is this: Except in some extraordinary circumstances, the maximum for the wife is one-half. That may be reduced to one-

1. Citing Gauger v. Gauger (1914), 157 Wis. 630, 147 N.W. 1075.

3. 27B C.J.S. Divorce §295(1) at p. 285: "The division of property or adjustment of property rights upon a divorce generally depends on the facts and circumstances of the particular case (citing eighteen states, including Wisconsin) and rests largely in the discretion of the court (citing twenty-three states, including Wisconsin)...."

> third or even less.... The general level to start from is one-third. Since the early suggestive guide in respect to the matter, it has been pretty well established that a clear third of the whole is a liberal allowance to the wife, subject to be increased or decreased according to special circumstances....[4]

Read as an entirety, it is clear that one-third to the wife was not laid down as either a maximum or a minimum. Phrases such as "extraordinary circumstances" and "subject to be increased or decreased" are not to be disregarded in analyzing what was said. The reference to one-half or more to the wife in some situations as well as the reference to one-third or less to the wife in other situations are both parts of the same "suggestive guide." We do not read the quote as establishing an exact formula or mandatory measuring stick for property division in divorce cases. We find in the full quotation a clear recognition that the formula to be followed in a particular case depends upon and derives from the material facts and factors present in such case. To extract the reference to either "one-half" or "one-third" as possible ratios is at least to shift emphasis and perhaps to distort meaning. The inbuilt flexibility of the 1914 suggestion is lost if a phrase or sentence therefrom is substituted for the full statement.

...

The division of the property of the divorced parties rests upon the concept of marriage as a shared enterprise or joint undertaking. It is literally a partnership, although a partnership in which contributions and equities of the partners may and do differ from individual case to individual case. In a brief marriage, particularly as to property which the husband brought to the marriage, one-third to the wife may be too liberal an allowance. In a long marriage, particularly as to property acquired by the parties during the marriage, a fifty-fifty division may well represent the mutuality of the enterprise. In determining the proportion of contribution by husband and by wife in the acquisition of property, more than economic factors are involved. We do not deal with two people with no more in common than two strangers or business associates. The contribution of a full-time homemaker-housewife to the marriage may well be greater or at least as great as those of the wife required by circumstances or electing by preference to seek and secure outside employment. The formula for division derives from the facts of the individual case. If it is argued that this approach gives great leeway and also places a heavy responsibility on trial courts in divorce cases, there is no gainsaying that fact. However, both flexibility and responsibility are called for by the endless variety of human situations that come to court in family cases. No two are exactly alike.

...

The application of the general concept and consideration of the specific factors involved in determining the fairness of the property division ordered in the case before us is no easy matter. In fact, it cannot be done because of gaps in both the trial court decision and its findings of facts. It is true that the sequence of events set forth in the record does give a general picture of the property holdings involved, and the manner of their acquisition, but it gives no more than that....

...

Additionally, neither the findings nor the written decision of the court indicate any of the factors considered and found material by the trial court in making the

4. Gauger v. Gauger, *supra*, at p. 633, 147 N.W. at p. 1077.

apportionment of the assets between the parties. If on review the equitableness of a division of property is to depend upon the material facts and factors present in the case, it follows that a firm foundation for such division must be laid by including in findings or decision the factors found relevant and considered by the judge in reaching his decision as to property division. Even if we were to revert to the starting point concept of one-third or one-half as a beginning, the special circumstances relied upon for ending up far from the starting point would have to be detailed to explain the variance. If the findings of fact or the written decision do not indicate the basis on which the property was divided, and the reasons for so doing, review of the fairness of the result reached become not just difficult, it becomes impossible.

...

Judgment reversed and remanded for further proceedings consistent with this opinion.

[*Editor's Note.* On remand, the trial court did not take additional testimony nor did it enter detailed findings of fact as to the division of property which was set at fifty percent of the marital estate to each spouse. Mr. Lacey appealed the trial court's decision. The Supreme Court of Wisconsin in *Lacey v. Lacey*, 61 Wis.2d 604, 213 N.W.2d 80 (1973), affirmed the trial court's 50–50 allocation of marital property.]

BROWN v. BROWN
District Court of Appeal of Florida
300 So.2d 719 (Fla. Dist. Ct. App. 1974)

RAWLS, Chief Judge.

The primary question posed by appellant-wife in this appeal from a final judgment dissolving the marriage of the parties is that of money and custody of the children....

In the year 1952, these parties entered into the holy estate of matrimony. When the coverture was consummated neither party possessed any estate of material value. At the outset of the marriage enterprise, the wife, a registered nurse, continued working and the husband, a graduate of the University of Florida (with a major in accounting), was employed. Not too long after this martial venture was launched, the husband received a promotion resulting in the parties moving to Lancaster, Pennsylvania, where the wife continued her nursing career until six weeks prior to their first child being born. At this point in time, the wife exchanged her career as a nurse for that of a mother and housewife.[1] During the next eighteen or so years, the husband successfully pursued his career as an accountant, reaching the top echelon of his profession upon earning the coveted title of "Certified Public Accountant." While the husband accumulated material wealth, the wife dutifully kept house and assumed the primary responsibility for raising and caring for the four male children born of this marriage.[2] When the

1. Other than working for a short period as a nurse in 1957, the wife has foregone her profession and practiced the time honored and revered profession of being a mother and housewife. The wife again worked outside of the home from October, 1964, through June, 1965, and the following two "tax seasons" to assist her husband in opening up a new accounting practice. Other than the above related "outside home" work activities, the wife has devoted her time and skills to being a housewife.

2. In 1973 the sons were 10, 13, 16 and 18 years of age.

marital partnership was dissolved after 21 years of coverture, the husband's financial statement reflected a net worth of $232,843.00, together with an annual earning capacity in the range of $36,000.00 to $40,000.00. The wife's material assets at the time of, and pursuant to, the judgment of dissolution when translated into money amounted to the following: 1) rehabilitative alimony — $6,000.00, one-half equity in residence — $3,000.00; one-half equity in beach cottage — $12,500.00; one-half interest in Hall note — $2,000.00; one-half interest in Jad note — $4,200.00;[3] aggregating the sum of $27,700.00.

We first consider the question of money and material goods. There are indications from the record of the proceedings below that members of the Bench and Bar consider that this Court has virtually eliminated alimony.[4] In addition, we have before us a factual situation which is still prevalent even in this modern day of women's liberation, *i.e.*, a wife who has foregone pursuing a professional career and the accumulation of a personal estate in order to be a full time mother and homemaker while the husband remains in the market place providing for the material needs of his family and accumulating a sizable personal estate. For these reasons, the time has come for us to pause and pursue an in-depth consideration of the law of alimony in Florida.

In order to fully explore the subject of alimony, the husband's testimony as to his mental attitude towards the future of the marital venture is material. We observe that the materiality is not by reason of "fault" or "no fault,"but is being considered in analyzing the financial status of each party of this marital partnership at the time of its inception and its dissolution. In answer to the question: When was it that you decided to leave? The husband answered, "1964. I made a vow to myself at that time and that vow was that if I ever made enough money that I could support her and those children and have enough groceries for myself, I was going to leave." This statement indicates the husband's motivation to accumulate wealth in his own name in order to prepare for the divorce he had long desired.[5]

For at least forty years prior to the recent enactments repealing "divorce" and instituting "dissolution of marriage" (commonly referred to as "no fault"), the courts awarded a divorced wife periodic alimony almost as a matter of constitutional right. In *Phelan v. Phelan*, 12 Fla. 449 (1868), the Supreme Court defined alimony as: "Permanent alimony is not a sum of money or a specific proportion of the husband's estate given absolutely to the wife. It is a continuous allotment of sums payable at regular periods for her support from year to year." The Court in further discussing alimony stated:

> The actual income of the husband appears from the cases to be as a general rule the precise fact to be regarded. 2 Hag. Con., 199, 201; 3 Hag. Ec., 472; 5 Eng. Ec., 186; 2 Philim., 40.
>
> But this is not a fixed and absolute rule, and there are circumstances which vary it. Before an allotment of permanent alimony is made, the ability of the husband should be made to appear as well as the other considerations which are to be estimated in connection with his faculties, in determining the amount.

3. Appellee husband cross-assigns as error this item.

4. The husband's lawyer declared to the trial judge, "Let's assume the district court of appeals virtually eliminated alimony."

5. The husband admitted that he had for more than one year prior to his testimony been engaged in an adulterous affair with another lady.

This definition of "permanent alimony" was reaffirmed by the Supreme Court in *Welsh v. Welsh*, 160 Fla. 380, 35 So.2d 6 (1948), where it is interesting to note that although she owned substantial proper in her own name and was working, the Court awarded her $150.00 per month periodic alimony. The Court observed in *Welsh* that Chapter 23,894, Acts of 1947, had been amended to permit the award of lump sum alimony but refused to apply same retroactively. So, at this point in our judicial construction of alimony, a wife was entitled to periodic alimony based upon her needs and her husband's ability to pay.

The next development in the law of alimony was the appearance of the doctrine of "special equity." As early as 1919 in *Carlton v. Carlton*, 78 Fla. 252, 83 So. 87 (1919), the Supreme Court in a per curiam opinion after noticing that the wife, mother of six children, had contributed generously in funds and by her personal exertion and industry through a long period of time to the acquisition and development of his home and other property and the establishment of his fortune, held that the wife possessed a special equity in the property which she aided in acquiring and possessing.

In *Heath v. Heath*, 103 Fla. 1071, 138 So. 796 (1932), the Supreme Court utilized the doctrine of special equity to relieve a wife from the harshness of the statutory prohibition of awarding alimony to an adulterous wife. Bottoming the decision in *Heath*, the Court stated:

> The provisions of section 4987, Comp. Gen. Laws, section 3195, Rev. Gen. St., to the effect that no alimony shall be granted to an adulterous wife, do not preclude the ascertainment and allowance by the court of an amount to the wife for her special equity in property and business of the husband toward which she is shown to have contributed materially in funds and industry through a period of years while the marriage remained undissolved.

...

As previously recited, lump sum alimony was statutorily authorized in 1947. In 1963 the legislature added the phrase "or both in its discretion" at the end of the last sentence of former Florida Statute 65.08.

In *Gordon v. Gordon*, 204 So.2d 734 (Fla.App.3rd 1967), the Third District Court of Appeal, in reviewing the dissolution of a marriage of 27 years, observed that the chancellor made provisions for the custody and support of three minor children. The Court next commented upon the relative material assets of the parties which reflected that the wife was possessed of $90,000.00 in assets while the husband had a net worth of approximately $60,000.00. In approving a lump sum alimony award to the wife of $5,000.00, the appellate court held that the chancellor abused his discretion in failing to reserve jurisdiction to modify the alimony awarded to the wife (upon a showing under F.S. §65.16) by providing for periodic payments in the future, if necessary.

...

In 1955 in *Kahn v. Kahn* 78 So.2d 367 (Fla. 1955), Justice Roberts, speaking for our Supreme Court, announced:

> Times have now changed. The broad, practically unlimited opportunities for women in the business world of today are a matter of common knowledge. Thus, in an era where the opportunities for self-support by the wife are so abundant, the fact that the marriage has been brought to an end

> because of the fault of the husband does not necessarily entitle the wife to be forever supported by a former husband who has little, if any, more economic advantages that she has.

This pronouncement marks the entry in the jurisprudence of this state of the concept of rehabilitative alimony. Rehabilitative means the restoration of property that has been lost. The concept of rehabilitative alimony appeared in the statutory scheme of this state in 1971 when the legislature made a major change in F.S. §61.08. The salient provisions are:

> 61.08... (1) ...the court may grant alimony to either party, which alimony may be rehabilitative or permanent in nature. In any award of alimony, the court may order periodic payment or payments in lump sum or both.
>
> ...
>
> (2) *In determining a proper award of alimony, the court may consider any factor necessary to do equity and justice between the parties.* [Emphasis supplied.]

In 1966, our sister court, the Third District Court of Appeal, in *Sommers v. Sommers*, 183 So.2d 744 (Fla. App. 3rd 1966),[6] clearly stated the rule that prevailed as to awarding alimony prior to the dissolution of marriage act in 1971 (Chapter 71-241, Laws of 1971) as:

> The accepted principles are that a divorced wife is entitled to alimony which will permit her to live in a manner commensurate with that provided by her husband during coverture, if he has the ability to pay.

An in-depth review of this Court's decisions after the 1971 statutory changes is now in order to determine the current status of alimony in our state.

In *Beard v. Beard*, 262 So.2d 269 (Fla. App. 1st 1972), the trial court found (as is probably true in more than 90 percent of marriage failures) that although neither party was without fault, "the preponderance of the equities lies with appellant husband and he is entitled to a divorce from appellee wife on the ground of habitual intemperance and indulgence in alcoholic beverages." Next, what did the trial court do in *Beard* as to the material assets accumulated during their 21-year partnership as husband and wife? The trial court awarded the wife the exclusive use of the marital home; the exclusive use of an automobile in her possession; one-half of a $15,900.00 joint savings account owned by the parties; a $1,400.00 savings account in the wife's name; and permanent period alimony of $100.00 per week. It is the last item which this Court reversed. After observing that the husband had a net income of $9,500.00 along with the custody and responsibility of supporting a minor child of the parties, we noted that payment of the periodic alimony would leave the husband the sum of $4,300.00 from which he would be required to purchase or rent a place of abode for himself and his minor daughter as well as pay all of their normal living expenses. At the same time, the wife had demonstrated her ability to support herself by having been employed in a supervisory position (with seven employees under her supervision) until sixty days prior to her instituting suit. The opinion carefully points out that:

---

6. Also see *Chestnut v. Chestnut*, 160 Fla. 83, 33 So.2d 730 (1948), wherein Justice Terrell, speaking for the Supreme Court, stated: "It [alimony] is awarded on the theory that marriage is a partnership to which the wife has contributed and when she withdraws from it she is entitled to reimbursement that she may not become a public charge."

> In view of the temporary impairment of her health at the time judgment was rendered, some months may have been required before she was able to completely overcome her drinking problem and regain her health sufficiently to enable her to return to work.... The elimination of alimony from the final judgment is predicated upon the conclusion that appellee has now had ample time to regain her health and again become employable but is without prejudice to her right to petition the court for a modification of the final judgment, as amended, upon a proper showing of a change of circumstances and a need for reasonable support not attributable to her own fault.

It is upon these facts that this Court stated:

> They [husband and wife] now occupy a position of equal partners in the family relationship resulting from marriage, and more often than not contribute a full measure to the economic well-being of the family unit. Whether the marriage continues to exist or is severed through the device of judicial decree, the woman continues to be as fully equipped as the man to earn a living and provide for her essential needs. The fortuitous circumstance created by recitation of the marriage vows neither diminishes her capacity for self-support nor does it give her a vested right in her husband's earnings for the remainder of her life.

Reversing an alimony award requiring a husband to support an alcoholic wife for the remainder of her life by contributing more than he would have remaining from the fruits of his labor to support himself and his minor daughter, does not appear to us as a decision that virtually eliminates alimony.

Thigpen v. Thigpen, 277 So.2d 583 (Fla. App. 1st 1973), is next. There, the parties had lived together for approximately 24 years. The wife had demonstrated her ability as an able office manager for some 15 years prior to the dissolvement of the marriage. The substantial material assets of the marital venture were *equally* divided between the parties. The husband was employed as a salesman at the time of the dissolution with an average take-home pay of approximately $750.00 per month. Appellee wife had declined two jobs during this same period of time due to an allergy she was suffering caused by use of cosmetics which affected her feet and prevented her from wearing dress shoes but not sandals or slides. In setting aside permanent alimony, payable monthly in the sum of $450.00, this Court held, inter alia:

> We have carefully considered the pertinent evidence contained in the record but fail to find any reasonable basis on which the alimony [periodic] award made to appellee can be sustained. The very heart of an alimony award is and always has been the need of the demanding spouse for support and the ability of the other spouse to respond. *The new concept of the marriage relation implicit in the so-called "no fault" divorce law enacted by the legislature in 1971 places both parties to the marriage on a basis of complete equality as partners — sharing equal rights and obligations in the marriage relationship and sharing equal burdens in the event of dissolution.* [Emphasis supplied.]

After this extensive (some readers might well add exhausting) review of the question of alimony, it is our considered judgment that a new day has been created by the 1971 legislative enactment and decisions construing same in the following respects: 1) Periodic alimony is no longer payable as nourishment or sustenance of wife or payable at regular periods for her support from year to year in the nature of obligation to a stranger (*Welsh v. Welsh, supra*). Periodic alimony is primarily payable from one spouse to another, based upon the need of the receiving spouse and upon the ability to pay by the contributing spouse, giving special attention to facts as to the advisability of rehabilitative alimony. Lump sum alimony is no longer frowned upon in adjusting the material wealth of the parties at the time of dissolution of the marriage. The overriding tenor of this Court's decisions in both *Beard, supra*, and *Thigpen, supra*,[7] is "a new day is born. Husband and wife are now truly partners in the marital venture sharing equal rights and obligations."

The ultimate question is now reached. How shall the material wealth of a marriage which is being dissolved be divided when one partner, the wife, has contributed her time to the marital home and children of the parties while the husband has pursued the accumulation of material goods. The evolution of the law of alimony that we have reviewed in length shows that today the contributions of each party to the accumulation of material assets must be considered in dissolving the marital partnership. Either spouse may contribute either by working in the market place or by working as a homemaker. The fact that in one marital venture a spouse is gainfully employed in the market place and pays a housekeeper to rear the children and keep house is not distinguishable from the spouse who devotes his or her full time to the profession of homemaker. The primary factual circumstance is each spouse's contribution to the marital partnership. In the case sub judice, the wife has been short changed. The wife has not been adequately compensated for the contribution that she made as a full time mother and homemaker to the equal partnership marriage. We hold that the trial court abused its discretion in awarding the wife a pittance of the material assets accumulated in the husband's name during 21 years. In so holding, we emphasize even though the cited authorities on the subject speak of "equal partners" and complete equality as partners, we are not engrafting upon the jurisprudence of this state the law of community property. On the question of alimony the judgment is reversed with instructions to the trial court to enter an award of lump sum alimony sufficient to compensate the wife for her contribution to the marriage.

We next turn our attention to the question of child custody. The trial court placed the custody of the four children with their mother with the right of the three oldest boys to live with their father if they so chose without further order of the court. Allowing minor children to pick and choose at their will the parent with whom they will reside only invites them to "play one parent against the other." Such conditions are not in the best interest of the child. The portion of the final judgment concerning the custody of the children is remanded with instructions that those children who are still minors shall be placed in the exclusive custody of the wife with visitation rights to the husband.

. . .

The case is remanded to the lower court for proceedings in accordance with this opinion.

. . .

7. It is noted the counsel for appellee in the instant cause was counsel for appellees in *Beard* and *Thigpen*.

BOYER, Judge (dissenting).

I respectfully dissent from the carefully and thoroughly prepared opinion of Chief Judge Rawls.

The law is well settled that courts should practice self discipline and refrain from entering into the legislative field: Further, the Supreme Court of Florida has clearly announced pre-emption unto itself of judicial innovations in the law. (*Hoffman v. Jones*, Sup. Ct. Fla. 1973, 280 So.2d 431)

Alimony came about during the era that women in general and wives in particular were placed on a pedestal by male chauvinists. Women apparently found being worshipped on a pedestal to be distasteful and commenced a virtual worldwide drive to be removed from their place of superiority to a position of equality. Why one enjoying a position of superiority would intentionally seek a lower position of equality eludes the writer, but it is a fact of social history. "Success" has been marked by a loss of many heretofore existing superior rights, among them being dower and alimony as a matter of right. The legislature, in its infinite wisdom, responding to the movement for women's liberation, adopted that which is commonly referred to as "no-fault divorce." Drastic changes in the law of domestic relations was thereby wrought. That act clearly and unambiguously provides for "rehabilitative alimony."

...

The majority opinion recites that we have before us a factual situation wherein the wife has foregone pursuing a professional career and the accumulation of a personal estate in order to be a fulltime mother and homemaker while the husband has remained in the market place providing for the material needs of the family and accumulating a sizable personal estate; arriving at the conclusion that "in the case sub judice, the wife has been shortchanged." Such recitations are, in my opinion, assumptions. The evidence does not necessarily lead to that conclusion. Just because a woman has borne children during a marriage does not mean that she is Whistler's mother. There is a vast difference between the physical act of bearing a child and the fact of being a mother as that term is generally eulogized and used in the traditional American concept. I do not here mean to malign the appellant in the case sub judice. She might well be the ideal mother from every standpoint. She might have also been the wife that every man dreams of. However there is nothing in the evidence of this cause to justify us so finding, or finding to the contrary. She may have contributed to the marriage "as a fulltime mother and homemaker" but on the other hand she may not have. The trial judge was in a much better position to make that determination than are we. For aught that we know the appellee may have had good cause to "await the day" that the children would be grown and the marriage relationship terminated.

...

In reviewing the final judgment appealed we should not overlook the unquestioned findings of the trial judge that the wife is a registered nurse and a real estate saleslady. It certainly appears to me that the $500 per month rehabilitative alimony plus the $500 per month child support was adequate.

In my view the majority opinion constitutes a substantial departure from this Court's holdings in *Beard v. Beard* and *Thigpen v. Thigpen*, both cited therein.

I must further dissent to the provision in the majority opinion instructing that the minor children be placed in the exclusive custody of the mother. Again, in my opinion, the record is not sufficient to justify that holding. If the case is to be reversed then the instruction to the trial judge should be to take such evidence as may be necessary to determine the proper custodian for the children, taking into account their best interests....

The findings and holdings of the trial court are fully sustained by the record. For us to hold otherwise is to substitute our judgment for his. He observed the parties and the witnesses. He also had an opportunity to observe the children.

I would affirm.

COMMENTS

The position of married women is perhaps nowhere more behind the times than in the legal treatment of the homemaker. Since the husband traditionally is entitled to consortium, namely services, society, and sexual relations, a homemaker is still often viewed as merely doing what the law requires of her. *Brown v. Brown*, in some respects a progressive opinion, used patronizing language in stating that "the wife dutifully kept house," while the husband was engaged in his career and in accumulating wealth. Any special compensation — for example, by separate contract benefiting the wife — may even be viewed as lacking consideration because of a preexisting legal duty. The same basic attitude results in the view that a woman as mere homemaker is not established as a partner in the legal sense. As in the small business cases, the wife, to be legally recognized as a partner, must engage in something more than keeping house — in other words, be active beyond the call of duty. It is the attorney's task to find these additional facts by taking an extensive and detailed history of both the marriage and the business.

Meanwhile, the courts have shown an increasing tendency to give greater recognition to the homemaker. In the exercise of judicial discretion, judges, aided by lawyers, have developed patterns of thought that may eventually evolve into rules. They refer to two methods of placing a value on the homemaker's economic contribution: "replacement value" and "opportunity lost." Replacement value indicates how much it would have cost to hire one or more persons, with all the necessary skills to raise children and run a household. United States Department of Labor statistics are used to determine these costs. Opportunity lost refers to the occupation the spouse would have pursued "but for" the marriage. To measure this value, it is necessary to determine the most rewarding occupation available to the spouse, given her education and special skills, at the time of and during the marriage.

In most cases, of course, it would be impracticable, if not impossible, to grant actual damages in these circumstances because the amounts involved would be prohibitively high. Courts therefore use the formulas of replacement value and opportunities lost to support a partnership position for the wife, or, by way of equitable distribution, to give her a substantial share of the marital assets.

Even though the judges in both *Lacey* and *Brown* used partnership language, they did not award the wife an equal share in accumulated assets. As the judge in *Lacey* pronounced, one third is the general level from which to start, although one half, and in rare instances more than that, is not entirely foreclosed. In *Brown*, although criticizing the lower court for not treating the wife as an "equal partner," the judge hastened to add that such equal treatment is not to be understood in the sense of community property.

Even in these relatively advanced opinions one is left with the discretion of the chancellor, who ordinarily may be inclined to give the wife less than half of the accumulated assets if she was "merely" a homemaker. The only way for women to avoid the risk of unfavorable exercise of judicial discretion is by antenuptial agreement. Of course, by extreme additional effort in marriage, a woman may bring about a situation that can be characterized as a business partnership; or she may suggest a move to the West Coast, where women's rights are better protected by community property law. The dissenting opinion of Judge Boyer in *Brown*, more than anything else, illustrates the depth of male frustration with the trend toward full recognition of wives as marital partners.

The recent legislative and judicial trend toward "equitable distribution" may, instead of granting relief from unfettered judicial discretion, increase the powers of the judge and expand the jurisdiction of the court. Equitable distribution increasingly subjects all property of the spouses to judicial distribution upon divorce, regardless of whether it was accumulated during the marriage through common effort or originated from other sources, such as inheritance. The adjective "equitable" injects potential consideration of conduct and thus of fault, and also invokes continued and even increased emphasis on judicial discretion. Whether or not equitable distribution favors homemakers may depend on personal preference of individual chancellors or the skills of attorneys who represent the parties. While these considerations are not adverse to the economic interests of the practicing bar, they may neglect the interests of the parties in the majority of divorces involving marriages of relatively short duration with minor children. *Brown*, which, together with *Canakaris v. Canakaris*, 382 So. 2d 1197 (Fla. 1980), paved the way for judicial equitable distribution in Florida, is somewhere in between. It did involve a marriage of twenty-one years' duration, but also minor children. Perhaps this made *Brown* suitable for laying the foundation for a principle of sweeping universality.

REFERENCE

Susan Westerberg Reppy, Comment, *The Development of Sharing Principles in Common Law Marital Property States*, 28 UCLA L. REV. 1269 (1981).

Marriage Partnership as a Liability

KENNEDY v. NELSON
Court of Appeals of Alabama
37 Ala. App.484, 70 So.2d 822 (1954)

CARR, Presiding Judge.

The plaintiff below brought suit against Guy Nelson and his wife, Mrs. Annie Ray Grisham Nelson, for work and labor done. The cause was tried without a jury, and the trial resulted in a judgment in favor of the plaintiff against Mr. Nelson, but in favor of the defendant, Mrs. Nelson. The plaintiff brings this appeal from the judgment in Mrs. Nelson's favor.

In material reviewable aspects the facts are not in dispute.

Mrs. Nelson was the sole owner of an eighty-two acre tract of land. She and her husband had lived on this farm for many years. Up until the year 1951 Mr. Nelson had looked after the farming and rental interests for his wife. Some disagreements arose over the management, and in 1951 Mrs. Nelson rented the place to her husband. The latter was to pay $100 a year for the pasture lands and one-third of the crops on the cultivated portion.

During the year 1952 the appellant contracted with Mr. Nelson to do some grading on the pasture lands. Mrs. Nelson did not in any manner participate in the plan, nor did she become a party to the agreement. In fact, the appellant did not know that Mrs. Nelson owned the farm until some time after the work was completed.

It appears that Mrs. Nelson knew the grading was in progress because the work was done not a great distance from her residence. The bill for the labor was mailed to Mr. Nelson, and he alone was pressed for payment.

Mr. Nelson did not consider the work satisfactorily done, and according to his claim he refused payment on this account. When it appeared that prompt payment would not be made, the appellant endeavored to get Mrs. Nelson to sign a note for the amount claimed. This she refused to do.

From this brief delineation of the evidence it is clear that if the appellant is entitled to recover against Mrs. Nelson this right must arise from the doctrine of principal and agent or from ratification of the contract.

We held in *Turner v. Rhodes*, 22 Ala. App. 426, 116 So. 412, that the relationship of husband and wife does not *per se* raise a presumption that the former acted as the agent of the latter.

Appellant's position is not strengthened by the mere fact that the property of the wife was benefitted by the improvements. *Fries v. Acme White Lead & Color Works*, 201 Ala. 613, 79 So. 45.

In other words, a party may choose the person with whom he deals. It may result that one has benefitted by the contract of another to which he is not a party, but the law will not imply a promise to pay for this gain which inures incidentally by the performance of the agreement.

A very comprehensive statement of the law is found in the early case of *Wadsworth v. Hodge*, 88 Ala. 500, 7 So. 194, 196:

> The contract must be either originally that of the wife, through herself or her authorized agent, or else the husband or other agent must assume to

> contract for her and in her own behalf, and such contract be subsequently ratified by her, with full notice or knowledge of its nature. In the absence of a contract of this character, no lien will attach to her property; and, where the credit is given solely to the husband, he alone is bound, although it may appear that the wife knew that the building or improvements were in process of erection on her land, and said nothing, or that she and other members of the family afterwards occupied the building as a dwelling.

The question of instant concern has been reviewed by our appellate courts in various aspects a number of times. We will discuss and cite some cases which bear analogous factual foundations to the case at bar.

In *Hawkins Lumber Co. v. Brown*, 100 Ala. 217, 14 So. 110, the suit was to recover for the price of lumber used in improving the dwelling on the property of the wife. The purchase of the material was made by the husband and credit was given to him solely. There was no evidence that in the transaction he undertook to act as the agent of his wife.

In response to a review the Supreme Court held that under these circumstances the statute did not create a lien upon the property of the owner for the price of the lumber.

In the case of *Hanchey v. Powell*, 171 Ala. 597, 55 So. 97, the vendor knew that lumber he sold was to be used for repairs on property owned by the wife. The court observed that the lumberman did not sell the material to the wife or to her husband as her agent, but it was sold to the latter individually, and under this state of facts the wife was not "originally or primarily liable for the debt...."

...In the case of *Womack v. Myrick Lumber Co.*, 200 Ala. 591, 76 So. 949, 950, the materialman furnished lumber to improve two dwellings on lots belonging to the wife of the purchaser. The account was stated on the vendor's books in the name of the husband, agent.

The court held that this was not conclusive of the matter, but it was essential to show that either the husband acted with authority as the agent of his wife or that "being fully advised of the facts, she, the owner, ratified the acts of R. J. Womack (husband) in the premises."

The court observed in *Fries v. Acme White Lead & Color Works*, [201 Ala. 613, 79 So. 48]:

> If there was no such contract in this case, no liability was assumed by appellant, and none attached, for which she may be subjected in this suit; for if by express contract credit was given solely to the husband he alone is bound, although it may appear that the wife knew that the building or improvements were in process of erection on her land, and said nothing, or that she and other members of the family afterwards occupied the building as a dwelling.

We are unable to find any evidence in this record which would authorize us to hold that Mrs. Nelson ratified the agreement between her husband and the appellant, and became liable for the debt on this account.

In this aspect the only proof which has any tendency to establish this doctrine is the fact that Mrs. Nelson knew the grading was in progress and that she took no steps to disclaim any liability for payment for the work.

According to the authorities, this alone is not sufficient.

...

Appellant urges that the long relationship between Mr. and Mrs. Nelson in the management of the latter's farm gave rise and application to the doctrine of implied agency.

We are, of course, faced with the testimony that this long standing relationship terminated in 1951.

This question seems to be answered adversely to the position of appellant in 41 C.J.S., *Husband and Wife*, §293(b), pages 777–778:

> Where the husband, in dealing with the wife's separate property, acts as her agent, persons dealing with him are bound to take notice of his authority as in the case of other agents, and are bound to inquire as to the extent of his authority; and persons having notice of the husband's agency will not be protected as to transactions with him hostile to her interest and beyond the apparent scope of his agency....
>
> Where one deals with the husband as principal, no fact of undisclosed agency appearing, the wife cannot be charged with liability; and it is not sufficient to charge the wife that the purchases were for the benefit of her separate estate.

...

As we have indicated, the case was tried without a jury. There is no indication that appellant's rights were infringed by the procedure.

It is well settled that in matters of this character the sound discretion of the trial judge is invoked. We are clear to the conclusion that we would be out of harmony with the authorities to declare that in the instant case this discretion was abused....

We have responded to the questions which are properly presented for our review.

It is ordered that the judgment below from which this appeal is taken be affirmed.

Affirmed.

NORTHAMPTON BREWERY CORPORATION v. LANDE

Superior Court of Pennsylvania

138 Pa. Super.235, 10 A.2d 583 (1939)

BALDRIGE, J.

This is an appeal from the order of Bluett, J., of the Municipal Court granting the prayer of the petitioner to charge the interest of the defendant, an alleged partner in a partnership with a debt owing the plaintiff.

Broadly stated, the question before us is whether a husband and wife may be partners in carrying on a business; more particularly, whether the court below was correct in holding the relationship existing between the appellant and her husband, in conducting a restaurant and grill at 732 Vine Street, Philadelphia, was that of partners rather than of tenants by entireties.

...

At common law, married women, lacking contract capacity generally, could not become partners. Modern legislation has removed almost entirely the legal incapacities of married women. In most jurisdictions they may become members of partnerships and even partners with their husbands. Crane on Partnership, page 32. There can be no doubt that under the existing law in this state a husband and wife may be partners in a business. Any previously existing incapacity of a married woman to contract in this respect has been removed by statute. This court, in *Loeb v. Mellinger*, 12 Pa. Super, 592, 597, held that a married woman can engage in a trade or business on her own account since the Act of June 8, 1893, P.L. 344, 48 P.S. §32. In *Italo-French Produce Co. v. Thomas*, 31 Pa. Super. 503, we stated that a married woman had the right, if she chose, to become a partner of her husband in a mercantile business, and be subject to the same rights and exposed to the same liabilities as any other member of the same partnership.

...

A partnership is defined under our Uniform Partnership Act of March 26, 1915, P.L. 18, §6, 59 P.S. §11, as "an association of two or more persons to carry on as co-owners a *business* for profit." (Italics supplied.) In ascertaining whether a partnership exists, it is necessary to consider all of the attending facts and circumstances, and, if the evidence is sufficient, it is for the jury's consideration.

A plain distinction exists between a partnership of a husband and wife and a tenancy of entireties, which is recognized by section 7 of our Uniform Partnership Act of 1915, supra, 59 P.S. §12, as follows: "In determining whether a partnership exists, these rules shall apply...(2) Joint tenancy, tenancy in common, *tenancy by the entireties*, joint property, common property, or part ownership does not of itself establish a partnership, whether such co-owners do or do not share any profits made by the use of the property." (Italics supplied.)

...[T]he difference between a tenancy by entireties and a partnership conducted by husband and wife as partners is that the partnership involves, in addition to co-ownership of property, the element of carrying on a business of commercial enterprise for profit.

...

The court below, without hearing any testimony under the petition, concluded that it had already adjudicated in the previous proceedings between the same parties that the relationship between Beatrice Lande and her husband in conducting the tap room and grill was that of partners. Accordingly, it made an order directing that a receiver be appointed to determine the value of the appellant's interest in the partnership. The appellant, in addition to contending that the parties were tenants by entireties only, alleges that the court below could not determine what the relationship was of her and her husband in conducting the grill without taking testimony. The learned judge below in his opinion stated that the question had already been adjudicated in this court in previous attachment proceedings when a considerable amount of testimony was taken and it was found that under the law a partnership did exist. A motion for a new trial prevailed in the attachment proceedings and the case was tried again before Judge Crane, who likewise, determined the existence of a partnership and found for the plaintiff against the garnishee. After the death of Judge Crane, a motion for a new trial was argued before Judge Glass, who, in a lengthy opinion, called attention to the fact that the record showed that

> David Lande...testified that the restaurant business conducted under the name of The Keg and Dave's Grill were both registered in the name of David Lande and Beatrice Lande...that both he and his wife signed the petition for registration under the Fictitious Name Act and that neither registration had been canceled;...that the liquor licenses at both addresses

are in the name of Beatrice Lande and David Lande; that those licenses have been renewed every year since 1936, and that both signed the petition for a liquor license and for the renewals...that bank accounts were opened in both names...that the leases to both places of business are in the names of both of them; that the money that went into each of the businesses aforesaid was borrowed from the banks by both himself and his wife, Beatrice Lande; that the income tax returns for 1936 and 1937 were joint returns of Beatrice and David Lande...that he draws and signs the checks and that Beatrice Lande, his wife, can if she wants to; that neither he nor his wife draw a salary.

There can be no dispute as to these facts and as to the manner in which both David Lande and Beatrice Lande conducted the grill and restaurant on Vine Street. The real dispute is to the legal conclusion to be drawn from these facts, namely, for the purpose of this case, were they partners or tenants by entireties? We think the trial court was entirely correct in treating the facts as already adjudicated....

...

The order is affirmed, at appellant's costs.

FARM BUREAU AGRICULTURAL CREDIT CORPORATION v. DICKE
Court of Appeals of Ohio
29 Ohio App. 2d.1, 277 N.E.2d 562 (1972)

GUERNSEY, Judge.

This is an appeal by the defendants Donald W. Dicke and his wife, Virginia, from a judgment in a declaratory judgment action determining the rights of the plaintiff credit corporation and said defendants to funds in the possession of the Sheriff of Auglaize County. It appears that on October 18, 1963,...the plaintiff took a cognovit judgment against Donald W. Dicke on a note of which he was the sole maker, issued execution thereon and that on October 19, 1963, the Sheriff attended a public sale of farm chattels which had been in possession of Donald W. Dicke and his wife, Virginia, where he attempted to levy, or succeeded in levying, execution against a part of the proceeds of sale in the hands of the auction clerk. These are the funds to which right of ownership is now disputed. The trial court held, in essence, that the chattels which were sold were the partnership property of Dicke and his wife, that the note upon which judgment had been taken was a partnership obligation, and that the funds derived from the sale of the partnership property were subject to the levy of execution on the judgment against Dicke.

...

Appellants' sixth assignment of error is that the trial court committed error in its decision in applying a theory of implied partnership. This we shall discuss together with the seventh assignment that the order of the court is against the manifest weight of the evidence and contrary to law. There was sufficient evidence of probative value with respect to the contributions of capital and labor, the manner of use of a joint bank account, and the frequent representations or acknowledgments, when borrowing money, of joint or common ownership of the chattels involved, that the farm business relationship between the appellants was that of a partnership and that the farm chattels sold at public sale were partnership property. On this state of the evidence we may not conclude otherwise as a matter of law and the fifth assignment of error must be found without merit.

However, the issue then resolves itself as being whether the plaintiff, having taken judgment individually against Donald W. Dicke, may levy execution on said judgment against partnership property owned by both Donald W. Dicke and his wife, Virginia, the funds produced by the sale of partnership chattels retaining the same character and being partnership funds....

We might conclude, notwithstanding that the plaintiff claims, and the trial court found, that the money which was loaned, evidenced by the obligation sued upon, was loaned for partnership use, that since the claim was merged in a judgment individually against Donald W. Dicke, it thereby became his sole obligation which could not be asserted against partnership property. We do not, however, have to rely on such conclusion, arrived at in such manner, for we may arrive at the same conclusion in a different manner.

R.C. §1775.08 prescribes among other things, that:

> (C) Unless authorized by the other partners..., one or more but less than all the partners have no authority to:
>
> ....
>
> (4) Confess a judgment;
>
> ....

This means, of course, that one partner, unless authorized, may not confess a judgment against the partnership, but does not preclude him from confessing a judgment against himself alone. It is likewise obvious that the mere existence of the partnership relation does not, in and of itself, extend the authority of the other partners to one partner to confess judgment. In other words, the authority is not implied by the partnership relationship but must be expressly granted or appear from other circumstances.

Here there is no evidence in the record of any authority expressly or otherwise granted by Virginia Dicke to her husband to confess judgment against their farming partnership and the plaintiff having taken a cognovit judgment against the husband, under such circumstances, may have recourse only against the individual property of the husband and not against partnership property. His interest in partnership property was subject, of course, to a charging order obtained in the manner prescribed in R.C. §1775.27, but not subject to a levy of execution in the manner here attempted.

We conclude that the trial court committed error as a matter of law prejudicial to the appellants in holding and declaring that the funds herein involved were subject to the levy of execution on plaintiff's judgment, that said levy was valid, and that the funds be paid to the plaintiff.

Judgment reversed.

COMMENTS

The conception of marriage as partnership can of course be a mixed blessing for women, as when, for example, they have higher income and assets than their husbands. Apart from this, lower-earning spouses (usually wives) become increasingly liable for marital debts under conceptions of partnership. They gain a vested interest in the partnership in exchange for the possibility of being liable to outsiders. *Northampton* involved a restaurant, jointly operated by husband and wife. The wife defended herself against the brewery's claims by stating that she was a tenant by the entireties rather than a partner and as such was not liable. The court disagreed and charged her interest in the partnership. This was a small business case; but if marriage is viewed as a pooling of resources for mutual profit, there is no reason why this holding could not be extended. In *Farm Bureau* a married woman who operated a farm jointly with her husband escaped liability on a promissory note signed by him, but only because of a mere procedural technicality.

Once the possibility is seen that a wife may be liable, conscious efforts may be made in marriage, parallel to those in business organizations, to avoid liability. It might be possible to operate the economic aspects of a marriage as a closed corporation. In *Kennedy*, the wife, as sole owner of an Alabama farm, changed her management contract with her husband into a lease. In a principal-agent or employment relationship, she would have been liable for the debts incurred by her husband; as a landlord she was not. Ancient conceptions of feudal law of property, shielding the landlord from liability for activities of the tenant, came to her aid.

As suggested above, marriage should be seen in the context of alternatives available in business, where it is always important to minimize liability. But litigation often becomes arrested in one legal theory, because attorneys have traditionally not been trained to think on multiple levels of analysis. The courts are then limited to whatever theory happens to be submitted to them in the pleadings.

Once a legal theory is chosen, further consequences flow from it. For example, in *Kennedy*, if the wife is classified as a landlord in a lease with her husband, her knowledge of what she saw becomes irrelevant. If the problem is seen as agency, then knowledge can become significant as ratification. The argument of a lease seems to have been facilitated in *Kennedy* by an express agreement between husband and wife. More problematic are the *Northampton* and *Farm Bureau* holdings, because they found partnership by implication. As always, the implied contract can be used as a judicial tool to apply public policy in a covert fashion that, in some instances, may approach legal fiction. The wife may be treated as if she were a partner for purposes of attaching personal liability to her or, on the positive side, to give her a better share in her husband's property as a matter of law.

REFERENCE

Walter O. Weyrauch, *Metamorphoses of Marriage*, 13 FAM. L. Q. 415 (1980).

Determining What Assets May be Divided as Marital Property

IN RE MARRIAGE OF GRUBB
Supreme Court of Colorado
745 P.2d 661 (Colo. 1987)

QUINN, Chief Justice.

The question in this case is whether a husband's interest in a vested employer-supported pension plan constitutes marital property subject to division upon dissolution of marriage when the receipt of benefits under the plan is contingent upon the husband's survival until the actual commencement of retirement. The court of appeals in *In re Marriage of Grubb*, 721 P.2d 1194 (Colo.App.1986), held that the husband's interest in the plan was not marital property. We reverse the judgment and remand the case for further proceedings.

I

The petitioner, Leisa T. Grubb (wife), and the respondent, William A. Grubb (husband), were married on April 5, 1950. They had one child who was emancipated prior to the commencement of the present dissolution proceeding. When the decree of dissolution was entered on February 28, 1984, the wife was 58 years of age and the husband was 60 years of age. The wife was unemployed at the time of the decree, having worked primarily as a mother and homemaker during the marriage. The husband has been employed by the Atlantic Richfield Company (ARCO) since February 2, 1948, and was earning approximately $92,000 per year at the time of the decree. Although the husband was eligible for retirement when the decree was entered, he testified that he was in good health and had no plans for retirement in the foreseeable future. ARCO has no mandatory retirement age.

During the course of his employment with ARCO, the husband participated in the Atlantic Richfield Retirement Plan (Plan). Under the terms of the Plan, the employee's retirement benefits become fully vested after the completion of ten years of service; and after fifteen years of service, the employee is eligible to retire at age 55 and receive 100% of the money in the Plan. Prior to 1974 the employees were required to make contributions to the Plan, but since that time the Plan has been employer-funded, with the employees being permitted to make voluntary contributions. Upon the employee's retirement or death, all employee contributions, plus interest, are unconditionally returned to the employee, the employee's estate, or beneficiary.

The employer contributions are kept separately from and are not intermingled with the employee contributions. The amount of the employer contributions is actuarially determined each year on a group basis, utilizing interest rates, mortality tables, turnover rates, ages of all Plan members, salary scales, and other factors. Employer contributions, in contrast to employee contributions, are "retirement qualified," which means that the employee must survive until the commencement of retirement in order to receive any payment. If the employee dies unmarried before retiring, only the employee contributions, plus interest, are paid to the employee's estate or the employee's beneficiary, even though the employee's right to benefits might have fully vested. Thus, although the employee has a vested right to payment after completing ten years of service, this right is subject to the requirement that the employee survive until the actual commencement of retirement. The employer contributions, therefore, have no cash or loan value prior to retirement, and cannot be sold, conveyed, pledged, garnished, or attached.

When the dissolution decree was entered, the husband had been employed by ARCO for 36 years and his right to retirement benefits was fully vested. He had made required and voluntary contributions which, with accrued interest, were valued at approximately $32,000, and ARCO had made employer contributions which, when added to the husband's contributions, brought the total value of the husband's interest in the Plan to approximately $250,000. As of the date of the dissolution decree, the husband, if he had chosen to retire at that time, would have been entitled to receive the total amount of employer contributions or, alternatively, a lifetime pension of approximately $2900 per month, calculated on the basis of several factors including his average annual salary during the last three years of employment.[1]

At the dissolution hearing, John Connell, a certified public accountant, estimated that the present value of the husband's interest in the Plan was approximately $250,000. He offered two reasons for this opinion. First, the husband would receive approximately that amount if he immediately retired. Second, according to Connell, if the husband elected to retire at age 65 (five years after the dissolution), he would be entitled to receive $37,759.63 per year. Based on the husband's life expectancy at age 65 of 14.05 years and expected benefits over that period of time of $530,523, Connell discounted the total benefits to a present value by using a seven per cent discount factor, and concluded that the present value of the husband's interest in the Plan was within ten percent of $250,000.

In contrast to Connell's opinion, Jerome Karsh, also a certified public accountant, estimated that the fair market value of the husband's interest in the plan was $32,000 — the amount of his required and voluntary contributions. Karsh based his opinion on the fact that the husband was not entitled to receive the employer contributions until the commencement of retirement.

Finding that "there [was] nothing speculative or uncertain about [the husband's] rights to the money" and that "he could if he wished, quit work and withdraw the money he ha[d] accumulated," the trial court concluded that the employer contributions to the Plan qualified as marital property. The court then valued the retirement benefits at $250,000, and awarded these benefits to the husband in addition to other property valued at $42,722. In order to equalize the award of the Plan to the husband, the court awarded various items of marital property to the wife and also ordered the husband to pay maintenance of $2,350 per month until further order of the court. The husband appealed, and the court of appeals reversed the judgment. It held that an employer-supported pension plan subject to divestment is not an item of marital property but rather is an economic resource to be received in the future and, hence, is merely a factor to be considered in fixing the amount of maintenance. *Grubb*, 721 P.2d at 1196. We thereafter granted the wife's petition for certiorari to consider whether the pension plan in this case qualifies as marital property under section 14-10-113(1), 6 C.R.S. (1973 & 1986 Supp.).

---

1. The amount of monthly pension is determined by a complex calculation which includes, in addition to the employee's annual salary during the last three years of employment, an annuity factor based on the employee's age at retirement, the employee's average annual Social Security tax base, the employee's total number of years of employment and age at retirement, the method chosen by the employee to receive payment of voluntary and required contributions, and whether a pension will be paid to a survivor upon the employee's death.

II

Under the Uniform Dissolution of Marriage Act, §§14-10-101 to -133, 6 C.R.S. (1973 & 1986 Supp.), the district court in a dissolution proceeding is required to:

> divide the marital property, without regard to marital misconduct, in such proportions as the court deems just after considering all relevant factors including:
>
> (a) The contribution of each spouse to the acquisition of the marital property, including the contribution of a spouse as homemaker;
>
> (b) The value of the property set apart to each spouse;
>
> (c) The economic circumstances of each spouse at the time the division of property is to become effective, including the desirability of awarding the family home or the right to live therein for reasonable periods to the spouse having custody of any children; and
>
> (d) Any increases or decreases in the value of the separate property of the spouse during the marriage or the depletion of the separate property for marital purposes.

§14-10-113(1), 6 C.R.S. (1973 & 1986 Supp.). Although the Uniform Act does not define the term "property," section 14-10-113(2), 6 C.R.S. (1973), states that "[f]or purposes of this article only" the term " 'marital property' means all property acquired by either spouse subsequent to the marriage except:"

> (a) Property acquired by gift, bequest, devise, or descent;
>
> (b) Property acquired in exchange for property acquired prior to the marriage or in exchange for property acquired by gift, bequest, devise, or descent;
>
> (c) Property acquired by a spouse after a decree of legal separation;
>
> (d) Property excluded by valid agreement of the parties.

...

A rule directed to the disposition of property in a dissolution proceeding can only be as sound as the economic reality which it attempts to service.... Retirement benefits, far from being a mere gratuity deriving from the employer's beneficence, are nothing less than a form of deferred compensation — that is, they are consideration for past services performed by the employee and constitute part of the compensation earned by the employee....

We recognize that a "vested" pension right must be distinguished from a "matured" pension right. "Vesting" occurs when an employee has completed the minimum terms of employment necessary to be entitled to receive retirement pay at some point in the future; a vested right "matures" when the employee reaches retirement age and elects to retire. *E.g., Johnson v. Johnson,* 131 Ariz. 38, 41 n. 2, 638 P.2d 705, 708 n. 2 (1981); *Brown,* 15 Cal.3d at 842, 544 P.2d at 563, 126 Cal.Rptr. at 637; *In re Marriage of Hunt,* 78 Ill.App.3d 653, 658, 397 N.E.2d 511, 515 (1979). The receipt of pension payments under a vested but unmatured pension plan is thus contingent on some future event. This contingency, however, does not render the plan so speculative as to remove it from the category of marital property.

While one might invoke the law of future interests to support an argument that a vested but unmatured pension right is a mere "expectancy" until such time as a right actually matures, a more persuasive argument, in our view, is that the employee's right derives from his contract of employment. Such a right is not a mere expectancy but, rather, is an enforceable contractual right that traditionally has been recognized as a *chose in action* and thus a form of property.... We find the controlling consideration to be that an employee who is fully vested under a pension plan has a *right* to receive payment at some time in the future. The mere existence of a future contingency does not downgrade that vested right to non-marital property even though receipt of payment under the plan might be contingent upon the employee surviving until the actual commencement of retirement. To exclude the employee's interest in a vested but as yet unmatured pension from the category of marital property not only ignores the true character of that interest as remuneration for past services but, more importantly, invites inequity, rather than equity, into the dissolution proceeding.

Any contingencies underlying the actual commencement of retirement under a pension plan should be taken into account, not when determining whether the pension plan is properly includable in the marital estate, but, rather, when the court disposes of marital property between the parties. *Deering*, 292 Md. at 129, 437 A.2d at 891. We thus hold that a spouse's interest in a vested but unmatured employer-supported pension plan, to the extent that such plan has been funded by employee and/or employer contributions during the course of a marriage, is marital property subject to equitable distribution in a dissolution proceeding.[2] Any statement or intimation to the contrary in our prior decisions in *Ellis* and *Mitchell* is hereby expressly disapproved.

...

IV

Turning to the facts of this case, there can be no question that the husband's contribution of $32,000 to the Plan was fully vested and fully matured. The husband also had a vested but unmatured right to the employer contributions, which right was subject to the condition that he survive until the actual commencement of his retirement. Both the husband's contributions to the Plan and the employer's contributions to the Plan, to the extent that they were made during the course of the marriage, constitute marital property within the meaning of section 14-10-113(2), 6 C.R.S. (1973), and the court of appeals erred in holding to the contrary.

...

We reverse the judgment of the court of appeals and remand the case to that court with directions to return the case to the district court for further proceedings consistent with the views herein expressed.

[Dissenting opinion omitted.]

2. Our holding is consistent with the vast majority of jurisdictions addressing this issue. *E.g.*, *Neal v. Neal*, 116 Ariz. 590, 570 P.2d 758 (1977)(community property jurisdiction); *Day v. Day*, 281 Ark. 261, 663 S.W.2d 719 (1984); *In re Marriage of Brown*, 15 Cal.3d 838, 544 P.2d 561, 126 Cal.Rptr. 633 (1976)(community property jurisdiction); *Clarke v. Clarke*, 443 So.2d 486 (Fla.Dist.App.1984); *In re Marriage of Hunt*, 78 Ill.App.3d 653, 34 Ill.Dec. 55, 397 N.E.2d 511 (1979); *In re Marriage of Schissel*, 292 N.W.2d 421 (Iowa 1980); *Foster v. Foster*, 589 S.W.2d 223 (Ky.App.1979); *Deering v. Deering*, 292 Md. 115, 437 A.2d 883 (1981); *Hatcher v. Hatcher*, 129 Mich.App. 753, 343 N.W.2d 498 (1983); *Taylor v. Taylor*, 329 N.W.2d 795 (Minn.1983); *Lynch v. Lynch*, 665 S.W.2d 20 (Mo.App.1983); *Hodgins v. Hodgins*, 126 N.H. 711, 497 A.2d 1187 (1985); *Weir v. Weir*, 73 N.J.Super. 130, 413 A.2d 638 (1980); *Copeland v. Copeland*, 91 N.M. 409, 575 P.2d 99 (1978); *Majauskas v. Majauskas*, 61 N.Y.2d 481, 463 N.E.2d 15, 474 N.Y.S.2d 699 (1984); *In re Marriage of Tjernlund*, 27 Or.App. 699, 557 P.2d 60 (1976); *Hansen v. Hansen* 273 N.W.2d 749 (S.D.1979); *Wilder v. Wilder*, 85 Wash.2d 364, 534 P.2d 1355 (1975); *Bloomer v. Bloomer*, 84 Wis.2d 124, 267 N.W.2d 235 (1978); *see generally* Annotation, *Pension or Retirement Benefits as Subject to Award or Division by Court in Settlement of Property Rights Between Spouses*, 94 A.L.R.3d 176 (1979).

SMITH v. LEWIS

Supreme Court of California

13 Cal. 3d 349, 530 P.2d 589, 118 Cal. Rptr. 621 (1975)

MOSK, Justice.

Defendant Jerome R. Lewis, an attorney, appeals from a judgment entered upon a jury verdict for plaintiff Rosemary E. Smith in an action for legal malpractice. The action arises as a result of legal services rendered by defendant to plaintiff in a prior divorce proceeding. The gist of plaintiff's complaint is that defendant negligently failed in the divorce action to assert her community interest in the retirement benefits of her husband.

Defendant principally contends, *inter alia*, that the law with regard to the characterization of retirement benefits was so unclear at the time he represented plaintiff as to insulate him from liability for failing to assert a claim therefor on behalf of his client.[1] We conclude defendant's appeal is without merit, and therefore affirm the judgment.

In 1943 plaintiff married General Clarence D. Smith. Between 1945 and his retirement in 1966 General Smith was employed by the California National Guard. As plaintiff testified, she informed defendant her husband "was paid by the state...it was a job just like anyone else goes to." For the first 16 years of that period the husband belonged to the State Employees' Retirement System, a contributory plan.[2] Between 1961 and the date of his retirement he belonged to the California National Guard retirement program, a noncontributory plan. In addition, by attending National Guard reserve drills he qualified for separate retirement benefits from the federal government, also through a noncontributory plan. The state and federal retirement programs each provide lifetime monthly benefits which terminate upon the death of the retiree. The programs make no allowance for the retiree's widow.

On January 1, 1967, the State of California began to pay General Smith gross retirement benefits of $796.26 per month. Payments under the federal program, however, will not begin until 1983, i.e., 17 years after his actual retirement, when General Smith reaches the age of 60. All benefits which General Smith is entitled to receive were earned during the time he was married to plaintiff.

On February 17, 1967, plaintiff retained defendant to represent her in a divorce action against General Smith. According to plaintiff's testimony, defendant advised her that her husband's retirement benefits were not community property. Three days later defendant filed plaintiff's complaint for divorce. General Smith's retirement benefits were not pleaded as items of community property, and therefore were not considered in the litigation or apportioned by the trial court. The divorce was uncontested and the interlocutory decree divided the minimal described community property and awarded Mrs. Smith $400 per month in alimony and child support. The final decree was entered on February 27, 1968.

---

1. Defendant alternatively contends the state and federal military retirement benefits in question cannot properly be characterized as community property, and hence his advice to plaintiff was correct. As will appear, the contention is manifestly untenable in light of recent decisions by this court. (*In re Marriage of Fithian* (1974) 10 Cal.3d 592, 111 Cal.Rptr. 369, 517 P.2d 449; *Waite v. Waite* (1972) 6 Cal.3d 461, 99 Cal.Rptr. 325, 492 P.2d 13; *Phillipson v. Board of Administration* (1970) 3 Cal.3d 32, 89 Cal.Rptr. 61, 473 P.2d 765.)

2. A contributory plan is one in which the member contributes to his retirement fund, normally through payroll deductions. A noncontributory plan is one in which no such contributions are made.

The State Employees' Retirement System is now referred to as the Public Employees' Retirement System (Gov.Code, § 20000 et seq.).

On July 17, 1968, pursuant to a request by plaintiff, defendant filed on her behalf a motion to amend the decree, alleging under oath that because of his mistake, inadvertence, and excusable neglect (Code Civ.Proc., §473) the retirement benefits of General Smith had been omitted from the list of community assets owned by the parties, and that such benefits were in fact community property. The motion was denied on the ground of untimeliness. Plaintiff consulted other counsel, and shortly thereafter filed this malpractice action against defendant.

Defendant admits in his testimony that he assumed General Smith's retirement benefits were separate property when he assessed plaintiff's community property rights. It is his position that as a matter of law an attorney is not liable for mistaken advice when well informed lawyers in the community entertain reasonable doubt as to the proper resolution of the particular legal question involved. Because, he asserts, the law defining the character of retirement benefits was uncertain at the time of his legal services to plaintiff, defendant contends the trial court committed error in refusing to grant his motions for nonsuit and judgment notwithstanding the verdict and in submitting the issue of negligence to the jury under appropriate instructions.[3]

The law is now settled in California that "retirement benefits which flow from the employment relationship, to the extent they have vested, are community property subject to equal division between the spouses in the event the marriage is dissolved." (*In re Marriage of Fithian* (1974) *supra*, 10 Cal.3d 592, 596, 111 Cal.Rptr. 369, 371, 517 P.2d 449, 451, citing *Waite v. Waite* (1972) *supra*, 6 Cal.3d 461, 99 Cal.Rptr. 325, 492 P.2d 13; *Phillipson v. Board of Administration* (1970) *supra*, 3 Cal.3d 32, 89 Cal.Rptr. 61, 473 P.2d 765; *Benson v. City of Los Angeles* (1963) 60 Cal.2d 355, 33 Cal.Rptr. 257, 384 P.2d 649; *French v. French* (1941) 17 Cal.2d 775, 112 P.2d 235; *Crossan v. Crossan* (1939) 35 Cal.App.2d 39, 94 P.2d 609.) Because such benefits are part of the consideration earned by the employee, they are accorded community treatment regardless of whether they derive from a state, federal, or private source, or from a contributory or non-contributory plan. (10 Cal.3d at p. 596, 111 Cal.Rptr. 369, 517 P.2d 449.) In light of these principles, it becomes apparent that General Smith's retirement pay must properly be characterized as community property.[4]

We cannot, however, evaluate the quality of defendant's professional services on the basis of the law as it appears today. In determining whether defendant exhibited the requisite degree of competence in his handling of plaintiff's divorce action, the crucial inquiry is whether his advice was so legally deficient when it was given that he may be found to have failed to use "such skill, prudence, and diligence as lawyers of ordinary skill and capacity commonly possess and exercise in

3. The jury was instructed as follows: "In performing legal services for a client in a divorce action an attorney has the duty to have that degree of learning and skill ordinarily possessed by attorneys of good standing, practicing in the same or similar locality and under similar circumstances."

"It is his further duty to use the care and skill ordinarily exercised in like cases by reputable members of his profession practicing in the same or a similar locality under similar circumstances, and to use reasonable diligence and his best judgment in the exercise of his skill and the accomplishment of his learning, in an effort to accomplish the best possible result for his client."

"A failure to perform any such duty is negligence."

"An attorney is not liable for every mistake he may make in his practice; he is not, in the absence of an express agreement, an insurer of the soundness of his opinions."

4. The fact General Smith will not receive any portion of the federal benefits until he reaches the age of 60 does not affect their community character. Though his right to the payments remained unmatured at the time of the divorce, it had fully vested. (*In re Marriage of Fithian* (1974) *supra*, 10 Cal.3d 592, 596, 111 Cal.Rptr. 369, 517 P.2d 449, fn. 2; *Williamson v. Williamson* (1962) 203 Cal.App.2d 8, 11, 21 Cal.Rptr. 164.)

the performance of the tasks which they undertake." (*Lucas v. Hamm* (1961) 56 Cal.2d 583, 591, 15 Cal.Rptr. 821, 825, 364 P.2d 685, 689.) We must, therefore examine the indicia of the law which were readily available to defendant at the time he performed the legal services in question.

The major authoritative reference works which attorneys routinely consult for a brief and reliable exposition of the law relevant to a specific problem uniformly indicated in 1967 that vested retirement benefits earned during marriage were generally subject to community treatment.[5] (See, e.g., Note, Pensions, and Reserve or Retired Pay, as Community Property, 134 A.L.R. 368; 15 Am.Jur.2d, Community Property, §46, p. 859; 38 Cal.Jur.2d, Pensions, §12, p. 325; 10 Cal.Jur.2d, Community Property, §25, p. 692; 1 Cal.Family Lawyer (Cont.Ed.Bar 1962) p. 111; 4 Witkin, Summary of Cal.Law (1960) pp. 2723–2724; cf. 41 C.J.S. Husband and Wife §475, p. 1010 & fn. 69 and 1967 Supp. p. 1011.) A typical statement appeared in The California Family Lawyer, a work with which defendant admitted general familiarity: "Of increasing importance is the fact that pension or retirement benefits are community property, even though they are not paid or payable until after termination of the marriage by death or divorce." (1 Cal.Family Lawyer, *supra*, at p. 111.)

Although it is true this court had not foreclosed all conflicts on some aspects of the issue at that time, the community character of retirement benefits had been reported in a number of appellate opinions often cited in the literature and readily accessible to defendant....

We are aware, moreover, of no significant authority existing in 1967 which proposed a result contrary to that suggested by the cases and the literature, or which purported to rebut the general statutory presumption, as it applies to retirement benefits, that all property acquired by either spouse during marriage belongs to the community. (Civ.Code, §5110, as amended Jan. 1, 1970; formerly Civ.Code, §164.)

On the other hand, substantial uncertainty may have existed in 1967 with regard to the community character of General Smith's *federal* pension. The above-discussed treatises reveal a debate which lingered among members of the legal community at that time concerning the point at which retirement benefits actually vest.[6] (See also Kent, *Pension Funds and Problems Under California Community Property Laws* (1950) 2 Stan.L.Rev. 447; Note, *Community Property: Division of Expectancies as Community Property at Time of Divorce* (1942) 30 Cal.L.Rev. 469.) Because the federal payments were contingent upon General Smith's survival to age 60, 17 years subsequent to the divorce, it could have been argued with some force that plaintiff and General Smith shared a mere expectancy interest in the future benefits. (See *French v. French* (1941) *supra*, 17 Cal.2d 775, 778, 112 P.2d 235; but see fn. 4, ante.) Alternatively, a reasonable contention could have been advanced in 1967 that federal retirement benefits were the personal entitlement of the employee spouse and were not subject to community division upon divorce in the absence of express congressional approval....

Of course, the fact that in 1967 a reasonable argument could have been offered to support the characterization of General Smith's federal benefits as separate

5. In evaluating the competence of an attorney's services, we may justifiably consider his failure to consult familiar encyclopedias of the law. (*People v. Ibarra* (1963) 60 Cal.2d 460, 465, 34 Cal.Rptr. 863, 386 P.2d 487.)

6. Indeed this debate may, to some extent, continue today. See, *e.g.*, *In re Marriage of Wilson* (1974) 10 Cal.3d 851, 112 Cal.Rptr. 405, 519 P.2d 165.

property does not indicate the trial court erred in submitting the issue of defendant's malpractice to the jury. The State benefits, the large majority of the payments at issue, were unquestionably community property according to all available authority and should have been claimed as such. As for the Federal benefits, the record documents defendant's failure to conduct any reasonable research into their proper characterization under community property law.[7] Instead, he dogmatically asserted his theory, which he was unable to support with authority and later recanted, that all noncontributory military retirement benefits, whether state or federal, were immune from community treatment upon divorce. The jury could well have found defendant's refusal to educate himself to the applicable principles of law constituted negligence which prevented him from exercising informed discretion with regard to his client's rights.

As the jury was correctly instructed, an attorney does not ordinarily guarantee the soundness of his opinions and, accordingly, is not liable for every mistake he may make in his practice. He is expected, however, to possess knowledge of those plain and elementary principles of law which are commonly known by well informed attorneys, and to discover those additional rules of law which, although not commonly known, may readily be found by standard research techniques. (*Lucas v. Hamm* (1961) 56 Cal.2d 583, 591, 15 Cal.Rptr. 821, 364 P.2d 685; *Lally v. Kuster* (1918) 177 Cal. 783, 786, 171 P. 961; *Floro v. Lawton* (1960) 187 Cal.App.2d 657, 673, 10 Cal.Rptr. 98; *Sprague v. Morgan* (1960) *supra*, 185 Cal.App.2d 519, 523, 8 Cal.Rptr. 347; *Armstrong v. Adams* (1929) 102 Cal.App. 677, 684, 283 P. 871.) If the law on a particular subject is doubtful or debatable, an attorney will not be held responsible for failing to anticipate the manner in which the uncertainty will be resolved. (See, e.g., *Sprague v. Morgan* (1960) *supra*.) But even with respect to an unsettled area of the law, we believe an attorney assumes an obligation to his client to undertake reasonable research in an effort to ascertain relevant legal principles and to make an informed decision as to a course of conduct based upon an intelligent assessment of the problem. In the instant case, ample evidence was introduced to support a jury finding that defendant failed to perform such adequate research into the question of the community character of retirement benefits and thus was unable to exercise the informed judgment to which his client was entitled. (See fn. 7, *ante*.)

...

...[N]o lawyer would suggest the property characterization of General Smith's retirement benefits to be so esoteric an issue that defendant could not reasonably have been expected to be aware of it or its probable resolution.... Certainly one of the central issues in any divorce proceeding is the extent and division of the community property. In this case the question reached monumental proportions, since General Smith's retirement benefits constituted the only significant asset

7. At trial defendant testified that prior to the division of property in the divorce action, he had assumed the retirement benefits were not subject to community treatment, despite the fact General Smith had already begun to receive payments from the state; that he did not at that time undertake any research on the point nor did he discuss the matter with plaintiff; that subsequent to the divorce plaintiff asked defendant to research the question whereupon defendant discovered the *French* case which contained dictum in support of plaintiff's position; that the *French* decision caused him to change his opinion and conclude "that the Supreme Court, when it was confronted with this (the language in *French*) may hold that it (vested military retirement pay) is community property." On the basis of *French* defendant filed his unsuccessful motion to amend the final decree of divorce to allow plaintiff an interest in the retirement benefits. Defendant admitted at trial, "I would have been very willing to assert it (a community interest) on her behalf had I known of the dictum in the *French* case at the time."

available to the community.[8] In undertaking professional representation of plaintiff, defendant assumed the duty to familiarize himself with the law defining the character of retirement benefits; instead, he rendered erroneous advice contrary to the best interests of his client without the guidance through research of readily available authority.

...

In any event, as indicated above, had defendant conducted minimal research into either hornbook or case law, he would have discovered with modest effort that General Smith's state retirement benefits were likely to be treated as community property and that his federal benefits at least arguably belonged to the community as well. Therefore, we hold that the trial court correctly denied the motions for non-suit and judgment notwithstanding the verdict and properly submitted the question of defendant's negligence to the jury under the instructions given. (See fn. 3, *ante.*) For the same reasons, the trial court correctly refused to instruct the jury at defendant's request that "he is not liable for being in error as to a question of law on which reasonable doubt may be entertained by well informed lawyers." Even as to doubtful matters, an attorney is expected to perform sufficient research to enable him to make an informed and intelligent judgment on behalf of his client.

...

The judgment is affirmed.

SAVIDES v. SAVIDES

Supreme Judicial Court of Massachusetts
400 Mass. 250, 508 N.E.2d 617 (1987)

LYNCH, Justice.

Joan L. Savides appeals from that part of the judgment of divorce of November 25, 1985, which determined the amount of the marital assets and divided them under G.L. c. 208, §34. The Probate Court judge ordered that the wife receive the former marital home (valued at approximately $130,000 as of the date of the divorce), plus $245,000. He also ordered that she receive $250 per week in support payments. We transferred the case to this court on our own motion. We affirm.

The Probate Court judge found the following facts: Edward K. Savides and Joan L. Savides were married in 1956 and thereafter lived together through 1974. In early 1974, both parties began extramarital relationships. In October, 1974, Edward left the marital residence and moved in with his paramour. At the same time Joan's paramour moved in with her. With the exception of a few months when Edward lived with Joan while recuperating from an illness, Joan's paramour lived with her through the date of the hearing in 1985. For all intents and purposes the parties' marriage terminated in October, 1974, at which time both ceased to hold themselves out to the community as a married couple, and there was no further marital relationship after that time.

Between 1974 and 1983, Edward paid all Joan's living expenses and until 1982 provided her with $100 per week for food. He also left a $62,000 savings account

8. It is undisputed that the only assets the parties had to show as community property after 24 years of marriage, aside from General Smith's retirement benefits, were an equity of $1,800 in a house, some furniture, shares of stock worth $2,800, and two automobiles on which money was owing.

with her, and Joan has had exclusive use of the marital home. In addition, Edward gave her money for travel, furnished her with a new motor vehicle, paid her medical expenses, and in general provided for her in a generous manner.

During the course of the marriage, Edward was engaged in automobile sales. He contributed all the finances to the marriage and through his investment skills and diligent work increased the parties' net worth. Joan was a homemaker and mother. Although she did not contribute financially to the estate of the parties, her contributions to the marriage were found equal to Edward's efforts up to October, 1974. After October, 1974, Joan contributed nothing to the acquisition of the assets. However, Edward's business grew substantially after October, 1974; at the time of the divorce his estate was valued at close to $5 million.

1. Findings. Joan argues that the Probate Court judge erred in finding the marriage to have effectively terminated in October, 1974. The uncontested facts demonstrate that both parties established separate relationships as described by the judge and ceased to hold themselves out to the community as husband and wife after October, 1974. None of the facts alluded to by the wife, most of which center around the husband's continuing generosity toward her after October, 1974, compels a finding that the marriage continued beyond that date. See Mass.R.Dom.Rel.P. 52(a).

2. Abuse of discretion. The wife also contends that the evidence establishes her right to an equitable division of the marital property as it existed at the time Edward filed his complaint for divorce (1983) rather than as of 1974. Our review of a judgment pursuant to G.L. c. 208, §34, proceeds under a two-step analysis. "First, we examine the judge's findings to determine whether all relevant factors in §34 were considered." The second part of our review requires us to determine "whether the reasons for the judge's conclusions are apparent in his findings and rulings." *Bowring v. Reid,* 399 Mass. 265, 267, 503 N.E.2d 966 (1987). *Redding v. Redding,* 398 Mass. 102, 107, 495 N.E.2d 297 (1986). Here the judge made findings on each of the factors enumerated in the statute as required. *Rice v. Rice,* 372 Mass. 398, 402–403, 361 N.E.2d 1305 (1977). In addition, a review of the judge's findings makes clear the rationale for the property division. The judge did not, as the wife suggests, assign the marital property solely by reference to the date of the parties' separation. The findings make clear that the judge did consider events after the parties' separation, including their relationship and the husband's greatly increased estate, but concluded that the wife's contribution to marital property ceased in October, 1974.

The equitable factors which are to be considered under §34 reflect a view of marriage as an implied partnership for the purposes of distribution of property.... In considering the increase in value of property after separation, it was not error for the judge to exclude the wife's participation in that increase where she made no contribution to the marriage after that time and the increase in value was solely attributable to the husband's efforts. See *Davidson v. Davidson,* 19 Mass.App.Ct. 364 (1985). Given the broad discretion conferred by §34, we cannot conclude that the Probate Court judge's determination as to the property division was "plainly wrong and excessive" as would be required for reversal. *Bowring v. Reid, supra,* 399 Mass. at 267, 503 N.E.2d 966. *Redding v. Redding, supra,* 398 Mass. at 107, 495 N.E.2d 297.

Judgment affirmed.

QUINN v. QUINN

Supreme Court of Rhode Island
512 A.2d 848 (R.I. 1986)

MURRAY, Justice.

This is an appeal by Thomas H. Quinn (husband) from an interlocutory decree entered in the Family Court granting the petition of Lois D. Quinn (wife) and the husband's cross-petition for absolute divorce on the grounds of irreconcilable differences. We affirm.

The parties were married on August 12, 1952. Two children, both of whom have since attained the age of majority, were born of the marriage. From 1952 until 1978 the Quinns resided in a twenty-room dwelling situated on sixteen acres of land on Woodside Avenue in the town of West Warwick. At the time of the marriage, the property was owned by Mr. Quinn's father, Patrick H. Quinn, who resided therein until his death in 1956. As the sole beneficiary of his father's estate, the husband inherited various parcels of real estate, including the Woodside Avenue property. Inherited assets also included a corporation, Phenix Mills, and other securities and personalty.

During the course of the marriage, Mr. Quinn sold several of the inherited parcels of realty. The proceeds were used to satisfy various financial obligations, including the cost of the children's education and miscellaneous household expenses. The husband would reinvest any surplus in money-market funds, stocks, and other securities. Mr. Quinn's testimony indicates that the investments that he made during the marriage involved a commingling of funds traceable to inherited assets with monies derived from other sources.

In 1977 the husband sold the Woodside Avenue property. The proceeds from the sale were placed in a certificate of deposit bearing the names of both parties. A smaller marital residence, located on Doyle Avenue in the city of Providence, was ultimately purchased with a portion of the funds. Title to the property was acquired by the parties as joint tenants.[1]

During the early years of their marriage, prior to the birth of the parties' first child, Mrs. Quinn was employed, part-time, in her husband's law office. Throughout the marriage, she also served as treasurer of Phenix Mills. In this capacity Mrs. Quinn maintained the corporation's books and records. In exchange for such services she received compensation in the amount of $100 per month. Upon the parties' separation in 1981, Mrs. Quinn was relieved of her duties as treasurer of Phenix Mills. Thereafter, the wife's sole source of income was her part-time employment in a hospital gift shop. Her earnings from this employment total approximately $80 per week.

By interlocutory decree entered on October 19, 1983, the Family Court granted both parties' petitions for absolute divorce on the grounds of irreconcilable differences. The trial justice found the husband's alcoholism to be the basis for the deterioration of the marital relationship. At trial Mrs. Quinn testified that Mr. Quinn began consuming excessive amounts of intoxicating beverages shortly before the birth of their first child and that such behavior continued throughout the marriage. On several occasions, the husband's alcoholism necessitated his hospitalization. The court found that the wife was not responsible for the breakdown

1. In his decision, the trial justice stated that the property was held in joint tenancy. However, Mrs. Quinn testified that the property was held in a tenancy by the entirety. We find such a discrepancy irrelevant to our determination of the issues before us.

of the marital relationship. Further, the trial justice credited her with being primarily responsible for the preservation of assets acquired during the marriage.

In addressing the economic issues presented, the court, after determining that the Doyle Avenue property was part of the marital estate, awarded all right, title, and interest therein to the wife.[2] The court found that the funds used to purchase the Doyle Avenue residence, although derived from the sale of the husband's inherited Woodside Avenue realty, had lost their character as inherited property. Specifically, the trial justice viewed the husband's placement of the proceeds from the sale of the Woodside Avenue property in a certificate of deposit bearing the names of both parties and the subsequent acquisition of the Doyle Avenue domicile in joint tenancy as indicative of an intent to confer the right of joint, equal ownership upon the wife.

Further, the court assigned to the wife all furnishings contained in the marital domicile. Although many of the furnishings had been acquired by the husband through inheritance, the court found that as a result of the placement and continuous use of such items in the marital domicile during nearly thirty years of marriage, they had lost their character as inherited property and had become part of the marital estate. However, the court found that other inherited furnishings, which the husband had placed in storage, had retained their inherited nature and therefore were not assignable as marital property.

The court determined that with the exception of certain shares of stock which were directly traceable to inherited investments, all securities held by Mr. Quinn were the result of commingling of inherited and noninherited assets and therefore were part of the marital estate. Accordingly, the trial justice ordered the husband to transfer to the wife one-half, or the cash equivalent thereof, of such securities.

The trial justice also concluded that the wife was entitled to retain ownership of three pieces of jewelry which, although initially acquired by the husband through inheritance, had remained in her possession throughout the course of the marriage.

In awarding alimony, the trial justice noted that, as a result of his earlier sale of Phenix Mills, the husband would receive installment payments of $3,506.70 per month over the succeeding forty-eight months. The court ordered the husband to pay to the wife, as alimony, one-half of each of such monthly payments. Thereafter, alimony would cease.

On appeal the husband challenges the trial court's determination that certain inherited property and assets traceable thereto had become part of the marital estate and were thus subject to distribution. Such an argument presents us with two issues. First, we must address whether such assets may, under any set of circumstances, lose their inherited nature and become part of the marital estate. If so, we must determine whether, under the facts presented, the trial court's determination was erroneous. For the reasons set forth below, we answer the first question propounded in the affirmative and respond negatively to the second.

Our equitable-distribution statute, G.L.1956 (1981 Reenactment) §15-5-16.1, as amended by P.L.1982, ch. 403, §1, provides in pertinent part as follows:

> Assignment of property. — In addition to or in lieu of an order to pay alimony made pursuant to a complaint for divorce, the court may assign to

2. However, the court found that all other realty held by the husband, having been acquired by inheritance, was not part of the marital estate and therefore not subject to distribution.

> either the husband or wife a portion of the estate of the other. In determining the nature and value of the property, if any, to be so assigned, the court after hearing the witnesses, if any, of each party, shall consider the length of the marriage, the conduct of the parties during the marriage, and the contribution of each of the parties in the acquisition, preservation, or appreciation in value of their respective estates, and the contribution and services of either party as a homemaker. The court may not assign property or an interest therein held in the name of one of the parties if said property was held by said party prior to the marriage, but may assign income which has been derived therefrom during the term of the marriage. The court also shall not assign property or an interest therein which has been transferred to one of the parties by inheritance before, during or after, the term of the marriage.

Equitable distribution is a three-step process. First, the trial justice must determine which of the parties' assets are marital property and which are nonmarital property. Second, the trial justice must consider the factors enumerated in §15-5-16.1. Third, he or she must distribute the marital property. *Lancellotti v. Lancellotti*, 481 A.2d 7, 10 (R.I.1984).

In conducting the first phase of this three-part analysis, the trial justice found that the marital domicile, although undisputably purchased with proceeds from the sale of the husband's inherited Woodside Avenue property, was part of the marital estate. In challenging this determination, the husband contends that neither the initial placement of the sale proceeds in a certificate of deposit held by the parties in joint tenancy nor the parties' subsequent joint acquisition of the Doyle Avenue property was indicative of any intent to grant the wife an interest in the property. We disagree.

When, during the course of a marriage, title to property for which one spouse has paid the purchase price is acquired in the names of both spouses, the transaction is presumed to be a gift or advancement for the benefit of the other spouse. *Matracia v. Matracia*, 119 R.I. 431, 435–36, 378 A.2d 1388, 1390 (1977). In addressing issues similar to those presently before us, courts in other jurisdictions have viewed the placement of one spouse's nonmarital assets or property traceable thereto in the names of both spouses as joint tenants or tenants by the entirety as bringing such assets into the marital estate. See, *e.g., Atkinson v. Atkinson*, 87 Ill.2d 174, 57 Ill.Dec. 567, 429 N.E.2d 465 (1981), *cert. denied*, 456 U.S. 905, 102 S.Ct. 1751, 72 L.Ed.2d 162 (1982); *Carter v. Carter*, 419 A.2d 1018 (Me.1980); *Ayars v. Ayars*, 50 Md.App. 93, 436 A.2d 490 (1981); *Madden v. Madden*, 336 Pa.Super. 552, 486 A.2d 401 (1984); *Bonnell v. Bonnell*, 117 Wis.2d 241, 344 N.W.2d 123 (1984). In so doing, courts have relied on the doctrine of transmutation. The doctrine, which represents an application of the presumption-of-gift principle discussed in *Matracia, supra,* refers to a change in character of property from separate to marital by an exercise of an actual intention objectively manifested. *Carter*, 419 A.2d at 1022. A transfer of nonmarital assets from one spouse to both spouses jointly, in the absence of clear and convincing evidence to the contrary, will be understood as evincing an intention to transfer the property to the marital estate. *Id.* We believe that the doctrine of transmutation is consistent with the recognition, afforded by §15-5-16.1, of marriage as a partnership. See *Lancellotti*, 481 A.2d at 9; *Wordell v. Wordell*, 470 A.2d 665, 667 (R.I.1984).

Applying the transmutation theory to the matter before us, we conclude that the trial justice correctly classified the Doyle Avenue domicile as marital property. Despite the husband's assertions to the contrary, we do not believe that the record evinces an intention that the realty, which was purchased with a portion of the proceeds from the sale of his inherited property, remain within his separate, nonmarital estate.

The proceeds from the sale of the husband's inherited Woodside Avenue property were first placed in a jointly held certificate of deposit. The record reveals that the parties initially disagreed over how the certificate should be titled. The wife sought joint ownership while the husband expressed a desire to retain the funds as his separate property. Ultimately, however, Mr. Quinn placed the funds in a joint account. Such action evinces his apparent consent to Mrs. Quinn's demand for an ownership interest in the funds. The record is devoid of any suggestion that the parties agreed or understood that the husband would retain sole ownership of the funds despite such placement. As the trial justice correctly held, the fact that the husband retained physical possession of the certificate is not determinative.

Further, when a portion of the funds was subsequently used to purchase the Doyle Avenue parcel, title to the realty was acquired by the parties as joint tenants. Such an act is consistent with, and indicative of, an intent that the parcel become part of the marital estate.

The presumption that the husband, by placing the property in joint tenancy, intended the wife to acquire an interest therein is particularly viable in view of the length of the parties' marriage and the assistance rendered by Mrs. Quinn throughout the course of the marital relationship. Acceptance of the husband's bare assertion that he lacked any donative intent and that he placed the property in joint ownership only for the purpose of convenience would lead to an inequitable result. It would permit a spouse owning what was initially nonmarital property, after exchanging and placing such property in joint names and after many years of marriage, to defeat the right of the other spouse in such assets. *Carter*, 419 A.2d at 1021 (citing *Conrad v. Bowers*, 533 S.W.2d 614, 622 (Mo.Ct.App.1975)).

Finally, to accept the husband's interpretation of §15-5-16.1, which he views as operating to forever preclude inclusion within the marital estate of any assets traceable to inherited property, would be contrary to clear legislative intent. The purpose of §15-5-16.1 is to effect a just and fair distribution of marital assets between the parties. *Wordell*, 470 A.2d at 667. To adopt the theory espoused by the husband would, in cases such as the one before us, require the court to ignore the parties' recognition of their marital partnership and their intentional creation of a joint tenancy. The noninheriting spouse, by being deprived of his or her rights as a joint tenant, would be left in a less equitable position than he or she would have been prior to the statute's enactment. *Carter*, 419 A.2d at 1022–23.

The husband also challenges the trial court's classification of certain securities contained in his investment portfolio as marital property. He argues that inherited assets served as the source of funds for such investments and that therefore the securities are not part of the marital estate. However, the trial justice determined that the securities were acquired through a commingling of inherited and noninherited assets. Such a finding is supported by Mr. Quinn's own testimony, which indicates that his investment funds represented a combination of proceeds from the sale of various parcels of inherited realty and noninherited monies, presumably derived from his engagement in the practice of law. When marital and nonmarital assets are commingled and then exchanged for other property, the newly acquired asset is marital property. *Anderson v. Anderson*, 584 S.W.2d 613 (Mo.Ct.App.1979). Therefore, the trial justice correctly classified the securities as part of the marital estate.

In challenging the trial court's characterization of all of the furnishings contained within the marital domicile as marital property, the husband relies on the uncontroverted evidence that he inherited many of the furnishings from his father. However, in view of the continuous, daily access to, and use of, such items by both parties throughout nearly thirty years of marriage, we believe that the trial justice correctly concluded that the furnishings had lost their character as inherited property.

In asserting that he did not intend to grant the wife an interest in the items, the husband refers us to his testimony that upon his father's death in 1956 the disputed furnishings were simply left in place in the Woodside Avenue domicile. He contends that such inaction should not be viewed as indicative of an intent to assimilate the property into the marital estate. We find such an argument to be unpersuasive, particularly in light of the fact that upon acquisition of a new marital domicile, the Doyle Avenue realty, the disputed items were placed and utilized therein.

The husband also contends that the trial justice erred in finding the wife had acquired, by gift, three pieces of jewelry which Mr. Quinn had inherited from his father. However, the record reveals that throughout the course of the marriage, the jewelry remained in the wife's possession with the husband's full knowledge and consent. Considered in view of the services and assistance provided by the wife during the marriage, such evidence was reasonably determined by the court to be indicative of a donative intent.

In addition to concluding that the trial justice did not commit error in classifying certain inherited property and assets traceable thereto as marital property, we find that the court's division of the marital estate did not constitute an abuse of discretion. Our review of the record reveals that the trial justice applied the guidelines set forth in §15-5-16.1 to, and engaged in a thoughtful examination of, the evidence before him.

...

For the reasons stated, the husband's appeal is denied and dismissed and the judgment appealed from is affirmed. The papers in the case are remanded to the Family Court.

COMMENTS

No-fault divorce and community property do not necessarily mean that all litigation is simple. In some jurisdictions, such as California, the emphasis may shift away from a determination of fault toward determining exactly what is the accumulated community property. The litigation of the issue of how to split the assets may be extremely bitter and protracted.

Community property cases have significance beyond community property jurisdictions. The same problems would arise if marriage is treated as partnership. Presumptions would operate in favor of equal division of partnership assets — for example, the presumption that property acquired during the marriage is partnership property, unless it can be traced to separate property. As marriage develops in the direction of partnership, California precedent becomes increasingly persuasive across the nation. It would be therefore recommendable in divorce litigation, regardless of what state is involved, to research the more complex questions also under California law. Since California appears to lead in development of family law, as for example in no-fault divorce and cohabitation contracts, it becomes an experimental field. Sometimes California precedent may be sufficiently persuasive elsewhere to bring about change.* Many states' treatment of marital property significantly mirrors the treatment of community property.

If a spouse's interest in his or her business or professional partnership (whether the partnership concerns law, medicine, dentistry, accounting, architecture, and so on) is treated as a marital asset for purposes of equitable distribution at dissolution, how is the fair value of the partnership to be determined and at what date? Needless to say, all the tools of discovery as well as valuation experts (often accountants) in the specialty of the partnership must be used. Such items as a partnership buy-out agreement, profit sharing and pension plans (both vested and nonvested), work in progress, accounts receivable, and good will need to be examined. It should be noted that lawyers may be reluctant to have their law partnership's finances scrutinized by another lawyer. Thus, an attempt to pursue a valuation of a law partnership could prompt an early negotiated settlement regarding the nonlawyer spouse's share in the martial property. Although *Savides* was unusual in the length of time between the initial separation and the final divorce and in the extent of the increase in the value of the husband's property, the importance of the date of valuation, illustrated in the case, is often important and must not be overlooked by lawyers.

Smith v. Lewis suggests, among other things, the possibility that family law practice may become an increasingly important target for legal malpractice lawsuits. Dissolution matters are often handled by lawyers in a routine fashion, with perhaps insufficient attention given to legal details, especially if the details are outside of the ordinary. To the extent that an individual practitioner handles family law matters on the side, together with a multitude of other litigation, the probability of slip-ups is increased. As *Smith v. Lewis* suggests, the damages may be substantial. Since malpractice claims are tried to juries, often not very sympathetic to a lawyer who has missed some point that could have been raised, insurance agents may be well advised to seek quick out-of-court settlements of such malpractice actions.

The fastest growing area of family law malpractice is likely to be cases that arise from litigants missing out on a claim against a marital or non-marital partner that could have been raised except for the oversight of the attorney who represented them, for example, failure to include certain assets which could have been discovered through diligent efforts but were not. Victims of these forms of malpractice

*For an illustration, see the reliance by the Supreme Court of Florida in *Posner v. Posner* (p. 50) on the law of California or the widespread reliance on *Marvin v. Marvin* (p. 214).

are more likely to be women than men. Once this gender dimension is added to the analysis, we can suspect that numerous issues of malpractice have been hidden from scrutiny and so far have not been raised in the courts or not even seen by the parties. It may be merely a matter of time before the hazards of practicing family law in a world of rapidly changing gender roles and expectations may gain major importance. Insofar as there is a depressed economic situation within the bar, the tendency toward increased malpractice litigation may be further accelerated.

Quinn illustrates the doctrine of transmutation. Notice in *Quinn* the judge's repeated references to the length of the marriage and references, sometimes more veiled, to the fault of the husband.

A difficult situation is created by the widespread refusal of courts to grant attorneys' fees during pre-trial discovery. Attorneys for wives complain that they are unable to prepare a case adequately unless they can spend the money to discover assets husband may have hidden. Attorneys may nevertheless be responsible for malpractice for failing to uncover such assets unless a specific waiver has been obtained from their clients.

REFERENCE

Carol S. Bruch, *The Definition and Division of Marital Property in California: Toward Parity and Simplicity*, 33 HASTINGS L.J. 769 (1982).

Chapter 2

Informal Marriage: State Withdrawal or State Intrusion?

THE LEGAL REACTION to informal cohabitation can be viewed as a key to an understanding of ceremonial marriage in its various forms. Throughout the Middle Ages, informal sexual unions prevailed. Form requirements were introduced by church and state as a means of asserting political power and controlling the population. At the Council of Trent in 1563, the Catholic Church, reacting to the threat of the Protestant Reformation, established ceremonial requirements for the validity of marriage: assistance of a priest and the presence of two or three witnesses after the publishing of the banns.

Much later, England, through Lord Hardwicke's Act of 1753, imposed comparable requirements for marriage; but informal cohabitation continued to exist, especially among the lower classes and in the colonies. The legal system reacted with indifference or tolerance so long as its value preferences were not infringed upon.

In American law, extralegal marital patterns were absorbed gradually into the legal system, and informal marriage has become more prevalent in all segments of the population than it was for generations. Its contemporary legal status is due to the creative imagination of practicing lawyers who pressed claims on behalf of women clients. Eventually their arguments were successful in the courts, and there is now enough data for legal theory.

The Dispensability of Marriage. A striking feature of marriage in the formal, legal sense is that, except as a symbol, it is decreasingly necessary. Each point discussed in Chapter 1 attests to this. The shift toward antenuptial agreements and marriage as partnership emphasizes individual autonomy and contract. In a resurrection of equitable maxims such as "equity considers as done what ought to be done" and proprietary theories of equitable conversion, parties to informal cohabitation may be considered to be in a quasi-marital state, at least for purposes of entitlements and property allocation. Consequently, whether a couple has been married under statutory requirements is increasingly irrelevant for the relation of the parties between themselves and also for governmental purposes of welfare and taxation.

On the other hand, what is done in fact also becomes the legal equivalent of what ought to be done in equity. To use the traditional frame of reference and language of a chancellor, if one behaves like a married person, regardless of whether one is married, he or she is taken by his or her word and treated as if married. And if an individual who ought to be married behaves like an unmarried person, he or she too is often treated as though married. This means that the legal effects of marriage, although sometimes for limited purposes, may be imposed on the parties if circumstances, as seen by the court, warrant it. In other words, the legal consequences of formal marriage and informal cohabitation are becoming more assimilated to each other. To some extent this means also an assimilation of form and substance because lacking the formality of marriage no longer necessarily results in the absence or loss of substantive rights. This evolution is facilitated because the courts seemingly make only ad hoc adjustments to remedy the hardships in specific cases pending before them, while gradually they affect the conceptions of marriage.

Common Law Marriage. From its inception in early American case law, it was never clear whether common law marriage was a matter of procedure or of substantive law of the family. Like the procedural presumption of marriage, it required cohabitation and repute of being married. Strictly considered, it was not really informal, since it had its own special form requirements. The substantive requirements of common law marriage, namely, cohabitation and repute, merged into the evidentiary requirements for any marriage, whether or not ceremonial and licensed. When the substantive aspects of common law marriage appeared to decline through legislative abolition in an increasing number of states, the "procedural marriage" by presumption survived and became important as a judicial remedy in hardship cases.

Common law marriage was often used in an ad hoc fashion many years after the fact of cohabitation. If an alleged husband and father had died, perhaps in war or in an industrial accident, and his purported wife and children claimed benefits as heirs or survivors, courts tended to be lenient and treat the claim as if there was a marriage. This was accomplished using the concept of common law marriage, if it was available under state law; otherwise the courts used the presumption of marriage.

Procedural Marriage and Other Escape Doctrines. Most Americans rely in their daily transactions on a presumption of marriage that often amounts to an irrebuttable legal fiction based on public policy. Marriage certificates are practically never required to be shown or recorded, not even in real estate transactions. In general, word of being married is accepted without question. If death intervenes, past cohabitation and repute of having been married will do in any American jurisdiction. Marriage certificates are often misplaced, and descendants would face an impossible task if they had to trace the marital history of their ancestors through documents. Whether there was a formal marriage or only informal cohabitation thus fades into insignificance.

Sometimes, of course, the evidence is clear that no formal marriage exists. It may be that the parties do not dispute this; they may never have intended a marriage and they may never have complied with any of the statutory requirements. Or the marriage may have been illegal because the two parties were too closely related to each other (incest) or because one of the parties was already married to someone else (bigamy). Even in these instances the courts, if "equity" warrants it, grant relief by applying a host of legal theories. They may rule that a party who is in bad faith is estopped to deny that he is married or, in some jurisdictions, they may talk of putative or de facto marriages.

An express agreement, enforced by the courts, may take the place of formal statutory marriage. Sometimes referred to as contract cohabitation, these agreements are more likely to be honored if they use the language of property. Since common law judges are traditionally property oriented, sexual cohabitation becomes less objectionable if it is presented in terms borrowed from the law of property rather than the law of personal service contracts. Personal services in the sphere of intimate relationships are still often stigmatized as prostitution. It is relatively easy to express the incidents of marriage, whether formal or not, in terms of landlord-tenant relationships, co-ownership, or perhaps even co-tenancy at will. Marriage as partnership is really only an application of these theories. It treats marriage, following the spirit of the Uniform Partnership Act, as a co-ownership for profit.

If an express agreement is missing, the courts may imply one. They may find a partnership for purposes of distribution of property, or they may apply theories of unjust enrichment or quasi-contract. They may imply a resulting trust, or impose a constructive trust. What started out as a barely concealed legal fiction, namely, treating the parties for limited purposes as if they were married, has in the decisions of modern courts increasingly come to approximate the reality of marriage. Considerations of fault and moral blame while still operative, are deemphasized.

Impact on Family Law. The legal consequences of this situation are manifold. They affect not only formal marriage but also the laws of the family and of inheritance. There is scarcely a situation today where it can be positively stated that a permanent sexual union is for all purposes void under the law. Also, under conceptions of privacy, standing to attack the validity of a relationship may be denied to all but the parties themselves. Death of a party, consequently, must heal any defect. Now that illegitimate children can inherit from their natural fathers, formal and informal marriage, except for ease or difficulty of proof, have essentially the same consequences. The underlying reasoning seems to be that if both formal and informal marriage are partnership, any marital cohabitation inevitably has proprietary consequences that must be recognized by the legal system like any other accumulation of wealth.

The main exception is same-sex couples, where negative views about homosexuality continue to create difficulties for unmarried couples. As of 1992, Denmark was the only country to provide a limited right to marry to couples of the same sex. Yet, even here changes can be observed in the United States also. Increasingly, homosexual unions may be recognized for some purposes. A handful of cities provide for some form of registration of "domestic partnerships," with at least some of the benefits that usually accompany marriage; and a slowly increasing number of courts provide protection of one form or another, such as a New York decision giving to the surviving partner of a same-sex union essentially the same protection against eviction from a rent-controlled apartment that the law provided to a heterosexual surviving partner.

The increasing recognition of informal marriages has created a seemingly infinite number of problems that are now being litigated in the courts. While common law marriage as a legal institution is relatively clear, its conceptual equivalents are hazy. How, for instance, does one enter a "procedural marriage" or, perhaps more importantly, how does one get out of it? Rebutting a presumption, if available, may become an alternative for divorce or dissolution. How can one avoid the consequences of an implied contract or partnership that in fact may never have been intended, but that now creates entitlements akin to those resulting from marriage? Obviously, in regard to their functions the evidentiary presumption of marriage is confused with the substantive implied contract of cohabitation.

What can be done to clarify the confusion that exists between engagement, common law marriage, and informal cohabitation? How can courts protect the reasonable expectations of the parties without opening the way for abuses? Just as in the past many actions for breach of promise to marry were thought to have been brought in bad faith, so too today will many allegations of contract cohabitation be thought to be brought in bad faith. The possibilities for abuse may be especially great where one member of a same-sex couple has chosen to avoid being identified as gay or lesbian, so that the cohabitation claim is also a form of "outing." The most obvious remedy in many cases would appear to be an express cohabitation contract that regulates and limits mutual property rights. Parties can avoid the consequences of marriage in any form by clearly establishing and periodically reaffirming their mutual intent; or, more simply, they may establish intimate relations without living together. The confusion of public records because of informal cohabitation is unavoidable and perhaps of little consequence. Social dynamics appear to be stronger than the capacity of the government to regulate.

Implications of social class continue to be present. Many of the current judicial theories on informal marriage appear to be tailored to the needs of the middle classes, as, for example, when these theories inject notions of property into marriage and the family. Moreover, it is the middle classes who find their way to lawyers, who, upon request, may draft a contract expressly regulating their informal cohabitation. However, if claims originate from the lower classes, in the absence of clearly established formal marriage or express contract, judges may impose a presumption of marriage, if one of the parties is deceased, or imply a contract, if they are both still alive. Thus it becomes increasingly clear that rules of evidence serve substantive functions. Furthermore, express contract and implied contract, although they share the same conceptual underpinning, are not necessarily part of the same social frame of reference. With express contract, party autonomy is more or less real, or at least a possibility; while with implied contract of cohabitation, party autonomy may have elements of a legal fiction judicially imposed upon the parties.

REFERENCES

Hans W. Baade, *The Form of Marriage in Spanish North America*, 61 CORNELL L. REV. 1 (1975).

David Daube, *Historical Aspects of Informal Marriage*, 25 REVUE INTERNATIONALE DES DROITS DE L'ANTIQUITE 95 (3e Serie 1978).

Note, *Marriage as Contract: Towards a Functional Redefinition of the Marital Status*, 9 COLUM. J.L. & SOC. PROBS. 607 (1973).

Marianne Hojgaard Pedersen, *Denmark: Homosexual Marriages and New Rules Regarding Separation and Divorce*, 30 J. FAM. L. 289 (1991).

Dieter D. Schwab, Eheschliessungsrecht und nichteheliche Lebensgemeinschaft — Eine rechtsgeschichtliche Skizze-, 1981 Zeitschrift für das gesamte Familienrecht 1151 (exhaustive treatment of sources from the Middle Ages and Antiquity).

A: COMMON LAW MARRIAGE

Substantive Versus Procedural Marriage (Marriage by Presumption)

CAMPBELL v. CHRISTIAN
Supreme Court of South Carolina
235 S.C. 102, 110 S.E.2d 1 (1959)

LEGGE, Justice.

James Woodrow Campbell, a resident of Anderson County, died on February 25, 1956. His will dated September 9, 1947 was offered for probate in the Probate Court for that county and was there contested by the appellant, Betty I. Campbell, upon the ground that it had been revoked by her marriage with Campbell on July 17, 1954. The Judge of that court admitted it to probate and held that the said marriage was invalid because the respondent Beulah Poole Campbell was then decedent's common-law wife....

...

Campbell was born on January 12, 1875, and was eighty-one years old at the time of his death in February, 1956. In February, 1894, when he was nineteen, his first child, Myrtis, was born to Emma Hickman, whom he never married. It should be said, in passing, that he supported Myrtis thereafter until her marriage in 1918, and that by his will, after provision for nine cash legacies aggregating $2,525, he left his residuary estate to her and his daughter Cornelia in equal shares and appointed both of them as executrices.

At some time prior to February, 1921, Campbell married Mattie Grey. They had no children.

While married to Mattie, Campbell had illicit relation with Beulah Poole, an illiterate, ignorant girl; and on November 18, 1921, she bore him a child. He was then forty-five, she fourteen.

On January 11, 1923, Mattie having died, Campbell married her niece, Gertrude. One child, Cornelia, was born to them on November 16, 1923. During this marriage, Campbell's relations with Beulah continued, with the result that she had two more children by him, one on January 28, 1925, the other on January 18, 1928. On December 10, 1927, he divorced Gertrude in a Florida proceeding, the validity of which is not in issue.

About a year after the divorce, Beulah came into his home and took the name of Campbell, and they lived together for more than twenty-four years, during which five children were born to them, one in 1931, one in 1932, one in 1935, one in 1938, and one in 1943. In the spring of 1954 he deserted her and moved to another house in the city of Anderson.

Shortly thereafter the appellant, who had been living in Georgia, came to Anderson. In response to a newspaper advertisement she entered Campbell's employ as cook and housekeeper, and on June 10, 1954, they executed a written contract to that effect, which, after reciting her agreement, in consideration of $15 per week and board and lodging, "to cook for J. Woodrow Campbell, keep his house clean, and attend to the washing and other household duties", proclaimed that "she will occupy a separate room and she will be known as an employee of J. Woodrow Campbell", and that "the relationship of employee and employer will be and is the only relationship which will exist between the parties thereto." On July 17, 1954, they drove across the Georgia line and the Ordinary of Hart County performed a ceremony purporting to unite them in holy wedlock. He was then seventy-nine, she forty-two.

There is in the record before us considerable evidence that from the time that Campbell took Beulah into his home, a year or so after his divorce from Gertrude, he and she lived together as husband and wife, and that they were so recognized in the community. An elderly neighbor, who had known Campbell throughout the latter's life, testified that "they lived openly as husband and wife"; that "he carried the children around with him and they went by the name of Campbell and went to school under the name of Campbell"; and that the general public considered them as man and wife. One of Campbell's sons testified, without objection, that when strangers came to the house Campbell, after introducing himself, would introduce Beulah as his wife. His daughter Myrtis testified that during the many years that Campbell and Beulah lived together she visited in their home and understood that they were married; and that the people of the community knew them as man and wife.

In evidence are the birth certificates of five of the children, from which we note the following:

1. That of the child born November 18, 1921, names Beulah Poole as its mother, does not name its father, and states that the child's parents were not married.
2. That of the child born January 28, 1925, names James Woodrow Campbell as its father and Beulah Poole as its mother, and states that the child's parents were not married.
3. That of the child born January 18, 1928, names the parents as Woodrow Campbell and Beulah Campbell, and states that they are married.
4. That of the child born June 8, 1935, names the parents as Woodrow Campbell and Beulah Campbell, and states that they are married.
5. That of the child born July 3, 1943, names the parents as James Woodrow Campbell and Beulah Poole, and states that they are married.

Appellant, contending that Beulah's own testimony shows the relationship between her and Campbell to have been that of concubinage, not common-law marriage, points to the following portions of it:

Q. You hadn't had any signed contract or anything at that time that you were his wife, did you?

A. No.

Q. And he never did tell you that you were his wife, did he?

A. I had sense enough to know that I didn't marry him.

Q. Both of you were not married then, were you?

A. No, we weren't married.

...

Q. Did you ever try to get him to take you to the preacher?

A. No, we talked about it but we never did get to it.

Q. Did you try to get him to?

A. No, I did not. I wasn't going to beg him. If he didn't want to marry me, I wasn't going to beg him.

...

Q. You don't think you had any right to take out a warrant against him for marrying Betty?

A. No, I didn't think that I did.

Q. That was because you didn't consider you and he were married?

A. That is right.

...

Q. Did you and he ever go to church together?

A. No, sir, he went to church sometimes and carried the children.

Q. He didn't take you?

A. I didn't go.

Q. Did you want to go?

A. Yes, sir, I would like to have gone some, but I didn't get to.

Q. And that is because you were uncertain about your relationship to him, weren't you?

A. Yes, sir.

Throughout the record of this case Beulah appears as a woman illiterate, uneducated, and of childlike simplicity. It is not improbable that when she made the statements above quoted she was thinking of a ceremonial, rather than actual, marriage. Nor is it improbable that she, like many others whose intellectual and social horizons are thus limited, had the notion that a marriage is not legal unless solemnized by a religious, or at least an official, ceremony. The trial judge did not discuss her testimony, and therefore we cannot say with certainty how he construed her statements as to nonmarriage; if he viewed them as referring to ceremonial marriage we could not condemn such inference as unreasonable. But whether he so viewed them or not, we do not think that they are conclusive of the issue. Against them stands evidence that after Campbell's divorce the relationship between him and Beulah, which theretofore had been illicit, underwent a fundamental change; that whereas before it they had lived separately, after it they resided together, openly and continuously, over a period of at least twenty-four years, during which they were known and recognized in the community as husband and wife; and that the children born to them during this cohabitation were declared to the public authorities charged with the duty of registering their births, as having been born in wedlock. In short, they are contradicted by the conduct and general repute of both parties over a period of many years.

> Assertions of both parties that their relation was one of open concubinage, or admission of nonmarriage by one party, fortified by strong circumstances, may suffice to overcome the presumption of their marriage from cohabitation and reputation. Such an admission by the parties does not suffice to overcome the presumption, however, where it is shown that the admission may well have been made with reference to a ceremonial marriage, and not uttered with the idea of negativing broadly the existence of the marital status....

Illicit relationship, though accompanied by cohabitation, is not transformed into the legal state of marriage by mere lapse of time. But mutual recognition of the marriage relation, at a time when the parties are able to enter into the marital contract, has long been accepted as ground for upholding the marriage. Where the evidence is in conflict, determination of the issue is for the trier of the facts....

In the case at bar there was ample evidence, to which we have already referred, to support the conclusion that after the barrier to their marriage had been removed by Campbell's divorce from Gertrude, he and Beulah entered into a new mutual agreement whereby their previously illicit relationship was terminated and a valid common-law marriage established. That Campbell some twenty-five years thereafter declared, in his application for a license to marry Betty, that he was not married, is of no legal consequence; for once his marriage to Beulah became complete, as the trial judge held it to be, no act or disavowal of it on his part could invalidate it....

...

...[I]t is rarely possible to fix precisely the time at which a common-law marriage may be said to have come into being. *Rodgers v. Herron*, 226 S.C. 317, 85 S.E.2d 104, 48 A.L.R.2d 1241. But it is clear from the evidence that it was entered into within a year or so after Campbell's divorce, which had been obtained on December 10, 1927. It would seem, then, that their illegitimate children living on May 2, 1951 became legitimate upon the approval that day of the Act of the General Assembly (47 Stat. at Large 265) now Section 20-5.1 of the 1952 Code.

Affirmed.

STUKES, C. J., and TAYLOR, OXNER and MOSS, JJ., concur.

THOMSON v. THOMSON

Kansas City Court of Appeals, Missouri
236 Mo. App. 1223, 163 S.W.2d 792 (1942)

SPERRY, Commissioner.

Martha S. Thomson, filed a claim in probate court seeking the statutory allowance of $400 for a widow, and an allowance for a year's maintenance and support, from the estate of Peter Thomson, deceased, whose widow she claims to be. Her claim was allowed for $400 absolute allowance and for $1,400 maintenance. Earl P. Thomson, a son of deceased and administrator of said estate, and Grace Richardson, a daughter of deceased, defendants, appealed to the circuit court. The cases were consolidated in circuit court, and a trial of the cause resulted in a judgment sustaining the allowances made by probate court. From that judgment both defendants prosecute their appeals to this court.

The sole question presented here is whether or not the evidence supports the judgment of the court to the effect that Martha S. Thomson, claimant, is the legal widow of Peter Thomson, deceased....

Peter Thomson and Anna George were married in 1894, and the two defendants herein are the children of that marriage. Anna George Thomson died in 1914, but her mother made her home with Thomson thereafter until her death in 1919. Earl came home from the army in 1918 and was introduced to claimant, under the name of Martha Evans, by his father. Grace also met claimant at about that time, at the Thomson home, and claimant was introduced to her also as Martha Evans. The Thomson family, then living at the home, consisted of Peter, Earl, Grace, the grandmother, and a housekeeper. Claimant did not live there but only came there occasionally. Grace was married and, shortly thereafter, on October 11, 1919, she left home. For a period of about ten years thereafter she did not return home but saw her father occasionally.

Claimant's sister testified in her behalf and stated that, from the date of her marriage in 1911, until 1930, she resided at Chicago, and only returned to Kansas City occasionally for visits to her sister and her father and mother; that their parents lived at 2510 Indiana, in Kansas City, where claimant and witness grew up; that she visited here in April, 1921, and was in the Thomson home; that claimant was living there at that time and was employed as housekeeper; that claimant was then the legal wife of one Fred C. Edelen who was living but was a mental case; that she requested claimant to move to and live in their father's home because their mother was ill; that deceased said: "Well, this will be her home some day," and that witness answered: "It isn't now because she has a living husband"; that claimant's name at that time was Edelen. The witness further testified that she returned to Chicago; that Fred C. Edelen committed suicide in May, 1921; that witness returned to Kansas City, on a visit, at about Christmas time, 1921: that she visited in the Thomson home and, while there at dinner with deceased and claimant, deceased said to her: "Well, kid, I finally got her to marry me"; that deceased talked with her several times about being married to claimant; that she told him that her wedding anniversary was August 7th, and deceased said: "Well, kid, I got you beat. My first anniversary was 8th of August, and I had another one, that is where I have got it over you, I was married in October, too." She stated that deceased and claimant accompanied witness and her husband on recreational trips out to parties and banquets almost weekly over a period of years and deceased always introduced claimant, and referred to her, as his wife and that she was so accepted and known among their friends and acquaintances; and that deceased and claimant were generally reputed to be husband and wife in the community in which they lived. She also testified that deceased and claimant made a number of trips to Canada to visit deceased's relatives and that she received mail from them while they were on such trips. She identified an envelope and letter which was addressed to claimant, and also a postal card addressed to her from Canada, as being in the handwriting of and signed by deceased. Said letter and card were placed in evidence and the letter closed as follows: "Your loving husband, Peter." The envelope was addressed to "Mrs. Peter Thomson, 1239 Ewing Ave., K. C. Mo." The postal card was signed "Your loving husband, Peter."

...

John B. Gage, mayor of Kansas City, testified to the effect that, as an attorney, deceased consulted him about preparation of a will for him; that he prepared a typewritten draft of such a will for deceased and at his request, which draft was offered in evidence and was identified as being the one prepared by witness. It bore date of 1938, but was never executed and was delivered by Mr. Gage, together with other papers belonging to deceased, to the administrator after death of Thomson. In the draft of the alleged will, which was in evidence, deceased's home at 1239 Ewing Avenue, Kansas City, was bequeathed to "my beloved wife, Martha S. Thomson," and provision for payment of certain trust funds was therein made "to my wife, Martha S. Thomson." It was further provided therein that such bequests were to be in lieu of "all dower and marriage rights she may have in my estate."

J. Francis O'Sullivan, a lawyer, testified that he lived for many years in the general vicinity of the Thomson home and that he had been employed by deceased to represent him as an attorney on different cases; that deceased introduced claimant to him as "Mrs. Thomson" and that the Thomsons were generally reputed to be husband and wife, in the neighborhood where they resided.

R. L. Dominick, vice-president of the Gate City National Bank, testified that deceased transacted business with the above mentioned bank, through the witness, for about 25 years; that claimant was introduced to him by deceased as "his wife"; that she had accompanied deceased to the bank and that she and deceased had executed deeds of trust, on real estate owned by deceased, as husband and wife; and he identified one such instrument which was executed by deceased and claimant, to the bank, in 1937, and which was signed by deceased and claimant, in witness' presence, as husband and wife, and was so acknowledged before a notary public who fully corroborated the testimony of Mr. Dominick. Mr. Dominick also identified one other such deed of trust, signed and acknowledged by deceased and claimant as husband and wife, which instrument was so executed in the presence of witness.

Mr. Hensley, vice-president of the Produce Exchange Bank, testified that he was formerly employed by the Gate City National Bank and, as notary public, took the acknowledgment of deceased and claimant, as husband and wife, to deeds of trust executed by them. He corroborated much of the testimony of Mr. Dominick.

Certain deed record books were identified and introduced in evidence. They disclosed that deceased and claimant had executed a number of deeds of trust on real estate, and had therein acknowledged themselves, under oath, to be husband and wife. One deed of trust, dated September 10, 1919, was signed by deceased and he acknowledged himself, under oath, to be single and unmarried. In a deed of trust dated November 24, 1923, deceased and claimant signed and acknowledged same as husband and wife, as they did in various others shown to have been executed in 1924, 1927, and 1937. All such instruments which were in evidence, and which bore date prior to 1921, were signed and acknowledged by deceased as a single person.

Dr. Fricke testified that he was the family physician of the Thomsons from 1937 until the death of deceased; that deceased introduced claimant to him in his office as his wife; that he treated claimant in the Thomson home; that he knew her as Mrs. Thomson; and that deceased and claimant were generally reputed to be husband and wife in the neighborhood where they resided.

Claimant was not permitted to testify in her own behalf, on objection as to any matter which occurred prior to issuance of the letters of administration.

On behalf of defendants Earl Thomson testified that his father "Asked me if I cared if he got married, I told him: 'No,' I says 'You didn't say anything when I told you I was going to get married. You told me I was twenty-one years old'... In 1921, just before I got married,... I was married October 19, 1921." He testified that his father never told him that he was married; that, in 1921, when Earl introduced his sister's brother-in-law to claimant, she said: "I beg your pardon, but it is Mrs. Thomson," that his father was in the house at the time but did not hear the conversation.

Grace Richardson testified that her father never told her he was married to claimant and that the people in the neighborhood did not believe they were married. She also gave testimony to the effect that while she and her father were visiting in the home of her father's sister in Canada the latter urged her to go home to her father's house; that the sister told deceased that, since he was married, claimant should invite witness to their home, and that deceased became angry, shook his cane at his sister and told her he would invite whom he pleased to live in his home.

Other witnesses testified to the effect that neighbors of the Thomsons questioned the fact of their marriage and denied that deceased had, to their knowledge or in their presence, introduced claimant as his wife, or had held her out as such. There was evidence which tended to prove that the marriage records of Jackson, Cass, and Lafayette counties contain no reference to a license having been issued for the marriage of claimant and deceased. No marriage license was offered in evidence and no witness testified regarding issuance of any; nor was there any evidence regarding the performance of any marriage ceremony.

It is claimant's contention that the evidence herein is sufficient to prove that deceased and claimant were married; and that the countervailing evidence was insufficient to overcome, or to seriously challenge such fact, so that the proof of marriage becomes conclusive.

Defendants contend that, at most, the evidence tended to establish a common law marriage and that common law marriages were outlawed by statute enacted in 1921, which statute became effective prior to the death of claimant's husband, Edelen, in May, 1921.... Therefore, if claimant's case rests on a common law marriage she may not prevail because until after March 31, 1921, she had a legal husband living and, hence, could not have entered into a valid common law marriage with deceased prior to that date.

Claimant did not attempt to prove by direct or by record evidence that a statutory marriage was entered into between herself and deceased. She contends that her evidence was sufficient to give rise to the presumption that she and deceased were married; that there was insufficient contradictory evidence to overcome said presumption; that said presumption became final; and that, since they were married, it is presumed that said marriage was legal according to the requirements of the laws of Missouri. Her position is that the same quantum and quality of evidence which proves a marriage, under the rule pertaining to presumption, proves a legal marriage, whatever may be the requirements of the law regulating marriages.

There is strong evidence tending to prove the fact that Thomson and claimant conducted themselves as husband and wife, that they so cohabited, and that the local repute was that they were married.

...

> Independent of any direct or documentary evidence, a marriage may be circumstantially established by the fact that a man and woman have for a considerable period of time openly cohabited as husband and wife and recognized and treated each other as such, so that they are generally reputed to be married among those who have come in contact with them. Such circumstances justify a finding that at the commencement of the cohabitation the parties actually entered into a marriage.... 38 C.J. page 1337.
>
> ...
>
> If a marriage in fact is established by evidence or admission, it is presumed to be regular and valid, and the burden of adducing evidence to the contrary rests on the party who attacks it, even though it involves the proving of a negative. 38 C.J. 1325, 1326.
>
> ...[W]here man and woman are living together as husband and wife, marriage should always be presumed.... A marriage which is once shown is presumed to have been in compliance with legal requirements as to its celebration. 35 Am. Jur. pages 303, 305.

There is strong circumstantial evidence tending to prove the marriage of claimant and deceased; and there is no substantial evidence, circumstantial or otherwise, tending to contradict the positive evidence of marriage. The fact that the records of Cass, Lafayette and Jackson counties failed to disclose the issuance of a license is wholly insufficient to overcome the proof of marriage here established by circumstantial evidence....

...Our statutes on marriage provide the procedure to be followed in order that a legal marriage may be entered into; but they do not provide that legal marriages can only be proved by offering evidence tending to establish the fact that such statutory steps were taken. Marriage statutes, such as ours, are intended to prescribe the manner by which legal marriages may be contracted; but they do not prescribe a rule of evidence by which marriages may be proved....

...

It would be most unwise to hold that a marriage cannot be proved except by the introduction of evidence tending to prove issuance of a license and performance of a ceremony. To so hold would be to render it utterly impossible for many couples who were so married to prove the legality of their relationship and the legitimacy of their children. All history teaches us that there is no permanency in the preservation of written records, and the present day bombing and total destruction of entire cities and towns, accompanied by the almost total extinction of the population of such places and the forced migration and dispersal of the survivors, constitute a cogent argument in support of the wisdom of the ancient rules of evidence which permit proof of marriage by evidence other than that of issuance of a license and proof of performance of a ceremony. Upon such proof, in that manner, of the fact of marriage, it follows that the presumption of legality must follow as a rule of necessity.

...

The judgment is affirmed.

GORDON v. RAILROAD RETIREMENT BOARD

United States Court of Appeals
696 F.2d 131 (D.C. Cir. 1983)

PER CURIAM:

By its decision in Docket No. 1813, the Railroad Retirement Board determined that Gertrude Gordon was not the legal widow of Samuel D. Gordon, the insured employee, and was, therefore, not entitled to widow's annuity benefits as authorized by Section 2(d)(1)(i) of the Railroad Retirement Act. 45 U.S.C. §231a(d). The Board found that Hattie M. Gordon was the legal widow and awarded the benefits to her.

The actual evidence before the Board is not in dispute, although the weight and legal significance of this evidence are vigorously contested. The relevant facts are as follows. Petitioner Gertrude Gordon married Samuel D. Gordon, by ceremony on February 16, 1952 in Prince George's County, Maryland. Gertrude and Samuel lived together for thirteen years, until Samuel's death in 1965. A child, Hortense, was born to the couple in 1952. Gertrude testified that she had no knowledge, at any time, of any previous marriage by Samuel, except for his first which ended in 1941 with the death of his wife.

Hattie Morris Gordon presented documentary proof that on June 26, 1943, two individuals bearing the same names as the applicant and deceased entered into a ceremonial marriage. Although the names on the documents correspond to the parties at issue, a discrepancy exists between the ages of the signatories to the certificate and the age (in 1943) of the Hattie and Samuel at issue herein. Hattie M. Gordon also asserts that she lived with Samuel in Knoxville, Tennessee from the time of their marriage in 1943 until 1952 when, she says, he moved to Washington, D.C. However, documentary and testimonial evidence reveals that Samuel Gordon lived in Washington, D.C. as early as 1944; and that he continued to reside in that city, periodically, until his marriage to Gertrude in 1952. Finally, Hattie M. Gordon asserts that she never obtained a divorce from Samuel and that she has no knowledge that he ever obtained one. A less than thorough search of the records of several jurisdictions, conducted by the Board, failed to produce any record of divorce.

To determine who is a "widow" within the meaning of the statute, Section 4 of the Railroad Retirement Act[1] directs that the law of the place of domicile at the time of death controls. In this case, the laws and jurisprudence of the District of Columbia control.

The District of Columbia courts have consistently recognized a strong presumption that the most recent marriage is valid. "While the presumption is not conclusive, it is one of the strongest in the law, and it is settled that the party attacking the second marriage has the burden of rebutting the presumption by strong, distinct, satisfactory, and conclusive evidence." *Johnson v. Young*, 372 A.2d 992, 994 (D.C.App.1977). This presumption is so strong that the District of Columbia courts have stated that in a "clash" between "the [presumption] favor-

---

1. Section 4 of the Act directs that the provisions of Section 216(h)(1)(A) of the Social Security Act control. Section 216(h)(1)(A) provides that:

> An applicant is the...widow of [an]...insured individual for purposes of this subchapter...if the courts of the State in which he was domiciled at the time of death...would find that such applicant and such insured individual were validly married...at the time he died.

42 U.S.C. §416(h)(1)(A).

ing the continuance of a valid ceremonial marriage [and] the other favoring the validity of the last marriage, it is generally held that the first must give way to the second." *Mayo v. Ford*, 184 A.2d 38, 41 (D.C.App. 1962).

Although the Board stated that it recognized and applied the aforediscussed presumption, it found that the presumption had been overcome. Specifically, the Board found that in 1943 a valid, ceremonial marriage occurred between the two individuals at issue, Hattie Morris and Samuel D. Gordon. Because no record of divorce or annulment was produced, the Board concluded that the valid marriage was never terminated. The Board found these facts sufficient to overcome the presumption of validity accorded the later marriage between Gertrude and Samuel Gordon. The Board acknowledged that conflicting evidence existed, but found "explanations" for these conflicts.

The Board erred by incorrectly applying the proper legal standard to the facts before it. Controlling law in the District of Columbia requires that the adversary prove by "strong, distinct, satisfactory, and conclusive evidence" that the most recent marriage is not valid. Such unequivocal evidence is required to overcome the strong presumption of validity accorded the most recent marriage. Where the evidence of rebuttal is contradictory, it does not overcome the presumption. *Johnson v. Young, supra,* at 994. The presumption "cannot be rebutted through a delicate balancing of equally plausible inferences." *Mayo v. Ford, supra,* at 41.

The presumed validity of the marriage between Gertrude Gordon and Samuel D. Gordon was not overcome by the conflicting evidence in support of the claim that an earlier undissolved marriage between Samuel and Hattie Morris remained valid. It was incumbent upon the party attacking the later marriage to prove its invalidity. No competent, reliable proof of the invalidity of the later marriage was produced by the Board or by Hattie Gordon. Due to this lack of proof, the later marriage prevails as valid.

The decision of the Board is reversed. Gertrude Gordon is declared the legal widow of Samuel D. Gordon and is, therefore, entitled to the widow's annuity benefits at issue.

COMMENTS

The facts of *Campbell* are not as unusual as one might think. In searching titles and determining whether real estate is marketable, complex facts concerning multiple possible marriages have to be analyzed. The lawyer has to delve into the past lives of people regardless of his or her personal moral beliefs or perhaps prejudices. *Campbell* involved a married 46-year-old impregnating a young teenager, barely half the age of his own daughter. The regional aspects of the case are less significant than might appear. The same problems arise in matters relating to inheritance or to land title in metropolitan centers. The case therefore has continuing significance.

Especially if the persons in issue are no longer alive, legal presumptions become important for untangling chaotic facts from the past. The possibility of common law marriage is closely interwoven with the possibility of applying presumptions of marriage. Common law marriage continues to be a factor even in jurisdictions that have legislatively abolished it. The persons involved may have lived temporarily in other jurisdictions that still recognize common law marriage. In view of the presumption of marriage they may even be presumed to have entered a valid marriage somehow and somewhere. Since ordinarily common law marriages were not abolished retroactively, the possibility of a common law marriage in the past, when it was still legal in a specific state, may be sufficient to cloud the title of real estate today.

Since the legal requirements for common law marriage and for the presumption of marriage are identical, namely, cohabitation and repute of being married, one may wonder how effective the abolition of common law marriage is. The presumption of marriage is available in all American jurisdictions, regardless of whether or not they still recognize common law marriage. *Thomson* arose in a jurisdiction, Missouri, that has not recognized common law marriage since 1921. Nevertheless, as a result of their long-standing cohabitation, the claimant widow and the decedent were presumed to be married. Even the claimant's failure to prove her marriage by documentary evidence did not harm her presumed marital status. The outcome was the same as it would have been had Missouri never tried to abolish common law marriage.

The same result may be reached whether or not any of the jurisdictions involved in a case recognize or once recognized common law marriage. The presumption of marriage and common law marriage are as a practical matter interchangeable in many situations. This has to be kept in mind in jurisdictions, such as Massachusetts, that do not recognize common law marriage. There too cohabitation and repute of being married may result in legal marriage. That this result is reached by way of presumption makes little practical difference. In fact, there are strategic advantages in arguing presumption rather than substantive law of marriage. Presumptions are based on popular feelings and predispositions reduced to rules of evidence. They carry considerable persuasive weight with the courts. The presumption of marriage, for example, is said to be one of the strongest in law. *Gordon* shows a court's strong reluctance to overturn a purported marriage, even when it may well have been bigamous. Essentially it is based on the presumption that people do not engage in immoral or illegal behavior. To what extent this presumption corresponds to reality is another question. The sexual mores have substantially changed, as illustrated by *Marvin v. Marvin* (p. 214), while the rules of evidence originate from another era with different customs that nevertheless are still effective in court.

REFERENCE

Walter O. Weyrauch, *Informal and Formal Marriage — An Appraisal of Trends in Family Organization*, 28 U. CHI. L. REV. 88 (1960).

Religious and Ethnic Factors

PARKINSON v. J. & S. TOOL COMPANY
Supreme Court of New Jersey
64 N.J. 159, 313 A.2d 609 (1974)

PASHMAN, J.

This is an appeal by Ruth Parkinson from a judgment of the Appellate Division which affirmed a denial of dependency benefits by the Judge of Compensation. Appellant, though not legally married, was living as husband and wife with decedent Richard Parkinson, who, it is conceded, died from an accident arising out of and in the course of his employment....

The sole issue is whether claimant is a "dependent" within the terms of N.J.S.A. 34:15-13(f) according to guidelines we enunciated in *Dawson v. Hatfield Wire & Cable Co.*, 59 N.J. 190, 280 A.2d 173 (1971).

Ruth and Richard Parkinson, lifelong Roman Catholics, were legally married before a Roman Catholic priest in 1927. Two children were born of this marriage which terminated in 1939 when Ruth obtained a divorce decree in the New Jersey courts. Richard thereupon left the state but returned in 1950 to resume life with Ruth and their children. Prior to doing so, and as a step toward remarriage, the couple visited the pastor of their local church, informed him of the divorce and requested that he remarry them. Consent to remarriage was withheld. The priest explained that they were "already married in the eyes of God." The couple accepted the priest's explanation, assumed they were married and resumed cohabitation. No civil ceremony followed.

Appellant testified that she understood the nature of her divorced status under the law, that she was no longer legally married. In the eyes of the Catholic Church, however, a religious ceremony lasts until death; only ecclesiastical authority can dissolve or annul the marriage. Monsignor Smith, an ecclesiastical attorney and expert on canon law, testified that the advice offered by the pastor, since deceased, would be the church's teaching as regards marriage. People reconciled after a divorce and returning to the same authority which married them initially is such an uncommon occurrence that most priests, even those more steeped in canon and civil law, are unqualified to grapple with its legal disposition. Since there is no canon covering these facts, even when proper advice is afforded, no new marriage occurs. On cross-examination, the Monsignor offered what would be his advice to such a couple: a "renewal of consent," *i.e.*, an expression of matrimonial consent by recalling their original marriage vows, coupled with obtaining a new marriage license. In the eyes of the church, it is not a new marriage, but merely a repetition of what already has occurred. It would suffice however for the civil authorities.

The Judge of Compensation found, however, that while the couple had remained married in the eyes of God, and recognized as a marital entity by the public, the civil authority, by virtue of the divorce, did not accept the remarriage. Accordingly, under strict statutory law, Ruth Parkinson did not qualify as a dependent for workmen's compensation benefits. The Appellate Division agreed and rejected appellant's contention that she qualifies as a *de facto* wife under *Dawson, supra.* For reasons hereinafter stated, we reverse, and remand to the Division of Workmen's Compensation for an award of death benefits.

The relevant Workmen's Compensation statute, N.J.S.A. 34:15-13(f) provides in part:

> The term "dependents" shall apply to and include any or all of the following who are dependent upon the deceased at the time of accident or the occurrence of occupational disease, or at the time of death, namely: ... wife....

Appellant concedes that she is not a lawful *de jure* widow, but respectfully urges that we accept her claim as a *de facto* widow, and therefore should be entitled to benefits under the reasoning we have set forth in *Dawson.* In that case, Mamie Dawson, legally married to decedent Charles Dawson in 1949, brought a dependency claim following his fatal work-connected injury. At the Compensation hearing, employer challenged Mamie's rights to dependency benefits, attacked her marriage as meretricious, and offered that decedent had previously been married in 1942, had fathered two children and had never secured a divorce. Dependency benefits were denied. The lower courts reasoned that a knowingly meretricious relationship is generally sufficient to defeat recovery. Justice Mountain, for the majority, fashioned an equitable result and reversed. He pointed out that the claimant entered her relationship in complete good faith, with no suspicion, let alone knowledge, of decedent's prior marriage. The couple had lived together in an open and unchallenged relationship as man and wife until decedent's death. The evidence was uncontradicted that Mamie Dawson had been dependent on decedent. It was only after the latter's death that employer challenged this relationship, and then only to be relieved of its dollar liability. We there concluded that the terms "wife" and "widow" as used in the statute include de facto widows where good faith coalesces with "...a *de facto* relationship of man and wife continuing unbroken over an extended period of years having had its genesis in a ceremonial marriage...." 59 N.J. 196, 280 A.2d 176.

The Appellate Division refused to apply the *Dawson* rationale because Ruth and Richard Parkinson lacked the "ceremonial" requisite. Justice Mountain stated in *Dawson*:

> ...We deem it significant that petitioner and decedent entered upon a ceremonial marriage, carrying with it, as all ceremonial marriages do in varying degree, elements of solemnity, publicity and prior deliberation not characteristic of a common law union. *Id.* at 196, 280 A.2d at 176.

Employer maintains that without the ceremonial marriage, *Dawson* is inapplicable, for otherwise the Court would be creating a paradox. It would allow claimant to use the legal system when it suits her — to secure a divorce and obtain compensation benefits — but to ignore it for purposes of the ceremonial marriage requirement. To employer, this would flout the fairness and equality of our system of laws.

We disagree. This position misreads both the underlying rationale of the marriage ceremony and the equitable policies we postulated in *Dawson.*

Solemnity, publicity, and deliberation distinguish a legitimate marriage ceremony from an illegitimate common law union. Inherent in the common law marriage are a non-recognition of the legal process, and a lack of commitment which often gives rise to an impermanent and ephemeral arrangement, such that economic support, let alone dependency, may be withheld randomly. The union, which in the eyes of the public remains an uncertainty, may dissolve at any time. Such a couple may not both use an identical surname, file joint tax returns, or be deemed an entity for census-taking, welfare or social security eligibility.

Oftentimes while they both may reside at one address, only one name may appear, and the other party may have legal residence elsewhere. Children of such union, moreover, might be deprived of parental guidance since they may never be certain who are their real parents. The Legislature and this Court have both declared that common law marriages are prohibited. N.J.S.A. 37:1-10[2]....

A different drama unfolds in the situation before us. Prior to resuming cohabitation in 1950, Ruth and Richard Parkinson, after some deliberation, visited a priest, expecting to arrange for a second church wedding. They had initiated the nuptial process with such a visit once before in 1927. As lifelong Roman Catholics, they were sensitively aware of this requirement. With but a limited sixth-grade parochial school education, however, Ruth was somewhat unsophisticated in understanding the interrelationship between the dual civil and religious mantles cloaking the priest. She had sufficient knowledge that the first ceremony performed by the priest was legally sanctioned. She had little reason to believe differently this time when informed that her marriage was still recognized "in the eyes of God." Words to this effect were expressed in the earlier marriage. Having been uttered by one legally considered an authoritative voice, Ruth and Richard accepted without question its plain and purported meaning. To all parties concerned, it was tantamount in both tenor and spirit to a veritable ceremony. Hence a re-affirmance of the earlier marriage was effectuated.

It has been contended that Ruth was opportune in utilizing the legal system. When she secured the divorce, she showed no hesitation in going to the courts; when she sought to remarry, she ignored the civil authorities. Such reasoning might be relevant if Ruth's legal status were at issue. But it is the "good faith wife" that concerns the Court. And nowhere has it been implied that petitioner lacked the reasonable and sincere belief in fulfilling this role, nor been suggested that she disregarded the duties and responsibilities of the marital institution.

Dawson speaks of good faith where the spouse thinks she is a wife, fulfills the role of a wife, is treated by the decedent as a wife, and is the dependent widow whom the Legislature seeks to aid. Her needs have been the same, and have arisen in the same way, as if the divorce had never occurred, and as if the priest had married them *de novo*. It is understandable that given Ruth Parkinson's limited sixth-grade education, she acted no differently than any one else in her position. When she wanted a divorce, she went to see a lawyer; when she wanted to get married, she went to see a priest. What could be more logical to a simple person with an inveterate Roman Catholic background? We do not question that for Ruth and Richard to be legally man and wife she would have had to comply with our marriage statute. That is not subject to argument. But she does not claim to have been a legal wife, rather a *de facto* one. Ruth Parkinson fulfills the good faith condition of the *de facto* spouse we have set forth in *Dawson.*

...

Ruth and Richard Parkinson withheld nothing from each other. No concealed impediments nor factors known to either party challenged otherwise legitimate aspects of the marriage. It was the priest, a third party, whose misguided decision proved inaccurate. Yet this marriage is devoid of any putative characteristics.

---

2. This statute says in part:

All common law marriages entered into after December 1, 1939 are invalid...and failure in any case to comply with both prerequisites (license and marriage performed by one authorized to solemnize marriages) which shall always be construed as mandatory and not merely directory, shall render the purported marriage absolutely void.

Therefore, both Ruth and Richard had the *bona fides*, if not the strict legal requirement; in *Dawson*, only the widow-claimant acted *bona fide*. Lack of strict legal requirements was not the fault of Ruth Parkinson. To deny her benefits for the unintentional mistake of another is seriously to penalize her for a wrong she did not wilfully commit. This is the very antithesis of the beneficent purposes for which our compensation statute speaks. We pointed out in *Dawson:*

> Workmen's Compensation legislation seeks to place upon industry the burden of bearing the loss inevitably resulting from accidents arising out of the business employment relationship...[when] such loss is occasioned by the work-connected death of an employee upon whom a wife — *or one living in such a relationship* — has been economically dependent.... The test of the relationship of husband and wife should not be quite the same in the context of this type of law, designed to supply a social need and to remedy a social evil, as in the area of familial law where questions of property, inheritance, legitimacy of offspring and the like rightly demand a more rigid adherence to conventional doctrine. (Emphasis added.)

59 N.J. at 196–197, 280 A.2d at 176.

...

Our equitable and humanitarian approach is predicated on a sensitive but frank awareness of the failings of the human being. By such a recognition we are insuring to the greatest extent possible the fulfillment of the high purposes of our socially important and ever broadening compensation act.

Reversed.

CLIFFORD, J. (dissenting).

...

The majority agrees that for petitioner and decedent to have "legally" been man and wife, they would have had to comply with the marriage statute. The language of that statute is "broad and sweeping" and its terms are "unusually peremptory," *Decunzo v. Edgye*, 19 N.J. 443, 450, 117 A.2d 508 (1955). However, the Court puts aside the legal requirements for the relationship of "wife" as one of those dependent upon the deceased workman at the time of the accident, N.J.S.A. 34:15-13(f), and again bestows its judicial blessing upon a de facto relationship on the authority of *Dawson v. Hatfield Wire & Cable Co.*, 59 N.J. 190, 280 A.2d 173 (1971).

I find no authority prior to *Dawson* for carving out a *de facto* marriage relationship for the singular purpose of creating a status entitling one to dependency benefits. Chief Justice Weintraub pointed out in his concurring opinion in *Dawson* that when the compensation statute speaks of a "wife," he assumed "for present purposes that a *de jure* wife was intended," 59 N.J. at 198, 280 A.2d at 177, but he was of the view that the employer lacked the necessary standing to challenge the validity of the ceremonial marriage in that case. Justice Francis, concurring and dissenting in part, likewise saw the doctrine of a *de facto* wife being accorded the status of a lawful wife for purposes of workmen's compensation as "contrary to the intention of the Legislature and the express language of the Workmen's Compensation Act," 59 N.J. at 200, 280 A.2d at 178. He said:

> Thus there comes into existence a *quasi*-marital status which was hitherto unknown to, and in fact contrary to, the law of our State, and which is

> to be employed in the administration of death benefits under the Workmen's Compensation Act. As I see the legislative intention under that act and under the public policy revealed by our marriage laws, a woman is either a legal wife or she is not a wife. Unless the parties are competent to marry and actually comply with the statutory ceremonial prerequisites, they do not become husband and wife regardless of the good faith attending their assumption of the relationship. To illustrate, no matter how fervently and sincerely a man and a woman agree to become husband and wife and to live together as such, in New Jersey they never acquire that status legally regardless of the length of time they live together. The Legislature has condemned common law marriage as "absolutely void." N.J.S.A. 37:1-10.

I agree with this perception of the legislative intention under the Workmen's Compensation Act.* It thus leads me to conclude that petitioner has failed to establish that she was the lawful wife of decedent. I therefore reach the same result as did the Judge of Compensation and the Appellate Division and would deny dependency benefits under N.J.S.A. 34:15-13.

FUNG DAI KIM AH LEONG v. LAU AH LEONG

United States Court of Appeals
27 F.2d 582 (9th Cir. 1928)

DIETRICH, Circuit Judge.

This is an appeal from a decree of the Supreme Court of Hawaii, affirming a dismissal by the circuit court of the appellant's bill of complaint, by which she sought to establish an interest in property held by the appellee. In the opinion below (29 Hawaii 770), may be found a comprehensive statement of the facts; for our purpose, details are unnecessary.

Both parties are of Chinese blood and nativity. In 1884 plaintiff, a girl 17 years old, came to Hawaii, where defendant was then residing, and after some negotiations a marriage was agreed upon and a wedding ceremony was held, all in accordance with Chinese customs, but without a license, as required by the laws of Hawaii. They immediately assumed, and thereafter for 35 years maintained, the relations of husband and wife. In the course of time the plaintiff bore to defendant 13 children, and, besides performing the domestic duties of a housewife, assisted him in carrying on his mercantile business. Success attended their joint efforts, with the result that at the time of the trial there was an accumulation of several hundred thousand dollars' worth of property. Following a decision of the Supreme Court of Hawaii in 1920 (*Parke v. Parke*, 25 Hawaii, 397), expressly overruling an earlier decision of that court and holding that a license was prerequisite to a valid marriage, defendant ceased to recognize plaintiff as his wife, and denied her any interest in the property accumulated during the long period they had lived together. That what was done would, in the absence of the territorial statute requiring a license, have constituted a valid common-law marriage, there can be no doubt, and that in believing they were living together in lawful wedlock they

*I should add that I also find Justice Francis's analysis and reasoning in *Dawson* compelling and would have been drawn to the same conclusion as he and on the same basis—that is, the strong presumption of validity of the second ceremonial marriage fortified by a presumption that the first marriage was terminated by divorce.

acted reasonably finds confirmation in the fact that not only was defendant advised by competent legal counsel that the marriage was valid, but such was the effect of a decision of the highest court of the territory. *Godfrey v. Rowland*, 16 Hawaii, 377.

Conceding that "there is great inherent justice in the complainant's claim," the Supreme Court was nevertheless of the opinion that the legal obstacles to its recognition are insurmountable. Under the civil law it was thought little difficulty would be encountered, but under the common law, which prevails in Hawaii, no basis for relief was found. There are but few reported decisions involving questions of the property rights of a putative wife, where for one reason or another the supposed marriage turns out to be void, but in the majority of those which have come to our attention relief of some character has been granted....

In these cases the principles invoked are not always the same, and, it may be conceded, in finding a basis for relief, some of them have put a strain upon statutory provisions the relevancy of which is not entirely obvious. But in all of them there is evinced a purpose to prevent a result so inherently wrong as to shock our common conception of fundamental justice.

Directly to the contrary is *Schmitt v. Schneider*, 109 Ga. 628, 35 S.E. 145. This was the only decision the court below found to be in point upon that side of the question, but the following may be cited as having some bearing in defendant's favor, though in the main they have to do with questions of the availability of certain specific remedies at law. *Bell v. Bennett*, 73 Ga. 784...; *De France v. Johnson* (C.C. Minn.) 26 F. 891. In the last case, strangely enough, the principle of estoppel was recognized as having efficacy to protect the innocent mortgagee, but not the putative wife, by whom the mortgage was given, though she was equally innocent.

The conclusion of the court below is made to rest upon a statutory provision prescribing as a rule of decision the common law of England, and the assumption that, however harsh and unjust the result, the plaintiff is without remedy under that law. This statute, first enacted in 1892 (section 5, c. 47, Session Laws of 1892), and, with slight amendment, now section 1, Rev. Laws of Hawaii 1925, provides that "the common law of England, as ascertained by English and American decisions, is declared to be the common law of the territory of Hawaii in all cases, except as otherwise expressly provided by the Constitution or laws of the United States, or by the laws of the territory, or fixed by Hawaiian judicial precedent, or established by Hawaiian usage," etc.

...

The precise case we have here could never have arisen under the common law of England, for under that law the parties would be husband and wife. Besides, plaintiff is seeking relief in a court of equity.... If, then, there is "great inherent justice in plaintiff's claim," for what reason shall a court of equity, invested with this broad power, hold itself incompetent to grant her a measure of relief? The parties were qualified to contract marriage; they agreed upon it, and actually established and for 35 years maintained the marital status. The plaintiff fully performed her agreement of marriage up to the point where, because of the law as then interpreted and the acts of defendant, it became impossible for her to go further. The contract of marriage turns out to be invalid only because of a failure to comply with a formality which at the time was not thought to be requisite. Had the parties entered into an understanding by which orally the plaintiff agreed to purchase and pay for, and defendant agreed to sell, a town lot, such an agreement might be invalid under the statute of frauds, for want of the requisite writing. But, if, pursuant to the agreement, plaintiff went into possession, improved the lot, and made the stipulated payments, a court of equity would afford her relief.

True, for reasons of public policy, as well as because of defendant's voluntary present disqualification, a court cannot compel performance to the extent of establishing the personal status originally contemplated; but because plaintiff is remediless in that respect, shall the court also deny her a measure of the pecuniary relief she here seeks? In decrees for separate support and maintenance, we have examples of relief respecting the economic side of the marital relation, without destroying the personal status established thereby. The common-law conception of marital unity by which the identity of the wife was merged into that of the husband has undergone a great change, in some jurisdictions recognized by statutory law, and almost universally by common understanding and ascent. If we assume that, as defendant contends, under the common law, in case of a void marriage, the putative wife was without remedy, we should not feel it incumbent to extend such a rule, the reasons for which no longer exist, to a specific case like this, which could never have arisen under the common law.

In common usage, equity protects relationships and vindicates rights not recognized in a court of law, and we are of the opinion that there is here substantial ground for the exercise of its jurisdiction. It may be that plaintiff cannot refer her right to any contractual or trust relation, within the strict legal definition of these terms; but that consideration is not conclusive, for otherwise there would be no place for the growing law of quasi contracts. Technically speaking, there was no partnership, no agreement of trust to cover the plaintiff's money contribution to the business enterprise, and no contract, express or implied, for compensation for her labor and service. But there was the underlying understanding, and the expectation, that she would receive a pecuniary benefit. She looked forward to support and maintenance in the years of her declining capacity to care for herself, which now have come upon her, and in certain contingencies to alimony, or dower. Owing to a mutual mistake of both parties respecting the fact of the existence of a valid marital status, the agreement cannot be fully executed, and plaintiff's expectations cannot be fully realized. We are inclined to think that this is such a mistake as warrants the interposition of a court of equity to grant appropriate relief. Pom. Eq. Juris. (4th Ed.) vol. 11, p. 1704 et seq., particularly pages 1731–1734, 1782; *Moore v. Shook*, 276 Ill. 47, 114 N.E. 592.

Quasi contractual obligations have been defined as "legal obligations arising without reference to the assent of the obligor, from the receipt of a benefit the retention of which is unjust, and requiring the obligor to make restitution." Woodward's Law of Quasi Contracts, p. 4; Maine's Ancient Law (4th Ed.) p. 344. The action upon such an obligation "lies for money paid by mistake, or upon a consideration which happens to fail, or for money got through imposition (express or implied).... In one word, the gist of this kind of action is that the defendant, upon the circumstances of the case, is obliged by the ties of natural justice and equity to refund the money." Woodward, *supra*, p. 4; and see, also, pages 295, 296; also *Moses v. McFarlen*, 2 Burr. 1005.

In commenting on *Cooper v. Cooper*, 147 Mass. 370, 17 N.E. 892, 9 Am.St.Rep. 721, cited *supra*, at pages 324 and 325 of Keener on Quasi Contracts, the learned author says:

> Had the plaintiff in this case surrendered to the defendant money or other chattels to which the defendant asserted a right because of his marital rights as husband, it does not seem possible that a court would hold that, because of the loss of the right to sue in tort by the death of the intestate, no claim could be asserted against his estate for the value so received by him. And yet in point of principle it is submitted that it is impossible to distinguish between the receipt of money or other property by the defendant and the receipt of services. The plaintiff whether she conferred a benefit on the intestate by rendering services, or by delivering to him money or other personal property, in either case parted with a right in rem under a mistaken supposition, induced by the fraud of the defendant, that the defendant was entitled thereto.

And

> whatever power, therefore, courts of equity possess to prevent and remove the consequences of fraud, they also possess in dealing with the effects of mistake.

Pom. Eq. Juris. (4th Ed.) vol. 11, pp. 1782, 1783.

As we have seen, by express statute the courts of Hawaii are clothed with wide equity jurisdiction, and more recently the court, from which comes *Cooper v. Cooper*, has said: "If our statutes had given jurisdiction of libels for nullity of marriage to courts having full equity powers, there might be some reason for holding that such courts could, as a condition of granting the relief prayed for, require that property brought by the defendant to the plaintiff should be restored to the former, or that an equitable division of any accumulated property should be made"....

We conclude that plaintiff is entitled to a measure of relief. Upon the question of what standard should be applied in determining the amount and character thereof, the decided cases, as already indicated, are not in harmony, and perhaps no specific general rule can be formulated. Each case must be adjudged in the light of its own peculiar facts and the local laws. Here, we think, it will be proper for the court in further proceedings to take into consideration the relative contributions of property, and of personal service in point of value, made by the two parties in the accumulation of the property standing in the defendant's name, the amount and value of such property at the time their de facto marital relations ceased, the amount of property accumulated by plaintiff during the same period and standing in her name, the local statutes affecting the marital relation and divorce, and alimony and dower, or other pecuniary interests of the wife, whether absolute or contingent, present or in expectancy....

By suggesting certain considerations, it is not to be inferred that upon further proceedings they should be deemed exclusive. The fact that during the period of cohabitation between the parties hereto the defendant entered into what now turns out to be a legal marriage with another woman may have some bearing upon the question, and other material circumstances may develop at the hearing affecting the equities.

Reversed, with directions for further proceedings not inconsistent herewith.

COMMENTS

Parkinson illustrates that religious factors can continue to have an impact on the contemporary secular law of marriage. Here the marriage of Roman Catholics continued to be recognized, at least for workmen's compensation purposes, although the parties had been divorced. The advice of the Catholic priest that they were still married "in the eyes of God," and consequently did not need to remarry, may appear to be shockingly irresponsible. Yet lawyers often render legal advice strictly on the basis of secular law and thereby invite misunderstanding in the parties, just as the priest in this case rendered advice strictly on the basis of church law, with serious consequences. Legal practice requires an awareness of the beliefs — whether based on religion or on popular conceptions of the law — of clients.

As in *Parkinson, Fung Dai Kim Ah Leong* shows the impact of religious, cultural and ethnic factors on adjudication. In both instances the wife thought herself to be married according to sincerely held beliefs. In *Fung Dai Kim Ah Leong* custom played the same kind of role that religion played in *Parkinson.* Each court was willing to treat the woman as having been in good faith, as a so-called "putative spouse," unaware of the legal requirements of marriage. Additional factors in *Fung Dai Kim Ah Leong* were thirty-five years of cohabitation as husband and wife with thirteen children, assistance in the successful business of the assumed "husband," and a change in judicial attitude toward informal marriage in Hawaii. Yet the true importance of the case lies in the fact that it was decided fifty years earlier than *Marvin v. Marvin* which appears at page 214; its reasoning closely paralleled, and to some extent went beyond, this well-publicized California holding. *Fung Dai Kim Ah Leong* is not referred to in *Marvin,* although it was actually decided in California, the Ninth Circuit Court of Appeals sitting in California and deciding appeals for the territorial Supreme Court of Hawaii. Uninhibited by local Hawaiian precedent, the federal court took an independent look at what it perceived to be the common law of quasi-marital cohabitation.

The Ninth Circuit Court of Appeals in 1928 suggested remedies for claims of women after prolonged cohabitation — for example, express or implied contract for compensation of labor and services; partnership; quasi-contract; unjust enrichment; and equitable relief for lost reasonable expectations relating to support, dower, alimony, or other pecuniary interests, whether absolute or contingent, present or inchoate. As in *Marvin,* the court concluded with a broad invocation of equitable powers, stressing that each case must be judged in the light of its own peculiar facts and that the remedies suggested in the opinion should not be deemed to be exclusive. Perhaps most startling and innovative is the comparison in *Fung Dai Kim Ah Leong* between marriage and real estate transactions. After implying that a de facto wife merits the same protection by estoppel theories as an innocent mortgagee, the court compared a marriage void for lack of form to an oral understanding to purchase land that might nevertheless be enforced in equity after part performance. Clearly, to paraphrase the language of the court in *Fung Dai Kim Ah Leong,* the plaintiff, after thirty-five years of cohabitation and thirteen children, should not be worse off than a grantee who "went into possession, improved the lot, and made the stipulated payments."

Parties may make mistakes not only about whether or not they are married, they may also erroneously believe themselves to be divorced. For example, it has occurred with some frequency that lawyers have issued a receipt reading "$50 for divorce" — meant to be a retainer for future legal action, but understood by the client to be a fee for divorce already obtained. In these instances, further prosecution of the case is then dropped because the party never reappears. In fact relying on the receipt, the party may have remarried. In other words, the possibility of error is ever present, but it can be controlled to some extent if the lawyer is aware of widespread common misunderstandings. Sometimes it is possible to cure past confusion and error with presumptions — for example, that the parties are married or that a divorce was somehow and somewhere obtained for a prior marriage. Since it is often impossible to overcome these presumptions, we really deal with legal fictions that are used to straighten out past facts. Sometimes a lenient statutory interpretation may help, as in *Parkinson,* especially in worker's compensation cases. But had the issue been inheritance of real property, the same court might have applied a more stringent test and ruled that no marriage existed. The use of presumptions adds a flexibility to the law that is often important in order to do justice in a particular case, but the practice also reduces the law's certainty and predictability.

Worker's Compensation

BURGESS CONSTRUCTION CO. v. LINDLEY

Supreme Court of Alaska
504 P.2d 1023 (Alaska 1972)

BOOCHEVER, Justice.

This is an appeal by Burgess Construction Company and Employers Commercial Union Companies, the employer and insurance carrier for the deceased workman, from the judgment of the superior court affirming the decision of the Alaska Workmen's Compensation Board that appellee was a surviving wife entitled to compensation benefits for the death of her husband in a job-related accident.

Appellee, Jeanne L. Lindley, was legally married to deceased in 1951 and had four children. In 1967, appellee obtained a divorce from Ronald Lindley and was awarded $75 per month in alimony. Appellee never remarried between her divorce and the death of Ronald Lindley. Ronald Lindley, subsequent to his divorce from appellee, remarried twice, and was divorced from each of these subsequent wives. In 1968, Jeanne and Ronald resumed living together but never went through another formal marriage ceremony. Appellee testified at the hearing that the only reason they did not marry again was because of financial inability to go outside of Ketchikan for a ceremony and the embarrassment that a ceremony in Ketchikan would cause their children and friends who were under the impression that they had in fact remarried. The couple lived together until the death of Ronald Lindley on December 10, 1970.

Appellants do not contest the fact of the accident or its job connection. They further concede the payment of benefits to the minor children. Their sole argument on appeal is that under AS 25.05.011[1] appellee was not legally married to deceased at the time of his death; and that therefore, appellee was not entitled to benefits under the workmen's compensation statutes as a "surviving wife."

...

No definition of the term "surviving wife" is provided by the workmen's compensation statute but the terms "married" and "widow" are defined by the Act. AS 23.30.265(15) provides

> "married" includes a person who is divorced but is required by the decree of divorce to contribute to the support of his former wife....

AS 23.30.265(21) provides

> "widow" includes only the decedent's wife living with or dependent for support upon him at the time of his death, or living apart for justifiable cause or by reason of his desertion at such a time....

It is clear under the statutory definition of "married" that the decedent, though divorced, was "married" for the purpose of the Workmen's Compensation Act, for the divorce decree required him to contribute to appellee's support. It follows that under the Act appellee would be regarded as his "surviving wife". She qualifies as a "widow" for she was living with decedent at the time of his death and was dependent upon him for support.[3]

Under the marital and domestic relations laws of the State of Alaska "[n]o person may be joined in marriage in this state until a license has been obtained for that purpose as provided in this chapter. No marriage performed in this state is valid without solemnization as provided in this chapter."[4] We have held that common law marriages are thus not valid in Alaska.[5] The subject case involves similar contentions to those ruled upon by the United States Court of Appeals for the Ninth Circuit in *Albina Engine & Machine Works v. O'Leary*[6] wherein the court stated:

> Neither the Oregon Workmen's Compensation Act nor the Longshoremen's and Harbor Workers' Act relate to or affect the marriage relationship as such. And the laws of the state regarding marriage are only

1. AS 25.05.011 provides:

Civil Contract. (a) Marriage is a civil contract requiring both a license and solemnization which may be entered into by

(1) a male who is 19 years of age or older with a female who is 18 years of age or older, who are otherwise capable, or

(2) those who qualify for a license under §171 of this chapter.

(b) No person may be joined in marriage in this state until a license has been obtained for that purpose as provided in this chapter. No marriage performed in this state is valid without solemnization as provided in this chapter.

3. The appellee, the appellants and the State of Alaska urged us to consider the equal protection argument which would result from the denial of benefits to a common law wife in such circumstances but we decline to consider this question at this time.

4. AS 25.05.011(b).

5. *Edwards v. Franke*, 364 P.2d 60, 63 (Alaska 1961).

6. 328 F.2d 877, 879 (1964).

> tangentially relevant as they may bear upon the existence of the status of "wife" or "widow" for the purpose of identifying recipients of benefits under these remedial statutes.
>
> The application of state domestic relations law, developed in other contexts, to the solution of problems under workmen's compensation statutes, produces results which at best have only a fortuitous relation to the remedial purposes of the compensation acts, and often are in direct conflict with them. When the state law does provide a definition of marital status deliberately shaped to compensation act purposes alone, there is no reason why that definition should not be applied under the federal statute in preference to one drawn from the state's general domestic relations law.

The *Albina* case is discussed in *Holland America Insurance Company v. Rogers*, 313 F.Supp. 314, 320 (N.D.Cal.1970) as follows:

> The *Albina* case reiterates the accepted approach to dealing with problems of marital relations: that marriage is not a monolithic institution, but consists instead of separate and severable incidents. Thus where the policy of a state may preclude its courts from "recognizing," say, a marriage of one man to two women, it may be permissible for both women to recover property from his estate on his death as his "wives," for recognizing a marriage for the purposes of the one incident would not violate the state's public policy as might recognition of it for other purposes. Similarly, in the instant case, this Court need not "recognize" the marriage of Angela Spies to Julian Spies in order to find that she is nonetheless entitled to at least some of the incidents of marriage, including the right to collect death benefits under a federal workmen's compensation law upon his death.

While, for some purposes, appellee would not have been recognized by the Alaska courts as married to the decedent, appellee qualifies for benefits as a "surviving wife" under terms of the Alaska Workmen's Compensation Act discussed above. The grant of benefits by the workmen's Compensation Board under the facts of this case is within the liberal humanitarian purposes of the Act[7] while a different reading of the statute would clearly frustrate this purpose.

The decision of the superior court is affirmed.

[Concurring opinion omitted.]

WEST v. BARTON-MALOW COMPANY

Supreme Court of Michigan

394 Mich. 334, 230 N.W.2d 545 (1975)

PER CURIAM.

The Appeal Board and the Court of Appeals erred in summarily relying upon *McDonald v. Kelly Coal Co.*, 335 Mich. 325, 55 N.W.2d 851 (1952) to deny plaintiff dependent's death benefits. *McDonald* is readily distinguishable from the instant case. A review of the particular facts in this case reveals that plaintiff was a dependent of the deceased within the meaning of Part II, §6 of the Workmen's Act.

---

7. *Gordon v. Burgess Constr. Co.*, 425 P.2d 602, 605 (Alaska 1967); *Holland America Ins. Co. v. Rogers*, 313 F.Supp. 314, 320 (N.D.Cal. 1970).

On January 9, 1967, Clarence West died as a result of injuries sustained in the course of his employment with Barton-Malow Construction Company. Plaintiff, Alzalee West, made claim for dependent's death benefits under the Workmen's Compensation Act.

For the 13 years preceding the death of Clarence West he and plaintiff resided together in the City of Detroit. During this time plaintiff held herself out as the wife of West and depended on him for her sole support. From the record there is no reason to doubt that West likewise considered plaintiff to be his wife. He depended on her to manage his household affairs and shared the wages he earned with her. A legal dispute arose in this case, however, because plaintiff and West were not formally wed, plaintiff remaining legally married to another man as a result of a short-lived marriage that took place in Texas in 1943.

Without elaborating on their specific rationales, both the Appeal Board and the Court of Appeals summarily concluded that *McDonald* barred Alzalee West's claim for relief.

McDonald v. Kelly Coal Co., supra, does not control the resolution of this action. In *McDonald* the claimants were a mother and her children who had been living with Milton McDonald for less than a year at the time of his death. In construing Part II, §6, the Court offered the following:

> We are of the opinion that in order to create a family relationship there must exist a condition devoid of moral turpitude. In the case at bar, the responsibility for the support of the two children rests upon their mother and father. Deceased had no such obligation. The tie that bound the children to deceased was the illicit relationship between their mother and deceased. Public policy does not sanction the payment of compensation arising out of meretricious cohabitation. We hold that plaintiffs were not members of deceased's family within the meaning of the Compensation Act.

335 Mich. 325, 330, 55 N.W.2d 851, 853.

The Court in *McDonald* was confronted with a relationship of short duration based on "meretricious cohabitation." In contrast, the facts of the present case reveal a long and continuing relationship with deceased and plaintiff treating each other, and holding themselves out to the public, as husband and wife. Plaintiff did secure an attorney in 1965 to commence divorce proceedings but no formal action had resulted by the date of the claim due to financial difficulties. A final judgment of divorce was obtained on June 2, 1967. If we read meretricious as the dictionary defines it — the relationship of a prostitute or a woman given to indiscriminate lewdness — we find no support whatsoever in the record for describing the relationship that existed between deceased and plaintiff as one based on meretricious cohabitation.

A proper resolution of this case demands that plaintiff's status be examined in terms of the words of, and the legislative purpose underlying, Part II, §6. In relevant part that section provides:

> In all other cases questions of dependency, in whole or in part, shall be determined in accordance with the fact, as the fact may be at the time of the injury. Where a deceased employee leaves a person wholly dependent upon him or her for support, said person shall be entitled to the whole death benefit.... *No person shall be considered a dependent unless he or she is a*

> *member of the family of the deceased employee*, or unless such person bears to said deceased employee the relation of husband or widow, or lineal descendant, or ancestor, or brother or sister. (Emphasis supplied.)

From a reading of the words of the statute it is evident that the Legislature did not intend to establish a strict definition of an eligible dependent. Instead, the Legislature employed words with expansive meanings and intended, we believe, to allow the administrative agency and the courts to interpret the statute in light of the individual factual situations that would arise.

An example of this type of construction that reflects the expansive nature of the words of Part II, §6 is found in the case of *Holmberg v. Cleveland-Cliffs Iron Co.*, 219 Mich. 204, 189 N.W. 26 (1922). In *Holmberg* this Court affirmed an award of dependent death benefits ruling that Mrs. Holmberg was a "dependent member" of her cousin's "family" because her cousin had provided monetary support to Mrs. Holmberg after her husband had abandoned her. The Court wrote:

> Was plaintiff a dependent member of Mr. Franzen's family at the time of his death? This court has had occasion, in insurance cases, to define the meaning of the term "member of the family," and has adopted the liberal view thereof. *Carmichael v. Benefit Ass'n*, 51 Mich. 494, 16 N.W.2d 871.
>
> In *Hosmer v. Welch*, 107 Mich. 470, 65 N.W. 280, it was stated:
>
> "The term 'family' is elastic, and will be liberally construed. It is not confined to a husband and wife and their children."

...

Turning to the facts of the case before us today, we are of the opinion that plaintiff is also an eligible dependent. Factually, plaintiff was totally dependent upon Clarence West for her support. Legally, we find that plaintiff fits within the scope of the statutory definition of an eligible dependent. She was, it is true, not legally married to deceased; however, the record indicates without contention that she did bear to Clarence West the relationship of a wife for the 13 years preceding his untimely death. During those years plaintiff was responsible for maintaining their household while deceased undertook the responsibility for furnishing them both with monetary support. In name and in outward appearance plaintiff and deceased were Mr. and Mrs. West.[3] From our reading of the record there is no evidence that would indicate that the propriety of their relationship was ever questioned by anyone except the compensation carrier herein.

In finding plaintiff to be an eligible dependent, it is not our intention to reduce by any degree the importance of the formalities surrounding marriage. Our concern rather is to effectuate the purpose of Part II, §6 of the Workmen's Compensation Act.

The Court of Appeals is reversed and this case remanded to the Workmen's Compensation Appeal Board for the entry of an order in conformity with today's opinion.

...

3. Plaintiff's actions also negate any inference that she intended to look to her first husband for support or to possibly claim any benefits that would flow to her as his legal wife. She commenced divorce proceedings against him while West was alive, but due to economic difficulties did not complete them before West died. Thereafter she did complete the divorce and consequently terminated any arguable claim that she might have had to her first husband's resources and future benefits.

FITZGERALD, Justice (dissenting).

In this case the majority finds that a woman legally married to one man is entitled to workmen's compensation benefits attributable to the death of another man as a member of that man's "family" under M.C.L.A. §412.6; M.S.A. §17.156. We are of the opinion that the public policy of this state will not sustain such strained interpretation.

Marriage to another while a former marriage is legally valid is prohibited by M.C.L.A. §551.5; M.S.A. §25.5. Such marriages, even if solemnized, are declared to be void by M.C.L.A. §552.1; M.S.A. §25.81. Plaintiff's deceased cohabiter had no legal obligation to support plaintiff. That plaintiff be "family" under the Workmen's Compensation Act is, in this state, a legal impossibility....

We cannot presage the impact of this decision upon the laws of this state, or other consequences which may flow from the Court's decision today. Suffice it to say, the decision represents a departure from legislatively established public policy which we cannot endorse.

POWELL v. ROGERS

United States Court of Appeals
496 F.2d 1248 (9th Cir. 1974)

SNEED, Circuit Judge:

The appellant, Ms. Mary Stewart Powell, brought this action pursuant to Section 21 of the Longshoreman's and Harbor Workers' Compensation Act, 33 U.S.C. 901 *et seq.*, before the Compensation Commission for the 13th Compensation District, which denied the appellant's claim for death benefits under the above Act as the "surviving wife" or "widow" of Mr. Amadee B. Powell. In the district court the Deputy Commissioner and the State Compensation Insurance Fund, the real party in interest, moved for summary judgment dismissing the appellant's action. A motion for summary judgment setting aside the Deputy Commissioner's order and finding that the appellant was entitled to judgment on her claim as a matter of law was also filed. The appellant's motion was denied and that of the Deputy Commissioner and the State Insurance Board was granted. This appeal resulted. Our jurisdiction rests on 28 U.S.C. 1291, while that of the district court flows from 33 U.S.C. 901.

In large part because of the appellant's commendable candor, there is no dispute about the facts. She and the decedent, Mr. Amadee B. Powell, lived together from 1955 until his death in 1969 but did not undergo a formal or ceremonial marriage. Three children were born of this union, and the entire household was supported by the decedent. During most of this period the decedent was lawfully married to another, a marriage of which the appellant was aware. This marriage was dissolved by divorce in 1965, but there occurred no ceremonial marriage by the Powells thereafter. In the words of the appellant, her marriage was legal "In the sight of God, yes; but in the sight of man, no."

The Deputy Commissioner found that the Powells lived together as man and wife in the States of California and Nevada, that death benefits should be paid on behalf of the three minor children to the appellant, their mother and natural guardian, but that no death benefits were payable to the appellant as a "surviving wife" or "widow." 33 U.S.C. 902(16) and 909.0

There is no escape from the conclusion that under these facts appellant was neither the lawful nor putative wife of the decedent under California or Nevada law. Lawful marriage requires the "issuance of a license and solemnization." Section 4100, California Civil Code. To be a putative spouse one must believe in good faith that he is a party to a valid marriage. *Vallera v. Vallera,* 21 Cal.2d 681, 134 P.2d 761 (1943); *Miller v. Johnson,* 214 Cal.App.2d 123, 29 Cal.Rptr. 251 (1963); *Union Bank & Trust Co. v. Gordon,* 116 Cal.App.2d 681, 254 P.2d 644 (1953); *In re Jackson's Estate,* 112 Cal.App.2d 16, 245 P.2d 684 (1952). The appellant had no such belief. Her status was that of a common law wife under circumstances in which neither state with which the Powells had relevant contacts recognize a common law marriage. Sections 4100, 4213, California Civil Code; Section 122.010, Nevada Revised Statutes, Vol. IV. The issue before us is whether Ms. Mary Stewart Powell under these circumstances can be considered a "surviving wife" or "widow" under the Longshoreman's and Harbor Workers' Compensation Act. We hold that she can not.

This Circuit has recognized, as it must, that the meaning of Sections 902(16) and 909 of the Act is a question of federal law. *Albina Engine and Machine Works v. O'Leary,* 328 F.2d 877 (9th Cir., 1964). However, this Circuit also has recognized that in the absence of a statutory definition of "surviving wife" or "widow" the applicable local law supplies the meaning of these terms. *Albina Engine and Machine Works v. O'Leary, supra; Bolin v. Marshall,* 76 F.2d 668 (9th Cir., 1935).

California law, while not recognizing the common law marriage, does employ the putative spouse doctrine generously. Thus, a putative wife is entitled to California workmen's compensation death benefits. *Neureither v. Workmen's Comp.* App. Bd., 15 Cal.App.3d 429, 93 Cal.Rptr. 162 (1971); *Brennfleck v. Workmen's Comp. App. Bd.,* 265 Cal.App.2d 738, 71 Cal.Rptr. 525 (1968). Quite properly, the putative spouse doctrine has been employed to permit such a spouse to qualify as a "surviving wife" under the Act here before us. *Holland America Insurance Co. v. Rodgers,* 313 F.Supp. 314 (D.C.N.D.Cal.1970). However, no case in California or Nevada has been found in which the common law wife has been extended the protection of the applicable workmen's compensation act, unless the common law marriage was validly created in a state which recognizes such marriages. *Tatum v. Tatum,* 241 F.2d 401 (9th Cir., 1957).

California also recognizes that the putative spouse is entitled to take by intestacy on the death of his spouse in the same manner as a validly married spouse. *In re Krone's Estate,* 83 Cal.App.2d 766, 189 P.2d 741 (1952); *Mazzenga v. Rosso,* 87 Cal.App.2d 790, 197 P.2d 770 (1948). *In re Krone's Estate* has been used to allow a putative wife to bring an action for the wrongful death of her putative husband. *Kunakoff v. Woods,* 166 Cal.App.2d 59, 332 P.2d 773 (1958). An agreement to pool earnings entered into by a putative spouse with the other member of the union has also been accorded the same protection that it would have received had there been a valid marriage. *Sancha v. Arnold,* 114 Cal.App.2d 772, 251 P.2d (1952).

In view of the failure of California and Nevada to recognize the common law marriage, and California's liberality in extending the equivalent of marital rights to a putative spouse, we are reluctant to depart from our practice of looking to the proper local law to provide the content of the terms "surviving wife" and "widow". To construe these terms to embrace the common law spouse to some extent would impose upon the residents of California and Nevada a form of marriage which they have rejected in favor of, at least in the case of California, the putative spouse doctrine. It is in this manner that the necessary melioration of the requirements of a valid marriage is accomplished.

It is urged upon us that both changing life styles and the cultural history of Blacks make necessary an interpretation of the Act that would recognize the rights of a surviving spouse of a common law marriage. This federal common law marriage, so to speak, would make uniform the application of the Act and eliminate from its administration the adventitious element of whether the law of a particular state recognized the common law marriage. These arguments are not without a certain appeal. We think, however, they more properly should be directed to Congress. Our view is strengthened by the fact that reliance on local law to supply the meaning of "surviving wife" and "widow" has existed since passage of the Act and Congress has not chosen to intervene. Whatever may be our desire to reform the law, it must be subordinate to our duty faithfully to interpret it in a reasonably consistent manner.

...

This holding can not be construed to mean that a common law marriage, as defined by federal law, is a "conjugal nexus" and that it alone is sufficient to qualify the claimant as a "surviving wife" or "widow." Such a meaning excessively extends the relatively narrow holding of the Supreme Court which, as a matter of fact, was designed to reject a holding of this Court which indicated that a claimant who was once a deserted wife remained one for the purposes of the Act although she had "remarried" another. 347 U.S. at 335. See *Moore Dry Dock Co. v. Pillsbury*, 169 F.2d 988 (9th Cir., 1948). It is for others to determine whether such an extension is desirable.

Affirmed.

B: OTHER INFORMAL MARRIAGES FOR LIMITED PURPOSES

Putative Marriage

HUPP v. HUPP

Court of Civil Appeals of Texas
235 S.W.2d 753 (Tex. Civ. App. 1950)

MCDONALD, Chief Justice.

According to the findings of the jury and the evidence in harmony with them, T. R. Hupp, now deceased, was at all times material to this suit married to Zula Hupp. At some time prior to the year 1936 T. R. Hupp became acquainted with the appellee, who will be referred to as Ann Hupp. It is Ann Hupp's claim that she and Hupp were married in 1936, she believing that T. R. Hupp and Zula Hupp had been divorced. T. R. Hupp and Ann moved to Texas, and lived together until his death in 1948. Through their joint efforts and contributions they accumulated property of the value of some twenty thousand dollars. In this suit, brought against Hupp's administrator, his heirs, and Zula Hupp, Ann Hupp seeks to recover judgment for one-half the value of said property, either on the theory that she was entitled thereto as the putative wife of T. R. Hupp, or on the theory that she and Hupp accumulated the property in a partnership or joint venture. Ann recovered judgment, and the defendants have appealed relying on seventeen points of error.

...

The jury found that there was not a ceremonial marriage between Ann and T. R. Hupp. Defendants argue that there cannot be a putative marriage where there has not been a ceremonial marriage. In other words, they say that a common law marriage, which would have been a valid marriage if one of the parties had not been married to another, cannot serve as the basis for asserting a putative marriage. The San Antonio Court of Civil Appeals declared in *Papoutsis v. Trevino*, Tex.Civ.App., 167 S.W.2d 777, writ dismissed, that "one asserting under a putative marriage cannot claim good faith in the absence of a ceremonial marriage attended by the formalities prescribed by law." See also, *In re Greathouse's Estate*, Tex.Civ.App., 184 S.W.2d 317. *Smith v. Smith*, 1 Tex. 621, 46 Am.Dec. 121, was relied on as authority for the pronouncement. We do not join in the view announced by the San Antonio Court. The Supreme Court, in *Smith v. Smith*, had before it a marriage relationship which began in 1830 and was governed by the laws of Mexico. The court referred to the fact that a common law marriage was not recognized in that jurisdiction, and said, among other things, that a claim of good faith could not be made under such circumstances in the absence of a ceremonial marriage. In the case then under review there had been in fact a ceremonial marriage. The facts of the three Court of Civil Appeals cases also cited in *Papoutsis v. Trevino* did not present the question now under discussion.

A putative marriage based on a common law marriage relationship was sustained in *Lawson v. Lawson*, 30 Tex.Civ.App. 43, 69 S.W. 246, writ refused, and the Supreme Court cited *Lawson v. Lawson*, without a hint of criticism, in *Barkley v. Dumke*, 99 Tex. 150, 87 S.W. 1147. The opinion in the latter case refers to the fact that *Smith v. Smith* was decided under the rules of the Spanish law, and not under the laws prevailing after Texas adopted the provisions of the common law in 1840....

While a different rule might well prevail under the Spanish law, which does not recognize what we know as common law marriages, every reason that exists for allowing relief to a party who has entered into a putative marriage relationship applies with equal force to the situation where the putative marriage was entered into as a common law marriage as where it was entered into pursuant to a marriage ceremony.

Defendants argue that the evidence was insufficient to warrant a finding that there was a partnership or a joint venture, that it was insufficient to show what property was subject to plaintiff's claims, if any she had, or the value of the accumulations resulting from the joint efforts and contributions of Ann and T. R. Hupp, or that certain items of property or money represented such accumulations, and complaint is made of the form of the issues submitted to the jury which inquired about some of such matters. Since we have no way of knowing what the proof may be on another trial, it would probably not be helpful to counsel or the trial court to discuss such questions against the background of the record now before us. We may, however, say this much: If there was a putative marriage, and if the proof does not show the amount of contributions or efforts of either party, the rule seems to be that each of the putative spouses is entitled to half of the joint accumulations. *Lawson v. Lawson, supra.* Attention of the parties is also called to the rule that partners are presumed equal where partnership is shown, and nothing more. *Johnston v. Ballard*, 83 Tex. 486, 18 S.W. 686; *Bivins v. Proctor*, 125 Tex. 137, 80 S.W.2d 307. It would be elemental that the person claiming to be a putative spouse or a partner would have the burden of identifying any particular piece of property as being a part of the accumulations of the parties during the putative marriage or partnership.

...

In answer to another contention made by defendants, we refer to the rule which permits proof of a marriage to be made by general repute as to the status of the parties in the neighborhood where they reside and are known. 28 Tex. Jur. 737. But it was not proper to endeavor to prove a divorce between T. R. Hupp and his first wife by the testimony of a witness that he had seen a copy of a divorce decree. If there was such a decree, a certified copy of it would ordinarily be the best evidence of it.

...

Reversed and remanded.

COMMENTS

Good faith is only one of many factors that may have an influence on determining a woman's claims after years of cohabitation. In *Burgess* and *West* the courts protected the financial interests of women who could not be said to have had a good faith belief that they were legally married. In *Burgess* there had been a legal marriage of sixteen years, resulting in four children, that ended in divorce. Although the claimant had never remarried, her former husband remarried and obtained divorces twice within a span of one year. After these two intervening marriages, the former spouses resumed living together without formal remarriage. In *West* the claiming woman, during the thirteen years of cohabitation, continued to be legally married to a different man with whom she had lived for only a short time. In both instances factors of social class and poverty seem to have been responsible, at least in part, for the fact that the parties continued to live for many years in relationships that had only the appearance of marriage.

The economic factors in the two cases give clues to why they were decided in favor of the women. They might have become public charges had they not won. In spite of the absence of good faith, the courts felt compelled to point out that the women were not really bad. Although not conforming to the laws of marriage and divorce, the woman in *Burgess* had in fact lived up to the traditional ideal of marriage to the same partner for life. The Supreme Court of Michigan defended the woman in *West* by pointing out that she did not fit the dictionary definition of "meretricious," namely being "a woman given to indiscriminate lewdness." Such tolerance cannot necessarily be expected from the courts. In fact, many courts have labeled as "meretricious" women who were no more "given to indiscriminate lewdness" than Alzalee West was. Judicial tolerance is more likely to be found in worker's compensation cases than in any other areas of law. There may seem to courts to be no reason that general welfare rather than worker's compensation funds should provide for the dependent of an injured or deceased worker simply because the worker and dependent were not married in a fully legal manner. The courts find a marriage for purposes of worker's compensation to avoid an unfair result. Yet the court in *Burgess* pointed out a truth of more general application that will be found frequently in this book, namely, that marriage can be valid for some purposes but not recognized for some others. Even a bigamous marriage can have some of the legal consequences of a regular marriage. According to the dissent in *West,* this is obviously a legal impossibility.

Hupp adds one more dimension to the question of who can be acting in good faith. The defense had claimed that the plaintiff could not be a "putative wife" because she had never attempted a licensed marriage. If this were the law, the realm of protected relationships would be drastically reduced. Courts are prone to leave avenues open for equitable relief, if they feel so inclined. Here we have the competing claims of wife no. 1 and wife no. 2 after the husband had died. While some legal rights of wife no. 1 from a continuing marriage appear to have been undisputed, wife no. 2 had helped in accumulating the property during years of apparent marital cohabitation. Whether she believed in good faith that the prior marriage had terminated in divorce is left open. The court indicated that she might be entitled to half of the property in any event, under a theory of either putative marriage or partnership.

Here, as is often the case, rules of evidence may not have been sufficiently explored by the lawyers. Unless there were clear facts to the contrary, plaintiff wife no. 2 could have claimed a presumption that her marriage was valid, and therefore that the prior marriage had been terminated by divorce. It would then have been incumbent upon wife no. 1 to overcome this presumption (that the later marriage was valid) by showing that no divorce had been obtained — an especially difficult, if not impossible, task in view of the fact that the presumption might even have covered the possibility of a divorce in a jurisdiction other than Texas, including neighboring Mexico. The presumption that a prior marriage had been terminated by divorce would even apply in favor of a subsequent common law marriage, as might have been the case here. Contemporary lawyers should be concerned with being liable under theories of malpractice for overlooking the possible application of a presumption in favor of their clients. The presumption, incidentally, would have excluded rights of wife no. 1 in the estate altogether.

REFERENCE

Hans W. Baade, *The Form of Marriage in Spanish North America*, 61 CORNELL L. REV. 1 (1975).

SOUSA v. FREITAS

California Court of Appeal

10 Cal.App.3d 660, 89 Cal.Rptr. 485 (1970)

DAVID, Associate Justice pro tem.

Plaintiff Maria Jacinto de Sousa, now some 82 years old, illiterate resident of Santo Espirito, on the island of Santa Maria, Azores, Republic of Portugal, was found by the trial court to be the lawful wife of Manuel Sousa Freitas at the time of his death. Hence, she was awarded a decree imposing a constructive trust as to her marital interest on the properties of his estate, as against Catherine E. Freitas, found to be only his putative wife, and the Bank of America National Trust & Savings Association, as executor. The appellants contest such determinations.

Three years after his marriage at Santo Espirito in 1908 and establishing their residence there, followed by the birth of a son, Manuel Joaquin de Sousa emigrated to California, and for a short period remitted small sums to his family. In 1915, Sousa secured a decree from the Superior Court of Alameda County changing his name to Manuel S. Freitas. Though it would seem that a wife or a child is a person vitally concerned, the Code of Civil Procedure, sections 1275–1279, inclusive, makes no provision for personal service of such an application upon them unless as a "near relative" when the father of a petitioner is not living (Code Civ.Proc., §1276). Maria, his wife, did not know of this change of name until long after 1916.

In 1916, Manuel S. Freitas secured a divorce from Maria S. Freitas, meaning Maria Jacinto Sousa. Service was made by publication, the affidavit stating the defendant lived in "Santa Maria, in the Republic of Portugal," though Manuel well knew Santa Maria was only the island on which his wife lived in Santo Espirito at the home they occupied together; and that there, his wife was not and never had been known as Maria Sousa Freitas. There is evidence that he was not there known as Freitas, contrary to his declaration for change of name. Her testimony was that he was always known as Sousa there.[1]

Testifying in the trial court for appellants, Manuel's brother bore the name of Sousa; and appellants' exhibits in the form of letters from the son of Manuel and Maria to his father show the complete home address as Azenka, Santo Espirito, Santa Maria, Portugal.

By reason of the name change and incomplete address the trial court is supported in the finding that Maria "had no notice or knowledge of said divorce action, was not served as a party to said action and was not a party to the judgment for divorce rendered in 1919. No other action was taken by either plaintiff or her said husband to terminate their marriage, and at all times until the date of death of said decedent, plaintiff believed that she was the legal wife of decedent; said plaintiff, not having been served with process in the aforementioned divorce action, had no opportunity to impose any valid and meritorious defense to any

---

1. In Spain, Portugal and in Latin-American countries, there is a custom whereby a child bears or may be known by the names of both father and mother, and the name of the mother, appearing last may be used as the family name; or is sometimes expressed only as an initial following the father's family name. Manuel Sousa was the son of Jose Joaquim de Sousa and Bernardina Jacinta de Freitas; and his cousin and wife Maria Jacinta de Sousa is the daughter of Manuel Joaquim de Sousa and Bernardina Jacinta de Chaves. Upon marriage, her surname (sire's name) remained Sousa; and although Freitas under the old custom might describe himself "Manuel Sousa de Freitas," the name Freitas still would not identify her in this island kingdom of cousins. On Santa Maria, there is testimony neither Manuel nor Maria was ever known by the name "Freitas." His brother testifying on the trial gave his surname as "Souza."

There were so many Maria Joaquin Sousas on Santa Maria—cousins bearing the same name—that Maria Sousa for better identity carried also her grandmother's name of Figueiredo. The son of Maria and Manuel Sousa, left with his mother when Manuel emigrated, also was called Jose Sousa Figueiredo.

It therefore seems inevitable that the identity of "Maria S. Freitas," without any designation of place of residence, whether town, locality or parish, on the island of Santa Maria, would be unknown. Thus whether by inadvertence or design, she was deprived of the notice that Code of Civil Procedure section 413 requires that "a copy of the summons and complaint to be forthwith deposited in the post office, directed to the person to be served, at his place of residence...."

"Residence" in this connection means the address at which letters would be most likely to reach the defendant....

cause of action for divorce which the decedent could or might have brought during his lifetime." The basis for Manuel's action was her alleged refusal to come to him in America; her claim is, that he did not send for her, nor provide the funds. This was a sufficient meritorious defense....

The trial court concluded that the plaintiff was not a party to nor bound by the change of name proceeding by her husband, and that the purported decree of divorce did not terminate her marriage because Manuel S. Freitas perpetrated extrinsic fraud on plaintiff by designating his defendant wife in the divorce proceedings as Maria S. Freitas. We have noted also the important variance in the address; but whether inadvertent or deliberate, the evidence would indicate that Maria might have received the summons had it been addressed in her proper name or in one which she recognized as her own or by which she was known in the community....

The trial court necessarily concluded that the marriage ceremony between Manuel S. Freitas and Catherine E. Afflech was invalid.[2]

But from December 29, 1919, until Manuel's death on August 4, 1962, Catherine E. Freitas lived with him in good faith, believing she was lawfully married to him. All of the property held by him at his death was the product of their joint efforts. Maria was not named in Manuel's will, which devised and bequeathed all of his estate to Catherine.

Therefore, we review the determinations of the trial court, relative to the trust imposed upon the estate, securing the rights therein declared in favor of plaintiff Maria Sousa.

These were (1) all of the property was community property of Manuel S. Freitas and Maria Jacinto Sousa, at the time of his death; (2) that as widow, Maria is the owner of an undivided one-half interest as a community interest in all of said real and personal property and income and proceeds thereof; (3) that as putative spouse Catherine is entitled to the other one-half of all such real and personal property with the proceeds and income thereof.

We are impelled to modify such findings and conclusions.

As against the other spouse or his heirs it is well settled that a woman who lives with a man as a wife in the belief a valid marriage exists is entitled to share in the property accumulated by them during its existence. The proportionate contribution of each is immaterial in this state, for the property is divided as community property would be upon dissolution of a valid marriage....

The putative wife's share is not community property. But what is the situation when the legally recognized spouse steps forward to assert her community property interest in and to the same property, as against the putative spouse? There is scant authority. In *Union Bank & Trust Co. v. Gordon* (1953) 116 Cal.App.2d 681, 254 P.2d 644, the "legal" spouse was estopped to assert her claim, since she herself had remarried in reliance upon the invalid divorce. In *Estate of Ricci* (1962) 201 Cal.App.2d 146, 19 Cal.Rptr. 739, where decedent apparently made no disposition of his community interest by will, the award of one-half to each of the legal and the putative spouses was affirmed. (There, the putative wife appealed, claiming the entire estate was the result of her joint efforts with decedent.) This was an equity decision, in the teeth of Probate Code section 201 under which the legal wife

2. We note that this marriage was on the day the divorce decree was signed, but on the day before it became effective by entry of judgment, no *nunc pro tunc* entry ever having been made; as well as the absence of valid service of summons and complaint on Maria Jacinto Sousa by publication.

would have inherited his portion. The trial court followed this precedent.

But here, the decedent already had by will vested his half of the community property in the defendant putative spouse, a valid disposition under Probate Code sections 201 and 201.5.

By definition, the one-half of the community property so devised was his; and did not include the other half to which the competing claims apply. Stated another way, in accordance with the views expressed by Professor William E. Burby in Family Law For California Lawyers, pages 359–360 (quoted in *Estate of Ricci, supra,* 201 Cal.App.2d 146, at pp. 148–149, 19 Cal.Rptr. 739, at p. 740): "It seems obvious that one-half of the property in question belongs to the putative spouse. The other half belongs to the legal community (husband and legally recognized spouse) and should be distributed as any other community property under the same circumstances." Under this analysis by the recognized expert in community property law, Catherine is entitled to one-half of the property in her own right; plus the half of the community property decedent was entitled to devise, or another one-quarter of the whole; and the plaintiff is entitled to one-quarter of the whole estate only. (*Blache v. Blache* (1945) 69 Cal.App.2d 616, 624, [160 P.2d 136.]) In effect, the innocent putative spouse was in partnership or a joint enterprise with her spouse, contributing her services — and in this case, her earnings — to the common enterprise. Thus, their accumulated property was held in effect in tenancy-in-common in equal shares. Upon death of the husband, only his half interest is considered as community property, to which the rights of the lawful spouse attach.[3] We do not undertake to state that this analysis would be equitable in all cases, but we are satisfied that it is under the facts here.[4]

The findings and conclusions are modified to state: (1) one-half of the property was community property of Manuel S. Freitas and Maria Jacinto Sousa, at the time of his death; and Maria Jacinto Freitas is the owner of an undivided one-fourth interest as a community interest in all of said real and personal property and income and proceeds thereof; (2) that as a putative spouse, Catherine is entitled to one-half of all such real and personal property and income and proceeds thereof; and as legatee and devisee of the deceased to an additional one-fourth thereof, being his disposition of his half interest in the community property, under Probate Code, sections 201 and 201.5.

...

As so modified the judgment is affirmed....

---

3. Various analogies have been drawn to characterize the nature of the property acquired during the putative marriage to protect the innocent de facto spouse. Consult: W. Q. de Funiak, PRINCIPLES OF COMMUNITY PROPERTY (1943) pages 124–132, section 56; FAMILY LAW FOR CALIFORNIA LAWYERS (1956) *supra,* chapter 13, William E. Burby, "Significant Aspects of Community Property Law," sections 5, 6, pages 359–361.

4. Some cases, based upon the Spanish law of community property have adopted the view that the lawful wife rightfully takes one-half and the putative wife one-half, leaving the husband nothing, upon the ground that by his conduct he has forfeited his community property rights in the community acquired during the putative marriage, as in Louisiana: *Waterhouse v. Star Land Co.* (1916) 139 La. 177, 71 So. 358, 359–360; *Fulton Bag & Cotton Mills v. Fernandez* (La.App.1935) 159 So. 339, 343. The court in *Estate of Ricci, supra,* 201 Cal.App.2d 146, 19 Cal.Rptr. 739, seems to have followed this rule, while in *Blache v. Blache, supra,* 69 Cal.App.2d 616, 624, 160 P.2d 136, it was not followed. Pursuant to Civil Code section 4452, operative January 1, 1970, property acquired during the putative marriage is termed "quasi-marital property" and is divided equally between the parties under Civil Code section 4800; but no resolution is made of the conflicting claims of the lawful and putative spouse.

Quasi-Contractual Marriage

SANGUINETTI v. SANGUINETTI

Supreme Court of California
9 Cal. 2d 95, 69 P.2d 845 (1937)

SEAWELL, Justice.

Plaintiff Angelina Sanguinetti and defendant Joe Sanguinetti were married on February 2, 1927, and separated on September 24, 1934. On October 8, 1934, plaintiff filed her complaint herein, setting forth two causes of action, the first for divorce on the ground of extreme cruelty, and the second for annulment based on the fact that at the time of her marriage to Sanguinetti she had a former husband living. Sanguinetti filed an answer and also a cross-complaint wherein he prayed for a divorce from plaintiff on the ground of her extreme cruelty and for an annulment. The court granted the defendant an annulment on his cross-complaint. It appears from the findings that plaintiff had married Antonio Depaoli on June 30, 1914, and on July 23, 1923, had procured an interlocutory decree of divorce from him. But at the time of her marriage to defendant herein, more than three years later, a final decree of divorce had not been entered and was not thereafter entered until January 12, 1934. The court herein found that both parties believed the second marriage legal, and that defendant did not know it was illegal until the filing of the complaint herein.

...

The court further held that plaintiff was entitled to recover from defendant the sum of $1,250 as the reasonable value of her services to defendant during the time they lived together, and that plaintiff was entitled to an equitable lien to secure payment of this sum on the defendant's San Francisco real property. Defendant appeals from this provision of the judgment....

...

...By her complaint plaintiff prayed for monthly alimony and that the San Francisco real property be assigned to her. She did not ask judgment for the value of her services, but their complaint contained a prayer for general relief. Upon an annulment plaintiff would not be entitled to alimony.... Since the appeal is on the judgment roll alone, it may be presumed in support of the judgment that plaintiff's right to recover for her services was made an issue in the trial by consent of the parties, and evidence introduced on said issue.... In an action for divorce or for annulment in the event the marriage sought to be dissolved by divorce has not been validly contracted, it is sound practice to dispose of the property rights of the parties in the same action, thus avoiding multiplicity of suits....

Where a "putative" marriage has existed, that is, where one or both parties to an invalid marriage have in good faith believed such marriage to be valid, upon an annulment or declaration of invalidity the courts will recognize the right of the de facto wife in property acquired by the parties through their joint efforts, and which would have been community property had the marriage been valid, and will make an equitable division of such property....

...But this is not the theory of recovery in the instant case. Here no joint property was found to exist. The recovery allowed plaintiff is for the reasonable value of her services rendered to her supposed husband. A legal wife upon divorce has no right to recover for services rendered in the maintenance of the joint domicile, but may obtain alimony for her future support in proper cases. The putative wife, as noted above, has no right to an allowance of alimony.

Where an invalid marriage has been procured by fraud of the de facto husband, who is aware of the invalidity of the marriage, the right of the wife who has acted in good faith to recover the reasonable value of her services over and above the value of the support and maintenance furnished her by her supposed husband, has been sustained in a number of jurisdictions, including this state....

The basis of recovery for services...is quasi-contractual. The supposed husband has been unjustly enriched by the amount by which the reasonable value of the services rendered to him by his de facto wife exceed the amount devoted by him to her support and maintenance. These services would not have been rendered but for a belief in the validity of the marriage and the continuance of the incidents of status incident to a valid marriage. It is just and equitable that the de facto husband should make compensation for what has been rendered to him under a mistaken belief in the validity of the marriage which was induced by his own fraud. The law raises the promise to pay in such cases. Cases in other jurisdictions which deny recovery to the de facto wife do so on the ground that as the wife never contemplated she should be paid, a contract will not be implied. *Cooper v. Cooper*, 147 Mass. 370, 17 N.E. 892, 9 Am.St.Rep. 721; *Cropsey v. Sweeney*, 27 Barb. (N.Y.) 310.

In the instant case, however, the invalidity of the marriage was due to no fraud or fault of the defendant. He was free to marry. Both parties believed their marriage in 1927 valid. A final decree of divorce was entered in plaintiff's action against her first husband on January 12, 1934, at which time plaintiff and defendant were living together as husband and wife. After entry of the final decree in plaintiff's action against her first husband, plaintiff and defendant were free to legalize their relationship of seven years' standing by contracting a valid marriage. The termination of said relationship cannot, therefore, fairly be said to arise from the invalidity of their marriage, but was due, rather, to circumstances existing at the time of their separation.

In the instant case both plaintiff and defendant alleged grounds for divorce, in addition to the invalidity of their marriage in 1927. During the seven-year period they lived together plaintiff rendered services for defendant, which, in view of the court's finding, we must assume exceeded by $1,250 the value of the maintenance and support supplied her by defendant.... To the extent that the value of plaintiff's services exceeded the value of the maintenance provided her, she has not received consideration therefor. She rendered these services in good faith under the belief that she was the wife of defendant, and in expectation of the continuing benefits of that status. If these continuing benefits were cut off, not because of the original invalidity of the marriage, but because the de facto husband committed acts of cruelty which if the marriage had been valid would constitute cause for divorce, we are of the view that the putative wife was entitled to be paid in so far as her services exceeded in value the support provided by her supposed husband.

...

It cannot be held that the court was without right to decree a lien for the amount of $1,250 awarded plaintiff on the San Francisco real property of defendant. Under section 140, Civil Code, the award of alimony in divorce actions may be decreed a lien on separate property of the husband.... There are no statutory provisions concerning the property rights of a putative wife. The judgment in the instant case is not for the division of joint property accumulated during the putative marriage, but for a sum found due plaintiff from defendant. Whether in a particular case a lien should be granted the putative wife is a matter to be determined by the trial court. Since the evidence is not before us, it cannot be held that the court below abused its discretion.

...The portion of the judgment appealed from by defendant is affirmed.

LAZZAREVICH v. LAZZAREVICH
California District Court of Appeal
88 Cal. App. 2d 708, 200 P.2d 49 (1948)

VALLEE, Justice.

Two appeals are pending in this nonjury case from a judgment rendered in favor of plaintiff in the sum of $2,350. Plaintiff appeals upon the judgment-roll. Defendant appeals upon a Settled Statement pursuant to rule 7(b), Rules on Appeal.

Plaintiff commenced the action on August 14, 1946. The first cause of action sought recovery of the reasonable value of work and services performed by plaintiff for defendant from July, 1935, to April, 1946, in maintaining a home for defendant and their son, "cooking for him, washing defendant's clothes, and performing the entire household services for defendant," during all of which period she "believed that she was the legal wife of defendant." The second cause of action sought recover of contributions made by plaintiff to the household expenses from January 17, 1943 to June 13, 1945, consisting of earnings received by plaintiff while employed in a defense plant and during the period she believed she was defendant's lawful wife. Defendant answered, denying generally all allegations of the complaint and alleging, as an affirmative defense, that the causes of action were barred by the statute of limitations. (Code Civ. Proc. §§337, 339.) He also alleged, as additional affirmative defenses, that the services rendered by plaintiff in his behalf were voluntarily rendered without any agreement or understanding that she would be compensated therefor; and that plaintiff had been fully compensated for all services rendered by her in his behalf.

The Settled Statement reveals the following facts: The parties were married in Los Angeles on March 18, 1921. One child, a daughter, was born, the issue of this marriage. Subsequently defendant (as plaintiff) filed an action for divorce in Los Angeles County. An interlocutory decree was granted the husband and entered on March 18, 1932. On September 6, 1933, without the husband's knowledge or request, his attorney had a final decree of divorce entered. Subsequent to the entry of the interlocutory decree and several months prior to the entering of the final decree, and thereafter, defendant continually sought a reconciliation with his wife. They became reconciled in July of 1935. Both parties testified that before the reconciliation occurred defendant informed plaintiff that no final decree had been entered. Defendant testified that he so believed and so informed plaintiff. The parties then took a trip to Reno, Nevada, the Pacific Northwest, and on their return stopped at Merced, California. While there, defendant made inquiry of the county clerk concerning the remarriage of the parties. He was informed that since no final decree had been entered in the divorce action no remarriage was necessary. This information defendant imparted to plaintiff. Thereafter, on April 23, 1936, a son was born to the parties. As an aftermath of domestic difficulties which arose between them, plaintiff, on August 1, 1945, consulted her attorney about a divorce. On August 10, 1945, she was informed by them that the court records disclosed the entry of a final decree of divorce on September 6, 1933. Plaintiff testified that she would not have lived with defendant if she had not believed that she was his wife. The parties remained separated from August 1, 1945, until October 1, 1945, when the plaintiff, upon the promise of defendant that he would remarry her if she would return to him, again became reconciled. They again separated on April 1, 1946. From July, 1935 on, defendant owned a half interest, as a partner, in Economy Plumbing Company. During the periods from July, 1935, to August, 1945, and from October, 1945, to April, 1946, plaintiff performed the usual household duties of a wife, excepting that during the period from January 17, 1943, until June 13, 1945, she worked in a defense plant. During this latter period she did not render to defendant the same amount of household services as she had when she was not employed, but during this period she contributed all of her salary, $172.50 a month, to the household expenses. It was agreed between the parties that plaintiff would contribute her salary to the living expenses and the money saved by defendant thereby would be put into War Bonds for their mutual benefit....

...The court concluded that: (1) plaintiff was entitled to recover the reasonable value of the services rendered for defendant during the period she lived with him under the mistaken belief that she was still married to him and for contributions made to him within that period, except that recovery for services rendered and for contributions made prior to August 14, 1944, was barred by the statute of limitations (Code Civ. Proc. §339, subd. 1); (2) plaintiff was entitled to a judgment in the amount of $625, being at the rate of $50 per month for a period of seven and one-half months between August 14, 1944, and April 1, 1946, and at the rate of $25 per month for a period of ten months within said period; (3) plaintiff was entitled to judgment in the sum of $1,725 for contributions made by her to defendant for a period of ten months between August 14, 1944, and April 1, 1946.

Upon his appeal defendant contends that the plaintiff is not entitled to a judgment for the value of her services or for contributions because she has received one-half of all the property acquired by the parties after their reconciliation and that he, therefore, has not been unjustly enriched. This contention is not tenable.

...

In view of the findings, which are not challenged here, that material misrepresentations as to the marital status of the parties were made by the defendant, we think the present case falls squarely within the principles set forth in section 40 of the Restatement of the Law of Restitution. This section reads in part: "A person who has rendered services to another...is entitled to restitution therefor if the services were rendered...(a) because of the fraud or material misrepresentation of the other..." In comment b the following appears:

> The rule stated in this Clause [(a)] is applicable both where the services are obtained by a consciously false statement and where they are the result of an innocent but material misstatement. The fact that the one rendering the services does not expect to be compensated therefor or otherwise to receive benefit is immaterial.... Where domestic services are rendered to a supposed spouse because of an innocent misrepresentation of marital status, the one rendering the services has the burden of proving that the services are of greater value than the benefits received.

...

The present action is one in *quantum meruit* seeking the recovery of the value of services rendered and contributions advanced by plaintiff during the putative marriage. The action is not one seeking an equitable division of whatever property, if any, may have been acquired by the parties during that period. The issue concerning an equitable division of the property was not presented by the pleadings or the evidence. While it is true, as defendant points out, that the Settled Statement shows there was some evidence that two parcels of real property acquired during this period now stand in the names of the parties jointly, there is nothing in the record before us to indicate the value of the property or the source or amount of the funds used to acquire the property. No attempt was made by defendant to go behind the joint tenancy and establish that it was the intention of the parties to hold the property as community property irrespective of the terms of the joint tenancy deed, (*Siberell v. Siberell*, 214 Cal. 767, 7 P.2d 1003; *Cummins v. Cummins*, 7 Cal.App.2d 294, 304, 46 P.2d 284), or that plaintiff received her interest in the joint tenancy property in compensation for services rendered, or that plaintiff did not acquire that interest by gift, or by devise, or from her own funds. In the absence of evidence that the property was acquired with community funds with the intention that it should remain community property, the joint tenancy stands as such, — the interest of each party being separate property. *Siberell v. Siberell, supra*; *Tomaier v. Tomaier*, 23 Cal.2d 754, 146 P.2d 905. The record before us is devoid of evidence indicating the amount of defendant's earnings during the period of the de facto marriage or the amount in his bank account. The meager evidence appearing in the Settled Statement, contrary to defendant's contention, reveals that there was little, if any, community property existing at the time the action was filed, defendant testifying that at the time of the trial he had less than $1,000. There is no evidence which would have warranted the trial court in finding that the services rendered by plaintiff prior to August 10, 1945, were voluntarily rendered without any agreement or understanding that she would be compensated therefor, or that she had been fully compensated therefor, or that she has received one-half of all the property acquired by the parties after their reconciliation in July, 1935. The trial court did not err in rendering judgment in favor of plaintiff for services rendered and for contributions advanced by her prior to August 10, 1945.

A different result must obtain as to services performed by plaintiff after August 10, 1945. As we have noted, the parties separated on August 1, 1945. On August 10, 1945, plaintiff discovered that the final decree of divorce had been entered on September 6, 1933. On October 1, 1945, she went to live with defendant and continued to do so until April 1, 1946. The essence of the right of a putative wife to recover for services rendered the putative husband is her belief in the validity of a marriage between them. After August 10, 1945, plaintiff was no longer an innocent, deluded, putative wife. She no longer believed that she was defendant's wife. She knew that she was not. The relationship between the parties was meretricious after October 1, 1945. Plaintiff was fully aware of the nature of the relationship. The fact that she returned to defendant upon his promise to remarry her is of no import. The "[e]quitable considerations arising from the reasonable expectation of the continuation of benefits attending the status of marriage entered into in good faith" which had existed prior to August 10, 1945, did not exist thereafter. *Vallera v. Vallera*, 21 Cal.2d 681, 685, 134 P.2d 761, 763. In the absence of an express agreement that plaintiff would be compensated for services performed after that date she has no right to compensation therefor....

The only point made by plaintiff on her appeal is that the court erred in concluding that she was barred by the statute of limitations from recovery for services rendered and advances made by her to defendant prior to "a date two years prior to the date of the commencement of her action." She argues that she should have judgment "for the reasonable value of all of the services rendered by her for respondent during the full period of 126 months, based upon the value of such services as found by the trial court, and for all of the advances made by appellant to respondent at the rate of $172.50 per month for a period of twenty-nine months"; that the statute of limitations did not begin to run until the cause of action accrued (Code Civ. Proc. §312), and that the action did not accrue until August 10, 1945, on which date she discovered that she was not legally married to defendant. The point is good.

...

The statute of limitations begins to run on a cause of action based on an implied or quasi-contract when the cause of action accrues, and depends largely on the facts of each particular case.... In commenting on *Cooper v. Cooper*, 147 Mass. 370, 17 N.E. 892, 9 Am.St.Rep. 721,...at pages 324 and 325 of Keener on Quasi Contracts, the learned author says:

> Had the plaintiff in this case surrendered to the defendant money or other chattels to which the defendant asserted a right because of his marital rights as husband, it does not seem possible that a court would hold that, because of the loss of the right to sue in tort by the death of the intestate, no claim could be asserted against his estate for the value so received by him. And yet in point of principle it is submitted that it is impossible to distinguish between the receipt of money or other property by the defendant and the receipt of services. The plaintiff whether she conferred a benefit on the intestate by rendering services, or by delivering to him money or other personal property, in either case parted with a right in rem under a mistaken supposition, induced by the fraud of the defendant, that the defendant was entitled thereto.

And

> whatever power, therefore, courts of equity possess to prevent and remove the consequences of fraud, they also possess in dealing with the effects of mistake. Pom. Eq. Juris. (4th Ed.) vol. 11, pp. 1782, 1783. *Fung Dai Kim Ah Leong v. Lau Ah Leong*, 9 Cir., 27 F.2d 582, 585.

...

Since the contributions made and advanced by the plaintiff and the services for which she seeks recovery prior to August 10, 1945, were rendered by her under the mistaken belief that the marriage had not been dissolved, it is obvious that her cause of action for services rendered and contributions advanced could not accrue until she discovered that the marriage had been dissolved. In a situation such as this, the law not only implies a promise to pay, but must, of necessity, imply a promise to pay at the termination of the services, occurring at the time of discovery of the fact that the marriage had been dissolved, which, in the instant case, occurred on August 10, 1945. While factually dissimilar, we believe this case falls within the principle announced in those cases holding that where there is an express or implied promise to pay on the termination of the services, the cause of action does not arise until the termination of the services and the statute of limitations does not bar any part of the period of continuous services....

The court found that plaintiff during a period of 126 months, from July 31, 1935, until April 1, 1946, performed work and services for defendant. The court also found that the reasonable value of the services performed during the period of 126 months was $50 a month for ninety-seven months and $25 a month for twenty-nine months. Plaintiff performed the services for which she is entitled to recover for 120 months prior to August 10, 1945, the date she discovered that the final decree of divorce had been entered September 6, 1933. As we hold that plaintiff is not entitled to recover for six months after August 10, 1945, for which the court found that the reasonable value of the services was $50 a month, the number of months that she performed services of the reasonable value for $50 a month is ninety-one months. Under the findings, plaintiff is entitled to recover the sum of $10,277.50 from defendant, as follows: For services rendered, $5,275.00, being ninety-one months at $50.00 a month and twenty-nine months at $25.00 a month; for contributions, $5,002.50, being twenty-nine months at $172.50.

The judgment is modified by striking therefrom the figures "$2350.00," and inserting in lieu thereof the figures "$10,277.50." As so modified, the judgment is affirmed, plaintiff to recover costs of appeal.

COMMENTS

Sousa, Sanguinetti, and *Lazzarevich* were cited as precedents in *Marvin v. Marvin* which appears at page 214 and thus are recognized as stepping-stones toward contract cohabitation and theories of equitable relief. In these three cases, the women believed in good faith that they were married, although in fact they were not. In *Marvin* there was cohabitation with some of the appearances of marriage, but no corresponding marital intent of the parties. Thus the cases come from opposite sides. *Sousa* shows the clearest case of good faith: an American woman having married an immigrant from the Portuguese Azores, relying on a California divorce he had secured from his wife who had stayed behind. The court's apparent confusion whether the divorce was obtained in 1916 or 1919 is probably based on a 1916 interlocutory divorce with no final decree entered until 1919. Although the court did not expressly state that the husband had committed fraud, the facts appear reasonably clear in this regard. Yet, the problem might also be the fault of the husband's first divorce lawyer: it may never have occurred to him to ask his client if he had previously used a different name and he may have simply assumed the first wife's last name was the same as her husband's. In 1916 the concept of divorce was so unknown in the Portuguese Azores that it is hard to imagine that proper notice to the first wife would have made any difference. The question before the court was whether the property after his death should be split equally between the two "wives" or whether the American wife, although her marriage of forty-three years proved to be void, was entitled to a larger share.

The court, applying partnership language to the void marriage, came to the conclusion that the good faith American wife was in any event entitled to half of the accumulated property as a partner, which means that only the remaining half was part of the estate and as such was to be split. Although the court talks in terms of a continuing Portuguese marriage, the opinion in effect gave greater rights, namely three fourths of the estate, to the American woman. As in many California cases dealing with conceptions of community property, *Sousa* is of potential interest to the rest of the nation. The same mathematics could be applied if marriage itself is viewed as partnership. A wife as "partner" could equally claim her own interest in the partnership, plus half of the remaining interest of the husband's estate. In other words, California cases can conceivably be used as precedents in non-community-property states, if the facts justify an argument based on partnership in jointly operated small businesses, for example.

While in *Sousa* the putative wife was treated as an entrepreneur who was primarily compensated by the profits from the joint venture, the women in *Sanguinetti* and *Lazzarevich* appeared to be in the role of domestic servants who, in the absence of a valid marital contract, could only be compensated under theories of unjust enrichment. In both instances it is probable that negligence of the attorneys brought about, or at least contributed to, the mistaken belief that a valid marriage existed. The duty is clearly upon the attorney, in any jurisdiction, to clarify with the parties what steps are necessary to secure a divorce and at what point they are free to remarry. *Lazzarevich* is a blatant case of insufficient communication between attorney and client, which today would be subject to a malpractice claim. Had California been a common law marriage jurisdiction the continued cohabitation of the parties, who did not realize that their divorce had become final, would have constituted a valid, new marriage. There is a further disturbing point about these cases, which is common to many cases dealing with marriage and divorce. The facts may have taken on an artificial clarity, due in the last analysis to the language the lawyers used in their pleadings. Had the lawyers in interviews with their clients been fully open to complexity rather than searching for clarity, the lawyers' presentation of the facts might have left room for presumptions. On the other hand, in all three cases relatively fixed legal consequences may have been dictated by the access to divorce records. Official documentary evidence may have precluded any possibility of doubt.

REFERENCE

Walter O. Weyrauch, *Informal and Formal Marriage — An Appraisal of Trends in Family Organization*, 28 U. CHI. L. REV. 88 (1960).

Marriage by Estoppel

EDGAR v. RICHARDSON
Supreme Court Commission of Ohio
33 Ohio St. 581 (1878)

ERROR to the District Court of Wood county.

The original action was brought in the Court of Common Pleas of Wood county, in 1866, by the plaintiff, William Edgar, to recover of the defendant, Fidelia Richardson, forty acres of land in her possession. The plaintiff averred, in his petition, that he was the owner of the land and entitled to its possession. The defendant answered, averring that her name is Fidelia Edgar, and denied the averments of the petition. At the trial a jury was waived, and the case was tried to the court which found the issues for the defendant, and rendered judgment in her favor....

The case, as disclosed by the bill of exceptions, is substantially, as follows: Both parties claim title under John Edgar who died childless and intestate. His title to the land was such that, under the statute, it descended to the wife, relict of the intestate. In 1841, he was married to Sarah Ann Dubbs, who survived him and conveyed the land to the plaintiff; this constitutes the plaintiff's title to the land.

To defeat this title, the defendant relies on the following facts: After the marriage of Edgar and Sarah Ann, they lived together about fourteen years, when Edgar took up his residence on the land in question, in Wood county; but his wife refused to live with him, and after about a year, applied in Lucas county for a divorce. Edgar opposed the divorce, and she was defeated. She then went away and remained for about three years, when she returned to her father's house, in the neighborhood of her husband, in Wood county, and said to her relatives and acquaintances that during her absence she had obtained a divorce, but then, and ever afterward, refused to tell where she was during that time. Edgar continued to reside on his farm, and Sarah Ann, soon after her return, made Toledo her place of residence, where she stated and caused it to be believed that she had obtained a divorce from John Edgar. After waiting a few years, Edgar desired to marry if he could be made certain that a divorce between him and Sarah Ann had been obtained. Accordingly, Edgar sent the father of Sarah Ann to Toledo to ascertain from her the truth about her having obtained a divorce. She assured her father that she went away and did not let Edgar know where she was, so that she could obtain a divorce from him, and did obtain a divorce, and showed him some papers to confirm it; and, on being told that Edgar desired to marry again, she said that she wished he would marry again. Soon after this occurred, Edgar communicated what he had done and the information obtained to Fidelia Richardson; thereupon, on the 28th day of May, 1862, he and Fidelia were married, and lived together as husband and wife until his death in 1866. About the same time that Edgar married Fidelia, Sarah Ann married one McKessick, with whom she has ever since lived as her husband. The plaintiff excepted to the admission of the evidence proving the statements of Sarah Ann about her having obtained a divorce from John Edgar.

To rebut the evidence introduced by the defendant, of the admissions of Sarah Ann that she had procured a divorce from Edgar, the plaintiff gave in evidence the deposition of Sarah Ann McKessick that she married John Edgar in 1841, and never was divorced from him.

. . .

DAY, J.

The errors assigned present two questions: 1. Did the court err in permitting the defendant to prove admissions of the grantor to the plaintiff, that she and her husband, John Edgar, were divorced; 2. If not, is the judgment unsustained by the law and the evidence.

1. The plaintiff sought to establish his title to the land in dispute through a deed to him from Sarah Ann Edgar; he was, therefore, in privity of estate with her; and, for that reason, her admissions before the conveyance, which would have been admissible against her had she been plaintiff in the action, were admissible against him. 1 Greenl. Ev., §189.

He could recover only upon the strength of her title, which depended solely upon her being the wife relict of John Edgar, deceased. To establish that fact, the plaintiff proved that Sarah Ann married Edgar in 1841, and that he died in 1846 without issue. The plaintiff rested on the presumption that she continued to be the wife of Edgar until his death. To rebut this presumption, the defendant was permitted to prove, by said Sarah Ann's admissions during the time she claimed to be Edgar's wife, that she had procured a divorce.

This evidence was objected to, on the ground that a divorce is a matter of record and cannot be proved by secondary evidence. This objection loses much of its force from the fact that the person who made the admissions, and whose interests were affected thereby, refused to disclose where the record could be obtained, thus putting it out of the power of the defendant to prove the alleged divorce by the record if it existed; therefore, the admissions of Sarah Ann, were, by reason of this concealment, the best evidence attainable by the defendant.

But admissions of a party relating to the contents of written instruments, in general, are not regarded as secondary evidence, and though they relate to a record, if the place where it can be obtained be concealed by the party, they should form no exception to the rule.

. . .

There was, then, no error in admitting the evidence of the admissions of Sarah Ann, the grantor of the plaintiff, made during her alleged coverture, tending to show that she was not the wife relict of John Edgar, deceased.

2. The remaining question arises upon the overruling of the motion for a new trial. The ground of the motion was, that the judgment was against the law and the evidence.

The plaintiff made a *prima facie* case, entitling him to recover. If, therefore, the judgment in favor of the defendant can be sustained at all, it must be upon the ground that the evidence was such as to warrant the court in holding, either that Sarah Ann was in law estopped from denying her declarations, that she was divorced from her husband, John Edgar, or that she had in fact obtained such divorce.

The court made no special finding of facts from the evidence; therefore, in looking to the evidence, we must, as a reviewing court, assume, in support of the judgment, the facts to be what the evidence would finally warrant the court to find as the facts of the case.

It is clear that Sarah Ann undertook, and intended to induce the belief, in whatever neighborhood she resided, that, during her absence of three years in parts unknown, she had obtained a divorce. It is also quite clear, that, after waiting in doubt about the matter for five years, John Edgar, desiring to marry again, if he might lawfully do so, sent her father to learn from her what he might rely upon as the truth about her having obtained a divorce; that she sent back to him assurances of having obtained a divorce; and that she intended to induce him to believe it, knowing that he might, in reliance on such belief, materially change his condition. The evidence further leaves the strong impression that both Edgar and Fidelia Richardson believed, and upon the faith of Sarah Ann's declarations consummated their marriage.

It is true that Sarah Ann had no direct communication with Fidelia; but she undoubtedly intended that her assurances of a divorce sent to Edgar should be communicated, as they in fact were, to the woman he desired to marry. The very object of such assurances was to induce his marriage; and, from the nature of the transaction, it must have been equally her intention that another should be influenced thereby.

Though Sarah Ann did not directly bring about the marriage of Edgar and Fidelia, the court was warranted in finding, from the evidence, that she induced them to believe that, as against any marital right of her's, they might lawfully marry.

Having acted upon her assurances, and in accordance with her expressed wishes, a strong case was made, which, but for reasons not affecting the substantial justice of the case, called for the application, as against her, of the principles of the law which would estop her from denying the truth of her declarations.

But, conceding that the declarations of Sarah Ann do not strictly rise to the degree of an estoppel, or cannot be regarded as conclusive, still the question remains, whether the court was clearly unwarranted in finding, from the evidence, that Sarah Ann had been divorced. This question is left to be determined solely upon her own acts and declarations during the alleged coverture, and her testimony in the case. But the point for our determination, as a reviewing court, arising upon this state of the case is, not whether such divorce had in fact been obtained, but whether a finding by the court below that it had, would be clearly unwarranted by the evidence.

In support of a finding that the divorce had been obtained, there are the declarations of Sarah Ann, strenuously persisted in during a series of years, that it had been obtained. These declarations are corroborated by undisputed facts. She tried to get a divorce with the knowledge of Edgar; after she was defeated by him, she went to parts unknown, avowedly for the purpose of getting a divorce; she was absent during a period sufficiently long to get it; she exhibited to her father papers to show that she had; she induced her husband to marry again; she married again herself. If not divorced, she knowingly was instrumental in bringing herself and her husband into a state of bigamy, and two other persons into that of adultery. Surely, since she concealed the place where the divorce was obtained, a stronger case to establish a divorce, as against her, could not be made. But now, to establish her heirship to the property of the decedent, she has, in a distant state, given her deposition that she never obtained a divorce. In the light of the evidence in the case, her testimony in a matter affecting her own interest cannot be regarded as conclusive.

Her declarations may not rise to the degree of an estoppel against her to deny the truth of her declarations. Nor was the court below estopped from regarding her declarations, supported by the corresponding acts of her life for many years, as more convincing than her testimony now given to win the estate left by the husband she deserted, and, if her declarations be not true, had fraudulently led into the belief that, as against any marital claim of her's, he might safely die intestate. We can not say that manifestly the court would not be warranted in finding in accordance with her declarations, corroborated by the acts of her life. Clearly such a finding would be supported by evidence — evidence, too, the truth of which Sarah Ann can not deny without impeaching her own credibility, and can deny only for the purpose of obtaining what, in justice, should be denied to her.

Since, then, the court of common pleas would not be clearly unwarranted in finding, from the evidence, a state of fact that would in law sustain its judgment in favor of the defendant, the judgment of the district court affirming that of the common pleas must be affirmed.

Judgment affirmed.

MASON v. MASON

District Court of Appeal of Florida
174 So.2d 620 (Fla. Dist. Ct. App. 1965)

PER CURIAM.

We adopt that portion of the opinion of the chancellor which is quoted below as the opinion of this court.

> THIS CAUSE came on to be heard on the Complaint of Plaintiff, LUCY DAVIS MASON, for Declaratory Relief, the Answer, Counterclaim and Cross-Claim of Defendant, SALLY MASON, the Answer to Counterclaim by Plaintiff, and the Answer of MARTIN W. GARY, Administrator Ad Litem of the Estate of WEARY M. MASON, deceased to Defendant's Cross-Claim, and the amendment to Answer of Defendant, SALLY MASON, and the Court having heard the testimony of the Parties and considered the evidence, the Court finds as follows:
>
> 1. That LUCY DAVIS MASON was married to the late WEARY M. MASON, on the 9th day of April, 1922, at Reddick, Florida; that a divorce suit was filed by WEARY M. MASON in the Circuit Court for Marion County, Florida, (Chancery No. 10936) against Plaintiff, but no Final Decree of Divorce was ever entered therein; that the marriage of Plaintiff to the said WEARY M. MASON was never dissolved by a Decree of Divorce prior to the death of the said WEARY M. MASON on or about February 3, 1962.
>
> 2. That Defendant SALLY MASON entered into a marriage with WEARY M. MASON during his lifetime on or about March 10, 1942, at Dade City, Florida in the innocent belief that the said MASON was a single man; that thereafter, said Defendant lived with the said MASON as his wife until his death on or about February 3, 1962.
>
> 3. That Plaintiff knew of the marriage of the late WEARY M. MASON to Defendant SALLY MASON, and that they were living together as husband and wife in Miami, Florida; that, notwithstanding said knowledge, Plaintiff

> asserted no rights or claims under her marriage to the late WEARY M. MASON during his lifetime.
>
> 4. That during the purported marriage of Defendant and the said MASON, the Defendant and the said MASON acquired the following properties in the names of the said MASON and Defendant as husband and wife, which were still so held at the time of the death of said MASON....
>
> ...
>
> 5. That the funds for the purchase and payment of said properties were contributed by the late WEARY M. MASON and Defendant, the Defendant having contributed substantial amounts from her own funds therefor, as well as having paid substantial sums from her own funds for improvements to the properties during the lifetime of the said MASON and since his death.
>
> ...
>
> [T]he late WEARY M. MASON led the Defendant, SALLY MASON, to enter into a marriage contract with him on March 10, 1942, to live with him and care for him, and to the taking of title to the above-described properties in their names as husband and wife, believing that they were in fact and in law husband and wife, and the said WEARY M. MASON was at the time of said marriage, at the time of the purchase of the properties above-described and at all times during his lifetime estopped to deny the validity of his marriage to the Defendant, and estopped to deny the right of said Defendant to take title to said properties by survivorship, which such estoppel is binding upon the Plaintiff as the heir-at-law of the said WEARY M. MASON.
>
> [B]y reason of the aforesaid estoppel, the titles to the above-described properties are declared vested in Defendant SALLY MASON....

See *Alexander v. Colston*, Fla.1953, 66 So.2d 673.

Affirmed.

WARNER v. WARNER

Supreme Court of Idaho

76 Idaho 399, 283 P.2d 931 (1955)

TAYLOR, Chief Justice.

The parties were married in November, 1947, and divorced in February, 1948; married again in November, 1948, and again divorced June 5, 1950. During the course of this second marriage they adopted a boy, who at the time of the trial herein was five years of age. By the decree of June 5, 1950, custody was awarded to the mother (appellant) and the father (respondent) was ordered to pay $20 per month for child support.

Shortly after this divorce, plaintiff moved to California and later married one Crim, who obtained a divorce from her in June, 1951. In the early spring of 1951, while plaintiff was married to Crim, defendant went to California and "I primarily looked her up to see Spence [the child], but, as all things happen, we became affiliated." He spent two or three weeks with the plaintiff on that occasion. She told him she would divorce Crim and return to Idaho. In August, 1951, she came back to Idaho and entered the employ of the defendant in a club which he had opened in American Falls. This club was closed in October. Whereupon, plaintiff took up residence with the defendant at the South Fork Lodge in Swan Valley. During the winter of '51–'52 they lived as man and wife in North Hollywood, California, defendant during that time being employed by Lockheed. In April, 1952, they separated and defendant returned to Idaho. In December, 1952, plaintiff married one McCarley in Ely, Nevada.

In March, 1953, defendant again went to Los Angeles to see the plaintiff. Concerning this visit he testified:

> I spent several weeks with her again as a family. When she wasn't at my place, I was at her place.... I asked her to come back to Idaho and try it again, that I thought we still had enough between us to warrant one more attempt.

She agreed and in April, 1953, they returned to the South Fork Lodge in Swan Valley, where they thereafter continuously lived together as husband and wife until this action was commenced in August, 1954. During this time they held themselves out to the public as husband and wife and introduced each other, and publicly referred to each other, as such. Plaintiff testified that before they returned from California she asked defendant to help her to get a divorce from McCarley; that defendant promised her if she would come back to him he would marry her; he would be kind to her and the boy and not beat her anymore; that he would share with her the property he then owned and any property thereafter acquired; that relying upon these promises she returned and lived with him as his wife; that he was good to her about a month after their return, but thereafter pursued his previous course of cruelty, slapping her and striking her with his fist; that on several occasions she asked him to enter into a ceremonial marriage and that "if I ever mentioned it he got mad, and usually slapped me around." As to the occasion which caused the final separation, she testified:

> Well, he — the last time he hit me he hit me in the head, and I couldn't hardly eat, or open my mouth, and he laughed and thought it was real funny, but it wasn't, and I decided that I am getting too old to take those beatings any longer, I can't take them.
>
> It knocked me down the last time he hit me. He hit me right here on the side of the head (Indicating). I had pains for about two months. I was even afraid he had injured me some way.

She did not leave immediately on this occasion, testifying:

> I thought I would wait and when he wasn't there and leave, I didn't want to get — He threatened to have — to beat me to where I wouldn't look presentable if I ever left, and I didn't — want to take that chance.

About a month later, while he was on a hunting trip, she left the home and commenced these proceedings. The court required the defendant to pay an attorney's fee of $150 and $75 for support of plaintiff pending the action.

About three weeks before the trial, having 'phoned plaintiff's father that he had come to see the child, the defendant went to the home of her parents in Twin Falls, Idaho, where plaintiff was then living. The plaintiff took the child out to meet him in the street rather than risk a disturbance in the house. Concerning this occasion she testified that he jerked her into his car, leaving the boy in the street, and drove down to his hotel and demanded that she go to his room to sign a paper. Upon her refusal, he said:

> All right, then, you take your choice, either I'll take you out in the country and beat the hell out of you, or you go in and do it.

Fearing him, she went to the room. As to what there occurred, she said:

> He wanted me to sign — write a letter and sign it calling this all off, and telling a bunch of — telling that it was a bunch of lies and everything, and I told him he could kill me first, so he just about did. He beat me up, and then left me in the hotel room with no money. I started down the street with my clothes half off, and some friend took me home. I was hysterical.
>
> ...[W]hen I finally got home they had to take me to the doctor, and I lost my voice for three days.

...

We also note as a part of this statement of facts that the defendant does not deny the beatings testified to by plaintiff.

The defendant testified that he did not know of the marriage to McCarley until after the parties had returned from California; that he had offered to help her to get a divorce in Idaho, but would not pay her expenses to California for that purpose. He denied any promise to share property with the plaintiff, and denied that he promised to marry her, and testified he did not consider her his wife. In conflict with this, he also testified:

> Q. Yes. And you — while you were there [California], and ever since, you have lived with her as husband and wife, haven't you?
>
> A. Yes, I believe it's been assumed by the public that we were man and wife.
>
> Q. Yes. And as a matter of fact, you held yourself out as man and wife since then, haven't you?
>
> A. I was proud to, yes.
>
> Q. Well, I am asking you if you haven't held yourself out as man and wife?
>
> A. Yes, I was proud to, yes.
>
> Q. ...So that when you testified a moment ago that her folks upon several times — "my wife has been taken from me several times by her folks," you considered Carmen as your wife, didn't you?
>
> A. Over a period of the last eight years, yes.
>
> Q. Yes, over a period of the last eight years you have considered her as your wife, that is correct, isn't it?
>
> A. When she wasn't, I have waited for her, I suppose.

...

The evidence is quite conclusive that these parties entered in to the relationship of marriage by mutual consent and by mutual assumption of marital rights, duties, and obligations, insofar as they were capable. The trial court made no contrary finding on this issue, but found that "plaintiff remains married" to McCarley and "that the parties are *in pari delicto* in this case." In its conclusions of law the court held:

> III. That plaintiff and defendant did not marry or become husband and wife under the common law on or about March 27, 1953, or at any time since because of plaintiff's incapacity to consent to such a marriage by reason of the plaintiff being, then and now, already married to one Olvis B. McCarley and that such a marriage would be illegal and void from the beginning.

It is apparent that the trial court based its judgment in this case entirely upon want of capacity in the plaintiff, not upon a lack of consent or mutual assumption of marital rights. The evidence as to the McCarley marriage consists of certified copy of the marriage certificate, and plaintiff's admission on the witness stand. Plaintiff testified that she believed that marriage had been dissolved "according to what I hear"; that she did not know where McCarley was; and that she did not think he knew where she was; and that she had not been served with process in any divorce proceedings by him. For aught that appears in this record that marriage could have been dissolved by action of McCarley either before these parties resumed marital relations in March, 1953, or during the time they lived together as husband and wife. If McCarley obtained a divorce before March, 1953, then there was no impediment to the marriage then agreed upon between these parties. If the impediment was removed during the period of their subsequent marital relationship, and they thereafter continued that relationship, then a common law marriage would result. *Huff v. Huff*, 20 Idaho 450, 118 P. 1080....

The evidence is wholly insufficient to show that the impediment to plaintiff's marriage was not removed by death or divorce. The record being silent on that question, the presumption of the validity of her marriage to defendant is not overcome.

...

> The presumption of marriage, from a cohabitation, apparently matrimonial, is one of the strongest presumptions known to the law. This is especially true in a case involving legitimacy. The law presumes morality, and not immorality; marriage, and not concubinage; legitimacy, and not bastardy. Where there is enough to create a foundation for the presumption of marriage, it can be repelled only by the most cogent and satisfactory evidence. *Hynes v. McDermott*, 91 N.Y. 451, at page 459, 43 Am.Rep. 677...

...

The case of *Thomey v. Thomey*, 67 Idaho 393, 181 P.2d 777, is in some respects parallel to this. There the parties entered into a common law marriage relationship, knowing that the plaintiff had a husband living. The defendant assured her that it "did not matter, that she could get a divorce later, and that whatever property was accumulated would belong jointly" to them. The parties lived together in such relationship for four years, at which time the wife procured a divorce from her first husband, after which they continued their relationship for nine years, without any marriage ceremony. The court held a common law marriage resulted. In that case the trial court concluded the defendant was estopped to deny the existence and validity of his marriage to the plaintiff, and its judgment was upheld by this court.

Here we think the defendant by his conduct is estopped to deny the validity of his marriage to plaintiff. It is evident that he wanted her to live with him as his wife. While the evidence is conflicting as to what, if any, promises he made to induce her to return, it is quite evident that he did persuade her to come back, and that his present denial of the marital relationship, and of any promise to share property, is actuated by his desire to deprive her of her property rights. It is also reasonable to conclude that she would not have returned without some inducement offered by him.... This conclusion of estoppel is further strengthened by defendant's conduct in living with the plaintiff as her husband after her divorce from Crim from about August, 1951, until April, 1952. Had it been in his interest to do so, he might have claimed a common law marriage arising out of this relationship as an impediment invalidating plaintiff's subsequent marriage to McCarley.

The fact that the relationship of the parties may have been meretricious in the beginning, or that they may have been in pari delicto, does not defeat her rights in the property accumulated during such relationship. A court of equity will protect the property rights of the parties in such cases, either according to their agreement in respect to property, or according to principles of equity and justice....

We conclude that the parties are husband and wife and that the plaintiff is entitled to a decree of divorce on the ground of extreme cruelty.

...

The judgment is reversed and the cause remanded with directions to enter judgment in conformity herewith.

COMMENTS

Marriage by estoppel belongs to the realm of legal fictions. The parties are treated as if they were married. The statement implies that in reality they are not. Sometimes, as in *Mason,* the party estopped with respect to one person to assert that no marriage exists may be legally married to another person. The application of estoppel to marriage may therefore lead to situations in which a husband appears to be married to two wives, or a wife to two husbands. In *Mason* the husband continued to be legally married to wife no. 1 while, according to the court's reasoning, he was estopped toward wife no. 2, who consequently could claim all rights as a widow. The *Mason* court also estopped wife no. 1 because she did not step forward to assert her rights from the marriage. In effect this means that wife no. 1 had an affirmative duty toward wife no. 2 to inform her that there never was a final divorce.

Mason invites speculation about the nature of estoppel. Assume, for example, that the husband had still been alive. Both he and wife no. 1 could have asked for a divorce, assuming other requirements were met, because they continued to be legally married to each other. On the other hand, neither he nor wife no. 2 could have obtained a divorce because they were in fact not married to one another. Wife no. 2 could ask for an annulment of marriage because of bigamy. The husband might be allowed to obtain an annulment because of the public interest in a clarification of status, but a number of jurisdictions would deny the husband the right to an annulment action because of his bad faith. It is questionable whether the husband would be estopped from raising the lack of marital status in the divorce action itself, although in regard to the economic consequences of marriage the estoppel theory would likely work in favor of wife no. 2. Both wife no. 1 and wife no. 2 would probably be entitled to support under theories of marriage and estoppel.

On the whole, estoppel seems to affect financial matters far more than it affects actual marital status. From that standpoint, talk about marriage by estoppel is a misnomer. Yet in actual litigation the lines are blurred, as for example in *Edgar* and *Warner.* In these cases marriage by estoppel and marriage by presumption are commingled, although conceptually this does not seem to make sense. Marriage by presumption results in real marriage, while estoppel is a mere fiction of marriage which in fact does not exist. On the other hand, a presumption, if practically irrebuttable, becomes a legal fiction too. For instance, in *Edgar,* wife no. 1 was caught in her own lie and treated as if she had obtained a divorce. By somewhat circular reasoning, the court treated her earlier statements that she had obtained a divorce as if they were true. In presuming the validity of the later marriage, they essentially raised a presumption of divorce which wife no. 1 failed to overcome. If she had submitted a divorce decree, she would have failed because she would not then have been married. Had she admitted to having lied, she would have been estopped to assert her marriage toward the bona fide wife no. 2. The overriding concern seems to be an understanding that the more recent wife has better rights, especially if the cohabitation is of some length. The rights of an original wife are somewhat improved if she is in good faith and was not remiss in asserting herself.

Essentially, these cases demonstrate that legal fictions can bring about just results under the appearance of marriage, regardless of the absence of legal marriage. Note also the overlap between estoppel and implied contract of cohabitation. The misrepresentation leading to estoppel can sometimes be viewed as a promise, and the reliance on the misrepresentation can be characterized as an acceptance. There is an element of artificiality in these legal distinctions, and they can be used interchangeably, provided the functional relationship is seen. *Warner* mentions promises that were made by the husband; it also applies a presumption of marriage and states that the defendant is estopped to deny the validity of his marriage. It even mentions that there might be a real common law marriage that invalidates an intervening marriage. The mere promise implies that there might have been a contract, but not necessarily a marriage. The presumption is a real marriage until overcome by contrary evidence. The estoppel implies that there was no marriage, but that the defendant is treated as if there were one. The common law marriage is a real marriage. The court therefore applied four conceptually independent theories, two of them implying that there was a marriage and two that there was not. The outcome of these contradictory theories was identical. The wife was entitled to a property settlement on a theory of marriage or, quasi-marriage.

Recent writing on domestic violence often refers to it as a problem that was hidden until the 1970s or 1980s and tend to restrict discussions to the responses of tort and criminal laws to it. Yet, divorce cases are filled with stories such as the one in *Warner.* On one hand, many wonder why women keep returning to violent men; on the other hand, as in *Warner,* the women who try to leave seem to receive little or no protection from anyone against serious and repeated acts of violence from the men who find and "reclaim" them. These topics are dealt with further in Chapter 3.

REFERENCES

Walter O. Weyrauch, *Informal and Formal Marriage — An Appraisal of Trends in Family Organization,* 28 U. CHI. L. REV. 88 (1960).

Developments in the Law — Legal Responses to Domestic Violence, 106 HARV. L. REV. 1498 (1993).

C: NON-MARITAL COHABITATION

Trial Marriage, Substitute for Marriage, or Holdover Marriage

PECK v. PECK
Supreme Judicial Court of Massachusetts
155 Mass. 479, 30 N.E. 74 (1892)

LATHROP, J.

This is a libel for divorce on the ground of desertion, filed February 2, 1891. The justice of the superior court who heard the case found that no valid marriage was proved and ordered the libel to be dismissed. The case comes before us on a report of the evidence, from which it appears that on October 5, 1877, the parties, having for three years before had their domicile in the state of California, executed the following contract at Portland, Or., which was witnessed by two persons:

> We, the undersigned, hereby enter into a copartnership on the basis of the true marriage relation. Recognizing love as the only law which should govern the sexual relationship, we agree to continue this partnership so long as mutual affection shall exist, and to dissolve it when the union becomes disagreeable or undesirable to either party. We also agree that all property that shall be acquired by mutual effort shall be equally divided on the dissolution of said copartnership. Should any children result from this union, we pledge ourselves to be mutually held and bound to provide them support whether the union continues or is dissolved.

It is further found that the parties thereafterwards lived together under said contract, and held themselves out to be husband and wife in the state of Oregon, for about three months; in California for about one year; in Iowa, for about three and a half years; in New York, for about three months, and at Boston, in this commonwealth, from 1886 to the time of the alleged desertion, on or about January 15, 1888, and that both said parties have resided in this state from desertion to the day of the filing of the libel; that the libelee was a spiritualist public speaker, who, on account of peculiar religious and business motives, and by consent of the libelant, retained the name of Mrs. H. S. Lake, the name of her former husband, who died before the year 1877, and there never was any ceremony, act, or solemnization of marriage between them, save as herein stated. The report also sets out the laws relating to marriage of the states of California, Oregon, Iowa, and New York, but does not refer us to any decisions of the courts of those states construing the laws set forth.

There is nothing in the law of California, where the parties had their domicile, or in the law of Oregon, where the contract was signed, which recognizes an agreement to live together, "so long as mutual affection shall exist," as a marriage contract. We have, therefore, no occasion to consider whether, by the law of either of those states, there can be a marriage by a mere contract, without a ceremony. There being no marriage, their subsequent cohabitation points only to the illegal contract under which it began. There is no room for any presumptions. We find nothing in the laws of the states where they lived together which recognizes such a cohabitation as a marriage.... Decree affirmed.

MARVIN v. MARVIN [I]

Supreme Court of California

18 Cal. 3d 660, 557 P.2d 106, 134 Cal. Rptr. 815 (1976)

TOBRINER, Justice.

During the past 15 years, there has been a substantial increase in the number of couples living together without marrying.[1] Such nonmarital relationships lead to legal controversy when one partner dies or the couple separates. Courts of Appeal, faced with the task of determining property rights in such cases, have arrived at conflicting positions: two cases (*In re Marriage of Cary* (1973) 34 Cal.App.3d 345, 109 Cal.Rptr. 862; *Estate of Atherley* (1975) 44 Cal.App.3d 758, 119 Cal.Rptr. 41) have held that the Family Law Act (Civ.Code, s 4000 *et seq.*) requires division of the property according to community property principles, and one decision (*Beckman v. Mayhew* (1975) 49 Cal.App.3d 529, 122 Cal.Rptr. 604) has rejected that holding....

We conclude: (1) The provisions of the Family Law Act do not govern the distribution of property acquired during a nonmarital relationship; such a relationship remains subject solely to judicial decision. (2) The courts should enforce express contracts between nonmarital partners except to the extent that the contract is explicitly founded on the consideration of meretricious sexual services. (3) In the absence of an express contract, the courts should inquire into the conduct of the parties to determine whether that conduct demonstrates an implied contract, agreement of partnership or joint venture, or some other tacit understanding between the parties. The courts may also employ the doctrine of quantum meruit, or equitable remedies such as constructive or resulting trusts, when warranted by the facts of the case.

In the instant case plaintiff and defendant lived together for seven years without marrying; all property acquired during this period was taken in defendant's

1. "The 1970 census figures indicate that today perhaps eight times as many couples are living together without being married as cohabited ten years ago." (Comment, *In re Cary: A Judicial Recognition of Illicit Cohabitation* (1974) 25 HASTINGS L.J. 1228.)

name. When plaintiff sued to enforce a contract under which she was entitled to half the property and to support payments, the trial court granted judgment on the pleadings for defendant, thus leaving him with all property accumulated by the couple during their relationship. Since the trial court denied plaintiff a trial on the merits of her claim, its decision conflicts with the principles stated above, and must be reversed.

1. The Factual Setting of This Appeal

Since the trial court rendered judgment for defendant on the pleadings, we must accept the allegations of plaintiff's complaint as true, determining whether such allegations state, or can be amended to state, a cause of action....

Plaintiff avers that in October of 1964 she and defendant "entered into an oral agreement" that while "the parties lived together they would combine their efforts and earnings and would share equally any and all property accumulated as a result of their efforts whether individual or combined." Furthermore, they agreed to "hold themselves out to the general public as husband and wife" and that "plaintiff would further render her services as a companion, homemaker, housekeeper and cook to...defendant."

Shortly thereafter plaintiff agreed to "give up her lucrative career as an entertainer [and] singer" in order to "devote her full time to defendant...as a companion, homemaker, housekeeper and cook;" in return defendant agreed to "provide for all of plaintiff's financial support and needs for the rest of her life."

Plaintiff alleges that she lived with defendant from October of 1964 through May of 1970 and fulfilled her obligations under the agreement. During this period the parties as a result of their efforts and earnings acquired in defendant's name substantial real and personal property, including motion picture rights worth over $1 million. In May of 1970, however, defendant compelled plaintiff to leave his household. He continued to support plaintiff until November of 1971, but thereafter refused to provide further support.

On the basis of these allegations plaintiff asserts two causes of action. The first, for declaratory relief, asks the court to determine her contract and property rights; the second seeks to impose a constructive trust upon one half of the property acquired during the course of the relationship.

Defendant demurred unsuccessfully, and then answered the complaint. Following extensive discovery and pretrial proceedings, the case came to trial.[2] Defendant renewed his attack on the complaint by a motion to dismiss. Since the parties had stipulated that defendant's marriage to Betty Marvin did not terminate until the filing of a final decree of divorce in January 1967, the trial court treated defendant's motion as one for judgment on the pleadings augmented by the stipulation.

2. When the case was called for trial, plaintiff asked leave to file an amended complaint. The proposed complaint added two causes of action for breach of contract against Santa Ana Records, a corporation not a party to the action, asserting that Santa Ana was an alter ego of defendant. The court denied leave to amend, and plaintiff claims that the ruling was an abuse of discretion. We disagree; plaintiff's argument was properly rejected by the Court of Appeal in the portion of its opinion quoted below.

No error was committed in denial of plaintiff's motion, made on the opening day set for trial, seeking leave to file a proposed amended complaint which would have added two counts and a new defendant to the action. As stated by plaintiff's counsel at the hearing, "[T]here is no question about it that we seek to amend the Complaint not on the eve of trial but on the day of trial."

...

After hearing argument the court granted defendant's motion and entered judgment for defendant. Plaintiff moved to set aside the judgment and asked leave to amend her complaint to allege that she and defendant reaffirmed their agreement after defendant's divorce was final. The trial court denied plaintiff's motion, and she appealed from the judgment.

2. PLAINTIFF'S COMPLAINT STATES A CAUSE OF ACTION FOR BREACH OF AN EXPRESS CONTRACT

In *Trutalli v. Meraviglia* (1932) 215 Cal. 698, 12 P.2d 430 we established the principle that nonmarital partners may lawfully contract concerning the ownership of property acquired during the relationship. We reaffirmed this principle in *Vallera v. Vallera* (1943) 21 Cal.2d 681, 685, 134 P.2d 761, 763, stating that "If a man and woman (who are not married) live together as husband and wife under an agreement to pool their earnings and share equally in their joint accumulations, equity will protect the interests of each in such property."

In the case before us plaintiff, basing her cause of action in contract upon these precedents, maintains that the trial court erred in denying her a trial on the merits of her contention. Although that court did not specify the ground for its conclusion that plaintiff's contractual allegations stated no cause of action,[3] defendant offers some four theories to sustain the ruling; we proceed to examine them.

Defendant first and principally relies on the contention that the alleged contract is so closely related to the supposed "immoral" character of the relationship between plaintiff and himself that the enforcement of the contract would violate public policy.[4] He points to cases asserting that a contract between nonmarital partners is unenforceable if it is "involved in" an illicit relationship.... A review of the numerous California decisions concerning contracts between nonmarital partners, however, reveals that the courts have not employed such broad and uncertain standards to strike down contracts. The decisions instead disclose a narrower and more precise standard: a contract between nonmarital partners is unenforceable only to the extent that it explicitly rests upon the immoral and illicit consideration of meretricious sexual services.

...

Although the past decisions hover over the issue in the somewhat wispy form of the figures of a Chagall painting, we can abstract from those decisions a clear and simple rule. The fact that a man and woman live together without marriage,

3. The colloquy between court and counsel at argument of the motion for judgment on the pleadings suggests that the trial court held the 1964 agreement violated public policy because it derogated the community property rights of Betty Marvin, defendant's lawful wife. Plaintiff, however, offered to amend her complaint to allege that she and defendant reaffirmed their contract after defendant and Betty were divorced. The trial court denied leave to amend, a ruling which suggests that the court's judgment must rest upon some other ground than the assertion that the contract would injure Betty's property rights.

4. Defendant also contends that the contract was illegal because it contemplated a violation of former Penal Code section 269a, which prohibited living "in a state of cohabitation and adultery." (§269a was repealed by Stats.1975, ch. 71, eff. Jan. 1, 1976.) Defendant's standing to raise the issue is questionable because he alone was married and thus guilty of violating section 269a. Plaintiff, being unmarried could neither be convicted of adulterous cohabitation nor of aiding and abetting defendant's violation. (See *In re Cooper* (1912) 162 Cal. 81, 85–86, 121 P. 318.)

The numerous cases discussing the contractual rights of unmarried couples have drawn no distinction between illegal relationships and lawful nonmarital relationships. (Cf. *Weak v. Weak* (1962) 202 Cal.App.2d 632, 639, 21 Cal.Rptr. 9 (bigamous marriage).) Moreover, even if we were to draw such a distinction — a largely academic endeavor in view of the repeal of section 269a — defendant probably would not benefit; his relationship with plaintiff continued long after his divorce became final, and plaintiff sought to amend her complaint to assert that the parties reaffirmed their contract after the divorce.

and engage in a sexual relationship, does not in itself invalidate agreements between them relating to their earnings, property, or expenses. Neither is such an agreement invalid merely because the parties may have contemplated the creation or continuation of a nonmarital relationship when they entered into it. Agreements between nonmarital partners fail only to the extent that they rest upon a consideration of meretricious sexual services. Thus the rule asserted by defendant, that a contract fails if it is "involved in" or made "in contemplation" of a nonmarital relationship, cannot be reconciled with the decisions.

The three cases cited by defendant which have declined to enforce contracts between nonmarital partners involved consideration that was expressly founded upon an illicit sexual services. In *Hill v. Estate of Westbrook,* [95 Cal.App.2d 599, 213 P.2d 727], the woman promised to keep house for the man, to live with him as man and wife, and to bear his children; the man promised to provide for her in his will, but died without doing so. Reversing a judgment for the woman based on the reasonable value of her services, the Court of Appeal stated that

> the action is predicated upon a claim which seeks, among other things, the reasonable value of living with decedent in meretricious relationship and bearing him two children.... The law does not award compensation for living with a man as a concubine and bearing him children.... As the judgment is, at least in part, for the value of the claimed services for which recovery cannot be had, it must be reversed.

(95 Cal.App.2d at p. 603, 213 P.2d at p. 730.) Upon retrial, the trial court found that it could not sever the contract and place an independent value upon the legitimate services performed by claimant. We therefore affirmed a judgment for the estate. (*Hill v. Estate of Westbrook* (1952) 39 Cal.2d 458, 247 P.2d 19.)

In the only other cited decision refusing to enforce a contract, *Updeck v. Samuel* (1964), 123 Cal.App.2d 264, 266 P.2d 822, the contract "was based on the consideration that the parties live together as husband and wife." (123 Cal.App.2d at p. 267, 266 P.2d at p. 824.) Viewing the contract as calling for adultery, the court held it illegal.[6]

The decisions in the *Hill* and *Updeck* cases thus demonstrate that a contract between nonmarital partners, even if expressly made in contemplation of a common living arrangement, is invalid only if sexual acts form an inseparable part of the consideration for the agreement. In sum, a court will not enforce a contract for the pooling of property and earnings if it is explicitly and inseparably based upon services as a paramour. The Court of Appeal opinion in *Hill,* however, indicates that even if sexual services are part of the contractual consideration, any *severable* portion of the contract supported by independent consideration will still be enforced.

---

6. Although not cited by defendant, the only California precedent which supports his position is *Heaps v. Toy* (1942) 54 Cal.App.2d 178, 128 P.2d 813. In that case the woman promised to leave her job, to refrain from marriage, to be a companion to the man, and to make a permanent home for him; he agreed to support the woman and her child for life. The Court of Appeal held the agreement invalid as a contract in restraint of marriage (Civ.Code, s 1676) and, alternatively, as "contrary to good morals" (Civ.Code, s 1607). The opinion does not state that sexual relations formed any part of the consideration for the contract, nor explain how — unless the contract called for sexual relations — the woman's employment as a companion and housekeeper could be contrary to good morals.

The alternative holding in *Heaps v. Toy, supra,* finding the contract in that case contrary to good morals, is inconsistent with the numerous California decisions upholding contracts between nonmarital partners when such contracts are not founded upon an illicit consideration, and is therefore disapproved.

The principle that a contract between nonmarital partners will be enforced unless expressly and inseparably based upon an illicit consideration of sexual services not only represents the distillation of the decisional law, but also offers a far more precise and workable standard than that advocated by defendant. Our recent decision in *In re Marriage of Dawley* (1976) 17 Cal.3d 342, 551 P.2d 323, offers a close analogy. Rejecting the contention that an antenuptial agreement is invalid if the parties contemplated a marriage of short duration, we pointed out in *Dawley* that a standard based upon the subjective contemplation of the parties is uncertain and unworkable; such a test, we stated, "might invalidate virtually all antenuptial agreements on the ground that the parties contemplated dissolution...but it provides no principled basis for determining which antenuptial agreements offend public policy and which do not." (17 Cal.3d 342, 352, 551 P.2d 323, 329.)

Similarly, in the present case a standard which inquires whether an agreement is "involved" in or "contemplates" a nonmarital relationship is vague and unworkable. Virtually all agreements between nonmarital partners can be said to be "involved" in some sense in the fact of their mutual sexual relationship, or to "contemplate" the existence of that relationship. Thus defendant's proposed standards, if taken literally, might invalidate all agreements between nonmarital partners, a result no one favors. Moreover, those standards offer no basis to distinguish between valid and invalid agreements. By looking not to such uncertain tests, but only to the consideration underlying the agreement, we provide the parties and the courts with a practical guide to determine when an agreement between nonmarital partners should be enforced.

Defendant secondly relies upon the ground suggested by the trial court: that the 1964 contract violated public policy because it impaired the community property rights of Betty Marvin, defendant's lawful wife. Defendant points out that his earnings while living apart from his wife before rendition of the interlocutory decree were community property under 1964 statutory law (former Civ.Code, §§169, 169.2) and that defendant's agreement with plaintiff purported to transfer to her a half interest in that community property. But whether or not defendant's contract with plaintiff exceeded his authority as manager of the community property (see former Civ.Code, §172), defendant's argument fails for the reason that an improper transfer of community property is not void *ab initio*, but merely voidable at the instance of the aggrieved spouse....

In the present case Betty Marvin, the aggrieved spouse, had the opportunity to assert her community property rights in the divorce action.... The interlocutory and final decrees in that action fix and limit her interest. Enforcement of the contract between plaintiff and defendant against property awarded to defendant by the divorce decree will not impair any right of Betty's, and thus is not on that account violative of public policy.

Defendant's third contention is noteworthy for the lack of authority advanced in its support. He contends that enforcement of the oral agreement between plaintiff and himself is barred by Civil Code section 5134, which provides that "All contracts for marriage settlements must be in writing...." A marriage settlement, however, is an agreement in contemplation of marriage in which each party agrees to release or modify the property rights which would otherwise arise from the marriage. (See *Corker v. Corker* (1891) 87 Cal. 643, 648, 25 P. 922.) The contract at issue here does not conceivably fall within that definition, and thus is beyond the compass of section 5134.[9]

Defendant finally argues that enforcement of the contract is barred by Civil Code section 43.5, subdivision (d), which provides that "No cause of action arises for...breach of a promise of marriage." This rather strained contention proceeds from the premise that a promise of marriage impliedly includes a promise to support and to pool property acquired after marriage (see *Boyd v. Boyd* (1964) 228 Cal.App.2d 374, 39 Cal.Rptr. 400) to the conclusion that pooling and support agreements not part of or accompanied by promise of marriage are barred by the section. We conclude that section 43.5 is not reasonably susceptible to the interpretation advanced by defendant, a conclusion demonstrated by the fact that since section 43.5 was enacted in 1939, numerous cases have enforced pooling agreements between nonmarital partners, and in none did court or counsel refer to section 43.5.

In summary, we base our opinion on the principle that adults who voluntarily live together and engage in sexual relations are nonetheless as competent as any other persons to contract respecting their earnings and property rights. Of course, they cannot lawfully contract to pay for the performance of sexual services, for such a contract is, in essence, an agreement for prostitution and unlawful for that reason. But they may agree to pool their earnings and to hold all property acquired during the relationship in accord with the law governing community property; conversely they may agree that each partner's earnings and the property acquired from those earnings remains the separate property of the earning partner.[10] So long as the agreement does not rest upon illicit meretricious consideration, the parties may order their economic affairs as they choose, and no policy precludes the courts from enforcing such agreements.

In the present instance, plaintiff alleges that the parties agreed to pool their earnings, that they contracted to share equally in all property acquired, and that defendant agreed to support plaintiff. The terms of the contract as alleged do not rest upon any unlawful consideration. We therefore conclude that the complaint furnishes a suitable basis upon which the trial court can render declaratory relief. (See 3 Witkin, Cal. Procedure (2d ed.) pp. 2335–2336.) The trial court consequently erred in granting defendant's motion for judgment on the pleadings.

3. Plaintiff's Complaint Can Be Amended To State a Cause of Action Founded Upon Theories of Implied Contract or Equitable Relief

As we have noted, both causes of action in plaintiff's complaint allege an express contract; neither assert any basis for relief independent from the contract. In *In re Marriage of Cary, supra,* 34 Cal.App.3d 345, 109 Cal.Rptr. 862, however, the Court of Appeal held that, in view of the policy of the Family Law Act, property accumulated by nonmarital partners in an actual family relationship should

9. Our review of the many cases enforcing agreements between nonmarital partners reveals that the majority of such agreements were oral. In two cases (*Ferguson v. Schuenemann, supra,* 167 Cal.App.2d 413, 334 P.2d 668; *Cline v. Festersen, supra,* 128 Cal.App.2d 380, 275 P.2d 149), the court expressly rejected defenses grounded upon the statute of frauds.

10. A great variety of other arrangements are possible. The parties might keep their earnings and property separate, but agree to compensate one party for services which benefit the other. They may choose to pool only part of their earnings and property, to form a partnership or joint venture, or to hold property acquired as joint tenants or tenants in common, or agree to any other such arrangement. (See generally Weitzman, *Legal Regulation of Marriage: Tradition and Change* (1974) 62 CAL.L.REV. 1169.)

be divided equally. Upon examining the *Cary* opinion, the parties to the present case realized that plaintiff's alleged relationship with defendant might arguably support a cause of action independent of any express contract between the parties. The parties have therefore briefed and discussed the issue of the property rights of a nonmarital partner in the absence of an express contract. Although our conclusion that plaintiff's complaint states a cause of action based on an express contract alone compels us to reverse the judgment for defendant, resolution of the *Cary* issue will serve both to guide the parties upon retrial and to resolve a conflict presently manifest in published Court of Appeal decisions.

Both plaintiff and defendant stand in broad agreement that the law should be fashioned to carry out the reasonable expectations of the parties. Plaintiff, however, presents the following contentions: that the decisions prior to *Cary* rest upon implicit and erroneous notions of punishing a party for his or her guilt in entering into a nonmarital relationship, that such decisions result in an inequitable distribution of property accumulated during the relationship, and that *Cary* correctly held that the enactment of the Family Law Act in 1970 overturned those prior decisions. Defendant in response maintains that the prior decisions merely applied common law principles of contract and property to persons who have deliberately elected to remain outside the bounds of the community property system.[11] *Cary*, defendant contends, erred in holding that the Family Law Act vitiated the force of the prior precedents.

As we shall see from examination of the pre-*Cary* decisions, the truth lies somewhere between the positions of plaintiff and defendant. The classic opinion on this subject is *Vallera v. Vallera, supra*, 21 Cal.2d 681, 134 P.2d 761. Speaking for a four-member majority, Justice Traynor posed the question: "whether a woman living with a man as his wife but with no genuine belief that she is legally married to him acquires by reason of cohabitation alone the rights of a co-tenant in his earnings and accumulations during the period of their relationship."… *Vallera* explains that "Equitable considerations arising from the reasonable expectation of the continuation of benefits attending the status of marriage entered into in good faith are not present in such a case." (P. 685, 134 P.2d p. 763.) In the absence of express contract, *Vallera* concluded, the woman is entitled to share in property jointly accumulated only "in the proportion that her funds contributed toward its acquisition." (P. 685, 134 P.2d p. 763.) Justice Curtis, dissenting, argued that the evidence showed an implied contract under which each party owned an equal interest in property acquired during the relationship.

The majority opinion in *Vallera* did not expressly bar recovery based upon an implied contract, nor preclude resort to equitable remedies. But *Vallera's* broad assertion that equitable considerations "are not present" in the case of a nonmar-

---

11. We note that a deliberate decision to avoid the strictures of the community property system is not the only reason that couples live together without marriage. Some couples may wish to avoid the permanent commitment that marriage implies, yet be willing to share equally any property acquired during the relationship; others may fear the loss of pension, welfare, or tax benefits resulting from marriage (see *Beckman v. Mayhew, supra*, 49 Cal.App.3d 529, 122 Cal.Rptr. 604). Others may engage in the relationship as a possible prelude to marriage. In lower socioeconomic groups the difficulty and expense of dissolving a former marriage often leads couples to choose a nonmarital relationship; many unmarried couples may also incorrectly believe that the doctrine of common law marriage prevails in California, and thus that they are in fact married. Consequently we conclude that the mere fact that a couple have not participated in a valid marriage ceremony cannot serve as a basis for a court's inference that the couple intend to keep their earnings and property separate and independent; the parties' intention can only be ascertained by a more searching inquiry into the nature of their relationship.

ital relationship (21 Cal.2d at p. 685, 134 P.2d 761) led the Courts of Appeal to interpret the language to preclude recovery based on such theories.[12]

Consequently, when the issue of the rights of a nonmarital partner reached this court in *Keene v. Keene* (1962) 57 Cal.2d 657, 21 Cal.Rptr. 593, 371 P.2d 329, the claimant forwent reliance upon theories of contract implied in law or fact. Asserting that she had worked on her partner's ranch and that her labor had enhanced its value, she confined her cause of action to the claim that the court should impress a resulting trust on the property derived from the sale of the ranch. The court limited its opinion accordingly, rejecting her argument on the ground that the rendition of services gives rise to a resulting trust only when the services aid in acquisition of the property, not in its subsequent improvement. (57 Cal.2d at p. 668, 21 Cal.Rptr. 593, 371 P.2d 329.) Justice Peters, dissenting, attacked the majority's distinction between the rendition of services and the contribution of funds or property; he maintained that both property and services furnished valuable consideration, and potentially afforded the ground for a resulting trust.

This failure of the courts to recognize an action by a nonmarital partner based upon implied contract, or to grant an equitable remedy, contrasts with the judicial treatment of the putative spouse. Prior to the enactment of the Family Law Act, no statute granted rights to a putative spouse. The courts accordingly fashioned a variety of remedies by judicial decision. Some cases permitted the putative spouse to recover half the property on a theory that the conduct of the parties implied an agreement of partnership of joint venture. (See *Estate of Vargas* (1974) 36 Cal.App.3d 714, 717–718, 111 Cal.Rptr. 779; *Sousa v. Freitas* (1970) 10 Cal.App.3d 660, 666, 89 Cal.Rptr. 485.) Others permitted the spouse to recover the reasonable value of rendered services, less the value of support received. (See *Sanguinetti v. Sanguinetti* (1937) 9 Cal.2d 95, 100–102, 69 P.2d 845.) Finally, decisions affirmed the power of a court to employ equitable principles to achieve a fair division of property acquired during putative marriage....

Thus in summary, the cases prior to *Cary* exhibited a schizophrenic inconsistency. By enforcing an express contract between nonmarital partners unless it rested upon an unlawful consideration, the courts applied a common law principle as to contracts. Yet the courts disregarded the common law principle that holds that implied contracts can arise from the conduct of the parties.[16] Refusing to enforce such contracts, the courts spoke of leaving the parties "in the position in which they had placed themselves" (*Oakley v. Oakley, supra,* 82 Cal.App.2d 188, 192, 185 P.2d 848, 850), just as if they were guilty parties "*in pari delicto.*"

---

12. The cases did not clearly determine whether a nonmarital partner could recover in *quantum meruit* for the reasonable value of services rendered. But when we affirmed a trial court ruling denying recovery in *Hill v. Estate of Westbrook, supra,* 39 Cal.2d 458, 247 P.2d 19, we did so in part on the ground that whether the partner "rendered her services because of expectation of monetary reward" (p. 462, 247 P.2d p. 21) was a question of fact resolved against her by the trial court — thus implying that in a proper case the court would allow recovery based on quantum meruit.

16. Contracts may be express or implied. These terms, however, do not denote different kinds on contracts, but have reference to the evidence by which the agreement between the parties is shown. If the agreement is shown by the direct words of the parties, spoken or written, the contract is said to be an express one. But if such agreement can only be shown by the acts and conduct of the parties, interpreted in the light of the subject-matter and of the surrounding circumstances, then the contract is an implied one.

(*Skelly v. Bristol Sav. Bank* (1893) 63 Conn. 83, 26 A. 474, 475, quoted in 1 Corbin, CONTRACTS (1963) p. 41.) Thus, as Justice Schauer observed in *Desny v. Wilder* (1956) 46 Cal.2d 715, 299 P.2d 257, in a sense all contracts made in fact, as distinguished from quasi-contractual obligations, are express contracts, differing only in the manner in which the assent of the parties is expressed and proved. (See 46 Cal.2d at pp. 735–736, 299 P.2d 257.)

Justice Curtis noted this inconsistency in his dissenting opinion in *Vallera,* pointing out that "if an express agreement will be enforced, there is no legal or just reason why an implied agreement to share the property cannot be enforced." (21 Cal.2d 681, 686, 134 P.2d 761, 764; see Bruch, *Property Rights of De Facto Spouses Including Thoughts on the Value of Homemakers' Services* (1976) 10 Family L.Q. 101, 117–121.) And in *Keene v. Keene, supra,* 57 Cal.2d 657, 21 Cal.Rptr. 593, 371 P.2d 329, Justice Peters observed that if the man and woman "were not illegally living together... it would be a plain business relationship and a contract would be implied." (Diss. opn. at p. 672, 21 Cal.Rptr. at p. 602, 371 P.2d at p. 338.)

Still another inconsistency in the prior cases arises from their treatment of property accumulated through joint effort. To the extent that a partner had contributed *funds* or *property,* the cases held that the partner obtains a proportionate share in the acquisition, despite the lack of legal standing of the relationship.... Yet courts have refused to recognize just such an interest based upon the contribution of services. As Justice Curtis points out, "Unless it can be argued that a woman's services as cook, housekeeper, and homemaker are valueless, it would seem logical that if, when she contributes money to the purchase of property, her interest will be protected, then when she contributes her services in the home, her interest in property accumulated should be protected." (*Vallera v. Vallera, supra,* 21 Cal.2d 681, 686–687, 134 P.2d 761, 764 (diss. opn.); see Bruch, *op. cit. supra,* 10 Family L.Q. 101, 110–114....

Thus as of 1973, the time of the filing of *In re Marriage of Cary, supra,* 34 Cal.App.3d 345, 109 Cal.Rptr. 862, the cases apparently held that a nonmarital partner who rendered services in the absence of express contract could assert no right to property acquired during the relationship. The facts of *Cary* demonstrated the unfairness of that rule.

Janet and Paul Cary had lived together, unmarried, for more than eight years. They held themselves out to friends and family as husband and wife, reared four children, purchased a home and other property, obtained credit, filed joint income tax returns, and otherwise conducted themselves as though they were married. Paul worked outside the home, and Janet generally cared for the house and children.

In 1971 Paul petitioned for "nullity of the marriage."[17] Following a hearing on that petition, the trial court awarded Janet half the property acquired during the relationship, although all such property was traceable to Paul's earnings. The Court of Appeal affirmed the award.

Reviewing the prior decisions which had denied relief to the homemaking partner, the Court of Appeal reasoned that those decisions rested upon a policy of punishing persons guilty of cohabitation without marriage. The Family Law Act, the court observed, aimed to eliminate fault or guilt as a basis for dividing marital property. But once fault or guilt is excluded, the court reasoned, nothing distinguishes the property rights of a nonmarital "spouse" from those of a putative spouse. Since the latter is entitled to half the "quasi marital property" (Civ.Code,

17. The Court of Appeal opinion in *In re Marriage of Cary, supra,* does not explain why Paul Cary filed his action as a petition for nullity. Briefs filed with this court, however, suggest that Paul may have been seeking to assert rights as a putative spouse. In the present case, on the other hand, neither party claims the status of an actual or putative spouse. Under such circumstances an action to adjudge "the marriage" in the instant case a nullity would be pointless and could not serve as a device to adjudicate contract and property rights arising from the parties' nonmarital relationship. Accordingly, plaintiff here correctly chose to assert her rights by means of an ordinary civil action.

§4452), the Court of Appeal concluded that, giving effect to the policy of the Family Law Act, a nonmarital cohabitator should also be entitled to half the property accumulated during an "actual family relationship." (34 Cal.App.3d at p. 353, 109 Cal.Rptr. 862.)[18]

Cary met with a mixed reception in other appellate districts. In *Estate of Atherley, supra,* 44 Cal.App.3d 758, 119 Cal.Rptr. 41, the Fourth District agreed with *Cary* that under the Family Law Act a nonmarital partner in an actual family relationship enjoys the same right to an equal division of property as a putative spouse. In *Beckman v. Mayhew, supra,* 49 Cal.App.3d 529, 122 Cal.Rptr. 604, however, the Third District rejected *Cary* on the ground that the Family Law Act was not intended to change California law dealing with nonmarital relationships.

If *Cary* is interpreted as holding that the Family Law Act requires an equal division of property accumulated in nonmarital "actual family relationships," then we agree with *Beckman v. Mayhew* that *Cary* distends the act. No language in the Family Law Act addresses the property rights of nonmarital partners, and nothing in the legislative history of the act suggests that the Legislature considered that subject.[19] The delineation of the rights of nonmarital partners before 1970 had been fixed entirely by judicial decision; we see no reason to believe that the Legislature, by enacting the Family Law Act, intended to change that state of affairs.

But although we reject the reasoning of *Cary* and *Atherley,* we share the perception of the *Cary* and *Atherley* courts that the application of former precedent in the factual setting of those cases would work an unfair distribution of the prop-

---

18. The court in *Cary* also based its decision upon an analysis of Civil Code section 4452, which specifies the property rights of a putative spouse. Section 4452 states that if the "court finds that either party or both parties believed in good faith that the marriage was valid, the court should declare such party or parties to have the status of a putative spouse, and shall divide, in accordance with Section 4800, that property acquired during the union...." Since section 4800 requires an equal division of community property, *Cary* interpreted section 4452 to require an equal division of the property of a putative marriage, so long as one spouse believed in good faith that the marriage was valid. Thus under section 4452, *Cary* concluded, the "guilty spouse" (the spouse who knows the marriage is invalid) has the same right to half the property as does the "innocent" spouse.

Cary then reasoned that if the "guilty" spouse to a putative marriage is entitled to one-half the marital property, the "guilty" partner in a nonmarital relationship should also receive one-half of the property. Otherwise, the court stated,

> We should be obliged to presume a legislative intent that a person, who by deceit leads another to believe a valid marriage exists between them, shall be legally guaranteed half of the property they acquire even though most, or all, may have resulted from the earnings of the blameless partner. At the same time we must infer an inconsistent legislative intent that two persons who, candidly with each other, enter upon an unmarried family relationship, shall be denied any judicial aid whatever in the assertion of otherwise valid property rights. (34 Cal.App.3d at p. 352, 109 Cal.Rptr. at p. 866.)

This reasoning in *Cary* has been criticized by commentators. (See Note, *op. cit., supra,* 25 HASTINGS L.J. 1226, 1234–1235; Comment, *In re Marriage of Carey* [sic]: *The End of the Putative-Meretricious Spouse Distinction in California* (1975) 12 San Diego L.Rev. 436, 444–446.) The Commentators note that Civil Code section 4455 provides that an "innocent" party to a putative marriage can recover spousal support, from which they infer that the Legislature intended to give only the "innocent" spouse a right to one-half of the quasi-marital property under section 4452.

We need not now resolve this dispute concerning the interpretation of section 4452. Even if *Cary* is correct in holding that a "guilty" putative spouse has a right to one-half of the marital property, it does not necessarily follow that a nonmarital partner has an identical right. In a putative marriage the parties will arrange their economic affairs with the expectation that upon dissolution the property will be divided equally. If a "guilty" putative spouse receives one-half of the property under section 4452, no expectation of the "innocent" spouse has been frustrated. In a nonmarital relationship, on the other hand, the parties may expressly or tacitly determine to order their economic relationship in some other manner, and to impose community property principles regardless of such understanding may frustrate the parties' expectations.

19. Despite the extensive material available on the legislative history of the Family Law Act neither *Cary* nor plaintiff cites any reference which suggests that the Legislature ever considered the issue of the property rights of nonmarital partners, and our independent examination has uncovered no such reference.

erty accumulated by the couple. Justice Friedman in *Beckman v. Mayhew, supra,* 49 Cal.App.3d 529 ,535, 122 Cal.Rptr. 604, also questioned the continued viability of our decisions in *Vallera* and *Keene;* commentators have argued the need to reconsider those precedents.[20] We should not, therefore, reject the authority of *Cary* and *Atherley* without also examining the deficiencies in the former law which led to those decisions.

The principal reason why the pre-*Cary* decisions result in an unfair distribution of property inheres in the court's refusal to permit a nonmarital partner to assert rights based upon accepted principles of implied contract or equity. We have examined the reasons advanced to justify this denial of relief, and find that none have merit.

First, we note that the cases denying relief do not rest their refusal upon any theory of "punishing" a "guilty" partner. Indeed, to the extent that denial of relief "punishes" one partner, it necessarily rewards the other by permitting him to retain a disproportionate amount of the property. Concepts of "guilt" thus cannot justify an unequal division of property between two equally "guilty" persons.[21]

Other reasons advanced in the decisions fare no better. The principal argument seems to be that "[e]quitable considerations arising from the reasonable expectation of...benefits attending the status of marriage...are not present [in a nonmarital relationship]." (*Vallera v. Vallera, supra,* 21 Cal.2d at p. 685, 134 P.2d 761, 763.) But, although parties to a nonmarital relationship obviously cannot have based any expectations upon the belief that they were married, other expectations and equitable considerations remain. The parties may well expect that property will be divided in accord with the parties' own tacit understanding and that in the absence of such understanding the courts will fairly apportion property accumulated through mutual effort. We need not treat nonmarital partners as putatively married persons in order to apply principles of implied contract, or extend equitable remedies; we need to treat them only as we do any other unmarried persons.[22]

The remaining arguments advanced from time to time to deny remedies to the nonmarital partners are of less moment. There is no more reason to presume that services are contributed as a gift than to presume that funds are contributed as a gift; in any event the better approach is to presume, as Justice Peters suggested, "that the parties intend to deal fairly with each other." (*Keene v. Keene, supra,* 57

---

20. See Bruch, *op. cit., supra,* 10 FAMILY L.Q. 101, 113; Article, *op. cit., supra,* 6 U.C. DAVIS L.REV. 354; Comment (1975) 6 GOLDEN GATE L.REV. 179, 197–201; Comment, *op. cit., supra,* 12 SAN DIEGO L.REV. 4356; Note, *op. cit., supra,* 25 HASTINGS L.J. 1226, 1246.

21. Justice Finley of the Washington Supreme Court explains:

> Under such circumstances (the dissolution of a nonmarital relationship), this court and the courts of other jurisdictions have, in effect, sometimes said, "We will wash our hands of such disputes. The parties should and must be left to their own devices, just where they find themselves." To me, such pronouncements seem overly fastidious and a bit fatuous. They are unrealistic and, among other things, ignore the fact that an unannounced (but nevertheless effective and binding) rule of law is inherent in any such terminal statements by a court of law. The unannounced but inherent rule is simply that the party who has title, or in some instances who is in possession, will enjoy the rights of ownership of the property concerned. The rule often operates to the great advantage of the cunning and the shrewd, who wind up with possession of the property, or title to it in their names, at the end of a so-called meretricious relationship. So, although the courts proclaim that they will have nothing to do with such matters, the proclamation in itself establishes, as to the parties involved, an effective and binding rule of law which tends to operate purely by accident or perhaps by reason of the cunning, anticipatory designs of just one of the parties.
>
> (*West v. Knowles* (1957) 50 Wash.2d 311, 311 P.2d 689, 692 (conc. opn.).)

22. In some instances a confidential relationship may arise between nonmarital partners, and economic transactions between them should be governed by the principles applicable to such relationships.

Cal.2d 657, 674, 21 Cal.Rptr. 593, 603, 371 P.2d 329, 339 (dissenting opn.); see Bruch, *op. cit., supra,* 10 Family L.Q. 101, 113.)

The argument that granting remedies to the nonmarital partners would discourage marriage must fail; as *Cary* pointed out, "with equal or greater force the point might be made that the pre-1970 rule was calculated to cause the income producing partner to avoid marriage and thus retain the benefit of all of his or her accumulated earnings." (34 Cal.App.3d at p. 353, 109 Cal.Rptr. at p. 866.) Although we recognize the well-established public policy to foster and promote the institution of marriage,...perpetuation of judicial rules which result in an inequitable distribution of property accumulated during a nonmarital relationship is neither a just nor an effective way of carrying out that policy.

In summary, we believe that the prevalence of nonmarital relationships in modern society and the social acceptance of them, marks this as a time when our courts should by no means apply the doctrine of the unlawfulness of the so-called meretricious relationship to the instant case. As we have explained, the nonenforceability of agreements expressly providing for meretricious conduct rested upon the fact that such conduct, as the word suggests, pertained to and encompassed prostitution. To equate the nonmarital relationship of today to such a subject matter is to do violence to an accepted and wholly different practice.

We are aware that many young couples live together without the solemnization of marriage, in order to make sure that they can successfully later undertake marriage. This trial period,[23] preliminary to marriage, serves as some assurance that the marriage will not subsequently end in dissolution to the harm of both parties. We are aware, as we have stated, of the pervasiveness of nonmarital relationships in other situations.

The mores of the society have indeed changed so radically in regard to cohabitation that we cannot impose a standard based on alleged moral considerations that have apparently been so widely abandoned by so many. Lest we be misunderstood, however, we take this occasion to point out that the structure of society itself largely depends upon the institution of marriage, and nothing we have said in this opinion should be taken to derogate from that institution. The joining of the man and woman in marriage is at once the most socially productive and individually fulfilling relationship that one can enjoy in the course of a lifetime.

We conclude that the judicial barriers that may stand in the way of a policy based upon the fulfillment of the reasonable expectations of the parties to a nonmarital relationship should be removed. As we have explained, the courts now hold that express agreements will be enforced unless they rest on an unlawful meretricious consideration. We add that in the absence of an express agreement, the courts may look to a variety of other remedies in order to protect the parties' lawful expectations.[24]

The courts may inquire into the conduct of the parties to determine whether that conduct demonstrates an implied contract or implied agreement of partnership or joint venture (see *Estate of Thornton* (1972) 81 Wash.2d 72, 499 P.2d 864),

23. Toffler, FUTURE SHOCK (Bantam Books, 1971) page 253.

24. We do not seek to resurrect the doctrine of common law marriage, which was abolished in California by statute in 1895. (See *Norman v. Thomson* (1898) 121 Cal. 620, 628, 54 P. 143; *Estate of Abate* (1958) 166 Cal.App.2d 282, 292, 333 P.2d 200.) Thus we do not hold that plaintiff and defendant were "married," nor do we extend to plaintiff the rights which the Family Law Act grants valid or putative spouses; we hold only that she has the same rights to enforce contracts and to assert her equitable interest in property acquired through her effort as does any other unmarried person.

or some other tacit understanding between the parties. The courts may, when appropriate, employ principles of constructive trust (see *Omer v. Omer* (1974) 11 Wash.App. 386, 523 P.2d 957) or resulting trust (see *Hyman v. Hyman* (Tex.Civ. App.1954) 275 S.W.2d 149). Finally, a nonmarital partner may recover in quantum meruit for the reasonable value of household services rendered less the reasonable value of support received if he can show that he rendered services with the expectation of monetary reward. (See *Hill v. Estate of Westbrook, supra,* 39 Cal.2d 458, 462, 247 P.2d 19.)[25]

Since we have determined that plaintiff's complaint states a cause of action for breach of an express contract, and, as we have explained, can be amended to state a cause of action independent of allegations of express contract,[26] we must conclude that the trial court erred in granting defendant a judgment on the pleadings.

The judgment is reversed and the cause remanded for further proceedings consistent with the views expressed herein.

CLARK, Justice (concurring and dissenting).

The majority opinion properly permits recovery on the basis of either express or implied in fact agreement between the parties. These being the issues presented, their resolution requires reversal of the judgment. Here, the opinion should stop.

This court should not attempt to determine all anticipated rights, duties and remedies within every meretricious relationship — particularly in vague terms. Rather, these complex issues should be determined as each arises in a concrete case.

The majority broadly indicates that a party to a meretricious relationship may recover on the basis of equitable principles and in *quantum meruit.* However, the majority fails to advise us of the circumstances permitting recovery, limitations on recovery, or whether their numerous remedies are cumulative or exclusive. Conceivably, under the majority opinion a party may recover half of the property acquired during the relationship on the basis of general equitable principles, recover a bonus based on specific equitable considerations, and recover a second bonus in quantum meruit.

The general sweep of the majority opinion raises but fails to answer several questions. First, because the Legislature specifically excluded some parties to a meretricious relationship from the equal division rule of Civil Code section 4452, is this court now free to create an equal division rule? Second, upon termination of the relationship, is it equitable to impose the economic obligations of lawful spouses on meretricious parties when the latter may have rejected matrimony to avoid such obligations? Third, does not application of equitable principles — necessitating examination of the conduct of the parties — violate the spirit of the Family Law Act of 1969, designed to eliminate the bitterness and acrimony resulting from the former fault system in divorce? Fourth, will not application of equitable principles reimpose upon trial courts the unmanageable burden of arbitrating domestic disputes? Fifth, will not a quantum meruit system of compensation

25. Our opinion does not preclude the evolution of additional equitable remedies to protect the expectations of the parties to a nonmarital relationship in cases in which existing remedies prove inadequate; the suitability of such remedies may be determined in later cases in light of the factual setting in which they arise.

26. We do not pass upon the question whether, in the absence of an express or implied contractual obligation, a party to a nonmarital relationship is entitled to support payments from the other party after the relationship terminates.

for services — discounted by benefits received — place meretricious spouses in a better position than lawful spouses? Sixth, if a quantum meruit system is to be allowed, does fairness not require inclusion of all services and all benefits regardless of how difficult the evaluation?

When the parties to a meretricious relationship show by express or implied in fact agreement they intend to create mutual obligations, the courts should enforce the agreement. However, in the absence of agreement, we should stop and consider the ramifications before creating economic obligations which may violate legislative intent, contravene the intention of the parties, and surely generate undue burdens on our trial courts.

By judicial overreach, the majority perform a nunc pro tunc marriage, dissolve it, and distribute its property on terms never contemplated by the parties, case law or the Legislature.

Marvin v. Marvin [II]
Superior Court of California
5 FAM. L. REP. 3077 (1979)

MARSHALL, J.

April 18, 1979

The Supreme Court in *Marvin v. Marvin* (1976) 18 C.3d 660, 665, 134 Cal. Rptr. 815, 557 P.2d 106, decided that an unmarried person may recover from a person, with whom the former had lived, in accordance with any written contract between them unless the agreement "rest[s] on an unlawful meretricious consideration." (p. 684.) That court also determined that a nonmarital partner may recover if the conduct of the couple was such that a trial court could imply therefrom either "an implied contract, agreement of partnership or joint venture, or some other tacit understanding between the parties." (pp. 665, 682.) Lacking evidence which would support any such finding, "[T]he courts may also employ the doctrine of quantum meruit, or equitable remedies such as constructive or resulting trusts, when warranted by the facts of the case." (pp. 665, 677, 682, 684.)

Finally, the Supreme Court declared that a nonmarital partner may recover in quantum meruit for the reasonable value of household services less the reasonable value of support received. (p. 684.) The action was remanded to the Superior Court where evidence has been taken in implementation of the above described decision. The last mentioned remedy, quantum meruit, need not be considered here inasmuch as the plaintiff has dismissed her fourth and fifth causes of action based on such ground.

The first three causes of action, amended to reflect the remedies described by the Supreme Court, allege contractual, express and implied and equitable bases for judgment in favor of plaintiff.

In order to comply with the Supreme Court mandate, the trial court collected all available evidence which might bear on the relationship established after defendant allegedly promised plaintiff half of his property or which might serve as a basis for a tacit agreement or for equitable relief.

FACTS

In June, 1964, the parties met while they both were working on a picture called "Ship of Fools," he as a star and she as a stand-in. (She also was employed as a singer at the "Little Club" in Los Angeles.) A few days after their first meeting, they lunched together, then dined together. In a short time they saw each other on a daily basis after work. Sexual intimacy commenced about 2 weeks after their first date. During these early meetings, there was much conversation about their respective marital problems. The defendant said that, although he loved his wife and children, communication between him and his spouse had failed and he was unhappy. Plaintiff said that her marriage had been dissolved but her husband sought reconciliation.

Plaintiff testified that defendant told her that as soon as two people sign "a piece of paper," (meaning a marriage certificate) they waved that paper at each other whenever any problem arose instead of attempting to settle the problem. Defendant allegedly said that a license is a woman's insurance policy and he did not like that. Defendant further stated to plaintiff that when two people loved each other, there is no need for a license. Plaintiff declared that she told him that she did not necessarily agree with him.

Plaintiff testified that she hoped to secure a part in "Flower Drum Song" and was to journey to New York City for that purpose, but defendant did not want her to go as, he said, it was hard to conduct a romance at long distance. She did not go to New York. She rented an apartment for approximately one month. Defendant stayed with her from time to time.

In October, 1964, the plaintiff rented and moved into a house. The defendant moved in with her although he also maintained a room at a nearby hotel and occasionally stayed at the home where he lived with his wife and children. Plaintiff told defendant that they were not "living together." His response was, "What does it mean when your blouse and my suit come back [from] to the cleaners together?" He inquired, "Does it mean that I live here?" She testified that she replied, "Well, I guess it does."

Defendant allegedly repeated again and again, his opinion that a piece of paper, a marriage certificate, is not needed by people in love. Plaintiff testified that at first she thought he was crazy and asked him to explain. She did not think it would work without the "paper." Defendant responded that marriage was lacking in communication and that he was unhappy about it.

The defendant went to San Blas, Mexico in November or December of 1964 for sport fishing. He later invited plaintiff to join him, which she did. There, the defendant allegedly told her that he was unhappily married, that he might be terminating his marriage, and that he and plaintiff could be together. She testified that she doubted his words. He declared again that a woman does not need a piece of paper, a marriage certificate, for security. He repeated his belief that whenever there was a misunderstanding, each waved the paper at each other instead of working hard at clearing up the misunderstanding. He allegedly said that he would never marry again because he did not like that kind of arrangement. He declared that he was almost positive that his marriage was not going to mend and asked whether plaintiff and defendant could share their lives. She inquired as to his meaning. He replied that after the divorce he would be left with only "the shirt on his back (and alimony)" but would she like to live on the beach. She initially responded she was going to New York. Two days later she asked defendant if he really thought living together without marriage would work out. He said that it would and she agreed to live with him.

Then defendant allegedly uttered the words which plaintiff contends constitute a contractual offer. He said, "what I have is yours and what you have is mine." She then accepted the alleged offer but declared that she had her own career and she did not want to depend on anyone. Defendant said that he had no objection to her career, that they still could share and build their lives. She told him that she loved him, that she would care for him and their home, and that she would cook and be his companion. She offered to learn how to fish, a sport of which he was quite fond, although she got seasick. He said that she would get over her seasickness.

The defendant was intoxicated in San Blas a "few times" to the point of losing control. She said that in subsequent years, 1965 and 1966, he lost control whenever he drank. She testified that she asked him to stop drinking and that he did not do so.

Defendant vigorously denies telling plaintiff, "what I have is yours and what you have is mine"; he declared that he never said he would support her for life and that he never stated "I'll take care of you always." He further denies saying that a marriage license is a piece of paper which stood in the way of working out problems. He testified that he decided to get a divorce from his wife after he arrived at his beach house, many months after his return from San Blas. During the examination of defendant under Evidence Code, Section 776, counsel for plaintiff read from defendant's deposition wherein defendant declared that he wanted a relationship of no responsibility and that the plaintiff agreed thereto.

The defendant rented and later purchased a house on the Malibu beach. Plaintiff moved in, bringing a bed, stereo equipment and kitchen utensils. A refrigerator and washing machine were purchased. She bought food, cooked meals for defendant, cleaned house (after the first year, she had the periodic help of a cleaning woman). On occasion, the couple had visitors and they in turn went together to the homes of friends. In the circle of their friends and their acquaintances in the theatrical world, the plaintiff was reputed not to be defendant's wife.

In the six years of their relationship, they did considerable traveling, over 30 months away from the beach house, for the most part on various film locations. Plaintiff usually accompanied the defendant except for the seven months devoted to the filming of "Dirty Dozen" in England (she visited him for about a month) and an exploratory trip to Micronesia preliminary to filming "Hell in the Pacific."

Plaintiff testified that her acquaintance with the theater began in 1957 as a dancer. She danced with several troupes. She states that she was a featured dancer in a group organized by Barry Ashton, who produced shows in Las Vegas. She further alleges that she was also a singer from about 1957 and appeared in nightclubs in several states and abroad. Her compensation was usually "scale," ranging from $285 to $400 a week. As to motion pictures, she served as "stand-in" or in background groupings until her appearance in "Synanon" (shortly after working in "Ship of Fools" where she met defendant) in which she spoke some lines but was not a featured performer.

After the parties moved into the beach house, plaintiff continued to have singing engagements, encouraged by the defendant who would frequently attend, bringing friends and buying drinks for them to lengthen their stay and thereby increase plaintiff's audience.

A decorator was hired to work on the beach house and, after some structural changes, a substantial amount of furniture was purchased. Plaintiff worked with the decorator; both consulted defendant on occasion as to the purchases and alterations.

In 1966, defendant contacted a friend in Hawaii and secured a singing engagement for plaintiff. Before she left for Hawaii, Santana Records, Inc., was organized by defendant and defendant paid for the recordation of four songs by plaintiff under the Santana label. With the assistance of her manager, Mimi Marleaux, plaintiff visited disc jockeys in Hawaii and promoted the record.

In that same year, 1966, defendant went to London to make a picture entitled, "Dirty Dozen." During his stay in England he wrote eight letters to plaintiff wherein he expressed affection for the plaintiff and looked forward to her coming to London. In one letter, Exhibit 13, he portrays an imaginary scene wherein he was "found guilty of robbing a 33-year-old cradle" and he answers the judge, "absolutely guilty, your honor.... Yes sir, I accept life with her, thank you your honor and the court. Will the jury please get out of that cradle!"

After the filming of "Dirty Dozen" and the parties' return to Malibu, Miss Marleaux allegedly was present in the Malibu house when defendant said, after plaintiff told Marleaux she was sorry she let her (Marleaux) down (by the slump in her career), "I don't know what you're worrying about. I'd always take care of you...."

While in Hawaii, plaintiff alleges that there was a ninth letter wherein defendant demanded that she give up her career, cut short her promotion of her record in Hawaii and come to London and if she did not the relationship would be ended. At one point in the suit, plaintiff declared that she could not locate the letter. She now contends that it was destroyed by defendant. Miss Marleaux recollects a telephone call by defendant to the same effect but defendant introduced bills which indicate he made no such call.

In March of 1967, defendant testified that he told plaintiff that she would have to prepare for separation and that she should learn a trade. The plaintiff responded that if he left her, she would reveal his fears, his worries to the public and his career would be destroyed. She also threatened suicide.

In 1967, the plaintiff accompanied defendant to Baker, Oregon, where the latter made a film called "Paint Your Wagon." The parties rented a house in Baker and established a joint bank account. Plaintiff signed most of the checks drawn on that account.

The plaintiff returned to Los Angeles while "Paint Your Wagon" was still being filmed in Oregon in order to confer with one of the defendant's attorneys, Louis L. Goldman. She asked him whether it would be any trouble to change her name to "Marvin" as their different names were embarrassing to her as well as defendant in a place like Baker. Goldman said if the change was approved by defendant, it was agreeable with him. She then requested him to arrange with defendant for the placement of some property or a lump sum in her name. She declared to him that she did not know whether the relationship would last forever, that she had talked to defendant about conveying the house to her but that he had absolutely said no. She requested Goldman to persuade defendant to do something for her. Goldman later telephoned plaintiff to inform her that defendant had refused to agree to any of her requests.

Goldman testified that plaintiff told him that neither she nor defendant wanted to get married, that each wanted to be free to come and go as they please and to terminate the relationship if they wished. The subject of defendant's frequent intoxication was discussed.

On cross-examination, plaintiff testified that they were "always very proud of the fact that nothing held us. We weren't — we weren't legally married." After the breakup she declared to an interviewer: "We used to laugh and feel a great warmth about the fact that either of us could walk out at anytime."

Following the completion of "Paint Your Wagon" (after additional work in Los Angeles), defendant made a picture entitled, "Hell in the Pacific" on the island of Palau in Micronesia. The parties again opened a joint account on location and drew funds therefrom for payment of food, clothing, etc. The plaintiff issued the greater number of checks.

She alleges that defendant introduced her as "Mrs. Marvin" although most of the American community on the island knew that they were not married, including the crew filming the picture and the cast. The defendant denies that he so introduced her.

The parties returned to Palau for a second sojourn. The parties enjoyed the fishing and the defendant supervised and assisted in the completion of a fishing boat which he hoped would vitalize the Palauan fishing industry. The parties talked to an architect about building a house, part of which they could occupy and part of which could be rented to visitors of Palau for the fishing.

Marriage was far from the thoughts of the parties. On the second visit to Palau plaintiff testified that defendant asked her to marry him but she thought he was joking and laughed. A few weeks later plaintiff allegedly asked defendant to marry her and he laughed.

On Palau, the parties met Richard Doughly, a member of the Peace Corps fishery department. Doughly testified that he had sexual relations with plaintiff approximately twenty times, on the island, and additional times later in Los Angeles and Tucson. Plaintiff vigorously denied this and claimed that Doughly was a homosexual, offering supporting witnesses. This in turn was vigorously denied by Doughly who also offered witnesses who would rebut such a charge. Doughly's testimony was corroborated by Carol Clark who testified that plaintiff admitted to her that she (plaintiff) had "an affair" with him.

Doughly's testimony is weakened by his denial of such relationship when defendant's counsel, A. David Kagon, first questioned him prior to the trial. He explained that he decided to tell the truth at the trial because he did not wish defendant to be railroaded and because he now was more willing to accept responsibility after he had recovered from a serious illness.

LaVerna Hogan, wife of the production manager of "Hell in the Pacific" accompanied plaintiff on a trip from Palau to Hawaii. They stayed overnight in Guam where plaintiff told Mrs. Hogan that she was to meet two men in Hawaii. Mrs. Hogan asked plaintiff why she was going to meet them in view of her relationship with defendant and plaintiff responded, "We (plaintiff and defendant) have an understanding. He does his thing and I do mine." Plaintiff denies any such Hawaiian meeting.

In 1969, defendant filmed "Monte Walsh" on locations approximately two hours from Tucson. He rented a house in Tucson for the ten to twelve weeks of shooting. Doughly secured employment in "Monte Walsh" as a dialogue coach and lived with the parties. A joint bank account was again opened and funded by Edward Silver, defendant's business manager. Plaintiff signed most of the checks.

At the end of the shooting of the pictures, "Hell in the Pacific," "Paint Your Wagon" and "Monte Walsh," the Palau, Baker and Tucson Joint bank accounts were closed and the balances transferred to defendant's account.

Plaintiff had a separate account in Malibu in which defendant's business manager deposited $400 per month for her personal use.

The plaintiff testified that in May, 1970, defendant left the Malibu beach house upon her request. Later, she was told by defendant's agent, Mishkin, that defendant wished that they separate (Mishkin had referred to a "divorce" but testified that he was mistaken in his use of the term). The plaintiff later sought and found defendant in La Jolla. There he told her, plaintiff alleges, that he would not give up drinking, that it was part of his life and that his relationship with plaintiff was no longer enjoyable because of her frequent admonitions as to his drinking.

In May, 1970, plaintiff went to the office of defendant's attorney, Goldman. He informed her that defendant wanted her out of the house and out of his life and that defendant would pay her $833 per month (net after deduction of taxes from a gross of $1050) for five years. Plaintiff testified that she told Goldman she could not exist on such a stipend. Goldman responded that defendant could not afford to pay more because of the alimony which he paid to his former wife. Plaintiff testified that she replied that defendant had promised to take care of her for life. Goldman, however, testified that she had simply thanked him for the arrangement and said that $833 would be enough for her needs.

She returned to the beach house but finally departed after an emotional confrontation with defendant and his attorney, Goldman and Kagon. Checks for $833 each began to arrive. According to defendant, the payments were made on condition that she removed herself from his life and not discuss with anyone anything she learned about defendant during their relationship. Defendant said that plaintiff thought this was fair. According to the plaintiff, the checks were stopped when defendant saw an item about him in one of the Hollywood columns. Defendant did send one more check but again stopped payment because, plaintiff declares, defendant was angered by her suit against Roberts. She told her attorney (then Howard L. Rosoff) to dismiss the action but, when no more checks came, she reversed her instructions. According to Goldman, plaintiff said she had nothing to do with the item in the column (re defendant's marriage to Pamela breaking up).

He testified that she also said that she would not do it again and to give her another chance. Goldman replied that defendant "was at the end of the road."...

The plaintiff filed an application dated March 26, 1970 to change her name to Michelle Triola Marvin. The verified application declared that she had been known professionally as "Marvin" and that she used the name in her acting and singing career.

Plaintiff stated in her deposition that she never used the name "Marvin" professionally. She now declares that she meant (in her application) that she used "Marvin" during her career but only socially.

The plaintiff also declared in her deposition that she had asked for a written agreement as to property shortly after moving into the beach house. Defendant allegedly said an agreement was being prepared but they did not need any papers. The plaintiff said they did. Plaintiff said nothing farther about the nonappearance of an agreement during 1968, 1969 and 1970.

The defendant stated in his deposition that he wanted a relationship of no responsibility and that the plaintiff agreed with him. On trips out of town, plaintiff was introduced on occasion as Michelle Marvin to avoid embarrassment in hotels, but defendant contends he never introduced her as *Mrs.* Marvin. Bills were rarely addressed to Mrs. Lee Marvin, but rather to Michelle Marvin. In the Malibu community and the actor-producer circles in which they moved, the couple's relationship was known not to be that of husband and wife.

The plaintiff testified that she never told the defendant that she would hold herself out as his wife, that the parties never used the terms "husband and wife," those words were not in their vocabulary and that they never used the word "homemaker."

Defendant testified that in the winter of 1969 plaintiff wanted him to finance a European trip at $10,000–$15,000 per month as the price for separation. Later, she offered to "get out of your (his) life for $50,000" and he would never hear from her again. Still later, she requested $100,000. Plaintiff denies that she made any such offer.

Rather than review the great number of allegations by plaintiff as to defendant's drinking to excess, it is enough to observe that defendant admits that he was frequently intoxicated. It is a reasonable inference therefrom that in such condition he needed care and that plaintiff provided it.

TESTIMONIAL INCONSISTENCIES

The weight of the testimony of the plaintiff is lessened by several inconsistencies.

Plaintiff claims to have had considerable help from Gene Kelly in the procurement of employment in "Flower Drum Song" in New York City. He however, denied that he hired plaintiff. He further testified that he never talked to plaintiff about "Flower Drum Song" in 1963 or 1964 and that at that time the play was not being performed in New York City. In later testimony plaintiff altered her allegation of employment by Kelly to an offer of letters of introduction by him. She also modified her declaration that she was going to New York City to appear in "Flower Drum Song" to say that she did not know whether it was then being performed on Broadway.

Plaintiff's contention of many weeks of employment of Playboy clubs in New York City, San Francisco and three other clubs and repeated in Chicago, Phoenix and San Francisco is countered by evidence from Playboy records of only one engagement, in Phoenix, and then for only two weeks. In fact, Noel Stein testified that the San Francisco club did not open until years after plaintiff's alleged engagement there. As for her allegations of employment by "Dino's Lodge" for 24 weeks in 1961 and 1962, its manager from 1958 on, Paul Wexler, declares that he recollects no employment of her by "Dino's Lodge" before 1965.

The testimony of plaintiff as to her right to compensation from Bobby Roberts, the producer of "Monte Walsh," contains three variations as to the type of compensation sought. At first she was to receive a Rolls Royce, then a 10% finders fee and lastly 50% of the producer's fee in return for informing Roberts as to the availability of the "Monte Walsh" script. Also, she testifies that she met Roberts and Landers in their offices on or about March 15,1968 whereas she was in Palau from Christmas of 1967 to April or May of 1968.

According to the records of Sears Roebuck, an account had been opened in the name of Lee Marvin (Exhibit 117; the application was signed by Betty Marvin, defendant's former wife). Plaintiff testified, however, that an account was opened by her with defendant present in the name of "Mr. and Mrs. Marvin" or Lee Marvin. Sears records do not list her on any application nor as an authorized signator (Exhibit 119).

Plaintiff testified that she "never had an apartment while I was with Lee." However, Exhibit 151 dated May 1, 1965 and signed by plaintiff is a lease of an apartment at 8633 West Knoll Drive, West Hollywood. Plaintiff contends she signed the lease on behalf of her manager, Mimi Marleaux, and that she, the plaintiff, had no belongings there nor did she make any rent payments. Yet, testimony by Marleaux reveals that plaintiff did have some clothes in the apartment and that she, Marleaux, had only stayed a month or two in the apartment. On cross-examination, plaintiff admitted that she may have paid the rent and on direct rebuttal she testified that she did pay the rent two or three times. Exhibit 186 indicates that a Continental Bank signature card signed on December 28, 1965 bore the West Knoll address as plaintiff's residence. At a later time, that address was crossed off and that of the Malibu Beach house was inserted.

Plaintiff testified that she asked defendant for a written agreement to protect her rights. The defendant responded that it was not necessary and she believed him. In her deposition, however, she stated that she continued to request such agreement.

LAW

IS THERE AN EXPRESS CONTRACT?

An express contract must be founded on a promise directly or indirectly enforceable at law. (1 Corbin on Contracts, §§11.) Every contract requires, *inter alia* the mutual consent of the parties. (Civil Code §§1550, 1565.)

A review of the extensive testimony clearly leads this court to the conclusion that no express contract was negotiated between the parties. Neither party entertained any expectations that the property was to be divided between them.

Further, before mutual consent can exist, an intent to contract must be present. Also, the meaning of the agreement must be ascertainable and both parties must have the same understanding of its meaning. *Merrit & Co.* (1959) 176 C.A. 2d 719, 1 Cal. Rptr. 500. The basic statement on which plaintiff relies is the one which she says (and defendant denies) was made by defendant at San Blas — "What I have is yours and what you have is mine."

Considering the circumstances from which it allegedly sprung, the lack of intent to make a contract is immediately apparent. In 1964–1965 defendant was married; he had considerable unresolved financial problems; he had repeatedly informed plaintiff that he did not believe in marriage because of the property rights which a wife thereby acquires. Plaintiff could not have understood that phrase to accord the same rights to one who was not defendant's wife. If those words had been spoken, they were not spoken under circumstances in which either party would be entitled to believe that an offer of a contract was intended. (See *Fowler v. Security Pacific Bank* (1956) 146 C.A.2d 37, 47, 303 P.2d 565.)

In addition, the meaning of the phrase is difficult to ascertain. Does it mean a sharing of future as well as presently owned property? Does it mean a sharing of the use of property or is title to be extended to both parties? Does it mean that all property is shared even though the relationship may be terminated in a week or weekend? These are all unanswered questions. It is more reasonable to conclude that the declaration is simply hyperbole typical of persons who live and work in the entertainment field. It was defendant's way of expressing his affection for the plaintiff. As the defendant testified, in his business terms of affection are bandied about freely; one "loves" everyone and calls everybody "sweetheart."

Also, after hearing defendant's views on marriage and noting his antagonism against a person acquiring any rights by means of a certificate of marriage, it is not reasonable to believe that plaintiff understood that defendant intended to give her such rights even without a certificate. Without intent to contract and with no clearly ascertainable meaning of the contractual phrase, no express contract exists.

During a meeting with Marleaux in the fall of 1966 and in the presence of the defendant, the plaintiff told Marleaux that she (plaintiff) was sorry she had let Marleaux down by not pursuing her career. Defendant then allegedly stated, "I don't know what you're worrying about. I'll always take care of you."

Corbin has this to say about remarks of that sort: "The law does not attempt the realization of every expectation that has been induced by a promise; the expectation must be a reasonable one. Under no system of law that has ever existed are all promises enforceable. The expectation must be one that most people would have, and the promise must be one that most people would perform." (Corbin on Contracts, p. 2 [West Pub. Co. 1852].) Surely plaintiff had no expectation that defendant would extend such care to her after separation, remembering defendant's antagonism to such automatic rights in a wife if the relationship failed (and to which she testified).

In addition, the phrase "I'll always take care of you" leaves many questions unanswered: Does defendant mean that plaintiff has the right to care even if separation is caused by plaintiff? What level of care? What if plaintiff marries, does the care continue? An offer as indefinite as this cannot be the basis of an enforceable contract (*Apablasa, supra* at 723).

Further, the alleged promise lacks mutuality; the plaintiff made no enforceable promise in response. Even if, *arguendo,* she had promised to forego her career, defendant could not have legally enforced such promise. (See *Mattei v. Hopper* (1959) 51 C.2d 119, 122, 330 P.2d 625.) Actually, plaintiff's career, never very brisk-paced, was sputtering and not because of any act of defendant; it came to an end unmourned and unattended by plaintiff who made no attempt to breathe life into it.

Doubt is cast upon the Marleaux testimony as to the alleged promise. The statement was allegedly made in the presence of Marleaux. The plaintiff testified that she remembers the event very clearly and that it was very important in her life. Yet in plaintiff's deposition of October, 1978, she was asked whether anyone other than the defendant was present and she responded, "I can't recall if anyone was present." (Deposition, p. 66, lines 19–23, read into the trial record at Vol. 30, p. 5490, lines 25–28, p. 5491, lines 1–3.)

The phrase, "Yes sir. I accept life with her, thank you. Your Honor, and the court" contained in Exhibit 13 (a letter written from London in 1966) adds no legal basis for a contract. It was a letter portraying an imaginary court scene from which one can infer the affection of defendant for plaintiff but from which one certainly cannot believe an offer of a contract was intended. (See *Fowler v. Security Pacific Bank, supra.*)

Is There an Implied Contract?

The conduct of the parties after the San Blas conversation certainly does not reveal any implementation of any contract nor does such conduct give rise to an implied contract. No joint bank accounts were established and no real property was placed in joint tenancy or tenancy in common. Plaintiff used a separate bank account for her allowance of $400 per month, her earnings from the Hawaii engagement and her settlement of the Roberts suit. When defendant bought real property, he placed it in his own name. Their tax returns were separate.

In plaintiff's letter to defendant dated November 2, 1971, (Ex. 67) she describes her activities after their separation, thanks defendant for his "financial help" (monthly payments for five years) and says nothing about any contract or agreement. In Ex. 155, a page from a book by plaintiff's counsel, he declares that plaintiff only asked him how to enforce defendant's promise to make payments pursuant to the five-year arrangement. Nothing was said then to counsel about any agreement to divide property. Plaintiff's attorney sent a letter to defendant's attorney, demanding recommencement of the payments for the five-year period. Plaintiff was quoted in an interview recorded in the Brenda Shaw article (Ex. 37) as follows: "We were always very proud of the fact that nothing really held us. We both agreed, and we were really pleased with the fact that you work harder at a relationship when you know that there is nothing really holding you." This evidence bars the finding of any contract.

The very fact that plaintiff pursued a claim for compensation from Roberts makes it plain that she expected no part of any earnings of defendant from the picture. Otherwise, why would she commence a lawsuit to recover a finder's fee or half of a producer's fee when she would have rights to half of the million dollars paid to defendant for the picture?[9]

The evidence does not support plaintiff's contention that she gave up her career in order to care for defendant and on his demand that she do so.

She claimed that defendant demanded that plaintiff give up her career and join him in London or else the relationship would end. Looking at the facts, she did go to London but remained only a few weeks. She declares that she returned because defendant was drinking heavily, and it was then too late to resume promotion of her record. Yet in her 1978 deposition she stated that she returned because her manager wanted her to come home to promote her record and in fact she did attempt to do so, but discovered that the radio stations were not interested. As for loss of momentum, in the promotion of her record by reason of her London trip, witnesses for defendant as well as one for plaintiff testified that no loss occurred. Contrary to any ultimatum, a witness for defendant declared that the latter expressed hope that she would have a successful career.

Plaintiff testified that the ultimatum was delivered to her by letter.[10]

However, her witness, Marleaux, declared that it came by way of telephone. One must doubt that the defendant issued an ultimatum (allegedly in the missing letter) demanding that plaintiff come to London when he writes in Ex. 12, "only a month and a half to go, w[h]oopee," indicating that plans for her coming to London had already been made by the parties.

The plaintiff's testimony as to defendant's drinking habits would indicate that he was virtually awash with alcohol. Yet during this same period, defendant starred in several major films, all demanding of him stamina, a high degree of alertness and verbal as well as physical concentration. Her portrayal of large-scale and all pervasive inebriation raises doubts as to her accuracy of observation.

An implied as well as an express agreement must be founded upon mutual consent. Such consent may be inferred from the conduct of the parties. Proof of introductions of plaintiff as Mrs. Marvin, and the occasional registrations at hotels as Mrs. Marvin and evidence of a relationship wherein plaintiff furnishes companionship, cooking and home care do not establish that defendant agreed to give plaintiff half of his property. Those services may be rendered out of love or affec-

9. After plaintiff and defendant separated, plaintiff testified she heard from Roberts many times. In her deposition (April 15, 1972, p. 44, lines 9–15) she said she never heard from Roberts after separation. Another inconsistency.

10. The letter has been allegedly destroyed by defendant although at first the plaintiff declared that it was missing.

tion and are indeed so rendered in a myriad of relationships between man and woman which are not contractual in nature. They may be consideration for a contract to receive property but the other elements of such contract remain to be established. Discussion of an equitable basis for an award because of homemaking services is to be found in a later portion of his opinion.

The change of name to Marvin appears to have had one motivation to avoid embarrassment when traveling. It ended the awkwardness occurring when, for example, plaintiff's passport was examined in customs. Coming at a time so close to the date of separation and after some indication of difficulties between the parties, the change of name does raise a question whether plaintiff sought relief from embarrassment or whether she wished to acquire the right to use defendant's name after separation.

The evidence of a contract as to property may be imputed from a change in the manner of holding, such as joint accounts, but not such joint accounts as were set up on the various filming locations (Tucson, Baker, Palau). These accounts were transient, employed solely for the convenience of attending to current needs away from California. The disposition of funds remaining after the film was completed underlined the single purpose of the accounts: upon completion the funds were placed not in a joint account in Los Angeles but in defendant's separate account.

Plaintiff's use of charge accounts certainly does not establish that defendant by his alleged consent to such use intended that half of his property be given to plaintiff.

Registering at hotels as Mr. and Mrs. Marvin does not indicate that defendant intended to give plaintiff one-half of the property. Such evidence may assist in proving a relationship which on its surface resembles marriage in areas away from home, but relationships resembling marriage may exist without any property arrangements. Hence more must be proved by a preponderance of evidence, that is, that plaintiff used the charge accounts *because defendant had agreed to give her half of the property.*

Plaintiff proved that she acted as companion and homemaker, that she prepared a number of defendant's meals and that she cleaned house or supervised a cleaning woman. That she did so in consideration of a contract, express, implied, or tacit, with respect to disposing of property, remains unproven. The existence of such property agreement has not been established by the requisite preponderance of the evidence. The decision of *In re Marriage of Cary* (1973) 34 Cal. App. 3d 345, 109 Cal. Rptr. 862 and *Estate of Atherley* (1975) 44 Cal. App.3d 758, 119 Cal. Rptr. 41 afford no comfort to the plaintiff as their facts distinguish them from the instant case. In *Cary*, the disputed property was placed in the joint names of both parties, joint income tax returns were filed, money was borrowed and business was conducted as husband and wife. In *Atherley*, both parties pooled earnings accumulated for 13 years and bought property as joint tenants. Both worked and contributed funds to the construction of improvements on land bought with such earnings. None of these facts were established in this case; there was no pooling of earnings, no property was purchased in joint names, and no joint income tax returns were executed. Joint accounts set up on filming locations were only used as convenient and transient methods of payment of bills with the balance returned to the separate account of the defendant when the film was completed.

As for pooling of earnings, the bulk of plaintiff's compensation for singing was used to pay her musician and arrangers. When she did achieve a net income in the Hawaiian engagement, she placed the money in her separate account. Defendant's income was deposited in his own bank account and used to buy property in his own name. This case therefore bears little resemblance either to *Cary* or *Atherley*.

Finding no contract, the testimony of Doughly is not evaluated as that relates to an alleged breach of contract.

It is clear that the parties came together because of mutual affection and not because of mutual consent to a contract. Nothing else, certainly no contract, kept them together and, when that affection diminished, they separated.

EQUITABLE REMEDIES

If no contract, express or implied, is to be found, the Supreme Court adjures the trial court to ascertain whether any equitable remedies are applicable. The high court suggests constructive and resulting trusts as well as quantum meruit. The court also declares: "Our opinion does not preclude the evolution of additional equitable remedies to protect the expectations of the parties to a nonmarital relationship in cases in which existing remedies prove inadequate; the suitability of such remedies may be determined in later cases in light of the factual setting in which they arise."[11]

The plaintiff has, by her dismissal of her fourth and fifth causes of action — both for quantum meruit — removed that remedy from the court's consideration.

If a resulting trust is to be established, it must be shown that property was intended by the parties to be held by one party in trust for the other and that consideration was provided by the one not holding title to purchase the property. As Witkin puts it, there must be "circumstances showing that the transferee (holder of title) was not intended to take the beneficial interest."[12]

No evidence has been adduced to show such consideration having been provided by the plaintiff to buy property.[13] It may be contended that as the defendant did not need to expend funds to secure homemaking services elsewhere, she thereby enhanced the financial base of the defendant and enabled him to increase his property purchases. (See Bruch, *supra*, p. 123.) Such alleged enhancement, however, would appear to be offset by the considerable flow of economic benefits in the other direction. Those benefits include payments for goods and services for plaintiff up to $72,900 for the period from 1967–1970 alone (Ex. 194). Exhibit 196 indicates that living expenses for the parties were $221,400 for the period from 1965 to 1970. Among such benefits were a Mercedes Benz automobile for plaintiff, fur coats, travel to London, Hawaii, Japan, Micronesia, and the pleasures of life on the California beach in frequent contact with many film and stage notables. Further, defendant made a substantial financial effort to launch plaintiff's career as a recording singer. No equitable basis for an expansion of the resulting trust theory is afforded in view of this evidence.

A constructive trust, pleaded in the second cause of action, is "equity's version of implied-in-law recovery" (see Bruch, *supra*, 125) based on unjust enrichment. This is a trust imposed to force restitution of something that in fairness and good conscience does not belong to its owner. (See Bruch, *supra*, p. 125). However, the defendant earned the money by means of his own effort, skill and reputation. The

---

11. *Marvin v. Marvin*, *supra* p. 684, footnote 25.

12. 7 Witkin, SUMMARY OF CALIF. LAW. §123, p. 5481.

13. Such establishment must be by clear and convincing proof. (G.G. Bogert and G.T. Bogert, HANDBOOK OF THE LAW OF TRUSTS, §74 at p. 279 (5th edition 1973); *Moulton v. Moulton* (1920) 182 Cal. 185, 187 p. 421; Bruch, *Property Rights of De Facto Spouses*, 10 FAMILY LAW QUARTERLY, P. 101.)

money was then invested in the properties now held by him. It cannot be said in good conscience that such properties do not belong to him.

As Witkin points out, such a trust is an equitable remedy imposed where a person obtains property by fraudulent misrepresentation or concealment or by some wrongful act.[14] No such wrongdoing can be elicited from the facts of this case.

Plaintiff contends that the Supreme Court by its opinion in *Marvin v. Marvin, supra,* requires that plaintiff receive a reasonable proportion of the property in defendant's name because of her performance of the homemaker, companion, cook and other wife-like functions even though no contract, express or implied, exists and even though no basis for a constructive or resulting trust can be found. To accede to such a contention would mean that the court would recognize each unmarried person living together to be automatically entitled by such living together, and performing spouse-like functions, to half of the property bought with the earnings of the other nonmarital partner. This is tantamount to recognition of common law marriages in California. As they were abolished in 1895, the Supreme Court surely does not mean to resurrect them by its opinion in *Marvin v. Marvin.*[15] The trial court's understanding of *Marvin v. Marvin* is that if there is mutual consent or proof of the mutual intent of the parties, by reason of their conduct or because of surrounding circumstances, to share the property or if the plaintiff directly participated in the procurement of or the nurturing of investments, or if there has been mutual effort (which will be discussed later) the property should be divided. None of these conditions pertains here.

While the Supreme Court directs under certain circumstances a fair apportionment of property even though there is no express or implied contract, it has imposed a condition, that such property be "accumulated through mutual effort." (p. 682.) Plaintiff declares that her work as homemaker, cook, and companion are "mutual effort."

The two cases cited as examples of mutual effort, *In re Marriage of Cary* (1973) 34 Cal.App.3d 345, 109 Cal. Rptr. 862 and *Estate of Atherley* (1975) 44 Cal.App.3d 758, 119 Cal. Rptr. 41, reveal considerably more involvement on accumulation of property. In the first place, Paul Cary and Janet Forbes (in *Cary, supra*) held themselves out to be husband and wife. That is not the case here. The reputation of the parties in the community in which they settled was not that they were a married couple. Not only did Cary and Forbes purchase a home, but they also borrowed money, obtained credit, and filed joint income tax returns. Four children were born to the couple. The children's birth certificates and school registration recorded them as Paul and Janet Cary. None of these facts are present in the instant case.

In *Atherley,* the parties, Harold and Annette, lived together for 22 years; after 14 years Harold divorced a prior wife ex parte in Juarez, Mexico and then married Annette in Reno, Nevada. Both were employed and pooled their earnings in various bank accounts. They had been advised by a Los Angeles attorney that the Mexican divorce was valid. Both contributed services to the construction of

14. Civil Code, §§2223, 2224: 7 Witkin. *Summary of Calif. Law,* §§131, 132, pp.5487, 5488.

15. Footnote 24 of *Marvin v Marvin, supra.* expressly denies any intent to revive the relationship:

> We do not seek to resurrect the doctrine of common law marriage. which was abolished in California by statute in 1885. (See *Norman v. Thomson* (1898) 121 Cal. 620, 628, [54 F. 143]; *Estate of Abate* (1958) 166 Cal.App.2d 282, 292 [333 P.2d 200].) Thus we do not hold that plaintiff and defendant were "married," nor do we extend to plaintiff the rights which the Family Law Act grants valid or putative spouses; we hold only that she has the same rights to enforce contracts and to assert her equitable interest in property acquired *through her effort* as does any other unmarried person. (emphasis added)

improvements on land purchased by them. Funds used to purchase both land and materials can be traced to their accumulated earnings. Two bank accounts were established with funds accumulated by Harold and Annette. Upon the sale of an improved parcel, a promissory note representing part of the sales price was held in joint tenancy. None of these facts is present in the instant case.[16]

In this case we have all assets bought solely with the earnings of the defendant. The plaintiff had no net earnings except from the Hawaiian engagement and those funds went into her own account. Plaintiff secured $750 from the settlement of her suit against Roberts and those funds also did not go into defendant's account. There were, on the other hand, funds that were expended by defendant to further Plaintiff's career. The defendant also persuaded a friend to employ plaintiff in Hawaii. He brought people to hear her sing and bought drinks to keep them in attendance. It was the plaintiff who stopped trying to sell her records and get singing engagements. The evidence does not establish that such cessation was caused by defendant.

It would be difficult to deem the singing career of plaintiff to be the "mutual effort" required by the Supreme Court. Certainly, where both wanted to be free to come and go without obligation, the basis of any division of property cannot be her "giving up" her career for him. It then can only be her work as cook, homemaker and companion that can be considered as plaintiff's contribution to the requisite "mutual effort." Yet, where $72,000 has been disbursed by defendant on behalf of plaintiff in less than six years, where she has enjoyed a fine home and travel throughout the world for about 30 months, where she acquired whatever clothes, furs and cars she wished and engaged in a social life amongst screen and stage luminaries, such services as she has rendered would appear to have been compensated. Surely one cannot glean from such services her participation in a "mutual effort" between the parties to earn funds to buy property as occurred in *Cary* and *Atherley, supra.*

The Supreme Court doubtless intended by the phrase "mutual effort" to mean the relationship of a man and woman who have joined together to make a home, who act together to earn and deposit such earnings in joint accounts, who pay taxes together, who make no effort to gain an advantage by reason of the association, (such as informing a producer of a script for a fee and taking defendant's name without his consent), who have children if possible and bring them up together. *Cary* and *Atherley* in fact demands more of the partners; they require participation in money-earning activities. Plaintiff's fund-raising put money in her own account.

To construe "mutual effort" to mean services as homemaker, cook and companion and nothing else[17] would be tantamount to the grant of the benefits of the Family Law Act to the nonmarital partner as well as to the married person. This the Supreme Court has refused to do. Therefore, one must seek and find in each case those additional factors which indicate the expenditure of "mutual effort," such as those present in *Cary* and *Atherley.* Such factors are not present in this case.

The court is aware that Footnote 25, *Marvin v. Marvin, supra* p. 684, urges the trial court to employ whatever equitable remedy may be proper under the cir-

---

16. Mere possession of property or the holding of title is not a determinant if standing alone. See *Marvin v. Marvin, supra* footnote 21, p. 682.

17. This is not to gainsay that an express or implied contract may be valid and enforceable where the consideration is ordinary homemaking services. (*Marvin v. Marvin, supra* footnote 5, p. 670)

cumstances. The court is also aware of the recent resort of plaintiff to unemployment insurance benefits to support herself and of the fact that a return of plaintiff to a career as a singer doubtful. Additionally, the court knows that the market value of defendant's property at time of separation exceeded $1,000,000.

In view of these circumstances, the court in equity awards plaintiff $104,000[18] for rehabilitation purposes so that she may have the economic means to re-educate herself and to learn new, employable skills or to refurbish those utilized, for example, during her most recent employment[19] and so that she may return from her status as companion of a motion picture star to a separate, independent but perhaps more prosaic existence.

MARVIN v. MARVIN [III]

California Court of Appeal, Second District
122 Cal.App.3d 871, 176 Cal.Rptr. 555 (1981)*

COBEY, Associate Justice.

Defendant, Lee Marvin, appeals from that portion of a judgment ordering him to pay to plaintiff, Michelle Marvin, the sum of $104,000, to be used by her primarily for her economic rehabilitation.

Defendant contends, among other things, that the challenged award is outside the issues of the case as framed by the pleadings of the parties (see Code Civ.Proc., §588) and furthermore lacks any basis in equity or in law.[1] We agree and will therefore modify the judgment by deleting therefrom the challenged award.

FACTS

This statement of facts is taken wholly from the findings of the trial court, which tried the case without a jury. The parties met in June 1964 and started living together occasionally in October of that year. They lived together almost continuously (except for business absences of his) from the spring of 1965 to May or June of 1970, when their cohabitation was ended at his insistence. This cohabitation was the result of an initial agreement between them to live together as unmarried persons so long as they both enjoyed their mutual companionship and affection.

More specifically, the parties to this lawsuit never agreed during their cohabitation that they would combine their efforts and earnings or would share equally in any property accumulated as a result of their efforts, whether individual or combined. They also never agreed during this period that plaintiff would relinquish her professional career as an entertainer and singer in order to devote her efforts full time to defendant as his companion and homemaker generally. Defendant did not agree during this period of cohabitation that he would provide all of plaintiff's financial needs and support for the rest of her life.

---

18. Plaintiff should be able to accomplish rehabilitation in less than two years. The sum awarded would be approximately equivalent to the highest scale that she ever earned as a singer, $1,000 per week, for two years.

19. While part of the funds may be used for living expenses, the primary intent is that they be employed for retraining purposes.

*Plaintiff's request for review was denied by the Supreme Court of California without comment. See *Los Angeles Times*, Oct. 8, 1981, Part II, at 3, col.6. Official Advance Sheets Number 29, October 27, 1981, Minutes, at 10.

1. Defendant challenges the constitutionality of the award on various grounds, but we will not reach the issues there raised because it is unnecessary to do so. (See *People v. Green* (1980) 27 Cal.3d 1, 50, 164 Cal.Rptr. 1, 609 P.2d 468; *People v. Kozden* (1974) 36 Cal.App.3d 918, 123, 111 Cal.Rptr. 826.)

Furthermore, the trial court specifically found that: (1) defendant has never had any obligation to pay plaintiff a reasonable sum as and for her maintenance;[2] (2) plaintiff suffered no damage resulting from her relationship with defendant, including its termination and thus defendant did not become monetarily liable to plaintiff at all; (3) plaintiff actually benefited economically and socially from the cohabitation of the parties, including payment by defendant for goods and services for plaintiff's sole benefit in the approximate amount of $72,900.00, payment by defendant of the living expenses of the two of them of approximately $221,400.00, and other substantial specified gifts;[3] (4) a confidential and fiduciary relationship never existed between the parties with respect to property; (5) defendant was never unjustly enriched as a result of the relationship of the parties or of the services performed by plaintiff for him or for them; (6) defendant never acquired any property or money from plaintiff by any wrongful act.

The trial court specifically found in support of its challenged rehabilitation award that the market value of defendant's property at the time the parties separated exceeded $1 million, that plaintiff at the time of the trial of this case had been recently receiving unemployment insurance benefits, that it was doubtful that plaintiff could return to the career that she had enjoyed before the relationship of the parties commenced, namely, that of singer, that plaintiff was in need of rehabilitation *i.e.*, to learn new employable skills, that she should be able to accomplish such rehabilitation in two years and that the sum of $104,000 was not only necessary primarily for such rehabilitation, but also for her living expenses (including her debts) during this period of rehabilitation, and that defendant had the ability to pay this sum forthwith.

Moreover, the trial court concluded as a matter of law that inasmuch as defendant had terminated the relationship of the parties and plaintiff had no visible means of support, "in equity," she had a right to assistance by defendant until she could become self-supporting. The trial court explained that it fixed the award at the highest salary that the plaintiff had ever earned, namely, $1,000 a week for two years, although plaintiff's salary had been at that level for only two weeks and she ordinarily had earned less than one-half that amount weekly.

DISCUSSION

1. The challenged rehabilitation award is not within the issues framed by the pleadings.

This is a judgment roll appeal in the sense that we have no transcript of the evidence taken at the apparently lengthy trial below. The issues in a lawsuit are, aside from those added by a pretrial order, either those framed by the pleadings or as expanded at trial. (See 4 Witkin, Cal. Procedure (2d ed. 1971) Trial, §336, p. 3138.) Here, however, since we do not have before us the evidence taken at trial and there was no pretrial order expanding the issues, we can look only to the pleadings to determine the issues between the parties.

Plaintiff's amended complaint, upon which this action went to trial, asks, with respect to the support of plaintiff by defendant, only that defendant be ordered to pay to plaintiff a reasonable sum per month as and for her support and mainte-

---

2. The judgment under appeal tracks this finding in the following language: "Defendant never had, and does not now have, the duty and obligation to pay to plaintiff a reasonable sum as and for her support and maintenance."

3. The trial court also found that "Defendant made a substantial financial effort to launch Plaintiff's career as a recording singer and to continue her career as a nightclub singer."

nance. Plaintiff did not ask in this basic pleading for any limited rehabilitative support of the type the trial court apparently on its own initiative subsequently awarded her. Consequently, the special findings of fact and conclusions of law in support of this award must be disregarded as not being within the issues framed by the pleadings. (See *Crescent Lumber Co. v. Larson* (1913) 166 Cal. 168, 171, 135 P. 502; *Gardiana v. Small Claims Court* (1976) 59 Cal.App.3d 412, 421, 130 Cal.Rptr. 675.) When this is done, the challenged portion of the judgment becomes devoid of any support whatsoever and therefore must be deleted.

2. In any event there is no equitable or legal basis for the challenged rehabilitative award.

The trial court apparently based its rehabilitative award upon two footnotes in the opinion of our Supreme Court in this case. (*Marvin v. Marvin* (1976) 18 Cal.3d 660, 134 Cal.Rptr. 815, 557 P.2d 106.) These are footnotes 25 and 26, which respectively read as follows:

> Our opinion does not preclude the evolution of additional equitable remedies to protect the expectations of the parties to a nonmarital relationship in cases in which existing remedies prove inadequate; the suitability of such remedies may be determined in later cases in light of the factual setting in which they arise. (*Id.* at p. 684, 134 Cal. Rptr. 815, 557 P.2d 106.)
>
> We do not pass upon the question whether, in the absence of an express or implied contractual obligation, a party to a nonmarital relationship is entitled to support payments from the other party after the relationship terminates. (*Id.* at p. 685, 134 Cal. Rptr. 815, 557 P.2d 106.)

There is no doubt that footnote 26 opens the door to a support award in appropriate circumstances. Likewise, under footnote 25, equitable remedies should be devised "to protect the expectations of the parties to a nonmarital relationship." The difficulty in applying either of these footnotes in the manner in which the trial court has done in this case is that, as already pointed out, the challenged limited rehabilitative award of the trial court is not within the issues of the case as framed by the pleadings and there is nothing in the trial court's findings to suggest that such an award is warranted to protect the expectations of *both* parties.

Quite to the contrary, as already noted, the trial court expressly found that plaintiff benefited economically and socially from her relationship with defendant and suffered no damage therefrom, even with respect to its termination. Furthermore, the trial court also expressly found that defendant never had any obligation to pay plaintiff a reasonable sum as and for her maintenance and that defendant had not been unjustly enriched by reason of the relationship or its termination and that defendant had never acquired anything of value from plaintiff by any wrongful act.

Furthermore, the special findings in support of the challenged rehabilitative award merely established plaintiff's need therefor and defendant's ability to respond to that need. This is not enough. The award, being nonconsensual in nature, must be supported by some recognized underlying obligation in law or in equity. A court of equity admittedly has broad powers, but it may not create totally new substantive rights under the guise of doing equity. (See *Rosenberg v. Lawrence* (1938) 10 Cal.2d 590, 594–595, 75 P.2d 1082; *Lande v. Jurisich* (1943) 59 Cal.App.2d 613, 618, 139 P.2d 657.)

The trial court in its special conclusions of law addressed to this point attempted to state an underlying obligation by saying that plaintiff had a right to assistance from defendant until she became self-supporting. But this special conclusion obviously conflicts with the earlier, more general, finding of the court that defendant has never had and did not then have any obligation to provide plaintiff with a reasonable sum for her support and maintenance and, in view of the already-mentioned findings of no damage (but benefit instead), no unjust enrichment and no wrongful act on the part of defendant with respect to either the relationship or its termination, it is clear that no basis whatsoever, either in equity or in law, exists for the challenged rehabilitative award. It therefore must be deleted from the judgment.[4]

DISPOSITION

The judgment under appeal is modified by deleting therefrom the portion thereof under appeal, namely, the rehabilitative award of $104,000 to plaintiff, Michelle Marvin. As modified it is affirmed. Costs on appeal are awarded to defendant, Lee Marvin.

POTTER, J., concurs.

KLEIN, Presiding Justice, dissenting.

I dissent.

This case was tried by the court sitting without a jury over a three-month period, during which time presumably extensive evidence was taken. The trial court was able to evaluate the parties and witnesses as they appeared and gave testimony. However, since the record on this appeal consists only of the judgment roll rather than a reporter's transcript, we do not know the extent and nature of the evidence presented, or whether the issues as framed by the pleadings were expanded during the trial.

We do know that at the conclusion of the trial, the trial court awarded Michelle $104,000 pursuant to finding number 26 that: "Plaintiff is in need of funds to be used in the course of rehabilitation, so that she may re-educate herself and learn new employable skills...," and finding number 27 that: "The sum of $104,000.00 is necessary primarily for rehabilitation and also living expenses and debts to be paid during such rehabilitation."

In her first amended complaint, Michelle pled as follows:

> That in order that Plaintiff would be able to devote her full time to Defendant Marvin as a companion, homemaker, housekeeper and cook, it was further agreed that Plaintiff would give up her lucrative career as an entertainer/singer.
>
> That in return, Defendant Marvin would provide for all of Plaintiff's financial support and needs for the rest of her life.

Michelle prayed for "such other relief as this Court deems just and proper."

We are also made aware of the fact that Marvin was paying Michelle monies on a monthly basis after their separation pursuant to some kind of an "arrangement."

---

4. We obviously disagree with our dissenting colleague regarding the clarity and consistency (with the judgment) of the trial court's special findings of fact and conclusions of law in support of the challenged rehabilitative award. There is no need to remand this case to the trial court for correction of these matters since the award itself is without support in either equity or law.

The trial court in its memorandum opinion recognizes that *Marvin v. Marvin* (1976) 18 Cal.3d 660, 134 Cal.Rptr. 815, 557 P.2d 106, "...urges the trial court to employ whatever equitable remedy may be proper under the circumstances."

Marvin v. Marvin, supra, at page 685, footnote 26, 134 Cal.Rptr. 815, 557 P.2d 106, specifically states: "We do not pass upon the question whether, in the absence of an express or implied contractual obligation, a party to a nonmarital relationship is entitled to support payments from the other party after the relationship terminates."

In finding number 3, the trial court herein concludes: "The parties did not enter into any agreement to the following effect: That Plaintiff would give up any career which she might have had, whether as an entertainer/singer, or in any other calling, in order to enable Plaintiff to devote her full time to Defendant as a companion, homemaker, housekeeper and cook of Defendant," the contents of which finding was echoed in finding numbers 6 and 7. In finding number 18(c), the trial court found that the plaintiff did not in fact give up her career at the defendant's request in order to devote her full time and attention to defendant's personal needs.

In view of all the evidence that the trial court had before it, including the plaintiff's sex, age, earning ability and career status, the length of the relationship, and other circumstances of the factual setting, *Marvin v. Marvin, supra,* seems to say that the trial court was authorized by way of remedy to provide support payments from the other party after the relationship terminated, provided it also found some equitable right to such a remedy. Apparently, this is what the trial court herein attempted to do in granting a support-type award for rehabilitation for a two-year period, which seemed to reinstate to some extent the prior "arrangement" the parties had.

However, it is the trial court's responsibility to provide findings of fact and conclusions of law which are consistent with the judgment in order that we may conduct proper appellate review. (*Spaulding v. Cameron* (1952) 38 Cal.2d 265, 270, 239 P.2d 625; *Kaiser Foundation Hospitals v. Workers' Comp. Appeals Bd.* (Fuchs)(1979) 91 Cal.App.3d 501, 506, fn. 5, 154 Cal.Rptr. 765; *Machado v. Machado* (1914) 26 Cal.App. 16, 18, 145 P. 738.)

Indeed, "'it is essential that [the trial court's findings of fact and conclusions of law] be sufficient in form and substance so that by reading them and referring to the record the parties can tell and this court can tell with reasonable certainty not only the theory upon which the [trial court] has arrived at its ultimate finding and conclusion but that the [trial court] has in truth found those facts which as a matter of law are essential to sustain its award.' (*Mercer-Fraser Co. v. Industrial Acc. Com.* [1953] 40 Cal.2d (102,) 124 [251 P.2d 955]." (*Kaiser Foundation Hospitals v. Workers' Comp. Appeals Bd.* (Fuchs), *supra,* 91 Cal.App.3d at p. 506, fn. 5, 154 Cal.Rptr. 765.)

As "it is impossible to reconcile this judgment with the findings..., it is clearly the duty of this court to reverse this judgment and remand the case to the trial court for... correction... of the [inconsistencies] in its findings [and conclusions] or its judgment or both." (*Machado v. Machado, supra,* 26 Cal.App. at p. 18, 145 P. 738; 6 Witkin, Cal. Procedure (2d ed. 1971) Appeal, §541, pp. 4482–4483.)

I would reverse the judgment and remand for further proceedings consistent with this dissent.

COMMENTS

Peck, decided eighty-four years earlier than *Marvin* by the Supreme Judicial Court of Massachusetts involved a clear case of contract cohabitation. The relationship was based on an express contract — witnessed and in writing — founded on love and terminable at the will of either party. The contract, styled as a partnership, provided for equal division of mutually acquired property and for mutual support obligations should there be children. In *Marvin,* on the other hand, the plaintiff alleged a mere oral contract which, ultimately, she could not prove. Her recovery, after the case was remanded to the trial court, was purely under the most general equitable considerations. (See pp. 240–41) Even this recovery was reversed on further appeal. (See *Marvin III,* p. 241.)

There are major procedural differences between *Peck* and *Marvin. Peck* involved a request for a divorce. It was dismissed because the contract the parties entered, calling for a partnership based on "the true marriage relation," strayed too far from the requirements for marriage at the time the case was decided. Moreover, there had been no further ceremony or solemnization, although the parties held themselves out as husband and wife. Whether any recovery would have been possible under contract was not in issue. In a sense, the woman had adhered to the contract by leaving after the union had become disagreeable to her. *Marvin,* on the other hand, was an action based on contract, not on marriage. Had the plaintiff requested a dissolution of marriage, her lawsuit would have been dismissed. It is unlikely that any form of recovery would have been possible in contract or equity under the facts recited in *Peck,* as the contract was probably against public policy in 1892. Yet, aside from its social-historical context, *Peck* is a much stronger case for contract cohabitation than *Marvin.*

It seems apparent from the tone of *Peck* that the judge intended to penalize both parties to what he considered an immoral contract. Yet, is there any way the court could penalize one party to the agreement without rewarding the other? In 1892 some courts considered it wise policy to deny divorce and force unhappy spouses to stay bound to one another, which presumably would have displeased both parties in *Peck,* but seemingly here the desertion of the (non)wife would have given the (non)husband a basis for divorce anyway. The actual effect of the court decree seems to have been to facilitate much of what the contract had intended — to allow the couple to break up if and when they wished.

Michelle Marvin was not attempting to establish or alter a marital status; the lawsuit was seeking economic recovery on the basis of the prior relationship. Why the male party in *Peck* filed a divorce action is less clear; perhaps it was brought to clarify his legal status. Since a valid marriage is a prerequisite to a divorce action, a dismissal of the request for lack of marriage can have some of the legal effects of a declaration of non-marital status. Yet if the plaintiff in *Peck* was merely interested in testing the validity of a possible marriage, it is still left unclear why he appealed the dismissal. Perhaps he was concerned primarily about the status of property in the various jurisdictions in which he and his companion had lived. Many of the states, including California, still recognized common law marriages in 1892. The plaintiff may also have been concerned about the full faith and credit effects of a judgment dismissing his complaint.

The significance of *Marvin* is somewhat affected by the way the case was pursued after the Supreme Court of California had reversed and remanded it "for further proceedings consistent with the views expressed herein." Trial courts frequently attempt to minimize the impact of an appellate reversal, trying to reach a decision as close as possible to their original holdings without incurring the danger of a renewed appeal. After extensive findings of fact that cover more than half his opinion, the trial judge came to the conclusion that none of the suggested remedies was supported by the facts as found — no express contract, no implied contract, no unjust enrichment, no resulting or constructive trust. He then seized upon footnote 25 of the mandating opinion of the Supreme Court of California, which contemplates the possibility of additional equitable remedies as they "may be determined in later cases in light of the factual setting in which they arise." In applying undefined equitable standards, the trial court awarded $104,000 to the plaintiff for rehabilitation purposes. Two short concluding paragraphs were felt to be sufficient for this result, although they contradict earlier portions of the opinion that question the veracity of the plaintiff. In effect, Michelle Marvin was awarded rights comparable to rehabilitative alimony, although no marriage existed. Whatever one may think of the logic of the trial court's decision, it may have been designed to prevent further appeals by permitting some recovery. Yet this hope proved to be unrealistic. (See p. 241)

Marvin emerges as an appellate opinion for the abstract proposition that cohabitation contracts are possible, although no such contract was found to exist in the specific case. To this the trial court added a remedy, erroneously as it seems, that has been called "palimony." Quite apart from the technical limits of stare decisis, three main consequences may acquire significance beyond California. First, parties may be induced to enter express cohabitation contracts to avoid the unlimited judicial discretion that could come into play if "additional equitable remedies" (footnote 25) were applicable. Second, in the absence of an express contract, the courts may imply one if they wish, since cohabitation always involves some consensus. A finding of an implied contract, based on facts relating to the conduct of the parties, would also be difficult to reverse on appeal. Obviously a great ideal of discretion would be involved. Third, the portion of the appellate opinion that permitted "additional equitable remedies," as demonstrated by the trial court opinion, could invite a judge's discretionary application of power in cohabitation cases. The question to be answered is: what does the *Marvin* result mean in terms of legal theory and practice?

An express contract of cohabitation is not likely to raise serious problems; courts will be increasingly inclined to enforce well-drafted ones. Since one of the many functions of express contracts of cohabitation may be to refute any presumption of marriage, as well as to limit judicial discretion, express contract may become an alternative available to the literate American middle classes. That is, if they choose not to protect or bind themselves by formal marriage, they will be able to order their financial dealings through written contractual stipulation.

On the other hand, implied contract, although viewed under contract theory as having the same conceptual basis as express contract, may break away from traditional theory and become a vehicle for subtly applying public policy through the legal fiction of an imposed consensual relationship. In other words, parties to cohabitation arrangements, based purely on ambiguous behavior and not on express agreement, may be treated by the courts as if they had entered a legal contract of cohabitation. Implied contract could thus become a tool for judicial intervention that allocates some of the social costs of a relationship to the appropriate party by way of contractual fiction. If this method appears too strained in an individual case, as in *Marvin,* the judge can still apply general equitable principles, although perhaps within limits, as indicated in the most recent appellate reversal. An ironic aspect of *Marvin* is that many couples have claimed as a reason for not getting married a desire to avoid the legal entanglement and costs of divorce in case the relationship fails; lawyers have once again refused to allow themselves to be made dispensable.

One further aspect of *Marvin* requires discussion, namely, the revived importance of fault, a possibility foreseen by Mr. Justice Clark in his concurring and dissenting opinion. He pointed out that any resort to equity necessitates an examination of the conduct of the parties, thus resurrecting the bitterness and acrimony of litigation that was common prior to the legislative adoption of no-fault divorce. The opinion of the trial court, following the mandate of the appellate court in *Marvin,* seemed to bear this out. The complete life patterns of the plaintiff and defendant were examined in detail, including alleged conduct of the plaintiff which, had there been a marriage, would have been adultery. Her defense was denial and an assertion that the alleged co-respondent was a homosexual. The trial court allowed the testimony under a theory that the sexual conduct of the plaintiff could amount to a breach of contract. While the court found that there was no contract and thus no breach, the testimony could nevertheless have been relevant under other headings, for instance, to prove that the plaintiff had not intended to be contractually bound or that she lacked clean hands for purposes of equitable remedies. It is possible therefore that evidence to demonstrate fault can be relevant in a breach of contract action based on nonmarital cohabitation, while the same evidence is excluded in California and elsewhere in a suit for no-fault divorce. Requiring a more stringent standard of conduct for cohabitation than for marriage lacks plausibility. We will see, however, that it is difficult to eradicate fault from human relations. There seems to be a strong emotional need to blame a party if a breakup occurs, regardless of whether there was or, as in *Marvin,* was not a marriage.

REFERENCES

Clare Dalton, *An Essay on the Deconstruction of Contract Doctrine,* 94 YALE L.J. 997, 1095 (1985).

Herma Hill Kay & Carol Amyx, *Marvin v. Marvin, Preserving the Options,* 65 CAL. L. REV. 937 (1977).

HEWITT v. HEWITT

Supreme Court of Illinois
77 Ill. 2d 49, 394 N.E.2d 1204 (1979)

UNDERWOOD, Justice:

The issue in this case is whether plaintiff Victoria Hewitt, whose complaint alleges she lived with defendant Robert Hewitt from 1960 to 1975 in an unmarried, family-like relationship to which three children have been born, may recover from him "an equal share of the profits and properties accumulated by the parties" during that period.

Plaintiff initially filed a complaint for divorce, but at a hearing on defendant's motion to dismiss, admitted that no marriage ceremony had taken place and that the parties have never obtained a marriage license. In dismissing that complaint the trial court found that neither a ceremonial nor a common law marriage existed; that since defendant admitted the paternity of the minor children, plaintiff need not bring a separate action under the Paternity Act (Ill.Rev.Stat. 1975, ch. 1063/4, par. 51 *et seq.*) to have the question of child support determined; and directed plaintiff to make her complaint more definite as to the nature of the property of which she was seeking division.

Plaintiff thereafter filed an amended complaint alleging the following bases for her claim: (1) that because defendant promised he would "share his life, his future, his earnings and his property" with her and all of defendant's property resulted from the parties' joint endeavors, plaintiff is entitled in equity to a one-half share; (2) that the conduct of the parties evinced an implied contract entitling plaintiff to one-half the property accumulated during their "family relationship"; (3) that because defendant fraudulently assured plaintiff she was his wife in order to secure her services, although he knew they were not legally married, defendant's property should be impressed with a trust for plaintiff's benefit; (4) that because plaintiff has relied to her detriment on defendant's promises and devoted her entire life to him, defendant has been unjustly enriched.

The factual background alleged or testified to is that in June 1960, when she and defendant were students at Grinnell College in Iowa, plaintiff became pregnant; that defendant thereafter told her that they were husband and wife and would live as such, no formal ceremony being necessary, and that he would "share his life, his future, his earnings and his property" with her; that the parties immediately announced to their respective parents that they were married and thereafter held themselves out as husband and wife; that in reliance on defendant's promises she devoted her efforts to his professional education and his establishment in the practice of pedodontia, obtaining financial assistance from her parents for this purpose; that she assisted defendant in his career with her own special skills and although she was given payroll checks for these services she placed them in a common fund; that defendant, who was without funds at the time of the marriage, as a result of her efforts now earns over $80,000 a year and has accumulated large amounts of property, owned either jointly with her or separately; that she has given him every assistance a wife and mother could give, including social activities designed to enhance his social and professional reputation.

The amended complaint was also dismissed, the trial court finding that Illinois law and public policy require such claims to be based on a valid marriage. The appellate court reversed, stating that because the parties had outwardly lived a conventional married life, plaintiff's conduct had not "so affronted public policy that she should be denied any and all relief" (62 Ill.App.3d 861, 869, 20 Ill.Dec. 476, 482, 380 N.E.2d 454, 460), and that plaintiff's complaint stated a cause of action on an express oral contract. We granted leave to appeal. Defendant apparently does not contest his obligation to support the children, and that question is not before us.

The appellate court, in reversing, gave considerable weight to the fact that the parties had held themselves out as husband and wife for over 15 years. The court noted that they lived "a most conventional, respectable and ordinary family life" (62 Ill.App.3d 861, 863, 20 Ill.Dec. 476, 478, 380 N.E.2d 454, 457) that did not openly flout accepted standards, the "single flaw" being the lack of a valid marriage. Indeed the appellate court went so far as to say that the parties had "lived within the legitimate boundaries of a marriage and family relationship of a most conventional sort" (62 Ill.App.3d 861, 864, 20 Ill.Dec. 476, 479, 380 N.E.2d 454, 457), an assertion which that court cannot have intended to be taken literally. Noting that the Illinois Marriage and Dissolution of Marriage Act (Ill.Rev.Stat.1977, ch. 40, par. 101 *et seq.*) does not prohibit nonmarital cohabitation and that the Criminal Code of 1961 (Ill.Rev.Stat.1977, ch. 38, par. 11-8(a)) makes fornication an offense only if the behavior is open and notorious, the appellate court concluded that plaintiff should not be denied relief on public policy grounds.

In finding that plaintiff's complaint stated a cause of action on an express oral contract, the appellate court adopted the reasoning of the California Supreme Court in the widely publicized case of *Marvin v. Marvin* (1976), 18 Cal.3d 660, 134 Cal.Rptr. 815, 557 P.2d 106, quoting extensively therefrom. In *Marvin*, Michelle Triola and defendant Lee Marvin lived together for 7 years pursuant to an alleged oral agreement that while "the parties lived together they would combine their efforts and earnings and would share equally any and all property accumulated as a result of their efforts whether individual or combined." (18 Cal.3d 660, 666, 134 Cal.Rptr. 815, 819, 557 P.2d 106, 110.) In her complaint she alleged that, in reliance on this agreement, she gave up her career as a singer to devote herself full time to defendant as "companion, homemaker, housekeeper and cook." (18 Cal.3d 660, 666, 134 Cal.Rptr. 815, 819, 557 P.2d 106, 110.) In resolving her claim for one-half the property accumulated in defendant's name during that period the California court held that "The courts should enforce express contracts between nonmarital partners except to the extent that the contract is explicitly founded on the consideration of meretricious sexual services" and that "In the absence of an express contract, the courts should inquire into the conduct of the parties to determine whether that conduct demonstrates an implied contract, agreement of partnership or joint venture, or some other tacit understanding between the parties. The courts may also employ the doctrine of quantum meruit, or equitable remedies such as constructive or resulting trusts, when warranted by the facts of the case." (18 Cal.3d 660, 665, 134 Cal.Rptr. 815, 819, 557 P.2d 106, 110.) The court reached its conclusions because:

> In summary, we believe that the prevalence of nonmarital relationships in modern society and the social acceptance of them, marks this as a time when our courts should by no means apply the doctrine of the unlawfulness of the so-called meretricious relationship to the instant case....
>
> ...

> The mores of the society have indeed changed so radically in regard to cohabitation that we cannot impose a standard based on alleged moral considerations that have apparently been so widely abandoned by so many.

18 Cal.3d 660, 683–84, 134 Cal.Rptr. 815, 831, 557 P.2d 106, 122.

It is apparent that the *Marvin* court adopted a pure contract theory, under which, if the intent of the parties and the terms of their agreement are proved, the pseudo-conventional family relationship which impressed the appellate court here is irrelevant; recovery may be had unless the implicit sexual relationship is made the explicit consideration for the agreement. In contrast, the appellate court here, as we understand its opinion, would apply contract principles only in a setting where the relationship of the parties outwardly resembled that of a traditional family. It seems apparent that the plaintiff in *Marvin* would not have been entitled to recover in our appellate court because of the absence of that outwardly appearing conventional family relationship.

The issue of whether property rights accrue to unmarried cohabitants can not, however, be regarded realistically as merely a problem in the law of express contracts. Plaintiff argues that because her action is founded on an express contract, her recovery would in no way imply that unmarried cohabitants acquire property rights merely by cohabitation and subsequent separation. However, the *Marvin* court expressly recognized and the appellate court here seems to agree that if common law principles of express contract govern express agreements between unmarried cohabitants, common law principles of implied contract, equitable relief and constructive trust must govern the parties' relations in the absence of such an agreement. (18 Cal.3d 660, 678, 134 Cal.Rptr. 815, 827, 557 P.2d 106, 118; 62 Ill.App.3d 861, 867–68, 20 Ill.Dec. 476, 380 N.E.2d 454.) In all probability the latter case will be much the more common, since it is unlikely that most couples who live together will enter into express agreements regulating their property rights. (Bruch, *Property Rights of De Facto Spouses, Including Thoughts on the Value of Homemakers' Services,* 10 Fam.L.Q. 101, 102 (1976).) The increasing incidence of nonmarital cohabitation referred to in *Marvin* and the variety of legal remedies therein sanctioned seem certain to result in substantial amounts of litigation, in which, whatever the allegations regarding an oral contract, the proof will necessarily involve details of the parties' living arrangements.

Apart, however, from the appellate court's reliance upon *Marvin* to reach what appears to us to be a significantly different result, we believe there is a more fundamental problem. We are aware, of course, of the increasing judicial attention given the individual claims of unmarried cohabitants to jointly accumulated property, and the fact that the majority of courts considering the question have recognized an equitable or contractual basis for implementing the reasonable expectations of the parties unless sexual services were the explicit consideration. (See cases collected in Annot., 31 A.L.R.2d 1255 (1953) and A.L.R.2d Later Case Service supplementing vols. 25 to 31.) The issue of unmarried cohabitants' mutual property rights, however, as we earlier noted, cannot appropriately be characterized solely in terms of contract law, nor is it limited to considerations of equity or fairness as between the parties to such relationships. There are major public policy questions involved in determining whether, under what circumstances, and to what extent it is desirable to accord some type of legal status to claims arising from such relationships. Of substantially greater importance than the rights of the immediate parties is the impact of such recognition upon our society and the institution of marriage. Will the fact that legal rights closely resembling those arising from conventional marriages can be acquired by those who deliberately choose to enter into what have heretofore been commonly referred to as "illicit" or "meretricious" relationships encourage formation of such relationships and weaken marriage as the foundation of our family-based society? In the event of death shall the survivor have the status of a surviving spouse for purposes of inheritance, wrongful death actions, workmen's compensation, etc.? And still more importantly: what of the children born of such relationships? What are their support and inheritance rights and by what standards are custody questions resolved? What of the sociological and psychological effects upon them of that type of environment? Does not the recognition of legally enforceable property and custody rights emanating from nonmarital cohabitation in practical effect equate with the legalization of common law marriage at least in the circumstances of this case? And, in summary, have the increasing numbers of unmarried cohabitants and changing mores of our society (Bruch, *Property Rights of De Facto Spouses Including Thoughts on the Value of Homemakers' Services*, 10 Fam.L.Q. 101, 102–03 (1976); Nielson, *In re Cary: A Judicial Recognition of Illicit Cohabitation*, 25 Hastings L.J. 1226 (1974)) reached the point at which the general welfare of the citizens of this State is best served by a return to something resembling the judicially created common law marriage our legislature outlawed in 1905?

Illinois' public policy regarding agreements such as the one alleged here was implemented long ago in *Wallace v. Rappleye* (1882), 103 Ill. 229, 249, where this court said: "An agreement in consideration of future illicit cohabitation between the plaintiffs is void." This is the traditional rule, in force until recent years in all jurisdictions. (See, *e.g., Gauthier v. Laing* (1950), 96 N.H. 80, 70 A.2d 207; *Grant v. Butt* (1941), 198 S.C. 298, 17 S.E.2d 689.) Section 589 of the Restatement of Contracts (1932) states, "A bargain in whole or in part for or in consideration of illicit sexual intercourse or of a promise thereof is illegal." See also 6A Corbin, Contracts sec. 1476 (1962), and cases cited therein.

It is true, of course, that cohabitation by the parties may not prevent them from forming valid contracts about independent matters, for which it is said the sexual relations do not form part of the consideration. (Restatement of Contracts secs. 589, 597 (1932); 6A Corbin, Contracts sec. 1476 (1962).) Those courts which allow recovery generally have relied on this principle to reduce the scope of the rule of illegality. Thus, California courts long prior to *Marvin* held that an express agreement to pool earnings is supported by independent consideration and is not invalidated by cohabitation of the parties, the agreements being regarded as simultaneous but separate. (See, e.g., *Trutalli v. Meraviglia* (1932), 215 Cal. 698, 12 P.2d 430; see also Annot., 31 A.L.R.2d 1255 (1953), and cases cited therein.) More recently, several courts have reasoned that the rendition of housekeeping and homemaking services such as plaintiff alleges here could be regarded as the consideration for a separate contract between the parties, severable from the illegal contract founded on sexual relations. (*Kozlowski v. Kozlowski* (1979), 80 N.J. 378, 403 A.2d 902; *Marvin v. Marvin* (1976), 18 Cal.3d 660, 670 n.5, 134 Cal.Rptr. 815, 822 n.5, 557 P.2d 106, 113 n.5; *Tyranski v. Piggins* (1973), 44 Mich.App. 570, 205 N.W.2d 595, 597; contra, *Rehak v. Mathis* (1977), 239 Ga. 541, 238 S.E.2d 81.) In *Latham v. Latham* (1976), 274 Or. 421, 547 P.2d 144, and *Carlson v. Olson* (Minn.1977), 256 N.W.2d 249, on allegations similar to those in this case, the Minnesota Supreme Court adopted *Marvin* and the Oregon court expressly held that agreements in consideration of cohabitation were not void, stating:

> We are not validating an agreement in which the only or primary consideration is sexual intercourse. The agreement here contemplated all the burdens and amenities of married life.

274 Or. 421, 427, 547 P.2d 144, 147.

The real thrust of plaintiff's argument here is that we should abandon the rule of illegality because of certain changes in societal norms and attitudes. It is urged that social mores have changed radically in recent years, rendering this principle of law archaic. It is said that because there are so many unmarried cohabitants today the courts must confer a legal status on such relationships. This, of course, is the rationale underlying some of the decisions and commentaries. (See, *e.g.*, *Marvin v. Marvin* (1976), 18 Cal.3d 660, 683, 134 Cal.Rptr. 815, 831, 557 P.2d 106, 122; *Beal v. Beal* (1978), 282 Or. 115, 577 P.2d 507; Kay & Amyx, *Marvin v. Marvin: Preserving the Options,* 65 Cal.L.Rev. 937 (1977).) If this is to be the result, however, it would seem more candid to acknowledge the return of varying forms of common law marriage than to continue displaying the naivete we believe involved in the assertion that there are involved in these relationships contracts separate and independent from the sexual activity, and the assumption that those contracts would have been entered into or would continue without that activity.

Even if we were to assume some modification of the rule of illegality is appropriate, we return to the fundamental question earlier alluded to: If resolution of this issue rests ultimately on grounds of public policy, by what body should that policy be determined? *Marvin,* viewing the issue as governed solely by contract law, found judicial policy-making appropriate. Its decision was facilitated by California precedent and that State's no-fault divorce law. In our view, however, the situation alleged here was not the kind of arm's length bargain envisioned by traditional contract principles, but an intimate arrangement of a fundamentally different kind. The issue, realistically, is whether it is appropriate for this court to grant a legal status to a private arrangement substituting for the institution of marriage sanctioned by the State. The question whether change is needed in the law governing the rights of parties in this delicate area of marriage-like relationships involves evaluations of sociological data and alternatives we believe best suited to the superior investigative and fact-finding facilities of the legislative branch in the exercise of its traditional authority to declare public policy in the domestic relations field. (*Strukoff v. Strukoff* (1979), 76 Ill.2d 53, 27 Ill.Dec. 762, 389 N.E.2d 1170; *Siegall v. Solomon* (1960), 19 Ill.2d 145, 166 N.E.2d 5.) That belief is reinforced by the fact that judicial recognition of mutual property rights between unmarried cohabitants would, in our opinion, clearly violate the policy of our recently enacted Illinois Marriage and Dissolution of Marriage Act. Although the Act does not specifically address the subject of nonmarital cohabitation, we think the legislative policy quite evident from the statutory scheme.

The Act provides:

> This Act shall be liberally construed and applied to promote its underlying purposes, which are to:
>
> (1) provide adequate procedures for the solemnization and registration of marriage;
>
> (2) strengthen and preserve the integrity of marriage and safeguard family relationships.

(Ill.Rev.Stat.1977, ch. 40, par. 102.)
We cannot confidently say that judicial recognition of property rights between unmarried cohabitants will not make that alternative to marriage more attractive by allowing the parties to engage in such relationships with greater security. As one commentator has noted, it may make this alternative especially attractive to persons who seek a property arrangement that the law does not permit to marital partners. (Comment, 90 Harv. L.Rev. 1708, 1713 (1977).) This court, for example, has held void agreements releasing husbands from their obligation to support their wives. (*Vock v. Vock* (1937), 365 Ill. 432, 6 N.E.2d 843; *VanKoten v. VanKoten* (1926), 323 Ill. 323, 154 N.E. 146; see also *Rhodes v. Rhodes* (1967), 82 Ill.App.2d 435, 225 N.E.2d 802; Restatement of Contracts sec. 587 (1932); Weitzman, *Legal Regulation of Marriage: Tradition and Change,* 62 Cal.L.Rev. 1169, 1259–63 (1974).) In thus potentially enhancing the attractiveness of a private arrangement over marriage, we believe that the appellate court decision in this case contravenes the Act's policy of strengthening and preserving the integrity of marriage.

The Act also provides: "Common law marriages contracted in this State after June 30, 1905 are invalid." (Ill. Rev. Stat. 1977, ch. 40, par. 214.) The doctrine of common law marriage was a judicially sanctioned alternative to formal marriage designed to apply to cases like the one before us. In *Port v. Port* (1873), 70 Ill. 484, this court reasoned that because the statute governing marriage did not "prohibit or declare void a marriage not solemnized in accordance with its provisions, a marriage without observing the statutory regulations, if made according to the common law, will still be a valid marriage." (70 Ill. 484, 486.) This court held that if the parties declared their present intent to take each other as husband and wife and thereafter did so a valid common law marriage existed. (*Cartwright v. McGown* (1887), 121 Ill. 388, 398, 12 N.E. 737.) Such marriages were legislatively abolished in 1905, presumably because of the problems earlier noted, and the above-quoted language expressly reaffirms that policy.

While the appellate court denied that its decision here served to rehabilitate the doctrine of common law marriage, we are not persuaded. Plaintiff's allegations disclose a relationship that clearly would have constituted a valid common law marriage in this State prior to 1905. The parties expressly manifested their present intent to be husband and wife; immediately thereafter they assumed the marital status; and for many years they consistently held themselves out to their relatives and the public at large as husband and wife. Revealingly, the appellate court relied on the fact that the parties were, to the public, husband and wife in determining that the parties living arrangement did not flout Illinois public policy. It is of course true, as plaintiff argues, that unlike a common law spouse she would not have full marital rights in that she could not, for example, claim her statutory one-third share of defendant's property on his death. The distinction appears unimpressive, however, if she can claim one-half of his property on a theory of express or implied contract.

Further, in enacting the Illinois Marriage and Dissolution of Marriage Act, our legislature considered and rejected the "no-fault" divorce concept that has been adopted in many other jurisdictions, including California. (See Uniform Marriage and Divorce Act secs. 302, 305.) Illinois appears to be one of three States retaining fault grounds for dissolution of marriage. (Ill.Rev.Stat.1977, ch. 40, par. 401; Comment, *Hewitt v. Hewitt, Contract Cohabitation and Equitable Expectations Relief for Meretricious Spouses,* 12 J. Mar. J. Prac. & Proc. 435, 452–53 (1979).)

Certainly a significantly stronger pro-marriage policy is manifest in that action, which appears to us to reaffirm the traditional doctrine that marriage is a civil contract between three parties — the husband, the wife and the State. (*Johnson v. Johnson* (1942), 381 Ill. 362, 45 N.E.2d 625; *VanKoten v. VanKoten* (1926), 323 Ill. 323, 154 N.E. 146.) The policy of the Act gives the State a strong continuing interest in the institution of marriage and prevents the marriage relation from becoming in effect a private contract terminable at will. This seems to us another indication that public policy disfavors private contractual alternatives to marriage.

Lastly, in enacting the Illinois Marriage and Dissolution of Marriage Act, the legislature adopted for the first time the civil law concept of the putative spouse. The Act provides that an unmarried person may acquire the rights of a legal spouse only if he goes through a marriage ceremony and cohabits with another in the good-faith belief that he is validly married. When he learns that the marriage is not valid his status as a putative spouse terminates; common law marriages are expressly excluded. (Ill. Rev. Stat. 1977, ch. 40, par. 305.) The legislature thus extended legal recognition to a class of nonmarital relationships, but only to the extent of a party's good-faith belief in the existence of a valid marriage. Moreover, during the legislature's deliberations on the Act *Marvin* was decided and received wide publicity. (See Note, 12 J. Mar. J. Prac. & Proc. 435, 450 (1979).) These circumstances in our opinion constitute a recent and unmistakable legislative judgment disfavoring the grant of mutual property rights to knowingly unmarried cohabitants. We have found no case in which recovery has been allowed in the face of a legislative declaration as recently and clearly enacted as ours. Even if we disagreed with the wisdom of that judgment, it is not for us to overturn or erode it. *Davis v. Commonwealth Edison Co.* (1975), 61 Ill.2d 494, 496–97, 336 N.E.2d 881.

Actually, however, the legislature judgment is in accord with the history of common law marriage in this country. "Despite its judicial acceptance in many states, the doctrine of common-law marriage is generally frowned on in this country, even in some of the states that have accepted it." (52 Am.Jur.2d 902 *Marriage* sec. 46 (1970).) Its origins, early history and problems are detailed in *In re Estate of Soeder* (1966), 7 Ohio App.2d 271, 220 N.E.2d 547, where that court noted that some 30 States did not authorize common law marriage. Judicial criticism has been widespread even in States recognizing the relationship. (See, *e.g., Baker v. Mitchell* (1941), 143 Pa.Super. 50, 54, 17 A.2d 738, 741, "a fruitful source of perjury and fraud..."; *Sorensen v. Sorensen* (1904), 68 Neb. 500, 100 N.W. 930.) "It tends to weaken the public estimate of the sanctity of the marriage relation. It puts in doubt the certainty of the rights of inheritance. It opens the door to false pretenses of marriage and the imposition on estates of suppositious heirs." 7 Ohio App.2d 271, 290, 220 N.E.2d 547, 561.

In our judgment the fault in the appellate court holding in this case is that its practical effect is the reinstatement of common law marriage, as we earlier indicated, for there is no doubt that the alleged facts would, if proved, establish such a marriage under our pre-1905 law. (*Cartwright v. McGown* (1887), 121 Ill. 388, 12 N.E. 737.) The concern of both the Marvin court and the appellate court on this score is manifest from the circumstance that both courts found it necessary to emphasize marital values ("the structure of society itself largely depends upon the institution of marriage" (*Marvin v. Marvin* (1976), 18 Cal.3d 660, 684, 134 Cal.Rptr. 815, 831, 557 P.2d 106, 122) and to deny any intent to "derogate from" (18 Cal.3d 660, 684, 134 Cal.Rptr. 815, 831, 557 P.2d 106, 122) or "denigrate" (*Hewitt v. Hewitt* (1978), 62 Ill.App.3d 861, 868, 20 Ill.Dec. 476, 380 N.E.2d 454) that institution. Commentators have expressed greater concern: "(T)he effect of these cases is to reinstitute common-law marriage in California after it has been abolished by the legislature." (Clark, *The New Marriage,* Williamette L.J. 441, 449 (1976).) "[*Hewitt*] is, if not a direct resurrection of common-law marriage contract principles, at least a large step in that direction." Reiland, *Hewitt v. Hewitt: Middle America, Marvin and Common-Law Marriage,* 60 Chi. B. Rec. 84, 88–90 (1978).

We do not intend to suggest that plaintiff's claims are totally devoid of merit. Rather, we believe that our statement in *Mogged v. Mogged* (1973), 55 Ill.2d 221, 225, 302 N.E.2d 293, 295, made in deciding whether to abolish a judicially created defense to divorce, is appropriate here:

> Whether or not the defense of recrimination should be abolished or modified in Illinois is a question involving complex public-policy considerations as to which compelling arguments may be made on both sides. For the reasons stated hereafter, we believe that these questions are appropriately within the province of the legislature, and that, if there is to be a change in the law of this State on this matter, it is for the legislature and not the courts to bring about that change.

We accordingly hold that plaintiff's claims are unenforceable for the reason that they contravene the public policy, implicit in the statutory scheme of the Illinois Marriage and Dissolution of Marriage Act, disfavoring the grant of mutually enforceable property rights to knowingly unmarried cohabitants. The judgment of the appellate court is reversed and the judgment of the circuit court of Champaign County is affirmed.

Appellate court reversed; circuit court affirmed.

BEAL v. BEAL

Supreme Court of Oregon

282 Or. 115, 577 P.2d 507 (1978)

HOWELL, Justice.

This is an appeal from a decree fixing the interests of the plaintiff, Raymond Beal, and the defendant, Barbara Beal, in a residence in Portland. The trial court found that the parties each owned an undivided one-half interest in the property. The plaintiff appeals.

As the Beals were not husband and wife at any time relevant to this suit, this is the first time this court has been asked to decide the principles to be applied in determining the property rights of the parties in property accumulated while they were living together unmarried.[1]

The parties were divorced in March, 1972. They entered into a land sale contract in April, 1972, to purchase the subject property for $22,500. The contract listed both parties' names as husband and wife. Raymond paid $500 of the $2,000 down payment and Barbara paid the balance of $1,500. The contract required monthly payments of $213.42, which included principal, interest and taxes. Barbara paid the first monthly payment, and Raymond has made all subsequent payments.

---

1. In *Latham and Latham,* 274 Or. 421, 547 P.2d 144 (1976), we held that an express agreement between two unmarried parties to share equally in real and personal property accumulated during the period they were living together as husband and wife was not void as against public policy.

After the purchase, the parties lived together in the house. Raymond worked steadily and Barbara was almost constantly employed. They had a joint savings account but maintained separate checking accounts. The parties added shades, storm windows and carpeting, and remodeled the kitchen. Barbara paid some of the costs, and some were paid from the joint savings account. Barbara's income was used for family expenses.

After living together for two years, Barbara moved out and Raymond remained, and he has made all monthly payments on the house.

Historically, courts have been reluctant to grant relief of any kind to a party who was involved in what was termed a "meretricious" relationship. Courts took the position that the parties had entered into a relationship outside the bounds of law, and the courts would not allow themselves to be used to solve the property disputes evolving from that relationship. Generally, the parties were left as they were when they came to court, with ownership resting in whoever happened to have title or possession at the time. The rationale was predicated on public policy or even an invocation of the clean hands doctrine....

While a majority of people still follow the marriage practice, many couples, both young and old, are living together without the benefit of a civil marriage. These situations create inheritance problems, questions concerning the relationship between parent and child and, as in the instant case, difficulty in dividing property when the relationship terminates. The problem with the previous judicial approach is well stated by the specially concurring opinion in *West v. Knowles*, 50 Wash.2d 311, 311 P.2d 689 (1957):

> "The majority opinion indicates that for ten years Bonnie West and Delmer Knowles lived together and were generally accepted as a married couple. However, they had never observed the usual conventions of (a) obtaining a marriage license and (b) formally exchanging marriage vows. Obviously, such a relationship is not generally approved by the mores of our society. It is not a relationship which is encouraged by the courts. Be that as it may, some of our citizens of the opposite sex occasionally become involved in a relationship such as that in the instant case.
>
> "Not infrequently, through the individual or joint efforts of the parties, such a couple acquires or accumulates property. Friction develops, the parties quarrel, and finally they terminate the unconventional or so-called meretricious relationship. Thereupon, a decided difference of opinion arises between them as to the ownership of certain items of property. Occasionally, the parties bring their dispute to the courts, seeking an authoritative settlement. Under such circumstances, this court and the courts of other jurisdictions have, in effect, sometimes said, 'We will wash our hands of such disputes. The parties should and must be left to their own devices, just where they find themselves.' To me, such pronouncements seem overly fastidious and a bit fatuous. They are unrealistic and, among other things, ignore the fact that an unannounced (but nevertheless effective and binding) rule of law is inherent in any such terminal statements by a court of law.
>
> "The unannounced but inherent rule is simply that the party who has title, or in some instances who is in possession, will enjoy the rights of ownership of the property concerned. The rule often operates to the great advantage of the cunning and the shrewd, who wind up with possession of

> the property, or title to it in their names, at the end of a so-called meretricious relationship. So, although the courts proclaim that they will have nothing to do with such matters, the proclamation in itself establishes, as to the parties involved, an effective and binding rule of law which tends to operate purely by accident or perhaps by reason of the cunning, anticipatory designs of just one of the parties." *West v. Knowles, supra* 50 Wash.2d at 315–16, 311 P.2d at 692.

...

We believe a division of property accumulated during a period of cohabitation must be begun by inquiring into the intent of the parties, and if an intent can be found, it should control that property distribution. While this is obviously true when the parties have executed a written agreement, it is just as true if there is no written agreement. The difference is often only the sophistication of the parties. Thus, absent an express agreement, courts should closely examine the facts in evidence to determine what the parties implicitly agreed upon....

More often than not, such an inquiry will produce convincing evidence of an intended division of property, but we recognize that occasionally the record will leave doubt as to the intent of the parties. In such cases, inferences can be drawn from factual settings in which the parties lived. Cohabitation itself can be relevant evidence of an agreement to share incomes during continued cohabitation. Additionally, joint acts of a financial nature can give rise to an inference that the parties intended to share equally. Such acts might include a joint checking account, a joint savings account, or joint purchases.

Here, the record supports the position that the parties intended to pool their resources for their common benefit during the time they lived together. This conclusion is supported by the defendant's testimony that she contributed her entire income to maintenance of the household. Further, she testified that she gave money on one occasion to the plaintiff to make the house payment. Neither party made any effort to keep separate accounts or to total their respective contributions for reimbursement purposes, and, although they had separate checking accounts, they had a joint savings account. Finally, the living arrangement itself is evidence that the parties intended to share their resources. Since the parties intended to pool their funds for payment of their obligations, they should be considered equal cotenants, except that Barbara is entitled to an offset of $500, representing the amount she paid over and above one-half of the down payment.

In summary, we hold that courts, when dealing with the property disputes of a man and a woman who have been living together in a nonmarital domestic relationship, should distribute the property based upon the express or implied intent of those parties.

In the instant case, the trial court found that both parties should have an undivided interest in the property. We believe that the parties should stand on an equal basis during the time they were living together, except that fairness dictates that Barbara should receive credit for the $500 additional she paid on the down payment.

However, a different situation exists after Barbara moved out of the residence in June, 1974. Raymond has continued to live in the house and has paid $7,469.70 in house payments from then until the time of trial, and he is continuing to make those payments. Since June, 1974, the parties have lived apart, maintained independent households, and have not contributed to each other's maintenance.

Since the parties have not lived together since June, 1974, their property rights after that date should be determined by the regular rules of cotenancy. As such, Barbara is obligated to reimburse plaintiff for 50 percent of the house payments made by him after June, 1974.

The question of whether the defendant is entitled to recover the reasonable rental value is also raised.[4] Normally, cotenants cannot charge one another for occupancy of the property in which they are part owners. This rule is subject to an exception when one cotenant's use of the property in fact excludes the other cotenant's use and enjoyment of it.

Here...the relationship of the parties was such that it apparently would have been impractical for the defendant to occupy the premises while the plaintiff was living there, and thus she is entitled to one-half of the fair rental value from June 1, 1974. Because the trial court made no findings on the issue of rental value and because no evidence was introduced on that point, we must remand the suit to the trial court.

Affirmed as modified, and remanded.

[Opinion by Justice Linde omitted.]

CHESTNUT v. CHESTNUT

Court of Appeals of Indiana
499 N.E.2d 783 (Ind. Ct. App. 1986)

RATLIFF, Judge.

Statement of the Case

Roger Murray Chestnut appeals the trial court's judgment distributing marital property, ordering child support payments, and awarding attorney fees. We affirm.

Facts

Beginning in 1979, Roger Murray Chestnut (Roger) and Patricia Mooney (Patricia) lived together in a house on Clarks Creek Road. Roger had purchased the house in 1970. In 1983, Roger and Patricia were married. At that time, Roger conveyed the Clarks Creek residence to Patricia and himself as tenants by the entireties. One year later, they had a child, Kathryn.

At the time of their marriage, Roger contributed $38,166 worth of assets consisting of the Clarks Creek Road property ($30,000), an automobile ($3000), tools ($3000), and personal property ($2166). All of Roger's assets were unencumbered. Patricia brought into the marriage $4,043 worth of assets consisting of an automobile ($1000), a certificate of deposit ($1043), personal property ($1050), and the cash value on life insurance ($950). Thus, the total assets as of the date of marriage were $42,209. From the figures above, Roger brought 90% of the assets while Patricia brought 10% into the marriage.

Roger's principal source of income came from rehabilitating homes and reselling them at a profit. However, the record is unclear as to when he started this enterprise. After their marriage, Roger and Patricia obtained a $22,000 loan

4. The trial court found that Raymond owed Barbara for her share of a reasonable rental value of the property. No evidence on that amount was introduced.

secured by a mortgage on the Clarks Creek Road property.[1] With the loan proceeds, they purchased a house in Mooresville. Roger used the excess money for financing, to buy materials to rehabilitate the Mooresville house, and to pay household expenses.

When this money was exhausted, Roger used his automobile as collateral for an additional loan of $2000 to pay household bills. Roger completed the Mooresville house in January of 1984 and began renting it for $400 per month.

Roger and Patricia mortgaged the Mooresville house for a $28,000 loan. Out of this money, Roger and Patricia made mortgage payments on their Clarks Creek Road home and two downpayments on a home on Franklin Street and a home in Plainfield. Rehabilitation materials were also purchased. The Plainfield house was obtained with a $22,000 mortgage. Roger sold the Franklin Street property in October of 1984 for a profit of $12,000. This amount was placed in a certificate of deposit (C.D.) along with $4000 which represented the remaining loan proceeds from the Mooresville loan. Roger used the C.D. to pay mortgage installments and household expenses. At the time of Roger and Patricia's separation, rehabilitation on the Plainfield home was substantially complete. Four months later, Roger rented the Plainfield house for $450 per month.

From 1979 through 1983, Roger was self-employed as a handyman and had little or no taxable income. This was the time period when Roger and Patricia cohabited prior to marriage. After they married in 1983 and throughout their marriage, Roger worked approximately 40 hours per week on rehabilitating the various properties.

From 1979 until the birth of Kathryn in 1984, Patricia worked six days a week at a hotel. Her annual earnings for that period ranged from $8000 to $13,400. With her income, Patricia paid for groceries, clothing, cleaning and other household expenses. During her days off, she worked with Roger on rehabilitating houses. In addition to her job, Patricia performed the homemaking chores. When Kathryn was born in 1984, Patricia and Roger jointly agreed that Patricia should quit her job at the hotel and look for another job. After Patricia looked for a job for two weeks, Roger convinced her to work full-time with him in the rehabilitation business. She did so until their separation.

After trial, the trial court divided and distributed the marital property. Roger got approximately $23,120 in assets as follows: the Clarks Creek Road property ($30,000 fair market value less outstanding mortgage of $21,700), $9000 from the sale proceeds of the Plainfield property, a 1976 Cutlass automobile ($3000 fair market value less lien of $1000), a GMC truck ($9000 fair market value less lien of $11,600), personal property ($2970), tools ($3000), a C.D. ($150 balance), and income tax refund proceeds ($300). Patricia received approximately $27,894 in assets as follows: the Mooresville property ($37,000 fair market value less outstanding mortgage of $27,900), personal property ($2150), a 1977 Dodge automobile ($1000), a C.D. ($400 balance), cash value of insurance ($950), taxes ($994), and the remaining sale proceeds from the Plainfield property ($49,500 fair market value less about 10% for commissions and selling expenses less outstanding mortgage of $22,250 less $9000 which goes to Roger). Thus, after the trial court's distribution, Roger received about 45% of the assets while Patricia received about 55%.

---

1. Roger and Patricia were co-makers on all loans secured by real estate mortgages. They took title to all real estate purchased as tenants by the entirety.

Additionally, the trial court ordered Roger to pay $45 per week for child support. The trial court further ordered Roger to pay $3000 to defray a portion of the costs of Patricia's attorney fees.

Issues

1. Whether the trial court abused its discretion in dividing the marital property.
2. Whether the trial court abused its discretion in ordering Roger to pay $45 per week as child support.
3. Whether the trial court abused its discretion in ordering Roger to pay $3000 for a portion of Patricia's attorney's fees.

Discussion and Decision

Issue One

In Indiana Code section 31-1-11.5-11(b), our legislature set forth five factors which a trial court must consider in arriving at a "just and reasonable" division of assets:

(1) The contribution of each spouse to the acquisition of the property, including the contribution of a spouse as a homemaker;

(2) The extent to which the property was acquired by each spouse prior to the marriage or through inheritance or gift;

(3) The economic circumstances of the spouse at the time the disposition of the property is to become effective,...;

(4) The conduct of the parties during the marriage as related to the disposition or dissipation of their property; and

(5) The earnings or earning ability of the parties as related to a final division of property and final determination of the property rights of the parties.

The trial court must consider all of these factors with none taking precedence over another. *Wright v. Wright* (1985), Ind.App., 471 N.E.2d 1240, 1244, *trans. denied.* There is a very strong presumption that the trial court considered all the evidence of record and applied the statutory factors. *In re Marriage of Mulvihill* (1984), Ind.App., 471 N.E.2d 10, 13.

...We will limit our review to a consideration of whether the trial court abused its discretion. *Taylor v. Taylor* (1982), Ind., 436 N.E.2d 56, 58; *Hoyle v. Hoyle* (1985), Ind.App., 473 N.E.2d 653, 657. As our supreme court held, "The trial court will be reversed only where the result reached is clearly against the logic and effect of the facts and circumstances before the court, including the reasonable inferences to be drawn therefrom." *Taylor,* at 58.

We hold that the trial court did not abuse its discretion in dividing the property between Roger and Patricia, despite the short duration of their marriage. Roger argues strenuously that the parties' period of premarital cohabitation should have no significance in the distribution of property and points to a lack of case authority in Indiana. However, there is support from our court which favors Patricia's argument. In *Glasgo v. Glasgo* (1980), Ind.App., 410 N.E.2d 1325, *trans. denied,* this court held that cohabitation can be a basis for distribution of assets under contractual and equitable principles....

In *Glasgo*, we reaffirmed the rule that "any contract in which sexual services serve as consideration are unenforceable and void as against public policy." *Id.* at 1331. However, this court refused to strictly apply this rule to all cohabitation relationships. Epithets such as "meretricious" or "illicit" "should be reserved for cases in which they are deserved." *Id.* at 1330. We held that the trial court could fashion relief in favor of the woman either under the theory of an implied contract or under principles of equity. *Id.* at 1332.

While *Glasgo* is factually distinguishable from the case under consideration, we are persuaded by its rationale. Roger and Patricia lived together a total of six years, four as premarital cohabitants and two as husband and wife. It would be against public policy to ignore Patricia's contribution during the period prior to marriage since she and Roger eventually married.... We therefore hold that the trial court could have considered Patricia's contributions during premarital cohabitation when it distributed the property upon dissolution. However, we reserve for another day the question of whether premarital cohabitation without subsequent marriage gives rise to potential relief.

During the four year period of cohabitation, Patricia worked six days a week and performed homemaking duties. With her income, she paid many of the household expenses. It was within the trial court's discretion to consider this evidence when distributing the marital assets under principles of equity.

Even if Patricia's contribution during premarital cohabitation is ignored, we still hold that the trial court did not abuse its discretion. Patricia's contribution as a homemaker and her help with Roger's rehabilitation business justify the trial court's division. Without her help, the real estate business would not have been possible since Patricia's job provided much of the necessary cash flow.

Also, the trial court could have concluded that Roger's earning ability exceeded his current earnings. Roger's completion of two years of college and his apparent skill and experience evince the possibility that Roger should have been making a better living for himself than he did. Given all of the statutory factors, we hold that Patricia's receipt of 55% of the assets after the two-year marriage was not an abuse of discretion.

Issue Two

Indiana Code section 31-1-11.5-12(a) specifies four factors which a trial court must consider when making an order for child support:

(1) The financial resources and needs of the custodial parent;

(2) Standard of living the child would have enjoyed had the marriage not been dissolved or had the separation not been ordered;

(3) Physical or mental condition of the child and his educational needs; and,

(4) Financial resources and needs of the non-custodial parent.

In Ind.Code §31-1-11.5-12(b), other factors are listed. In reviewing a trial court's order for child support, we will reverse only if there is an abuse of discretion. *Branstad v. Branstad* (1980), Ind.App., 400 N.E.2d 167, 169.

In light of the evidence at trial which indicated that it cost $75 to $85 per week to raise Kathryn, exclusive of shelter and health care, we hold that the trial court's order for Roger to pay $45 per week was not an abuse of discretion. We reject Roger's ludicrous argument that had the marriage not dissolved, Kathryn would have been raised in a "spartan, frontier-style environment." Appellant's Brief at 35.

We also reject Roger's claim that the trial court's division of the assets leaves him nothing with which to pay $45 per week. Roger received $23,120 in unencumbered assets and had the apparent ability and expertise to earn income. *Reffeitt v. Reffeitt* (1981), Ind.App., 419 N.E.2d 999, 1003–04.

Issue Three

Indiana Code section 31-1-11.5-16 allows the trial court to assess reasonable attorney's fees against one party in a divorce proceeding. The determination of payment of costs and attorney fees lies within the sound discretion of the trial court. We will reverse only upon a showing of a clear abuse of discretion. *McDaniel v. McDaniel* (1964), 245 Ind. 551, 562, 201 N.E.2d 215, 220; *McBride v. McBride* (1981), Ind.App., 427 N.E.2d 1148, 1152.

In the case under consideration, the trial court ordered Roger to pay $3000 in monthly installments of $200. At the time of trial, Patricia had incurred about $4600 in attorney's fees. Roger alleges that the trial court's order was excessive in light of his financial status after the dissolution. However, we refuse to substitute our judgment for that of the trial court. Roger not only had the resources to pay the fees but also had the ability to engage in gainful employment. *Planert v. Planert* (1985), Ind.App., 478 N.E.2d 1251, 1254. Therefore, the trial court did not abuse its discretion.

Judgment affirmed.

COMMENTS

Hewitt and *Beal* take decidedly different positions on the issue of the legal treatment of non-marital cohabitation. Some would argue that *Hewitt* focuses broadly on public policy while *Beal* deals more realistically with issues of fairness between the parties. Should it make any difference that the couple in *Beal* had previously been married to one another, while in *Hewitt* the couple never married? Might the public policy of Illinois have been less offended by post-decree cohabitation of a divorced couple than by simple non-marital cohabitation?

Yet, regarding public policy, one might profitably ask whose decision it was in *Hewitt* not to get married, and who benefitted from that decision. Assuming the court accurately stated the moral view of the people of Illinois, it is important to consider in what sense the Illinois Supreme Court decision can be said to be upholding morality and supporting married life. Suppose a young man in the same position as Robert Hewitt (that is, an unmarried college student, also an expectant father) were to read the decision in *Hewitt.* Would you expect the decision to discourage him from engaging in a so-called "illicit" relationship? The court's decision seems to have given Robert just what he wanted — the comforts and pleasures of married life for as long as he wished without the obligations that generally accompany marriage. Does the court intend to suggest that Illinois public policy would consider it better for the father in the case to abandon his pregnant girlfriend?

One might say that the "illicit" relationship already took place in *Hewitt,* before Victoria Hewitt became pregnant. If the court endorses the view that women are responsible for "morality" — that men will seek sexual relations and that it is up to "nice" girls to say "no" until they are married — then the decision penalizing the woman and her (and Robert's) children might make a kind of sense. But of course such a decision offers men as great a positive incentive to engage in such behavior as it offers women a negative incentive to refrain from it. Often, men make more of the decisions regarding sexual relations than women do — a grim example being "date rape." Thus, it might be more appropriate to discourage the men's aggressiveness than to increase the incentive on women to refuse sexual relations — a refusal that too often can be ignored or met with outright violence.

The *Beal* court pointed out, quoting from the 1957 *West v. Knowles* case, that it is impossible for courts really to take no position — that any decision courts make regarding the property of unmarried cohabitants will establish a legal rule by which the couple can order their lives. The court suggests that a rule refusing to divide the property of unmarried cohabitants (such as that followed by *Hewitt*) may reward the "cunning and shrewd" who get possession of the property or get title to it placed in their own name. In *Hewitt* the male who increased his earning capacity with the help of a woman he refused to marry was rewarded while the female who presumably cared for children and did everything that might be expected of a good wife (except to convince Robert to enter a valid marriage with her) was penalized.

It should be noted that the *Hewitt* relationship began in 1960 in Iowa where common law marriage was recognized. Victoria Hewitt's initial pleading in the trial court was a complaint for divorce, alleging that she and Robert Hewitt had lived as husband and wife in Iowa. The trial judge found that "the parties had never lived together in the State of Iowa and that there was no common law marriage which the [Illinois] court might recognize" (*Hewitt v. Hewitt*, 62 Ill.App.3d 861, 380 N.E.2d 454 (1978)). Had a common law marriage been found to have taken place in Iowa, a sister state would normally recognize the status because of the rule that a marriage valid where formed is ordinarily valid everywhere. When clients seek legal advice about breach of a cohabitation contract, lawyers should be particularly careful to elicit as much information as possible about the history of their client's relationship with his or her cohabiting partner, when and where it was formed, and where they lived because of the possibility of the existence of a common law marriage in some state.

Many couples live together for some period of time before they formally get married. *Chestnut* demonstrates the importance of a lawyer in a dissolution action examining whether there was pre-marital cohabitation which might affect property division. This is particularly relevant if the formal marriage relationship is of short duration following a long period of time when the couple lived together and pooled their resources, but were not formally married.

REFERENCES

Susan Estrich, REAL RAPE (1987)
Robin Warshaw, I NEVER CALLED IT RAPE (1988)

Partnership, Joint Venture, or Joint Enterprise

POOLE v. SCHRICHTE
Supreme Court of Washington
39 Wash. 2d 558, 236 P.2d 1044 (1951)

HILL, Justice.

The respondent, Irene M. Poole, and the appellant, Herbert A. Schrichte, lived together without the formality of a marriage ceremony, from 1935 to 1941 in Chicago and from 1941 to 1947 in Seattle. The present action is to determine their respective interests in a tavern and certain household furniture and personal property in Mr. Schrichte's possession.

In January, 1942, they combined their limited resources to acquire a beauty shop, which Mrs. Poole operated under the name of "Crosley Beauty Salon." (Their resources were then so limited that Mrs. Poole had to borrow fifty dollars to help pay the first month's rent.) During 1942, 1943 and part of 1944, Mr. Schrichte worked as a railroad switchman. In his spare time he constructed living quarters in back of the beauty shop, assisted Mrs. Poole in its business management, and did maintenance work in connection with its operation.

She opened a bank account, which will be referred to as the "Crosley account," and into it went the proceeds from the operation of the beauty shop and Mr. Schrichte's earnings, and the funds so deposited were used for their living expenses and for the operation of the shop. Mrs. Poole alone could write checks on this account.

In June, 1944, Mr. Schrichte sustained an injury that marked the termination of his employment with the railroad. In August of that year they made a three-thousand-dollar payment from the Crosley account on the purchase of a tavern, and borrowed ten thousand dollars to pay the balance of the purchase price. The loan was secured by two chattel mortgages, one on the fixtures and equipment in the beauty shop and one on the fixtures and equipment in the tavern. The bill of sale to the tavern, the lease, and the liquor licenses were in Mr. Schrichte's name, as was a bank account that was opened with six hundred dollars from the Crosley account and into which most of the tavern proceeds went. Checks signed "Herbert A. Schrichte, by Mrs. Herbert A. Schrichte" were honored on the tavern account.

For almost two years, until the beauty shop was sold in 1946, she ran the salon while he ran the saloon. Both before and after the sale of the beauty shop, because of Mr. Schrichte's frequent asthmatic seizures, which necessitated trips to Arizona, California, Canada and eastern Washington for relief, Mrs. Poole devoted considerable time to the tavern's operation and business management.

They purchased a house in January, 1946. The down payment and some of the monthly payments on the mortgage were made from the proceeds of the tavern. When the beauty shop was sold, some $1,534 from the proceeds of the sale was used to accelerate the payments on the house, and the remainder, like the proceeds from the operation of the shop, was used for living expenses. The Crosley account was closed in September, 1947, the balance in the account, $844, finding its way into the tavern account.

Differences arose between the parties and they separated October 9, 1947. He testified, "She left me"; her testimony was that he "threw me out bag and baggage.... He hit me until I couldn't walk, and I had to go to the hospital." A friend of hers testified that when Mrs. Poole left the hospital, "She was in bad condition. Her mouth was swollen and her face was in a bad mess."

Under those circumstances, the separation justifiably terminated any attempt by Mrs. Poole to participate in the operation of the tavern.

She instituted the present action to establish her interest in the tavern and in the household furniture and personal property which remained in Mr. Schrichte's possession. The trial court gave her a judgment for five thousand dollars against Mr. Schrichte in lieu of a half interest in the tavern and the profits thereof subsequent to her exclusion from any participation in its operation, and also gave her a half interest in the furniture and personal property. He has appealed.

The theory of both parties as to the proper disposition of this case stems from the fact of their cohabitation, concededly meretricious in its inception in Chicago in 1935, as Mrs. Poole had not at that time secured a final divorce from her second husband.

...

We have here a situation in which, if the parties to this action had not been living together, there would be no question but that Mrs. Poole had at least a one-half interest in the tavern. Her rights do not stem from cohabitation or the meretricious relationship, but from the fact that the proceeds from the beauty shop she operated clearly constituted a larger proportion of the Crosley account than did Mr. Schrichte's earnings as a railroad switchman. The undisputed testimony is that the money that went into the down payment on the tavern was at least half hers; that her credit was pledged to make its purchase possible, and that she assisted in its operation during Mr. Schrichte's frequent illnesses and absences from the city. The other payments on the purchase price came from the operation of the tavern. We know of no rule of law or equity that says that if she lived with Mr. Schrichte knowing that she was not married to him, she thereby forfeited her interest in the tavern because he had the foresight to see that the legal title thereto stood in his name.

The evidence establishes here a joint venture if not a partnership between the parties so far as their interests in the tavern are concerned. Their social relationships, legal or illegal, moral or immoral, are not material on this phase of the case. Mr. Schrichte chose to exclude Mrs. Poole from any voice in the operation of the tavern, and that she has made no contribution to its operation since October, 1947, is his fault, not hers. We would, therefore, not have allowed him the sum of $1,372 with which the trial court credited him for his services to the joint venture in the operation of the tavern.

Mr. Schritche urges that the trial court having found that he was entitled to $39.80 a month for his services in the operation of the tavern and Mrs. Poole not having appealed from that finding, the law of the case is that he is entitled to compensation for his services to the joint venture; and that it is obvious that $39.80 a month is an arbitrary and not an adequate allowance, and, since he is entitled to compensation, the case should be remanded for the taking of evidence as to the value of his services. The argument is that we should not only perpetuate what we conceive to be error in allowing Mr. Schrichte any compensation for his services, but we should remand the case so that the error might be augmented.

In an equity case the trial is *de novo* in this court, and, although the trial court's findings are given great weight, we do, so far as necessary, make our own findings and draw our own conclusions, and certainly we are not bound to perpetuate error. ...

We fail to see how the trial court could have found Mrs. Poole's interest in the business and her share of the proceeds to be less than five thousand dollars. She seemingly is satisfied with that amount, or at least does not cross-appeal from the judgment awarding it to her. That portion of the trial court's judgment will therefore be affirmed.

It could likewise be affirmed on the theory adopted by Mrs. Poole and the trial court, *i.e.*, that she had actually believed that there was a common-law marriage and that in such a situation, although she was mistaken, a court of equity will protect the rights of the innocent party in the property accumulated by the joint efforts of both. While some skeptics might be dubious as to the good faith of Mrs. Poole, since there is no common-law marriage in either Illinois or Washington, the experienced trial judge was convinced that she believed she was married, and he so found; and he, though doubtless gallant, is not entirely naive and unacquainted with the ways of the world. After an examination of the record, we are agreed that there is credible evidence to support that finding and to establish that Mrs. Poole is an innocent party within the rule and that under such circumstances a court of equity will protect the rights of an innocent party in the property accumulated by the joint efforts of both.

...

The judgment is affirmed in its entirety.

IRELAND v. FLANAGAN
Court of Appeals of Oregon
51 Ore. App. 837, 627 P.2d 496 (1981)

WARREN, Judge.

Plaintiff brought this suit in equity seeking: (1) an award of a one-half interest in a house held in the name of defendant and occupied by the parties during the period of their relationship; and (2) an accounting from defendant for her exclusive use of the property from the time the parties ceased living together. The basis of her complaint was that the parties, during their period of cohabitation, had an express oral agreement whereby they agreed to pool all of their assets for their joint benefit. Defendant generally denied plaintiff's allegations and counterclaimed for payment of plaintiff's share of certain debts, which were allegedly jointly incurred during their relationship, and for recovery of an article of defendant's personal property. The trial court denied any relief; only plaintiff appeals.

The facts of this case are sharply contested. Regarding the parties' financial arrangement, plaintiff testified:

A. After we moved in together, we sat down and discussed financial things and decided, for convenience sake and because, in essence, we were going to have a long relationship together and a marriage, we would pool our resources.

Q. Did you expressly agree in those terms?

A. Yes, we did.

Q. What did you mean by pooling your resources?

A. Whatever I had was hers; whatever she had was mine. And that included, money, cars, furniture, whatever it was.

In obtaining the $7,000 down payment for the purchase of the house, plaintiff testified that defendant secured a $5,000 loan from her credit union and plaintiff sold her automobile for $2,000.

On direct examination, plaintiff testified that they planned to purchase the house in both names if at all possible and that it was not until they went to sign the closing papers at the escrow office that they discovered that both names did not appear on the contract. Nevertheless, they decided that defendant should sign the papers as written and that they would be corrected at another time. Thereafter, the parties on numerous occasions discussed changing title to both names, but, as plaintiff put it, they "never got around to doing it." On cross-examination, however, an excerpt from plaintiff's May 14, 1979, deposition was read into the record in which plaintiff had testified that, near to the time they purchased the house, they decided to take title solely in defendant's name in order to provide her with a tax shelter for her higher wages.

Defendant's testimony regarding the nature of the parties' agreement as to the house was punctuated with inconsistencies. The essence of her testimony was that the parties had an express oral agreement to pool their resources, each paying fifty percent of everything, and if plaintiff contributed her fifty percent of the house payments, then when the house was sold, plaintiff would get fifty percent of the equity. At one point in her testimony, defendant admitted that plaintiff had contributed $2,000 from the sale of plaintiff's automobile toward the $7,000 down payment on the house; at another point, defendant stated that plaintiff had contributed nothing to the house and that the automobile which allegedly was sold by plaintiff for her $2,000 contribution was not owned by plaintiff, but by defendant.

Several witnesses, including mutual friends of the parties, the escrow agent who prepared the papers on the house and the seller of the house, corroborated plaintiff's testimony that the parties bought the house together. One witness testified that defendant had expressly stated that the house was owned by both parties and that, in the event plaintiff's and defendant's relationship terminated, the house and other jointly-owned property would "be split right down the middle."

Both parties testified to the fact that they maintained a joint checking account, a joint savings account and a safety deposit box and that they had joint loans and two joint credit cards. They testified that their practice was to deposit their paychecks into their joint checking account and from this account to pay their bills, including the house payment. Defendant, moreover, admitted that plaintiff had in fact made most of the numerous, substantial household improvements plaintiff had claimed.

Upon the termination of their relationship, defendant moved out of the house in August, 1978. However, in October, 1978, defendant returned after plaintiff had vacated the premises.

The trial court made findings of fact: (1) both plaintiff and defendant are unreliable witnesses whose testimony is false in parts and is unreliable in parts unless corroborated by other evidence; (2) they agreed to pool their assets for their joint use during the period of their relationship, which terminated on August 31, 1978; (3) on about March 1, 1977, defendant purchased a house and assumed the mortgage; (4) plaintiff contributed $2,000 toward the total down payment for the property of $7,000; (5) pursuant to their agreement the property was used by the parties jointly during their relationship; (6) plaintiff occupied the premises with defendant until August 31, 1978; (7) during her occupancy, plaintiff expended some labor in improvements to the premises and some money was jointly expended by the parties for materials and labor for these improvements; (8) debts for these improvements were incurred in the name of defendant only; and (9) the relationship of the parties, as construed by the parties themselves, imposed upon them a moral obligation to provide for the other, similar to the relationship of husband and wife.

The trial court concluded that the law presumes that plaintiff's contributions toward defendant's purchase and improvement of the residence were gifts from plaintiff to defendant; that this presumption may be overcome only by evidence of the most convincing and satisfactory kind; that plaintiff's evidence failed to overcome the presumption of a gift; that plaintiff did not sustain her burden of proving that defendant promised to convey any legal or equitable interest in said real property to plaintiff, other than the right to use the property jointly with defendant during the time of their relationship; that defendant is not estopped to deny plaintiff's claims; that defendant is not legally required to account to plaintiff for her use of the property after the termination of their relationship; and that plaintiff does not owe defendant any of the sums alleged in defendant's counterclaims. Thereupon, the court denied relief to either party.

Although the trial court held that plaintiff failed to overcome the legal presumption that her contributions toward the purchase and improvements to the house were gifts from plaintiff to defendant, neither party pleaded or argued that plaintiff's contributions were gifts. Instead, this theory was proffered gratuitously by the trial court. It has no applicability here. The general rule is, rather, that a party seeking to establish the existence of a gift must prove its existence by clear and convincing evidence. *Carpenter v. Carpenter,* 153 Or. 584, 601, 602, 56 P.2d 305, 57 P.2d 1098, 58 P.2d 507 (1936). An exception applies when there is a transfer of property from a parent, or one standing *in loco parentis,* to a child; such a transfer is presumptively a gift. *Ingersoll v. Ingersoll,* 263 Or. 376, 379, 502 P.2d 598 (1972). There is obviously no parent/child relationship here, and defendant's argument that *in loco parentis* cases are applicable is unpersuasive.

...

...[I]n the present case we find that during the parties' relationship they intended to pool their resources for their mutual benefit. In purchasing the house, the parties intended joint ownership. Title was taken in defendant's name for the sole purpose of providing her with a tax shelter. Thus, we conclude that the parties should be considered equal co-tenants. Although the parties here are members of the same sex, we believe that the principles articulated in *Beal v. Beal,* [282 Or. 115, 577 P.2d 507 (1978)] are equally applicable....

...[W]e further find that since October 1, 1978, plaintiff has not contributed toward the house payments. Therefore, defendant is entitled to reimbursement by plaintiff for 50% of the house payments made by defendant after October 1, 1978. *Beal v. Beal, supra* 282 Or. at 123–24, 577 P.2d 507. Moreover, because defendant's occupancy of the property excluded plaintiff's use and enjoyment thereof, plaintiff as a co-tenant is entitled to recover one-half of its fair rental value from October 1, 1978. The evidence was that the fair rental value of the property as of August 1, 1978, was $275 per month and that its fair rental value as of August 1, 1979, was $325 per month. Plaintiff is entitled to recover from defendant one-half of the reasonable rental value of the premises, less a credit of $1500 and a credit for one-half of the mortgage payments made by the defendant since October 1, 1978.

Reversed and remanded for entry of a decree in conformity with this opinion.

Express, Resulting, or Constructive Trust

OMER v. OMER
Court of Appeals of Washington
11 Wash. App. 386, 523 P.2d 957 (1974)

PEARSON, Chief Judge.

This is an action by plaintiff, Helen Omer, claiming an interest in several parcels of real property held in the name of defendant, Daniel Omer, her former husband. From a decree awarding plaintiff a one-half interest in each of the parcels as tenant in common, defendant appeals.

...

The relationship of plaintiff and defendant was stated by the trial court to be "technically" meretricious. The wisdom of this denomination is apparent from a consideration of the established facts.

The parties were married in Israel in 1949. During the course of their marriage, they had two children. In 1959, at the urging of Daniel Omer, at that time employed by the United States embassy in Israel, the parties were divorced. It was the stated opinion of the defendant that the divorce would facilitate the entry of the parties and their children into the United States. Subsequent to this divorce, the parties continued to live together as husband and wife in Israel.

In early 1963, the plaintiff came to New York. The defendant arrived in New York with the children the following year. The parties lived together in New York and operated together a luncheonette in that city. Both parties further entered into sham marriages to expedite their plans to obtain United States citizenship. (These marriages were terminated after the parties obtained citizenship.)

The defendant moved to Washington some time later. The record discloses that at his request, the plaintiff remained in New York with the children and regularly sent portions of her earnings to him in this state. He assured her that he was building a "paradise" for the family here, that she must continue to work and remit money to him, and in no event to disclose their relationship to third parties so as to impair naturalization prospects.

The trial court found that the plaintiff had difficulty with the English language, and that she was reliant upon the defendant for guidance and advice.

At various times while plaintiff remained in New York, the children came to Washington and resided with their father. Eventually, the plaintiff moved to Washington. The parties continued to live together here; Mrs. Omer continued to work and to turn paychecks over to the defendant.

Throughout this period, the defendant acquired the parcels of real estate which are the subject of this action. In 1969 the relationship between the parties deteriorated seriously; plaintiff was abused and rejected by the defendant, and she eventually brought this action, seeking a division of the real property.

The trial court found that from the time of the divorce until 1969, the intent of the parties was to further the interests of their family community. Telling in this connection was the testimony of the children that they were unaware until 1969 that their parents were, in fact, not married. In light of this intent, and the labors and contributions made by the plaintiff in furtherance of it, the trial court entered this finding of fact:

> That the property mentioned above was acquired through the joint efforts, by the plaintiff and by the defendant, in which they combined their earnings and accumulations of labor and their skills, and the funds contributed by the plaintiff were used by the defendant in the acquisition and the payment of the properties mentioned and were so intended to be used.

The settlement of property rights arising out of meretricious relationships has had a busy history in this state. It has generally involved two classes of cases: (1) those involving the claim of a meretricious "spouse" against the estate of the deceased partner to the relationship who held title to assets acquired during the relationship (*Creasman v. Boyle*, 31 Wash.2d 345, 196 P.2d 835 (1948)); and (2) those, like the one at bench, involving the claim by a meretricious spouse who has become estranged from the one who holds title to property acquired during the relationship. *West v. Knowles*, 50 Wash.2d 311, 311 P.2d 689 (1957). Aside from the obvious difficulty in proving the claim where one party is deceased, there appears little other reason to differentiate between the rules applicable to the two classes of cases. See *In re Estate of Thornton*, 81 Wash.2d 72, 499 P.2d 864 (1972).

Much of the history has recently been reviewed by the Supreme Court in *Humphries v. Riveland*, 67 Wash.2d 376, 407 P.2d 967 (1965) and *In re Estate of Thornton, supra.* We offer a brief summary of that history by first considering the rule enunciated in *Creasman v. Boyle, supra,* which poses a difficult hurdle to an equitable adjustment of the property rights of meretricious spouses. In *Creasman* the Supreme Court at 351 of 31 Wash.2d, at 838 of 196 P.2d established the following legal presumption

> [P]roperty acquired by a man and a woman not married to each other, but living together as husband and wife, is not community property, and, *in the absence of some trust relation,* belongs to the one in whose name the legal title to the property stands.

Because of the harshness of the announced rule, certain theories have been established as exceptions. In many instances these theories require fictional applications. Examples are (1) implied partnership or joint venture, *In re Estate of Thornton, supra;* (2) constructive trust, *Humphries v. Riveland, supra*; (3) resulting trust, *Walberg v. Mattson*, 38 Wash.2d 808, 232 P.2d 827 (1951); (4) express or implied contract (to make a will), *In re Estate of Thornton, supra;* and (5) community property interest arising out of a long-term stable meretricious relationship, *In re Estate of Thornton, supra.*

Without intending to unduly generalize, it appears from our review of the cases that if the joint efforts of the meretricious spouses relates to a business enterprise of some kind, an implied partnership affords the most viable theory of recovery. *Poole v. Schrichte*, 39 Wash.2d 558, 236 P.2d 1044 (1951); *In re Estate of Thornton, supra.* Otherwise, the party seeking to establish the claim usually must rely on either a constructive trust theory with its requirement of fraud, overreaching, or inequitable conduct, *Humphries v. Riveland, supra,* or a resulting trust theory with its requirement that the parties must have intended one party would hold the property in trust for the other who furnished the consideration for its purchase. See *Creasman v. Boyle, supra*; *Walberg v. Mattson, supra.* Proof of these theories must meet the clear, cogent, and convincing standard of proof, as an additional hurdle. *Manning v. Mount St. Michael's*, 78 Wash.2d 542, 477 P.2d 635 (1970); *Humphries v. Riveland, supra.*

A theory which would appear to involve the least fictional analysis has so far not been adopted in this state. That theory would recognize that certain meretricious relationships of long and durable standing may give rise to community property rights similar to those which prevail between married persons. See *In re Estate of Thornton, supra,* where the Supreme Court expresses some reluctance to continue resistance to this theory, but still declines to overrule or modify *Creasman v. Boyle, supra.*

The case at bench affords cogent reasons for supporting plaintiff's claim by analogy to the community property laws. Here the parties appear to have been divorced solely for the expediency of gaining entry to and citizenship in this country. In all other respects they lived together, raised a family and acquired property through joint efforts and money, as though they were in fact married.

If, in passing upon this type of case, the court is truly exercising its inherent power to do justice between the parties, and is not making its judgment on the basis that the relationship is illicit, as many of the cases suggest, it seems unwise that we should require proof of some fictional relationship by clear, cogent and convincing evidence in order to escape the consequences of a rigid legal presumption. This approach may deny, rather than achieve justice between the parties. See both dissents in *Humphries v. Riveland, supra*; see *In re Estate of Thornton, supra.*

It seems to us that a better approach would be to let proof of the relationship itself, its purpose, duration, stability, and so forth, determine the merits of the claim, and then, if warranted by the facts, hold that the community property laws should be applied by analogy to determine the rights of the parties.

If our trial courts were free of rigid doctrinal analysis, legal presumptions, high standards of proof and so forth, and could make determinations on the basis of the facts and equity of the particular case, it is our opinion that a just result could be achieved more often than it is presently.

Since *In re Estate of Thornton, supra* compels adherence to the traditional approach, we now reach the question of whether or not the facts as found by the trial court are sufficient to justify the conclusion it reached. In other words, do those findings support either a constructive trust or an implied partnership, to justify the division of property decreed?

Perhaps the simplest theory for affirming the judgment would be for us to hold that the finding quoted above relating to the joint efforts of the parties is sufficient to establish an implied partnership or joint venture and rely upon the statements pertaining to that theory as enunciated in *In re Estate of Thornton, supra.*

The difficulty we have with this simplistic approach is that the parties clearly did not either expressly or impliedly intend a business relationship. The clear thrust of the findings was that the non-marital status of the parties were conceived by defendant and carried out under his direction for the sole purpose of allowing his family the benefits of United States immigration and citizenship. But for that purpose, the parties would not have divorced in Israel nor entered into sham marriages in this country. The property was acquired by the joint efforts of the parties with that goal in mind and with the ultimate goal of remarriage when citizenship was achieved.

Without rejecting an implied partnership out of hand, other findings convince us to affirm the judgment on a theory of constructive trust. The real intention of the parties appears in finding of fact 8:

> That while the property was taken in the name of the defendant it was the intent of the parties that the property would be shared both by the

> plaintiff and the defendant when they would once again be reunited as husband and wife in this country, as they had been in Israel once their citizenship was acquired.

Inasmuch as the trial court also found that defendant initiated and directed the changes in marital status, allegedly to further the goal of United States citizenship, and since plaintiff followed his advice and directions and contributed to the goals with labor and money, it would be grossly inequitable to deny her the relief sought.

It was stated by Justice Cardozo that "A constructive trust is the formula through which the conscience of equity finds expression." *Beatty v. Guggenheim Exploration Co.*, 225 N.Y. 380, 386, 122 N.E. 378, 380 (1919). A further amplification of the doctrine appears in *Proctor v. Forsythe,* 4 Wash.App. 238, 242, 480 P.2d 511, 514 (1971):

> A constructive trust arises where a person holding title to property is subject to an equitable duty to convey it to another on the ground that he would be unjustly enriched if he were permitted to retain it. Restatement of Restitution §160 (1937). Our court has noted that constructive trusts are those which arise purely by construction of equity and are entirely independent of any actual or presumed intention of the parties and are often directly contrary to such intention. They are entirely in invitum and are forced upon the conscience of the trustee for the purpose of working out right and justice or frustrating fraud.

Carkonen v. Alberts, 196 Wash. 575, 83 P.2d 899, 135 A.L.R. 209 (1938). This description of the doctrine of constructive trusts describes rather well the circumstances of this case and we believe the findings of the trial court justify its application.

It is true, there is no specific finding of fraud or misrepresentation or overreaching. There is, however, a clear element of unconscionability inherent in the findings of the trial court which, in our view, justifies application of the doctrine of constructive trust.

Judgment affirmed.

SULLIVAN v. ROONEY

Supreme Judicial Court of Massachusetts
404 Mass. 160, 533 N.E.2d 1372 (1989)

WILKINS, Justice.

This case is another, in what appears likely to be an increasing number of cases, concerned with unraveling the property interests of two unmarried people who became disaffected after living together for a long time as if husband and wife. Here, we conclude that the defendant holds a one-half interest in residential premises in Reading in constructive trust for the plaintiff. We thus affirm the judgment entered in the Probate and Family Court directing the defendant to convey the premises to the plaintiff and himself as tenants in common.

We recite the facts from the judge's findings, supplemented in certain respects by the defendant's testimony and by testimony of the plaintiff, to whose truthfulness the defendant admitted at trial. The parties had had a thirteen or fourteen-year relationship, during seven of which they lived together and were engaged to be married at some indefinite future date. The plaintiff gave up her position as a flight attendant in order to maintain a home for the defendant. In 1977, while they were living in an apartment in Medford, they discussed buying a house, and, after some months of searching, they settled on purchasing the Reading home of the defendant's sister and her husband. Each thought of the transaction as a joint purchase of a home that would belong to both of them. On the way to the Registry of Deeds for the passing of papers, the defendant told the plaintiff that, in order to get 100% Veterans' Administration financing, he would have to take title in his name alone. The deed was so recorded.

The parties lived together in the Reading house from January, 1978, to December, 1980, when the defendant, a career army officer who had been admitted to the bar of the Commonwealth, was transferred to Washington, D.C. While living in Reading, the defendant worked full-time during the day as an R.O.T.C. instructor and attended law school at night. He paid the mortgage obligations, taxes, utilities, and insurance on the house. The plaintiff, a waitress, put all her earnings and savings into the house, paying for the food and household supplies and for much of the furniture. She did all the housework, the decorating, and the entertaining of the defendant's colleagues. The defendant promised at various times to place the property in joint ownership, but he never did.

In June, 1982, the plaintiff agreed, on the defendant's urging, to join the defendant in the Washington, D.C. area, where again she kept house while he paid their expenses. The defendant told the plaintiff that they should rent out the Reading house rather than sell it, so they would have a home to go back to in a few years and to which they could retire. After a year, the plaintiff, unhappy in Virginia, moved back to Massachusetts. The relationship deteriorated, and the two separated in late 1983. The plaintiff wished to move back into what she considered her home, the house in Reading, but the defendant told her she could not because it was rented.

In 1984, the plaintiff brought this action to obtain title to the house as tenant in common with the defendant. The judge found that the defendant had promised to convey joint title at the time of the purchase, that he had reiterated that promise on several occasions up through early 1984 (when he told the plaintiff to send him a deed to sign), and that he admitted to having made these promises. The judge further found that, in reliance on these promises, the plaintiff was induced to stay in the relationship, to contribute her earnings and services, and to give up her home to move to Virginia. The judge also found that the plaintiff had made these contributions to her detriment, because she gave up her position as a flight attendant and lost career opportunities and job benefits. The judge ruled that the defendant would be unjustly enriched if he were allowed to keep sole title to the house. The judgment ordered the defendant to convey to the plaintiff a half-interest in the house. We transferred the defendant's appeal here.

We are unable to identify the principle of law on which the judge relied in awarding the plaintiff a tenancy in common in the Reading property. The judge's rulings of law speak of compensation for services and a "quantum meruit theory." Even if we were to recognize that the plaintiff was entitled to recover the fair value of her services, without offsetting the value of her services against the fair value of the defendant's contributions during their relationship, there are no findings, nor any evidence that would warrant findings, concerning the fair value of the plaintiff's services or the fair value of one-half of the equity in the Reading property at the time of the trial.

The plaintiff argues here that the defendant's oral promises to give her one-half the property are enforceable in the circumstances despite the defendant's reliance on the Statute of Frauds, and, alternatively, that the defendant holds one-half the property on a constructive trust in favor of the plaintiff. We accept the plaintiff's argument that the evidence and the judge's findings demonstrate that the judgment should be upheld on the theory of a constructive trust.

The judge's unchallenged findings of fact demonstrate that there was a fiduciary relationship between the parties and that the defendant violated his fiduciary duty to the plaintiff. Equitable principles impose a constructive trust on property to avoid the unjust enrichment of a party who violates his fiduciary duty and acquires that property at the expense of the person to whom he owed that duty. See *Barry v. Covich*, 332 Mass. 338, 342–343, 124 N.E.2d 921 (1955); *Hatton v. Meade*, 23 Mass.App.Ct. 356, 363, 502 N.E.2d 552 (1987). Here the plaintiff was less educated (a high school graduate) and less experienced (she is a waitress) than the defendant (a career army officer attending law school at the time of the purchase of the house). She relied on him over a long period in important matters. See *Kelly v. Kelly*, 358 Mass. 154, 156, 260 N.E.2d 659 (1970). That reliance was reasonable, and the defendant knew of and accepted the plaintiff's trust in him. See *Hatton v. Meade, supra* 23 Mass.App.Ct. at 365, 502 N.E.2d 552, which has many factual parallels to this case. See also *Markell v. Sidney B. Pfeifer Found., Inc.*, 9 Mass.App.Ct. 412, 443–444, 402 N.E.2d 76 (1980).

It would be unjust not to impose a constructive trust in this case. The plaintiff gave up her career as a flight attendant and undertook to maintain a home for the defendant while he advanced his career. She contributed her earnings and services to the home. The defendant's assurances to the plaintiff that they would own the property together (although title would be taken only in his name), his later promises to transfer title to joint ownership, and the plaintiff's reasonable reliance on those promises made by one in whom she reasonably placed special confidence call for the imposition of a constructive trust in the plaintiff's favor on one-half the Reading property.

Judgment affirmed.

Property Transaction, Specific Performance, and Suit to Quiet Title

TYRANSKI v. PIGGINS
Court of Appeals of Michigan
44 Mich. App. 570, 205 N.W.2d 595 (1973)

LEVIN, Presiding Judge.

The plaintiff, Mrs. Helen Tyranski, commenced this action in January, 1970, claiming that she was entitled to a house located on Blue Skies Avenue, Livonia, Michigan, which was held in the name of Alfred P. Lattavo. Mr. Lattavo had died in October, 1969.

At the conclusion of the trial, the judge, who sat without a jury, found that Mrs. Tyranski was entitled to the house and its furnishings. A judgment was entered for specific performance of an oral agreement the judge found Lattavo had made with Mrs. Tyranski to convey the house to her.

The defendant, the ancillary administrator of Lattavo's estate, does not, on appeal, dispute the claimed oral agreement. He contends that the judge should have refused to enforce the agreement because of the meretricious relationship of the parties. We affirm.

Lattavo, who traveled frequently in connection with his trucking business, met Mrs. Tyranski in 1963, while she was working as a cocktail waitress. They were attracted to one another and shortly thereafter began living together in Mrs. Tyranski's rented Detroit home, and later in an apartment. After they had been living together for nearly four years, Lattavo had the Blue Skies house built. There is evidence that tends to show that $10,000 of the required funds was contributed by Mrs. Tyranski. Mrs. Tyranski decorated the house and selected the furniture. They lived together in the Blue Skies home from 1967 until Lattavo's death.

Lattavo had married Rosella Lattavo in 1941. He made trips to their home in Canton throughout the period of his relationship with Mrs. Tyranski, though by 1967 he spent only a few days a month in Canton. The rest of the time he spent in Livonia.

Mrs. Tyranski is a married woman and the mother of two children. She has been separated from her husband for many years, but never secured a divorce. Lattavo acted as a father to her children, and gave away her daughter, Laura, in marriage. While Lattavo was in Michigan, he and Mrs. Tyranski lived together as man and wife, and at least one mutual friend testified that she knew Mrs. Tyranski as "Mrs. Lattavo."

Rosella Lattavo testified that she did not learn about Mrs. Tyranski or the Blue Skies house until she went to an attorney to file for a divorce and had her husband investigated in August, 1969.

The issue is whether Mrs. Tyranski's claim under the agreement is defeated by the meretricious relationship.

While the parties illicitly cohabited over a period of years, that does not render all agreements between them illegal. Professor Corbin and the drafters of the Restatement of Contracts both write that while bargains in whole or in part in consideration of an illicit relationship are unenforceable, agreements between parties to such a relationship with respect to money or property will be enforced if the agreement is independent of the illicit relationship.[1]

Neither these authorities nor the large body of case law in other jurisdictions — there is no Michigan authority dealing with this precise issue — articulate a guideline for determining when the consideration will be regarded as "independent", and when it is so coupled with the meretricious acts that the agreement will not be enforced. A pattern does, however, emerge upon reading the cases.

Neither party to a meretricious relationship acquires, by reason of cohabitation alone, rights in the property accumulations of the other during the period of the relationship. But where there is an express agreement to accumulate or transfer property following a relationship of some permanence and an additional consideration in the form of either money or of services, the courts tend to find an independent consideration.

Thus, a plaintiff who can show an actual contribution of money, pursuant to an agreement to pool assets and share accumulations, will usually prevail. Services, such as cooking meals, laundering clothes, "caring" for the decedent through sickness, have been found to be adequate and independent considerations in cases where there was an express agreement.

1. 6A Corbin, CONTRACTS, §1476, p. 622; 2 RESTATEMENT CONTRACTS, §§589, 597, pp. 1098, 1108.

An express agreement to convey the Blue Skies house was established by testimony at the trial. There was also evidence that Mrs. Tyranski had "changed the tenor of her life" in performance of the agreement so as to make reasonable the inference that there was such an agreement. See *In re Cramer's Estate*, 296 Mich. 44, 49, 295 N.W. 553 (1941).

Mrs. Tyranski cleaned the house, did the marketing, cooked the food, did Mr. Lattavo's personal laundry, and acted as his hostess. She cared for him when he was sick, especially during the last year and a half of his life when his condition required greater attention and care. There was also the evidence of the $10,000 claimed to have been contributed by Mrs. Tyranski to Lattavo in April or May of 1967.

It has been said that "equity does not demand that its suitors shall have led blameless lives." *Loughran v. Loughran*, 292 U.S. 216, 229, 54 S.Ct. 684, 689, 78 L.Ed. 1219, 1227 (1934). The Michigan case law is in accord. In *Burns v. Stevens*, 236 Mich. 447, 452–453, 210 N.W. 483, 485 (1926), the plaintiff (the man) and the defendant (the woman) lived together for three years. They made a $1,000 down payment on a cottage. They signed a land contract "jointly." After the man tired of the woman, he brought suit claiming the cottage was his property and that her name was put on the contract to secure repayment to her of $400 she had advanced. He sought to have her interest in the contract declared to be a mortgage. In upholding the trial court's determination in his favor, the Michigan Supreme Court said:

> [T]he rule that if the parties to a suit are *in pari delicto* a court of equity will leave them where they have placed themselves should not be here applied.... The question to be determined in this case...is whether the party acquired an interest in the property or a security for the money advanced. *The manner in which they were then living is immaterial to the issue* except in its bearing upon the weight to be given to their testimony. The doors of courts are not closed to people who lead immoral lives when contracts between them untainted with illegality or fraud are involved. (Emphasis supplied.)

...

Where a meretricious relationship has already been entered upon, to penalize one of the parties by striking down their otherwise lawful promises, will not undo the relationship, nor is it likely to discourage others from entering upon such relationships. It appears on examination of the cases that the courts have, on various theories, allotted to the woman a share of the property in cases thought to be meritorious. We are persuaded, as was the trial judge, that this is such a case.

Affirmed....

TRUTALLI v. MERAVIGLIA

Supreme Court of California
215 Cal. 698, 12 P.2d 430 (1932)

CURTIS, J.

This appeal is taken upon the judgment roll alone. The action was brought by plaintiff to quiet his title to certain real property situated in the city and county of San Francisco. The defendant answered, and, in addition to her answer, filed a cross-complaint in which she claimed to be the owner of an undivided one-half of said real property, and also the owner of an undivided one-half of another parcel of land situated in the county of Santa Clara. Each of said two parcels of real property stood upon the public records in the name of the plaintiff who claimed to be the sole owner of the same. The court made findings of fact upon which judgment was entered in favor of the defendant upon her cross-complaint. Two of these findings are as follows:

> II.
>
> That in the year nineteen sixteen (1916) the plaintiff and defendant, without the performance of a marriage ceremony, agreed to become and live together and assume the marital relation between themselves and the world, as husband and wife; that thereupon said plaintiff and defendant did assume said marital relation openly, publicly and notoriously, and were known to the public in general, and their friends in particular, as husband and wife, living and cohabiting together as such, and so continued until the latter part of the year nineteen twenty-seven (1927); that during said time there were born to plaintiff and defendant, as the issue of said cohabitation, two (2) children, to-wit: Alma, a girl, of the age of twelve (12) years, and Disma, a girl, of the age of eleven (11) years.
>
> III.
>
> That it was mutually agreed by and between the plaintiff and defendant herein, upon the making and entering into of said agreement set forth in paragraph one (1) herein, that the defendant would perform all the necessary household services, and that all monies derived by either, or both, of said parties would be paid to the plaintiff to be invested by him for the benefit of both parties from time to time; and that all property, real and personal, acquired by said plaintiff should be held by him for the joint benefit of the said parties, each having an undivided one-half (½) interest therein.

The court further found: "Finding V. That as a result of the joint efforts of plaintiff and defendant, under and by virtue of said agreement, and while they were living and cohabiting together as husband and wife, the plaintiff purchased, with funds accumulated through the joint efforts of plaintiff and defendant," the real property described in said cross-complaint.

Plaintiff now seeks to set aside this judgment in favor of the defendant on the ground that the agreement under which said parties acquired said real property was based upon an immoral consideration, and is therefore unenforceable against either party thereto. We do not so understand the findings. The agreement to live together as husband and wife without the formality of a marriage ceremony is set forth in finding II, quoted above. The agreement to invest their separate earnings for their joint benefit, and that all property so acquired should be owned by them jointly, is set forth in finding III. While the court found that the parties agreed "upon the making and entering into" the agreement of cohabitation that they would invest their earnings in property to be held jointly by them, it did not find that this latter agreement was a part of, or that it was in any manner connected with, their agreement to unlawfully cohabit together. The two agreements, although made at the same time, are separate and distinct contracts, and neither is made dependent upon the other. Therefore it cannot be said that the consideration of the latter agreement was the unlawful cohabitation assented to in the agreement set forth in finding II. It clearly appears from finding III that the consideration of plaintiff's agreement to hold all property for their joint benefit, which was acquired by their joint efforts, was the agreement on defendant's part that all moneys earned by her should be paid to plaintiff and invested by him in property of which each party was to be the owner of an undivided half.

...

The authorities cited by plaintiff and relied upon by him in support of his contention that the agreement upon which the defendant relies was based upon an immoral consideration are not applicable to the facts in the present action. They simply hold, as stated by the plaintiff in his brief, "that agreeing to live and cohabit together as man and wife, without the performance of a marriage ceremony constitutes an illegal and immoral consideration for the basis of a contract, and is, therefore, a void consideration." There is no question but that this statement of law is correct, but, as we have shown, the facts as found by the court in this action do not bring this case within the principles of law there enunciated.

...

The judgment is affirmed.

COMMENTS

Poole, Ireland, Omer and *Sullivan* illustrate the infinite variety of fact and law attendant upon nonmarital cohabitation.

In *Poole,* parties of modest means joined their resources to acquire a beauty shop and a tavern. The business ventures may have facilitated the findings that there was "a joint venture if not a partnership" or a bona fide marital relationship. The alternative reasoning made it immaterial whether the parties actually believed themselves to be married. *Omer* and *Tyranski* involve meretricious relationships. *Omer* concerns cohabitation and pooling of resources between parties who had formerly been married in Israel, and who had obtained a divorce, thereafter entering sham marriages to facilitate immigration and naturalization in the United States. That this entails a conspiracy under federal law did not seem to disturb the Washington State courts, which gave the former wife the full protection of equity. This decision was also cited in *Marvin.* Perhaps its most outstanding feature is that it gives a full enumeration of legal theories in support of claims based on cohabitation and, at the same time, recognizes the fictitious character of these remedies. Yet the court concluded by finding a constructive trust, perhaps the most fictitious alternative of all, although it is a well established equitable remedy in cases of fraud or, as here, where fraud is not alleged between the parties.

Tyranski, by comparison, was based on a common occurrence — a relationship between two parties already married to other persons. Since no divorces were argued, the cohabitation was found to be illegal under traditional views. Nevertheless the trial judge granted specific performance on an oral contract to convey title to land, thus benefiting a woman who knew that she was married to somebody else and that her now-deceased cohabitant had also been married.

Factors of social class were implied in the facts, the deceased apparently having been a teamster and the plaintiff a cocktail waitress. Since the two families of the deceased were in different locations, the facts are reminiscent of cases in which common law marriage or a presumption of marriage arose, although the possibility of presumption of divorce was not in issue in *Tyranski.* Obviously, specific performance of the agreement underlying the cohabitation would not have been possible, but death changed the relationship to a purely proprietary one.

Property was also involved in *Trutalli,* a cohabitation of eleven years, short of marriage, resulting in two children. The mere assumption that a contract to live together may violate public policy does not necessarily invalidate a contract relating to property, although it may have been made simultaneously. The parallel contracts can be viewed as "separate and distinct," provided of course that the court considers them so. Apart from this the case relates to the fundamental problem of how such relationships should be terminated. The term "nonmarital cohabitation" seems to imply that mere factual termination is sufficient, but this is not necessarily true if issues of property are involved. Divorce or dissolution is not available because the parties are not legally married. The male party's suit to quiet title in *Trutalli* can be viewed as a functional equivalent to an action for annulment of marriage. The theory of the complaint is that there was no valid agreement to begin with, and that the unjustified claims of the woman clouded title in real property. The woman's cross-complaint, on the other hand, proceeded under a theory that some aspects of the relationship were valid and permitted splitting the mutually acquired assets. Seen in this light, the cross-complaint is similar to a request for divorce. The possibilities of legally adjudicated termination are infinite. If there is the possibility of a "marriage by presumption," for example, evidence can be introduced to rebut the presumption. The results of successful introduction of evidence may be comparable to those of divorce. The presence of children, as in *Trutalli* is always a complicating factor. Obviously, a custody dispute, as well as requests for support, may ensue. Here, too, the functional differences between marriage and nonmarital cohabitation are fewer than may initially appear.

Ireland can be viewed as a rather straight-forward application of the principles enunciated in *Beal* to a case involving two women, instead of a man and a woman. Although the relationship seemingly lasted only about a year and a half, there was significant evidence of an intent to form a long-term commitment. Moreover, unlike many of the heterosexual cases, one could not argue in *Ireland,* if they wanted to be treated like a married couple, then why didn't they just get married? The trial opinion, overturned on appeal, could also be argued to be supportive of same-sex couples. The basis on which the trial court refused relief was an alleged legal presumption that plaintiff's contribution to the purchase of and improvements to the home were gifts to the defendant. The trial court had also held that the parties' relationship imposed upon them a moral obligation to provide for one another "similar to the relationship of husband and wife."

Sullivan v. Rooney illustrates a case in which the probate judge clearly saw an inequity but did not state a theory of the case that was convincing to the Supreme

Judicial Court. That court preferred to characterize the issue as one of whether a constructive trust had been created instead of the requirements of an enforceable promise. The case underscores the importance of fashioning a specific remedy and arguing for that remedy instead of arguing (or in the case of a judge, deciding a case) on vague principles of equity.

Protection of and Discrimination against Cohabitation

COOPER v. FRENCH
Supreme Court of Minnesota
460 N.W.2d 2 (Minn. 1990)

YETKA, Justice.

Appellant was found guilty of discrimination by an administrative law judge to whom a complaint filed with the Department of Human Rights was referred for hearing. Appellant had refused to rent his property to one Susan Parsons because she planned to live there with her fiance. A trial de novo before the district court was denied, and the court of appeals affirmed the action of the administrative law judge. French was ordered to pay $368.50 in compensatory damages to Parsons, $400 for mental anguish and suffering, and $300 civil penalties. We reverse the administrative law judge and the court of appeals.

A summary of the facts are as follows:

French owned and occupied a two-bedroom house ("subject property") in Marshall, Minnesota, until moving to a house he purchased in the country. While attempting to sell the subject property, French rented it to both single individuals and married couples. From January to March 1988, French advertised the subject property as being available for rent. On February 22, 1988, French agreed to rent the property to Parsons and accepted a $250 check as a security deposit.

Shortly thereafter, French decided that Parsons had a romantic relationship with her fiance, Wesley Jenson, and that the two would likely engage in sexual relations outside of marriage on the subject property. On February 24, 1988, French told Parsons that he had changed his mind and would not rent the property to her because unmarried adults of the opposite sex living together were inconsistent with his religious beliefs. French is a member of the Evangelical Free Church in Marshall, and his beliefs include that an unmarried couple living together or having sexual relations outside of marriage is sinful. Despite being questioned by French, neither Parsons nor Jenson told French whether they were planning to have sexual relations on the subject property. The record is in dispute as to whether appellant had knowledge of Parsons' intended sexual activity with her fiance, but Parsons did not deny such an intent when queried by French. Even if they would not have had sexual relations on the property, French believes that living together constitutes the "appearance of evil" and would not have rented to them on that basis. French admits that if Parsons had been married to Jenson, he would not have objected renting to them.

Parsons filed a charge of discrimination against French with respondent department alleging that French committed marital status discrimination in violation of the Minnesota Human Rights Act (MHRA) when he refused to rent the subject property to her because she planned to live there with her fiance. Following an investigation, the department issued a complaint against French.

An administrative law judge granted the department partial summary judgment on the issue of liability, ruling that French violated the act's (Minn.Stat. §363.03, subd. 2(1)(a)(1986)) prohibition of marital status discrimination by refusing to rent the subject property to Parsons because she was single and living with her fiance and rejected French's defenses. Following a hearing on damages, the judge found French liable to Parsons for $368.50 in compensatory damages and $400.00 in mental anguish and suffering. In addition, the judge assessed a civil penalty of $300 to be paid to the State of Minnesota by French, but declined to award punitive damages. French's motion for a trial de novo in district court was denied.

After issuing French a writ of certiorari, a court of appeals panel affirmed that French discriminated against Parsons because of her marital status in violation of the Human Rights Act and that neither the free exercise of religion nor any of French's other arguments provided a defense. We granted French's petition for further review.

On an appeal from summary judgment, we ask two questions: (1) whether there are any genuine issues of material fact and (2) whether the lower courts erred in their application of the law.

Initially the department must establish a prima facie case of discrimination. *State ex rel. McClure v. Sports & Health Club, Inc.*, 370 N.W.2d 844, 849 (Minn. 1985), *appeal dismissed*, 478 U.S. 1015, 106 S.Ct. 3315, 92 L.Ed.2d 730 (1986). We must examine whether appellant's refusal to rent to Parsons constituted a prima facie violation of the Human Rights Act's prohibition of marital status discrimination. The act provides in relevant part:

> It is an unfair discriminatory practice:
>
> (1) For an owner, lessee...
>
> (a) to refuse to sell, rent, or lease...any real property because of race, color, creed, religion, national origin, sex, marital status, status with regard to public assistance, disability, or familial status.

...

I. THE DEFINITION OF "MARITAL STATUS"

The administrative law judge (ALJ) found that appellant refused to rent to Parsons because she "was single and planned to cohabit with another person of the opposite sex." The version of the MHRA in effect at the time the alleged discrimination occurred and when the charge was filed did not contain a definition of the term "marital status." See Minn.Stat. §363.01 (1987 Supp.).

...

The MHRA was amended in 1973 to add the prohibition against discrimination on the basis of "marital status." Act of May 24, 1973, ch. 729, §3, 1973 Minn.Laws 2158, 2162 (codified at Minn.Stat. §363.03, subd. 2 (1988)). This court, in construing the term "marital status" has consistently looked to the legislature's policy of discouraging the practice of fornication and protecting the institution of marriage. See *Kraft, Inc. v. State ex rel. Wilson*, 284 N.W.2d 386, 388 (Minn.1979)(8-0 decision). *Kraft* presented the question of whether an employer's anti-nepotism policy constituted marital status discrimination within the meaning of the MHRA. *Id.* at 387–88. In answering this question in the affirmative, Chief Justice Sheran stated:

> Endorsing a narrow definition of marital status and uncritically upholding an employment policy such as respondent's *could discourage similarly situated employees from marrying.* In a locale where a predominant employer enforced such a policy, economic pressures might lead two similarly situated individuals to forsake the marital union and *live together in violation of Minn.Stat. §609.34* [fornication statute]. Such an employment policy would thus undermine the *preferred status enjoyed by the institution of marriage.*
>
> *In view of these considerations,* we hold the employment policy of respondent presumptively invalid under Minn.Stat. §363.03, subd. 1.

Kraft, 284 N.W.2d at 388 (emphasis added)(footnote omitted). The *Kraft* court unanimously concluded that the fornication statute was a valid expression of Minnesota public policy. Moreover, the *Kraft* court did not ignore the destructive practical effect of a contrary ruling simply because there was no direct evidence of fornication. It is easy to see that, but for these important public policies, the *Kraft* decision would have been different.

. . .

Respondent makes the surprising suggestion that the fornication statute no longer expresses this state's public policy because "it has fallen into complete disuse." Not only is such a notion of implied repeal unprecedented, it is factually mistaken. See *State v. Ford,* 397 N.W.2d 875 (Minn.1986). In *Ford,* an educator was charged with fornication in connection with consensual sex acts with 16-year-old students. *Id.* at 876–77. Although the educator entered into a plea bargain agreement pursuant to which he pleaded guilty to different charges, there was no suggestion by anyone that the fornication statute was a nullity.

. . .

The legislative history of this subdivision indicates that the legislature did not intend to extend the protection of the MHRA to unmarried, cohabiting couples in the area of housing....

. . .

Other courts which have addressed the same issue have considered their state's policy with respect to fornication as expressed in statutory law. See *Foreman v. Anchorage Equal Rights Comm'n,* 779 P.2d 1199, 1201–02 (Alaska 1989); *Mister v. A.R.K. Partnership,* 197 Ill.App.3d 105, 113–14, 143 Ill.Dec. 166, 171, 553 N.E.2d 1152, 1157 (1990). The facts in *Mister* were virtually identical to the instant case except the record was silent as to the defendants' alleged religious beliefs. *See Mister,* 197 Ill.App.3d at 107–10, 143 Ill.Dec. at 167–68, 553 N.E.2d at 1153–54 (1990). In *Mister,* the court held that the Illinois Human Rights Act's prohibition against discrimination on the basis of sex or marital status does not include a landlord's refusal to rent an apartment to unmarried persons of the opposite sex. *Mister,* 197 Ill.App.3d at 116–17, 143 Ill.Dec. at 173, 553 N.E.2d at 1159. In ascertaining legislative intent, the court observed that:

> Plaintiffs' interpretation of the Act would have us conclude that the legislature intended to protect from discrimination those individuals who choose to cohabit with a person of the opposite sex without entering into marriage. The fornication statute, as it existed when plaintiffs attempted

> to rent the apartments, evidenced this State's policy against such a practice. We believe plaintiffs' interpretation of the Act is in conflict with the longstanding policy reflected by the fornication statute. Statutory provisions relating to the same subject matter should be construed harmoniously where possible....
>
> Such a stance [by this court] expresses neither approval nor disapproval of discreet cohabitation;couples who wish to live together without being married can certainly still do so, but they must *find a landlord who does not object to the arrangement. The Act's failure to protect such couples from "discrimination" merely evidences the legislature's hesitancy to require landlords to acquiesce.*

197 Ill.App.3d at 114–15, 143 Ill.Dec. at 171–72, 553 N.E.2d at 1157–58 (emphasis added).

Similarly, in *Foreman,* the Alaska Supreme Court, in ascertaining its legislature's intent as to the meaning of "marital status," relied entirely on the fact that Alaska's fornication statute had been repealed 11 years earlier in concluding that protection for unmarried, cohabiting couples was included. *Foreman v. Anchorage Equal Rights Comm'n,* 779 P.2d at 1201–02. At the very least, before the state imposes sanctions on French, it must repeal the fornication statute.

...

It is simply astonishing to me that the argument is made that the legislature intended to protect fornication and promote a lifestyle which corrodes the institutions which have sustained our civilization, namely, marriage and family life. If the legislature intended to protect cohabiting couples and other types of domestic partners, it would have said so. The legislative history of this statute indicates that an attempt to do this was defeated by a substantial majority of the Minnesota House of Representatives. It is not the role of this court, especially in light of the foregoing analysis, to read such protections into the MHRA.

...

...[W]e interpret the Minnesota Constitution as requiring a more stringent burden on the state; it grants far more protection of religious freedom than the broad language of the United States Constitution. Pursuant to this analysis, we conclude that the state has failed to sustain its burden in demonstrating a sufficiently compelling interest.

It appears that we have now reached the stage in Minnesota constitutional law where the religious views of a probable majority of the Minnesota citizens are being alleged by a state agency to violate state law. Today we have a department of state government proposing that, while French has sincere religious beliefs and those beliefs are being infringed upon by the Human Rights Act, the state, nevertheless, has an interest in promoting access to housing for cohabiting couples which overrides French's right to exercise his religion.

Respondent characterizes the state's interest as "eliminating *pernicious* discrimination, including marital status discrimination." We are not told what is so pernicious about refusing to treat unmarried, cohabiting couples as if they were legally married. The state does not even attempt to reconcile this notion with this court's express recognition of the "preferred status" of the institution of marriage in *Kraft*.... There are numerous other contexts in which cohabiting couples are not legally entitled to the same treatment as married couples. A prime example is found in the area of employee life and health insurance benefits, a subject which is also regulated by the MHRA. See Minn.Stat. §363.03, subd. 1(2)(c)(1989 Supp.). Other examples are found in the laws governing intestate succession and the rules of evidence governing the privilege for marital communications. Is the argument now being made that these too are "*pernicious*" discrimination? If they are, surely it is the role of the legislature to make whatever changes are necessary.

How can there be a compelling state interest in promoting fornication when there is a state statute on the books prohibiting it? See Minn.Stat. §609.34 (1988). Moreover, if the state has a duty to enforce a statute in the least restrictive way to accommodate religious beliefs, surely it is less restrictive to require Parsons to abide by the law prohibiting fornication than to compel French to cooperate in breaking it. Rather than grant French an exemption from the MHRA, the state would rather grant everyone an exemption from the fornication statute. Such a result is absurd.

...

There are certain moral values and institutions that have served western civilization well for eons.... This generation does not have a monopoly on either knowledge or wisdom. Before abandoning fundamental values and institutions, we must pause and take stock of our present social order: millions of drug abusers; rampant child abuse; a rising underclass without marketable job skills; children roaming the streets; children with only one parent or no parent at all; and children growing up with no one to guide them in developing any set of values. How can we expect anything else when the state itself contributes, by arguments of this kind, to further erosion of fundamental institutions that have formed the foundation of our civilization for centuries?

...We find that, on statutory grounds and on the grounds of the Minnesota Constitution, French was within his rights in refusing to rent to Parsons.

...

SIMONETT, Justice (concurring as to Part I).

I join Part I of the court's opinion. Because the issue of statutory construction is dispositive here, I do not reach the constitutional questions.

POPOVICH, Chief Justice (dissenting).

I respectfully dissent. Precedent establishes the refusal to rent real property to an unmarried woman because she would be living with her fiance is a prima facie violation of the Minnesota Human Rights Act's (MHRA) prohibition of marital status discrimination. I believe the majority misconstrues legislative history, public policy and the facts presented to reach a result contrary to this court's interpretation of the MHRA.

...

III.

Enforcement of the provision of the Human Rights Act against French violates neither the federal due process or equal protection clauses. Appellant argues "due process/equal protection rights will protect *any landlord*" who objects to people of the opposite sex living together. (Emphasis added.) French summarily asks us to find a violation of these provisions because the Act "seeks to penalize an individual who is seeking only to exercise a fundamental right." In substance, appellant argues even if it is not against your religious beliefs for persons of the opposite sex to live together, you can still discriminate against these people if you personally disagree with them living together. This basically amounts to a facial attack on the Act's prohibition of marital status discrimination.

Not only has appellant failed to identify what fundamental right is violated, but he was provided a full administrative hearing prior to being assessed a penalty. Preventing discrimination certainly is a legitimate government purpose necessary to survive a facial due process or equal protection challenge. *Sports & Health Club*, 370 N.W.2d at 853 (compelling state interest in preventing marital status discrimination); *AFSCME Councils 6, 14, 65 & 96 v. Sundquist*, 338 N.W.2d 560, 574 (Minn.1983)(rational basis needed to satisfy due process or equal protection challenge). French's equal protection and due process challenges lack merit.

IV.

Discriminating against unmarried individuals living with members of the opposite sex is neither the cause or the solution to societal woes. The majority's decision rejects the reasoned precedents of this court. Unless the legislature acts differently or until those cases are overruled, we are obliged to follow clear, established precedent in this state.

WAHL, Justice.

I join the dissent of Chief Justice Popovich.

KEITH, Justice.

I join the dissent of Chief Justice Popovich.

MacGREGOR v. UNEMPLOYMENT INSURANCE APPEALS BOARD

Supreme Court of California

37 Cal. 3d 205, 689 P.2d 453, 207 Cal. Rptr. 823 (1984)

REYNOSO, Justice.

When a worker leaves her employment to accompany her "nonmarital partner" to another state in order to maintain the familial relationship they have established with their child does she voluntarily leave work with good cause within the meaning of the statute governing eligibility for unemployment insurance benefits? We left open the possibility that a claimant might show good cause in such circumstances when we decided *Norman v. Unemployment Ins. Appeals Bd.* (1983) 34 Cal.3d 1, 192 Cal.Rptr. 134, 663 P.2d 904, less than two years ago. We now hold that Patricia MacGregor has established that her quitting was motivated by the need to preserve the family she had established with her nonmarital partner and their child, and that this need constituted good cause for her voluntary departure from work. We therefore affirm the judgment of the Santa Clara County Superior Court ordering the Unemployment Insurance Appeals Board to reconsider its decision and to award benefits to plaintiff if she meets other eligibility requirements.

Plaintiff Patricia MacGregor worked as a waitress at the Ramada Inn in Santa Clara, California from July 7, 1978 through December 31, 1979. On January 1, 1980, she began a six-month pregnancy leave of absence. According to the terms of her leave, she was to return to work in June of 1980.

MacGregor was engaged to and lived with Dick Bailey, the father of her expected child. Their daughter Leanna was born February 29, 1980. The three continued to live together as a family. Bailey acknowledged that he was Leanna's father.

In April, Bailey decided the family should move to New York to live with and care for his 76-year-old father.... Bailey's father asked if Bailey, MacGregor and their daughter would come to live with and care for him. In May MacGregor informed her employer that she would not be returning to work.

MacGregor, Bailey and their daughter moved into Bailey's father's home in June. When MacGregor was unable to find work, she applied for unemployment insurance benefits. Her claim was referred to the California Employment Development Department (Department), which determined that she had quit voluntarily without good cause and was thus ineligible for benefits. (Unemp.Ins. Code, §1256.)

MacGregor appealed this decision.... The judge determined MacGregor had left her most recent work voluntarily without good cause and was thus disqualified from receiving benefits. Although the judge found evidence in the record indicating that Bailey had to return to New York to care for his father who was ill, the judge concluded that "it [was] not apparent why it was essential for the claimant to follow." Since there was no marriage, no plans to marry at a certain future date, and no assurance the relationship would continue for any particular period of time, the judge found there was no family unit to be preserved.

MacGregor again appealed. The California Unemployment Insurance Appeals Board (Board) adopted as its own the administrative law judge's decision and statement of facts and reasons. Plaintiff then sought a writ of mandate from the Santa Clara Superior Court pursuant to Code of Civil Procedure section 1094.5.

After considering the record of the administrative proceeding, the superior court found plaintiff had good cause for leaving her employment. The court found as facts that MacGregor had lived with Bailey for three years, that she and Bailey had established a family unit with their child, that Bailey had decided to move to New York, and that plaintiff had chosen to leave her employment and relocate to New York in order to maintain and preserve their family unit. The court concluded that these underlying facts established good cause for plaintiff's quitting pursuant to section 1256 and that she was therefore entitled to receive benefits if otherwise qualified.

The court issued a peremptory writ of mandate directing the Board to set aside its decision and to reconsider its action in light of the court's findings of fact and conclusions of law. The Board appealed. While the Board's appeal was pending, this court decided *Norman v. Unemployment Insurance Appeals Board, supra,* 34 Cal.3d 1, 192 Cal.Rptr. 134, 663 P.2d 904.

...

Whether or not there is "good cause" within the meaning of section 1256 is a question of law (*Norman v. Unemployment Ins. Appeals Bd., supra,* 34 Cal.3d 1, 6, 192 Cal.Rptr. 134, 663 P.2d 904) which must be answered in relation to the particular facts of each case. (*Cal. Portland Cement Co. v. Cal. Unemp. Ins. Appeals Bd.* (1960) 178 Cal.App.2d 263, 274, 3 Cal.Rptr. 37.) Good cause may exist for reasons which are personal and not connected to the employment situation (*id.* at p. 272, 3 Cal.Rptr. 37), but those reasons must be imperative and compelling in nature. (*Evenson v. Unemployment Ins. Appeals Bd.* (1976) 62 Cal.App.3d 1005, 1016, 133 Cal.Rptr. 488.) Several Courts of Appeal have defined "good cause" as used in section 1256 to mean "such a cause as justifies an employee's voluntarily leaving the ranks of the employed;... such a cause as would, in a similar situation, reasonably motivate the average able-bodied and qualified worker to give up his or her employment with its certain wage rewards in order to enter the ranks of the unemployed. (81 C.J.S. Social Security and Public Welfare, §167, p. 253.)" (*Evenson v. Unemployment Ins. Appeals Bd., supra,* 62 Cal.App.3d at p. 1016, 133 Cal.Rptr. 488; *Zorrero v. Unemployment Ins. Appeals Bd.* (1975) 47 Cal.App.3d 434, 120 Cal.Rptr. 855.)

Precedent decisions of the Board have long recognized that the circumstances attendant upon a worker's decision to leave employment in order to accompany a spouse and family to a new home may be so compelling as to constitute good cause for quitting within section 1256....

In 1982 the Legislature added the fourth paragraph to section 1256 which recognizes that the desire to preserve a marital relationship, or a relationship in which marriage is imminent, may constitute good cause within the meaning of the statute. The Legislature explicitly stated that the amendment was intended to overturn the Court of Appeal decision in *Norman v. Unemployment Ins. Appeals Bd.* (which had found good cause based on a nonmarital relationship) and to "endorse the policy of the Employment Development Department, as expressed in its regulations, which distinguishes persons who are married or whose marriage is imminent from others in determining whether a person has left his or her most recent work without good cause...." (Stats.1982, ch. 1073 §13, pp. 3873–3874.)

...

It is apparent from the *Norman* decision's treatment of the subject that the presumption which attaches to a couple that is legally married is not the exclusive means of demonstrating good cause based on compelling family circumstances. Regulations of the Department itself recognize the "existing or prospective marital status of the claimant" as but one of three kinds of domestic obligations which might compel a person to leave work with good cause. (Cal.Admin.Code, tit. 22, §1256-9, *et seq.*)

The decisions of the administrative law judge and the Board in this case rested on the lack of a legally recognized marriage between MacGregor and Bailey, ignoring the existence of any family unit. When reviewing a decision of the Board on a petition for writ of mandate, however, the superior court must exercise its independent judgment on the evidence in the administrative record. (Code Civ.Proc., §1094.5; *Interstate Brands v. Unemp. Ins. App. Bd.* (1980) 26 Cal.3d 770, 163 Cal.Rptr. 619, 608 P.2d 707.) The court may make its own findings and conclusions based on the evidence before it. (*Thomas v. California Emp. Stab. Com.* (1952) 39 Cal.2d 501, 504, 247 P.2d 561.) These conclusions will be upheld on appeal if they are supported by substantial evidence. (*Rowe v. Hansen* (1974) 41 Cal.App.3d 512, 518–519, 116 Cal.Rptr. 16.)

The evidence here amply supports the trial court's findings that MacGregor had "established a family unit consisting of herself, her fiance and their child" and that she "chose to relocate to New York with her fiance and their child in order to maintain and preserve their family unit." The record shows that MacGregor and Bailey had maintained a common household for over two years prior to the birth of their daughter. When the child was born the parents received her into that home and gave her Bailey's surname. It is clear that both MacGregor and Bailey intend to and do provide a stable and secure home for their daughter.

It is difficult to conceive of a more fundamental familial relationship than one which is created when two parents establish a home with their natural child. According to Black's Law Dictionary, "family" "most commonly refers to group of persons consisting of parents and children;..." (5th ed. 1979.)... This court has recognized that "the family is the basic unit of our society, the center of the personal affections that ennoble and enrich human life. It channels biological drives that might otherwise become socially destructive; it ensures the care and education of children in a stable environment; it establishes continuity from one generation to another; it nurtures and develops the individual initiative that distinguishes a free people." (*De Burgh v. De Burgh* (1952) 39 Cal.2d 858, 863, 864, 250 P.2d 598.)

The Legislature has explicitly recognized that the legal relationship between a child and his or her parents is not dependent upon the existence of a marriage between the parents....

Leanna was only two months old when Bailey decided his father's illness required him to move to New York. The need for MacGregor to follow — which the administrative law judge could not fathom — is in our view manifest. The intimate nature of the family bond among these three individuals would have been forever altered had MacGregor decided that she, or she and Leanna, should not accompany Bailey to New York.

The Board's arguments here, like the administrative decisions below, focus on the lack of a legal marriage relationship between plaintiff and Bailey. The Board urges that leaving work to join a spouse should be deemed good cause only where there is a marriage to be preserved. This rule, according to the Board, is consistent with the public policy favoring marriage and with laws which afford special benefits and protections to that institution. (*E.g.*, Civ.Code, §242 [duty to support spouse]; Code Civ.Proc., §1730, *et seq.* [establishing conciliation procedures]; *Cohen v. Cohen* (1946) 73 Cal.App.2d 330, 335–336, 166 P.2d 622 [law will not recognize contract with the object of dissolving marriage].) The rule would also avoid the difficulties and dangers which would accompany a requirement that administrative agencies and the courts make individualized determination of the "true nature" of intimate personal relationships.

...Today we reaffirm the principle that the lack of a legally recognized marriage does not prevent a claimant from demonstrating that compelling familial obligations provided good cause for leaving employment.

The state's policy in favor of maintaining secure and stable relationships between parents and children is equally as strong as its interest in preserving the institution of marriage. The Legislature has declared that the rights and obligations of parents and children exist regardless of the marital status of the parents. (Civ.Code, §7002.) The purposes of the conciliation statutes relied on by the Board include the protection of the rights of children as well as the protection of the institution of matrimony. (Code Civ.Proc., §1730.) The courts have recognized the family as a basic unit of our society. (*De Burgh v. De Burgh, supra,* 39 Cal.2d 858, 863–864, 250 P.2d 598.)

...

...Prior decisions of the board recognize that even if one spouse's reason for relocating appears arbitrary, the importance of preserving the marital or familial relationship may provide good cause for the other spouse's decision to follow....

In this case the decisions of the administrative law judge and the Board conceded that Bailey had a good reason for relocating: the care of his elderly and ill father. This would constitute a compelling circumstance under the Department's own regulations. (22 Cal.Admin.Code., tit. 22, §1256-11(c)(2).) The trial court found as matters of fact that Bailey made the decision to move and that plaintiff chose to go with him in order to preserve their family unit. The court's findings are supported by substantial, credible and competent evidence. (*Rowe v. Hansen, supra,* 41 Cal.App.3d 512, 116 Cal.Rptr. 16.) The conclusion that MacGregor had "such a cause as would, in a similar situation, reasonably motivate the average able-bodied and qualified worker to give up his or her employment with its certain wage rewards in order to enter the ranks of the unemployed" is entirely consistent with the laws and public policies of the State of California.

As the record clearly supports the trial court's finding that plaintiff had good cause for leaving work, the judgment is affirmed.

ELDEN v. SHELDON

Supreme Court of California

46 Cal. 3d 267, 758 P.2d 582, 250 Cal. Rptr. 254 (1988)

MOSK, Justice.

Plaintiff Richard Elden appeals from a judgment of dismissal after the trial court sustained, without leave to amend, defendants' demurrer to his complaint alleging causes of action for negligent infliction of emotional distress and loss of consortium.

The issue presented is whether plaintiff, who witnessed the tortious injury and death of the person with whom he shared a cohabitant relationship allegedly akin to a marital relationship, may recover damages for loss of consortium and negligent infliction of emotional distress. We conclude that he may not.

The facts pleaded are few and not in dispute. In December 1982, plaintiff and Linda Eberling were both involved in an automobile accident allegedly caused by defendant Sheldon's negligence. Plaintiff, a passenger in Eberling's car, sustained serious personal injuries. Eberling was thrown from the car and died a few hours later. Plaintiff filed an action against Sheldon and the owner of the automobile he was driving (defendants), alleging that at the time of the accident plaintiff had an "unmarried cohabitation relationship with the decedent...which was both stable and significant and parallel to a marital relationship." The complaint set forth three causes of action. The first sought recovery for plaintiff's own injuries, the second for negligent infliction of emotional distress which he suffered as a result of witnessing the injury of his "de facto spouse," and in the third cause of action he sought recovery for loss of consortium. Defendants demurred to the last two causes of action on the ground that plaintiff was not legally married to Eberling at the time of the accident. The trial court sustained the demurrer without leave to amend and entered judgment of dismissal. Plaintiff appeals.

I. NEGLIGENT INFLICTION OF MENTAL DISTRESS

The first issue is whether plaintiff can maintain a cause of action for negligent infliction of emotional distress based on the fact that he witnessed the injury to Eberling, his alleged de facto spouse.

In the landmark decision of *Dillon v. Legg* (1968) 68 Cal.2d 728, 69 Cal.Rptr. 72, 441 P.2d 912, this court first held that a bystander who was not himself in danger of injury from an accident may recover damages for negligent infliction of emotional distress as the result of witnessing an accident in which another was injured by the defendant's negligence....

We suggested three guidelines, based on the plaintiff's physical, temporal and relational proximity to the primary victim at the time of the accident, to determine whether liability was reasonably foreseeable: "(1) Whether plaintiff was located near the scene of the accident as contrasted with one who was a distance away from it. (2) Whether the shock resulted from a direct emotional impact upon plaintiff from the sensory and contemporaneous observance of the accident, as contrasted with learning of the accident from others after its occurrence. (3) Whether plaintiff and the victim were closely related, as contrasted with an absence of any relationship or the presence of only a distant relationship." (*Id.* at pp. 740–741, 69 Cal.Rptr. 72, 441 P.2d 912.) We further advised that no "immutable rule" could replace a case-by-case determination of the foreseeability of serious mental distress to the plaintiff.

These guidelines have been applied with varying degrees of flexibility. Some courts have extended the *Dillon* holding to close relations who did not visually witness the injury-causing event and to those who arrived soon after impact.... Others have denied recovery because plaintiff first learned of the injury from a third party, even though he was present or nearby when the injury-causing conduct occurred...or because the plaintiffs arrived at the scene of the accident a few minutes after it occurred....

...

With regard to the third prong of the *Dillon* foreseeability test, i.e., whether the plaintiff and the victim were closely related, the cases have refused to extend recovery to friends or distant relatives of the injured person....

...

A few cases have allowed recovery if the plaintiff and victim shared a relationship that was the functional and emotional equivalent of a nuclear family relationship. In *Leong v. Takasaki* (1974) 55 Hawaii 398, 520 P.2d 758, 766, a child successfully stated a cause of action for emotional distress after he witnessed an automobile strike his stepfather's mother, with whom he allegedly shared a very close relationship.

And in *Mobaldi v. Regents of University of California* (1976) 55 Cal.App.3d 573, 127 Cal.Rptr. 720 (disapproved on other grounds in *Baxter v. Superior Court* (1977) 19 Cal.3d 461, 466, fn. 4, 138 Cal.Rptr. 315, 563 P.2d 871), a foster mother was allowed to recover damages for emotional distress after she watched hospital personnel negligently administer a fatal dose of glucose solution to her foster child. Plaintiff held the child in her arms as he went into convulsions and became comatose, suffering irreversible brain damage.

The *Mobaldi* court reasoned that it is "[t]he emotional attachments of the family relationship and not legal status [that] are...relevant to foreseeability." (55 Cal.App.3d at p. 582, 127 Cal.Rptr. 720.) Although the plaintiff did not share a biological relationship with the child, their relationship possessed all the attributes of a natural parent-child relationship "except those flowing as a matter of law." (*Id.* at p. 583, 127 Cal.Rptr. 720.) The child had lived under plaintiff's care for three years, since he was five months old. Plaintiff had attempted to formally adopt the child, only to be frustrated by a county policy against the adoption of seriously ill children. The child was baptized and given the surname of his foster parents. The fact that the plaintiff and child were "closely related" also was known to some personnel at the medical center, who referred to the two as "mother and child."

Plaintiff relies on *Mobaldi, supra,* 55 Cal.App.3d 573, 127 Cal.Rptr. 720, and on *Ledger v. Tippitt* (1985) 164 Cal.App.3d 625, 210 Cal.Rptr. 814, which extended the reasoning in *Mobaldi* to allow recovery for emotional distress to a plaintiff who was not married to her injured partner. The plaintiff in Ledger observed another motorist stab her fiance in the chest following a verbal altercation. She rushed to his aid, and he died in her arms moments later. The couple began living together 2 years before the incident, when plaintiff was 15½ years old and her fiance was 19. They had a son, and they planned to marry but were twice frustrated in their attempt to do so. Plaintiff also claimed to be economically dependent on the decedent.

The *Ledger* court held that "it is foreseeable, as a matter of law..., that when defendant drew his knife, and stabbed Richard...the woman a few feet distant seated in the vehicle was likely a loved one who would suffer extreme emotional distress when Richard died in her arms." (164 Cal.App.3d at p. 646, 210 Cal.Rptr. 814.)

Defendants, on the other hand, cite *Drew v. Drake* (1980) 110 Cal.App.3d 555, 168 Cal.Rptr. 65, which reached the opposite result on facts similar to the instant matter. The plaintiff in that case witnessed the death of her companion in an automobile accident. She claimed damages for emotional trauma, alleging that she had lived for three years as his de facto spouse. In affirming the dismissal of the suit for failure to state a cause of action, the court reasoned that emotional distress to a spouse or a parent "meets the *Dillon* test because it is reasonably foreseeable that a person standing in such close relationship to the injured person may be present and suffer intense distress.... To allow persons standing in a 'meaningful relationship' (to use a contemporary colloquialism) to recover for emotional distress resulting in physical injury would abandon the *Dillon* requirement that '[t]he courts...mark out the areas of liability, excluding the remote and unexpected.'" (*Id.* at p. 557, 168 Cal.Rptr. 65.) The *Drew* court distinguished *Mobaldi* on the ground that there hospital personnel actually "knew the nature of the relationship" between the child and plaintiff, and therefore her mental distress was reasonably foreseeable. (*Id.* at p. 558, 168 Cal.Rptr. 65.)

Plaintiff argues that the injury to him was foreseeable under the guidelines set forth in *Dillon, supra,* 68 Cal.2d 728, 69 Cal.Rptr. 72, 441 P.2d 912. Relying on the holdings in *Ledger, supra,* 164 Cal.App.3d 625, 210 Cal.Rptr. 814, and *Mobaldi, supra,* 55 Cal.App.3d 573, 127 Cal.Rptr. 720, he asserts that he should have been allowed the opportunity to show that he met the "closely related" prong of the *Dillon* test by proof that he and his partner had a de facto marriage. The basis of his claim of foreseeability is that in recent years there has been a marked increase in the number of unmarried cohabitants, and therefore it is foreseeable that two persons occupying the same vehicle may be unmarried cohabitants whose relationship parallels that of a legally married couple.

We have no quarrel with the factual premise of plaintiff's position. There can be no doubt that the last two decades have seen a dramatic increase in the number of couples who live together without formal marriage, that some of these couples are bound by emotional ties as strong as those that bind formally married partners, and that they may share financial resources and expenses in the same manner as married couples. It may well be also that the number of such households has increased to the point that emotional trauma suffered by a partner in such an arrangement from injury to his companion cannot be characterized as "unexpected or remote." Nevertheless, we conclude, for the reasons stated below, that an unmarried cohabitant may not recover damages for emotional distress based on such injury.

Although *Dillon* stresses foreseeability of the risk as the "chief element in determining whether defendant owes a duty to...plaintiff" (68 Cal.2d at p. 740, 69

Cal.Rptr. 72, 441 P.2d 912), it recognizes that policy considerations may dictate a cause of action should not be sanctioned no matter how foreseeable the risk. This proposition is self-evident. It is manifest, for example, that a mother will suffer severe emotional trauma from the death or serious injury of her child in an accident whether or not she is present at the scene. The same would often be true of very close friends. Yet recovery of damages for such trauma is not allowed (*Justus v. Atchison, supra,* 19 Cal.3d 564, 139 Cal.Rptr. 97, 565 P.2d 122; *Kately v. Wilkinson, supra,* 148 Cal.App.3d 576, 195 Cal.Rptr. 902) for the sound reason that the consequences of a negligent act must be limited in order to avoid an intolerable burden on society.... *Borer v. American Airlines, Inc.* (1977) 19 Cal.3d 441, 138 Cal.Rptr. 302, 563 P.2d 858, applied this principle in rejecting a claim for loss of consortium made by the children of a woman killed in an airplane accident. A majority of this court held that foreseeable injury to a legally recognized relationship does not necessarily give rise to a cause of action, and that "social policy must at some point intervene to delimit liability." (*Id.* at p. 446, 138 Cal.Rptr. 302, 563 P.2d 858.) *Baxter v. Superior Court, supra,* 19 Cal.3d 461, 138 Cal.Rptr. 315, 563 P.2d 871, a companion case, held that the parents of an injured child are also not entitled to recover for loss of consortium.

There are several policy reasons to justify rejection of plaintiff's claim that he should be allowed to recover damages for emotional distress.

First, the state has a strong interest in the marriage relationship; to the extent unmarried cohabitants are granted the same rights as married persons, the state's interest in promoting marriage is inhibited. In a recent case holding that the wrongful death statute does not unfairly discriminate against unmarried partners, it was said: "Unmarried cohabitants with enforceable contracts for support clearly differ as a class from spouses and putative spouses. Spouses receive special consideration from the state, for marriage is a civil contract 'of so solemn and binding a nature... that the consent of the parties alone will not constitute marriage...the consent of the state is also required.'... Marriage is accorded this degree of dignity in recognition that '[t]he joining of the man and woman in marriage is at once the most socially productive and individually fulfilling relationship that one can enjoy in the course of a lifetime.'... Consonant therewith, the state is most solicitous of the rights of spouses.... The state affords similar protection to certain putative relationships in recognition of the good faith in which the innocent party undertook to marry.... Unmarried cohabitants receive no similar solicitous statutory protection, nor should they; such would impede the state's substantial interest in promoting and protecting marriage." (*Nieto v. City of Los Angeles* (1982) 138 Cal.App.3d 464, 470–471, 188 Cal.Rptr. 31.)

This policy in favor of formal marriage was expressed in the abolition of common law marriage in 1895..., and it has been reaffirmed in numerous cases since that time....

Our emphasis on the state's interest in promoting the marriage relationship is not based on anachronistic notions of morality. The policy favoring marriage is "rooted in the necessity of providing an institutional basis for defining the fundamental relational rights and responsibilities of persons in organized society." (*Laws v. Griep* (Iowa 1983) 332 N.W.2d 339, 341.) Formally married couples are granted significant rights and bear important responsibilities toward one another which are not shared by those who cohabit without marriage. For example, a detailed set of statutes governs the requirements for the entry into and termination of marriage and the property rights which flow from that relationship

(Civ.Code, §4000 et seq.), and the law imposes various obligations on spouses, such as the duty of support (*id.* §§242, 244). Plaintiff does not suggest a convincing reason why cohabiting unmarried couples, who do not bear such legal obligations toward one another, should be permitted to recover for injuries to their partners to the same extent as those who undertake these responsibilities.

A second basis for our determination is that the allowance of a cause of action in the circumstances of this case would impose a difficult burden on the courts. It would require a court to inquire into the relationship of the partners to determine whether the "emotional attachments of the family relationship" existed between the parties (*Mobaldi, supra,* 55 Cal.App.3d at p. 582, 127 Cal.Rptr. 720), and whether the relationship was "stable and significant" (*Butcher v. Superior Court* (1983) 139 Cal.App.3d 58, 70, 188 Cal.Rptr. 503). *Butcher,* which will be discussed *infra* in connection with the cause of action for loss of consortium, suggested that the stability of a cohabitation relationship could be established by evidence of its duration, whether the parties had a contract, the degree of economic cooperation, the exclusivity of sexual relationships, and whether the couple had children. In *Norman v. Unemployment Ins. Appeals Board, supra,* 34 Cal.3d 1, 8–10, 192 Cal.Rptr. 134, 663 P.2d 904, we commented on the "difficult problems of proof" involved in determining whether a relationship is equivalent to a marriage. Authorities in this state and elsewhere have rejected the *Butcher* test as inviting "mischief and inconsistent results."...

A determination whether a partner in an unmarried cohabitation relationship may recover damages for emotional distress based on such matters as the sexual fidelity of the parties and their emotional and economic ties would require a court to undertake a massive intrusion into the private life of the partners. Further, application of these factors would not provide a sufficiently definite and predictable test to allow for consistent application from case to case.

The final justification for our conclusion is advanced in *Borer, supra,* 19 Cal.3d 441, 138 Cal.Rptr. 302, 563 P.2d 858, i.e., the need to limit the number of persons to whom a negligent defendant owes a duty of care.... This need is especially urgent in relation to damages for negligent infliction of emotional distress resulting from injury to another. "[I]f recovery [for mental distress] is to be permitted, there must be some limitation. It would be an entirely unreasonable burden on all human activity if the defendant who has endangered one man were to be compelled to pay for the lacerated feelings of every other person disturbed by reason of it, including every bystander shocked at an accident, and every distant relative of the person injured, as well as his friends. And obviously the danger of fictitious claims, and the necessity of some guarantee of genuineness, are even greater here than before." (Prosser, Law of Torts (3d ed. 1964) §55, pp. 353–354.)

As we have seen, the cases have generally limited recovery of damages for mental distress to the immediate family of the injured person, but a few have extended their holdings to allow recovery by a bystander who had the "functional and emotional equivalent" of a nuclear family relationship with the injured person. Thus, recovery has been allowed to a foster mother whose relationship with her foster child was similar to that of a parent (*Mobaldi, supra,* 55 Cal.App.3d 573, 127 Cal.Rptr. 720), and a step grandmother who was like a natural grandmother to the injured child (*Leong v. Takasaki, supra,* 520 P.2d 758). And in *Ledger, supra,* 164 Cal.App.3d 625, 210 Cal.Rptr. 814, an unmarried cohabiting partner was allowed to recover such damages.

We decline to follow the rationale of these decisions for to do so would result in the unreasonable extension of the scope of liability of a negligent actor. The need to draw a bright line in this area of the law is essential, as Dean Prosser has observed. The temptation to give legal effect to close emotional ties between unrelated or distantly related persons is often strong, for it cannot be denied that in some cases such relationships offer as much affection, support and solace as is provided by immediate family members, and that the emotional trauma suffered as the result of injury to a person in such a relationship may be as devastating as that suffered by a member of the immediate family. Yet we cannot draw a principled distinction between an unmarried cohabitant who claims to have a de facto marriage relationship with his partner and de facto siblings, parents, grandparents or children. The "problems of multiplication of actions and damages" that would result from such an extension of liability (*Borer, supra,* 19 Cal.3d at p. 448, 138 Cal.Rptr. 302, 563 P.2d 858) would place an intolerable burden on society.

We hold that plaintiff failed to state a cause of action for negligent infliction of emotional distress and that, therefore, the trial court did not err in sustaining the demurrer to the second cause of action. We disapprove the holding of *Ledger, supra,* 164 Cal.App.3d 625, 210 Cal.Rptr. 814, and language in *Mobaldi, supra,* 55 Cal.App.3d 573, 127 Cal.Rptr. 720, insofar as they are inconsistent with our conclusion.

II. Loss of Consortium

We come, then, to plaintiff's claim that he is entitled to recover for loss of consortium even though he and the decedent had never married. *Rodriguez v. Bethlehem Steel Corp.* (1974) 12 Cal.3d 382, 404–405, 115 Cal.Rptr. 765, 525 P.2d 669, held that a married person whose spouse has been injured by the negligence of a third party may recover for loss of consortium; that is, loss of conjugal society, comfort, affection, companionship and sexual relations. Plaintiff asks that we extend the holding of this case to unmarried cohabiting couples with a "stable and significant relationship… parallel to a marital relationship." We decline to do so.

In *Borer* this court cautioned that judicial recognition of a cause of action for loss of consortium "must be narrowly circumscribed." (19 Cal.3d at p. 444, 138 Cal.Rptr. 302, 563 P.2d 858.) We advanced as reasons for this policy the intangible nature of the loss, the difficulty of measuring damages, and the possibility of an unreasonable increase in the number of persons who would be entitled to sue for the loss of a loved one. (See also *Baxter v. Superior Court, supra,* 19 Cal.3d 461, 138 Cal.Rptr. 315, 563 P.2d 871.) Subsequent cases, almost without exception, both in this jurisdiction and in others, have refused to extend such a cause of action to unmarried cohabitants. These cases hold that the right to recover for loss of consortium is founded on the relationship of marriage, and absent such a relationship the right does not exist.

The sole exception in this state is *Butcher v. Superior Court, supra,* 139 Cal.App.3d 58, 188 Cal.Rptr. 503. There, the parties had never married but had lived together for almost 12 years, had 2 children, filed joint income tax returns, and maintained joint bank accounts. The Court of Appeal reasoned that the injury to the plaintiff was foreseeable, the damage was not too indirect, remote or speculative, and the argument for limiting liability made in *Borer, supra,* 19 Cal.3d 441, 138 Cal.Rptr. 302, 563 P.2d 858, in the context of loss of parent-child consortium was not convincing where a de facto spousal relationship was alleged. It concluded that if plaintiff proved at trial that the relationship of the parties was stable and significant and the equivalent of a de facto marriage, she could recover damages for loss of consortium.

Contrary to plaintiff's assertion, the *Butcher* decision has not been followed in California. Two federal district courts have allowed a recovery for loss of consortium even though the couples were not married, but the holdings were based on their expectation that state law would recognize such an action. In both cases, the prediction proved to be unfounded.

In addition to the virtual absence of authority to support plaintiff's position, some of the factors recited above in our discussion of the cause of action for negligent infliction of emotional distress apply equally to plaintiff's claim for loss of consortium. That is, the state's interest in promoting the responsibilities of marriage and the difficulty of assessing the emotional, sexual and financial relationship of cohabiting parties to determine whether their arrangement was the equivalent of a marriage, reinforce our conclusion that the trial court did not err in upholding the demurrer to the third cause of action. We disapprove *Butcher, supra,* 139 Cal.App.3d 58, 188 Cal.Rptr. 503, insofar as it is contrary to our conclusion.

Neither the holding nor the policies underlying our decision in *Marvin v. Marvin, supra,* 18 Cal.3d 660, 134 Cal.Rptr. 815, 557 P.2d 106, support a different conclusion. That case permits unmarried cohabiting couples to enforce express or implied contracts relating to a division of property or support, and holds that a court may employ equitable doctrines such as quantum meruit to compensate a homemaking partner for services rendered. The decision also holds that the Family Law Act (Civ.Code, §4000 et seq.), which includes provisions for the division of marital property, does not apply to unmarried partners. In overruling prior decisions which denied even contract recovery to a partner in a cohabitation relationship on the ground that such an arrangement was immoral, we commented on the increase in the number of cohabiting couples and the change in society's perception of their status. We concluded, "we cannot impose a standard based on alleged moral considerations that have apparently been so widely abandoned by so many." (18 Cal.3d at p. 684, 134 Cal.Rptr. 815, 557 P.2d 106.) It is evident from what we say above that our determination here is not based on a value judgment regarding the morality of unmarried cohabitation relationships.

The judgment is affirmed.

LUCAS, C.J., and PANELLI, ARGUELLES, EAGLESON AND KAUFMAN, JJ., concur.

BROUSSARD, Justice, dissenting.

I dissent.

Bolstered by the self-evident proposition that tortfeasors' liability must be limited, the majority decide that a plaintiff who witnessed the tortious injury of the woman with whom he shared a stable and significant relationship but to whom he was not married, may not state a cause of action for negligent infliction of emotional distress or loss of consortium. They concede that this artificial limitation has no relationship to the nature or foreseeability of the plaintiff's injury, factors usually considered important in defining the perimeters of tort liability. Rather, they posit that the "no marriage — no recovery" rule is justified for policy reasons. One need barely scratch the surface of these purported policies to discover their hollowness. The convenience and certainty of a foolproof bright line is not sufficient to justify denying recovery to an entire class of deserving plaintiffs on the arbitrary ground of marital status.

Negligent Infliction of Emotional Distress

In *Dillon v. Legg* (1968) 68 Cal.2d 728, 69 Cal.Rptr. 72, 441 P.2d 912, we were faced with the same general question posed by this case — the circumstances under which a plaintiff who is injured upon witnessing the tortious injury of another may recover damages against the tortfeasor. We acknowledged the need to limit liability and reiterated the well-accepted maxim that one's duty is limited by the risk which his or her negligent conduct foreseeably entails. (*Id.* at p. 739, 69 Cal.Rptr. 72, 441 P.2d 912.) We further observed that foreseeability depends upon the circumstances presented by each case and "no immutable rule can establish the extent of that obligation for every circumstance of the future." (*Id.* at p. 740, 69 Cal.Rptr. 72, 441 P.2d 912.) Recognizing the need for a principled yet flexible framework for limiting liability, we offered guidelines for determining foreseeability in a given case. These guidelines were based on the plaintiff's physical, temporal and relational proximity to the primary victim at the time of the accident.

It is in the context of defining foreseeability that the relationship between the primary victim and the plaintiff is relevant. *Dillon* observed that a defendant is more likely to foresee the emotional injury of a nearby person who is closely related to the primary victim than he or she is to foresee injury of an unrelated or distantly related bystander. (*Id.* at p. 741, 69 Cal.Rptr. 72, 441 P.2d 912.)

The majority do not conclude that the plaintiff was unrelated or distantly related to his injured lover. Nor do they challenge the general proposition that the sheer number of unmarried cohabitants in our society makes it foreseeable that injury of an adult will result in emotional suffering by his or her intimate partner. Given the widespread reality and acceptance of unmarried cohabitation, a reasonable person would not find the plaintiff's emotional trauma to be "remote and unexpected." This should end the inquiry. The parties' closeness is only pertinent to foreseeability; once foreseeability is established, the nature of their relationship has no logical connection to the plaintiff's legal standing.

Even if there were some relevant purpose other than assessing foreseeability to inquire into the relationship between the plaintiff and the victim, there is no rational reason to limit recovery to married persons. The majority nevertheless dredge up boilerplate policy arguments to justify denying relief to deserving but unmarried plaintiffs.

A. The State's Interest in Marriage

The majority contend that the state's interest in the institution of marriage is inhibited to the extent unmarried persons are granted the same rights as married persons. It is difficult to fathom how granting relief to a person who is already injured, regardless of marital status, will detract from society's interest in marriage. Presumably, a person who would not otherwise choose to marry would not be persuaded to do so in order to assure his or her legal standing in a future personal injury action should that person have the misfortune of witnessing the serious injury of his or her spouse. Moreover, no one proposes any new restrictions on the recovery of married plaintiffs. Marriage would maintain its preferential status since married persons are presumed to be "closely related" for the purposes of *Dillon.* Rather, the proposal is merely to elevate unmarried cohabitants to a neutral status by permitting them to prove on a case-by-case basis that their relationship is equivalent in all relevant respects to a good marriage and equally deserving of legal protection.

We have acknowledged that society benefits from the stability and structure provided by the institution of marriage. (*Marvin v. Marvin* (1976) 18 Cal.3d 660, 684, 134 Cal.Rptr. 815, 557 P.2d 106; *Norman v. Unemployment Ins. Appeals Bd.* (1983) 34 Cal.3d 1, 9, 192 Cal.Rptr. 135, 663 P.2d 904.) The Legislature has expressed the state's policy favoring formal marriage in statutes governing the solemnization of marriage (Civ.Code, §§4100-4309), and in statutes defining the rights and responsibilities of spouses (Civ.Code, §§5100-5138). "The state's policy in favor of marriage, however, does not imply a corresponding policy *against* nonmarital relationships." (*Norman, supra,* 34 Cal.3d at p. 14, 192 Cal.Rptr. 135, 663 P.2d 904 (dis. opn. of Broussard, J.).) Nor does it imply that the values underlying the state's interest in marriage flourish only within the confines of that institution.

Nevertheless, the majority cling to the untenable notion that only married couples can create families which promote society's interests. They treat tort recovery as a benefit stemming from the marital compact as if only those persons who choose to marry have any legitimate expectation that the law recognize the value of their relationships or the depth of their feelings. Not only are these assumptions offensive, but they ignore the reality of our evolving social fabric and the corresponding accommodations made in both statutory and decisional law.

While the marital relationship is accompanied by a well-defined set of legal rights and obligations, the law also protects analogous rights and obligations voluntarily undertaken by unmarried cohabitants. (*Marvin, supra,* 18 Cal.3d 660, 134 Cal.Rptr. 815, 557 P.2d 106.) And the Legislature has granted unmarried cohabitants the equivalent legal rights provided marital couples in the fields of housing, credit and family relations. Depriving unmarried persons of compensation for injuries in tort no more advances the state's interest in marriage than would restrictions on their acquisition of housing or credit. The trend in this state is toward *removing* legal distinctions based on marital status that serve only to burden the unmarried without advancing some corresponding societal interest.

B. BURDEN ON THE COURTS

The majority next express concern that courts would be unduly burdened by a standard which required them to determine whether the plaintiff has met his or her burden of proving that his or her relationship is "stable and significant." In the past, this court — including the author of the majority opinion — has soundly rejected the argument that compensation should be denied to all plaintiffs because of the difficulty of determining which plaintiffs are deserving and how much they deserve. (*Rodriguez v. Bethlehem Steel* (1974) 12 Cal.3d 382, 401–404, 115 Cal.Rptr. 765, 525 P.2d 669; *Dillon, supra,* 68 Cal.2d at pp. 742–743, 69 Cal.Rptr. 72, 441 P.2d 912.)

The capability of courts and juries to make sensitive factual determinations is regularly demonstrated in cases, like this one, in which loss of consortium is alleged. There the trier of fact must calculate the amount of damages sustained by the plaintiff due to the intangible loss of relational interests that include love, companionship, emotional support, society and sexual relations.... This assessment often requires consideration of evidence concerning the quality and nature of the plaintiff's relationship with his or her partner before and after the partner's injury.... Whether the purpose is to determine legal standing or to assess the measure of damages, the same inquiry concerning the plaintiff's relationship is made and the same kind of evidence properly considered.

...

C. Limitation of Liability

The majority's final justification for denying recovery is that liability must stop somewhere. As a general proposition, I agree that a line must be drawn. However, I do not share in the majority's enthusiasm for crude, bright lines. In my view, recovery should not be cut off on arbitrary, definitional grounds but on functional grounds that correspond with real loss. "As the commentators have suggested, the problem should be solved by the application of the principles of tort, not by the creation of exceptions to them. Legal history shows that artificial islands of exceptions, created from the fear that the legal process will not work, usually do not withstand the waves of reality and, in time, descend into oblivion." (*Dillon, supra,* 68 Cal.2d at p. 747, 69 Cal.Rptr. 72, 441 P.2d 912.)

Only tortfeasors lucky enough to have injured a de facto rather than a de jure spouse benefit from a bright line based on marriage. An approach that grants recovery to those plaintiffs foreseeably and genuinely injured by a negligent defendant's acts both advances the goals of tort compensation and sufficiently limits liability. To that end, a standard based on the significance and stability of the plaintiff's relationship is workable and fair.

The majority's prediction of an ever-expanding class of "closely related" plaintiffs is just as empty now as it was in *Dillon, supra,* 68 Cal.2d at pp. 743–748, 69 Cal.Rptr. 72, 441 P.2d 912 and *Rodriguez, supra,* 12 Cal.3d at pages 402–403, 115 Cal.Rptr. 765, 525 P.2d 669. "The teaching of those cases is that the rights of a proposed new class of tort plaintiffs should be forthrightly judged on their own merits, rather than by indulging in gloomy speculation on where it will all end." (*Borer, supra,* 19 Cal.3d at p. 460, 138 Cal.Rptr. 302, 563 P.2d 858, (dis. opn. of Mosk, J.).)

Loss of Consortium

In addition to mental distress from witnessing the death of his loved one, plaintiff allegedly suffered the distinct injury of lost consortium. For the same policy reasons utilized to deny recovery under the first theory, the majority denies recovery under the second theory as well. In addition to the policies of certainty, judicial convenience and the state's interest in promoting marriage, the majority fall back on the well-worn argument that extending liability to unmarried cohabitants is not supported by precedent. (But see *Butcher, supra,* 139 Cal.App.3d 58, 188 Cal.Rptr. 503; *Bulloch, supra,* 487 F.Supp. 1078.)

For many years, this court and others relied on the lack of precedent to refuse to extend the cause of action for lost consortium to women.... Relying on the Legislature to update the law, the court clung to the common law rule which denied legal standing to women despite the crumbled foundation upon which the rule rested. The old rule defined consortium only in terms of the husband's property interest in his wife as chattel. Because the husband owed no services to his wife and the wife had no independent legal identity, she suffered no legally cognizable loss when her husband was injured....

When the Legislature failed to correct this artifact of medieval mentality, we eliminated the inequality by entirely abolishing the common law cause of action for lost consortium. (*West v. City of San Diego* (1960) 54 Cal.2d 469, 475–478, 6 Cal.Rptr. 289, 353 P.2d 929.) Finally, in *Rodriguez v. Bethlehem Steel, supra,* 12 Cal.3d 382, 115 Cal.Rptr. 765, 525 P.2d 669, we resurrected the common law action for lost consortium and made the remedy available to both men and women. Recognizing the inherent capacity of the common law to adjust to evolving social realities, we announced the obvious — that a wife's loss of consortium was in every respect equivalent to that of a husband, and equally worthy of compensation. (*Ibid.*)

The majority, however, ignore the lesson of *Rodriguez* and retreat to the unfortunate pattern of refusing to acknowledge the obsolescence of assumptions upon which existing law is based. As noted, the notion that a valid legal marriage is a prerequisite to a cause of action for lost consortium has its origin in a proprietary entitlement theory that viewed marriage as vesting in the husband a property interest in his wife's services.... But the law no longer regards women as property nor consortium as limited to the services owed by women to their husbands. The modern view regards consortium as a package of relational interests, including love, companionship, emotional support, and sexual relations. The marital status of the plaintiff has no more bearing on his or her standing to claim injury to these interests than does age or socioeconomic status. Accordingly, there is no principled reason to perpetuate the fiction that only marital partners suffer compensable loss of consortium.

By failing to harmonize the law with present societal conditions, the majority abdicate the court's responsibility for the upkeep of the common law. As we observed in *Rodriguez, supra,* 12 Cal.3d 382, 394, 115 Cal.Rptr. 765, 525 P.2d 669, "'The inherent capacity of the common law for growth and change is its most significant feature. Its development has been determined by the social needs of the community which it serves. It is constantly expanding and developing in keeping with advancing civilization and the new conditions and progress of society, and adapting itself to the gradual change of trade, commerce, arts, inventions, and the needs of the country.'... But that vitality can flourish only so long as the courts remain alert to their obligation and opportunity to change the common law when reason and equity demand it."

Conclusion

For the reasons stated, I would reverse the decision of the trial court and direct it to give plaintiff an opportunity to prove his causes of action for negligent infliction of emotional distress and loss of consortium.

MEDLEY v. STRONG

Appellate Court of Illinois

200 Ill. App. 3d 488, 558 N.E.2d 244 (1990)

Justice LINN delivered the opinion of the court:

Plaintiff, Carolyn Medley, seeks damages against defendant doctors and hospitals for their alleged negligence in treating her lover and companion of ten years, Oscar Medley. In the course of his medical treatment for a condition of the penis, complications set in that resulted in its amputation. She seeks to recover damages for loss of consortium.

The trial court granted defendants' motion to dismiss her claim on the grounds that she lacked legal capacity, under section 2-219(a)(2) of the Code of Civil Procedure, to maintain the action. (Ill.Rev.Stat.1987, ch. 110, par. 2- 619(a)(2).) On appeal, she argues that under general, common law principles of tort liability, and in light of the increasing numbers of persons who cohabit without marriage, she should be allowed to maintain her action despite her lack of marital status.

We affirm the trial court.

Background

Oscar and Carolyn Medley had been living together and representing themselves as married for ten years before Oscar's injuries. In August 1986 Oscar sought treatment for priapism, which is defined as an abnormal, painful, and continued erection of the penis due to disease. He was referred to defendant Larry Strong, M.D., an employee of defendant Urology Associates. He was admitted to defendant Hyde Park Community Hospital, where he stayed until September 5, 1986. According to the complaint, Dr. Strong failed to perform surgery to reduce the priapism and instead attempted manual compression of the penis and then attempted further compression by using a blood pressure cuff.

During his stay in the hospital, Oscar Medley developed non-viable tissue and ulceration of the penis. According to the complaint, Dr. Strong did not intervene and treat the condition.

Defendant Evelyn Currie, M.D., a hematologist, consulted on the case. She allegedly failed to appreciate the significance of laboratory data and failed to give necessary information to nursing and medical personnel who were treating Medley. Plaintiff alleges that she recommended or ordered medical approaches that were based on a "misassessment" of Medley's medical, clinical, and laboratory history.

Plaintiff further alleges that the nurses responsible for Medley's treatment were negligent in using a blood pressure cuff on his penis, which contributed to and aggravated the injury. In addition, the nurses allegedly failed to notify the treating physicians of the developing infection in Medley's penis. Although Medley's white blood cell count had become elevated, he was discharged from the hospital without further laboratory testing and without proper medication and instruction for follow-up care.

Plaintiff further alleges that on September 20, 1986, Medley was admitted to defendant Mercy Hospital and Medical Center, under the care of Dr. Paul Carryon, who was employed by defendant William's Clinic. Medley suffered from respiratory distress and "necrotic penis." He was discharged on September 30, 1986. According to the complaint, during his stay at this hospital he was not given appropriate treatment and testing, and his doctor failed to offer any treatment when Medley developed a second opening on the underside of the penis, on September 26.

Dr. Carryon called upon Dr. Currie, the same hematologist who previously had examined Medley. According to plaintiff, she again failed to appreciate the significance of the data and recommended inappropriate treatment.

The complaint alleges negligence on the part of all named defendants, as a result of which Medley underwent a penectomy, or surgical amputation, and additional surgeries and treatments. His claimed damages and losses are not in issue in this appeal, however; it is Carolyn Medley's claim for loss of consortium that must be considered.

Opinion

Carolyn Medley's claim is for an injury that is recognized in Illinois and other States as arising out of the marriage relation. In fact, the case on which she relies, *Dini v. Naiditch* (1960), 20 Ill.2d 406, 170 N.E.2d 881, recognized that "the husband and wife have equal rights in the *marriage relation* which should receive equal protection of the law." (20 Ill.2d at 424, 170 N.E.2d at 889–90 (emphasis added).) The court stated that "[c]onsortium...includes, in addition to material services, elements of companionship, felicity and sexual intercourse, all welded into a conceptualistic unity." 20 Ill.2d 406, 427, 170 N.E.2d 881, 891.

We agree with Carolyn that but for the lack of a marriage license, she would state a viable cause of action and could recover whatever amount of damages she could prove were proximately caused by defendants' negligence.

We do not agree, however, that we can expand common law tort principles to allow her a cause of action that is defined in marital terms. Since 1905, Illinois has not recognized common law marriage (see Ill.Rev.Stat.1987, ch. 40, par. 214) and the Illinois Supreme Court has expressly reaffirmed the State's strong, continuing interest in the institution of marriage. (*Hewitt v. Hewitt* (1979), 77 Ill.2d 49, 31 Ill.Dec. 827, 394 N.E.2d 1204.) The statutory rights of married people include interests in marital property, support obligations, inheritance rights, and the entitlement to sue for wrongful death of the spouse. Unmarried cohabitants do not have these protections, either by statute or by common law, since de facto marriages are not legally recognized.

In *Hewitt v. Hewitt,* the Illinois Supreme Court held, in the clearest possible terms, that unmarried cohabitants (even those in long-term, stable relationships), are entitled to no legal protection for claims that depend on the cohabitation itself. The court held that the Illinois Marriage and Dissolution of Marriage Act (Ill.Rev.Stat.1987, ch. 40, pars. 101 *et seq.*) embodied the legislative preference for marriage by refusing to accord legal status to claims for marriage-like relationships that would, in effect, reactivate common law marriages.

The result in *Hewitt* was particularly harsh in light of its facts. Mrs. Hewitt had devoted 15 years of her life to establishing a home and raising the parties' three children. She had borrowed money from her parents and otherwise facilitated her "husband's" ability to develop a lucrative practice of pedodontia. Even the parents of the parties believed that the two were married. Since they had not complied with the marriage laws of the State, however, the court held that Mrs. Hewitt could not claim any property rights based on the cohabitational relationship itself. Nor could she enforce an express oral contract. In a discussion of contract principles, moreover, the court noted that agreements based on sexual services are void for want of legal consideration and that Illinois courts would not enforce what in effect are private contracts for marriage-like relationships.

Carolyn attempts to distinguish *Hewitt* as involving claims between the cohabiting parties only, as distinguished from tort claims against third parties. She states that traditional principles of tort liability are satisfied because she is a foreseeable plaintiff to whom the defendants owed a duty of care.

We believe that this approach ignores the legislature's pre-emptive regulation of rights and obligations integral to marriage and marriage-like relationships. We also find unpersuasive Carolyn's attempt to narrow the consortium claim — and thus the issue under review — to the point where we look only at the sexual injury as a distinct injury to Carolyn's relationship with Oscar and pretend that the public policy concerns regarding the integrity of marriage do not apply. Her argument that the times have changed and the laws have not kept up with the changes may be well-taken, but they are not ultimately relevant in this case. The object here is not to re-examine Illinois public policy on marriage as opposed to other relationships or to slay the draconic notion of women as chattel. That already has been done, in *Hewitt* and in *Dini v. Naiditch,* respectively.

Certainly, statistical data may reveal that many people in the United States do, have, or will cohabit without marriage. In Illinois, tort law gives them whatever protections and rights that are commonly enjoyed by all other people, except for torts that are specifically designed to compensate for injuries to the relationship between spouses.

Moreover, loss of consortium damages belong to the restricted group of claims that arise from injuries to other persons, rather than from direct, physical injury to the claimants themselves. We do not mean to denigrate Carolyn's own, separate suffering or to imply that her injury is insignificant. Claims involving loss of consortium or loss of society should not be indiscriminately expanded, however; otherwise all who claim a sexual relationship, friendship, or some other close relationship with the injured or deceased party could recover damages for their losses....

The only apparent limit on Carolyn's theory is that the claimant have regular sexual relations with the person whose sexual abilities are impaired through the negligence of a third party. If we recognize such claims, outside the context of marriage, we would be creating a situation in which multiple partners of an injured person may sue. We hesitate to create new classes of claimants, under the rubric of "foreseeable plaintiffs," as Carolyn suggests. Whether all potential plaintiffs in such cases would be "foreseeable" or not is open to question; legally married spouses, in contrast, are foreseeable plaintiffs by definition.

Even if we were to hold that Carolyn is a foreseeable plaintiff under the facts of this case we question the soundness of permitting an action to be based on a tort duty that has been found only in the context of interspousal relationships. The more a relationship resembles a long-term, stable marriage, the more it looks like common law marriage, which is legally invalid in Illinois. The more a relationship is viewed as purely sexual, the more plaintiffs may emerge from the bedrooms into the courts. We doubt, in fact, that common law principles support any relief based on loss of sexual services, given historical prohibitions against these relations outside of marriage. Current codifications of such laws even criminalize some types of sexual activities. Therefore, whether we focus narrowly on sexual injury or more broadly on loss of companionship and material services, we find no support for creating a tort claim based on lost sexual services.

...

Carolyn's argument that many people live together or have relations outside of marriage does not, therefore, persuade us that this fact alone justifies the recognition of such a tort. If we were to adopt the "evolving social reality" theory advanced here we would be usurping the legislative function to an unprecedented degree. Judicial modification of judge-made law is appropriate where the purpose of the modification is to correct mistakes or entomb anachronisms. For example, in *Skinner v. Reed-Prentice Division Package Machinery Co.* (1977), 70 Ill.2d 1, 13, 15 Ill.Dec. 829, 374 N.E.2d 437, the Illinois Supreme Court recognized that America's historic, blanket ban on contribution among tortfeasors was based on an erroneous expansion of the original English rule that no intentional tortfeasor should be allowed to recover against others for the consequences of his deliberate acts. (See also *Gerill v. Jack L. Hargrove Builders, Inc.* (1989), 128 Ill.2d 179, 203, 131 Ill.Dec. 155, 538 N.E.2d 530.) Another example is *Dini v. Naiditch* (1960), 20 Ill.2d 406, 170 N.E.2d 881. There the supreme court condemned the historical view of women as chattel, which let their male "owners" recover compensation for injuries to their wives, as for damaged goods. The court simply raised women's rights for loss of consortium to the level of the pre-existing rights of men.

...[T]he Illinois appellate court has already barred a claim for loss of consortium when the cohabitants were unmarried at the time of the alleged injuries, but intended to marry and did in fact marry at a later time. (*Sostock v. Reiss* (1980), 92 Ill.App.3d 200, 47 Ill.Dec. 781, 415 N.E.2d 1094.) In *Sostock,* the husband sought damages for loss of consortium dating from the time of the marriage. The court rejected his claim because he was not the lawful spouse at the time the accident occurred.

We find no basis to depart from the reasoning of Sostock and the other pertinent authorities and conclude that the trial court properly dismissed those counts of the complaint that consisted of Carolyn Medley's loss of consortium claims. Accordingly, we affirm.

Affirmed.

McMORROW, P.J., and JOHNSON, J., concur.

SAN FRANCISCO RECOGNITION OF DOMESTIC PARTNERS LAW
Section 121

SEC. 121.1 PURPOSE. The purpose of this ordinance is to create a way to recognize intimate committed relationships, including those of lesbians and gay men who otherwise are denied the right to identify partners with whom they share their lives. All costs of registration must be covered by fees to be established by ordinance. (Add by Proposition K, 11/6/90)

SEC. 121.2 DEFINITIONS.

(a) Domestic Partnership. Domestic Partners are two adults who have chose to share one another's lives in an intimate and committed relationship of mutual caring, who live together, and who have agreed to be jointly responsible for basic living expenses incurred during the Domestic Partnership. They must sign a Declaration of Domestic Partnership, and establish the partnership under Section 121.3 of this chapter.

(b) "Live Together." "Live together" means that two people share the same living quarters. It is not necessary that the legal right to possess the quarters be in both of their names. Two people may live together even if one or both have additional living quarters. Domestic Partners do not cease to live together if one leaves the shared quarters but intends to return.

(c) "Basic Living Expenses." "Basic living expenses" means the cost of basic food and shelter. It also includes the expenses which are paid at least in part by a program or benefit for which the partner qualified because of the domestic partnership. The individuals need not contribute equally or jointly to the cost of these expenses as long as they agree that both are responsible for the costs.

(d) "Declaration of Domestic Partnership." A "Declaration of Domestic Partnership" is a form provided by the County Clerk. By signing it, two people agree to be jointly responsible for basic living expenses which they incur during the domestic partnership and that this agreement can be enforced by anyone to whom those expenses are owed. They also state under penalty of perjury that they met the definition of domestic partnership when they signed the statement that neither is married, that they are not related to each other in a way which would bar marriage in California, and that neither had a different domestic partner less than six months before they signed. This last condition does not apply if the previous domestic partner died. The form will also require each partner to provide a mailing address. (Added by Proposition K, 11/6/90)

SEC. 121.3. ESTABLISHING A DOMESTIC PARTNERSHIP.

(a) Methods.

Two persons may establish a Domestic Partnership by either:

(1) Presenting a signed Declaration of Domestic Partnership to the County Clerk, who will file it and give the partners a certificate showing that the Declaration was filed; or

(2) Having a Declaration of Domestic Partnership notarized and giving a copy to the persons who witnessed the signing (who may or may not be the notary).

(b) Time Limitation. A person cannot become a member of a Domestic Partnership until at least six months after any other Domestic Partnership of which he or she was a member ended. This does not apply if the earlier domestic partnership ended because one of the members died.

(c) Residence Limitation. The County Clerk will only file Declaration of Partnership if:

(1) The partners have a residence in San Francisco; or

(2) At least one of the partners works in San Francisco. (Added by Proposition K, 11/6/90)

SEC. 121.4 ENDING DOMESTIC PARTNERSHIPS.

(a) When the Partnership Ends. A Domestic Partnership ends when:

(1) One partner sends the other a written notice that he or she has ended the partnership; or

(2) One of the partners dies; or

(3) One of the partners marries or the partners no longer live together.

(b) Notice the Partnership Has Ended.

(1) To Domestic Partners. When a Domestic Partnership ends, at least one of the partners must sign a notice saying that the partnership has ended. The notice must be dated and signed under penalty of perjury. If the Declaration of Domestic Partnership was filed with the County Clerk, the notice must be filed with the clerk; otherwise, the notice must be notarized. The partner who signs the notice must send a copy to the other partner.

(2) To Third Parties. When a Domestic Partnership ends, a Domestic Partner who has given a copy of a Declaration of Domestic Partnership to any third party, (or, if that partner has died, the sur-

viving member of a domestic partnership) must give that third party a notice signed under penalty of perjury stating the partnership has ended. The notice must be sent within 60 days of the end of the domestic partnership.

(3) Failure to Give Notice. Failure to give either of the notices required by this subsection will neither prevent nor delay termination of the Domestic Partnership. Anyone who suffers any loss as a result of failure to send either of these notices may sue for actual losses. (Added by Proposition K 11/6/90)

SEC 121.5 COUNTY CLERK'S RECORDS.

(a) Amendments to Declarations. A Partner may amend a Declaration of Domestic Partnership filed with County Clerk at any time to show a change in his or her mailing address.

(b) New Declarations of Domestic Partnership. No person who has filed a Declaration of Domestic Partnership with the County Clerk may file another Declaration of Domestic Partnership until six months after a notice the partnership has ended has been filed. However, if the Domestic Partnership ended because one of the partners died, a new Declaration may be filed anytime after the notice the partnership ended is filed.

(c) Maintenance of County Clerk's Records. The County Clerk will keep a record of all Declarations of Domestic Partnership, amendments to Declarations of Domestic Partnership and all notices that a partnership has ended. The records will be maintained so that amendments and notices a partnership has ended, are filed with the Declaration of Domestic Partnership which they apply.

(d) Filing Fees. The Board of Supervisors will set the filing fee for Declarations of Domestic Partnership and Amendments. No fee will be charged for notice that a partnership has ended. The fees charged must cover the city's cost of administering this ordinance. (Added by Proposition-K, 11/6/90)

SEC. 121.6 LEGAL EFFECT OF DECLARATION OF DOMESTIC PARTNERSHIP.

(a) Obligations. The obligations of domestic partners to each other are those described by the definition.

(b) During the Rights and Duties. If a domestic partnership ends, the partners incur no further obligations to each other. (Added by Proposition K, 11/6/90)

SEC. 121.7 CODIFICATION. Upon adoption, the Clerk of the Board shall codify this amendment into the San Francisco Administrative Code. (Added by Proposition K, 11/6/90)

COMMENTS

Most people tend to view questions regarding the treatment of gay men and lesbians to involve conflicts between strict morality or moralistic rejection of so-called "homosexual lifestyles" on one hand, and on the other hand, tolerance and basic civil rights of individuals who happen to have a non-majority sexual orientation. Opponents of "gay rights" may appeal to various religious teachings, to "traditional values" or to decency. They sometimes characterize homosexuality as an affront or challenge to heterosexuality and often emphasize the *choice* gay people make regarding their sexual practices.

Supporters of gay rights are more likely to focus on studies suggesting a very early, involuntary setting of one's sexual orientation and to deemphasize the differences between people who happen to have different sexual orientations. Same-sex couples have many of the same goals as heterosexual couples, the same affection, commitments and problems. The major differences, according to this view, are that heterosexual couples receive a variety of economic and social benefits, especially if they get married, while same-sex couples suffer economic and social discrimination and are not allowed to marry one another.

Perhaps the issue is nowhere more clearly framed than in the question whether same-sex couples should be allowed to marry or to raise children. To opponents, the proposal is sometimes seen as preposterous. According to this view, it would destroy the meaning of marriage and be an unfair burden on the children whose lives might be ruined forever. To supporters, the denial to gay men and lesbians of the right to marry a person of the same sex is an unjustified discrimination as well as bad social policy. Heterosexual couples produce children more easily — and indeed often produce children unintentionally, some of whom remain unwanted — but there is no reliable evidence that they raise children any better. Some suggest a long history of same-sex couples, especially women, raising children in shared households, and no one thinking twice about their sexual practices. Many courts now overlook a parent's sexual orientation in awarding custody of children between mother and father, and according to this view, courts should take the next step. Child custody is discussed further in Chapter 5.

We have already noted the decreasing importance of formal marriage with respect to the legal treatment of heterosexual couples. As more opposite-sex couples choose not to get married, increasing numbers of same-sex couples are seeking legal recognition of their relationships. The efforts of same-sex couples to establish their right to choose to get married are discussed in Chapter 4.

However, an increasing number of people find this framing of the issues to be inadequate. Feminists often associate "homophobia" with sexism in general and an insistence on rigid gender roles. An attack on male dominance may entail an attack on some macho conceptions of heterosexuality. The "traditional values" that conservatives sometimes contrast with the "gay lifestyle" often include the devaluation of women or at least a valuation restricted to women's limited traditional roles as supportive wife and self-sacrificing mother. A number of politically-active gay men and lesbians have questioned whether they should be trying to be included in marriage or should rather seek to abolish marriage and replace it with other forms of shared relationships.

REFERENCE

Marc A. Fajer, *Can Two Real Men Eat Quiche Together? Storytelling, Gender-Role Stereotypes, and Legal Protection for Lesbians and Gay Men*, 46 U. OF MIAMI L. REV. 511 (1992).

Chapter 3

Toward Equality in Marriage

FOR CENTURIES CHRISTIANITY, together with many other religions, taught that women were inferior to men and that God wished for husbands to dominate their wives. Minority views within the major religions have long disputed these assertions and have interpreted much of the Bible to support their more egalitarian views. As the United States formed its legal system, it was greatly influenced by the English law of the time, under which wives were radically subordinated to husbands, a subordination only slightly softened by the doctrines devised by courts of equity.

A major trend over the past two centuries has been toward greater equality in marriage. This greater equality has generally taken the form of allowing the wife more autonomy within the marriage. While women have benefitted from this increased autonomy, some observers believe that the solidarity of "the family" has suffered. It is striking how few reforms have aimed directly at allowing wives greater say in family decisions — democratizing the family — rather than just at allowing wives to opt out of decisions made by the husband, such as the "family" domicile. Instead of just allowing a wife to keep her "own" name, for example, perhaps the couple should choose a new family name. Moreover, after two centuries of laws requiring or encouraging the family to adopt the husband's name, perhaps it would not be inappropriate to have at least one century of laws encouraging the family to adopt the wife's name.

Most commentators support the trend toward increasing equality within marriage. Less consensus exists, however, about what greater equality in marriage really means and about who should bear the brunt of the disruption during the period of readjustment. For example, some commentators justify paying little or no alimony to "traditional" wives at divorce by the assertion that times are changing and wives should no longer suppress their own economic viability for the sake of their husband and they should no longer expect to be able to rely on their husband for a life-time of economic support. Others suggest that greater equality can be achieved without making older vulnerable women suffer.

Interestingly, most assume that the former inequality was functional and that the present requires different rules from the past because of societal changes. They also seem to think that the inequality was basically caused by societal inequality or at least that the laws that discriminated against women merely reflected this preexisting inequality.

As the materials in this chapter will show, however, the state has played a major role in establishing and maintaining inequality between husbands and wives in the past and continues to do so today, if in perhaps more subtle ways. The changes that have come about do have something to do with broad societal changes — the automation of housekeeping chores and changes in the organization of the economy resulting in more women working at paid employment outside the home. They have as much or more, however, to do with political struggles of women and supportive men.

A: The Common Law Background: Reducing State-Imposed Inequality and Dependency

Property Ownership and Control

ROBINSON v. TROUSDALE COUNTY
Supreme Court of Tennessee
516 S.W.2d 626 (Tenn. 1974)

HENRY, Justice.

This is an inverse condemnation suit involving the nature of the estate of tenancy by the entireties under Tennessee law and the common law disability of coverture.

Petitioners, husband and wife, sued Trousdale County for damages for the taking of certain real estate owned by them as tenants by the entirety, for the purpose of widening a public road adjacent to their property, and for incidental damages.

The answer of Trousdale County, among other defenses, asserts that petitioners are barred from seeking compensation and damages by virtue of a deed, executed by the husband alone, conveying the property involved to Trousdale County, in fee simple.

...

The trial judge held that the husband was estopped to claim any damage because of the deed; that there were no incidental damages, and allowed the wife Five Hundred Thirty Dollars ($530.00) as actual damages for the value of the land taken.

All parties prayed and perfected appeals to the Court of Appeals.

That court affirmed the judgment of the trial court in all respects except as to the ownership and disposition of the money ($530.00), representing the value of the land. The court directed (1) that this sum be held by the Clerk of the trial court and invested by him during the joint married lives of petitioners; (2) that should the husband die first, the entire recovery would be paid to the wife; (3) that should the wife die first the entire recovery would be paid to Trousdale County, and (4) in the event of a divorce, it would be distributed equally between the wife and Trousdale County.

All parties have petitioned this Court for certiorari. We granted the petition of the wife with argument limited to the disposition of the recovery.

...

Our investigation leads us to the conclusion that the decisional law of Tennessee, not only is nebulous and confusing, but is in substantial conflict and out of harmony with justice, reason and logic.

We, therefore, propose to clarify the law by a clear, comprehensive and definitive opinion.

...

In *In re Guardianship, Plowman*, 217 Tenn. 487, 398 S.W.2d 721 (1966), the Court held that a husband was not obligated to account to the wife for rents and profits collected by him from real property owned as tenants by the entirety. ...The Court...makes this unusual observation:

> To permit the wife to demand an accounting of rents collected by her husband on property owned by them as tenants by the entirety by suit at law would disrupt and injure the marriage relationship and would be of little, if any, benefit to the wife. It would, no doubt, bring an end to the relationship. 217 Tenn. at 493, 398 S.W.2d at 723.

We are constrained to doubt that any such dire and disastrous consequences would ensue if the wife were accorded equal legal status as opposed to being made legally subservient and subordinate to her husband. This is but a judicially decreed recognition of the traditional pattern of married women being forced into a subservient and supportive role that is inherently unequal, patently unfair, and at variance with the concept of equality mandated by contemporary standards of justice.

...

We do not believe that the common law disability of coverture has any sanction in our jurisprudence or any relevance in our society. At best it is outmoded; at worst oppressive and degrading.

...

To put the present law in proper perspective, let us assume that a husband and wife, having no other assets whatsoever, simultaneously inherit the sum of $250,000.00 each and that they pool their inheritances and purchase an apartment house, taking title as tenants by the entirety. The rental income starts coming in. The husband, the dominant tenant, appropriates all rental income and expends it in accordance with his desires, without the consent of the wife and over her protest. Short of resorting to the divorce courts, she has no legal remedy. One does not have to be a "Women's Libber" or even have an educated conscience, or anything beyond an elemental sense of justice to grasp the patent unfairness of such a situation. It is not only archaic; it is gross and unconscionable.

...

The fact that Tennessee clings to the common law concept of coverture casts a shadow of doubt upon the intellectual consistency of our approach to the whole area of equality of the sexes, and points up the need for bringing this phase of our law into harmony with modern thinking.

We hold that the Married Women's Act (Ch. 26, Acts of 1913), fully and effectively eradicated the common law disability of coverture and that the amendatory act, Chapter 126, Acts of 1919, did not have the legal effect of restoring it.

We abolish the last vestige of the common law disability of coverture in Tennessee.

We do not abolish the estate of tenancy by the entirety, but we strip it of the artificial and archaic rules and restrictions imposed at the common law, and we fully deterge it of its deprivations and detriments to women and fully emancipate them from its burdens.

From this date forward each tenant shall have a joint right to the use, control, incomes, rents, profits, usufructs and possession of property so held, and neither may sell, encumber, alienate or dispose of any portion thereof except his or her right of survivorship, without the consent of the other. Any unilateral attempt will be wholly and utterly void at the instance of the aggrieved tenant and any prospective purchaser, transferee, lessee, mortgagee and the like will act at his peril.

Lastly we reach the matter of the ownership of the fund now in the Registry of the Court. The husband conveyed his right of expectancy. The County has acquired the needed land for the public road. The result is that all parties in this case have received their just desserts except Mrs. Robinson. She gets the money.

It results that the judgment of the Court of Appeals...is modified and affirmed, and this cause is remanded to the Circuit Court of Trousdale County for the distribution of the fund.

The costs of this cause are taxed against Trousdale County.

FONES, C.J., and COOPER, BROCK and HARBISON, JJ., concur.

HENRY, Justice (concurring).

I wrote the main opinion to reflect the unanimous views of the Court.

While I am in full accord with the conclusions we have reached on the common law disability of coverture and share with my colleagues a sense of pride in this progressive action, I am convinced that we should have based our decision to a substantial extent, on constitutional grounds.

...

I would hold that the application of the common law disability of coverture is violative of Section 1 of the Fourteenth Amendment to the Constitution of the United States in that married women are "citizens" of the United States and the application of this doctrine deprives them of their property without due process of law, and denies them the equal protection of the law. Moreover, said doctrine is an invidious and "suspect" classification based upon sex and marital status, and is predicated on no rational basis, and abridges their right to acquire, enjoy, lease, hold, own and benefit from their own property.

I would hold, for the same reasons, that the application of this doctrine is violative of Article 1, Section 8, of the Constitution of the State of Tennessee, in that it operates to deprive married women of their property and abridges their rights and privileges as citizens of the State, contrary to the law of the land.

D'ERCOLE v. D'ERCOLE

United States District Court

407 F. Supp. 1377 (D. Mass. 1976)

TAURO, District Judge.

This is an action brought under 42 U.S.C. §1983 in which the plaintiff seeks declaratory and injunctive relief for deprivation of rights allegedly secured to her under the Fifth and Fourteenth Amendments. Jurisdiction is claimed under 28 U.S.C. §1343(3) and (4).

Basically, plaintiff's complaint states that the common law concept of tenancy by the entirety, as formulated and enforced by case law, and as recognized by the statutes of the Commonwealth of Massachusetts, deprives her of due process and equal protection of the law in that it gives the defendant, her husband, the right of possession and control during his lifetime of their home, owned by them as tenants by the entirety. Defendant's position is that plaintiff's complaint fails to state a claim upon which relief can be granted. Fed.R.Civ.P. 12(b)(6).

I

The plaintiff and the defendant have been married for some thirty five years. In November of 1962 they bought a residence at 61 Stone Road, Waltham, Massachusetts, for $20,000. The percentage of down payment provided by each party for the home is disputed. Plaintiff used her own funds to purchase some $3500 in new furnishings for the home at the time of purchase. She has been steadily employed during the entire thirty five years of her marriage and, by agreement with the defendant, assumed financial responsibility for all household expenses, except for mortgage payments and real property taxes....

In 1971, the plaintiff and defendant determined they could no longer live together. When the defendant refused to leave the marital home, plaintiff departed, moving to a relative's home where she still resides.

Proceedings for legal separation and for divorce are now pending in the Middlesex County Probate Court. The defendant husband is seeking a divorce. The plaintiff wife is seeking a separation and is vehemently opposing the divorce on factual issues and because of religious beliefs.

Defendant has refused to share the marital home with plaintiff by allowing her sole occupancy for part of the year, by selling the house and dividing the proceeds, by paying plaintiff her share in the equity of the house, or by renting the premises and dividing the proceeds. In support of his position, defendant points out that the property in question is held under a tenancy by the entirety, which gives both him and the plaintiff an indefeasible right of survivorship, but gives him exclusive right to possession and control in his lifetime. He has stated that he will grant plaintiff one-half the equity in the house if she will grant him an uncontested divorce.[4]

II

When two or more persons wish to hold property together in Massachusetts they may select one of three common law forms of ownership: the tenancy in common, joint tenancy or tenancy by the entirety.

The tenancy in common is the holding of land "by several and distinct titles."

> Each tenant owns an undivided fraction, being entitled to an interest in every inch of the property. With respect to third persons the entire tenancy constitutes a single entity. There is no right of survivorship as between tenants in common. Upon the death of a tenant in common his undivided interest in the property is transferred to his heirs or devisees, subject to liens, claims and dower.

28 Mass.Practice (Park) §125, at 119–120. (Footnotes omitted.) There is a presumption in favor of the tenancy in common over the joint tenancy as a matter of construction in Massachusetts. Each tenant in common has a right to free usage of the whole parcel and may freely convey out his share of the property to a third

4. Divorce would, in any case, terminate the tenancy by the entirety and thus allow the plaintiff to seek partition of the property.... Separation, even when ratified by a formal decree, does not end the tenancy by the entirety.

party, who then becomes a tenant in common in relation to the remaining cotenants.

The joint tenancy is "a single estate in property owned by two or more persons under one instrument or act."

> A joint tenancy is similar to a tenancy in common in that all tenants have an equal right to possession, but the joint tenants hold the property by one joint title and in one right, whereas the tenants in common hold by several titles or by one title and several rights.
>
> The joint tenancy differs also in that there is a right of survivorship in a joint tenancy but not in a tenancy in common. On the death of one of the joint tenants his interest does not descend to his heirs or pass under his will as in a tenancy in common.... The widow of the deceased tenant has no dower rights and his creditors have no claim against the enlarged interest of the surviving tenants.

28 Mass.Practice (Park) §126, at 121–122. (Footnotes omitted). A joint tenant may convey out his share in the property via a legal partition. See Mass.Gen.L. ch. 241, §1.

The tenancy by the entirety is designed particularly for married couples and may be employed only by them. Until 1973 unless there was clear language to the contrary a conveyance to a married couple was presumed to create a tenancy by the entirety. This form of property ownership differs from the joint tenancy in two respects. First, each tenant has an indefeasible right of survivorship in the entire tenancy, which cannot be defeated by any act taken individually by either spouse during his or her lifetime. There can be no partition. Second, the spouses do not have an equal right to control and possession of the property. The husband during his lifetime has paramount rights in the property. In the event of divorce the tenancy by the entirety becomes a tenancy in common unless the divorce decree reflects that a joint tenancy is intended.

III

The stage was set for the instant case by this court's decision in *Klein v. Mayo*, 367 F.Supp. 583 (1973) *aff'd*, 416 U.S. 953, 94 S.Ct. 1964, 40 L.Ed.2d 303 (1974). In *Klein* a three-judge panel heard a challenge to the constitutionality of Mass.Gen.L. ch. 241, §1. This statute states that:

> Any person, except a tenant by the entirety, owning a present undivided legal estate in land, not subject to redemption, shall be entitled to have partition in the manner hereinafter provided.

The plaintiff in that case was in precisely the same position as the present plaintiff, having separated from her husband without dissolving her marriage and desiring an equal share in their property, which was held under a tenancy by the entirety. She contended that, given the bias of the tenancy by the entirety, the quoted statute barring partition discriminated against her on the basis of sex. In ordering judgment for the defendant, *Klein* separated the issue of partition from the issue of any underlying bias in the common law tenancy by the entirety. Finding that partition was equally unavailable to men and women holding property by the entirety, the court concluded that the challenged statute was non-discriminatory, while leaving open the possibility of future direct challenges to the tenancy by the entirety itself.

> The statute which is the subject of plaintiff's complaint deals solely with the right to partition, and that right is denied to both husbands and wives. The issue concerning right to possession and control is separate and distinct from that concerning the right to partition.
>
> We are mindful that, in the future, certain common-law aspects of tenancy by the entirety may be subject to judicial review in the light of recent decisions concerning sex discrimination....We are mindful as well that such a challenge may or may not be met by the fact that tenancy by the entirety is but one option open to married persons, and is in no way compelled by the state.

367 F.Supp. 586.

This action presents the challenge referred to in *Klein*, a direct attack on the common law tenancy by the entirety. No challenge to a statute is involved here. Plaintiff's original claim for an order of partition and sale by this court has been waived. Plaintiff asks this court to "restrain and enjoin the defendant from collecting any rents or profits from the above described premises," and to "restrain and enjoin the defendant from continuing to exercise exclusive possession and control over the above described premises."

IV

Defendant has not contested the court's jurisdiction in this case,[8] but defends on the merits, contending that the Massachusetts' tenancy by the entirety does not discriminate against women.

As was conceded in *Klein*, the common law concept of tenancy by the entirety is male oriented.

> It is true that the only Massachusetts tenancy tailored exclusively for married persons appears to be balanced in favor of males. There is no equivalent female-biased tenancy, nor is there a "neutral" married persons' tenancy providing for indefeasible survivorship but not vesting paramount lifetime rights in the male. Married couples may, it is true, elect a joint tenancy, a tenancy in common, or a sole tenancy. However, the survivorship feature of a joint tenancy may be destroyed by partition. A wife who wants the security of indefeasible survivorship can achieve it only by means of a male-dominated tenancy. 367 F.Supp. at 585.

But, the dispositive issue is not merely whether the tenancy by the entirety favors males. Rather, the issue is whether it does so in a manner that creates a constitutionally impermissible classification. On the specific facts of this case, this court holds that tenancy by the entirety, being but one option open to married persons seeking to take title in real estate, is constitutionally permissible.

It may be possible in some future case for a plaintiff wife to demonstrate factually that a selection of tenancy by the entirety was made through coercion, igno-

8. An issue might have been raised as to the existence of state action in this case, but in any event this court concludes that the tenancy by the entirety is a "custom or usage" enforced by the "persistent practices of state officials" sufficient to satisfy the state action prerequisite for suits brought under 42 U.S.C. §1983.... The presumption favoring the tenancy by the entirety in property holdings by married persons has been upheld by a line of Massachusetts cases, unbroken until 1973, when the presumption was eliminated by statute.... The presumption in favor of tenancies by the entirety was eliminated by an amendment to Mass.Gen.L. ch. 184, §7, April 23, 1973, ch. 210 of the Acts of 1973.

In addition, as noted above, the common law tenancy by the entirety is enforced in the Commonwealth by Mass.Gen.L. ch. 241, §1, which bars partition of property so held.

rance or misrepresentation. But no such facts were presented here, nor does plaintiff advance such a theory. Rather, this record makes almost inescapable the conclusion that plaintiff freely entered into a contract along with her husband in 1961, selecting one among several options open to her. Events have not transpired as she expected and now she seeks to revise the terms of her contract, because she now feels that her husband got the better end of the bargain.

Without greater justification than plaintiff's unsubstantiated allegations of prejudice, this court will not declare unconstitutional a form of property ownership selected by and presently relied upon by thousands of Massachusetts residents, including this plaintiff and defendant. As was noted in *Klein*,

> [t]he state does not compel husbands and wives to hold their property as tenants by the entirety. Undoubtedly, that choice is knowingly made in many instances despite or even, perhaps, because of its male oriented aspects. The choice would have been the same whether or not alternatives were available.

Id. at 585.

The Commonwealth permits tenancy by the entirety as one available option of property ownership. The plaintiff now complains of its consequences. But, as indicated in *Klein*, this is not to say that other married women would not prefer a vehicle giving husbands the right to possession, while at the same time foreclosing the possibility of partition, thereby preserving the family homestead even during bitter but temporary periods of separation.

This case is readily distinguishable from *Reed v. Reed*, 404 U.S. 71, 92 S.Ct. 251, 30 L.Ed.2d 225 (1971). There, the challenged statute barred forever a wife from acting as administratrix of her child's estate if her husband sought appointment as administrator. Here, the plaintiff has made her own choice. The state did not compel her current status....

...

The court orders entry of judgement for the defendant.

COMMENTS

The common law courts of England ruled that upon marriage any property to which the wife held title would automatically pass to her husband. One might wonder why such a drastic transfer of power from wives to husbands and systematic impoverishment of married women was not viewed as state intervention. Instead, this dramatic state imposition of male dominance was widely accepted in the United States as a matter of course. Until the passage of the Married Women's Property Acts last century, these rules went unchallenged. Individual wealthy families could circumvent some of the harshness of the doctrine, for example, through the use of trusts giving women about to be wed the beneficial interest in property to which legal title was placed in a trustee. Upon the woman's marriage, title to such property would remain in the trustee and the woman would continue to be the beneficiary of the trust after her marriage. These evasions reduced some of the pressure that otherwise might have been exerted on the rule, but they proved inadequate to reduce to a tolerable level the injustice worked in individual cases. A financially irresponsible husband could make life extraordinarily difficult for his wife and children. Beginning in 1839 in Mississippi, state legislatures enacted Married Women's Property Acts, which provided a variety of protections to wives from the common law rules empowering husbands and enabled families to protect property from the creditors of the husband. During most of the nineteenth century state courts interpreted the acts narrowly and left in place other inequalities of the common law.

In *Robinson*, the Tennessee court eliminated the sexism from the common law rules relating to tenancies by the entirety, or, as the court put it, stripped tenancy by the entirety of "the artificial and archaic rules and restrictions imposed at the common law." The federal court in Massachusetts refused to do the same. Rather, *D'Ercole* treated the matter under the rubric of consent. Of course, because of the presumption operating in Massachusetts until 1973 that a married couple took property as tenants by the entirety, many married couples affected by the court's decision never in fact considered the matter or would have decided to hold their property in this unequal manner. Quite aside from this issue, however, the *D'Ercole* court failed to consider the constitutionality of the law providing preferential treatment to couples willing to put up with the inequality of tenancy by the entirety. The only way to achieve indefeasible survivorship was to adopt a tenancy by the entirety. When one spouse dies, the surviving spouse automatically becomes sole owner of property held under a tenancy by the entirety, without the property passing through probate or being subject to delays and taxes. Upon divorce, the court will divide property held by the entirety, but as long as a marriage continues, the wife has no right to control the property and no right of partition. There is no tenancy in Massachusetts that gives the married couple the same benefits upon the death of one spouse without providing also for the superior power of the husband.

Interspousal Immunity

KLEIN v. KLEIN

Supreme Court of California

58 Cal. 2d 692, 376 P.2d 70, 26 Cal. Rptr. 102 (1962)

PETERS, Justice.

This case involves the rule of interspousal immunity for personal torts. In this respect it is similar to *Self v. Self*, 26 Cal.Rptr. 97, 376 P.2d 65. The instant case, however, unlike the *Self* case, involves a negligent tort rather than an intentional one. We are of the opinion that insofar as interspousal liability for tort is concerned there is no logical or legal reason for drawing a distinction between the two, and that for that reason, the rule announced in *Self v. Self*, *supra*, is here controlling.

In the instant case, Thelma Klein filed her complaint against Joseph Klein on January 5, 1962. The complaint contains two causes of action. The first alleges that for some time prior to April 15, 1961, defendant owned and possessed a certain pleasure boat; that on April 15, 1961, plaintiff and defendant were married; that plaintiff has no right, title or interest in the pleasure boat; that on July 8, 1961, defendant invited plaintiff on the boat for a fishing trip; that after the trip was completed and the boat moored, plaintiff commenced to clean the exterior of the pleasure boat with the approval and consent of defendant; that defendant knew that the exterior deck of the boat was covered with a covering that when wet became so slippery and slick that it was difficult to maintain footing thereon; that in cleaning the pleasure boat it was necessary for plaintiff to use the exterior deck; that defendant knew that this was so; that prior to plaintiff walking on the exterior deck, defendant with full knowledge that plaintiff would have to use that deck, and contrary to his former practices and customs, did so negligently, carelessly and recklessly cause water to be placed on certain parts of the boat so that water ran down over the exterior deck so that it was not safe to walk on; that plaintiff while walking on the deck fell and broke her leg as a proximate result of the defendant's negligence.

The second cause of action is predicated upon the same facts as the first except that it is alleged that defendant, knowing plaintiff would walk upon the deck in question, failed to warn her of the slippery and unsafe condition of which he had knowledge.

The defendant demurred to this complaint on several grounds, among which was the alleged incapacity of the plaintiff to sue defendant because of the marital status of the parties. The demurrer was sustained without leave to amend on the ground that one spouse may not sue the other in California for a personal tort. Judgment was entered in favor of defendant and the plaintiff has appealed.

In *Self v. Self, supra*, 26 Cal.Rptr. 97, 376 P.2d 65, it was held that because the reasons for the rule of interspousal immunity for torts no longer exists, and because of certain legislative changes in recent years, that rule should be abandoned.

Respondent contends that even if the rule of *Peters v. Peters*, 156 Cal. 32, 103 P. 219, 23 L.R.A.,N.S., 699, is to be abandoned as to intentional torts, it should be retained as to negligent torts. It is argued that to permit tort actions based on negligence to be maintained between spouses will cause the courts to be inundated with trifling suits, will tend to destroy conjugal harmony, and, because of the possibility of insurance, will encourage collusion, fraud and perjury. These arguments are not convincing. Similar arguments were advanced in the *Self* case as reasons for maintaining the old rule as to intentional torts and such arguments were there found not to be convincing. They are not any more convincing here. It is our opinion that the logical and legal reasons set forth in the *Self* case that cause us to abandon the old rule as to intentional torts apply with equal force to negligent torts.

...

The argument about inundating the courts with trifling suits is palpably unsound. We have not been informed that such result has followed in any of the 18 states that have repudiated the old rule. In response to this same argument, in *Spellens v. Spellens*, 49 Cal.2d 210, 317 P.2d 613, Justice Schauer, in his concurring and dissenting opinion, at page 241, at page 632 of 317 P.2d, stated: "The court should not decline to entertain a meritorious action against a spouse...because of the dubious apprehension that in some future case trifling domestic difficulties may became the subject of litigation." That is a sound argument.

The contention that there may be insurance involved, and that to permit such actions in such cases will encourage collusion, fraud and perjury, is also not convincing. Such arguments should be advanced to the Legislature, and not to the courts. Where such a danger is made clear to the Legislature it has not been slow to act.[1]

It is, of course, fundamental in the law of torts that any person proximately injured by the act of another, whether that act be willful or negligent, should, in the absence of statute or compelling reasons of public policy, be compensated. The possibility of fraud or perjury exists to some degree in all cases. But we do not deny a cause of action to a party because of such a danger. There is no contention that any collusion is involved in the present case. When, as and if that issue does arise in future cases the courts are equipped to meet it. As was said in *Emery v. Emery*, 45 Cal.2d 421, 289 P.2d 218, a case that held that an unemancipated minor could sue his minor brother or sister and parent for an intentional tort (pp. 431–432, 289 P.2d p. 224–225):

> Defendants' second argument, that tort actions between minor brothers and sisters will encourage fraud and collusion, is based on assumptions opposite from those on which their first argument is based. This argument assumes that the action is not in reality directed against the minor brother or sister of the plaintiff, but is in fact directed at his liability insurer. If this assumption is correct, maintenance of such a tort action would not disturb the family peace and harmony; on the contrary, the "domestic harmony will not be disrupted so much by allowing the action as by denying it." (PROSSER ON TORTS (2d ed.) 677.) Moreover, although defendants' statement that the existence of insurance, of which there is no evidence in the present case, "gives no cause of action where one did not exist before" is correct, by the same token the mere possibility of fraud or collusion because of the possible existence of liability insurance does not warrant immunity from liability where it would otherwise exist. The interest of the child in freedom from personal injury caused by the tortious conduct of others is sufficient to outweigh any danger of fraud or collusion. As the Supreme Court of Washington said in reply to the same argument in a case involving an analogous situation (action by a child to recover for injuries caused by its parent's negligent operation of a truck for business purposes), "The courts may and should take cognizance of fraud and collusion when found to exist in a particular case. However, the fact that there may be greater opportunity for fraud or collusion in one class of cases than another does not warrant courts of law in closing the door to all cases of that class. Courts must depend upon the efficacy of the judicial processes to ferret out the meritorious from the fraudulent in particular cases. *Rozell v. Rozell, supra* (281 N.Y. 106, 22 N.E.2d 254, 123 A.L.R. 1015). If those processes prove inadequate, the problem becomes one for the Legislature. …Courts will not immunize tortfeasors from liability in a whole class of cases because of the possibility of fraud, but will depend upon the legislature to deal with the problem as a question of public policy." *Borst v. Borst, supra*, 41 Wash.2d 642, 653–654, 251 P.2d 149, 155.

This is a complete answer to the contentions of respondent. It would be a sad commentary on the law if we were to admit that the judicial processes are so inef-

1. Thus the Legislature enacted the guest law, now section 17158, Vehicle Code, abolishing causes of action by guests in an automobile against the host for simple negligence, but retaining such an action based on the intoxication or willful misconduct of the host.

fective that we must deny relief to a person otherwise entitled simply because in some future case a litigant may be guilty of fraud or collusion. Once that concept were accepted, then all causes of action should be abolished. Our legal system is not that ineffectual.

It is true that in some respects the law has drawn a distinction between intentional and negligent torts. It has been held in California that a child may sue his parent for an intentional tort, contrary to the common law rule, but may not sue him for a negligent tort. (*Emery v. Emery, supra*, 45 Cal.2d 421, 289 P.2d 218 (a case involving an intentional tort); *Trudell v. Leatherby*, 212 Cal. 678, 300 P. 7 (a case denying to a minor any recovery against a defendant who was standing in the position of one *in loco parentis*); *Gillett v. Gillett*, 168 Cal.App.2d 102, 335 P.2d 736 (a case involving an intentional tort); *Perkins v. Robertson*, 140 Cal.App.2d 536, 295 P.2d 972 (a case involving both an intentional and negligent tort).)

But, because these cases have made a distinction between the two types of tort in the parent-child relationship, there is no logical basis for extending the distinction to the husband-wife relationship. As already pointed out, as to such relationship, the doctrines of identity of the persons, and of maintenance of the sanctity of the home, are no longer applicable. This being so, and there being no other argument to the contrary that is convincing, we are of the view that the rule of *Self v. Self, supra*, is here applicable.

Judgment reversed.

SCHAUER, Justice (dissenting).

While I concur in the adoption of the rule of interspousal liability for intentional torts to the person announced in *Self v. Self*, Cal., 26 Cal.Rptr. 97, 376 P.2d 65, I believe it ill-advised for this court to undertake to extend that rule to interspousal liability for simple negligence. Inherent in every assertion of the latter liability are opportunities and incentives for and hence probabilities of collusion and fraud far more real than those involved in claims based on intentional torts. For this among other reasons, if the proposed extension is to become law it should be so declared by the Legislature after proper study of the problem and formulation of such specific rules as may be found necessary to protect all parties....

...

Indeed, judicial interference in this sensitive area of substantive law may well have the opposite effect: *e.g.*, within a few months after the Supreme Court of Illinois judicially abrogated in that state the common law rule of interspousal immunity in an action based on "wilful and wanton" conduct resulting in an automobile accident (*Brandt v. Keller* (1953) 413 Ill. 503, 109 N.E.2d 729) the Illinois Legislature reinstated the immunity rule as to all personal torts between spouses, enacting that "neither husband nor wife may sue the other for a tort to the person committed during coverture." (Ill.Rev.Stats.1953, ch. 68, §1; see *Hindman v. Holmes* (1955, 4 Ill.App.2d 279) 124 N.E.2d 344, 345.)...

...

The distinction in this regard between intentional torts and negligent torts is a valid one, grounded on hard facts. Accident liability policies do not ordinarily insure against intentionally inflicted injuries, and hence the incentives for trumped up actions against insurers based on intentional tort are few or nonexistent. But negligent injuries offer a fertile field for conjugal collusion and fraud. The wife to take as example the suspiciously frequent case is shaken up in an automobile accident caused by the husband's inattentive driving. Perhaps, on reflection, she discovers symptoms of a whiplash injury. An action for damages is brought nominally against the husband who, being insured, stands only to gain by losing and hence willingly plays the role of defendant. The resultant judgment for the "plaintiff" wife is collected from the "defendant" husband's insurer, and provides a tidy sum which both spouses may then enjoy as the fruits of conjugal cooperation. Or, conversely, the husband sues the wife for injuries allegedly caused when he slipped on a highly polished kitchen floor, tripped over the wife's mop, or suffered a similar household mishap. The variations on this theme are limited only by the ingenuity of the parties and the patience of the insurance company.

...

For the reasons stated I would affirm the judgment.

G.L. v. M.L.

Superior Court of New Jersey
228 N.J. Super. 566, 550 A.2d 525 (1988)

KRAFTE, J.S.C.

Do sexual relations between spouses constitute "marital or nuptial privileges" under *Merenoff v. Merenoff*, 76 N.J. 535, 388 A.2d 951 (1978), thereby entitling any sexual tort committed by one spouse upon the other to interspousal immunity? This court finds that they do not.

The plaintiff in this matter filed for divorce on November 2, 1984. Included in her complaint were four separate counts for personal injury alleging that her husband, the defendant, transmitted genital herpes to her during their marriage. The defendant's insurance carrier, defending against the negligence claim and the defendant's attorney in the matrimonial proceeding defending against the intentional tort claim now join together in bringing a motion for summary judgement dismissing the personal injury counts.

Our highest court examined and incorporated the history and nature of interspousal immunity in *Merenoff v. Merenoff*, 76 N.J. at 539–547, 388 A.2d 951 and abrogated the doctrine regarding tortious conduct stating, "...where personal injuries are tortiously inflicted by one spouse upon another, it is just and fair that compensation in appropriate circumstances be afforded the wronged and injured party and, to this end, a suit be allowed to effectuate such recovery." *Id.* at 557, 388 A.2d 95. The *Merenoff* court recognized that there was a range of activity in a marital relationship, characterized as "special matters of privacy and familiarity" beyond the reach of the law of torts because they "fall outside the bounds of a definable and enforceable duty of care" and are encompassed by a marital or nuptial privilege. *Id.* at 557, 388 A.2d 95. These areas were not left intact, however, were seen as potential exceptions to the otherwise abrogated doctrine and were to be ultimately defined and developed on a case-by-case basis by future courts. *Id.* at 557, 388 A.2d 951.

...

In the present action, the plaintiff alleges that the defendant continued to have sexual relations with her even after discovering that he had herpes, the result of an extramarital relationship. It is argued by the defendant that sexual intercourse between spouses is by its very nature an act which falls within the scope of a marital or nuptial privilege and therefore his conduct should be shielded from liability. This Court does not agree. It is unconscionable that a person could escape liability for infecting a spouse with genital herpes or other sexually transmitted disease by merely claiming that the transmission occurred during privileged sexual relations of marriage. As early as *Crowell v. Crowell*, 180 N.C. 516, 105 S.E. 206 (Sup.Ct.1920), *reh. den.* 181 N.C. 66, 106 S.E. 149 (Sup.Ct.1921), courts began to recognize a cause of action in tort for the transmission of veneral disease to one's spouse.

Defendant misconstrues the meaning of marital privilege and furthermore destroyed any that may have existed by his own intentional involvement in an extramarital relationship. Defendant cannot simultaneously breach his marital relationship by engaging in extramarital intercourse, and claim nuptial immunity for consequences flowing from his own wilful and intentional conduct. It is a "...sound principle of law, and certainly approved in morals, although a man may have a legal right to do a given thing, yet he forfeits that right when he voluntarily and deliberately places himself in a position where it becomes impossible for him to exercise it without hurt or injury to another." *Crowell v. Crowell*, 106 S.E. at 149–150. Contagion of sexually transmitted diseases was clearly not contemplated by the *Merenoff* court to be barred from personal injury suits through the use of interspousal immunity. Moreover, the court was concerned with judicial neutrality toward married persons and did not intend to create a shield for one spouse as against the other. "And the right to bring a lawsuit for compensation for wrongful injury is an option or choice that ought not be denied a person solely because of marriage." *Merenoff*, 76 N.J. at 557, 388 A.2d 951.

As to the intentional aspect of the personal injury claim, it is clear that the abolition of the interspousal immunity doctrine pertains to intentional tortious conduct as well as conventional negligence. *Tevis v. Tevis*, 79 N.J. 422, 426, 400 A.2d 1189 (1979). Plaintiff first observed symptoms of the herpes simplex virus on defendant's body in February 1983, but accepted his explanations to the contrary. Defendant argued that he never intended to inflict the plaintiff with herpes as he was never officially diagnosed until 1987, almost three years after the filing of the complaint. However defendant admitted in his deposition that he told plaintiff of his extramarital affair prior to the couple's separation. It was also stated by the parties' former housekeeper that defendant told plaintiff that he had contracted herpes as a result of this affair and was sorry to have infected her. Defendant has since denied this conversation. Regardless, the intentional act was not that of knowingly transmitting herpes to plaintiff but, rather, it was the act of sexual intercourse with the plaintiff after sexual relations with someone else with whom he carried on a two year relationship. Such behavior on defendant's part placed plaintiff at risk of physical harm.

There remains a duty of care to one's spouse and the threat of physical harm cannot be excused. "Consent to sexual intercourse vitiated by one partner's fraudulent concealment of the risk of infection with venereal disease is equally applicable today, whether or not partners involved are married to each other." *Kathleen K. v. Robert B.*, 150 Cal.App.3d 992, 198 Cal.Rptr. 273, 277 (Ct.App.1984)....

...

This court holds that the marital privilege of sexual relations does not include immunity to personal injury suits between spouses based upon the transmittal of a sexual disease. Motion for summary judgement is denied as to all counts of the personal injury claim. Plaintiff will submit an appropriate order.

COMMENTS

As early as 1920 when *Crowell*, cited in *G.L. v. M.L.*, was decided, cases in the United States began to allow wives to sue their husband under certain circumstances. Although the language of the early cases sounds strikingly old-fashioned, the ideas behind them were much like those expressed in the more recent case of *G.L. v. M.L.* Before the widespread availability and use of penicillin and other antibiotics, many sexually transmitted diseases, such as syphilis and gonorrhea, were extremely serious, even when promptly treated. They may have been feared in some of the same ways that AIDS is feared at the present time.

Klein represents the trend toward abolishing the vestiges of marital immunity by judicial decree. State legislatures are traditionally reluctant to change the law in this area, partly because of an effective insurance lobby; the common law disabilities of married women in bringing actions for damages against their husbands have therefore continued, except where the courts have taken the initiative. Marital immunity illustrates the persistence of common law theories of marriage which, although based on religious dogma and the economic needs of feudal times, sometimes resurface in modern times, changed in appearance but with similar legal effects.

One of these ancient conceptions was the ideal of marital unity, based on the legal fiction that husband and wife are one. At one time the doctrine of merger at marriage led commentators to suggest that for a person to sue his spouse would be tantamount to suing himself. Thus, it seems particularly fitting that one of the earliest immunity cases, cited in *Klein*, bore the name "*Self v. Self*." A conventional view is that this theory rendered a lawsuit by the wife against the husband based on tort or contract inconceivable; and in the earlier days of the law's evolution, common law judges had no opportunity to think about the problem resulting from this fact. Thus, strictly speaking, neither issues of marital immunity nor questions of policy were involved. The disability of the wife resulted from the nature of marriage and from logic and reason as they were then perceived.

This view overlooks the strong role of the government, through the courts, in disempowering married women. As Oliver Wendell Holmes is famous for pointing out, the life of the law has not been logic, but experience. Male judges found it easy to decide that "logic" and "reason" required decisions that gave men a great deal of power over their wives. (Notice how easily the dissenting judge in *Klein* assumed that husbands drove cars and wives mopped and waxed floors.)

The passage of Married Women's Property Acts brought about new legal fictions, such as treating married women in regard to their separate property as if they were unmarried. The first such statute, passed in 1839 in Mississippi, applied only to white women, and made a specific reference to removing women's disabilities in the exercise of ownership of slaves. At that time, divorce was difficult or impossible for women, even if they had the misfortune to be married to hopeless drunks who squandered all their money. Under the common law, the husband owned and had control over all property of the wife and could thus keep her in perpetual poverty. One theory about how a state like Mississippi happened to be the first to pass a Married Woman's Property Act is that many of the state legislators happened to reside, while the legislature was in session, in a boarding house run by one such unfortunate wife, and she was either in risk of losing or actually lost the boarding house due to the financial irresponsibility of her estranged drunken husband.

Although the policies behind these statutes broadened as they spread across the country, judges tended to interpret them strictly on the basis that they were in derogation of common law. Thus tort actions by a wife against her husband were not covered because they related not to property but to choses in action, while marital immunity was invoked to prevent a wife from suing her husband, even though she could sue outsiders. When the concept of immunity lost its persuasive power, social policies such as the maintenance of marital peace or, as expressed in *Klein*, conjugal harmony and the sanctity of the home rose to the fore and led to the same results.

Closer examination of these social policies reveals that they hardly convey a true picture. The lawyer for the defendant husband, who raised these arguments by way of demurrer or motion to dismiss was in fact representing the interests of an insurance company that would have to pay if the plaintiff wife were to prevail against her husband. Insurance contracts contained clauses that the insured had to collaborate with the lawyer furnished by the company in case of a claim. Although the interests of the husband and the insurance company would seem in fact to conflict, defense lawyers were permitted to argue the virtues of marital peace for the ulterior purpose of avoiding liability on the insurance policy.

Compared to this legal situation, the latest arguments for preserving the disabilities of married women are bluntly to the point and coincide with the views expressed in the dissenting opinion in *Klein*. According to this view, lawsuits by wives against husbands encourage collusion, perjury, and fraud to the detriment of insurance companies. Of course, this issue is not likely to arise in the case of intentional torts by a husband against his wife, since intentional torts are rarely if ever covered by insurance. Thus, this argument, like that of the insurance lawyer representing the husband in *Klein*, emphasizes the analytical distinction between intentional and negligent torts. There remains the power of insurance companies to include clauses in their policies specifically excluding liability in case of injury to a spouse or other specified members of the family. Whether such clauses should be valid and enforceable depends on one's views on freedom of contract and contracts of adhesion.

The lesson to be learned is that legal concepts sometimes acquire a life of their own that enables them to persevere in spite of drastic changes in social conditions and underlying policies. Indeed, they sometimes appear to be independent even of the logic or rationality of any given period of time. Of course, the chain of events depicted here does not mean that older notions, such as unity of husband and wife, marital immunity, the maintenance of marital peace, and the prevention of fraud and collusion to the detriment of insurers, are totally without effect. All of them are to some extent still viable and can be argued by lawyers in appropriate cases, depending on whom they are representing. The courts, especially on the trial level, may still give them some weight. Since the vast majority of all accident cases result in a negotiated settlement, all the theories on marital disabilities may play some role in the context of negotiations. In other words, in their pretrial negotiations lawyers are still likely to argue those legal theories that might persuade a conservative trial judge, even if those theories may not succeed in the relatively rare appeals in matters of this kind.

The picture that emerges is complex. That the law on the books differs from the law in action is no surprise. Less obvious is that the law in action has several levels. In *Klein*, for example, the trial court adhered to the notion that one spouse cannot sue the other for a personal tort. On the appellate level a more progressive court permitted such an action. A lawyer would be ill-advised to overlook the attitudes of the lower courts. Even after *Klein*, in settlement negotiations defense lawyers are likely to argue the view of marriage espoused by the lower court and by the dissenting judge on appeal, while plaintiff lawyers can counter with reference to the Supreme Court of California.

REFERENCES

Elizabeth Gasper Brown, *Note, Husband and Wife — Memorandum on the Mississippi Women's Law of 1839*, 42 MICH. L. REV. 1110 (1944).

Carl W. Tobias, *Interspousal Tort Immunity in America*, 23 GA. L. REV. 359 (1989).

Identity

STUART v. BOARD OF SUPERVISORS
Court of Appeals of Maryland
266 Md. 440, 295 A.2d 223 (1972)

MURPHY, Chief Judge.

Mary Emily Stuart and Samuel H. Austell, Jr., were married in Virginia on November 13, 1971 and, shortly thereafter, took up residence in Columbia, Howard County, Maryland. In accordance with the couple's oral antenuptial agreement, Stuart continued, after the marriage, to use and be exclusively known by her birth given ("maiden") name and not by the legal surname of her husband.

On March 2, 1972, Stuart undertook to register to vote in Howard County in her birth given name. After disclosing to the registrar that she was married to Austell but had consistently and nonfraudulently used her maiden name, she was registered to vote in the name of Mary Emily Stuart.

On March 16, 1972 the Board of Supervisors of Elections for Howard County notified Stuart by letter that since under Maryland law "a woman's legal surname becomes that of her husband upon marriage," she was required by Maryland Code, Article 33, §3-18(c) to complete a "Request for Change of Name" form or her registration would be cancelled. Stuart did not complete the form and her registration was cancelled on April 4, 1972.

Stuart promptly challenged the Board's action by two petitions filed in the Circuit Court for Howard County, the first entitled "Petition to correct (the voter) registry," and the second "Petition to restore name to registry of voters in Howard County." In each petition Stuart maintained that she was properly registered to vote in her birth given name, that being her true and correct name; that under the English common law, in force in Maryland, a wife could assume the husband's name if she desired, or retain her own name, or be known by any other name she wished, so long as the name she used was not retained for a fraudulent purpose; and that since the only name she ever used was Mary Emily Stuart the Board had no right to cancel her voter registration listed in that name.

...Evidence was adduced showing that the oral antenuptial agreement between Stuart and Austell that she would retain her maiden name was a matter of great importance to both parties. Stuart testified that her marriage to Austell was "based on the idea that we're both equal individuals and our names symbolize that." There was evidence that prior to the marriage lawyers were consulted on the parties' behalf who indicated that Stuart had the right to retain her own name after the marriage. Stuart testified, and Austell corroborated her testimony, that she would not have gotten married "if...[the marriage] would have jeopardized my name." She testified that after the marriage she continued to use her own name on charge accounts, on her driver's license and Social Security registration and in "every legal document I've ever had." "Everybody" she said, "knows me by the name Mary Stuart."

There was evidence showing that the practice of the Board requiring a married woman to use the surname of her husband dated back to 1936; that the practice was a uniform one throughout the State and was adopted to provide some trail of identification to prevent voter fraud; that if a married woman could register under different names the identification trail would be lost; and that the only exception permitted to the requirement that married women register under their husbands' surnames was if the name was changed by court order.

By opinion filed May 10, 1972, Judge Mayfield concluded "that a person may adopt and use any name chosen in the absence of fraudulent intent or purpose"; that the use by Stuart of her maiden name was without fraudulent intent or purpose; that it is the law of Maryland that "the use by the wife of the husband's surname following marriage, while the same have been initially based upon custom and usage, is now based on the common law of England, which law has been duly adopted as the law of this State"; that under the provisions of the Code, Article 33, §3-18(a)(3) clerks of courts, as therein designated, are required to notify Boards of Supervisors of Elections of the "present names" of females over the age of eighteen years residing within the State "whose names have been changed by marriage"; that by subsection (c) of §3-18, the Boards, upon being advised of a "change of name by marriage," are required to give notification "that such...change of name by marriage...has been reported to the board, and shall require the voter to show cause within two weeks...why his registration should not be cancelled"; that §3-18 appeared "to be in conformity with the common law," as espoused in such cases as *People ex rel. Rago v. Lipsky*, 327 Ill.App. 63, 63 N.E.2d 642 (1945) and *Forbush v. Wallace*, 341 F.Supp. 217 (M.D.Ala.1971), *aff'd per curiam* 405 U.S. 970, 92 S.Ct. 1197, 31 L.Ed.2d 246 (1972); that the "statutory requirements (of §3-18) are in accordance with the law which says that upon marriage the wife takes the surname of her husband"; that the provisions of §3-18 do not deprive Stuart of her right to use her maiden name, nor of her right to vote, but require only that she "register to vote under her 'legal' name,...based upon the broad general principle of the necessity for proper record keeping and the proper and most expedient way of identifying the person who desires to vote."

From the court's order denying her petitions to correct the voter registry and to restore her name thereto, Stuart has appealed. She claims on appeal, as she did below, that a woman's surname upon marriage does not become that of her husband by operation of the common law in force in Maryland and that nothing in the provisions of §3-18(a)(3) and (c) mandates a contrary result.

What constitutes the correct legal name of a married woman under common law principles is a question which has occasioned a sharp split of authorities, crystallized in the conflicting cases of *State ex rel. Krupa v. Green*, 114 Ohio App. 497, 177 N.E.2d 616 (1961), relied upon by Stuart, and *People ex rel. Rago v. Lipsky*, *supra*, adopted by the lower court as its principal authority for denying the petitions. *Green* approved the voter registration of a married woman in her birth given name which she had openly, notoriously and exclusively used subsequent to her marriage, and held that she could use that name as a candidate for public office. The court held:

> It is only *by custom*, in English speaking countries, that a woman, upon marriage, adopts the surname of her husband in place of the surname of her father. *Id.* 177 N.E.2d at 619 (Emphasis in original.)

Lipsky refused to allow a married woman to remain registered to vote under her birth given name on the basis of

> ...the long-established custom, policy and rule of the common law among English-speaking peoples whereby a woman's name is changed by marriage and her husband's surname becomes *as a matter of law* her surname. *Id.* 63 N.E.2d at 645 (Emphasis supplied.)

...

We think the lower court was wrong in concluding that the principles enunciated in *Lipsky* represent the law of Maryland. We have heretofore unequivocally recognized the common law right of any person, absent a statute to the contrary, to "adopt any name by which he may become known, and by which he may transact business and execute contracts and sue or be sued." *Romans v. State*, 178 Md. 588, 597, 16 A.2d 642, 646. In the context of the name used in an automobile liability insurance contract, we approved the consistent nonfraudulent use by a married woman of a surname other than that of her lawful husband in *Erie Insurance Exchange v. Lane*, 246 Md. 55, 227 A.2d 231. Citing with approval *Everett v. Standard Acc. Ins. Co.*, 45 Cal.App. 332, 187 P. 996 (1919), we summarized its holding as follows:

> The court...held that because the insured had been known as Everett for twenty-two years before the policy was issued, a representation that his name was Everett was not a misrepresentation, although his name before had been Cowie, since a man may lawfully change his name without resorting to legal proceedings and by general usage or habit acquire another.

Erie 246 Md. at 62–63, 227 A.2d at 236. If a married woman may lawfully adopt an assumed name (which, in *Erie*, was neither her birth given name nor the name of her lawful husband) without legal proceedings, then we think Maryland law manifestly permits a married woman to retain her birth given name by the same procedure of consistent, nonfraudulent use following her marriage. In so concluding, we note that there is no statutory requirement in the Code, in either Article 62 (Marriages) or Article 45 (Husband and Wife), that a married woman adopt her husband's surname.[3] Consistent with the common law principle referred to in the Maryland cases, we hold that a married woman's surname does not become that of her husband where, as here, she evidences a clear intent to consistently and nonfraudulently use her birth given name subsequent to her marriage. Thus, while under *Romans*, a married woman may choose to adopt the surname of her husband — this being the long-standing custom and tradition which has resulted in the vast majority of married women adopting their husbands' surnames as their own — the mere fact of the marriage does not, as a matter of law, operate to establish the custom and tradition of the majority as a rule of law binding upon all.

From a study of the English authorities cited to us by the parties and amici curiae, we believe the rule we enunciate today is founded upon the English common law incorporated into the laws of Maryland by Article 5 of the Maryland Declaration of Rights. The question of English common law was considered by the Ohio Court of Appeals in *State ex rel. Krupa v. Green*, *supra*, 177 N.E.2d at 619:

> In England, from which came our customs with respect to names, a woman is permitted to retain her maiden surname upon marriage if she so desires.
>
> M. Turner-Samuels, in his book on "The Law of Married Women" at page 345, states:
>
>> In England, custom has long since ordained that a married woman takes her husband's name. This practice is not invariable; not compellable by law.... A wife may continue to use her maiden, married, or any other name she wishes to be known by....
>
> ...

Other English text writers have expressed a similar view of English law:

> In England (followed by the United States of America) practice has crept in, though apparently comparatively recently, for a woman upon marriage to merge her identity in that of her husband, and to substitute his name for her father's acquiring the new surname by repute. C. Ewen, A History of British Isles 391 (London 1931)

To the same effect see 19 Halsbury's Laws of England 829 (3d 1957):

> 1350. Assumption by wife of husband's name. When a woman on her marriage assumes, as she usually does in England, the surname of her husband in substitution for her father's name, it may be said that she acquires a new name by repute. The change of name is in fact, rather than in law, a consequence of the marriage.... (Footnotes omitted.)

Under the common law of Maryland, as derived from the common law of England, Mary Emily Stuart's surname thus has not been changed by operation of law to that of Austell solely by reason of her marriage to him. On the contrary, because of her

3. Compare Hawaii Rev.Stat., Title 31, §574-1 (1968): "Every married woman shall adopt her husband's name as a family name." Hawaii appears to be the only state with a statutory provision determinative of the issue.

exclusive, consistent, nonfraudulent use of her maiden name, she is entitled to use the name Mary Emily Stuart unless there is a statute to the contrary....

Nothing in the language of §3-18(a)(3) or (c) purports to compel all married women to register to vote in their husbands' surname. Since Mary Emily Stuart did not undergo a "change of name by marriage," this Section merely requires her to show cause to the Board that she consistently and nonfraudulently used her birth given name rather than her husband's surname following marriage....

In light of our disposition of the common law issue, we find it unnecessary to reach the constitutional issues raised by the appeal.

Order dismissing petitions vacated....

SMITH, Judge.

I would affirm.

I do not see a constitutional issue in this case other than that of judicial legislation.

...

It is interesting to note that in 1931 the Attorney General was asked to advise "as to the proper name to be used by a Catholic Sister or a Brother in a religious order when registering for voting purposes." In 16 Op. Atty. Gen. 144 (1931), he replied:

> The law requires the giving of the correct legal name, and until a person's name has been changed in the manner provided by law, this name should be given when applying for registration purposes. *Id.* at 144.

2 Bishop, Marriage, Divorce and Separation §1622 (1891), states:

> The rule of law and custom is familiar, that marriage confers on the woman the husband's surname.

...

In re Kayaloff, 9 F.Supp. 176 (S.D.N.Y.1934), is interesting in this regard. There a married woman was seeking naturalization. She was a musician "known professionally by her maiden name." She feared that she might possibly suffer financial loss if her naturalization certificate showed her surname to be that of her husband. She saw another problem in that a discrepancy would exist between her musical union card and her naturalization certificate. The court, after stating that "[t]he union card should conform to the naturalization certificate rather than that the latter should yield to the union card," said:

> Under the law of New York, as pronounced in *Chapman v. Phoenix National Bank*, 85 N.Y. 437, a woman, at her marriage, takes the surname of her husband. "That," it was there said, "becomes her legal name, and she ceases to be known by her maiden name. By that name she must sue and be sued, make and take grants and execute all legal documents. Her maiden surname is absolutely lost, and she ceases to be known thereby." *Id.* 9 F.Supp. at 176.

The exact point here involved was before the court in *People ex rel. Rago v. Lipsky*, 327 Ill.App. 63, 63 N.E.2d 642 (1945). Antonia E. Rago, admitted to the bar of Illinois in 1938, married MacFarland in 1944. She was admitted to practice under the name of Rago in the federal courts in Chicago and before the Supreme Court of the United States, in addition to the Illinois courts. She practiced under the name of Rago. She claimed that her husband expressly approved of her plans to continue her practice of law and her other business affairs under the name of Rago. She sought to register under that name and challenged a provision of the Illinois law which provided that any registered voter who changed her name by marriage should "be required to register anew and authorize the cancellation of the previous registration." In holding that she was obliged to register under her married name, the court said:

> Notwithstanding petitioner's contention to the contrary, it is well settled by common-law principles and immemorial custom that a woman upon marriage abandons her maiden name and takes the husband's surname, with which is used her own given name. *Id.* 327 Ill. at 67, 63 N.E.2d at 644.

...

I am not impressed by the comment, citing *Romans v. State*, 178 Md. 588, 597, 16 A.2d 642 (1940), that a person has a common law right, absent a statute to the contrary, to "adopt any name by which he may become known, and by which he may transact business and execute contracts and sue or be sued." Rather, the question is, as I see it, what the General Assembly meant in the registration laws when "name" was mentioned.

It is conceded by all concerned that the uniform practice in Maryland has been for a married woman to register under the surname of her husband. This is in accordance with what I understand to be the authorities on the subject of name. It certainly is in accordance with custom. Therefore, I believe that to permit a married woman to register under a surname other than that of her husband she must either go through the process of having her name changed or the General Assembly must so provide. A holding to the contrary is in my humble opinion judicial legislation which is forbidden by the Maryland Declaration of Rights.

SYDNEY v. PINGREE

United States District Court
564 F. Supp. 412 (S.D. Fla. 1982)

GONZALEZ, District Judge.

THIS CAUSE has come before the court upon cross motions for summary judgment.

The plaintiffs in this case, Chris Ledbetter, Dean Skylar, and their son Sydney, bring this suit pursuant to 42 U.S.C. §1983 and the First, Fifth, Ninth and Fourteenth Amendments to the United States Constitution, to determine the constitutionality of Florida Statute §382.16(5). Because the plaintiffs allege that Sydney was conceived and born in wedlock, this case presents only the question of the constitutionality of §382.16(5)(a). This section provides that a child conceived and born in wedlock shall be given the surname of his father on his birth certificate.

In April 1982, plaintiffs Ledbetter and Skylar requested permission from the Department of Health and Rehabilitative Services of the State of Florida to use the name "Skybetter", a combination of the parents' surnames, as their child's surname. The Department of Health and Rehabilitative Services denied the plaintiffs' request, relying on Florida Statute §382.16(5).

On June 6, 1982, plaintiff Ledbetter gave birth to plaintiff Sydney. The following day plaintiff Skylar completed the birth certificate application form using "Skybetter" as the child's surname. Because the child's surname was different from that of his father, the application was not accepted by the hospital official responsible for transmitting birth certificate information to the Office of Vital Statistics. To this date, plaintiff Sydney has no officially recognized surname and no birth certificate has been issued to the child.

The plaintiffs seek a declaratory judgment that Florida Statute §382.16(5) is unconstitutional, an injunction enjoining the defendants from enforcing the statute and from enacting similarly unconstitutional statutes, a mandatory injunction requiring the defendants to issue a birth certificate to Plaintiff Sydney with the surname chosen by his parents, and other appropriate relief.

Our first inquiry is whether the statute in question intrudes upon a constitutionally protected right of the plaintiffs. Following the reasoning of the United States Supreme Court in *Roe v. Wade*, 410 U.S. 113, 93 S.Ct. 705, 35 L.Ed.2d 147 (1973), this court concludes that the due process clause of the Fourteenth Amendment protects the plaintiffs' right to choose the name of their child from arbitrary state action.

The Court's decision in *Roe v. Wade* and other privacy cases, *e.g. Griswold v. Connecticut*, 381 U.S. 479, 85 S.Ct. 1678, 14 L.Ed.2d 510 (1965); *Loving v. Virginia*, 388 U.S. 1, 87 S.Ct. 1817, 18 L.Ed.2d 1010 (1967), hold that the liberty component of the due process clause of the Fourteenth Amendment encompasses a freedom of choice in certain matters of marriage and procreation. *See Florida Women's Medical Clinic, Inc., et al., v. Jim Smith, et al.*, 536 F.Supp. 1048, at 1052–1053 (S.D.Fla.1982). This constitutional right of liberty and privacy is broad enough to include the right of parents to choose a name for their child. *Jech v. Burch*, 466 F.Supp. 714, 719 (D.Hawaii 1979).

Since parents have a constitutionally protected right to choose the name of their child, the state must at least show that any intrusion on that right has a reasonable relationship to some state purpose. The state has failed to show any reasonable justification for intruding on the parents' right; thus it is unnecessary for this court to determine whether something more than a reasonable relationship must be shown.

In conclusion, the court having found that there is a constitutional right of parents to choose the name of their child, and the state having shown no reasonable justification for impinging upon that right, the court holds that Florida Statute §382.16(5)(a), which requires that a child conceived and born in wedlock shall be given the father's surname, is unconstitutional.

It is accordingly

ORDERED AND ADJUDGED as follows:

1) That the Plaintiffs' Motion for Summary Judgment be and the same is hereby GRANTED.

2) That the Defendants' Motion for Summary Judgment be and the same is hereby DENIED.

3) That Plaintiffs shall submit a proposed form of final judgment.

D. R. S. v. R. S. H.
Court of Appeals of Indiana
412 N.E.2d 1257 (Ind. Ct. App. 1980)

BUCHANAN, C.J.

...

D.R.S. is the unwed mother of a one-year-old child, J. Ten days after J.'s birth, D.R.S. and the biological father, R.S.H., jointly filed a Voluntary Petition to Establish Paternity.

At the hearing, the parties stipulated that R.S.H. was the child's father and that he would pay child support of twenty-five dollars per week. The parties asked the court to allocate medical expenses associated with the child's birth, to establish visitation rights for the non-custodial father, and to determine whether J. should retain his mother's maiden name or take the surname of his father.

After the trial judge indicated that he would be inclined to reduce support payments if the name were not changed, D.R.S. testified that she would forego all support if J. retained her surname. She maintained that because she has no plans to marry and would retain her maiden name even if she were to marry, there would be no potential for confusing J. She also testified that J.'s retention of her name would promote consistency because J. would be living with her.

R.S.H. testified that he had paid some support since J.'s birth and that he would be willing to pay one-half of the medical expenses already incurred along with one-half of all future medical bills not covered by insurance. He stated that he wished to have J. bear his surname.

The court ordered that R.S.H. pay twenty-five dollars per week as support, that he have visitation rights, that the parties split the costs of the action and medical expenses, and that J. subsequently be known by his father's surname.

ISSUE

D.R.S. raises one issue: Was the court's order changing the child's surname contrary to law, against the evidence, or an abuse of discretion?

DECISION

...D.R.S. contends that the court's action was erroneous because the law provides that an illegitimate child is to carry the mother's name, and there was no evidence to support a change of name. Hence, she maintains that the court abused its discretion in ordering the change. R.S.H. responds that the law vests the court in a paternity action with the power to effect such a change.

...The court's action in changing the child's name was neither contrary to law, against the evidence, nor an abuse of discretion.

D.R.S. leans heavily on certain Indiana statutes as preventing the trial judge from requiring J. to bear the name of his father. There is no Indiana case law on this precise point.

Her main reliance is on Ind. Code §31-4-1-8, which deals with the court's powers in a paternity proceeding. That section of the law simply authorizes the parents of a child born out of wedlock to file a voluntary joint petition requesting that the court establish the child's paternity and make provision for its support. The court, after conducting a hearing, is to "make a finding and enter judgment and make an order in accordance therewith." *Id.* Ind. Code §31-4-1-19, covering the order in a paternity action, provides that "[if] the verdict or finding be against the defendant, the court shall enter a judgment against him, and make an order which shall make adequate provision for the support of the child, taking into consideration the needs of the child and the ability of the defendant to pay." D.R.S. argues that because the law on paternity actions is silent with respect to judicial discretion in general and name changes in particular, the legislature did not intend to authorize changing the child's name in paternity proceedings. In short, she interprets these sections as an exclusive statement of the court's powers in a paternity action, namely, to determine the issues of paternity and support.

D.R.S. construes other Indiana statutes as not permitting name changes in paternity actions. Ind. Code §16-1-16-15 (1976), covering vital statistics, specifies that "[a] child born illegitimate shall be *recorded* under the name of the mother" (emphasis supplied). Other sections of the law authorize a change of surname and birth record for an illegitimate child following its parents' marriage. These statutes, she says, taken together, amount to a legislative directive that an illegitimate child may assume the paternal surname *only* if its parents marry.

We decline to give the statutes the restrictive interpretation which D.R.S. proposes. It is true that neither Ind. Code §31-4-1-8, which creates and prescribes the mode of proceeding in a paternity action, nor Ind. Code §31-4-1-19, which describes the order to be entered in such an action, authorizes a change in the child's name. It is equally true, however, that neither provision proscribes changing the child's name in the context of a paternity proceeding. Those sections of the law which authorize a change of name and birth record after the parents of an illegitimate child marry do not purport to make marriage a condition precedent to changing the name or to provide the exclusive method for appending the unwed father's surname to the child. The use of the word "recorded" in Ind. Code §16-1-16-15 (1976), which requires that an illegitimate child be recorded under its mother's name, refers only to the filing of a birth certificate with the local health officers: While this statute may be viewed as supporting the position that an illegitimate child traditionally takes its mother's name at *birth*, it does not implicitly or explicitly prohibit a subsequent judicial determination that the child's surname should be changed to that of its father. It seems to be designed to reach those situations in which only the mother is involved.

...

Bearing in mind the emerging protection of the unmarried father's parental rights, as well as the underlying purpose of the action to establish paternity, namely, to advance the child's best interests, we turn to a discussion of the law regarding name changes.

At common law and today, in the absence of a statute to the contrary, an individual may change his name at will so long as the change is not effect for a fraudulent purpose. *Petition of Hauptly* (1974), 262 Ind. 150, 312 N.E.2d 857...Ind. Code §34-4-6-1 (1976) provides a procedure by which a name change may be accomplished by court decree. The statute does not repeal the common law rule; it merely furnishes an additional method of effecting a name change.... In *Petition of Hauptly, supra,* our supreme court set forth the responsibility of a court hearing a petition for a change of name:

> The only duty of the trial court upon the filing of such a petition is to determine that there is no fraudulent intent involved. Once having so found, we hold that it is an abuse of judicial discretion to deny any application for a change of name under the statute.

262 Ind. at 153, 312 N.E.2d at 860.

Although Indiana law covers name changes in general, no Indiana court has previously considered the question whether a child's name should be changed over the objection of one of the parents. The problem has arisen in other jurisdictions, however, usually in the context of a mother's petition to change her child's surname from that of her former spouse (the child's biological father) to that of her present spouse. In several cases, the divorced mother has sought leave to change her child's name to her maiden name...or to append her maiden name to the children's paternal surname.... Courts have reached conflicting results. Nevertheless, all agree that the welfare of the child is the paramount consideration in deciding whether a child's name should be changed over the opposition of one parent.... In determining whether a change of name will promote the child's best interests, courts look to various factors.

First, significant consideration is given to the father's interest in having his child bear the paternal surname in accordance with tradition.... [T]he West Virginia Supreme Court [in *Petition of Harris*, 236 S.E.2d 426 (1977)] listed various practical considerations in support of the custom:

> For example, a surname common to both parent and child makes it easier to demonstrate a legal relationship for the purpose of qualifying for benefits with the Social Security Administration upon the death of the father, as an heir in the event of intestate succession, or as the beneficiary of certain types of group insurance policies such as "G.I. Insurance" where the beneficiaries are established by law unless specifically changed by the insured.
>
> In addition, in areas where families live in a given county for successive generations, a family name may be a substantial financial asset. A well-regarded and trusted member of a community may pass on to his children a certain presumption with regard to honor, integrity and fair dealing based upon the conduct of the parents. Regardless of the relationship between the parents, this can be a valuable asset to the children. It may give the children a substantial edge in life when they seek credit, employment, or admission to tightly controlled union, trade, or professional groups. *Of course, all of these benefits could theoretically pass through the female line as well as the male line, but it is not customary. People expect children to bear the surname of their fathers, and as the circuit judge in one of the cases before us so ably pointed out, a child's bearing a woman's maiden name does give fair indication that the child is illegitimate. This may not be the way things ought to be; however, at this stage of our development, it is the way things are....*

236 S.E. 2d. at 429 (emphasis supplied).

Although the case involved a divorced mother's petition to change her son's name to her maiden name, many of the factors enumerated by the court in *Petition of Harris* apply with equal force to the offspring of divorced and unmarried parents, particularly in view of the increasing legislative and judicial recognition of the rights of illegitimate children.

Upholding the tradition of having a child bear the paternal surname promotes the child's welfare not only in a pragmatic way but also in a more subtle, but equally important, fashion: retention of the paternal surname strengthens the father-child relationship.... In *Robinson v. Hansel*, *supra*, the court explained that

> [s]ociety has a strong interest in the preservation of the parental relationship. Even though a divorce decree may terminate a marriage, courts have traditionally tried to maintain and to encourage continuing parental relationships. The link between a father and child in circumstances such as these is uncertain at best, and a change of name could further weaken, if not sever, such a bond.

302 Minn. at 35–36, 223 N.W.2d at 140.

The father-child bond is even more tenuous in the case of an unwed father who has never lived with his child and thus has lacked the opportunity to discharge his paternal responsibilities on a day-to-day basis than in the case of a father whose ongoing relationship with his child has been interrupted by divorce. Hence, society's interest in sustaining the custom of having the child bear the paternal surname is particularly urgent when the situation involves a child born out of wedlock.

It is true that some decisions have afforded minimal consideration to the father's interest in having his child bear the paternal surname. Many of the cases have involved egregious conduct on the part of the father....

In a few cases the assumption of the stepfather's surname has been allowed despite the absence of wrongdoing on the part of the natural father; the courts seem to have been influenced by the child's own preference for the change....

In this case, the father, R.S.H., has not engaged in misconduct which might justify forfeiture of his interest in having J. bear the paternal surname — as has been customary. We have said that the siring of an illegitimate child is not, in itself, a crime. *J.E.G. v. C.J.E.* (Ct.App. 1977), 360 N.E.2d 1030.

R.S.H. has already made payments for the support of J., has testified to his willingness to provide support in the future, and has indicated his desire to exercise visitation rights. J. is not of sufficient age and maturity to voice a preference for or against the proposed change of surname; hence, those cases in which the father's interest has been diminished by virtue of an older child's choice of name are inapplicable. Changing J.'s name to that of his natural father would be consistent with the public policy favoring preservation of the father-child relationship. And, perhaps more importantly, such a change avoids a "fair indication that the child is illegitimate." *Petition of Harris, supra.*

Despite the foregoing rationale, D.R.S. insists that the child should carry the maternal surname because J. will be living with her. Several courts have rejected the argument that a child should forfeit the paternal surname to lessen maternal inconvenience or confusion; the father's interest in having the child bear the paternal surname is deemed more significant than the mother's interest in avoiding embarrassment....

Our decision is not intended to suggest that a mother has no interest in her child's name....

...

...[W]e conclude that when, as here, there is evidence that a natural father acknowledges and supports his child born out of wedlock, takes an interest in the child's welfare, and is not guilty of such wrongdoing as would render retention of his name positively deleterious to the child, requiring the child to bear his surname is not an abuse of discretion.

...

Judgment affirmed

[Judge SULLIVAN's concurring opinion is omitted.]

SHIELDS, Judge, dissenting.

I agree with the majority opinion as I interpret it as holding the trial court had the authority to change J.'s surname if it found, in its discretion, the change in surname was in the child's best interest. However, thereafter I disagree with the majority.

Mother has been employed for over a year and a half as director of operations of a company. She earns $14,500 annually. As of the date of the hearing, she personally has paid in full medical expenses required by the child of over $1,300. She presently carries medical insurance covering the child. She agreed to forego all child support if the child retains her name. Her reason for asking the child's name not be changed is:

> A.... First of all, I am single. I was never married to the defendant, do not intend to be married to the defendant. Should I ever marry again, it is my intention to retain my maiden name. Therefore, I feel that [J.] will never be confused by having the name changed. I feel that — well, [R.S.H.] feels that he will wonder why he doesn't have his father's name and it is my intent to explain the situation to him and that I feel it is best that our names be consistent since he will be living with me.
>
> THE COURT: How do you know that you won't lose custody of him and that he won't go to the father?
>
> THE WITNESS: I beg your pardon.
>
> THE COURT: How do you know that at some point and time in the next eighteen years that you couldn't lose custody and that the custody could go to the father and then there would be confusion.
>
> THE WITNESS: That's always a possibility but I don't feel that my behavior would warrant lose [sic] of custody.
>
> THE COURT: Okay. Go ahead.

Father has paid an unspecified amount of support since the child's birth. He has been employed as a waiter at one restaurant for one and one-half weeks where he anticipates an income of $200 a week. He was previously employed as a waiter for a month at another restaurant. He is willing to pay $25 per week support and is willing to pay one-half of the child's medical bills, past and future, not covered by insurance. His reason for asking the child's name be changed to his is:

> Q. And, would you tell me what name you would like the child to have?
>
> A. [J.C.S.H.]
>
> Q. You would like the child to bear your name?
>
> A. Yes.

In reciting the evidence I have set forth all the evidence presented on the issue of the child's surname, including any evidence that relates to the majority's discussion of the policy considerations involved. However, I wish to make clear that I seriously question the validity of several of these policy considerations.

(1) Traditional use of paternal surname.

This tradition is valid only for legitimate children. The tradition for illegitimate children is that they bear the mother's surname.

(2) Use of paternal surname facilitates establishment of paternal relationship for claims to Social Security benefits, intestate succession, and insurance benefits.

An illegitimate child whose paternity is established may claim Social Security benefits through mother as well as father and may be the beneficiary of certain types of mother's group insurance policies as well as father's where beneficiaries are established by law unless specifically changed by the insured. For purposes of intestate succession an illegitimate child may only inherit through the maternal line unless the child's paternity has been established by law during the lifetime of the father or the putative father marries the mother and acknowledges the child as his own. IC 29-1-2-7 (Burns Code Ed.).

(3) Substantial financial asset of paternal surname.

There is no evidence in this case as to whether or not the paternal surname would indeed constitute an asset to child. I would point out that in today's society there is no just reason to assume the maternal surname will not be as substantial a financial asset as the paternal surname.

(4) Mother's maiden name is an indication of illegitimacy.

The use of mother's maiden name is not an indication of illegitimacy without knowledge that, in fact, the surname is the mother's maiden name. People who know the mother well enough to know her maiden name will doubtless also know whether she has ever been married and whether the child is illegitimate. Others, who do not know mother so well, will not be aware that the name shared by mother and child is actually mother's maiden name and will not be surprised by the fact that mother and child have the same surname. Rather, a child bearing a different name from the mother is as likely, if not more so, to raise inquiry as to the circumstances resulting in the name discrepancy.

(5) Retention of paternal surname strengthens father-child relationship.

In a paternity action there generally is no such relationship; in fact, the relationship is vigorously denied. It is one that is to be established. If a name is important to the strengthening of the father-son relationship, it is just as logical to say it is important to strengthening the mother-son relationship.

(6) Wrongdoing on the part of the father.

I agree with the reasoning of this policy statement as far as it goes; however, this consideration should be extended to encompass the wrongdoing of either parent. In this case there is no evidence as to wrongdoing on the part of either parent.

(7) Child's preference.

I feel this is an important consideration, but it is irrelevant in this case due to the infancy of the child and the lack of evidence presented.

(8) Quid pro quo for obligation of support and maintenance.

This argument assumes the father alone will support the child and completely ignores the fact the mother has a coexisting obligation. IC 31-4-1-2 (Burns Code Ed.). In this case the evidence shows the child will be living

> with the mother who will bear the primary obligation for support. In addition, this policy consideration deals with the interest of the parent in having the child bear his or her name rather than the best interest of the child which is the determining criterion.

In reviewing the above factors it is important to observe they are derived from cases in which a mother sought to change her child's surname from that of her former spouse and the child's biological father, a situation so factually different as to make the factors of questionable validity.

The only evidence presented on the policy consideration which I find to be relevant to the ultimate question — the best interest of the child — is the mother's testimony as set forth above. Father presented no evidence as to the best interest of the child.

Furthermore, in light of the judge's commentary I am forced to reach the opinion that consideration of the child's best interest in this particular proceeding was undermined by the personal opinion of the trial court expressed on the record as follows:

> [Counsel for D.R.S.]: Judge, maybe for the record we should enter our stipulation so Your Honor knows what we have agreed to at this point.
>
> THE COURT: Alright. Fine.
>
> [Counsel for D.P.S.]: For the record, the parties have stipulated...
>
> [Counsel for D.P.S.]: And, subject to the Court approval, he will pay $25.00 per week as child support.... At issue will be the allocation of the medical bills, the visitation and the name of the child, Your Honor.
>
> THE COURT: What do you mean, "the name of the child"?
>
> [Counsel for D.R.S.]: The present name of the child is [J.C.S.] and [D.R.S.] wants the baby to retain her name and [R.S.H.] wants the baby to take his name.
>
> THE COURT: I would take a very dim view on the amount of support if the name is not changed.
>
> [Counsel for D.R.S.]: On the amount of the support?
>
> THE COURT: Uh huh.
>
> [Counsel for D.R.S.]: I am not following you.
>
> THE COURT: Well, I imagine my award so far as the amount the defendant is to pay for support is going to be substantially less if the father doesn't have the right to have that child have his name. If you want me to take a five-minute recess, you might want to discuss that with your client.
>
> [Counsel for D.R.S.]: No, that would not pose any problem with us, Your Honor, and we would be willing to let the Court set the amount of child support.
>
> THE COURT: Because I absolutely think it is absolutely wrong. I am violently opposed to it. If they want to play women's lib, then let them call it all by themselves.
>
> [Evidence concluded.]

> THE COURT: ...The support order will be as agreed to at $25.00 per week.
>
> THE COURT: Well, this women's lib thing just makes me furious and I will put it on the record.

Therefore, I find the trial court abused its discretion in ordering the child's surname changed.

I vote to reverse and remand for a new trial.

COMMENTS

As long as women adopted their husband's name at marriage, no one particularly questioned the common law rule allowing the non-fraudulent use of any name one wished. Movie stars and other well-known women often retained their own names without raising any controversy. When women began to retain their own names in the late 1960s and 1970s, however, as part of the movement for freedom and equality for women, civil servants across the country began to challenge the legality of the practice.

The changed position of women in marriage has found expression in extensive litigation relating to their right to retain their birth names. The result has been increased recognition of that right by federal authorities in the context of filing joint income tax returns or obtaining passports and by many state authorities in other contexts. The practice became more broadly recognized socially in 1984 when Geraldine Ferraro, the first major party candidate for vice-president to be a female, was married to a man with a different last name. On occasion, however, there continue to be difficulties that are harder to fight. For example, joint income tax returns under different last names may be returned by the computers for a closer check, increasing the likelihood of an I.R.S. audit. Hillary Rodham adopted her husband's name — Clinton — when he was fighting to regain the governorship of Arkansas. (After his election to a first term as President, she reinserted "Rodham" as a middle name.) A married couple with different last names may in practice be required to prove their marital status when other couples, where the wife adopted the husband's surname, would not be so required. Moreover, because every state has the power to develop its own notions of the local common law on marital names, there is the problem of fifty-one separate laws of marital names, with different lines of reasoning applied in individual cases. Thus, some states permit variations of the husband's and wife's names in hyphenated form, while other jurisdictions still adhere to the custom that the wife takes the husband's name upon marriage.

In a nation with a high degree of mobility, differences in the law of marital names pose problems. State authorities are often inclined, mainly with respect to voter registration and issuance of driver's licenses, to impose local law on women who have married elsewhere. A married woman could thus face the dilemma of the common law in a particular state being retroactively applied to her and to a marriage contracted in another jurisdiction at an earlier time. State administrative agencies, as well as the courts, are prone to overlook the questions of conflict of laws in this area. Attorneys representing married women in mandamus actions of this sort, perhaps in their zeal to get a ruling on local law, do not argue the conflict of laws question, namely, the right of women not to have different names imposed on them when they cross borders after marriage.

Stuart involved a marriage contracted in Virginia, after which the husband and wife moved to Maryland; yet the question of Virginia law on marital names was never examined. Similarly, in *Davis v. Roos*, 326 So.2d 226 (Fla. Dist. Ct. App. 1976), the court did not even mention the marriage locale of the petitioning wife although the record disclosed that she was originally from Oklahoma and had, after her marriage, legally retained her birth name in Michigan, her state of domicile before moving to Florida. Neither the Florida Department of Highway Safety and Motor Vehicles nor the court checked whether the wife was entitled to retain her birth name under some out-of-state common law. The attorney for the petitioning wife reported that he had never thought of attempting to apply the laws of the state where the marriage took place, and that he had never seen this point argued in cases from other jurisdictions. Although this matter illustrates the unconscious preference for local rules, which counteracts the impact of conflict of laws in family law, it also demonstrates that conflicts are still perceived as being professorial law, at least in large segments of legal practice.

Increasingly it is accepted that a woman may use any name she wishes, with or without her husband's approval. Some states, such a Massachusetts, avoid many administrative problems and avoid sexism by simply asking on the marriage license form what surname each person wishes to use after marriage.

If a married woman may retain her birth name or a new form, such as a hyphenated combination of the husband's and the wife's last names, the question arises as to what names should be given to children. Those states where the question has been addressed have concluded that any name is permissible under common law, even an entirely new one, as long as its adoption does not result in fraud or deceit.

The possibility that children may be given any surname of the parents' choice seems to have inflamed some legislatures even more than the right of women to retain their birth names after marriage. The statute found unconstitutional in *Sydney v. Pingree* was a hasty legislative response to the opinion of the Attorney General of Florida of December 21, 1976, implying that any name was permissible as long as there was no intent to defraud. Some see lurking behind the question of names fundamental value choices relating to the nature of marriage and the balance of power between mothers and fathers.

The trial judge in *D.R.S. v. R.S.H.* clearly believed that important value choices were at stake in deciding to change the name of child from the mother's to the father's at the request of the father and over the strenuous objection of the mother. The tradition of paternal control seemed stronger to him that the tradition that children born to unmarried women bear their mother's names.

REFERENCES

Priscilla Ruth McDougall, *The Right of Women to Determine Their Own Names Irrespective of Marital Status,* 1 FAM. L. REP. 4005 (1974).

Frances Olsen, *The Family and the Market: A Study of Ideology and Legal Reform,* 96 HARV. L. REV. 1497, 1533 and note 134 (1983).

Personal Safety

WARREN v. STATE

Supreme Court of Georgia

255 Ga. 151, 336 S.E.2d 221 (1985)

SMITH, Justice.

"When a woman says I do, does she give up her right to say I won't?"[1] This question does not pose the real question, because rape[2] and aggravated sodomy are not sexual acts of an ardent husband performed upon an initially apathetic wife,[3] they are acts of violence that are accompanied with physical and mental abuse and often leave the victim with physical and psychological damage that is almost always long lasting.[4] Thus we find the more appropriate question: When a woman says "I do" in Georgia does she give up her right to State protection from the violent acts of rape and aggravated sodomy performed by her husband. The answer is no.[5] We affirm.

---

1. Griffin, *In 44 States, It's Legal to Rape Your Wife,* 21 Student Lawyer. Another question posed is: "But if you can't rape your wife, who[m] can you rape?" Freeman, *"But If You Can't Rape Your Wife, Who[m] Can You Rape?"*: The Marital Rape Exemption Re-examined. 15 FAMILY LAW QUARTERLY (1981).

2. "As one author has observed, people have 'trouble with rape' because: [T]he mention of rape makes us all uneasy — for different reasons depending on who we are. It makes men uneasiest of all perhaps, and usually brings forth an initial response of nervous laughter or guffaw-evoking jokes. After all, as far as the normal, but uninformed, man knows, rape is something he might suddenly do himself some night if life becomes too dull. It isn't, of course, but he knows too little about it to realize that.

On the other hand, the thoughtful normal man, after hearing the details of a forcible rape, finds it difficult to believe.... He knows that all thoughts of sex — which he equates with fun, romance, and mutual admiration — would leave him if the woman were *really* struggling to get free.... He does not realize that, to the rapist, the act is not 'love,' nor ardor, and usually not even passion; it is a way of debasing and degrading a woman.... This gives rise to the commonly held view that: 'There is no such thing as rape.'... To most women, [rape] is almost as unreal as it is to most men because they themselves have not experienced it, and few people who have done so are in the habit of talking about it....

At the same time, an occasional newspaper story about a particularly brutal rape-murder makes all women shudder. They wonder if it could possibly happen to them, and if it did, how would they react...." (Emphasis in original.) Massaro, *Experts, Psychology, Credibility, and Rape: The Rape Trauma Syndrome Issue and Its Implications for Expert Psychological Testimony,* 69 MINN. L.R. 395, 399 n. 27 (1985).

3. Georgia has recognized both spouses' right to say "I won't" under the domestic law, by providing that before refusal of sexual intercourse rose to the level of cruel treatment in divorce, the refusal had to be "a denial, that...was wilful, persistent and without justification and done with an intent to cast him off as a husband completely and forever." *Harkness v. Harkness,* 228 Ga. 184, 185, 184 S.E.2d 566 (1971).

4. "When you have been intimately violated by a person who is supposed to love and protect you, it can destroy your capacity for intimacy with anyone else. Moreover, many wife victims are trapped in a reign of terror and experience repeated sexual assaults over a period of years. When you are raped by a stranger you have to live with a frightening memory. When you are raped by your husband, you have to live with your rapist." NATIONAL CENTER ON WOMEN AND FAMILY LAW, CLEARING HOUSE REVIEW, November, 1984, citing Dr. David Finkelhor's testimony and statement in support of H.B. 516 to remove spousal exemption to sexual assault offenses to the Judiciary Committee, New Hampshire State Legislature (Mar. 25, 1981), p. 745.

5. It would be incongruous to find both spouses have a right under the domestic law to refuse a normal and mutual satisfying function of married life, and at the same time find that wives have no protection under the criminal law in the event their husbands engage in the violent conduct defined as rape.

The appellant, Daniel Steven Warren, was indicted by a Fulton County Grand Jury for the rape and aggravated sodomy of his wife. They were living together as husband and wife at the time. The appellant filed a pre-trial general demurrer and motion to dismiss the indictment. After a hearing, the motions were denied. The appellant...filed an application for an interlocutory appeal which was granted by this court.

1. The appellant asserts that there exists within the rape statute an implicit marital exclusion that makes it legally impossible for a husband to be guilty of raping his wife.

Until the late 1970's there was no real examination of this apparently widely held belief. Within the last few years several jurisdictions have been faced with similar issues and they have decided that under certain circumstances a husband can be held criminally liable for raping his wife. See *Commonwealth v. Chretien*, Mass., 417 N.E.2d 1203 (1981); *State v. Smith*, 85 N.J. 193, 426 A.2d 38 (1981); *Smith v. State*, Fla.App., 401 So.2d 1126 (1981); *People v. DeStefano*, 121 Misc.2d 113, 467 N.Y.S.2d 506 (Co.Ct.1983); *State v. Rider*, 449 So.2d 903 (Fla.App. 3 Dist.1984); *Weishaupt v. Commonwealth*, 227 Va. 389, 315 S.E.2d 847 (1984); *People v. Liberta*, 64 N.Y.2d 152, 485 N.Y.S.2d 207, 474 N.E.2d 567 (Ct.App.1984).

What is behind the theory and belief that a husband could not be guilty of raping his wife? There are various explanations for the rule and all of them flow from the common law attitude toward women, the status of women and marriage.

Perhaps the most often used basis for the marital rape exemption is the view set out by Lord Hale[6] in 1 Hale P.C. 629. It is known as Lord Hale's contractual theory. The statement attributed to Lord Hale used to support the theory is: "but a husband cannot be guilty of a rape committed by himself upon his lawful wife, for by their mutual matrimonial consent and contract the wife hath given up herself in this kind unto her husband which she cannot retreat."

There is some thought that the foundation of his theory might well have been the subsequent marriage doctrine of English law, wherein the perpetrator could, by marrying his victim, avoid rape charges. It was thus argued as a corollary, rape within the marital relationship would result in the same immunity.[7]

Another theory stemming from medieval times is that of a wife being the husband's chattel or property. Since a married woman was part of her husband's property, nothing more than a chattel, rape was nothing more than a man making use of his own property.

A third theory is the unity in marriage or unity of person theory that held the very being or legal existence of a woman was suspended during marriage, or at least was incorporated and consolidated into that of her husband. In view of the fact that there was only one legal being, the husband, he could not be convicted of raping himself.

These three theories have been used to support the marital rape exemption. Others have tried to fill the chasm between these three theories with justifications

6. Hale was Chief Justice of the Court of King's Bench from 1671 until 1675 when he resigned at age 66, one year before his death. A book based on his manuscripts was published in 1736, and the first American edition of the book was published in America in 1847, 1 M. Hale, Pleas of the Crown. Although we could not find a Georgia case that cited Hale's implied consent theory, we found a case that gives us a glimpse into Hale's world of more than three hundred years ago. "In 2 P.C. 290, this great judge and illustrious author says, 'But of all difficulties in evidence, there are two sorts of crimes that give the greatest difficulty, namely, rapes and witchcraft,...'" *Smith v. State*, 77 Ga. 705, 712 (1886).

7. The laws in America changed that doctrine, "[t]he general rule apart from statute is that the subsequent marriage of the parties is no bar to a prosecution for rape. [Cit.]..." 9 A.L.R. 339.

for continuing the exemption in the face of changes in the recognition of women, their status, and the status of marriage. Some of the justifications include: Prevention of fabricated charges; Preventing wives from using rape charges for revenge; Preventing state intervention into marriage so that possible reconciliation will not be thwarted. A closer examination of the theories and justifications indicates that they are no longer valid, if they ever had any validity.

Hale's implied consent theory was created[8] at a time when marriages were irrevocable and when all wives promised to "love, honor, and obey" and all husbands promised to "love, cherish, and protect until death do us part." Wives were subservient to their husbands, her identity was merged into his, her property became his property, and she took his name for her own.

There have been dramatic changes in women's rights and the status of women and marriage. Today our State Constitution provides that, "no person shall be deprived of life, *liberty*, or property except by due process," (Emphasis supplied.) Art. I, §I, Par. I, and "protection to *person* and property is the paramount duty of government and shall be impartial and complete. No person shall be denied the equal protection of the laws." (Emphasis supplied.) Art. I, §I, Par. II. Our State Constitution also provides that each spouse has a right to retain his or her own property. Art. I, §I, Par. XXVII. Our statutory laws provide that, "[t]he rights of citizens include, *without limitation*, the following: (1) The right of *personal security*, [and] (2) The right of *personal liberty*..." (Emphasis supplied.) OCGA §1-2-6. Women in Georgia "are entitled to the privilege of the elective franchise and have the right to hold any civil office or perform any civil function as fully and completely as do male citizens." OCGA §1-2-7. Couples who contemplate marriage today may choose either spouse's surname or a combination of both names for their married surname, OCGA §19-3-33.1. No longer is a wife's domicile presumed to be that of her husband, OCGA §19-2-3 and no longer is the husband head of the family with the wife subject to him. OCGA §19-3- 8. Marriages are revocable without fault by either party, OCGA §19-5-3(13); either party, not just the husband, can be required to pay alimony upon divorce, OCGA §19-6-1; and both parties have a joint and several duty to provide for the maintenance, protection, and education of their children, OCGA §19-7-2. Couples may write antenuptial agreements in which they are able to decide, prior to marriage, future settlements, OCGA §19-3-62; and our legislature has recognized that there can be violence in modern family life and it has enacted special laws to protect family members who live in the same household from one another's violent acts, Ga.L.1981, 880; OCGA §19-13-1 *et seq.*

Today, many couples write their own marriage vows in which they specifically decide the terms of their marriage contract. Certainly no normal woman who falls in love and wishes "'to marry, establish a home and bring up children'...a central part of the *liberty* protected by the Due Process Clause, [Cits.]" (Emphasis supplied.) *Zablocki v. Redhail*, 434 U.S. 374, 384, 98 S.Ct. 673, 679, 54 L.Ed.2d 618 (1978), would knowingly include an irrevocable term to her revocable marriage contract that would allow her husband to rape her. Rape "is highly reprehensible, both in a moral sense and in its almost total contempt for the personal integrity

8. Hale cited no legal authority for his proposition, "[t]hus the marital exemption rule expressly adopted by many of our sister states has its [origin] in a bare, extra-judicial declaration made some 300 years ago. Such a declaration cannot itself be considered a definite and binding statement of the common law, although legal commentators have often restated the rule since the time of Hale without evaluating its merits, [cits.]" *State v. Smith*, 85 N.J. 193, 426 A.2d 38, 41 (1981).

and autonomy of the female victim.... Short of homicide, it is the 'ultimate violation of self.'" *Coker v. Georgia*, 433 U.S. 584, 599, 97 S.Ct. 2861, 2869, 53 L.Ed.2d 982 (1977). It is incredible to think that any state would sanction such behavior by adding an implied consent term *to all marriage contracts* that would leave *all* wives with no protection under the law from the "ultimate violation of self," *Coker, supra*, 97 S.Ct. at 2869, simply because they choose to enter into a relationship that is respected and protected by the law. The implied consent theory to spousal rape is without logical meaning, and *obviously conflicts* with our Constitutional and statutory laws and our regard for all citizens of this State.

One would be hard pressed to argue that a husband can rape his wife because she is his chattel. Even in the darkest days of slavery when slaves were also considered chattel, rape was defined as "the carnal knowledge of a female whether free or slave, forcibly and against her will." Georgia Code, §4248, p. 824 (1863). Both the chattel and unity of identity rationales have been cast aside. "Nowhere in the common law world — [or] in any modern society — is a woman regarded as chattel or demeaned by denial of a separate legal identity and the dignity associated with recognition as a whole human being." *Trammel v. United States*, 445 U.S. 40, 52, 100 S.Ct. 906, 913, 63 L.Ed.2d 186 (1980).

We find that none of the theories have any validity. The justifications likewise are without efficacy. There is no other crime we can think of in which *all of the victims are denied protection* simply because someone might fabricate a charge; there is no evidence that wives have flooded the district attorneys with revenge filled trumped-up charges,[9] and once a marital relationship is at the point where a husband rapes his wife, state intervention is needed for the wife's protection.[10]

There never has been an expressly stated marital exemption included in the Georgia rape statute. Furthermore, our statute never included the word "unlawful" which has been widely recognized as signifying the incorporation of the common law spousal exclusion. *Commonwealth v. Chretien*, 388 Mass. 123, 417 N.E.2d 1203, 1208 (1981). A reading of the statute indicates that there is no marital exclusion. "A person commits the offense of rape when he has carnal knowledge of a female forcibly and against her will." OCGA §16-6- 1. We need not decide whether or not a common law marital exemption became part of our old statutory rape law,[11] because the rape statute that was similar to the common law

---

9. "'[E]mbittered and vengeful wives are not rushing to their District Attorney to falsely claim rape in order to gain leverage on their husbands in a divorce. Victims are very reluctant to report the crime.' (Letter from Peter F. Sandrock, Jr., District Attorney, Benton County, Oregon, to The Women's History Research Center, Berkeley, Calif. (July 7, 1980).)" *People v. De Stefano*, 121 Misc.2d 113, 467 N.Y.S.2d 506, 515 (Co.Ct.1983). Furthermore, studies show that the average person finds alleged husband-wife rapes the lowest in credibility, 69 MINN.L.R. n. 63 at 408, and juries convict only 3 of 42 rape suspects in simple rapes, i.e., where there is only one assailant, he is known by the victim, and there is no evidence of extrinsic violence. 69 MINN.L.R. 395, *supra* n. 52 at 405.

10. The state intervenes in cases of assault, OCGA §§16-5-20; 16-5-21 and battery OCGA §§16-5-23; 16-5-24, and in other forms of family violence, OCGA §19-13-1 et seq., and we have recognized that assault and battery are involved in rape. *Hardy v. State*, 159 Ga.App. 854, 285 S.E.2d 547 (1981).

11. If a common law implied consent theory had attached to our earlier statutory crime of rape, it could not have survived because it conflicts with our Constitution and statutory laws. "Courts are organized and established to administer the laws of the land. In their decisions, they are bound to observe and protect those *paramount* laws which they are sworn to *support*. The laws of Georgia may be thus graduated, with reference to their obligation or authority. 1st, The Constitution of the United States. 2nd, Treaties entered into by the Federal Government before, or since, the adoption of the Constitution. 3rd, Laws of the United States, made in pursuance of the Constitution. 4th, The Constitution of the State. 5th, The Statutes of the State. 6th, Provincial Acts that were in force and binding on the 14th day of May, 1776, so far as they are not contrary to the Constitution, laws and form of government of the State. 7th, The Common Law of England, and such of the Statute Laws as were usually in force before the revolution, with the foregoing limitation. It is the peculiar

definition[12] was specifically repealed in 1968, Ga.L. 1968, p. 1338, and our new broader statute, OCGA §16-6-1, was enacted in its place which plainly on its face includes a husband.[13]

...

[The court also found that there is no implicit marital exclusion within the aggravated sodomy statute.]

Judgment affirmed.

All the Justices concur.

COMMENTS

The common expression "rule of thumb" is thought by many to be left over from the days in which the state formally empowered husbands to beat their wives. The husband's thumb provided the measure of the size branch a man could use to "chastise" or "correct" his wife. The practice has been very slow to die.

The formal empowerment of husbands has generally never been considered state intervention into the marital relationship. Yet, of course, these rules did represent significant state intervention into the power relations between husband and wife. Even after the criminal law ceased formally to exempt husbands from the normal operation of criminal prohibitions of personal violence, the general refusal to prosecute combined with doctrines of family tort immunity to leave husbands with the practical power to beat their wives. The notion of husbands' entitlement was replaced with notions of family privacy and references to the state policy against divorce and in favor of reconciliation. This notion — that exempting family violence from the normal deterrence of criminal law will increase the likelihood of reconciliation — continues to have some adherents, despite a striking lack of empirical evidence for any such effect. A more recent justification for continuing a de facto immunity for battering husbands is a kind of "assumption of risk" argument. The fact that the wife seeks reconciliation or that she does not leave the relationship is used to suggest that she does not really want the protection of the law.

One factor that tends to encourage change in this area is a growing recognition that domestic violence often spills into broader violence. Well publicized cases in which the perpetrator of multiple murders began by abusing his wife leads some to hope that preventing wife abuse will come to be seen as an important element of general crime prevention. A large percentage of the young men jailed for violent

---

11. *Continued*

province of the Court to ascertain and declare when any two of these several species of law conflict with each other; and then it follows, as a matter of course, that the less must yield to the *greater.*" *Flint River Steamboat Company v. Foster,* 5 Ga. 194, 204 (1848).

12. "Rape is the carnal knowledge of a female, forcibly and against her will."

13. When our Criminal Code was revised, the drafters relied upon the Illinois Criminal Code and the Model Penal Code. Both Codes included within their rape statutes an explicit marital exemption. "A male person...who has sexual intercourse with a female, not his wife, by force and against her will commits rape." Ill.Rev.Stat. §11.1; "A male who has sexual intercourse with a female not his wife is guilty of rape if;..." Section 213.1 Model Penal Code. Our Legislature could have, but did not, include the words "not his wife." They chose instead to add the words "A person," which broadens the statute and which is in keeping with the enunciated purposes of the code. OCGA §16-1-2.

assault acted against a man committing domestic violence against the young man's mother. When he was a candidate for President, it became widely known, for example, that Bill Clinton as a young man confronted his step-father to stop the abuse of his mother. If the state is not willing to protect women for the sake of the women themselves, perhaps it will protect them as one might protect a canary in a mine — as the first warning sign of a broader danger.

REFERENCE

Frances Olsen, *The Family and the Market: A Study of Ideology and Legal Reform*, 96 HARV. L. REV. 1497 (1983).

Freedom of Movement

MASSACHUSETTS STALKING LAW
1992

Be it enacted by the Senate and House of Representatives in General Court assembled, and by the authority of the same, as follows:

Chapter 265 of the General Laws is hereby amended by adding the following section:

Section. 43. (a) Whoever willfully, maliciously, and repeatedly follows or harasses another person and who makes a threat with the intent to place that person in imminent fear of death or serious bodily injury shall be guilty of the crime of stalking and shall be punished by imprisonment in the state prison for not more than five years or by a fine of not more than one thousand dollars, or imprisonment in the house of correction for not more than two and one-half years or both.

(b) Whoever commits the crime of stalking in violation of a temporary or permanent vacate, restraining, or no-contact order or judgment issued pursuant to sections eighteen, thirty-four B, or thirty-four C of Chapter two hundred and eight; or section thirty-two of Chapter two hundred and nine; or sections three, four, or five of Chapter two hundred and nine A; or sections fifteen or twenty of Chapter two hundred and nine C; or a temporary restraining order or preliminary or permanent injunction issued by the superior court, shall be punished by imprisonment in a jail or the state prison for not less than one year and not more than five years. No sentence imposed under the provisions of this subsection shall be less than a mandatory minimum term of imprisonment of one year.

A prosecution commenced hereunder shall not be placed on file or continued without a finding, and the sentence imposed upon a person convicted of violating any provision of this subsection shall not be reduced to less than the mandatory minimum term of imprisonment as established herein, nor shall said sentence of imprisonment imposed upon any person be suspended or reduced until such person shall have served said mandatory term of imprisonment.

A person convicted of violating any provision of this subsection shall not, until he shall have served the mandatory minimum term of imprisonment established herein, be eligible for probation, parole, furlough, work release or receive any deduction from his sentence for good conduct under sections one hundred and twenty-nine, one hundred and twenty-nine C and one hundred and twenty-nine D of Chapter one hundred and twenty-seven; provided, however, that the commissioner of correction may, on the recommendation of the warden, superintendent, or other person in charge of a correctional institution, grant to said offender a temporary release in the custody of an officer of such institution for the following purposes only: to attend the funeral of next of kin or spouse; to visit a critically ill close relative or spouse; or to obtain emergency medical services unavailable at said institution. The provisions of section eighty-seven of chapter two hundred and seventy-six relating to the power of the court to place certain offenders on probation shall not apply to any person seventeen years of age or over charged with a violation of this subsection. The provisions of section thirty-one of chapter two hundred and seventy-nine shall not apply to any person convicted of violating any provision of this subsection.

(c) Whoever, after having been convicted of the crime of stalking, commits a second subsequent such crime shall be punished by imprisonment in a jail or the state prison for not less than two years and not more than ten years. No sentence imposed under the provisions of this subsection shall be less than a mandatory minimum term of imprisonment of two years.

A prosecution commenced hereunder shall not be placed on file or continued without a finding, and the sentence imposed upon a person convicted of violating any provision of this subsection shall not be reduced to less than the mandatory minimum term of imprisonment as established herein, nor shall said sentence of imprisonment imposed upon any person be suspended or reduced until such person shall have served said mandatory term of imprisonment.

A person convicted of violating any provision of this subsection shall not, until he shall have served the mandatory minimum term of imprisonment established herein, be eligible for probation, parole, furlough, work release or receive any deduction from his sentence for good conduct under sections one hundred and twenty-nine, one hundred and twenty-nine C and one hundred and twenty-nine D of chapter one hundred and twenty-seven; provided, however, that the commissioner of correction may, on the recommendation of the warden, superintendent, or other person in charge of a correctional institution, grant to said offender a temporary release in the custody of an officer of such institution for the following purposes only: to attend the funeral of next of kin or spouse; to visit a critically ill close relative or spouse; or to obtain emergency medical services unavailable at said institution. The provisions of section eighty-seven of chapter two hundred and seventy-six relating to the power of the court to place certain offenders on probation shall not apply to any person seventeen years of age or over charged with a violation of this subsection. The provisions of section thirty-one of chapter two hundred and seventy-nine shall not apply to any person convicted of violating any provision of this section.

(d) For the purposes of this section, "harasses" means a knowing and willful pattern of conduct or series of acts over a period of time directed at a specific person, which seriously alarms or annoys the person. Said conduct must be such as would cause a reasonable person to suffer substantial emotional distress.

COMMENTS

The common law gave husbands the power to control their wife's movements. He chose the marital domicile and her domicile was changed by operation of law. He was entitled to imprison her in his house, or elsewhere. Anyone offering hospitality or assistance to a wife against his wishes could be sued by the husband.

The policy behind the stalking laws represents a dramatic shift. Wives are given a degree of control over the physical movements of their estranged husbands or other people who pose a demonstrable threat to them. The stalking laws may be seen as a kind of memorial to several women who were dramatically murdered by men who had "stalked" them for some time before the murders. It may be hard for most of us to imagine how threatening a stalker — whether known or a stranger — can be to the person targeted. Probably this lack of imagination contributes to the constitutional challenges, thus far largely unsuccessful, that have been launched against stalking laws in several states. Other forms of terrorism, such as airplane hijacking, have not created nearly as many victims and nevertheless have been understood to justify passenger searches and other greater intrusions into civil liberties with fewer objections from civil libertarians.

The Double Standard of Sexual Morality

Another way in which the state has long intervened into the marital relationship and structured family relations is by reinforcing the double standard of sexual morality. While some would argue that the double standard hurts both men and women — men by making sex a scarce commodity and women by inhibiting their sexual freedom — it also ensures that sex is organized to please and benefit men. In the old days, the double standard encouraged men to have multiple sex partners and gain sexual experience, while it divided women between "good" women, who had to be chaste virgins until they married and then monogamous wives, and "bad" women who were available to men and were penalized in multiple ways for that availability. For example, if a woman were not married, her children were stigmatized as "illegitimate," and criminal laws against rape generally protected only women of "chaste" character. The racism of the double standard is evident in court decisions on rape that as late as the twentieth century presume African-American women to be unchaste. Although often overlooked, the role of the state was crucial in encouraging and maintaining this double standard. Although the double standard has been considerably "softened" it remains and the state continues to reinforce it in its "softer" form.

Early definitions of adultery ignored sexual relations between married men and unmarried women; the crime, just like the sin, was to have sexual relations with someone else's wife. The wife as well as her paramour might be blamed, but the wrong was based on the woman's marital status, not the man's. The wife's adultery was one of the earliest grounds upon which a man could obtain a divorce, and until most recent years a husband's adultery was treated as no wrong or as a wrong only if it were flagrant and repeated, whereas a single "indiscretion" by a woman was treated as a serious transgression. For the adulterous wife to take careful precautions against pregnancy provided no excuse or mitigation; the husband's desire to be sure of his parentage provided a convenient excuse for demanding sexual exclusivity. In contrast, a husband was relatively mildly blamed if his extramarital affairs produced "bastard" children that he was then (at least in theory) obliged to support until their maturity, at the expense of his wife and her children. A newlywed husband could sometimes obtain an annulment if the wife were found to be "unchaste" and more certainly if she were pregnant by another man at the time of the marriage. No similar out was provided for the new wife who discovered her husband had concealed his sexual relations with or impregnation of another woman.

A husband was entitled to his wife's sexual and domestic services and could recover for lost "consortium" if some third party were to deprive him of them, as for example by accidentally injuring the wife. Initially a wife had no similar entitlement. The loss of her husband was seen to entail a loss of financial support, but no loss of consortium. Some courts would grant a woman an annulment if the husband refused ever to have sexual intercourse with her or a divorce if he steadfastly refused to impregnate her or even to try, but she had no grounds for complaint if he merely made no effort to please her sexually. He had the right to engage in sexual intercourse with her; her legal right was limited to *requesting* he refrain from exercising his rights on particular occasions, and many wives felt constrained to justify or explain their request, for example by claims of a headache or other physical impairment. A wife's wish to avoid pregnancy was not seen to justify her in putting off intercourse until a less fertile time of the month, even if pregnancy would endanger her life.

This attitude is evidenced in law as late as the early 1970s. A married couple sought to join the *Roe v. Wade* litigation on the basis that the wife's medical condition made most forms of birth control counter-indicated and pregnancy inadvisable. The statute under scrutiny so restricted the availability of abortion to the wife that she and her husband asserted that it restricted their "marital happiness." The Court ignored their implication that they were refraining from sexual intercourse and denied standing. Their objection to the anti-abortion statute was deemed "too speculative" until such time as the wife actually became pregnant. In other words, the U.S. Supreme Court assumed that a woman would continue to have unrestricted sexual intercourse with her husband, even if effective birth control were impossible and pregnancy would endanger her health.

GRISWOLD v. CONNECTICUT

United States Supreme Court
381 U.S. 479 (1965)

Mr. Justice DOUGLAS delivered the opinion of the Court.

Appellant Griswold is Executive Director of the Planned Parenthood League of Connecticut. Appellant Buxton is a licensed physician and a professor at the Yale Medical School who served as Medical Director for the League at its Center in New Haven — a center open and operating from November 1 to November 10, 1961, when appellants were arrested.

They gave information, instruction, and medical advice to *married persons* as to the means of preventing conception. They examined the wife and prescribed the best contraceptive device or material for her use. Fees were usually charged, although some couples were serviced free.

The statutes whose constitutionality is involved in this appeal are §§53-32 and 54-196 of the General Statutes of Connecticut (1958 rev.). The former provides:

> Any person who uses any drug, medicinal article or instrument for the purpose of preventing conception shall be fined not less than fifty dollars or imprisoned not less than sixty days nor more than one year or be both fined and imprisoned.

Section 54-196 provides:

> Any person who assists, abets, counsels, causes, hires or commands another to commit any offense may be prosecuted and punished as if he were the principal offender.

The appellants were found guilty as accessories and fined $100 each, against the claim that the accessory statute as so applied violated the Fourteenth Amendment. The Appellate Division of the Circuit Court affirmed. The Supreme Court of Errors affirmed that judgment. 151 Conn. 544, 200 A.2d 479....

...

Coming to the merits, we are met with a wide range of questions that implicate the Due Process Clause of the Fourteenth Amendment.... We do not sit as a super-legislature to determine the wisdom, need, and propriety of laws that touch economic problems, business affairs, or social conditions. This law, however, operates directly on an intimate relation of husband and wife and their physician's role in one aspect of that relation.

The association of people is not mentioned in the Constitution nor in the Bill of Rights. The right to educate a child in a school of the parents' choice — whether public or private or parochial — is also not mentioned. Nor is the right to study any particular subject or any foreign language. Yet the First Amendment has been construed to include certain of those rights.

By *Pierce v. Society of Sisters*, [268 U.S. 510 (1925)], the right to educate one's children as one chooses is made applicable to the States by the force of the First and Fourteenth Amendments. By *Meyer v. State of Nebraska*, [262 U.S. 390 (1923)], the same dignity is given the right to study the German language in a private school. In other words, the State may not, consistently with the spirit of the First Amendment, contract the spectrum of available knowledge....

In *NAACP v. State of Alabama*, 357 U.S. 449, 462, 78 S.Ct. 1163, 1172, we protected the "freedom to associate and privacy in one's associations," noting that freedom of association was a peripheral First Amendment right. Disclosure of membership lists of a constitutionally valid association, we held, was invalid "as entailing the likelihood of a substantial restraint upon the exercise by petitioner's members of their right to freedom of association." *Ibid.* In other words, the First Amendment has a penumbra where privacy is protected from governmental intrusion. In like context, we have protected forms of "association" that are not political in the customary sense but pertain to the social, legal, and economic benefit of the members. *NAACP v. Button*, 371 U.S. 415, 430–431, 83 S.Ct. 328, 336–337....

Those cases involved more than the "right of assembly" — a right that extends to all irrespective of their race or idealogy. *De Jonge v. State of Oregon*, 299 U.S. 353, 57 S.Ct. 255, 81 L.Ed. 278. The right of "association", like the right of belief (*West Virginia State Board of Education v. Barnette*, 319 U.S. 624, 63 S.Ct. 1178), is more than the right to attend a meeting; it includes the right to express one's attitudes or philosophies by membership in a group or by affiliation with it or by other lawful means. Association in that context is a form of expression of opinion; and while it is not expressly included in the First Amendment its existence is necessary in making the express guarantees fully meaningful.

The foregoing cases suggest that specific guarantees in the Bill of Rights have penumbras, formed by emanations from those guarantees that help give them life and substance. See *Poe v. Ullman*, 367 U.S. 497, 516–522, 81 S.Ct. 1752, 6 L.Ed.2d 989 (*dissenting opinion*). Various guarantees create zones of privacy. The right of association contained in the penumbra of the First Amendment is one, as we have seen. The Third Amendment in its prohibition against the quartering of soldiers "in any house" in time of peace without the consent of the owner is another facet of that privacy. The Fourth Amendment explicitly affirms the "right of the people to be secure in their persons, houses, papers, and effects, against unreasonable searches and seizures." The Fifth Amendment in its Self-Incrimination Clause enables the citizen to create a zone of privacy which government may not force him to surrender to his detriment. The Ninth Amendment provides: "The enumeration in the Constitution, of certain rights, shall not be construed to deny or disparage others retained by the people."

The Fourth and Fifth Amendments were described in *Boyd v. United States*, 116 U.S. 616, 630, 6 S.Ct. 524, 532, 29 L.Ed. 746, as protection against all governmental invasions "of the sanctity of a man's home and the privacies of life." We recently referred in *Mapp v. Ohio*, 367 U.S. 643, 656, 81 S.Ct. 1684, 1692, 6 L.Ed.2d 1081, to the Fourth Amendment as creating a "right to privacy, no less important than any other right carefully and particularly reserved to the people." See Beaney, *The Constitutional Right to Privacy*, 1962 SUP.CT.REV. 212; Griswold, *The Right to be Let Alone*, 55 NW.U.L.REV. 216 (1960).

...

The present case, then, concerns a relationship lying within the zone of privacy created by several fundamental constitutional guarantees. And it concerns a law which, in forbidding the use of contraceptives rather than regulating their manufacture or sale, seeks to achieve its goals by means having a maximum destructive impact upon that relationship. Such a law cannot stand in light of the familiar principle, so often applied by this Court, that a "governmental purpose to control or prevent activities constitutionally subject to state regulation may not be achieved by means which sweep unnecessarily broadly and thereby invade the area of protected freedoms." *NAACP v. Alabama*, 377 U.S. 288, 307, 84 S.Ct. 1302, 1314, 12 L.Ed.2d 325. Would we allow the police to search the sacred precincts of marital bedrooms for telltale signs of the use of contraceptives? The very idea is repulsive to the notions of privacy surrounding the marriage relationship.

We deal with a right of privacy older than the Bill of Rights — older than our political parties, older than our school system. Marriage is a coming together for better or for worse, hopefully enduring, and intimate to the degree of being sacred. It is an association that promotes a way of life, not causes; a harmony in living, not political faiths; a bilateral loyalty, not commercial or social projects. Yet it is an association for as noble a purpose as any involved in our prior decisions.

Reversed.

Mr. Justice GOLDBERG, whom the CHIEF JUSTICE and Mr. Justice BRENNAN join, concurring.

...

My Brother STEWART, while characterizing the Connecticut birth control law as "an uncommonly silly law," *post*, at 1705, would nevertheless let it stand on the ground that it is not for the courts to "substitute their social and economic beliefs for the judgment of legislative bodies, who are elected to pass laws." *Post*, at 1705....

The logic of the dissents would sanction federal or state legislation that seems to me even more plainly unconstitutional than the statute before us. Surely the Government, absent a showing of a compelling subordinating state interest, could not decree that all husbands and wives must be sterilized after two children have been born to them. Yet by their reasoning such an invasion of marital privacy would not be subject to constitutional challenge because, while it might be "silly," no provision of the Constitution specifically prevents the Government from curtailing the marital right to bear children and raise a family. While it may shock some of my Brethren that the Court today holds that the Constitution protects the right of marital privacy, in my view it is far more shocking to believe that the personal liberty guaranteed by the Constitution does not include protection against such totalitarian limitation of family size, which is at complete variance with our constitutional concepts. Yet, if upon a showing of a slender basis of rationality, a law outlawing voluntary birth control by married persons is valid, then, by the same reasoning, a law requiring compulsory birth control also would seem to be valid. In my view, however, both types of law would unjustifiably intrude upon rights of marital privacy which are constitutionally protected.

...

Although the Connecticut birth-control law obviously encroaches upon a fundamental personal liberty, the State does not show that the law serves any "subordinating [state] interest which is compelling" or that it is "necessary...to the accomplishment of a permissible state policy." The State, at most, argues that there is some rational relation between this statute and what is admittedly a legitimate subject of state concern — the discouraging of extra-marital relations. It says that preventing the use of birth-control devices by married persons helps prevent the indulgence by some in such extra-marital relations. The rationality of this justification is dubious, particularly in light of the admitted widespread availability to all persons in the State of Connecticut, unmarried as well as married, of birth-control devices for the prevention of disease, as distinguished from the prevention of conception, see *Tileston v. Ullman*, 129 Conn. 84, 26 A.2d 582. But, in any event, it is clear that the state interest in safeguarding marital fidelity can be served by a more discriminately tailored statute, which does not, like the present one, sweep unnecessarily broadly, reaching far beyond the evil sought to be dealt with and intruding upon the privacy of all married couples....

Finally, it should be said of the Court's holding today that it in no way interferes with a State's proper regulation of sexual promiscuity or misconduct. As my Brother HARLAN so well stated in his dissenting opinion in *Poe v. Ullman, supra,* 367 U.S. at 553, 81 S.Ct. at 1782.

> Adultery, homosexuality and the like are sexual intimacies which the State forbids...but the intimacy of husband and wife is necessarily an essential and accepted feature of the institution of marriage, an institution which the State not only must allow, but which always and in every age it has fostered and protected. It is one thing when the State exerts its power either to forbid extra-marital sexuality...or to say who may marry, but it is quite another when, having acknowledged a marriage and the intimacies inherent in it, it undertakes to regulate by means of the criminal law the details of that intimacy.
>
> ...

ROE v. WADE

United States Supreme Court
410 U.S. 113 (1973)

Mr. Justice BLACKMUN delivered the opinion of the Court.

...

The Texas statutes that concern us here are Arts. 1191–1194 and 1196 of the State's Penal Code, Vernon's Ann. P.C. These make it a crime to "procure an abortion," as therein defined, or to attempt one, except with respect to "an abortion procured or attempted by medical advice for the purpose of saving the life of the mother." Similar statutes are in existence in a majority of the States.

...

The American law. In this country, the law in effect in all but a few States until mid-19th century was the pre-existing English common law. Connecticut, the first State to enact abortion legislation, adopted in 1821 that part of Lord Ellenborough's Act that related to a woman "quick with child." The death penalty was not imposed. Abortion before quickening was made a crime in that State only in 1860. In 1828, New York enacted legislation that, in two respects, was to serve as a model for early anti-abortion statutes. First, while barring destruction of an unquickend fetus as well as a quick fetus, it made the former only a misdemeanor, but the latter second-degree manslaughter. Second, it incorporated a concept of therapeutic abortion by providing that an abortion was excused if it "shall have been necessary to preserve the life of such mother, or shall have been advised by two physicians to be necessary for such purpose." By 1840, when Texas had received the common law, only eight American States had statutes dealing with abortion. It was not until after the War Between the States that legislation began generally to replace the common law. Most of these initial statutes dealt severely with abortion after quickening but were lenient with it before quickening. Most punished attempts equally with completed abortions. While many statutes included the exception for an abortion thought by one or more physicians to be necessary to save the mother's life, that provision soon disappeared and the typical law required that the procedure actually be necessary for that purpose.

Gradually, in the middle and late 19th century the quickening distinction disappeared from the statutory law of most States and the degree of the offense and the penalties were increased. By the end of the 1950's a large majority of the jurisdictions banned abortion, however and whenever performed, unless done to save or preserve the life of the mother. The exceptions, Alabama and the District of Columbia, permitted abortion to preserve the mother's health. Three States permitted abortions that were not "unlawfully" performed or that were not "without lawful justification," leaving interpretation of those standards to the courts. In the past several years, however, a trend toward liberalization of abortion statutes has resulted in adoption, by about one-third of the States, of less stringent laws.

It is thus apparent that at common law, at the time of the adoption of our Constitution, and throughout the major portion of the 19th century, abortion was viewed with less disfavor than under most American statutes currently in effect. Phrasing it another way, a woman enjoyed a substantially broader right to terminate a pregnancy than she does in most States today. At least with respect to the early stage of pregnancy, and very possibly without such a limitation, the opportunity to make this choice was present in this country well into the 19th century. Even later, the law continued for some time to treat less punitively an abortion procured in early pregnancy.

The position of the American Medical Association. The anti-abortion mood prevalent in this country in the late 19th century was shared by the medical profession. Indeed, the attitude of the profession may have played a significant role in the enactment of stringent criminal abortion legislation during that period.

...

The position of the American Public Health Association. In October 1970, the Executive Board of the APHA adopted Standards for Abortion Services...:

> a. Rapid and simple abortion referral must be readily available through state and local public health departments, medical societies, or other non-profit organizations.

...

The position of the American Bar Association. At its meeting in February 1972 the ABA House of Delegates approved, with 17 opposing votes, the Uniform Abortion Act that had been drafted and approved the preceding August by the Conference of Commissioners on Uniform State Laws.

...

VIII

The Constitution does not explicitly mention any right of privacy. In a line of decisions, however, going back perhaps as far as *Union Pacific R. Co. v. Botsford*, 141 U.S. 250, 251, 11 S.Ct. 1000, 1001, 35 L.Ed. 734 (1891), the Court has recognized that a right of personal privacy, or a guarantee of certain areas or zones of privacy, does exist under the Constitution. In varying contexts, the Court or individual Justices have, indeed, found at least the roots of that right in the First Amendment, *Stanley v. Georgia*, 394 U.S. 557, 564, 89 S.Ct. 1243, 1247, 22 L.Ed.2d 542 (1969); in the Fourth and Fifth Amendments, *Terry v. Ohio*, 392 U.S. 1, 8–9, 88 S.Ct. 1868, 1872–1873, 20 L.Ed.2d 889 (1968), *Katz v. United States*, 389 U.S. 347, 350, 88 S.Ct.

507, 510, 19 L.Ed.2d 576 (1967); *Boyd v. United States*, 116 U.S. 616, 6 S.Ct. 524, 29 L.Ed. 746 (1886), see *Olmstead v. United States*, 277 U.S. 438, 478, 48 S.Ct. 564, 572, 72 L.Ed. 944 (1928)(Brandeis, J., dissenting); in the penumbras of the Bill of Rights, *Griswold v. Connecticut*, 381 U.S., at 484–485, 85 S.Ct., at 1681–1682; in the Ninth Amendment, *id.*, at 486, 85 S.Ct. at 1682 (GOLDBERG, J., concurring); or in the concept of liberty guaranteed by the first section of the Fourteenth Amendment, see *Meyer v. Nebraska*, 262 U.S. 390, 399, 43 S.Ct. 625, 626, 67 L.Ed. 1042 (1923). These decisions make it clear that only personal rights that can be deemed "fundamental" or "implicit in the concept of ordered liberty,"...are included in this guarantee of personal privacy. They also make it clear that the right has some extension to activities relating to marriage, *Loving v. Virginia*, 388 U.S. 1, 12, 87 S.Ct. 1817, 1823, 18 L.Ed.2d 1010 (1967); procreation, *Skinner v. Oklahoma*, 316 U.S. 535, 541–542, 62 S.Ct. 1110, 1113–1114, 86 L.Ed. 1655 (1942); contraception, *Eisenstadt v. Baird*, 405 U.S., at 453–454, 92 S.Ct., at 1038–1039; *id.*, at 460, 463–465, 92 S.Ct. at 1042, 1043–1044 (WHITE, J., concurring in result); family relationships, *Prince v. Massachusetts*, 321 U.S. 158, 166, 64 S.Ct. 438, 442, 88 L.Ed. 645 (1944); and child rearing and education, *Pierce v. Society of Sisters*, 268 U.S. 510, 535, 45 S.Ct. 571, 573, 69 L.Ed. 1070 (1925); *Meyer v. Nebraska, supra.*

This right of privacy, whether it be founded in the Fourteenth Amendment's concept of personal liberty and restrictions upon state action, as we feel it is, or, as the District Court determined, in the Ninth Amendment's reservation of rights to the people, is broad enough to encompass a woman's decision whether or not to terminate her pregnancy. The detriment that the State would impose upon the pregnant woman by denying this choice altogether is apparent. Specific and direct harm medically diagnosable even in early pregnancy may be involved. Maternity, or additional offspring, may force upon the woman a distressful life and future. Psychological harm may be imminent. Mental and physical health may be taxed...by child care. There is also the distress, for all concerned, associated with the unwanted child, and there is the problem of bringing a child into a family already unable, psychologically and otherwise, to care for it. In other cases, as in this one, the additional difficulties and continuing stigma of unwed motherhood may be involved. All these are factors the woman and her responsible physician necessarily will consider in consultation.

On the basis of elements such as these, appellant and some *amici* argue that the woman's right is absolute and that she is entitled to terminate her pregnancy at whatever time, in whatever way, and for whatever reason she alone chooses. With this we do not agree. Appellant's arguments that Texas either has no valid interest at all in regulating the abortion decision, or no interest strong enough to support any limitation upon the woman's sole determination, are unpersuasive. The Court's decisions recognizing a right of privacy also acknowledge that some state regulation in areas protected by that right is appropriate. As noted above, a State may properly assert important interests in safeguarding health, in maintaining medical standards, and in protecting potential life. At some point in pregnancy, these respective interests become sufficiently compelling to sustain regulation of the factors that govern the abortion decision. The privacy right involved, therefore, cannot be said to be absolute. In fact, it is not clear to us that the claim asserted by some *amici* that one has an unlimited right to do with one's body as one pleases bears a close relationship to the right of privacy previously articulated in the Court's decisions. The Court has refused to recognize an unlimited right of this kind in the past....

We, therefore, conclude that the right of personal privacy includes the abortion decision, but that this right is not unqualified and must be considered against important state interests in regulation....

Where certain "fundamental rights" are involved, the Court has held that regulation limiting these rights may be justified only by a "compelling state interest."

...

IX

The District Court held that the appellee failed to meet his burden of demonstrating that the Texas statute's infringement upon Roe's rights was necessary to support a compelling state interest, and that, although the appellee presented "several compelling justifications for state presence in the area of abortions," the statutes outstripped these justifications and swept "far beyond any areas of compelling state interest." 314 F.Supp., at 1222–1223. Appellant and appellee both contest that holding. Appellant, as has been indicated, claims an absolute right that bars any state imposition of criminal penalties in the area. Appellee argues that the State's determination to recognize and protect prenatal life from and after conception constitutes a compelling state interest. As noted above, we do not agree fully with either formulation.

A. The appellee and certain *amici* argue that the fetus is a "person" within the language and meaning of the Fourteenth Amendment. In support of this, they outline at length and in detail the well-known facts of fetal development. If this suggestion of personhood is established, the appellant's case, of course, collapses, for the fetus' right to life would then be guaranteed specifically by the Amendment. The appellant conceded as much on reargument. On the other hand, the appellee conceded on reargument that no case could be cited that holds that a fetus is a person within the meaning of the Fourteenth Amendment.

The Constitution does not define "person" in so many words. Section 1 of the Fourteenth Amendment contains three references to "person." The first, in defining "citizens," speaks of "persons" born or naturalized in the United States." The word also appears both in the Due Process Clause and in the Equal Protection Clause. "Person" is used in other places in the Constitution: in the listing of qualifications for Representatives and Senators, Art, I, §2, cl. 2, and §3, cl. 3; in the Apportionment Clause, Art. I, §2, cl. 3; in the Migration and Importation provision, Art. I, §9, cl. 1; in the Emoulument Clause, Art, I, §9, cl. 8; in the Electors provisions, Art. II, §1, cl. 2, and the superseded cl. 3; in the provision outlining qualifications for the office of President, Art. II, §1, cl. 5; in the Extradition provisions, Art. IV, §2, cl. 2, and the superseded Fugitive Slave Clause 3; and in the Fifth, Twelfth, and Twenty-second Amendments, as well as in §§2 and 3 of the Fourteenth Amendment. But in nearly all these instances, the use of the word is such that it has application only postnatally. None indicates, with any assurance, that it has any possible prenatal application.

All this, together with our observation, that throughout the major portion of the 19th century prevailing legal abortion practices were far freer than they are today, persuades us that the word "person," as used in the Fourteenth Amendment, does not include the unborn. This is in accord with the results reached in those few cases where the issue has been squarely presented.

...

This conclusion, however, does not of itself fully answer the contentions raised by Texas, and we pass on to other considerations.

B. The pregnant woman cannot be isolated in her privacy. She carries an embryo and, later, a fetus, if one accepts the medical definitions of the developing young in the human uterus. See *Dorland's Illustrated Medical Dictionary* 478–479, 547 (24th ed. 1965). The situation therefore is inherently different from marital intimacy, or bedroom possession of obscene material, or marriage, or procreation, or education, with which *Eisenstadt* and *Griswold*, *Stanley*, *Loving*, *Skinner* and *Pierce* and *Meyer* were respectively concerned. As we have intimated above, it is reasonable and appropriate for a State to decide that at some point in time another interest, that of health of the mother or that of potential human life, becomes significantly involved. The woman's privacy is no longer sole and any right of privacy she possesses must be measured accordingly.

Texas urges that, apart from the Fourteenth Amendment, life begins at conception and is present throughout pregnancy, and that, therefore, the State has a compelling interest in protecting that life from and after conception. We need not resolve the difficult question of when life begins. When those trained in the respective disciplines of medicine, philosophy, and theology are unable to arrive at any consensus, the judiciary, at this point in the development of man's knowledge, is not in a position to speculate as to the answer.

It should be sufficient to note briefly the wide divergence of thinking on this most sensitive and difficult question. There has always been strong support for the view that life does not begin until live birth. This was the belief of the Stoics. It appears to be the predominant, though not the unanimous, attitude of the Jewish faith. It may be taken to represent also the position of a large segment of the Protestant community, insofar as that can be ascertained; organized groups that have taken a formal position on the abortion issue have generally regarded abortion as a matter for the conscience of the individual and her family. As we have noted, the common law found greater significance in quickening. Physicians and their scientific colleagues have regarded that event with less interest and have tended to focus either upon conception, upon live birth, or upon the interim point at which the fetus becomes "viable," that is, potentially able to live outside the mother's womb, albeit with artificial aid. Viability is usually placed at about seven months (28 weeks) but may occur earlier, even at 24 weeks. The Aristotelian theory of "mediate animation," that held sway throughout the Middle Ages and the Renaissance in Europe, continued to be official Roman Catholic dogma until the 19th century, despite opposition to this "ensoulment" theory from those in the Church who would recognize the existence of life from the moment of conception. The latter is now, of course, the official belief of the Catholic Church. As one brief *amicus* discloses, this is a view strongly held by many non-Catholics as well, and by many physicians. Substantial problems for precise definition of this view are posed, however, by new embryological data that purport to indicate that conception is a "process" over time, rather than an event, and by new medical techniques such as menstrual extraction, the "morning-after" pill, implantation of embryos, artificial insemination, and even artificial wombs.

In areas other than criminal abortion, the law has been reluctant to endorse any theory that life, as we recognize it, begins before live birth or to accord legal rights to the unborn except in narrowly defined situations and except when the rights are contingent upon live birth. For example, the traditional rule of tort law denied recovery for prenatal injuries even though the child was born alive. That rule has been changed in almost every jurisdiction. In most States, recovery is said to be permitted only if the fetus was viable, or at least quick, when the injuries were sustained, though few courts have squarely so held. In a recent development, generally opposed by the commentators, some States permit the parents of a stillborn child to maintain an action for wrongful death because of prenatal injuries. Such an action, however, would appear to be one to vindicate the parents' interest and is thus consistent with the view that the fetus, at most, represents only the potentiality of life. Similarly, unborn children have been recognized as acquiring rights or interests by way of inheritance or other devolution of property, and have been represented by guardians *ad litem*. Perfection of the interests involved, again, has generally been contingent upon live birth. In short, the unborn have never been recognized in the law as persons in the whole sense.

X

In view of all this, we do not agree that, by adopting one theory of life, Texas may override the rights of the pregnant woman that are at stake. We repeat, however, that the State does have an important and legitimate interest in preserving and protecting the health of the pregnant woman, whether she be a resident of the State or a non-resident who seeks medical consultation and treatment there, and that it has still *another* important and legitimate interest in protecting the potentiality of human life. These interests are separate and distinct. Each grows in substantiality as the woman approaches term and, at a point during pregnancy, each becomes "compelling."

With respect to the State's important and legitimate interest in the health of the mother, the "compelling" point, in the light of present medical knowledge, is at approximately the end of the first trimester. This is so because of the now-established medical fact,...that until the end of the first trimester mortality in abortion may be less than mortality in normal childbirth. It follows that, from and after this point, a State may regulate the abortion procedure to the extent that the regulation reasonably relates to the preservation and protection of maternal health. Examples of permissible state regulation in this area are requirements as to the qualifications of the person who is to perform the abortion; as to the licensure of that person; as to the facility in which the procedure is to be performed, that is, whether it must be a hospital or may be a clinic or some other place of less-than-hospital status; as to the licensing of the facility; and the like.

This means, on the other hand, that, for the period of pregnancy prior to this "compelling" point, the attending physician, in consultation with his patient, is free to determine, without regulation by the State, that, in his medical judgment, the patient's pregnancy should be terminated. If that decision is reached, the judgment may be effectuated by an abortion free of interference by the State.

With respect to the State's important and legitimate interest in potential life, the "compelling" point is at viability. This is so because the fetus then presumably has the capability of meaningful life outside the mother's womb. State regulation protective of fetal life after viability thus has both logical and biological justifications. If the State is interested in protecting fetal life after viability, it may go so far as to proscribe abortion during that period, except when it is necessary to preserve the life or health of the mother.

Measured against these standards, Art. 1196 of the Texas Penal Code, in restricting legal abortions to those "procured or attempted by medical advice for the purpose of saving the life of the mother," sweeps too broadly. The statute makes no distinction between abortions performed early in pregnancy and those performed later, and it limits to a single reason, "saving" the mother's life, the legal justification for the procedure. The statute, therefore, cannot survive the constitutional attack made upon it here.

XI

To summarize and to repeat:

1. A state criminal abortion statute of the current Texas type, that excepts from criminality only a *life-saving* procedure on behalf of the mother, without regard to pregnancy stage and without recognition of the other interests involved, is violative of the Due Process Clause of the Fourteenth Amendment.

(a) For the stage prior to approximately the end of the first trimester, the abortion decision and its effectuation must be left to the medical judgment of the pregnant woman's attending physician.

(b) For the stage subsequent to approximately the end of the first trimester, the State, in promoting its interest in the health of the mother, may, if it chooses, regulate the abortion procedure in ways that are reasonably related to maternal health.

(c) For the stage subsequent to viability, the State in promoting its interest in the potentiality of human life may, if it chooses, regulate, and even proscribe, abortion except where it is necessary, in appropriate medical judgment, for the preservation of the life or health of the mother.

...

It is so ordered.

Affirmed in part and reversed in part.

Mr. Justice STEWART, concurring.

...

Mr. Justice REHNQUIST, dissenting.

...

WEBSTER v. REPRODUCTIVE HEALTH SERVICES
United States Supreme Court
492 U.S. 490 (1989)

Chief Justice REHNQUIST announced the judgement of the Court and delivered the opinion of the Court with respect to Parts I, II-A, II-B, and II-C, and an opinion with respect to Parts II-D and III, in which Justice WHITE and Justice KENNEDY join.

This appeal concerns the constitutionality of a Missouri statute regulating the performance of abortions....

I.

...The Act consisted of 20 provisions, 5 of which are now before the Court. The first provision, or preamble, contains "findings" by the state legislature that "[t]he life of each human being begins at conception," and that "unborn children have protectable interests in life, health, and well-being." The Act further requires that all Missouri laws be interpreted to provide unborn children with the same rights enjoyed by other persons, subject to the Federal Constitution and this Court's precedents. Among its other provisions, the Act requires that prior to performing an abortion on any woman whom a physician has reason to believe is 20 or more weeks pregnant, the physician ascertain whether the fetus is viable by performing "such medical examinations and tests as are necessary to make a finding of the gestational age, weight, and lung maturity of the unborn child." The Act also prohibits the use of public employees and facilities to perform or assist abortions not necessary to save the mother's life, and it prohibits the use of public funds, employees, or facilities for the purpose of "encouraging or counseling" a woman to have an abortion not necessary to save her life.

...

II.

Decision of this case requires us to address four sections of the Missouri Act: (a) the preamble; (b) the prohibition on the use of public facilities or employees to perform abortions; (c) the prohibition on public funding of abortion counseling; and (d) the requirement that physicians conduct viability test prior to performing abortions. We address these *seriatim.*

A

...

...[T]he preamble does not by its terms regulate abortion.... *Roe v. Wade* "implies no limitation on the authority of a State to make a value judgement favoring childbirth over abortion." The preamble can be read simply to express that sort of value judgement.

We think the extent to which the preamble's language might be used to interpret other state statutes or regulations is something that only the courts of Missouri can definitively decide. State law has offered protections to unborn children in tort and probate law, and §1.205.2 can be interpreted to do no more than that.... It will be time enough for federal courts to address the meaning of the preamble should it be applied to restrict the activities of appellees in some concrete way.... We therefore need not pass on the constitutionality of the Act's preamble.

B.

Section 188.210 provides that "[i]t shall be unlawful for any public employee within the scope of his employment to perform or assist an abortion, not necessary to save the life of the mother," while §188.215 makes it "unlawful for an public facility to be used for the purpose of performing or assisting an abortion not necessary to save the life of the mother." The Court of Appeals held that these provisions contravened this Court's abortion decisions. 851 F.2d, at 1082–1083. We take the contrary view.

As we said earlier this Term in *DeShaney v. Winnebago County Dept. of Social Services,* 489 U.S. 189, 196, 109 S.Ct. 998, 1003, 103 L.Ed. 2d 249 (1989), "our cases have recognized that the Due Process Clauses generally confer no affirmative right to governmental aid, even where such aid may be necessary to secure life, liberty, or property interests of which the government itself may not deprive the individual." In *Maher v. Roe,* [432 U.S. 464 (1977)], the Court upheld a Connecticut welfare regulation under which Medicaid recipients received payments for medical services related to childbirth, but not for nontherapeutic abortions. The Court rejected the claim that this unequal subsidization of childbirth and abortion was impermissible under *Roe v. Wade....* Relying on *Maher,* the Court in *Poelker v. Doe,* 432 U.S. 519, 521, 97 S.Ct. 2391, 2392 (1977), held that the city of St. Louis committed "no constitutional violation...in electing, as a policy choice, to provide publicly financed hospital services for childbirth without providing corresponding services for nontherapeutic abortions."

More recently, in *Harris v. McRae*, 448 U.S. 297, 100 S.Ct. 2671, 65 L.Ed.2d 784 (1980), the Court upheld "the most restrictive version of the Hyde Amendment," *id.*, at 325, n. 27, 100 S.Ct. at 2692, n. 27, which withheld from States federal funds under the Medicaid program to reimburse the costs of abortions, "'except where the life of the mother would be endangered if the fetus were carried to term.'" *Ibid.* (quoting Pub.L. 94–439, §209, 90 Stat. 1434). As in *Maher* and *Poelker*, the Court required only a showing that Congress' authorization of "reimbursement for medically necessary services generally, but not for certain medically necessary abortions" was rationally related to the legitimate governmental goal of encouraging childbirth. 448 U.S., at 325, 100 S.Ct., at 2692–93.

The Court of Appeals distinguished these cases on the ground that "[t]o prevent access to a public facility does more than demonstrate a political choice in favor of childbirth; it clearly narrows and in some cases forecloses the availability of abortion to women." 851 F.2d. at 1081....

We think that this analysis is much like that which we rejected in *Maher, Poelker*, and *McRae*. As in those cases, the State's decision here to use public facilities and staff to encourage childbirth over abortion "places no governmental obstacle in the path of a woman who chooses to terminate her pregnancy." *McRae*, 448 U.S., at 315, 100 S.Ct., at 2687. Just as Congress' refusal to fund abortions in *McRae* left "an indigent woman with at least the same range of choice in deciding whether to obtain a medically necessary abortion as she would have had if Congress had chosen to subsidize no health care costs at all," *id.*, at 317, 100 S.Ct., at 2688, Missouri's refusal to allow public employees to perform abortions in public hospitals leaves a pregnant woman with the same choices as if the State had chosen not to operate any public hospitals at all. The challenged provisions only restrict a women's ability to obtain an abortion to the extent that she chooses to use a physician affiliated with a public hospital. The circumstance is more easily remedied, and thus considerably less burdensome, than indigency, which "may make it difficult — and in some cases, perhaps, impossible — for some women to have abortions" without public funding. *Maher*, 432 U.S., 474, 97 S.Ct., at 2383....

The Court of Appeals sought to distinguish our cases on the additional ground that "[t]he evidence here showed that all of the public facility's costs in providing abortion services are recouped when the patient pays." 851 F.2d, at 1083. Absent any expenditure of public funds, the court thought that Missouri was "expressing" more than "its preference for childbirth over abortions," but rather was creating an "obstacle to exercise of the right to choose an abortion [that could not] stand absent a compelling state interest." *Ibid.* We disagree.

Maher, Poelker, and *McRae* all support the view that the State need not commit any resources to facilitate abortions, even if it can turn a profit by doing so....

C.

The Missouri Act contains three provisions relating to "encouraging or counseling a woman to have an abortion not necessary to save her life." Section 188.205 states that public employees cannot, within the scope of their employment, engage in such speech; and §188.215 forbids such speech in public facilities. The Court of Appeals did not consider §188.205 separately from §§188.210 and 188.215. It held that all three provisions were unconstitutionally vague and that "the ban on using public funds, employees, and facilities to encourage or counsel a woman to have an abortion is an unacceptable infringement of the woman's fourteenth amendment right to choose an abortion after receiving the medical information necessary to exercise the right knowingly and intelligently." 851 F.2d, at 1079.

Missouri has chosen only to appeal the Court of Appeals' invalidation of the public funding provision, §188.205. *See* Juris. Statement I-II. A threshold question is whether this provision reaches primary conduct, or whether it is simply an instruction to the State's fiscal officers not to allocate funds for abortion counseling. We accept, for the purposes of decision, the State's claim that §188.205 "is not directed at the conduct of any physician or health care provider, private or public," but "is directed solely at those persons responsible for expending public funds."

Appellees contend that they are not "adversely" affected under the State's interpretation of §188.205, and therefore that there is no longer a case or controversy before us on this question. Brief for Appellees 31-32. Plaintiffs are masters of their complaints and remain so at the appellate stage of a litigation. A majority of the Court agrees with appellees that the controversy over §188.205 is now moot, because appellees' argument amounts to a decision to no longer seek a declaratory judgement that §188.205 is unconstitutional and accompanying declarative relief. We accordingly direct the Court of Appeals to vacate the judgement of the District Court with instructions to dismiss the relevant part of the complaint.

D.

Section 188.029 of the Missouri Act provides:

> Before a physician performs an abortion on a woman he has reason to believe is carrying an unborn child of twenty or more weeks gestational age, the physician shall first determine if the unborn child is viable by using and exercising that degree of care, skill, and proficiency commonly exercised by the ordinarily skillful, careful, and prudent physician engaged in similar practice under the same or similar conditions. In making this determination of viability, the physician shall perform or cause to be performed such medical examinations and tests as are necessary to make a finding of the gestational age, weight, and lung maturity of the unborn child and shall enter such findings and determination of viability in the medical record of the mother.

...[T]he parties disagree over the meaning of this statutory provision. The State emphasizes the language of the first sentence, which speaks in terms of the physician's determination of viability being made by the standards of ordinary skill in the medical profession. Appellees stress the language of the second sentence, which prescribes such "tests as are necessary" to make a finding of gestational age, fetal weight, and lung maturity.

The Court of Appeals read §188.029 as requiring that after 20 weeks "doctors *must* perform tests to find gestational age, fetal weight and lung maturity."...

...

We think the viability testing provision makes sense only if the second sentence is read to require only those tests that are useful to making subsidiary findings as to viability. If we construe this provision to require a physician to perform those tests needed to make the three specified findings *in all circumstances*, including when the physician's reasonable professional judgement indicates that the tests would be irrelevant to determining viability or even dangerous to the mother and the fetus, the second sentence of §188.029 would conflict with the first sentence's *requirement* that a physician apply his reasonable professional skill and judgement. It would also be incongruous to read this provision, especially the word "necessary," to require performance of tests irrelevant to the expressed statutory purpose of determining viability. It thus seems clear to us that the Court of Appeals' construction of §188.029 violates well-accepted canons of statutory interpretation used in the Missouri courts....

The viability-testing provision of the Missouri Act is concerned with promoting the State's interest in potential human life rather than in maternal health. Section 188.029 creates what is essentially a presumption of viability at 20 weeks, which the physician must rebut with tests indicating that the fetus is not viable prior to performing an abortion. It also directs the physician's determination as to viability by specifying consideration, if feasible, of gestational age, fetal weight, and lung capacity. The District Court found that "the medical evidence is uncontradicted the a 20-week fetus is *not* viable," and that "23 1/2 to 24 weeks gestation is the earliest point in pregnancy where a reasonable possibility of viability exists." But it also found that there may be a 4-week error in estimating gestational age, which supports testing at 20 weeks.

...

In *Colautti v. Franklin*, 439 U.S. 379 (1979), upon which appellees rely, the Court held that a Pennsylvania statute regulating the standard of care to be used by a physician performing an abortion of a possibly viable fetus was void for vagueness. But in the course of reaching that conclusion, the Court reaffirmed its earlier statement in *Planned Parenthood of Central Missouri v. Danforth*, 428 U.S. 52, 64 (1976), that "the determination of whether a particular fetus is viable is, and must be, a matter for the judgement of the responsible attending physician." The dissent, ignores the statements in *Colautti* that "neither the legislature nor the courts may proclaim one of the elements entering into the ascertainment of viability — be it weeks of gestation or fetal weight or any other single factor — as the determination of when the State has a compelling interest in the life or health of the fetus." To the extent that §188.029 regulates the method for determining viability, it undoubtedly does superimpose state regulation on the medical determination of whether a particular fetus is viable. The Court of Appeals and the District Court thought it unconstitutional for this reason. To the extent the viability tests increase the cost of what are in fact second-trimester abortions, their validity may also be questioned under *Akron*, where the Court held that a requirement that second trimester abortions must be performed in hospitals was invalid because it substantially increased the expense of those procedures.

We think that the doubt cast upon the Missouri statute by these cases is not so much a flaw in the statute as it is a reflection of the fact that the rigid trimester analysis of the course of a pregnancy enunciated in *Roe* has resulted in subsequent cases like *Colautti* and *Akron* making constitutional law in this area a virtual Procrustean bed....

Stare decisis is a cornerstone of our legal system, but it has less power in constitutional cases, where save for constitutional amendments, this Court is the only body able to make needed changes. We have not refrained from reconsideration of a prior construction of the Constitution that has proved "unsound in principle and unworkable in practice." We think the *Roe* trimester framework falls into that category.

In the first place, the rigid *Roe* framework is hardly consistent with the notion of a Constitution cast in general terms, as ours is, and usually speaking in general principles, as ours does. The key elements of the *Roe* framework — trimesters and viability — are not found in the text of the Constitution or in any place else one would expect to find a constitutional principle. Since the bounds of the inquiry are essentially indeterminate, the result has been a web of legal rules that have become increasingly intricate, resembling a code of regulations rather than a body of constitutional doctrine....

In the second place, we do not see why the State's interest in protecting potential human life should come into existence only at the point of viability, and that there should therefore be a rigid line allowing state regulation after viability but prohibiting it before viability. The dissenters in *Thornburgh*, writing in the context of the *Roe* trimester analysis, would have recognized this fact by positing against the "fundamental right" recognized in *Roe*, the State's "compelling interest" in protecting potential human life throughout pregnancy. "[T]he State's interest, if compelling after viability, is equally compelling before viability." *Thornburgh*, 476 U.S., at 795 (WHITE, J., dissenting).

The tests that §188.029 requires the physician to perform are designed to determine viability. The State here has chosen viability as the point at which its interest in potential human life must be safeguarded. It is true that the tests in question increase the expense of abortion, and regulate the discretion of the physician in determining the viability of the fetus. Since the tests will undoubtedly show in many cases that the fetus is not viable, the tests will have been performed for what were in fact second-trimester abortions. But we are satisfied that the requirement of these tests permissibly furthers the State's interest in protecting potential human life, and we therefore believe §188.029 to be constitutional.

The dissent...accuses us, *inter alia*, of cowardice and illegitimacy in dealing with "the most politically divisive domestic legal issue of our time." There is no doubt that our holding today will allow some governmental regulation of abortion that would have been prohibited under the language of cases such as *Colautti v. Franklin*, 439 U.S. 379 (1979), and *Akron v. Akron Center for Reproductive Health Inc., supra.* But the goal of constitutional adjudication is surely not to remove inexorably "politically divisive" issues from the ambit of the legislative process, whereby the people through their elected representatives deal with matters of concern to them. The goal of constitutional adjudication is to hold true the balance between that which the Constitution puts beyond the reach of the democratic process and that which it does not. We think we have done that today. Justice BLACKMUN's suggestion...that legislative bodies, in a Nation where more than half of our population is women, will treat our decision today as an invitation to enact abortion regulations reminiscent of the Dark Ages not only misreads our views but does scant justice to those who serve in such bodies and the people who elect them.

III.

Both appellants and the United States as *amicus curiae* have urged that we overrule our decision in *Roe v. Wade.* The facts of the present case, however, differ from those at issue in *Roe.* Here Missouri has determined that viability is the point at which its interest in potential human life must be safeguarded. In *Roe*, on the other hand, the Texas statute criminalized the performance of *all* abortions, except when the mother's life was at stake. This case affords us no occasion to revisit the holding of *Roe*, which was that the Texas statute unconstitutionally infringed the right to an abortion derived from the Due Process Clause, and we leave it undisturbed. To the extent indicated in our opinion, we would modify and narrow *Roe* and succeeding cases.

Because none of the challenged provisions of the Missouri Act properly before us conflict with the Constitution, the judgement of the Court of Appeals is

Reversed.

Justice O'CONNOR, concurring in part and concurring in the judgement.

...

In its interpretation of Missouri's "determination of viability" provision. Mo.Rev.Stat. §188.029 (1986), the plurality has proceeded in a manner unnecessary to deciding the question at hand. I agree with the plurality that it was plain error for the Court of Appeals to interpret the second sentence of Mo.Rev.Stat. §188.029 as meaning that "doctors *must* perform tests to find gestational age, fetal weight, and lung maturity." (emphasis in original)...

Unlike the plurality, I do not understand these viability testing requirements to conflict with any of the Court's past decisions concerning state regulation of abortion....

It is clear to me that requiring the performance of examinations and tests useful to determining whether a fetus is viable, when viability is possible, and when it would not be medically imprudent to do so, does not impose an undue burden on a women's abortion decision. On this ground alone I would reject the suggestion that §188.029 as interpreted is unconstitutional. More to the point, however, just as I see no conflict between §188.029 and *Colautti* or any decision of this Court concerning a State's ability to give effect to its interest in potential life, I see no conflict between §188.029 and the Court's opinion in *Akron*. The second-trimester hospitalization requirement struck down in *Akron* imposed, in the majority's view, "a heavy, and unnecessary, burden," more than doubling the cost of "women's access to a relatively inexpensive, otherwise accessible, and safe abortion procedure." By contrast, the cost of examinations and tests that could usefully and prudently be performed when a woman is 20–24 weeks pregnant to determine whether the fetus is viable would only marginally, if at all, increase the cost of an abortion. . . .

Moreover, the examinations and tests required by §188.029 are to be performed when viability is possible. This feature of §188.029 distinguishes it from the second-trimester hospitalization requirement struck down by the *Akron* majority. As the Court recognized in *Thornburgh*, the State's compelling interest in potential life postviability renders its interest in determining the critical point of viability equally compelling. Under the Court's precedents, the same cannot be said for the *Akron* second-trimester hospitalization requirement. As I understand the Court's opinion in *Akron*, therefore, the plurality's suggestion today that *Akron* casts doubt on the validity of §188.029, even as the Court has interpreted it, is without foundation and cannot provide a basis for reevaluating *Roe*. Accordingly, because the Court of Appeals misinterpreted Mo.Rev.Stat. §188.029, and because, properly interpreted, §188.029 is not inconsistent with any of this Court's prior precedents, I would reverse the decision of the Court of Appeals.

In sum, I concur in Parts I, II-A, II-B, and II-C of the Court's opinion and concur in the judgement of part II-D.

Justice SCALIA, concurring in part and concurring in the judgement.

I join Parts I, II-A, II-B, and II-C of the opinion of The CHIEF JUSTICE. As to Part II-D, I share Justice BLACKMUN's view, that it effectively would overrule *Roe v. Wade*, 410 U.S. 113 (1973). I think that should be done, but would do it more explicitly. Since today we contrive to avoid doing it, and indeed to avoid almost any decision of national import, I need not set forth my reasons....

...

Justice O'CONNOR's assertion...that a "'fundamental rule of judicial restraint'" requires us to avoid reconsidering Roe, cannot be taken seriously....

...

The real question...is whether there are valid reasons to go beyond the most stingy possible holding today. It seems to me there are not only valid but compelling ones. Ordinarily, speaking no more broadly than is absolutely required avoids throwing settled law into confusion; doing so today preserves a chaos that is evident to anyone who can read and count....

It was an arguable question whether §188.029 of the Missouri law contravened this Court's understanding of *Roe v. Wade,** and I would have examined *Roe* rather than examining the contravention....

Of the four courses we might have chosen today — to reaffirm *Roe*, to overrule it explicitly, to overrule it *sub silentio*, or to avoid the question — the last is the least responsible. On the question of the constitutionality of §188.029, I concur in the judgement of the Court and strongly dissent from the manner in which it has been reached.

Justice BLACKMUN, with whom Justice BRENNAN and Justice MARSHALL join, concurring in part and dissenting in part.

Today, *Roe v. Wade*, 410 U.S. 113 (1973), and the fundamental constitutional right of women to decide whether to terminate a pregnancy, survive but are not secure. Although the Court extricates itself from this case without making a single, even incremental, change in the law of abortion, the plurality and Justice SCALIA would overrule *Roe* (the first silently, the other explicitly) and would return to the States virtually unfettered authority to control the quintessentially intimate, personal, and life-directing decision whether to carry a fetus to term. Although today, no less than yesterday, the Constitution and the decisions of this Court prohibit a State from enacting laws that inhibit women from the meaningful exercise of that right, a plurality of the Court implicitly invites every

---

* ...

Justice O'CONNOR would...uphold the law because it "does not impose an undue burden on a woman's abortion decision."... The fact that the challenged regulation is less costly than what we struck down in *Akron* tells us only that we cannot decide the present case on the basis of that earlier decision. It does not tell us whether the present requirement is an "undue burden," and I know of no basis for determining that this particular burden (or any other for that matter) is "due." One could with equal justification conclude that it is not. To avoid the question of *Roe v. Wade's* validity, with the attendant costs that this will have for the Court and for the principles of self-governance, on the basis of a standard that offers "no guide but the Court's own discretion," *Baldwin v. Missouri*, 281 U. S. 586, 595 (1930)(Holmes, J., dissenting), merely adds to the irrationality of what we do today.

Similarly irrational is the new concept that Justice O'CONNOR introduces into the law in order to achieve her result, the notion of a State's "interest in potential life when viability is possible."... Since "viability" means the mere possibility (not the certainty) of survivability outside the womb, "possible viability" must mean the possibility of a possibility of survivability outside the womb. Perhaps our next opinion will expand the third trimester into the second even further, by approving state action designed to take account of "the chance of possible viability."

state legislature to enact more and more test cases, in the hope that sometime down the line the Court will return the law of procreative freedom to the severe limitations that generally prevailed in this country before January 22, 1973. Never in my memory has a plurality announced a judgement of this Court that so foments disregard for the law and for our standing decisions.

Nor in my memory has a plurality gone about its business in such a deceptive fashion. At every level of its review, from its effort to read the real meaning out of the Missouri statute, to its intended evisceration of precedents and its deafening silence about the constitutional protections that it would jettison, the plurality obscures the portent of its analysis. With feigned restraint, the plurality announces that its analysis leaves *Roe* "undisturbed," albeit "modif[ied] and narrow[ed]." But this disclaimer is totally meaningless. The plurality opinion is filled with winks, and nods, and knowing glances to those who would do away with *Roe* explicitly, but turns a stone face to anyone in search of what the plurality conceives as the scope of a woman's right under the Due Process Clause to terminate a pregnancy free from the coercive and brooding influence of the State. The simple truth is that *Roe* would not survive the plurality analysis, and that the plurality provides no substitute for *Roe*'s protective umbrella.

I fear for the future. I fear for the liberty and equality of the millions of women who have lived and come of age in the 16 years since *Roe* was decided. I fear for the integrity of, and public esteem for, this Court.

. . .

. . . [R]ather than arguing that the text of the Constitution makes no mention of the right to privacy, the plurality complains that the critical elements of the *Roe* framework — trimesters and viability — do not appear in the Constitution and are, therefore, somehow inconsistent with a Constitution cast in general terms. Were this a true concern, we would have to abandon most of our constitutional jurisprudence. As the plurality well knows, or should know, the "critical elements" of countless constitutional doctrines nowhere appear in the Constitution's text. The Constitution makes no mention, for example, of the First Amendment's "actual malice" standard for proving certain libels, *See New York Times v. Sullivan*, 376 U.S. 254 (1964), or of the standard for determining when speech is obscene. *See Miller v. California*, 413 U.S. 15 (1973). Similarly, the Constitution makes no mention of the rational-basis test, or the specific verbal formulations of intermediate and strict scrutiny by which this Court evaluates claims under the Equal Protection Clause. The reason is simple. Like the *Roe* framework, these tests or standards are not and do not purport to be, rights protected by the Constitution. Rather, they are judge-made methods for evaluating and measuring the strength and scope of constitutional rights or for balancing the constitutional rights of individuals against the competing interests of the government.

With respect to the *Roe* framework, the general constitutional principle, indeed the fundamental constitutional right, for which it was developed is the right to privacy, *see, e.g., Griswold v. Connecticut*, 381 U.S. 479 (1965), a species of "liberty" protected by the Due Process Clause, which under our past decisions safeguards the right of women to exercise some control over their own role in procreation. As we recently reaffirmed in *Thornburgh v. American College of Obstetricians and Gynecologists*, 476 U.S. 747 (1986), few decisions are "more basic to individual dignity and autonomy" or more appropriate to that "certain private sphere of individual liberty" that the Constitution reserves from the intrusive reach of government than the right to make the uniquely personal, intimate, and self-defining decision whether to end a pregnancy. It is this general principle, the "'moral fact that a person belongs to himself and not others nor to society as a whole,'" *id.*, at 777, n. 5 (STEVENS, J., concurring), that is found in the Constitution. The trimester framework simply defines and limits that right to privacy in the abortion context to accommodate, not destroy, a State's legitimate interest in protecting the health of pregnant women and in preserving potential human life. Fashioning such accommodations between individual rights and the legitimate interests of government, establishing benchmarks and standards with which to evaluate the competing claims of individuals and government, lies at the very heart of constitutional adjudication. To the extent that the trimester framework is useful in this enterprise, it is not only consistent with constitutional interpretation, but necessary to the wise and just exercise of this Court's paramount authority to define the scope of constitutional rights.

. . .

Finally, the plurality asserts that the trimester framework cannot stand because the State's interest in potential life is compelling throughout pregnancy, not merely after viability. The opinion contains not one word of rationale for its view of the State's interest. This "it-is-so-because-we-say-so" jurisprudence constitutes nothing other than an attempted exercise of brute force; reason, much less persuasion, has no place.

In answering the plurality's claim that the State's interest in the fetus is uniform and compelling throughout pregnancy, I cannot improve upon what Justice STEVENS has written:

> I should think it obvious that the State's interest in the protection of an embryo — even if that interest is defined as "protecting those who will be citizens"... — increases progressively and dramatically as the organism's capacity to feel pain, to exercise pleasure, to survive, and to react to its surroundings increases day by day. The development of a fetus — and pregnancy itself — are not static conditions, and the assertion that the government's interest is static simply ignores this reality... [U]nless the religious view that a fetus is a "person" is adopted...there is a fundamental and well-recognized difference between a fetus and a human being; indeed, if there is not such a difference, the permissibility of terminating the life of a fetus could scarcely be left to the will of the state legislatures. And if distinctions may be drawn between a fetus and a human being in terms of state of interest in their protection — even though the fetus represents one of "those who will be citizens" — it seems to me quite odd to argue that distinctions may not also be drawn between the state interest in protecting the freshly fertilized egg and the state interest in protecting the 9-month-gestated, fully sentient fetus on the eve of birth. Recognition of this distinction is supported not only by logic, but also by history and by our shared experiences. *Thornburgh*, 476 U.S., at 778–779 (footnotes omitted).

See also *Roe*, 410 U.S. at 129–147.

For my own part, I remain convinced, as six other Members of this Court 16 years ago were convinced, that the *Roe* framework, and the viability standard in particular, fairly, sensibly, and effectively functions to safeguard the constitutional liberties of pregnant women while recognizing and accommodating the State's interest in potential human life. The viability line reflects the biological facts and truths of fetal development; it marks that threshold moment prior to which a fetus cannot survive separate from the woman and cannot reasonably and objectively be regarded as a subject of rights or interests distinct from, or paramount to, those of the pregnant woman. At the same time, the viability standard takes account of the undeniable fact that as the fetus evolves into its postnatal form, and as it loses its dependence on the uterine environment, the State's interest in the fetus' potential human life, and in fostering a regard for human life in general, becomes compelling. As a practical matter, because viability follows "quickening" — the point at which a woman feels movement in her womb — and because viability occurs no earlier than 23 weeks gestational age, it establishes an easily applicable standard for regulating abortion while providing a pregnant woman ample time to exercise her fundamental right with her responsible physician to terminate her pregnancy. Although I have stated previously for a majority of this Court that "[c]onstitutional rights do not always have easily ascertainable boundaries," to seek and establish those boundaries remains the special responsibility of this Court. *Thornburgh*, 476 U.S., at 771. In *Roe*, we discharged that responsibility as logic and science compelled. The plurality today advances not one reasonable argument as to why our judgement in that case was wrong and should be abandoned.

...

Justice STEVENS, concurring in part and dissenting in part.

...

In my opinion the preamble to the Missouri statute is unconstitutional for two reasons. To the extent that it has substantive impact on the freedom to use contraceptive procedures, it is inconsistent with the central holding in *Griswold*. To the extent that it merely makes "legislative findings without operative effect," as the State argues, it violates the Establishment Clause of the First Amendment. Contrary to the theological "finding" of the Missouri Legislature, a woman's constitutionally protected liberty encompasses the right to act on her own belief that — to paraphrase St. Thomas Aquinas — until a seed has acquired the powers of sensation and movement, the life of a human being has not yet begun.

PLANNED PARENTHOOD v. CASEY

United States Supreme Court
112 S.Ct. 2791 (1992)

Justice O'CONNOR, Justice KENNEDY, and Justice SOUTER announced the judgment of the Court and delivered the opinion of the Court with respect to Parts I, II, III, V-A, V-C, and VI, an opinion with respect to Part V-E, in which Justice STEVENS joins, and an opinion with respect to Parts IV, V-B, and V-D.

I

Liberty finds no refuge in a jurisprudence of doubt. Yet 19 years after our holding that the Constitution protects a woman's right to terminate her pregnancy in its early stages, *Roe v. Wade*, that definition of liberty is still questioned. Joining the respondents as amicus curiae, the United States, as it has done in five other cases in the last decade, again asks us to overrule *Roe*....

At issue...are five provisions of the Pennsylvania Abortion Control Act of 1982 as amended in 1988 and 1989.... The Act requires that a woman seeking an abortion give her informed consent prior to the abortion procedure, and specifies that she be provided with certain information at least 24 hours before the abortion is performed. §3205. For a minor to obtain an abortion, the Act requires the informed consent of one of her parents, but provides for a judicial bypass option if the minor does not wish to or cannot obtain a parent's consent. §3206. Another provision of the Act requires that, unless certain exceptions apply, a married woman seeking an abortion must sign a statement indicating that she has notified her husband of her intended abortion. §3209. The Act exempts compliance with these three requirements in the event of a "medical emergency," which is defined in §3203 of the Act.... In addition..., the Act imposes certain reporting requirements on facilities that provide abortion services....

...[T]he petitioners...brought this suit seeking declaratory and injunctive relief. Each provision was challenged as unconstitutional on its face. The District Court held all the provisions at issue here unconstitutional.... The Court of Appeals for the Third Circuit affirmed in part and reversed in part, upholding all of the regulations except for the husband notification requirement. 947 F.2d 682 (1991). We granted *certiorari*....

...

After considering the fundamental constitutional questions resolved by *Roe*, principles of institutional integrity, and the rule of stare decisis, we are led to conclude this: the essential holding of *Roe v. Wade* should be retained and once again reaffirmed.

...*Roe*'s essential holding, the holding we reaffirm, has three parts. First is a recognition of the right of the woman to choose to have an abortion before viability and to obtain it without undue interference from the State. Before viability, the State's interests are not strong enough to support a prohibition of abortion or the imposition of a substantial obstacle to the woman's effective right to elect the procedure. Second is a confirmation of the State's power to restrict abortions after fetal viability, if the law contains exceptions for pregnancies which endanger a woman's life or health. And third is the principle that the State has legitimate interests from the outset of the pregnancy in protecting the health of the woman and the life of the fetus that may become a child. These principles do not contradict one another; and we adhere to each.

II

Constitutional protection of the woman's decision to terminate her pregnancy derives from the Due Process Clause of the Fourteenth Amendment. It declares that no State shall "deprive any person of life, liberty, or property, without due process of law." The controlling word in the case before us is "liberty." Although a literal reading of the Clause might suggest that it governs only the procedures by which a State may deprive persons of liberty, for at least 105 years..., the Clause has been understood to contain a substantive component as well, one "barring certain government actions regardless of the fairness of the procedures used to implement them."...

...

Our law affords constitutional protection to personal decisions relating to marriage, procreation, contraception, family relationships, child rearing, and education. *Carey v. Population Services International*, 431 U.S., at 685, 97 S.Ct., at 2016. Our cases recognize "the right of the *individual*, married or single, to be free from unwarranted governmental intrusion into matters so fundamentally affecting a person as the decision whether to bear or beget a child." *Eisenstadt v. Baird, supra,* 405 U.S., at 453, 92 S.Ct., at 1038 (emphasis in original). Our precedents "have respected the private realm of family life which the state cannot enter." *Prince v. Massachusetts,* 321 U.S. 158, 166, 64 S.Ct. 438, 442, 88 L.Ed. 645 (1944). These matters, involving the most intimate and personal choices a person may make in a lifetime, choices central to personal dignity and autonomy, are central to the liberty protected by the Fourteenth Amendment. At the heart of liberty is the right to define one's own concept of existence, of meaning, of the universe, and of the mystery of human life. Beliefs about these matters could not define the attributes of personhood were they formed under compulsion of the State.

These considerations begin our analysis of the woman's interest in terminating her pregnancy but cannot end it, for this reason: though the abortion decision may originate within the zone of conscience and belief, it is more than a philosophic exercise. Abortion is a unique act. It is an act fraught with consequences for others: for the woman who must live with the implications of her decision; for the persons who perform and assist in the procedure; for the spouse, family, and society which must confront the knowledge that these procedures exist, procedures some deem nothing short of an act of violence against innocent human life; and, depending on one's beliefs, for the life or potential life that is aborted. Though abortion is conduct, it does not follow that the State is entitled to proscribe it in all instances. That is because the liberty of the woman is at stake in a sense unique to the human condition and so unique to the law. The mother who carries a child to full term is subject to anxieties, to physical constraints, to pain that only she must bear. That these sacrifices have from the beginning of the human race been endured by woman with a pride that ennobles her in the eyes of others and gives to the infant a bond of love cannot alone be grounds for the State to insist she make the sacrifice. Her suffering is too intimate and personal for the State to insist, without more, upon its own vision of the woman's role, however dominant that vision has been in the course of our history and our culture. The destiny of the woman must be shaped to a large extent on her own conception of her spiritual imperatives and her place in society.

It should be recognized, moreover, that in some critical respects the abortion decision is of the same character as the decision to use contraception, to which *Griswold v. Connecticut, Eisenstadt v. Baird,* and *Carey v. Population Services International,* afford constitutional protection. We have no doubt as to the correctness of those decisions. They support the reasoning in *Roe* relating to the woman's liberty because they involve personal decisions concerning not only the meaning of procreation but also human responsibility and respect for it. As with abortion, reasonable people will have differences of opinion about these matters. One view is based on such reverence for the wonder of creation that any pregnancy ought to be welcomed and carried to full term no matter how difficult it will be to provide for the child and ensure its well-being. Another is that the inability to provide for the nurture and care of the infant is a cruelty to the child and an anguish to the parent. These are intimate views with infinite variations, and their deep, personal character underlay our decisions in *Griswold, Eisenstadt,* and *Carey.* The same concerns are present when the woman confronts the reality that, perhaps despite her attempts to avoid it, she has become pregnant.

...

III

A

The obligation to follow precedent begins with necessity, and a contrary necessity marks its outer limit....[T]he very concept of the rule of law underlying our own Constitution requires such continuity over time that a respect for precedent is, by definition, indispensable.... At the other extreme, a different necessity would make itself felt if a prior judicial ruling should come to be seen so clearly as error that its enforcement was for that very reason doomed.

...[W]hen this Court reexamines a prior holding, its judgment is customarily informed by a series of prudential and pragmatic considerations designed to test the consistency of overruling a prior decision with the ideal of the rule of law, and to gauge the respective costs of reaffirming and overruling a prior case. Thus, for example, we may ask whether the rule has proved to be intolerable simply in defying practical workability...; whether the rule is subject to a kind of reliance that would lend a special hardship to the consequences of overruling and add inequity to the cost of repudiation...; whether related principles of law have so far developed as to have left the old rule no more than a remnant of abandoned doctrine...; or whether facts have so changed or come to be seen so differently, as to have robbed the old rule of significant application or justification....

So in this case we may inquire whether *Roe*'s central rule has been found unworkable; whether the rule's limitation on state power could be removed without serious inequity to those who have relied upon it or significant damage to the stability of the society governed by the rule in question; whether the law's growth in the intervening years has left *Roe*'s central rule a doctrinal anachronism discounted by society; and whether *Roe*'s premises of fact have so far changed in the ensuing two decades as to render its central holding somehow irrelevant or unjustifiable in dealing with the issue it addressed.

1

Although *Roe* has engendered opposition, it has in no sense proven "unworkable"....

2

...Since the classic case for weighing reliance heavily in favor of following the earlier rule occurs in the commercial context..., where advance planning of great precision is most obviously a necessity, it is no cause for surprise that some would find no reliance worthy of consideration in support of *Roe*.

...Abortion is customarily chosen as an unplanned response to the consequence of unplanned activity or to the failure of conventional birth control, and except on the assumption that no intercourse would have occurred but for *Roe*'s holding, such behavior may appear to justify no reliance claim.... This argument would be premised on the hypothesis that reproductive planning could take virtually immediate account of any sudden restoration of state authority to ban abortions.

To eliminate the issue of reliance that easily, however, one would need to limit cognizable reliance to specific instances of sexual activity. But to do this would be simply to refuse to face the fact that for two decades of economic and social developments, people have organized intimate relationships and made choices that define their views of themselves and their places in society, in reliance on the availability of abortion in the event that contraception should fail. The ability of women to participate equally in the economic and social life of the Nation has been facilitated by their ability to control their reproductive lives. See, *e.g.*, R. Petchesky, Abortion and Woman's Choice 109, 133, n. 7 (rev. ed. 1990). The Constitution serves human values, and while the effect of reliance on *Roe* cannot be exactly measured, neither can the certain cost of overruling *Roe* for people who have ordered their thinking and living around that case be dismissed.

3

No evolution of legal principle has left *Roe*'s doctrinal footings weaker than they were in 1973....

...

...The original holding resting on the concurrence of seven Members of the Court in 1973 was expressly affirmed by a majority of six in 1983, see *Akron v. Akron Center for Reproductive Health, Inc.*, 462 U.S. 416, 103 S.Ct. 2481, 76 L.Ed.2d 687 (1983)(*Akron I*), and by a majority of five in 1986, see *Thornburgh v. American College of Obstetricians and Gynecologists*, 476 U.S. 747, 106 S.Ct. 2169, 90 L.Ed.2d 779 (1986), expressing adherence to the constitutional ruling despite legislative efforts in some States to test its limits. More recently, in *Webster v. Reproductive Health Services*, 492 U.S. 490, 109 S.Ct. 3040, 106 L.Ed.2d 410 (1989), although two of the present authors questioned the trimester framework in a way consistent with our judgment today..., a majority of the Court either decided to reaffirm or declined to address the constitutional validity of the central holding of *Roe*....

...

4

We have seen how time has overtaken some of *Roe*'s factual assumptions: advances in maternal health care allow for abortions safe to the mother later in pregnancy than was true in 1973, see *Akron I, supra,* 462 U.S., at 429, n. 11, 103 S.Ct., at 2492, n. 11, and advances in neonatal care have advanced viability to a point somewhat earlier.... But these facts go only to the scheme of time limits on the realization of competing interests, and the divergences from the factual premises of 1973 have no bearing on the validity of *Roe*'s central holding, that viability marks the earliest point at which the State's interest in fetal life is constitutionally adequate to justify a legislative ban on nontherapeutic abortions. The soundness or unsoundness of that constitutional judgment in no sense turns on whether viability occurs at approximately 28 weeks, as was usual at the time of *Roe*, at 23 to 24 weeks, as it sometimes does today, or at some moment even slightly earlier in pregnancy, as it may if fetal respiratory capacity can somehow be enhanced in the future....

5

The sum of the precedential inquiry to this point shows *Roe*'s underpinnings unweakened in any way affecting its central holding. While it has engendered disapproval, it has not been unworkable. An entire generation has come of age free to assume *Roe*'s concept of liberty in defining the capacity of women to act in society, and to make reproductive decisions; no erosion of principle going to liberty or personal autonomy has left *Roe*'s central holding a doctrinal remnant; *Roe* portends no developments at odds with other precedent for the analysis of personal liberty; and no changes of fact have rendered viability more or less appropriate as the point at which the balance of interests tips. Within the bounds of normal *stare decisis* analysis, then, and subject to the considerations on which it customarily turns, the stronger argument is for affirming *Roe*'s central holding, with whatever degree of personal reluctance any of us may have, not for overruling it.

B

[The Court contrasts *Roe* with two cases that it considered properly overruled, *Lochner v. New York*, 198 U.S. 45, 25 S.Ct. 539, 49 L.Ed. 937 (1905), and *Plessy v. Ferguson*, 163 U.S. 537, 16 S.Ct. 1138, 41 L.Ed. 256 (1896). *Lochner* (and *Adkins v. Children's Hospital*, 261 U.S. 525, 43 S.Ct. 394, 67 L.Ed. 785 (1923)) was properly overruled because the Depression demonstrated to most people that *Lochner* and the cases following it "rested on fundamentally false factual assumptions about the capacity of a relatively unregulated market to satisfy minimal levels of human welfare.... [T]he clear demonstration that the facts of economic life were different from those previously assumed warranted the repudiation of the old law." Although *Plessy*, the case that established the "separate but equal" doctrine that was overruled by *Brown v. Board of Education*, "was wrong the day it was decided," it was also significant that "[s]ociety's understanding of the facts...in 1954 was...fundamentally different from the basis claimed for the decision in 1896." The Court pointed out that "the *Plessy* Court's explanation for its decision was so clearly at odds with the facts apparent to the Court in 1954 that the decision to reexamine *Plessy* was on this ground alone not only justified but required."]

...Because neither the factual underpinnings of *Roe*'s central holding nor our understanding of it has changed (and because no other indication of weakened precedent has been shown) the Court could not pretend to be reexamining the prior law with any justification beyond a present doctrinal disposition to come out differently from the Court of 1973. To overrule prior law for no other reason than that would run counter to the view repeated in our cases, that a decision to overrule should rest on some special reason over and above the belief that a prior case was wrongly decided....

C

...

The need for principled action to be perceived as such is implicated to some degree whenever this, or any other appellate court, overrules a prior case....

...

...Where...the Court decides a case in such a way as to resolve the sort of intensely divisive controversy reflected in *Roe* and those rare, comparable cases, its decision has a dimension that the resolution of the normal case does not carry. It is the dimension present whenever the Court's interpretation of the Constitution calls the contending sides of a national controversy to end their national division by accepting a common mandate rooted in the Constitution.

The Court is not asked to do this very often, having thus addressed the Nation only twice in our lifetime, in the decisions of *Brown* and *Roe*. But when the Court does act in this way, its decision requires an equally rare precedential force to counter the inevitable efforts to overturn it and to thwart its implementation. Some of those efforts may be mere unprincipled emotional reactions; others may proceed from principles worthy of profound respect. But whatever the premises of opposition may be, only the most convincing justification under accepted standards of precedent could suffice to demonstrate that a later decision overruling the first was anything but a surrender to political pressure, and an unjustified repudiation of the principle on which the Court staked its authority in the first instance....

The country's loss of confidence in the judiciary would be underscored by an equally certain and equally reasonable condemnation for another failing in overruling unnecessarily and under pressure. Some cost will be paid by anyone who approves or implements a constitutional decision where it is unpopular, or who refuses to work to undermine the decision or to force its reversal. The price may be criticism or ostracism, or it may be violence. An extra price will be paid by those who themselves disapprove of the decision's results when viewed outside of constitutional terms, but who nevertheless struggle to accept it, because they respect the rule of law. To all those who will be so tested by following, the Court implicitly undertakes to remain steadfast, lest in the end a price be paid for nothing. The promise of constancy, once given, binds its maker for as long as the power to stand by the decision survives and the understanding of the issue has not changed so fundamentally as to render the commitment obsolete. From the obligation of this promise this Court cannot and should not assume any exemption when duty requires it to decide a case in conformance with the Constitution. A willing breach of it would be nothing less than a breach of faith, and no Court that broke its faith with the people could sensibly expect credit for principle in the decision by which it did that.

...Like the character of an individual, the legitimacy of the Court must be earned over time. So, indeed, must be the character of a Nation of people who aspire to live according to the rule of law.... If the Court's legitimacy should be undermined, then, so would the country be in its very ability to see itself through its constitutional ideals. The Court's concern with legitimacy is not for the sake of the Court but for the sake of the Nation to which it is responsible.

The Court's duty in the present case is clear. In 1973, it confronted the already-divisive issue of governmental power to limit personal choice to undergo abortion, for which it provided a new resolution based on the due process guaranteed by the Fourteenth Amendment. Whether or not a new social consensus is developing on that issue, its divisiveness is no less today than in 1973, and pressure to overrule the decision, like pressure to retain it, has grown only more intense. A decision to overrule *Roe*'s essential holding under the existing circumstances would address error, if error there was, at the cost of both profound and unnecessary damage to the Court's legitimacy, and to the Nation's commitment to the rule of law. It is therefore imperative to adhere to the essence of *Roe*'s original decision, and we do so today.

IV

...

The woman's right to terminate her pregnancy before viability is the most central principle of *Roe v. Wade.* It is a rule of law and a component of liberty we cannot renounce.

...

Roe established a trimester framework to govern abortion regulations....

...

We reject the trimester framework, which we do not consider to be part of the essential holding of *Roe.* See *Webster v. Reproductive Health Services, supra*, 492 U.S., at 518, 109 S.Ct., at 3056 (opinion of REHNQUIST, C.J.); *id.*, at 529, 109 S.Ct., at 3062 (O'CONNOR, J., concurring in part and concurring in judgment)(describing the trimester framework as "problematic"). Measures aimed at ensuring that a woman's choice contemplates the consequences for the fetus do not necessarily interfere with the right recognized in *Roe*, although those measures have been found to be inconsistent with the rigid trimester framework announced in that case. A logical reading of the central holding in *Roe* itself, and a necessary reconciliation of the liberty of the woman and the interest of the State in promoting prenatal life, require, in our view, that we abandon the trimester framework as a rigid prohibition on all previability regulation aimed at the protection of fetal life. The trimester framework suffers from these basic flaws: in its formulation it misconceives the nature of the pregnant woman's interest; and in practice it undervalues the State's interest in potential life, as recognized in *Roe*.

...[N]ot every law which makes a right more difficult to exercise is, *ipso facto*, an infringement of that right....

...Numerous forms of state regulation might have the incidental effect of increasing the cost or decreasing the availability of medical care, whether for abortion or any other medical procedure. The fact that a law which serves a valid purpose, one not designed to strike at the right itself, has the incidental effect of making it more difficult or more expensive to procure an abortion cannot be enough to invalidate it. Only where state regulation imposes an undue burden on a woman's ability to make this decision does the power of the State reach into the heart of the liberty protected by the Due Process Clause....

...

The very notion that the State has a substantial interest in potential life leads to the conclusion that not all regulations must be deemed unwarranted. Not all burdens on the right to decide whether to terminate a pregnancy will be undue. In our view, the undue burden standard is the appropriate means of reconciling the State's interest with the woman's constitutionally protected liberty.

The concept of an undue burden has been utilized by the Court as well as individual members of the Court, including two of us, in ways that could be considered inconsistent.... Because we set forth a standard of general application to which we intend to adhere, it is important to clarify what is meant by an undue burden.

A finding of an undue burden is a shorthand for the conclusion that a state regulation has the purpose or effect of placing a substantial obstacle in the path of a woman seeking an abortion of a nonviable fetus. A statute with this purpose is invalid because the means chosen by the State to further the interest in potential life must be calculated to inform the woman's free choice, not hinder it. And a statute which, while furthering the interest in potential life or some other valid state interest, has the effect of placing a substantial obstacle in the path of a woman's choice cannot be considered a permissible means of serving its legitimate ends....

...

V

The Court of Appeals applied what it believed to be the undue burden standard and upheld each of the provisions except for the husband notification requirement. We agree generally with this conclusion, but refine the undue burden analysis in accordance with the principles articulated above. We now consider the separate statutory sections at issue.

A

Because it is central to the operation of various other requirements, we begin with the statute's definition of medical emergency. Under the statute, a medical emergency is "[t]hat condition which, on the basis of the physician's good faith clinical judgment, so complicates the medical condition of a pregnant woman as to necessitate the immediate abortion of her pregnancy to avert her death or for which a delay will create serious risk of substantial and irreversible impairment of a major bodily function." 18 Pa.Cons.Stat. (1990). §3203.

...

...[T]he Court of Appeals...stated: "we read the medical emergency exception...to assure that compliance with [Pennsylvania's] abortion regulations would not in any way pose a significant threat to the life or health of a woman."... [A]s construed by the Court of Appeals, the medical emergency definition imposes no undue burden on a woman's abortion right.

B

We next consider the informed consent requirement. 18 Pa. Cons.Stat.Ann. §3205. Except in a medical emergency, the statute requires that at least 24 hours before performing an abortion a physician inform the woman of the nature of the procedure, the health risks of the abortion and of childbirth, and the "probable gestational age of the unborn child." The physician or a qualified nonphysician must inform the woman of the availability of printed materials published by the State describing the fetus and providing information about medical assistance for childbirth, information about child support from the father, and a list of agencies which provide adoption and other services as alternatives to abortion....

...

...It cannot be questioned that psychological well-being is a facet of health. Nor can it be doubted that most women considering an abortion would deem the impact on the fetus relevant, if not dispositive, to the decision. In attempting to ensure that a woman apprehend the full consequences of her decision, the State furthers the legitimate purpose of reducing the risk that a woman may elect an abortion, only to discover later, with devastating psychological consequences, that her decision was not fully informed. If the information the State requires to be made available to the woman is truthful and not misleading, the requirement may be permissible.

We also see no reason why the State may not require doctors to inform a woman seeking an abortion of the availability of materials relating to the consequences to the fetus, even when those consequences have no direct relation to her health. An example illustrates the point. We would think it constitutional for the State to require that in order for there to be informed consent to a kidney transplant operation the recipient must be supplied with information about risks to the donor as well as risks to himself or herself.... [W]e permit a State to further its legitimate goal of protecting the life of the unborn by enacting legislation aimed at ensuring a decision that is mature and informed, even when in so doing the State expresses a preference for childbirth over abortion....

...

Whatever constitutional status the doctor-patient relation may have as a general matter, in the present context it is derivative of the woman's position. The doctor-patient relation does not underlie or override the two more general rights under which the abortion right is justified: the right to make family decisions and the right to physical autonomy.... [A] requirement that a doctor give a woman certain information as part of obtaining her consent to an abortion is, for constitutional purposes, no different from a requirement that a doctor give certain specific information about any medical procedure.

...

Our analysis of Pennsylvania's 24-hour waiting period...requires us to reconsider the premise behind the decision in *Akron* I invalidating a parallel requirement.... The idea that important decisions will be more informed and deliberate if they follow some period of reflection does not strike us as unreasonable, particularly where the statute directs that important information become part of the background of the decision..... In theory, at least, the waiting period is a reasonable measure to implement the State's interest in protecting the life of the unborn, a measure that does not amount to an undue burden.

Whether the mandatory 24-hour waiting period is nonetheless invalid because in practice it is a substantial obstacle to a woman's choice to terminate her pregnancy is a closer question. The findings of fact by the District Court indicate that because of the distances many women must travel to reach an abortion provider, the practical effect will often be a delay of much more than a day because the waiting period requires that a woman seeking an abortion make at least two visits to the doctor. The District Court also found that in many instances this will increase the exposure of women seeking abortions to "the harassment and hostility of anti-abortion protestors demonstrating outside a clinic." 744 F.Supp., at 1351. As a result, the District Court found that for those women who have the fewest financial resources, those who must travel long distances, and those who have difficulty explaining their whereabouts to husbands, employers, or others, the 24-hour waiting period will be "particularly burdensome." *Id.*, at 1352.

These findings are troubling in some respects, but they do not demonstrate that the waiting period constitutes an undue burden. We do not doubt that, as the District Court held, the waiting period has the effect of "increasing the cost and risk of delay of abortions".... Yet, as we have stated, under the undue burden standard a State is permitted to enact persuasive measures which favor childbirth over abortion, even if those measures do not further a health interest....

We also disagree with the District Court's conclusion that the "particularly burdensome" effects of the waiting period on some women require its invalidation. A particular burden is not of necessity a substantial obstacle. Whether a burden falls on a particular group is a distinct inquiry from whether it is a substantial obstacle even as to the women in that group. And the District Court did not conclude that the waiting period is such an obstacle even for the women who are most burdened by it. Hence, on the record before us, and in the context of this facial challenge, we are not convinced that the 24-hour waiting period constitutes an undue burden.

...

C

Section 3209 of Pennsylvania's abortion law provides, except in cases of medical emergency, that no physician shall perform an abortion on a married woman without receiving a signed statement from the woman that she has notified her spouse that she is about to undergo an abortion. The woman has the option of providing an alternative signed statement certifying that her husband is not the man who impregnated her; that her husband could not be located; that the pregnancy is the result of spousal sexual assault which she has reported; or that the woman believes that notifying her husband will cause him or someone else to inflict bodily injury upon her. A physician who performs an abortion on a married woman without receiving the appropriate signed statement will have his or her license revoked, and is liable to the husband for damages.

The District Court heard the testimony of numerous expert witnesses, and made detailed findings of fact regarding the effect of this statute. These included: "...The vast majority of women consult their husbands prior to deciding to terminate their pregnancy.... The 'bodily injury' exception could not be invoked by a married woman whose husband, if notified, would, in her reasonable belief, threaten to (a) publicize her intent to have an abortion to family, friends or acquaintances; (b) retaliate against her in future child custody or divorce proceedings; (c) inflict psychological intimidation or emotional harm upon her, her children or other persons; (d) inflict bodily harm on other persons such as children, family members or other loved ones; or (e) use his control over finances to deprive of necessary monies for herself or her children.... Studies reveal that family violence occurs in two million families in the United States. This figure, however, is a conservative one that substantially understates (because battering is usually not reported until it reaches life-threatening proportions) the actual number of families affected by domestic violence. In fact, researchers estimate that one of every two women will be battered at some time in their life.... A wife may not elect to notify her husband of her intention to have an abortion for a variety of reasons, including the husband's illness, concern about her own health, the imminent failure of the marriage, or the husband's absolute opposition to the abortion.... The required filing of the spousal consent form would require plaintiff-clinics to change their counseling procedures and force women to reveal their most intimate decision-making on pain of criminal sanctions. The confidentiality of these revelations could not be guaranteed, since the woman's records are not immune from subpoena.... Women of all class levels, educational backgrounds, and racial, ethnic and religious groups are battered.... Wife-battering or abuse can take on many physical and psychological forms. The nature and scope of the battering can cover a broad range of actions and be gruesome and torturous.... Married women, victims of battering, have been killed in Pennsylvania and throughout the United States.... Battering can often involve a substantial amount of sexual abuse, including marital rape and sexual mutilation.... In a domestic abuse situation, it is common for the battering husband to also abuse the children in an attempt to coerce the wife.... Mere notification of pregnancy is frequently a flashpoint for battering and violence within the family. The number of battering incidents is high during the pregnancy and often the worst abuse can be associated with pregnancy.... The battering husband may deny parentage and use the pregnancy as an excuse for abuse.... Secrecy typically shrouds abusive families. Family members are instructed not to tell anyone, especially police or doctors, about the abuse and violence. Battering husbands often threaten their wives or her children with further abuse if she tells an outsider of the violence and tells her that nobody will believe her. A battered woman, therefore, is highly unlikely to disclose the violence against her for fear of retaliation by the abuser.... Even when confronted directly by medical personnel or other helping professionals, battered women often will not admit to the battering because they have not admitted to themselves that they are battered.... A woman in a shelter or a safe house unknown to her husband is not 'reasonably likely' to have bodily harm inflicted upon her by her batterer, however her attempt to notify her husband pursuant to section 3209 could accidentally disclose her whereabouts to her husband. Her fear of future ramifications would be realistic under the circumstances.... Marital rape is rarely discussed with others or reported to law enforcement authorities, and of those reported only few are prosecuted.... It is common for battered women to have sexual intercourse with their husbands to avoid being battered. While this type of coercive sexual activity would be spousal sexual assault as defined by the Act, many women may not consider it to be so and others would fear disbelief.... The marital rape exception to section 3209 cannot be claimed by women who are victims of coercive sexual behavior other than penetration. The 90-day reporting requirement of the spousal sexual assault statute...further narrows the class of sexually abused wives who can claim the exception, since many of these women may be psychologically unable to discuss or report the rape for several years after the incident.... Because of the nature of the battering relationship, battered women are unlikely to avail themselves of the exceptions to section 3209 of the Act, regardless of whether the section applies to them." 744 F.Supp., at 1360–1362.

These findings are supported by studies of domestic violence. The American Medical Association (AMA) has published a summary of the recent research in this field, which indicates that in an average 12-month period in this country, approximately two million women are the victims of severe assaults by their male partners. In a 1985 survey, women reported that nearly one of every eight husbands had assaulted their wives during the past year. The AMA views these figures as "marked underestimates," because the nature of these incidents discourages women from reporting them, and because surveys typically exclude the very poor, those who do not speak English well, and women who are homeless or in institutions or hospitals when the survey is conducted. According to the AMA, "[r]esearchers on family violence agree that the true incidence of partner violence is probably *double* the above estimates; or four million severely assaulted women per year. Studies suggest that from one-fifth to one-third of all women will be physically assaulted by a partner or ex-partner during their lifetime." AMA Council on Scientific Affairs, Violence Against Women 7 (1991)(emphasis in original). Thus on an average day in the United States, nearly 11,000 women are severely assaulted by their male partners. Many of these incidents involve sexual assault. *Id.*, at 3-4; Shields & Hanneke, *Battered Wives' Reactions to Marital Rape*, in The Dark Side of Families: Current Family Violence Research 131, 144 (D. Finkelhor, R. Gelles, G. Hataling, & M. Straus eds. 1983). In families where wife-beating takes place, moreover, child abuse is often present as well. Violence Against Women, *supra*, at 12.

Other studies fill in the rest of this troubling picture. Physical violence is only the most visible form of abuse. Psychological abuse, particularly forced social and economic isolation of women, is also common. L. Walker, The Battered Woman Syndrome 27-28 (1984). Many victims of domestic violence remain with their abusers, perhaps because they perceive no superior alternative. Herbert, Silver, & Ellard, *Coping with an Abusive Relationship: I. How and Why do Women Stay?*, 53 J. Marriage & the Family 311 (1991). Many abused women who find temporary refuge in shelters return to their husbands, in large part because they have no other source of income. Aguirre, *Why Do They Return? Abused Wives in Shelters*, 30 J. Nat. Assn. of Social Workers 350, 352 (1985). Returning to one's abuser can be dangerous. Recent Federal Bureau of Investigation statistics disclose that 8.8% of all homicide victims in the United States are killed by their spouse. Mercy & Saltzman,

Fatal Violence Among Spouses in the United States, 1976-85, 79 Am.J.Public Health 595 (1989). Thirty percent of female homicide victims are killed by their male partners. *Domestic Violence: Terrorism in the Home, Hearing before the Subcommittee on Children, Family, Drugs and Alcoholism of the Senate Committee on Labor and Human Resources*, 101st Cong., 2d Sess., 3 (1990).

The limited research that has been conducted with respect to notifying one's husband about an abortion, although involving samples too small to be representative, also supports the District Court's findings of fact. The vast majority of women notify their male partners of their decision to obtain an abortion. In many cases in which married women do not notify their husbands, the pregnancy is the result of an extramarital affair. Where the husband is the father, the primary reason women do not notify their husbands is that the husband and wife are experiencing marital difficulties, often accompanied by incidents of violence. Ryan & Plutzer, *When Married Women Have Abortions: Spousal Notification and Marital Interaction*, 51 J. Marriage & the Family 41, 44 (1989).

This information and the District Court's findings reinforce what common sense would suggest. In well-functioning marriages, spouses discuss important intimate decisions such as whether to bear a child. But there are millions of women in this country who are the victims of regular physical and psychological abuse at the hands of their husbands. Should these women become pregnant, they may have very good reasons for not wishing to inform their husbands of their decision to obtain an abortion. Many may have justifiable fears of physical abuse, but may be no less fearful of the consequences of reporting prior abuse to the Commonwealth of Pennsylvania. Many may have a reasonable fear that notifying their husbands will provoke further instances of child abuse; these women are not exempt from §3209's notification requirement. Many may fear devastating forms of psychological abuse from their husbands, including verbal harassment, threats of future violence, the destruction of possessions, physical confinement to the home, the withdrawal of financial support, or the disclosure of the abortion to family and friends. These methods of psychological abuse may act as even more of a deterrent to notification than the possibility of physical violence, but women who are the victims of the abuse are not exempt from §3209's notification requirement. And many women who are pregnant as a result of sexual assaults by their husbands will be unable to avail themselves of the exception for spousal sexual assault, §3209(b)(3), because the exception requires that the woman have notified law enforcement authorities within 90 days of the assault, and her husband will be notified of her report once an investigation begins. §3128(c). If anything in this field is certain, it is that victims of spousal sexual assault are extremely reluctant to report the abuse to the government; hence, a great many spousal rape victims will not be exempt from the notification requirement imposed by §3209.

The spousal notification requirement is thus likely to prevent a significant number of women from obtaining an abortion. It does not merely make abortions a little more difficult or expensive to obtain; for many women, it will impose a substantial obstacle. We must not blind ourselves to the fact that the significant number of women who fear for their safety and the safety of their children are likely to be deterred from procuring an abortion as surely as if the Commonwealth had outlawed abortion in all cases.

Respondents attempt to avoid the conclusion that §3209 is invalid by pointing out that it imposes almost no burden at all for the vast majority of women seeking abortions. They begin by noting that only about 20 percent of the women who obtain abortions are married. They then note that of these women about 95 percent notify their husbands of their own volition. Thus, respondents argue, the effects of §3209 are felt by only one percent of the women who obtain abortions. Respondents argue that since some of these women will be able to notify their husbands without adverse consequences or will qualify for one of the exceptions, the statute affects fewer than one percent of women seeking abortions. For this reason, it is asserted, the statute cannot be invalid on its face. See Brief for Respondents 83-86. We disagree with respondents' basic method of analysis.

The analysis does not end with the one percent of women upon whom the statute operates; it begins there. Legislation is measured for consistency with the Constitution by its impact on those whose conduct it affects.... The proper focus of constitutional inquiry is the group for whom the law is a restriction, not the group for whom the law is irrelevant.

...The unfortunate yet persisting conditions we document above will mean that in a large fraction of the cases in which §3209 is relevant, it will operate as a substantial obstacle to a woman's choice to undergo an abortion. It is an undue burden, and therefore invalid.

This conclusion is in no way inconsistent with our decisions upholding parental notification or consent requirements.... Those enactments, and our judgment that they are constitutional, are based on the quite reasonable assumption that minors will benefit from consultation with their parents and that children will often not realize that their parents have their best interests at heart. We cannot adopt a parallel assumption about adult women.

We recognize that a husband has a "deep and proper concern and interest...in his wife's pregnancy and in the growth and development of the fetus she is carrying." *Danforth, supra,* at 69, 96 S.Ct., at 2841.... If this case concerned a State's ability to require the mother to notify the father before taking some action with respect to a living child raised by both, therefore, it would be reasonable to conclude as a general matter that the father's interest in the welfare of the child and the mother's interest are equal.

Before birth, however, the issue takes on a very different cast. It is an inescapable biological fact that state regulation with respect to the child a woman is carrying will have a far greater impact on the mother's liberty than on the father's. The effect of state regulation on a woman's protected liberty is doubly deserving of scrutiny in such a case, as the State has touched not only upon the private sphere of the family but upon the very bodily integrity of the pregnant woman. *Cf. Cruzan v. Director, Missouri Dept. of Health,* 497 U.S., at 281, 110 S.Ct., at — —. The Court has held that "when the wife and the husband disagree on this decision, the view of only one of the two marriage partners can prevail. Inasmuch as it is the woman who physically bears the child and who is the more directly and immediately affected by the pregnancy, as between the two, the balance weighs in her favor." *Danforth, supra,* 428 U.S., at 71, 96 S.Ct., at 2842. This conclusion rests upon the basic nature of marriage and the nature of our Constitution: "[T]he marital couple is not an independent entity with a mind and heart of its own, but an association of two individuals each with a separate intellectual and emotional makeup. If the right of privacy means anything, it is the right of the *individual,* married or single, to be free from unwarranted governmental intrusion into matters so fundamentally affecting a person as the decision whether to bear or beget a child." *Eisenstadt v. Baird,* 405 U.S., at 453, 92 S.Ct., at

1038 (emphasis in original). The Constitution protects individuals, men and women alike, from unjustified state interference, even when that interference is enacted into law for the benefit of their spouses.

There was a time, not so long ago, when a different understanding of the family and of the Constitution prevailed. In *Bradwell v. Illinois*, 16 Wall. 130, 21 L.Ed. 442 (1873), three Members of this Court reaffirmed the common-law principle that "a woman had no legal existence separate from her husband, who was regarded as her head and representative in the social state; and, notwithstanding some recent modifications of this civil status, many of the special rules of law flowing from and dependent upon this cardinal principle still exist in full force in most States." *Id.*, at 141 (Bradley J., joined by Swayne and Field, JJ., concurring in judgment). Only one generation has passed since this Court observed that "woman is still regarded as the center of home and family life," with attendant "special responsibilities" that precluded full and independent legal status under the Constitution. *Hoyt v. Florida*, 368 U.S. 57, 62, 82 S.Ct. 159, 162, 7 L.Ed.2d 118 (1961). These views, of course, are no longer consistent with our understanding of the family, the individual, or the Constitution.

...For the great many women who are victims of abuse inflicted by their husbands, or whose children are the victims of such abuse, a spousal notice requirement enables the husband to wield an effective veto over his wife's decision. Whether the prospect of notification itself deters such women from seeking abortions, or whether the husband, through physical force or psychological pressure or economic coercion, prevents his wife from obtaining an abortion until it is too late, the notice requirement will often be tantamount to the veto found unconstitutional in *Danforth*. The women most affected by this law — those who most reasonably fear the consequences of notifying their husbands that they are pregnant — are in the gravest danger.

The husband's interest in the life of the child his wife is carrying does not permit the State to empower him with this troubling degree of authority over his wife. The contrary view leads to consequences reminiscent of the common law. A husband has no enforceable right to require a wife to advise him before she exercises her personal choices. If a husband's interest in the potential life of the child outweighs a wife's liberty, the State could require a married woman to notify her husband before she uses a postfertilization contraceptive. Perhaps next in line would be a statute requiring pregnant married women to notify their husbands before engaging in conduct causing risks to the fetus. After all, if the husband's interest in the fetus' safety is a sufficient predicate for state regulation, the State could reasonably conclude that pregnant wives should notify their husbands before drinking alcohol or smoking. Perhaps married women should notify their husbands before using contraceptives or before undergoing any type of surgery that may have complications affecting the husband's interest in his wife's reproductive organs. And if a husband's interest justifies notice in any of these cases, one might reasonably argue that it justifies exactly what the *Danforth* Court held it did not justify — a requirement of the husband's consent as well. A State may not give to a man the kind of dominion over his wife that parents exercise over their children.

Section 3209 embodies a view of marriage consonant with the common-law status of married women but repugnant to our present understanding of marriage and of the nature of the rights secured by the Constitution. Women do not lose their constitutionally protected liberty when they marry. The Constitution protects all individuals, male or female, married or unmarried, from the abuse of governmental power, even where that power is employed for the supposed benefit of a member of the individual's family. These considerations confirm our conclusion that §3209 is invalid.

D

We next consider the parental consent provision....

...

The only argument made by petitioners respecting this provision and to which our prior decisions do not speak is the contention that the parental consent requirement is invalid because it requires informed parental consent. For the most part, petitioners' argument is a reprise of their argument with respect to the informed consent requirement in general, and we reject it for the reasons given above....

E

...

For each abortion performed, a report must be filed identifying: the physician (and the second physician where required); the facility; the referring physician or agency; the woman's age; the number of prior pregnancies and prior abortions she has had; gestational age; the type of abortion procedure; the date of the abortion; whether there were any pre-existing medical conditions which would complicate pregnancy; medical complications with the abortion; where applicable, the basis for the determination that the abortion was medically necessary; the weight of the aborted fetus; and whether the woman was married, and if so, whether notice was provided or the basis for the failure to give notice. Every abortion facility must also file quarterly reports showing the number of abortions performed broken down by trimester. See 18 Pa.Cons.Stat. §§3207, 3214 (1990). In all events, the identity of each woman who has had an abortion remains confidential.

In *Danforth*, 428 U.S., at 80, 96 S.Ct., at 2846, we held that recordkeeping and reporting provisions "that are reasonably directed to the preservation of maternal health and that properly respect a patient's confidentiality and privacy are permissible." We think that under this standard, all the provisions at issue here except that relating to spousal notice are constitutional. Although they do not relate to the State's interest in informing the woman's choice, they do relate to health. The collection of information with respect to actual patients is a vital element of medical research, and so it cannot be said that the requirements serve no purpose other than to make abortions more difficult. Nor do we find that the requirements impose a substantial obstacle to a woman's choice. At most they might increase the cost of some abortions by a slight amount. While at some point increased cost could become a substantial obstacle, there is no such showing on the record before us.

...

VI

Our Constitution is a covenant running from the first generation of Americans to us and then to future generations. It is a coherent succession. Each generation must learn anew that the Constitution's written terms embody ideas and aspirations that must survive more ages than one. We accept our responsibility not to retreat from interpreting the full meaning of the covenant in light of all of our precedents. We invoke it once again to define the freedom guaranteed by the Constitution's own promise, the promise of liberty.

...

[Appendix omitted.]

Justice STEVENS, concurring in part and dissenting in part.

The portions of the Court's opinion that I have joined are more important than those with which I disagree. I shall therefore first comment on significant areas of agreement, and then explain the limited character of my disagreement.

I

The Court is unquestionably correct in concluding that the doctrine of stare decisis has controlling significance in a case of this kind.... The societal costs of overruling *Roe* at this late date would be enormous. *Roe* is an integral part of a correct understanding of both the concept of liberty and the basic equality of men and women.

...

II

My disagreement with the joint opinion begins with its understanding of the trimester framework established in *Roe.* Contrary to the suggestion of the joint opinion, ante, at 2823, it is not a "contradiction" to recognize that the State may have a legitimate interest in potential human life and, at the same time, to conclude that that interest does not justify the regulation of abortion before viability (although other interests, such as maternal health, may). The fact that the State's interest is legitimate does not tell us when, if ever, that interest outweighs the pregnant woman's interest in personal liberty. It is appropriate, therefore, to consider more carefully the nature of the interests at stake.

First, it is clear that, in order to be legitimate, the State's interest must be secular; consistent with the First Amendment the State may not promote a theological or sectarian interest....

...[T]he interest in protecting potential life is not grounded in the Constitution. It is, instead, an indirect interest supported by both humanitarian and pragmatic concerns....

In counterpoise is the woman's constitutional interest in liberty.... "Our whole constitutional heritage rebels at the thought of giving government the power to control men's minds." *Stanley v. Georgia,* 394 U.S. 557, 565, 89 S.Ct. 1243, 1248, 22 L.Ed.2d 542 (1969). The same holds true for the power to control women's bodies.

The woman's constitutional liberty interest also involves her freedom to decide matters of the highest privacy and the most personal nature.... A woman considering abortion faces "a difficult choice having serious and personal consequences of major importance to her own future — perhaps to the salvation of her own immortal soul." *Thornburgh,* 476 U.S., at 781, 106 S.Ct., at 2189. The authority to make such traumatic and yet empowering decisions is an element of basic human dignity. As the joint opinion so eloquently demonstrates, a woman's decision to terminate her pregnancy is nothing less than a matter of conscience.

Weighing the State's interest in potential life and the woman's liberty interest, I agree with the joint opinion that the State may "'expres[s] a preference for normal childbirth,'" that the State may take steps to ensure that a woman's choice "is thoughtful and informed," and that "States are free to enact laws to provide a reasonable framework for a woman to make a decision that has such profound and lasting meaning." Ante, at 2818. Serious questions arise, however, when a State attempts to "persuade the woman to choose childbirth over abortion." Ante, at 2821. Decisional autonomy must limit the State's power to inject into a woman's most personal deliberations its own views of what is best. The State may promote its preferences by funding childbirth, by creating and maintaining alternatives to abortion, and by espousing the virtues of family; but it must respect the individual's freedom to make such judgments.

...

In my opinion...§§3205(a)(2)(i)-(iii) of the Pennsylvania statute are unconstitutional. Those sections require a physician or counselor to provide the woman with a range of materials clearly designed to persuade her to choose not to undergo the abortion. While the State is free...to produce and disseminate such material, the State may not inject such information into the woman's deliberations just as she is weighing such an important choice.

Under this same analysis, §§3205(a)(1)(i) and (iii) of the Pennsylvania statute are constitutional. Those sections, which require the physician to inform a woman of the nature and risks of the abortion procedure and the medical risks of carrying to term, are neutral requirements comparable to those imposed in other medical procedures. Those sections indicate no effort by the State to influence the woman's choice in any way. If anything, such requirements enhance, rather than skew, the woman's decisionmaking.

III

The 24-hour waiting period required by §§3205(a)(1)-(2) of the Pennsylvania statute raises even more serious concerns. Such a requirement arguably furthers the State's interests in two ways, neither of which is constitutionally permissible.

First, it may be argued that the 24-hour delay is justified by the mere fact that it is likely to reduce the number of abortions, thus furthering the State's interest in potential life. But such an argument would justify any form of coercion that placed an obstacle in the woman's path. The State cannot further its interests by simply wearing down the ability of the pregnant woman to exercise her constitutional right.

Second, it can more reasonably be argued that the 24-hour delay furthers the State's interest in ensuring that the woman's decision is informed and thoughtful. But there is no evidence that the mandated delay benefits women or that it is necessary to enable the physician to convey any relevant information to the patient. The mandatory delay thus appears to rest on outmoded and unacceptable assumptions about the decisionmaking capacity of women. While there are well-established and consistently maintained reasons for the State to view with skepticism the ability of minors to make decisions, see *Hodgson v. Minnesota*, 497 U.S. 417, 449, 110 S.Ct. 2926, — —, 111 L.Ed.2d 344 (1990), none of those reasons applies to an adult woman's decisionmaking ability. Just as we have left behind the belief that a woman must consult her husband before undertaking serious matters, see ante, at 2830–2831, so we must reject the notion that a woman is less capable of deciding matters of gravity. *Cf. Reed v. Reed*, 404 U.S. 71, 92 S.Ct. 251, 30 L.Ed.2d 225 (1971).

...

Part of the constitutional liberty to choose is the equal dignity to which each of us is entitled. A woman who decides to terminate her pregnancy is entitled to the same respect as a woman who decides to carry the fetus to term. The mandatory waiting period denies women that equal respect.

IV

In my opinion, a correct application of the "undue burden" standard leads to the same conclusion concerning the constitutionality of these requirements. A state-imposed burden on the exercise of a constitutional right is measured both by its effects and by its character: A burden may be "undue" either because the burden is too severe or because it lacks a legitimate, rational justification.

The 24-hour delay requirement fails both parts of this test. The findings of the District Court establish the severity of the burden that the 24-hour delay imposes on many pregnant women. Yet even in those cases in which the delay is not especially onerous, it is, in my opinion, "undue" because there is no evidence that such a delay serves a useful and legitimate purpose. As indicated above, there is no legitimate reason to require a woman who has agonized over her decision to leave the clinic or hospital and return again another day....

The counseling provisions are similarly infirm. Whenever government commands private citizens to speak or to listen, careful review of the justification for that command is particularly appropriate.... [T]he information requirements in §3205(a)(1)(ii) and §§3205(a)(2)(i)-(iii) do not serve a useful purpose and thus constitute an unnecessary — and therefore undue — burden on the woman's constitutional liberty to decide to terminate her pregnancy.

Accordingly, while I disagree with Parts IV, V-B, and V-D of the joint opinion,[8] I join the remainder of the Court's opinion.

Justice BLACKMUN, concurring in part, concurring in the judgment in part, and dissenting in part.

I join parts I, II, III, V-A, V-C, and VI of the joint opinion of Justices O'CONNOR, KENNEDY, and SOUTER, *ante.*

Three years ago, in *Webster v. Reproductive Health Serv.*, 492 U.S. 490, 109 S.Ct. 3040, 106 L.Ed.2d 410 (1989), four Members of this Court appeared poised to "cas[t] into darkness the hopes and visions of every woman in this country" who had come to believe that the Constitution guaranteed her the right to reproductive choice. *Id.*, at 557, 109 S.Ct., at 3077 (BLACKMUN, J., dissenting).... All that remained between the promise of *Roe* and the darkness of the plurality was a single, flickering flame. Decisions since Webster gave little reason to hope that this flame would cast much light.... But now, just when so many expected the darkness to fall, the flame has grown bright.

I do not underestimate the significance of today's joint opinion. Yet I remain steadfast in my belief that the right to reproductive choice is entitled to the full protection afforded by this Court before *Webster.* And I fear for the darkness as four Justices anxiously await the single vote necessary to extinguish the light.

I

Make no mistake, the joint opinion of Justices O'CONNOR, KENNEDY, and SOUTER is an act of personal courage and constitutional principle. In contrast to previous decisions in which Justices O'CONNOR and KENNEDY postponed reconsideration of *Roe v. Wade,* 410 U.S. 113, 93 S.Ct. 705, 35 L.Ed.2d 147 (1973), the authors of the joint opinion today join Justice STEVENS and me in concluding that "the essential holding of *Roe* should be retained and once again reaffirmed." Ante, at 2804. In brief, five Members of this Court today recognize that

8. Although I agree that a parental-consent requirement (with the appropriate bypass) is constitutional, I do not join Part V-D of the joint opinion because its approval of Pennsylvania's informed parental-consent requirement is based on the reasons given in Part V-B, with which I disagree.

"the Constitution protects a woman's right to terminate her pregnancy in its early stages." *Id.*, at 2803.

...

II

Today, no less than yesterday, the Constitution and decisions of this Court require that a State's abortion restrictions be subjected to the strictest of judicial scrutiny. Our precedents and the joint opinion's principles require us to subject all non-de minimis abortion regulations to strict scrutiny. Under this standard, the Pennsylvania statute's provisions requiring content-based counseling, a 24-hour delay, informed parental consent, and reporting of abortion-related information must be invalidated.

A

...

State restrictions on abortion violate a woman's right of privacy....

...

A State's restrictions on a woman's right to terminate her pregnancy also implicate constitutional guarantees of gender equality. State restrictions on abortion compel women to continue pregnancies they otherwise might terminate. By restricting the right to terminate pregnancies, the State conscripts women's bodies into its service, forcing women to continue their pregnancies, suffer the pains of childbirth, and in most instances, provide years of maternal care. The State does not compensate women for their services; instead, it assumes that they owe this duty as a matter of course. This assumption — that women can simply be forced to accept the "natural" status and incidents of motherhood — appears to rest upon a conception of women's role that has triggered the protection of the Equal Protection Clause.... The joint opinion recognizes that these assumptions about women's place in society "are no longer consistent with our understanding of the family, the individual, or the Constitution." *Ante*, at 2831.

B

The Court has held that limitations on the right of privacy are permissible only if they survive "strict" constitutional scrutiny — that is, only if the governmental entity imposing the restriction can demonstrate that the limitation is both necessary and narrowly tailored to serve a compelling governmental interest....

Roe implemented these principles through a framework that was designed "to insure that the woman's right to choose not become so subordinate to the State's interest in promoting fetal life that her choice exists in theory but not in fact," [*Danforth*], at 2818....

In my view, application of this analytical framework is no less warranted than when it was approved by seven Members of this Court in *Roe*. Strict scrutiny of state limitations on reproductive choice still offers the most secure protection of the woman's right to make her own reproductive decisions, free from state coercion. No majority of this Court has ever agreed upon an alternative approach. The factual premises of the trimester framework have not been undermined, see *Webster*, 492 U.S., at 553, 109 S.Ct., at 3075 (BLACKMUN, J., dissenting), and the *Roe* framework is far more administrable, and far less manipulable, than the "undue burden" standard adopted by the joint opinion.

...

In sum, *Roe*'s requirement of strict scrutiny as implemented through a trimester framework should not be disturbed. No other approach has gained a majority, and no other is more protective of the woman's fundamental right. Lastly, no other approach properly accommodates the woman's constitutional right with the State's legitimate interests.

C

Application of the strict scrutiny standard results in the invalidation of all the challenged provisions. Indeed, as this Court has invalidated virtually identical provisions in prior cases, *stare decisis* requires that we again strike them down.

...

III

At long last, the CHIEF JUSTICE and those who have joined him admit it. Gone are the contentions that the issue need not be (or has not been) considered. There, on the first page, for all to see, is what was expected: "We believe that *Roe* was wrongly decided, and that it can and should be overruled consistently with our traditional approach to *stare decisis* in constitutional cases." *Post,* at 2855. If there is much reason to applaud the advances made by the joint opinion today, there is far more to fear from the CHIEF JUSTICE's opinion.

The CHIEF JUSTICE's criticism of *Roe* follows from his stunted conception of individual liberty.... He argues that the record in favor of a right to abortion is no stronger than the record in *Michael H. v. Gerald D.*, 491 U.S. 110, 109 S.Ct. 2333, 105 L.Ed.2d 91 (1989), where the plurality found no fundamental right to visitation privileges by an adulterous father, or in *Bowers v. Hardwick*, 478 U.S. 186, 106 S.Ct. 2841, 92 L.Ed.2d 140 (1986), where the Court found no fundamental right to engage in homosexual sodomy, or in a case involving the "firing of a gun...into another person's body." *Post,* at 2859. In the CHIEF JUSTICE's world, a woman considering whether to terminate a pregnancy is entitled to no more protection than adulterers, murderers, and so-called "sexual deviates."[11] Given the CHIEF JUSTICE's exclusive reliance on tradition, people using contraceptives seem the next likely candidate for his list of outcasts.

Even more shocking than the CHIEF JUSTICE's cramped notion of individual liberty is his complete omission of any discussion of the effects that compelled childbirth and motherhood have on women's lives. The only expression of concern with women's health is purely instrumental — for the CHIEF JUSTICE, only women's psychological health is a concern, and only to the extent that he assumes that every woman who decides to have an abortion does so without serious consideration of the moral implications of their decision. *Post,* at 2867-2868. In short, the CHIEF JUSTICE's view of the State's compelling interest in maternal health has less to do with health than it does with compelling women to be maternal.

...

IV

In one sense, the Court's approach is worlds apart from that of the CHIEF JUSTICE and Justice SCALIA. And yet, in another sense, the distance between the two approaches is short — the distance is but a single vote.

---

11. Obviously, I do not share the CHIEF JUSTICE's views of homosexuality as sexual deviance. See *Bowers,* 478 U.S., at 202–203 n. 2 (BLACKMUN, J., dissenting). 106 S.Ct., at 2849–2850 n. 2 (BLACKMUN, J., dissenting).

I am 83 years old. I cannot remain on this Court forever, and when I do step down, the confirmation process for my successor well may focus on the issue before us today. That, I regret, may be exactly where the choice between the two worlds will be made.

Chief Justice REHNQUIST, with whom Justice WHITE, Justice SCALIA, and Justice THOMAS join, concurring in the judgment in part and dissenting in part.

The joint opinion, following its newly-minted variation on stare decisis, retains the outer shell of *Roe v. Wade*, 410 U.S. 113, 93 S.Ct. 705, 35 L.Ed.2d 147 (1973), but beats a wholesale retreat from the substance of that case. We believe that *Roe* was wrongly decided, and that it can and should be overruled . . . .

. . .

The joint opinion of Justices O'CONNOR, KENNEDY, and SOUTER cannot bring itself to say that *Roe* was correct as an original matter, but the authors are of the view that "the immediate question is not the soundness of *Roe's* resolution of the issue, but the precedential force that must be accorded to its holding." Ante, at 2817. Instead of claiming that *Roe* was correct as a matter of original constitutional interpretation, the opinion therefore contains an elaborate discussion of stare decisis. This discussion of the principle of stare decisis appears to be almost entirely dicta, because the joint opinion does not apply that principle in dealing with *Roe*. *Roe* decided that a woman had a fundamental right to an abortion. The joint opinion rejects that view. *Roe* decided that abortion regulations were to be subjected to "strict scrutiny" and could be justified only in the light of "compelling state interests." The joint opinion rejects that view. *Ante*, at 2817–2818; see *Roe v. Wade*, *supra*, 410 U.S., at 162–164, 93 S.Ct., at 731–732. *Roe* analyzed abortion regulation under a rigid trimester framework, a framework which has guided this Court's decisionmaking for 19 years. The joint opinion rejects that framework. *Ante*, at 2818.

...While purporting to adhere to precedent, the joint opinion instead revises it. *Roe* continues to exist, but only in the way a storefront on a western movie set exists: a mere facade to give the illusion of reality....

. . .

Taking the joint opinion on its own terms, we doubt that its distinction between *Roe*, on the one hand, and *Plessy* and *Lochner*, on the other, withstands analysis. The joint opinion acknowledges that the Court improved its stature by overruling *Plessy* in *Brown* on a deeply divisive issue. And our decision in *West Coast Hotel*, which overruled *Adkins v. Children's Hospital*, *supra*, and *Lochner*, was rendered at a time when Congress was considering President Franklin Roosevelt's proposal to "reorganize" this Court and enable him to name six additional Justices in the event that any member of the Court over the age of 70 did not elect to retire. It is difficult to imagine a situation in which the Court would face more intense opposition to a prior ruling than it did at that time, and, under the general principle proclaimed in the joint opinion, the Court seemingly should have responded to this opposition by stubbornly refusing to reexamine the *Lochner* rationale, lest it lose legitimacy by appearing to "overrule under fire." *Ante*, at 2815.

. . .

The joint opinion also agrees that the Court acted properly in rejecting the doctrine of "separate but equal" in *Brown*. In fact, the opinion lauds *Brown* in comparing it to *Roe*. *Ante*, at 2815. This is strange, in that under the opinion's "legitimacy" principle the Court would seemingly have been forced to adhere to its erroneous decision in *Plessy* because of its "intensely divisive" character. To us, adherence to *Roe* today under the guise of "legitimacy" would seem to resemble more closely adherence to *Plessy* on the same ground....

...

We...think that the correct analysis is that set forth by the plurality opinion in *Webster.* A woman's interest in having an abortion is a form of liberty protected by the Due Process Clause, but States may regulate abortion procedures in ways rationally related to a legitimate state interest....

...

The question...is therefore whether the spousal notification requirement rationally furthers any legitimate state interests. We conclude that it does. First, a husband's interests in procreation within marriage and in the potential life of his unborn child are certainly substantial ones.... The State itself has legitimate interests both in protecting these interests of the father and in protecting the potential life of the fetus, and the spousal notification requirement is reasonably related to advancing those state interests. By providing that a husband will usually know of his spouse's intent to have an abortion, the provision makes it more likely that the husband will participate in deciding the fate of his unborn child, a possibility that might otherwise have been denied him. This participation might in some cases result in a decision to proceed with the pregnancy. As Judge Alito observed in his dissent below, "[t]he Pennsylvania legislature could have rationally believed that some married women are initially inclined to obtain an abortion without their husbands' knowledge because of perceived problems — such as economic constraints, future plans, or the husbands' previously expressed opposition — that may be obviated by discussion prior to the abortion." 947 F.2d, at 726 (Alito, J., concurring in part and dissenting in part).

The State also has a legitimate interest in promoting "the integrity of the marital relationship." 18 Pa.Cons.Stat. §3209(a)(1990). This Court has previously recognized "the importance of the marital relationship in our society." *Planned Parenthood of Central Mo. v. Danforth, supra,* 428 U.S., at 69, 96 S.Ct., at 2841. In our view, the spousal notice requirement is a rational attempt by the State to improve truthful communication between spouses and encourage collaborative decisionmaking, and thereby fosters marital integrity.... The spousal notice provision will admittedly be unnecessary in some circumstances, and possibly harmful in others, but "the existence of particular cases in which a feature of a statute performs no function (or is even counterproductive) ordinarily does not render the statute unconstitutional or even constitutionally suspect." *Thornburgh v. American College of Obstetricians and Gynecologists,* 476 U.S., at 800, 106 S.Ct., at 2199 (WHITE, J., dissenting). The Pennsylvania Legislature was in a position to weigh the likely benefits of the provision against its likely adverse effects, and presumably concluded, on balance, that the provision would be beneficial. Whether this was a wise decision or not, we cannot say that it was irrational. We therefore conclude that the spousal notice provision comports with the Constitution....

[Opinion of Justice SCALIA, concurring in the judgment in part and dissenting in part omitted.]

COMMENTS

Griswold and *Roe v. Wade* are frequently referred to as extending the constitutional right of privacy as emanating from the "penumbras" of the First, Third, Fourth, Fifth, and Ninth Amendments. The privacy rights of married persons to use contraceptives as proclaimed in *Griswold* were later extended to cover the rights of unmarried persons to receive contraceptive information. This extension was not necessarily dictated by any inherent logic, since *Griswold* emphasized in its concluding paragraphs the fundamental nature of the marriage relationship and did not address itself to the rights of unmarried persons at all. Rather, the Court's opinions seemed to be based on value choices — quite independent of and perhaps incidentally contrary to more traditional views of marriage and procreation — that ultimately favor the equality of women in their relations to men. But we are less concerned here with the constitutional ramifications of these cases than with their possible impact on marriage and the family.

The tensions between the institution of marriage and the rights of individuals are accentuated by the later extension of privacy, supported by the Fourteenth Amendment's command that personal liberty not be denied without due process of law, to cover the various phases and aspects of abortion. Again we are dealing with implicit value choices that lie deeper than the text of the opinions in *Roe v. Wade* and in its companion case *Doe v. Bolton*, 410 U.S. 179 (1973). In *The Brethren* (1979), Woodward and Armstrong give an account of the tortuous ways in which the majority opinions in *Roe* and *Doe* were assigned to and drafted by Justice Blackmun. The original draft memorandum did not even contain a reference to a constitutional right of privacy. Later drafts incorporated suggestions from other Justices in an effort to accommodate them and gain their votes. Originally, only the viability of the fetus was accepted by Justice Blackmun as a factor limiting abortion. Reference to trimesters of pregnancy was included at a later phase in an effort to gain the vote of Chief Justice Burger. The majority opinions were thus less the product of a cohesive intellectual effort, and more in the nature of a political compromise. This may be to some extent typical of many opinions of collegial courts, but the patchwork quality has been more observed and criticized in these lengthy abortion decisions.

Because of their compromise language based on underlying but not fully articulated value preferences, it was probably inevitable that the abortion decisions spawned further controversy, especially over the question of whether public funds should be made available for abortions in case of poverty. Strong opinions on both sides have been voiced by Catholics and Protestants and by scholars. Although statistics on abortions vary regionally and may not be fully reliable, it has been estimated by Wood and Durham that the number of abortions probably exceeds the number of live births in the United States. Psychoanalyst Erik Erikson has deplored the trend toward smaller families, which he characterizes as a repression of the urge to procreate. According to Erikson, the repression of the urge to procreate, like the earlier repression of sexuality, could lead to emotional harm on a large scale.

In the years since Erikson wrote, his thesis has come under a variety of attacks. For example, recent work by Michel Foucault challenges the basic assertion that there *has* been sexual repression, while some radical feminists have catalogued the emotional harm caused by the unleashing of male sexuality in a society of gender hierarchy. Population studies suggest that increasing family size, without radically decreasing the number of families, would lead to ecological disaster. The Western industrialized world has devoted much energy to trying to reduce the population growth rate in the less developed parts of the world.

More important to some, however, than the specific holdings in the contraception and abortion decisions are their indirect consequences for marriage and the family. The cases may have significance, at least for argumentative purposes, in areas that have nothing to do with abortion. The penumbra of privacy rights established by *Griswold* is a prime illustration. *Eisenstadt v. Baird* (see p. 395) held that married and unmarried persons cannot be treated differently in regard to contraceptive articles. The Supreme Court of New Jersey in *Application of Ellen Gaulkin* (see p. 428) dealt with the question of whether the wife of a judge could be a candidate for public office. The court referred to the holding in *Eisenstadt* that even in marriage two individuals, each with a separate intellectual and emotional makeup, can be distinguished. Consequently, the court reasoned, the wife could have legitimate career goals apart from her husband. *Planned Parenthood v. Danforth* (428 U.S. 52 (1976)), which overturned a requirement that married women obtain spousal consent before they obtain an abortion, could be used to modify the laws of child support. The argument has been made by husbands that they should not be required to support an unwanted child since the wife and not the husband had control over the choice to carry the pregnancy to term. The husband might grant that he should pay the costs of an abortion, because he caused the pregnancy; but why should he pay for the costs of the child? Similar arguments are raised by unmarried men to avoid paying support for their unwanted children.

The constitutionality of statutes that irrebuttably presume the husband to be the father of a child could also be questioned because the privacy rights of married women weaken the control of husbands over procreation. Is it consistent to require spousal consent for artificial insemination, as is provided in many states, while spousal consent is irrelevant for abortion decisions?

From a feminist perspective, very different questions are raised. Is it consistent for the state to place roadblocks in the way to abortion, encouraging the birth of unwanted children, but at the same time to deny women access to artificial insemination unless the child would be wanted by her husband? Why do men believe they should control procreation, especially when so many of them show so little responsibility for the children produced with their sperm? As one feminist asked, why do men think they should be able to control women's bodies when men cannot even control their own bodies and do not seem very inclined to control their own sexuality?

Organized religious groups, political groups and others opposed the *Roe v. Wade* decision from the beginning. Defense for the decision was slower to develop.

Some of the people who had spearheaded the movement to reform abortion law turned their attention to other issues, such as the involuntary sterilization of poor and minority women that was all too common in the 1970s. Efforts to overturn *Roe* through a constitutional amendment were unsuccessful, but other ways were found to chip away at the decision. Public funding for abortion was cut off, and clinics and doctors who did abortions were targeted for lawsuits, boycotts and violence.

From 1980 through 1992, anti-abortionists found an ally in the White House. During the four years before that, President Jimmy Carter, though in some ways supportive of women's right to choose, had opposed public funding for abortion. Beginning in 1980, there was a concerted campaign to overturn *Roe* through changing the personnel of the U.S. Supreme Court. Although it was denied that any "litmus test" was required of judicial appointments, no one was named to the Supreme Court who was on record supporting *Roe.* Nevertheless, Supreme Court Justices are appointed for life and can be influenced by the wisdom or insults of other Justices, a period of reflection, law review articles, their law clerks, and so forth. Justice Kennedy, shortly after voting in *Webster v. Health Services* essentially to overturn *Roe,* joined a three-person block with Justices O'Connor and Souter in *Casey* to reaffirm *Roe* and to retain all the traces of it that *Webster* left standing. There are clear indications that some members of the Court are concerned with the public perception of the Court as an institution and wish to avoid the Court seeming to base decisions on shifting majorities rather than on reason and precedent. The 1993 replacement of Justice White, who dissented in *Roe* and voted in favor of any virtually abortion restriction, with Justice Ruth Bader Ginsberg, the second woman to join the Court and a jurist sensitive to precedent and to issues of sex discrimination, is likely to influence the Court's decisions in this and other areas.

Equally divergent perspectives exist regarding the influence that these questions have on the nature of marriage, the legal consequences of nonmarital relations, and the nature of the state's role. Some would argue that these cases involve fundamental questions relating to freedom from state intrusion. Of course, it still has to be determined whether the autonomy of the marital institution or of the individuals who participate in it is concerned, and the case law must seem to be ambivalent when it speaks of privacy both of marriage and of the individual; nevertheless, it may seem clear to these observers that many important decisions within the sphere of intimate relations have been surrendered by the State. The inquiry into what is left for assertion of State power can thus be viewed as related to the expanding boundary of private autonomy. Alternatively, the "ambivalence" about individual autonomy or group autonomy may be seen to reflect a basic incoherence in the notion of privacy. *Casey* marks a clear shift in the Court's recognition that access to abortion involves issues of gender equality as well as privacy.

REFERENCES

John Hart Ely, *The Wages of Crying Wolf: A Comment on Roe v. Wade,* 82 YALE L.J. 920 (1973).

E.H. Erikson, Address, 31st Congress of the International Psycho-Analytical Association (Aug. 3, 1979), quoted in Adams, *Erikson Sees Psychological Danger in Trend of Having Fewer Children,* N.Y. TIMES, Aug. 4,1979, at 17, col. 3.

Michel Foucault, THE HISTORY OF SEXUALITY, VOLUME 1: AN INTRODUCTION (1978).
John Thomas Noonan, A PRIVATE CHOICE: ABORTION IN AMERICA IN THE SEVENTIES (1979).
Frances Olsen, *Unraveling Compromise*, 103 HARV. L. REV. 105 (1989).
Frances Olsen, *A Finger to the Devil: Abortion, Privacy, and Equality*, DISSENT 377 (Summer, 1991).
Laurence J. Tribe, *The Supreme Court 1972 Term Foreword Toward a Model of Roles in the Due Process of Life and Law*, 87 HARV. L. REV. 1 (1973).

Sexual Behavior Outside of Marriage

EISENSTADT v. BAIRD
United States Supreme Court
405 U.S. 438 (1972)

Mr. Justice BRENNAN delivered the opinion of the Court.

Appellee William Baird was convicted at a bench trial in the Massachusetts Superior Court under Massachusetts General Laws Ann., c. 272, §21, first, for exhibiting contraceptive articles in the course of delivering a lecture on contraception to a group of students at Boston University and, second, for giving a young woman a package of Emko vaginal foam at the close of his address.[1] The Massachusetts Supreme Judicial Court unanimously set aside the conviction for exhibiting contraceptives on the ground that it violated Baird's First Amendment rights, but by a four-to-three vote sustained the conviction for giving away the foam. *Commonwealth v. Baird*, 355 Mass. 746, 247 N.E.2d 574 (1969). Baird subsequently filed a petition for a federal *writ of habeas corpus*, which the District Court dismissed. 310 F.Supp. 951 (1970). On appeal, however, the Court of Appeals for the First Circuit vacated the dismissal and remanded the action with directions to grant the writ discharging Baird. 429 F.2d 1398 (1970). This appeal by the Sheriff of Suffolk County, Massachusetts, followed....We Affirm.

Massachusetts General Laws Ann., c. 272, §21, under which Baird was convicted, provides a maximum five-year term of imprisonment for "whoever...gives away...any drug, medicine, instrument or article whatever for the prevention of conception," except as authorized in §21A. Under §21A, "[a] registered physician may administer to or prescribe for any married person drugs or articles intended for the prevention of pregnancy or conception. [And a] registered pharmacist actually engaged in the business of pharmacy may furnish such drugs or articles to any married person presenting a prescription from a registered physician."... As interpreted by the State Supreme Judicial Court, these provisions make it a felony for anyone, other than a registered physician or pharmacist acting in accordance with the terms of §21A, to dispense any article with the intention that it be used for the prevention of conception. The statutory scheme distinguishes among three distinct classes of distributee — *first*, married persons may obtain contraceptives to prevent pregnancy, but only from doctors or druggists on prescription; *second*,

1. The Court of Appeals below described the recipient of the foam as "an unmarried adult woman." 429 F.2d 1398, 1399 (1970). However, there is no evidence in the record about her marital status.

single persons may not obtain contraceptives from anyone to prevent pregnancy; and, *third*, married or single persons may obtain contraceptives from anyone to prevent, not pregnancy, but the spread of disease....

The legislative purposes that the statute is meant to serve are not altogether clear. In *Commonwealth v. Baird, supra*, the Supreme Judicial Court noted only the State's interest in protecting the health of its citizens: "[T]he prohibition in §21," the court declared, "is directly related to" the State's goal of "preventing the distribution of articles designed to prevent conception which may have undesirable, if not dangerous, physical consequences," 355 Mass., at 753, 247 N.E.2d, at 578. In a subsequent decision, *Sturgis v. Attorney General*, 358 Mass. 37, 260 N.E.2d 687, 690 (1970), the court, however, found "a second and more compelling ground for upholding the statute" — namely, to protect morals through "regulating the private sexual lives of single persons."[3] The Court of Appeals, for reasons that will appear, did not consider the promotion of health or the protection of morals through the deterrence of fornication to be the legislative aim. Instead, the court concluded that the statutory goal was to limit contraception in and of itself — a purpose that the court held conflicted "with fundamental human rights" under *Griswold v. Connecticut*, 381 U.S. 479, 85 S.Ct. 1678, 14 L.Ed.2d 510 (1965), where this Court struck down Connecticut's prohibition against the use of contraceptives as an unconstitutional infringement of the right of marital privacy. 429 F.2d, at 1401–1402.

We agree that the goals of deterring premarital sex and regulating the distribution of potentially harmful articles cannot reasonably be regarded as legislative aims of §§21 and 21A. And we hold that the statute, viewed as a prohibition on contraception *per se*, violates the rights of single persons under the Equal Protection Clause of the Fourteenth Amendment.

I

We address at the outset appellant's contention that Baird does not have standing to assert the rights of unmarried persons denied access to contraceptives because he was neither an authorized distributor under §21A nor a single person unable to obtain contraceptives....

...

II

The basic principles governing application of the Equal Protection Clause of the Fourteenth Amendment are familiar. As the CHIEF JUSTICE only recently explained in *Reed v. Reed*, 404 U.S. 71, 75–76, 92 S.Ct. 251, 253, 30 L.Ed.2d 225 (1971):

> In applying that clause, this Court has consistently recognized that the Fourteenth Amendment does not deny to States the power to treat different classes of persons in different ways.... The Equal Protection Clause of that amendment does, however, deny to States the power to legislate that different treatment be accorded to persons placed by a statute into different classes on the basis of criteria wholly unrelated to the objective of that statute. A classification "must be reasonable, not arbitrary, and must rest

3. Appellant suggests that the purpose of the Massachusetts statute is to promote marital fidelity as well as to discourage premarital sex. Under §21A, however, contraceptives may be made available to married persons without regard to whether they are living with their spouses or the uses to which the contraceptives are to be put. Plainly the legislation has no deterrent effect on extramarital sexual relations.

> upon some ground of difference having a fair and substantial relation to the object of the legislation, so that all persons similarly circumstanced shall be treated alike." *Royster Guano Co. v. Virginia*, 253 U.S. 412, 415, 40 S.Ct. 560, 64 L.Ed. 989 (1920).

The question for our determination in this case is whether there is some ground of difference that rationally explains the different treatment accorded married and unmarried persons under Massachusetts General Laws Ann., c. 272, §§21 and 21A.[7] For the reasons that follow, we conclude that no such ground exists.

First. Section 21 stems from Mass. Stat.1879, c. 159, §1, which prohibited without exception, distribution of articles intended to be used as contraceptives. In *Commonwealth v. Allison*, 227 Mass. 57, 62, 116 N.E. 265, 266 (1917), the Massachusetts Supreme Judicial Court explained that the law's "plain purpose is to protect purity, to preserve chastity, to encourage continence and self restraint, to defend the sancity of the home, and thus to engender in the State and nation a virile and virtuous race of men and women." Although the State clearly abandoned that purpose with the enactment of §21A, at least insofar as the illicit sexual activities of married persons are concerned, see n. 3, *supra*, the court reiterated in *Sturgis v. Attorney General, supra*, that the object of the legislation is to discourage premarital sexual intercourse. Conceding that the State could, consistently with the Equal Protection Clause, regard the problems of extramarital and premarital sexual relations as "[e]vils...of different dimensions and proportions, requiring different remedies," *Williamson v. Lee Optical Co.*, 348 U.S. 483, 489, 75 S.Ct. 461, 465, 99 L.Ed. 563 (1955), we cannot agree that the deterrence of premarital sex may reasonably be regarded as the purpose of the Massachusetts law.

It would be plainly unreasonable to assume that Massachusetts has prescribed pregnancy and the birth of an unwanted child as punishment for fornication, which is a misdemeanor under Massachusetts General Laws Ann., c. 272, §18. Aside from the scheme of values that assumption would attribute to the State, it is abundantly clear that the effect of the ban on distribution of contraceptives to unmarried persons has at best a marginal relation to the proffered objective. What Mr. Justice Goldberg said in *Griswold v. Connecticut, supra*, 381 U.S., at 498, 85 S.Ct., at 1689, 14 L.Ed.2d 510 (concurring opinion), concerning the effect of Connecticut's prohibition on the use of contraceptives in discouraging extramarital sexual relations, is equally applicable here. "The rationality of this justification is dubious, particularly in light of the admitted widespread availability to all persons in the State of Connecticut, unmarried as well as married, of birth-control devices for the prevention of disease, as distinguished from the prevention of conception." See also *id.*, at 505–507, 85 S.Ct., at 1689 (WHITE, J., concurring in judgment). Like Connecticut's laws, §§21 and 21A do not at all regulate the distribution of contraceptives when they are to be used to prevent, not pregnancy, but the spread of disease. *Commonwealth v. Corbett*, 307 Mass. 7, 29 N.E.2d 151 (1940), cited with approval in *Commonwealth v. Baird*, 355 Mass., at 754, 247 N.E.2d, at 579. Nor, in making contraceptives available to married persons without regard to their intended use, does Massachusetts attempt to deter married per-

---

7. Of course, if we were to conclude that the Massachusetts statute impinges upon fundamental freedoms under Griswold, the statutory classification would have to be not merely rationally related to a valid public purpose but necessary to the achievement of a compelling state interest. *E.g., Shapiro v. Thompson*, 394 U.S. 618, 89 S.Ct. 1322, 22 L.Ed.2d 600 (1969); *Loving v. Virginia*, 388 U.S. 1, 87 S.Ct. 1817, 18 L.Ed.2d 1010 (1967). But just as in *Reed v. Reed*, 404 U.S. 71, 92 S.Ct. 251, 30 L.Ed.2d 225 (1971), we do not have to address the statute's validity under that test because the law fails to satisfy even the more lenient equal protection standard.

sons from engaging in illicit sexual relations with unmarried persons. Even on the assumption that the fear of pregnancy operates as a deterrent to fornication, the Massachusetts statute is thus so riddled with exceptions that deterrence of premarital sex cannot reasonably be regarded as its aim.

Moreover, §§21 and 21A on their face have a dubious relation to the State's criminal prohibition on fornication. As the Court of Appeals explained, "Fornication is a misdemeanor (in Massachusetts), entailing a thirty dollar fine, or three months in jail. Massachusetts General Laws Ann. c. 272, §18. Violation of the present statute is a felony, punishable by five years in prison. We find it hard to believe that the legislature adopted a statute carrying a five-year penalty for its possible, obviously by no means fully effective, deterrence of the commission of a ninety-day misdemeanor." 429 F.2d, at 1401. Even conceding the legislature a full measure of discretion in fashioning means to prevent fornication, and recognizing that the State may seek to deter prohibited conduct by punishing more severely those who facilitate than those who actually engage in its commission, we, like the Court of Appeals, cannot believe that in this instance Massachusetts has chosen to expose the aider and abetter who simply gives away a contraceptive to 20 times the 90-day sentence of the offender himself. The very terms of the State's criminal statutes, coupled with the *de minimis* effect of §§21 and 21A in deterring fornication, thus compel the conclusion that such deterrence cannot reasonably be taken as the purpose of the ban on distribution of contraceptives to unmarried persons.

Second. Section 21A was added to the Massachusetts General Laws by Stat. 1966, c. 265, §1. The Supreme Judicial Court in *Commonwealth v. Baird, supra,* held that the purpose of the amendment was to serve the health needs of the community by regulating the distribution of potentially harmful articles. It is plain that Massachusetts had no such purpose in mind before the enactment of §21A. As the Court of Appeals remarked, "Consistent with the fact that the statute was contained in a chapter dealing with 'Crimes Against Chastity, Morality, Decency and Good Order,' it was cast only in terms of morals. A physician was forbidden to prescribe contraceptives even when needed for the protection of health. *Commonwealth v. Gardner,* 1938, 300 Mass. 372, 15 N.E.2d 222." 429 F.2d, at 1401. Nor did the Court of Appeals "believe that the legislature (in enacting §21A) suddenly reversed its field and developed an interest in health. Rather, it merely made what it thought to be the precise accommodation necessary to escape the *Griswold* ruling." *Ibid.*

Again, we must agree with the Court of Appeals. If health were the rationale of §21A, the statute would be both discriminatory and overbroad. Dissenting in *Commonwealth v. Baird,* 355 Mass., at 758, 247 N.E.2d, at 581, Justices Whittemore and Cutter stated that they saw "in §21 and §21A, read together, no public health purpose. If there is need to have physician prescribe (and a pharmacist dispense) contraceptives, that need is as great for unmarried persons as for married persons." The Court of Appeals added: "If the prohibition (on distribution to unmarried persons)...is to be taken to mean that the same physician who can prescribe for married patients does not have sufficient skill to protect the health of patients who lack a marriage certificate, or who may be currently divorced, it is illogical to the point of irrationality." 429 F.2d, at 1401.[8] Furthermore, we must join the Court of Appeals in noting that not all contraceptives are potentially dan-

8. Appellant insists that the unmarried have no right to engage in sexual intercourse and hence no health interest in contraception that needs to be served. The short answer to this contention is that the same devices the distribution of which the State purports to regulate when their asserted purpose is to forestall pregnancy are available without any controls whatsoever so long as their asserted purpose is to prevent the spread of

gerous.[9] As a result, if the Massachusetts statute were a health measure, it would not only invidiously discriminate against the unmarried, but also be overbroad with respect to the married, a fact that the Supreme Judicial Court itself seems to have conceded in *Sturgis v. Attorney General*, Mass., 260 N.E.2d at 690, where it noted that "it may well be that certain contraceptive medication and devices constitute no hazard to health, in which event it could be argued that the statute swept too broadly in its prohibition." "In this posture," as the Court of Appeals concluded, "it is impossible to think of the statute as intended as a health measure for the unmarried, and it is almost as difficult to think of it as so intended even as to the married." 429 F.2d, at 1401.

But if further proof that the Massachusetts statute is not a health measure is necessary, the argument of Justice Spiegel, who also dissented in *Commonwealth v. Baird*, 355 Mass., at 759, 247 N.E.2d, at 582, is conclusive: "It is at best a strained conception to say that the Legislature intended to prevent the distribution of articles 'which may have undesirable, if not dangerous, physical consequences.' If that was the Legislature's goal, §21 is not required" in view of the federal and state laws *already* regulating the distribution of harmful drugs. We conclude, accordingly, that, despite the statute's superficial earmarks as a health measure, health, on the face of the statute, may no more reasonably be regarded as its purpose than the deterrence of premarital sexual relations.

Third. If the Massachusetts statute cannot be upheld as a deterrent to fornication or as a health measure, may it, nevertheless, be sustained simply as a prohibition on contraception? The Court of Appeals analysis "led inevitably to the conclusion that, so far as morals are concerned, it is contraceptives *per se* that are considered immoral — to the extent that *Griswold* will permit such a declaration." 429 F.2d, at 1401–1402. The Court of Appeals went on to hold, *id.*, at 1402:

> To say that contraceptives are immoral as such, and are to be forbidden to unmarried persons who will nevertheless persist in having intercourse, means that such persons must risk for themselves an unwanted pregnancy, for the child, illegitimacy, and for society, a possible obligation of support. Such a view of morality is not only the very mirror image of sensible legislation; we consider that it conflicts with fundamental human rights. In the absence of demonstrated harm, we hold it is beyond the competency of the state.

We need not and do not, however, decide that important question in this case because, whatever the rights of the individual to access to contraceptives may be, the rights must be the same for the unmarried and the married alike.

If under *Griswold* the distribution of contraceptives to married persons cannot be prohibited, a ban on distribution to unmarried persons would be equally impermissible. It is true that in *Griswold* the right of privacy in question inhered

---

8. *Continued*

disease. It is inconceivable that the need for health controls varies with the purpose for which the contraceptive is to be used when the physical act in all cases is one and the same.

9. The Court of Appeals stated, 429 F.2d, at 1401:

> [W]e must take notice that not all contraceptive devices risk "undesirable…[or] dangerous physical consequences." It is 200 years since Casanova recorded the ubiquitous article which, perhaps because of the birthplace of its inventor, he termed a "redingote anglais." The reputed nationality of the condom has now changed, but we have never heard criticism of it on the side of health. We cannot think that the legislature was unaware of it, or could have thought that it needed a medical prescription. We believe the same could be said of certain other products.

in the marital relationship. Yet the marital couple is not an independent entity with a mind and heart of its own, but an association of two individuals each with a separate intellectual and emotional makeup. If the right of privacy means anything, it is the right of the *individual*, married or single, to be free from unwarranted governmental intrusion into matters so fundamentally affecting a person as the decision whether to bear or beget a child. See *Stanley v. Georgia*, 394 U.S. 557, 89 S.Ct. 1243, 22 L.Ed.2d 542 (1969).[10] See also *Skinner v. Oklahoma ex rel. Williamson*, 316 U.S. 535, 62 S.Ct. 1110, 86 L.Ed. 1655 (1942); *Jacobson v. Massachusetts*, 197 U.S. 11, 29, 25 S.Ct. 358, 362, 49 L.Ed. 643 (1905).

...

On the other hand, if *Griswold* is no bar to a prohibition on the distribution of contraceptives, the State could not, consistently with the Equal Protection Clause, outlaw distribution to unmarried but not to married persons. In each case the evil, as perceived by the State, would be identical, and the underinclusion would be invidious.... We hold that by providing dissimilar treatment for married and unmarried persons who are similarly situated, Massachusetts General Laws Ann., c. 272, §§21 and 21A, violate the Equal Protection Clause. The judgment of the Court of Appeals is affirmed.

Affirmed.

[Justice DOUGLAS filed a separate concurring opinion in which he expressed the view that the case was "a simple First Amendment case."]

...

Mr. Justice WHITE, with whom Mr. Justice BLACKMUN joins, concurring in the result.

...

I assume that a State's interest in the health of its citizens empowers it to restrict to medical channels the distribution of products whose use should be accompanied by medical advice. I also do not doubt that various contraceptive medicines and article are properly available only on prescription, and I therefore have no difficulty with the Massachusetts court's characterization of the statute at issue here as expressing "a legitimate interest in preventing the distribution of articles designed to prevent conception which may have undesirable, if not dangerous, physical consequences." *Id.*, at 753, 247 N.E.2d, at 578. Had Baird distributed a supply of the so-called "pill," I would sustain his conviction under this statute. Requiring a prescription to obtain potentially dangerous contraceptive material may place a substantial burden upon the right recognized in *Griswold*, but that burden is justified by a strong state interest and does not, as did the statute at issue in *Griswold*, sweep unnecessarily broadly or seek "to achieve its goals by means having a maximum destructive impact upon" a protected relationship. *Griswold v. Connecticut*, 381 U.S., at 485, 85 S.Ct., at 1682.

---

10. In *Stanley*, 394 U.S., at 564, 89 S.Ct., at 1247, the Court stated:

> [A]lso fundamental is the right to be free, except in very limited circumstances, from unwanted governmental intrusions into one's privacy.
>
> "The makers of our Constitution undertook to secure conditions favorable to the pursuit of happiness. They recognized the significance of man's spiritual nature, of his feelings and of his intellect. They knew that only a part of the pain, pleasure and satisfactions of life are to be found in material things. They sought to protect Americans in their beliefs, their thoughts, their emotions, and their sensations. They conferred, as against the Government, the right to be let alone — the most comprehensive of rights and the right most valued by civilized man." *Olmstead v. United States*, 277 U.S. 438, 478, 48 S.Ct. 564, 572, 72 L.Ed. 944 (1928)....

Baird, however, was found guilty of giving away vaginal foam. Inquiry into the validity of this conviction does not come to an end merely because some contraceptives are harmful and their distribution may be restricted. Our general reluctance to question a State's judgment on matters of public health must give way where, as here, the restriction at issue burdens the constitutional rights of married persons to use contraceptives. In these circumstances we may not accept on faith the State's classification of a particular contraceptive as dangerous to health. Due regard for protecting constitutional rights requires that the record contain evidence that a restriction on distribution of vaginal foam is essential to achieve the statutory purpose, or the relevant facts concerning the product must be such as to fall within the range of judicial notice.

Neither requirement is met here. Nothing in the record even suggests that the distribution of vaginal foam should be accompanied by medical advice in order to protect the user's health. Nor does the opinion of the Massachusetts court or the State's brief filed here marshal facts demonstrating that the hazards of using vaginal foam are common knowledge or so incontrovertible that they may be noticed judicially. On the contrary, the State acknowledges that Emko is a product widely available without prescription. Given *Griswold v. Connecticut*, *supra*, and absent proof of the probable hazards of using vaginal foam, we could not sustain appellee's conviction had it been for selling or giving away foam to a married person. Just as in *Griswold*, where the right of married persons to use contraceptives was "diluted or adversely affected" by permitting a conviction for giving advice as to its exercise, *id.*, at 481, 85 S.Ct., at 1679, so here, to sanction a medical restriction upon distribution of a contraceptive not proved hazardous to health would impair the exercise of the constitutional right.

That Baird could not be convicted for distributing Emko to a married person disposes of this case. Assuming, *arguendo*, that the result would be otherwise had the recipient been unmarried, nothing has been placed in the record to indicate her marital status. The State has maintained that marital status is irrelevant because an unlicensed person cannot legally dispense vaginal foam either to married or unmarried persons. This approach is plainly erroneous and requires the reversal of Baird's conviction; for on the facts of this case, it deprives us of knowing whether Baird was in fact convicted for making a constitutionally protected distribution of Emko to a married person.

...

[Chief Justice BURGER's dissent is omitted.]

FADGEN v. LENKNER

Supreme Court of Pennsylvania
469 Pa. 272, 365 A.2d 147 (1976)

JONES, Chief Justice.

Appellee, James T. Fadgen, brought an action in trespass against appellant, George Lenkner, based upon the theory of criminal conversation. The complaint alleged that appellee and one Bonnie Hoch Fadgen were married in 1972 and that during the period of this marriage, the appellant, without the consent of appellee Fadgen, criminally conversed with Ms. Fadgen.

...

This Court last reviewed an action similar to the one presently at bar in 1959. In *Karchner v. Mumie*, 398 Pa. 13, 156 A.2d 537 (1959), the Court upheld a jury verdict in favor of the plaintiff-wife based upon the tort of criminal conversation where appellant-defendant had sought reversal on the ground that the cause of action as developed at common law was only available to married men as against an erring spouse's paramour. The Court reasoned that the Married Women's Property Act of June 8, 1893, P.L. 344, *as amended* by the Act of May 17, 1945, P.L. 625, mandated the extension to married women of the right to bring such an action on their own behalf....

It is clear, however, that that first step directed towards fusing the ancient with the "modern" of 1959 was not sufficient revitalization such as to weather the rapid legal and societal changes witnessed over the past fifteen years. We might look back and well appreciate that, absent the benefit of attitudes reflected in the passage of the Equal Rights Amendment, the Court in 1959 nevertheless laudably rejected the fictitious notion that a wife, like a servant, was the personal property (chattel as it were) of the husband and that an action in criminal conversation was a right sacrosanct to none but the master. Still, the Court's extension to married women of the right to bring such a cause of action only delayed what today demands; that is, the total abolition of a pious yet unrighteous cause of action.

...

One of several civil actions directed at protecting against intentional interferences with the marital relationship,[4] criminal conversation comes closest in form to a strict liability tort. The cause of action is made out upon plaintiff's proof that while married to plaintiff, plaintiff's spouse and the defendant engaged in at least a single act of sexual intercourse without the consent of plaintiff.... There are but two possible complete defenses to the action: one, obviously, is an outright denial by the defendant of having had any such relation with plaintiff's spouse; the other occurs upon proof that the Plaintiff consented to the adulterous relation. Prosser, Law of Torts, §124, at p. 879 (Fourth Ed. 1971)....

It is no defense to the action, however, that the plaintiff's spouse consented nor in fact that the spouse was the aggressor or seducer. *Sieber v. Pettit*, 200 Pa. 58, 49 A. 763 (1901); *During v. Hastings*, 183 Pa. 210, 38 A. 627 (1897). As to the former, it was thought at common law that a wife was not competent to give her consent so as to defeat her husband's interest. *Tinker v. Colwell*, 193 U.S. 473, 483, 24 S.Ct. 505, 48 L.Ed. 754 (1903).[5] As to the justification for eliminating the defense that the wife initiated and pursued the adulterous relationship, in addition to the belief at common law that she was incapable of prejudicing her husband's rights, the law burdensomely presuming the superiority of men over women chastised:

> The man who breaks up the home of his neighbor by debauching his wife, rendering his children worse than motherless, is not excused because he is weak, and, being tempted by the woman, falls.

Seiber v. Pettit, 200 Pa. 58 at 67, 49 A. 763 (1901).

---

4. See Note, *The Case for Retention of Causes of Action for Intentional Interference with the Marital Relationship*, 48 NOTRE DAME LAWYER, 426, 427 (1972), wherein the author posits that statutory and judicial abolition of the tort actions known as "alienation of affections" and "enticement" is uncalled for and unfairly undermines the marriage institution. However, the author shows no like sympathy for criminal conversation. *Id.* at 433–34.

5. Prosser, citing 8 Holdsworth, History of English Law, 2d Edition 1937, 430, provides us with the following choice tidbit: "...it was considered that she was no more capable of giving a consent which would prejudice the husband's interests than was his horse." Prosser, *supra*, at 875.

> ...it is but the old cowardly excuse set up by the first man, "The woman gave me of the tree, and I did eat." It did not save from the penalty the first defendant, and cannot, under the law, save this one.

Id. at p. 69, 49 A. at 765.... Moreover, a man could not plead ignorance of the marital status of the adulterer: "A man who has sexual relations with a woman, not his wife, assumes the risk that she is married. Even her misrepresentation that she is single affords the offender no defense to liability for criminal conversation...." *Antonelli v. Xenakis, supra,* 363 Pa. at 378, 69 A.2d at 103.

We, of course, in no way condone sexual promiscuity and continue to hold the institution of marriage in the highest regard. However, the reasoning developed at common law behind stripping a defendant of all defenses to an action in criminal conversation, save the plaintiff's consent, no longer merits endorsement.

Damages alleged in an action for criminal conversation are compensatory, covering injury to the plaintiff's social position, disgrace in the community where he or she lives or was in business and dishonor to plaintiff and plaintiff's family.... "And, a single act of adultery is sufficient to entitle the husband of the woman to damages in an action against the adulterer for criminal conversation even though the husband sustains no further loss: *Antonelli v. Xenakis, supra,* 363 Pa. at 377, 69 A.2d 102; Restatement of Torts, §683, Comment c; §685, Comment b." *DiSanti v. Cassidy, supra,* 63 Pa. D & C 2d at 9. Punitive damages have been held to be appropriate as well.... Computations for the type of injury alleged here is always inexact and as Blackstone warned "usually very large and exemplary." This is so not only by virtue of the abstract nature of the injuries alleged but is further exacerbated by the emotion-laden nature of the proceedings....

...Prosser succinctly summarizes:

> Those actions for interference with domestic relations which carry an accusation of sexual misbehavior — that is to say, criminal conversation, seduction, and to some extent alienation of affections — have been peculiarly susceptible to abuse. Together with the action for breach of promise to marry, it is notorious that they have afforded a fertile field for blackmail and extortion by means of manufactured suits in which the threat of publicity is used to force a settlement. There is good reason to believe that even genuine actions of this type are brought more frequently than not with purely mercenary or vindictive motives; that it is impossible to compensate for such damage with what has derisively been called "heartbalm"; that people of any decent instincts do not bring an action which merely adds to the family disgrace; and that no preventive purpose is served, since such torts seldom are committed with deliberate plan.

Prosser, *supra,* at 887 and authorities cited therein.

We in no way intend to infer such motives on the part of the appellee in the instant case by pointing to the potential abuses to which this action is susceptible. However, we believe the cause of action itself is an anachronism and that in today's society it is unreasonable to impose upon a defendant such harsh results without affording any real opportunity to interject logically valid defenses on the merits such as the role of the plaintiff's spouse in the adulterous relationship or the quality of the plaintiff's marriage prior to the occurrence of the acts constituting the tort.

The total abolition of this cause of action is well within the bounds of our judicial powers. In fact, it is our duty to so act with regard to court-made rules where "reason and a right sense of justice recommend it." *Ayala v. Philadelphia Board of Public Education*, 453 Pa. 584, 600, 305 A.2d 877, 885 (1973)....

...As we said in *Flagiello v. Pennsylvania Hospital* 417 Pa. 486, 208 A.2d 193 (1965), quoting Justice Cardozo:

> "[W]hen a rule, after it has been duly tested by experience, has been found to be inconsistent with the sense of justice or with the social welfare, there should be less hesitation in frank avowal and full abandonment.... There should be greater readiness to abandon an untenable position when the rule to be discarded may not reasonably be supposed to have determined the conduct of the litigants, and *particularly when in its origin it was the product of institutions or conditions which have gained a new significance or development with the progress of the years.*" (Emphasis added).

Id. at 514, 208 A.2d at 207.

> "Precedent speaks for the past; policy for the present and the future. The goal which we seek is a blend which takes into account in due proportion the wisdom of the past and the needs of the present."

Ayala v. Philadelphia Board of Public Education, *supra*, 453 Pa. at 603–04, 305 A.2d at 887.

The Order of the court below is vacated and the case remanded for the entry of judgment in favor of the appellant. The civil cause of action based upon the tort of criminal conversation is hereby abolished.

...

MANDERINO, Justice (concurring).

I concur in the result reached by the majority opinion because I believe that result mandated by the decisions of the United States Supreme Court in *Roe v. Wade*, 410 U.S. 113, 93 S.Ct. 705, 35 L.Ed.2d 147 (1973), in which the court held that the right of privacy was broad enough to preclude interference by the state in a woman's decision whether or not to terminate her pregnancy, and in *Cleveland Board of Education v. La Fleur*, 414 U.S. 632, 94 S.Ct. 791, 39 L.Ed.2d 52 (1974). In the latter case the court stated its recognition "...that freedom of personal choice in matters of marriage and family life is one of the liberties protected by the Due Process Clause of the Fourteenth Amendment." *Id.* at 639, 94 S.Ct. at 796, 39 L.Ed.2d at 60. If a married man or woman chooses to engage in sexual activity with one other than his or her spouse, I believe such a choice is protected by the right to privacy guaranteed by the Constitution and there is no "compelling state interest" involved which would justify the state's limiting the exercise of such rights....

I also comment on the dissenting opinion of Mr. Justice Roberts. By "abolishing" the cause of action for criminal conversation, the majority at last recognizes that one's spouse no longer suffers a compensable injury when the other engages in sexual activity outside the marriage relationship. Such a recognition is long overdue. In fact, I believe that were we to apply Mr. Justice Roberts' three part inquiry the result would be the same: (1) society no longer has any interest in protecting one spouse against extramarital sexual activity by the other; (2) since there is no longer any interest to protect, there has been no invasion of such interest; and (3) no injury has resulted.

...

ROBERTS, Justice (dissenting).

I dissent. The majority totally abolishes the cause of action for criminal conversation without any statutory or any other authority for doing so other than its own inclinations that the tort is an "anachronism." I cannot agree that the marital relationship — which has been protected in this Commonwealth for more than two centuries — is no longer deserving of the protection of our law.

. . .

The true inquiry here should be: (1) Is there an interest which society should protect? (2) Has there been an invasion of that interest which cannot be excused or justified? (3) Has the invasion produced an injury for which the law can provide a remedy?

The first inquiry has been answered in the affirmative for more than two hundred years. Whether the interest is no longer worthy of protection is a public policy decision only the Legislature should make. Since a legally protected interest exists and an invasion of that interest has been admitted in this case, the trial court should determine whether the invasion can be excused or justified. Likewise, the trial court should determine whether the injury sustained is one for which the court should provide a remedy.

The judgment on that issue of liability should be affirmed and the case remanded to the trial court for a determination of damages.

[Justice POMEROY's dissenting opinion omitted.]

COMMENTS

The common law action for criminal conversation has been abolished by legislation in a number of states, together with the causes of action for alienation of affection, seduction, and breach of contract to marry. The stated legislative concern in all instances is the danger that punitive and excessive jury verdicts might lead to extortion. The fact that the legislatures were predominantly male, as were the defendants in such actions, may have played an important role in the decisions. *Fadgen* follows this pattern of abolition; but this time we have a court abolishing a common law action in tort as no longer appropriate to contemporary conditions.

The Equal Protection Clause did not necessarily mandate this result. In fact, an earlier Pennsylvania Supreme Court case, *Karchner v. Mumie*, cited in *Fadgen*, in 1959 extended the cause of action that under common law was available only to men, and permitted married women to recover from the paramours of their husbands. Thus, equal protection could mean extension to both spouses rather than abolition as to either. In *Fadgen*, however, the majority opinion seemed to recognize an inherent power of the courts to abolish such judge-made law, regardless of precedent, if it "is no longer in accord with modern realities."

The reasoning of Justice Manderino in his concurring opinion, referring to freedom of choice, privacy, and the liberties protected by the Due Process Clause of the Fourteenth Amendment, accords with contemporary legal theory. The reference to abortion appears to some particularly apt: If a woman, whether married or not, has a privacy right to have an abortion, perhaps her freedom of choice and individual privacy also covers choice of sexual partner. *Fadgen* did not actually make such drastic pronouncements; it merely abolished a common law cause of action against an outsider intervening in the marriage. The concurring opinion, in response to the dissenting opinion of Justice Roberts, seems to say that the rights of privacy of married women (and consequently of married men) prevail over other considerations, and that, since society no longer has an interest in protecting one spouse against extramarital sexual activity by the other, one can no longer speak of any injury that has resulted. Obviously this view of marriage, although not accepted by a large segment of the general public, seems to some people to be a logical consequence of the reasoning in the abortion decisions.

Fadgen is conventionally seen as a liberal, pro-woman decision, with its rhetoric about women no longer being men's property, and so forth. It could also be seen in a different light. The earlier case of *Karchner v. Mumie* had extended criminal conversation recovery to women (thus making husbands the "property" of wives in a somewhat similar manner as wives were the "property" of husbands). The tort of criminal conversation therefore had the arguably gender-neutral effect of giving one spouse a protectable interest in the sexual exclusivity of the other spouse. One could see the Pennsylvania Supreme Court's decision to be an indication that men would rather give up the right to sue men who cuckold them than to allow their wives to sue the husbands' lovers or to let any woman claim exclusive rights over their sexuality. It should be remembered that all forms of adultery regulation used to be gender-skewed to the disadvantage of women, and thus women had a greater stake in changing or abolishing the laws against adultery. If, as the old stereotype would have it, men in our society are less committed to monogamy than women are, then presumably men now get more out of a permissive attitude toward adultery than women do.

A question not addressed in *Fadgen* is whether husband or wife may have remedies other than criminal prosecution and damages for criminal conversation. In light of *Bauman v. Bauman*, 250 N.Y. 382, 165 N.E. 819 (1929), it is unlikely that an injunction against the intervening outsider is possible. While in the past injunctive relief was denied on the ground that no property rights were involved and that conduct which merely injures a person's feelings cannot be restrained, *Fadgen* gave sufficient cues as to contemporary limitations on injunctive relief: the change of conditions in the relations of husband and wife, freedom of choice and rights of privacy of either spouse, and a declining social concern with intimate relations.

An interesting problem arises if husband and wife are viewed as partners in more than one sense — perhaps with respect to a jointly owned and operated business. Interference by an outsider in a business relationship continues to be subject to a cause of action in tort for damages as well as injunctive relief. Traditional legal theory would probably justify this result by arguing that the marital and business interests can be treated separately. In reality, as we have seen in prior chapters, it becomes increasingly difficult to make such a distinction. The same remedies that have declined within the realm of the family and marriage have survived in business as interference with contract, although both originate from the same historical source — the protection in Roman law of the paterfamilias from outside interference. It would be interesting to see whether the Supreme Court of Pennsylvania would adhere to the reasoning in *Fadgen* if an outsider were to interfere in a husband-and-wife operated business by alienating one of the partners from the other.

REFERENCES

Kenneth L. Karst, *The Freedom of Intimate Association*, 89 YALE L.J. 624 (1980).
William Lloyd Prosser, HANDBOOK OF THE LAW OF TORTS 929–931 (4th ed. 1971).

BOWERS v. HARDWICK

United States Supreme Court
478 U.S. 186 (1986)

Justice WHITE delivered the opinion of the Court.

In August 1982, respondent Hardwick (hereafter respondent) was charged with violating the Georgia statute criminalizing sodomy[1] by committing that act with another adult male in the bedroom of respondent's home. After a preliminary hearing, the District Attorney decided not to present the matter to the grand jury unless further evidence developed.

Respondent then brought suit in the Federal District Court, challenging the constitutionality of the statute insofar as it criminalized consensual sodomy.[2] He asserted that he was a practicing homosexual, that the Georgia sodomy statute, as administered by the defendants, placed him in imminent danger of arrest, and that the statute for several reasons violates the Federal Constitution. The District Court granted the defendants' motion to dismiss for failure to state a claim, relying on *Doe v. Commonwealth's Attorney for the City of Richmond*, 403 F.Supp. 1199 (ED Va.1975), which this Court summarily affirmed, 425 U.S. 901, 96 S.Ct. 1489, 47 L.Ed.2d 751 (1976).

A divided panel of the Court of Appeals for the Eleventh Circuit reversed....

We agree with petitioner that the Court of Appeals erred, and hence reverse its judgment.

---

1. Georgia Code Ann. §16-6-2 (1984) provides, in pertinent part, as follows:

(a) A person commits the offense of sodomy when he performs or submits to any sexual act involving the sex organs of one person and the mouth or anus of another....

(b) A person convicted of the offense of sodomy shall be punished by imprisonment for not less than one nor more than 20 years....

2. John and Mary Doe were also plaintiffs in the action. They alleged that they wished to engage in sexual activity proscribed by §16-6-2 in the privacy of their home, *App.* 3, and that they had been "chilled and deterred" from engaging in such activity by both the existence of the statute and Hardwick's arrest. *Id.*, at 5. The District Court held, however, that because they had neither sustained, nor were in immediate danger of sustaining, any direct injury from the enforcement of the statute, they did not have proper standing to maintain the action. *Id.*, at 18. The Court of Appeals affirmed the District Court's judgment dismissing the Does' claim for lack of standing, 760 F.2d 1202, 1206–1207 (CA11 1985), and the Does do not challenge that holding in this Court.

The only claim properly before the Court, therefore, is Hardwick's challenge to the Georgia statute as applied to consensual homosexual sodomy. We express no opinion on the constitutionality of the Georgia statute as applied to other acts of sodomy.

This case does not require a judgment on whether laws against sodomy between consenting adults in general, or between homosexuals in particular, are wise or desirable. It raises no question about the right or propriety of state legislative decisions to repeal their laws that criminalize homosexual sodomy, or of state-court decisions invalidating those laws on state constitutional grounds. The issue presented is whether the Federal Constitution confers a fundamental right upon homosexuals to engage in sodomy and hence invalidates the laws of the many States that still make such conduct illegal and have done so for a very long time. The case also calls for some judgment about the limits of the Court's role in carrying out its constitutional mandate.

We first register our disagreement with the Court of Appeals and with respondent that the Court's prior cases have construed the Constitution to confer a right of privacy that extends to homosexual sodomy and for all intents and purposes have decided this case. The reach of this line of cases was sketched in *Carey v. Population Services International*, 431 U.S. 678, 685, 97 S.Ct. 2010, 2016, 52 L.Ed.2d 675 (1977). *Pierce v. Society of Sisters*, 268 U.S. 510, 45 S.Ct. 571, 69 L.Ed. 1070 (1925), and *Meyer v. Nebraska*, 262 U.S. 390, 43 S.Ct. 625, 67 L.Ed. 1042 (1923), were described as dealing with child rearing and education; *Prince v. Massachusetts*, 321 U.S. 158, 64 S.Ct. 438, 88 L.Ed. 645 (1944), with family relationships; *Skinner v. Oklahoma ex rel. Williamson*, 316 U.S. 535, 62 S.Ct. 1110, 86 L.Ed. 1655 (1942), with procreation; *Loving v. Virginia*, 388 U.S. 1, 87 S.Ct. 1817, 18 L.Ed.2d 1010 (1967), with marriage; *Griswold v. Connecticut, supra*, and *Eisenstadt v. Baird, supra*, with contraception; and *Roe v. Wade*, 410 U.S. 113, 93 S.Ct. 705, 35 L.Ed.2d 147 (1973), with abortion. The latter three cases were interpreted as construing the Due Process Clause of the Fourteenth Amendment to confer a fundamental individual right to decide whether or not to beget or bear a child. *Carey v. Population Services International, supra*, 431 U.S., at 688–689, 97 S.Ct., at 2017–2018.

Accepting the decisions in these cases and the above description of them, we think it evident that none of the rights announced in those cases bears any resemblance to the claimed constitutional right of homosexuals to engage in acts of sodomy that is asserted in this case. No connection between family, marriage, or procreation on the one hand and homosexual activity on the other has been demonstrated, either by the Court of Appeals or by respondent. Moreover, any claim that these cases nevertheless stand for the proposition that any kind of private sexual conduct between consenting adults is constitutionally insulated from state proscription is unsupportable. Indeed, the Court's opinion in *Carey* twice asserted that the privacy right, which the *Griswold* line of cases found to be one of the protections provided by the Due Process Clause, did not reach so far. 431 U.S., at 688, n. 5, 694, n. 17, 97 S.Ct., at 2018, n. 5, 2021, n. 17.

Precedent aside, however, respondent would have us announce, as the Court of Appeals did, a fundamental right to engage in homosexual sodomy. This we are quite unwilling to do. It is true that despite the language of the Due Process Clauses of the Fifth and Fourteenth Amendments, which appears to focus only on the processes by which life, liberty, or property is taken, the cases are legion in which those Clauses have been interpreted to have substantive content, subsuming rights that to a great extent are immune from federal or state regulation or proscription. Among such cases are those recognizing rights that have little or no textual support in the constitutional language. *Meyer*, *Prince*, and *Pierce* fall in this category, as do the privacy cases from *Griswold* to *Carey*.

Striving to assure itself and the public that announcing rights not readily identifiable in the Constitution's text involves much more than the imposition of the Justices' own choice of values on the States and the Federal Government, the Court has sought to identify the nature of the rights qualifying for heightened judicial protection. In *Palko v. Connecticut*, 302 U.S. 319, 325, 326, 58 S.Ct. 149, 151, 152, 82 L.Ed. 288 (1937), it was said that this category includes those fundamental liberties that are "implicit in the concept of ordered liberty," such that "neither liberty nor justice would exist if [they] were sacrificed." A different description of fundamental liberties appeared in *Moore v. East Cleveland*, 431 U.S. 494, 503, 97 S.Ct. 1932, 1937, 52 L.Ed.2d 531 (1977)(opinion of POWELL, J.), where they are characterized as those liberties that are "deeply rooted in this Nation's history and tradition." *Id.*, at 503, 97 S.Ct., at 1938 (POWELL, J.). See also *Griswold v. Connecticut*, 381 U.S., at 506, 85 S.Ct., at 1693.

It is obvious to us that neither of these formulations would extend a fundamental right to homosexuals to engage in acts of consensual sodomy. Proscriptions against that conduct have ancient roots. See generally, *Survey on the Constitutional Right to Privacy in the Context of Homosexual Activity*, 40 U. Miami L.Rev. 521, 525 (1986). Sodomy was a criminal offense at common law and was forbidden by the laws of the original thirteen States when they ratified the Bill of Rights. In 1868, when the Fourteenth Amendment was ratified, all but 5 of the 37 States in the Union had criminal sodomy laws. In fact, until 1961, all 50 States outlawed sodomy, and today, 24 States and the District of Columbia continue to provide criminal penalties for sodomy performed in private and between consenting adults. See *Survey*, U.Miami L.Rev., supra, at 524, n. 9. Against this background, to claim that a right to engage in such conduct is "deeply rooted in this Nation's history and tradition" or "implicit in the concept of ordered liberty" is, at best, facetious.

Nor are we inclined to take a more expansive view of our authority to discover new fundamental rights imbedded in the Due Process Clause. The Court is most vulnerable and comes nearest to illegitimacy when it deals with judge-made constitutional law having little or no cognizable roots in the language or design of the Constitution. That this is so was painfully demonstrated by the face-off between the Executive and the Court in the 1930's, which resulted in the repudiation much of the substantive gloss that the Court had placed on the Due Process Clauses of the Fifth and Fourteenth Amendments. There should be, therefore, great resistance to expand the substantive reach of those Clauses, particularly if it requires redefining the category of rights deemed to be fundamental. Otherwise, the Judiciary necessarily takes to itself further authority to govern the country without express constitutional authority. The claimed right pressed on us today falls far short of overcoming this resistance.

Respondent, however, asserts that the result should be different where the homosexual conduct occurs in the privacy of the home. He relies on *Stanley v. Georgia*, 394 U.S. 557, 89 S.Ct. 1243, 22 L.Ed.2d 542 (1969), where the Court held that the First Amendment prevents conviction for possessing and reading obscene material in the privacy of one's home: "If the First Amendment means anything, it means that a State has no business telling a man, sitting alone in his house, what books he may read or what films he may watch." *Id.*, at 565, 89 S.Ct., at 1248.

Stanley did protect conduct that would not have been protected outside the home, and it partially prevented the enforcement of state obscenity laws; but the decision was firmly grounded in the First Amendment. The right pressed upon us here has no similar support in the text of the Constitution, and it does not qualify for recognition under the prevailing principles for construing the Fourteenth Amendment. Its limits are also difficult to discern. Plainly enough, otherwise illegal conduct is not always immunized whenever it occurs in the home. Victimless crimes, such as the possession and use of illegal drugs, do not escape the law where they are committed at home. *Stanley* itself recognized that its holding offered no protection for the possession in the home of drugs, firearms, or stolen goods. *Id.*, at 568, n. 11, 89 S.Ct., at 1249, n. 11. And if respondent's submission is limited to the voluntary sexual conduct between consenting adults, it would be difficult, except by fiat, to limit the claimed right to homosexual conduct while leaving exposed to prosecution adultery, incest, and other sexual crimes even though they are committed in the home. We are unwilling to start down that road.

Even if the conduct at issue here is not a fundamental right, respondent asserts that there must be a rational basis for the law and that there is none in this case other than the presumed belief of a majority of the electorate in Georgia that homosexual sodomy is immoral and unacceptable. This is said to be an inadequate rationale to support the law. The law, however, is constantly based on notions of morality, and if all laws representing essentially moral choices are to be invalidated under the Due Process Clause, the courts will be very busy indeed. Even respondent makes no such claim, but insists that majority sentiments about the morality of homosexuality should be declared inadequate. We do not agree, and are unpersuaded that the sodomy laws of some 25 States should be invalidated on this basis.[8]

Accordingly, the judgment of the Court of Appeals is Reversed.

[C.J. BURGER's concurring opinion omitted.]

[J. POWELL's concurring opinion omitted.]

Justice BLACKMUN, with whom Justice BRENNAN, Justice MARSHALL, and Justice STEVENS join, dissenting.

...I believe we must analyze Hardwick's claim in the light of the values that underlie the constitutional right to privacy. If that right means anything, it means that, before Georgia can prosecute its citizens for making choices about the most intimate aspects of their lives, it must do more than assert that the choice they have made is an "abominable crime not fit to be named among Christians." *Herring v. State*, 119 Ga. 709, 721, 46 S.E. 876, 882 (1904).

...

The Court concludes today that none of our prior cases dealing with various decisions that individuals are entitled to make free of governmental interference "bears any resemblance to the claimed constitutional right of homosexuals to engage in acts of sodomy that is asserted in this case." *Ante*, at 190–191. While it is true that these cases may be characterized by their connection to protection of the family, see *Roberts v. United States Jaycees*, 468 U.S. 609, 619, 104 S.Ct. 3244, 3250, 82 L.Ed.2d 462 (1984), the Court's conclusion that they extend no further than this

8. Respondent does not defend the judgment below based on the Ninth Amendment, the Equal Protection Clause, or the Eighth Amendment.

boundary ignores the warning in *Moore v. East Cleveland*, 431 U.S. 494, 501, 97 S.Ct. 1932, 1936, 52 L.Ed.2d 531 (1977)(plurality opinion), against "clos[ing] our eyes to the basic reasons why certain rights associated with the family have been accorded shelter under the Fourteenth Amendment's Due Process Clause." We protect those rights not because they contribute, in some direct and material way, to the general public welfare, but because they form so central a part of an individual's life. "[T]he concept of privacy embodies the 'moral fact that a person belongs to himself and not others nor to society as a whole.'" *Thornburgh v. American College of Obstetricians & Gynecologists*, 476 U.S., at 777, n. 5, 106 S.Ct., at 2187, n. 5 (STEVENS, J., concurring), quoting Fried, *Correspondence*, 6 Phil. & Pub. Affairs 288–289 (1977). And so we protect the decision whether to marry precisely because marriage "is an association that promotes a way of life, not causes; a harmony in living, not political faiths; a bilateral loyalty, not commercial or social projects." *Griswold v. Connecticut*, 381 U.S., at 486, 85 S.Ct., at 1682. We protect the decision whether to have a child because parenthood alters so dramatically an individual's self-definition, not because of demographic considerations or the Bible's command to be fruitful and multiply. *Cf. Thornburgh v. American College of Obstetricians & Gynecologists, supra*, 476 U.S., at 777, n. 6, 106 S.Ct., at 2188, n. 6 (STEVENS, J., concurring). And we protect the family because it contributes so powerfully to the happiness of individuals, not because of a preference for stereotypical households. *Cf. Moore v. East Cleveland*, 431 U.S., at 500–506, 97 S.Ct., at 1936–1939 (plurality opinion). The Court recognized in *Roberts*, 468 U.S., at 619, 104 S.Ct., at 3250, that the "ability independently to define one's identity that is central to any concept of liberty" cannot truly be exercised in a vacuum; we all depend on the "emotional enrichment from close ties with others." *Ibid.*

Only the most willful blindness could obscure the fact that sexual intimacy is "a sensitive, key relationship of human existence, central to family life, community welfare, and the development of human personality," *Paris Adult Theatre I v. Slaton*, 413 U.S. 49, 63, 93 S.Ct. 2628, 2638, 37 L.Ed.2d 446 (1973); see also *Carey v. Population Services International*, 431 U.S. 678, 685, 97 S.Ct. 2010, 2016, 52 L.Ed.2d 675 (1977). The fact that individuals define themselves in a significant way through their intimate sexual relationships with others suggests, in a Nation as diverse as ours, that there may be many "right" ways of conducting those relationships, and that much of the richness of a relationship will come from the freedom an individual has to *choose* the form and nature of these intensely personal bonds. See Karst, *The Freedom of Intimate Association*, 89 Yale L.J. 624, 637 (1980); cf. *Eisenstadt v. Baird*, 405 U.S. 438, 453, 92 S.Ct. 1029, 1038, 31 L.Ed.2d 349 (1972); *Roe v. Wade*, 410 U.S., at 153, 93 S.Ct., at 726.

In a variety of circumstances we have recognized that a necessary corollary of giving individuals freedom to choose how to conduct their lives is acceptance of the fact that different individuals will make different choices. For example, in holding that the clearly important state interest in public education should give way to a competing claim by the Amish to the effect that extended formal schooling threatened their way of life, the Court declared: "There can be no assumption that today's majority is 'right' and the Amish and others like them are 'wrong.' A way of life that is odd or even erratic but interferes with no rights or interests of others is not to be condemned because it is different." *Wisconsin v. Yoder*, 406 U.S. 205, 223–224, 92 S.Ct. 1526, 1537, 32 L.Ed.2d 15 (1972). The Court claims that its decision today merely refuses to recognize a fundamental right to engage in homosexual sodomy; what the Court really has refused to recognize is the fundamental interest all individuals have in controlling the nature of their intimate associations with others.

...

COMMENTS

When the question is characterized to be "whether the Federal Constitution confers a fundamental right upon homosexuals to engage in sodomy," the result seems understandable, if not foreordained. Yet, would most people really say that the Federal Constitution confers a fundamental right upon unwed women to use vaginal foam? Nothing prevents such a characterization of the *Eisenstadt* case. The *Bowers* Court avoided the question of the constitutionality of the sodomy laws as applied to married couples; thus, it could be said that the Court avoided deciding whether the Federal Constitution confers upon married people a fundamental right to engage in sodomy. In particular, it might be difficult to determine exactly what phrases in the Constitution conferred such a right upon a heterosexual man without conferring the same right upon a homosexual man. In fact, it might seem odd to say that the Federal Constitution confers upon married people a fundamental right to engage in French kissing, but it is also hard to think that the Court would uphold any law that attempted to specify how married couples could or could not kiss. Surely such a law would be found to be a constitutional violation, presumably of their right to privacy.

Of course, sodomy violates the religious or moral beliefs of many more people than French kissing does. But to return to the *Eisenstadt* example, using birth control has been considered terribly immoral. Centuries of Christian writers have compared birth control to murder. Yet, the right to use birth control has been guaranteed by the Constitution, and guaranteed to unmarried as well as to married people.

A number of courts have interpreted *Bowers v. Hardwick* to mean that the Constitution offers no protection to the *status* of being a homosexual, as well as offering no protection to certain sexual behavior engaged in by homosexuals. The distinction between status (or desire) and behavior gained increased attention in 1993 during the debate over "gays in the military."

At the moment it appears that the Constitution protects unmarried heterosexual behavior considerably more than it protects the behavior of same-sex couples. Many of the protections denied by the courts, however, are being achieved through the political process. Of course, what the electorate gives, the electorate can also take away if the moral climate or fashion changes.

REFERENCES:

Beverly Wilding Harrison, OUR RIGHT TO CHOOSE (1983).

Phyllis Coleman, *Who's Been Sleeping in My Bed? You and Me, and the State Makes Three*, 24 IND. L. REV. 399 (1991).

Comment, History, *Homosexuality and Political Values: Searching for the Hidden Determinants of Bowers v. Hardwick*, 97 YALE L.J. 1073 (1988).
Note, *From This Day Forward: A Feminine Moral Discourse on Homosexual Marriage*, 97 YALE L.J. 1783 (1988).
Note, *The Miscegenation Analogy: Sodomy Law as Sex Discrimination*, 98 YALE L.J. 145 (1988).
Janet E. Halley, *The Politics of the Closet: Towards Equal Protection for Gay, Lesbian, and Bisexual Identity*, 36 UCLA L. REV. 915 (1989).
Note, *Bowers v. Hardwick: An Incomplete Constitutional Analysis*, 65 N.C. L. REV. 1100 (1987).
Hannah Schwarzchild, *Same-Sex Marriage and Constitutional Privacy: Moral Threat and Legal Anomaly.* 4 BERKELEY WOMEN'S L.J. 94 (1988–89).
Marc A. Fajer, *Can Two Men Eat Quiche Together? Storytelling, Gender Role Stereotypes, and Legal Protection for Lesbians and Gay Men*, 46 U. MIAMI L. REV. 511 (1992).

B: STATE ROLE IN PROMOTING OR MODERATING GENDER-ROLE STEREOTYPES

Wives and Mothers in the Labor Force

CLEVELAND BOARD OF EDUCATION v. LaFLEUR

United States Supreme Court
414 U.S. 632 (1974)

Mr. Justice STEWART delivered the opinion of the Court.

The respondents in No. 72-777 and the petitioner in No. 72-1129 are female public school teachers. During the 1970–1971 school year, each informed her local school board that she was pregnant; each was compelled by a mandatory maternity leave rule to quit her job without pay several months before the expected birth of her child. These cases call upon us to decide the constitutionality of the school boards' rules.

I

Jo Carol LaFleur and Ann Elizabeth Nelson, the respondents in No. 72-777, are junior high school teachers employed by the Board of Education of Cleveland, Ohio. Pursuant to a rule first adopted in 1952, the school board requires every pregnant school teacher to take maternity leave without pay, beginning five months before the expected birth of her child. Application for such leave must be made no later than two weeks prior to the date of departure. A teacher on maternity leave is not allowed to return to work until the beginning of the next regular school semester which follows the date when her child attains the age of three months. A doctor's certificate attesting to the health of the teacher is a prerequisite to return; an additional physical examination may be required. The teacher on maternity leave is not promised re-employment after the birth of the child; she is merely given priority in reassignment to a position for which she is qualified. Failure to comply with the mandatory maternity leave provisions is ground for dismissal.[1]

Neither Mrs. LaFleur nor Mrs. Nelson wished to take an unpaid maternity leave; each wanted to continue teaching until the end of the school year.[2] Because of the mandatory maternity leave rule, however, each was required to leave her job in March 1971.[3] The two women then filed separate suits in the United States District Court for the Northern District of Ohio under 42 U.S.C. §1983, challenging the constitutionality of the maternity leave rule. The District Court tried the cases together, and rejected the plaintiffs' arguments. 326 F.Supp. 1208. A divided panel of the United States Court of Appeals for the Sixth Circuit reversed, finding the Cleveland rule in violation of the Equal Protection Clause of the Fourteenth Amendment.[4] 465 F.2d 1184.

The petitioner in No. 72-1129, Susan Cohen, was employed by the School Board of Chesterfield County, Virginia. That school board's maternity leave regulation requires that a pregnant teacher leave work at least four months prior to the expected birth of her child. Notice in writing must be given to the school board at least six months prior to the expected birth date. A teacher on maternity leave is declared re-eligible for employment when she submits written notice from a physician that she is physically fit for re-employment, and when she can give assurance that care of the child will cause only minimal interference with her job responsibilities. The teacher is guaranteed re-employment no later than the first

---

1. The Cleveland rule provides:

Any married teacher who becomes pregnant and who desires to return to the employ of the Board at a future date may be granted a maternity leave of absence without pay.

APPLICATION A maternity leave of absence shall be effective not less than *five (5) months before the expected date* of the normal birth of the child. Application for such leave shall be forwarded to the Superintendent at least *two (2) weeks before the effective date of the leave of absence.* A leave of absence without pay shall be granted by the Superintendent for a period not to exceed *two (2) years.*

REASSIGNMENT A teacher may return to service from maternity leaves not earlier than the *beginning* of the regular school semester which follows the child's age of *three (3) months.* In unusual circumstances, exceptions to this requirement may be made by the Superintendent with the approval of the Board. *Written* request for return to service from maternity leave must reach the Superintendent at least six (6) weeks prior to the beginning of the semester when the teacher expects to resume teaching and shall be accompanied by a doctor's certificate stating the health and physical condition of the teacher. The Superintendent may require an additional physical examination.

When a teacher qualifies to return from maternity leave, she shall have priority in reassignment to a vacancy for which she is qualified under her certificate, but she shall not have prior claim to the exact position she held before the leave of absence became effective.

A teacher's failure to follow the above rules for maternity leave of absence shall be construed as termination of contract or as grounds for dismissal. (Emphasis in original.)

2. Mrs. LaFleur's child was born on July 28, 1971; Mrs. Nelson's child was born during August of that year.

3. Effective February 1, 1971, the Cleveland regulation was amended to provide that only teachers with one year of continuous service qualified for maternity leave; teachers with less than one year were required to resign at the beginning of the fifth month of pregnancy. Since Mrs. Nelson had less than a year of service at the time she notified her principal that she was pregnant, the school board originally required her to resign her teaching position. The school board has since conceded that the February 1 amendment did not apply to Mrs. Nelson, since it was enacted after her contract of employment was executed. Pursuant to that concession, the board has placed Mrs. Nelson, like Mrs. LaFleur, on mandatory leave.

4. Chief Judge Phillips filed a separate opinion, dissenting in part and concurring in part. He felt that the portion of the challenged regulation requiring maternity leave at the beginning of the fifth month of pregnancy was constitutional; he agreed with the majority, however, that the three-month post-delivery waiting period before becoming eligible to return to teaching was unconstitutional.

day of the school year following the date upon which she is declared re-eligible.[5]

Mrs. Cohen informed the Chesterfield County School Board in November 1970, that she was pregnant and expected the birth of her child about April 28, 1971.[6] She initially requested that she be permitted to continue teaching until April 1, 1971.[7] The school board rejected the request, as it did Mrs. Cohen's subsequent suggestion that she be allowed to teach until January 21, 1971, the end of the first school semester. Instead, she was required to leave her teaching job on December 18, 1970. She subsequently filed this suit under 42 U.S.C. §1983 in the United States District Court for the Eastern District of Virginia. The District Court held that the school board regulation violates the Equal Protection Clause, and granted appropriate relief. 326 F.Supp. 1159. A divided panel of the Fourth Circuit affirmed, but, on rehearing *en banc*, the Court of Appeals upheld the constitutionality of the challenged regulation in a 4–3 decision. 474 F.2d 395.

We granted certiorari in both cases, 411 U.S. 947, 93 S.Ct. 1921, 36 L.Ed.2d 408, in order to resolve the conflict between the Courts of Appeals regarding the constitutionality of such mandatory maternity leave rules for public school teachers.[8]

---

5. The Chesterfield County rule provides:

MATERNITY PROVISIONS

a. Notice in writing must be given to the School Board at least six (6) months prior to the date of expected birth.

b. Termination of employment of an expectant mother shall become effective at least four (4) months prior to the expected birth of the child. Termination of employment may be extended if the superintendent receives written recommendations from the expectant mother's physician and her principal, and if the superintendent feels that an extension will be in the best interest of the pupils and school involved.

c. Maternity Leave

(1) Maternity leave must be requested in writing at the time of termination of employment.

(2) Maternity leave will be granted only to those persons who have a record of satisfactory performance.

(3) An individual will be declared eligible for re-employment when she submits written notice from her physician that she is physically fit for full-time employment and when she can give full assurance that care of the child will cause minimal interference with job responsibilities.

(4) Re-employment will be guaranteed no later than the first day of the school year following the date that the individual was declared eligible for re-employment.

(5) All personnel benefits accrued, including seniority, will be retained during maternity leave unless the person concerned shall have accepted other employment.

(6) The school system will have discharged its responsibility under this policy after offering re-employment for the first vacancy that occurs after the individual has been declared eligible for re-employment.

6. Mrs. Cohen's child was in fact born on May 2.

7. Unlike the Cleveland rule, n. 1, *supra*, the Chesterfield County regulation allows the superintendent of schools to extend a teacher's employment beyond the normal cutoff date, if he determines that such action is in the best interests of the students and school involved. See n. 5, *supra*.

8. Apart from the cases here under review, there are at least three other reported federal appellate opinions dealing with the constitutionality of mandatory maternity leave regulations. Compare *Green v. Waterford Board of Education*, 473 F.2d 629 (CA2), and *Buckley v. Coyle Public School System*, 476 F.2d 92 (CA10)(both invalidating mandatory leave rules for pregnant public school teachers) with *Schattman v. Texas Employment Comm'n*, 459 F.2d 32 (CA5)(upholding a leave policy of a state agency).

For opinions of the district courts dealing with mandatory maternity leaves, see, *e.g.*, *Heath v. Westerville Board of Education*, 345 F.Supp. 501 (SD Ohio); *Pocklington v. Duval County School Board*, 345 F.Supp. 163 (MD Fla.); *Bravo v. Board of Education of the City of Chicago*, 345 F.Supp. 155 (ND Ill.); *Williams v. San Francisco Unified School District*, 340 F.Supp. 438 (ND Cal.); *Seaman v. Spring Lake Park Independent School District*, 363 F.Supp. 944 (Minn.); *Monell v. Department of Social Services*, 357 F.Supp. 1051 (SDNY).

Cf. Struck v. Secretary of Defense, 460 F.2d 1372 (CA9), vacated and remanded to consider the issue of mootness 409 U.S. 1071, 93 S.Ct. 676, 34 L.Ed.2d 660; *Gutierrez v. Laird*, 346 F.Supp. 289 (DC); *Robinson v. Rand*, 340 F.Supp. 37 (Colo.)(all dealing with Air Force regulations requiring separation of pregnant personnel).

The practical impact of our decision in the present cases may have been somewhat lessened by several recent developments. At the time that the teachers in these cases were placed on maternity leave, Title VII of the Civil Rights Act of 1964, 78 Stat. 253, 42 U.S.C. §2000e *et seq.*, did not apply to state agencies and educational institutions. 42 U.S.C. §§2000e(b) and 2000e-1. On March 24, 1972, however, the Equal Employment Opportunity

II

This Court has long recognized that freedom of personal choice in matters of marriage and family life is one of the liberties protected by the Due Process Clause of the Fourteenth Amendment. *Roe v. Wade*, 410 U.S. 113, 93 S.Ct. 705, 35 L.Ed.2d 147; *Loving v. Virginia*, 388 U.S. 1, 12, 87 S.Ct. 1817, 1823, 18 L.Ed.2d 1010; *Griswold v. Connecticut*, 381 U.S. 479, 85 S.Ct. 1678, 14 L.Ed.2d 510; *Pierce v. Society of Sisters*, 268 U.S. 510, 45 S.Ct. 571, 69 L.Ed. 1070; *Meyer v. Nebraska*, 262 U.S. 390, 43 S.Ct. 625, 67 L.Ed. 1042. See also *Prince v. Massachusetts*, 321 U.S. 158, 64 S.Ct. 438, 88 L.Ed. 645; *Skinner v. Oklahoma*, 316 U.S. 535, 62 S.Ct. 1110, 86 L.Ed. 1655. As we noted in *Eisenstadt v. Baird*, 405 U.S. 438, 453, 92 S.Ct. 1029, 1038, 31 L.Ed.2d 349, there is a right "to be free from unwarranted governmental intrusion into matters so fundamentally affecting a person as the decision whether to bear or beget a child."

By acting to penalize the pregnant teacher for deciding to bear a child, overly restrictive maternity leave regulations can constitute a heavy burden on the exercise of these protected freedoms. Because public school maternity leave rules directly affect "one of the basic civil rights of man," *Skinner v. Oklahoma, supra*, 316 U.S., at 541, 62 S.Ct., at 1113, the Due Process Clause of the Fourteenth Amendment requires that such rules must not needlessly, arbitrarily, or capriciously impinge upon this vital area of a teacher's constitutional liberty. The question before us in these cases is whether the interests advanced in support of the rules of the Cleveland and Chesterfield County School Boards can justify the particular procedures they have adopted.

The school boards in these cases have offered two essentially overlapping explanations for their mandatory maternity leave rules. First, they contend that the firm cutoff dates are necessary to maintain continuity of classroom instruction, since advance knowledge of when a pregnant teacher must leave facilitates the finding and hiring of a qualified substitute. Secondly, the school boards seek to justify their maternity rules by arguing that at least some teachers become physically incapable of adequately performing certain of their duties during the latter part of pregnancy. By keeping the pregnant teacher out of the classroom during these final months, the maternity leave rules are said to protect the health of the teacher and her unborn child, while at the same time assuring that students have a physically capable instructor in the classroom at all times.[9]

---

8. *Continued.*

Act of 1972 amended Title VII to withdraw those exemptions. Pub.L. 92-261, 86 Stat. 103. Shortly thereafter, the Equal Employment Opportunity Commission promulgated guidelines providing that a mandatory leave or termination policy for pregnant women presumptively violates Title VII. 29 CFR §1604.10, 37 Fed.Reg. 6837. While the statutory amendments and the administrative regulations are, of course, inapplicable to the cases now before us, they will affect like suits in the future.

In addition, a number of other federal agencies have promulgated regulations similar to those of the Equal Employment Opportunity Commission, forbidding discrimination against pregnant workers with regard to sick leave policies. See, *e.g.*, 5 CFR §630.401(b)(Civil Service Commission); 41 CFR §60-20.3(g)(Office of Federal Contract Compliance). See generally Koontz, *Childbirth and Child Rearing Leave: Job-Related Benefits*, 17 N.Y.L.F. 480, 487–490; Comment, *Love's Labors Lost: New Conceptions of Maternity Leaves*, 7 HARV.CIV. RIGHTS-CIV.LIB.L.REV. 260, 280–281. We, of course, express no opinion as to the validity of any of these regulations.

9. The records in these cases suggest that the maternity leave regulations may have originally been inspired by other, less weighty, considerations. For example, Dr. Mark C. Schinnerer, who served as Superintendent of Schools in Cleveland at the time the leave rule was adopted, testified in the District Court that the rule had been adopted in part to save pregnant teachers from embarrassment at the hands of giggling schoolchildren; the cutoff date at the end of the fourth month was chosen because this was when the teacher "began to show." Similarly, at least several members of the Chesterfield County School Board thought a mandatory leave rule was justified in order to insulate schoolchildren from the sight of conspicuously pregnant women. One

It cannot be denied that continuity of instruction is a significant and legitimate educational goal. Regulations requiring pregnant teachers to provide early notice of their condition to school authorities undoubtedly facilitate administrative planning toward the important objective of continuity. But, as the Court of Appeals for the Second Circuit noted in *Green v. Waterford Board of Education*, 473 F.2d 629, 635:

> Where a pregnant teacher provides the Board with a date certain for commencement of leave...that value [continuity] is preserved; an arbitrary leave date set at the end of the fifth month is no more calculated to facilitate a planned and orderly transition between the teacher and a substitute than is a date fixed closer to confinement. Indeed, the latter...would afford the Board more, not less, time to procure a satisfactory long-term substitute. (Footnote omitted.)

Thus, while the advance-notice provisions in the Cleveland and Chesterfield County rules are wholly rational and may well be necessary to serve the objective of continuity of instruction, the absolute requirements of termination at the end of the fourth or fifth month of pregnancy are not. Were continuity the only goal, cutoff dates much later during pregnancy would serve as well as or better than the challenged rules, providing that ample advance notice requirements were retained. Indeed, continuity would seem just as well attained if the teacher herself were allowed to choose the date upon which to commence her leave, at least so long as the decision were required to be made and notice given of it well in advance of the date selected.[10]

In fact, since the fifth or sixth month of pregnancy will obviously begin at different times in the school year for different teachers, the present Cleveland and Chesterfield County rules may serve to hinder attainment of the very continuity objectives that they are purportedly designed to promote. For example, the beginning of the fifth month of pregnancy for both Mrs. LaFleur and Mrs. Nelson occurred during March of 1971. Both were thus required to leave work with only a few months left in the school year, even though both were fully willing to serve through the end of the term.[11] Similarly, if continuity were the only goal, it seems ironic that the Chesterfield County rule forced Mrs. Cohen to leave work in mid-December 1970 rather than at the end of the semester in January, as she requested.

We thus conclude that the arbitrary cutoff dates embodied in the mandatory leave rules before us have no rational relationship to the valid state interest of preserving continuity of instruction. As long as the teachers are required to give substantial advance notice of their condition, the choice of firm dates later in

---

9. *Continued*

member of the school board thought that it was "not good for the school system" for students to view pregnant teachers, "because some of the kids say, my teacher swallowed a water melon, things like that."

The school boards have not contended in this Court that these considerations can serve as a legitimate basis for a rule requiring pregnant women to leave work; we thus note the comments only to illustrate the possible role of outmoded taboos in the adoption of the rules. Cf. *Green v. Waterford Board of Education*, 473 F.2d, at 635 ("Whatever may have been the reaction in Queen Victoria's time, pregnancy is no longer a dirty word").

10. It is, of course, possible that either premature childbirth or complications in the latter stages of pregnancy might upset even the most careful plans of the teacher, the substitute, and the school board. But there is nothing in these records to indicate that such emergencies could not be handled, as are all others, through the normal use of the emergency substitute teacher process. See *Green, supra*, at 635–636.

11. Indeed, it is somewhat difficult to view the Cleveland mandatory leave rule as seriously furthering the goal of continuity, since the rule requires only two weeks' advance notice before the leave is to commence.

pregnancy would serve the boards' objectives just as well, while imposing a far lesser burden on the women's exercise of constitutionally protected freedom.

The question remains as to whether the cutoff dates at the beginning of the fifth and sixth months can be justified on the other ground advanced by the school boards — the necessity of keeping physically unfit teachers out of the classroom. There can be no doubt that such an objective is perfectly legitimate, both on educational and safety grounds. And, despite the plethora of conflicting medical testimony in these cases, we can assume, *arguendo*, that at least some teachers become physically disabled from effectively performing their duties during the latter stages of pregnancy.

The mandatory termination provisions of the Cleveland and Chesterfield County rules surely operate to insulate the classroom from the presence of potentially incapacitated pregnant teachers. But the question is whether the rules sweep too broadly. See *Shelton v. Tucker*, 364 U.S. 479, 81 S.Ct. 247, 5 L.Ed.2d 231. That question must be answered in the affirmative, for the provisions amount to a conclusive presumption that every pregnant teacher who reaches the fifth or sixth month of pregnancy is physically incapable of continuing. There is no individualized determination by the teacher's doctor — or the school board's — as to any particular teacher's ability to continue at her job. The rules contain an irrebuttable presumption of physical incompetency, and that presumption applies even when the medical evidence as to an individual woman's physical status might be wholly to the contrary.

As the Court noted last Term in *Vlandis v. Kline*, 412 U.S. 441, 446, 93 S.Ct. 2230, 2233, 37 L.Ed.2d 63, "permanent irrebuttable presumptions have long been disfavored under the Due Process Clause of the Fifth and Fourteenth Amendments." In *Vlandis*, the Court declared unconstitutional, under the Due Process Clause of the Fourteenth Amendment, a Connecticut statute mandating an irrebuttable presumption of nonresidency for the purposes of qualifying for reduced tuition rates at a state university. We said in that case, *id.*, at 452, 93 S.Ct., at 2236:

> [I]t is forbidden by the Due Process Clause to deny an individual the resident rates on the basis of a permanent and irrebuttable presumption of nonresidence, when that presumption is not necessarily or universally true in fact, and when the State has reasonable alternative means of making the crucial determination.

Similarly, in *Stanley v. Illinois*, 405 U.S. 645, 92 S.Ct. 1208, 31 L.Ed.2d 551, the Court held that an Illinois statute containing an irrebuttable presumption that unmarried fathers are incompetent to raise their children violated the Due Process Clause. Because of the statutory presumption, the State took custody of all illegitimate children upon the death of the mother, without allowing the father to attempt to prove his parental fitness. As the Court put the matter:

> It may be, as the State insists, that most unmarried fathers are unsuitable and neglectful parents. It may also be that Stanley is such a parent and that his children should be placed in other hands. But all unmarried fathers are not in this category; some are wholly suited to have custody of their children. *Id.*, at 654, 92 S.Ct., at 1214 (footnotes omitted).

Hence, we held that the State could not conclusively presume that any particular unmarried father was unfit to raise his child; the Due Process Clause required a more individualized determination. See also *United States Dept. of Agriculture v. Murry*, 413 U.S. 508, 93 S.Ct. 2832; *id.*, at 514–517, 93 S.Ct., at 2836–2837 (concurring opinion); *Bell v. Burson*, 402 U.S. 535, 91 S.Ct. 1586, 29 L.Ed.2d 90; *Carrington v. Rash*, 380 U.S. 89, 85 S.Ct. 775, 13 L.Ed.2d 675.

These principles control our decision in the cases before us. While the medical experts in these cases differed on many points, they unanimously agreed on one — the ability of any particular pregnant woman to continue at work past any fixed time in her pregnancy is very much an individual matter.[12] Even assuming, *arguendo*, that there are some women who would be physically unable to work past the particular cutoff dates embodied in the challenged rules, it is evident that there are large numbers of teachers who are fully capable of continuing work for longer than the Cleveland and Chesterfield County regulations will allow. Thus, the conclusive presumption embodied in these rules, like that in *Vlandis*, is neither "necessarily [nor] universally true," and is violative of the Due Process Clause.

The school boards have argued that the mandatory termination dates serve the interest of administrative convenience, since there are many instances of teacher pregnancy, and the rules obviate the necessity for case-by-case determinations. Certainly, the boards have an interest in devising prompt and efficient procedures to achieve their legitimate objectives in this area. But, as the Court stated in *Stanley v. Illinois, supra*, 405 U.S., at 656, 92 S.Ct., at 1215:

> [T]he Constitution recognizes higher values than speed and efficiency. Indeed, one might fairly say of the Bill of Rights in general, and the Due Process Clause in particular, that they were designed to protect the fragile values of a vulnerable citizenry from the overbearing concern for efficiency and efficacy that may characterize praiseworthy government officials no less, and perhaps more, than mediocre ones. (Footnote omitted.)

While it might be easier for the school boards to conclusively presume that all pregnant women are unfit to teach past the fourth or fifth month or even the first month, of pregnancy, administrative convenience alone is insufficient to make valid what otherwise is a violation of due process of law.[13] The Fourteenth Amendment requires the school boards to employ alternative administrative

---

12. There were three medical witnesses in the Cleveland case: Dr. Sarah Marcus and Dr. Veners Rutenbeigs (Mrs. Nelson's obstetrician), who testified on behalf of the respondents, and Dr. William C. Weir, the petitioners' expert. While Dr. Weir generally disagreed with his colleagues on the potential effects of pregnancy on a teacher's job performance, he noted that each pregnancy was an individual matter, and should be prescribed for as such. Similarly, the two medical experts in the Chesterfield County case, Dr. Leo J. Dunn and Dr. David C. Forrest, testified that each particular pregnancy must be managed as an individual matter. Cf. R. Benson, HANDBOOK OF OBSTETRICS & GYNECOLOGY, 109 (4th ed. 1971); Curran, *Equal Protection of the Law: Pregnant School Teachers*, 285 NEW ENGLAND J. MEDICINE, 336; Comment, *Mandatory Maternity Leave of Absence Policies — An Equal Protection Analysis*, 45 TEMP.L.Q. 240, 245.

13. This is not to say that the only means for providing appropriate protection for the rights of pregnant teachers is an individualized determination in each case and in every circumstance. We are not dealing in these cases with maternity leave regulations requiring a termination of employment at some firm date during the last few weeks of pregnancy. We therefore have no occasion to decide whether such regulations might be justified by considerations not presented in these records — for example, widespread medical consensus about the "disabling" effect of pregnancy on a teacher's job performance during these latter days, or evidence showing that such firm cutoffs were the only reasonable method of avoiding the possibility of labor beginning while some teacher was in the classroom, or proof that adequate substitutes could not be procured without at least some minimal lead time and certainty as to the dates upon which their employment was to begin.

means, which do not so broadly infringe upon basic constitutional liberty, in support of their legitimate goals.[14]

We conclude, therefore, that neither the necessity for continuity of instruction nor the state interest in keeping physically unfit teachers out of the classroom can justify the sweeping mandatory leave regulations that the Cleveland and Chesterfield County School Boards have adopted. While the regulations no doubt represent a good-faith attempt to achieve a laudable goal, they cannot pass muster under the Due Process Clause of the Fourteenth Amendment, because they employ irrebuttable presumptions that unduly penalize a female teacher for deciding to bear a child.

III

In addition to the mandatory termination provisions, both the Cleveland and Chesterfield County rules contain limitations upon a teacher's eligibility to return to work after giving birth. Again, the school boards offer two justifications for the return rules — continuity of instruction and the desire to be certain that the teacher is physically competent when she returns to work. As is the case with the leave provisions, the question is not whether the school board's goals are legitimate, but rather whether the particular means chosen to achieve those objectives unduly infringe upon the teacher's constitutional liberty.

Under the Cleveland rule, the teacher is not eligible to return to work until the beginning of the next regular school semester following the time when her child attains the age of three months. A doctor's certificate attesting to the teacher's health is required before return; an additional physical examination may be required at the option of the school board.

The respondents in No. 72-777 do not seriously challenge either the medical requirements of the Cleveland rule or the policy of limiting eligibility to return to the next semester following birth. The provisions concerning a medical certificate or supplemental physical examination are narrowly drawn methods of protecting the school board's interest in teacher fitness; these requirements allow an individualized decision as to the teacher's condition, and thus avoid the pitfalls of the presumptions inherent in the leave rules. Similarly, the provision limiting eligibility to return to the semester following delivery is a precisely drawn means of serving the school board's interest in avoiding unnecessary changes in classroom personnel during any one school term.

The Cleveland rule, however, does not simply contain these reasonable medical and next-semester eligibility provisions. In addition, the school board requires the mother to wait until her child reaches the age of three months before the return rules begin to operate. The school board has offered no reasonable justification for this supplemental limitation, and we can perceive none. To the extent that the three-month provision reflects the school board's thinking that no mother is fit to return until that point in time, it suffers from the same constitutional deficiencies that plague the irrebuttable presumption in the termination rules.[15] The

---

14. The school boards have available to them reasonable alternative methods of keeping physically unfit teachers out of the classroom. For example, they could require the pregnant teacher to submit to medical examination by a school board physician, or simply require each teacher to submit a current certification from her obstetrician as to her ability to continue work. Indeed, when evaluating the physical ability of a teacher to *return* to work, each school board in this case relies upon precisely such procedures. See nn. 1 and 5, *supra;* see also text, *infra*, at 800–801.

15. It is clear that the factual hypothesis of such a presumption — that no mother is physically fit to return to work until her child reaches the age of three months — is neither necessarily nor universally true. See

presumption, moreover, is patently unnecessary, since the requirement of a physician's certificate or a medical examination fully protects the school's interests in this regard. And finally, the three-month provision simply has nothing to do with continuity of instruction, since the precise point at which the child will reach the relevant age will obviously occur at a different point throughout the school year for each teacher.

Thus, we conclude that the Cleveland return rule, insofar as it embodies the three-month age provision, is wholly arbitrary and irrational, and hence violates the Due Process Clause of the Fourteenth Amendment. The age limitation serves no legitimate state interest, and unnecessarily penalizes the female teacher for asserting her right to bear children.

We perceive no such constitutional infirmities in the Chesterfield County rule. In that school system, the teacher becomes eligible for re-employment upon submission of a medical certificate from her physician; return to work is guaranteed no later than the beginning of the next school year following the eligibility determination.[16] The medical certificate is both a reasonable and narrow method of protecting the school board's interest in teacher fitness, while the possible deferring of return until the next school year serves the goal of preserving continuity of instruction. In short, the Chesterfield County rule manages to serve the legitimate state interests here without employing unnecessary presumptions that broadly burden the exercise of protected constitutional liberty.

IV

For the reasons stated, we hold that the mandatory termination provisions of the Cleveland and Chesterfield County maternity regulations violate the Due Process Clause of the Fourteenth Amendment, because of their use of unwarranted conclusive presumptions that seriously burden the exercise of protected constitutional liberty. For similar reasons, we hold the three-month provision of the Cleveland return rule unconstitutional.

Accordingly, the judgment in No. 72-777 is affirmed; the judgment in No. 72-1129 is reversed, and the case is remanded to the Court of Appeals for the Fourth Circuit for further proceedings consistent with this opinion.

It is so ordered.

Mr. Justice DOUGLAS concurs in the result.

---

15. *Continued.*

R. Benson, *supra*, n. 12, at 209 (patient may return to "full activity or employment" if course of progress up to fourth or fifth week is normal). Cf. Comment, *Love's Labors Lost: New Conceptions of Maternity Leaves*, 7 HARV.CIV.RIGHTS-CIV.LIB.L.REV., at 262 n. 11, 287 n. 145.

Of course, it may be that the Cleveland rule is based upon another theory — that new mothers are too busy with their children within the first three months to allow a return to work. Viewed in that light, the rule remains a conclusive presumption, whose underlying factual assumptions can hardly be said to be universally valid.

16. The Virginia rule also requires that the teacher give assurance that care of the child will not unduly interfere with her job duties. While such a requirement has within it the potential for abuse, there is no evidence on this record that the assurance required here is anything more than that routinely sought by employers from prospective employees — that the worker is willing to devote full attention to job duties. Nor is there any evidence in this record that the school authorities do not routinely accept the woman's assurance of her ability to return.

Mr. Justice POWELL, concurring in the result.

I concur in the Court's result, but I am unable to join its opinion. In my view these cases should not be decided on the ground that the mandatory maternity leave regulations impair any right to bear children or create an "irrebuttable presumption." It seems to me that equal protection analysis is the appropriate frame of reference.

These regulations undoubtedly add to the burdens of childbearing. But certainly not every government policy that burdens childbearing violates the Constitution. Limitations on the welfare benefits a family may receive that do not take into account the size of the family illustrate this point. See *Dandridge v. Williams*, 397 U.S. 471, 90 S.Ct. 1153, 25 L.Ed.2d 491 (1970). Undoubtedly Congress could, as another example, constitutionally seek to discourage excessive population growth by limiting tax deductions for dependents. That would represent an intentional governmental effort to "penalize" childbearing. See *ante*, at 796. The regulations here do not have that purpose. Their deterrent impact is wholly incidental. If some intentional efforts to penalize childbearing are constitutional, and if *Dandridge, supra*, means what I think it does, then certainly these regulations are not invalid as an infringement of any right to procreate.

I am also troubled by the Court's return to the "irrebuttable presumption" line of analysis of *Stanley v. Illinois*, 405 U.S. 645, 92 S.Ct. 1208, 31 L.Ed.2d 551 (1972)(POWELL, J., not participating), and *Vlandis v. Kline*, 412 U.S. 441, 93 S.Ct. 2230, 37 L.Ed.2d 63 (1973). Although I joined the opinion of the Court in *Vlandis* and continue fully to support the result reached there, the present cases have caused me to re-examine the "irrebuttable presumption" rationale. This has led me to the conclusion that the Court should approach that doctrine with extreme care. There is much to what Mr. Justice REHNQUIST says in his dissenting opinion, *post*, at 660, about the implications of the doctrine for the traditional legislative power to operate by classification. As a matter of logic, it is difficult to see the terminus of the road upon which the Court has embarked under the banner of "irrebuttable presumptions." If the Court nevertheless uses "irrebuttable presumption" reasoning selectively, the concept at root often will be something else masquerading as a due process doctrine. That something else, of course, is the Equal Protection Clause.

These cases present precisely the kind of problem susceptible of treatment by classification. Most school teachers are women, a certain percentage of them are pregnant at any given time, and pregnancy is a normal biological function possessing, in the great majority of cases, a fairly well defined term. The constitutional difficulty is not that the boards attempted to deal with this problem by classification. Rather, it is that the boards chose irrational classifications.

A range of possible school board goals emerge from the cases. Several may be put to one side. The records before us abound with proof that a principal purpose behind the adoption of the regulations was to keep visibly pregnant teachers out of the sight of schoolchildren.[1] The boards do not advance this today as a legitimate objective, yet its initial primacy casts a shadow over these cases. Moreover, most of the after-the-fact rationalizations proposed by these boards are unsupported in the records. The boards emphasize teacher absenteeism, classroom discipline, the safety of schoolchildren, and the safety of the expectant mother and her unborn child. No doubt these are legitimate concerns. But the boards have

1. See, *e.g.*, *ante*, at 641, n. 9.

failed to demonstrate that these interests are in fact threatened by the continued employment of pregnant teachers.

To be sure, the boards have a legitimate and important interest in fostering continuity of teaching. And, even a normal pregnancy may at some point jeopardize that interest. But the classifications chosen by these boards, so far as we have been shown, are either counterproductive or irrationally overinclusive even with regard to this significant, nonillusory goal. Accordingly, in my opinion these regulations are invalid under rational-basis standards of equal protection review.[2]

In speaking of continuity of teaching, the boards are referring in part to their valid interest in reducing the number of times a new teacher is assigned to a given class. It is particularly appropriate to avoid teacher turnover in the middle of a semester, since continuity in teaching approach, as well as teacher-pupil relationships, is otherwise impaired. That aspect of the Cleveland regulation limiting a teacher's eligibility to return to the classroom to the semester following delivery, which the Court approves, *ante*, at 649, rationally serves this legitimate state interest. But the four-and five-months prebirth leave periods of the two regulations and the three-month post-birth provision of the Cleveland regulation do not. As the Court points out, *ante*, at 642–643, such cutoff points are more likely to prevent continuity of teaching than to preserve it. Because the cutoff dates occur throughout the school year, they inevitably result in the removal of many capable teachers from the classroom in the middle or near the end of a semester, thus provoking the disruption the boards hope to avoid.

The boards' reference to continuity of teaching also encompasses their need to assure constant classroom coverage by teachers who are up to the task. This interest is obviously legitimate. No one disputes that a school board must concern itself with the physical and emotional capabilities of its teachers. But the objectionable portions of these regulations appear to be bottomed on factually unsupported assumptions about the ability of pregnant teachers to perform their jobs. The overwhelming weight of the medical testimony adduced in these cases is that most teachers undergoing normal pregnancies are quite capable of carrying out their responsibilities until some ill-defined point a short period prior to term. Certainly the boards have made little effort to contradict this conclusion. Thus, it appears that by forcing all pregnant teachers undergoing a normal pregnancy from the classroom so far in advance of term, the regulations compel large numbers of able-bodied teachers to quit work.[3] Once more, such policies inhibit, rather than further, the goal of continuity of teaching. For no apparent reason, they remove teachers from their students and require the use of substitutes.

The boards' reliance on the goal of continuity of teaching also takes into account their obvious planning needs. Boards must know when pregnant teachers will temporarily cease their teaching responsibilities, so that substitutes may be scheduled to fill the vacancies. And, planning requires both notice of pregnancy and a fixed termination date. It appears, however, that any termination date serves

2. I do not reach the question whether sexbased classifications invoke strict judicial scrutiny, *e.g.*, *Frontiero v. Richardson*, 411 U.S. 677, 93 S.Ct. 1764, 36 L.Ed.2d 583 (1973), or whether these regulations involve sex classifications at all. Whether the challenged aspects of the regulations constitute sex classifications or disability classifications, they must at least rationally serve some legitimate articulated or obvious state interest. While there are indeed some legitimate state interests at stake here, it has not been shown that they are rationally furthered by the challenged portions of these regulations.

3. Teachers who undergo abnormal pregnancies may well be disabled, either temporarily or for a substantial period. But as I read the Court, boards may deal with abnormal pregnancies like any other disability. *Ante*, at 642, n. 10.

the purpose.[4] The choice of a cutoff date that produces several months of forced unemployment is thus wholly unnecessary to the planning of the boards. Certainly nothing in the records of these cases is to the contrary.

For the above reasons, I believe the linkage between the boards' legitimate ends and their chosen means is too attenuated to support those portions of the regulations overturned by the Court. Thus, I concur in the Court's result. But I think it important to emphasize the degree of latitude the Court, as I read it, has left the boards for dealing with the real and recurrent problems presented by teacher pregnancies. Boards may demand in every case "substantial advance notice of [pregnancy]...." *Ante*, at 643. Subject to certain restrictions, they may require all pregnant teachers to cease teaching "at some firm date during the last few weeks of pregnancy...." *Id.*, at 647 n. 13.[5] The Court further holds that boards may in all cases restrict reentry into teaching to the outset of the school term following delivery. *Id.*, at 649.

In my opinion, such class-wide rules for pregnant teachers are constitutional under traditional equal protection standards.[6] School boards, confronted with sensitive and widely variable problems of public education, must be accorded latitude in the operation of school systems and in the adoption of rules and regulations of general application. *E.g., San Antonio Independent School District v. Rodriguez*, 411 U.S. 1, 42–43, 93 S.Ct. 1278, 1301–1302, 36 L.Ed.2d 16 (1973). A large measure of discretion is essential to the effective discharge of the duties vested in these local, often elective, governmental units. My concern with the Court's opinion is that, if carried to logical extremes, the emphasis on individualized treatment is at war with this need for discretion. Indeed, stringent insistence on individualized treatment may be quite impractical in a large school district with thousands of teachers.

But despite my reservations as to the rationale of the majority, I nevertheless conclude that in these cases the gap between the legitimate interests of the boards and the particular means chosen to attain them is too wide. A restructuring generally along the lines indicated in the Court's opinion seems unavoidable. Accordingly, I concur in its result.

Mr. Justice REHNQUIST, with whom the CHIEF JUSTICE joins, dissenting.

The Court rests its invalidation of the school regulations involved in these cases on the Due Process Clause of the Fourteenth Amendment, rather than on any claim of sexual discrimination under the Equal Protection Clause of that Amendment. My Brother STEWART thereby enlists the Court in another quixotic

---

4. One may question, however, whether planning needs are well served by the mere two-week gap between notice and departure set forth in the Cleveland regulation. The brief notice the Cleveland board has allowed itself casts some doubt on that board's reliance on planning needs.

5. The Court's language does not specify a particular prebirth cutoff point, and we need not decide that issue, as these boards have attempted to support only four- and five-month dates. In light of the Court's language, however, I would think that a four-week prebirth period would be acceptable. I do not agree with the Court's view of the stringent standards a board must meet to justify a reasonable prebirth cutoff date. See *ante*, at 647 n. 13. Nothing in the Constitution mandates the heavy burden of justification the Court has imposed on the boards in this regard. If school boards must base their policies on a "widespread medical consensus...," the "only reasonable method..." for accomplishing a goal, or a demonstration that needed services will otherwise be impossible to obtain, *ibid.*, they may be seriously handicapped in the performance of their duties.

6. As the Court notes, these cases arose prior to the recent amendment extending Title VII of the Civil Rights Act of 1964, 42 U.S.C. §2000e *et seq.*, to state agencies and educational institutions. Pub.L. 92-261, 86 Stat. 103. See *ante*, at 639 n 8. Like the Court, I do not address the impact of Title VII on mandatory maternity leave regulations.

engagement in his apparently unending war on irrebuttable presumptions. In these cases we are told that although a regulation "requiring a termination of employment at some firm date during the last few weeks of pregnancy," *ante*, at 647 n. 13, might pass muster, the regulations here challenged requiring termination at the end of the fourth or fifth month of pregnancy violate due process of law.

As the CHIEF JUSTICE pointed out in his dissent last year in *Vlandis v. Kline*, 412 U.S. 441, 93 S.Ct. 2230, 37 L.Ed.2d 63, "literally thousands of state statutes create classifications permanent in duration, which are less than perfect, as all legislative classifications are, and might be improved on by individualized determinations...." *Id.*, at 462, 93 S.Ct., at 2241. Hundreds of years ago in England, before Parliament came to be thought of as a body having general lawmaking power, controversies were determined on an individualized basis without benefit of any general law. Most students of government consider the shift from this sort of determination, made on an *ad hoc* basis by the King's representative, to a relatively uniform body of rules enacted by a body exercising legislative authority, to have been a significant step forward in the achievement of a civilized political society. It seems to me a little late in the day for this Court to weigh in against such an established consensus.

Countless state and federal statutes draw lines such as those drawn by the regulations here which, under the Court's analysis, might well prove to be arbitrary in individual cases. The District of Columbia Code, for example, draws lines with respect to age for several purposes. The Code requires that a person to be eligible to vote be 18 years of age,[1] that a male be 18 and a female be 16 before a valid marriage may be contracted,[2] that alcoholic beverages not be sold to a person under the age of 21 years,[3] or beer or light wines to any person under the age of 18 years.[4] A resident of the District of Columbia must be 16 years of age to obtain a permit to operate a motor vehicle,[5] and the District of Columbia delegate to the United States Congress must be 25 years old.[6] Nothing in the Court's opinion clearly demonstrates why its logic would not equally well sustain in challenge to these laws from a 17-year-old who insists that he is just as well informed for voting purposes as an 18-year-old, from a 20-year-old who insists that he is just as able to carry his liquor as a 21-year-old, or from the numerous other persons who fall on the outside of lines drawn by these and similar statutes.

More closely in point is the jeopardy in which the Court's opinion places long-standing statutes providing for mandatory retirement of government employees. Title 5 U.S.C. §8335 provides with respect to Civil Service employees:

> (a) Except as otherwise provided by this section, an employee who becomes 70 years of age and completes 15 years of service shall be automatically separated from the service....

It was pointed out by my Brother STEWART only last year in his concurring opinion in *Roe v. Wade*, 410 U.S. 113, 168, 93 S.Ct. 705, 734, 35 L.Ed.2d 147, that

1. D.C.Code Ann. §1-1102 (1973).
2. *Id.*, §30-103.
3. *Id.*, §25-121.
4. *Ibid.*
5. *Id.*, §40-301.
6. *Id.*, §1-291(b)(2).

"the 'liberty' protected by the Due Process Clause of the Fourteenth Amendment covers more than those freedoms explicitly named in the Bill of Rights.... Cf. ...*Truax v. Raich*, 239 U.S. 33, 41, 36 S.Ct. 7, 60 L.Ed. 131." In *Truax v. Raich*, the Court said:

> It requires no argument to show that the right to work for a living in the common occupations of the community is of the very essence of the personal freedom and opportunity that it was the purpose of the Amendment to secure. 239 U.S. 33, 41, 36 S.Ct. 7, 10, 60 L.Ed. 131 (1915).

Since this right to pursue an occupation is presumably on the same lofty footing as the right of choice in matters of family life, the Court will have to strain valiantly in order to avoid having today's opinion lead to the invalidation of mandatory retirement statutes for governmental employees. In that event federal, state, and local governmental bodies will be remitted to the task, thankless both for them and for the employees involved, of individual determinations of physical impairment and senility.

It has been said before, *Williamson v. Lee Optical Co.*, 348 U.S. 483, 75 S.Ct. 461, 99 L.Ed. 563 (1955), but it bears repeating here: All legislation involves the drawing of lines, and the drawing of lines necessarily results in particular individuals who are disadvantaged by the line drawn being virtually indistinguishable for many purposes from those individuals who benefit from the legislative classification. The Court's disenchantment with "irrebuttable presumptions," and its preference for "individualized determination," is in the last analysis nothing less than an attack upon the very notion of lawmaking itself.

The lines drawn by the school boards in the city of Cleveland and Chesterfield County in these cases require pregnant teachers to take forced leave at a stage of their pregnancy when medical evidence seems to suggest that a majority of them might well be able to continue teaching without any significant possibility of physical impairment. But, so far as I am aware, the medical evidence also suggests that in some cases there may be physical impairment at the stage of pregnancy fastened on by the regulations in question, and that the probability of physical impairment increases as the pregnancy advances. If legislative bodies are to be permitted to draw a general line anywhere short of the delivery room, I can find no judicial standard of measurement which says the ones drawn here were invalid. I therefore dissent.

PHILLIPS v. MARTIN MARIETTA

United States Supreme Court
400 U.S. 542 (1971)

...

Mr. Justice MARSHALL, concurring.

While I agree that this case must be remanded for a full development of the facts, I cannot agree with the Court's indication that a "bona fide occupational qualification reasonably necessary to the normal operation of" Martin Marietta's business could be established by a showing that some women, even the vast majority, with pre-school-age children have family responsibilities that interfere with job performance and that men do not usually have such responsibilities. Certainly, an employer can require that all of his employees, both men and women, meet minimum performance standards, and he can try to insure compliance by requiring parents, both mothers and fathers, to provide for the care of their children so that job performance is not interfered with.

But the Court suggests that it would not require such uniform standards. I fear that in this case, where the issue is not squarely before us, the Court has fallen into the trap of assuming that the Act permits ancient canards about the proper role of women to be a basis for discrimination. Congress, however, sought just the opposite result.

By adding the prohibition against job discrimination based on sex to the 1964 Civil Rights Act Congress intended to prevent employers from refusing "to hire an individual based on stereotyped characterizations of the sexes." Equal Employment Opportunity Commission, Guidelines on Discrimination Because of Sex, 29 CFR §1604.1(a)(i)(ii). See *Bowe v. Colgate-Palmolive Co.*, 416 F.2d 711 (CA7 1969); *Weeks v. Southern Bell Tel. & Tel. Co.*, 408 F.2d 228 (CA5 1969). Even characterizations of the proper domestic roles of the sexes were not to serve as predicates for restricting employment opportunity. The exception for a "bona fide occupational qualification" was not intended to swallow the rule.

That exception has been construed by the Equal Employment Opportunity Commission, whose regulations are entitled to "great deference," *Udall v. Tallman*, 380 U.S. 1, 16, 85 S.Ct. 792, 801, 13 L.Ed.2d 616 (1965), to be applicable only to job situations that require specific physical characteristics necessarily possessed by only one sex.[3] Thus the exception would apply where necessary "for the purpose of authenticity or genuineness" in the employment of actors or actresses, fashion

---

3. The Commission's regulations provide:

Sex as a bona fide occupational qualification.

(a) The Commission believes that the bona fide occupational qualification exception as to sex should be interpreted narrowly. Labels — ,"Men's jobs" and "Women's jobs" — tend to deny employment opportunities unnecessarily to one sex or the other.

(1) The Commission will find that the following situations do not warrant the application of the bona fide occupational qualification exception:

(i) The refusal to hire a woman because of her sex, based on assumptions of the comparative employment characteristics of women in general. For example, the assumption that the turnover rate among women is higher than among men.

(ii) The refusal to hire an individual based on stereotyped characterizations of the sexes. Such stereotypes include, for example, that men are less capable of assembling intricate equipment; that women are less capable of aggressive salesmanship. The principle of non- discrimination requires that individuals be considered on the basis of individual capacities and not on the basis of any characteristics generally attributed to the group.

(iii) The refusal to hire an individual because of the preferences of co-workers, the employer, clients or customers except as covered specifically in subparagraph (2) of this paragraph.

(iv) The fact that the employer may have to provide separate facilities for a person of the opposite sex will not justify discrimination under the bona fide occupational qualification exception unless the expense would be clearly unreasonable.

(2) Where it is necessary for the purpose of authenticity or genuineness, the Commission will consider sex to be a bona fide occupational qualification, *e.g.*, an actor or actress.

(b)(1) Many States have enacted laws or promulgated administrative regulations with respect to the employment of females. Among these laws are those which prohibit or limit the employment of females, e.g., the employment of females in certain occupations, in jobs requiring the lifting or carrying of weights exceeding certain prescribed limits, during certain hours of the night, or for more than a specified number of hours per day or per week.

(2) The Commission believes that such State laws and regulations, although originally promulgated for the purpose of protecting females, have ceased to be relevant to our technology or to the expanding role of the female worker in our economy. The Commission has found that such laws and regulations do not take into account the capacities, preferences, and abilities of individual females and tend to discriminate rather than protect. Accordingly, the Commission has concluded that such laws and regulations conflict with Title VII of the Civil Rights Act of 1964 and will not be considered a defense to an otherwise established unlawful employment practice or as a basis for the application of the bona fide occupational qualification exception. 29 CFR §1604.1.

models, and the like. If the exception is to be limited as Congress intended, the Commission has given it the only possible construction.

When performance characteristics of an individual are involved, even when parental roles are concerned, employment opportunity may be limited only by employment criteria that are neutral as to the sex of the applicant.

APPLICATION OF ELLEN GAULKIN

Supreme Court of New Jersey
69 N.J. 185, 351 A.2d 740 (1976)

HUGHES, C.J.

This application for the review and relaxation of an administrative policy enunciated by the Court is somewhat unusual in nature. It was initiated by a petition filed by one affected by the policy, Mrs. Ellen Gaulkin, wife of a Judge of the New Jersey Superior Court. In a most appropriate way she had sought the views of the Supreme Court as to the propriety of her intended candidacy for public office in view of her husband's judicial position. Upon the expression of our negative opinion, she acceded for the time, although disagreeing with it, and reserved the right to contest further. She is properly here now, as are the *amici* who have also briefed and argued the cause, which in itself is not adversarial in nature. *Cf. In re National Broadcasting Co.*, 64 N.J. 476, 317 A.2d 695 (1974). Through its chairman the Supreme Court's Advisory Committee on Professional Ethics joined in argument for explication of the reasons relevant to the origin and existence of the policy. There has been no adjudicatory hearing as such, nor indeed is such hearing necessary where the Court is exercising legislatively its constitutional power to formulate court rules and policy. *Cf. American Trial Lawyers Assoc. v. New Jersey Supreme Court*, 66 N.J. 258, 330 A.2d 350 (1974).

I

Since 1948, when the judicial system created by Article VI of the 1947 Constitution came into existence, judges and others officially associated with that court system have been wholly divorced from involvement in partisan or other political activity, as a necessary sacrifice for the sake of judicial integrity and the public appearance thereof. This separation is thought in this State (all judges in New Jersey are appointed) to be indispensable to public confidence in the courts and their probity, impartiality, disinterested objectivity and freedom from outside pressures in their dealing with causes coming before them. Such public confidence in judicial integrity is the foundation (along with Constitution and law) of our courts' power, influence and acceptance as necessary instruments in the effective administration of justice.

In recognition of that concept the people of New Jersey, in adopting our present Constitution, reposed in the New Jersey Supreme Court, a non-political entity, exclusive responsibility for the making of rules concerning practice and procedure in the courts thereby created, and for the admission and discipline of those admitted to the practice of the law. N.J.Const. (1947), Art. VI, §II, par. 3....

It was to implement this mandate that our Court perceived the need for extension of the judge's disqualification from political involvement to include that of the spouse. (To avoid confusion, this opinion will refer to the wife or husband of a judge as the "non-judicial spouse.")

In reaffirming this policy the present Court, through a letter to Judge Gaulkin on December 31, 1973, opined that the candidacy for public office of his spouse represented "a form of political activity which would, unintentionally but seriously, affect public confidence in the judicial system." This was then our position despite an assurance that such candidacy would not involve the typical indicia of political campaigns, such as association with a slate, or acceptance of campaign financing, or solicitation of endorsements, and Mrs. Gaulkin's further belief that her tenure and its incidents would not be subversive of the policy of the Court.

...

II

It goes without saying that our system of government is predicated upon the premise that every citizen shall have the right to engage in political activity. It is a basic freedom enshrined in the First Amendment.... This important right (except of course for the private exercise of the voting franchise) is relinquished by our judges upon ascendancy to the bench. In this state, at least, it has been clearly established that courts do not belong in politics, that the independence of the judiciary depends upon that separation, and that political ties and debts and their accommodation would demean and degrade the courts and ultimately corrupt them....

...

III

But the years which demonstrated the wisdom of this basic policy have also wrought other changes bearing upon the question now directly before us, namely, whether and to what extent the proscription of all political activity on the part of a judge should extend to the non-judicial spouse.

We focus first upon the trend of modern law which reflects society's realistic appreciation of the independence of both spouses in marriage and more specifically represents modern awareness and sensitivity to individual freedoms, rights, responsibilities and development. A married woman in New Jersey has the right to own property individually, N.J.S.A. 37:2-12; is liable for debts contracted in her own name, N.J.S.A. 37:2-10; may enter into a partnership with her husband, N.J.S.A. 37:2-16.1; may even enter into a criminal conspiracy with him, *State v. Pittman*, 124 N.J.Super. 334, 338–40, 306 A.2d 500 (Law Div. 1973); may testify in court against her husband in certain cases, *Evid. R.* 23(2); and is not compelled to assume her husband's surname as her legal name, *In re Application of Lawrence*, 133 N.J.Super. 408, 412, 337 A.2d 49 (App.Div.1975). The coexistence of separate and different interests in an ongoing marriage has also been recognized. In *Immer v. Risko*, 56 N.J. 482, 267 A.2d 481 (1970), the Court limited the doctrine of interspousal immunity in a woman's negligence action against a defendant who became her husband. The Court rejected the assumption that interspousal tort actions would inevitably disrupt marital harmony. (*Id.* at 488–90, 267 A.2d 481). See also *Small v. Rockfeld*, 66 N.J. 231, 241, 330 A.2d 335 (1974). In *King v. Greene*, 30 N.J. 395, 412, 153 A.2d 49 (1959), the Court held that a wife's interest in property held in a tenancy by the entirety could be alienated. We notice too that the evolving recognition of individual spousal interests has resulted in their being viewed as well from the perspective of the male and his role as husband and father. He too is being relieved of the consequences of being fitted into a stereotypic mold. See, *e.g.*, *Weinberger v. Wiesenfeld*, 420 U.S. 636, 95 S.Ct. 1225, 43 L.Ed.2d 514 (1975); *Stanley v. Illinois*, 405 U.S. 645, 92 S.Ct. 1208, 31 L.Ed.2d 551 (1972).

All of this bespeaks a realist appreciation of the marriage relationship and the nature of the partnership it embodies:

> [T]he marital couple is not an independent entity with a mind and heart of its own, but an association of two individuals each with a separate intellectual and emotional makeup. [*Eisenstadt v. Baird*, 405 U.S. 438, 453, 92 S.Ct. 1029, 1038, 31 L.Ed.2d 349, 362 (1972)].

And so it is with an appreciation of the emergence and the social and legal recognition of spousal autonomy and retention of separate identities and interests, notwithstanding the sympathetic relationship of an ongoing marriage, that we turn to the question of spousal political activity, as seen by others in the judicial and professional world.

IV

The record before us indicates that no other American jurisdiction, whether by a court having administrative responsibility for the conduct of judges, a judicial ethics commission, or otherwise, has ever undertaken to forbid or limit spousal public or political activity, with the exception of the Association of the Bar of the City of New York, Committee on Professional Ethics, whose Opinion No. 865, 20 *Record of N.Y.C.B.A.* 52 (1965), sought to control political activity of a judge's spouse. It is pointed out to us that such opinion has never been cited with approval in any opinion or other writing since. On the contrary, in voluminous writings of recent years concerning judicial ethics there does not seem to be the slightest suggestion that any prohibition of a spouse's service in or candidacy for public office is either necessary or appropriate....

...

Ours, then, has been a conspicuously minority position, designed however to meet a plain exigency, namely, the need to extricate our courts from the sort of pre-1948 entanglements to which we have referred. It reflected as well our determination, to which we still firmly adhere, not to move one inch from the principle of total separation of the judiciary itself from involvement, directly or indirectly, in political activities.

Upon the most careful reconsideration, however, we no longer see any confirmed justification for extending that prohibition to the non-judicial spouse. The reasoning supporting extension of the basic policy was based upon our perception that the spousal political activity would seem to embroil the judge in politics, because of an inevitable public belief that the publicly stated views of the political spouse would or must implicate the fundamental thinking of the judge and the court represented by that judge.

In light of the strong admonitions of Canon 7 adjuring the abstention by the judge from political activity and the Court's undoubted power and determination to enforce such a rule vigorously, we express doubt that spousal political activity *per se* would involve the judge in the political stream. Where a court is dealing with a First Amendment right (here the political involvement of the non-judicial spouse), fears that its exercise will have undesirable consequences cannot inhibit judicial vindication thereof....

As to the community's perception of the spouse's exercise of that right, emerging concepts of spousal independence and autonomy in activities, development, interests, rights and responsibilities lead us to appraise our earlier assessment of probable public discernment and sophistication as no longer realistic. Furthermore, certain disqualification provisions under the Code provide an avenue for appropriate withdrawal of the judge from any matter which would or could embarrass the court, an implicit burden always resting on the judge to be vigilant in detecting possible impropriety or the likelihood of public appearance thereof....

Additionally, our previous position now lacks a persuasive ring when we consider the impact on our judicial system of the publicly expressed views of the wife or husband of a judge as stated in the political forum, and those of a non-judicial spouse who is, let us say, an author, playwright, lecturer, newspaper editor or the like. The former would seem no more invidious than the latter. And one can hardly suppose that the latter, ordinarily, could come within the orbit of legitimate spousal control or judicial concern.

V

We think we have been explicit enough to indicate that while we now see the need and justice of withdrawing the Court's previous disapproval of spousal political involvement, which we do by this opinion, we are equally determined that every precaution shall be taken to assure that the judiciary itself shall continue its careful separation from direct or indirect involvement in politics. We consider that certain amenities of life, and perhaps even some legal rights, have to be sacrificed or curtailed for the larger purpose of avoiding the fact or appearance of participation by the judge in the political effort of a spouse. The administration of justice must be free of such appearance, as well as the fact.... Thus, for instance, despite the theory of *Painter. v. Painter*, 65 N.J. 196, 320 A.2d 484 (1974), recognizing the contribution of both spouses to the marital assets, we would regard the use of any part thereof in the political forum as degrading to the court and plainly within the reach of the adjuration that the judge abstain from politics. Such assets normally are marked by a lack of an identifiable interest of either spouse, thus at least suggesting indirect involvement of the judge. The use of the marital home for a political or fund-raising meeting or the making of political contributions from the common family funds would come within this objection. The ordinary courtesy of the judge in accompanying his or her spouse to a political gathering of any kind, or being seen as a political adviser, would have to be foregone. The making of political contributions to the campaign of a spouse of a judge by attorneys or litigants who are or may be involved in practice before that judge would be particularly offensive from an ethical standpoint. A myriad of other circumstances apt to involve the judge or give the public appearance of such political involvement may be imagined, but need not here be enumerated. Suffice it to say that notwithstanding the present relaxation of the policy with regard to the non-judicial spouse, the Court will be vigilant and will deal most strenuously with respect to any encroachment, actual or apparent, of politics upon the judiciary of New Jersey.

...

ABA COMMITTEE on ETHICS and PROFESSIONAL RESPONSIBILITY FORMAL OPINION 340*

September 23, 1975

Where both husband and wife are lawyers but they are not practicing in association with one another, they are not necessarily prohibited from representing different interests or from being associated with firms representing differing interests. Like all lawyers, they must obey all disciplinary rules; a particular situation may be inherently difficult because of the close relationship between husband and wife. In any situation where a client or potential client might question the loyalty of the lawyer representing him, the situation should be fully explained to the client and the question of acceptance or continuance of representation left to the client for decision.

Where both husband and wife are lawyers but they are not practicing in association with one another, may they or their firms represent differing interests?

This question, in varying forms, has been presented to this Committee with some frequency recently. Some firms apparently have been reluctant to employ one spouse-lawyer where that person's husband or wife is, or may soon be, practicing with another firm in the same city or area. On the other hand, some law schools have expressed disapproval of the practice by some firms in their hiring practices of attaching grave importance to the fact that the law student under consideration is married to a lawyer or a law student. Some law firms are concerned whether a law firm is disqualified, by reason of its employment of one spouse, to represent a client opposing an interest represented by another law firm that employs the husband or wife of the inquiring firm's associate. Some of the circumstances bearing on this question include whether the fee of either firm is contingent, whether the disputed matter is one of negotiation or litigation, and whether the married lawyer in question will or will not actually be working on the particular matter. Another variation of the problem is the situation in which a governmental agency, such as a district attorney or an attorney general, is the employer of either the husband or the wife, and the spouse is associated with a law firm in the same community.

The problem undoubtedly will arise with increasing frequency and in different settings, for it is a fact of modern society that women are entering the profession in increasing numbers and that increasing numbers of these women are married to lawyers. Clearly, today it is not uncommon for husband and wife lawyers to be practicing in different offices in the same city, and the current enrollment of women in law schools indicates that women lawyers will constitute a greater percentage of the bar in the future than now.

It is not necessarily improper for husband-and-wife lawyers who are practicing in different offices or firms to represent differing interests. No disciplinary rule expressly requires a lawyer to decline employment if a husband, wife, son, daughter, brother, father, or other close relative represents the opposing party in negotiation or litigation. Likewise, it is not necessarily improper for a law firm having a married partner or associate to represent clients whose interests are opposed to

---

*Excerpted from *Recent Ethics Opinions*, September 23, 1975, copyright of 1975. American Bar Association, National Center for Professional Responsibility.

those of other clients represented by another law firm with which the married lawyer's spouse is associated as a lawyer.

A lawyer whose husband or wife is also a lawyer must, like every other lawyer, obey all disciplinary rules, for the disciplinary rules apply to all lawyers without distinction as to marital status. We cannot assume that a lawyer who is married to another lawyer necessarily will violate any particular disciplinary rule, such as those that protect a client's confidences, that proscribe neglect of a client's interest, and that forbid representation of differing interests. Yet it also must be recognized that the relationship of husband and wife is so close that the possibility of an inadvertent breach of a confidence or the unavoidable receipt of information concerning the client by the spouse other than the one who represents the client (for example, information contained in a telephoned message left for the lawyer at home) is substantial. Because of the closeness of the husband-and-wife relationship, a lawyer who is married to a lawyer must be particularly careful to observe the suggestions and requirements of EC 4-1, EC 4-5, EC 5-1, EC 5-2, EC 5-3, EC 5-7, DR 4-101, and DR 5-101.

Even though the representation by husband and wife of opposing parties is not a violation of any disciplinary rule, the possibility of a violation of DR 5-101, in particular, is real and must be carefully considered in each instance. If the interest of one of the marriage partners as attorney for an opposing party creates a financial or personal interest that reasonably might affect the ability of a lawyer to represent fully his or her client with undivided loyalty and free exercise of professional judgment, the employment must be declined. We cannot assume, however, that certain facts, such as a fee being contingent or varying according to results obtained, necessarily will involve a violation of DR 5-101(A). In some instances the interest of one spouse in the other's income resulting from a particular fee may be such that professional judgment may be affected, while in other situations it may not be; the existence of such interest is a fact determination to be made in each individual case. Wherever one spouse is disqualified under DR 5-101(A), the entire firm is disqualified under DR 5-105(D).[1]

In any event, the advice contained in EC 5-3 and EC 5-16 is apropos; the lawyer should advise the client of all circumstances that might cause one to question the undivided loyalty of the law firm and let the client make the decision as to its employment. If the client prefers not to employ a law firm containing a lawyer whose spouse is associated with a firm representing an opposing party, that decision should be respected.

The views expressed in this opinion are consistent with the views expressed by other committees in regard to the close relationships of opposing lawyers. For example, it has been held that a father and son may represent opposite sides in litigation: See Opinion 19 (January 23, 1963), Professional Ethics Committee of the Kansas Bar Association; Opinion 48, Missouri Advisory Opinions. In its Opinion No. 170 (1970), the New Jersey Advisory Committee on Professional Ethics held it is not improper for a lawyer to represent an indigent when the lawyer's brother is employed by the prosecutor's office.[2]

---

1. As amended February, 1974, DR 5-105(D) provides: "If a lawyer is required to decline employment or to withdraw from employment under a Disciplinary Rule, no partner, or associate, or any other lawyer affiliated with him or his firm, may accept or continue such employment."

2. But see Opinion No. 288 (1974) of the New Jersey Advisory Committee on Professional Ethics which held that a "wife should not be permitted to practice criminal defense law in New Jersey while her husband is" a deputy attorney general assigned to the Appellate Section of the Division of Criminal Justice.

Accordingly, we conclude that a law firm employing a lawyer whose spouse is a lawyer associated with another local law firm need not fear consistent or mandatory disqualification when the two firms represent opposing interests; yet it is both proper and necessary for the firm always to be sensitive to both the possibility of disqualification and the wishes of its clients. Marriage partners who are lawyers must guard carefully at all times against inadvertent violations of their professional responsibilities arising by reason of the marital relationship.

COMMENTS

The Application of Ellen Gaulkin and the American Bar Association Committee on Ethics and Professional Responsibility Formal Opinion No. 340 present matters in a nonadversary context, and are seemingly narrow in scope. *Gaulkin* dealt with the issue of whether the wife of a New Jersey judge may run for public office, specifically, seek election to the Weehawken Board of Education. Opinion 340 was concerned with the question whether husband and wife, both lawyers but not associated with each other may represent opposing interests. In addition to these issues, there are numerous other problems posed by dual career marriages. Husband and wife may find themselves professors on the same law faculty or they may be prevented from such employment by formal or informal antinepotism policies. While protege relationships do not result in automatic exclusion marriage often does.

Even if there is no legal restriction against activities of husband and wife within the same professional and occupational context it may still be customary to exclude one of the spouses — usually the wife — from employment. The implication is that marriage may result in an appearance of undue influence or at least the possibility of corruption. While this reasoning is contemporary, it results in disabilities similar to those incurred by married women under archaic beliefs that merged the wife's individuality into the husband's. Under somewhat less ancient conceptions, a wife was presumed not to have a mind of her own, but to be under coercion by her husband. None of this conforms to the realities of modern life, but the persistence of the effect illustrates a frequent occurrence in family law: that older policies, though they may take a different form, remain essentially unchanged or are modified only slowly.

Progress may also have negative implications. Referring to *Eisenstadt v. Baird*, *Gaulkin* stressed that marriage is not an independent entity but an association of two individuals "each with a separate intellectual and emotional makeup." Both in *Gaulkin* and in Opinion 340 marriage is referred to as partnership, following an aggregate, rather than an entity, theory of partnership. Some fear that such emphasis on the individual in marriage may mean that husband and wife grow apart and that the centrifugal forces in modern marriage tend to result in dissolution, winding up of the marital business, and distribution of assets. A situation can be reached in marriage in which legally the spouses are no longer identified by a common name or abode, do not want to have children, do not share common interests or property, and are not in any sense liable for each other. If all these factors coincide, we have a marriage in name only, yet as an institution it still is legally recognized, more so than cohabitation arrangements of sometimes considerable mutual involvement. This state of affairs could become an issue of significance to legislators and to judges in their lawmaking role. It could result in extreme reactions: a return to traditional conceptions of marriage with all its negative connotations; or the opposite, a weakening of traditional marriage, perhaps even a further encouragement of nonmarital cohabitation. More likely a compromise will become institutionalized. Examples for more extreme positions in regard to marriage can be found in the laws of Illinois and California, while other states try to work out a compromise.

REFERENCES

Katherine Bird, *Lawyer Couples: After the Honeymoon is Over, Can They Live and Work Together?*, CALIF. LAW., Sept. 1981, at 26.

Kenneth L. Karst, *The Freedom of Intimate Association*, 89 YALE L.J. 624 (1980).

Herma Hill Kay, *Legal and Social Impediments to Dual Career Marriages*, 12 U.C. DAVIS L. REV. 207 (1979).

ELKUS v. ELKUS

New York Supreme Court

182 A.D. 2d 45, 588 N.Y.S.2d 138 (1992)

SULLIVAN, Justice.

This appeal is from an order which permits the mother, their primary caretaker, to relocate the two children of the marriage, ages 14 and 12, from their present home on Long Island, easily accessible to the father, who faithfully exercises his visitation rights, to California so that the mother can spend more time with her new husband, who resides there and cannot relocate.

The parties, after a 17-year marriage, were divorced by judgment, entered on September 18, 1990 pursuant to a stipulation of settlement, which provided for joint custody of their two daughters. Within three months, the mother, an internationally renowned opera and concert singer, whose annual gross earnings approximate $800,000, remarried and, shortly afterward, moved to relocate the children to Alameda, California, in the San Francisco Bay area, where her new husband resides with his 17-year old daughter from a prior marriage. The father, who earns approximately $90,000 yearly and has inherited wealth, opposed the application on the ground that he and the two children had a close relationship which would be jeopardized by a move to California; over the previous year and one-half, he visited them in the rented Long Island former marital home every other weekend and twice during the week.

After a hearing, review of the guardian's report and an *in camera* interview with the children, who, with the father and the guardian *ad litem*, opposed the proposed relocation, the court denied the application, finding that relocation was against the children's best interests. The court noted that the children opposed relocation for many reasons, that the mother's scheduled operatic engagements for the next year required extended absences from California and that, since the mother had no plans to hire a housekeeper, her new husband would be the children's primary caretaker. The court, however, indicated its willingness to grant permission for such a move at the end of the school year, in June 1992 — when the older child would have graduated from junior high school — on a showing that the children had been properly prepared for the move. This court affirmed. (*Elkus v. Elkus*, 180, A.D.2d 444, 580 N.Y.S.2d 652.)

The mother subsequently took steps to ameliorate the court's concerns. At significant financial sacrifice, she rearranged her professional schedule to minimize her absences from California, and she took the children to a therapist to prepare them for the move. In addition, the mother offered to assume financial responsibility for visitation-related expenses, including airfare, telephone calls and a rental apartment for the father in the Bay area, found suitable educational facilities for the children in California and hired a housekeeper to care for them during her absences.

Despite these efforts, the children continued to oppose relocation. A second guardian *ad litem*, appointed after a charge of bias was asserted by the mother against the original guardian on the second application to relocate the children, independently opposed relocation, citing the danger of jeopardizing the children's close relationship with the father, the importance to the children of their friends, teachers and social relationships, the mother's frequent absences due to her career commitments and the possibility of friction between the children and the new husband's 17-year old daughter.

A court-appointed child psychiatrist, who conducted extensive interviews with the children, the parents, the new husband and the guardian concluded that their best interests would be served by their remaining on Long Island. He expressed the view that relocating the children in California would lead to "the disruption of their lives, the loss of the stabilizing aspects of their friends and school, and the loss of their regular and frequent contact with their father." In reaching his determination, the psychiatrist found that the parents' divorce led to a greater need for the children to seek stability elsewhere, in this case with friends and school, and that during the mother's absences it was the father who had been present and available to them.

Despite the opposition of the children, father, guardian and court-appointed child psychiatrist, the court, after a hearing, granted the motion to relocate, finding that the children and their stepsister had spent more time together since the prior application and that the schools chosen for the children in California would be academically superior to the one presently attended on Long Island. The court took note of the mother's agreement to cancel some of her European appearances, and her hiring of a housekeeper. Under such circumstances, the court held, there was "no compelling reason for [the children] to remain here." Since, in our view, the court applied an improper standard and the requisite standard of exceptional circumstance justifying relocation has not been met, we reverse.

The predominant concern where child custody is at issue is "the ultimate best interest of the child." (*Matter of Nehra v. Uhlar*, 43 N.Y.2d 242, 248, 401 N.Y.S.2d 168, 372 N.E.2d 4.) Since, "[w]henever possible, the best interests of a child lie in being nurtured by both natural parents" (*Hemphill v. Hemphill*, 169 A.D.2d 29, 32, 572 N.Y.S.2d 689, *appeal dismissed*, 78 N.Y.2d 1070, 576 N.Y.S.2d 216, 582 N.E.2d 599), a custodial parent may not remove a child of the marriage outside the locale where the non-custodial parent resides unless the custodial parent proves that there are exceptional circumstances or pressing concerns for the welfare of the custodial parent or the child which warrant relocation....

While "the obligations of a new marriage may legitimately, if rarely, require even 'a dramatic change of locale'"..., the mere fact of remarriage, without more, will not constitute an exceptional circumstance....

That the mother's new husband resides in California and cannot relocate and that the move will be advantageous to her career are insufficient, in the absence of a showing of economic necessity or other exceptional circumstances to justify relocation of the children. In granting the mother's motion to relocate, the hearing court relied on *Hemphill v. Hemphill, supra,* 169 A.D.2d 29, 572 N.Y.S.2d 689, in which a divided court granted an application for relocation. While the *Hemphill* decision signifies a somewhat generous view of the custodial parent's right to relocate, the court did not purport to establish any new standard for determinations of this kind. Rather, the result turned on a question of economic necessity, the relocating parent being economically dependent on the new spouse with no alternative but to move, and the fact that the children were no strangers to long-distance visitation. Those circumstances are not present here. While relocation to California may be advantageous to the mother's career, she specifically represented at the second hearing that if relocation were denied she would remain in the New York area as the children's primary custodian.

Furthermore, the mother's frequent absences necessitated by her professional engagements are an important consideration in any best interests assessment, underscoring the significance of the children's relationship with their father and the stabilizing influence of their friends, school and surroundings.

We note also the hearing court's failure to address the reasons advanced by the guardians and court-appointed psychiatrist for opposing relocation, all of which revolved around the general rule that disfavors distant geographic relocations tending to frustrate the objective of regular contact with both parents. For example, both guardians and the expert, as well as the children, expressed the view that the new husband was not an adequate substitute for the proximity of and frequent contact with the father, especially during the mother's absences. Neither the availability of a housekeeper in California nor the mother's offer to defray the expenses of the father's visitation adequately addresses that concern. The quality of the father's visitation can only suffer when frequency and flexibility are diminished.

Instead of addressing this and other concerns, the court relied upon factual findings which are insufficient to uphold its determination and, in some instances, do not find record support. For instance, the court's statement that "there is no real disagreement that the schools chosen for the children in California" are academically superior to the children's school in Long Island is unsupported by any proof other than the self-serving testimony of the mother, who did not attend any classes at the California school under consideration. In fact, the older child, who "excels in math" and who did visit the California school, was under the impression that "no accommodation would be made there for her advanced math level." The court also found that both children get along "much better" with their stepsister since the initial determination. While the older child did tell the guardian that "she likes the stepsister more after spending a day with her at [her] high school" during a trip to Alameda, she was "still opposed to moving to California."

The court's findings that the father has not "created any kind of home life for the children" and has "made no attempt" to move from his studio apartment in Manhattan to an apartment to accommodate the children either in Manhattan or Long Island failed to take into account the father's motions for primary custody at both relocation hearings and his deliberate efforts to fit himself into the children's lives rather than make theirs part of his. He has visited the children at least two evenings during the week and spent the greater part of alternate weekends with them. When the mother has had to travel, he has visited with the children almost every night.

Relocation to California would not only limit the frequency of visitation, but would have an adverse effect on the nature and quality of the father's relationship with the children. While the father's visitation in New York has harmoniously blended with the children's lives and activities, visitation in California, 3,000 miles away, would necessarily be sporadic; moreover, it would be taking place in an alien environment that would take the children out of their daily routine. Rather than supportive, the visits would be disruptive. In such circumstances, the mother has failed to demonstrate a compelling reason or exceptional circumstances to justify relocation to California.

Finally, although we affirmed the denial of the mother's original application to relocate for the reasons stated by the IAS court, which, in denying the motion, held that "unless circumstances change substantially, the children should be permitted to move to California after [the 1991–1992] school year", our consideration of the issue whether relocation is now warranted is not foreclosed, since the determination of this issue was not necessary to the prior order denying relocation and was not decided on the prior appeal.

Accordingly, the order of the Supreme Court, New York County...entered May 18, 1992, which, *inter alia*, modified the decision of the court, dated April 30, 1992, to provide that the decision constitute the order of the court and directed the parties to settle a subsequent order regarding visitation, and the order of the same court and justice, dated April 30, 1992, which granted plaintiff's application to relocate with the parties' children to Alameda, California, should be reversed, on the law and the facts and in the exercise of discretion, without costs or disbursements, and the motion to relocate denied.

All concur.

BROWN v. BROWN

Supreme Court of Appeals of West Virginia
184 W.Va. 627, 403 S.E.2d 29 (1991)

PER CURIAM:

This case is before this Court upon the appeal of Martha Young Brown from an order of the Circuit Court of Monongalia County entered on May 25, 1990, which awarded custody of the parties' two children to the appellee, Jo Baily Brown, and denied the appellant's request for one-half of the appellee's pension. The appellant contends that the circuit court abused its discretion in awarding the appellee custody of the children, and also maintains that she is entitled to one-half of the appellee's pension. We find that the circuit court abused its discretion in awarding appellee custody of the children, and therefore, we reverse the circuit court solely on this issue. In all other respects, the order of the circuit court is affirmed.

The parties were married on March 1, 1980. Two children were born as issue of the marriage, Emily, who is now age six, and Ben, who is now age four. Now and throughout the marriage, the appellee has been employed as a librarian at West

Virginia University. The appellant was employed by the Dominion Post newspaper until October of 1987, at which time she ceased working to devote her time to her studies at the West Virginia University College of Law.

During the summer of 1989, while the appellant was living with her two children in Pittsburgh and working as a summer associate at Buchanan Ingersoll, the parties separated. On September 6, 1989, the appellant filed a complaint against the appellee seeking a divorce on the grounds of irreconcilable differences, and custody of the parties' two children. In his answer to the complaint, the appellee also alleged that irreconcilable differences had arisen between the parties, and sought custody of the children.

The appellant subsequently filed a motion for relief *pendente lite.* Upon hearing the sworn testimony of each of the parties, the family law master entered a temporary order on October 6, 1989, awarding the appellant custody of the two children. Following the final hearing on March 6, 1990, the family law master entered a recommended decision finding that the appellant was the primary caretaker, and awarding her custody of the parties' two children.

The appellee then petitioned the circuit court for a review of the family law master's recommended decision. By order dated May 25, 1990, the circuit court reversed that decision and found the appellee to be the primary caretaker of the parties' children. The circuit court also ruled that the appellant was not entitled to one-half of the appellee's pension. The appellant appealed that order. We issued a stay of the order of the circuit court pending a decision by this Court on appeal.

I

The first issue before us is whether the circuit court abused its discretion in awarding custody of the parties' two children to the appellee on the grounds that he was the primary caretaker of the children. The appellant asserts that the family law master, after presiding over two hearings, correctly determined that she was the primary caretaker of the children. The appellee contends that the circuit court was correct in finding that the family law master's determination that the appellant was the primary caretaker was unsupported by substantial evidence. Both parties claim to be the primary caretaker.

This Court has consistently recognized, in child custody disputes, that the welfare of the child can best be served by placing the child in the custody of the primary caretaker if he or she is fit, as we stated in syllabus point 2 of *David M. v. Margaret M.*, 182 W.Va. 57, 385 S.E.2d 912 (1989):

> With reference to the custody of very young children, the law presumes that it is in the best interest of such children to be placed in the custody of their primary caretaker, if he or she is fit. Syllabus point 2, *Garska v. McCoy*, 167 W.Va. 59, 278 S.E.2d 357 (1981).

We defined the "primary caretaker" in syllabus point 3 of *David M. v. Margaret M., supra:*

> The "primary caretaker" is the parent who has taken primary responsibility for, *inter alia*, the performance of the following caring and nurturing duties of a parent: (1) preparing and planning of meals; (2) bathing, grooming and dressing; (3) purchasing, cleaning, and care of clothes; (4) medical care, including nursing and trips to physicians; (5) arranging for social interaction among peers after school, *i.e.* transporting to friends'

houses or, for example, to girl or boy scout meetings; (6) arranging alternative care, *i.e.* babysitting, day-care, etc.; (7) putting child to bed at night, attending to child in the middle of the night, waking child in the morning; (8) disciplining, *i.e.* teaching general manners and toilet training; (9) educating, *i.e.* religious, cultural, social, etc.; and, (10) teaching elementary skills, *i.e.* reading, writing and arithmetic.

In the two separate hearings before the family law master, only the appellant and appellee testified.[1] The appellant testified that, when her daughter Emily was born, she took a six-month leave of absence from her employment at the Dominion Post newspaper to stay at home and care for Emily. The parties then agreed upon a schedule whereby the appellant would stay at home with Emily until 1:00 p.m., at which time Emily would be cared for by a babysitter while the appellant would go to work. The appellee would then relieve the babysitter when he finished work, and would care for Emily until the appellant finished working at 9:30 p.m. The appellant further testified that she returned home during her work schedule to nurse Emily, and to have dinner with the family. The appellant also took a six-month leave of absence after the birth of her son Benjamin, and then followed the same schedule described above.

During the summer of 1989, while the appellant was a summer associate at Buchanan Ingersoll, she lived in Pittsburgh at her mother-in-law's home with Emily and Benjamin. The children were cared for by a babysitter while the appellant worked. The parties separated that summer, and the appellee visited with the children on weekends.

The appellant also testified that, when she and the children returned to Morgantown in August of 1989, the parties continued to live in the same home. The parties then agreed that the appellant would care for the children on Monday and Wednesday evenings, and the appellee would care for them on Tuesday and Thursday evenings. The appellant also agreed to allow the appellee to have breakfast with the children on Monday and Wednesday mornings, and to take them to school on those days. The appellant testified that the parties alternated the weekends they would separately care for the children.

The appellee testified that he shared child care responsibilities from the time Emily was born in August of 1984. The appellee acknowledged that, during the appellant's maternity leave with each child, the appellant had almost exclusive child care responsibilities. The appellee stated that, prior to the separation, he prepared dinner for the family in the evenings while the appellant worked, and bathed and put the children to bed.

The appellee also testified that his child care and financial responsibilities dramatically increased when the appellant entered law school and ceased working at the Dominion Post. The appellee stated that he performed "virtually all of the grocery shopping," and that the appellant was responsible for all of the laundry. Although the appellant arranged for the children's schooling, the appellee testified that he was more involved with "[car pooling] and attending board meetings the first week of each of their schools." The appellee believed that he has much more time to spend with the children than the appellant because his schedule is much more flexible.

---

1. We pointed out, in *David M. v. Margaret M.*, 182 W.Va. at 68, 385 S.E.2d at 924, that "generally the question of which parent, if either, is the primary caretaker of minor children in a divorce proceeding is to be proven with lay testimony from the parties themselves and from teachers, relatives and neighbors."

Following the hearings before the family law master, a recommended decision was entered in which the family law master concluded that, although either party would be fit to have custody of the children, custody should be awarded to the appellant.[2] The appellee appealed this decision to circuit court.

Upon reviewing the recommended decision of the family law master, the circuit court was bound to follow the scope of judicial review set forth in *W. Va. Code*, 48A-4-10(c) [1990], which provides:

> (c) The circuit court shall examine the recommended order of the master, along with the findings and conclusions of the master, and may enter the recommended order, may recommit the case, with instructions, for further hearing before the master or may, in its discretion, enter an order upon different terms, as the ends of justice may require. The circuit court shall not follow the recommendation, findings, and conclusions of a master found to be:
>
> (1) Arbitrary, capricious, an abuse of discretion, or otherwise not in conformance with the law;
>
> (2) Contrary to constitutional right, power, privilege, or immunity;
>
> (3) In excess of statutory jurisdiction, authority, or limitations, or short of statutory right;
>
> (4) Without observance of procedure required by law;
>
> (5) Unsupported by substantial evidence; or
>
> (6) Unwarranted by the facts.

In the case now before us, the circuit court concluded that the family law master's decision was "arbitrary and capricious," and awarded custody to the appellee. The circuit court appeared to base this decision on the fact that the appellant is working for a large law firm, and will rely on a babysitter to care for her children while she is at work.[3]

Pursuant to the provisions of *W. Va. Code*, 48A-4-10(c) [1990], the circuit court "may, in its discretion, enter an order upon different terms, *as the ends of justice*

---

2. The family law master explained at the final hearings:

> I have set [sic] here and listened to both the mother and the father, I don't really like to call them plaintiff and defendant because its certainly obvious to me that this [sic] is no question that both parties have a great deal of love and affection for their children and that's not held against either party. There isn't any question that both parties are fit parties when it comes to their children. Mr. Brown has not been the average father that's in front of this court, I mean he has like I say done yomens [sic] duties. He's taken care of his children, he's bathed them, he's fed them, he's cleaned, he's done all the things that a caring parent and a primary caretaker does. So has his wife, so has the mother done those things.

The family law master went on to say:

> Mr. Brown's testimony was that he played with them and cared for them and that he bathed them is more or less an arrangement between the parties and this was his job as opposed to taking an active part.... I found that Mrs. Brown was more the chief he was an [I]ndian that did a tremendous amount of work and is a tremendous and dutiful father. But the directions in the way the things were set up is the primary caretaker if you are looking for a percentage on this I would doubt that I could, I would probably set it at 52 to 48% as close as you can get.

3. In its memorandum order, the circuit court made the following observation:

> The Court recognizes the plaintiff's employment as one filled with much opportunity and demand. However, lucrative careers often do not leave much room for flexibility. The Court respects the plaintiff's desire to devote after hours to the children, but recognizes the practical aspects of that expressed intention. The law profession is by no means comparable to any 9:00 a.m. to 5:00 p.m. job. The profession requires the availability and time flexibility that the plaintiff claims she will not sacrifice for the sake of the children. On the other hand, she plans to hire a live-in nanny to care for the children while she works. There seems to be an inconsistency with wanting to devote after hours at home with the children and hiring a full-time, live-in nanny.

may require." (emphasis added). However, we believe that the circuit court abused its discretion in reversing the family law master's decision on the grounds that it was "arbitrary and capricious," and in ordering that the appellee be awarded custody. The family law master presided over two hearings, during which time he had the opportunity to hear the parties' testimony, and to observe their demeanor. The evidence indicated that the parties shared child-rearing responsibilities, and that both of the parents were fit to care for the children. Although both parents in this case took active roles in raising their children, there was substantial evidence to support the family law master's determination that the appellant was the primary caretaker, and that the children should remain in the appellant's custody. Furthermore, the record indicates that the childrens' maternal and paternal grandparents live in Pittsburgh where the appellant is employed, and has established a home. Moreover, the children have been in the care of their mother since birth, and since the separation of the parties.[4] The family law master's decision to award custody to the appellant was not "arbitrary and capricious," and "the ends of justice" did not require the circuit court to enter an order upon different terms. Thus, for the foregoing reasons, we shall reverse the circuit court on this issue.

II

The next issue we must consider is whether the circuit court abused its discretion in denying the appellant's request for one-half of the appellee's pension, which is an amount of $3,761.83. The appellant avers that she is entitled to one-half of the pension the appellee accumulated during their ten-year marriage because she worked throughout the marriage, and performed homemaker and child care services. The appellee contends that, under the factors set forth in *W.Va.Code*, 48-2-32(c) [1984], the circuit court correctly determined that the appellant was not entitled to one-half of the appellee's pension.

The circuit court, in the absence of a valid agreement, must assume that all marital property is to be divided equally. However, the circuit court may alter this distribution upon consideration of the factors enumerated by this Court in syllabus point 1 of *Somerville v. Somerville*, 179 W.Va. 386, 369 S.E.2d 459 (1988):

> In the absence of a valid agreement, the trial court in a divorce case shall presume that all marital property is to be divided equally between the parties, but may alter this distribution, without regard to fault, based on consideration of certain statutorily enumerated factors, including: (1) monetary contributions to marital property such as employment income, other earnings, and funds which were separate property; (2) nonmonetary contributions to marital property, such as homemaker services, child care services, labor performed without compensation, labor performed in the actual maintenance or improvement of tangible marital property, or labor performed in the management or investment of assets which are marital property; (3) the effect of the marriage on the income-earning abilities of the parties, such as contributions by either party to the education or training of the other party, or foregoing by either party of employment or education; or (4) conduct by other party that lessened the value of the marital property. *W.Va.Code*, §48-2-32(c)(1986).

4. After the separation, the appellee did live with the appellant and their children for a brief period from the time the appellant and her children returned from Pittsburgh at the end of the summer of 1989 until the first hearing in October of 1989.

If the circuit court determines to distribute any marital property in a manner other than equally, the circuit court must specifically state the reasons for such division as we pointed out in syllabus point 3 of *Somerville, supra*: "An order directing a division of marital property in any way other than equally must make specific reference to factors enumerated in §48-2-32(c), and the facts in the record that support application of those factors."

In the case now before us, the circuit court observed that the appellee is a librarian who earns $25,000 a year, whereas the appellant, as an attorney, earns an annual salary of $57,000. The circuit court believed that the appellee had contributed to the appellant's legal education, both directly and indirectly, thereby substantially increasing her income-earning ability. Thus, as its reasons for denying the appellant one-half of the appellee's pension accumulated during the marriage, the circuit court stated that the appellee had: (1) made substantial contributions as a homemaker and provider of child care services; (2) foregone opportunities to increase his income-earning capacity in order to provide child care services; and (3) indirectly contributed to the appellant's law school education by caring for the children while she attended school.

Upon review of the record before us, we find evidence that the appellee made substantial contributions to the home by providing homemaker and child care services throughout the marriage. The evidence further indicates that the appellee's financial burden and child care responsibilities significantly increased when the appellant ceased working and attended law school. It appears from the record that the appellee contributed directly and indirectly to the appellant's legal education, which substantially increased the appellant's income-earning ability. Therefore, we conclude that the trial court did not abuse its discretion in determining that the family law master failed to consider the specific language of *W.Va.Code*, 48-2-32(c), and to allow the appellee's contributions to offset the appellant's interest in his pension.

Thus, for the reasons stated herein, we conclude that the order of the Circuit Court of Monongalia County entered on May 25, 1990, shall be affirmed, in part, and reversed, in part.

Affirmed, in part; reversed, in part.

COMMENTS

Elkus and *Brown* illustrate some of the problems faced by women who try to combine the roles of wife, mother and professional. In *Elkus* the travel imposed by the mother's career as an opera singer was used as a partial basis for the court restricting her ability to be a wife to her new husband. Insofar as more divorced mothers than divorced fathers have custody of the children, restrictions on the rights of a custodial parent to relocate adversely affect more women and benefit more men.

The problems of coordinating the plans of mother and father may radically increase after divorce. Whatever conflicting pressures exist within a marriage are likely to be greater after a break-up. Often during the on-going marriage the family moved one or more times to further the father's work or career opportunities and the mother may feel strong social or economic pressures to return to an earlier domicile. Sometimes the marriage break-up alone is enough to make one spouse or the other wish to leave the area.

Some ex-husbands feel frustrated by their loss of control over their ex-wife and use the children to try to control her. Other ex-husbands feel unfairly limited in their career opportunities by their desire to remain close to children no longer in their custody. On occasion, non-custodial fathers have petitioned courts to force their ex-wives to continue to follow them in their career moves so that they can maintain their relationship with their children without extensive travel. It is often easier for the father than for the mother to claim economic necessity because courts are likely to take his job and career interests more seriously and because the father is more likely than the mother to have a well-paying job with geographic demands. While fathers may be seen as appropriately ambitious, mothers are often seen as selfish and "unmotherly" if they wish to pursue a career move that inconveniences their children or ex-husband.

The women's movement has long advocated a more active role for fathers in child-rearing. Much economic inequality and some family disruption is attributed to the unequal share of parental responsibilities that usually falls upon women. The *Brown* case points up both the positive and the negative aspects of shared child-rearing. On the positive side, Jo's active role as a parent facilitated Martha's work on the newspaper as well as her decision to go to law school and become a lawyer, and it is likely to have been good for the children. A major disadvantage from Martha's point of view is that she almost lost custody upon divorce. Although the family law master recommended in favor of her custody, the circuit court reversed, and she retained custody only through an appeal to her state supreme court. A further disadvantage is that losing custody is almost undoubtedly more difficult for Jo than it would have been for a less involved father. The period of uncertainty regarding custody is likely to have increased the strain of the divorce on the children. It may be harder for children if they must lose everyday contact with either parent when both parents have shared in their raising. On the other hand, when children are raised primarily by one parent, it is especially difficult for them if they are placed in the other parent's custody, which sometimes happens, or if they are virtually abandoned by their inactive parent who does not bother to exercise visitation rights when denied custody, which all too often happens. Overall, it seems better for couples to share child-rearing more equally during an on-going marriage, but one should not overlook the problems raised — problems that may be inevitable as long as we continue our pattern of raising children in a mobile society in unstable nuclear families.

Husbands Who Keep House and Fathers Who Care for Children

STATE ex rel. WATTS v. WATTS

Family Court, City of New York
77 Misc. 2d 178, 350 N.Y.S.2d 285 (1973)

SYBIL HART KOOPER, Judge.

The Family Court is now vested with original jurisdiction to determine custody of children (Chapter 535 of the Laws of 1972 amending section 651 of the Family Court Act). This is such an action between the mother and father of three infant children who are each suing for custody.

Although in theory, a father has an equal right with the mother to the custody of his children, in well over ninety percent of the cases adjudicated, the mother is awarded custody. (The Right of Children in Modern American Family Law, Drinan)

Yet, sound application of the "best interests of the child" criteria requires that the court not place a greater burden on the father in proving suitability for custody than on the mother.

Application of a presumption favoring the mother violates the law of New York State. Both section 240 of the Domestic Relations Law, dealing with custody of children in matrimonial actions and section 70 of the Domestic Relations Law, dealing with *habeas corpus* for a child detained by a parent provides in relevant part:

> In all cases there shall be no *prima facie* right to the custody of the child in either parent, but the court shall determine solely what is for the best interest of the child, and what will best promote its welfare and happiness....

...

Until recently, however, there has been a pattern of at least cursory invocation by the courts in New York and elsewhere, of the presumption that children of tender years, all other things being equal, should be given into the custody of their mother. In fact, this approach to deciding custody cases, since the Domestic Relations Law was amended to forbid such preference, constitutes judicial error — error, moreover, which does not promote the best interests of the children involved. As Foster and Freed, authors of the comprehensive treatise *Law and the Family*, New York, Vol. 2 (1967) stated:

> The statutory mandate in practice is ignored and instead of equality as between the parents, the mother's claim to the child is paramount. In reality instead of "best interests of the child" serving as the test, the "unfitness" rule which was designed to serve in all custody contests between parents and non-parents is being applied....

The "tender years presumption" is actually a blanket judicial finding of fact, a statement by a court that, until proven otherwise by the weight of substantial evidence, mothers are always better suited to care for young children than fathers. This flies in the face of the legislative finding of fact underlying the explicit command of section 240 and section 70 of the Domestic Relations Law, that the best interests of the child are served by the court's approaching the facts of the particular case before it without sex preconceptions of any kind.

However, the trend in legislation, legal commentary, and judicial decisions is away from the "tender years presumption."

Recent amendments of the Domestic Relations Law of several other states have codified as explicitly as New York the view that the child's best interest requires that neither parent have preference. In Florida, for example, the relevant provision, effective July 1, 1971, states:

> The court shall award custody and visitation rights of minor children of the parties as a part of proceeding for dissolution of marriage in accordance with the best interests of the child. Upon considering all relevant factors, the father of the child shall be given the same consideration as the mother in determining custody. Fla.Stat. 61.13(2), F.S.A. (1971).

Wisconsin's law also revised in 1971, provides in relevant part:

> In determining the parent with whom a child shall remain, the court shall consider all facts in the best interest of the child and shall not prefer one parent over the other solely on the basis of the sex of the parent. Wis.Stat. 247.24(3)(1971).

Colorado Rev.Stats. 46-1-5(7) provides:

> No party shall be presumed to be able to serve the best interests of the child better than any other party because of sex.

Legal scholars advocate this evenhanded approach with near virtual unanimity.... Evidence that the courts are taking long strides toward abandoning the "tender years presumption" in favor of an unbiased consideration of the best interests of the children solely on the basis of the individual characteristics and relationships of the parents and children involved is found in the large number of recent custody cases in which the parents were treated equally and the father prevailed....

Apart from the question of legality, the "tender years presumption" should be discarded because it is based on outdated social stereotypes rather than on rational and up-to-date consideration of the welfare of the children involved.

The simple fact of being a mother does not, by itself, indicate a capacity or willingness to render a quality of care different from that which the father can provide. The traditional and romantic view, at least since the turn of the century, has been that nothing can be an adequate substitute for mother love.

> For a boy of such tender years nothing can be an adequate substitute for mother love — for that constant ministration required during the period of nurture [she] can give because...in her alone is service expressed in terms of love. She alone has the patience and sympathy required to mold and soothe the infant mind in its adjustment to its environment. The difference between fatherhood and motherhood in this respect is fundamental, and the law should recognize it unless offset by undesirable traits in the mother.

(*Jenkins v. Jenkins*, 173 Wis. 592, 181 N.W. 826, 827, 1921).

Later decisions have recognized that this view is inconsistent with informed application of the best interests of the child doctrine and out of touch with contemporary thought about child development and male and female stereotypes.

In *Garrett v. Garrett* (464 S.W.2d 740, 742, Mo.App., 1971), the court stated:

> The rule giving the mother preferential right to custody is considerably softened by the realization that "all things never are exactly equal" and is predicated upon the acts of motherhood — not *the fact of motherhood.* Likewise, the rule will yield if the welfare of the children demands it, because this is not a presumption of law but a simple fact of life gleaned from human experience, and the courts are not timid in entrusting children into their father's care and custody when their best interests will be served thereby. (Citations omitted and emphasis added.)

Eminent psychologists and anthropologists, including Margaret Mead, have also acknowledged and asserted that both female and male parents are equally able to provide care and perform child-rearing functions.

> At present, the specific biological situation of the continuing relationship of the child to the biological mother and its need for care by human beings are being hopelessly confused in the...insistence that the child and mother or mother surrogate must never be separated; that all separation even for a few days is ultimately damaging and that if long enough it does irreversible damage. This is a mere and subtle form of anti-feminism which men — under the guise of exalting the importance of maternity — are tying women more tightly to their children than has been thought necessary since the invention of bottle feeding and baby carriages.

Margaret Mead, *Some Theoretical Considerations of the Problems of Mother-Child Separation,* 24 Amer.Jrl. of Orthopsychiatry 24 (1954).

Studies of maternal deprivation have shown that the essential experience for the child is that of mothering — the warmth, consistency and continuity of the relationship rather than the sex of the individual who is performing the mothering function. (See, *e.g.,* R. A. Spitz and Katherine Wolf, *Anaclitic Depression,* Psychoanalytic Study of the Child, 1946, pages 313–342; Leon J. Yarrow, *Maternal Deprivation: Toward an Empirical and Conceptual Reevaluation,* Psychological Bull., 58, 1961.)

Finally, application of the "tender years presumption" would deprive respondent of his right to equal protection of the law under the Fourteenth Amendment to the United States Constitution.

...Recent decisions of the Supreme Court of the United States make clear that differential treatment on the basis of sex of the kind created by the "tender years presumption" is "suspect" and therefore subject to the strictest judicial scrutiny. In *Frontiero v. Richardson* (411 U.S. 677, 93 S.Ct. 1764, 1770, 36 L.Ed.2d 583, 1973) the court made explicit the incurable flaw in rules of law which accord different treatment to men and women on the basis of rigid and outdated sexual stereotypes:

> Since sex, like race and national origin, is an immutable characteristic determined solely by the accident of birth, the imposition of special disabilities upon the members of a particular sex because of their sex would seem to violate "the basic concept of our system that legal burdens should bear some relationship to individual responsibility...." And what differentiates sex from such nonsuspect statutes as intelligence or physical disability, and aligns it with the recognized suspect criteria, is that the sex

characteristic frequently bears no relation to ability to perform or to contribute to society.

The message of *Frontiero* is clear: persons similarly situated, whether male or female, must be accorded evenhanded treatment by the law. Legislative classifications may legitimately take account of need or ability; they may not be premised on unalterable sex characteristics that bear no necessary relationship to the individual's need, ability or life situation....

Classifications subject to "strict scrutiny" under the Fourteenth Amendment pass constitutional muster only if a "compelling state interest" requires their existence. (See *Frontiero v. Richardson*, 411 U.S. at 682, 93 S.Ct. at 1768, 36 L.Ed.2d at 589; *McLaughlin v. Florida*, 379 U.S. 184, 85 S.Ct. 283, 13 L.Ed.2d 222, 1964; *Loving v. Virginia*, 388 U.S. 1, 87 S.Ct. 1817, 18 L.Ed.2d 1010, 1967.) The "best interests" of the child might well qualify as such a compelling state interest if, in fact, it were served by the "tender years presumption." But since, as has been shown, the presumption does not in fact serve the child's interests, it does not constitute a compelling state interest justifying the different treatment of parents on the basis of sex. Thus the "tender years presumption" in addition to its other faults, works an unconstitutional discrimination against the respondent.

In this connection, even before *Frontiero*, the Federal District Court for the Southern District of New York indicated that governmental authorities could not, without violating the Fourteenth Amendment, make employee leaves for the purpose of caring for newborn infants available to mothers unless they also make them available to fathers. (*Danielson v. Board of Higher Education of the City of New York*, 358 F.Supp. 22, S.D.N.Y., 1972.) Ruling on a motion to dismiss, the court held that the Board of Higher Education of the City of New York's policy of granting such leaves only to mothers but not to fathers presented a colorable constitutional claim. The case was not pushed to a final decision because the board changed its policies to make such leave available for men.

Arbitrary assumptions about which spouse is better suited to care for young children are no more permissible in the case at bar then they are in the child care leave situation just described.

This court, in arriving at its decision, has applied one criteria only — the best interests of the children.

Having listened to all the testimony, having read all the medical reports and records and having observed the demeanor and responses of the parties on the witness stand, this court concludes that it is in the best interests of the children for them to be in their father's custody.

DANIELSON v. BOARD OF HIGHER EDUCATION

United States District Court
358 F. Supp. 22 (S.D.N.Y. 1972)

MOTLEY, District Judge.

This is an action by Ross Danielson, a lecturer in sociology at City College, a branch of the City University of New York. Mr. Danielson's challenge is to the constitutionality of defendants' maternity leave provision on its face and as applied. The essence of Danielson's claim is that women faculty members are permitted to take a leave of absence in connection with pregnancy, up to three semesters, for the purpose, among others, of caring for a new born infant, without adversely affecting their tenure rights, but the same child care leave privilege is denied to men.

This action is also brought by Mr. Danielson's wife, Susan Danielson, who is a lecturer in English at Lehman College, another branch of the City University of New York. Her challenge is to the constitutionality of defendants' refusal to treat her 12-day leave, during which she gave birth to a child, as sick leave.

Defendants are the Board of Higher Education which governs the City University of New York, the chairman of that Board, the chancellor of the University, the president of City College, and the dean of faculties of Lehman College.

...

The action is presently before the court on the motion of plaintiffs for summary judgment in their favor and the motion of defendants to dismiss or, alternatively, for summary judgment in their favor. Defendants have moved to dismiss the complaint on two grounds: 1) the court lacks jurisdiction of the subject matter and, 2) the complaint fails to state a claim upon which relief may be granted. For the reasons set forth below, the motion to dismiss is denied. The motions for summary judgment are also denied on the ground that there are several disputed issues of fact.

Mr. Danielson commenced teaching in the City College in the fall semester of 1969. His wife, Susan Danielson, who was teaching at Lehman College at the same time became pregnant in the early spring of 1970. Upon discovering her pregnancy, Susan and her husband discussed the matter at great length. They weighed the options available to them with respect to the care of their child and the pursuit of their respective careers. They decided that Susan would continue her teaching duties throughout her pregnancy and after childbirth. Then, for at least the first six months after the child was born, Mr. Danielson would stay home and assume the primary responsibility for the care of their infant. Susan Danielson consulted her physician who assured her that such conduct on her part would in no way be injurious to her health.

Mr. Danielson then made every effort to obtain "parental leave of absence" from City College. He claims such "parental leave" is available for women faculty members pursuant to Article XIII, Section 13.4, of the By-Laws of the Board of Higher Education and should be equally available to men.

...

On or about December 21, 1970 Mr. Danielson learned that the president's Review Committee had rejected his application without stating any reason. Mr. Danielson appealed to the chancellor of the University and the chairman of the Board of Higher Education but received no reply to his letters.

Ross Danielson took a leave during the spring 1971 semester and alleges he assumed primary responsibility for the care of his child. His wife resumed her teaching duties. His application for maternity leave was treated as a resignation. Thus, although he was rehired for the fall 1971 term, the computation of his continuous service time has been affected.

Susan Danielson, who had a right to do so, did not request the maternity leave permitted under Section 13.4. The president's office, however, sent her a form for such leave on numerous occasions. Maternity leaves which are granted under Section 13.4 are leaves without pay. If Mrs. Danielson had chosen to take maternity leave as of September 1, 1970 and had requested the one year extension, she could have remained away from her post until February 1, 1972 without loss of accrued time towards tenure requirements. It appears that no doctor's certificate in support of her request for extension would have been required. However, there is no proof one way or the other on this question. During this time away from her position, Mrs. Danielson apparently would have been free to devote all her time to the care of her newborn infant or, it appears, she could also have worked on her Ph.D. But, again, there is no firm proof one way or the other on this crucial question.

Defendants say that "...Ross Danielson might have obtained a leave for special purposes under Section 13.6 if he so requested, for the purpose of taking care of his child." (Defendants' Brief, p. 18.) They also assert that "If any parent desires to take leave solely for childrearing purposes, they must proceed under By-Law §13.6, leave for special purposes." (*Id.* p. 24.)

Section 13.6b provides: "On the recommendation of the relevant departmental committee concerned with appointments, the relevant college committee and the president, the Board may grant to members of the instructional staff leaves of absence for special purposes such as study, writing, research, the carrying out of a creative project or a public service of reasonable duration. Such leaves shall be *without* pay." (Emphasis added.)

Mr. Danielson was not advised of this "administrative procedure...available to accommodate him" prior to suit. (*Id* pp. 18–19.) Such leave, of course, does affect the computation of the five years of continuous service required for tenure.

It should be noted also that defendants' statement, that any parent who desires leave "solely" for childrearing purposes may apply for same under Section 13.6, does not square with defendants' assertion on the same page of their brief (p. 24) which reads as follows: "Defendant's By-Law provides a mother with the option to recuperate from pregnancy. If she utilizes this leave period to also care for her child, this is her own determination." This latter statement is consistent with the former if the former refers to women who desire to take child-care leave unconnected with childbirth. Thus from reading defendants' brief, it is clear to this court that defendants have not made up their collective minds as to what their child-care leave policies really are in the face of this men's liberation request for equal treatment with women.

Consequently, summary judgment cannot be granted for either party. Not only is it unclear what defendants' policies really are, but the central fact is plainly in dispute, *i.e.*, whether women faculty members are permitted leaves up to three semesters under Section 13.4 to care for their newborn children when there is no unusual medical disability resulting from the birth of the child and, during this period, may also do work toward a Ph.D. degree without loss of time served, as it relates to tenure.

Mrs. Danielson made arrangements with other teachers to cover her classes during her brief leave for the birth of her child. She was absent from work for 12 days, from December 8, 1970 to December 23, 1970. She requested that her absence be credited against her allotted sick leave with pay. Instead of treating her absence as sick leave, Lehman College recorded the leave as a "special leave without pay for emergency purposes (maternity)." The special leave section, Section 13.6a, provides for special leaves for personal emergencies of not more than 10 working days *with pay* at the discretion of the president. Despite the express terms of this provision, Mrs. Danielson was not paid.

Again it is clear defendants were confused about their own policy. Mrs. Danielson's claim that the leave which she took should be treated as any other illness is disputed by defendants on the ground that pregnancy is not an illness. With respect to Mrs. Danielson's claim we thus have another central disputed issue of fact, *i.e.*, whether the period immediately following childbirth unattended by other complications is a medical disability or illness for which a woman is entitled to sick leave. Mrs. Danielson's claim for sick leave pay is a claim which has been previously recognized by a federal court, *Cohen v. Chesterfield County School Board*, 326 F.Supp. 1159 (E.D.Va.1971), and has been bolstered by recently adopted Rules and Regulations of the Equal Employment Opportunity Commission. 37 Fed.Reg. 6837 (April 5, 1972).

On this motion to dismiss it is only necessary to determine whether Mr. and Mrs. Danielson's allegations raise "colorable" constitutional claims....

Mr. Danielson's primary claim is that his right to equal protection of the laws has been violated by defendants' refusal to extend to him the same childcare leave privilege which they extend to women solely because he is a man. He claims that by so discriminating against men who seek to fully participate in the care of their children, defendants are effectively denying men the right to play a full and equal role in their families. He then argues that the fact that child care has traditionally been considered women's work is no more an answer here than were the use of such sex stereotypes in an attempt to bar women from certain kinds of employment.... He also argues that he and other men are perfectly capable of caring for infant children and have a right to elect to do so without arbitrary interference with this choice by the state.

Very recently, the Supreme Court ruled that a state may not arbitrarily prefer men over women similarly situated in determining appointments to positions of administrator of decedent's estates. *Reed v. Reed*, 404 U.S. 71, 92 S.Ct. 251, 30 L.Ed.2d 225 (1971). There the Court ruled that where the state provides that different treatment be accorded to persons similarly situated, such a classification is subject to scrutiny under the equal protection clause. The Court held that a classification must be reasonable, not arbitrary, and must rest upon some ground of difference having a fair and substantial relation to the object of the legislation, so that all persons similarly circumstanced shall be treated alike. If upon a trial it is proved that the purpose of Section 13.4 leave is to give women an opportunity to care for infant children, and since it is not claimed that Mr. Danielson is incapable of such child care, then Mr. Danielson would have presented at least a "colorable" constitutional claim. Whether he will succeed with his claim is another matter not here decided.

...

For all of the foregoing reasons, the motions for summary judgement and to dismiss are denied.

...

PFOHL v. PFOHL

District Court of Appeal of Florida
345 So.2d 371 (Fla. Dist. Ct. App. 1977)

HUBBART, Judge.

This is an action for dissolution of marriage in which the husband was awarded lump sum and rehabilitative alimony as well as attorneys' fees. The wife appeals and the husband cross appeals, raising questions which go to the propriety and sufficiency of such awards.

On May 28, 1966, the parties were married. At the time of the marriage, the wife owned a one third interest in a trucking company given to her by her father, which interest she sold in 1972 for seven million dollars. The husband had no assets going into the marriage except for a one half interest in one hundred shares of Sears Roebuck stock. He had been employed for four and one half years as a toy salesman for Strombecker Toy Co. earning a salary of approximately $9,000–$10,000 a year plus expenses and bonus. He resigned this job after one and a half years of marriage to satisfy the wife's wishes. She did not like his traveling which was necessary to pursue his line of work, and refused to move to New York with him to accept a promotion. Prior to the marriage, he had finished three years of college and received an honorable discharge from the marines. The couple had two sons, now ages 8 and 2.

The parties lived a life of extreme luxury and comfort during a marriage which lasted nine years prior to the parties' final separation. The wife supported the family at first through contributions from her father, and from 1972–75 from her own separate estate.

Both the husband and wife had an unlimited joint checking account. Both had access to the wife's extensive properties: a one hundred acre farm in Elgin, Illinois, purchased for $500,000; a five bedroom house in Chicago; and two homes in Bal Harbour, Florida, purchased for $140,000 and $60,000 respectively. Both had access to a six bedroom home and an eighty acre farm in Crystal Lake, Illinois, in which the wife gave the husband one half interest.

The husband had all the major credit cards with unlimited credit plus charge accounts at many luxury stores where he regularly shopped. He maintained extensive clothing in their Florida and Illinois homes. Several times each year he paid substantial entry fees so he could participate in celebrity golf tournaments such as the Bob Hope and Andy Williams Classics.

The parties were members of seven luxury country clubs in Chicago and Miami for which the wife paid substantial initial membership sums and all the subsequent dues and bills incurred. They traveled extensively throughout the country and the world, and because of the wife's substantial interest in race horses, routinely traveled to the Kentucky Derby and other races in New York, California and Illinois. They were attended by servants in their homes in Florida and Illinois. They entertained extensively at home and various clubs at which they were members. They had full access to the seventy-five foot family yacht on which they maintained a full crew, contributing $3,000 a month to the operation of the vessel. In addition, they had two late model Cadillacs, a Buick stationwagon and a speedboat.

The husband estimated that his living expenses during the marriage were over $5,000 a month. The wife estimated that the family's total monthly living expenses were approximately $15,000 including income taxes. The wife could not have provided the foregoing fantasy-land existence for the husband on anything less than enormous resources. At the time of the final hearing, she had a net worth of $4,250,000 including cash and marketable securities of $3,325,000 plus an annual net income of $200,000.

During the marriage the husband dabbled, but never seriously participated in various business ventures provided by his wife's family. He was a figurehead president of the Antioch Insurance Agency for four years. Following this venture, he was a treasurer and director in the Antioch Savings and Loan Association from which he was eventually removed for failure to attend meetings.

The parties ceased living together as husband and wife on May 6, 1975. At that time the wife forbade the husband to return to their home in Florida or to live in any other of her properties. She removed his clothes therefrom and the husband has remained unemployed living with friends at a drastically reduced living style ever since. He unsuccessfully sought employment on several occasions in Florida and Chicago. There is evidence that the husband presently suffers from a mental disorder requiring professional treatment, but that at 37 he is in excellent physical health.

At the time of the dissolution, the husband held the following assets, all provided to him by the wife during the marriage: an undivided one half interest in an eighty acre farm in Crystal Lake, Illinois, his interest valued at $160,000; a 1974 and 1975 Cadillac valued together at a total of $12,000; and a twenty-five foot power boat valued at $6,000. In addition, he leaves the marriage with his original one half interest in one hundred shares of Sears Roebuck stock valued at $6,000 and an 80 percent ownership interest in a Ft. Lauderdale lounge known as the "Filling Station." The husband owes the wife $60,000 for the purchase of this lounge which at the time of the final hearing was up for sale for $110,000. He, therefore, has approximately $200,000 in assets, almost all of which are non-liquid and non-income producing.

The wife filed a petition for dissolution of marriage seeking the dissolution of the marriage, custody of the parties' two minor children and an adjudication of her rights as to the $60,000 loan which she had made to the husband. The husband answered denying that the marriage was irretrievably broken as well as the allegations concerning the loan. He requested alimony, attorneys fees and suit monies. The wife replied denying the husband's need for alimony, suit monies, and attorneys fees, which reply was amended to assert adultery as a defense to his claim for alimony, suit monies and attorneys fees.

...

The major question presented for review is whether it is an abuse of discretion in a dissolution of marriage action for a trial court to award the husband $30,000 in lump sum alimony and $5,000 a month rehabilitative alimony for 18 months when: (1) the wife has a net worth of $4,250,000; (2) the parties shared an extremely high standard of living at first supported by the wife based on contributions to her from her father and thereafter based entirely on her own wealth during a nine year marriage; (3) the husband is 37 years old, unemployed with limited employment skills, in good physical, but impaired mental health, and in possession of approximately $200,000 assets most of which were received during the marriage from the wife.

Both parties contend that the trial judge abused his discretion. The wife argues that the husband is not entitled to any alimony; the husband argues that the amount of lump sum alimony is inadequate and that permanent, rather than rehabilitative alimony should have been awarded. We reject all these contentions and hold that the alimony awards herein were well within the discretion of the trial judge to make under the circumstances of this case....

Alimony has been traditionally considered an allowance which a husband is required to make in order to maintain his wife in the event of separation or divorce and is based on the common law obligation of a husband to support his wife. *Floyd v. Floyd*, 91 Fla. 910, 108 So. 896 (1926). In determining the amount of such alimony, the courts have established two criteria: (1) the husband's ability to pay, and (2) the needs of the wife, taking into consideration the standard of living shared by the parties to the marriage. *Sisson v. Sisson*, 336 So.2d 1129 (Fla.1976); *Firestone v. Firestone*, 263 So.2d 223 (Fla.1972)....

Quite properly, these are criteria of the broadest nature, not susceptible to a precise formula automatically translatable into dollars and cents. We are dealing with a tragically human problem which touches peoples' lives during a period of immense personal crisis. One cannot dispense substantial justice in such explosive cases as if the answer lies in a computer or a rigid rule book. Mathematical exactness is neither possible nor desirable. The trial court of necessity has a wide discretion to apply the established criteria in fashioning a fair and equitable alimony award in the infinite variety of cases which come before it. Absent a showing that the trial court exercised this discretion arbitrarily or unfairly, alimony awards made pursuant to such criteria must be sustained on appeal....

The so-called "no fault" divorce law enacted by the Florida Legislature in 1971, represents a significant, but not totally radical departure from the historic conception of alimony. Section 61.08, Florida Statutes (1975) provides as follows:

> (1) In a proceeding for dissolution of marriage, the court may grant alimony to either party, which alimony may be rehabilitative or permanent in nature. In any award of alimony, the court may order periodic payments or payments in lump sum or both. The court may consider the adultery of a spouse and the circumstances thereof in determining whether alimony shall be awarded to such spouse and the amount of alimony, if any, to be awarded to such spouse.
>
> (2) In determining a proper award of alimony, the court may consider any factor necessary to do equity and justice between the parties.

Under this statute, it is provided for the first time that a wife may be required to support her husband through alimony payments. This is in keeping with the current social trend toward establishing a more equitable relationship between the sexes. The First District Court of Appeal pointed out in *Beard v. Beard*, 262 So.2d 269 (Fla.1st DCA 1972):

> In this era of women's liberation movements and enlightened thinking, we have almost universally come to appreciate the fallacy of treating the feminine members of our society on anything but a basis of complete equality with the opposite sex. Any contrary view would be completely anachronistic. In this day and time, women are well educated and trained in the arts, sciences, and professions as are their male counterparts. The law properly protects them in their right to independently acquire, encumber, accumulate, and alienate property at will. They now occupy a position of equal partners in the family relationship resulting from marriage, and more often than not contribute a full measure to the economic well-being of the family unit.

Id. at 271–72.

The First District Court of Appeal further elaborated on this theme in *Thigpen v. Thigpen*, 277 So.2d 583 (Fla.1st DCA 1973) as follows:

> The new concept of marriage relation implicit in the so-called "no fault" divorce law enacted by the legislature in 1971 places both parties to the

> marriage on a basis of complete equality as partners sharing equal rights and obligations in the marriage relationship and sharing equal burdens in the event of dissolution. *Id.* at 585.

Although this historic change in alimony law is far-reaching and we have not yet chartered its full effects, we can at least begin by stating that a husband's entitlement to alimony must stand on the same criteria as that of a wife. *Lefler v. Lefler*, 264 So.2d 112 (Fla.4th DCA 1972). To be entitled to alimony, the husband must show a financial ability by the wife to pay for such an award coupled with a demonstrated need of the husband for support, taking into consideration the standard of living shared by the parties to the marriage.

Although in most marriages, the husband remains the sole provider of the family, with the wife making the home and raising the children, if any, an increasing number of marriages do not fit this mold. In some marriages, both parties work and jointly support the family, although the degree of support by either party may vary. In others, the wife is the sole support of the family unit with the husband fulfilling some non-economic role. It is in these non-traditional type marriages where the question of alimony for the husband may arise.

In the instant case, we are faced with such a non-traditional type of marriage. Although neither party did any serious work to financially support the family unit, the wife, rather than the husband, was the sole provider in this marriage. The husband resigned his employment at the request of the wife to live a life of luxury with his wife and family. Such fabulous wealth on the part of a woman who supports a marriage in which the husband is of modest means is not unknown in our society, but it certainly presents a case of unusual dimensions which we think the trial judge handled most reasonably upon the marriage's dissolution under the traditional criteria for awarding alimony.

...

As to the first criterion for awarding alimony, it is undisputed that the wife easily has the financial ability to pay for the alimony award in this case. She has a financial worth in excess of $4,000,000 and regularly maintains a checking account considerably greater than the total $120,000 alimony award for the husband. The award is therefore immune from attack as being beyond the financial means of the wife....

As to the second criterion for awarding alimony, the lump sum and rehabilitative alimony awards herein were commensurate with the need of the husband for temporary, although not permanent support, taking into consideration the standard of living shared by the parties to the marriage. The husband's limited employment opportunities, his impaired mental condition, and the very high standard of living to which the wife accustomed the husband to live during the marriage, are all critical factors in sustaining the trial court's exercise of discretion in fashioning the alimony award in this case.

The husband was a toy salesman for six years earning a modest salary which job he gave up at the request of the wife to devote full time to his life with the wife and family after a year and a half of marriage. Save for this limited service mainly as a figurehead in the businesses of his wife's family, he has been out of the employment market for the last seven and a half years of the marriage. At the time of the final hearing, he was unemployed, living with friends at a drastically reduced life style, having unsuccessfully attempted on a number of occasions to obtain employment, since the wife barred him from the marital homes. This impairment in a spouse's otherwise modest employment capacities caused in part by the supporting spouse's insistence that such work be terminated in favor of the family is a significant factor in sustaining an alimony award. *Brook v. Brook*, 289 So.2d 766 (Fla.3d DCA 1974).

Added to this, is the husband's impaired mental condition. According to the uncontradicted testimony of an industrial psychologist, Dr. Marquit, the husband is suffering from a mental disorder which will require at least a year of intensive psychotherapy at considerable expense. He further testified that at present the husband is ill-suited for the employment market. We are in no position to second guess the trial judge's acceptance of this testimony based on his personal evaluation of Dr. Marquit as well as that of the husband. Certainly it is not beyond the realm of reasonable inference for the trial judge to have concluded that the husband's nine years of leisure class idleness followed by an abrupt end to his male cinderella existence when the wife literally threw him out of her home, at least partially brought on his current mental problems for which some period of rehabilitation is necessary. Such mental impairment, although temporary rather than permanent in nature, is a significant factor in sustaining an alimony award. *Baker v. Baker*, 229 So.2d 276 (Fla.3d DCA 1974).

The husband's financial needs must also be measured in part by taking into consideration the extremely high standard of living to which the wife accustomed the husband through nine years of marriage.... The wife accustomed the husband to a life style which costs over $5,000 a month to maintain during a marriage which can hardly be described as a "marry in June and sue the following September" situation. *Firestone v. Firestone, supra.* In view of this fact, we cannot say that the limited eighteen month rehabilitative alimony plus lump sum alimony fashioned by the trial judge herein was an abuse of discretion. It was reasonably commensurate with the parties' high life style without at the same time creating an unreasonable charge on the wife for the rest of her life.

The wife argues that she accustomed the husband to such a high life style based on money she received from her father. It is true that the wife supported the marriage at first through contributions from the wife's father, but from 1972–1975 she supported the family unit entirely from her own separate estate. In our judgment, it is irrelevant how the wife lawfully acquired the money on which she supported the husband and family. The fact is she supported the family unit, not the husband. And despite the wife's protests, a high standard of living remains a significant factor in setting an alimony award, which result is unchanged by the fact that the paying spouse acquired his or her wealth by gift or inheritance....

Rehabilitative alimony has been awarded to supplement means already available in an amount reasonably required during the post-marriage period to maintain a spouse until he or she in the exercise of reasonable efforts and endeavors is in a position of self support. *Cann v. Cann*, 334 So.2d 325 (Fla.1st DCA 1976). It necessarily presupposes the potential for self support which is presently impaired. *Reback v. Reback*, 296 So.2d 541 (Fla.3d DCA 1974). Lump sum alimony has been awarded as a payment of a definite sum or property in the nature of a final property settlement which serves a reasonable purpose such as rehabilitation or where the marriage's duration or the parties' financial position would make such an award advantageous to both parties.... The alimony awards herein fit these traditional patterns and purposes for alimony.

The wife argues that the husband's $200,000 in assets acquired mainly by gift from the wife during the marriage, disqualifies the husband from receiving any alimony. We disagree. Although this is a significant factor in upholding the trial court's refusal to make the alimony permanent, we cannot say that this compels the result urged by the wife, particularly in view of the husband's demonstrated need for temporary, rehabilitative support. Except for the Sears stock, the husband's assets are non-income producing. And it has been held that a spouse is not required to deplete capital assets in order to maintain a prior standard of living. *Gordon v. Gordon*, 204 So.2d 734 (Fla.3d DCA 1967). Moreover, alimony awards have been upheld where the spouse seeking alimony possessed assets comparable to that of the husband in this case. *Harrison v. Harrison*, 314 So.2d 812 (Fla.3d DCA 1975).

The wife throughout these proceedings has attacked the husband's life style as parasitic and has warned that he should not be able to parlay such an existence into a $120,000 alimony award. The same criticism could be made of a good many wives who upon dissolution of a tragically flawed marriage have received alimony awards. We pass no judgment on the morality or social value of the marriage herein. Many Americans might very well regard the conduct of either party to this marriage with some cynicism. The work ethic is, after all, deeply ingrained in our mores. But we must take the marriage as we find it without passing judgment on the life style of either party. In a free society, there is room enough for many kinds of marriages, including this one. If and when such a marriage dissolves, it must be accorded equal treatment according to the standards for determining alimony set for all marriage dissolutions.

Moreover, the limited nature of the alimony awards herein should allay any fears that it will encourage any type of parasitic conduct. The husband has hardly been given a meal ticket for life; he has been given a temporary and limited assist to rehabilitate himself to a position of eventual self-support based on a demonstrated need. In this, we can find no abuse of discretion....

Turning now to the husband's cross appeal, we are not persuaded that the husband's demonstrated needs are so great that the trial court abused its discretion in refusing to make the alimony award permanent rather than rehabilitative and in refusing to award a greater lump sum alimony. As the wife accurately points out, the husband is a relatively young, well-educated man of 37, has excellent physical health although temporarily impaired mental health, has $200,000 in assets of his own, has some employment skills if only limited ones, and lives alone without custody of the parties' two children. We can see no reason why he could not properly rehabilitate himself within eighteen months with the alimony awarded herein.... In the event that substantial rehabilitation does not occur by the end of eighteen months despite the husband's reasonable and diligent efforts, the husband can petition the court for modification of the alimony award. Section 61.14 Florida Statutes (1975); *Lee v. Lee*, 309 So.2d 26 (Fla.2d DCA 1975)....

The second question presented for review is whether it is an abuse of discretion in a dissolution of marriage action for a trial judge to set a $30,000 attorneys fee to be paid by the wife for the husband's attorneys where: (1) the wife has a net worth of $4,250,000; (2) the husband has a net worth of $200,000; (3) the husband's attorneys secure lump sum and rehabilitative alimony for the husband worth $120,000; (4) the husband attorneys are eminent counsel who spent one hundred working hours plus twenty more hours of associate and law clerk time preparing for a unique, but not protracted or unduly complex litigation; and (5) the expert testimony puts a reasonable attorneys fee at $30,000.

The wife contends that she should not be required to pay the fee and that in any event, the fee was excessive. We reject these contentions and hold that the award of attorneys fees was well within the discretion of the trial judge to set under the circumstances of this case.

...

Affirmed.

COMMENTS

Watts, *Danielson*, and *Pfohl* all deal with the changed position of men in marriage and the family. In order to understand these cases, it is important to consider a world view strongly held by some men: The excessive rights of married men under common law were accompanied by an excessive imposition of legal burdens. For example, since the husband acquired the property of his wife at marriage, it followed that he had an absolute duty to support her, as she had no property left to contribute to the costs of the marriage. Under these rules, formulated in England, it would have been considered illogical that a wife could ever be obligated to support her husband or herself. A case like *Pfohl* would have been a factual and legal impossibility. Absolute divorce was not available then, and even if there had been a divorce from bed and board, the husband, who retained control over the marital assets, would have been exclusively responsible for support. In reality the dichotomy between rights and duties of the husband proved to be artificial, because what appeared to be his rights were inseparable from the responsibilities flowing from his status within the family.

From a "men's rights" perspective, the father's position with respect to his children was governed by somewhat different perceptions. He was historically perceived to have all the rights and duties toward them, but nineteenth century English legislation established the rights of mothers to custody. Thus, as far as children were concerned, the father lost many of his rights but ordinarily continued to be burdened with the duty to support his children as well as his wife.

In America, while it seems to some men that women acquired more and more rights because women's dependent position was increasingly understood to be socially undesirable, the duties of husbands and fathers remained relatively unchanged. Men were primarily responsible for the burdens of marriage while at the same time they lost much of their preferred status. In the public mind too, and in the minds of elected state court judges, men were still expected to live up to their responsibilities. Not inconsequentially, according to this view, society was and still is rightly inclined to grant men higher wages, with the implicit understanding that the bonus will be applied to the care of dependents. We thus face an irregular legal situation in which married men, having lost their absolute rights, are burdened with severe disabilities within the family. At the same time women continue to be subjected to discrimination in the labor market. This view provides the context for the assertion in *Danielson* that the issue of women's liberation is complemented by an issue of men's liberation that is of at least equal weight but less visible.

The Equal Rights Amendment, which became quite controversial during the 1970s, would have provided that "Equality of rights under the law shall not be denied or abridged by the United States or by any State on account of sex." Such a legal statement would provide a vehicle for removing the disabilities of both men and women. Some of the opposition against adoption of the ERA originated from the traditional feeling that men ought to be made to live up to their responsibilities. It is an economic reality that they can do so more effectively if they retain their favored position for higher earnings and better career opportunities than those available to women.

Both men and women sometimes argue that as job opportunities for women improve, the social climate will slowly change in favor of also giving men more equal rights. This will mean fewer financial burdens for men resulting from marriage. If men share more equally in child care, they can expect to have more rights with respect to child custody in the case of marital failure. It is this kind of process that some would see at work in *Watts*, *Danielson*, and *Pfohl*. Some expect the process will cause substantial and prolonged strain because it runs counter to traditional roles of men and women and to traditional perspectives on marriage, the family, and social institutions. The hostile attitude of the defendant Board of Education in *Danielson* against the argument of the husband and father requesting "maternity leave" is symptomatic. It is not accidental that the opinion in *Watts* was written by a female judge. The strong language disfavoring the presumption benefiting the mother would perhaps have been less likely to emerge had the judge been a man; a male judge might have feared that his motives would be found suspect.

On the other hand, a number of women dispute these assertions. They argue that men receive inordinate credit for the minor concessions they have made to women. Men's salaries continue to be fifty percent higher than women's, and women continue to do a disproportionate share of housework and other unpaid labor. As a result, women and their children make up the largest group living in poverty. The only "severe disability" men are burdened with in the family is the loss of the absolute rights they used to enjoy but which were never justified (nor indeed exercised by civilized men).

The language in *Watts* referring to the best interest of the child obscures more than it enlightens. It has strong emotional appeal, but in fact invites decisions according to prevailing social stereotypes of sex roles. According to some men, this is a fact borne out by the situation in most states. In spite of widespread statutory provisions that the father shall be given the same consideration as the mother in determining custody, the trial courts have continued to grant custody to the mother in the overwhelming number of cases. The statutory invocation of "the best interest of the child," combined with the statement that "all relevant factors" must be considered, effectively resulted in a continuation of the judicial preference for mothers.

According to some women, however, the sex role stereotype issue often works in favor of fathers. It is taken for granted that a mother will care for her children, and courts hold it against women if they pursue a career, or even if they work in the labor market to support their children. (See *Elkus v. Elkus, supra* at p.435.) Men, however, are given huge amounts of credit for any time they spend with their children. Even if the father begins spending time with the children only as the marriage begins to break up, the judge will typically consider him a fully adequate father, equally entitled to custody as the mother. Many would argue that the main reason that women get custody of children is that women continue to do most child care. Most fathers do not seek sole custody and would not want to be fully responsible for caring for their children. Even in contested cases, a father's claim for custody may be motivated as much by strategic and competitive considerations as by an actual desire to have custody of the children. These and other custody issues are discussed more fully in Chapter 5.

The interpretation given by the New York court in *Watts* to Florida's child custody provision did not correspond to Florida practice. This is only one illustration of the inclination of the courts in common law jurisdictions to continue established judicial patterns regardless of legislative efforts to bring about change.

Even *Pfohl,* granting substantial rehabilitative alimony to the husband, is in fact not as progressive a decision as it appears to be. Had the husband instead of the wife been a multimillionaire, with other facts reversed, namely, the wife being unemployable because of a mental disorder requiring professional treatment, there may be little doubt that the court would have granted her substantially higher alimony payments, perhaps of a permanent nature, than were granted in this case to the husband. In other words, although the trend is toward greater equality of the spouses, even the more advanced decisions often fall short of that goal.

REFERENCE

Frances Olsen, *The Politics of Family Law,* 2 J. L. & INEQUALITY 1 (1984).

C: Beyond Individualism and Gender-Blind Equality

No-Fault Divorce and Gender-Blind Equality

ORR v. ORR
United States Supreme Court
440 U.S. 268 (1979)

Mr. Justice BRENNAN delivered the opinion of the Court.

The question presented is the constitutionality of Alabama alimony statutes which provide that husbands, but not wives, may be required to pay alimony upon divorce.[1]

On February 26, 1974, a final decree of divorce was entered, dissolving the marriage of William and Lillian Orr. That decree directed appellant, Mr. Orr, to pay appellee, Mrs. Orr, $1,240 per month in alimony. On July 28, 1976, Mrs. Orr initiated a contempt proceeding in the Circuit Court of Lee County, Ala., alleging that Mr. Orr was in arrears in his alimony payments. On August 19, 1976, at the hearing on Mrs. Orr's petition, Mr. Orr submitted in his defense a motion requesting that Alabama's alimony statutes be declared unconstitutional because they authorize courts to place an obligation of alimony upon husbands but never upon wives. The Circuit Court denied Mr. Orr's motion and entered judgment against him for $5,524, covering back alimony and attorney fees. Relying solely upon his federal constitutional claim, Mr. Orr appealed the judgment. On March 16, 1977, the Court of Civil Appeals of Alabama sustained the constitutionality of the Alabama statutes, 351 So.2d 904. On May 24, the Supreme Court of Alabama granted Mr. Orr's petition for a writ of certiorari, but on November 10, without court opinion, quashed the writ as improvidently granted. 351 So.2d 906. We noted probable jurisdiction, 436 U.S. 924, 98 S.Ct. 2817, 56 L.Ed.2d 767 (1978). We now hold the challenged Alabama statutes unconstitutional and reverse.

. . .

II

In authorizing the imposition of alimony obligations on husbands, but not on wives, the Alabama statutory scheme "provides that different treatment be accorded...on the basis of...sex; it thus establishes a classification subject to

---

1. The statutes, Ala.Code, Tit. 30 (1975), provide that:

§30-2-51. If the wife has no separate estate or if it be insufficient for her maintenance, the judge, upon granting a divorce, at his discretion, may order to the wife an allowance out of the estate of the husband, taking into consideration the value thereof and the condition of his family.

§30-2-52. If the divorce is in favor of the wife for the misconduct of the husband, the judge trying the case shall have the right to make an allowance to the wife out of the husband's estate, or not make her an allowance as the circumstances of the case may justify, and if an allowance is made, it must be as liberal as the estate of the husband will permit, regard being had to the condition of his family and to all the circumstances of the case.

§30-2-53. If the divorce is in favor of the husband for the misconduct of the wife and if the judge in his discretion deems the wife entitled to an allowance, the allowance must be regulated by the ability of the husband and the nature of the misconduct of the wife.

The Alabama Supreme Court has held that "there is no authority in this state for awarding alimony against the wife in favor of the husband.... The statutory scheme is to provide alimony only in favor of the wife." *Davis v. Davis*, 279 Ala. 643, 644, 189 So.2d 158, 160 (1966).

scrutiny under the Equal Protection Clause," *Reed v. Reed*, 404 U.S. 71, 75, 92 S.Ct. 251, 253, 30 L.Ed.2d 225 (1971). The fact that the classification expressly discriminates against men rather than women does not protect it from scrutiny. *Craig v. Boren*, 429 U.S. 190, 97 S.Ct. 451, 50 L.Ed.2d 397 (1976). "To withstand scrutiny" under the Equal Protection Clause, "'classifications by gender must serve important governmental objectives and must be substantially related to achievement of those objectives.'" *Califano v. Webster*, 430 U.S. 313, 316–317, 97 S.Ct. 1192, 1194, 51 L.Ed.2d 360 (1977). We shall, therefore, examine the three governmental objectives that might arguably be served by Alabama's statutory scheme.

Appellant views the Alabama alimony statutes as effectively announcing the State's preference for an allocation of family responsibilities under which the wife plays a dependent role, and as seeking for their objective the reinforcement of that model among the State's citizens. *Cf. Stern v. Stern*, 165 Conn. 190, 332 A.2d 78 (1973). We agree, as he urges, that prior cases settle that this purpose cannot sustain the statutes.[9] *Stanton v. Stanton*, 421 U.S. 7, 10, 95 S.Ct. 1373, 1376, 43 L.Ed.2d 688 (1975), held that the "old notio[n]" that "generally it is the man's primary responsibility to provide a home and its essentials," can no longer justify a statute that discriminates on the basis of gender. "No longer is the female destined solely for the home and the rearing of the family, and only the male for the marketplace and the world of ideas," *id.*, at 14–15, 95 S.Ct., at 1378. See also *Craig v. Boren*, *supra*, 429 U.S., at 198, 97 S.Ct., at 457. If the statute is to survive constitutional attack, therefore, it must be validated on some other basis.

The opinion of the Alabama Court of Civil Appeals suggests other purposes that the statute may serve. Its opinion states that the Alabama statutes were "designed" for "the wife of a broken marriage who needs financial assistance," 351 So.2d, at 905. This may be read as asserting either of two legislative objectives. One is a legislative purpose to provide help for needy spouses, using sex as a proxy for need. The other is a goal of compensating women for past discrimination during marriage, which assertedly has left them unprepared to fend for themselves in the working world following divorce. We concede, of course, that assisting needy spouses is a legitimate and important governmental objective. We have also recognized "[r]eduction of the disparity in economic condition between men and women caused by the long history of discrimination against women...as...an important governmental objective," *Califano v. Webster*, 430 U.S., at 317, 97 S.Ct., at 1194. It only remains, therefore, to determine whether the classification at issue here is "substantially related to achievement of those objectives." *Ibid.*[10]

Ordinarily, we would begin the analysis of the "needy spouse" objective by considering whether sex is a sufficiently "accurate proxy," *Craig v. Boren*, 429 U.S.,

9. Appellee attempts to buttress the importance of this objective by arguing that while "[t]he common law stripped the married woman of many of her rights and most of her property,...it attempted to partially compensate by giving her the assurance that she would be supported by her husband." Brief for Appellee 11-12. This argument, that the "support obligation was imposed by the common law to compensate the wife for the discrimination she suffered at the hands of the common law," *id.*, at 11, reveals its own weakness. At most it establishes that the alimony statutes were part and parcel of a larger statutory scheme which invidiously discriminated against women, removing them from the world of work and property and "compensating" them by making their designated place "secure." This would be reason to invalidate the entire discriminatory scheme — not a reason to uphold its separate invidious parts. But appellee's argument is even weaker when applied to the facts of this case, as Alabama has long ago removed, by statute, the elements of the common law appellee points to as justifying further discrimination. See Ala.Const., Art. X, §209 (married women's property rights).

10. Of course, if upon examination it becomes clear that there is no substantial relationship between the statutes and their purported objectives, this may well indicate that these objectives were not the statutes' goals in the first place. See Ely, *The Centrality and Limits of Motivation Analysis*, 15 SAN DIEGO L.REV. 1155 (1978).

at 204, 97 S.Ct., at 460, for dependency to establish that the gender classification rests "upon some ground of difference having a fair and substantial relation to the object of the legislation," *Reed v. Reed, supra,* 404 U.S., at 76, 92 S.Ct., at 254. Similarly, we would initially approach the "compensation" rationale by asking whether women had in fact been significantly discriminated against in the sphere to which the statute applied a sex-based classification, leaving the sexes "not similarly situated with respect to opportunities" in that sphere, *Schlesinger v. Ballard,* 419 U.S. 498, 508, 95 S.Ct. 572, 577, 42 L.Ed.2d 610 (1975). Compare *Califano v. Webster, supra,* 430 U.S., at 318, 97 S.Ct., at 1195, and *Kahn v. Shevin,* 416 U.S. 351, 353, 94 S.Ct. 1734, 1736, 40 L.Ed.2d 189 (1974), with *Weinberger v. Wiesenfeld,* 420 U.S. 636, 648, 95 S.Ct. 1225, 1233, 43 L.Ed.2d 514 (1975).[11]

But in this case, even if sex were a reliable proxy for need, and even if the institution of marriage did discriminate against women, these factors still would "not adequately justify the salient features of" Alabama's statutory scheme, *Craig v. Boren, supra,* 429 U.S., at 202–203, 97 S.Ct., at 459–460. Under the statute, individualized hearings at which the parties' relative financial circumstances are considered already occur. See *Russell v. Russell,* 247 Ala. 284, 286, 24 So.2d 124, 126 (1945); *Ortman v. Ortman,* 203 Ala. 167, 82 So. 417 (1919). There is no reason, therefore, to use sex as a proxy for need. Needy males could be helped along with needy females with little if any additional burden on the State. In such circumstances, not even an administrative-convenience rationale exists to justify operating by generalization or proxy.[12] Similarly, since individualized hearings can determine which women were in fact discriminated against *vis-a-vis* their husbands, as well as which family units defied the stereotype and left the husband dependent on the wife, Alabama's alleged compensatory purpose may be effectuated without placing burdens solely on husbands. Progress toward fulfilling such a purpose would not be hampered, and it would cost the State nothing more, if it were to treat men and women equally by making alimony burdens independent of sex. "Thus, the gender-based distinction is gratuitous; without it, the statutory scheme would only provide benefits to those men who are in fact similarly situated to the women the statute aids," *Weinberger v. Wiesenfeld, supra,* 420 U.S., at 653, 95 S.Ct., at 1236, and the effort to help those women would not in any way be compromised.

Moreover, use of a gender classification actually produces perverse results in this case. As compared to a gender-neutral law placing alimony obligations on the spouse able to pay, the present Alabama statutes give an advantage only to the financially secure wife whose husband is in need. Although such a wife might have to pay alimony under a gender-neutral statute, the present statutes exempt her from that obligation. Thus, "[t]he [wives] who benefit from the disparate treatment are those who were...nondependent on their husbands," *Califano v.*

11. We would also consider whether the purportedly compensatory "classifications in fact penalized women," and whether "the statutory structure and its legislative history revealed that the classification was not enacted as compensation for past discrimination." *Califano v. Webster,* 430 U.S., at 317, 97 S.Ct., at 1194.

12. It might be argued that Alabama's rule at least relieves the State of the administrative burden of actions by husbands against their wives for alimony. However, when the wife is also seeking alimony, no savings will occur, as a hearing will be required in any event. But even when the wife is willing to forgo alimony, it appears that under Alabama law savings will still not accrue, as Alabama courts review the financial circumstances of the parties to a divorce despite the parties' own views — even when settlement is reached. See *Russell v. Russell,* 247 Ala. 284, 286, 24 So.2d 124, 126 (1945). Even were this not true, and some administrative time and effort were conserved, "[t]o give a mandatory preference to members of either sex...merely to accomplish the elimination of hearings on the merits, is to make the very kind of arbitrary legislative choice forbidden by the Equal Protection Clause," *Reed v. Reed,* 404 U.S. 71, 76, 92 S.Ct. 251, 254, 30 L.Ed.2d 225 (1971).

Goldfarb, 430 U.S. 199, 221, 97 S.Ct. 1021, 1034, 51 L.Ed.2d 270 (1977)(STEVENS, J., concurring in judgment). They are precisely those who are not "needy spouses" and who are "least likely to have been victims of...discrimination," *ibid.*, by the institution of marriage. A gender-based classification which, as compared to a gender-neutral one, generates additional benefits only for those it has no reason to prefer cannot survive equal protection scrutiny.

Legislative classifications which distribute benefits and burdens on the basis of gender carry the inherent risk of reinforcing the stereotypes about the "proper place" of women and their need for special protection. *Cf. United Jewish Organizations v. Carey*, 430 U.S. 144, 173–174, 97 S.Ct. 996, 1013–1014, 51 L.Ed.2d 229 (1977)(concurring opinion). Thus, even statutes purportedly designed to compensate for and ameliorate the effects of past discrimination must be carefully tailored. Where, as here, the State's compensatory and ameliorative purposes are as well served by a gender-neutral classification as one that gender classifies and therefore carries with it the baggage of sexual stereotypes, the State cannot be permitted to classify on the basis of sex. And this is doubly so where the choice made by the State appears to redound — if only indirectly — to the benefit of those without need for special solicitude.

III

Having found Alabama's alimony statutes unconstitutional, we reverse the judgment below and remand the cause for further proceedings not inconsistent with this opinion. That disposition, of course, leaves the state courts free to decide any questions of substantive state law not yet passed upon in this litigation. *Indiana ex rel. Anderson v. Brand*, 303 U.S. 95, 109, 58 S.Ct. 443, 450, 82 L.Ed. 685 (1938); C. Wright, Federal Courts, at 544. See *South Dakota v. Opperman*, 428 U.S. 364, 396, 96 S.Ct. 3092, 3110, 49 L.Ed.2d 1000 (1976)(MARSHALL, J., dissenting); *United Air Lines, Inc. v. Mahin*, 410 U.S., at 632, 93 S.Ct., at 1192; *California v. Green*, 399 U.S. 149, 169–170, 90 S.Ct. 1930, 1940–1941, 26 L.Ed.2d 489 (1970); *Schuylkill Trust Co. v. Pennsylvania*, 302 U.S. 506, 512, 58 S.Ct. 295, 297, 82 L.Ed. 392 (1938); *Georgia R. & Elec. Co. v. Decatur*, 297 U.S. 620, 623–624, 56 S.Ct. 606, 607, 80 L.Ed. 925 (1936). Therefore, it is open to the Alabama courts on remand to consider whether Mr. Orr's stipulated agreement to pay alimony, or other grounds of gender-neutral state law, bind him to continue his alimony payments.

Reversed and remanded.

COMMENTS

No-fault divorce, which is discussed further in Chapter 4, is the culmination of a long struggle over the grounds for divorce. This struggle for easier divorce was closely associated with the struggle for the rights of women, in part because strict divorce laws historically operated more harshly upon women than men. For example, a single act of adultery by the wife would provide grounds for divorce while in many states a husband's adultery would have to be repeated or flagrant to provide grounds. Similarly, if the couple separated over a dispute regarding where to live, the wife and not the husband would be said to have deserted. Moreover, men have historically had more resources than women and thus been more able than women to avoid the devastating effects of an unhappy marriage. Many commentators, however, claim that no-fault divorce has backfired for women, especially in the area of alimony.

Before the wide-spread adoption of no-fault divorce, there was a complex relationship between marital fault and alimony. Alimony was sometimes seen as akin to damages for the husband's breach of the marriage contract, or as a penalty levied against the husband because of his marital fault. Many states would deny any alimony to a wife if a divorce were granted to the husband on the basis of the wife's fault, regardless of her need and regardless of the financial equities. Although fault-based divorces were sometimes granted over the strenuous objection of one of the spouses, the more common practice was for the husband and wife to agree to an uncontested divorce, sometimes on fabricated grounds. Although collusion between the parties would technically empower the court to deny the divorce, in practice uncontested divorces were routinely granted. Before no-fault divorce, the spouse who wanted out of a marriage might need to "buy" the consent and cooperation of the other spouse through a generous financial settlement. A wife who wanted a divorce in order to marry another man would easily consent to no alimony, since alimony would traditionally terminate upon her remarriage in any event. A husband who was anxious to change wives might be forced to agree to pay his ex-wife quite generous alimony before she would agree to file for divorce. No-fault divorce has had the effect of taking this power away from women.

With the adoption of no-fault divorce, courts and commentators have sought new conceptual bases for alimony or spousal support. Notions of gender equality and partnership or sharing principles in marriage do not necessarily mean that upon divorce the couple should divide the property and then be economically independent from one another. As discussed in Chapter 1, the parties may leave a marriage with very different abilities to support themselves and fulfill their obligations to their children. Periodic payments after divorce may be justified, indeed may be necessary to achieve a fair economic situation in individual cases. Although such payments are more likely to be paid from the ex-husband to the ex-wife, there will no doubt also be exceptions in which justice would require payments from the ex-wife to the ex-husband.

Orr v. Orr is generally considered to be a good opinion supporting equality. Because alimony is an individualized, case-by-case decision, there is no justification for refusing categorically to consider alimony, or spousal support, for men. Statistically, fewer men will qualify for alimony than women, but in those few cases in which the man should receive continued support, it seems very difficult to argue against it, unless one simply rejects gender equality altogether.

Perhaps the situation is more complicated than this. The formal equality mandated by *Orr* means that husbands can ask for alimony or threaten to do so as a negotiation tool, perhaps discouraging women from seeking alimony in cases in which justice would call for payments from the husband to the wife.

Wife-Battering, Self-Defense, Special Injunctions

PEOPLE v. CAMERON

California Court of Appeal, Fifth District
53 Cal.App.3d 786, 126 Cal.Rptr. 44 (1975)

THOMPSON, Associate Justice (Assigned).

Defendant herein was convicted by a jury of violation of section 273d of the Penal Code (infliction by a husband of corporal injury upon his wife). Defendant admitted a prior conviction of receiving stolen property (Pen.Code §496). Defendant was sentenced to state prison. He appeals.

The domestic situation from which this criminal charge arose is unremarkable. Defendant Jack Cameron and his wife Joyce, a bride of one month, were participating is a social affair with another couple who were having dinner with them at the Cameron apartment. Shortly after midnight Jack and Joyce offered to drive their friends, the Walkers, back to their motel. On the way defendant stopped his car and was unable to start it. Joyce and her friends decided to take a taxi home while Jack remained with his vehicle to repair it.

Joyce went to bed and fell asleep. At about 2:00 a.m. she was awakened by her husband who had seized her by a breast and was twisting it. Jack told Joyce that he intended to hurt her and thereupon slapped and kicked her and threw her off the bed. He told Joyce that he had once knocked a woman's teeth out because she talked too much and since she (Joyce) did not listen he was going to have to "fix" her ears so she would never hear again. Defendant continued to strike and shake Joyce and kicked her after he had jerked her off the bed onto the floor. In the course of the melee Joyce's nose was broken, her left ear was cut requiring considerable surgical intervention. Her face and body bore marks of trauma.

The affray concluded by defendant's forcibly dragging his wife into the bathroom and placing her under the shower after having torn off her nightgown.

Joyce's eleven year old daughter, who had been awakened by the commotion, ran next door to get help for her mother. The authorities were called and defendant was arrested.

Defendant at all times contended that he had slapped his wife only once and the remainder of the injuries had been caused by her falling against a sewing machine.

There was testimony that both husband and wife had been drinking but the arresting officers concluded that neither was intoxicated.

...

Defendant's chief reliance for a reversal is his assertion that Penal Code section 273d is unconstitutional.[1] He makes a threefold argument in support of his contention: (1) that said section 273d denies a defendant equal protection of the law in that it applies only to married men who assault their wives and not to unmarried men who assault their paramours nor to wives who assault their husbands;

---

1. Penal Code section 273d reads as follows:

> Any husband who willfully inflicts upon his wife corporal injury resulting in a traumatic condition, and any person who willfully inflicts upon any child any cruel or inhuman corporal punishment or injury resulting in a traumatic condition, is guilty of a felony, and upon conviction thereof shall be punished by imprisonment in the state prison for not more than 10 years or in the county jail for not more than one year.

(2) that the definition of the crime in Penal Code section 273d is impermissibly vague; and (3) that the punishment provided for the crime is cruel and unusual.

...

...[I]n the instant case we are not confronted with discrimination relative to employment or morality. We are rather concerned with one of the most troublesome and yet most fundamental relationships in our social structure, marriage, and while, of course, one marriage partner is of necessity a female, the more fundamental consideration is that she is a wife and oftentimes a mother. The voluminous laws relating to such matters arising out of the marital relationship such as property rights, child custody, etc., demonstrate the vital interest of the state in marriage relationships. The observable effect of broken homes upon juvenile delinquency emphasizes society's concern with the preservation of marriage.

...

We think the conclusion inescapable that wives as an object of abuse by their spouses are a class distinctly set apart by the conditions under which their abuse customarily occurs. The first and most obvious distinction is that women are physically less able to defend themselves against their husbands than vice versa. National statistics show that the average adult male is 28 pounds heavier and five inches taller than the average adult female. No competent prize fight manager would send a much smaller combatant into the ring against a much larger opponent, especially to face such opponent without the benefit of a referee or the restraining influence of an audience.

It is indisputable that the overwhelming number of encounters between husbands and wives take place in the home, usually late at night and after the consumption of alcohol by one or both of the parties. Except in cases of rape or other serious felonies the male does not ordinarily attack a female not his wife. Society places strong restraints upon unchivalrous conduct by a male toward the female in a social setting. But such chivalry appears to lose its efficacy at the threshold, especially if the husband comes home filled with the tension of his work and often a few beers and confronts a vituperative wife. Given this milieu physical confrontation is not unpredictable and quite predictable is the outcome, that the husband's fists are more damaging than the wife's tongue, however sharp.

The argument is made that no special legislation is needed to protect wives inasmuch as an assaultive husband can be charged under Penal Code section 245(a) with assault by force and means likely to produce great bodily injury if the severity of the injury warrants such a charge, or otherwise with assault and battery.

Such an argument loses much of its persuasive effect when we consider the realities of the situation. When a husband assaults his wife it is usually late at night and frequently out of the presence of witnesses except, as in this case, in front of a helpless and disturbed child. The officer responding to the call for help, as in this case, must determine whether a felony or a misdemeanor has been committed. If he determines that a misdemeanor has been committed he is powerless to effect an arrest, inasmuch as it was not committed in his presence, unless the wife makes a citizens arrest, a most unlikely course of action. He must therefore leave the wife in the home wherein the beating took place. The wife's options are not very satisfactory. She is almost forced to remain at home since her opportunities to flee are usually severely limited. The husband may have the car; there may be children in the home to be considered; and the unaccompanied female at night is greeted with suspicion if not refusal of admission by hotel and motel clerks who fear not only her possible profession but if convinced of her true plight are fearful of her being followed by a vengeful husband who would create a scene.

Another factor we believe worthy of consideration is that, unlike most assaults charged under Penal Code section 245(a), a wife beating is usually accomplished with fists and kicking as in this case. The severity of the injuries are therefore not always capable of instant diagnosis. Internal injuries and even broken limbs may not immediately evidence themselves. Except for the provisions of Penal Code section 273d an officer responding to a wife beating case would ordinarily, in the exercise of caution and to avoid a charge of false arrest, only arrest the husband under the provisions of Penal Code section 245(a) in extreme cases. Even the infliction upon a wife of considerable traumatic injury would tend to be treated by the arresting officer as a misdemeanor which would produce the consequences of the wife's being left in the home to face possible further aggregation. But an officer given the alternative of arresting for a felony under the provisions of section 273d may do so when he observes traumatic injury. The skepticism in general with which domestic embroglios are viewed tends to insure that an arresting officer will not abuse his power.

What we have heretofore said as to the seriousness of the problem is reinforced by the overriding interest of the state in preserving the institution of marriage and particularly so when children are involved. The state has a greater interest in deterring crimes which disrupt the marriage relationship than in other classes of crime. While we realize that the deterrent effect of any particularly prescribed punishment is difficult to evaluate it is a rational assumption that at least some men may be restrained from inflicting injury upon their wives if such conduct may lead to a felony conviction. It may also be inferrable that some wives (a declining number) may submit to some corporal abuse by their husbands without seeking police intervention, but are unwilling to accept the infliction of trauma. A reminder to their husbands that the law does not only not tolerate the infliction of wife beatings but may in fact impose prison terms therefore may not only deter such conduct but may thereby preserve the marriage by curbing the male aggressiveness. While this cause and effect relationship may be imprecise, the law does not, and cannot, require an irrefutable cause and effect relationship between crime and punishment.

Admittedly the number of laws in civil and criminal fields in this state, in other states, and in federal jurisdictions in which sex is a significant factor is diminishing. But in each instance wherein a law which makes a distinction between males and females has been held constitutional some rational basis has been found to exist for the discrimination practiced....

...

The argument is made that Penal Code section 273d is impermissibly uninclusive because it does not provide greater punishment for a wife who beats her husband than is true of the reverse.

...

...*Russell v. Carleson* (1973), 36 Cal.App.3d 334, 111 Cal.Rptr. 497 ([hearing denied] by the Supreme Court April 17, 1974[),]...a case factually similar to our own...[involved] a constitutional attack...upon a provision...that an unrelated adult male living with a family receiving or applying for aid to dependent children "shall be required to make a financial contribution to the family...."

...

The court, while recognizing that the law was to a degree discriminatory, said 36 Cal.App.3d at p. 344, 111 Cal.Rptr. at 503: "The Legislature could justifiably have determined that there were more spouseless AFDC mothers than AFDC fathers, and that a greater threat of diversion of the grant was therefor posed by cohabiting UAMs (unrelated adult males) than by unrelated adult females or by adult relatives; hence plaintiffs' claimed denial of equal protection falls. The Legislature could properly have assigned a greater priority or urgency to UAM legislation than to comparable legislation in other areas...."

We think it abundantly apparent that percentagewise the number of wives who assault their husbands under the definition of such assault in section 273d of the Penal Code is far smaller than the number of AFDC families who have either adult unrelated females or related males living with them. The Attorney General cites us to statistics from the Staff Report submitted to the National Commission on the Causes and Prevention of Violence (Vol. II, p. 301) which indicate that 273d type assaults committed by husbands upon wives as opposed to assaults committed by wives upon husbands approach the ratio of 15 to one (93.3 percent to 6.7 percent).

...

In conclusion upon this point we do not wish to be understood as saying that section 273d could not with justification be made applicable to the reverse situation, namely assaults by wives upon husbands. In fact, with the modern trend of greater independence and assertiveness on the part of the female the legislature perhaps would be well advised to give recognition to this fact. By making section 273d applicable to both spouses it might be expected that the state would be affording some additional protection to the marital state. We merely conclude that its failure to do so does not for the reasons we have advanced, vitiate the constitutionality of section 273d as it presently stands.

Defendant's argument that section 273d of the Penal Code is unconstitutionally vague may be quickly disposed of. The language complained of, namely, "corporal injury resulting in a traumatic condition" appears to pose no difficulty of interpretation. The language, particularly in the context of this case is crystal clear. Defendant was advised that he had wilfully inflicted injury to the body of plaintiff producing a traumatic condition, *i.e.*, bruises, abrasions, a cut ear and a broken nose. The court was well able to define the offense for the jury. For example, he instructed that a "traumatic condition is an abnormal condition of the living body produced by violence."

The test set forth in *People v. Anderson* (1972), 29 Cal.App.3d 551, 561, 105 Cal.Rptr. 664, 670, is squarely met. We quote: "If an accused can reasonably understand by the terms of the statute that his conduct is prohibited, the statute is not vague. [Citation.]"

Defendant's remaining contention that the punishment imposed by section 273d of the Penal Code constitutes cruel and unusual punishment has been fully answered by the recent case of *People v. Wingo* (1975), 14 Cal.3d 169, 534 P.2d 1001. *Wingo* held in effect that the Adult Authority must within a reasonable time fix the maximum in any given case, and if the Adult Authority either fails within a reasonable time to fix the maximum sentence or fixes an unreasonable term, defendant may seek relief by way of *habeas corpus*. Penal Code section 273d on its face permits a wide range of sentences, from one to ten years, to cover a wide range of behavior, and until the court is otherwise advised it is presumed that the Adult Authority will fix a term reasonably commensurate under the circumstances.

The judgment is affirmed.

[Concurring and dissenting opinions omitted.]

PEOPLE v. LIBERTA

Court of Appeals of New York

64 N.Y. 2d 152, 474 N.E.2d 567, 485 N.Y.S. 2d 207 (1984)

WACHTLER, Judge.

The defendant, while living apart from his wife pursuant to a Family Court order, forcibly raped and sodomized her in the presence of their 2½ year old son. Under the New York Penal Law a married man ordinarily cannot be prosecuted for raping or sodomizing his wife. The defendant, however, though married at the time of the incident, is treated as an unmarried man under the Penal Law because of the Family Court order. On this appeal, he contends that because of the exemption for married men, the statutes for rape in the first degree (Penal Law, §130.35) and sodomy in the first degree (Penal Law, §130.50), violate the equal protection clause of the Federal Constitution (U.S. Const., 14th Amdt.). The defendant also contends that the rape statute violates equal protection because only men, and not women, can be prosecuted under it.

I

Defendant Mario Liberta and Denise Liberta were married in 1978. Shortly after the birth of their son, in October of that year, Mario began to beat Denise. In early 1980 Denise brought a proceeding in the Family Court in Erie County seeking protection from the defendant. On April 30, 1980 a temporary order of protection was issued to her by the Family Court. Under this order, the defendant was to move out and remain away from the family home, and stay away from Denise. The order provided that the defendant could visit with his son once each weekend.

On the weekend of March 21, 1981, Mario, who was then living in a motel, did not visit his son. On Tuesday, March 24, 1981 he called Denise to ask if he could visit his son on that day. Denise would not allow the defendant to come to her house, but she did agree to allow him to pick up their son and her and take them both back to his motel after being assured that a friend of his would be with them at all times. The defendant and his friend picked up Denise and their son and the four of them drove to defendant's motel.

When they arrived at the motel the friend left. As soon as only Mario, Denise, and their son were alone in the motel room, Mario attacked Denise, threatened to kill her, and forced her to perform fellatio on him and to engage in sexual intercourse with him. The son was in the room during the entire episode, and the defendant forced Denise to tell their son to watch what the defendant was doing to her.

The defendant allowed Denise and their son to leave shortly after the incident. Denise, after going to her parents' home, went to a hospital to be treated for scratches on her neck and bruises on her head and back, all inflicted by her husband. She also went to the police station, and on the next day she swore out a felony complaint against the defendant. On July 15, 1981 the defendant was indicted for rape in the first degree and sodomy in the first degree.

II

Section 130.35 of the Penal Law provides in relevant part that "A male is guilty of rape in the first degree when he engages in sexual intercourse with a female...by forcible compulsion." "Female," for purposes of the rape statute, is defined as "any female person who is not married to the actor" (Penal Law, §130.00, subd. 4).

Section 130.50 of the Penal Law provides in relevant part that "a person is guilty of sodomy in the first degree when he engages in deviate sexual intercourse with another person...by forcible compulsion.. "Deviate sexual intercourse" is defined as "sexual conduct between persons not married to each other consisting of contact between the penis and the anus, the mouth and penis, or the mouth and the vulva" (Penal Law, §130.00, subd. 2). Thus, due to the "not married" language in the definitions of "female" and "deviate sexual intercourse", there is a "marital exemption" for both forcible rape and forcible sodomy. The marital exemption itself, however, has certain exceptions. For purposes of the rape and sodomy statutes, a husband and wife are considered to be "not married" if at the time of the sexual assault they "are living apart...pursuant to a valid and effective: (i) order issued by a court of competent jurisdiction which by its terms or in its effect requires such living apart, or (ii) decree or judgment of separation, or (iii) written agreement of separation" (Penal Law, §130.00, subd. 4).

Defendant moved to dismiss the indictment, asserting that because he and Denise were still married at the time of the incident[1] he came within the "marital exemption" to both rape and sodomy. The People opposed the motion, contending that the temporary order of protection required Mario and Denise to live apart, and they in fact were living apart, and thus were "not married" for purposes of the statutes. The trial court granted the defendant's motion and dismissed the indictment, concluding that the temporary order of protection did not require Mario and Denise to live apart from each other, but instead required only that he remain away from her, and that therefore the "marital exemption" applied.

...The Appellate Division held that a Family Court order of protection is within the scope of "[an] order...which by its terms or in its effect requires such living apart" even though it is directed only at a husband, and thus found that Mario and Denise were "not married" for purposes of the statute at the time of the incident.

The defendant was then convicted of rape in the first degree and sodomy in the first degree and the conviction was affirmed by the Appellate Division, 100 A.D.2d 741, 473 N.Y.S.2d 636. Defendant asserts on this appeal that the temporary order of protection is not the type of order which enables a court to treat him and Denise as "not married" and that thus he is within the marital exemption. Defendant next asserts, assuming that because of the Family Court order he is treated just as any unmarried male would be, that he cannot be convicted of either rape in the first degree or sodomy in the first degree because both statutes are unconstitutional. Specifically, he contends that both statutes violate equal protection because they burden some, but not all males (all but those within the "marital exemption"), and that the rape statute also violates equal protection for burdening only men, and not women. The lower courts rejected the defendant's constitutional arguments, finding that neither statute violated the equal protection clause in the Fourteenth Amendment. Although we affirm the conviction of the defendant, we do not agree with the constitutional analysis of the lower courts and instead conclude that the marital and gender exemptions must be read out of the statutes prohibiting forcible rape and sodomy.

...

...[T]he defendant was properly found to have been statutorily "not married" to Denise at the time of the rape.

1. The defendant and Denise were divorced several months after the assault in the motel room.

IV

The defendant's constitutional challenges to the rape and sodomy statutes are premised on his being considered "not married" to Denise and are the same challenges as could be made by any unmarried male convicted under these statutes. The defendant's claim is that both statutes violate equal protection because they are underinclusive classifications which burden him, but not others similarly situated (see Tribe, American Constitutional Law, p. 997). A litigant has standing to raise this claim even though he does not contend that under no circumstances could the burden of the statute be imposed upon him.... This rule of standing applies as well to a defendant in a criminal prosecution who, while conceding that it is within the power of a State to make criminal the behavior covered by a statute, asserts that the statute he is prosecuted under violates equal protection because it burdens him but not others....

A. THE MARITAL EXEMPTION

...[U]nder the Penal Law a married man ordinarily cannot be convicted of forcibly raping or sodomizing his wife. This is the so-called marital exemption for rape.... The assumption, even before the marital exemption was codified, that a man could not be guilty of raping his wife, is traceable to a statement made by the 17th century English jurist Lord Hale, who wrote: "[T]he husband cannot be guilty of a rape committed by himself upon his lawful wife, for by their mutual matrimonial consent and contract the wife hath given up herself in this kind unto her husband, which she cannot retract" (1 Hale, History of Pleas of the Crown, p. 629). Although Hale cited no authority for his statement it was relied on by State Legislatures which enacted rape statutes with a marital exemption and by courts which established a common-law exemption for husbands.

The first American case to recognize the marital exemption was decided in 1857 by the Supreme Judicial Court of Massachusetts, which stated in dictum that it would always be a defense to rape to show marriage to the victim (*Commonwealth v. Fogerty*, 74 Mass. 489). Decisions to the same effect by other courts followed, usually with no rationale or authority cited other than Hale's implied consent view. In New York, a 1922 decision noted the marital exemption in the Penal Law and stated that it existed "on account of the matrimonial consent which [the wife] has given, and which she cannot retract" (*People v. Meli*, 193 N.Y.S. 365, 366 [Sup.Ct.]).

...

We find that there is no rational basis for distinguishing between marital rape and nonmarital rape. The various rationales which have been asserted in defense of the exemption are either based upon archaic notions about the consent and property rights incident to marriage or are simply unable to withstand even the slightest scrutiny. We therefore declare the marital exemption for rape in the New York statute to be unconstitutional.

Lord Hale's notion of an irrevocable implied consent by a married woman to sexual intercourse has been cited most frequently in support of the marital exemption ("Equal Protection Considerations", *supra*, n. 6, 16 N.Eng.L.Rev., at p. 21). Any argument based on a supposed consent, however, is untenable. Rape is not simply a sexual act to which one party does not consent. Rather, it is a degrading, violent act which violates the bodily integrity of the victim and frequently causes severe, long-lasting physical and psychic harm.... To ever imply consent to such an act is irrational and absurd. Other than in the context of rape statutes, marriage has never been viewed as giving a husband the right to coerced intercourse on demand.... Certainly, then, a marriage license should not be viewed as a license for a husband to forcibly rape his wife with impunity. A married woman has the same right to control her own body as does an unmarried woman.... If a husband feels "aggrieved" by his wife's refusal to engage in sexual intercourse, he should seek relief in the courts governing domestic relations, not in "violent or forceful self-help" (*State v. Smith*, 85 N.J. 193, 206, 426 A.2d 38).

The other traditional justifications for the marital exemption were the common-law doctrines that a woman was the property of her husband and that the legal existence of the woman was "incorporated and consolidated into that of the husband" (1 Blackstone's Commentaries [1966 ed.], p. 430.... Both these doctrines, of course, have long been rejected in this State. Indeed, "[n]owhere in the common-law world — [or] in any modern society — is a woman regarded as chattel or demeaned by denial of a separate legal identity and the dignity associated with recognition as a whole human being" (*Trammel v. United States*, 445 U.S. 40, 52, 100 S.Ct. 906, 913, 63 L.Ed.2d 186).

Because the traditional justifications for the marital exemption no longer have any validity, other arguments have been advanced in its defense. The first of these recent rationales, which is stressed by the People in this case, is that the marital exemption protects against governmental intrusion into marital privacy and promotes reconciliation of the spouses, and thus that elimination of the exemption would be disruptive to marriages. While protecting marital privacy and encouraging reconciliation are legitimate State interests, there is no rational relation between allowing a husband to forcibly rape his wife and these interests. The marital exemption simply does not further marital privacy because this right of privacy protects consensual acts, not violent sexual assaults.... Just as a husband cannot invoke a right of marital privacy to escape liability for beating his wife, he cannot justifiably rape his wife under the guise of a right to privacy.

Similarly, it is not tenable to argue that elimination of the marital exemption would disrupt marriages because it would discourage reconciliation. Clearly, it is the violent act of rape and not the subsequent attempt of the wife to seek protection through the criminal justice system which "disrupts" a marriage.... Moreover, if the marriage has already reached the point where intercourse is accomplished by violent assault it is doubtful that there is anything left to reconcile.... This, of course, is particularly true if the wife is willing to bring criminal charges against her husband which could result in a lengthy jail sentence.

Another rationale sometimes advanced in support of the marital exemption is that marital rape would be a difficult crime to prove. A related argument is that allowing such prosecutions could lead to fabricated complaints by "vindictive" wives. The difficulty of proof argument is based on the problem of showing lack of consent. Proving lack of consent, however, is often the most difficult part of any rape prosecution, particularly where the rapist and the victim had a prior relationship.... Similarly, the possibility that married women will fabricate complaints would seem to be no greater than the possibility of unmarried women doing so.... The criminal justice system, with all of its built-in safeguards, is presumed to be capable of handling any false complaints. Indeed, if the possibility of fabricated complaints were a basis for not criminalizing behavior which would otherwise be sanctioned, virtually all crimes other than homicides would go unpunished.

The final argument in defense of the marital exemption is that marital rape is not as serious an offense as other rape and is thus adequately dealt with by the possibility of prosecution under criminal statutes, such as assault statutes, which provide for less severe punishment. The fact that rape statutes exist, however, is a recognition that the harm caused by a forcible rape is different, and more severe, than the harm caused by an ordinary assault.... Under the Penal Law, assault is generally a misdemeanor unless either the victim suffers "serious physical injury" or a deadly weapon or dangerous instrument is used (Penal Law, §§120.00, 120.05, 120.10). Thus, if the defendant had been living with Denise at the time he forcibly raped and sodomized her he probably could not have been charged with a felony, let alone a felony with punishment equal to that for rape in the first degree.

Moreover, there is no evidence to support the argument that marital rape has less severe consequences than other rape. On the contrary, numerous studies have shown that marital rape is frequently quite violent and generally has *more* severe, traumatic effects on the victim than other rape....

...

B. THE EXEMPTION FOR FEMALES

Under the Penal Law only males can be convicted of rape in the first degree. Insofar as the rape statute applies to acts of "sexual intercourse", which, as defined in the Penal Law (see Penal Law, §130.00) can only occur between a male and a female, it is true that a female cannot physically rape a female and that therefore there is no denial of equal protection when punishing only males for forcibly engaging in sexual intercourse with females. The equal protection issue, however, stems from the fact that the statute applies to males who forcibly rape females but does not apply to females who forcibly rape males.

Rape statutes historically applied only to conduct by males against females, largely because the purpose behind the proscriptions was to protect the chastity of women and thus their property value to their fathers or husbands.... New York's rape statute has always protected only females, and has thus applied only to males (see Penal Law, §130.35; 1909 Penal Law, §2010; 1881 Penal Code, tit. X, ch. II, §278)....

A statute which treats males and females differently violates equal protection unless the classification is substantially related to the achievement of an important governmental objective.... This test applies whether the statute discriminates against males or against females.... The People bear the burden of showing both the existence of an important objective and the substantial relationship between the discrimination in the statute and that objective.... This burden is not met in the present case, and therefore the gender exemption also renders the statute unconstitutional.

The first argument advanced by the People in support of the exemption for females is that because only females can become pregnant the State may constitutionally differentiate between forcible rapes of females and forcible rapes of males. This court and the United States Supreme Court have upheld statutes which subject males to criminal liability for engaging in sexual intercourse with underage females without the converse being true.... The rationale behind these decisions was that the primary purpose of such "statutory rape" laws is to protect against the harm caused by teenage pregnancies, there being no need to provide the same protection to young males....

There is no evidence, however, that preventing pregnancies is a primary purpose of the statute prohibiting forcible rape, nor does such a purpose seem likely.... Rather, the very fact that the statute proscribes "forcible compulsion" shows that its overriding purpose is to protect a woman from an unwanted, forcible, and often violent sexual intrusion into her body.... Thus, due to the different purposes behind forcible rape laws and "statutory" (consensual) rape laws, the cases upholding the gender discrimination in the latter are not decisive with respect to the former, and the People cannot meet their burden here by simply stating that only females can become pregnant.

The People also claim that the discrimination is justified because a female rape victim "faces the probability of medical, sociological, and psychological problems unique to her gender". This same argument, when advanced in support of the discrimination in the statutory rape laws, was rejected by this court..., and it is no more convincing in the present case....

Finally, the People suggest that a gender-neutral law for forcible rape is unnecessary, and that therefore the present law is constitutional, because a woman either cannot actually rape a man or such attacks, if possible, are extremely rare. Although the "physiologically impossible" argument has been accepted by several courts...it is simply wrong. The argument is premised on the notion that a man cannot engage in sexual intercourse unless he is sexually aroused, and if he is aroused then he is consenting to intercourse. "Sexual intercourse" however, "occurs upon any penetration, however slight" (Penal Law, §130.00); this degree of contact can be achieved without a male being aroused and thus without his consent.

As to the "infrequency" argument, while forcible sexual assaults by females upon males are undoubtedly less common than those by males upon females this numerical disparity cannot by itself make the gender discrimination constitutional. Women may well be responsible for a far lower number of all serious crimes than are men, but such a disparity would not make it permissible for the State to punish only men who commit, for example, robbery....

...The fact that the act of a female forcibly raping a male may be a difficult or rare occurrence does not mean that the gender exemption satisfies the constitutional test. A gender-neutral law would indisputably better serve, even if only marginally, the objective of deterring and punishing forcible sexual assaults. The only persons "benefitted" by the gender exemption are females who forcibly rape males. As the Supreme Court has stated, "[a] gender-based classification which, as compared to a gender-neutral one, generates additional benefits only for those it has no reason to prefer cannot survive equal protection scrutiny" (*Orr v. Orr...*).

Accordingly, we find that section 130.35 of the Penal Law violates equal protection because it exempts females from criminal liability for forcible rape.

V

Having found that the statutes for rape in the first degree and sodomy in the first degree are unconstitutionally underinclusive, the remaining issue is the appropriate remedy for these equal protection violations. When a statute is constitutionally defective because of underinclusion, a court may either strike the statute, and thus make it applicable to nobody, or extend the coverage of the statute to those formerly excluded....

...

Though our decision does not "create a crime," it does, of course, enlarge the scope of two criminal statutes. We recognize that a court should be reluctant to expand criminal statutes, due to the danger of usurping the role of the Legislature, but in this case overriding policy concerns dictate our following such a course in light of the catastrophic effect that striking down the statutes and thus creating a hiatus would have.... Courts in other States have in numerous cases applied these same principles in eliminating an unconstitutional exception from a criminal statute and thereby enlarging the scope of the statute. The decision most similar factually to the present one comes from the Alaska Supreme Court in *Plas v. State*, 598 P.2d 966 (Alaska). That court addressed an equal protection challenge by a female prostitute to a statute which criminalized prostitution, and defined it as a female offering her body for sexual intercourse for hire. The court agreed with the defendant that the statute violated equal protection because it covered only females, but chose to remedy this underinclusion by striking the definition, thereby expanding the statute to cover any person who engaged in prostitution, and affirmed her conviction.

The defendant cannot claim that our decision to retain the rape and sodomy statutes, and thereby affirm his conviction, denies him due process of the law. The due process clause of the Fourteenth Amendment requires that an accused have had fair warning at the time of his conduct that such conduct was made criminal by the State (see *Bouie v. City of Columbia*, 378 U.S. 347, 84 S.Ct. 1697, 12 L.Ed.2d 894). Defendant did not come within any of the exemptions which we have stricken, and thus his conduct was covered by the statutes as they existed at the time of his attack on Denise.

Neither can it be said that by the affirmance of his conviction the defendant is deprived of a constitutionally protected right to equal protection. The remedy chosen by our opinion is to extend the coverage of the provisions for forcible rape and sodomy to all those to whom these provisions can constitutionally be applied. While this remedy does treat the defendant differently than, for example, a married man who, while living with his wife, raped her prior to this decision, the distinction is rational inasmuch as it is justified by the limitations imposed on our remedy by the notice requirements of the due process clause (U.S. Const., 14th Amdt.), and the prohibition against *ex post facto* laws (U.S. Const., art. I, §10). Thus, for purposes of choosing the proper remedy, the defendant is simply not similarly situated to those persons who were not within the scope of the statutes as they existed prior to our decision.

To reverse the defendant's conviction would mean that all those persons now awaiting trial for forcible rape or sodomy would be entitled to dismissal of the indictment. Indeed if we were to reverse no person arrested for forcible rape or sodomy prior to the date of this decision could be prosecuted for that offense, and every person already convicted of forcible rape or sodomy who raised the equal protection challenge would be entitled to have the conviction vacated. As the equal protection clause does not require us to reach such a result, we decline to do so.

Accordingly, the order of the Appellate Division should be affirmed.

Order affirmed.

COMMENTS

Sexual and physical assaults by husbands upon wives were legally condoned for many years. As women demanded that rape be recognized as a serious and violent crime, one state after another began to enact limited "marital rape" legislation similar to that challenged in *Liberta.* The New York statute made fairly clear its basis for limiting the marital rape exemption — a couple living apart under certain circumstances ought to be considered "not married." Many of the most horrendous cases of husbands raping their wives occurred when the couple was legally separated but not yet divorced, so legislation dealing with these cases was politically expedient and lessened the pressure for more sweeping change. This statute and others like it were frequently very limited in that they continued to allow a husband to force intercourse upon his wife; they just recognized that there was a gap between women who should be treated as married and the legal definition of "wife." Some state statutes approached this gap from the other direction also and extended the marital exemption to unmarried cohabitants.

Opinions on the wisdom and justice of totally abolishing the marital exemption for rape, as *Liberta* did on constitutional grounds, have varied widely. One California state legislator is infamous for allegedly asking, "If you can't rape your wife, who can you rape?" Some have argued that while naturally a man should not force intercourse upon his wife, the solution is not simply to pass a law against it. The criminal law is not a practical or effective way to deal with this difficult social problem. A different approach rejects this characterization of the issue. The question is rather whether an exception should be made to the normal criminal law. No sensible social policy is served by a special rule allowing husbands to rape their wives. One could ask, "If women aren't safe from being raped by their husbands, from whom can they be safe?" One response to the California state legislator is: "If a woman can't shoot her abusive husband, whom can she shoot?"

Insofar as the domination of wives by husbands has been encouraged by law, equality is served by simple state withdrawal. For many abuses suffered by wives, a solution is for the law simply to afford to married people the same treatment afforded to unmarried people. For a variety of reasons, however, certain abuses can be remedied more effectively by state recognition of the marital relationship. Some states have enacted laws specifically designed to reduce domestic battery. The statute upheld in *Cameron* is such a provision. Notice that the judge suggests that it might be good if the legislature were to equally criminalize assaults by a wife upon a husband but refuses to find any constitutional necessity for doing so. Would the *Liberta* court have decided this issue differently? Is the analysis of either judge mistaken?

Cameron describes well some of the problems faced by women who are abused by their husbands. Every state now provides for some form of restraining order, such as that obtained by Denise Liberta. As *Liberta* illustrates, however, these restraining orders may not protect abused wives, especially when young children are involved and if courts require the wife to facilitate the husband's visitation, as in *Liberta.* Some states have diversion programs under which abusive husbands must participate in counseling to avoid jail; other states have experimented with mandatory jail sentences. A study conducted in Minnesota in 1981 and 1982 suggested that jailing abusive husbands, even just overnight, signaled social disapproval of abuse and significantly reduced recidivism rates. Some people look to the seeming intractability of the problem of domestic violence and see the limits of what the law can achieve. Others look to the failures of the law and question whether society is really committed to stopping wife beating. Should one worry about a judge who characterizes Jack's unprovoked beating of Joyce one month into their marriage, from which the criminal charge in *Cameron* arose, as "unremarkable"?

REFERENCE

The Minneapolis Domestic Violence Experiment, discussed in Amy Eppler, *Battered Women and the Equal Protection Clause: Will the Constitution Help Them When the Police Won't?*, 95 YALE L. J. 788, 791 note 16 (1985) and in *Arrest Deters Domestic Violence*, 20 TRIAL (Number 8), p. 83–84 (August, 1984).

Interference in Marriage

GATES v. FOLEY

Supreme Court of Florida
247 So.2d 40 (Fla. 1971)

ADKINS, Justice.

...

Plaintiff, Hilda I. Gates, sued the Defendant, alleging that the Defendant negligently operated his automobile causing a collision with an automobile operated by the husband of Plaintiff. It is further alleged that as a result of the accident Plaintiff's husband was rendered totally disabled and the Plaintiff claimed damages for "the loss of consortium and other services from her said husband."

In other words, a wife is suing for damages for loss of consortium as a result of injuries to her husband proximately caused by the negligence of the Defendant which rendered the husband totally disabled.

A motion to dismiss the complaint was granted on the ground that it failed to state a cause of action. Plaintiff appealed from the final judgment of dismissal. The District Court of Appeal affirmed the judgment.

At common law the wife could not maintain such an action. In 1950 the United States District Court of Appeal for the District of Columbia decided *Hitaffer v. Argonne Company*, 87 U.S.App.D.C. 57, 183 F.2d 811, 23 A.L.R.2d 1366, *cert. den.* 340 U.S. 852, 71 S.Ct. 80, 95 L.Ed. 624 in which the Court updated the common law of the District of Columbia by acknowledging a cause of action in the wife for loss of consortium.

This Court, in *Ripley v. Ewell*, 61 So.2d 420 (Fla.1952), rejected the reasoning in the *Hitaffer* case and followed the common law doctrine.

...

Since *Hitaffer v. Argonne Company, supra*, a flood of authorities in other jurisdictions have overturned the common law rule and, on various grounds, allowed the wife to recover for loss of consortium.

Moreover, the overwhelming legal literature favors the position that the wife should have such a cause of action where the husband does.[2]

...

It should be specifically noted that the suit is for "loss of consortium" and not loss of support or earnings which the husband might recover in his own right. We are only concerned with loss of consortium, by which is meant, the companionship and fellowship of husband and wife and the right of each to the company, cooperation and aid of the other in every conjugal relation. Consortium means much more than mere sexual relation and consists, also, of that affection, solace, comfort, companionship, conjugal life, fellowship, society and assistance so necessary to a successful marriage. *Lithgow v. Hamilton*, 69 So.2d 776 (Fla.1954).

As discussed in *Ripley v. Ewell, supra*, Fla.Stat. §2.01, F.S.A., adopts the common law of England. The Court recognized the principle that if the inability of the wife to recover in a case of this kind is due to some reason of the common law which has disappeared, the rule denying her the right to maintain the action may have disappeared with it. This principle is a part of the common law which was adopted by the Florida Statute.

The law is not static. It must keep pace with changes in our society, for the doctrine of *stare decisis* is not an iron mold which can never be changed. Holmes, in his The Common Law (1881), p. 5, recognizes this in the following language:

> The customs, beliefs, or needs of a primitive time establish a rule or a formula. In the course of centuries the customs, belief, or necessity disappear, but the rule remains. The reason which gave rise to the rule has been forgotten, and ingenious minds set themselves to inquire how it is to be accounted for. Some ground of policy is thought of, which seems to explain it and to reconcile it with the present state of things; and then the rule adapts itself to the new reasons which have been found for it, and [enters] on a new career. The old form receives a new content, and in time even the form modifies itself to fit the meaning which it has received.

It may be argued that any change in this rule should come from the Legislature. No recitation of authority is needed to indicate that this Court has not been backward in overturning unsound precedent in the area of tort law. Legislative action could, of course, be taken, but we abdicate our own function, in a field peculiarly nonstatutory, when we refuse to reconsider an old and unsatisfactory court-made rule.

...

2. 1 Harper & James, TORTS, §8.9, p. 641–643 (1956); Prosser, TORTS 916–19 (3rd ed. 1964); Holbrook, *The Change in the Meaning of Consortium*, 22 MICH.L.REV. 1 (1923); Lippman, *The Breakdown of Consortium*, 30 COLUM.L.REV. 651, 664–68 (1930); Simone, *The Wife's Action for Loss of Consortium — Progress or No?*, 4 ST. LOUIS U.L.J. 424 (1957); Kinaird, *Right of Wife to Sue for Loss of Consortium Due to Negligent Injury to Her Husband*, 35 KY.L.J. 220, 223 (1946); Foster, *Relational Interests of the Family*, 1962, U.ILL.L.F. 493, 525–27 (1962); Note, *Judicial Treatment of Negligent Invasion of Consortium*, 61 COLUM.L.REV. 1341, 1352–57 (1961); Friedman, *Consortium as an "Interest" in the Law of Torts*, 32 CAN.B.REV. 1065 (1954); Brett, *Consortium and Servitium*, A HISTORY AND SOME PROPOSALS (Pts. 1–3, 29 Austl.L.J. 321, 389, 428 (1955); 64 HARV.L.REV. 672 (1951); 39 CORNELL L. Q. 761 (1954); 39 MICH.L.REV. 820 (1941); 55 MICH.L.REV. 721 (1957); 1 U.C.L.A.L.REV. 223 (1954); 20 FORDHAM L.REV. 342 (1951); 41 GEO.L.J. 443 (1953); 86 A.L.R.2D 1184 (1960); 23 A.L.R.2D 1366 (1950).

The recent changes in the legal and societal status of women in our society force[] us to recognize a change in the doctrine with which this opinion is concerned. The Florida Constitution (1968) contained the following significant clauses:

> All natural persons are equal before the law. Article 1, Section 2.
>
> No person shall be deprived of life, liberty or property without due process of law. Article 1, Section 9.
>
> The courts shall be open to every person for redress of any injury, and justice shall be administered without sale, denial or delay. Article 1, Section 21.
>
> There shall be no distinction between married women and married men in the holding, control, disposition, or encumbering of their property, both real and personal. Article 10, Section 5.

Prior to the 1968 revision, the Florida Constitution always contained a provision that *all men* are equal before the law (Fla.Const., Declaration of Rights, §1 (1885)); and that every person could have a remedy for injury done *him* by due course of law (Fla.Const., Declaration of Rights §4 (1885)).

The Florida Legislature has enacted the married woman's property act (Fla.Stat., Ch. 708, F.S.A.), and the United States Congress has passed the Civil Rights Act (U.S.C.A. Title 42, Ch. 21). Discrimination on the basis of sex has been proscribed by the United States Congress. U.S. Code Title 42, §2000e *et seq.*

So it is that the unity concept of marriage has in a large part given way to the partner concept whereby a married woman stands as an equal to her husband in the eyes of the law. By giving the wife a separate equal existence, the law created a new interest in the wife which should not be left unprotected by the courts. Medieval concepts which have no justification in our present society should be rejected. We therefore hold that deprivation to the wife of the husband's companionship, affection and sexual relation (or consortium, as above defined) constitutes a real injury to the marital relationship and one which should be compensable at law if due to the negligence of another.

A husband, of course, has a cause of action for loss of consortium of his wife when she suffers personal injury through the negligence of another, *Busby v. Winn & Lovett Miami, Inc.*, 80 So.2d 675 (Fla.1955). No reasonable suggestion can be offered any longer to explain the disparity in the spouses' relative rights to secure damages for loss of consortium. No reasonable distinctions may be made between the wife's claim for negligent impairment of consortium and a similar claim by her husband. As consortium is defined above, the interests of the husband and wife are the same and it necessarily follows that negligent impairment of those interests by an outsider ought to have the same legal consequences.

...

The intangible segments of the elements comprising a cause of action for loss of consortium are equally precious to both husband and wife. The classification by sex formerly made by this Court discriminates unreasonably and arbitrarily against women and must be abolished. We recede from *Riley v. Ewell, supra.*

There are practical difficulties in allowing a consortium action, especially with respect to retrospective application. The problem has not troubled other courts seriously and may be easily resolved. Where there is a cause of action brought by the injured husband pending, the wife's consortium action, if not time barred, may be joined with her husband's claim, or, if separate suit has been filed, consolidated for the purpose of trial. The Defendant has the right to request joinder of the wife as a proper party to an action brought by her husband, if she has not filed suit in her own behalf. Where the husband's cause of action has been terminated by adverse judgment on the merits, this should bar the wife's cause of action for consortium.

The rule that we now recognize is that the wife of a husband injured as a proximate result of the negligence of another shall have a right of action against that same person for her loss of consortium. We further hold that her right of action is a derivative right and she may recover only if her husband has a cause of action against the same defendant. This means that the tort-feasor was negligent and the husband was free from contributory negligence.

In such actions by the wife, the trial court should carefully caution the jury that any loss to the wife of her husband's material support is fully compensated by any award to him for impairment of his lost earning and that the wife is entitled to recover only for loss of consortium as defined in this opinion.

The decision of the District Court of Appeal is quashed and the cause is remanded to that court with instructions to further remand same to the trial court for further proceedings not inconsistent with this opinion.

It is so ordered.

COMMENTS

Gates deals with the question of whether a wife, too, is entitled to an action for loss of consortium based on an injury to her husband by a third person. At common law only the husband was permitted such recovery if his wife were injured. It is not clear whether the disability of the wife was procedural or substantive in nature. She could not have a cause of action in her own name. Perhaps her injury of loss of consortium of her husband was not perceived to be distinguishable from the injury to the husband. Perhaps, since she had no rights for services and comfort against her husband, she could not claim loss of such rights against a third person who had injured her husband. The husband, of course, could always sue for his own damages as well as for damages to the extent that his wife was injured. In any event, there was concern at a later phase of the law's development that extension of recovery might result in double compensation.

A more realistic picture emerges if we look at the problems from the perspective of attorney strategies. The plaintiff's attorney has a natural interest in having as many causes of action against the wrongdoer as possible. Furthermore, if multiple counts are permissible, recovery is likely to be higher than for a single count. The defendant's attorney, on the other hand, is interested in keeping the causes of action and the counts at the lowest level possible. Thus, the question of whether the husband and wife can sue separately, each on multiple counts, is possibly related not so much to the nature of the marital relationship but to how much protection should be given to the outsider who causes an injury to either spouse. Under contemporary conditions these questions are related to policies sometimes referred to as socialization of risks. Should the parties to a marriage absorb at least part of the risk of injury, or should the risk be distributed, with the aid of insurance companies, to a large group of persons? Equality of spouses has little bearing on this fundamental problem. If equal treatment were the only issue, it would have been possible, for example, to abolish the cause of action for loss of consortium by both the husband and the wife. By not pursuing this solution, an implicit choice was made by the legislature and the courts that preferred wide distribution of the risk of injury to letting the risk fall on the marital unit.

The question of what is to be contained in an action for loss of consortium and how to avoid double recovery of husband and wife is related to the basic problem of allocation of risks. Instead of viewing "consortium" purely as a single item of recovery, the inclination has been, even when the action could be brought only by the husband, to break consortium down into multiple components, each with a separate count of damages. Although sometimes reduced to loss of society, services, and sexual rights, other losses might be added, such as loss of love, companionship, affection, comfort, and solace. Each of these items may enlarge claims of both husband and wife. While the right for services is retained, perhaps in a form of legal fiction, other rights, such as those for sexual relations, may be regarded by insurance companies as encouraging dual recovery for both husband and wife.

Additional complications may arise because some claims can traditionally be raised only by the husband because of his duty to support the wife. Thus, if the wife has medical bills, it would be the duty of the husband to pay them, and he is entitled to demand compensation whether in fact he pays them or not. If the wife inadvertently claims damages that fall under the husband's duty to support, her claim could be subject to a motion to dismiss. Many jurisdictions, including Florida in *Gates*, also view the cause of action as derivative. Contributory negligence of the husband in causing an accident would therefore negate the wife's recovery. Or, if today comparative negligence of the husband is at issue, it could affect the wife's recovery in the same degree.

An interesting aspect of *Gates* is its value as precedent. It is cited less for its holding than for its dictum. Once the right of married women to recover for loss of consortium is judicially recognized, the need to cite the opinion for this purpose will dissipate. The most durable part of the opinion, and the most frequently cited, is the paragraph proclaiming "that the unity concept of marriage has in large part given way to the partner concept whereby a married woman stands as an equal to her husband in the eyes of the law." *Gates* could, however become a stepping-stone toward recognition of rights of children for loss of consortium if one or both parents were injured.

Chapter 4

State Control Over Entry into and Exit from Marriage

A MAJOR FORM OF STATE CONTROL over family life, often not considered to be state intervention in the family, is the power states assert to grant or deny a marriage license and to deny recognition to attempted marriages that have not met the state requirements. A related and perhaps equally important power is the state's authority to refuse divorce or to control the conditions of divorce.

There appears to be agreement, at least among politicians seeking election, that the state should promote family values. Considerably less agreement exists regarding what family values are and about what the state should do to promote them. A popular liberal view is that one of the most important things the state should do to promote family values is to avoid intervening in the family — that is, to leave the family alone. Conservatives often share the view that the state should avoid intervening in the family, especially should avoid doing anything to undermine parental authority. Liberals and conservatives often differ about what constitutes "non-intervention" in particular cases: for example, if a young girl were to run away from her parents and go to live with her aunt. Should the child be returned to her parents, or would that be state intervention? Should an inquiry first be made why the girl ran away and whether the parents are better able than the aunt to raise the child, or would that be state intervention? Insofar as everyone involved is part of the same extended family, should the state refuse to become involved at all? The traditional response has been to order the child returned to the parents unless the state is convinced that the parents are unfit, in which case the state would "intervene" and not force the child's return. A nineteenth century English case actually suggested that it would be "intervention" unless the state ordered the mother to turn her children over to their father when the parents separated.

Clearly, the notion of "state intervention in the family" makes sense only if there is a preexisting notion of what a family is and which members should have what authority over which other members. Questions about what it means to "intervene" in the family implicate disputes over what constitutes a family and who should have what power within the family. If a same-sex couple is a family, then a state rule that allowed the parents rather than the same-sex partner to determine funeral arrangements if one partner died might be seen as state intervention. Some have considered it state intervention to prosecute a man for using force to restrain his wife, for raping her, or for beating her — and that the state, if it does intervene, must do so as circumspectly as possible.

The notion that state intervention in the family should be approached with caution and sensitivity is generally employed in a manner that reinforces traditional power relations within the family. No one suggested that Lorena Bobbett, who attracted nation-wide attention in 1993 when she cut off the penis of her husband, had thereby engaged in a very private sex act and that the state should not intervene in the family — or even that the state should proceed cautiously. Indeed, at about the same time, prosecutors in California were refusing to drop charges against another woman who had castrated her allegedly abusive husband, although the couple had since reconciled and the husband wanted charges dropped.

The materials in this book have examined many of the direct and indirect ways that state regulations affect family life. This chapter explores another aspect of the state's relationship to the family — state efforts to limit marriage and divorce and constitutional limits upon those efforts.

REFERENCE

Frances Olsen, *The Myth of State Intervention in the Family*, 18 MICH. J. OF L. REFORM 835 (1985).

A: FREEDOM TO MARRY AS A FUNDAMENTAL HUMAN RIGHT

LOVING v. VIRGINIA

United States Supreme Court
388 U.S. 1 (1967)

Mr. Chief Justice WARREN delivered the opinion of the Court.

This case presents a constitutional question never addressed by this Court: whether a statutory scheme adopted by the State of Virginia to prevent marriages between persons solely on the basis of racial classifications violates the Equal Protection and Due Process Clauses of the Fourteenth Amendment....

In June 1958, two residents of Virginia, Mildred Jeter, a Negro woman, and Richard Loving, a white man, were married in the District of Columbia pursuant to its laws. Shortly after their marriage, the Lovings returned to Virginia and established their marital abode in Caroline County. At the October Term, 1958, of the Circuit Court of Caroline County, a grand jury issued an indictment charging the Lovings with violating Virginia's ban on interracial marriages. On January 6, 1959, the Lovings pleaded guilty to the charge and were sentenced to one year in jail; however, the trial judge suspended the sentence for a period of 25 years on the condition that the Lovings leave the State and not return to Virginia together for 25 years. He stated in an opinion that:

> Almighty God created the races white, black, yellow, malay and red, and he placed them on separate continents. And but for the interference with his arrangement there would be no cause for such marriages. The fact that he separated the races shows that he did not intend for the races to mix.

After their convictions, the Lovings took up residence in the District of Columbia. On November 6, 1963, they filed a motion in the state trial court to vacate the judgment and set aside the sentence on the ground that the statutes which they had violated were repugnant to the Fourteenth Amendment. The motion not having been decided by October 28, 1964, the Lovings instituted a class action in the United States District Court for the Eastern District of Virginia requesting that a three-judge court be convened to declare the Virginia antimiscegenation statutes unconstitutional and to enjoin state officials from enforcing their convictions. On January 22, 1965, the state trial judge denied the motion to vacate the sentences, and the Lovings perfected an appeal to the Supreme Court of Appeals of Virginia. On February 11, 1965, the three-judge District Court continued the case to allow the Lovings to present their constitutional claims to the highest state court.

The Supreme Court of Appeals upheld the constitutionality of the antimiscegenation statutes and, after modifying the sentence, affirmed the convictions. The Lovings appealed this decision....

The two statutes under which appellants were convicted and sentenced are part of a comprehensive statutory scheme aimed at prohibiting and punishing interracial marriages. The Lovings were convicted of violating §20-58 of the Virginia Code:

> *Leaving State to evade law.* If any white person and colored person shall go out of this State, for the purpose of being married, and with the intention of returning, and be married out of it, and afterwards return to and reside in it, cohabiting as man and wife, they shall be punished as provided in §20-59, and the marriage shall be governed by the same law as if it had been solemnized in this State. The fact of their cohabitation here as man and wife shall be evidence of their marriage.

Section 20-59, which defines the penalty for miscegenation, provides:

> *Punishment for marriage.* If any white person intermarry with a colored person, or any colored person intermarry with a white person, he shall be guilty of a felony and shall be punished by confinement in the penitentiary for not less than one nor more than five years.

Other central provisions in the Virginia statutory scheme are §20-57, which automatically voids all marriages between "a white person and a colored person" without any judicial proceeding, and §§20-54 and 1-14 which, respectively, define "white persons" and "colored persons and Indians" for purposes of the statutory prohibitions.[4] The Lovings have never disputed in the course of this litigation that Mrs. Loving is a "colored person" or that Mr. Loving is a "white person" within the meanings given those terms by the Virginia statutes.

---

4. Section 20-54 of the Virginia Code provides:

> *Intermarriage prohibited; meaning of term "white persons."* It shall hereafter be unlawful for any white person in this State to marry any save a white person, or a person with no other admixture of blood than white and American Indian. For the purpose of this chapter, the term "white person" shall apply only to such person as has no trace whatever of any blood other than Caucasian; but persons who have one-sixteenth or less of the blood of the American Indian and have no other non-Caucasic blood shall be deemed to be white persons. All laws heretofore passed and now in effect regarding the intermarriage of white and colored persons shall apply to marriages prohibited by this chapter.
>
> Va.Code Ann. §20-54 (1960 Repl.Vol.).
>
> The exception for persons with less than one-sixteenth "of the blood of the American Indian" is apparently accounted for, in the words of a tract issued by the Registrar of the State Bureau of Vital Statistics, by "the desire of all to recognize as an integral and honored part of the white race the descendants of John Rolfe and Pocahontas...." Plecker, *The New Family and Race Improvement,* 17 VA.HEALTH BULL., Extra No. 12, at 25-26 (New Family Series No. 5, 1925), cited in Wadlington, *The Loving Case: Virginia's Anti-Miscegenation Statute in Historical Perspective,* 52 VA.L.REV. 1189, 1202, n. 93 (1966).

Section 1-14 of the Virginia Code provides:

> *Colored persons and Indians defined.* Every person in whom there is ascertainable any Negro blood shall be deemed and taken to be a colored person, and every person not a colored person having one fourth or more of American Indian blood shall be deemed an American Indian; except that members of Indian tribes existing in this Commonwealth having one fourth or more of Indian blood and less than one sixteenth of Negro blood shall be deemed tribal Indians.
>
> Va.Code Ann. §1-14 (1960 Repl.Vol.).

Virginia is now one of 16 States which prohibit and punish marriages on the basis of racial classifications.[5] Penalties for miscegenation arose as an incident to slavery and have been common in Virginia since the colonial period.[6] The present statutory scheme dates from the adoption of the Racial Integrity Act of 1924, passed during the period of extreme nativism which followed the end of the First World War. The central features of this Act, and current Virginia law, are the absolute prohibition of a "white person" marrying other than another "white person," a prohibition against issuing marriage licenses until the issuing official is satisfied that the applicants' statements as to their race are correct, certificates of "racial composition" to be kept by both local and state registrars, and the carrying forward of earlier prohibitions against racial intermarriage.

I

In upholding the constitutionality of these provisions in the decision below, the Supreme Court of Appeals of Virginia referred to its 1955 decision in *Naim v. Naim,* 197 Va. 80, 87 S.E.2d 749, as stating the reasons supporting the validity of these laws. In *Naim,* the state court concluded that the State's legitimate purposes were "to preserve the racial integrity of its citizens," and to prevent "the corruption of blood," "a mongrel breed of citizens," and "the obliteration of racial pride," obviously an endorsement of the doctrine of White Supremacy. *Id.*, at 90, 87 S.E.2d, at 756. The court also reasoned that marriage has traditionally been subject to state regulation without federal intervention, and, consequently, the regulation of marriage should be left to exclusive state control by the Tenth Amendment.

While the state court is no doubt correct in asserting that marriage is a social relation subject to the State's police power, *Maynard v. Hill,* 125 U.S. 190, 8 S.Ct. 723, 31 L.Ed. 654 (1888), the State does not contend in its argument before this Court that its powers to regulate marriage are unlimited notwithstanding the commands of the Fourteenth Amendment. Nor could it do so in light of *Meyer v. State of Nebraska,* 262 U.S. 390, 43 S.Ct. 625, 67 L.Ed. 1042 (1923), and *Skinner v. State of Oklahoma,* 316 U.S. 535, 62 S.Ct. 1110, 86 L.Ed. 1655 (1942). Instead, the State argues that the meaning of the Equal Protection Clause, as illuminated by the statements of the Framers, is only that state penal laws containing an interracial element as part of the definition of the offense must apply equally to whites and Negroes in the sense that members of each race are punished to the same degree. Thus, the State contends that, because its miscegenation statutes punish equally both the white and the Negro participants in an interracial marriage, these

5. After the initiation of this litigation, Maryland repealed its prohibitions against interracial marriage, Md.Laws 1967, c. 6, leaving Virginia and 15 other States with statutes outlawing interracial marriage: Alabama, Ala.Const., Art. 4, §102, Ala.Code, Tit. 14, §360 (1958); Arkansas, Ark.Stat.Ann. §55-104 (1947); Delaware, Del.Code Ann., Tit. 13, §101 (1953); Florida, Fla.Const., Art. 16, §24, F.S.A., Fla.Stat. §741.11 (1965) F.S.A.; Georgia, Ga.Code Ann. §53-106 (1961); Kentucky, Ky.Rev.Stat.Ann. §402.020 (Supp.1966); Louisiana, La.Rev.Stat. §14:79 (1950); Mississippi, Miss.Const., Art. 14, §263, Miss.Code Ann. §459 (1956); Missouri, Mo.Rev.Stat. §451.020 (Supp.1966), V.A.M.S.; North Carolina, N.C.Const., Art. XIV, §8, N.C.Gen.Stat. §14-181 (1953); Oklahoma, Okla.Stat., Tit. 43, §12 (Supp.1965); South Carolina, S.C.Const., Art. 3, §33, S.C.Code Ann. §20-7 (1962); Tennessee, Tenn.Const., Art. 11, §14, Tenn.Code Ann. §36-402 (1955); Vernon's Ann.Texas, Tex.Pen.Code, Art. 492 (1952); West Virginia, W.Va.Code Ann. §4697 (1961).

Over the past 15 years, 14 States have repealed laws outlawing interracial marriages: Arizona, California, Colorado, Idaho, Indiana, Maryland, Montana, Nebraska, Nevada, North Dakota, Oregon, South Dakota, Utah, and Wyoming.

The first state court to recognize that miscegenation statutes violate the Equal Protection Clause was the Supreme Court of California. *Perez v. Sharp,* 32 Cal.2d 711, 198 P.2d 17 (1948).

6. For a historical discussion of Virginia's miscegenation statutes, see Wadlington, *supra,* n. 4.

statutes, despite their reliance on racial classifications do not constitute an invidious discrimination based upon race. The second argument advanced by the State assumes the validity of its equal application theory. The argument is that, if the Equal Protection Clause does not outlaw miscegenation statutes because of their reliance on racial classifications, the question of constitutionality would thus become whether there was any rational basis for a State to treat interracial marriages differently from other marriages. On this question, the State argues, the scientific evidence is substantially in doubt and, consequently, this Court should defer to the wisdom of the state legislature in adopting its policy of discouraging interracial marriages.

Because we reject the notion that the mere "equal application" of a statute containing racial classifications is enough to remove the classifications from the Fourteenth Amendment's proscription of all invidious racial discriminations, we do not accept the State's contention that these statutes should be upheld if there is any possible basis for concluding that they serve a rational purpose....

...

...We have rejected the proposition that the debates in the Thirty-ninth Congress or in the state legislatures which ratified the Fourteenth Amendment supported the theory advanced by the State, that the requirement of equal protection of the laws is satisfied by penal laws defining offenses based on racial classifications so long as white and Negro participants in the offense were similarly punished. *McLaughlin v. State of Florida*, 379 U.S. 184, 85 S.Ct. 283, 13 L.Ed.2d 222 (1964).

The State finds support for its "equal application" theory in the decision of the Court in *Pace v. State of Alabama*, 106 U.S. 583, 1 S.Ct. 637, 27 L.Ed. 207 (1883). In that case, the Court upheld a conviction under an Alabama statute forbidding adultery or fornication between a white person and a Negro which imposed a greater penalty than that of a statute proscribing similar conduct by members of the same race. The Court reasoned that the statute could not be said to discriminate against Negroes because the punishment for each participant in the offense was the same. However, as recently as the 1964 Term, in rejecting the reasoning of that case, we stated "*Pace* represents a limited view of the Equal Protection Clause which has not withstood analysis in the subsequent decisions of this Court." *McLaughlin v. Florida, supra*, 379 U.S. at 188, 85 S.Ct. at 286. As we there demonstrated, the Equal Protection Clause requires the consideration of whether the classifications drawn by any statute constitute an arbitrary and invidious discrimination. The clear and central purpose of the Fourteenth Amendment was to eliminate all official state sources of invidious racial discrimination in the States....

There can be no question but that Virginia's miscegenation statutes rest solely upon distinctions drawn according to race. The statutes proscribe generally accepted conduct if engaged in by members of different races. Over the years, this Court has consistently repudiated "[d]istinctions between citizens solely because of their ancestry" as being "odious to a free people whose institutions are founded upon the doctrine of equality." *Hirabayashi v. United States*, 320 U.S. 81, 100, 63 S.Ct. 1375, 1385, 87 L.Ed. 1774 (1943). At the very least, the Equal Protection Clause demands that racial classifications, especially suspect in criminal statutes, be subjected to the "most rigid scrutiny," *Korematsu v. United States*, 323 U.S. 214, 216, 65 S.Ct. 193, 194, 89 L.Ed. 194 (1944), and, if they are ever to be upheld, they must be shown to be necessary to the accomplishment of some permissible state objective, independent of the racial discrimination which it was the object of the

Fourteenth Amendment to eliminate. Indeed, two members of this Court have already stated that they "cannot conceive of a valid legislative purpose...which makes the color of a person's skin the test of whether his conduct is a criminal offense." *McLaughlin v. Florida, supra,* 379 U.S. at 198, 85 S.Ct. at 292, (STEWART, J., joined by DOUGLAS, J., concurring).

There is patently no legitimate overriding purpose independent of invidious racial discrimination which justifies this classification. The fact that Virginia prohibits only interracial marriages involving white persons demonstrates that the racial classifications must stand on their own justification, as measures designed to maintain White Supremacy.[11] We have consistently denied the constitutionality of measures which restrict the rights of citizens on account of race. There can be no doubt that restricting the freedom to marry solely because of racial classifications violates the central meaning of the Equal Protection Clause.

II

These statutes also deprive the Lovings of liberty without due process of law in violation of the Due Process Clause of the Fourteenth Amendment. The freedom to marry has long been recognized as one of the vital personal rights essential to the orderly pursuit of happiness by free men.

Marriage is one of the "basic civil rights of man," fundamental to our very existence and survival. *Skinner v. State of Oklahoma,* 316 U.S. 535, 541, 62 S.Ct. 1110, 1113, 86 L.Ed. 1655 (1942). See also *Maynard v. Hill,* 125 U.S. 190, 8 S.Ct. 723, 31 L.Ed. 654 (1888). To deny this fundamental freedom on so unsupportable a basis as the racial classifications embodied in these statutes, classifications so directly subversive of the principle of equality at the heart of the Fourteenth Amendment, is surely to deprive all the State's citizens of liberty without due process of law. The Fourteenth Amendment requires that the freedom of choice to marry not be restricted by invidious racial discriminations. Under our Constitution, the freedom to marry or not marry, a person of another race resides with the individual and cannot be infringed by the State.

These convictions must be reversed. It is so ordered.

Reversed.

COMMENTS

Loving and *Maynard v. Hill* (p. 78) are interrelated. *Maynard* proclaims marriage as the most important relation in life, while *Loving* speaks of marriage as a basic civil right and a fundamental freedom. Consequently, *Loving* is more frequently invoked when freedom from restrictive legislation is claimed. *Maynard,* on the other hand, retains practical value for the support of such legislation. The very importance of marriage for society was viewed as making it subject to state regulation. Although this injects an element of contradiction between the two

11. Appellants point out that the State's concern in these statutes, as expressed in the words of the 1924 Act's title, "An Act to Preserve Racial Integrity," extends only to the integrity of the white race. While Virginia prohibits whites from marrying any nonwhite (subject to the exception for the descendants of Pocahontas), Negroes, Orientals, and any other racial class may intermarry without statutory interference. Appellants contend that this distinction renders Virginia's miscegenation statutes arbitrary and unreasonable even assuming the constitutional validity of an official purpose to preserve "racial integrity." We need not reach this contention because we find the racial classifications in these statutes repugnant to the Fourteenth Amendment, even assuming an even-handed state purpose to protect the "integrity" of all races.

cases, they are frequently cited in the same breath. For example, whenever an attempt is made to broaden the concept of marriage to include categories earlier excluded, such as marriage between close relatives or members of the same sex, both cases tend to be cited. For the time being, the power of the state to regulate and prohibit is likely to prevail.

The importance of *Loving* should not, however, be seen in its ability to support a winning argument in court. In our view, its function is to signal potential changes in the law of marriage. These changes favor the increased autonomy of the parties and the decline of state involvement in marriage. There are other, more indirect, consequences of *Loving*: for instance, when the courts uphold contract cohabitation between parties who would be prohibited from marrying. In other words, the power of the state to regulate marriage, following *Maynard*, is likely to be strictly construed and not necessarily extended to cover nonmarital cohabitation. If formal and informal marriage are viewed as being functionally related, the more permissive message of *Loving* seems to prevail over restrictive state regulation insofar as informal marriage is concerned.

Compared to these fundamental questions, the problem of interracial marriage that gave rise to *Loving* appears to be of less significance. Since *Loving*, although the process took some time and sometimes new litigation, antimiscegenation statutes have been repealed or ruled unconstitutional in all states. The question of interracial marriage continues, however, to have social significance. Racial classifications are still treated as relevant. In some states information on race, ostensibly for identification, is requested for driver's licenses and applications for marriage licenses. Racial classifications continue to be legally relevant, if only for purposes of proving illegal discrimination and for remedies to that discrimination, including affirmative action. Nevertheless, the state statutes defining race referred to in *Loving* have all been repealed; and most racial classifications, for example, in the United States Census, appear to be based today on self-classification. To a large extent, individuals belong to the racial group they say they belong to.

Race continues to be treated as relevant in child custody matters and in placing children in foster care and for adoption. Thus the impact of *Loving* on race relations so far is limited. As long as discrimination and de facto segregation continue, it is likely that racial patterns will form the bases of legal arguments. In light of the continued relevance of issues of racism, the decision of the California Supreme Court in *Perez v. Sharp*, 32 Cal.2d 711, 198 P.2d 17 (1948), should be read together with *Loving*. *Perez* held the California antimiscegenation statute to be unconstitutional almost twenty years before the ruling of the United States Supreme Court and with reasoning that has not lost its poignancy.

REFERENCES

Kenneth L. Karst, *The Freedom of Intimate Association*, 89 YALE L.J. 624 (1980).
Kenneth L. Karst, BELONGING TO AMERICA (1989).
Walter Wadlington, *The Loving Case: Virginia's Anti-Miscegenation Statute in Historical Perspective*, 52 VA. L. REV. 1189 (1966).

ZABLOCKI v. REDHAIL

United States Supreme Court
434 U.S. 374 (1978)

Mr. Justice MARSHALL delivered the opinion of the Court.

At issue in this case is the constitutionality of a Wisconsin statute, Wis. Stat. §§245.10(1), (4), (5)(1973), which provides that members of a certain class of Wisconsin residents may not marry, within the State or elsewhere, without first obtaining a court order granting permission to marry. The class is defined by the statute to include any "Wisconsin resident having minor issue not in his custody and which he is under obligation to support by any court order or judgment." The statute specifies that court permission cannot be granted unless the marriage applicant submits proof of compliance with the support obligation and, in addition, demonstrates that the children covered by the support order "are not then and are not likely thereafter to become public charges." No marriage license may lawfully be issued in Wisconsin to a person covered by the statute, except upon court order; any marriage entered into without compliance with §245.10 is declared void; and persons acquiring marriage licenses in violation of the section are subject to criminal penalties.

After being denied a marriage license because of his failure to comply with §245.10, appellee brought this class action under 42 U.S.C. §1983, challenging the statute as violative of the Equal Protection and Due Process Clauses of the Fourteenth Amendment and seeking declaratory and injunctive relief. The United States District Court for the Eastern District of Wisconsin held the statute unconstitutional under the Equal Protection Clause and enjoined its enforcement....

Appellee Redhail is a Wisconsin resident who, under the terms of §245.10, is unable to enter into a lawful marriage in Wisconsin or elsewhere so long as he maintains his Wisconsin residency. The facts, according to the stipulation filed by the parties in the District Court, are as follows. In January 1972, when appellee was a minor and a high school student, a paternity action was instituted against him in Milwaukee County Court, alleging that he was the father of a baby girl born out of wedlock on July 5, 1971. After he appeared and admitted that he was the child's father, the court entered an order on May 12, 1972, adjudging appellee the father and ordering him to pay $109 per month as support for the child until she reached 18 years of age. From May 1972 until August 1974, appellee was unemployed and indigent, and consequently was unable to make any support payments.

On September 27, 1974, appellee filed an application for a marriage license with appellant Zablocki, the County Clerk of Milwaukee County, and a few days later the application was denied on the sole ground that appellee had not obtained a court order granting him permission to marry, as required by §245.10. Although appellee did not petition a state court thereafter, it is stipulated that he would not have been able to satisfy either of the statutory prerequisites for an order granting permission to marry. First, he had not satisfied his support obligations to his illegitimate child, and as of December 1974 there was an arrearage in excess of $3,700. Second, the child had been a public charge since her birth, receiving benefits under the Aid to Families with Dependent Children program. It is stipulated that the child's benefit payments were such that she would have been a public charge even if appellee had been current in his support payments.

On December 24, 1974, appellee filed his complaint in the District Court, on behalf of himself and the class of all Wisconsin residents who had been refused a marriage license pursuant to §245.10(1) by one of the county clerks in Wisconsin. Zablocki was named as the defendant, individually and as representative of a class consisting of all county clerks in the State. The complaint alleged, among other things, that appellee and the woman he desired to marry were expecting a child in March 1975 and wished to be lawfully married before that time. The statute was attacked on the grounds that it deprived appellee, and the class he sought to represent of equal protection and due process rights secured by the First, Fifth, Ninth, and Fourteenth Amendments to the United States Constitution.

...

...Since our past decisions make clear that the right to marry is of fundamental importance, and since the classification at issue here significantly interferes with the exercise of that right, we believe that "critical examination" of the state interests advanced in support of the classification is required....

The leading decision of this Court on the right to marry is *Loving v. Virginia*, 388 U.S. 1, 87 S.Ct. 1817, 18 L.Ed.2d 1010 (1967). In that case, an interracial couple who had been convicted of violating Virginia's miscegenation laws challenged the statutory scheme on both equal protection and due process grounds. The Court's opinion could have rested solely on the ground that the statutes discriminated on the basis of race in violation of the Equal Protection Clause. *Id.*, at 11-12, 87 S.Ct., at 1823-1824. But the Court went on to hold that the laws arbitrarily deprived the couple of a fundamental liberty protected by the Due Process Clause, the freedom to marry. The Court's language on the latter point bears repeating:

> The freedom to marry has long been recognized as one of the vital personal rights essential to the orderly pursuit of happiness by free men.
>
> Marriage is one of the "basic civil rights of man," fundamental to our very existence and survival.

Id., at 12, 87 S.Ct., at 1824, quoting *Skinner v. Oklahoma ex rel. Williamson*, 316 U.S. 535, 541, 62 S.Ct. 1110, 1113, 86 L.Ed. 1655 (1942).

Although *Loving* arose in the context of racial discrimination, prior and subsequent decisions of this Court confirm that the right to marry is of fundamental importance for all individuals. Long ago, in *Maynard v. Hill*, 125 U.S. 190, 8 S.Ct. 723, 31 L.Ed. 654 (1888), the Court characterized marriage as "the most important relation in life," *id.*, at 205, 8 S.Ct., at 726, and as "the foundation of the family and of society, without which there would be neither civilization nor progress," *id.*, at 211.

...

More recent decisions have established that the right to marry is part of the fundamental "right of privacy" implicit in the Fourteenth Amendment's Due Process Clause. In *Griswold v. Connecticut*, 381 U.S. 479, 85 S.Ct. 1678, 14 L.Ed.2d 510 (1965), the Court observed:

> We deal with a right of privacy older than the Bill of Rights — older than our political parties, older than our school system. Marriage is a coming together for better or for worse, hopefully enduring, and intimate to the degree of being sacred. It is an association that promotes a way of life, not causes; a harmony in living, not political faiths; a bilateral loyalty, not commercial or social projects. Yet it is an association for as noble a purpose as any involved in our prior decisions.

...

It is not surprising that the decision to marry has been placed on the same level of importance as decisions relating to procreation, childbirth, child rearing, and family relationships. As the facts of this case illustrate, it would make little sense to recognize a right of privacy with respect to other matters of family life and not with respect to the decision to enter the relationship that is the foundation of the family in our society. The woman whom appellee desired to marry had a fundamental right to seek an abortion of their expected child, see *Roe v. Wade, supra*, or to bring the child into life to suffer the myriad social, if not economic, disabilities that the status of illegitimacy brings, see *Trimble v. Gordon*, 430 U.S. 762, 768-770, and n. 13, 97 S.Ct. 1459, 1464-1465 (1977); *Weber v. Aetna Casualty & Surety Co.*, 406 U.S. 164, 175-176, 92 S.Ct. 1400, 1406-1407, 31 L.Ed.2d 768 (1972). Surely, a decision to marry and raise the child in a traditional family setting must receive equivalent protection. And, if appellee's right to procreate means anything at all, it must imply some right to enter the only relationship in which the State of Wisconsin allows sexual relations legally to take place.

By reaffirming the fundamental character of the right to marry, we do not mean to suggest that every state regulation which relates in any way to the incidents of or prerequisites for marriage must be subjected to rigorous scrutiny. To the contrary, reasonable regulations that do not significantly interfere with decisions to enter into the marital relationship may legitimately be imposed. See *Califano v. Jobst*, 434 U.S. 47, 98 S.Ct. 95, 54 L.Ed.2d 228, n. 12, *infra*. The statutory classification at issue here, however, clearly does interfere directly and substantially with the right to marry.

Under the challenged statute, no Wisconsin resident in the affected class may marry in Wisconsin or elsewhere without a court order, and marriages contracted in violation of the statute are both void and punishable as criminal offenses. Some of those in the affected class, like appellee, will never be able to obtain the necessary court order, because they either lack the financial means to meet their support obligations or cannot prove that their children will not become public charges. These persons are absolutely prevented from getting married. Many others, able in theory to satisfy the statute's requirements, will be sufficiently burdened by having to do so that they will in effect be coerced into forgoing their right to marry. And even those who can be persuaded to meet the statute's requirements suffer a serious intrusion into their freedom of choice in an area in which we have held such freedom to be fundamental.[12]

When a statutory classification significantly interferes with the exercise of a fundamental right, it cannot be upheld unless it is supported by sufficiently important state interests and is closely tailored to effectuate only those interests.... Appellant asserts that two interests are served by the challenged statute: the per-

---

12. The directness and substantiality of the interference with the freedom to marry distinguish the instant case from *Califano v. Jobst*, 434 U.S. 47, 98 S.Ct. 95, 54 L.Ed.2d 228. In *Jobst*, we upheld sections of the Social Security Act providing, *inter alia*, for termination of a dependent child's benefits upon marriage to an individual not entitled to benefits under the Act. As the opinion for the Court expressly noted, the rule terminating benefits upon marriage was not "an attempt to interfere with the individual's freedom to make a decision as important as marriage." 434 U.S., at 54, 98 S.Ct., at 99. The Social Security provisions placed no direct legal obstacle in the path of persons desiring to get married, and — notwithstanding our Brother REHNQUIST's imaginative recasting of the case, see dissenting opinion, *post*, at 692 — there was no evidence that the laws significantly discouraged, let alone made "practically impossible," any marriages. Indeed, the provisions had not deterred the individual who challenged the statute from getting married, even though he and his wife were both disabled. See *Califano v. Jobst*, 434 U.S., at 48, 98 S.Ct., at 96. See also 434 U.S., at 57, n. 17, 98 S.Ct., at 101 (because of availability of other federal benefits, total payments to the Jobsts after marriage were only $20 per month less than they would have been had Mr. Jobst's child benefits not been terminated).

mission-to-marry proceeding furnishes an opportunity to counsel the applicant as to the necessity of fulfilling his prior support obligations; and the welfare of the out-of-custody children is protected. We may accept for present purposes that these are legitimate and substantial interests, but, since the means selected by the State for achieving these interests unnecessarily impinge on the right to marry, the statute cannot be sustained.

There is evidence that the challenged statute, as originally introduced in the Wisconsin Legislature, was intended merely to establish a mechanism whereby persons with support obligations to children from prior marriages could be counseled before they entered into new marital relationships and incurred further support obligations. Court permission to marry was to be required, but apparently permission was automatically to be granted after counseling was completed. The statute actually enacted, however, does not expressly require or provide for any counseling whatsoever, nor for any automatic granting of permission to marry by the court, and thus it can hardly be justified as a means for ensuring counseling of the persons within its coverage. Even assuming that counseling does take place — a fact as to which there is no evidence in the record — this interest obviously cannot support the withholding of court permission to marry once counseling is completed.

With regard to safeguarding the welfare of the out-of-custody children, appellant's brief does not make clear the connection between the State's interest and the statute's requirements. At argument, appellant's counsel suggested that, since permission to marry cannot be granted unless the applicant shows that he has satisfied his court-determined support obligations to the prior children and that those children will not become public charges, the statute provides incentive for the applicant to make support payments to his children. Tr. of Oral Arg. 17-20. This "collection device" rationale cannot justify the statute's broad infringement on the right to marry.

First, with respect to individuals who are unable to meet the statutory requirements, the statute merely prevents the applicant from getting married, without delivering any money at all into the hands of the applicant's prior children. More importantly, regardless of the applicant's ability or willingness to meet the statutory requirements, the State already has numerous other means for exacting compliance with support obligations, means that are at least as effective as the instant statute's and yet do not impinge upon the right to marry. Under Wisconsin law, whether the children are from a prior marriage or were born out of wedlock, court-determined support obligations may be enforced directly via wage assignments, civil contempt proceedings, and criminal penalties. And, if the State believes that parents of children out of their custody should be responsible for ensuring that those children do not become public charges, this interest can be achieved by adjusting the criteria used for determining the amounts to be paid under their support orders.

There is also some suggestion that §245.10 protects the ability of marriage applicants to meet support obligations to prior children by preventing the applicants from incurring new support obligations. But the challenged provisions of §245.10 are grossly underinclusive with respect to this purpose, since they do not limit in any way new financial commitments by the applicant other than those arising out of the contemplated marriage. The statutory classification is substantially overinclusive as well: Given the possibility that the new spouse will actually better the applicant's financial situation, by contributing income from a job or otherwise, the statute in many cases may prevent affected individuals from improving their ability to satisfy their prior support obligations. And, although it is true that the applicant will incur support obligations to any children born during the contemplated marriage, preventing the marriage may only result in the children being born out of wedlock, as in fact occurred in appellee's case. Since the support obligation is the same whether the child is born in or out of wedlock, the net result of preventing the marriage is simply more illegitimate children.

The statutory classification created by §§245.10(1), (4), (5) thus cannot be justified by the interests advanced in support of it. The judgment of the District Court is, accordingly,

Affirmed.

[Chief Justice BURGER's concurring opinion omitted.]

...

Mr. Justice STEVENS, concurring in the judgment.

Because of the tension between some of the language in Mr. Justice MARSHALL's opinion for the Court and the Court's unanimous holding in *Califano v. Jobst*, 434 U.S. 47, 98 S.Ct. 95, 54 L.Ed.2d 228, 1977, a further exposition of the reasons why the Wisconsin statute offends the Equal Protection Clause of the Fourteenth Amendment is necessary.

When a State allocates benefits or burdens, it may have valid reasons for treating married and unmarried persons differently. Classification based on marital status has been an accepted characteristic of tax legislation, Selective Service rules, and Social Security regulations. As cases like *Jobst* demonstrate, such laws may "significantly interfere with decisions to enter into the marital relationship." *Ante*, at 681. That kind of interference, however, is not a sufficient reason for invalidating every law reflecting a legislative judgment that there are relevant differences between married persons as a class and unmarried persons as a class.[1]

A classification based on marital status is fundamentally different from a classification which determines who may lawfully enter into the marriage relationship. The individual's interest in making the marriage decision independently is sufficiently important to merit special constitutional protection. See *Whalen v. Roe*, 429 U.S. 589, 599-600, 97 S.Ct. 869, 876-877, 51 L.Ed.2d 64. It is not, however, an interest which is constitutionally immune from evenhanded regulation. Thus, laws prohibiting marriage to a child, a close relative, or a person afflicted with venereal disease, are unchallenged even though they "interfere directly and substantially with the right to marry." *Ante*, at 681. This Wisconsin statute has a different character.

Under this statute, a person's economic status may determine his eligibility to enter into a lawful marriage. A noncustodial parent whose children are "public charges" may not marry even if he has met his court-ordered obligations. Thus, within the class of parents who have fulfilled their court-ordered obligations, the

---

1. In *Jobst*, we pointed out that "it was rational for Congress to assume that marital status is a relevant test of probable dependency...." We had explained:

> Both tradition and common experience support the conclusion that marriage is an event which normally marks an important change in economic status. Traditionally, the event not only creates a new family with attendant new responsibilities, but also modifies the pre-existing relationships between the bride and groom and their respective families. Frequently, of course, financial independence and marriage do not go hand in hand. Nevertheless, there can be no question about the validity of the assumption that a married person is less likely to be dependent on his parents for support than one who is unmarried.

Ante, at 53, 98 S.Ct., at 99.

rich may marry and the poor may not. This type of statutory discrimination is, I believe, totally unprecedented, as well as inconsistent with our tradition of administering justice equally to the rich and to the poor.

The statute appears to reflect a legislative judgment that persons who have demonstrated an inability to support their offspring should not be permitted to marry and thereafter to bring additional children into the world. Even putting to one side the growing number of childless marriages and the burgeoning number of children born out of wedlock, that sort of reasoning cannot justify this deliberate discrimination against the poor.

The statute prevents impoverished parents from marrying even though their intended spouses are economically independent. Presumably, the Wisconsin Legislature assumed (a) that only fathers would be affected by the legislation, and (b) that they would never marry employed women. The first assumption ignores the fact that fathers are sometimes awarded custody, and the second ignores the composition of today's work force. To the extent that the statute denies a hard-pressed parent any opportunity to prove that an intended marriage will ease rather than aggravate his financial straits, it not only rests on unreliable premises, but also defeats its own objectives.

These questionable assumptions also explain why this statutory blunderbuss is wide of the target in another respect. The prohibition on marriage applies to the noncustodial parent but allows the parent who has custody to marry without the State's leave. Yet the danger that new children will further strain an inadequate budget is equally great for custodial and non-custodial parents, unless one assumes (a) that only mothers will ever have custody and (b) that they will never marry unemployed men.

Characteristically, this law fails to regulate the marriages of those parents who are least likely to be able to afford another family, for it applies only to parents under a court order to support their children. Wis.Stat. §245.10(1)(1973). The very poorest parents are unlikely to be the objects of support orders. If the State meant to prevent the marriage of those who have demonstrated their inability to provide for children, it overlooked the most obvious targets of legislative concern.

In sum, the public-charge provision is either futile or perverse insofar as it applies to childless couples, couples who will have illegitimate children if they are forbidden to marry, couples whose economic status will be improved by marriage, and couples who are so poor that the marriage will have no impact on the welfare status of their children in any event. Even assuming that the right to marry may sometimes be denied on economic grounds, this clumsy and deliberate legislative discrimination between the rich and the poor is irrational in so many ways that it cannot withstand scrutiny under the Equal Protection Clause of the Fourteenth Amendment.

[Dissenting opinion of Justice REHNQUIST omitted.]

COMMENTS

The statute involved in *Zablocki* had little chance of surviving constitutional attack. It was a clear illustration of what Professor Jacobus tenBroek has called a dual system of family law: one law for the reasonably affluent and a separate law for the poor. Even more significant than the outcome in this specific case, however, is the reasoning of the Court. It exemplifies the evolution of the legal treatment of marriage toward its recognition as a "fundamental right."

Maynard v. Hill (p. 78), *Loving v. Virginia* (p. 484), and *Griswold v. Connecticut* (p. 350) are cited by the Court as way stations in this development. In their facts, these cases were quite unrelated. *Maynard* dealt with legislative divorce under frontier conditions, *Loving* with interracial marriage, and *Griswold* with the use of contraceptives in marriage. But they all incidentally stressed the importance of marriage as a social institution. It is perhaps not accidental that those portions of U.S. Supreme Court opinions that are traditionally classified as obiter dicta are often cited as significant statements in the evolution of law. They are the more speculative parts of the reasoning, not strictly essential to the exact point to be adjudicated, which tends to be narrow in scope and sometimes confined to one jurisdiction. Transcending, as they do, the case at hand, the speculative portions are just the ones likely to prove important in a wider context.

Related to the use of obiter dicta are the many hypotheticals employed by the Court. These hypotheticals go beyond the scope of the actual controversy and expand the factual basis of the decision. The hypotheticals are not necessarily phrased as such but appear in the opinion as a mere process of reasoning that tests the statute under attack. The Court asks, for example, to assume as a thinking construct that the children to be supported were born of a prior marriage rather than out of wedlock. The Court also asks what would happen if the applicant for a marriage license were to take on new financial commitments other than those arising from the contemplated marriage. Suppose further, Justice Marshall hypothesizes in the majority opinion, that the new spouse will actually better the applicant's financial situation; would that not improve his ability to satisfy prior support obligations? Similar veiled hypotheticals are contained in the concurring opinions and the dissenting opinion of Justice Rehnquist.

On one hand, the U.S. Supreme Court uses restraint in the exercise of its jurisdiction; on the other hand, once jurisdiction is taken, it broadens the scope of inquiry, also in regard to its factual basis, by the use of hypotheticals. While hypotheticals as analytical devices may well be introduced by the Court itself, they can also originate in the argument of counsel. They are thus an important tool of persuasion, especially in novel questions of law where precedent is scant or missing.

Zablocki, in conjunction with *Califano v. Jobst*, 434 U.S. 47 (1977), may lead to a reexamination of restrictions on marriage. It would be wrong to assume, however, that recognition of marriage as a fundamental human right is firmly settled. *Zablocki* resulted in six separate opinions, each different in respect to the standard of review, ranging from "critical examination" in Justice Marshall's opinion to a test of minimal rationality in Justice Rehnquist's dissent. If the assumption is correct that state involvement in marriage is likely to decrease rather than increase, it is probable that critical examination of state regulations of marriage will prevail, as it did in the majority opinion of Justice Marshall, although this standard may still fall short of "strict scrutiny." The standards may also vary from case to case depending on what kind of regulation of marriage is involved. Even restrictions on marriage by persons of the same sex (see pp. 537–568) may be reexamined.

REFERENCES

Note, *Zablocki v. Redhail: Due Process or Equal Protection?*, 12 U.C. DAVIS L. REV. 165 (1979).

Jacobus tenBroek, *California's Dual System of Family Law: Its Origin, Development, and Present Status* (pts. 1 & 2), 16 STAN. L. REV. 257, 900 (1964); (pt. 3), 17 STAN. L. REV. 614 (1965).

Walter O. Weyrauch, *Dual Systems of Family Law: A Comment*, 54 CAL. L. REV. 781 (1966).

B: STATE EFFORTS TO LIMIT MARRIAGE

Form Requirements: Mandamus

F.A. Marriage License
District Court of Pennsylvania
4 Pa. D. & C.2d 1 (1955)

KLEIN, P. J., and LEFEVER, J., May 19, 1955.

Application for a marriage license was filed by the applicants on April 30, 1955. It appears from the statements made by the female applicant (herein referred to as F.A.), that she was a mental patient in St. Mary's Hospital, Philadelphia, for a period of two months in 1951.

Mr. MacDonnell, assistant orphans' court clerk, pursuant to the provisions of section 9 of The Marriage Law of August 22, 1953, P.L. 1344, 48 PS §1, *et seq*, refused to issue the license and certified the matter to this court for hearing.

This is the first time that this court has been asked to construe the provisions of the new marriage law, pertaining to the issuance of a marriage license to a person who has been afflicted with mental illness within a period of five years prior to the date of application for the license.

...

The legislature has thus placed a great social responsibility on the orphans' court. It is our duty to determine whether "it is for the best interest of such applicant and the general public to issue the license." Yet, the statute contains no criteria, standards or rules for determining this fact; and no definition of crucial terms used in the statute. This is perhaps necessary, for the broad discretion vested in the courts, will enable them, in true common-law tradition, to progress with the advances of science in this difficult and inexact field of law and medicine and decide each case on its own facts.

A vast, hazy shadowland exists between mental health and mental illness. The gradations of abnormalities are as varied and diffused as the merging colors of the rainbow. The most illustrious and respected psychiatrists often disagree radically in their opinions with respect to the sanity of an individual.

The following extract from the *Encyclopedia Britannica*, vol. 12, p. 383 (14th ed.) points up the difficulty very sharply:

> INSANITY. This term ordinarily connotes more or less severe unsoundness of mind. Though its loose usage is almost synonymous with mental disease, scientifically the term should only be applied to the mental condition of an individual who, through socially inefficient conduct, has to be placed under supervision and control. The mind is the mechanism by means of which we adapt adequately to our environment and when, through its derangement, conduct is exhibited which the community looks upon as evidence of disease and as implying irresponsibility, the individual concerned is said to be insane and the law steps in to certify him as such. Strictly speaking, then, insanity is really a social and legal term and not medical. Mental illness is a broad concept which may include very efficient members of society. No satisfactory definition can therefore be arrived at, since it would be necessary to define what we mean by sanity, which would involve us in equal difficulties.

The phrase "an inmate of an institution for weakminded, insane, or persons of unsound mind" is, likewise, subject to interpretation. Institutions for the insane are no longer regarded merely as places in which persons of unsound mind are confined as custodial cases to rid the general public of their troublesome presence. Today, great progress is being made toward curing the mentally sick and the establishments in which they are housed are usually called "hospitals." In fact, many general hospitals have departments set aside for the care of the mentally sick. Furthermore, in present day usage the word "inmate" has been generally replaced by the more charitable word "patient." The language of the statute is general, but we believe that the legislature intended to include all cases in which the applicant has been hospitalized for treatment of some form of mental illness or deficiency in any mental institution, including a general hospital which conducts a department for the care of the mentally sick.

Basically, the problem which confronts us is one for the medical profession. A diagnosis by judicial decree should not be made except with the advice, and upon the recommendation of, trained psychiatrists.

The statute does not in so many words state that an applicant who has been in a mental institution must be cured permanently at the time the application is made. However, because the issuance of a license to a person who is weak-minded, insane or of unsound mind is absolutely prohibited by the statute, the legislature must have intended that a license is to be issued only to a person who has been completely cured of his mental illness or whose condition has so improved that he can be expected to lead a normal life and to take his place in society without serious risk to himself or to the community generally.

Leading members of the medical profession freely admit that the science of caring for the mentally ill is in its infancy. Much research and investigation has been undertaken recently which has resulted in tremendously enhancing the chances of curing or, at least, improving the condition of persons suffering from mental sickness.

It seems clear that under no circumstances should a marriage license be issued to persons having a mental deficiency of severe degree, *e.g.*, an idiot or imbecile. It is also apparent that persons suffering irremedial brain injury or deteriorating organic brain syndromes which are of progressive or irreversible nature, *e.g.*, senile dementia, should not be permitted to marry.

On the other hand, many persons who are unable to cope with the intense pressures of the modern age, suffer what is commonly designated as "mental breakdowns" and are institutionalized. Most of these people respond favorably to therapy; many are completely cured. These obviously are the persons whom the legislature intended to benefit primarily and furnish no serious problem when they apply for marriage licenses.

The real difficulties arise with respect to persons who suffer moderate mental deficiency or who have been hospitalized because of the more serious mental illnesses, such as manic-depressive psychosis, schizophrenia (dementia praecox), post-partum psychosis, and involutional melancholia. Although many of these cases are completely hopeless, a great number show marked improvement under modern therapy, such as shock treatment, psychotherapy, and the use of newly discovered drugs. Some of these persons are able to leave the mental hospitals and, at least temporarily, take their places in society as useful citizens. Some apparently have complete remission from their malady. Whether they have recovered sufficiently to assume the responsibilities of marriage presents an extremely delicate question.

No general rule can be handed down. Each case is *sui generis* and must be decided upon its own facts. The discretion vested in the orphans' court must be carefully exercised in order to protect not only the applicants and their issue, but the general public as well.

Three preliminary requirements seem to be indicated in every case before a license should issue: (1) Full disclosure must be made to both applicants of all of the details of the case history of the applicant who has been mentally afflicted; (2) the court must be satisfied that such applicant has recovered sufficiently to adjust normally to the problems of everyday living, particularly those arising from the marriage relationship, and (3) the court must be reasonably assured that if children are born of the marriage, such children will be normal, healthy children, free from the taint of mental illness or deficiency.

With these principles in mind, let us examine the factual situation existing in the present case.

...

F.A. is 30 years of age. She was graduated from a Catholic parochial grade school and attended Little Flower High School for two years. She left school when she was about 17 years old and took a job in a hosiery mill, "sewing on piece-work." She continued in the hosiery industry until, apparently, the pressure of "piece-work" caused her to have a mental breakdown. She was hospitalized at St. Mary's Hospital in Philadelphia for a period of eight weeks with a diagnosis of dementia praecox. While in the hospital she received a full course of electric shock treatments, following which she received treatments as an out-patient until December 1953, when she was pronounced well. It appears, further, from the testimony that since her discharge from the hospital she has managed the household of her invalid sister satisfactorily and efficiently and has given no evidence of any recurrence of her malady.

...

After a careful study of the record in this case we make the following findings of fact:

1. That St. Mary's Hospital, Philadelphia, is an institution for persons who are insane or of unsound mind, within the purview of The Marriage Law of 1953;

2. That F.A. was an inmate of the mental department of that institution from April 16, 1951, to June 16, 1951;

3. That F.A. was an out-patient of the mental department of that institution from June 1951 until December 1953, when she was discharged as cured;

4. That F.A. is not at this time weak-minded, insane, or a person of un-sound mind;

5. That the male applicant is fully aware of the entire history of F.A.'s mental illness, and

6. That there is no compelling evidence that children, if any, born of this marriage will be mentally deficient or predisposed to mental illness.

This is a borderline case and we confess that we are beset with doubts. However, life at its very best is uncertain. Probably in a strictly disciplined society persons of defective mentality would be deprived of the blessings of matrimony. This, however, is an imperfect world. It is difficult to foretell the unhappy consequences which might result from our refusing to issue a marriage license in this case in view of the fact that the marriage banns have been posted, and all of the arrangements for the marriage have been made. The applicants are obviously in love with each other. If they cannot be married in this State, they may be tempted to live together without the benefit of marriage, or to seek a marriage license in another State where the restrictions are less stringent. Under all of the existing circumstances, we are of the opinion that it is for the best interest of the applicants and the general public to issue the marriage license.

COMMENTS

F.A. Marriage License is similar to a mandamus proceeding, although it is governed by local state statute and seems to have been initiated ex officio. Many states still require aggrieved parties who are refused a marriage license to file a formal action. There are other possibilities as well. Sometimes a lower-level judge, before refusing to issue a license may request an opinion of the state attorney general on the legal issues involved. Indeed, much law on questions relating to marriage licenses is hidden away in poorly indexed opinions of state attorneys general. Such matters are perceived not to be genuine judicial activities, but rather administrative tasks delegated in part to the courts. These are artificial classifications, and many activities of state attorneys general are quasi-judicial. According to the Pennsylvania statute in question, the judicial nature of the proceedings is more openly recognized.

Substantively, *F.A. Marriage License* is a mixture of archaic and progressive notions. While ultimately directing the clerk of the court to issue a marriage license in spite of the medical history of the female applicant, it did so only after elaborate and strained reasoning, using dated classifications such as "mental breakdown" and "dementia praecox." The court also appears to have been concerned about the fact that the applicant received "a full course of electric shock treatments." The classifications of the statute itself in reference to the weak-minded, insane, or persons of unsound mind are behind the times. On the other hand, the court recognized that no strict demarcations exist between mental health and illness and that, in the last analysis, insanity is more a social and legal term than a medical term. However, following the general judicial inclination, this progressive reasoning is only a preface to the statement that each case is sui generis and must be decided on its own facts. In effect this means that judicial discretion, rather than the actual language of the legislature, governs the outcome. More likely than not, as in this case, the marriage license will be granted.

Nevertheless, the opinion is retrogressive in many respects. The factual account of the seventeen-year-old working girl who, while sewing on piecework in a hosiery mill, had a mental breakdown, sounds as if it had been written in the nineteenth century. The court maximized language that stigmatizes persons who have been hospitalized and received shock treatment in mental institutions. That such stigmatization persists was demonstrated, within a political context, in the McGovern-Eagleton presidential campaign in 1972. When it became known that Senator Eagleton had a history of psychiatric treatment, he withdrew from the ticket. As recently as 1988, the allegation that the Democratic nominee for President, Governor Michael Dukakis, had seen a psychiatrist required specific denial. The requirements implicit in the findings of fact set forth by the court for issuance of a marriage license must also have a chilling effect on the parties and on future applicants. The court ungraciously told the female applicant that she was not "at this time" insane and that there was "no compelling evidence" that her children would be mentally deficient. The court also established a requirement that the other applicant, here the male party, must be fully informed of all the details of the medical history. It is conceivable that the process itself will encourage many parties to withdraw their request for a license or to decide to refrain from having children. Perhaps this was a calculated risk that the court was willing to take. Yet many states do not inquire into the mental conditions of the applicants at all, and severe character defects are usually not relevant to the capacity to marry.

Apart from the statutory requirements in Pennsylvania, the capacity to marry seems to imply a capacity to contract, at least in many jurisdictions. Yet even in this respect a minimum level of understanding, less than in ordinary contracts, appears to be considered sufficient. What is important, however, is the context in which this issue is likely to be raised. It would probably not be raised upon application for a marriage license, but more likely if the issue is divorce or annulment of a marriage already entered. Except in a rare instance like *F.A. Marriage License*, a license is usually granted without delay. The minor court officials who accept and process applications are not likely to ask searching questions and generally decide in favor of the couple. Mental institutions have been known to avoid potential complications by releasing patients who express an intention to marry. Much of the recommended procedure consists of treating patients as normally as possible and includes sex education and preparation for relationships that may result in marriage.

Thus inertia and design may lead to the common practical result that licenses to marry can be obtained without difficulty. As indicated above, the question of the capacity to marry is somewhat more likely to be raised successfully after the fact of marriage in the context of dissolution or annulment of marriage. The standards in such cases are not necessarily identical with those that apply, at least in theory, to the application for a marriage license. This is also the phase where attorneys are more likely to become involved.

REFERENCES

August de Belmont Hollingshead, & Frederick C. Redlich, SOCIAL CLASS AND MENTAL ILLNESS: A COMMUNITY STUDY (1958).

Note, *The Right of the Mentally Disabled to Marry: A Statutory Evaluation*, 15 J. FAM. L. 463 (1976–1977).

Annulment

WILKINS v. ZELICHOWSKI
Supreme Court of New Jersey
26 N.J. 370, 140 A.2d 65 (1958)

JACOBS, J.

...

The plaintiff and the defendant were domiciled in New Jersey as were their respective parents. They ran away from New Jersey to marry and they chose Indiana because they believed "it was the quickest place." The Indiana statutes provide that "females of the age of sixteen" are capable of marriage although they also provide that where the female is within the age of 18 the required marriage license shall not be issued without the consent of her parents. See Burns, Indiana Statutes Annotated, §§44-101, 44-202. After their marriage in Indiana on April 23, 1954 the plaintiff and defendant returned immediately to New Jersey where they set up their home. On February 22, 1955 the plaintiff bore the defendant's child. On April 22, 1955 the defendant, having been convicted on several independent charges of automobile theft, was sent to Bordentown Reformatory where he was still confined at the time of the hearing in the Chancery Division. On January 4, 1956 the plaintiff filed her annulment complaint under N.J.S. 2A:34-1(e), N.J.S.A., which provides that a judgment of nullity may be rendered on the wife's application upon a showing that she was under the age of 18 years at the time of her marriage and that the marriage has not been "confirmed by her after arriving at such age"; the statute also provides that where a child has been born there shall be no judgment of nullity unless the court is of the opinion that the judgment "will not be against the best interests of the child." Although the defendant was duly served he did not file any answer and he chose not to contest the plaintiff's proceeding.

The plaintiff's evidence adequately established that she was 16 years of age when she was married and that she did not confirm her marriage after she had reached 18 years of age and the Chancery Division expressly found that an annulment would be "for the best interests of the child"; nevertheless it declined to grant the relief sought by the plaintiff on the ground that the marriage was valid in Indiana and should therefore, under principles of the conflict of laws, not be nullified by a New Jersey court because of the plaintiff's non-age. In reaching the same result the Appellate Division recognized that the Chancery Division had ample power to nullify the Indiana marriage of the New Jersey domiciliaries (N.J.S. 2A:34-1(e), N.J.S.A.; *Scularekes v. Gullett*, 106 N.J.Eq. 369, 371, 150 A. 826 (Ch.1930); *In re Olcott*, 141 N.J.Eq. 8, 11, 55 A.2d 820 (Ch.1947)) but expressed the view that comity dictated that it should not take such action unless there was an imperative New Jersey policy (which it did not find) against marriages of 16-year-old females....

...

The vigor of New Jersey's policy against marriages by persons under the prescribed age is evidenced not only by the breadth of the statutory language but also by the judicial decisions....

It is undisputed that if the marriage between the plaintiff and the defendant had taken place here, the public policy of New Jersey would be applicable and the plaintiff would be entitled to the annulment; and it seems clear to us that if New Jersey's public policy is to remain at all meaningful it must be considered equally applicable though their marriage took place in Indiana. While that State was interested in the formal ceremonial requirements of the marriage it had no interest whatever in that marital status of the parties. Indeed, New Jersey was the only State having any interest in that status, for both parties were domiciled in New Jersey before and after the marriage and their matrimonial domicile was established here. The purpose in having the ceremony take place in Indiana was to evade New Jersey's marriage policy and we see no just or compelling reason for permitting it to succeed....

In the *Cunningham* case (206 N.Y. 341, 99 N.E. 848) the New York Court of Appeals annulled a marriage between New York residents who married outside the state to evade New York's age policy; the court expressed the view that the marriage was "repugnant to our public policy and legislation, and in view of the fact that the parties were, and ever since have been, residents of this state, our courts have the power to relieve the plaintiff by annulling the marriage." In the *Mitchell* case (63 Misc. 580, 117 N.Y.S. 676), the New York Supreme Court annulled a Canadian marriage of New York residents because the plaintiff was under the age of 18 at the time of her marriage; Justice Wheeler found that there was ample power in the New York court to annul the marriage though it was valid under Canadian law; in the course of his opinion he stressed that the New York Legislature had "seen fit in its wisdom to discourage marriages contracted by immature persons" and had provided for "the annulment of such marriages under certain circumstances and conditions," and he concluded that there would be neither reason nor justification for judicially permitting New York residents to evade the Legislature's age policy and defeat annulments contemplated by it.

...

...We are not here concerned with a collateral attack on an Indiana marriage or with a direct attack on an Indiana marriage between domiciliaries of Indiana or some state other than New Jersey. We are concerned only with a direct and timely proceeding, authorized by the New Jersey statute (N.J.S. 2A:34-1(e), N.J.S.A.), by an underage wife for annulment of an Indiana marriage between parties who have at all times been domiciled in New Jersey. We are satisfied that at least in this situation the strong public policy of New Jersey (see Restatement, Conflict of Laws §132(b), comment b) requires that the annulment be granted. The annulment will not render the plaintiff's child illegitimate (N.J.S. 2A:34-20, N.J.S.A.) and, as the Chancery Division found, it will be for his best interests. The annulment will also serve the plaintiff's best interests for it will tend to reduce the tragic consequences of her immature conduct and unfortunate marriage. The Legislature has clearly fixed the State's policy in her favor and has granted her the right to apply for a judgment nullifying her marriage; we know of no considerations of equity or justice or overriding principles of the law which would lead us to deprive her of the relief she seeks under the circumstances she presents....

Reversed.

...

COMMENTS

Wilkins has significance beyond the jurisdiction of New Jersey. It exemplifies a problem that may occur in various forms in any state, although the problem doenot pose itself as severely as it does in *Wilkins.* The issue is whether marriages contracted elsewhere to avoid local restrictions are to be recognized in the domiciliary state of the parties. Nevada, for example, is not only a state where people used to go for easy divorces, but also a jurisdiction attracting "migratory marriages." Most couples choose the state in which they will marry on convenience or social grounds — to be with friends and family or perhaps to avoid friends and family. Some people may consider it objectionable to be married by a judge or a minister, or they may wish to avoid burdensome formal restrictions such as waiting periods. Other people seek out-of-state marriage because their home state would not allow them to marry one another at all. A state's interest in having marriages of domiciliaries performed within its borders is substantially less than its interest in having a say in prospective divorces. Consequently, in many instances no question as to the validity of a marriage contracted out-of-state is likely to be raised. Usually a marriage valid where performed will be valid everywhere.

Teenage runaway marriages in neighboring states have long posed special problems. In a typical situation the young parties leave their home state for a day or two and falsify their ages across the border. Whether the neighboring laws are more lenient than the laws regarding the capacity to marry at home then becomes irrelevant. The license-granting officials in border towns are often less than ardent about checking whether requirements under their own laws have been complied with. Of course, criminal prosecution of applicants who falsify their ages in order to avoid restrictions of parental consent is theoretically possible. Such prosecution, however, would have to take place where the crime has been committed, and parties to a runaway marriage ordinarily leave the neighboring jurisdiction soon thereafter. The home state cannot prosecute because the crime was not committed there.

The question of whether a crime was committed and, if so, whether it can realistically be prosecuted anywhere, has to be distinguished from the issue of whether a valid marriage has been contracted at the place where the license was obtained. In *Wilkins*, for example, even under Indiana law a falsification of age must have occurred to avoid consent of the parents, at least in regard to the young woman. If Indiana authorities had been concerned with the matter, they might have concluded that the statutory requirements are merely directory and thus do not affect the validity of the marriage. Thus the marriage of the parties may have been valid under Indiana law regardless of what position is taken by New Jersey thereafter. *Wilkins* does not address itself to this problem because it assumes that only New Jersey had an interest in this matter. Probably no further complication arose because of the situation of the parties. In fact, the husband's being in a reformatory for automobile theft may have facilitated granting the annulment. Had the parties been of different social status, the legal issue of whether the Indiana marriage was to be recognized in New Jersey, not to mention other jurisdictions, might not have been as clearly decided in favor of an annulment. That the marriage had taken place four years earlier in another state and had resulted in the birth of a child could also be of significance.

Many states do not have legislation dealing with the possibility of annulment in case of underage marriages. On the other hand, many states do have statutes that provide for emancipation of minors upon marriage. Even a voidable marriage, since it is valid until voided, would have this effect. This could have a bearing on who has standing to sue for an annulment. It also could have a bearing on whether an annulment is possible at all. One could take the position that age requirements themselves, just as requirements for parental consent, are merely directory and that, in case of actual marriage, original common law should govern. That could mean that marriages are fully valid if the common law requirements of twelve years for the female party and fourteen years for the male party are met. We do not take the position that these arguments would necessarily prevail in any given jurisdiction. It could speak, however, for obtaining judicial dissolutions in runaway marriages of this kind before any new marriage is entered. Such precautionary divorces have functions comparable to actions in real property law to remove a cloud and to clear title. In other words, it is important for lawyers to realize that cases of this nature can never be clear enough, for practical purposes, to disregard what has taken place in another jurisdiction simply because that jurisdiction supposedly had no interest in the matter.

In the light of these problems *Wilkins* can be viewed as an effort to clear the record. The state statute did authorize an annulment action. Yet, at least in some cases of this nature the alternative of a divorce action may be more appropriate. In this instance, it would have conflicted less with possible interests of the state of Indiana in the integrity of its public records. Although complications are not likely to arise in the present case, they may arise if the states involved are in closer proximity and if property is involved. Not infrequently the validity of an underage marriage and of subsequent proceedings to avoid its consequences comes up years later in an inheritance situation. It should also be remembered that in *Wilkins* the husband was apparently in no position to answer. The case was therefore not truly contested. A lawyer representing the plaintiff should also consider, in counseling a party whether to file for annulment or divorce, that the full faith and credit consequences of an annulment might not be as clear as those of a divorce.

As seen from these perspectives, *Wilkins* is less persuasive than its strong pronouncement of policy makes it appear. The case also loses significance because of a change in mores. The need for marriage, and consequently the need to run away to neighboring jurisdictions for purposes of getting married, has declined. As unmarried cohabitation has increased and as parents have placed fewer restrictions on their adolescent children, the problem of teenage marriage has decreased and been replaced in public consciousness by the problem of teenage pregnancy. While these alternatives short of marriage may result in as many legal complications as underage marriage, they are of a different nature.

REFERENCE

Hans W. Baade, *Marriage and Divorce in American Conflicts Law: Governmental-Interests Analysis and the Restatement (Second)*, 72 COLUM. L. REV. 329 (1972).

BILOWIT v. DOLITSKY

Superior Court of New Jersey
124 N.J. Super. 101, 304 A.2d 774 (1973)

MCKENZIE, J.C.C.

On the representation of defendant that he was a practicing Orthodox Jew, plaintiff married him on January 23, 1971. Thereafter plaintiff discovered that defendant did not in fact adhere to the tenets of Orthodox Judaism and had misrepresented his religious connections to plaintiff because he was in love with her, wished to marry her, and was aware that she would not marry him otherwise. The marriage was admittedly consummated. Plaintiff seeks an annulment, and her cause of action is not contested.

Our courts have long required a more substantial quantum of fraud to entitle a party to an annulment where the marriage has been consummated than where it has not. Any kind of fraud which would render a contract voidable may be the basis for the annulment of a marriage similarly infected....

Where the marriage has been consummated, the fraud of defendant will entitle plaintiff to an annulment only when the fraud is of an extreme nature, going to one of the essentials of marriage....

As to what constitutes the "essentials" of the marriage relation, it has been observed that the guidelines are vague and not fully delineated by our decisional law.... This is as it should be. What is essential to the relationship of the parties in one marriage may be of considerably less significance in another. For this reason a determination of whether a fraud goes to the essentials of the marriage must rest upon the facts in each case....

Here plaintiff, corroborated by her rabbi, testified that she has been a deeply religious Orthodox Jew throughout her life. Her beliefs were made known to defendant and he, representing himself to be an Orthodox Jew, agreed to follow the requirements of that religion. As testified to by the rabbi, they are many and far-reaching, touching virtually all aspects of everyday life. Although for a few weeks following the marriage defendant adhered to them, it soon became apparent that he was not in fact an Orthodox Jew, and never sincerely intended to follow that religion. Plaintiff promptly separated from him.

The reported cases on this subject are meager. In both *Akrep v. Akrep*, 1 N.J. 268, 63 A.2d 253 (1949), and *Nocenti v. Ruberti*, 17 N.J.Misc. 21, 3 A.2d 128 (Ch.1933), our courts granted annulments where the defendant misrepresented his intention to enter into a religious ceremony of marriage following the civil ceremony. However, in both cases the marriage was not consummated.

Numerous cases in New York indicate that annulments have been granted under circumstances similar to those in the instant case.... This court is aware, however, that these decisions were reported during the period preceding the reform of the New York divorce law, and this court is satisfied that under the circumstances they should not be given great weight here at this time....

...

...To plaintiff the religious beliefs and convictions of her husband were essential to her marriage. She could not have properly performed the duties of a wife and mother, following the rules and teachings of her faith, without the support of a husband holding the same beliefs. Defendant, having substantially and knowingly misrepresented the same to her, and plaintiff having relief thereon in entering into the marriage, this court holds the fraud to which plaintiff was subjected to be "gross and far-reaching"....

That a subjective test may render more difficult the fact-finding process of the court should not prevent a litigant from obtaining relief where justice dictates. Our requirement that the fraud alleged must be proved by clear and convincing evidence should be noted....

A judgment for annulment of the marriage will be entered.

KOBER v. KOBER

Court of Appeals of New York

16 N.Y.2d 191, 211 N.E.2d 817, 264 N.Y.S.2d 364 (1965)

VAN VOORHIS, Judge.

This is an annulment suit. The question is one of pleading. The appeal presents solely whether the second cause of action in the wife's amended complaint is sufficient in law....

The material portions of this cause of action allege that the parties were married at New York City on June 28, 1963 (this annulment action was begun April 22, 1964) and that at and before the marriage the defendant husband falsely and fraudulently concealed from the plaintiff that he had been an officer in the German Army and a member of the Nazi party during World War II, and "was fanatically anti-Semitic; that he believed in, advocated, approved and even applauded Hitler's 'Final Solution' of the Jewish question, namely the extermination of the Jewish people; and that he would require plaintiff to 'weed out' all of her Jewish friends and to cease socializing with them." The next paragraph alleges that plaintiff married defendant believing him to be without fanatic anti-Semitism and without the belief that the Jewish people should be exterminated, "all of which he had at the date thereof, and during the marriage and all of which he expressed after and during the marriage so as to make the marital relationship unworkable." The next paragraph further alleges: "That plaintiff relied on defendant's apparent normal character, high moral beliefs and absence of fanatic anti-Semitism and would not have married him had she known prior to the aforementioned marriage that the defendant had been a member of the Nazi Party, was fanatically anti-Semitic, believed that all Jews should be exterminated, and that he would require plaintiff to cease socializing with all her Jewish friends, and had the defendant not been guilty of said fraudulent concealment."

A pleading, the sufficiency of which is being tested, "is deemed to allege whatever can be implied from its statements by fair intendment and the whole of it must be considered." (*Howard Stores Corp. v. Pope*, 1 N.Y.2d 110, 114, 150 N.Y.S.2d 792, 796, 134 N.E.2d 63, 66.) All of the allegations, for the purpose of such a motion, must be assumed to be true, and the cause of action must stand....

Bearing these principles in mind, we hold that this portion of the amended complaint states a cause of action. In *Shonfeld v. Shonfeld* (260 N.Y. 477, 184 N.E. 60) an annulment was granted...where the [husband] had stated that he was in no position to marry because he was not able to make a living, in response to which the defendant [wife] had stated fraudulently that, if it was merely a matter of sufficient money to establish him in a business of his own, she had enough, if such an opportunity presented itself. The opportunity did arise, but she refused to advance the money before marriage, and the trial court had found as facts that the representations thus made were false, were believed and relied upon, and induced the plaintiff's consent to the marriage, and that if they had not been made he would not have consented. The case reached this court in the posture that a decree of annulment had been refused upon the ground that these representations did not go "to the essence of the marriage contract."

The decree was granted in this court upon the ground that, if the true facts had been known to the husband, he would not have entered into the marriage. "The obligation of a husband to support a wife is no less lightly to be entered into than the other obligations of the marital relation. The ability to support is correspondingly important.... The business which defendant's mythical money was to establish was plaintiff's only prospect of supporting her. The misrepresentation was not a mere exaggeration or misstatement of her means or prospects, which might or might not be an incentive to marriage. It was a definite statement of an existing fact without which, as defendant clearly understood, no marriage was presently practicable" (*supra*, p. 482, 184 N.E. p. 62).

The development of the law of annulment was reviewed, the court pointing out (pp. 476-480, 184 N.E. p. 61) that the fraud need no longer "necessarily concern what is commonly called the essentials of the marriage *relation* — the rights and duties connected with cohabitation and consortium attached by law to the marital status. (*di Lorenzo v. di Lorenzo, supra* (174 N.Y. 467, 67 N.E. 63); *Beard v. Beard*, 238 N.Y. 599, 144 N.E. 908; *Domschke v. Domschke*, 138 App.Div. 454, 122 N.Y.S. 892). Any fraud is adequate which is 'material, to that degree that, had it not been practiced, the party deceived would not have consented to the marriage' (*di Lorenzo v. di Lorenzo, supra*, p. 471 of 174 N.Y., 67 N.E. 63, 64), and is 'of such a nature as to deceive an ordinarily prudent person.' (*Id.*, page 474 of 174 N.Y., 67 N.E. 63, 65.)" (See *Woronzoff-Daschkoff v. Woronzoff-Daschkoff*, 303 N.Y. 506, 511, 104 N.E.2d 877, 880). Although it is not enough to show merely that one partner married for money and was disappointed (*Woronzoff-Daschkoff v. Woronzoff-Daschkoff, supra*, 303 N.Y. p. 512, 104 N.E.2d p. 880), and the decisions upon the subject of annulment of marriage have not always been uniform, there have been circumstances where misrepresentation of love and affection, with intention to make a home, were held sufficient (*Schinker v. Schinker*, 271 App.Div. 688, 68 N.Y.S.2d 470), likewise in case of fraudulent misrepresentations concerning the legitimacy of children of the wife by a supposedly prior marriage (*Domschke v. Domschke*, 138 App.Div. 454, 122 N.Y.S. 892), or concerning prior marital status (*Smith v. Smith*, 273 App.Div. 987, 77 N.Y.S.2d 902). Concealment of prior marital status was held to be sufficient in *Costello v. Costello* (155 Misc. 28, 279 N.Y.S. 303), concealment of affliction with tuberculosis in *Yelin v. Yelin* (142 Misc. 533, 255 N.Y.S. 708) and *Sobol v. Sobol* (88 Misc. 277, 150 N.Y.S. 248); failure to reveal treatment of a mental disorder (schizophrenia, catatonic type) was held to be enough in *Schaeffer v. Schaeffer* (20 Misc.2d 662, 192 N.Y.S.2d 275); material misrepresentation of age in *Tacchi v. Tacchi* (47 Misc.2d 996, 195 N.Y.S.2d 892); fraudulent promise to become a United States citizen in *Siecht v. Siecht*, Sup. (41 N.Y.S.2d 393), where after years of married life the husband learned that his wife was a member of the Deutsche Bund and that her failure to become a citizen had been deliberate because of disloyalty to the United States. In *Laage v. Laage* (176 Misc. 190, 26 N.Y.S.2d 874), an annulment was granted to a wife by reason of the husband's false representation that he was a naturalized American citizen, after she had stated to him that she would not marry a German-born alien. In *Brillis v. Brillis* (207 Misc. 104, 137 N.Y.S.2d 32, affd. 3 A.D.2d 662, 158 N.Y.S.2d 780), a marriage was annulled where the evidence established that the defendant did not intend, at the time when he induced plaintiff's consent to the marriage, to establish a home for his wife and to support her, and that his purpose in entering into the marriage, unknown to plaintiff, was to facilitate his re-entry into the United States from Greece as a nonquota immigrant. In *Harris v. Harris* (201 App.Div. 880, 193 N.Y.S. 936), an annulment was granted on account of the concealment by the husband of previous criminal activities. A recent annulment suit in this court was *Sophian v. Von Linde* (22 A.D.2d 34, 253 N.Y.S.2d 496, affd. 16 N.Y.2d 785, 262 N.Y.S.2d 505, 209 N.E.2d 823 (July 9, 1965)). Although a third cause of action was sustained that the defendant misrepresented his intentions to have normal sexual relations with his wife, the first cause of action was also sustained (see opinion at Appellate Division, p. 35, 253 N.Y.S.2d p. 497) based on misrepresentation by the defendant of his age, origin and ancestry. We affirmed, notwithstanding the dissent of two Justices at the Appellate Division based on *Lapides v. Lapides* (254 N.Y. 73, 80, 171 N.E. 911) and other decisions holding or purporting to hold that misrepresentations of the nature alleged in the *Sophian* first cause of action were not vital to the marriage relationship.

Marriage is a civil contract (Domestic Relations Law, §10) and, as stated in *Shonfeld v. Shonfeld* (*supra*, 260 N.Y. p. 479, 184 N.E. p. 61): "The essentials of marriage as a civil contract are, therefore, (a) consent by (b) parties having statutory capacity to give it. Any lack in those essentials makes the marriage void (Domestic Relations Law, §§5 and 6) or voidable (*Id.* §7). If either party consents by reason of fraud there is no reality of consent. Hence the marriage is voidable (*Id.* §7, subd. 4) and an action may be maintained to annul it."

Under these principles, if the facts stated in the second cause of action of this amended complaint are true (as we are bound to assume for the purposes of this appeal), the trier of the fact might well conclude that there was no reality to the consent of plaintiff to this marriage. Allowing the pleading the broad construction to which it is entitled under the law, defendant had not merely been a member of the Nazi party and an officer in the German Army during World War II, which in themselves would be insufficient to sustain an annulment, but also, as an individual, he was fanatically anti-Semitic and supported the extermination of the Jewish people. In spite of the fact that he believed in, advocated and approved such genocide, he nevertheless, during courtship, according to the complaint, maintained an "apparent...absence of fanatic anti-Semitism" from which it would appear that, if true, he put on a false front to obtain plaintiff's hand in that he dissembled his genocidal beliefs by seemingly associating agreeably with Jews.

Plaintiff alleges that she relied on this, and would not have married him had she known his true nature, in these respects, which he manifested "after and during the marriage so as to make the marital relationship unworkable."

These allegations go beyond merely requiring "a wife, in order to preserve marital harmony, to give up friendships which she had made in the past", or asking the courts to "lay down a viable line of separation between political and philosophical views too extreme to be concealed during the courting relationship from those not so extreme which may be concealed intentionally or inadvertently without impairing the agreement to marry" as said by the Appellate Division majority (22 A.D.2d, p. 471, 256 N.Y.S.2d p. 618). A fanatical conviction, to be effectuated where possible through the mobilization of superior force, that a race or group of people living in the same community should be put to death as at Auschwitz, Belsen, Dachau or Buchenwald, evinces a diseased mind and makeup which parallels the ground for annulment stated in subdivision (c) of section 140 of the Domestic Relations Law, where a party to the marriage is an idiot or lunatic.

The continuation of defendant's addiction to this anti-social and fanatical objective after and during marriage, which had been concealed and inferentially misrepresented during courtship, would so plainly make the marital relationship unworkable in this jurisdiction, where the marriage was contracted, that it would depart from the realities to conclude that it was not essential to this married relationship, or that, to defendant's knowledge, plaintiff would have consented to the marriage without its concealment. At least the trier of the fact could so find if evidence is adduced to sustain the allegations of the second cause of action in this pleading....

We are not called upon at this stage of the litigation to determine whether plaintiff will succeed in establishing these allegations at the trial. She should not be denied her day in court, however, on the basis that it could not be found at the trial that the facts alleged, if established by evidence, would go to the essence of her consent to marry him.

The order appealed from should be reversed and that of Special Term reinstated, without costs.

...

COMMENTS

Bilowit illustrates some of the problems of actions for annulment of marriage as distinguished from divorce actions. The plaintiff wife proceeded under a theory that her marriage was void. The title of the case in the official reports reflects this theory. It is styled "*Anne Bilowit, falsely known as Ann Dolitsky v. Michael Dolitsky.*" The findings of the court are largely based on her pleadings and testimony, corroborated by her rabbi, that she had always been a deeply religious Orthodox Jew, and that the defendant husband induced her to marry by the fraudulent representation that he also was an Orthodox Jew. The outcome of the case, the entering of a judgment for annulment, may have been influenced by the fact that the husband did not contest the suit. As a result several issues that could have been raised remained in the dark, and others were somewhat summarily disposed of by the court in favor of the plaintiff wife. Although the point was not argued, an inference from the case is that the husband was in fact Jewish but, after an unsuccessful attempt of a few weeks to follow the requirements of orthodoxy, discontinued his efforts. This factor, if the case had been contested, could have affected the outcome in a direction of not permitting an annulment, perhaps under a theory that the plaintiff had not satisfied her burden of proof that a misrepresentation had taken place prior to marriage.

A traditional difference between actions for annulment and for divorce is that the grounds for annulment must have occurred prior to the marriage, such as preexisting insanity or fraud, often combined with an allegation that as a result marital consent has been impaired. Divorce, on the other hand, conceptually requires grounds that have occurred after marriage. In *Bilowit* this distinction could mean viewing the unsuccessful attempt of the husband to conform to orthodox customs in two contradictory ways, either as an attempted cover-up of a preexisting fraud or as a good-faith but failed attempt to live up to a marital promise. Only in the former situation of an attempted cover-up could the annulment action succeed. Since wrongdoing cannot be presumed, any uncertainty of fact ordinarily would have to be interpreted in favor of the husband. However, in practice the chancellor in equity, having jurisdiction in annulment actions, can do as he pleases, for example, by taking the position that the evidence submitted by the plaintiff wife was sufficient to prove her allegations. There is yet an additional difficulty to overcome, mentioned by the court, namely, whether the fraud was of an extreme nature going to the essentials of marriage.

This language, sometimes referred to as the Massachusetts rule, originates from *Reynolds v. Reynolds*, 85 Mass. (3 Allen) 605 (1862). It took the position followed in many jurisdictions that no misrepresentation as to character, fortune, health, or temper would support an annulment of the marriage, once it is executed. Rather, the misrepresentation must go to the essence of marriage, not to mere personal traits or attributes. A certain degree of misrepresentation, consequently, is considered excusable by *Reynolds*, and perhaps even permissible so that a person may be able, so to speak, to be rehabilitated from past weaknesses or misconduct through marriage. The startling aspect of this holding, which in *Reynolds* was meant to apply to sexual misconduct of women, is that it seems to establish at least an excuse to lie, provided that the misrepresentation does not go to the essence of marriage. The essence in turn was perceived mainly in terms of procreation. Although this holding has been criticized, it could be defended under traditional views of marriage. Basically it assumed that certain forms of misrepresentation are likely to occur in courtship when both parties are inclined to present themselves in the most favorable light. If any untruth in this context could lead to annulment actions at a later time, many marriages would be in jeopardy from the start. To translate this view into terms of contract law, it is like saying that materiality of the misrepresentation is lacking.

Bilowit, while purporting to apply the test of essentiality of misrepresentation, extends it to include matters of intense belief or feeling. Conceivably this could cover not only strongly felt religious beliefs but also personal predispositions of a less laudable nature. In this regard, courts are likely to reflect whatever might be considered in a given community as going to the essence of marriage. The more dubious aspects of such annulments are, however, somewhat mitigated by changed attitudes toward courtship. In fact this may mean that the rule as such — that the misrepresentation must go to the essentials of marriage — remains unchanged in form but is slowly given a different substantive content. The availability of no-fault divorce may also result in a change of approach and reasoning. A court in a situation comparable to *Bilowit* could, for example, take the position today that the allegations of the complaint merely state character flaws of the defendant husband, and the plaintiff consequently should be limited to claiming irretrievable breakdown of marriage. To avoid the need for filing new complaints, attorneys are inclined to combine requests for annulment with alternative requests for dissolution of marriage. A judge faced with these alternatives is likely to grant divorce rather than an annulment, simply because it appears to be the more customary remedy. Requests for annulment alone are rare and often involve cases in which one party, because of strong feelings, is particularly aggrieved. Perhaps also annulments are brought so that an effort can be made to revive a pension or social security benefits from a previous marriage.

Other reasons may speak in favor of abolishing annulment actions altogether. It is impossible to void long-term contractual relations retroactively. Too many factors may have changed from the time when the contract was entered. Thus even in case of annulment or rescission, a de facto relationship remains which in one form or other must be legally recognized. Courts and the legislatures have, for instance, provided that children should not become illegitimate in case of annulment. Furthermore, most defects in the marriage contract are increasingly viewed as resulting not in void marriages, but in marriages valid until voided. Thus, the differences between annulment and divorce decrease to the point that it becomes arguable as a matter of policy that dissolution for irretrievable breakdown of marriage should be the only available remedy. In effect this means that policies on marriage, as perceived by the state, lose ground and that the fate of the marriage increasingly depends on the parties themselves.

Kober has to be understood in the context of New York law which at the time permitted divorce only for adultery. This conservative approach resulted in judicial extension of annulment grounds. Whether any other jurisdiction would follow the reasoning in *Kober* appears to be doubtful. Yet an attempt could be made today if someone unknowingly married a person whose political views were so extreme as to evidence mental instability.

REFERENCES

Winston P. Nagan, *Conflict of Laws: Group Discrimination and the Freedom to Marry — A Policy Science Prologue to Human Rights Decisions*, 21 HOW. L.J. 1 (1978).

Willis L.M. Reese, *Marriage in American Conflict of Laws*, 26 INT'L & COMP. L.Q. 952 (1977).

Age Requirement

SHORT v. HOTALING

New York Supreme Court
32 Misc. 2d 933, 225 N.Y.S.2d 53 (1962)

BENJAMIN BRENNER, Justice.

The father and guardian *ad litem* of the infant wife seeks to annul her marriage, pursuant to section 7, subdivision 1 of the Domestic Relations Law. In the exercise of the discretion provided by that section, I believe that the dissolution here sought would not be in the public interest nor that of the married couple.

The facts as adduced upon the trial are as follows: In October of 1960, after dating one another for about a year, the girl, then 16, and the boy, then 19, eloped and married in the State of Virginia. On their return the following day, the parents of the boy accepted the situation, but not so the parents of the girl, who refused to allow them to stay in their home on the night of their return. After an unsuccessful attempt to separate them, the father suggested that the couple stay at a hotel, and on the following night both he and his wife brought them to another hotel to spend a second night together. Thereafter, the father finally prevailed upon his daughter to separate from her husband, to continue attendance at high school and remain at home. He unsuccessfully sought to prosecute the husband for abduction and, when, on a subsequent occasion, the couple contrived to be together at the home of the boy's parents, he again sought a solution through criminal action.

The couple cohabited at the time of their elopement as well as on the nights they stayed at the hotels. They probably also cohabited at the home of the husband's parents. Despite his disclaimer of knowledge, the further consummation of the marriage at the hotels should reasonably have been anticipated by the father. The husband is now of age and has taken part in the alteration of his parent's home to create a separate, if not a legally independent basement apartment, thus hopefully readying it for its prospective use by himself and his wife. He is capable of substantial earnings and, at the trial, appeared to me to be an upright, responsible individual who is most anxious to take on the burdens of married life and, when reunited, to adequately support his wife. So desirous is he of pleasing her and her parents that he has indicated a willingness to convert from Protestantism to Catholicism when so reunited. His love for her was freely professed in open court. The young lady, for her part, has made like professions of love for the husband. She appears to be quite dutiful, is now graduating high school and, except for the elopement and her understandable impatience, she has in large part exercised considerable restraint and complied with the wishes of her parents.

The marital status should be upheld, when the underaged persons involved show willingness and capacity for enduring marital life and for the building of a family unit (*Magee v. Nealon*, 108 Misc. 396, 177 N.Y.S. 517). This is the very discretion mandated by the section and repeatedly exercised in favor of validity when the circumstances so required.... It is also to be noted that while parental consent was here lacking, the consummation of the marital relationship was furthered by the father and mother of the wife when they suggested that the couple spend several nights together at hotels. This, it seems to me, constituted a measure of ratification of the matrimonial status (*Magee v. Nealon, supra*).

We know from our experience in the matrimonial courts that maturity of body alone is no sure foundation for a satisfactory marriage. What is needed is maturity of both body and mind, which quite often does occur in the case of a youthful couple while sometimes absent in people of age. Where it is present, as it is here, though it be a marriage without parental consent, the marriage deserves to be sustained.

Mindful as I am of all the reasons advanced by the father for the abrogation of the marriage, and giving due consideration to the duty of a parent to guide his child and to prevent her from an improvident marriage, I nevertheless find that the evidence presented by him upon trial offers little more than mere non-age and relentless opposition to the husband, which alone form no basis for the action.... This couple has now been forcefully parted for some fifteen months. Evidence usually needed to annul for non-age, similar to that which constitutes grounds for a decree of divorce or separation, does not exist. Nor do the circumstances warrant their continued enforced separation. They have already been sorely tried and they plainly deserve to put their marriage to the ultimate test of a single residence without parental interference, for which, in the light of their heartbreaking experience, they deserve the whole-hearted support of all involved.

The defendant is therefore entitled to a dismissal of the complaint. The motion for a counsel fee to him is denied.

Enter judgment accordingly.

LOVATO v. EVANS

District Court of Utah (3d District)
1 FAM. L. REP. 2848 (1975)

CROFT, J.

Plaintiff, 19 years old and not previously married, applied for a marriage license in the Salt Lake County Clerk's office which license was refused because plaintiff was a male under the age of 21 years and did not have the consent of his father, mother, or guardian to the marriage as required by Section 30-1-9 UCA as amended. Plaintiff asks the court to declare that section unconstitutional and to order defendants to issue a marriage license to plaintiff.

In 1975 the Legislature amended the statute on minority of children to read as follows: "The period of minority extends in males and females to the age of eighteen years, but all minors obtain their majority by marriage. It is further provided that courts in divorce actions may order support to age 21."

The legislature did not amend Section 30-1-9 which since statehood has fixed the age of applying for a marriage license without parental consent at 18 for females and 21 for males.

Prior to the 1975 amendment, Section 15-2-1 fixed the period of minority in males at 21 years and in females at 18. With respect to this statute the Supreme Court of the United States on April 15, 1975 ruled in *Stanton v. Stanton*, 43 L.Ed.2d 689, that in the context of child support the classification effectuated by Section 15-2-1 denied equal protection of the laws, as guaranteed by the Fourteenth Amendment. The *Stanton* case involved only the question of child support in divorce cases. The court said the test in *Stanton* was whether the difference in sex between children warranted the distinction in a father's obligation to support boys to 21 but girls only until 18 as drawn in Section 15-2-1 (before 1975 amendment). In reaching its conclusion that it did not, the court in *Stanton* said the section imposes "criteria wholly unrelated to the objective of that statute" for the need of support was equally great for girls as for boys.

In *Stanton* the court said it had held in *Reed v. Reed*, 404 U.S. 71.30 L.Ed.2d 225, that an Idaho statute (preference to males over females in probate matters) accorded different treatment on the basis of sex and that it "thus establishes a classification subject to scrutiny under the Equal Protection Clause."...

It thus appears that the test here, then, is whether the difference in sex between children warrants the distinction in the requirement of parental consent to a marriage of a male under 21 when it is required only for females under 18. In other words, is this classification "reasonable, not arbitrary" and does the classification "rest upon some ground of difference having a fair and substantial relation to the objection of the legislation?"

Undoubtedly, convincing arguments may be advanced on either side of the controversy. As one sits upon the bench of this court and witnesses the daily parade of divorce cases that are handled by the court, one longs for a means of making the stability of the home stronger and the marriage ties more lasting. But statistics in the past show that the divorce rate in Utah exceeds the national average and thus it does not appear that if the "object of the legislation" in Section 30-1-9 was to bring stability into marriage, it has achieved that goal....

If Section 30-1-9 be held constitutional, this case would thus appear to put a premium upon falsifying one's age when the required written consent is not forthcoming, for he who lies about his age and gets a license, even though he may be guilty of perjury (Sec. 30-1-10), may thus enter into a valid marriage while he who truthfully admits to being "under age" cannot get a license without the written consent and thus cannot marry. This hardly smacks of "equal protection," or at least of the kind that ought to exist....

As a judge I strongly oppose legislation by judicial fiat and I do not look lightly upon declaring existing statutes unconstitutional, particularly those of long standing. The Supreme Court of this state, or the United States or the legislature, should ultimately decide this question, but as a judge I cannot do other than declare the law as I believe it to be and to thus rule accordingly.

It is therefore my opinion that Section 30-1-9 denies equal protection of the law to males between the ages of 18 and 21 and is therefore unconstitutional and that the plaintiff is entitled to the relief prayed for in his complaint, subject, however, to a stay of one month from entry of judgment pending possible appeal by the defendants.

COMMENTS

A number of questions relating to teenage marriages, especially in the area of conflict of laws, were dealt with in *Wilkins v. Zelichowski* (see p. 502). Much in these cases depends on the wording used in an individual state statute establishing age limits for marriage. If such statutes use language to the effect that a state official or judge shall not issue a license unless certain requirements in regard to age and parental consent are met, it seems clear that no absolute bar to marriage is established. Such language appears to be directed toward the issuing officials who may be subject to state sanctions if they violate their obligations. To the extent that such statutes are silent, the traditional common law limits of twelve years of age for the female party to marriage and fourteen for the male may still apply. Even parental consent may be viewed as being irrelevant to the validity of a marriage, although it may be relevant to the question of whether the issuing official has violated his obligations. Popular opinion treats the age requirements for marriage as more important than statutes and case law necessarily do.

The practical power of parents and the state to "terminate" an underage marriage by physical separation of the parties should be distinguished from the legal validity of the marriage. In *Short* the teenage bride's father succeeded in separating her from her husband, although there was an initial period of cohabitation in hotel rooms. The father attempted sanctions, but without success. Even so, the practical power of the police to break up marriages should not be underestimated. Realistically, much erroneous parental and official behavior may acquire all appearances of law because there is no effective power to challenge it. In *Short* an unusually persistent young couple combined their efforts with those of a benevolent court to overcome practical obstacles to the marriage.

In many jurisdictions a parent's standing to sue for annulment on behalf of his or her child would be questionable, but New York has a statute that empowers the parent to bring such an action. The action failed not on procedural grounds, but because of the ways the facts were perceived by the court. The young woman's parents facilitated the consummation of marriage by permitting the couple to stay in a hotel together. Consummation, although the judge did not say it explicitly, involves sexual intercourse, which was presumed by the court in these circumstances. The courts have traditionally been inclined to give special weight to such consummation of marriage. Thus what may make the difference between a marriage subject to annulment and one that continues to be valid is the act of the parties that is presumed to have taken place in the privacy of the bedroom. Because of the continued legal significance of sexual intercourse in a marital context, attorneys should still inquire about this aspect in their interviews with clients. In *Short* the father's ratification was an additional concept in sustaining the marriage. Although the parties, at the time in question, did not have the power to ratify, the father himself ratified their conduct. Nevertheless it should not be overlooked that the court viewed the actions of the parties to the marriage in the most favorable light. Factors that could have spoken against them were neglected, for example, that in all probability the parties committed perjury in Virginia about their respective ages.

No perjury was committed in *Lovato.* The plaintiff, who had apparently remained in his home jurisdiction of Utah, had stated his proper age at all times. The objective of the suit was to declare that the different treatment of males and females in Utah in regard to parental consent is unconstitutional because it violates the Equal Protection Clause. In permitting the action, the Utah court set the stage for a broader national trend, namely, making the requirements of age for marriage equal for males and females. Any effort to apply the common law age limits of twelve for females and fourteen for males could be similarly challenged on constitutional grounds.

Yet again, both *Short* and *Lovato* appear somewhat dated in other respects. The behavior of the parties to the marriages no longer corresponds to contemporary mores. Young adults are more inclined to delay marriage regardless of the legal or constitutional situation. Consummation of marriage is also a dated concept because sexual intercourse prior to marriage is frequent. Although "consummation" continues to be stressed by the courts, it increasingly acquires elements of a legal fiction that, as in *Short,* facilitates reaching an equitable result.

REFERENCE

Lynn Wardle, *Rethinking Marital Age Restrictions,* 21 J. FAM. LAW 1 (1983).

Prisoner's Marriage

In re CARRAFA

California Court of Appeal
77 Cal.App.3d 788, 143 Cal.Rptr. 848 (1978)

REYNOSO, Associate Justice.

Petitioner, Victor Carrafa, an inmate at Folsom State Prison, by his *habeas corpus* proceeding challenges the actions of the Department of Corrections ("Department"). The Department has prohibited at least temporarily, his marriage with his fiancee, Joan Vibbard.

The right to marry is a statutorily recognized fundamental constitutional guarantee. The right was impermissibly infringed. Prison authorities erroneously ruled that denial of general visitation rights to the bride also justified the denial of the marriage request. We conclude that the Department must permit petitioner's marriage. Prison security may properly be considered by the Department in making arrangements for the ceremony.

Petitioner requested permission to marry his fiancee. The request, dated May 23, 1977, was to marry on June 29, the date already set for weddings. Permission was denied.

On June 4, 12 days after the request, a pistol and other contraband were found in prison. Petitioner was immediately placed in an isolated security unit. The next day he was informed in writing that he had been placed in the security unit pending the investigation. Prison authorities later advised petitioner that his "lock-up" was for his protection; they had received information that his murder was planned by other inmates. After 15 days, on June 20, petitioner was placed back in the general prison population.

Petitioner's fiancee's visitation rights were suspended apparently between June 20 and June 28. On the 28th she was advised in writing that the suspension was "due to information leading us to believe that you were involved [in] the smuggling of a firearm and narcotics" into prison. The suspension was also based on falsification of her residence address on the "visiting questionnaire."

Two further letters from prison authorities to petitioner's fiancee explained the suspension. During the investigation, according to a July 15 letter, "reliable information" revealed that she, Joan Vibbard, was involved in the introduction of large amounts of marijuana to the prison. Further, the method of introduction (hiding marijuana in prison service vehicle tire) was the same as that used to introduce the pistol. Secondly, the pistol found by prison authorities had been serviced prior to its introduction to prison. The repair "tag" listed Sharon Smith as the person who had the gun serviced. During that period the same address was used by Joan Vibbard. On July 25 yet another letter was sent. She was advised that she could not visit the prison until the investigation was complete. The letter explained that the investigation dealt with the "smuggling of a gun" and that she was "implicated" as being possibly involved.

In addition to the explanations contained in the letters, the record reveals that prison authorities had other information. They considered the inmate, whom they believed to be involved in the gun incident, petitioner's "associate." Further, no person by the name of Sharon Smith had been found who lived at the address listed on the "tag" at the time the pistol was serviced.

The petition to marry, as previously indicated, was denied. The letter sent Joan Vibbard dated July 25 also responded to her complaint that she has been unable to marry petitioner. She was told that she could renew her application to marry when her visitation rights were restored. The date of the actual denial is July 29, 1977; petitioner's uncontradicted assertion is that he was not advised until August 19. The denial appears on the bottom of the internal memorandum recommending approval of the "marriage request" the denial reads: "Denied. Bride not approved visitor."

Meanwhile, on July 27, petitioner filed a writ of *habeas corpus* before the Superior Court of Sacramento County. The writ was denied August 11, 1977. The petition for writ of *habeas corpus* before this court followed. As of December 15, the date of oral argument, permission to marry had apparently not been granted.

The right of prisoners to marry has been codified (Pen.Code, §§2600-2601.) Section 2601 declares: "Notwithstanding any other provision of law, each such person shall have the following civil rights: [...] (f) [t]o marry." Our Supreme Court has explained the historical setting of this statutory declaration: "We have, in this state, 'long since abandoned the medieval concept of strict "civil death" and have replaced it with statutory provisions seeking to insure that the civil rights of those convicted of crime be limited only in accordance with legitimate penal objectives.' [Citation omitted.] To that end, the Legislature, in 1968, amended the 'Civil Death' statute, section 2600, to provide that certain basic rights be retained by prisoners." (*In re Van Geldern* (1971) 5 Cal.3d 832, 836, 97 Cal.Rptr. 698, 700, 489 P.2d 578, 580.)

The right to marry is a fundamental constitutional right. (*Perez v. Sharp* (1948) 32 Cal.2d 711, 714, 198 P.2d 17; *Loving v. Virginia* (1967) 388 U.S. 1, 12, 87 S.Ct. 1817, 18 L.Ed.2d 1010, 1018.) The codification of that right emphasizes its fundamental nature. "The civil rights set forth in section 2600 are fundamental guarantees which may not arbitrarily be infringed." (*In re Van Geldern, supra,* 5 Cal.3d 832, 836, 97 Cal.Rptr. 698, 700, 489 P.2d 578, 580.)

A prisoner may not be deprived of such a right except "as is necessary in order to provide for the reasonable security of the institution in which he is confined and for the reasonable protection of the public." (Pen.Code, §2600.) Such a limitation is not a "straightjacket limiting the ability of the prison authorities to deal with institutional realities." (*In re Van Geldern, supra,* at p. 837, 97 Cal.Rptr. at p. 700, 489 P.2d at p. 580.) Rather "[v]alid and compelling institutional considerations may necessitate certain *limited inroads* upon the exercise of the prisoner's civil rights." (*Ibid.*; emphasis added.)

However, when state action infringes a fundamental right of the petitioner, the state action can be upheld only if necessary to effect an overriding governmental interest. The government must show that its interest cannot be satisfied by alternative methods less restrictive of the individual right abridged. Otherwise, the infringement must fail. (*Payne v. Superior Court* (1976) 17 Cal.3d 908, 914, 132 Cal.Rptr. 405, 553 P.2d 565.) As we explain below, the government has failed to meet that burden.

The Department argues that it is not depriving petitioner of the right to marry. Rather the marriage is delayed only until the conclusion of a pending investigation. The delay, the Department argues, is essential to prison security.

We disagree. We deal with the reality that delay prevents exercise of that right. (See *In re Harrell, supra,* 2 Cal.3d 675, 703, 87 Cal.Rptr. 504, 470 P.2d 640.) Denial of petitioner's right to marry does not appear to be the only alternative available to the state in protecting its legitimate interest in prison security. First, his fiancee indicated her willingness to submit to a body search and noncontact visits if that would improve prison security. Thus, the possibility of smuggled contraband is virtually eliminated. Second, the mere fact of marriage does not preclude the Department from excluding the marriage partner if it believes that there is a legitimate security risk. (Cal.Admin. Code, tit. 15, §3176.) The Department has failed to demonstrate the unavailability of any reasonable alternative to protect prison security.

As indicated, a spouse may be excluded when appropriate. Thus, we draw a clear distinction, not recognized by the Department in this case, between the right to marry and the right of visitation. The right to marry may not be impinged or delayed unless security is endangered at the time and place of the marriage. Visitation rights are quite another matter.

A writ of *habeas corpus* will issue directing the Department of Corrections to permit petitioner's marriage under such circumstances as will respect prison security.

TURNER v. SAFLEY
United States Supreme Court
482 U.S. 78 (1987)

Justice O'CONNOR delivered the opinion of the Court.

This case requires us to determine the constitutionality of regulations promulgated by the Missouri Division of Corrections relating to inmate marriages and inmate-to-inmate correspondence. The Court of Appeals for the Eighth Circuit, applying a strict scrutiny analysis, concluded that the regulations violate respondents' constitutional rights. We hold that a lesser standard of scrutiny is appropriate in determining the constitutionality of the prison rules. Applying that standard, we uphold the validity of the correspondence regulation, but we conclude that the marriage restriction cannot be sustained.

...

In support of the marriage regulation, petitioners first suggest that the rule does not deprive prisoners of a constitutionally protected right. They concede that the decision to marry is a fundamental right under *Zablocki v. Redhail*, 434 U.S. 374, 98 S.Ct. 673, 54 L.Ed.2d 618 (1978), and *Loving v. Virginia* 388 U.S. 1, 87 S.Ct. 1817, 18 L.Ed.2d 1010 (1967), but they imply that a different rule should obtain "in...a prison forum." See *Brief for Petitioners*, 38, n. 6. Petitioners then argue that even if the regulation burdens inmates' constitutional rights, the restriction should be tested under a reasonableness standard. They urge that the restriction is reasonably related to legitimate security and rehabilitation concerns.

We disagree with petitioners that *Zablocki* does not apply to prison inmates. It is settled that a prison inmate "retains those [constitutional] rights that are not inconsistent with his status as a prisoner or with the legitimate penological objectives of the corrections system." *Pell v. Procunier, supra*, 417 U.S., at 822, 94 S.Ct., at 2804. The right to marry, like many other rights, is subject to substantial restrictions as a result of incarceration. Many important attributes of marriage remain, however, after taking into account the limitations imposed by prison life. First, inmate marriages, like others, are expressions of emotional support and public commitment. These elements are an important and significant aspect of the marital relationship. In addition, many religions recognize marriage as having spiritual significance; for some inmates and their spouses, therefore, the commitment of marriage may be an exercise of religious faith as well as an expression of personal dedication. Third, most inmates eventually will be released by parole or commutation, and therefore most inmate marriages are formed in the expectation that they ultimately will be fully consummated. Finally, marital status often is a precondition to the receipt of government benefits (*e.g.*, Social Security benefits), property rights (*e.g.*, tenancy by the entirety, inheritance rights), and other, less tangible benefits (*e.g.*, legitimation of children born out of wedlock). These incidents of marriage, like the religious and personal aspects of the marriage commitment, are unaffected by the fact of confinement or the pursuit of legitimate corrections goals.

Taken together, we conclude that these remaining elements are sufficient to form a constitutionally protected marital relationship in the prison context. Our decision in *Butler v. Wilson*, 415 U.S. 953, 94 S.Ct. 1479, 39 L.Ed.2d 569 (1974), summarily affirming *Johnson v. Rockefeller*, 365 F.Supp. 377 (SDNY 1973), is not to the contrary. That case involved a prohibition on marriage only for inmates sentenced to life imprisonment; and, importantly, denial of the right was part of the punishment for crime. See *id.*, at 381-382 (Lasker, J., concurring in part and dissenting in part)(asserted governmental interest of punishing crime sufficiently important to justify deprivation of right); see generally *Mandel v. Bradley*, 432 U.S. 173, 176, 97 S.Ct. 2238, 2240, 53 L.Ed.2d 199 (1977)("Because a summary affirmance is an affirmance of the judgment only, the rationale of the affirmance may not be gleaned solely from the opinion below").

The Missouri marriage regulation prohibits inmates from marrying unless the prison superintendent has approved the marriage after finding that there are compelling reasons for doing so. As noted previously, generally only pregnancy or birth of a child is considered a "compelling reason" to approve a marriage. In determining whether this regulation impermissibly burdens the right to marry, we note initially that the regulation prohibits marriages between inmates and civilians, as well as marriages between inmates.... Although not urged by respondents, this implication of the interests of nonprisoners may support application of the *Martinez* standard, because the regulation may entail a "consequential restriction on the [constitutional] rights of those who are not prisoners." See *Procunier v. Martinez*, 416 U.S., at 409, 94 S.Ct., at 1809. We need not reach this question, however, because even under the reasonable relationship test, the marriage regulation does not withstand scrutiny.

Petitioners have identified both security and rehabilitation concerns in support of the marriage prohibition. The security concern emphasized by petitioners is that "love triangles" might lead to violent confrontations between inmates.... With respect to rehabilitation, prison officials testified that female prisoners often were subject to abuse at home or were overly dependent on male figures, and that this dependence or abuse was connected to the crimes they had committed.... The superintendent at Renz, petitioner William Turner, testified that in his view, these women prisoners needed to concentrate on developing skills of self-reliance...and that the prohibition on marriage furthered this rehabilitative goal. Petitioners emphasize that the prohibition on marriage should be understood in light of Superintendent Turner's experience with several ill-advised marriage requests from female inmates....

We conclude that on this record, the Missouri prison regulation, as written, is not reasonably related to these penological interests. No doubt legitimate security concerns may require placing reasonable restrictions upon an inmate's right to marry, and may justify requiring approval of the superintendent. The Missouri regulation, however, represents an exaggerated response to such security objectives. There are obvious, easy alternatives to the Missouri regulation that accommodate the right to marry while imposing a *de minimis* burden on the pursuit of security objectives. See, *e.g.*, 28 CFR §551.10 (1986)(marriage by inmates in federal prison generally permitted, but not if warden finds that it presents a threat to security or order of institution, or to public safety). We are aware of no place in the record where prison officials testified that such ready alternatives would not fully satisfy their security concerns. Moreover, with respect to the security concern emphasized in petitioners' brief — the creation of "love triangles" — petitioners have pointed to nothing in the record suggesting that the marriage regulation was viewed as preventing such entanglements. Common sense likewise suggests that there is no logical connection between the marriage restriction and the formation of love triangles: surely in prisons housing both male and female prisoners, inmate rivalries are as likely to develop without a formal marriage ceremony as with one. Finally, this is not an instance where the "ripple effect" on the security of fellow inmates and prison staff justifies a broad restriction on inmates' rights — indeed, where the inmate wishes to marry a civilian, the decision to marry (apart from the logistics of the wedding ceremony) is a completely private one.

Nor, on this record, is the marriage restriction reasonably related to the articulated rehabilitation goal. First, in requiring refusal of permission absent a finding of a compelling reason to allow the marriage, the rule sweeps much more broadly than can be explained by petitioners' penological objectives. Missouri prison officials testified that generally they had experienced no problem with the marriage of male inmates,...and the District Court found that such marriages had routinely been allowed as a matter of practice at Missouri correctional institutions prior to adoption of the rule, 586 F.Supp., at 592. The proffered justification thus does not explain the adoption of a rule banning marriages by these inmates. Nor does it account for the prohibition on inmate marriages to civilians. Missouri prison officials testified that generally they had no objection to inmate-civilian marriages...and Superintendent Turner testified that he usually did not object to the marriage of either male or female prisoners to civilians.... The rehabilitation concern appears from the record to have been centered almost exclusively on female inmates marrying other inmates or ex-felons; it does not account for the ban on inmate-civilian marriages.

Moreover, although not necessary to the disposition of this case, we note that on this record the rehabilitative objective asserted to support the regulation itself is suspect. Of the several female inmates whose marriage requests were discussed by prison officials at trial, only one was refused on the basis of fostering excessive dependency. The District Court found that the Missouri prison system operated on the basis of excessive paternalism in that the proposed marriages of all female inmates were scrutinized carefully even before adoption of the current regulation — only one was approved at Renz in the period from 1979-1983 — whereas the marriages of male inmates during the same period were routinely approved. That kind of lopsided rehabilitation concern cannot provide a justification for the broad Missouri marriage rule.

It is undisputed that Missouri prison officials may regulate the time and circumstances under which the marriage ceremony itself takes place.... On this record, however, the almost complete ban on the decision to marry is not reasonably related to legitimate penological objectives. We conclude, therefore, that the Missouri marriage regulation is facially invalid.

...

[Discussion of the constitutionality of the correspondence regulation is omitted.]

COMMENTS

In re Carrafa deals with the power of prison authorities to prohibit prisoners from marrying. To be distinguished is the question of the extent to which existing marriages are affected by conviction or imprisonment. *In re Carrafa* represents the modern view, emphasizing the prisoner's civil rights including his fundamental right to marry. California was more progressive in these respects than other American jurisdictions, many of which, until the Supreme Court decision in *Turner v. Safley*, upheld the right of prison authorities to refuse their consent to a prisoner's marriage virtually without review. A state statute, changed in 1968, facilitated the liberal decision in *Carrafa*. The more restrictive traditional view, expressed with a certain grimness, can be found in *In re Goalen*, 30 Utah 2d 27, 512 P.2d 1028 (1973), *cert. denied*, 414 U.S. 1148 (1974). An extreme, unlitigated case occurred in Florida, where two death-row inmates, Jessie Tafero and Sonia Jacobs, requested permission to marry. The petitioners, who had lived together for about three years, desired to legitimate their young child. The petition was denied by the Department of Offender Rehabilitation because, it was said, the marriage would serve no useful purpose and would be an inappropriate expenditure of tax money.

Somewhat related policy questions are involved in regard to the impact of conviction for crime on marriages. Throughout much of our history, conviction of a felony has been a special divorce ground. *In re Carrafa* mentions the concept of "civil death," which used to be applied to prisoners who had received a life term. Under this theory such prisoners not only were prohibited from marrying, but their existing marriages were perceived to be terminated. In spite of the changes signaled by *Turner v. Safley,* America's sentencing practices remain among the harshest in the Western world.

The result in *Turner v. Safley* was facilitated by the facts of the case. Because the prison officials regularly denied women prisoners' requests to marry while routinely granting similar requests from male prisoners, the Court was more easily able to find "excessive paternalism." Justice Stevens, in an opinion not reproduced here, pointed out that under the majority opinion, "an inmate...may marry another inmate, but may not carry on the courtship leading to the marriage by correspondence. " *Id.* at n. 15 (Stevens, J. concurring in part and dissenting in part). A traditional view is that marriage encourages men to settle down and become law-abiding, while the effect of marriage upon a woman is considered to depend upon the character of the man she intends to marry. While it is important to combat such sexist stereotypes, it is also striking what a high percentage of women in jail have been abused by their male partner and are in jail for a crime committed with him, for him, or against him. Testimony of "battered women's syndrome," widely admitted into trials in which a woman is charged with killing a man she asserts had regularly beaten her, is just beginning to be admissible when the woman is charged with a separate crime and raises the defense of duress.

A lawyer has to be concerned not merely with the law in his or her own jurisdiction but also with the legal myths, sometimes quite unsupported, that exist in the population. Perhaps as a result of theories of "civil death," many people believe that a felony conviction for a lengthy prison term frees the other party from marital obligations. The presumption of death after seven years' absence is also erroneously thought to be applicable in such cases if the conviction is for a term longer than seven years. Sometimes spouses remarry on the basis of a mistaken understanding of the law. Some authors have written in this context about "common law divorce," which is not actual law but a popular myth. This so-called "prison divorce" is only one illustration among many of how persons, because of their misinterpretation of law, feel free to remarry. It is the lawyer's obligation to be aware of the actual legal situation and at the same time of the ways in which it is reflected in the minds of clients who, in these kinds of cases, may well be from a lower-educated stratum of society.

REFERENCES

Meredith Blake, *A Call for the Extension of Expert Testimony on Battered Woman Syndrome to the Defense of Duress,* (Unpublished Manuscript, 1994)(on file in the UCLA Law Library).

Virginia S. Jordan, *The Doctrine of Common Law Divorce,* 14 U. FLA. L. REV. 264 (1962).

Shields, *Prison Director Bans Death Row Wedding,* GAINESVILLE SUN, Feb. 3, 1977, Sec. D at 1, col. 3.

Mental Competence

LARSON v. LARSON
Appellate Court of Illinois
141 Ill. App. 2d 467, 192 N.E.2d 594 (1963)

CROW, Presiding Justice.

This is an appeal by the plaintiff, Sidney F. Larson, from a decree dismissing a suit for want of equity on a complaint for annulment of a marriage between the plaintiff and the defendant, Myrtle Larson.

...

The pertinent evidence offered by the plaintiff disclosed that the plaintiff was 48 years of age and the defendant 39 years of age on March 21, 1950, the date of the marriage. The plaintiff had known the defendant for about two years, but had known her well for only about one month before the marriage. During that period he noticed nothing abnormal about her. He knew nothing of her having any mental disability, if she had any. A few months after the marriage the defendant once in a while thought police officers were watching her, although they were not. During the following months she thought the house was wired with electricity from which she was receiving electric shocks, but the house was not so wired. In the middle of the night some times she thought she heard people running around on the roof and around the house, but there were no people on the roof or around the house. In the night time on one occasion she ran to a neighbor's house where she was not known, and the police brought her home. The plaintiff thought it was a nervous condition. She ran away a second time. She was then committed to Elgin State Hospital for treatment on July 22, 1952, by the Winnebago County Court as a mentally ill person, incapable of managing and caring for her own estate. She was there about four months. Subsequently, on March 17, 1954, the County Court of Winnebago County, on the defendant's petition, found that she had recovered from her mental illness and was capable of caring for her own estate and restored her to all her civil rights. The plaintiff said she got along good for awhile. But, on November 9, 1956, she was again committed by the County Court of Winnebago County to the Elgin State Hospital, again as a mentally ill person. During the time between the first discharge and the second commitment, March 17, 1954 and November 9, 1956, she accused the plaintiff of having women around, when he did not, and sometimes said the police were watching her. Sometimes when the plaintiff came home from work she chased him with a broom. Once she locked him out of the house. The defendant had previously been married to another party and had been divorced by him on the ground of desertion in 1942. The plaintiff lived with the defendant as husband and wife until she was committed to the Hospital in 1952, and thereafter whenever she was at intervals permitted to come home on week-ends, and again after she was restored in 1954 and until the second commitment in 1956, and again thereafter when she was at times given conditional discharges on week-ends at home.

Dr. Curt Steffen, called as a witness on behalf of the plaintiff, testified that he was a physician and surgeon specializing in mental disorders. He had never personally examined or treated Mrs. Larson. She was diagnosed by some other doctor or doctors as a schizophrenic (apparently at the time of the 1952 or 1956 commitments), and, from an hypothetical question which took certain evidentiary facts into account alleged to have taken place before and after her marriage, he said all of her symptoms appeared to be schizophrenic symptoms, persecution ideas, delusions, and depressions. Such a psychosis usually starts earlier in life than 39 years of age he said. With this type of psychosis, he said, patients have so-called lucid intervals. Those intervals may last for months or even for years and then they go back into depression or insanity. Very few schizophrenics are cured, he said. They may be discharged from a hospital but after a time they have attacks again and have to be recommitted. He said he would assume she had been mentally sick for quite a while but she might not have had such outspoken symptoms that a layman would be able to recognize such as insanity. She might be all right for two years — a layman's cure. Outspoken symptoms usually come on very gradually. During the cross-examination, the doctor was asked:

> Q. Then is it your opinion, Doctor, that a schizophrenic can never be cured?
>
> A. I would say — I wouldn't say never, but I would say it is a rarity if they can ever cure a schizophrenic completely.
>
> . . .
>
> Q. Then is it your opinion a schizophrenic is in the way of medically always insane?
>
> A. One doesn't have to be insane. There are a lot of symptoms between sanity and insanity, and you cannot just say sane and insane. It might be legally all right, but medically it is very difficult to say.

A brother of the defendant's first husband (from whom she was divorced in 1942, 8 years before the present marriage) said that while she was married to his brother she would about once a year just flare up, not talk to anyone, and run off and leave her family. He said she just didn't act normally. Once after she was married to the plaintiff Larson this witness said she came to the witness' home and accused his oldest son of improprieties towards her — that was in 1958. He said at one Christmas time she was good one day and not the next. He had no trouble with her.

It is this medical testimony and the other evidence referred to that the plaintiff insists is sufficient evidence of insanity of the defendant on March 21, 1950 to justify decreeing an annulment of the marriage.

When the celebration of a marriage is shown, the contract of marriage, the capacity of the parties, and, in fact, everything necessary to the validity of the marriage, in the absence of proof to the contrary, will be presumed; the burden of proof was upon the plaintiff to show the marriage was invalid; to enable a party legally to contract a marriage he or she must be capable of understanding the nature of the act. *Flynn et al. v. Troesch et al.* (1940) 373 Ill. 275, 26 N.E.2d 91. When a marriage is shown the law raises a strong presumption in favor of its validity, and the burden is upon the party objecting thereto to prove such facts and circumstances as necessarily establish its invalidity; there is no clear dividing line between competency and incompetency, and each case must be judged by its own peculiar facts; the parties must have sufficient mental capacity to enter into the status, but proof of lack of mental capacity must be clear and definite; if the party possesses sufficient mental capacity to understand the nature, effect, duties, and obligations of the marriage contract into which he or she is entering, the marriage contract is binding, as long as they are otherwise legally competent to enter into the relation. *Ertel v. Ertel* (1942) 313 Ill.App. 326, 40 N.E.2d 85. A marriage contract will be invalidated by the want of consent of capable persons; it requires the mutual consent of two persons of sound mind, and if at the time one is mentally incapable of giving an intelligent consent to what is done, with an understanding of the obligations assumed, the solemnization is a mere idle ceremony — they must be capable of entering understandingly into the relation.... It is impossible to prescribe a definite rule by which the mental condition as to sanity or insanity in regard to a marriage can in every case be tested; the question is not altogether of brain quantity or quality in the abstract, but whether the mind could and did act rationally regarding the precise thing in contemplation — marriage — and the particular marriage in dispute — not whether his or her conduct was wise, but whether it proceeded from a mind sane as respects the particular thing done....

The decree here is not contrary to the manifest weight of the evidence or to the law. Prior to and at the time of the marriage the plaintiff noticed nothing abnormal about the defendant. There is no evidence that any of the unusual things she thought and did some months after the marriage had also occurred prior to and at the time of the marriage. Her first commitment to Elgin State Hospital was in 1952, more than two years after the marriage. In 1954 she was found to have recovered and was restored to all her civil rights. She got along good for awhile thereafter. Her second commitment was in 1956, more than four and one-half years after the marriage. The plaintiff continued to live regularly with the defendant as husband and wife except for such times as she was actually physically confined at the Hospital. The doctor who testified had never examined, or treated the defendant and his entire testimony is based, necessarily, on an hypothetical question. The ostensible diagnosis was evidently made by another or other doctors, who were not available or did not testify here. No doctor, nurse, or attendant at the Hospital who might have observed, examined, or treated her testified. In this doctor's opinion, even, a patient of that type may have lucid intervals for months or years — she may not have had any symptoms which a layman would recognize as insanity — she might be all right for years — and he would not say a patient of such type could never be cured. Even he said such a patient might be legally all right — not legally insane — though medically it may be very difficult to say. The other witness' testimony was either quite remote in point of time, or related to an incident eight years after the marriage, or had to do with matters having no great legal significance.

The plaintiff has not satisfied the burden or proving, clearly and definitely, that the defendant was an "insane person" at the particular time of this marriage, March 21, 1950 — that she was at that time incapable of understanding the nature of the act, that she had insufficient mental capacity to enter into the status and understand the nature, effect, duties, and obligations of the marriage contract, that she was mentally incapable of giving an intelligent, understanding consent, or that her mind could not and did not act rationally regarding the precise thing in contemplation, marriage, and this particular marriage in dispute.

The decree is correct and it will be affirmed.

COMMENTS

Theoretically, as the court states in *Larson*, marriage requires the mutual consent of two persons of sound mind; otherwise the solemnization of marriage "is a mere idle ceremony." Yet the capacity to contract is not necessarily identical with the capacity to marry; a more lenient standard may be applied to the latter. Furthermore, the substantive requirement of insanity of one of the spouses for purposes of an annulment action is not necessarily identical with the psychiatric conceptions of mental illness. Thus considerable diversification in analysis is possible. A person may be sane for purposes of entering a marriage, but not necessarily for entering a major contract of a commercial nature; and the medical characterization may vary for either legal classification. The legal conceptions of insanity are also, as are many legal terms, based on an implicit dichotomy of reasoning — that a person either is or is not sane for a particular purpose. As the expert stated in *Larson*, medical judgment is more tentative for a variety of reasons, one of which being that doctors are not concerned with solving specific issues. Further complications arise, as in *Larson*, from the psychiatric classification of schizophrenia, which includes a wide range of human behavior.

Although legal and medical classifications may vary in an individual case as well as in general, courts have developed procedural devices that facilitate an adjustment between differing professional judgments in law and medicine. In *Larson*, for example, the court concluded that the plaintiff had not satisfied the burden of proof that the defendant was "clearly and definitely" an insane person. A rule of evidence, rather than a substantive legal rule of insanity, permitted the court to reach a conclusion that can be compared in its tentative nature to the substantive medical diagnosis. While the evaluation of the psychiatric condition of the defendant wife remained inconclusive, for legal purposes a definite outcome of the litigation was still assured: the plaintiff lost. The lesson to be learned for legal analysis is that controversies have to be analyzed in their totality, including all aspects of substantive and procedural law. To the practicing lawyer this reflects the common experience that except for appellate strategy it does not matter whether it is on procedural grounds or on substantive ones that a case is won or lost.

There is also an aspect of laches in *Larson*. More than ten years had elapsed after the marriage. The defendant wife had been in and out of mental hospitals and, during this time, cohabitation between her and the plaintiff husband had taken place. Contrary to older views, even if one assumes that the wife was insane at the time of marriage, the marriage would be considered to be merely voidable. This means in effect that the marriage was valid, and continued to be valid after the husband had lost his remedy of annulment by his conduct. The court did not stress this point, but it may have helped in coming to the conclusion that the complaint was to be dismissed. Here too there is a procedural side of a related nature. The plaintiff's lawyer had prepared the case poorly. He tried to prove his case by posing hypothetical questions to an expert who had never examined the defendant wife. Obviously better evidence was available but he neglected to pursue it. For example, he could have requested the doctors and nurses who had actually treated the wife to testify.

Today an additional aspect has to be considered: the impact of grounds for dissolution of marriage on annulment actions. Conceptually the two types of remedies have nothing to do with each other because dissolution arises from facts that occur after a marriage has been entered while annulment actions relate to facts prior to marriage. Nevertheless, courts can hardly overlook that even in no-fault jurisdictions a dissolution of marriage for insanity is regularly possible only if very specific and stringent statutory conditions have been met. If in comparison annulment were easily available without such conditions, plaintiffs could choose this avenue in an effort to avoid the pitfalls of dissolution, especially the obligation to support one's ex-spouse. This does not mean of course that the same conditions have to be met in annulment actions that apply to divorce for insanity, but a court may again use stringent standards of proof as a means of reaching similar results.

Incestuous Marriage

ISRAEL v. ALLEN

Supreme Court of Colorado
195 Colo. 263, 577 P.2d 762 (1978)

PRINGLE, Chief Justice.

This is an appeal from a decision of the District Court of Jefferson County holding a provision of the Colorado Uniform Marriage Act unconstitutional as violative of equal protection of the laws. We affirm.

Plaintiffs, Martin Richard Israel and Tammy Lee Bannon Israel, are brother and sister related by adoption and are not related by either the half or the whole blood.

Raymond Israel (the natural father of Martin Richard Israel) and Sylvia Bannon (the natural mother of Tammy Lee Bannon Israel) were married on November 3, 1972. At the time of their marriage, Martin was 18 years of age and was living in the State of Washington; Tammy was 13 years of age and was living with her mother in Denver, Colorado. Raymond Israel adopted Tammy on January 7, 1975.

Plaintiffs desire to be married in the State of Colorado. Defendant, Clerk and Recorder of Jefferson County, however, denied plaintiffs a license to marry based on section 14-2-110(1)(b), C.R.S.1973:

> *Prohibited marriages.* (1) The following marriages are prohibited:...(b) A marriage between an ancestor and a descendant or between a brother and sister, whether the relationship is by the half or the whole blood or by adoption....

A complaint seeking declaratory relief was filed in the district court. The district court found that marriage is a fundamental right and that no compelling state interest is furthered by prohibiting marriage between a brother and sister related only by adoption. Thus, the court held that that part of section 14-2-110(1)(b) which prohibited the marriage of a brother and sister by adoption was unconstitutional as a denial of equal protection and, therefore, severed from the statute the words "or by adoption."

I

At the outset, there is an issue as to whether or not marriage is a fundamental right in Colorado. See, *Beeson v. Kiowa County School District*, Colo.App., 567 P.2d 801 (1977). If it is, defendant must show a compelling state interest in order to justify the unequal treatment of adopted brothers and sisters under the statute. Since we find, however, that the provision prohibiting marriage between adopted children fails even to satisfy minimum rationality requirements, we need not determine whether a fundamental right is infringed by this statute.

While the practice of adoption is an ancient one, the legal regulation of adoptive relationships in our society is strictly statutory in nature. The legislative intent in promulgating statutes concerning adoption was, in part, to make the law affecting adopted children in respect to equality of inheritance and parental duties *in pari materia* with that affecting natural children. It is clear, however, that adopted children are not engrafted upon their adoptive families for all purposes. See, *e.g.*, the criminal incest statute, section 18-6-301, C.R.S.1973, which does not include sexual relationships between adopted brother and sister.

Nonetheless, defendant argues that this marriage prohibition provision furthers a legitimate state interest in family harmony. See, section 14-2-102(2)(a), C.R.S.1973. We do not agree. As the instant case illustrates, it is just as likely that prohibiting marriage between brother and sister related by adoption will result in family discord.[2] While we are not, strictly speaking, dealing with an affinity based relationship in this case,[3] we find the following analysis equally applicable to the situation presently before us:

> According to the English law, relationship by affinity was an impediment to marriage to the same extent and in the same degree of consanguinity. While this principle, derived from the ecclesiastically administered canon law, still strongly persists in England, in the United States the statutory law governing the marriage relationship nowhere so sweepingly condemns the marriage of persons related only by affinity.... The objections that exist against consanguineous marriages are not present where the relationship is merely by affinity. The physical detriment to the offspring of persons related by blood is totally absent. The natural repugnance of people toward marriages of blood relatives, that has resulted in well-nigh universal moral condemnation of such marriages, is quite generally lacking in application to the union of those related only by affinity. It is difficult to construct any very logical case for the prohibition of marriage on grounds of affinity... 1 *Vernier, American Family Laws* 183.

We hold that it is just as illogical to prohibit marriage between adopted brother and sister.

II

Defendant next argues that the trial court erred in its holding that the provision of section 14-2-110(1)(b), C.R.S.1973, in question here is severable from that

2. Plaintiff's parents filed affidavits indicating that they had no objection to the proposed marriage and, in fact, were in favor of the marriage. In addition, Bishop Evans of the Roman Catholic Archdiocese of Denver filed an affidavit stating that the Church had no objection to the proposed marriage.

3. An affinity based relationship is that which one spouse because of marriage has to blood relatives of the other. BLACK'S LAW DICTIONARY (4th ed.).

portion of section 14-2-110(1)(b), C.R.S.1973, prohibiting marriage between a brother and sister related by the half or whole blood. We disagree.

. . .

The prohibition against marriage between a brother and sister related by the half or whole blood is complete in itself and in no way depends upon the stricken provision. Thus, the trial court did not err in holding that this statute was severable.

The judgment of the district court is affirmed.

In re MEW and MLB
Pennsylvania Court of Common Pleas
4 Pa. D. & C.3d 51, 3 FAM. L. REP. 2602 (1977)

The question to be determined on this record is whether two persons who are unrelated by blood but who become brother and sister by reason of an adoption of the male applicant by the natural mother of the female applicant may lawfully obtain a license to marry under the provisions of "The Marriage Law," Act of August 22, 1953, P.L. 1344, Sec. 5, 48 P.S. 1-5....

...[T]here being no specific statutory prohibition of a marriage between two persons who are brother and sister by adoption, we come face to face with the proposition as to whether this relationship constitutes an impediment which bars the issuance of a marriage license in Pennsylvania.

The policy of the law of the Commonwealth is to impose upon adopted children all of the rights and duties of a natural child of an adoptive parent or parents. Correspondingly, an adopted child has imposed upon him or her all of the obligations and disabilities which accompany the relationship of parent and child....

The hearing judge, in the case at bar, perceives the present application for a license to marry to be an entirely different problem than the one presented in *Enderle,* [1 D.&C. 2d 114]. Here the applicants are brother and sister by reason the male applicant's adoption by the mother of the female applicant. While the applicants did not live and grow up together in the same household from early childhood, they have for at least part of their lives lived together as brother and sister in the family residence of their respective parents. An important consideration in this case is the integrity of the family which the law has a duty to protect. To authorize and encourage marriages of brothers and sisters by adoption would undermine the fabric of family life and would be the antithesis of the social aims and purposes which the adoption process is intended to serve.

The hearing judge holds that an adoption imposes on an adopted child a constructive relationship with the natural children of his adoptive parent equal to a relationship by consanguinity. In these circumstances the Court is obliged to sustain the action of the Clerk of the Orphan's Court Division, who has refused to issue a marriage license in this case. — BOYLE, J.

Concurrence: I agree with the result reached by Judge Boyle and join in his decree sustaining the refusal of the requested marriage license. Here, as in *Enderle,* 1 D&C 2nd 114, there appears at first blush no reason to prevent the marriage of the above applicants since their relationship arises from adoption and is not based on consanguinity. There are, however, other complex facets inherent in this matter, one of which concerned both Judge Boyle and Judge Klein, Judge Klein expressing his concern by stating that the sanctity of the home should be maintained and there should not be competition for sexual companionship between members of the same household or family, while Judge Boyle indicated that the duty of the law is to protect the integrity of the family with the law not encouraging marriages of brothers and sisters by adoption as this would undermine the family life and be antithesis of the adoption process purpose.

To this I would add my concern that if this license is granted, the marriage code will have preference over the adoption act. The adoption act makes the applicants brother and sister and since a man may not marry his sister, to hold that the marriage code means only a man and his sister by blood, would make the adoption process meaningless for the purposes of marriage. A person should not be able to consent to an adoption, receive the benefits of an adoption and then pretend that the adoption does not exist or does not affect the family relationship all for the purpose of obtaining a marriage license. — ZAVARELLA, J.

Dissent: The majority deny the parties the right to marry on the ground that the marriage "would undermine the fabric of family life and would be the antithesis of the social aim and purposes which the adoption process is intended to serve."

I do not believe that this would follow if a license were to be issued in the case at bar. Prior to the wedding above referred to, the parties were as strangers to each other. The fact that they lived in the same household for "a short period" in 1973 does not in my judgment make them "*de facto*" brother and sister. This is not a case where a male infant and a female infant were adopted and raised to maturity by the adopting parents in the same household. In a case of this nature the reasoning of the majority might be applicable.

The parties are not related by blood or affinity. Therefore, there is in law no obstacle to their marriage.

The purpose of the adoption law is to provide a secure home and loving parents to a child not wanted, or abandoned by his natural parents. I do not believe it should be construed in such a manner as to prevent a marriage between two persons, who, I believe, are legally entitled to marry. Therefore, I dissent. — MCKENNA, J.

In re MAY'S ESTATE

Court of Appeals of New York
305 N.Y. 486, 114 N.E.2d 4 (1953)

LEWIS, Chief Judge.

In this proceeding, involving the administration of the estate of Fannie May, deceased, we are to determine whether the marriage in 1913 between the respondent Sam May and the decedent, who was his niece by the half blood which marriage was celebrated in Rhode Island, where concededly such marriage is valid is to be given legal effect in New York where statute law declares incestuous and void a marriage between uncle and niece. Domestic Relations Law, §5, subd. 3, McK.Consol. Laws.

The question thus presented arises from proof of the following facts: The petitioner Alice May Greenberg, one of six children born of the Rhode Island marriage of Sam and Fannie May, petitioned in 1951 for letters of administration of the estate of her mother Fannie May, who had died in 1945. Thereupon, the respondent Sam May, who asserts the validity of his marriage to the decedent, filed an objection to the issuance to petitioner of such letters of administration upon the ground that he is the surviving husband of the decedent and accordingly, under section 118 of the Surrogate's Court Act, he has the paramount right to administer her estate. Contemporaneously with, and in support of the objection filed by Sam May, his daughter Sirel Lenrow and his sons Harry May and Morris B. May who are children of the challenged marriage filed objections to the issuance of letters of administration to their sister, the petitioner, and by such objections consented that letters of administration be issued to their father Sam May.

The petitioner, supported by her sisters Ruth Weisbrout and Evelyn May, contended throughout this proceeding that her father is not the surviving spouse of her mother because, although their marriage was valid in Rhode Island, the marriage never had validity in New York where they were then resident and where they retained their residence until the decedent's death.

The record shows that for a period of more than five years prior to his marriage to decedent the respondent Sam May had resided in Portage, Wisconsin; that he came to New York in December, 1912, and within a month thereafter he and the decedent both of whom were adherents of the Jewish faith went to Providence, Rhode Island, where, on January 21, 1913, they entered into a ceremonial marriage performed by and at the home of a Jewish rabbi. The certificate issued upon that marriage gave the age of each party as twenty-six years and the residence of each as "New York, N.Y." Two weeks after their marriage in Rhode Island the respondent May and the decedent returned to Ulster County New York, where they lived as man and wife for thirty-two years until the decedent's death in 1945. Meantime the six children were born who are parties to this proceeding.

A further significant item of proof to which more particular reference will be made was the fact that in Rhode Island on January 21, 1913, the date of the marriage here involved, there were effective statutes which prohibited, the marriage of an uncle and a niece, *excluding*, however, those instances of which the present case is one where the marriage solemnized is between persons of the Jewish faith within the degrees of affinity and consanguinity allowed by their religion.

In Surrogate's Court, where letters of administration were granted to the petitioner, the Surrogate ruled that although the marriage of Sam May and the decedent in Rhode Island in 1913 was valid in that State, such marriage was not only void in New York as opposed to natural law but is contrary to the provisions of subdivision 3 of section 5 of the Domestic Relations Law. Accordingly the Surrogate concluded that Sam May did not qualify in this jurisdiction for letters of administration as the surviving spouse of the decedent.

...

We regard the law as settled that, subject to two exceptions presently to be considered, and in the absence of a statute expressly regulating within the domiciliary State marriages solemnized abroad, the legality of a marriage between persons *sui juris* is to be determined by the law of the place where it is celebrated. *Van Voorhis v. Brintnall*, 86 N.Y. 18, 24....

In *Van Voorhis v. Brintnall*, *supra*, the decision turned upon the civil status in this State of a divorced husband and his second wife whom he had married in Connecticut to evade the prohibition of a judgment of divorce which, pursuant to New York law then prevailing, forbade his remarriage until the death of his former wife. In reaching its decision, which held valid the Connecticut marriage there involved, this court noted the fact that in the much earlier case of *Decouche v. Savetier*, 1817, 3 Johns.Ch. 190, 211, Chancellor Kent had recognized the general principle "...that the rights dependent upon nuptial contracts, are to be determined by the *lex loci*." Incidental to the decision in *Van Voorhis v. Brintnall, supra*, which followed the general rule that "...recognizes as valid a marriage considered valid in the place where celebrated", *Id.*, 86 N.Y. at page 25, this court gave careful consideration to, and held against the application of two exceptions to that rule *viz.*, cases within the prohibition of positive law; and cases involving polygamy or incest in a degree regarded generally as within the prohibition of natural law.

We think the Appellate Division in the case as bar rightly held that the principle of law which ruled *Van Voorhis v. Brintnall* and kindred cases cited, *supra*, was decisive of the present case and that neither of the two exceptions to that general rule is here applicable.

The statute of New York upon which the appellants rely is subdivision 3 of section 5 of the Domestic Relations Law which, insofar as relevant to our problem, provides:

> §5. *Incestuous and void marriages*
>
> A marriage is incestuous and void whether the relatives are legitimate or illegitimate between either:
>
> 1. ...
>
> 2. ...
>
> 3. An uncle and niece or an aunt and nephew.
>
> If a marriage prohibited by the foregoing provisions of this section be solemnized it shall be void, and the parties thereto shall each be fined not less than fifty nor more than one hundred dollars and may, in the discretion of the court in addition to said fine, be imprisoned for a term not exceeding six months. Any person who shall knowingly and wilfully solemnize such marriage, or procure or aid in the solemnization of the same, shall be deemed guilty of a misdemeanor and shall be fined or imprisoned in like manner.

Although the New York statute quoted above declares to be incestuous and void a marriage between an uncle and a niece and imposes penal measures upon the parties thereto, it is important to note that the statute does not by express terms regulate a marriage solemnized in another State where, as in our present case, the marriage was concededly legal. In the case at hand, as we have seen, the parties to the challenged marriage were adherents of the Jewish faith which, according to Biblical law and Jewish tradition made the subject of proof in this case permits a marriage between an uncle and a niece; they were married by a Jewish rabbi in the State of Rhode Island where, on the date of such marriage in 1913 and ever since, a statute forbidding the marriage of an uncle and a niece was expressly qualified by the following statutory exceptions appearing in 1913 in Rhode Island General Laws, tit. XXIV, ch. 243, §§4, 9; now tit. XXXVI, ch. 415, §§4, 9:

> §4. The provisions of the preceding sections shall not extend to, or in any way affect, any marriage which shall be solemnized among the Jews, within the degrees of affinity or consanguinity allowed by their religion.

...

As section 5 of the New York Domestic Relations Law (quoted *supra*) does not expressly declare void a marriage of its domiciliaries solemnized in a foreign State where such marriage is valid, the statute's scope should not be extended by judicial construction. *Van Voorhis v. Brintnall, supra*, 86 N.Y. at page 33. Indeed, had the Legislature been so disposed it could have declared by appropriate enactment that marriages contracted in another State — which if entered into here would be void — shall have no force in this State.... Although examples of such legislation are not wanting, we find none in New York which serve to give subdivision 3 of section 5 of the Domestic Relations Law extraterritorial effectiveness. *Van Voorhis v. Brintnall, supra*, 86 N.Y. at pages 25–37. Accordingly, as to the first exception to the general rule that a marriage valid where performed is valid everywhere, we conclude that, absent any New York statute expressing clearly the Legislature's intent to regulate within this State marriages of its domiciliaries solemnized abroad, there is no "positive law" in this jurisdiction which serves to interdict the 1913 marriage in Rhode Island of the respondent Sam May and the decedent.

As to the application of the second exception to the marriage here involved — between persons of the Jewish faith whose kinship was not in the direct ascending or descending line of consanguinity and who were not brother and sister we conclude that such marriage, solemnized, as it was, in accord with the ritual of the Jewish faith in a State whose legislative body has declared such a marriage to be "good and valid in law," was not offensive to the public sense of morality to a degree regarded generally with abhorrence and thus was not within the inhibitions of natural law.

...

The decree [granting Sam May letters of administration] should be affirmed, with one bill of costs to respondents, payable out of the estate.

DESMOND, Judge (dissenting).

It is fundamental that every State has the right to determine the marital status of its own citizens, *Maynard v. Hill*, 125 U.S. 190, 8 S.Ct. 723, 31 L.Ed. 654.... Exercising that right, New York has declared in section 5 of the Domestic Relations Law that a marriage between uncle and niece is incestuous, void and criminal. Such marriages, while not within the Levitical forbidden degrees of the Old Testament, have been condemned by public opinion for centuries...and are void, by statute in (it would seem) forty-seven of the States of the Union (all except Georgia,...and except, also, that Rhode Island, one of the forty-seven, exempts from its local statute "any marriage which shall be solemnized among the Jews, within the degrees of affinity or consanguinity allowed by their religion", Gen.L. of R.I., ch. 415, §4). It is undisputed here that this uncle and niece were both domiciled in New York in 1913, when they left New York for the sole purpose of going to Rhode Island to be married there, and that they were married in that State conformably to its laws (see above) and immediately returned to New York and ever afterwards resided in this State. That Rhode Island marriage, between two New York residents, was, in New York, absolutely void for any and all purposes, by positive New York law which declares a strong public policy of this State....

The general rule that "a marriage valid where solemnized is valid everywhere" (see Restatement, Conflict of Laws, §121) does not apply. To that rule there is a proviso or exception, recognized, it would seem, by all the States, as follows: "unless contrary to the prohibitions of natural law or the express prohibitions of a statute."... New York, as a sovereign State with absolute powers over the marital status of its citizens, has enacted such legislation, but we, by this decision, are denying it efficacy.

...This court's opinion in the *Van Voorhis* case, while stating the general rule that the validity of a marriage depends on the law of the place of marriage, noted that there are exceptions thereto in cases of incest, within the prohibition of natural law, and "prohibition by positive law". 86 N.Y. at page 26. Section 5 of the Domestic Relations Law, the one we are concerned with here, lists the marriages which are "incestuous and void" in New York, as being those between parent and child, brother and sister, uncle and niece, and aunt and nephew. All such misalliances are incestuous, and all, equally, are void. The policy, language, meaning and validity of the statute are beyond dispute. It should be enforced by the courts.

...

COMMENTS

Israel and *In re MEW* deal not with incest as traditionally understood, that is, as prohibitions against marriage in case of consanguinity or affinity, but with statutory prohibitions against marriage between adopted siblings. As in affinity, questions of genetics are not involved because adoption does not involve a blood relationship. *Israel* permitted a marriage when the relationship of brother and sister resulted from adoption. *MEW* came to the opposite conclusion. There the court viewed the integrity of the family to be at stake. Inevitably this raises questions of conflict of laws since two different jurisdictions, Colorado and Pennsylvania, were involved. A question that may arise is, what effects should be given to a "migratory marriage"? For example, could the adoptive brother and sister in *MEW* go from Pennsylvania to Colorado to marry, and would their out-of-state marriage in the more liberal jurisdiction of Colorado be recognized if they were to return to Pennsylvania? A further question could arise if they were to leave Colorado for a third jurisdiction. Actually, these questions are simplistic and unanswerable unless further facts are given.

Most discussions of incest do not differentiate sufficiently between the numerous factual and legal variations that are possible. Obviously, legal characterizations of incest do not necessarily coincide with social understanding. The social understanding of incest is sometimes narrower, sometimes broader, than the legal prohibitions. Society may be tolerant toward marriages between cousins, but statutes may prohibit them. Although society may disapprove of stepfather-stepdaughter relationships, some jurisdictions, such as Florida, may prohibit marriages only in case of consanguinity. With the increased incidence of cohabitation without marriage, legal prohibitions of step-parent and step-child marriage may be too narrow to prevent marriage of a child to an adult who has lived in a parental relationship with that child or has assumed such a relationship even if that adult has not actually lived with the child or the child's parent for a sustained period of time. Woody Allen's relationship with Mia Farrow's daughter raised no genetic problems and was not incestuous by any conventional definition, yet the disapproval felt by many people was the same disapproval they feel for incest. Many felt that Woody Allen was taking unfair advantage of the daughter and betraying the trust placed in him. Many focused on the fact that Mia Farrow and Woody Allen were together the parents of two younger children and disapproved the family disruption.

To the variables of legal policies and social understandings others should be added. The outcome of cases, regardless of statutory language, may depend on whether and to what degree consanguinity is involved or whether affinity is merely established by marriage. Whether the marriage establishing the relationship still exists or has been terminated by death or divorce may make a difference. Yet a close relationship, such as that between stepfather and stepdaughter, may be considered a continuing impediment, even if the mother has died. In adoption it may make a difference whether the issue involves a parent and adoptive child, a brother and adoptive sister, or cousins who are merely related by adoption. Even more remote, and thus not necessarily effective in the courts, might be prohibitions of marriage if affinity established only by adoption is involved. Thus a marriage between a woman and the adoptive brother of her deceased husband may technically be prohibited. Yet courts may be inclined to grant relief under reasoning similar to that in *Israel*.

In *May's Estate*, three of the daughters of Sam and Fannie May sought to declare their parent's marriage void (and thus to bastardize themselves), while the two sons and one daughter supported their father's petition. Even if Sam and Fannie had been brother and sister, it is difficult to see what positive purpose would be served now, fifty years later, by declaring their marriage void. Neither does it make full sense, however, to suggest that incestuous marriages are all right unless someone lodges a timely objection.

As illustrated by *May's Estate*, the outcome of cases is further influenced by the purpose of the litigation. In applying the same statute, courts may be more stringent in permitting a marriage than in declaring it valid once it has been entered. It may be more difficult to enter an incestuous marriage than to stay in it. As in ordinary contract law, the level of execution can have a bearing on whether a marriage contract is upheld. It does make a difference when a marriage entered in violation of law has lasted for many years and has resulted in children and in the accumulation of property as to whether it is void for any purpose. Such a union may be upheld, as if it had been merely voidable, if the only issue is whether a past real estate transaction is valid after the death of both spouses. In this case cohabitation is no longer a problem, and courts may relax legislative prohibitions (see *Johnson v. Landefeld*, 138 Fla. 511, 189 So. 666 (1939)). It is not likely that an incestuous marriage would have been permitted upon mandamus action. It also may have resulted in criminal prosecution during the life of the parties. Whether an incestuous marriage is absolutely void or merely voidable — in other words, valid until annulled — cannot be answered in the abstract.

Although nearly everybody agrees that close blood relationships should be absolutely prohibited in marriage and sexual relations, the volume of civil litigation relating to incest is not concerned with these. Leaving criminal cases aside, the courts are involved in matters relating to adoption (as in *Israel* and *MEW*), to affinity relationships established by marriage, and to attempted marriages between cousins, between aunt and nephew, or uncle and niece (as in *May's Estate*). It may become necessary for a lawyer then to delve into the underlying considerations of policy. Strong religious and social taboos are involved. Further considerations have been added, many of them relating to bygone times. It is no longer a matter of survival to establish a wide network of relationships through marriage outside the family or clan. Genetic considerations — for example, that incestuous marriages may result in defective offspring — have no bearing on relationships based on affinity and adoption. Even in the case of marriages between cousins, genetic theories are not conclusive. In the last analysis it is the taboo itself, whether or not it conforms to scientific knowledge, that provides the justification.

Nevertheless, any of the theories on incest is valid enough for a legal argument, especially in borderline cases. In other words, scientific evidence is good for argumentation, but the decision is likely to be made on another level. It is not the practicing lawyer's task to resolve deeply controversial matters beyond the resolution of a specific case at hand.

REFERENCES

William J. Goode, THE FAMILY 24 (1964).

Claude Levi-Strauss, *The Family,* in MAN, CULTURE AND SOCIETY 261, 276–278, (Shapiro ed. 1956).

Margaret Mead, *Anomalies in American Post-Divorce Relationships,* in DIVORCE AND AFTER 97, 106–112 (1970).

Frederic P. Storke, *The Incestuous Marriage — Relic of the Past,* 36 U. COLO. L. REV. 473 (1964).

Sex

M.T. v. J.T.

Superior Court of New Jersey
140 N.J. Super 77, 355 A.2d 204 (1976)

HANDLER, J.A.D.

This appeal presents the portentous problem of how to tell the sex of a person for marital purposes. Involved is a postoperative transsexual, born a male but now claiming to be a female.

The case started inauspiciously enough when plaintiff M.T. filed a simple complaint in the Juvenile and Domestic Relations Court for support and maintenance. The legal issue sharpened dramatically when defendant J.T. interposed the defense that M.T. was a male and that their marriage was void. Following a hearing the trial judge determined that plaintiff was a female and that defendant was her husband, and there being no fraud, ordered defendant to pay plaintiff $50 a week support. Notice of appeal was then filed by defendant.

A careful recapitulation of the testimony is appropriate. M.T. testified that she was born a male. While she knew that she had male sexual organs she did not know whether she also had female organs. As a youngster she did not participate in sports and at an early age became very interested in boys. At the age of 14 she began dressing in a feminine manner and later began dating men. She had no real adjustment to make because throughout her life she had always felt that she was a female.

Plaintiff first met defendant in 1964 and told him about her feelings about being a woman. Sometime after that she began to live with defendant. In 1970 she started to go to Dr. Charles L. Ihlenfeld to discuss the possibility of having an operation so that she could "be physically a woman." In 1971, upon the doctor's advice, she went to a surgeon who agreed to operate. In May of that year she underwent surgery for the removal of male sex organs and construction of a vagina. Defendant paid for the operation. Plaintiff then applied to the State of New York to have her birth certificate changed.

On August 11, 1972, over a year after the operation, plaintiff and defendant went through a ceremonial marriage in New York State and then moved to Hackensack. They lived as husband and wife and had intercourse. Defendant supported plaintiff for over two years when, in October 1974, he left their home. He has not supported plaintiff since.

Dr. Ihlenfeld, plaintiff's medical doctor with a specialty in gender identity, was accepted as an expert in the field of medicine and transsexualism. A transsexual, in the opinion of this expert, was "a person who discovers sometime, usually very early in life, that there is a great discrepancy between the physical genital anatomy and the person's sense of self-identity as a male or as a female.... [T]he transsexual is one who has a conflict between physical anatomy and psychological identity or psychological sex." Usually sexual anatomy was "normal" but for some reason transsexuals did not see themselves as members of the sex their anatomy seemed to indicate. According to Dr. Ihlenfeld, there are different theories to explain the origin of that conflict. There was, however, "very little disagreement" on the fact that gender identity generally is established "very, very firmly, almost immediately, by the age of 3 to 4 years." He defined gender identity as "a sense, a total sense of self as being masculine or female..."; it "pervades one's entire concept of one's place in life, of one's place in society and in point of fact the actual facts of the anatomy are really secondary...."

The doctor first saw and examined plaintiff in September 1970 and took a medical history from her. She told him that she had always felt like a woman and was living like a woman. She wanted sex reassignment surgery as well as treatments and hormones so that she could end the conflict she was feeling, "confronted with a male body," in order to live her life completely as the woman she thought herself to be. Dr. Ihlenfeld diagnosed her as a transsexual. He knew of no way to alter her sense of her own feminine gender identity in order to agree with her male body, and the only treatment available to her was to alter the body to conform with her sense of psyche gender identity. That regimen consisted of hormone treatment and sex reassignment surgery. Dr. Ihlenfeld recommended such an operation and treated plaintiff both before and after it.

The examination of plaintiff before the operation showed that she had a penis, scrotum and testicles. After the operation she did not have those organs but had a vagina and labia which were "adequate for sexual intercourse" and could function as any female vagina, that is, for "traditional penile/vaginal intercourse." The "artificial vagina" constructed by such surgery was a cavity, the walls of which are lined initially by the skin of the penis, often later taking on the characteristics of normal vaginal mucosa; the vagina, though at a somewhat different angle, was not really different from a natural vagina in size, capacity and "the feeling of the walls around it." Plaintiff had no uterus or cervix, but her vagina had a "good cosmetic appearance" and was "the same as a normal female vagina after a hysterectomy." Dr. Ihlenfeld had seen plaintiff since the operation and she never complained to him that she had difficulty having intercourse. So far as he knew, no one had tested plaintiff to find out what chromosomes she had. He knew that plaintiff had had silicone injections in her breasts; he had treated her continuously with female hormones to demasculinize her body and to feminize it at the same time. In the doctor's opinion plaintiff was a female; he no longer considered plaintiff to be a male since she could not function as a male sexually either for purposes of "recreation or procreation."

Plaintiff also produced Charles Annicello, a psychologist who worked at the gender identity clinic of the Johns Hopkins University Hospital. He was qualified as an expert in transsexualism. This witness demonstrated through slides the various methods by which scientists define whether a person is male or female. The witness said that transsexualism represented only one sexual variant although it was not known whether its cause was chromosomal, gonadal, or hormonal. Annicello expressed the opinion that if a person had a female psychic gender and underwent a sex reassignment operation, that person would be considered female although no person is "absolutely" male or female.

Dr. Richard M. Samuels, a Ph.D. with a specialty in behavioral therapy and sexual dysfunctions, testified as an expert in psychology as it related to transsexualism. His definition of a transsexual was essentially the same as that given by the prior experts: "someone whose physical anatomy does not correspond to their [*sic*] sense of being, to their [*sic*] sense of gender." He also acknowledged that it was not known what caused that condition but he believed that it was probably a combination of neurological, chromosomal and environmental factors. Some psychological changes are noted following a sex reassignment operation. Thus, a transsexual was often depressed preoperatively, but after the operation he or she lived a "fuller and richer life" and was better able to overcome obstacles in employment, housing, social security and welfare benefits; a sense of satisfaction and relief was felt since the body was now in line with the psyche. For Dr. Samuels the most important factor in determining whether a person should have a sex reassignment operation was how consistently the patient lived in the chosen gender role. A sex reassignment operation did not determine a person's gender. After a transsexual underwent a sex reassignment operation to remove male organs, Dr. Samuels would characterize that person as a female.

Defendant called as an expert witness Dr. T, a medical doctor who was defendant's adoptive father. Over plaintiff's objection he was allowed to testify as an expert. Dr. T classified sex at birth according to sexual anatomy. He described a female as "a person who has female organs in an anatomical sense, who has a vagina and a uterus and ovaries or at least has had them." The witness had heard all of the prior testimony and he said that in his opinion plaintiff was still a male because she did not have female organs. He did believe, however, that transsexuals existed and that they were people who had "the mental and emotional reactions of the opposite sex." On cross-examination Dr. T reiterated that it was the anatomy alone which determined the real sex of an individual and that gender in contrast to sex was not a significant factor. Although he was "very sympathetic to any male person" who had "the emotional and mental reactions of a female," since he knew that it was "very annoying," he still did not believe that that was determinative.

The trial judge made careful findings of fact on this evidential record. He accepted the testimony concerning M.T.'s personal and medical history as related by her and her doctor. He noted that defendant knew of her condition and cooperated in her sex reassignment surgery. The parties married in New York and subsequently consummated their marriage by engaging in sexual intercourse. The judge also found that defendant later deserted plaintiff and failed to support her.

Drawing from the opinions of the experts the judge defined a transsexual as "an individual anatomically of one sex who firmly believes he belongs to the other sex." He enumerated the seven factors considered generally relevant to the determination of sex. According to the judge, a preoperative transsexual would appropriately be classified according to his anatomical sex. After a successful sex reassignment operation, however, "psychological sex and anatomical sex become consistent as to outward appearances." The judge ruled that plaintiff was of the female psychic gender all her life and that her anatomical change through surgery required the conclusion that she was a female at the time of the marriage ceremony. He stated:

> It is the opinion of the court that if the psychological choice of a person is medically sound, not a mere whim, and irreversible sex reassignment surgery has been performed, society has no right to prohibit the transsexual from leading a normal life. Are we to look upon this person as an exhibit in a circus side show? What harm has said person done to society? The entire area of transsexualism is repugnant to the nature of many persons within our society. However, this should not govern the legal acceptance of a fact....

Defendant's basic and continuing contention is that the marriage between him and plaintiff was a nullity because plaintiff was a male at the time of the ceremony. We disagree with this position and affirm the decision of the lower court.

We accept — and it is not disputed — as the fundamental premise in this case that a lawful marriage requires the performance of a ceremonial marriage of two persons of the opposite sex, a male and a female. Despite winds of change, this understanding of a valid marriage is almost universal....

There is not the slightest doubt that New Jersey follows the overwhelming authority.[1]...

The issue must then be confronted whether the marriage between a male and a postoperative transsexual, who has surgically changed her external sexual anatomy from male to female, is to be regarded as a lawful marriage between a man and a woman.

An English case, *Corbett v. Corbett*, 2 W.L.R. 1306, 2 All E.R. 33 (P.D.A.1970) appears to be the only reported decision involving the validity of marriage of a true post operative transsexual and a male person. The judge there held that the transsexual had failed to prove that she had changed her sex from male to female. The court subscribed to the opinion of the medical witnesses that "the biological

---

1. No issue was raised below or on appeal as to the state law applicable to this case. Our courts would generally look to the law of the place of the marriage ceremony to determine its validity unless contrary to public policy. *Booker v. James Spence Iron Foundry*, 80 N.J.Super. 68, 77-78, 192 A.2d 860 (App.Div.1963); *Winn v. Wiggins*, 47 N.J.Super. 215, 220, 135 A.2d 673 (App.Div.1957). We have examined independently the statutory law of the State of New York (New York Domestic Relations Law, §§5 through 25) and are satisfied that by its literal terms the marriage in this case would not by statute be prohibited. The current decisional law of New York, discussed infra, is not dispositive of the legal issue as to whether this marriage would be void or voidable in that state. Hence, we are free to apply the law of the State of New Jersey.

sexual constitution of an individual is fixed at birth (at the latest), and cannot be changed, either by the natural development of organs of the opposite sex, or by medical or surgical means. The respondent's operation, therefore, cannot affect her true sex." 2 W.L.R. at 1323. It felt that three tests for sex should be used, the chromosomal, gonadal and genital, and when these were congruent sex for purposes of marriage should be determined accordingly. *Id.* at 1325. And, in view of the "essentially hetero-sexual character" of marriage, the test to determine sex must be biological, "for even the most extreme degree of transsexualism in a male or the most severe hormonal imbalance which could exist in a person with male chromosomes, male gonads, and male genitalia, cannot reproduce a person who is naturally capable of performing the essential role of a woman in marriage." *Id.* at 1324-1325. Based upon an assumed distinction between "sex" and "gender," the court held that "marriage is a relationship which depends on sex and not on gender." *Id.* at 1325. In addition, the judge was mindful that the marriage was unstable, brief and the sexual exchange between the parties — the husband was a transvestite — was ambivalent. He concluded on alternative grounds that the marriage had not been, and indeed could not be, consummated.

We cannot join the reasoning of the *Corbett* case. The evidence before this court teaches that there are several criteria or standards which may be relevant in determining the sex of an individual. It is true that the anatomical test, the genitalia of an individual, is unquestionably significant and probably in most instances indispensable. For example, sex classification of an individual at birth may as a practical matter rely upon this test. For other purposes, however, where sex differentiation is required or accepted, such as for public records, service in the branches of the armed forces, participation in certain regulated sports activities, eligibility for types of employment and the like, other tests in addition to genitalia may also be important. Comment, *Transsexualism, Sex Reassignment Surgery, and the Law,* 56 Cornell L.Rev. 963, 992-1002 (1971).

Against the backdrop of the evidence in the present record we must disagree with the conclusion reached in *Corbett* that for purposes of marriage sex is somehow irrevocably cast at the moment of birth, and that for adjudging the capacity to enter marriage, sex in its biological sense should be the exclusive standard. On this score the case has not escaped critical review. Comment, *supra,* 56 Cornell L.Rev. at 1003-1007; Note, *Transsexuals in Limbo,* 31 Md.L.Rev. 236, 244 (1971).

Our departure from the *Corbett* thesis is not a matter of semantics. It stems from a fundamentally different understanding of what is meant by "sex" for marital purposes. The English court apparently felt that sex and gender were disparate phenomena. In a given case there may, of course, be such a difference. A preoperative transsexual is an example of that kind of disharmony, and most experts would be satisfied that the individual should be classified according to biological criteria. The evidence and authority which we have examined, however, show that a person's sex or sexuality embraces an individual's gender, that is, one's self-image, the deep psychological or emotional sense of sexual identity and character. Indeed, it has been observed that the "psychological sex of an individual," while not serviceable for all purposes, is "practical, realistic and humane." Comment, *supra,* 56 Cornell L.Rev. at 969-970; *Cf. In re Anonymous,* 57 Misc.2d 813, 293 N.Y.S.2d 834, 837 (Civ.Ct.1968).

The English court believed, we feel incorrectly, that an anatomical change of genitalia in the case of a transsexual cannot "affect her true sex." Its conclusion was rooted in the premise that "true sex" was required to be ascertained even for marital purposes by biological criteria. In the case of a transsexual following surgery, however, according to the expert testimony presented here, the dual tests of anatomy and gender are more significant. On this evidential demonstration, therefore, we are impelled to the conclusion that for marital purposes if the anatomical or genital features of a genuine transsexual are made to conform to the person's gender, psyche or psychological sex, then identity by sex must be governed by the congruence of these standards.

Implicit in the reasoning underpinning our determination is the tacit but valid assumption of the lower court and the experts upon whom reliance was placed that for purposes of marriage under the circumstances of this case, it is the sexual capacity of the individual which must be scrutinized. Sexual capacity or sexuality in this frame of reference requires the coalescence of both the physical ability and the psychological and emotional orientation to engage in sexual intercourse as either a male or a female.

Other decisions touching the marital status of a putative transsexual are not especially helpful. *Anonymous v. Anonymous*, 67 Misc.2d 982, 325 N.Y.S.2d 499 (Sup.Ct.1971), cited by defendant, held a marriage a nullity, but there the two persons had never had sexual intercourse and had never lived together. Although it was claimed that respondent was a transsexual and had had an operation to remove his male organs after the marriage, there was no medical evidence of this. In *B. v. B., supra*, a female transsexual had had a hysterectomy and mastectomy but had not received any male organs and was incapable of performing sexually as a male. He had then married a normal female who later sued for an annulment on the ground that he had defrauded her by not informing her of his transsexualism and of the operation. The judge there held that even if defendant were a male and trapped in the body of a female, his attempted sex reassignment surgery had not successfully released him from that body.

Anonymous v. Weiner, 50 Misc.2d 380, 270 N.Y.S.2d 319 (Sup.Ct. 1966), sustained the refusal by the New York City Board of Health to amend a sex designation on a birth certificate. The court acquiesced in the view of the administrative agency that "male-to-female transsexuals are still chromosomally males while ostensibly females and that the desire of the transsexual for 'concealment of a change of sex...is outweighed by the public interest for protection against fraud.'" 270 N.Y.S.2d at 322. To reiterate, the chromosomal test of sex in this context is unhelpful. The potential for fraud, feared by the court, moreover, is effectively countered by the apt observation of the trial judge here: "The transsexual is not committing a fraud upon the public. In actuality she is doing her utmost to remove any false facade." Further, we note the *Weiner* case was sharply criticized in *In re Anonymous, supra*, which ordered a change to a female name for a post-operative transsexual. The court concluded that the chromosomal test recommended by the New York Academy of Medicine and adopted by the court in *Weiner* was unrealistic and inhumane. It said:

> It has been suggested that there is some middle ground between the sexes, a "no-man's land" for those individuals who are neither truly "male" nor truly "female." Yet the standard is much too fixed for such far-out theories. Rather the application of a simple formula could and should be the test of gender, and that formula is as follows: Where there is disharmony between the psychological sex and the anatomical sex, the social sex or gender of the individual will be determined by the anatomical sex. Where, however, with or without medical intervention, the psychological

> sex and the anatomical sex are harmonized, then the social sex or gender of the individual should be made to conform to the harmonized status of the individual and, if such conformity requires changes of a statistical nature, then such changes should be made. Of course, such changes should be made only in those cases where physiological orientation is complete. [293 N.Y.S.2d at 837]

...

In sum, it has been established that an individual suffering from the condition of transsexualism is one with a disparity between his or her genitalia or anatomical sex and his or her gender, that is, the individual's strong and consistent emotional and psychological sense of sexual being. A transsexual in a proper case can be treated medically by certain supportive measures and through surgery to remove and replace existing genitalia with sex organs which will coincide with the person's gender. If such sex reassignment surgery is successful and the postoperative transsexual is, by virtue of medical treatment, thereby possessed of the full capacity to function sexually as a male or female, as the case may be, we perceive no legal barrier, cognizable social taboo, or reason grounded in public policy to prevent that person's identification at least for purposes of marriage to the sex finally indicated.

In this case the transsexual's gender and genitalia are no longer discordant; they have been harmonized through medical treatment. Plaintiff has become physically and psychologically unified and fully capable of sexual activity consistent with her reconciled sexual attributes of gender and anatomy. Consequently, plaintiff should be considered a member of the female sex for marital purposes. It follows that such an individual would have the capacity to enter into a valid marriage relationship with a person of the opposite sex and did do so here. In so ruling we do no more than give legal effect to a *fait accompli*, based upon medical judgment and action which are irreversible. Such recognition will promote the individual's quest for inner peace and personal happiness, while in no way disserving any societal interest, principle of public order or precept of morality.

Accordingly, the court below correctly determined that plaintiff at the time of her marriage was a female and that defendant, a man, became her lawful husband, obligated to support her as his wife. The judgment of the court is therefore affirmed.

BAEHR v. LEWIN

Supreme Court of Hawaii
74 Haw. 530, 852 P.2d 44 (1993)

LEVINSON, Judge, in which MOON, Chief Judge, joins.

...

I. Background

On May 1, 1991, the plaintiffs filed a complaint for injunctive and declaratory relief in the Circuit Court of the First Circuit, State of Hawaii, seeking, *inter alia*: (1) a declaration that Hawaii Revised Statutes (HRS) §572-1 (1985) — the section of the Hawaii Marriage Law enumerating the ["r]equisites of [a] valid marriage contract" — is unconstitutional insofar as it is construed and applied by the [Department of Health (DOH)] to justify refusing to issue a marriage license on the sole basis that the applicant couple is of the same sex; and (2) preliminary and permanent injunctions prohibiting the future withholding of marriage licenses on that sole basis.

...

...[Director of the DOH John C.] Lewin urged that the plaintiffs' complaint failed to state a claim upon which relief could be granted for the following reasons: (1) the state's marriage laws "contemplate marriage as a union between a man and a woman"; (2) because the only legally recognized right to marry "is the right to enter a heterosexual marriage, [the] plaintiffs do not have a cognizable right, fundamental or otherwise, to enter into state-licensed homosexual marriages";[11] (3) the state's marriage laws do not "burden, penalize, infringe, or interfere in any way with the [plaintiffs'] private relationships"; (4) the state is under no obligation "to take affirmative steps to provide homosexual unions with its official approval"; (5) the state's marriage laws "protect and foster and may help to perpetuate the basic family unit, regarded as vital to society, that provides status and a nurturing environment to children born to married persons" and, in addition, "constitute a statement of the moral values of the community in a manner that is not burdensome to [the] plaintiffs"; (6) assuming the plaintiffs are homosexuals (a fact not pleaded in the plaintiffs' complaint), they "are neither a suspect nor a quasi-suspect class and do not require heightened judicial solicitude"; and (7) even if heightened judicial solicitude is warranted, the state's marriage laws "are so removed from penalizing, burdening, harming, or otherwise interfering with [the] plaintiffs and their relationships and perform such a critical function in society that they must be sustained."

...

The circuit court...filed its order granting Lewin's motion for judgment on the pleadings on the basis that Lewin was "entitled to judgment in his favor as a matter of law" and dismissing the plaintiffs' complaint with prejudice. The plaintiffs' timely appeal followed.

II. Judgment of the Pleadings Was Erroneously Granted

A complaint should not be dismissed for failure to state a claim unless it appears beyond doubt that the plaintiff can prove no set of facts in support of his or her claim that would entitle him or her to relief.... We must therefore view a plaintiff's complaint in a light most favorable to him or her in order to determine whether the allegations contained therein could warrant relief under any alternative theory.... For this reason, in reviewing the circuit court's order dismissing the plaintiffs' complaint in this case, our consideration is strictly limited to the allegations of the complaint, and we must deem those allegations to be true....

A. The Circuit Court Made Evidentiary Findings of Fact

Notwithstanding the absence of any evidentiary record before it, the circuit court's October 1, 1991 order granting Lewin's motion for judgment on the pleadings contained a variety of findings of fact. For example, the circuit court "found" that: (1) HRS §572-1 "does not infringe upon a person's individuality or lifestyle

11. "Homosexual" and "same-sex" marriages are not synonymous; by the same token, a "heterosexual" same-sex marriage is, in theory, not oxymoronic. A "homosexual" person is defined as "[o]ne sexually attracted to another of the same sex." Taber's Cyclopedic Medical Dictionary 839 (16th ed. 1989). "Homosexuality" is "sexual desire or behavior directed toward a person or persons of one's own sex." Webster's Encyclopedic Unabridged Dictionary of the English Language 680 (1989). Conversely, "heterosexuality" is "[s]exual attraction for one of the opposite sex," Taber's Cyclopedic Medical Dictionary at 827, or "sexual feeling or behavior directed toward a person or persons of the opposite sex." Webster's Encyclopedic Unabridged Dictionary of the English Language at 667. Parties to "a union between a man and a woman" may or may not be homosexuals. Parties to a same-sex marriage could theoretically be either homosexuals or heterosexuals.

decisions, *and none of the plaintiffs has provided testimony to the contrary*"; (2) HRS §572-1 "does not...restrict [or] burden...the exercise of the right to engage in a homosexual lifestyle"; (3) Hawaii has exhibited a "history of tolerance for all peoples and their cultures"; (4) "*the plaintiffs have failed to show* that they have been ostracized or oppressed in Hawaii and have opted instead to rely on a general statement of historic problems encountered by homosexuals which may not be relevant to Hawaii"; (5) "homosexuals in Hawaii have not been relegated to a position of 'political powerlessness.'... *[T]here is no evidence* that homosexuals and the homosexual legislative agenda have failed to gain legislative support in Hawaii"; (6) *the "[p]laintiffs have failed to show* that homosexuals constitute a suspect class for equal protection analysis under [a]rticle I, [s]ection 5 of the Hawaii State Constitution;" (7) "the issue of whether homosexuality constitutes an immutable trait has generated much dispute in the relevant scientific community";[14] and (8) HRS §572-1 "is obviously designed to promote the general welfare interests of the community by sanctioning traditional man-woman family units and procreation." (Emphasis added.)

Although not expressly denominated as such, the circuit court's order also contained a number of conclusions of law. These included: (1) "[t]he right to enter into a homosexual marriage is not a fundamental right protected by [a]rticle I, [s]ection 6 of the Hawaii State Constitution"; (2) the right to be free from the denial of a person's civil rights or from discrimination in the exercise thereof because of "sexual orientation [is]...covered under [a]rticle I, [s]ection 5 of the State Constitution"; (3) HRS §572-1 "permits heterosexual marriages but not homosexual marriages" and "does not violate the due process clause of [a]rticle I, [s]ection 5 of the Hawaii State Constitution"; (4) HRS §572-1 "represents a legislative decision to extend the benefits of lawful marriage only to traditional family units which consist of male and female partners"; (5) "[b]ecause [entering into a] homosexual marriage [is not] a fundamental [constitutional] right..., the provisions of section 572-1 do not violate the due process clause of [a]rticle I, [s]ection 5 of the Hawaii State Constitution"; (6) "[h]omosexuals do not constitute a 'suspect class' for purposes of equal protection analysis under [a]rticle I, [s]ection 5 of the Hawaii State Constitution"; (7) "a group must have been subject to purposeful, unequal treatment or have been relegated to a position of political powerlessness in order to be considered a 'suspect class' for the purposes of constitutional analysis"; (8) "[a] law which classifies on the basis of race deserves the utmost judicial scrutiny because race clearly qualifies as a suspect classification. The same cannot be convincingly said with respect to homosexuals as a group"; (9) "the classification created by section 572-1 must meet only the rational relationship test"; (10)

14. For the reasons cited *infra* in this opinion, it is irrelevant, for purposes of the constitutional analysis germane to this case, whether homosexuality constitutes "an immutable trait" because it is immaterial whether the plaintiffs, or any of them, are homosexuals. Specifically, the issue is not material to the equal protection analysis set forth in section II.C of this opinion *infra* at 57–67. Its resolution is unnecessary to our ruling that HRS §572-1, both on its face as applied, denies same-sex couples access to the marital status and its concomitant rights and benefits. Its resolution is also unnecessary to our conclusion that it is the state's regulation of access to the marital status, on the basis of the applicants' sex, that gives rise to the question whether the applicant couples have been denies the equal protection of the laws in violation of article I, section 5 of the Hawaii Constitution. *See infra* at 58–63. And, in particular, it is immaterial to the excercise of "strict scrutiny" review, *see infra* at 63–67, inasmuch as we are unable to perceive any conceivable relevance of the issue to the ultimate conclusion of law — which, in the absence of further evidentiary proceedings, we cannot reach at this time — regarding whether HRS §572-1 furthers compelling state interests and is narrowly drawn to avoid unnecessary abridgements of constitutional rights. *See infra* at 67–68.

In light of the above, we disagree with Chief Judge Burns's position that "questions whether heterosexuality, homosexuality, bisexuality, and asexuality are 'biologically fated' are relevant questions of fact." Concurring opinion at 3. This preoccupation seems simply to restate the immaterial question whether sexual orientation is an "immutable trait."

"[t]he classification of section 572-1 meets the rational relationship test"; (11) "[s]ection 572-1 is clearly a rational, legislative effort to advance the general welfare of the community by permitting only heterosexual couples to legally marry"; and, finally, (12) Lewin "is entitled to judgment in his favor as a matter of law[.]"

In reviewing the circuit court's order on appeal, as noted above, we must deem all of the *factual* allegations of the plaintiffs' complaint as true or admitted...and, in the absence of an evidentiary record, ignore all of the circuit court's findings of fact.... Ultimately, our task on appeal is to determine whether the circuit court's order, stripped of its improper factual findings, supports its conclusion that Lewin is entitled to judgment as a matter of law and, by implication, that it appears beyond doubt that the plaintiffs can prove no set of facts in support of their claim that would entitle them to relief under any alternative theory....

We conclude that the circuit court's order runs aground on the shoals of the Hawaii Constitution's equal protection clause and that, on the record before us, unresolved factual questions preclude entry of judgment, as a matter of law, in favor of Lewin and against the plaintiffs. Before we address the plaintiffs' equal protection claim, however, it is necessary as a threshold matter to consider their allegations regarding the right to privacy (and, derivatively, due process of law) within the context of the record in its present embryonic form.

B. The Right to Privacy Does Not Include a Fundamental Right to Same-Sex Marriage.

It is now well established that "'a right to personal privacy, or a guarantee of certain areas or zones of privacy,' is implicit in the United States Constitution."... And article I, section 6 of the Hawaii Constitution expressly states that "[t]he right of the people to privacy is recognized and shall not be infringed without the showing of a compelling state interest." Haw. Const. art. I, §6 (1978). The framers of the Hawaii Constitution declared that the "privacy concept" embodied in article I, section 6 is to be "treated as a fundamental right[.]"...

When article I, section 6 of the Hawaii Constitution was being adopted, the 1978 Hawaii Constitutional Convention, acting as a committee of the whole, clearly articulated the rationale for its adoption:

> By amending the Constitution to include a separate and distinct privacy right, it is the intent of your Committee to insure that privacy is treated as a fundamental right for purposes of constitutional analysis.... This right is similar to the privacy right discussed in cases such as *Griswold v. Connecticut*, [381 U.S. 479, 85 S.Ct. 1678, 14 L.Ed.2d 510 (1965)], *Eisenstadt v. Baird*, [405 U.S. 438, 92 S.Ct. 1029, 31 L.Ed.2d 349 (1972)], *Roe v. Wade*, etc. It is a right that, though unstated in the federal Constitution, emanates from the penumbra of several guarantees of the Bill of Rights. Because of this, there has been some confusion as to the source of the right and the importance of it. As such, it is treated as a fundamental right subject to interference only when a compelling state interest is demonstrated. By inserting clear and specific language regarding this right into the Constitution, your Committee intends to alleviate any possible confusion over the source of the right and the existence of it.

Comm.Whole Rep. No. 15, 1 Proceedings, at 1024. This court cited the same passage in *Mueller*, 66 Haw. at 625-26, 671 P.2d at 1357-58, in an attempt to determine the "intended scope of privacy protected by the Hawaii Constitution." *Id.* at 626, 671 P.2d at 1358. We ultimately concluded in *Mueller* that the federal cases cited by the Convention's committee of the whole should guide our construction of the intended scope of article I, section 6. *Id.*

Accordingly, there is no doubt that, at a minimum, article I, section 6 of the Hawaii Constitution encompasses all of the fundamental rights expressly recognized as being subsumed within the privacy protections of the United States Constitution. In this connection, the United States Supreme Court has declared that "the right to marry is part of the fundamental 'right of privacy' implicit in the Fourteenth Amendment's Due Process Clause." *Zablocki v. Redhail*, 434 U.S. 374, 384, 98 S.Ct. 673, 680, 54 L.Ed.2d 618 (1978). The issue in the present case is, therefore, whether the "right to marry" protected by article I, section 6 of the Hawaii Constitution extends to same-sex couples. Because article I, section 6 was expressly derived from the general right to privacy under the United States Constitution and because there are no Hawaii cases that have delineated the fundamental right to marry, this court, as we did in *Mueller*, looks to federal cases for guidance.

...

...[T]he federal construct of the fundamental right to marry — subsumed within the right to privacy implicitly protected by the United States Constitution — presently contemplates unions between men and women. (...[T]his is hardly surprising inasmuch as such unions are the only state-sanctioned marriages currently acknowledged in this country.)

Therefore, the precise question facing this court is whether we will extend the present boundaries of the fundamental right of marriage to include same-sex couples, or, put another way, whether we will hold that same-sex couples possess a fundamental right to marry. In effect, as the applicant couples frankly admit, we are being asked to recognize a new fundamental right....

... In the case that first recognized a fundamental right to privacy, *Griswold v. Connecticut*, 381 U.S. 479, 85 S.Ct. 1678, 14 L.Ed.2d 510 (1965),... Justice Goldberg observed that judges "determining which rights are fundamental" must look not to "personal and private notions," but

> to the "traditions and [collective] conscience of our people" to determine whether a principle is "so rooted [there]...as to be ranked as fundamental." ... The inquiry is whether a right involved "is of such a character that it cannot be denied without violating those 'fundamental principles of liberty and justice which lie at the base of all our civil and political institutions'...."

Id. at 493, 85 S.Ct. at 1686-87 (Goldberg, J., concurring) (citations omitted).

Applying the foregoing standards to the present case, we do not believe that a right to same-sex marriage is so rooted in the traditions and collective conscience of our people that failure to recognize it would violate the fundamental principles of liberty and justice that lie at the base of all our civil and political institutions. Neither do we believe that a right to same-sex marriage is implicit in the concept of ordered liberty, such that neither liberty nor justice would exist if it were sacrificed. Accordingly, we hold that the applicant couples do not have a fundamental constitutional right to same-sex marriage arising out of the right to privacy or otherwise.

Our holding, however, does not leave the applicant couples without a potential remedy in this case. As we will discuss below, the applicant couples are free to press their equal protection claim. If they are successful, the State of Hawaii will no longer be permitted to refuse marriage licenses to couples merely on the basis that they are of the same sex. But there is no fundamental right to marriage for same-sex couples under article I, section 6 of the Hawaii Constitution.

C. Inasmuch as the Applicant Couples Claim That the Express Terms of HRS §572-1, which Discriminates against Same-Sex Marriages, Violate Their Rights under the Equal Protection Clause of the Hawaii Constitution, the Applicant Couples Are Entitled to an Evidentiary Hearing to Determine Whether Lewin Can Demonstrate that HRS §572-1 Furthers Compelling State Interests and Is Narrowly Drawn to Avoid Unnecessary Abridgments of Constitutional Rights.

...[T]he circuit court erred when it concluded, *as a matter of law*, that: (1) homosexuals do not constitute a "suspect class" for purposes of equal protection analysis under article I, section 5 of the Hawaii Constitution;[17] (2) the classification created by HRS §572-1 is not subject to "strict scrutiny," but must satisfy only the "rational relationship" test; and (3) HRS §572-1 satisfies the rational relationship test because the legislature "obviously designed [it] to promote the general welfare interests of the community by sanctioning traditional man-woman family units and procreation."

1. Marriage is a state-conferred legal partnership status, the existence of which gives rise to a multiplicity of rights and benefits reserved exclusively to that particular relation.

...

The applicant couples correctly contend that the DOH's refusal to allow them to marry on the basis that they are members of the same sex deprives them of access to a multiplicity of rights and benefits that are contingent upon that status. Although it is unnecessary in this opinion to engage in an encyclopedic recitation of all of them, a number of the most salient marital rights and benefits are worthy of note. They include: (1) a variety of state income tax advantages, including deductions, credits, rates, exemptions, and estimates, under HRS chapter 235 (1985 and Supp.1992); (2) public assistance from and exemptions relating to the Department of Human Services under HRS chapter 346 (1985 and Supp.1992); (3) control, division, acquisition, and disposition of community property under HRS chapter 510 (1985); (4) rights relating to dower, curtesy, and inheritance under HRS chapter 533 (1985 and Supp.1992); (5) rights to notice, protection, benefits, and inheritance under the Uniform Probate Code, HRS chapter 560 (1985 and Supp.1992); (6) award of child custody and support payments in divorce proceedings under HRS chapter 571 (1985 and Supp.1992); (7) the right to spousal support pursuant to HRS §572-24 (1985); (8) the right to enter into premarital agreements under HRS chapter 572D (Supp.1992); (9) the right to change of name pursuant to HRS §574-5(a)(3)(Supp.1992); (10) the right to file a nonsupport action under HRS chapter 575 (1985 and Supp.1992); (11) post-divorce rights relating to support and property division under HRS chapter 580 (1985 and Supp.1992); (12) the benefit of the spousal privilege and confidential marital communications pursuant to Rule 505 of the Hawaii Rules of Evidence (1985); (13) the benefit of the exemption of real property from attachment or execution under HRS chapter 651 (1985); and (14) the right to bring a wrongful death action under HRS chapter 663 (1985 and Supp.1992). For present purposes, it is not disputed that the applicant couples would be entitled to all of these marital rights and benefits, but for the fact that they are denied access to the state-conferred legal status of marriage.

17. For the reasons stated *infra* in this opinion, it is irrelevant, for purposes of the constitutional analysis germane to this case, whether homosexuals constitute a "suspect class" because it is immaterial whether the plaintiffs, or any of them, are homosexuals. See *supra* note 14.

2. HRS §572-1, on its face, discriminates based on sex against the applicant couples in the exercise of the civil right of marriage, thereby implicating the equal protection clause of article I, section 5 of the Hawaii Constitution.

Notwithstanding the state's acknowledged stewardship over the institution of marriage, the extent of permissible state regulation of the right of access to the marital relationship is subject to constitutional limitations or constraints.... It has been held that a state may deny the right to marry only for compelling reasons....

The equal protection clauses of the United States and Hawaii Constitutions are not mirror images of one another. The fourteenth amendment to the United States Constitution somewhat concisely provides, in relevant part, that a state may not "deny to any person within its jurisdiction the equal protection of the laws." Hawaii's counterpart is more elaborate. Article I, section 5 of the Hawaii Constitution provides in relevant part that "[n]o person shall...be denied the equal protection of the laws, *nor be denied the enjoyment of the person's civil rights or be discriminated against in the exercise thereof because of* race, religion, *sex*, or ancestry." (Emphasis added.) Thus, by its plain language, the Hawaii Constitution prohibits state-sanctioned discrimination against any person in the exercise of his or her civil rights on the basis of sex.

"The freedom to marry has long been recognized as one of the vital personal rights essential to the orderly pursuit of happiness by free [people]." *Loving*, 388 U.S. at 12, 87 S.Ct. at 1824. So "fundamental" does the United States Supreme Court consider the institution of marriage that it has deemed marriage to be "one of the 'basic civil rights of [men and women.]'" *Id.* (quoting *Skinner*, 316 U.S. at 541, 62 S.Ct. at 1113).

...

Relying primarily on four decisions construing the law of other jurisdictions, Lewin contends that "the fact that homosexual [sic — actually, same-sex][22] partners cannot form a state-licensed marriage is not the product of impermissible discrimination" implicating equal protection considerations, but rather "a function of their biologic inability as a couple to satisfy the definition of the status to which they aspire." Lewin's answering brief at 21. Put differently, Lewin proposes that "the right of persons of the same sex to marry one another does not exist because marriage, by definition and usage, means a special relationship between a man and a woman." *Id.* at 7. We believe Lewin's argument to be circular and unpersuasive.

Two of the decisions upon which Lewin relies are demonstrably inapposite to the appellant couples' claim. In *Baker v. Nelson*, 291 Minn. 310, 191 N.W.2d 185 (1971), appeal dismissed, 409 U.S. 810, 93 S.Ct. 37, 34 L.Ed.2d 65 (1972), the questions for decision were whether a marriage of two persons of the same sex was authorized by state statutes and, if not, whether state authorization was compelled by various provisions of the United States Constitution, including the fourteenth amendment. Regarding the first question, the *Baker* court arrived at the same conclusion as have we with respect to HRS §572-1: by their plain language, the Minnesota marriage statutes precluded same-sex marriages. Regarding the second question, however, the court merely held that the United States Constitution was not offended; apparently, no state constitutional questions were raised and none were addressed.

---

22. See *supra* note 11.

De Santo v. Barnsley, 328 Pa.Super. 181, 476 A.2d 952 (1984), is also distinguishable. In *De Santo*, the court held only that common law same-sex marriage did not exist in Pennsylvania, a result irrelevant to the present case. The appellants sought to assert that denial of same-sex common law marriages violated the state's equal rights amendment, but the appellate court expressly declined to reach the issue because it had not been raised in the trial court.

Jones v. Hallahan, 501 S.W.2d 588 (Ky.Ct.App.1973), and *Singer v. Hara*, 11 Wash.App. 247, 522 P.2d 1187, review denied, 84 Wash.2d 1008 (1974), warrant more in-depth analysis. In *Jones*, the appellants, both females, sought review of a judgment that held that they were not entitled to have a marriage license issued to them, contending that refusal to issue the license deprived them of the basic constitutional rights to marry, associate, and exercise religion freely. In an opinion acknowledged to be "a case of first impression in Kentucky," the Court of Appeals summarily affirmed, ruling as follows:

> Marriage was a custom long before the state commenced to issue licenses for that purpose.... [M]arriage has always been considered as a union of a man and a woman....
>
> It appears to us that appellants are prevented from marrying, not by the statutes of Kentucky or the refusal of the County Clerk...to issue them a license, but rather by their own incapability of entering into a marriage as that term is defined.
>
> ...
>
> In substance, the relationship proposed by the appellants does not authorize the issuance of a marriage license because what they propose is not a marriage.

501 S.W.2d at 589-90.

Significantly, the appellants' equal protection rights — federal or state — were not asserted in *Jones*, and, accordingly, the appeals court was relieved of the necessity of addressing and attempting to distinguish the decision of the United States Supreme Court in *Loving*. *Loving* involved the appeal of a black woman and a caucasian man (the Lovings) who were married in the District of Columbia and thereafter returned to their home state of Virginia to establish their marital abode. 388 U.S. at 2, 87 S.Ct. at 1819. The Lovings were duly indicted for and convicted of violating Virginia's miscegenation laws,[23] which banned interracial marriages. *Id.*[24] In his sentencing decision, the trial judge stated, in substance, that Divine Providence had not intended that the marriage state extend to interracial unions:

> Almighty God created the races white, black, yellow, malay and red, and he placed them on separate continents. And but for the interference with

23. Virginia's miscegenation laws "arose as an incident to slavery and [were] common...since the colonial period." 388 U.S. at 6, 87 S.Ct. at 1820-21. It is noteworthy that one of the "central provisions" of the statutory miscegenation scheme *automatically voided* all marriages between "a white person and a colored person" without the need for any judicial proceeding. *Id.* at 4, 87 S.Ct. at 1820.

24. As of 1949, the following thirty of the forty-eight states banned interracial marriages by statute: Alabama; Arizona; Arkansas; California; Colorado; Delaware; Florida; Georgia; Idaho; Indiana; Kentucky; Louisiana; Maryland; Mississippi; Missouri; Montana; Nebraska; Nevada; North Carolina; North Dakota; Oklahoma; Oregon; South Carolina; South Dakota; Tennessee; Texas; Utah; Virginia; West Virginia; and Wyoming. 388 U.S. at 6 n. 5, 87 S.Ct. at 1820 n. 5. When the Lovings commenced their lawsuit on October 28, 1964, sixteen states still had miscegenation laws on the books. *Id.* at 3, 6 n. 5, 87 S.Ct. at 1819, 1820 n. 5. The first state court to recognize that miscegenation statutes violated the right to the equal protection of the laws was the Supreme Court of California in *Perez v. Sharp*, 32 Cal.2d 711, 198 P.2d 17 (1948). 388 U.S. at 6 n. 5, 87 S.Ct. at 1820-21 n. 5.

> his arrangement there would be no cause for such marriages. The fact that he separated the races shows that *he did not intend for the races to mix.*

Id. at 3, 87 S.Ct. at 1819 (quoting the trial judge)(emphasis added).

The Lovings appealed the constitutionality of the state's miscegenation laws to the Virginia Supreme Court of Appeals, which, inter alia, upheld their constitutionality and affirmed the Lovings' convictions. *Id.* at 3-4, 87 S.Ct. at 1819.[25] The Lovings then pressed their appeal to the United States Supreme Court. *Id.*

In a landmark decision, the United States Supreme Court, through Chief Justice Warren, struck down the Virginia miscegenation laws on both equal protection and due process grounds. The Court's holding as to the former is pertinent for present purposes:

> [T]he Equal Protection Clause requires the consideration of whether the classifications drawn by any statute constitute an arbitrary and invidious discrimination....
>
> There can be no question but that Virginia's miscegenation statutes rest solely upon distinctions drawn according to race. *The statutes proscribe generally accepted conduct* if engaged in by members of different races.... At the very least, the Equal Protection Clause demands that racial classifications...be subjected to the "most rigid scrutiny,"...and, if they are ever to be upheld, *they must be shown to be necessary to the accomplishment of some permissible state objective, independent of the racial discrimination which it was the object of the Fourteenth Amendment to eliminate....*
>
> There is patently no legitimate overriding purpose independent of invidious discrimination which justifies this classification.... We have consistently denied the constitutionality of measures which restrict the rights of citizens on account of race. There can be no doubt that restricting the freedom to marry solely because of racial classifications violates the central meaning of the Equal Protection Clause.

Id. at 10-12, 87 S.Ct. at 1823 (emphasis added and citation omitted).[26]

The facts in *Loving* and the respective reasoning of the Virginia courts, on the one hand, and the United States Supreme Court, on the other, both discredit the reasoning of *Jones* and unmask the tautological and circular nature of Lewin's argument that HRS §572-1 does not implicate article I, section 5 of the Hawaii Constitution because same sex marriage is an innate impossibility. Analogously to Lewin's argument and the rationale of the *Jones* court, the Virginia courts declared that interracial marriage simply could not exist because the Deity had deemed such a union intrinsically unnatural, 388 U.S. at 3, 87 S.Ct. at 1819, and, in effect, because it had theretofore never been the "custom" of the state to recognize mixed

---

25. See *Loving v. Commonwealth,* 206 Va. 924, 147 S.E.2d 78 (1966). The Virginia Supreme Court of Appeals, however, modified as "so unreasonable as to render the sentences void" the trial court's twenty-five year suspension of the Lovings' jail sentences "upon the condition that they leave the...state 'at once and...not return together or at the same time to [the]...state for a period of twenty-five years.'" *Id.* at 930, 147 S.E.2d at 82-83. The Virginia high court deemed it sufficient that the Lovings be prohibited from "again cohabit[ing] as man and wife in [the] state" in order to achieve the objectives of "securing the rehabilitation of the offender[s and] enabling [them] to repent and reform so that [they] may be restored to a useful place in society." *Id.* at 930, 147 S.E.2d at 83.

26. As we have noted in this opinion, unlike the equal protection clause of the fourteenth amendment to the United States Constitution, article I, section 5 of the Hawaii Constitution, *inter alia,* expressly prohibits discrimination against persons in the exercise of their civil rights on the basis of sex.

marriages, marriage "always" having been construed to presuppose a different configuration. With all due respect to the Virginia courts of a bygone era, we do not believe that trial judges are the ultimate authorities on the subject of Divine Will, and, as *Loving* amply demonstrates, constitutional law may mandate, like it or not, that customs change with an evolving social order.

Singer v. Hara, 11 Wash.App. 247, 522 P.2d 1187, *review denied*, 84 Wash.2d 1008 (1974), suffers the same fate as does *Jones*. In *Singer*, two males appealed from a trial court's order denying their motion to show cause by which they sought to compel the county auditor to issue them a marriage license. On appeal, the unsuccessful applicants argued that: (1) the trial court erred in concluding that the Washington state marriage laws prohibited same-sex marriages; (2) the trial court's order violated the equal rights amendment to the state constitution; and (3) the trial court's order violated various provisions of the United States Constitution, including the fourteenth amendment.

The Washington Court of Appeals affirmed the trial court's order, rejecting all three of the appellants' contentions. Predictably, and for the same reasons that we have reached the identical conclusion regarding HRS §572-1, the *Singer* court determined that it was "apparent from a plain reading of our marriage statutes that the legislature has not authorized same-sex marriages." *Id.* at 249, 522 P.2d at 1189. Regarding the appellants' federal and state claims, the court specifically "[did] not take exception to the proposition that *the Equal Protection Clause of the Fourteenth Amendment requires strict judicial scrutiny of legislative attempts at sexual discrimination.*" *Id.* at 261, 522 P.2d at 1196 (emphasis added).[27] Nevertheless, the *Singer* court found no defect in the state's marriage laws, under either the United States Constitution or the state constitution's equal rights amendment, based upon the rationale of *Jones*: "[a]ppellants were not denied a marriage license because of their sex; rather, they were denied a marriage license because of the nature of marriage itself." *Id.* As in *Jones*, we reject this exercise in tortured and conclusory sophistry.

3. Equal Protection Analysis under Article I, Section 5 of the Hawaii Constitution

"Whenever a denial of equal protection of the laws is alleged, as a rule our initial inquiry has been whether the legislation in question should be subjected to 'strict scrutiny' or to a 'rational basis' test."... This court has applied "strict scrutiny" analysis to "'laws classifying on the basis of suspect categories or impinging upon fundamental rights expressly or impliedly granted by the [c]onstitution,'" in which case the laws are "'presumed to be unconstitutional[28] unless the state shows compelling state interests which justify such classifications,'"...and that the laws are "narrowly drawn to avoid unnecessary abridgments of constitutional rights."...

By contrast, "[w]here 'suspect' classifications or fundamental rights are not at issue, this court has traditionally employed the rational basis test." *Id.* at 393, 629

27. Accordingly, but for the fact that the *Singer* court was unable to discern sexual discrimination in the state's marriage laws, it would have engaged in a "strict scrutiny" analysis. See *infra* at 63-64.

28. The presumption of statutory constitutionality, to which Judge Heen refers at 8 of his dissenting opinion, does not apply to laws, which, on their face, classify on the basis of suspect categories. *Washington v. Fireman's Fund Ins. Cos.*, 68 Haw. 192, 199, 708 P.2d 129, 134 (1985), cert. denied, 476 U.S. 1169, 106 S.Ct. 2890, 90 L.Ed.2d 977 (1986) on which the dissent relies, is not authority to the contrary inasmuch as the statute in question did not involve any suspect categories and was reviewed under the "rational basis" standard.

P.2d at 112. "Under the rational basis test, we inquire as to whether a statute rationally furthers a legitimate state interest."... "Our inquiry seeks only to determine whether any reasonable justification can be found for the legislative enactment."...

As we have indicated, HRS §572-1, on its face and as applied, regulates access to the marital status and its concomitant rights and benefits on the basis of the applicants' sex. *See infra* at 60-61. As such, HRS §572-1 establishes a sex-based classification.

...

In light of...the presence of article I, section 3 — the Equal Rights Amendment — in the Hawaii Constitution, ...we hold that sex is a "suspect category" for purposes of equal protection analysis under article I, section 5 of the Hawaii Constitution[33] and that HRS §572-1 is subject to the "strict scrutiny" test. It therefore follows, and we so hold, that (1) HRS §572-1 is presumed to be unconstitutional (2) unless Lewin, as an agent of the State of Hawaii, can show that (a) the statute's sex-based classification is justified by compelling state interests and (b) the statute is narrowly drawn to avoid unnecessary abridgements of the applicant couples' constitutional rights.

4. The dissenting opinion misconstrues the holdings and reasoning of the plurality.

We would be remiss if we did not address certain basic misconstructions of this opinion appearing in Judge Heen's dissent. First, we have *not* held, as Judge Heen seems to imply, that (1) the appellants "have a 'civil right' to a same sex marriage[,]" (2) "the civil right to marriage must be accorded to same sex couples[,]" and (3) the applicant couples "have a right to a same sex marriage[.]" Dissenting opinion at 70-71. These conclusions would be premature. We have, however, noted that the United States Supreme Court has recognized for over fifty years that marriage is a basic civil right. *See supra* at 60-61. That proposition is relevant to the prohibition set forth in article I, section 5 of the Hawaii Constitution against discrimination in the exercise of a person's civil rights, *inter alia*, on the basis of sex. *See id.* at 60.

Second, we have *not* held, as Judge Heen also seems to imply, that HRS §572-1 "unconstitutionally discriminates against [the applicant couples] who seek a license to enter into a same sex marriage[.]" Dissenting opinion at 70. Such a holding would likewise be premature at this time. What we *have* held is that, on its face and as applied, HRS §572-1 denies same-sex couples access to the marital status and its concomitant rights and benefits, thus implicating the equal protection clause of article I, section 5. *See supra* at 60.

We understand that Judge Heen disagrees with our view in this regard based on his belief that "HRS §572-1 treats everyone alike and applies equally to both sexes[,]" with the result that "neither sex is being *granted* a right or benefit the other does not have, and neither sex is being *denied* a right or benefit that the other has." Dissenting opinion at 71-72 (emphasis in original). The rationale underlying Judge Heen's belief, however, was expressly considered and rejected in Loving:

> Thus, the State contends that, because its miscegenation statutes punish equally both the white and the Negro participants in an interracial marriage, these statutes, despite their reliance on racial classifications do not

33. Our holding in this regard is *not*, as the dissent suggests, "[t]hat Appellants are a 'suspect class.'" Dissenting opinion at 72.

> constitute an invidious discrimination based upon race.... [W]e reject the notion that the mere "equal application" of a statute containing racial classifications is enough to remove the classifications from the Fourteenth Amendment's proscriptions of all invidious discriminations.... In the case at bar,...we deal with statutes containing racial classifications, and the fact of equal application does not immunize the statute from the very heavy burden of justification which the Fourteenth Amendment has traditionally required of state statutes drawn according to race.

388 U.S. at 8, 87 S.Ct. at 1821-22. Substitution of "sex" for "race" and article I, section 5 for the fourteenth amendment yields the precise case before us together with the conclusion that we have reached.

As a final matter, we are compelled to respond to Judge Heen's suggestion that denying the appellants access to the multitude of statutory benefits "conferred upon spouses in a legal marriage...is a matter for the legislature, which can express the will of the populace in deciding whether such benefits should be extended to persons in [the applicant couples'] circumstances." Dissenting opinion at 74. In effect, we are being accused of engaging in judicial legislation. We are not. The result we reach today is in complete harmony with the *Loving* Court's observation that any state's powers to regulate marriage are subject to the constraints imposed by the constitutional right to the equal protection of the laws....

III. Conclusion

Because, for the reasons stated in this opinion, the circuit court erroneously granted Lewin's motion for judgment on the pleadings and dismissed the plaintiffs' complaint, we vacate the circuit court's order and judgment and remand this matter for further proceedings consistent with this opinion. On remand, in accordance with the "strict scrutiny" standard, the burden will rest on Lewin to overcome the presumption that HRS §572-1 is unconstitutional by demonstrating that it furthers compelling state interests and is narrowly drawn to avoid unnecessary abridgements of constitutional rights....

Vacated and remanded.

JAMES S. BURNS, Intermediate Court of Appeals Chief Judge, concurs in the result.

JAMES S. BURNS, Intermediate Court of Appeals Chief Judge, concurring.

...

The marriage at issue in this case is the marriage specifically authorized by Hawaii's statutes. My label for this marriage is the "Hawaii Civil Law Marriage." The issue is whether the Hawaii constitution permits the State to discriminate against same-sex couples by extending the right to enter into a Hawaii Civil Law Marriage to opposite-sex couples and not to same-sex couples.

The Hawaii Constitution mandates, in article I, section 3, that "[e]quality of rights under the law shall not be denied or abridged by the State on account of sex." It also mandates, in article I, section 5, that "[n]o person shall be...denied the equal protection of the laws,...or be discriminated against in the exercise thereof because of...sex[.]" Thus, any State action that discriminates against a person because of his or her "sex" is subject to strict scrutiny.

As used in the Hawaii constitution, to what does the word "sex" refer? In my view, the Hawaii constitution's reference to "sex" includes all aspects of each person's "sex" that are "biologically fated." The decision whether a person when born will be a male or a female is "biologically fated." Thus, the word "sex" includes the male-female difference. Is there any other aspect of a person's "sex" that is "biologically fated"?

In March 1993, the *Cox News Service* reported in relevant part as follows:

> The issue of whether people become homosexuals because of "nature or nurture" is one of the most controversial subjects scientists have confronted in recent years.
>
> ...
>
> Until the middle 1980s, the prevailing view among most scientists was that homosexual "tendencies" were mostly the result of upbringing....
>
> ...
>
> Later, researchers at the Salk Institute in San Diego found anatomical differences between homosexual and heterosexual men in parts of the brain noted for differences between men and women.
>
> Theories gravitate to the role of male sex hormones.
>
> ...

The Honolulu Advertiser, March 9, 1993, at A8, col. 1.

In March 1993, the Associated Press reported in relevant part as follows:

> CHICAGO — Genes appear to play an important role in determining whether women are lesbians, said a researcher who found similar results among gay men.
>
> ...
>
> "I think we're dealing with something very complex, perhaps the interaction between hormones, the environment and genetic components," [Roger] Gorski [an expert in biological theories of homosexuality] said yesterday.
>
> ...

The Honolulu Advertiser, March 12, 1993, at A-24, col. 1.

On the other hand, columnist Charles Krauthammer reports as follows:

> It is natural, therefore, that just as parents have the inclination and right to wish to influence the development of a child's character, they have the inclination and right to try to influence a child's sexual orientation. Gay advocates argue, however, that such influence is an illusion. Sexual orientation, they claim, is biologically fated and thus entirely impervious to environmental influence.
>
> Unfortunately, as E.L. Pattullo, former director of Harvard's Center for the Behavioral Sciences, recently pointed out in Commentary magazine, the scientific evidence does not support such a claim....
>
> ...

The Honolulu Advertiser, May 2, 1993, at B2, cols. 3, 4 and 5.

If heterosexuality, homosexuality, bisexuality, and asexuality are "biologically fated[,]" then the word "sex" also includes those differences. Therefore, the questions whether heterosexuality, homosexuality, bisexuality, and asexuality are "biologically fated" are relevant questions of fact which must be determined before the issue presented in this case can be answered. If the answers are yes, then each person's "sex" includes both the "biologically fated" male-female difference and the "biologically fated" sexual orientation difference, and the Hawaii constitution probably bars the State from discriminating against the sexual orientation difference by permitting opposite-sex Hawaii Civil Law Marriages and not permitting same-sex Hawaii Civil Law Marriages. If the answers are no, then each person's "sex" does not include the sexual orientation difference, and the Hawaii constitution may permit the State to encourage heterosexuality and discourage homosexuality, bisexuality, and asexuality by permitting opposite-sex Hawaii Civil Law Marriages and not permitting same-sex Hawaii Civil Law Marriages.

WALTER M. HEEN, Intermediate Court of Appeals Judge, dissenting.

I dissent. Although the lower court judge may have engaged in "verbal overkill" in arriving at his decision, the result he reached was correct and should be affirmed....

I agree with the plurality's holding that Appellants do not have a fundamental right to a same sex marriage protected by article I, §6 of the Hawaii State Constitution.

However, I cannot agree with the plurality that (1) Appellants have a "civil right" to a same sex marriage; (2) Hawaii Revised Statutes (HRS) §572-1 unconstitutionally discriminates against Appellants who seek a license to enter into a same sex marriage; (3) Appellants are entitled to an evidentiary hearing that applies a "strict scrutiny" standard of review to the statute; and (4) HRS §572-1 is presumptively unconstitutional. Moreover, in my view, Appellants' claim that they are being discriminatorily denied statutory benefits accorded to spouses in a legalized marriage should be addressed to the legislature.

1

Citing *Loving*..., the plurality holds that Appellants have a civil right to marriage. I disagree....

Loving is simply not authority for the plurality's proposition that the civil right to marriage must be accorded to same sex couples. *Loving* points out that the right to marriage occupies an extremely venerated position in our society. So does every other case discussing marriage. However, the plaintiff in *Loving* was not claiming a right to a same sex marriage. *Loving* involved a marriage between a white male and a black female whose marriage, which took place in Washington, D.C., was refused recognition in Virginia under that state's miscegenation laws.

...

2

HRS §572-1 treats everyone alike and applies equally to both sexes. The effect of the statute is to prohibit same sex marriages on the part of professed or non-professed heterosexuals, homosexuals, bisexuals, or asexuals, and does not effect an invidious discrimination.[3]

The constitutional guarantee of equal protection of the laws means that no person or class of persons shall be denied the same privileges and benefits under

3. Appellants' sexual preferences or lifestyles are completely irrelevant. Although the plurality appears to recognize the irrelevance, the real thrust of the plurality opinion disregards the true import of the statute. The statute treats everyone alike and applies equally to both sexes.

the laws that are enjoyed by other persons or other classes of persons in like circumstances....

HRS §572-1 does not establish a "suspect" classification based on gender[4] because all males and females are treated alike. A male cannot obtain a license to marry another male, and a female cannot obtain a license to marry another female. Neither sex is being *granted* a right or benefit the other does not have, and neither sex is being *denied* a right or benefit that the other has.

...

...HRS §572-1 does not discriminate on the basis of gender. The statute applies equally to all unmarried persons, both male and female, who desire to enter into a legally recognized marriage. Thus, no evidentiary hearing is required.

...

3

Since HRS §572-1 is not invidiously discriminatory and Appellants are not members of a suspect class, this court should not require an evidentiary hearing. Neither should this court mandate that HRS §572-1 be subjected to the "strict scrutiny" test. If anything, Appellants' challenge subjects the statute only to the "rational basis" test. Estate of Coates v. Pacific Engineering, 71 Haw. 358, 791 P.2d 1257 (1990). Thus, the issue is whether the statute rationally furthers a legitimate state interest. *Id.* There is no question that such a rational relationship exists; therefore, the statute is a constitutional exercise of the legislature's authority.

In my view, the purpose of HRS §572-1 is analogous to the purpose of Washington's marriage license statute as stated in *Singer, supra.*

> In the instant case, it is apparent that the *state's refusal to grant a license allowing the appellants to marry one another is not based upon appellantsstatus as males, but rather it is based upon the state's recognition that our society as a whole views marriage as the appropriate and desirable forum for procreation and the rearing of children.... [M]arriage exists as a protected legal institution primarily because of societal values associated with the propagation of the human race. Further, it is apparent that no same-sex couple offers the possibility of the birth of children by their union. Thus the refusal of the state to authorize same sex marriage results from such impossibility of reproduction rather than from an invidious discrimination "on account of sex."* Therefore, the definition of marriage as the legal union of one man and one woman is permissible as applied to appellants, notwithstanding the prohibition contained in the ERA, because it is founded upon the unique physical characteristics of the sexes and appellants are not being discriminated against because of their status as males per se.[8]

Id. 11 Wash.App. at 259-60, 522 P.2d at 1195 (emphasis and footnote added). The court in *Singer* was considering the case in the light of that state's Equal Rights Amendment (identical to article I, §3 of the Hawaii State Constitution). The Washington court's reasoning is pertinent, in my view, to Appellants' claim in the case at hand and supports the constitutionality of the statute.

---

4. The plurality recognizes that the U.S. Supreme Court does not recognize sex or gender as a "suspect" classification, and thus gender has not historically been afforded the elevated "strict scrutiny" standard of review.

8. Since, in my view, the purpose of HRS §572-1 is to promote and protect propagation, the concern expressed in Chief Judge Burns' concurring opinion as to whether the statute discriminates against persons who may be genetically impelled to homosexuality does not cause the statute to be invidiously discriminatory.

4

Furthermore, I cannot agree with the plurality that HRS §572-1 is presumptively unconstitutional.

The general rule is that every statute is presumed to be constitutional, and the party challenging the law on constitutional grounds has the heavy burden of overcoming this presumption....

...

In my view, the statute's classification is clearly designed to promote the legislative purpose of fostering and protecting the propagation of the human race through heterosexual marriages and bears a reasonable relationship to that purpose. I find nothing unconstitutional in that.

5

Appellants complain that because they are not allowed to legalize their relationships, they are denied a multitude of statutory benefits conferred upon spouses in a legal marriage. However, redress for those deprivations is a matter for the legislature, which can express the will of the populace in deciding whether such benefits should be extended to persons in Appellants' circumstances. Those benefits can be conferred without rooting out the very essence of a legal marriage.[10] This court should not manufacture a civil right which is unsupported by any precedent, and whose legal incidents — the entitlement to those statutory benefits — will reach beyond the right to enter into a legal marriage and overturn long standing public policy encompassing other areas of public concern. This decision will have far-reaching and grave repercussions on the finances and policies of the governments and industry of this state and all the other states in the country.

...

COMMENTS

The transsexual marriage in *M.T. v. J.T.* basically conformed to a heterosexual pattern, which may well be why it was recognized when a same-sex marriage would not have been. An extraordinary procedure was necessary to bring about full physical gender change, described in unusual detail by the court. The male sexual organs were removed and an artificial vagina was surgically created. The trial judge found, as a matter of fact, that the plaintiff was a female. The appellate judge had no trouble consistently referring to the plaintiff as "she." Nevertheless it is possible that the case also had elements of estoppel. The defendant, after having paid for the operation prior to marriage, was in a bad position to raise the issue that the marriage was void. In other words, although the court did not use an estoppel rationale, it may have felt for this particular litigation that the defendant was precluded from raising the issue of homosexual marriage and should support the plaintiff as if she were a woman and his wife. If the issue of homosexual marriage had been raised prior to marriage — perhaps in a mandamus action upon refusal of a clerk to grant a marriage license — it is probable that such refusal would have been upheld.

10. I note that a number of municipalities across the country have adopted domestic partnership ordinances that confer such benefits on the domestic partners as the municipalities have authority to grant. Note: *A More Perfect Union: A Legal And Social Analysis Of Domestic Partnership Ordinances*, 92 COLUM.L.REV. 1164 (1992).

There is no certainty that other courts would treat a transsexual marriage as any different from an attempt to enter a homosexual union. For example, in the English case *Corbett v. Corbett*, [1970] 2 All E.R. 33, [1970] 2 W.L.R. 1306, a marriage was annulled because, in the opinion of the court, the participants in a transsexual union continued to be of the male sex. Indeed many courts, because of the ambiguity of the term "homosexual," may treat "transsexual" as a mere subspecies of homosexuality rather than recognizing legal effects of the operation. Courts have also been disinclined to recognize sex change operations of women. (See, *e.g.*, *B. v. B.*, 355 N.Y.S.2d 712 (1974).) It appears that conceptual problems related to language precede the legal characterizations. In *Corbett*, for instance, the court referred to the respondent by the male pronoun "he" up to the recital of the operation in the statement of facts, thereafter as "she." It recognized the operation as effective for linguistic purposes, but not for the legal purposes of marriage.

For many years courts summarily rejected arguments in favor of same-sex marriage. The problems judges encountered in dealing with a theory of homosexual marriage are related to language. *Jones v. Hallahan*, cited in *Baehr v. Lewin*, relied primarily on *Webster's* and other dictionaries as authorities for its decision on what constitutes marriage. The justification for this procedure was seen in the need to determine "common usage." Since common usage appeared to exclude any definition of marriage other than one limited to a union between a man and a woman, the court concluded that no constitutional issue was involved. *Webster's* is not concerned with the question whether a particular usage is constitutionally objectionable, or even discriminatory. A problem of linguistics becomes even more visible if one attempts to determine who is homosexual.

If there are conceptual difficulties with the terms "marriage" and "homosexual," there are greater difficulties with the combined term "homosexual marriage." Coming at the matter from a traditional direction, the tendency is strong, as illustrated by *Hallahan* and other cases cited in *Baehr*, to view such a combination as an absurdity. If the discussion were to stop at this point, the constitutional issue would indeed never be reached. Yet there have always been legal "homosexual marriages," if we agree to use this term for two persons of different sexes who are homosexually inclined and marry each other as a social accommodation. These unions may, of course, include affection and even procreation, and are not perceived as being homosexual. They seem to conform, at least outwardly, to the traditional heterosexual pattern. In fact, they include all the heterosexuality that the law asks for. Whether further pressure to conform is necessary or desirable is a matter to be examined, but it was not reached in *Hallahan* or most other cases. Whether further pressure is constitutional is sure to be examined further in subsequent cases.

Since most courts seem to rely more on traditional community values opposing homosexuality than on an exhaustive exploration of the underlying issues in given cases, constitutional attacks on prohibitions of homosexual marriages are likely to continue. The imperfections of language provide a further stimulus for continued efforts at clarification. In spite of *Bowers v. Hardwick*, further litigation relating to homosexual marriage is likely to take place and rely on *Zablocki v. Redhail* (p. 490), where Justice Marshall, in speaking for the majority, declared "that the decision to marry has been placed on the same level of importance as decisions relating to procreation, childbirth, child-rearing, and family relationships." Both courts and legislatures have shown an increasing inclination to embrace a larger segment of human relationships, perhaps in an effort to "domesticate" and stabilize these relationships. One of the questions to be asked is whether society is aided by laws that facilitate more stable human associations. Another task is to ascertain the shifting community values in regard to marriage. As illustrated by the materials in Chapter 2, supra, marriage and nonmarriage are not the only alternatives. Contractual cohabitation is an additional alternative that, short of marriage, could lend stability to the relationships of homosexual persons. It is likely that such contracts, express or implied, between persons of the same sex will be recognized, or at least recognized sooner than same-sex marriage. The notion of "domestic partnership" seems to avoid some of the conceptual problems that have plagued the notion of homosexual marriage. Legislative efforts to recognize domestic partnerships, such as the San Francisco Ordinance reproduced supra (p. 304), are sometimes politically feasible and sometimes not.

Some same-sex couples have used adoption law to obtain a certain degree of legal recognition for a homosexual relationship. In adult adoptions there is typically no substantive evaluation of best interests as found in child adoptions. As long as there is no obvious fraud (such as a lawyer attempting to be adopted by a wealthy octogenarian for purposes of inheritance) or a violation of a criminal statute (such as incest laws), a judge ordinarily does not inquire into matters other than whether the person being adopted is younger than the person adopting and whether the parties have technically complied with adoption laws.

It is too early to tell how significant an effect *Baehr* will have. It was a fairly narrow decision, based on the Hawaii constitution, but the approach the court took was considerably different from prior courts and may well influence future decisions. In addition, some other states have provisions in their constitutions similar to the Hawaiian. In any event, if any one state comes to permit same-sex marriages, interesting questions of conflict of laws will arise. While some states are likely to refuse any recognition to same-sex marriages, other states may decide to recognize same-sex marriages that are valid where performed, even if the state recognizing the marriage would not have allowed the marriage to take place within its own borders. Thus, for example, a couple married in Hawaii might be legally married in New York, California, and Massachusetts but have no legal relationship in New Hampshire or Florida. Even if a degree of uniformity and security of status could be achieved by a Supreme Court ruling — for example, that Full Faith and Credit had to be given to same-sex marriages — it is likely that many other countries throughout the world would refuse recognition to U.S. same-sex marriages. Issues relating to conflict of laws are discussed further in Chapter 6.

REFERENCES

Rhonda R. Rivera, *Our Straight-Laced Judges: The Legal Position of Homosexual Persons in the United States*, 30 HASTINGS L.J. 799 (1979).

Claudia A. Lewis, Note, *From This Day Forward: An Feminine Moral Discourse on Homosexual Marriage*, 97 YALE L.J. 1793 (1988).

Note, *Developments in the Law: Sexual Orientation and the Law*, 102 HARV. L. REV. 1511 (1989).

Katherine Shaw Spaht, *Revision of the Law of Marriage: One Baby Step Forward*, 48 LA. L. REV. 1131 (1988).

Hannah Schwarzchild, *Same-Sex Marriage and Constitutional Privacy*, 4 BERKELEY WOMEN'S L.J. 94 (1988–1989).

Marc A. Fajer, *Can Two Men Eat Quiche Together? Storytelling, Gender-Role Stereotypes, and Legal Protection for Lesbians and Gay Men*, 46 U. MIAMI L. REV. 511, 564–570 (1992).

BRASCHI v. STAHL ASSOCIATES COMPANY

Court of Appeals of New York
74 N.Y. 2d 201, 543 N.E.2d 49 (1989)

TITONE, Judge.

In this dispute over occupancy rights to a rent-controlled apartment, the central question to be resolved on this request for preliminary injunctive relief (see, CPLR 6301) is whether appellant has demonstrated a likelihood of success on the merits (see, *Grant Co. v. Srogi*, 52 N.Y.2d 496, 517, 438 N.Y.S.2d 761, 420 N.E.2d 953) by showing that, as a matter of law, he is entitled to seek protection from eviction under New York City Rent and Eviction Regulations 9 NYCRR 2204.6(d)(formerly New York City Rent and Eviction Regulations §56[d]). That regulation provides that upon the death of a rent-control tenant, the landlord may not dispossess "either the surviving spouse of the deceased tenant or some other member of the deceased tenant's *family* who has been living with the tenant" (emphasis supplied). Resolution of this question requires this court to determine the meaning of the term "family" as it is used in this context.

I

Appellant, Miguel Braschi, was living with Leslie Blanchard in a rent-controlled apartment located at 405 East 54th Street from the summer of 1975 until Blanchard's death in September of 1986. In November of 1986, respondent, Stahl Associates Company, the owner of the apartment building, served a notice to cure on appellant contending that he was a mere licensee with no right to occupy the apartment since only Blanchard was the tenant of record. In December of 1986 respondent served appellant with a notice to terminate informing appellant that he had one month to vacate the apartment and that, if the apartment was not vacated, respondent would commence summary proceedings to evict him.

Appellant then initiated an action seeking a permanent injunction and a declaration of entitlement to occupy the apartment. By order to show cause appellant then moved for a preliminary injunction, pendente lite, enjoining respondent from evicting him until a court could determine whether he was a member of Blanchard's family within the meaning of 9 NYCRR 2204.6(d). After examining the nature of the relationship between the two men, [the] Supreme Court concluded that appellant was a "family member" within the meaning of the regulation and, accordingly, that a preliminary injunction should be issued. The court based this decision on its finding that the long-term interdependent nature of the 10-year relationship between appellant and Blanchard "fulfills any definitional criteria of the term 'family.'"

The Appellate Division reversed, concluding that section 2204.6(d) provides noneviction protection only to "family members within traditional, legally recognized familial relationships" (143 A.D.2d 44, 45, 531 N.Y.S.2d 562). Since appellant's and Blanchard's relationship was not one given formal recognition by the law, the court held that appellant could not seek the protection of the noneviction ordinance. After denying the motion for preliminary injunctive relief, the Appellate Division granted leave to appeal to this court, certifying the following question of law: "Was the order of this Court, which reversed the order of the Supreme Court, properly made?" We now reverse.

...

The present dispute arises because the term "family" is not defined in the rent-control code and the legislative history is devoid of any specific reference to the noneviction provision. All that is known is the legislative purpose underlying the enactment of the rent-control laws as a whole.

Rent control was enacted to address a "serious public emergency" created by "an acute shortage in dwellings," which resulted in "speculative, unwarranted and abnormal increases in rents" (L.1946 ch. 274, codified, as amended, at McKinney's Uncons.Laws of N.Y. §8581 *et seq*). These measures were designed to regulate and control the housing market so as to "prevent exactions of unjust, unreasonable and oppressive rents and rental agreements and to forestall profiteering, speculation and other disruptive practices tending to produce threats to the public health...[and] to prevent uncertainty, hardship and dislocation" (*id.*). Although initially designed as an emergency measure to alleviate the housing shortage attributable to the end of World War II, "a serious public emergency continues to exist in the housing of a considerable number of persons" (*id.*). Consequently, the Legislature has found it necessary to continually reenact the rent-laws, thereby providing continued protection to tenants.

To accomplish its goals, the Legislature recognized that not only would rents have to be controlled, but that evictions would have to be regulated and controlled as well (*id.*). Hence, section 2204.6 of the New York City Rent and Eviction Regulations (9 NYCRR 2204.6), which authorizes the issuance of a certificate for the eviction of persons occupying a rent-controlled apartment after the death of the named tenant, provides, in subdivision (d), noneviction protection to those occupants who are either the "surviving spouse of the deceased tenant or *some other member of the deceased tenant's family* who has been living with the tenant [of record]" (emphasis supplied). The manifest intent of this section is to restrict the landowners' ability to evict a narrow class of occupants other than the tenant of record. The question presented here concerns the scope of the protections provided. Juxtaposed against this intent favoring the protection of tenants, is the over-all objective of a gradual "transition from regulation to a normal market of free bargaining between landlord and tenant" (*see, e.g.*, Administrative Code of City of New York §26-401). One way in which this goal is to be achieved is "vacancy decontrol," which automatically makes rent-control units subject to the less rigorous provisions of rent stabilization upon the termination of the rent-control tenancy (9 NYCRR 2520.11[a]; 2521.1[a][1]).

Emphasizing the latter objective, respondent argues that the term "family member" as used in 9 NYCRR 2204.6(d) should be construed, consistent with this State's intestacy laws, to mean relationships of blood, consanguinity and adoption in order to effectuate the over-all goal of orderly succession to real property. Under this interpretation, only those entitled to inherit under the laws of intestacy would be afforded noneviction protection (see, EPTL 4-1.1). Further, as did the Appellate Division, respondent relies on our decision in *Matter of Robert Paul P.*, 63 N.Y.2d 233, 481 N.Y.S.2d 652, 471 N.E.2d 424, arguing that since the relationship between appellant and Blanchard has not been accorded legal status by the Legislature, it is not entitled to the protections of section 2204.6(d), which, according to the Appellate Division, applies only to "family members within traditional, legally recognized familial relationships" (143 A.D.2d 44, 45, 531 N.Y.S.2d 562). Finally, respondent contends that our construction of the term "family member" should be guided by the recently enacted noneviction provision of the Rent Stabilization Code (9 NYCRR 2523.5 [a], [b][1], [2])....

However, as we have continually noted, the rent-stabilization system is different from the rent-control system in that the former is a less onerous burden on the property owner, and thus the provisions of one cannot simply be imported into the other.... Respondent's reliance on *Matter of Robert Paul P. (supra)* is also misplaced, since that case, which held that one adult cannot adopt another where none of the incidents of a filial relationship is evidenced or even remotely intended, was based solely on the purposes of the adoption laws...and has no bearing on the proper interpretation of a provision in the rent-control laws.

We also reject respondent's argument that the purpose of the noneviction provision of the rent-control laws is to control the orderly succession to real property in a manner similar to that which occurs under our State's intestacy laws (EPTL 4-1.1, 4-1.2). The noneviction provision does not concern succession to real property but rather is a means of protecting a certain class of occupants from the sudden loss of their homes. The regulation does not create an alienable property right that could be sold, assigned or otherwise disposed of and, hence, need not be construed as coextensive with the intestacy laws. Moreover, such a construction would be inconsistent with the purposes of the rent-control system as a whole, since it would afford protection to distant blood relatives who actually had but a superficial relationship with the deceased tenant while denying that protection to unmarried lifetime partners.

...

...[W]e conclude that the term family, as used in 9 NYCRR 2204.6(d), should not be rigidly restricted to those people who have formalized their relationship by obtaining, for instance, a marriage certificate or an adoption order. The intended protection against sudden eviction should not rest on fictitious legal distinctions or genetic history, but instead should find its foundation in the reality of family life. In the context of eviction, a more realistic, and certainly equally valid, view of a family includes two adult lifetime partners whose relationship is long term and characterized by an emotional and financial commitment and interdependence. This view comports both with our society's traditional concept of "family" and with the expectations of individuals who live in such nuclear units.... In fact, *Webster's Dictionary* defines "family" *first* as "a group of people united by certain convictions or common affiliation" (*Webster's Ninth New Collegiate Dictionary* 448 [1984]).... Hence, it is reasonable to conclude that, in using the term "family," the Legislature intended to extend protection to those who reside in households having all of the normal familial characteristics. Appellant Braschi should therefore be afforded the opportunity to prove that he and Blanchard had such a household.

This definition of "family" is consistent with both of the competing purposes of the rent-control laws: the protection of individuals from sudden dislocation and the gradual transition to a free market system. Family members, whether or not related by blood, or law who have always treated the apartment as their family home will be protected against the hardship of eviction following the death of the named tenant, thereby furthering the Legislature's goals of preventing dislocation and preserving family units which might otherwise be broken apart upon eviction.[3] This approach will foster the transition from rent control to rent stabilization by drawing a distinction between those individuals who are, in fact, genuine family members, and those who are mere roommates...or newly discovered relatives hoping to inherit the rent-controlled apartment after the existing tenant's death.

The determination as to whether an individual is entitled to noneviction protection should be based upon an objective examination of the relationship of the parties. In making this assessment, the lower courts of this State have looked to a number of factors, including the exclusivity and longevity of the relationship, the level of emotional and financial commitment, the manner in which the parties have conducted their everyday lives and held themselves out to society, and the reliance placed upon one another for daily family services (see, *e.g.*, *Athineos v. Thayer*, N.Y.L.J., Mar. 25, 1987, at 14, col. 4 [Civ.Ct., Kings County], *aff'd.* N.Y.L.J., Feb. 9, 1988, at 15, col. 4 [App. Term, 2d Dept.] [orphan never formally adopted but lived in family home for 34 years]; *2-4 Realty Assocs. v. Pittman*, 137 Misc.2d 898, 902, 523 N.Y.S.2d 7 [two men living in a "father-son" relationship for 25 years]; *Zimmerman v. Burton*, 107 Misc.2d 401, 404, 434 N.Y.S.2d 127 [unmarried heterosexual life partner]; *Rutar Co. v. Yoshito*, No. 53042/79 [Civ.Ct., N.Y. County] [unmarried heterosexual life partner]; *Gelman v. Castaneda*, NYLJ, Oct. 22, 1986, at 13, col. 1 [Civ.Ct., N.Y. County] [male life partners]). These factors are most helpful, although it should be emphasized that the presence or absence of one or more of them is not dispositive since it is the totality of the relationship as evidenced by the dedication, caring and self-sacrifice of the parties which should, in the final analysis, control. Appellant's situation provides an example of how the rule should be applied.

Appellant and Blanchard lived together as permanent life partners for more than 10 years. They regarded one another, and were regarded by friends and family, as spouses. The two men's families were aware of the nature of the relationship, and they regularly visited each other's families and attended family functions together, as a couple. Even today, appellant continues to maintain a relationship with Blanchard's niece, who considers him an uncle.

In addition to their interwoven social lives, appellant clearly considered the apartment his home. He lists the apartment as his address on his driver's license and passport, and receives all his mail at the apartment address. Moreover, appellant's tenancy was known to the building's superintendent and doormen, who viewed the two men as a couple.

---

3. We note, however, that the definition of family that we adopt here for purposes of the noneviction protection of the rent-control laws is completely unrelated to the concept of "functional family," as that term has developed under this court's decisions in the context of zoning ordinances.... Those decisions focus on a locality's power to use its zoning powers in such a way as to impinge upon an individual's ability to live under the same roof with another individual. They have absolutely no bearing on the scope of noneviction protection provided by section 2204.6(d).

Financially, the two men shared all obligations including a household budget. The two were authorized signatories of three safe-deposit boxes, they maintained joint checking and savings accounts, and joint credit cards. In fact, rent was often paid with a check from their joint checking account. Additionally, Blanchard executed a power of attorney in appellant's favor so that appellant could make necessary decisions — financial, medical and personal — for him during his illness. Finally, appellant was the named beneficiary of Blanchard's life insurance policy, as well as the primary legatee and coexecutor of Blanchard's estate. Hence, a court examining these facts could reasonably conclude that these men were much more than mere roommates.

Inasmuch as this case is before us on a certified question, we conclude only that appellant has demonstrated a likelihood of success on the merits, in that he is not excluded, as a matter of law, from seeking noneviction protection. Since all remaining issues are beyond this court's scope of review, we remit this case to the Appellate Division so that it may exercise its discretionary powers in accordance with this decision.

Accordingly, the order of the Appellate Division should be reversed and the case remitted to that court for a consideration of undetermined questions. The certified question should be answered in the negative.

[Concurring opinion by Judge BELLACOSA omitted.]

[Dissenting opinion by Judge SIMONS omitted.]

COMMENTS

Braschi reduces to some extent the disadvantages suffered by same-sex couples who are not allowed to marry one another. The difficulty it presents to courts is that it would seem to require complicated case-by-case determinations of the nature of a relationship. This difficulty is avoided by the enactment of registration statutes such as that in San Francisco (see supra p. 304) and other cities.

The trial court in *Braschi* looked to the "long-term interdependent nature of the 10-year relationship" and concluded that it "fulfill[ed] any definitional criteria for the term 'family'." The couple had interwoven social lives and a relationship marked by "dedication, caring and self-sacrifice." The court also referred to the household as having "all the normal familial characteristics." It seems clear that a couple not married is held to a higher standard than that to which a married couple would be held.

An interesting aspect of the case is what it says and implies about the expectations of family life. Families should be characterized by sacrifice and sharing. There should be an emotional and financial commitment and interdependence. One might wonder how many existing families would fully satisfy the criteria *Braschi* identifies. Although it is rare for a marriage to be challenged, in certain cases, such as immigration, the benefits given married people are valuable enough that the government has tried to determine which couples, although legally married, should be denied the benefits on the basis that the marriage is a sham.

DANISH LEGISLATION ON SAME-SEX MARRIAGE, 1989

LAW ON REGISTERED PARTNERSHIP

We, MARGRETHE THE FIRST, by the Grace of God Queen of Denmark, do proclaim: The Parliament has adopted and We have assented to the following law:

§1. Two people of the same sex can have their partnership registered.

REGISTRATION

§2. The Marriage Act chapter 1 and §12 and §13, subsection 1 and subsection 2, 1st clause, apply equally to the registering of partnerships, except as provided in subsection 2.

Subsection 2. Registration of partnership can occur only if both partners or one of them has a permanent residence in this country and Danish citizenship.

Subsection 3. Regulations regarding the procedure for registration of partnership, including the examination whether the requirements for registration are met, shall be set by the Minister of Justice.

LEGAL CONSEQUENCES

§3. The registering of a partnership has, with the exceptions provided in §4, the same legal effect as entering a marriage

Subsection 2. Provisions in Danish legislation which deal with marriage and married parties shall apply equally to registered partnerships and registered partners.

§4. Regulations on adoption that apply to a married couple do not apply to registered partnership.

Subsection 2. Child custody law §13, 3rd clause, and §15, subsection 3, which apply to married couples do not apply to registered partnerships.

Subsection 3. Provisions in Danish law, which contain special rules for one party in a marriage, dependent upon the sex of the party, do not apply to registered partnership.

Subsection 4. Provisions in international treaties do not apply to registered partnerships, unless the...parties [to the treaty] agree to go along with it.

DISSOLUTION

§5. The Marriage Act Chapters 3, 4 and 5 and Administration of Justice Law Chapter 42 apply equally to the dissolution of a registered partnership, except as provided in subsections 2 and 3.

Subsection 2. The Marriage Act §46 does not apply to the dissolution of registered partnerships.

Subsection 3. Notwithstanding the Administration of Justice Law §448c, a registered partnership can always be dissolved in this country.

COMING INTO FORCE

§6. The law comes into force the 1st of October, 1989.

§7.The law does not apply to the Faroe Islands or Greenland, but can by Royal proclamation be set into force in whole or in part in these areas, with any changes the special conditions dictate.

Given in Christianborg Castle, the 7th June 1989

Under our Royal Hand and Seal

MARGRETHE R.

COMMENTS

Under the 1989 law in Denmark, the parties to a registered partnership have the same legal status as married couples, with a few exceptions. The procedure for creating a registered partnership resembles a civil marriage. The same laws regarding bigamy, property, inheritance rights, taxation, dissolution, maintenance, and so forth, that apply to marriage apply also to registered partnerships. As with marriage, there is no requirement that parties to a registered partnership share a household or have sexual relations. Danish marriage law includes certain sex-specific provisions, such as laws presuming the husband to be father of any child born during a marriage and provisions making the husband responsible for certain debts incurred by his wife. Under §4 Subsection 3 of the Danish act, these provisions are inapplicable to registered partners. Lesbians in a registered partnership are not presumed to be together the parents of a child born to one of them.

Registered partners are not allowed to have common custody of a child and cannot together adopt a child. A same-sex partner therefore cannot adopt his or her partner's child, when an otherwise similarly-situated heterosexual partner would be entitled to a step-parent adoption. In addition, because it is expected that other countries will refuse to recognize Danish Registered Partnerships, the law requires Danish citizenship and permanent residence of one party to a registered partnership. Nevertheless, interesting and complex conflict-of-laws issues will arise; for example, if a party to a Danish registered partnership attempts to enter a marriage with a party of the opposite sex in any country that refuses to recognize Danish registered partnerships, such marriage would be valid where performed but presumably invalid in Denmark.

The Danish law was enacted through the active and effective lobbying of the Danish National Organization for Gays and Lesbians (LBL), originally founded in 1948 as "The Association of 1948." The only major compromises made in the legislation was its failure to allow adoption and the inability, at present, of those who wish to have their same-sex unions celebrated officially by the church. Because Denmark has a state church (Lutheran), the decision regarding the church's stance toward same-sex unions depends primarily upon democratic processes.

The situation of religion in the United States is quite different, in some ways better and in some ways worse. The separation of church and state, mandated by the Constitution, means that many separate struggles over the issue of who may marry whom will be carried out church-by-church. In recent years increasing numbers of religious same-sex marriages have been celebrated in the United States. Some of these marriages do, and others do not have the approval of the higher church authorities. The general public has only a limited ability to influence the decisions and activities of their own church officials and almost no influence over the policies of other religions, whether to enforce a basic moral code, to promote tolerance, or to encourage free choice for all between homosexuality, heterosexuality, bisexuality and asexuality.

REFERENCES

Michael Elmer and Marianne Lund Larsen, *Nye love: familieretlige lovaendringer i 1989*, 72 JURISTEN 126 (1990).

Linda Nielsen, *Family Rights and the "Registered Partnership" in Denmark*, 4 INTERNATIONAL JOURNAL OF LAW AND THE FAMILY 297 (1990).

Number (Bigamous Marriage)

DAVIS v. DAVIS
Supreme Court of Texas
521 S.W.2d 603 (Tex. 1975)

REAVLEY, Justice.

Charles Davis was killed by shipwreck in the Sea of Java on December 24, 1970, at the age of 36 years. The Probate Court of Chambers County, where the administration of his estate is pending, is in possession of the small amount of his personal property, together with wages due from his employer, Reading & Bates Offshore Drilling Company, and the proceeds of a group accidental death insurance policy which was purchased by that employer and issued a few days prior to the death of Charles. The insurer has paid $51,031.38 into the registry of the Chambers County Court. This litigation will determine the heirship of Charles Davis and the manner of division of this property.

Charles married Mary Nell in Liberty County in 1966, and in 1967 he departed for Australia without her on an assignment with Reading & Bates. After a year or so in Australia he was in Iran briefly, and then in August of 1968 he was assigned to Singapore. On October 2, 1968, a Buddhist wedding ceremony was performed to unite Charles and Nancy, and they lived together as man and wife in Singapore from that time until his death. Approximately one month after his death, both Mary Nell and Nancy gave birth to daughters.

This controversy ensues over the status and rights of Mary Nell and Nancy, and of the daughter of each. The County Probate Court held that Nancy was the lawful widow of Charles and that both of these daughters were entitled to inherit as children of Charles. The District Court, after an appeal and de novo trial without a jury, decided that Mary Nell was the widow, that Nancy was the putative wife, but that the daughter born to Mary Nell after the death of Charles was not his child and was not entitled to inherit any portion of his estate. The Court of Civil Appeals agreed that Mary Nell was the lawful widow and that her daughter was not the child of Charles, but it held that Nancy was not the putative wife at the time of the death of Charles. 507 S.W.2d 841. The only difference between the District Court and the Court of Civil Appeals in the division of the property was in the allotment to Nancy. What did not go to Nancy, under either judgment, went one-half to Mary Nell and the remaining one-half in equal parts to the children of Charles. The District Court awarded Nancy one-half of the wages due and the insurance proceeds; the Court of Civil Appeals judgment gave her nothing. Both Courts ruled that Mary Nell's daughter was not the child of Charles, and both ruled that Nancy's daughter inherited as a child of Charles. Even though the Court of Civil Appeals held that Nancy's putative status was terminated prior to the death of Charles, that holding would not prevent the daughter from being a legitimate child of their marriage. V.A.T.S. Probate Code, §42.

Nancy is here contending that she is the lawful widow or, at least, that she was the putative wife. Mary Nell's daughter contends that she is the legitimate child of Charles.

We hold, first, that Nancy was not the lawful widow of Charles. While it is initially presumed that Charles and Mary Nell were divorced prior to the wedding ceremony between Charles and Nancy..., the evidence presented by Mary Nell was legally adequate to rebut that presumption. It is shown that the records in Chambers and Liberty Counties reflect no divorce between them, that the records of the State of Queensland, Australia, show no divorce during the period from September 1, 1967 to December 31, 1970, and that the records in Singapore show no divorce between them during that same period. It is not necessary in order to rebut the presumption that Mary Nell prove the nonexistence of divorce in every jurisdiction where proceedings could have been possible; it is only necessary to rule out those proceedings where Charles might reasonably have been expected to have pursued them.... The trial court was entitled to find that there had been no divorce between Charles and Mary Nell and that Mary Nell was therefore his lawful widow.

We next hold that Nancy was the putative wife of Charles. A written contract of marriage (the Chinese document and the English translation), signed by Charles and Nancy, together with her father and another witness, certifying the marriage as being solemnized on October 2, 1968, was placed in evidence. Nancy and two other witnesses testified to the full formality of the ceremony, which was held in the home of her parents with all of her family participating and with twenty persons in attendance. For more than two years thereafter, and until the date of his death, Charles and Nancy lived together as man and wife. Nancy testified that Charles told her of his previous marriage but also assured her that he was divorced and free to marry her. The evidence clearly warrants the finding that Nancy entered this relationship in good faith. The attorney for Mary Nell, however, having proved that official Singapore records show no registration of this marriage prior to the death of Charles, contends that the marriage was entirely void and of no legal effect under Singapore law. He placed in evidence photographic copies of a portion of the pages of what appears to be an official publication of the law of the Republic of Singapore. There was no pleading as to the law of Singapore, nor do these pages establish the total effect of that law as it pertains to Nancy and Charles. Even if there had been an adequate pleading and if we assume that these copies faithfully reflect some of the pages of an official publication, on this record the Texas courts cannot determine that the total law of Singapore would brand the relationship of Nancy and Charles as meretricious. See generally: Thomas, *Proof of Foreign Law in Texas*, 25 Sw.L.J. 554 (1971).

The Court of Civil Appeals has held that even though Nancy may have become the putative wife of Charles at the outset and continued in that relationship for two years thereafter, at a time prior to his death she was put on notice that he was not divorced from Mary Nell — where-upon her putative standing terminated. The evidence on this point turns on the following testimony by Nancy:

Q: Now, during — well — subsequent to April 2, 1968 and before December 23, 1970, you learned, did you not, that Mary Nell Davis was trying to get a divorce from Charles Davis?

A: I didn't learn nothing of that.

Q: Well, you remember you (sic) asking that question on your deposition?

A: You asking me whether I received —

Q: No ma'am, I didn't ask you if you received it. I asked you if you learned that Mary Nell Davis was trying to get a divorce from Charles?

A: I learned it.

Q: Yes.

A: I know it.

The interrogation on the occasion of Nancy's deposition, which was introduced at the trial by the lawyer for Nancy to show a waiver of the dead man's statute, does not throw much light on this matter except for her statements that she knew that Charles was asked to sign a paper which came in the mail at a time when she was pregnant with the child born after the death of Charles. This testimony does not establish conclusively her lack of good faith. In the first place, it is not clear when Nancy understood that Mary Nell was "trying to get a divorce." She appreciated the facts as of the time of the trial, but it is not clear that she did so prior to the death of Charles. And even if she knew that these were divorce papers, it does not necessarily follow that Nancy had any reason to believe that Charles had been dishonest with her and had not obtained a prior divorce from Mary Nell. Before we charge Nancy with bad faith or impose upon her a duty to investigate matters, we must take into account that she was in Singapore and not in Texas, that she knew nothing of Texas law, and that she was a 20 year old Chinese woman who had always lived in Singapore and was then expecting a child by a husband who had given her no reason to believe that he had another wife. The trial court was entitled to find in her favor; we hold that the record does not conclusively establish her lack of good faith.

As a putative wife Nancy is entitled to the same right in the property acquired during her marital relationship with Charles as if she were a lawful wife.... In her case it will be half of the wages owed by the employer at the date of his death as well as half of the proceeds from the insurance policy which was furnished by the employer as an incident of the employment.

This brings us to the question of the legitimacy of Mary Nell's daughter who was born a month after the death of Charles. We agree with the Court of Civil Appeals that impossibility of access between Charles and Mary Nell, during the time when this child might have been conceived, has not been proved unless we consider the testimony to that effect by Mary Nell herself. Whether her testimony may be considered depends on whether we apply the Rule of Lord Mansfield, so-called because it was Lord Mansfield in *Goodright v. Moss*, 98 Eng.Rep. 1257 who said in 1777 that husband and wife "shall not be permitted to say after marriage that they had no connection and therefore that the offspring is spurious." This rule has been applied to exclude testimony to facts that would bastardize one's own child as of the time of birth.... It has even been used to exclude testimony on the ground that the effect would not be in accord with the innocence of married persons....

...

Rules that exclude evidence bearing directly on the truth to be determined ought not to survive without very good cause. The testimony of a spouse on the matter of non-access by the other spouse is, subject to the usual tests of credibility, clearly the best evidence of that fact. The present case is one where all of the testimony establishes beyond any reasonable doubt that Mary Nell's daughter is not the child of Charles. Then why should the courts refuse to accept the truth? And is there not a valid objection to allowing the child of another father to inherit part of this estate? Some courts have said that the Rule is required for the protection of the child. This may or may not be its consequence. It may be harmful to the interest of the child....

...The system and tradition that we call the "common law" is not a body of law which evolved within historic England or a bygone age to stand immutable ever afterward. It is the guide and governance of this Court today — in the absence of a mandate of the Constitution or statute. Learned Hand said that our common law is "a combination of custom and its successive adaptations. The judges receive it and profess to treat it as authoritative, while they gently mould it the better to fit changed ideas." THE SPIRIT OF LIBERTY p. 52 (1952). "This flexibility and capacity for growth and adaptation is the peculiar boast and excellence of the common law." *Hurtado v. California,* 110 U.S. 516, 530, 4 S.Ct. 111, 118, 28 L.Ed. 232 (1884). "[A]s life is always in flux, so the common law, which is merely life's explanation as the lawyer and the judge, law's spokesmen, are always making it, must also be." Hutcheson, *The Common Law of the Constitution,* 15 Tex.L.Rev. 317, 319 (1937).

...

It does not follow that this Court, or any court, is entitled to apply or not apply the rules of law according to preference in the individual case. Those who depend upon the law require continuity and predictability. If the administration of justice is to be effective in the trial courts, the rules must not be constantly shuffled. The appellate court must always start with the rule of precedent and either apply it faithfully or modify the rule if it is not consistent with the prevailing customs and precepts of the legal profession and of the community, giving particular attention to that portion of the community most concerned and affected by the rule.

If Lord Mansfield's Rule were one that had been counted upon in the planning of property rights, it should be left to the Legislature to change. That is no obstacle in this case. The Rule has never prevented proof of non-access of spouses for a determination of illegitimacy of a child born or conceived during wedlock. The exclusion has only applied to testimony by the spouses themselves. Proof of illegitimacy has been made more difficult, but there is no rule of law that prevents the fact from being shown if other evidence is available. Regarding blindfolds on triers of fact with disfavor, and finding no justification for perpetuating this decree by Lord Mansfield, we hold that testimony of non-access between man and woman is admissible from any witness knowledgeable of the fact.

The judgment of the Court of Civil Appeals is reversed; the judgment of the District Court is affirmed.

COMMENTS

The substantive question of bigamy is often related to procedural questions, in particular in the application of presumptions. (Some aspects of this problem have been discussed earlier in the comments on *Campbell v. Christian,* p. 161, *Thomson v. Thomson,* p. 164 and *Parkinson v. J. & S. Tool Company,* p. 172.) Rules relating to the putative wife, as well as the possibility of presumptions, were raised in connection with *Sousa v. Freitas* (p. 191), *Sanguinetti v. Sanguinetti* (p. 195), and

Lazzarevich v. Lazzarevich (p. 197). Whether bigamy was committed, with all the consequences of an illegal relationship, depends largely on questions of proof. In *Davis*, both the presumption of divorce and the conception of a putative wife are based on an underlying presumption of innocence. Whether this presumption, in its various manifestations, was overcome is left essentially to the discretion of the fact finder. Thus *Davis* refers repeatedly to the powers of the trial court, and mentions specifically that it "was entitled" to find in the second wife's favor. The Supreme Court of Texas was sympathetic to the twenty-year-old second wife who had always lived in Singapore. It was less sympathetic to the first who, as the court was willing to accept, had conceived a child from another man.

It is customary to view substantive law and procedure separately. Analytically this is justified and necessary, yet in legal practice the questions of whether a given case contains the substantive elements of bigamy and whether bigamy can be proven are blurred. Failure on either level results in a finding of no bigamy. As in *Davis*, courts indeed have a proclivity to resolve controversies on an evidentiary level. An argument of a lawyer that stresses the evidentiary aspects of the case — for example, the application of presumptions — has a good chance of persuading the court. In effect this means exactly what the Supreme Court of Texas is disclaiming in another context when discussing the Rule of Lord Mansfield (spouses "shall not be permitted to say after marriage that they had no connection and therefore that the offspring is spurious"), that is, that application of the rule of law depends on the court's preference in an individual case. Translating this premise and applying it to *Davis*, we see that the questions of whether the presumption of divorce is or is not applied, whether Nancy was a putative wife, and whether the child from the first marriage is presumed to be legitimate depend on what weight is given to the specific circumstances — in other words, on the preference of the court in this individual case.

REFERENCE

Walter O. Weyrauch, *Law as Mask — Legal Ritual and Relevance*, 66 CALIF. L. REV. 699 (1978).

REYNOLDS v. UNITED STATES

United States Supreme Court
98 U.S. 145 (1878)

Error to the Supreme Court of the Territory of Utah.

This is an indictment found in the District Court for the third judicial district of the Territory of Utah, charging George Reynolds with bigamy, in violation of section 5352 of the Revised Statutes, which, omitting its exceptions, is as follows:

> Every person having a husband or wife living, who marries another, whether married or single, in a Territory, or other place over which the United States have exclusive jurisdiction, is guilty of bigamy, and shall be

punished by a fine of not more than $500, and by imprisonment for a term of not more than five years.

...

...[T]he district attorney, after proving that the defendant had been married...to Mary Ann Tuddenham, offered to prove his subsequent marriage to one Amelia Jane Schofield during the lifetime of said Mary....

...

...The jury found him guilty, as charged in the indictment; and the judgment...rendered by the District Court...having been affirmed by the Supreme Court of the Territory, he sued out this writ of error.

...

Mr. Chief Justice WAITE delivered the opinion of the court.

The assignments of error, when grouped, present the following questions:—

...

5. Should the accused have been acquitted if he married the second time, because he believed it to be his religious duty?

...

On the trial, the plaintiff in error, the accused, proved that at the time of his alleged second marriage he was, and for many years before had been, a member of the Church of Jesus Christ of Latter-Day Saints, commonly called the Mormon Church, and a believer in its doctrines; that it was an accepted doctrine of that church "that it was the duty of male members of said church, circumstances permitting, to practise polygamy;... that this duty was enjoined by different books which the members of said church believed to be of divine origin, and among others the Holy Bible, and also that the members of the church believed that the practice of polygamy was directly enjoined upon the male members thereof by the Almighty God, in a revelation to Joseph Smith, the founder and prophet of said church; that the failing or refusing to practise polygamy by such male members of said church, when circumstances would admit, would be punished, and that the penalty for such failure and refusal would be damnation in the life to come." He also proved "that he had received permission from the recognized authorities in said church to enter into polygamous marriage;...that Daniel H. Wells, one having authority in said church to perform the marriage ceremony, married the said defendant on or about the time the crime is alleged to have been committed, to some woman by the name of Schofield, and that such marriage ceremony was performed under and pursuant to the doctrines of said church."

Upon this proof he asked the court to instruct the jury that if they found from the evidence that he "was married as charged — if he was married — in pursuance of and in conformity with what he believed at the time to be a religious duty, that the verdict must be 'not guilty.'" This request was refused, and the court did charge "that there must have been a criminal intent, but that if the defendant, under the influence of a religious belief that it was right, — under an inspiration, if you please, that it was right, — deliberately married a second time, having a first wife living, the want of consciousness of evil intent — the want of understanding on his part that he was committing a crime — did not excuse him; but the law inexorably in such case implies the criminal intent."

Upon this charge and refusal to charge the question is raised, whether religious belief can be accepted as a justification of an overt act made criminal by the law of the land....

Congress cannot pass a law for the government of the Territories which shall prohibit the free exercise of religion. The first amendment to the Constitution expressly forbids such legislation. Religious freedom is guaranteed everywhere throughout the United States, so far as congressional interference is concerned. The question to be determined is, whether the law now under consideration comes within this prohibition.

...

Polygamy has always been odious among the northern and western nations of Europe, and, until the establishment of the Mormon Church, was almost exclusively a feature of the life of Asiatic and of African people. At common law, the second marriage was always void (2 Kent, Com. 79), and from the earliest history of England polygamy has been treated as an offence against society....

By the statute of 1 James I. (c. 11), the offence, if committed in England or Wales, was made punishable in the civil courts, and the penalty was death. As this statute was limited in its operation to England and Wales, it was at a very early period re-enacted, generally with some modifications, in all the colonies. In connection with the case we are now considering, it is a significant fact that on the 8th of December, 1788, after the passage of the act establishing religious freedom, and after the convention of Virginia had recommended as an amendment to the Constitution of the United States the declaration in a bill of rights that "all men have an equal, natural, and unalienable right to the free exercise of religion, according to the dictates of conscience," the legislature of that State substantially enacted the statute of James I., death penalty included, because, as recited in the preamble, "it hath been doubted whether bigamy or poligamy be punishable by the laws of this Commonwealth." 12 Hening's Stat. 691. From that day to this we think it may safely be said there never has been a time in any State of the Union when polygamy has not been an offence against society, cognizable by the civil courts and punishable with more or less severity. In the face of all this evidence, it is impossible to believe that the constitutional guaranty of religious freedom was intended to prohibit legislation in respect to this most important feature of social life. Marriage, while from its very nature a sacred obligation, is nevertheless, in most civilized nations, a civil contract, and usually regulated by law. Upon it society may be said to be built, and out of its fruits spring social relations and social obligations and duties, with which government is necessarily required to deal. In fact, according as monogamous or polygamous marriages are allowed, do we find the principles on which the government of the people, to a greater or less extent, rests....

In our opinion, the statute immediately under consideration is within the legislative power of Congress.... This being so, the only question which remains is, whether those who make polygamy a part of their religion are excepted from the operation of the statute. If they are, then those who do not make polygamy a part of their religious belief may be found guilty and punished, while those who do, must be acquitted and go free. This would be introducing a new element into criminal law. Laws are made for the government of actions, and while they cannot interfere with mere religious belief and opinions, they may with practices. Suppose one believed that human sacrifices were a necessary part of religious worship, would it be seriously contended that the civil government under which he lived could not interfere to prevent a sacrifice? Or if a wife religiously believed it was her duty to burn herself upon the funeral pile of her dead husband, would it be beyond the power of the civil government to prevent her carrying her belief into practice?

So here, as a law of the organization of society under the exclusive dominion of the United States, it is provided that plural marriages shall not be allowed. Can a man excuse his practices to the contrary because of his religious belief? To permit this would be to make the professed doctrines of religious belief superior to the law of the land, and in effect to permit every citizen to become a law unto himself. Government could exist only in name under such circumstances.

...

Judgment affirmed.

In re DALIP SINGH BIR'S ESTATE

California District Court of Appeal

83 Cal. App. 2d 256, 188 P.2d 499 (1948)

ADAMS, Presiding Justice.

Dalip Singh Bir, a native of India, died intestate in San Joaquin County on April 18, 1945, and respondent Florence Boyes was appointed and qualified as administratrix of his estate. On April 4, 1947, two women named Harnam Kaur and Jiwi, both residents of India, joined in a petition to determine heirship, alleging in their petition:

> That your petitioners were, at the time of the death of the deceased herein, the legally wedded wives of said deceased, having lawfully married said deceased in the Punjab over 50 years ago whilst all parties were domiciled in Punjab Province, British India, according to the law and manner of the Jat community, in which province and community said marriages are lawful and valid. As said widows of deceased, petitioners are entitled to distribution of his estate.

Their petition further alleged that the residue of the estate consists of approximately $1,450 in cash and that in India petitioners would be entitled to share equally in the estate.

The record before us contains the following stipulation signed by counsel for the respective parties:

> It is hereby stipulated between counsel for the petitioners and the Administratrix herein, that the Petition for Determination of Heirship of Harnam Kaur and Jiwi was presented to the court as a joint petition requesting solely a judgment of an undivided one-half interest to each petitioner as the legal widows of Dalip Singh Bir, and that the judgment rendered was based upon said petition as so amended in open court, and the findings of fact and conclusions of law heretofore rendered may be deemed the final judgment herein denying said petition.

The trial court found that decedent, while domiciled in the Punjab Province of India, there married and was possessed of two wives, the petitioners above named, and that petitioners were legal spouses of decedent under the laws of the Punjab Province of India; that thereafter decedent emigrated to the United States and established residence in California, and that the money belonging to his estate was community property; that neither of said marriages had been dissolved prior to decedent's death but that no satisfactory proof was introduced as to which of the marriages was first performed.

Upon these findings of fact the trial court concluded that under the laws of California and the public policy thereof, only the first wife of decedent can be recognized as his legal widow. It therefore entered an order continuing the matter awaiting proof as to which of the marriages was first performed and which of the two petitioners was the initial wife of decedent. From that order the two wives have appealed.

Appellants rely on the provisions of section 63 of the Civil Code which reads:

> All marriages contracted without this state, which would be valid by the laws of the country in which the same were contracted are valid in this state.

In The Conflict of Laws, by Beale (1935), Vol. 2, page 666, the text reads:

> The American courts both those of the United States and those of Canada, have been much more liberal than those of England in recognizing and giving effect to a polygamous marriage or to a marriage which permits free divorce. Thus they have recognized a marriage of native tribes, and have given widows of polygamous marriages the legal rights of a widow.... Thus in a case decided in British Columbia it appeared that a Chinaman, domiciled in China, and legally having two wives under the law of China, died while temporarily in British Columbia, leaving property there. By his will he left the property to his two wives. The question was whether the succession duty should be that due on a gift to a wife. Held, that it should be: that, he being validly married by the law of his domicile, the validity of the marriage should be recognized in matters of succession.

The Canadian case above referred to is *Yew v. Attorney General for British Columbia,* 1 Dominion Law Reports 1166, British Columbia Court of Appeal (1923); and in that case many cases on the subject are cited. The conclusion there reached was that the law of China controlled, and since that law permitted the decedent to have more than one wife, the wives had the civil status of wives in China and must be so recognized in Canada in all matters of succession to property in respect to movables.

...

Polygamous marriages among Indians have been held valid, and in *Rogers v. Cordingley et al.,* 212 Minn. 546, 4 N.W.2d 627, 629, the court said:

> *Hallowell v. Commons,* 8 Cir., 210 F. 793, recognizes even polygamous marriages contracted by Indians according to their laws, and cites with approval from *Ortley v. Ross,* 78 Neb. 339, 110 N.W. 982, 983:
>
> > Now, it is contended by appellants that, as the alleged marriage between the father and mother of the plaintiff was polygamous, it was neither valid in the state of Minnesota, where the parties then resided, nor in the state of Nebraska, to which they subsequently removed. This contention would be well founded if this marriage had taken place between citizens of the United States in any state of the Union. But a different rule prevails with reference to the marriages of Indians, who are members of a tribe recognized and treated with as such by the

> United States government; for it has always been the policy of the general government to permit the Indian tribes as such to regulate their own domestic affairs, and to control the intercourse between the sexes by their own customs and usages.

To the same effect are numerous cases cited in the *Rogers* case. See, also, 38 C.J., p. 1278. Since polygamous marriages between tribal Indians are given validity for purposes of succession, it would seem there is no reason why the polygamous marriages in the instant case should not be held valid for succession purposes.

A good illustration will be found in Illustration 1 to section 134 of Restatement of the Law, Conflict of Laws, at page 202:

> A, domiciled in state X, validly marries B and C in X. By the law of Y, a polygamous marriage is void. A brings B and C to state Y; Y *may refuse to permit him to cohabit with them.* A and B die; Y may grant a widow's allowance to C. (Italics added.)

Succession of Caballero v. Executor et al., 24 Ann. 573, was a case where deceased, Caballero, lived with a Negro woman in Louisiana and had several children by her. Prior to his death he married the Negro woman in Havana, Cuba, where marriages between whites and Negroes are valid, and thus legitimated the children. From Cuba he moved with his family to Spain where his children remained. Upon Caballero's death a dispute arose as to inheritance, the executor of decedent's will claiming the children were illegitimate since Louisiana declared all marriages between whites and Negroes to be void. The court held in favor of a child claimant as to her right to succeed to her father's estate on the theory that the marriage in Havana, Cuba, was valid in Louisiana in so far as the right to succeed to decedent's property was concerned. The court said:

> We understand the rule to be well settled that marriages valid by the laws of the country where they are entered into, are held valid in any other country to which the parties may remove, unless there exists, from reasons of public policy, in the country to which they remove, some impediment by the laws of that country, or that such marriages are in derogation of good morals. In such exceptional cases comity could not be invoked to recognize their validity. How stands the matter in regard to the rights of Mrs. Conte, the plaintiff in this case? Here we may notice that this person, after her parents removed from Louisiana to Spain, never returned to Louisiana to live, and that she is a subject of the government of Spain. At the time of her legitimation by the marriage of her parents, marriage between white persons and free persons of color was prohibited by our law. The Louisiana law would not have recognized as valid in Louisiana the marriage of Caballero in Havana.... Thus far would our law have extended and had effect when Caballero returned to Louisiana, but no further. Its edict, so far as it bore upon his marriage, was of local and limited effect. It existed for a purpose local and special in this country. That purpose could not have been more effectually carried out by withholding from persons abroad, legitimate by the laws of the country where they lived, *the right of inheriting property* in this State.... The policy of this State had no broader extent, because there was no reason why it should have. (Italics added.)

The decision of the trial court was influenced by the rule of "public policy"; but that rule, it would seem, would apply only if decedent had attempted to cohabit with his two wives in California. Where only the question of descent of property is involved, "public policy" is not affected. It was so held in the *Succession of Caballero, supra.* On the authority of Beale on Conflict of Laws, *Yew v. Attorney General of British Columbia* and *Succession of Caballero, supra,* the two wives of decedent should share equally in the money in question. No case has been found that is opposed to those authorities. True, there are cases holding invalid polygamous marriages entered into in places where such marriages are legal, but in each such case found, all the parties were living and no question of succession to property was considered. Therefore, it would seem that the above cited authorities which actually considered the right of succession and granted such succession in cases growing out of marriages legal where entered into but illegal in the place where probate proceedings are being had, are controlling. "Public policy" would not be affected by dividing the money equally between the two wives, particularly since there is no contest between them and they are the only interested parties.

The order appealed from is therefore reversed with directions to the trial court to enter a decree in accordance with the views herein expressed.

COMMENTS

Polygamy is often seen as an issue dividing West from East, Christian from Muslim, or modern civilization from olden, less civilized times. Some have understood the issue in gendered terms: "Monogamy is woman's doctrine, as polygamy is man's." (Matilda Joslyn Gage, at 188.) None of these characterizations seems accurate, perhaps in part because polygamy is a complex, multi-faceted practice, which takes different forms at different times and in different cultures. Some groups in the East oppose polygamy more strongly than groups in the West; polygamy has its Muslim opponents, and the Mormons in the United States are widely assumed, rightly or wrongly, to support polygamy.

Polygamy has from time to time in our history been considered a moral question of enormous importance. In England and some states in the U.S., it was a capital offense. *Reynolds* gives some suggestion of the moral tone of some anti-polygamy rhetoric. As divorce has become easier and restrictions on remarriage have been essentially abolished — and indeed some have characterized the American system as one of *serial* polygamy — opposition to polygamy has also decreased. *Dalip Bir's Estate* illustrates a more tolerant view of polygamy, at least when practiced elsewhere and after the husband's death. Some groups in the United States practice polygamy more or less openly, and only occasionally are they interfered with (although, of course, this "occasional" interference can seem quite intrusive to those it affects). It is possible that polygamy can in fact be achieved legally, so to speak, if a marriage is entered with only one wife and the other women by mutual consent enter the arrangement without going through the formalities of a licensed marriage. Any cohabitation contract for such a de facto polygamous relationship, especially if specific reference to the sexual aspects of the relationship were made, would likely be void as against public policy; but that would simply make the contract unenforceable, not prevent the relationship. By one estimate, over 50,000 people were living in polygamous families in the Rocky Mountain states in 1991.

The social effects of polygamy are complicated. Many in the United States associate polygamy with the exploitation of women, but others would argue that there is no necessary connection. Indeed, some argue that polygamy is great for women, because there are more of them to share the work. Few of these polygamy supporters would argue, however, that polyandry is terrific for men because there are more of them to share the work.

Mormons traditionally objected to governmental efforts to prevent polygamy. They asserted that Christianity long supported polygamy and pointed out that nothing in the Old or New Testament opposes it. Christian tolerance for polygamy has been alluded to both in defenses of the practice and in attacks on it. For example, it has been pointed out that Jacob fathered children by four women: Leah, Rachel, Bilhah and Zilpah. Although one or two may have been considered concubines, at least two were his wives. The twelve sons of Jacob, born of the different women, were all equally made patriarchs of the Tribes of Israel. One can feel a certain sympathy for the claim of one Mormon: "Had Jacob lived now, the judges would have sent spies, spotters and deputy marshals after him, and if caught would have sent him to the penitentiary." (Quoted in Matilda Joslyn Gage, at 181.)

Matilda Joslyn Gage, a nineteenth-century critic of polygamy, referred to polygamy as "a component part of Christianity" and asserted:

> Although like the fagot and the stake, under the light of advancing civilization it has somewhat fallen into disrepute with the majority of men and women, yet its renewal as an underlying principle of a new christian sect need not be a subject of astonishment. (P. 190.)

It appears that the so-called Branch Davidians, who came to wide attention during the stand-off and shoot-out in Waco, Texas in 1993, practiced a form of polygamy, with the leader of the group claiming a large, perhaps indeterminate group of girls and women as his wives. Some American's support for the war to defend Kuwait against the Iraqi invasion of 1990 was dampened when it became known that members of the Kuwaiti leadership had several wives.

REFERENCES

Matilda Joslyn Gage, WOMAN, CHURCH & STATE (1893, republished 1980).
Dirk Johnson, *Polygamists Emerge From Secrecy*, N.Y. TIMES, April 9, 1991 at A.22, col. 1.

VILLAGE OF BELLE TERRE v. BORAAS

United States Supreme Court
416 U.S. 1 (1974)

Mr. Justice DOUGLAS delivered the opinion of the Court.

Belle Terre is a village on Long Island's north shore of about 220 homes inhabited by 700 people. Its total land area is less than one square mile. It has restricted land use to one-family dwellings excluding lodging houses, boarding houses, fraternity houses, or multiple-dwelling houses. The word "family" as used in the ordinance means, "[o]ne or more persons related by blood, adoption, or marriage, living and cooking together as a single housekeeping unit, exclusive of household servants. A number of persons but not exceeding two (2) living and cooking together as a single housekeeping unit though not related by blood, adoption, or marriage shall be deemed to constitute a family."

Appellees, the Dickmans, are owners of a house in the village and leased it in December 1971 for a term of 18 months to Michael Truman. Later Bruce Boraas became a colessee. Then Anne Parish moved into the house along with three others. These six are students at nearby State University at Stony Brook and none is related to the other by blood, adoption, or marriage. When the village served the Dickmans with an "Order to Remedy Violations" of the ordinance, the owners plus three tenants thereupon brought this action under 42 U.S.C. §1983 for an injunction and a judgment declaring the ordinance unconstitutional....

...

The present ordinance is challenged on several grounds: that it interferes with a person's right to travel; that it interferes with the right to migrate to and settle within a State; that it bars people who are uncongenial to the present residents; that it expresses the social preferences of the residents for groups that will be congenial to them; that social homogeneity is not a legitimate interest of government; that the restriction of those whom the neighbors do not like trenches on the newcomers' rights of privacy; that it is of no rightful concern to villagers whether the residents are married or unmarried; that the ordinance is antithetical to the Nation's experience, ideology, and self-perception as an open, egalitarian, and integrated society.

We find none of these reasons in the record before us. It is not aimed at transients. *Cf. Shapiro v. Thompson*, 394 U.S. 618, 89 S.Ct. 1322, 22 L.Ed.2d 600. It involves no procedural disparity inflicted on some but not on others such as was presented by *Griffin v. Illinois*, 351 U.S. 12, 76 S.Ct. 585, 100 L.Ed. 891. It involves no "fundamental" right guaranteed by the Constitution, such as voting, *Harper v. Virginia State Board*, 383 U.S. 663, 86 S.Ct. 1079, 16 L.Ed.2d 169; the right of association, *NAACP v. Alabama ex rel. Patterson*, 357 U.S. 449, 78 S.Ct. 1163, 2 L.Ed.2d 1488; the right of access to the courts, *NAACP v. Button*, 371 U.S. 415, 83 S.Ct. 328, 9 L.Ed.2d 405; or any rights of privacy, *cf. Griswold v. Connecticut*, 381 U.S. 479, 85 S.Ct. 1678, 14 L.Ed.2d 510; *Eisenstadt v. Baird*, 405 U.S. 438, 453-454, 92 S.Ct. 1029, 1038-1039, 31 L.Ed.2d 349. We deal with economic and social legislation where legislatures have historically drawn lines which we respect against the charge of violation of the Equal Protection Clause if the law be "reasonable, not arbitrary" (quoting *Royster Guano Co. v. Virginia*, 253 U.S. 412, 415, 40 S.Ct. 560, 561, 64 L.Ed. 989) and bears "a rational relationship to a (permissible) state objective." *Reed v. Reed*, 404 U.S. 71, 76.

It is said, however, that if two unmarried people can constitute a "family," there is no reason why three or four may not. But every line drawn by a legislature leaves some out that might well have been included. That exercise of discretion, however, is a legislative, not a judicial, function.

It is said that the Belle Terre ordinance reeks with an animosity to unmarried couples who live together. There is no evidence to support it; and the provision of the ordinance bringing within the definition of a "family" two unmarried people belies the charge.

The ordinance places no ban on other forms of association, for a "family" may, so far as the ordinance is concerned, entertain whomever it likes.

The regimes of boarding houses, fraternity houses, and the like present urban problems. More people occupy a given space; more cars rather continuously pass by; more cars are parked; noise travels with crowds.

A quiet place where yards are wide, people few, and motor vehicles restricted are legitimate guidelines in a land-use project addressed to family needs. This goal is a permissible one.... The police power is not confined to elimination of filth, stench, and unhealthy places. It is ample to lay out zones where family values, youth values, and the blessings of quiet seclusion and clean air make the area a sanctuary for people.

...

Reversed.

...

Mr. Justice MARSHALL, dissenting.

This case draws into question the constitutionality of a zoning ordinance of the incorporated village of Belle Terre, New York, which prohibits groups of more than two unrelated persons, as distinguished from groups consisting of any number of persons related by blood, adoption, or marriage, from occupying a residence within the confines of the township. Lessor-appellees, the two owners of a Belle Terre residence, and three unrelated student tenants challenged the ordinance on the ground that it establishes a classification between households of related and unrelated individuals, which deprives them of equal protection of the laws. In my view, the disputed classification burdens the students' fundamental rights of association and privacy guaranteed by the First and Fourteenth Amendments. Because the application of strict equal protection scrutiny is therefore required, I am at odds with my Brethren's conclusion that the ordinance may be sustained on a showing that it bears a rational relationship to the accomplishment of legitimate governmental objectives.

...

...Zoning officials properly concern themselves with the uses of land — with, for example, the number and kind of dwellings to be constructed in a certain neighborhood or the number of persons who can reside in those dwellings. But zoning authorities cannot validly consider who those persons are, what they believe, or how they choose to live, whether they are Negro or white, Catholic or Jew, Republican or Democrat, married or unmarried.

My disagreement with the Court today is based upon my view that the ordinance in this case unnecessarily burdens appellees' First Amendment freedom of association and their constitutionally guaranteed right to privacy....

...Constitutionally protected privacy is, in Mr. Justice Brandeis' words, "as against the Government, the right to be let alone...the right most valued by civilized man." *Olmstead v. United States*, 277 U.S. 438, 478, 48 S.Ct. 564, 572, 72 L.Ed. 944 (1928)(dissenting opinion). The choice of household companions — of whether a person's "intellectual and emotional needs" are best met by living with family, friends, professional associates, or others — involves deeply personal considerations as to the kind and quality of intimate relationships within the home. That decision surely falls within the ambit of the right to privacy protected by the Constitution....

The instant ordinance discriminates on the basis of just such a personal lifestyle choice as to household companions. It permits any number of persons related by blood or marriage, be it two or twenty, to live in a single household, but it limits to two the number of unrelated persons bound by profession, love, friendship, religious or political affiliation, or mere economics who can occupy a single home. Belle Terre imposes upon those who deviate from the community norm in their choice of living companions significantly greater restrictions than are applied to residential groups who are related by blood or marriage, and compose the established order within the community. The village has, in effect, acted to fence out those individuals whose choice of lifestyle differs from that of its current residents.

...

A variety of justifications have been proffered in support of the village's ordinance. It is claimed that the ordinance controls population density, prevents noise, traffic and parking problems, and preserves the rent structure of the community and its attractiveness to families. As I noted earlier, these are all legitimate and substantial interests of government. But I think it clear that the means chosen to accomplish these purposes are both overinclusive and underinclusive, and that the asserted goals could be as effectively achieved by means of an ordinance that did not discriminate on the basis of constitutionally protected choices of lifestyle. The ordinance imposes no restriction whatsoever on the number of persons who may live in a house, as long as they are related by marital or sanguinary bonds — presumably no matter how distant their relationship. Nor does the ordinance restrict the number of income earners who may contribute to rent in such a household, or the number of automobiles that may be maintained by its occupants. In that sense the ordinance is underinclusive. On the other hand, the statute restricts the number of unrelated persons who may live in a home to no more than two. It would therefore prevent three unrelated people from occupying a dwelling even if among them they had but one income and no vehicles. While an extended family of a dozen or more might live in a small bungalow, three elderly and retired persons could not occupy the large manor house next door. Thus the statute is also grossly overinclusive to accomplish its intended purposes.

...

... I would find the challenged ordinance unconstitutional. But I would not ask the village to abandon its goal of providing quiet streets, little traffic, and a pleasant and reasonably priced environment in which families might raise their children. Rather, I would commend the village to continue to pursue those purposes but by means of more carefully drawn and even-handed legislation.

I respectfully dissent.

FRAMBACH v. DUNIHUE

District Court of Appeal of Florida
419 So.2d 1115 (Fla. Dist. Ct. App. 1982)

FRANK D. UPCHURCH, Jr., Judge.

The Frambachs appeal from a judgment awarding Dunihue an undivided one-half interest in their property. Two pieces of property were titled in the Frambachs' names. In parcel A the court imposed a resulting trust. In parcel B, the court determined that Dunihue was entitled to a one-half interest as an "equitable lien and equitable interest." By this appeal, the Frambachs question only the court's ruling as to parcel B on which their home was located.

The history of this case is an amazing account of human relationships. Why people who for many years had demonstrated an incredible ability to solve their disputes would ultimately end up in litigation is mystifying.

Dunihue was a widower with seven children to raise ranging in age from three to eleven. The Frambachs lived nearby with their four children. Contact between the parties started when Mrs. Frambach, a devoted churchwoman, asked if she could take the Dunihue children to church. She later became a babysitter and took care of the Dunihue children sometimes at their home and sometimes at hers for which she was paid $25.00 per week.

This arrangement continued for a few months. In September, 1960, the Frambachs and the Dunihues waited out a hurricane in the Frambachs' home. The Frambachs' house was small (a bedroom, living room and kitchen, 600 square feet in all) and had no inside plumbing. As fate would have it, the relationships which developed as the storm howled proved so interesting and the two families so congenial that the Frambachs and Dunihues decided to see if the two families could live together.

Dunihue set out to enlarge the house. A bedroom and bath were added and various improvements made. As the years passed, Mrs. Frambach had another child and for a time, until the Dunihue children began to move out, fifteen people (three adults and twelve children) lived in the house. Mrs. Frambach ran the household, did the cooking, and saw that the children cleaned, helped with the washing, and did such chores as were required and within their capabilities.

Both Dunihue and the Frambachs were employed. Dunihue on several occasions obtained employment for Mr. Frambach and their earnings were not substantially different, although Dunihue had the larger income. The Frambachs and Dunihue each had a bank account into which they deposited their respective earnings. Mrs. Frambach wrote checks on both accounts and decided in large measure which account would be used to pay a particular bill. Dunihue's characterization of the arrangement was probably the most appropriate, that it was just one family and whatever money was available was used wherever it was most needed. Very often the three shopped together for clothes, furniture, and automobiles.

Improvements in the home continued to be made. Dunihue's contributions to these improvements undoubtedly were the most valuable although everyone assisted. At the time of this litigation, the value of the home had appreciated to approximately $65,000. The court received considerable testimony of Dunihue's contributions to the improvements, but very little evidence was adduced as to the value of the services received by Dunihue and his family.

This arrangement lasted for nineteen years until the last of the Dunihue children were grown and gone. The relationship was suddenly terminated when Mrs. Frambach called Dunihue at work and told him to come get his things and get out. He was given thirty minutes to comply. The reason for the sudden end to the friendship was not clear.

After being ejected from the Frambachs' home, Dunihue brought suit to impose an equitable lien on the property. Dunihue claimed that the Frambachs had promised him a place to live for the rest of his life in exchange for his work. He further alleged that he had relied on this promise and that the Frambachs will be unjustly enriched at his expense if he is not compensated for his work. The Frambachs denied that they had made any such promise to Dunihue claiming that without the improvements it would have been impossible to house that many people.

The trial court determined that the two families had operated as a single family. While emphasizing that he was not making such an inference, the judge opined that the association of the parties was almost as close as though there had been a single wife and two husbands. The court then found that the pooling of assets and commingling of everything into a common pot was to assure Dunihue that he would have a home as long as he lived and that it would award Dunihue an equitable lien in the home. Regarding the amount of the lien, the court stated the following:

> They did start out with a thousand-dollar equity, the [Frambachs]. But in effect because of the way they treated everything through the years, they really are just as though this was a divorce. And we are dividing up the property between a wife that had two husbands, so to speak. That's why I think the only fair thing to do is to make them tenants in common right down the middle. So that's my judgment.

As a general rule, a court of equity may give restitution to a plaintiff and prevent the unjust enrichment of a defendant by imposing a constructive trust or by imposing an equitable lien upon the property in favor of the plaintiff. Restatement of Restitution §§160-161 (1937). However, where the plaintiff makes improvements upon the land of another under circumstances which entitle him to restitution, he is entitled only to an equitable lien upon the land and he cannot charge the owner of the land as constructive trustee and compel the owner to transfer the land to him. Restatement of Restitution §161, Comment a. Neither a constructive trust nor a resulting trust arises in favor of a person who pays no part of the purchase price even though he pays for improvements on the property. 5 Scott, The Law of Trusts, §§455.7,472 (3d ed. 1967). The person does not become, in whole or in part, a beneficial owner of the property although he may be entitled to reimbursement.

In the present case, the court, in effect, determined that the Frambachs held an undivided one-half interest in the property in trust for Dunihue. However, there was no evidence of a promise or agreement to deed a portion of the Frambachs' property to Dunihue in return for the improvements. Nor has Dunihue alleged that he actually paid a part of the purchase price. In these circumstances, Dunihue was not entitled to have a constructive trust imposed on the property. We therefore reverse the award to Dunihue of a tenancy in common and remand the cause for further consideration.

Upon remand, the trial court should determine the value of the respective contributions of Dunihue and the Frambachs. This can be accomplished by calculating the fair market value of the improvements attributable to Dunihue and the fair market value of the services rendered by the Frambachs to him during the nineteen years the parties lived together. In the alternative, the court could determine the cost to Dunihue for his labor, services and material in making the improvements as compared to the cost to the Frambachs of providing services to Dunihue. We suspect that, under either measure, the contributions of the parties will be equal. However, if the court finds that Dunihue's contributions exceed the value of the benefits received by him from the Frambachs, an equitable lien in this amount should be imposed to prevent the unjust enrichment of the Frambachs.

Reversed and Remanded.

COMMENTS

The definition of the "family" is of concern to legislatures on all levels. It is an important tool in administering a variety of government welfare programs, although sometimes legislatures prefer the terms "household" or "cohabitation." The definition must depend on the purposes of the individual legislation — whether, for example, food stamps or zoning is involved. A further complication arises because more often than not the legislative history is not recorded and the purposes of the legislation are thus left to speculation. In the case of federal legislation we have clues; but in *Belle Terre* it is difficult if not impossible to ascertain what deliberations resulted in the specific wording of the ordinance of a small Long Island community of 700 people. Not unlikely, the ordinance was copied wholly or in part from some other ordinance, which in turn was copied from some preexisting form. Seemingly minor but nonetheless significant changes may have been made to adjust the form to local conditions, for instance, the proximity of a state university. The changes might have tried to cope with the influx of students and the fear that neighborhoods would deteriorate. Justice Douglas considered this fear legitimate.

Regardless of whether any forms were used, the defining of the "family" for zoning purposes, as for any other purpose, is a difficult task of drafting. Since, in the absence of a clear legislative history, any interpretation at a later stage must be left to the actual wording and speculation about the context, an ordinance of this nature is inevitably over-inclusive or under-inclusive, depending on the ways it is examined. The *Belle Terre* ordinance permits two unmarried people to constitute a family for zoning purposes. It is reasonably clear that unmarried cohabitation between a man and a woman is covered by the wording of the statute; but difference in sex does not seem to be required. The wording implies that the ordinance is directed against living arrangements of students and "hippie communes," but not against same-sex couples or other groups of two.

Constitutional adjudication necessarily proceeds from the wording of a statute or ordinance as a given fact. While this furnishes, as in *Belle Terre*, an important guideline to legal practice, it does not solve the problem of a lawyer who is requested to draft an ordinance of this kind. Only after it is clear what groups of persons are to be excluded and who is to be included in a definition of the family can the question be asked whether the wording is acceptable under constitutional standards. A lawyer who tried to combine the two steps would be likely to neglect either the wishes of the community (assuming that they can be identified) or constitutional demands.

Returning to the speculative underlying purposes of the *Belle Terre* ordinance, like most zoning regulations it was probably concerned more with property values than with anyone's idea of morality. In the vicinity of any university campus so-called "student ghettos" can be found. These ghettos have a tendency to spread. Their visual impact has some unique features, partly due to the transient nature of their occupants. The campus atmosphere tends to attract elements considered even less desirable and stable than students. There is potential for drug dealing and a lack of supervision of premises. Buildings deteriorate until they are finally condemned.

As pointed out by Justice Marshall, an ordinance can legitimately concern itself with these matters. To use a definition of the family within this context — that of regulating the external appearance of a neighborhood — may well be a subterfuge to reach a result that could be more appropriately reached by direct language. Yet the courts have permitted the use of definitions of the family for regulatory purposes that have little to do with the conception of the family as such. (See also *Palo Alto Tenants Union v. Morgan*, 321 F. Supp. 908 (N.D. Cal. 1970), *aff'd per curiam*, 487 F.2d 883 (9th Cir. 1973).)

States often grant a higher degree of protection to their citizens than is constitutionally provided for on the federal level. The rising cost of housing might also have influenced the Supreme Court of California in *City of Santa Barbara v. Adamson*, 27 Cal.3d 123, 610 P.2d 436,164 Cal. Rptr. 539 (1980). In that case twelve unrelated persons were living in a large, 6,231 square foot house. They regarded themselves as a family. In its definition of the family for purposes of residential zoning, the city ordinance included only a group not to exceed five unrelated persons living together as a single housekeeping unit. By a narrow majority, the court held the ordinance invalid, as applied to the appellants, because it violated their broadly construed privacy rights, expressly protected in Article I of the California Constitution.

At one time it was disputed whether there could be a real "family" without a father, mother and at least one child. In particular, single mothers living with their children were considered by some not to constitute a family. The strongest indication that a change had occurred may be the flap over Vice President Dan Quayle's campaign attack on the television sit-com character Murphy Brown. The candidate had intended to suggest that positive representations of unwed motherhood would tend to undermine morality. His statements were widely interpreted as an attack on unwed mothers and their families. Democrats and Republicans almost tripped over each other rushing to affirm the validity of mother-child(ren) families.

American courts sometimes take a common-sense approach and recognize the reality of family arrangements they would not allow if they had the power to prevent them. This is a possible explanation of *Braschi* (p. 561) and of *Dalip Bir's Estate* (p. 575).

Frambach v. Dunihue is a remarkable case, especially the trial court's decision. While emphasizing that he was "not making such an inference," the trial judge suggested that he was treating the case as though it involved polyandry and a divorce from one of the two husbands. The judge asserted that "the only fair thing to do is to make them tenants in common right down the middle," and then proceeded to award one of the men half the property. It is not clear whether the judge in this quotation refers only to the men, discounting the woman and leaving her out of the property division altogether. He might have included all three in the quotation but considered Mr. and Mrs. Frambach one person (in the best Blackstonian tradition) entitled together to one share. If the three of them were tenants in common, each should be entitled to one-third share.

To the best of our knowledge, *Frambach* has never before appeared in a family law casebook, probably in large part because its headnotes make no reference to family law. A variety of interesting cases not headnoted as "family law" may possibly begin to appear more frequently in literature on family law, with the increased use of computers in research. The difference between using headnotes for research and using computer searches for particular words and phrases is only one of many changes that computers may make in law.

REFERENCES

Thomas H. Kagy, *City of Santa Barbara v. Adamson: An Associational Right of Privacy and the End of Family Zones*, 69 CALIF. L. REV. 1052 (1981).
Kenneth L. Karst, *The Freedom of Intimate Association*, 89 YALE L.J. 624 (1980).
Note, *Developments in the Law — The Constitution and the Family*, 93 HARV. L. REV. 1156 (1980).
Frances Olsen, *The Impact of Computerization on the Legal System and on Legal Reasoning*, in HIGH-TECHNOLOGY AND LAW: A CRITICAL APPROACH 101 (András Sajó & Ferenc B. Petrik, eds. Budapest, Hungary, 1989).

C: DIVORCE: THE LIMITS OF STATE CONTROL

Fault, Filing Fees, Residency Requirements

Divorce was not generally available in the American colonies or later in the United States. The few divorces that occurred were granted by special legislation and usually to wealthy men (as in *Maynard v. Hill*, supra p. 78) or to free a woman from a prior marriage so that she could marry some wealthy or influential man (as in *Ponder v. Graham*, supra p. 74). Legislatures granted divorces as a favor or privilege; there was no question of a *right* to divorce. As the number of legislative divorces increased and as they became more routine, pressure slowly mounted to transfer the divorce power from the legislatures to the courts, which was done by early divorce legislation.

Divorces were granted to an "innocent" party against a party who was found to be at fault in his or her marital behavior. Statutes would specify certain grounds for divorce, and statutes and court decisions established defenses against these grounds. If the defendant in a divorce action refused to appear in court or defaulted, no default judgment would issue, as in a typical civil case. Instead, there would be a court hearing at which the judge would have to be convinced that proper grounds for divorce existed. Some states even designated a public official whose job it was to dispute otherwise unchallenged divorce cases.

Throughout most of the nineteenth and twentieth centuries, divorce was a matter of lively public concern and debate. There was wide agreement that in certain egregious cases, a divorce was the least destructive alternative. But most people also believed that if divorce were made too easy, marriage in general would suffer. Different states worked out different statutory schemes and a variety of judicial approaches to divorce. Certain states became notorious for being particularly lenient in granting divorces. These states were seen by some as their only escape from impossible marriages, but seen by divorce opponents as "divorce mills." States wishing to avoid such a designation or generally to avoid attracting divorce litigants from other states imposed residency requirements for divorce. These typically required that a divorce litigant be a resident of the state for twelve consecutive months prior to the filing of the petition for divorce. Some residence requirements were more stringent, some less. Nevada required residency for six weeks, and many suspected that the term was chosen by local motels and other economic interests who wished to enjoy six weeks of patronage by those coming to Nevada to obtain a divorce.

No-fault divorce was the final result of a long process of slow liberalization of divorce. Before no-fault was officially recognized, in actual practice more and more courts were granting divorces in cases in which the parties essentially manufactured grounds or lied about grounds to obtain an uncontested divorce where the marriage had simply broken down. Restrictive laws served mainly to increase the costs of divorce and to add an unfortunate hypocrisy to the process. Thus no-fault divorce was seen by many less as a loosening of the grounds for divorce and more as an honest acknowledgement of what was already taking place. "Migratory divorce" is discusses further in Chapter 6.

The notion that a person might have a *right* to divorce has developed rather slowly. In *Boddie v. Connecticut* (401 U.S. 371 (1971)) the United States Supreme Court ruled that the state of Connecticut could not enforce a court filing fee that would prevent indigent litigants from seeking divorce. The Court was careful to limit its holding. It did not require Connecticut to permit divorce, but once the State has chosen to allow its citizens to obtain divorces, it cannot enforce a filing fee requirement to bar indigent people.

Now, an indigent person has a right to file for divorce *in forma pauperis*, and a right to remarry even if he or she has failed to support a child (*Zablocki v. Redhail*, supra at p. 490). The state cannot limit who can marry based on race (*Loving v. Virginia*, supra at p. 484) and possibly not based on sex or gender, at least in some states. (*Baehr v. Lewin*, supra at p. 543.) If someone can divorce wife number 1 and marry wife number 2, why should he not be able to marry wife number 2 without divorcing wife number 1, especially if all parties agree to the arrangement? Certainly many incest laws can be attacked as unconstitutional. Is there a sensible and principled place to draw the line? Or does a line need to be drawn?

"Pure" No-Fault Reasoning and Its Consequences for Distribution of Assets

MANNING v. MANNING*
Supreme Court of Georgia
237 Ga. 746, 229 S.E.2d 611 (1976)

PER CURIAM.

This appeal by the wife is from a summary judgment entered in Bibb Superior Court which granted a divorce at the request of the husband on the ground that the marriage was irretrievably broken. The wife opposed the grant of the divorce. She denied the marriage was irretrievably broken and denied that there were no prospects for a reconciliation. The wife sought to have the trial court deny a divorce and also sought a jury trial on this issue. We affirm the grant of the divorce by the trial judge as we find this case is controlled by *Harwell v. Harwell*, 233 Ga. 89, 209 S.E.2d 625 (1974), and *McCoy v. McCoy*, 236 Ga. 633, 225 S.E.2d 682 (1976).

The husband filed an affidavit in support of the motion for summary judgment seeking a divorce. In it, the husband swore, in pertinent part, as follows: "The separation between us is complete and permanent. I am unwilling to live with the defendant [wife] at the present time. I am unwilling, and I refuse, to live with her at any time in the future. There is no possibility whatever of a reconciliation ever taking place between us. The marriage... is irretrievably broken."

This affidavit by the husband which was submitted to the trial judge brought the case squarely within the language of McCoy that, "Just as it takes two consenting parties to make a contract, it takes two consenting parties to make a reconciliation. Just as one party cannot make a contract, one party cannot make a marriage or a reconciliation thereof." We find no error, as there was no issue for a jury to decide on the question of the divorce.

Judgment affirmed.

ON MOTION FOR REHEARING

Appellant insists in a vigorous motion for rehearing that we have overlooked the provisions of Code Ann. §30-109, and *Williford v. Williford*, 230 Ga. 543, 198 S.E.2d 181 (1973) which, if applied, would require a different judgment in this case. In *Williford*, the husband sought a divorce on the grounds of desertion and cruel treatment by the wife. The wife did not ask for a divorce and sought to have a divorce denied to the husband because of his alleged adultery and cruel treatment.

The majority of this court is of the opinion that the Code section and decision noted above have no application in this no-fault divorce case. The rule urged by appellant and recognized by this court in fault ground divorce cases is that the court (or jury) is authorized to refuse a divorce to the party seeking the divorce when the evidence shows such party is guilty of adultery. Code Ann. §30-109 allows the opposite party to show "the conduct of the party suing" for divorce and *Williford* holds that such evidence authorizes, but does not require, the court (or jury) to refuse a divorce in these circumstances.

*[Overruled by *Dickson v. Dickson*, 238 Ga. 672, 235 S.E.2d 479 (1977)]

These authorities have no application to no-fault divorce cases which this court has held involve only whether "either or both parties are unable or refuse to cohabit and there are no prospects for a reconciliation." *Harwell v. Harwell*, 233 Ga. 89, 91, 209 S.E.2d 625, 627 (1974). In summary, a majority of this court thinks that the traditional rules which have been applied in fault ground divorce cases should not be applied when the divorce is granted on the no-fault ground.

Motion for rehearing denied.

GUNTER, Justice (concurring specially).

In this case the husband filed a complaint for divorce against his wife; he alleged that their marriage was irretrievably broken; the wife filed responsive pleadings in which she denied the irretrievable brokenness of the marriage; she further affirmatively alleged: "...contrary to the allegations of the plaintiff in the complaint, the marriage between the plaintiff and defendant is not irretrievably broken, and further that there are reasonable prospects for a reconciliation between the parties"; by counterclaim the wife sought temporary and permanent alimony for her separate support and maintenance irrespective of whether a divorce was granted; by counterclaim she also sought the vesting of fee simple title in her to the family residence and all furniture and furnishings situated therein; she alleged that she was entitled to be awarded temporary and permanent alimony for her support and maintenance because the parties were living separate and apart, and that the separation was caused by the misconduct of the husband in that he "wilfully and without just cause abandoned defendant against her wishes"; and she further alleged that her entitlement to temporary and permanent alimony was based on the fact that her husband "in the past wilfully and repeatedly inflicted and continues to inflict mental pain and anguish upon defendant such as reasonably justifies defendant's being apprehensive of danger to her life, limb and health."

The husband filed a motion for summary judgment on the sole issue of the irretrievable brokenness of the marriage; he filed a supporting affidavit set forth in part in the court's opinion; the wife filed an opposing affidavit in which she testified that "she personally knows that the marriage between herself and William S. Manning is not irretrievably broken inasmuch as a reconciliation may be possible between deponent and her said husband"; and she concluded her opposing affidavit by testifying that "she desires and is willing to reconcile and continue the marriage between the plaintiff and herself."

The husband contended that on the basis of the pleadings and affidavits he was entitled to a judgment in his favor as a matter of law on the issue of the irretrievable brokenness of the marriage. The wife contended that the issue of irretrievable brokenness was one of fact for determination by a jury, and that it could not be resolved on motion for summary judgment.

The trial judge granted the husband's motion for summary judgment on this sole issue, and he reserved for future determination the issues with respect to alimony and division of property. The wife has appealed, and her sole contention here is that the issue of irretrievable brokenness, a fact issue, was erroneously decided as a matter of law by the trial judge on a motion for summary judgment.

As I read the pleadings and affidavits in this case, there is no issue of fact as to the irretrievable brokenness of this marriage. In *Harwell v. Harwell*, 233 Ga. 89, 209 S.E.2d 625 (1974) this court said: "An 'irretrievably broken' marriage is one where either or both parties are unable or refuse to cohabit and there are no prospects for a reconciliation." P. 91, 209 S.E.2d p. 627.

In *McCoy v. McCoy*, 236 Ga. 633, 225 S.E.2d 682 (1976), this court said:

> In the case before us, we make explicit that which was implicit in *Harwell*, to wit: where one of the parties to a marriage refuses to cohabit with the other and testifies that the marriage is irretrievably broken, the fact that the other party maintains hope for a reconciliation will not support a finding under *Harwell* that there are "prospects for a reconciliation." Just as it takes two consenting parties to make a contract, it takes two consenting parties to make a reconciliation. Just as one party cannot make a contract, one party cannot make a marriage or a reconciliation thereof. If the General Assembly had intended that the thirteenth ground for divorce be consensual, it would have provided that "The parties agree that the marriage is irretrievably broken."

P. 634, 225 S.E.2d p. 683.

Under the verified pleadings and the affidavits of record in this case by both parties, there are no real or practical prospects for a reconciliation. Stripped of all conclusions that project a mere glimmer of hope at reconciliation, this record eliminates any fact issue on the subject of irretrievable brokenness, and the trial judge correctly granted summary judgment on this issue.

I therefore concur in the judgment of affirmance.

INGRAM, Justice (concurring specially).

I concur in the judgment not because I think it is right but because it is based on case law decided by a majority of this court and I am bound by it. This court now holds that the mere assertion by one of the parties to a marriage that the marriage is irretrievably broken is sufficient not just to authorize, but to require the grant of a divorce.

Obviously, I think the court has gone too far in giving expression to this ground of divorce. Without repeating what I have said in previous dissents in these cases, I feel I must point out that the result in this case classically illustrates how generally beneficent legislation can be distorted beyond all reasonable intendment by judicial construction. Perhaps I am wrong, but I thought the primary purpose behind the addition of the no-fault ground for divorce was to cleanse our divorce law of the hypocrisy we previously indulged in the use of cruel treatment as a ground for divorce by parties who wanted a quiet, decent and friendly termination of their marriage without attacking one another in the process.

In other words, I see the use of the no-fault ground as a good and honest solution for ending a marriage where both parties agree it is finished, and in cases where one of the parties asserts the marriage is over and the other tacitly admits it by failing to contest it. What I find difficult to accept is this court's implicit holding that there can never be any serious judicial inquiry about prospects for reconciliation.[1] To my mind, this encourages divorce and is inconsistent with the state's traditional, and I think wise, policy of encouraging efforts toward resolution of

---

1. Intellectual candor compels me to note that the present decision by this court seems to fit an existing trend in divorce law. There is evidence of "the diminishing willingness of the state(s) to be involved in the matter of marriage termination" as a corollary to the states' "gradual divestment of its marriage regulation business." *Marriage and The States: The Withering Away of Marriage*, Professor Mary Ann Glendon, VIRGINIA LAW REVIEW, Vol. 62, May, 1976, No. 4, pp. 703-706. Even so, I maintain that this is such a fundamental issue of profound public importance that it should be decided in the General Assembly rather than in this court on a case by case basis.

domestic disputes through reconciliation and continuation of the marriage, particularly where there are children.

I do not believe that anyone could reasonably foresee that the addition of the no fault ground for divorce by the legislature would lead this court to deny a party the opportunity to have this issue presented to a jury in a proper case. But, it has happened in this case. In effect, this court holds here that where one party says there are no prospects for reconciliation and the other one says there are, the court has no alternative except to grant a divorce. This is too cold and hard for me to accept because the message it conveys is that our society has no interest in preserving marriages, but, on the contrary, encourages one of the parties to end it quickly and officially on the slightest caprice by merely asserting the marriage is irretrievably broken and without ever appearing in court to prove it. I see little difference between this and permitting one of the parties to write "Canceled" on the marriage license and mail it in to the judge of the probate court. If we have come to that, then I think the legislature ought to say so in plain and unmistakable language.

The judgment we have previously required trial judges to use in deciding these cases has been removed from them. I cannot agree this was intended merely by adding the no fault ground, but I concur in the judgment in this case as our decisions require it.

[Justice HILL's dissenting opinion omitted.]

COMMENTS

Manning is included in this book although it was overruled by decision of the Supreme Court of Georgia in *Dickson v. Dickson*, 235 S.E.2d 479 (1977). It expresses most clearly a fundamental problem in no-fault divorce, present to various degrees in other jurisdictions: how to interpret a legislative clause that requires proof that a marriage is "irretrievably broken." The standard of interpretation could relate to external factors determinable by the fact finder according to more or less objective criteria or it could be purely subjective, that is, entirely dependent on the petitioner's state of mind. *Manning* took the extreme position that, in case of appropriate pleading supported by an affidavit of the petitioner, the court has no choice but to grant the dissolution. The opposing affidavit of the respondent wife, who believed in the possibility of reconciliation, could not shake the husband's express determination to end the marriage. Fault was to have no relevance whatsoever; and summary judgment on the pleadings, according to this view, had to be given to the petitioner regardless of whether or not he was to blame. The court apparently differentiated between facts and feelings, and found that the petitioner's subjective view of the state of his marriage entitled him to a judgment as a matter of law.

The opposite interpretation had been made three years earlier by the Supreme Court of Florida in *Ryan v. Ryan* (see p. 83). The court posited that the judge should not act merely as a ministerial officer who accepts the magic words "irretrievably broken" from the petitioner, but should inquire objectively into what happened in the marriage. Inquiries into the causes of marital breakdown inevitably lead to resurrection of the fault concept, if only in an adumbrated form.

This was demonstrated, again in Florida, in *McClelland v. McClelland*, (p. 603) where the court permitted the petitioner to plead adultery as the cause of an irretrievably broken marriage.

Georgia itself retreated from its initial conception of "pure" no-fault, expressed in *Manning*. In *Dickson* the court held that a respondent can counter the pleadings of the petitioner by an affidavit that the marriage is not irretrievably broken because, for instance, the petitioner has shown prospects for reconciliation. The internal state of mind thus becomes a disputed issue to be resolved by the fact-finder. In spite of the radical holding of *Manning*, Georgia has never entirely abandoned considerations of fault. It has retained the traditional divorce grounds based on fault in addition to the new ground of irretrievable breakdown of marriage. Since in mixed jurisdictions of this kind fault and no-fault can be linked together in the same proceedings by way of petition and counterclaim, it appears analytically to be difficult to eliminate fault altogether, especially in view of the consequences of dissolution, financial and otherwise.

It is possible to differentiate between jurisdictions that adhere to a relatively pure concept of no-fault dissolution and those that have more or less openly reestablished considerations of fault. Mostly, rather than a dichotomy of fault and no-fault jurisdictions, we face various degrees of judicial adjustment to legislative demands. Perhaps one should ask why it is so difficult to eradicate considerations of fault in the dissolution of marriage. On a superficial level it appears that judges have resented what they may view as legislative intrusion upon their prerogatives. Clearly judges do not want to be subservient to the demands of the petitioner but prefer to have a say in the matter that has been brought before them or at least, in these cases, the power to inquire into the causes of irretrievable breakdown of marriage. However, the reasons for the continued emphasis on or need for moral blame in connection with divorce are deeper. In particular, considerations of fault and moral blame have economic consequences in the vast majority of cases that are bargained over in lawyers' offices and then merely processed through the courts.

Complete eradication of fault interferes in this bargaining process and is likely to lead to financial complications. The nature of these complications is hinted at in *Manning* in the concurring opinion of Justice Gunter. By way of counterclaim the respondent wife had asked for temporary and permanent alimony and for title in the family home and all furniture. It was not accidental that she raised misconduct of the husband petitioner in this context. Indeed in terms of social functions, fault may be related to considerations of a proprietary nature. In this connection, perhaps *Manning* had to be overruled because it did not consider adequately the proprietary consequences of granting a petitioner for dissolution of marriage a judgment on his pleadings alone. The misgivings about these pleadings are further accentuated if consideration is given to their nature and to the problem of the extent to which obviously fictitious pleadings and affidavits should be taken at face value by the courts. The language in the husband's sworn affidavit was clearly not his, but that of the lawyer who, with distinct legal and financial consequences in mind, supplied words that were then regarded by the court as the client's. The language used is deliberately meant to foreclose any possibility of reconciliation, regardless of any argument the respondent wife might make. If a lawyer is to prevail with this strategy, as he did in *Manning*, it must affect not only the dissolution as such but, more importantly, its proprietary consequences.

REFERENCES

Susan Westerberg Reppy, Comment, *The End of Innocence: Elimination of Fault in California Divorce Law*, 17 UCLA L. REV. 1306 (1970).

Robert H. Mnookin & Lewis Kornhauser, *Bargaining in the Shadow of the Law: The Case of Divorce*, 88 YALE L.J. 950 (1979).

In re MARRIAGE OF WILLIAMS
Supreme Court of Iowa
199 N.W.2d 339 (Iowa 1972)

MASON, Judge.

Elmer Williams, respondent, appeals from decree entered in dissolution of marriage proceedings brought under the provisions of what is now chapter 598, The Code, 1971.

...The revised statute makes the breakdown of the marriage the sole basis for termination of the marital relationship and eliminates the specific categories of fault grounds enumerated in section 598.8, The Code, 1966, as a standard for granting dissolution.

...

...[O]nly those propositions which deal with that portion of the decree ordering alimony and support payments by respondent remain for consideration. These assignments are closely related. Perhaps it will tend to a better understanding of the problem if respondent's fourth proposition is considered first.

...After entry of the decree of dissolution, defendant filed motion asking the court to include in its findings a determination of whether petitioner had committed acts of adultery while married to respondent, had been dating a named individual during this period and had written and received letters from the person with whom she was inferentially accused of committing adultery....

The trial court denied the motion on the basis that if it were to comply with the request, it would be necessary in fairness to the petitioner to also enlarge the findings to detail misconduct on respondent's part and any testimony by respondent deemed by the court to be untrue. In its order the court made this statement:

> The court did determine that fault lay with both parties, although perhaps more heavily upon the petitioner than upon the respondent and did accord fault some consideration in its determination of..., support and alimony, and property division.

In his second assignment respondent contends the property settlement and alimony and support payments are not equitable since the award does not take into account petitioner's fault for the marriage breakdown. In this connection respondent argues that although chapter 598, The Code, 1971, would seem, in effect, to remove the element of fault as a basis for dissolution of the marriage, nothing in the statute removes from the court's consideration the conduct of the spouses and particularly that of the guilty party as a criterion in determining the equitable disposition of property.

I. In support of his position respondent relies on *Schantz v. Schantz*, 163 N.W.2d 398, 405 (Iowa 1968), which was decided at a time divorces were based on the fault grounds enumerated in section 598.8, The Code, 1966. The opinion sets forth several factors as a suggested aid to trial courts in adjusting the rights and obligations of the parties upon judicial termination of the marriage relationship. *Loc. cit.* 163 N.W.2d at 405. Before listing the factors to be evaluated, the court gave this caveat:

> This court has also repeatedly taken the position that in resolving the troublesome problem inherent in awarding alimony and effecting a distribution of property rights, *many factors* must be considered. See *Gerk v. Gerk*, Iowa, 158 N.W.2d 656, and citations.
>
> Use of the following general formula may be helpful in arriving at an equitable determination of financial or property rights and obligations of the parties to a divorce action, though each element is not always present or important. (emphasis supplied)

The court then proceeds to set forth five premarital criteria and ten postmarital criteria which will not be repeated here.

Fault was never the sole criterion for an award or property settlement or an allowance of alimony or support under our previous statute. True, it did enter into the determination along with other factors.

The issue presented by this appeal is what, if any, consideration fault of the spouses is to be given in awarding property settlement, alimony or support payments under the revised statute.

This is a matter of first impression for this court. The courts of other jurisdictions which have adopted no-fault divorce statutes have not considered the precise problem so far as our research discloses.

...

Originally, the Divorce Laws Study Committee of Iowa in its report said that all evidence should be permitted in determining marital breakdown. The committee specifically mentioned certain kinds of evidence which were to be included in the scope of review:

> 1. Commission of adultery; 2. Willful desertion without reasonable cause for a period of two years; 3. Conviction of a felony after the marriage; 4. Chronic alcoholism; 5. Inhuman treatment affecting physical or mental well-being; 6. Incurable mental illness for a continuous period of three years immediately preceding the filing of the action, requiring confinement to an institution, home, or other facility and based upon the testimony of a qualified member of the medical profession that such spouse is incurably mentally ill; 7. Pregnancy of the wife at the time of the marriage, unknown by the husband, by a person other than the husband; 8. That the spouses have voluntarily lived entirely separate for three years next preceding the commencement of the action; and 9. The existence of an illegitimate child or children of one of the spouses, then living, which was unknown to the other spouse at the time of the marriage.

Peters, *Iowa Reform of Marriage Termination*, 20 Drake L. Rev. 211, 215-216. The legislature, however, declined to follow its recommendation, electing, instead, to eliminate fault grounds. One writer suggests this be interpreted as an attempt to truly effectuate the purpose of the modern approach to divorce. Note, *The No Fault Concept: Is This the Final Stage in the Evolution of Divorce?*, 47 Notre Dame Law. 959, 969 (1972).

The first paragraph of section 598.17 makes breakdown of the marriage relationship the sole basis for termination of the marriage. The decree neither favors a petitioner nor is against a respondent. It acts only upon the status of the parties with relation to one another and consists in the granting of a judgment of dissolution of the marriage.

The second paragraph of this section directs that the division of assets of the parties, support or maintenance of either spouse be "based on competent and relevant evidence." It does not specifically prohibit the use of fault evidence. This might logically be interpreted as leaving the court some flexibility in individual cases in arriving at a proper adjustment of the rights and obligations of the parties upon judicial termination of the marriage.

The contents of the petition for dissolution of marriage are specifically set out in subparagraph 7 of section 598.5, The Code, 1971, in this manner:

> 7. Allege that there has been a breakdown of the marriage relationship to the extent that the legitimate objects of matrimony have been destroyed and there remains no reasonable likelihood that the marriage can be preserved.

The statute does not allow for the introduction of fault grounds in the petition.

Since the statute does not provide any specific guidelines, we turn to the efforts of legal writers in this field who have commented on similar no-fault dissolution statutes enacted in other jurisdictions as an aid in construing our statute. In addition to those already cited, we have examined: Clark, *Divorce Policy and Divorce Reform*, 42 Colo.L.Rev. 403 (1971); Tenney, *Divorce Without Fault: The Next Step*, 46 Neb.L.Rev. 24 (1967); Comment, 17 U.C.L.A.L.Rev. 1306 (1969-1970); Hayes, *California Divorce Reform: Parting is Sweeter Sorrow*, 56 A.B.A.J. 660; Walker, *Beyond Fault: An Examination of Patterns of Behavior in Response to Present Divorce Laws*, 10 J.Fam.L. 267 (1971). An article, *The New California Divorce Law*, 1969, by Walter T. Winter is of interest.

In addition to Iowa, California (Calif. Civ.Code sections 4500-40); Florida (Florida Statutes, Title 6, chapter 61); Idaho (chapter 6, Title 32, Idaho Code); Michigan (Michigan Comp.Laws Ann. section 552.6 (Supp.1971)); New Jersey (N.J.Rev.Stat. section 2A:34-2 (Supp.1972)) and West Virginia (W.Va.Code chapter 48), are among the states that have taken steps to revise their state laws governing divorce.

California was the first to make the move in 1969 followed by Iowa and Michigan in 1970. The Florida statute became effective July 1, 1971; Idaho in February 1971 and New Jersey, September 1971. The West Virginia statute was partially rewritten by the 1969 legislature.

These statutes vary from state to state with Michigan's being the most similar to the Iowa statute upon which it based the format of its law for the new dissolution of marriage procedure. They each present problems of interpretation and administration.

In criticizing the various enactments, authors of the legal periodicals referred to, *supra*, agree the most significant aspect of the new law is the attempt to eliminate the notion of fault or marital guilt from marital dissolution proceedings, and to substitute the marital-breakdown approach as a standard for granting dissolution. Generally, they maintain the marital-breakdown approach does away "with the hypocrisy of the fault approach, and, more importantly, it can be used to limit the bitterness and emotional stress associated with the fault system." 47 Notre Dame Law. at 970. The writer in another place in the cited note expresses the view that it was the hope of the legislatures this approach would eliminate the finger-pointing and thus reduce the bitterness and conflict.

These and other expressions found in the cited materials make it clear the overriding legislative purpose of the dissolution act is to remove fault-based standards for termination of marriages.

...

However, respondent's argument that the conduct of the spouses and particularly that of the guilty party has not been removed as a criterion in determining the equitable disposition of property remains. He directs attention to the fourth factor of the post-marital criteria, "conduct of the spouses and particularly that of the guilty party", as listed in the *Schantz* opinion....

...

Unless the purpose of this enactment as determined from legislative history in the report of the Divorce Study Committee is to be defeated, the "guilty party" concept must be discarded as a factor for consideration in providing an award or an allowance of alimony or support money.

The author of the comment in 17 U.C.L.A.L.Rev. at 1316-1317, expresses the belief, "Alimony, now called 'support,' will be determined by fairness rather than fault. Three factors must be taken into account: (a) the duration of the marriage, (b) the ability of the supported spouse to engage in gainful employment, and (c) the economic condition of the parties."

...

In order to carry out this obvious legislative intent and give effect to the object sought to be accomplished, we hold not only the "guilty party" concept must be eliminated but evidence of the conduct of the parties insofar as it tends to place fault for the marriage breakdown on either spouse must also be rejected as a factor in awarding property settlement or an allowance of alimony or support money. Usually both spouses contribute to a breakdown of the marital relations which makes necessary an adjustment of their rights and obligations. In other words, evidence bearing on the fourth factor listed in the *Schantz* decision of postmarital criteria is not admissible on this issue.

...

II. Having arrived at the conclusion that fault is not a factor to be considered in awarding property settlement or an allowance of alimony under chapter 598, The Code, 1971, we proceed to consider respondent's other contention that the award was otherwise inequitable and unjust since it leaves him in an almost impossible financial position in view of his mortgage indebtedness.

...

Our examination of the record discloses that petitioner has had virtually no job training and at time of trial was employed part time as a nurses' aide at a rate of $1.65 per hour. She estimated her earnings at approximately $25 per week and the cost of a babysitter for their ten-year-old daughter at $10. Respondent, a skilled journeyman carpenter, is capable of earning in excess of $4.00 per hour. In 1969 he earned approximately $9000 as a carpenter and approximately $8500 in 1970.

The gross income from the apartment house building was $100 per month per rented unit and there had been no problem in keeping three units occupied. Respondent was living in the fourth unit. In addition to payment of taxes and insurance premiums, monthly payments of $221 on principal and interest were required by the mortgage on this property. The insurance premiums were $150 per year and the taxes were just a few dollars less than $800, including the curb and gutter tax. Tenants in the apartments are furnished some utilities which run approximately $87 per month.

Taxes on the personal residence where petitioner resides are $404 and insurance, $47.50. Monthly payments on this mortgage were $84.84.

. . .

Respondent was ordered to pay as alimony and for the support of their minor daughter the sum of $200 per month commencing June 15, 1971. These payments were to cease when Tamela reached the age of 18 or sooner died, married or became self-supporting. However, termination of such payments was not to take place as long as Tamela was in full-time attendance at an accredited college, university or trade school, the period of such attendance not to exceed four years in any event and should be continuous following graduation from high school, vacation periods excepted.

Occupancy of the personal residence of the parties was awarded to petitioner with respondent being required to maintain the same, pay taxes, insurance premiums and principal and interest payments coming due on the mortgage on this residence.

Respondent was awarded the use and income from the apartment house building, being required to maintain the same, pay taxes, insurance premiums and mortgage payments.

Use of the properties by the parties was to terminate at the same time as payments of alimony and support money. Upon termination of the use and maintenance of the properties, the same were to be sold and after the payment of expenses, proceeds were to be divided 25 percent to petitioner and 75 percent to respondent.

Provision was made for the distribution of the net proceeds from the sale of these properties in the event either party should die prior to the termination date as fixed.

. . .

In summary, respondent is required under the terms of the court's decree to make the following annual payments on both pieces of real estate until the termination date fixed therein: taxes $1204, insurance $197.50, and mortgage loans $3670. In addition there is an estimated utility bill of $1044. Taxes and insurance premiums are, of course, approximate figures. Added to this amount are alimony and support money payments of $2400 per year. He is thus required to pay $8515.50. To do this he has his income of approximately $9000 as a carpenter and rent of $3600 from the three apartment units assuming they remain occupied. Subtracting the payments required of him from this $12,600, respondent is left with the sum of $4084.50.

Respondent was given stocks and bonds of approximately $1675 and was required to pay a bank note of $700, attorney fees and court costs.

We appreciate that this does not leave respondent with much money. On the other hand, petitioner is furnished a residence for herself and daughter with the taxes and insurance being paid by respondent. She has $200 per month to maintain herself and child in addition to such income as she is able to produce. We also realize that under the terms of the decree the respondent cannot use the real estate during the period payments are required in any financial transactions. This court has said many times under the old divorce statute that there is seldom enough money to support two families in these situations. It appears in this case the same is true.

In our de novo review of this record we have eliminated any consideration of the fault concept and reached our determination on the basis of the criteria otherwise suggested in *Schantz v. Schantz*, 163 N.W.2d at 405 and conclude that respondent's contention the decree was inequitable and unjust as it related to the division of property and alimony and support payments is without merit under the circumstances presented by this record.

Except for the monthly payments of alimony and support money the adjudication of the rights and obligations of the parties relating to the distribution of their property rights was just and fair.

As to those payments, we believe the decree should be modified by striking the provision requiring respondent to pay $200 per month as alimony and for the support of Tamela and that in lieu thereof the decree provide respondent make monthly payments of $100 as alimony with a further sum of $100 as support for Tamela. The decree insofar as it fixes the dates and conditions under which said payments are to continue shall remain unchanged.

. . .

Except as modified with respect to an allocation of a definite amount for alimony and support money and the additional allowances made herein, the decree is affirmed.

. . .

UHLENHOPP, Justice (dissenting from division I but concurring in result).

The question is whether the parties' *conduct* with respect to each other — not merely "fault" for the marital breakdown — may be considered as one factor on the issue of fair and equitable alimony. ("Alimony" is used here in the broad sense to include both property division and monetary payments.)

The question may be brought into focus by two rather extreme but not rare examples, in which all factors are equal except the parties' conduct. In one, the husband in frequent fits of rage visits violent physical abuse on his blameless wife and children, eventually driving them from the home by his cruelty. In the other, the wife carries on with a paramour, frequently spending nights and weekends with him to the knowledge of the blameless husband and children. Is the court to be allowed to know these facts along with the other equities in the case in deciding upon a fair adjustment of the parties' financial rights and obligations? Or is the court to function in a vacuum so far as the parties' conduct is concerned? Compare facts in *Caldwell v. Caldwell*, 5 Wis.2d 146, 92 N.W.2d 356, with *Manske v. Manske*, 6 Wis.2d 605, 95 N.W.2d 401.

. . .

Does the change in the basis for terminating marriage — from specified wrongs to irretrievable marital breakdown — constitute an enactment by implication that the parties' conduct shall no longer be considered on alimony?

Domestic relations cases ordinarily involve three main issues: dissolution of the marriage, child custody, and alimony. The legislature made a basic change in the law on the first issue, but it did not deal or purport to deal with the latter two.

The issue of custody is governed by what is in the best interest of the children. *Utter v. Utter*, 261 Iowa 683, 155 N.W.2d 419. The new act did not abolish that rule, nor did the act provide that the parties' conduct cannot be considered in determining the children's best interest.

Similarly, the issue of alimony is governed by what is just, fair, and equitable between the parties. The new act did not abolish that rule either, nor did it provide that the parties' conduct cannot be considered in determining what is a just, fair, and equitable adjustment of their financial affairs. The parties' conduct is just as relevant today as it was yesterday in resolving the custody and alimony issues. If evidence of that conduct also happens to disclose the cause of the marital breakdown, that is merely incidental.

Decreeing alimony is not as mechanical as fixing the award in other no-fault proceedings such as workmen's compensation, where the scale of payments is set by statute. In domestic relations cases, adjustment of the parties' financial rights and obligations is much more delicate and imprecise. The proceeding is in equity, and "the equities on both sides are to be considered.... A court of equity is a court of conscience; it seeks to do justice and equity between all parties; it seeks to strike a balance of convenience as between litigants; and *it looks at the whole situation.*" 30 C.J.S. Equity §89 at 976, 978-979. (Italics added.)

Under the new act, the chancellor is searching as he was before for a fair, just, and equitable determination of the parties' financial rights and duties. In that search he still needs to be placed in the position of the parties and to know what they know. To do equity, he still needs to be allowed to see the full picture.

Finally, a rule against considering the parties' conduct will not work in practice. Thus in a case involving a custody contest, a chancellor hearing evidence that the wife is living with another man will in fact be unable to blot that evidence from his mind when he comes to the alimony issue. The law in books and the law in action will not be the same. In the absence of direction by the legislature, courts of equity should continue to be permitted, in word as well as in fact, to consider the parties' conduct in decreeing alimony. They should continue to weigh all the equities.

...

COMMENTS

In re Williams illustrates the strains that result from the introduction of no-fault divorce into jurisdictions, such as California and Iowa, that have traditionally been governed by conceptions of fault in marital breakdown. It becomes apparent that in practice, moral blame is related less to marital ethics than to issues of allocation of property. In this context the dominant position of the husband under common law should be recalled. As soon as absolute divorce through the courts was made available, it became necessary to create equitable means to provide for formerly married women. Since by virtue of marriage husbands owned or controlled most of the property, women, especially in long-term marriages, would have been left with little or nothing after divorce. Fault as a concept, even if it sometimes resulted in punitive awards, gave the chancellor the power to grant alimony and distribute property according to equitable standards.

Specifically, the concept of fault has been useful as an equitable tool for balancing the power of men in divorce proceedings by findings in favor of women.

Other factors helped bring about this result. Statistically women were petitioners in divorce proceedings more often than men, although their husbands often instigated the filing of complaints. Also, cultural patterns, perhaps from the Puritan heritage, tended to fix the blame for marital breakdown on men.

Since pure no-fault divorce more often than not works to the disadvantage of women when accompanied by mere rehabilitative alimony or none at all and an unclear situation in regard to marital property, it will take considerable time and experimentation to bring about adjustments. The most obvious solution might be to give women a vested right in marital property, perhaps an equal share as now existing in community-property states, or as a possibility in equitable distribution jurisdictions. Experience in California indicates, however, that mandatory equal distribution of community property does not necessarily relieve the acrimony of marital disputes. The emphasis shifts from blame to determining exactly what constitutes half of the assets. If equitable distribution governs, marital behavior becomes relevant, as pointed out in *Williams*, and considerations of fault are resurrected. Complex problems of bookkeeping arise. Questions are raised as to what assets are marital and how and at what point in the litigation these assets should be valued. (See Chapter 1, *supra.*) Divorce practice increasingly acquires aspects of business practice, and the emotional factors, at least outwardly, lose in significance.

Williams illustrates another problem of a pure no-fault approach in a non-community-property jurisdiction like Iowa. A strict elimination of any consideration of fault, especially if the marital assets are limited, may put the relatively blameless party in an untenable financial position. In *Williams*, it appears to have been the wife who benefitted from no-fault. Testimony about her alleged adultery could not be considered at all, while her husband continued to be burdened with alimony and support obligations with hardly enough left for himself to live on. More usual is the reverse situation: A husband after a twenty-year marriage with limited assets demands his freedom. In this context, substantial obligations he may face appear to be more palatable; at least they were brought about by his own actions. *Williams* illustrates this difficulty of disregarding behavior altogether, even good behavior. It leaves the impression of an inequitable and unfair result. Yet the invocation of equity seems to reestablish fault, at least in the phase when the consequences of dissolution are to be considered.

Many no-fault jurisdictions choose a compromise that permits consideration of some fault. Or they may recognize, as does Florida so-called "special equities"; or they may consider, as does Massachusetts, "conduct of the parties" possibly leading to a reward for unusual efforts beyond the call of ordinary marital duties or to a penalty in cases in which the conduct of the spouse involved the wasting of assets (e.g., gambling) or physical absence from the home. To the extent that rights in marital property are "vested," they are not subject to the limitations that apply to alimony. Yet a pattern can be discerned. The inchoate rights resulting from marriage, like the possibility of alimony, are declining in importance. Even lump-sum alimony, where permitted, increasingly acquires the characteristics of equitable property distribution. Increasingly in the typical case, both husband and wife may, after divorce, be left with nothing but their capacity to work and a portion of whatever assets can be found. Whether community property or equitable distribution laws are adopted, courts appear to be decreasingly important. Even under fault regimes, the grounds for a divorce were largely bargaining tools. Today the real decisions are likely to be made in lawyers' offices by way of complex property settlements or, at an earlier stage, by antenuptial agreements. That cohabitation short of marriage does not necessarily avoid these questions has already been discussed in connection with *Marvin v. Marvin* (see Comments at pp. 347–348).

The problem posed by *Williams* remains unresolved. What should be done if the martial assets are insufficient to support two separate households? None of the traditional civil enforcement remedies seem to be practical (e.g., voluntary wage assignments, mandatory wage withholding, liens, security or a bond to guarantee payment, setoff of tax refunds, registration of support orders in another state), and criminal prosecution under nonsupport laws has been ineffective. Statistics indicate that males on the whole do not pay support or alimony. If they pay at all, they discontinue after a short period. Five years after divorce most males do not pay anything and enforcement has been unrealistic in most cases. Consequently the financial position of males improves by divorce, because, regardless of what the courts say, they are effectively rid of obligations (publicized enforcement attempts in individual cases notwithstanding). The overwhelming burden of divorce continues to fall on women, especially if they have custody of minor children, as is usually the case. Thus *Williams* is an irregular case, and we do not know how Mr. Williams was in fact financially situated, apart from what the court said about his plight.

To the extent that members of the original family unit are in financial distress, with the government increasingly unwilling to assume the burden of such families, marriage can be a speculative investment that does not pay off. The same applies to a former spouse who, in addition to having to live on insufficient assets, is often in a poor position to enter the job market.

REFERENCES

Lenore J. Weitzman, *The Economics of Divorce: Social and Economic Consequences of Property, Alimony and Child Support Awards*, 28 UCLA L. REV. 1181, 1211, 1249–56 (1981).

Lenore J. Weitzman & Ruth B. Dixon, *The Alimony Myth: Does No-Fault Divorce Make a Difference?*, 14 FAM. L.Q. 141, 172–79 (1980).

Lingering Concepts of Fault

McCLELLAND v. McCLELLAND

District Court of Appeal of Florida
318 So.2d 160 (Fla. Dist. Ct. App. 1975)

SMITH, Judge.

Confronted with an unresolved conflict between decisions of two sister District Courts of Appeal,[1] we are asked to determine whether, in the consideration of a petition for dissolution of marriage and for alimony, child custody and child support, a trial court may hear evidence of allegedly persistent adultery by a respondent husband who seeks no alimony for himself and who does not deny that the marriage is irretrievably broken. Affirming the trial judge, we hold that the court may properly consider such evidence for the light it sheds on the condition of the marriage and on the equities of the necessary financial adjustment to be made between the parties.

The petition for dissolution filed by Ms. McClelland, appellee here, alleged:

> 7. Petitioner alleges that the Respondent has been involved in adulterous relationships for many years. The Petitioner has implored the Respondent to cease these activities, and even now he is engaged in an adulterous relationship. Although the Petitioner would gladly reconcile with the Respondent if he would cease his immoral behavior, he has indicated he does not intend to do so, and the Petitioner thus is reluctantly forced to conclude that the marriage is irretrievably broken.

Responding, appellant William J. McClelland admitted that the marriage is broken and moved to strike as irrelevant all of the quoted allegations except the last six words. The trial court denied that motion and the husband appealed from the interlocutory order. Appellant's answer seeks neither alimony (as to which see §61.08(1), F.S.1973) nor child custody and it does not dispute that the marriage is broken. Appellant therefore complains that a foray into the matter of his alleged adultery is not only irrelevant but also potentially destructive of the legislative goals to promote the amicable settlement of the marriage dispute and to minimize the hurt inflicted by the legal process itself. Secs. 61.001(2)(b), (c), F.S.1973.

...

It is evident that the principal issue to be determined by the trial judge in this case, should he agree with the parties that the marriage is irretrievably broken, is the nature and the amount of alimony. Because in making these determinations the trial judge will be guided by evidence of the need of the demanding spouse for support and the ability of the other to respond [*Thigpen v. Thigpen*], 277 So.2d 583 (Fla.App.1st, 1973)], the District Court of Appeal, Third District, held that a trial judge properly excluded evidence of a respondent husband's adultery when considering whether and in what amount the wife should receive alimony. "Here the wife hoped to obtain alimony," the Court observed, "by showing her husband's adultery." *Escobar v. Escobar*, 300 So.2d 702, 703 (Fla.App.3rd, 1974). It may be that our Ms. McClelland is similarly motivated and that, while pleading that the marriage is broken for grave cause from which even now she seeks relief short of

1. *Pro v. Pro*, 300 So.2d 288 (Fla.App.4th, 1974) and *Escobar v. Escobar*, 300 So.2d 702 (Fla.App.3rd, 1974).

dissolution, her real intention is to be compensated and to punish her husband financially for his past offenses.

But we must give face value to appellee's declared reluctance to seek dissolution. Although husband and wife may agree in pleadings that the marriage is irretrievably broken, the statute does not require a circuit judge sitting with the historic discretion of a chancellor to find that to be a fact simply because the parties have said so. Secs. 61.011, 61.052(2)(a), F.S.1973. Such a finding remains a judicial act; and it follows, even in the absence of a pleaded issue on the subject, that the court may consider at least some evidence of whether the marriage is irretrievably broken. The Court must therefore be permitted to learn from the parties the depth of the breach and, inevitably, its cause....

While there is no contest in this case that Ms. McClelland shall have custody of the minor children, the award of custody is also a judicial act which is not woodenly to be performed as stipulated by the parents. For that act also discretion must be informed; and evidence of a parent's persistent adultery could be pertinent to the inquiry.

Finally, we agree with the District Court of Appeal, Fourth District, that evidence of adulterous activities may be pertinent to the questions of alimony. *Pro v. Pro*, 300 So.2d 288 (Fla.App.4th, 1974). The legislative mandate is that the court "consider any factor necessary to do equity and justice between the parties" in respect to alimony. Sec. 61.08(2), F.S. 1973.

We do not share appellant's apprehension that the trial court's decision will resurrect a system of divorce based on fault and, with it, all of the old agonies of accusation and recrimination. The trial judge in this case cautioned against "an unlimited foray into the details" of the alleged adultery and indicated a determination to restrict the inquiry "within reasonable bounds." It is unnecessary, undesirable and improper for the trial judge "to sit and hear every jit and jot of testimony offered by a party as to the other's misconduct" [*Oliver v. Oliver*, 285 So.2d 638, 641, (Fla.App.4th, 1973)], and there are no circuit judges who, remembering such experiences, will now willingly relive them. "It is enough," the District Court, Fourth District, held in *Oliver* in connection with alimony questions, "that he simply get a broad picture and understanding of the relative equities and factors necessary to do justice."

The interlocutory appeal is dismissed.

McALLISTER v. McALLISTER

District Court of Appeal of Florida
345 So.2d 352 (Fla. Dist. Ct. App. 1977)

LETTS, Judge.

This appeal stems from a dissolution of marriage in which the wife of a successful doctor received a $500.00 per month award of permanent alimony.

This cause is reversed in part.

The McAllisters were married in 1951 while he was a medical student and she an employed pharmacist. The record reflects that the wife worked, to assist her husband finish school,[1] for over a year after the marriage, and almost immediately thereafter, bore the first of four children. Subsequently, until now, she pursued the

1. It is not reflected in the record that he could not have finished his education but for her earnings.

outmoded profession of housewife and mother, only once working during a vacation period, in 24 years of marriage. Upon receiving his medical degree, the husband commenced to build a medical practice, equipping his office with the aid of a loan secured by the meager inherited stocks and bonds owned by the wife. His practice became successful and Doctor McAllister's 1973 corporate income tax return, for his single P.A., reflected a gross income of over $200,000. Moreover, his personal return for that same year, even after his accountants had done with their computations, reflected a payment to himself of a $75,000 salary. By contrast, the wife's income from dividends and interest totalled less than $2,200 in that same year.

The record reflects that Doctor McAllister is a good father, 49 years old and a man's man, who goes elk hunting in Wyoming, dove shooting in Mexico, fishing, belongs to the yacht club and enjoys many skiing excursions. Vacations have included several trips to the Bahamas, Canada and to Europe. He breeds horses, co-owns cattle, and he himself claims that his monthly personal living expenses add up to over $2,600. There can be no doubt that he enjoys a style of living and social prestige which, by the rest of society's standards, must be termed both generous and glamorous, and which can continue completely unaffected by the permanent alimony award in the court below. The wife, on the other hand, aged 48, although also able bodied and capable of employment, will, in terms of permanent alimony awarded, be receiving only $500.00 per month, plus her private income of $175.00, for a grand total, before taxes, of $675.00 per month, plus whatever she can earn. She claims her knowledge of pharmacology is so outdated that she cannot resume her former profession, but regardless of the truth of this, there is no suggestion that she cannot procure work. (Pharmacologists are paid $6.00 per hour, according to the record). The wife, apparently, has latterly continued her education, part-time, and now holds a degree in anthropology from Florida Atlantic University, but neither she, nor any of her graduate classmates, have been able to secure a job in this field.

The final judgment, insofar as alimony is concerned, awarded the wife $500.00 a month rehabilitative alimony for five years, and $500.00 a month permanent alimony, until his death or her remarriage. In addition, she was given possession of the house for five years (she was already the owner of record of an undivided one-half thereof and her assets were used to collateralize a second mortgage when it was purchased) and the husband required to pay the mortgage and taxes during that period, which he can deduct. At the end of the five years, the house is to be sold and the proceeds equally divided.

The foregoing recitation of facts and circumstances in the case now before us, is laborious and detailed; however, we find it neither a waste of time nor paper, because we would hope by this opinion to help clarify the law regarding alimony where a breakup of a long term family marriage is involved, and we perceive a tendency by some trial courts, to undercompensate the wife. It would appear that, in some instances at the trial level, the result has very much hinged upon the luck of the draw depending upon which division in the courthouse gets the case; however, we see no such variation at the appellate level, where the recent case law on this kind of long term family marriage breakup has been reasonably uniform....

The history of the change in alimony concept, up through the new dissolution of marriage law and beyond, is best set forth by Judge Rawls in the case of *Brown v. Brown*, 300 So.2d 719 (Fla.1st DCA 1974), and we see no purpose to repeat it here. Suffice it to say that reasonable permanent alimony still lives, especially, in dissolutions involving the long time role of a mother and housewife.

Alimony is traditionally predicated on three criteria: (1) the ability of the husband to pay it, (2) the needs of the wife compared to reasonable expectations from her own income, and (3) the standard of living enjoyed by the wife during marriage. *Caracristi v. Caracristi*, 324 So.2d 634 (Fla.2nd DCA 1976). In turn, these three criteria have, in developing case law, been supplemented by six more: (4) the length of the marriage; (5) the number of children. (Included in this category should be the extent to which the wife has been required to do the actual housework and perform the chore of raising the children, *vis a vis* the amount of outside domestic assistance paid for by the husband;)(6) the relative health and physical condition of both the wife and the husband, and (7) the extent of the contribution by the wife to her husband's successful career.

An eighth factor considered by the courts concerns the conduct, or misconduct, of the parties during the marriage. *Oliver v. Oliver*, 285 So.2d 638 (Fla.4th DCA 1973). This particular category is cited with some reluctance, (although in the light of case law, it would be remiss to exclude it) for we recognize that, inevitably, a consideration of conduct involves a retrogression back to the fault concept and away from no-fault; however, in *Oliver* the Court was careful to point out that the extent of such evidence should be limited, at the trial judge's discretion. Moreover, in *Oliver*, it would appear that the misconduct was gross, for the wife claiming alimony was all the time drunk, repeatedly threatened to kill her husband and made no effort whatever to keep house. The *Oliver* court permitted such testimony to be considered by the chancellor below on the basis of Florida Statute §61.08(2)(1975), which says:

> In determining a proper award of *alimony*, the court may consider *any factor necessary to do equity* and justice between the parties. (emphasis supplied).

By contrast, there is no suggestion in the record now before us of any misconduct by Dr. McAllister, but likewise, there is no indication that Mrs. McAllister was other than a good spouse. At all events, we would urge that evidence of misconduct be limited to gross situations such as existed in *Oliver*, with no mitigating circumstances, otherwise, as was conceded in that case, we will return to the very type of "...often sordid and provocative testimony of fault...that lead to the enactment of the so-called no-fault dissolution of marriage chapter." *Id.* at 640.

Finally, there is a ninth catch all consideration set forth in *Kennedy v. Kennedy*, 303 So.2d 629 (Fla.1974), where the Supreme Court said that while alimony should not result in one spouse having to "...pass automatically from misfortune to prosperity, neither should a good [spouse] suffer a shocking change from prosperity to misfortune."

In the case now before us, we find all nine of these criteria present, in one form or another, although we quickly point out that the list is intended only as exemplary and neither exclusive nor demanding of the presence of all nine. Mrs. McAllister contributed to the early success of her healthy husband, who is well able to provide support, was married to him for 24 years, enjoyed a high standard of living and community prestige as his wife, will need financial help desperately at the end of five years, and bore her husband four children. By including the number of children as one of the nine significant factors, we do not mean to promote child bearing as an indirect form of future planning in order to insure alimony.

After all, child support payments are more appropriate for that; however, it is axiomatic that a husband is a willing participant in the very existence of offspring, and their pre-and post-natal presence, in significant numbers, is a formidable obstacle to the mother pursuing a more financially rewarding career.

The award of permanent alimony in this case was $6,000 per year. The tax laws permit a deduction for that and the award will only actually cost Doctor McAllister half that sum, which in net effect, will hardly discomfit his life style by more than the sacrifice of one elk hunting trip to Wyoming a year. His wife, by contrast, will be devastated, and Mrs. McAllister, her children now adult, (the last is 18 this year), is left with little but her memories. Such is neither just, nor proper, nor is it the law of this State. Indeed, a ruling to the contrary would require society to re-classify the traditional all-American concept of Mom and apple pie and re-label it a most hazardous occupation that all young girls should be dissuaded from.

It is normally not our function to set the amount of the award, but in a case such as this, the trial court must allow a wife to continue with some semblance of her former standards while at the same time ensuring that the husband is not strapped so that his incentive to strive forward and his lust for life are seriously impaired. By so ruling, we do not intend to lend support to the though that a middle aged healthy woman need not go out to work. In our society, today, women, more often than not, are required to work until retirement and there is no reason to excuse Mrs. McAllister from doing the same just because her former position allowed her to follow a more traditional role. On the other hand, it must be remembered that at her age and level of earning experience, Mrs. McAllister is unlikely to become a great financial success story, and in all probability she will not achieve other than a very modest income.

Accordingly, mere rehabilitative alimony is not enough; however, the award of reasonable permanent periodic alimony does not forever enslave the husband, because significantly changed circumstances, either his or hers, are well settled in the law as a basis for later modification thereof. As was said in *Wilson v. Wilson*, 279 So.2d 893 (Fla.4th DCA 1973), "Nil prospects to the contrary notwithstanding, if she should somehow blossom into a financially productive member of society and other material changes occur, the husband can obtain a trial court review of the award."

We therefore reverse and direct an increase in the permanent periodic alimony from $500.00 to $1,000.00 per month during the first five years encompassed by the judge's final order. At the end of said period, after, and not before, the house has been sold and the husband no longer required to pay the mortgage payments and taxes on the house, the permanent periodic alimony shall be increased to $1,500.00 per month, until his death or her remarriage. The $500.00 per month rehabilitative alimony is hereby cancelled.

In so holding, we recognize that this decision does little more than repeat the same award as was made by the trial court, except that the total sum arrived at is permanent, rather than a combination of permanent and rehabilitative. Such a similar result is reached by us in deference to the trier of the fact who was out there on the firing line, which we were not; however we would comment that the award is low.

...

In all other respects, the final judgment is affirmed.

In re MARRIAGE OF SOMMERS
Supreme Court of Kansas
246 Kan. 652, 792 P.2d 1005 (1990)

McFARLAND, Justice:

This is a divorce action in which the petitioner husband appeals from the division of property, award of maintenance, and allowance of attorney fees made by the trial court. The Court of Appeals affirmed the trial court in an unpublished opinion pursuant to Supreme Court Rule 7.042 (1989 Kan.Ct.R.Annot. 35), said opinion being filed on November 22, 1989. 782 P.2d 1259.

We granted review to determine the issue of whether it was proper for the trial court to admit evidence of fault and to consider fault in the division of property and awards of maintenance and attorney fees where the divorce was sought and granted on the ground of incompatibility (K.S.A. 60-1601[a][1]).

The parties, Donald and Tepin, were married on May 16, 1970. On March 15, 1971, and on September 14, 1972, respectively, the parties' two children were born. The trial court granted a divorce on the ground of incompatibility on February 13, 1989. The balance of the issues were taken under advisement. On March 16, 1989, the trial court entered its memorandum opinion which provided, *inter alia*:

1. joint custody of the children with Tepin to be the custodial parent;
2. child support to be paid by Donald in the amount of $411 per month per child;
3. Tepin to be awarded 45 percent of Donald's retirement benefits with the U.S. Postal Service;
4. Tepin to be awarded the family residence subject to the indebtedness thereon;
5. Tepin to be awarded maintenance of $500 per month for 100 months;
6. Donald to pay the marital indebtedness other than that on the residence, the motor vehicles of Tepin and their son, Alan, and to Montgomery Ward; and
7. Donald to pay $1,000 on Tepin's attorney fees.

Over Donald's objection, evidence was admitted that he was having an extramarital affair with a named individual. In its March 16 memorandum opinion, the trial court stated, in part:

> The Court specifically finds that the primary cause of the destruction of the marriage was the Petitioner's involvement with [name deleted], which the Court finds relevant to the issue of maintenance. The Court finds that the Petitioner entered into this relationship, irrespective of any fault on part of the Respondent. The Court further finds that an award of maintenance should be made to the Petitioner not only because of this factor, but because of the totality of all the factors in this case, including, but not limited to: the length of marriage (19 years); the past, present, and future income producing ability of the parties, which the evidence clearly indicates is favorable to the Petitioner; the division of the property and division of debts awarded to the Respondent; and the need to adequately provide for the children.
>
> . . .

In determining this division of property, the Court has taken into account the ages of the parties, the duration of the marriage, the property owned by the parties, their present and future earning capacities, the time, source and manner of acquisition of property, family ties and obligations, the allowance of maintenance or lack thereof, dissipation of assets, and such other factors this Court considered necessary all as required by K.S.A.1988 Supp. 60-1610(b)(1).

Kansas law, of course, does not require equal split of all property acquired during marriage but rather gives the Court discretion to consider all the property to arrive at a just and reasonable division.

...

...Most importantly, and first and foremost, is that the Respondent, in this case, has been married to the Petitioner for many years, was a good and responsible housewife, and contributed to the accumulation of the marital property. The Petitioner in this case now decides, after having taken up with another woman, specifically [name deleted], that he no longer desires to live with, support, and be a good husband to the Respondent in this case.

While this Court recognizes that this is a no-fault divorce case, nonetheless, there is still some room in these cases for fault, the fault lies with the Petitioner and that matter can appropriately be taken into account by the Court in making an equitable division of property and the Court has done so.

K.S.A. 60-1601(a) provides:

> The district court shall grant a decree of divorce or separate maintenance for any of the following grounds: (1) Incompatibility; (2) failure to perform a material marital duty or obligation; or (3) incompatibility by reason of mental illness or mental incapacity of one or both spouses.

K.S.A.1989 Supp. 60-1610(b)(1) provides in pertinent part:

> In making the division of property the court shall consider the age of the parties; the duration of the marriage; the property owned by the parties; their present and future earning capacities; the time, source and manner of acquisition of property; family ties and obligations; the allowance of maintenance or lack thereof; dissipation of assets; *and such other factors as the court considers necessary* to make a just and reasonable division of property. (Emphasis supplied.)

Donald contends that the trial court's admission of evidence of fault (his alleged marital infidelity) and the consideration thereof in determining the financial aspects of the dissolution of the marriage was improper and contrary to the concept of incompatibility as a no-fault ground for divorce. It should be noted that Donald has consistently denied the existence of the alleged marital infidelity. Tepin contends that such evidence was properly considered as it falls within the purview of the non-specified "such other factors" phrase of K.S.A.1989 Supp. 60-1610(b)(1).

...

In the case before us, much evidentiary time was spent in seeking to prove the alleged infidelity. The "other woman" was called as a witness. Tepin proved to the court's satisfaction that her claims of marital infidelity were true. The trial court specifically stated it considered marital infidelity on the part of Donald in resolving the financial matters. The clear inference is that the trial court penalized Donald for his fault in making its findings relative to the financial aspects involved in the dissolution of the marriage. But for his fault, the resolution of the financial aspects would, presumably, have been more favorable to Donald. Was this error? We believe so.

...

We conclude that in domestic relations actions it was the legislative intent that, in all but extremely gross and rare situations, financial penalties are not to be imposed by a trial court on a party on the basis of fault. There is difficulty in establishing rigid rules relative thereto. For purposes of consideration of the financial aspects of the dissolution of a marriage, the term fault must be confined to a term of art relative to a ground for dissolution of the marriage and penalties arising therefrom. Certain conduct might be a fault ground and also be a circumstance properly to be considered in making a determination relative to financial matters. For illustration, let us say that because of the husband's mental abuse of the wife she is so emotionally impaired that her earning capacity is affected. Certainly, the court should consider this in its determination of a fair and equitable award. The court, in such circumstances, is not imposing a penalty for fault but is considering the circumstances of the parties as they exist and making its award based on such existing circumstances and the likely future results arising therefrom. For another example, let us say that each party is requesting the court to award the family dog to him or her. Evidence that one spouse has cruelly abused the dog in the past and only seeks it to further hurt the other spouse, who has great affection for the animal, should certainly be presented to the court and considered by the court in its division of property. Again, such evidence is not evidence of fault as a term of art, but is evidence necessary to the making of an appropriate division of property. For a final example, let us say we have a physician who because of alcoholism or drug abuse is on a downward professional spiral. The physician's income is high now, but the circumstances show that this income level is not likely to continue. The trial court should have this information before it. It might well conclude that the physician's future ability to pay adequate maintenance and child support is highly questionable and that it would be more provident to award a greater than usual share of the marital property to the custodial spouse. Again, such action would not be a penalty for fault, but rather would be based upon a realistic evaluation of the parties' circumstances, future income, and needs.

It is difficult to conceive of any circumstances where evidence of marital infidelity would be a proper consideration in the resolution of the financial aspects of a marriage. Consideration of such evidence could result only on a decision of whether or not to impose a penalty for such conduct, as it does not relate to the present or future financial circumstances of the parties or the award of any particular property.

We believe that this interpretation of K.S.A.1989 Supp. 60-1610(b)(1) is consistent with its language that the court should, in making its division of property, consider "such other factors as the court considers necessary to make a just and reasonable division of property," and the legislative history of its enactment. Fault, as a term of art, is not to be considered in the determination of the financial aspects of the dissolution of the marriage, nor should a penalty be imposed as a result of such consideration. The only exception would be some rare and unusual situation where a party's conduct is so gross and extreme that failure to penalize therefor would, itself, be inequitable.

This interpretation should also be consistent with the legislative intent that marriage dissolutions occur with minimal hostility and vituperation. The decision to seek a divorce on the grounds of incompatibility or on fault should not be made on the basis that an allegation of fault might result in a party being awarded a greater share of the parties accumulated hoard of nuts or a lesser share of accumulated debts.

We conclude that the trial court erred in admitting evidence of fault (Donald's alleged infidelity) and in considering the same in its resolution of the financial aspects of the dissolution of the marriage. Accordingly, the case must be remanded for redetermination of these matters without consideration of fault....

...

COMMENTS

While *Sommers* is Kansas's effort to ignore marital fault, *McClelland* and *McAllister*, from the supposedly no-fault jurisdiction of Florida, illustrate the resurrection of fault by judicial interpretation of the dissolution statute. This development in Florida was initiated by a decision of the Florida State Supreme Court in *Ryan v. Ryan* (see p. 83), which encouraged judicial inquiry into the causes of irretrievable breakdown of marriage. The cases also illustrate that the return to fault is dictated by economic considerations, namely, the amount of alimony to be awarded and the equitable distribution of property. Moral considerations appear to be secondary, although the preference of the judges for traditional values regarding marriage and the family is made quite clear, for example, in the ways husband and wife are described by the court in *McAllister*. This was a "good marriage," with the wife performing the traditional role of homemaker and mother; her conduct was considered laudable. The husband was not depicted as a bad person, although fault is hinted at and, under the facts as pointed out by the court, he appeared to be less than generous with his wife.

McClelland more directly permits the pleading of adultery in a no-fault jurisdiction for three reasons: (1) the chancellor should continue to have discretionary powers in establishing why a marriage is irretrievably broken; (2) adultery and other fault could be relevant in custody of children; (3) the legislature had empowered the courts to "consider any factor necessary to do equity and justice between the parties." *Sommers* disagrees that marital fault should be considered necessary to do equity and justice between the parties and would have the judge disregard marital fault in determining financial awards.

In spite of *McClelland* and *Ryan*, the position of lower courts in Florida is not uniform. Some judges continue to permit motions to strike pleadings based on fault concepts. *McClelland* mentions such a litigation, in which the trial judge properly excluded evidence of the husband's adultery because the pleadings introduced such facts solely for purposes of obtaining alimony. Although the court felt some discomfort about the wife's motivations in the instant case, it concluded that her pleadings had to be taken at face value. She had stated that she would gladly have reconciled if the respondent had ceased his immoral behavior, and that she brought this action reluctantly after the respondent had failed to do so. Reality, however, may be more complex than these pleadings indicate. As discussed in connection with *Manning v. Manning* (see p. 589), pleadings often contain a fictitious element. Rather than giving the genuine reasons for a client's complaint, they reflect the language of the lawyer, who paraphrases legal requirements. The pleadings in *McClelland* could have been skillfully designed to inject adultery into the discussion and to preclude its being stricken as irrelevant under the no-fault statute. Certainly after *McClelland* attorneys would be aware that it is advisable to plead fault with an appearance of hesitation combined with fictitious offers of reconciliation. Judges, on the other hand, may listen to such pleadings if they feel like it. More often than not, they will be so inclined if the marriage in question is of some duration and if substantial economic factors are involved.

The most important effect of cases like *McClelland* and *McAllister* is that they shift proceedings even further from the courts and into lawyers' offices, where all the fault will be discussed in an effort to reach an agreement. Adultery is a good example. According to divorce statistics, it was rarely used by the courts in granting divorces except in New York, where until 1967 it was the sole ground for divorce. More often the threat to file a divorce action based on adultery was used for purposes of pressure in divorce negotiations or, as sometimes stated from the husband's perspective, for purposes of extortion. Even if the pleadings referred to adultery, they usually contained other divorce grounds, and the claim of adultery could still be withdrawn from consideration. The main effect of *McClelland* is to permit the continued use of adultery and other traditional divorce grounds as bargaining tools in a jurisdiction that seemingly adheres to an irretrievable breakdown standard. Only if the negotiations fail, in a small minority of cases, will it become necessary to plead adultery or other fault as alleged reasons for an irretrievably broken marriage. As in *McClelland*, such pleading is likely to be fictitious to the extent that it tries to avoid the consequences of pure no-fault in regard to alimony and property distribution.

McAllister, which is less visibly concerned with fault, exemplifies a different trend, in which the court can go into the elaborate marital history only because the petitioner has pleaded it. Because the "equities" continue to be relevant, they must be pleaded in great detail, often using the same style and reasoning that was customary before no-fault divorce. In effect this means that the content of the negotiations between the participating lawyers spills over into the pleadings because the negotiations outside of the court have not been successful. It would be a mistake to reproach lawyers for this state of affairs. They perform a valuable and necessary social function, and in continuing to apply conceptions of fault in their negotiations and pleadings, they act under the direction of cases like *McClelland* and *McAllister*. In the last analysis conceptions of moral blame still seem to be needed emotionally, although the underlying issues are more often than not economic.

It is an interesting question whether the rule expressed in *Sommers*, making fault such as marital infidelity irrelevant to the issue of maintenance and the division of property, is more likely to benefit men as a group or women as a group.

Historically, the effect fault has had on the economic consequences of divorce has been devastating for some women — with women found to have committed a single act of adultery denied any alimony even if their contribution to the marriage left them with no marketable skills or earning capacity. A man's adultery often did not increase his alimony obligation, especially if it was only an occasional adulterous act and not a pattern. If, as is often asserted, husbands commit more adultery than wives, the refusal to admit such evidence today may be more beneficial to men than to women.

Defenses Against Fault

NARDONE v. NARDONE
Superior Court of New Jersey
134 N.J. Super. 478, 341 A.2d 698 (1975)

MCKENZIE, J.C.C., Temporarily Assigned.

The parties were married July 2, 1949. In June 1971 defendant wife advised plaintiff husband that she was involved in an adulterous relationship with the co-respondent. The relationship continued until June 1972, when plaintiff joined defendant in inviting the co-respondent to reside with them. The co-respondent and defendant occupied the master bedroom while plaintiff slept in another bedroom in the house. About January, 1974 plaintiff moved from the marital home to Pennsylvania after accepting employment in that state. At no time did plaintiff object to the relationship between defendant and the co-respondent, and in fact it is clear that he consented to it impliedly, if not expressly.

Is plaintiff entitled to a judgment for divorce on the grounds of adultery based on the above circumstances?

The 1971 revision of our Divorce Law was based primarily on the present-day concept that the viability of the marriage, rather than the assessment of fault, should be the principal factor to be considered in determining whether a marriage should be dissolved.... Accordingly, in addition to the introduction of the non-fault ground for divorce based on separation (N.J.S.A. 2A:34-2(d)), the Legislature abolished the defenses of condonation, recrimination and unclean hands in divorce cases. N.J.S.A. 2A:34-7.

Previously, connivance in or consent to the adulterous conduct of the wife was a bar to the right of the husband to obtain a divorce on adultery grounds. This rule was grounded on the premise that it was the duty of a husband "to protect his wife's fair name, and to see that she was not improperly led into temptation." *Atha v. Atha*, 94 N.J.Eq. 692, 121 A. 301 (Ch.1923); *aff'd* 95 N.J.Eq. 275, 122 A. 926 (E. & A.1923). A husband who failed to perform his duty to so protect his wife was held to have unclean hands, barring him from the relief to which he would otherwise be entitled. See *Bingenheimer v. Bingenheimer*, 2 N.J. 284, 66 A.2d 327 (1949).

In abolishing the unclean hands doctrine, the Legislature has adopted the view that to withhold relief in such circumstances is simply the infliction of punishment by the State.... Clearly the marriage is not "less dead" because the husband does not object to the wife's adultery. *Volenti non fit injuria* is now substantially inapplicable in the field of divorce law.

Plaintiff is granted a judgment for divorce.

MOGGED v. MOGGED

Supreme Court of Illinois
55 Ill. 2d 221, 302 N.E.2d 293 (1973)

UNDERWOOD, Chief Justice:

The circuit court of Iroquois County entered a decree of divorce in favor of both parties on the grounds of mental cruelty....

In his complaint, plaintiff Roy Mogged alleged that his wife, defendant Wilma Mogged, was guilty of extreme and repeated mental cruelty. Defendant filed an answer denying the allegations of the complaint and counterclaimed for divorce from plaintiff alleging that plaintiff had been guilty of extreme and repeated mental cruelty toward her. After hearing a portion of the plaintiff's case, which included examination of the defendant as an adverse witness, the trial judge called a halt to the proceedings, over plaintiff's objection, and granted a decree of divorce to each party after stating that it was his opinion that both parties were at fault and that nothing would be accomplished by hearing further testimony.

On appeal by the plaintiff, the appellate court held that the evidence heard by the trial court was sufficient to establish extreme and repeated mental cruelty on the part of each party and stated that "the real question involved...is whether the doctrine of recrimination in Illinois...should be maintained inviolate, thus automatically precluding the divorce of parties who have each been guilty of marital misconduct of equal stature toward the other, or whether that doctrine must be reexamined, and, in the light of present day reality, be rejected as unsound." (5 Ill.App.3d at 583, 284 N.E.2d at 664.) The court answered this question by concluding that the doctrine of recrimination should not be applied in those cases where, in the exercise of sound judicial discretion, it would be unwarranted. In affirming the trial court, the appellate court held further that the trial judge did not err in exercising his discretion in favor of the dual decree of divorce.

...

The doctrine of recrimination has been the subject of extensive analysis and commentary over the years with most writers recommending its modification or abolition.... Also, some courts have re-examined their States' respective divorce laws and have found them susceptible of an interpretation which modified and limited the previous application of the doctrine. Notable in this respect is the decision of the California Supreme Court in *DeBurgh v. DeBurgh* (1952), 39 Cal.2d 858, 250 P.2d 598, where that court analyzed in depth the origin and development of the doctrine as well as the public-policy considerations involved. The court concluded that the California statute which was then in existence did not require the automatic application of the doctrine of recrimination but instead left to the discretion and duty of the trial judge "to determine whether or not the fault of the plaintiff in a divorce action is to be regarded as 'in bar' of the plaintiff's cause of divorce based upon the fault of the defendant." (39 Cal.2d at 871, 250 P.2d at 605.) The court went on to state that dual divorces were permissible in appropriate circumstances. The Florida Supreme Court in *Stewart v. Stewart* (1946), 158 Fla. 326, 328, 29 So.2d 247, 249, has also held that "[t]he application of the doctrine of recrimination like the doctrine of clean hands is a matter of sound judicial discretion dependent upon public policy, public welfare and the exigencies of the case at bar." Other courts have reached similar conclusions.... We also note that in the Uniform Marriage and Divorce Act (1970), sec. 303(e), the National Conference of Commissioners on Uniform State Laws has recommended abolition of recrimination as a defense in divorce proceedings.

In Illinois, recrimination has long been recognized as a bar to divorce. (See *Davis v. Davis* (1857), 19 Ill. 333.) After adoption of the 1874 Divorce Act (Rev.Stat.1874, ch. 40, par. 1 et seq.), which is the basis of our existing act, this court reaffirmed the doctrine. (*Bast v. Bast* (1876), 82 Ill. 584.) The subject was reviewed again in *Duberstein v. Duberstein* (1897), 171 Ill. 133, where the court defined the doctrine in the following terms:

> "A party charged with cruelty may justify himself or herself by showing that the other party was equally to blame.... The law is for the relief of an oppressed party, and the courts will not interfere in quarrels where both parties commit reciprocal excesses and outrages."... Divorce is a remedy provided for an innocent party; (5 Am. & Eng. Ency. of Law, 825, note 6); so that, when each party has committed a cause for divorce, the causes being of the same statutory character, neither can complain of the other.

(171 Ill. at 144-145.) The court concluded that when parties are *in pari delicto* they must be left to themselves....

Whether or not the defense of recrimination should be abolished or modified in Illinois is a question involving complex public-policy considerations as to which compelling arguments may be made on both sides. For the reasons stated hereafter, we believe that these questions are appropriately within the province of the legislature, and that, if there is to be a change in the law of this State on this matter, it is for the legislature and not the courts to bring about that change.

...

...What we stated in *Maki v. Frelk* (1968), 40 Ill.2d 193, 196-197, 239 N.E.2d 445, 447, is pertinent here: "Where it is clear that the court has made a mistake it will not decline to correct it, even though the rule may have been re-asserted and acquiesced in for long number of years. (*Neff v. George*, 364 Ill. 306, 4 N.E.2d 388.) No person has a vested right in any rule of law entitling him to insist that it shall remain unchanged for his benefit. (*Grasse v. Dealer's Transport Co.*, 412 Ill. 179, 190, 106 N.E.2d 124.) But when a rule of law has once been settled, contravening no statute or constitutional principle, such rule ought to be followed unless it can be shown that serious detriment is thereby likely to arise prejudicial to public interests.... The rule of *stare decisis* is founded upon sound principles in the administration of justice, and rules long recognized as the law should not be departed from merely because the court is of the opinion that it might decide otherwise were the question a new one...."

Furthermore, we believe it is significant that over a period of almost one hundred years during which the doctrine of recrimination as enunciated in the *Duberstein* case has been established law of this State our legislature has in no manner acted to either abolish or modify the doctrine, although it has limited its application. This occurred most recently in 1967 when the legislature amended the Act by the addition of section 8a, which provides: "In every action for a divorce commenced on or after the effective date of this amendatory Act of 1967, the fault or conduct of the plaintiff, unless raised by the pleadings, is not a bar to the action nor a proper basis for the refusal of a decree of divorce." (Ill.Rev.Stat.1971, ch. 40, par. 9a.) This provision, while limiting the application of the defense of recrimination, clearly recognizes its existence and contemplates its application in cases such as the one before us where recriminatory conduct on the part of the plaintiff is raised by the pleadings.

...

Accordingly, the judgments of the appellate court and the circuit court of Iroquois County are reversed. It seems appropriate, however, in view of the fact that the action of the trial court prevented the parties from completing the presentation of evidence, to afford an opportunity for the submission of such additional pleadings and evidence, if any, as the parties may desire and the trial court deems appropriate. We accordingly remand the cause to the circuit court of Iroquois County.

Reversed and remanded.

KLUCZYNSKI, Justice (dissenting):

I would affirm the judgment of the appellate court. It is my opinion that the trial court in its sound discretion should decide whether a recriminatory defense is permissible based solely upon the facts of each case....

...

In a comment in the *Journal of Family Law*, the trend toward abolition or modification of the recrimination doctrine was examined. The author stated,

> Whatever value may be gained in the application of the "clean hands" doctrine in mutual fault divorces, it must be weighed against the ramifications of denial of relief. It must be remembered that if relief is denied, the state is in effect forcing two people to live together after they have decided that their continued relationship is no longer viable. It is very conceivable that this forced relationship could lead to increased hatred between parties, fostering of adulterous relationships, and destruction of home life to the detriment of the children.

Albers, *Judicial Discretion and the Doctrine of Recrimination* (1972), 11 J.Fam.L. 737, 739.

...

The majority remands to afford the parties an opportunity to introduce any additional evidence despite their recognition that the findings that both parties committed wrongs of an equal stature is adequately established by the present record. It is unclear what the majority contemplates. Additional evidence of mental cruelty would be useless for it has been determined that if both parties are guilty of positive acts of the same statutory nature, recrimination must bar a divorce. (*Garrett v. Garrett*, 252 Ill. 318, 322, 96 N.E. 882) To say now that a divorce should be granted to the party who might ultimately be determined to have occasioned a lesser degree of mental cruelty would be to adopt the concept of comparative rectitude, which was designed to ameliorate the harsh injustice created by recrimination.... This doctrine has not previously been applied in Illinois.

Thus it would appear that in order to obtain a divorce in this jurisdiction one of the present parties must plead and prove a ground for divorce not subject to a recriminatory defense of mental cruelty or have the opposing party acquiesce in the divorce by voluntarily amending the pleadings to exclude the allegation of a recriminatory defense. The former seems unlikely at this juncture, the latter might be subject to criticism as a product of collusion.

...The doctrine of recrimination is rooted in antiquity and has attained its initial status by judicial action. The present authorities are extremely critical of the harsh, unjust ramifications of this outmoded concept. Finally, our present Divorce Act does not preclude judicial modification or limitation of the doctrine, and the intent of recent legislative action can be reasonably interpreted as contrary to the strict application adopted by the majority.

This case is particularly appropriate to the comments of Justice Oliver Wendell Holmes. "It is revolting to have no better reason for a rule of law than that so it was laid down in the time of Henry IV. It is still more revolting if the grounds upon which it was laid down have vanished long since, and the rule simply persists from blind imitation of the past." *The Path of the Law*, 10 Harv.L.Rev. 457, 469 (1897).

SIMONSON v. SIMONSON

Appellate Court of Illinois
128 Ill. App. 2d 39, 262 N.E.2d 326 (1970)

STAMOS, Presiding Justice.

Defendant appeals from a decree that awarded plaintiff a divorce based upon mental cruelty, denied defendant a divorce based upon desertion and awarded custody of their six year old daughter to plaintiff. The decree also directed defendant to pay the sum of $40.00 per week to plaintiff for child support and provided that the court retain jurisdiction to hear evidence regarding alimony.

Defendant argues the following contentions:

(1) There is a total lack of evidence that defendant's conduct caused plaintiff's life or health to be endangered;

(2) Plaintiff condoned all of the acts complained of;

(3) Plaintiff's departure and her living separate and apart from defendant were unjustified and entitled defendant to a decree of divorce on the grounds of desertion;

(4) The court abused its discretion in awarding custody of their child to plaintiff; and

(5) Plaintiff failed to allege and prove lack of provocation.

Plaintiff's complaint alleged fifteen specific allegations of defendant's conduct toward plaintiff that allegedly caused her severe and extreme mental anguish. It was further alleged that as a result plaintiff suffered a severe breakdown that required her hospitalization and placed her in great fear for her mental and physical well being.

Defendant answered and denied each specific allegation of misconduct toward plaintiff; that if the allegations were true, they were all condoned by plaintiff and are of themselves glaring evidence of the emotional instability and mental incapacity of plaintiff and not sufficient to establish a cause of action for mental cruelty.

The allegations and proof of defendant's misconduct, with the exception of a few instances, related to a period of time of approximately a year before the parties separated. The parties were married on May 11, 1961, after a 4 month courtship and separated on August 30, 1967.

Plaintiff testified and also called upon next door neighbors, a family friend and two treating psychiatrists to testify in support of her allegations.

Defendant testified and denied each accusation of misconduct toward defendant and related general and specific instances of his devotion, affection and concern for plaintiff and his efforts to accommodate her personality. A salesman who frequented the parties' home and delicatessen testified that defendant always treated plaintiff with respect and decency and never cursed or abused her.

Plaintiff's evidence revealed that defendant criticized plaintiff in public and private regarding her housekeeping abilities, repeatedly boasted about his premarital relations, unfavorably compared plaintiff with these other women, struck her with a rolled up newspaper on the face and head causing her great pain and twisted her leg on another occasion causing her great pain and anguish. The evidence further revealed that defendant called her "nuts" threatening to send her to the "nut house," advised others that plaintiff was "nuts," constantly cursed and swore at plaintiff repeatedly telling her to return to Norway, constantly remained out late at night, possessed and publicly displayed pornographic pictures and magazines in her presence, refused to introduce plaintiff as his wife and constantly caused her humiliation and embarrassment before their friends, relatives, customers and employees at defendant's delicatessen store.

Plaintiff testified that shortly after her marriage she realized her husband was a personality with three sides and that she had made a bad marriage, but endeavored to make it work although she was very unhappy because he mistreated her.

In 1964 plaintiff developed nervousness and on medical advice took tranquilizers and sleeping pills for a few days. She had no further difficulty until February, 1967, when plaintiff became very nervous and experienced vomiting spells and diarrhea. She lost her appetite, became nauseous, suffered from insomnia and began to lose weight. She prevailed upon her mother-in-law to drive her to the Edgewater Hospital, and testified that she did not have anyone else to assist her and could not rely upon defendant. After a two week period of hospitalization it was determined that plaintiff was in need of psychiatric care to prevent her "anxiety reactions" and was referred to the Northwestern University Clinic for examination and treatment. Plaintiff made some visits to the clinic during the summer of 1967 but felt she was not being helped. Plaintiff testified that during this period of her illness, she pleaded with defendant on her knees and implored him to at least treat her as his friend. She told defendant that she was desperate and needed his help, but defendant laughed and threatened her with incarceration in an institution for the mentally ill. Plaintiff testified that defendant's threat was the "biggest scare" in her life.

In September, 1967, plaintiff's condition had not improved and she prevailed upon her sister-in-law to drive her to Billings Hospital where plaintiff was hospitalized and treated in the psychiatric clinic for six weeks. Her symptoms were similar to those she exhibited in February, 1967, and her condition was diagnosed as "depressive reaction" for which she was afforded treatment. It was the opinion of the psychiatrists that her marital difficulties were a major contributor to the need for hospitalization. Two other emotional events in plaintiff's life they deemed significant were plaintiff's miscarriage in August, 1966, and the fact that her daughter in February, 1967, attained the same age that plaintiff had when plaintiff's first sibling was born. Plaintiff was discharged from the hospital on October 26, 1967.

After plaintiff's separation from defendant in August, 1967, and her subsequent hospital care, she was greatly improved and exhibited none of the symptoms for which she was given treatment. Her mood was considerably improved and the psychiatric impairment was minimal. Plaintiff was also examined on July 25, 1968, and no evidence of any psychiatric disorder was discovered.

During her hospitalization the psychiatrists discerned that plaintiff was a person who tended to keep resentment to herself, not being open and expressive about it, with a tendency to handle stressful relationships, inner distresses and nervousness by pleasantness and carefree amiability.

There is no dispute that plaintiff suffered a mental illness that required her hospitalization on more than one occasion. Plaintiff's condition was diagnosed as "depressive reaction." Defendant contends that there is a total lack of evidence that his conduct caused plaintiff's mental health to be endangered, but that plaintiff was a victim of her own frail personality and emotional instability. Defendant further contends that none of his conduct, that plaintiff complains about, if true, would be sufficient to meet the legal requirement for mental cruelty.

In *Hayes v. Hayes*, 117 Ill.App.2d 211 at page 215, 254 N.E.2d 288 at page 290 the court expressed the following language we find appropriate to the case at bar:

> . . .
>
> "Whether certain acts will constitute physical or mental cruelty still depends upon the total factual background surrounding the conduct under question. This includes the particular emotional and personal makeup of the parties and the varying circumstances under which any of the incidents occurred that may have given rise to the acts." *Stanard v. Stanard*, 108 Ill.App.2d 240, 247 N.E.2d 438 (1969). In this case the emotional makeup of the plaintiff must be considered in determining the effect of the conduct of defendant in providing grounds for the mental cruelty allegation. Plaintiff's testimony, taken with the psychiatrist's reports, furnish an adequate basis for the court's findings.

We find that the evidence in the case at bar is sufficient to establish that defendant has been guilty of extreme and repeated mental cruelty. (Ill.Rev.Stat., ch. 40 §1 (1967)).

Defendant contends that the continued cohabitation and sexual relations of the parties constituted condonation of defendant's alleged misconduct. Condonation is a question of intent to be shown by words and deeds that reflect full, free and voluntary forgiveness and continued cohabitation will not necessarily amount to condonation. *Collinet v. Collinet*, 31 Ill.App.2d 72, 78, 175 N.E.2d 659. Plaintiff in the case at bar testified that she engaged in sexual relations, relied upon by defendant as condonation, against her wishes and that she was afraid of him.

In *Rasgaitis v. Rasgaitis*, 347 Ill.App. 477, at page 482, 107 N.E.2d 273, at page 275, the court said: "The law will not presume that a wronged wife condones the actions of her guilty husband simply because the difficulty of finding another place to live, the welfare of her child, and other factors beyond her control, force her to remain temporarily in the same house with him." Condonation is an affirmative defense which defendant pleaded but failed to prove by a preponderance of the evidence.

In view of the foregoing, defendant's contention that plaintiff's departure and her living separate and apart were unjustified and entitled defendant to a decree of divorce on grounds of desertion, is of no merit.

The Chancellor elicited an opinion from one of plaintiff's psychiatrists that plaintiff was capable of caring for her minor child. The Chancellor also asked questions of the same witness which revealed that the witness was not surprised to learn that plaintiff filed a separate maintenance action while she was hospitalized. Defendant complains and contends that the answers were both bottomed on conversations the witness had with plaintiff and were hearsay and should not have been admitted into evidence. We find no error in the admission of an expression of the medical opinion and as to the other point, we observe that it was on defendant's own motion that voluminous medical records of both the Edgewater Hospital and the University of Chicago Hospitals and Clinics were received into evidence. These exhibits reflected countless recitations of conversations plaintiff had with the witness and other medical personnel regarding her illness, treatment, prognosis, symptoms and her marital disharmony and discontent. We also note that defendant's cross-examination prior to the Chancellor's questions delved into conversations this psychiatrist had with plaintiff regarding her marital difficulties.

There is no evidence in the record that would justify this court in finding that the Chancellor abused his discretion in awarding custody of the minor child to plaintiff. The psychiatric testimony established that plaintiff was not emotionally unstable but had in fact recovered from her illness and was clearly able to function and assume responsibility for the care of her minor child. The paramount consideration in determining custody is the welfare and best interest of the child. *Nye v. Nye*, 411 Ill. 408, 105 N.E.2d 300. We cannot set aside this award unless it was entered against the manifest weight of the evidence....

Defendant contends that plaintiff's complaint lacks an essential element in failing to allege a lack of provocation and thus does not state a cause of action and that therefore, the complaint may be successfully attacked on appeal as not justifying the decree. *Stanard v. Stanard*, 108 Ill.App.2d 240, 247 N.E.2d 438.

...

In the case at bar plaintiff's evidence more than adequately depicted that defendant's misconduct was not caused or provoked by plaintiff and defendant averred and adduced evidence and conducted his cross-examination on the theory that the acts and misconduct of purported extreme and repeated mental cruelty charged by plaintiff never occurred — a theory which, by its nature, is inconsistent with a defense of provocation.

...

The judgment is affirmed.

COMMENTS

The continued significance of fault and moral blame, even in many no-fault jurisdictions, raises the question of the extent to which these residual conceptions are related to the original, now seemingly abolished, divorce grounds (e.g., adultery, desertion, extreme cruelty). It also must be examined whether any of the traditional defenses has survived, and if so in what form. Obviously, as long as courts continue to discuss adultery, as in *McClelland* (see p. 603), or talk about facts that may be the equivalent of mental cruelty, as in *McAllister* (see p. 604), lawyers will have to be concerned with what now constitutes adultery or cruelty, even though they practice in a no-fault divorce jurisdiction. They also will have to be concerned with the kinds of defenses that are still available even though those defenses, such as condonation, collusion, connivance, recrimination, and unclean hands, may have been legislatively abolished.

Because of the difficulties involved in eliminating conceptions of fault altogether, it is submitted that an effective law practice in any jurisdiction must include a knowledge of the traditional divorce grounds and the defenses, regardless of what a given statute states. Even in apparently pure no-fault jurisdictions fault may resurface, for example, in custody proceedings involving children. And even in community-property jurisdictions such as California, which first legislated on no-fault divorce, a judge may be moved by the equities of a case in determining what is half of such property. In any event, the traditional definitions of fault grounds and defenses continue to be relevant for divorce negotiations. More important, failure to inform a client of the potential continuing relevance of adultery and other fault grounds may constitute malpractice (although the client may find it difficult to meet the burden of proof in the malpractice action). From this perspective the mechanical application of no-fault statutes in some law firms, in which paraprofessionals record the history of the marriage and fill in form pleadings in the interest of low-cost divorce and rapid turnover, is dangerous and may backfire, with suits eventually being brought against lawyers.

To the extent that a given jurisdiction has retained traditional divorce grounds in addition to a newly adopted no-fault statute, it is clear that preexisting case law on adultery, cruelty, and so on, as well as in regard to the defenses, continues to be applicable. Not quite so clear is what happens in such mixed jurisdictions if fault and no-fault grounds are linked together in the same proceedings by way of petition and counterclaim. Even though logic seems to dictate that no-fault prevail in such situations, it is more likely that fault will spill over into the whole proceeding with all the defenses then still available.

Even more complex is the situation if a no-fault divorce jurisdiction has legislatively abolished all defenses, but insists judicially that fault continues to be relevant (see *Ryan*, p. 83, and *McClelland*, p. 603). In *McClelland* it was made clear that courts should be interested only in the broad picture of why the marriage is irretrievably broken and refrain from going into details. Actual proof of sexual intercourse, as was necessary under the traditional divorce ground of adultery, or minute establishment of "reasonable apprehension of bodily harm," as under the divorce ground of cruelty, may no longer be required. Yet if moral blame has a bearing on the outcome, the traditional defenses must continue to be available in some form to the person who is accused of misconduct. *Ryan* makes it clear as to how this is to come about. Accordingly, not only is the chancellor permitted to continue to inquire into fault by asking why the marriage is irretrievably broken, but the respondent must have the right to demonstrate why it is not. The breakdown standard implicitly incorporates the possibility of fault and the traditional defenses against it. The legislative abolition of these defenses is, however, not entirely ineffective. What has been binding law has probably now become discretionary. The judge is not likely to refer expressly to condonation, collusion, connivance, recrimination, and unclean hands, because that might lead to a reversal on appeal. Instead he or she will state as a finding of fact that the marriage is or is not irretrievably broken.

If the husband was facilitating the adultery of his wife, a judge might at least theoretically continue to deny relief even in a no-fault jurisdiction. More likely, as in *Nardone*, a dissolution will be granted. If husband and wife have an "open marriage" or both engage consensually in "swinging" (having sexual relations outside marriage), a judge could, without reference to recrimination, deny their request for dissolution because the marriage is not irretrievably broken. A more natural course of events would be for the judge to give a moral lecture to the parties and grant the request. In either case the fault of the parties and the nature of their defenses have a definite bearing on the remaining equities of the requests, particularly in regard to alimony, property distribution, and child custody.

It should be remembered that the opinions in *Mogged* and *Simonson* originated in Illinois at the time when the state had not yet adopted no-fault divorce. The traditional defenses were still fully in force. Yet even with respect to recrimination, the approach of the Supreme Court of Illinois in *Mogged* was not as orthodox as it appears. In its concluding paragraph the majority opinion remanded the case to the trial court to facilitate additional pleadings and evidence by the parties, which in effect amounted to an implicit invitation to the lawyers to engage in negotiations about the divorce grounds and defenses. The outcome of this litigation may thus be similar to that in a no-fault jurisdiction, although probably at a much higher cost. Yet it seems clear that the Supreme Court of Illinois perceived its primary function in this case to be one of maintaining principle.

Simonson injected the problem of mental health, which can come up in multiple fashions. In this instance it was used to demonstrate the extreme and repeated mental cruelty of the husband, which resulted in a "depressive reaction." It could also have been used as a defense by the wife that, because of her condition, she could not be cruel or commit desertion, nor could she commit any other act based on fault. She could also have used mental illness as a reply to the husband's defense that she had "condoned," in other words, forgiven, his misconduct by continuing to live and have sexual relations with him. Condonation would also require legal capacity at the time in question. In addition, mental illness could have an impact on alimony, equitable distribution of property, and child custody. Had this been a no-fault jurisdiction, the pleadings could have been quite similar in an effort to show irretrievable breakdown of marriage, although express reference to condonation might have been avoided. Continued sexual intercourse, if voluntary, could show that a marriage is salvageable. Hence lawyers in any jurisdiction should continue to include in their check list inquiry about intercourse and when it last took place.

An additional problem with mental illness may arise in some no-fault jurisdictions. California and Florida, for example, have two dissolution grounds, one based on ordinary breakdown of marriage, the other on mental illness. The question of how the two grounds relate to each other could arise. For instance, if a husband were to bring a request for dissolution of marriage in Florida, based on the alleged mental incompetence of his wife, he would have to satisfy specific statutory requirements, for example, that the wife must have been adjudged incompetent for a preceding period of at least three years. If such adjudication is missing or if it is less than three years in the past, could the husband base his request for dissolution on the first ground, namely that his marriage is "irretrievably broken"? It can be argued that the wife, in such an instance, could defend herself by stating that an action must satisfy the requirements of the ground based on mental illness. Assuming this defense prevails, the first ground should really read, "The marriage is irretrievably broken, unless the other party is mentally incompetent, in which case the petitioner must proceed under the requirements of that ground." Yet this interpretation injects a further element of residual fault into the statute: that the respondent in a no-fault action must be legally competent, that is, responsible for the breakdown of marriage. Whether actual litigation will often reach such a level of conceptual refinement is doubtful. Attorneys are likely to proceed under a simple theory of breakdown of marriage in cases of mental illness. However, if a lawyer who represents an insane person does not raise the conceptual problems resulting from mental incompetence, the lawyer may become susceptible to substantial claims of malpractice.

REFERENCES

Susan Westerberg Reppy, Comment, *The End of Innocence: Elimination of Fault in California Divorce Law*, 17 UCLA L. REV. 1306 (1970).

Herma Hill Kay, *An Appraisal of California's No-Fault Divorce Law*, 75 CAL. L. REV. 291 (1987).

Herma Hill Kay, *Beyond No-Fault — New Directions in Divorce Reform*, in Stephen D. Sugarman and Herma Hill Kay, eds. DIVORCE REFORM AT THE CROSSROADS 6 (1990).

Controlling Divorce and Post-Divorce Life Through Alimony

DAKIN v. DAKIN

Supreme Court of Washington
62 Wash. 2d 687, 384 P.2d 639 (1963)

HUNTER, Judge.

Olcott W. Dakin, the husband (defendant), appeals from a decree awarding a divorce to Catherine M. Dakin, his wife (plaintiff), and dismissing his cross complaint for divorce with prejudice.

Olcott and Catherine Dakin were married at Watertown, New York, in 1936. They moved to Seattle where the defendant worked at various jobs until, in 1957, he purchased a small transfer and storage company. The plaintiff also obtained employment during this period in various positions within the general field of social work.

The defendant is presently the president and manager of three transfer businesses. He purchased Chesley Transfer Company, Inc., in 1957 and, shortly thereafter, organized Chesley Overseas, Inc. Later, he bought Yukon Transfer Company which, unlike the other two companies, is a sole proprietorship. These three businesses are one-man businesses which completely depend upon the defendant's attention.

In 1939, the plaintiff invited Karen Frolund, a co-worker at the Welfare Department, to be a guest at her home. After Karen married in 1941, the two families remained close friends and saw each other often. Sometime in 1948 (approximately), the defendant commenced seeing Karen privately despite the fact the plaintiff previously had remonstrated his excessive attentions to her. From 1949 on, the defendant and Karen secretly met at various locations in and around Seattle to prevent the plaintiff from discovering their relationship. Despite the couple's caution, the plaintiff suspected that her husband was meeting another woman and accused him of it. The defendant denied her accusations and, in rebuff, told her she was obsessed with jealousy.

In the fall of 1957, the defendant and Karen told the plaintiff that they had been in love with each other for nine years. They requested her to give the defendant a divorce, but she refused to do so. Despite her refusal, the defendant continued to live, off and on, with the plaintiff. Sometimes he abused her, both physically and mentally; other times he was very attentive and kind. During this period, however, the defendant kept up his relationship with Karen. This conduct left the plaintiff in a state of emotional turmoil.

Mr. and Mrs. Dakin separated permanently in 1959, in which year the defendant agreed to pay to the plaintiff $300 per month for temporary support money provided a divorce action was commenced prior to February 18, 1960.

...

The trial court found that the plaintiff should be granted a decree of divorce and that the defendant's cross complaint for divorce should be dismissed with prejudice; that the plaintiff should be given the family residence and vacant lot, together with certain household furnishings, an automobile, $7,500 in cash and alimony in the amount of $300 per month until she should remarry or die; that the defendant should be given the interests in the transfer businesses, his separate property, and the remaining community property; and that the defendant should be required to maintain the life insurance until the plaintiff should remarry or die, to pay certain debts, and to pay $1,000 as reasonable attorneys' fees as well as $400 for suit money previously allowed. A decree of divorce incorporating the above findings was entered from which the defendant appeals.

The defendant assigns error to the trial court's awarding of $300 per month as alimony for the plaintiff until she marries or dies.

...

...He argues that, if justified at all, the plaintiff should be granted alimony of a temporary nature to be received during the period of her readjustment and rehabilitation and no longer.

The criterion adopted by this court for the allowance of alimony includes two factors: (1) the necessities of the wife, and (2) the financial ability of the husband....

...

The record shows that the plaintiff has no children to support or care for; that she was 53 years of age at the commencement of this action; that she was extremely nervous and upset at the time of the trial; but, otherwise, she is an able-bodied woman; that, because of her past condition, she has been unable to maintain steady employment; that she attended teacher's college for two years and taught school for four years thereafter; and that she has had considerable experience as a social worker, although no formal training.

It is the policy of this state to place a duty upon the wife to gain employment, if possible. In *Morgan v. Morgan*, [59 Wash. 2d 639, 369 P.2d 516 (1962)] we said:

> Alimony is not a matter of right. When the wife has the ability to earn a living, it is not the policy of the law of this state to give her a perpetual lien on her divorced husband's future income. *Warning v. Warning*, 40 Wash.2d 903, 247 P.2d 249 (1952); *Lockhart v. Lockhart*, 145 Wash. 210, 259 P. 385 (1927).

We are of the opinion that the plaintiff in the instant case should not receive alimony until her remarriage or until her death. We think that she should be encouraged to rehabilitate herself and that, within a reasonable period, she may become self-supporting. Although she may have been nervous and upset prior to her decree of divorce, there is no evidence which indicates this condition is of a permanent nature. Except for this condition, she appears to be an able-bodied woman capable of future employment. We conclude that alimony should be awarded which is adequate for the purpose of providing for her during her transitional period. We cannot say, under the state of this record, what this period should be. Therefore, the trial court should be in a position to modify or terminate the alimony upon competent proof of changed conditions, if any, that may be established at future modification hearings. The divorce decree is therefore modified by awarding the plaintiff alimony in the amount of $300 per month until further order of the court.

...

The judgment of the trial court is affirmed as modified by this opinion which provides that the alimony award shall be in the sum of $300 per month until further order of the court.

...

COMMENTS

Alimony awards are essentially discretionary decisions. This realization has several consequences that are sometimes overlooked. Alimony controversies are won or lost on the trial court level. As in a case of a jury verdict, a judge's or chancellor's decision can be attacked only if it is clearly unreasonable, is unsupported by sufficient findings of fact, or involves an abuse of discretion. Appellate judges are prone to rule that since trial judges have observed the parties, heard their testimony, and studied their financial statements firsthand, their decisions should ordinarily be upheld. Knowing this, it is relatively easy for a trial judge to inject sufficient findings of fact into the trial record to support his decision and make it immune to appeal. On the other hand, it is exactly this discretionary power of the trial judge that encourages divorce settlements between the parties. By such settlement agreement, the parties avoid the risks of judicial discretion.

Some settlement agreements do not avoid judicial discretion, but in effect reflect it. For example, in jurisdictions which hold pre-trial conferences, the judge may suggest informally what he or she perceives to be an appropriate award. This suggestion, although not binding in fact, sets the boundaries in which the settlement will be reached.

Trial judges appear to be uneasy with an unfettered exercise of discretionary powers. They often develop their own rules regarding the exercise of their discretion. To the extent that patterns of judicial discretion have become settled in a given jurisdiction — for example in regard to need for alimony and ability to pay it — exercise of discretion may be restricted by precedent. The legislative trend in this area, as in child support (see Chapter 5) has been toward standardized guidelines that further limit discretion. Most important is the adoption in some states of the Uniform Marriage and Divorce Act (see Appendix) and provisions similar to the Act. Section 308 of that act sets out factors to be considered in making an assignment of property, including the husband's ability to pay and the wife's needs; conduct of the parties; duration of the marriage; standard of living during the marriage; age and health of the spouses; financial resources; needs for education or training; and contributions of each party to the marriage. Fault of the parties continues to be significant, even if the courts no longer acknowledge it openly under conceptions of no-fault divorce. This does not mean that the courts will necessarily articulate that fault had any relevance; more likely they will not do so, because such articulation could encourage appeals.

Since the circumstances of a marriage are usually relevant for alimony claims, regardless of whether the divorce is based on the no-fault concept, good or bad conduct can be pleaded. Even if *Dakin* had been decided today, the plaintiff wife could have set forth her husband's conduct which resulted in her extreme nervousness and perhaps continued need for medical attention. On the other hand, her own "fault" may have a bearing too, even though it may not fit into traditional categories of improper conduct. For more than a decade she was "sleeping on her rights," apparently being unusually gullible, although her friend Karen carried on an affair with her husband. Some judges may be influenced by such conduct under some theory that the wife brought the marital problem upon herself, although they would be unwise to express such an opinion because it could lead to an appeal for an abuse of discretion.

The legislative regulation of alimony and the assignment of property also has an important effect on lawyers conducting divorce negotiations and preparing for litigation. These statutory requirements furnish a check list of factors for purposes of organizing the case.

The concept of "rehabilitative alimony" grew out of the exercise of judicial discretion. *Dakin* illustrates early judicial demands that women should participate in their rehabilitation after divorce. No statute was needed for this pronouncement. The wife's needs and the husband's limited financial ability, in the court's view, made it desirable that she be self-supporting after a reasonable period. Once the concept of "rehabilitation" had been judicially developed, it could be legislatively adopted. No-fault divorce legislation provided an opportunity to make rehabilitative alimony the norm rather than the exception. Of course, this opened the door to no alimony at all in the many cases in which judicial discretion or the divorce settlement results in a decision that no rehabilitation is needed.

The shift from permanent to rehabilitative alimony has, however, a deeper meaning. It relates to the evolution of marriage toward a contractual relationship. Permanent alimony was part of a husband's obligation to support his wife, even after divorce. By requiring divorced women to become self-supporting, their status in marriage is altered. They lose some of the traditional characteristics of wives and acquire those of employees. Dissolution of marriage, on the other hand, acquires characteristics of breach of contract. For over a century employees dismissed from their contracts without sufficient justification have been under a duty to mitigate damages. In other words, they had to seek other employment in an effort to keep the damages low. Thus the concept of mitigation of damages, which seems archaic under modern conditions, has been revived in the context of marriage and divorce as "rehabilitative alimony." Underlying this revival are economic conditions that affect the nature of marriage and the status of women. However, if a married woman is more than a mere employee of sorts, namely, a person with an equal share in a marital partnership, the concept of "rehabilitative alimony" does not seem to fit. In this case, her status is more akin to that of an entrepreneur. If the marriage fails, the venture did not succeed. In that case there is no need to rehabilitate the wife because she carried her own risk. (For a very different kind of analysis of risk, however, see supra at pp. 92–93.) To carry the analogy further, she may not be granted severance pay unless it was bargained for prior to marriage in an antenuptial agreement. Division of property then becomes the only remaining issue.

REFERENCE

Frances Olsen, *The Family and the Market: A Study of Ideology and Legal Reform*, 96 HARV. L. REV. 1497 (1983).

LEPIS v. LEPIS
Supreme Court of New Jersey
83 N.J. 139, 416 A.2d 45 (1980)

PASHMAN, J.

Long after the bonds of matrimony are dissolved, courts of equity are frequently called upon to reassess the persisting obligations of financial support. This case presents for review the standards and procedures for modifying support and maintenance arrangements after a final judgment of divorce.

The parties were married in 1961 and had three children. After a period of marital discord, on January 8, 1974, the wife obtained from the Superior Court, Chancery Division, a judgment of divorce on grounds of desertion. The court incorporated as part of the judgment a detailed agreement governing property distribution, alimony, child custody and support.

Under the terms of the agreement, the wife retained all the household items and "any and all other tangible personal property" located at the marital home. She received title to the marital home and the husband's two-year old automobile. Upon entry of a final judgment of divorce and judicial ratification of the agreement, the husband would make a single payment of $22,000 "in settlement of the Wife's claim to her right for equitable distribution and any other support claims of the Wife now or at any time in the future except as provided herein."

The agreement permitted the wife to retain custody of the children and provided flexible visitation provisions. The husband agreed to pay $120 per week for alimony and $210 per week for child support $70 per week for each unemancipated child. A child's attendance at college, business or trade school would not terminate support payments. The husband was obligated to maintain health insurance for the wife until her death or remarriage and for each child until emancipated. He was also responsible for all necessary medical, dental and prescription drug expenses of the children and for the wife's medical, dental and prescription drug expenses in excess of $50 per illness. The husband promised to pay all expenses for four years of college or professional education for each child. If a child lived away at school, child support would be reduced by some "appropriate" amount.

Looking to future uncertainties, the agreement sought to remove some of them from consideration if questions regarding modification arose. It specified that the presence or absence of separate earnings by the wife, or changes in the husband's income, would be irrelevant to a decision to alter or halt the husband's payments. The agreement also contained a provision governing modification by consent:

> This Agreement shall not be varied, modified or annulled by the Husband or the Wife except by written instrument voluntarily executed and acknowledged by both.

On February 1, 1978, plaintiff moved to modify the support and alimony provisions of the agreement. She sought increased support for herself and the three children, a single, additional payment of $1,500 for household repairs and furniture, and counsel fees. Plaintiff also sought production of defendant's 1976 and 1977 income tax returns before a hearing on the modification motion. The trial court denied the motion without requiring defendant to disclose actual earnings. Plaintiff's request for counsel fees was also denied.

Plaintiff appealed from these rulings to the Appellate Division on April 19, 1978. On the following day she filed a notice of motion for rehearing of her motion for modification. Defendant responded by filing a notice of cross-motion for counsel fees and costs on the ground that plaintiff's motion for rehearing was frivolous. The trial court denied a rehearing, noting that by virtue of the pending appeal the court lacked jurisdiction to grant it. Because the application for a rehearing was clearly without merit, the court granted defendant's cross-motion for counsel fees. Plaintiff sought review in the Appellate Division of this second determination which was consolidated with her earlier appeal.

In an unreported opinion, the Appellate Division reversed the trial court's dispositions. The court held that "[o]nly after the discovery process is complete should the former wife's application for increased alimony and child support be determined." The Appellate Division concluded that refusing discovery of defendant's income despite plaintiff's showing of increased need "effectively denied her any opportunity to prove changed circumstances...." Since the court viewed plaintiff's application as requiring further examination, it held that the award of counsel fees was premature. It therefore vacated the trial court's orders and remanded the cause with directions to order production of all tax returns of defendant since 1973.

This Court granted defendant's petition for certification. 81 N.J. 281, 405 A.2d 826 (1979). We now affirm. Before addressing whether the summary rejection of plaintiff's claims was proper, we first discuss the effect of a consensual agreement upon the court's power to modify obligations of support and maintenance. Secondly, we examine generally what constitutes "changed circumstances" so as to warrant a modification of those obligations. We then consider the procedures that a court should employ when passing upon a modification petition particularly the allocation of the burdens of proof and the conditions for compelling production of tax returns. Finally, we apply the results of this analysis to the facts of the present case.

I. Modification of Spousal Agreements

The equitable power of the courts to modify alimony and support orders at any time is specifically recognized by N.J.S.A. 2A:34-23:

> Pending any matrimonial action brought in this State or elsewhere, or after judgment of divorce or maintenance, whether obtained in this State or elsewhere, the court may make such order as to the alimony or maintenance of the parties, and also as to the care, custody, education and maintenance of the children, or any of them, as the circumstances of the parties and the nature of the case shall render fit, reasonable and just, and require reasonable security for the due observance of such orders.... Orders so made may be revised and altered by the court from time to time as circumstances may require.

As a result of this judicial authority, alimony and support orders define only the present obligations of the former spouses. Those duties are always subject to review and modification on a showing of "changed circumstances."...

Divorcing spouses have often attempted to temper the flexibility of the court's power to modify with greater predictability by entering into separation agreements. In the past, such agreements have had significant and varying impact on the availability of post-judgment modification. Specific performance of spousal support agreements was once thought to be barred by the flexible approach to modification embodied in N.J.S.A. 2A:34-23. *Apfelbaum v. Apfelbaum*, 111 N.J.Eq. 529, 162 A. 543 (E & A 1932). Although not specifically enforceable, such agreements could be regarded by the court as relevant to the issue of support, and could be incorporated in a divorce decree. "The fact that [a] court took over the terms of the contract did not impair the power of the court to alter such provisions to accord with the equity of unfolding circumstance." *Corbin v. Mathews*, 129 N.J.Eq. 549, 554, 19 A.2d 633, 635 (E & A 1941). The agreement was said to merge into the divorce decree, thereby losing its contractual nature....

The rule against specific enforcement was later rejected by this Court in *Schlemm v. Schlemm*, 31 N.J. 557, 158 A.2d 508 (1960). That decision recognized that apart from its statutory authority, the Superior Court may exercise its "highly flexible" remedial powers to enforce the terms of interspousal support agreements "to the extent that they are just and equitable." *Id.* at 581-582, 158 A.2d at 522. Later decisions continued to recognize the courts' power to modify such agreements "upon a showing of changed circumstances." *Berkowitz v. Berkowitz*, 55 N.J. 564, 569, 264 A.2d 49, 52 (1970); see *Gulick v. Gulick*, 113 N.J.Super. 366, 370, 273 A.2d 792 (Ch.Div.1971). The rule which developed, however, required that "[a] far greater showing of changed circumstances must be made before the court can modify a separation agreement than need be shown to warrant the court amending an order for alimony or support." *Schiff v. Schiff*, 116 N.J.Super. 546, 561, 283 A.2d 131, 139 (App.Div.1971), *certif. den.* 60 N.J. 139, 286 A.2d 512 (1972).

Applying the "same standard that is applied by courts of equity to the specific enforcement of contracts in other fields[,]" the Appellate Division in *Schiff* held that modification of a spousal agreement required a showing of changed circumstances "such as to convince the court that to enforce the agreement would be *unconscionable*." 116 N.J.Super. at 561, 283 A.2d at 139 (emphasis supplied). "Subsequent events which should have been in contemplation of the parties as possible contingencies when they entered into the contract [would] not excuse performance." *Id.* Although this standard was never expressly adopted by the Supreme Court, it has been followed by lower courts.[1]...

In *Smith v. Smith*, 72 N.J. 350, 371 A.2d 1 (1977), this Court considered whether the *Schiff* standard applied when the trial court was effecting equitable distribution of marital property pursuant to N.J.S.A. 2A:34-23. Noting that "support payments are intimately related to equitable distribution" and that "trial judges should have the utmost leeway and flexibility in determining what is just and equitable in making allocations of marital assets," we disapproved of the *Schiff* rule:

> Henceforth the extent of the change in circumstances, whether urged by plaintiff or defendant, shall be the same, regardless of whether the support payments being questioned were determined consensually or by judicial decree. In each case the court must determine what, in the light of all the facts presented to it, is equitable and fair, giving due weight to the strong public policy favoring stability of arrangements. [72 N.J. at 360, 371 A.2d at 6].

The rule announced in *Smith* is fully applicable when considering post-judgment modification. Consensual agreements and judicial decrees should be subject to the same standard of "changed circumstances." Initially it might appear that this rule would diminish the advantages of separation and property settlement agreements, since they would provide no greater certainty or stability than a judicial determination. However, granting a greater degree of permanence to negotiated agreements would tend to make them a riskier arrangement for spouses who are likely to be harmed by changed circumstances. Typically, they have been spouses who are economically dependent; they generally have been wives with custody of children. Often consensual agreements would not be in their best interests if only "unconscionable" circumstances would warrant modification.[2] As we recognized in rejecting Schiff, contract principles have little place in the law of domestic relations. See *Smith*, 72 N.J. at 360, 371 A.2d 1.

When we first upheld the specific enforceability of spousal agreements in *Schlemm*, we relied on the flexible power of equity to enforce such agreements only to the extent that they were fair and equitable. Similarly, the terms of such agreements should receive continued enforcement without modification only so long as they remain fair and equitable. The equitable authority of a court to modify support obligations in response to changed circumstances, regardless of their source, cannot be restricted. *Smith*, 72 N.J. at 360, 371 A.2d 1; *Berkowitz*, 55 N.J.

1. The *Schiff* rule, however, was not extended to modification of child support provisions. See *Clayton v. Muth*, 144 N.J.Super. 491, 366 A.2d 354 (Ch.Div.1976).

2. Commentators have addressed similar arguments to the *Schiff* rule of unconscionability. See Skoloff, *Schiff—Unconscionable Obstacle to Matrimonial Settlements*, 99 N.J.L.J. 553 (1976)("The undue burden placed on counsel as well as the parties by this *Schiff* requirement is itself unconscionable.... The result: a decided chilling effect on the negotiation of such agreements...." Id. at 553-566); Meth, *Matrimonial Arbitration*, 99 N.J.L.J. 409 (1976)(noting that the impossibility of providing for every future contingency made "*Schiff* seem like a voice from a very ivory tower." *Id.*).

at 569, 264 A.2d 49; *Schlemm*, 31 N.J. at 581, 158 A.2d 508; *Parmly*, 125 N.J.Eq. at 548, 5 A.2d 789. We therefore find no reason to distinguish between judicial decrees and consensual agreements when "changed circumstances" call for the modification of either.

II. Changed Circumstances

The parties here disagree over what constitutes "changed circumstances" sufficient to justify modification of alimony and child support. Plaintiff claims that her detailed demonstration of the increased needs resulting from maturation of the children and severe inflation justifies discovery of defendant's tax returns. Such increased needs and her husband's substantiated ability to pay would, according to plaintiff, constitute "changed circumstances" warranting upward modification of alimony and child support. Defendant responds that an increase in the cost of living and the "normal wear and tear" alleged here does not even entitle plaintiff to discovery of his present earnings. He argues that the increase in need alleged, even if coupled with proof of his increased ability to pay, would not constitute "changed circumstances." According to defendant, plaintiff's position and the Appellate Division disposition are contrary to prior caselaw and will result in an avalanche of unwarranted petitions for modification.

The frequency with which courts are called upon to make or modify support awards needs no documentation. The lack of uniformity in their approaches and predictability in their decisions is similarly widely recognized. See generally Note, "Modification of Spousal Support: A Survey of a Confusing Area of the Law," 17 *J.Fam.Law* 711 (1979). In part, the inability to predict dispositions is responsible for the volume of modification motions. The solution to the problem of predictability would be a just accommodation of the power of the courts to adjust support obligations with the desirable features of stable arrangements and spousal cooperation. We conclude such an accommodation is possible through an approach linking the notion of "changed circumstances" to the initial support determination, be it judicial or consensual. This case presents an appropriate opportunity for us to clarify the proper set of coordinated standards.

A. The Elements of "Changed Circumstances"

The supporting spouse's obligation is mainly determined by the quality of economic life during the marriage, not bare survival. The needs of the dependent spouse and children "contemplate their continued maintenance at the standard of living they had become accustomed to prior to the separation." *Khalaf v. Khalaf*, 58 N.J. 63, 69, 275 A.2d 132, 135 (1971); see *Bonanno v. Bonanno*, 4 N.J. 268, 274, 72 A.2d 318 (1950).[3]

> The amount is not fixed *solely* with regard, on the one hand, to the actual needs of the wife, nor, on the other, to the husband's actual means. There should be taken into account the physical condition and social position of the parties, the husband's property and income (including what he could derive from personal attention to business), and also the separate property and income of the wife. Considering all these and any other factors bearing upon the question, the sum is to be fixed at what the wife would have the right to expect as support if living with her husband.

3. These cases actually phrased this entitlement in terms of what a husband owes a wife. As we will discuss below, this is no longer a sound statement of contemporary domestic relations law. See *infra* at 53, 54.

[*Bonanno*, 4 N.J. at 274, 72 A.2d at 320-21 (quoting *Dietrick v. Dietrick*, 88 N.J.Eq. 560, 561-562, 103 A. 242 (E & A 1917))]

In accordance with this general principle, courts have recognized "changed circumstances" that warrant modification in a variety of settings. Some of them include

(1) an increase in the cost of living,...

(2) increase or decrease in the supporting spouse's income,...

(3) illness, disability or infirmity arising after the original judgment,...

(4) the dependent spouse's loss of a house or apartment,...

(5) the dependent spouse's cohabitation with another,[4]...

(6) subsequent employment by the dependent spouse,...

(7) changes in federal income tax law....

Courts have consistently rejected requests for modification based on circumstances which are only temporary or which are expected but have not yet occurred....

When children are involved, an increase in their needs whether occasioned by maturation, the rising cost of living or more unusual events has been held to justify an increase in support by a financially able parent.... Their emancipation and employment may warrant reduction in their support....

This review of New Jersey decisions reveals the factors that a court of equity must assess when determining whether the former marital standard of living is being maintained. When support of an economically dependent spouse is at issue, the general considerations are the dependent spouse's needs, that spouse's ability to contribute to the fulfillment of those needs, and the supporting spouse's ability to maintain the dependent spouse at the former standard. The decision to modify child support requires a similar examination of the child's needs and the relative abilities of the spouses to supply them.

Our analysis makes clear that "changed circumstances" are not limited in scope to events that were unforeseeable at the time of divorce. This is particularly obvious in cases involving modification of child support orders, where maturation is cited as justifying an increase in support by a financially able parent. See, *e.g.*, *Shaw v. Shaw*, [138 N.J. Super. 436, 351 A.2d 374]. The supporting spouse has a continuing obligation to contribute to the maintenance of the dependent spouse at the standard of living formerly shared. So long as this duty continues, objective notions of foreseeability what the parties or the court could or should have foreseen are all but irrelevant. The proper criteria are whether the change in circumstance is continuing and whether the agreement or decree has made explicit provision for the change. An increase in support becomes necessary whenever changed circumstances substantially impair the dependent spouse's ability to maintain the standard of living reflected in the original decree or agreement. Conversely, a decrease is called for when circumstances render all or a portion of support received unnecessary for maintaining that standard. After finding that the dependent spouse cannot maintain the original standard of living, the court must consider the extent to which the supporting spouse's ability to pay permits modification.

4. If the dependent spouse remarries, the court must modify any order or judgment to eliminate the alimony obligation on application by the supporting spouse, N.J.S.A. 2A:34-25; see *Sharpe v. Sharpe*, 109 N.J.Super. 410, 263 A.2d 490 (Ch.Div.1970).

If the existing support arrangement has in fact provided for the circumstances alleged as "changed," it would not ordinarily be "equitable and fair," *Smith*, 72 N.J. at 360, 371 A.2d 1, to grant modification. For example, although a spouse cannot maintain the marital standard of living on the support payments received, this would not ordinarily warrant modification if it were shown that a single large cash payment made at the time of divorce was included with the express intention of meeting the rising cost of living.[6] In other cases, the equitable distribution award — which we have recognized is intimately related to support, *id.* — might have been devised to provide a hedge against inflation. The same might be true with respect to child support. A lump sum payment or a trust established for the benefit of the children could be shown to have been designed to cover the certain eventuality of increasing needs.

B. Judicial Provision for Changed Circumstances

As a practical matter, spousal agreements have great potential for ensuring the desired degree of stability in support arrangements.... Such agreements have traditionally been more comprehensive and particularized than court orders, and thus more carefully tailored to the peculiar circumstances of the parties' lives.[7] In view of the current economic conditions and the changing social structure of the family particularly with regard to women's roles, *cf. Orr v. Orr*, 440 U.S. 268, 99 S.Ct. 1102, 59 L.Ed.2d 306 (1979), courts, too, should make greater efforts to provide in advance for change. This would enhance the stability of judicially fashioned arrangements and make unnecessary a return to court. The power to distribute property equitably should be exercised to relieve the strain of total reliance on support payments for financial security. See *Rothman v. Rothman*, 65 N.J. 219, 229, 320 A.2d 496 (1974); see also *Smith*, 72 N.J. at 360, 371 A.2d 1; *Painter v. Painter*, 65 N.J. 196, 218, 320 A.2d 484 (1974). Courts have refused to consider an alimony award in isolation; the earnings received from investments funded by an equitable distribution award have been considered when determining the adequacy of the dependent spouse's income. *Esposito v. Esposito*, 158 N.J.Super. 285, 300, 385 A.2d 1266 (App.Div.1978). "As a result of the equitable distribution plaintiff will have available a substantial capital fund to invest in order to produce additional income." *Lavene v. Lavene*, 162 N.J.Super. at 203, 392 A.2d at 629.

A closer look should also be taken at the supported spouse's ability to contribute to his or her own maintenance, both at the time of the original judgment and on applications for modification.[8] The fact that our State's alimony and support statute is phrased without reference to gender, N.J.S.A. 2A:34-23, will accomplish little if judicial decision making continues to employ sexist stereotypes. The

6. Of course under the standard for modification stated in *Smith*, should such a provision later prove inadequate, the court is free to require greater support if it is warranted in the light of prevailing circumstances. See 72 N.J. at 360, 371 A.2d 1.

7. For examples of separation and property settlement agreements, see G. Skoloff, FAMILY LAW PRACTICE 330-349 (1976 ed.); 11 D. Herr, NEW JERSEY PRACTICE MARRIAGE, DIVORCE AND SEPARATION §789 (3d ed. 1963) and §793.7 (Supp.1978). See also *Berkowitz*, 55 N.J. at 569-570, 264 A.2d 49. In that case the parties provided that on the wife's remarriage the husband would convey his interest in the residence to the wife in return for cancellation of his obligations regarding it. They also made financial arrangements for the children's attendance at college away from home and a consequent reduction in child support. The court therefore denied the husband's motion for reduction of child support on grounds of the wife's remarriage: "[A]ll of the alleged 'changed circumstances' were envisioned by the parties and *dealt with* specifically in the Agreement." *Id.* at 570, 264 A.2d at 52 (Emphasis supplied).

8. At times courts have found it necessary to assess the supporting spouse's ability to pay without regard to current earnings to determine fair and equitable support. See, *e.g.*, *Hess v. Hess*, 134 N.J.Eq. 360, 35 A.2d 677 (E & A 1944). The same should be done when the supported spouse's earning potential is an issue.

extent of actual economic dependency, not one's status as a wife, must determine the duration of support as well as its amount....[9]

Not only the realities of the marketplace, but also the constitutional guarantee of "the equal protection of the laws," U.S.Const., Amend. XIV, compels this approach. It is no longer permissible to ground the law of domestic relations in the "'old notio[n]' that 'generally it is the man's primary responsibility to provide a home and its essentials.'" *Orr v. Orr*, 440 U.S. at 279-280, 99 S.Ct. at 1112, 59 L.Ed.2d at 319 (quoting *Stanton v. Stanton*, 421 U.S. 7, 10, 95 S.Ct. 1373, 1375, 43 L.Ed.2d 688, 692 (1975)). "No longer is the female destined solely for the home and the rearing of the family, and only the male for the marketplace and the world of ideas." *Orr*, 440 U.S. at 280, 99 S.Ct. at 1112, 59 L.Ed.2d at 319 (quoting *Stanton*, 421 U.S. at 14-15, 95 S.Ct. at 1377-1378); see *Taylor v. Louisiana*, 419 U.S. 522, 535 n.17, 95 S.Ct. 692, 700 n.17, 42 L.Ed.2d 690 (1975); *Craig v. Boren*, 429 U.S. 190, 198, 97 S.Ct. 451, 457, 50 L.Ed.2d 397 (1976). The law must be concerned with the economic realities of contemporary married life, not a model of domestic relations that provided women with security in exchange for economic dependence and discrimination. This does not mean that relative economic dependence when proven is irrelevant to the determination of support obligations. But a court of equity cannot rely on antiquated presumptions; gender is no longer a permissible proxy for economic need. See *Orr*, 440 U.S. at 281, 99 S.Ct. at 1112, 59 L.Ed.2d at 320. The need for support must be assessed with a view towards the earning capacity of the individual woman in the marketplace.

Careful consideration of all these factors at the time of divorce and at the time modification is sought will eventually reduce the necessity for otherwise well-founded postjudgment applications. It may also lessen the need for plenary hearings on modification motions. We are confident that any increased expenditure of judicial time necessitated by this expanded inquiry will be more than offset by savings from a reduced need for modification hearings.

III. Procedural Guidelines

The parties here disagree on the proper procedure for courts to follow on modification motions. In particular they dispute both the necessity and the elements of a *prima facie* showing of changed circumstances prior to discovery of the respondent's financial status. We therefore think it appropriate to explain procedures to be followed in the postjudgment setting.

The party seeking modification has the burden of showing such "changed circumstances" as would warrant relief from the support or maintenance provisions involved. *Martindell*, 21 N.J. at 353, 122 A.2d 352. A *prima facie* showing of changed circumstances must be made before a court will order discovery of an ex-spouse's financial status. When the movant is seeking modification of an alimony award, that party must demonstrate that changed circumstances have substantially impaired the ability to support himself or herself. This requires full disclosure of

9. In *Arnold v. Arnold*, 167 N.J.Super. 478, 401 A.2d 261 (App.Div.1979), the Appellate Division concluded that in the absence of unusual facts, automatic cutoff dates for alimony should be avoided. While we disapprove of the general approach in *Arnold*, the trial court in that case made no investigation of the nature of the wife's employment potential, and for this reason the 30-month limitation was justifiably seen as arbitrary. Careful and explicit factfinding on the earning ability of the dependent spouse is of paramount importance in such cases.

We do not share the view that only unusual cases will warrant the "rehabilitative alimony" approach. We note that other states permit such awards. See, e.g., Fla.Stat.Ann. §61.08 (West Supp.1979); Haw.Rev.Stat.Ann. §580-47 (Supp.1979). See also Cal.Civ.Code §4806 (Supp.1980)(court may withhold support allowance to a party who is "earning his or her own livelihood"); Ind.Code Ann. §31-1-11.5-9 (Burns 1979)(prohibiting maintenance of party unless he or she is physically or mentally incapable of supporting himself or herself).

the dependent spouse's financial status, including tax returns. When the movant is seeking modification of child support, the guiding principle is the "best interests of the children." See *Hallberg v. Hallberg*, 113 N.J.Super. 205, 209, 273 A.2d 389 (App.Div.1971); *Clayton v. Muth*, 144 N.J.Super. at 493, 366 A.2d 354. A *prima facie* showing would then require a demonstration that the child's needs have increased to an extent for which the original arrangement does not provide.

Only after the movant has made this *prima facie* showing should the respondent's ability to pay become a factor for the court to consider. Therefore, once a *prima facie* case is established, tax returns or other financial information should be ordered. We recognize that individuals have a legitimate interest in the confidentiality of their income tax returns. However, without access to such reliable indicia of the supporting spouse's financial ability, the movant may be unable to prove that modification is warranted. Similarly, without knowledge of the financial status of both parties, the court will be unable to make an informed determination as to "what, in light of all the [circumstances] is equitable and fair." *Smith*, 72 N.J. at 360, 371 A.2d at 6. Courts have recognized that discovery and inspection of income tax returns should only be permitted for good cause.... Because financial ability of the supporting spouse may be crucial to the proper disposition of a motion for modification, we conclude that a *prima facie* showing of changed circumstances meets this good cause standard. We also recognize, however, that the financial information of other individuals may be necessarily involved, as where the supporting spouse has remarried and filed joint returns with the new spouse. In such circumstances the court should follow the procedure outlined by the court in *DeGraaff* [163 N.J.Super. 578, 395 A.2d 525 (App.Div. 1978)]: the trial judge should examine the tax return *in camera* and excise irrelevant matters before giving the return to the plaintiff. 163 N.J.Super. at 583, 395 A.2d 525.

Once the above steps have been completed, the court must decide whether to hold a hearing. Although equity demands that spouses be afforded an opportunity to seek modification, the opportunity need not include a hearing when the material facts are not in genuine dispute. We therefore hold that a party must clearly demonstrate the existence of a genuine issue as to a material fact before a hearing is necessary.... Without such a standard, courts would be obligated to hold hearings on every modification application. The application of the equitable principles we have outlined does not require elaborate procedures in every case. Courts should be free to exercise their discretion to prevent unnecessary duplication of proofs and arguments. The volume of postjudgment litigation provides additional, practical support for this approach.

In determining whether a material fact is in dispute, a court should rely on the supporting documents and affidavits of the parties. Conclusory allegations would, of course, be disregarded. Only statements to which a party could testify should be considered. Thus, if the sole dispute centered around the supporting spouse's earnings, the disclosure of income tax returns might render a hearing unnecessary.

IV. The Present Motion for Modification

Applying the foregoing standards and guidelines to the facts of this case, we conclude that the Appellate Division was correct in reversing the trial court's denial of plaintiff's motion and directing production of defendant's tax returns. Plaintiff has alleged with specificity the increases in her own and her children's needs caused by substantial inflation and the rising cost of supporting growing children. These changes in circumstances will apparently continue. They clearly warrant court inquiry into whether plaintiff's ability to maintain herself and her children has been substantially impaired.

By reason of plaintiff's *prima facie* showing, defendant should be required to disclose the requested evidence of his income, subject to the protections outlined above. See *supra* at 55. On remand, the trial court must then determine, among other things, whether the earlier agreement, as incorporated in the divorce judgment, provided for the present circumstances. Since the record clearly discloses genuine disputes as to material facts other than defendant's earnings, a hearing will be necessary.

As defendant points out, the agreement provided that the increased income of either spouse "shall not be a consideration to change or modify the support and maintenance payments for the Wife or the Wife and children." This might appear to be a valid accommodation of contingencies which otherwise would support modification based on "changed circumstances" the wife's post-divorce employment or an increase in the husband's earnings. But as we have stated, the court is not bound by such provisions. It should scrutinize carefully the dependent spouse's ability to contribute to her own and her children's maintenance. The court must determine whether there has been substantial impairment of their ability to maintain the standard of living to which they are entitled.

Plaintiff, who was a teacher before her marriage, holds a Master's degree in Speech Communication and is continuing her education towards earning a Ph.D. She contends, however, that she has been unable to find substantial employment to bridge the gap between needs and expenses, and that employment in positions for which she is substantially overqualified would diminish her self image or esteem. Defendant asserts that plaintiff has unreasonably restricted her choice of employment fields. He points out that plaintiff's background and age and the children's maturity and attendance in school make her failure to find full-time employment while continuing her education unreasonable. These disputes must be addressed by the trial court on remand.

Defendant alleges that a $22,000 lump sum payment to plaintiff incorporated in their agreement should be recognized as the agreed means for covering the increased needs which plaintiff alleges especially with respect to repairs to her present home. Whether this amount should be so considered is a question of fact for the court. While the supported spouse need not completely deplete savings to qualify for increased support, see *Capodanno v. Capodanno*, 58 N.J. 113, 118, 275 A.2d 441 (1971); *Khalaf*, 58 N.J. at 70, 275 A.2d 132; *Martindell*, 21 N.J. at 354, 122 A.2d 352, neither can that spouse be permitted unilaterally to designate her funds, as plaintiff attempts to do here, for the children's college education. This is so particularly in light of defendant's obligation under the agreement to pay for the expense of higher education. Any contention that the defendant will not perform this duty must be rejected as premature. When and if such college expenses arise and defendant fails to fulfill his obligation, a court is free to order defendant to make the required payments.[12]

. . .

[Discussion of child support and counsel fees has been omitted.]

For the foregoing reasons, the judgment of the Appellate Division is affirmed. The matter is remanded for further proceedings in accordance with this opinion.

12. If circumstances have changed in such a way that requiring defendant to pay for college would no longer be equitable and fair, the court also remains free to alter the prior arrangement. See *Rufner v. Rufner*, 131 N.J.Eq. at 196, 24 A.2d 180; see also *Khalaf*, 58 N.J. at 71-72, 275 A.2d 132.

GOTTSEGEN v. GOTTSEGEN
Supreme Judicial Court of Massachusetts
397 Mass. 617, 492 N.E.2d 1133 (1986)

ABRAMS, Justice.

We hold that in a judgment for divorce, a judge of the Probate Court may not order the termination of alimony on the occurrence of an event unrelated to the recipient spouse's need for alimony or the supporting spouse's ability to pay.

On December 11, 1980, the plaintiff, Sandra L. Gottsegen, filed a complaint for divorce in the Probate and Family Court on the ground of irretrievable breakdown of her marriage to the defendant, Robert S. Gottsegen. G.L. c. 208, §1A. A judge of the Probate Court entered a judgment of divorce *nisi* on August 3, 1981. On October 12, 1983, the plaintiff filed a complaint for civil contempt against the defendant for violation of the August 3, 1981, order. The judge dismissed the complaint, but awarded counsel fees to the plaintiff. Both parties appealed. The plaintiff then retained new counsel and, on April 24, 1984, moved for relief from the judgment of divorce under Mass.R.Dom.Rel.P. 60(b)(1975), and concurrently moved for leave to take discovery, for an evidentiary hearing, and for reference to a master. The judge allowed the defendant's motion to strike the various motions, and denied the plaintiff's subsequent motion for reconsideration. The plaintiff appealed the allowance of the motion to strike. The appeals were consolidated. We transferred the case here on our own motion. We now affirm the rulings on the motion for relief under rule 60(b) and on counsel fees. We vacate and remand the ruling on contempt.

Before the plaintiff filed for divorce, she and the defendant executed a separation agreement. Under art. V.3 of the separation agreement, the parties agreed to request the Probate Court to incorporate the terms of the agreement into a final judgment of divorce. They further agreed that if the court did so, the provisions of art. III of the agreement ("Financial Arrangements Relating to Wife") would be merged in the judgment, but that the remaining provisions would survive as an independent contract. In the judgment of divorce *nisi*, the court ordered that the agreement be made a part of the judgment. The clauses here in controversy derive from art. III of the agreement which, by the terms of the agreement, merged into the judgment and did not survive. They therefore have no legal significance independent of the divorce judgment. See *Knox v. Remick*, 371 Mass. 433, 435, 358 N.E.2d 432 (1976). *Cf. Bell v. Bell*, 16 Mass.App.Ct. 188, 190, 459 N.E.2d 109 (1983)(agreement survives judgment and has independent significance), rev'd on other grounds, 393 Mass. 20, 468 N.E.2d 859 (1984).

Paragraph A.1 of art. III of the judgment requires the defendant to pay the plaintiff $812.50 per month for her support and maintenance. Paragraph A.5 of art. III provides that, "[i]n the event of the wife's remarriage (as hereinafter defined) at any time prior to the fifth (5th) anniversary of the date of execution hereof, the husband's support obligation...shall thereupon terminate and be substituted by an obligation to pay to the wife, or for her benefit, for her support and maintenance" $30,000, at the rate of $833.33 per month for three years. Paragraph A.9 provides, "The remarriage of the wife shall, for purposes of this Agreement, be deemed to include her cohabitation with the same unrelated man with whom the wife has a romantic relationship for more than two (2) consecutive months."

1. *The civil contempt complaint.* In early 1983, the defendant began to suspect that the plaintiff was cohabiting with one L.W. After confirming his suspicions

through personal observation and the report of a private investigator, the defendant concluded that the plaintiff had been cohabiting with L.W. for more than two consecutive months. On July 15, 1983, he commenced making monthly payments of $833.33, pursuant to the remarriage and cohabitation clauses of the agreement.

The plaintiff responded to the changed alimony payments by filing a complaint for civil contempt. The defendant denied that he was in contempt of the divorce judgment. He counterclaimed to request a judgment declaring that the plaintiff had remarried pursuant to paragraph A.9 of art. III of the agreement and determining the date of the remarriage and his further alimony obligations. The parties stipulated that the plaintiff had a romantic relationship with L.W. The judge found that, during the seven-week period from April 17 through June 5, 1983, the plaintiff and L.W. spent the night together on an average of at least 5.5 nights per week, including one period of seventeen consecutive nights. The judge made detailed findings about the plaintiff's and L.W.'s living, social, and financial arrangements, including the following: "40. [L.W.] and Mrs. Gottsegen have never represented to be man and wife, even on over night trips. 41. Mrs. Gottsegen receives no financial support from Mr. [L.W.] except [that] he pays for about 85% of the cost of eating out. Mrs. Gottsegen provided no financial support to [L.W.]. 42. Mrs. Gottsegen and [L.W.] have no joint assets of any kind. 43. Mrs. Gottsegen and [L.W.] maintain separate residences. 44. There is a continuing need for alimony for Mrs. Gottsegen." The judge concluded that the plaintiff and L.W. were cohabiting for more than two consecutive months within the terms of the cohabitation clause,[3] and that the remarriage provisions should take effect as of June 1, 1983. He concluded by finding the defendant not in contempt.

We begin our analysis by considering briefly the history of judicial jurisdiction over alimony. In England, questions of divorce and alimony were not within the jurisdiction of the common law courts, but instead were decided by the ecclesiastical courts, applying canon law. 1 LEGAL PAPERS OF JOHN ADAMS 281 (L. Wroth & H. Zobel 1965).[4] Because there was no alimony jurisdiction at common law, this court early held that the power to grant alimony was wholly statutory. *Davol v. Davol*, 13 Mass. 264, 264-265 (1816). See *Orlandella v. Orlandella*, 370 Mass. 225, 227, 347 N.E.2d 665 (1976); *Parker v. Parker*, 211 Mass. 139, 141, 97 N.E. 988 (1912). In 1692, the provincial Legislature vested jurisdiction over all questions of marriage and divorce in the Governor and Council. Province Laws 1692-1693, c. 25, §4. In 1695, the justices of the Superior Court of Judicature were empowered to assign to a wife whose marriage had been nullified by reason of consanguinity "such reasonable part of the estate of her late [i.e., former] husband as in their discretion the circumstances of the estate may admit." Province Laws 1695-1696, c. 2, §3.[5] By St.1785, c. 69, §7, the Legislature enacted comprehensive legislation

3. We need not decide whether "cohabitation," as used in this divorce judgment, encompasses an arrangement in which the parties are together on an almost daily basis and frequently eat meals together, even though they maintain separate residences and neither mingle financial assets nor support each other financially.

4. The ecclesiastical courts granted two types of divorce decree: absolute divorce *(a vinculo matrimonii*, "from the bonds of matrimony") when the marriage was a nullity because of defects such as consanguinity or impotence; and divorce from bed and board (*a mensa et thoro*) when the grounds were adultery, cruelty, and the like. 1 LEGAL PAPERS OF JOHN ADAMS, *supra* at 281, 282. In the latter case, the marriage itself was considered valid and unbreakable. The legal effect was that of a decree for separation and maintenance, and the husband was required to pay alimony under the theory that "since the marriage still existed, he was merely continuing to perform the duty of support which he would have had in normal course." *Id.* at 282, 283.

5. The act also provided for criminal penalties in the case of incestuous marriage: "such man and woman so convicted shall be set upon the gallows by the space of an hour, with a rope about their neck and the other end cast over the gallows, and in the way from thence to the common [gaol] shall be severely whipped, not

regulating marriage and divorce, and directed that all questions of divorce and alimony be heard by the Supreme Judicial Court. The act set out several grounds for divorce — more limited than are available today — and provided for property settlement and alimony that varied according to the grounds for divorce.[6] The property settlement and alimony scheme reflected the necessity of providing support for women who, by social convention and traditional property law, were usually dependent on their husbands.

In *Holbrook v. Comstock*, 16 Gray 109, 110 (1860), this court defined alimony as "that portion of the husband's estate which is allowed [the wife] for her present subsistence and livelihood."[7] In subsequent years, as the Legislature gradually expanded the conditions in which alimony could be granted, see *Parker v. Parker*, 211 Mass. 139, 141-143, 97 N.E. 988 (1912), the support purposes behind alimony remained constant. Thus, in *Topor v. Topor*, 287 Mass. 473, 192 N.E. 52 (1934), we stated, "The word 'alimony' as used in our statutes carries the meaning of money or property which under order of court a husband provides for the support and maintenance of his wife and such minor children as are committed to her custody.... From the nature of the word 'alimony' support or maintenance of the recipient is an essential element."... *Id.* at 475, 192 N.E. 52.

Throughout this period, the amount of alimony to be granted lay in the "just and reasonable" discretion of the court. While mere subsistence may have been the minimum to which the wife was entitled, the court could grant greater sums depending on the property and capacity of the husband. *Graves v. Graves*, 108 Mass. 314, 321 (1871). By 1916, it was clear that support and maintenance comprehended "the condition in life of the parties and their mode of living," *Brown v. Brown*, 222 Mass. 415, 417, 111 N.E. 42 (1916), which, the court later explained, meant "maintain[ing] her and the family according to the property and condition in life of her husband." *Coe v. Coe*, 313 Mass. 232, 236, 46 N.E.2d 1017 (1943), quoting *Jordan Marsh Co. v. Cohen*, 242 Mass. 245, 249, 136 N.E. 350 (1922).

In 1974, the Legislature substantially revised the statutory treatment of alimony. G.L. c. 208, §34, as appearing in St.1974, c. 565. See generally *Bianco v. Bianco*, 371 Mass. 420, 358 N.E.2d 243 (1976). The amendment made alimony available to either party, depending on the needs and circumstances of the case. The statute now requires the court, in determining the amount of alimony, to consider "the length of the marriage, the conduct of the parties during the marriage, the age, health, station, occupation, amount and sources of income, vocational skills, employability, estate, liabilities and needs of each of the parties and the

---

5. *Continued*

exceeding forty stripes each; also every person so offending shall forever after wear a capital I of two inches long and proportionable bigness, cut out in cloth of a contrary colour to their cloaths, and sewed upon their upper garments on the outside of their arm or on their back in open view." Province Laws 1695-1696, c. 2, §2. Thus did the provincial authorities ensure punishment for incestuous marriage consistent with punishment for adultery. See Province Laws 1694-1695, c. 5, §2; N. Hawthorne, THE SCARLET LETTER (1850).

6. For example, in cases of absolute divorce, the statute required that the wife be restored to all her lands, tenements and hereditaments, and all or part of her personal estate held by the husband, but made no provision for alimony. See *Davol v. Davol, supra.*

7. Compare the ecclesiastical definition of alimony: "that proportion of the Husband's Estate, which the Wife sues in the Ecclesiastical Court, to have allowed her for her present subsistence and livelyhood, according to Law, upon any such separation from her Husband, as is not caused by her own *elopement or Adultery*" (emphasis in original). 1 LEGAL PAPERS OF JOHN ADAMS, *supra* at 284 n. 19, quoting J. Godolphin, REPERTORIUM CANONICUM 508 (3d ed. 1687). See also *Cole v. Cole*, 142 Ill. 19, 25-27, 31 N.E. 109 (1892). Ecclesiastical principles formerly were an important source of law for interpreting and applying the alimony statutes in this Commonwealth. See, *e.g.*, *Graves v. Graves*, 108 Mass. 314, 321 (1871); *Davol v. Davol*, 13 Mass. 264, 265 (1816); 1 LEGAL PAPERS OF JOHN ADAMS, *supra* at 283.

opportunity of each for future acquisition of capital assets and income." G.L. c. 208, §34 (1984 ed.). The statute affords the judge considerable discretion, but also defines the scope of that discretion by requiring the judge to consider all the factors set forth by the statute. *Bianco v. Bianco, supra* at 423, 358 N.E.2d 243.

Despite these changes, §34 does *not* alter the fundamental purpose of alimony: to provide economic support to the dependent spouse. As the Appeals Court recently noted, "[t]he focus of any financial award must include 'the crucial issue in an alimony dispute, namely, the [spouse's] need for support and maintenance in relationship to the respective financial circumstances of the parties.'" *Grubert v. Grubert*, 20 Mass.App.Ct. 811, 819, 483 N.E.2d 100 (1985), quoting *Partridge v. Partridge*, 14 Mass.App.Ct. 918, 919, 436 N.E.2d 447 (1982). Thus, the statutory authority of a court to award alimony continues to be grounded in the recipient spouse's need for support and the supporting spouse's ability to pay. A court may not limit alimony for reasons unrelated to its statutory base. See *Levine v. Levine*, 394 Mass. 749, 752 n. 4, 477 N.E.2d 402 (1985). *Accord, Mitchell v. Mitchell*, 418 A.2d 1140, 1143 (Me.1980); *Marriage of Grove*, 280 Or. 341, 354, 571 P.2d 477 (1977); *Overson v. Overson*, 125 Wis.2d 13, 17-18, 370 N.W.2d 796 (Ct.App.1985). Any event that triggers a change in alimony must bear some relation to the financial circumstances of the parties.

We turn now to the precise issue here presented: whether the judge properly ordered in the original judgment that alimony be terminated on the wife's "cohabitation with the same unrelated man with whom the wife has a romantic relationship for more than two (2) consecutive months." A divorced spouse has no right to exercise control over a former spouse's life, and a court may not attempt to create such a right through the alimony provisions of a divorce judgment.[8]... Thus, the Probate Court may not in the original divorce judgment order alimony to be terminated on mere cohabitation.[9]

Nevertheless, the court may later modify the original judgment if the petitioner demonstrates a material change of circumstances. *Schuler v. Schuler*, 382 Mass. 366, 368, 416 N.E.2d 197 (1981), and cases cited. The court "may make any judgment relative [to the modification of the original judgment] which it might have made in the original action." G.L. c. 208, §37 (1984 ed.). Thus, if the supporting spouse shows

8. The judge's lack of discretion to order alimony terminated on mere cohabitation does not prevent a divorcing couple from including such a provision in a separation agreement that survives the entry of the divorce judgment. In *Bell v. Bell*, 393 Mass. 20, 468 N.E.2d 859 (1984), cert. denied, — - U.S. — —, 105 S.Ct. 1392, 84 L.Ed.2d 782 (1985), this court affirmed the dismissal of a contempt complaint brought by the recipient spouse, on the ground that, under the terms of an independent, surviving separation agreement, *Bell v. Bell*, 16 Mass.App.Ct. 188, 190, 459 N.E.2d 109 (1983), she had "liv[ed] together with a member of the opposite sex, so as to give the outward appearance of marriage." *Bell v. Bell*, 393 Mass. at 21, 468 N.E.2d 859. The court thereby allowed the defendant husband to raise the surviving agreement as a bar to the contempt proceeding. See *Knox v. Remick*, 371 Mass. 433, 438, 358 N.E.2d 432 (1976).

As we discussed *supra*, the cohabitation provisions of the separation agreement in this case did not survive as an independent contract. There is no agreement to be enforced in a contract action, only a court order enforceable in an action for contempt. The original court order for which enforcement is sought must have been within the court's discretion when made. As our discussion of the history of alimony jurisdiction, *supra*, makes clear, the court's discretion in ordering alimony is limited to the economic — not the social — circumstances of the parties. The parties cannot by their own agreement confer discretion on a court to issue an order not otherwise within its statutory authority. Where, as here, the sole issue raised is one of authority under the statute, the intent of the parties is irrelevant.

9. If the parties submit such a clause to the court for incorporation in the judgment, as was done in this case, the court should inform the parties that such an order is beyond the scope of its discretion. The court may then allow the parties an opportunity to renegotiate a proposed order to present to the court, or may incorporate in the judgment some or all of the allowable portion of the agreement. Nothing in today's decision, however, disturbs our holding in *Moore v. Moore*, 389 Mass. 21, 23-24, 448 N.E.2d 1255 (1983), that the Probate Court may not order that a separation agreement shall not survive when the parties clearly intended that it should.

that, as a result of cohabitation, the recipient spouse's economic circumstances have materially changed, then the court may alter or eliminate alimony. However, a judge may not modify a judgment solely on the basis of a finding of cohabitation. Such an order is not within the court's discretion under G.L. c. 208, §34.[10] Most State courts that have considered the issue are in accord with our conclusion....

In this case, there are no grounds for modification of the original alimony award. The judge made detailed findings on the financial arrangements between the plaintiff and L.W. He found that neither the plaintiff nor L.W. supported the other, with the exception of L.W.'s payment of about 85% of the cost of dining out; that they have no joint assets of any kind; that they maintain separate residences; and that there is a continuing need for alimony by the plaintiff. These findings could not support a conclusion of material change of circumstances sufficient to justify modification of the original judgment.

We conclude that the judge's dismissal of the complaint for contempt on factors unrelated to the financial circumstances of the parties is error and that the judge's findings do not otherwise warrant a modification of the judgment. We therefore vacate the dismissal of the complaint for contempt and remand that portion of the case for proceedings consistent with this opinion.[11] To prevent any confusion, we order the judgment to be modified by striking paragraph A.9 of art. III, pursuant to our equitable power under G.L. c. 211, §3 (1984 ed.). See *Moore v. Moore*, 389 Mass. 21, 26, 448 N.E.2d 1255 (1983).

...

3. *Conclusion*.... The inclusion of the cohabitation clause in the original judgment is beyond the scope of the Probate Court's discretion and should be struck from the judgment. Because the provisions of art. III in the *Gottsegen* agreement did not survive, the judgment of dismissal of the plaintiff's complaint for contempt on factors unrelated to the financial circumstances of the parties is error. That judgment is therefore vacated and the case is remanded to the Probate Court for further proceedings consistent with this opinion.

So ordered.

HENNESSEY, C.J. (concurring).

I concur, but I wish to emphasize that this case does not overrule the princi-

---

10. Under §34, the court may consider the parties' conduct during the marriage as one factor in determining an alimony award, but may not base the award only on a spouse's blameworthy conduct. See *Rice v. Rice*, 372 Mass. 398, 401, 361 N.E.2d 1305 (1977). After a divorce is final, a court may not condition alimony on either party's subsequent conduct. See *Zildjian v. Zildjian*, 8 Mass.App.Ct. 1, 17, 391 N.E.2d 697 (1979). Nor may a judge penalize either spouse for companionship with another person after the divorce is final.

11. The plaintiff also argues that enforcement of the cohabitation clause violates her rights under the Federal Constitution and the Massachusetts Declaration of Rights. Because that argument was not raised below, we do not reach or decide any of the constitutional issues.

On cross-appeal, the defendant argues that the judge erred in determining the plaintiff's date of remarriage under the terms of the judgment. In light of our disposition of the plaintiff's appeal, we need not consider this aspect of the cross-appeal. The defendant also argues on cross-appeal that the probate judge erred in awarding $4,000.00 in fees to the plaintiff's trial counsel in the contempt proceeding. Under Mass.R.Dom.Rel.P. 46 (1975), the defendant was obliged to "make[ ] known to the court...his objection to the action of the court and his grounds therefor." Although the defendant filed a motion for reconsideration after the judge's decision, there is no indication on the record that the defendant objected to the plaintiff's motion for counsel fees at the time the award was made. Therefore, the issue was not preserved for appeal. *Cassamasse v. J.G. Lamotte & Son, Inc.*, 391 Mass. 315, 320, 461 N.E.2d 785 (1984). Even if it had been, there is no showing — particularly in light of our disposition of the contempt complaint — that the award is incommensurate with an objective evaluation of the services performed or that the judge otherwise abused his discretion. *Ross v. Ross*, 385 Mass. 30, 38-39, 430 N.E.2d 815 (1982). See *Grubert v. Grubert*, 20 Mass.App.Ct. 811, 819-820 & n. 15, 483 N.E.2d 100 (1985).

ples of *Bell v. Bell*, 393 Mass. 20, 468 N.E.2d 859 (1984). In *Bell*, we held that the parties were bound by the clear language of their separation agreement, which provided that alimony would cease if the wife cohabited with another man. *Id.* at 23, 468 N.E.2d 859. I have no doubt that, even in the absence of an agreement, the fact of such arrangement is an appropriate circumstance to be considered by the court in setting or modifying a support order. In this case, however, (1) under the terms of the agreement between the parties, the provision as to cohabitation did not survive the judgment of divorce, and (2) the judge found in substance that the wife's arrangement with another man did not affect her need for support. The judge thus relied on a condition which is irrelevant to the need for support under G.L. c. 208, §34. The principles of *Bell* are not affected.

[Justice NOLAN's dissenting opinion is omitted.]

COMMENTS

Lepis illustrates a conservative approach to the relation between divorce settlements and alimony decrees. According to this case, judicial discretion continues to prevail over the power of the parties to regulate their affairs by contract. In view of the fact that in any jurisdiction, regardless of its classification as conservative or liberal in divorce matters, the overwhelming majority of dissolutions are bargained for, the court's pronouncements in *Lepis* appear to be more ceremonial than real. On the other hand, court opinions still furnish the signposts for the bargaining that takes place between the parties or, between the lawyers representing them.

From this perspective it might be interesting to consider what effect an opinion like *Lepis* might have on the process of divorce bargaining in that jurisdiction. Obviously, a husband may be less inclined to make a large payment in settlement of his wife's future claims. Thus the result of *Lepis* does not necessarily favor the recipients of alimony and support, although the case seems to protect the rights of a divorced wife and of children. Yet leaving the matter entirely to the courts and to their relatively unpredictable discretion may not be in the best interest of either party. In the future, after a husband argues *Lepis* as a reason for not making a large payment "in settlement," the wife's lawyer may be willing to make concessions in order to avoid the negative consequences of *Lepis* for his client. Clearly, a married woman may prefer to receive a fixed sum of money or other property allocation at divorce rather than depend on judicial discretion in future requests for modification of alimony. The issue for the negotiations in lawyers' offices is, what concessions can still be validly made by a married woman in a post-*Lepis* situation?

Since the court in *Lepis* seems to foreclose any binding force of agreements provided they have merged into a divorce decree — at least to the extent that they appear to oust the court of jurisdiction or interfere with the power of the court to modify alimony and support obligations — lawyers for both husband and wife may be willing to try to prevent such merger, conceivably by not incorporating the divorce settlement in the decree. Of course, it could not then be enforced by contempt measures but only by ordinary contractual remedies. A further alternative is to avoid the language of alimony and support altogether in the settlement and refer only to mutual allocation of property rights. Since property rights "vest" upon execution of the settlement, it would be difficult for a court to modify what appears to be a certain and final situation proprietary in nature. Needless to say, the lawyer for the husband will attempt to use as much property language as possible, while the lawyer representing the wife will try to retain reference to "alimony and support." Sometimes this may bring about a compromise that deliberately confounds the language in the agreement, for instance, referring to "lump-sum property" or to real estate transfer as "alimony." In spite of the strong language in *Lepis*, it appears that the courts' power is limited.

Quite generally, the concept of alimony is waning and with it the protective discretionary powers of the courts. What we then have is a trend towards equitable distribution of proprietary rights leading to increased negotiations between lawyers. Since the development is in flux, it continues to be possible, for the time being, to argue *Lepis* considerations even in jurisdictions other than New Jersey if not in court, then in negotiations with opposing counsel.

Gottsegen illustrates the difficulty in labelling an approach "liberal" or "conservative." Like *Lepis*, *Gottsegen* appears to reduce the contractual freedom of the parties, and in this sense is conservative. Yet in its refusal to penalize the ex-wife's sexual relations, it is liberal. The effect is quite limited, however, insofar as the court indicates that as long as a separation agreement is not merged into the decree, it is enforceable, including the penalties for cohabitation. Thus, after *Gottsegen*, lawyers may simply draft agreements so that non-cohabitation clauses are not merged into the decree. This result may make women like Mrs. Gottsegen worse off because their ex-husbands can use contractual remedies to enforce the non-cohabitation clause as a contract and the payee will not have the benefit of enforcement mechanisms beyond contract remedies, which have been notoriously inadequate in the domestic field.

Non-cohabitation clauses tend to be quite unfair and to serve few if any legitimate purposes. Usually they extend the ex-husband's control over his wife beyond the marriage and may deprive an ex-spouse of needed financial support. One can trace their origin to traditional rules that provided alimony obligations cease upon the wife's remarriage. (The husband's remarriage would not increase his obligation and might decrease it.) It was assumed that the new husband would support the woman, and it seemed fair for the ex-husband to be relieved of his obligation. Moreover, remarrying was an assertion of independence inconsistent with the image of a dependent ex-wife deserving of alimony. If the new husband was in fact unable to support her, she was seen simply as having made a foolish choice — and she should live with it. To be an ex-wife was itself a status which was compromised by remarriage.

As non-marital cohabitation lost some of its stigma, ex-husbands were concerned that their ex-wife would choose to cohabit instead of marrying so as to keep alimony coming in. Almost all non-cohabitation clauses are imposed against women, and they are agreed to during a time of stress, often a time when the woman may fully expect to have nothing further to do with any man. Perhaps such non-cohabitation clauses should be void as against public policy or presumptively unenforceable because inherently oppressive.

Many people in the midst of a divorce grossly underestimate the likelihood that they will want to seek or be able to find a new partner. Thus, women may agree to non-cohabitation clauses without any adequate compensation in the bargaining process and without thinking to seek a similar non-cohabitation agreement from the husband.

Some state legislatures and courts have extended the rule that alimony ceases upon remarriage to include that alimony ceases also upon cohabitation. The modern trend, however, is to consider the reality of the situation. Cohabitation may be the basis for modification of spousal support, but only if the cohabitation changes the needs of the payee. Some would argue that the same rule should be applied also to remarriage. For example, if an ex-wife who received support from her ex-husband chose to marry a man who was receiving support from his ex-wife, both support awards should continue and at most be modified slightly to reflect the lower living expenses of the new couple. Others, however, feel marriage should cut off all periodic support payments, whether or not the remarriage changes actual need.

Chapter 5

Children — Raising the Next Generation

THE LEGAL POSITION of children has been controversial through the ages and continues to be so today. As we shall see, the decisional law reflects a number of conflicting theories, each rooted in historical antecedents.

At one time, the legal status of children was not greatly different from the status of slaves or of wives. Slaves were emancipated (but continued to be exploited in other manners), and the status of wives slowly changed to what could now be considered close to the status of a partner with her husband. The status of children has not gone through any sudden change, but it is in a state of flux. All of us have been children in the past, and many have strong views about the proper status of children.

With the decrease of farms and other family-run businesses and the advent of compulsory schooling and laws against child labor, children lost the economic value they once had. The non-economic value placed on children seems if anything to be rising. At one time, it was relatively easy to adopt a young baby in good health and of about whatever shade of skin and hair the adoptive parents wished. Now, although there continue to be many children unsuccessfully seeking adoptive homes and many unwanted children, there is also a great deal of talk of a "baby shortage." The general understanding is that at least young children are in great demand and that there is an excess of parents wishing to adopt and raise children. Some infertile couples spend thousands of dollars trying to achieve a pregnancy.

Complicating factors in regard to children are introduced by the evolution of marriage toward contract and partnership. If marriage is viewed as contractual in nature, it is obvious that children do not participate as parties to the agreement; they are born into it. Thus, at least under traditional views, they appear to be excluded from any remedy as not being in privity of contract. In considering this theory of the position of children, it is important to note that the concept of privity has been slowly eroded in many areas of law, for example, in the protection of the consumer. Of course, the parallels between consumer protection and "best interests of the child" are hardly explicitly acknowledged by the courts.

If the courts increasingly treat marriage as a partnership — that is, as a co-ownership for profit between parties presumed to be equal who deal with each other at arm's length — then children acquire new and sometimes contradictory characteristics. They are "assets" of the marriage to be fought over in case of dissolution; they are also, in a sense, a "product" of marriage; and, if it comes to their protection as persons, they are "consumers" of marriage regardless of lack of privity of contract. They are rarely seen as co-partners.

Children are a common locus of struggle between men and women. Last century some courts openly used children to keep unwilling partners in unhappy marriages. During an ongoing marriage, many disputes center on how children shall be raised and on whether or how much of the everyday work of child-rearing shall be shared by men. Upon divorce, children may be the objects of strategic negotiation or of sincere custody battles. Children are all too often abandoned at divorce, both emotionally and financially. The largest group in poverty in the United States is children and single mothers. The same father who lavishes money and attention on the children of a new family may renege on support obligations and neglect children from a prior marriage.

Children are our most valued possessions, the subjects of our warmest affections, and the objects of our worst neglect. Thus we witness conflicting trends in the law according to which children are increasingly recognized as persons, while at the same time they continue to be treated as if they were chattels or consumer goods to be enjoyed or discarded.

A: The Status of Childhood: Caught Between Parents and the State

Education: Protection Against State Imposition

MEYER v. NEBRASKA
United States Supreme Court
262 U.S. 390 (1923)

Mr. Justice McREYNOLDS delivered the opinion of the Court.

Plaintiff in error was tried and convicted in the district court for Hamilton county, Nebraska, under an information which charged that on May 25, 1920, while an instructor in Zion Parochial School he unlawfully taught the subject of reading in the German language to Raymond Parpart, a child of 10 years, who had not attained and successfully passed the eighth grade. The information is based upon "An act relating to the teaching of foreign languages in the state of Nebraska," approved April 9, 1919 [Laws 1919, c. 249], which follows:

> Section 1. No person, individually or as a teacher, shall, in any private, denominational, parochial or public school, teach any subject to any person in any language than the English language.
>
> Sec. 2. Languages, other than the English language, may be taught as languages only after a pupil shall have attained and successfully passed the eighth grade as evidenced by a certificate of graduation issued by the county superintendent of the county in which the child resides.

...

The Supreme Court of the state affirmed the judgment of conviction.... And it held that the statute forbidding this did not conflict with the Fourteenth Amendment, but was a valid exercise of the police power. The following excerpts from the opinion sufficiently indicate the reasons advanced to support the conclusion:

> The salutary purpose of the statute is clear. The Legislature had seen the baneful effects of permitting foreigners, who had taken residence in this country, to rear and educate their children in the language of their native land. The result of that condition was found to be inimical to our own safety. To allow the children of foreigners, who had emigrated here, to be taught from early childhood the language of the country of their parents was to rear them with that language as their mother tongue. It was to educate them so that they must always think in that language, and, as a consequence, naturally inculcate in them the ideas and sentiments foreign to the best interests of this country. The statute, therefore, was intended not only to require that the education of all children be conducted in the English language, but that, until they had grown into that language and until it had become a part of them, they should not in the schools be taught any other language. The obvious purpose of this statute was that the English language should be and become the mother tongue of all children reared in this state. The enactment of such a statute comes reasonably within the police power of the state.

The problem for our determination is whether the statute as construed and applied unreasonably infringes the liberty guaranteed to the plaintiff in error by the Fourteenth Amendment: "No state…shall deprive any person of life, liberty, or property, without due process of law."

While this court has not attempted to define with exactness the liberty thus guaranteed, the term has received much consideration and some of the included things have been definitely stated. Without doubt, it denotes not merely freedom from bodily restraint but also the right of the individual to contract, to engage in any of the common occupations of life, to acquire useful knowledge, to marry, establish a home and bring up children, to worship God according to the dictates of his own conscience, and generally to enjoy those privileges long recognized at common law as essential to the orderly pursuit of happiness by free men.… The established doctrine is that this liberty may not be interfered with, under the guise of protecting the public interest, by legislative action which is arbitrary or without reasonable relation to some purpose within the competency of the state to effect. Determination by the Legislature of what constitutes proper exercise of police power is not final or conclusive but is subject to supervision by the courts. *Lawton v. Steele*, 152 U. S. 133, 137, 14 Sup. Ct. 499, 38 L. Ed. 385.

The American people have always regarded education and acquisition of knowledge as matters of supreme importance which should be diligently promoted.… Corresponding to the right of control, it is the natural duty of the parent to give his children education suitable to their station in life; and nearly all the states, including Nebraska, enforce this obligation by compulsory laws.

Practically, education of the young is only possible in schools conducted by especially qualified persons who devote themselves thereto. The calling always has been regarded as useful and honorable, essential, indeed, to the public welfare. Mere knowledge of the German language cannot reasonably be regarded as harmful. Heretofore it has been commonly looked upon as helpful and desirable. Plaintiff in error taught this language in school as part of his occupation. His right thus to teach and the right of parents to engage him so to instruct their children, we think, are within the liberty of the amendment.

…

It is said the purpose of the legislation was to promote civic development by inhibiting training and education of the immature in foreign tongues and ideals before they could learn English and acquire American ideals, and "that the English language should be and become the mother tongue of all children reared in this state." It is also affirmed that the foreign born population is very large, that certain communities commonly use foreign words, follow foreign leaders, move in a foreign atmosphere, and that the children are thereby hindered from becoming citizens of the most useful type and the public safety is imperiled.

That the state may do much, go very far, indeed, in order to improve the quality of its citizens, physically, mentally and morally, is clear; but the individual has certain fundamental rights which must be respected. The protection of the Constitution extends to all, to those who speak other languages as well as to those born with English on the tongue. Perhaps it would be highly advantageous if all had ready understanding of our ordinary speech, but this cannot be coerced by methods which conflict with the Constitution — a desirable end cannot be promoted by prohibited means.

...

The desire of the Legislature to foster a homogeneous people with American ideals prepared readily to understand current discussions of civic matters is easy to appreciate. Unfortunate experiences during the late war and aversion toward every character of truculent adversaries were certainly enough to quicken that aspiration. But the means adopted, we think, exceed the limitations upon the power of the state and conflict with rights assured to plaintiff in error. The interference is plain enough and no adequate reason therefor in time of peace and domestic tranquility has been shown.

The power of the state to compel attendance at some school and to make reasonable regulations for all schools, including a requirement that they shall give instructions in English, is not questioned. Nor has challenge been made of the state's power to prescribe a curriculum for institutions which it supports. Those matters are not within the present controversy. Our concern is with the prohibition approved by the Supreme Court. *Adams v. Tanner, supra,* [244 U. S. 594, 37 Sup. Ct. 662, 61 L. Ed. 1336, L. R. A. 1917F, 1163, Ann. Cas. 1917D, 973], pointed out that mere abuse incident to an occupation ordinarily useful is not enough to justify its abolition, although regulation may be entirely proper. No emergency has arisen which renders knowledge by a child of some language other than English so clearly harmful as to justify its inhibition with the consequent infringement of rights long freely enjoyed. We are constrained to conclude that the statute as applied is arbitrary and without reasonable relation to any end within the competency of the state.

As the statute undertakes to interfere only with teaching which involves a modern language, leaving complete freedom as to other matters, there seems no adequate foundation for the suggestion that the purpose was to protect the child's health by limiting his mental activities. It is well known that proficiency in a foreign language seldom comes to one not instructed at an early age, and experience shows that this is not injurious to the health, morals or understanding of the ordinary child.

The judgment of the court below must be reversed and the cause remanded for further proceedings not inconsistent with this opinion.

Reversed.

PIERCE v. SOCIETY OF SISTERS
United States Supreme Court
268 U.S. 510 (1925)

Mr. Justice McREYNOLDS delivered the opinion of the Court.

...

The challenged act, effective September 1, 1926, requires every parent, guardian, or other person having control or charge or custody of a child between eight and sixteen years to send him "to a public school for the period of time a public school shall be held during the current year" in the district where the child resides; and failure so to do is declared a misdemeanor. There are exemptions — not specially important here — for children who are not normal, or who have completed the eighth grade, or whose parents or private teachers reside at considerable distances from any public school, or who hold special permits from the county superintendent. The manifest purpose is to compel general attendance at public schools by normal children, between eight and sixteen, who have not completed the eight grade. And without doubt enforcement of the statute would seriously impair, perhaps destroy, the profitable features of appellees' business and greatly diminish the value of their property.

Appellee the Society of Sisters is an Oregon corporation, organized in 1880, with power to care for orphans, educate and instruct the youth, establish and maintain academies or schools, and acquire necessary real and personal property. It has long devoted its property and effort to the secular and religious education and care of children, and has acquired the valuable good will of many parents and guardians. It conducts interdependent primary and high schools and junior colleges, and maintains orphanages for the custody and control of children between eight and sixteen. In its primary schools many children between those ages are taught the subjects usually pursued in Oregon public schools during the first eight years. Systematic religious instruction and moral training according to the tenets of the Roman Catholic Church are also regularly provided....

After setting out the above facts, the Society's bill alleges that the enactment conflicts with the right of parents to choose schools where their children will receive appropriate mental and religious training, the right of the child to influence the parents' choice of a school, the right of schools and teachers therein to engage in a useful business or profession, and is accordingly repugnant to the Constitution and void. And, further, that unless enforcement of the measure is enjoined the corporation's business and property will suffer irreparable injury.

Appellee Hill Military Academy is a private corporation organized in 1908 under the laws of Oregon, engaged in owning, operating, and conducting for profit an elementary, college preparatory, and military training school for boys between the ages of five and twenty-one years....

...

No question is raised concerning the power of the state reasonably to regulate all schools, to inspect, supervise and examine them, their teachers and pupils; to require that all children of proper age attend some school, that teachers shall be of good moral character and patriotic disposition, that certain studies plainly essential to good citizenship must be taught, and that nothing be taught which is manifestly inimical to the public welfare.

The inevitable practical result of enforcing the act under consideration would be destruction of appellees' primary schools, and perhaps all other private primary schools for normal children within the state of Oregon. Appellees are engaged in a kind of undertaking not inherently harmful, but long regarded as useful and meritorious. Certainly there is nothing in the present records to indicate that they have failed to discharge their obligations to patrons, students, or the state. And there are no peculiar circumstances or present emergencies which demand extraordinary measures relative to primary education.

Under the doctrine of *Meyer v. Nebraska*, 262 U. S. 390, 43 S. Ct. 625, 67 L. Ed. 1042, 29 A.L.R. 1146, we think it entirely plain that the Act of 1922 unreasonably interferes with the liberty of parents and guardians to direct the upbringing and education of children under their control. As often heretofore pointed out, rights guaranteed by the Constitution may not be abridged by legislation which has no reasonable relation to some purpose within the competency of the state. The fundamental theory of liberty upon which all governments in this Union repose excludes any general power of the state to standardize its children by forcing them to accept instruction from public teachers only. The child is not the mere creature of the state; those who nurture him and direct his destiny have the right, coupled with the high duty, to recognize and prepare him for additional obligations.

Appellees are corporations, and therefore, it is said, they cannot claim for themselves the liberty which the Fourteenth Amendment guarantees. Accepted in the proper sense, this is true. *Northwestern Life Ins. Co. v. Riggs*, 203 U.S. 243, 255, 27 S.Ct. 126, 51 L.Ed. 168, 7 Ann.Cas. 1104; *Western Turf Association v. Greenberg*, 204 U.S. 359, 363, 27 S.Ct. 384, 51 L.Ed. 520. But they have business and property for which they claim protection. These are threatened with destruction through the unwarranted compulsion which appellants are exercising over present and prospective patrons of their schools. And this court has gone very far to protect against loss threatened by such action....

...

Generally, it is entirely true, as urged by counsel, that no person in any business has such an interest in possible customers as to enable him to restrain exercise of proper power of the state upon the ground that he will be deprived of patronage. But the injunctions here sought are not against the exercise of any *proper* power. Plaintiffs asked protection against arbitrary, unreasonable, and unlawful interference with their patrons and the consequent destruction of their business and property....

The suits were not premature. The injury to appellees was present and very real, not a mere possibility in the remote future. If no relief had been possible prior to the effective date of the act, the injury would have become irreparable. Prevention of impending injury by unlawful action is a well-recognized function of courts of equity.

The decrees below are *affirmed*.

WISCONSIN v. YODER

United States Supreme Court
406 U.S. 205 (1972)

Mr. Chief Justice BURGER delivered the opinion of the Court.

On petition of the State of Wisconsin, we granted the writ of certiorari in this case to review a decision of the Wisconsin Supreme Court holding that respondents' convictions for violating the State's compulsory school-attendance law were invalid under the Free Exercise Clause of the First Amendment to the United States Constitution made applicable to the States by the Fourteenth Amendment. For the reasons hereafter stated we affirm the judgment of the Supreme Court of Wisconsin.

Respondents Jonas Yoder and Wallace Miller are members of the Old Order Amish religion, and respondent Adin Yutzy is a member of the Conservative Amish Mennonite Church. They and their families are residents of Green County, Wisconsin. Wisconsin's compulsory school-attendance law required them to cause their children to attend public or private school until reaching age 16 but the respondents declined to send their children, ages 14 and 15, to public school after they complete the eighth grade. The children were not enrolled in any private school, or within any recognized exception to the compulsory-attendance law, and they are conceded to be subject to the Wisconsin statute.

On complaint of the school district administrator for the public schools, respondents were charged, tried, and convicted of violating the compulsory-attendance law in Green County Court and were fined the sum of $5 each.[3] Respondents defended on the ground that the application of the compulsory-attendance law violated their rights under the First and Fourteenth Amendments.[4] The trial testimony showed that respondents believed, in accordance with the tenets of Old Order Amish communities generally, that their children's attendance at high school, public or private, was contrary to the Amish religion and way of life. They believed that by sending their children to high school, they would not only expose themselves to the danger of the censure of the church community, but, as found by the county court, also endanger their own salvation and that of their children. The State stipulated that respondents' religious beliefs were sincere.

In support of their position, respondents presented as expert witnesses scholars on religion and education whose testimony is uncontradicted. They expressed their opinions on the relationship of the Amish belief concerning school attendance to the more general tenets of their religion, and described the impact that compulsory high school attendance could have on the continued survival of Amish communities as they exist in the United States today. The history of the Amish sect was given in some detail, beginning with the Swiss Anabaptists of the 16th century who rejected institutionalized churches and sought to return to the early, simple, Christian life de-emphasizing material success, rejecting the competitive spirit, and seeking to insulate themselves from the modern world. As a result of their common heritage, Old Order Amish communities today are characterized by a fundamental belief that salvation requires life in a church commu-

3. Prior to trial, the attorney for respondents wrote the State Superintendent of Public Instruction in an effort to explore the possibilities for a compromise settlement. Among other possibilities, he suggested that perhaps the State Superintendent could administratively determine that the Amish could satisfy the compulsory-attendance law by establishing their own vocational training plan similar to one that has been established in Pennsylvania. Supp.App. 6. Under the Pennsylvania plan, Amish children of high school age are required to attend an Amish vocational school for three hours a week, during which time they are taught such subjects as English, mathematics, health, and social studies by an Amish teacher. For the balance of the week, the children perform farm and household duties under parental supervision, and keep a journal of their daily activities. The major portion of the curriculum is home projects in agriculture and homemaking . See generally J. Hostetler & G. Huntington, CHILDREN IN AMISH SOCIETY: SOCIALIZATION AND COMMUNITY EDUCATION, c. 5 (1971). A similar program has been instituted in Indiana. *Ibid.* See also Iowa Code §299.24 (1971); Kan.Stat.Ann. §72—1111 (Supp. 1971).

The Superintendent rejected this proposal on the ground that it would not afford Amish children "substantially equivalent education" to that offered in the schools of the area. Supp.App. 6.

4. The First Amendment provides: "Congress shall make no law respecting an establishment of religion, or prohibiting the free exercise thereof...."

nity separate and apart from the world and worldly influence. This concept of life aloof from the world and its values is central to their faith.

A related feature of Old Order Amish communities is their devotion to a life in harmony with nature and the soil, as exemplified by the simple life of the early Christian era that continued in America during much of our early national life. Amish beliefs require members of the community to make their living by farming or closely related activities. Broadly speaking, the Old Order Amish religion pervades and determines the entire mode of life of its adherents. Their conduct is regulated in great detail by the *Ordnung*, or rules, of the church community. Adult baptism, which occurs in late adolescence, is the time at which Amish young people voluntarily undertake heavy obligations, not unlike the Bar Mitzvah of the Jews, to abide by the rules of the church community.

Amish objection to formal education beyond the eighth grade is firmly grounded in these central religious concepts. They object to the high school, and higher education generally, because the values they teach are in marked variance with Amish values and the Amish way of life; they view secondary school education as an impermissible exposure of their children to a "worldly" influence in conflict with their beliefs. The high school tends to emphasize intellectual and scientific accomplishments, self-distinction, competitiveness, worldly success, and social life with other students. Amish society emphasizes informal learning-through-doing; a life of "goodness," rather than a life of intellect; wisdom, rather than technical knowledge, community welfare, rather than competition; and separation from, rather than integration with, contemporary worldly society.

Formal high school education beyond the eighth grade is contrary to Amish beliefs, not only because it places Amish children in an environment hostile to Amish beliefs with increasing emphasis on competition in class work and sports and with pressure to conform to the styles, manners, and ways of the peer group, but also because it takes them away from their community, physically and emotionally, during the crucial and formative adolescent period of life. During this period, the children must acquire Amish attitudes favoring manual work and self-reliance and the specific skills needed to perform the adult role of an Amish farmer or housewife. They must learn to enjoy physical labor. Once a child has learned basic reading, writing, and elementary mathematics, these traits, skills, and attitudes admittedly fall within the category of those best learned through example and "doing" rather than in a classroom. And, at this time in life, the Amish child must also grow in his faith and his relationship to the Amish community if he is to be prepared to accept the heavy obligations imposed by adult baptism. In short, high school attendance with teachers who are not of the Amish faith — and may even be hostile to it — interposes a serious barrier to the integration of the Amish child into the Amish religious community. Dr. John Hostetler, one of the experts on Amish society, testified that the modern high school is not equipped, in curriculum or social environment, to impart the values promoted by Amish society.

The Amish do not object to elementary education through the first eight grades as a general proposition because they agree that their children must have basic skills in the "three R's" in order to read the Bible, to be good farmers and citizens, and to be able to deal with non-Amish people when necessary in the course of daily affairs. They view such a basic education as acceptable because it does not significantly expose their children to worldly values or interfere with their development in the Amish community during the crucial adolescent period. While Amish accept compulsory elementary education generally, wherever possible they have established their own elementary schools in many respects like the small local schools of the past. In the Amish belief higher learning tends to develop values they reject as influences that alienate man from God.

On the basis of such considerations, Dr. Hostetler testified that compulsory high school attendance could not only result in great psychological harm to Amish children, because of the conflicts it would produce, but would also, in his opinion, ultimately result in the destruction of the Old Order Amish church community as it exists in the United States today. The testimony of Dr. Donald A. Erickson, an expert witness on education, also showed that the Amish succeed in preparing their high school age children to be productive members of the Amish community. He described their system of learning through doing the skills directly relevant to their adult roles in the Amish community as "ideal" and perhaps superior to ordinary high school education. The evidence also showed that the Amish have an excellent record as law-abiding and generally self-sufficient members of society.

Although the trial court in its careful findings determined that the Wisconsin compulsory school-attendance law "does interfere with the freedom of the Defendants to act in accordance with their sincere religious belief" it also concluded that the requirement of high school attendance until age 16 was a "reasonable and constitutional" exercise of governmental power, and therefore denied the motion to dismiss the charges. The Wisconsin Circuit Court affirmed the convictions. The Wisconsin Supreme Court, however, sustained respondents' claim under the Free Exercise Clause of the First Amendment and reversed the convictions....

I

There is no doubt as to the power of a State, having a high responsibility for education of its citizens, to impose reasonable regulations for the control and duration of basic education. See, *e.g.*, *Pierce v. Society of Sisters*, 268 U.S. 510, 534, 45 S.Ct. 571, 573, 69 L.Ed. 1070 (1925). Providing public schools ranks at the very apex of the function of a State. Yet even this paramount responsibility was, in *Pierce*, made to yield to the right of parents to provide an equivalent education in a privately operated system.... As that case suggests, the values of parental direction of the religious upbringing and education of their children in their early and formative years have a high place in our society. See...*Meyer v. Nebraska*, 262 U.S. 390, 43 S.Ct. 625, 67 L.Ed. 1042 (1923); ... Thus, a State's interest in universal education, however highly we rank it, is not totally free from a balancing process when it impinges on fundamental rights and interests, such as those specifically protected by the Free Exercise Clause of the First Amendment, and the traditional interest of parents with respect to the religious upbringing of their children so long as they, in the words of *Pierce*, "prepare (them) for additional obligations." 268 U.S., at 535, 45 S.Ct., at 573.

...

II

We come then to the quality of the claims of the respondents concerning the alleged encroachment of Wisconsin's compulsory school-attendance statute on their rights and the rights of their children to the free exercise of the religious beliefs they and their forbears have adhered to for almost three centuries. In evaluating those claims we must be careful to determine whether the Amish religious faith and their mode of life are, as they claim, inseparable and interdependent. A way of life, however virtuous and admirable, may not be interposed as a barrier to reasonable state regulation of education if it is based on purely secular considerations; to have the protection of the Religion Clauses, the claims must be rooted in religious belief. Although a determination of what is a "religious" belief or practice entitled to constitutional protection may present a most delicate question, the very concept of ordered liberty precludes allowing every person to make his own standards on matters of conduct in which society as a whole has important interests. Thus, if the Amish asserted their claims because of their subjective evaluation and rejection of the contemporary secular values accepted by the majority, much as Thoreau rejected the social values of his time and isolated himself at Walden Pond, their claims would not rest on a religious basis. Thoreau's choice was philosophical and personal rather than religious, and such belief does not rise to the demands of the Religion Clauses.

...

III

Neither the findings of the trial court nor the Amish claims as to the nature of their faith are challenged in this Court by the State of Wisconsin. Its position is that the State's interest in universal compulsory formal secondary education to age 16 is so great that it is paramount to the undisputed claims of respondents that their mode of preparing their youth for Amish life, after the traditional elementary education, is an essential part of their religious belief and practice. Nor does the State undertake to meet the claim that the Amish mode of life and education is inseparable from and a part of the basic tenets of their religion — indeed, as much a part of their religious belief and practices as baptism, the confessional, or a sabbath may be for others.

...

The State advances two primary arguments in support of its system of compulsory education. It notes, as Thomas Jefferson pointed out early in our history, that some degree of education is necessary to prepare citizens to participate effectively and intelligently in our open political system if we are to preserve freedom and independence. Further, education prepares individuals to be self-reliant and self-sufficient participants in society. We accept these propositions.

However, the evidence adduced by the Amish in this case is persuasively to the effect that an additional one or two years of formal high school for Amish children in place of their long-established program of informal vocational education would do little to serve those interests. Respondents' experts testified at trial, without challenge, that the value of all education must be assessed in terms of its capacity to prepare the child for life. It is one thing to say that compulsory education for a year or two beyond the eighth grade may be necessary when its goal is the preparation of the child for life in modern society as the majority live, but it is quite another if the goal of education be viewed as the preparation of the child for life in the separated agrarian community that is the keystone of the Amish faith. See *Meyer v. Nebraska*, 262 U.S., at 400, 43 S.Ct., at 627, 67 L.Ed. 1042.

The State attacks respondents' position as one fostering "ignorance" from which the child must be protected by the State. No one can question the State's duty to protect children from ignorance but this argument does not square with the facts disclosed in the record. Whatever their idiosyncrasies as seen by the majority, this record strongly shows that the Amish community has been a highly successful social unit within our society, even if apart from the conventional "mainstream." Its members are productive and very law-abiding members of society; they reject public welfare in any of its usual modern forms. The Congress itself recognized their self-sufficiency by authorizing exemption of such groups as the Amish from the obligation to pay social security taxes.

It is neither fair nor correct to suggests that the Amish are opposed to education beyond the eighth grade level. What this record shows is that they are opposed to conventional formal education of the type provided by a certified high school because it comes at the child's crucial adolescent period of religious development. Dr. Donald Erickson, for example, testified that their system of learning-by-doing was an "ideal system" of education in terms of preparing Amish children for life as adults in the Amish community, and that "I would be inclined to say they do a better job in this than most of the rest of us do." As he put it, "These people aren't purporting to be learned people, and it seems to me the self-sufficiency of the community is the best evidence I can point to — whatever is being done seems to function well."

We must not forget that in the Middle Ages important values of the civilization of the Western World were preserved by members of religious orders who isolated themselves from all worldly influences against great obstacles. There can be no assumption that today's majority is "right" and the Amish and others like them are "wrong." A way of life that is odd or even erratic but interferes with no rights or interests of others is not to be condemned because it is different.

The State, however, supports its interest in providing an additional one or two years of compulsory high school education to Amish children because of the possibility that some such children will choose to leave the Amish community, and that if this occurs they will be ill-equipped for life. The State argues that if Amish children leave their church they should not be in the position of making their way in the world without the education available in the one or two additional years the State requires. However, on this record, that argument is highly speculative. There is no specific evidence of the loss of Amish adherents by attrition, nor is there any showing that upon leaving the Amish community Amish children, with their practical agricultural training and habits of industry and self-reliance, would become burdens on society because of educational shortcomings. Indeed, this argument of the State appears to rest primarily on the State's mistaken assumption, already noted, that the Amish do not provide any education for their children beyond the eighth grade, but allow them to grow in "ignorance." To the contrary, not only do the Amish accept the necessity for formal schooling through the eighth grade level, but continue to provide what has been characterized by the undisputed testimony of expert educators as an "ideal" vocational education for their children in the adolescent years.

There is nothing in this record to suggest that the Amish qualities of reliability, self-reliance, and dedication to work would fail to find ready markets in today's society. Absent some contrary evidence supporting the State's position, we are unwilling to assume that persons possessing such valuable vocational skills and habits are doomed to become burdens on society should they determine to leave the Amish faith, nor is there any basis in the record to warrant a finding that an additional one or two years of formal school education beyond the eighth grade would serve to eliminate any such problem that might exist.

...

IV

Finally, the State, on authority of *Prince v. Massachusetts*, argues that a decision exempting Amish children from the State's requirement fails to recognize the substantive right of the Amish child to a secondary education, and fails to give due regard to the power of the State as *parens patriae* to extend the benefit of secondary education to children regardless of the wishes of their parents....

This case, of course, is not one in which any harm to the physical or mental health of the child or to the public safety, peace, order, or welfare has been demonstrated or may be properly inferred. The record is to the contrary,...

Contrary to the suggestion of the dissenting opinion of Mr. Justice DOUGLAS, our holding today in no degree depends on the assertion of the religious interest of the child as contrasted with that of the parents. It is the parents who are subject to prosecution here for failing to cause their children to attend school, and it is their right of free exercise, not that of their children, that must determine Wisconsin's power to impose criminal penalties on the parent. The dissent argues that a child who expresses a desire to attend public high school in conflict with the wishes of his parents should not be prevented from doing so. There is no reason for the Court to consider that point since it is not an issue in the case. The children are not parties to this litigation. The State has at no point tried this case on the theory that respondents were preventing their children from attending school against their expressed desires, and indeed the record is to the contrary. The State's position from the outset has been that it is empowered to apply its compulsory-attendance law to Amish parents in the same manner as to other parents — that is, without regard to the wishes of the child. That is the claim we reject today.

Our holding in no way determines the proper resolution of possible competing interests of parents, children, and the State in an appropriate state court proceeding in which the power of the State is asserted on the theory that Amish parents are preventing their minor children from attending high school despite their expressed desires to the contrary. Recognition of the claim of the State in such a proceeding would, of course, call into question traditional concepts of parental control over the religious upbringing and education of their minor children recognized in this Court's past decisions. It is clear that such an intrusion by a State into family decisions in the area of religious training would give rise to grave questions of religious freedom comparable to those raised here and those presented in *Pierce v. Society of Sisters*, 268 U.S. 510, 45 S.Ct. 571, 69 L.Ed. 1070 (1925). On this record we neither reach nor decide those issues.

The State's argument proceeds without reliance on any actual conflict between the wishes of parents and children. It appears to rest on the potential that exemption of Amish parents from the requirements of the compulsory-education law might allow some parents to act contrary to the best interests of their children by foreclosing their opportunity to make an intelligent choice between the Amish way of life and that of the outside world. The same argument could, of course, be made with respect to all church schools short of college. There is nothing in the record or in the ordinary course of human experience to suggest that non-Amish parents generally consult with children of ages 14–16 if they are placed in a church school of the parents' faith.

Indeed it seems clear that if the State is empowered, as *parens patriae*, to "save" a child from himself or his Amish parents by requiring an additional two years of compulsory formal high school education, the State will in large measure influence, if not determine, the religious future of the child. Even more markedly than in *Prince*, therefore, this case involves the fundamental interest of parents, as contrasted with that of the State, to guide the religious future and education of their children. The history and culture of Western civilization reflect a strong tradition of parental concern for the nurture and upbringing of their children. This primary role of the parents in the upbringing of their children is now established beyond debate as an enduring American tradition. If not the first, perhaps the most significant statements of the Court in this area are found in *Pierce v. Society of Sisters*....

The duty to prepare the child for "additional obligations," referred to by the Court, must be read to include the inculcation of moral standards, religious beliefs, and elements of good citizenship. *Pierce*, of course, recognized that where nothing more than the general interest of the parent in the nurture and education of his children is involved, it is beyond dispute that the State acts "reasonably" and constitutionally in requiring education to age 16 in some public or private school meeting the standards prescribed by the State.

However read, the Court's holding in *Pierce* stands as a charter of the rights of parents to direct the religious upbringing of their children. And, when the interests of parenthood are combined with a free exercise claim of the nature revealed by this record, more than merely a "reasonable relation to some purpose within the competency of the State" is required to sustain the validity of the State's requirement under the First Amendment. To be sure, the power of the parent, even when linked to a free exercise claim, may be subject to limitation under *Prince* if it appears that parental decisions will jeopardize the health or safety of the child, or have a potential for significant social burdens. But in this case, the Amish have introduced persuasive evidence undermining the arguments the State has advanced to support its claims in terms of the welfare of the child and society as a whole....

In the face of our consistent emphasis on the central values underlying the Religion Clauses in our constitutional scheme of government, we cannot accept a *parens patriae* claim of such all-encompassing scope and with such sweeping potential for broad and unforeseeable application as that urged by the State.

V

For the reasons stated we hold...that the First and Fourteenth Amendments prevent the State from compelling respondents to cause their children to attend formal high school to age 16.... It cannot be overemphasized that we are not dealing with a way of life and mode of education by a group claiming to have recently discovered some "progressive" or more enlightened process for rearing children for modern life.

Aided by a history of three centuries as an identifiable religious sect and a long history as a successful and self-sufficient segment of American society, the Amish in this case have convincingly demonstrated the sincerity of their religious beliefs, the interrelationship of belief with their mode of life, the vital role that belief and daily conduct play in the continued survival of Old Order Amish communities and their religious organization, and the hazards presented by the State's enforcement of a statute generally valid as to others. Beyond this, they have carried the even more difficult burden of demonstrating the adequacy of their alternative mode of continuing informal vocational education in terms of precisely those overall interests that the State advances in support of its program of compulsory high school education. In light of this convincing showing, one that probably few other religious groups or sects could make, and weighing the minimal difference between what the State would require and what the Amish already accept, it was incumbent on the State to show with more particularity how its admittedly strong interest in compulsory education would be adversely affected by granting an exemption to the Amish....

...

Affirmed.

Mr. Justice POWELL and Mr. Justice REHNQUIST took no part in the consideration or decision of this case.

Mr. Justice STEWART, with whom Mr. Justice BRENNAN joins, concurring.

This case involves the constitutionality of imposing criminal punishment upon Amish parents for their religiously based refusal to compel their children to attend public high schools. Wisconsin has sought to brand these parents as criminals for following their religious beliefs, and the Court today rightly holds that Wisconsin cannot constitutionally do so.

This case in no way involves any questions regarding the right of the children of Amish parents to attend public high schools, or any other institutions of learning, if they wish to do so. As the Court points out, there is no suggestion whatever in the record that the religious beliefs of the children here concerned differ in any way from those of their parents....

Mr. Justice WHITE, with whom Mr. Justice BRENNAN and Mr. Justice STEWART join, concurring.

Cases such as this one inevitably call for a delicate balancing of important but conflicting interests. I join the opinion and judgment of the Court because I cannot say that the State's interest in requiring two more years of compulsory education in the ninth and tenth grades outweighs the importance of the concededly sincere Amish religious practice to the survival of that sect.

This would be a very different case for me if respondents' claim were that their religion forbade their children from attending any school at any time and from complying in any way with the educational standards set by the State. Since the Amish children are permitted to acquire the basic tools of literacy to survive in modern society by attending grades one through eight and since the deviation from the State's compulsory-education law is relatively slight, I conclude that respondents' claim must prevail, largely because "religious freedom — the freedom to believe and to practice strange and, it may be, foreign creeds — has classically been one of the highest values of our society." *Braunfeld v. Brown*, 366 U.S. 599, 612, 81 S.Ct. 1144, 1150, 6 L.Ed.2d 563 (1961)(BRENNAN, J., concurring and dissenting).

The importance of the state interest asserted here cannot be denigrated, however.... As recently as last Term, the Court reemphasized the legitimacy of the State's concern for enforcing minimal educational standards. *Lemon v. Kurtzman*, 403 U.S., 602, 613, 91 S.Ct. 2105, 2111, 29 L.Ed.2d 745 (1971). *Pierce v. Society of Sisters*, 268 U.S. 510, 45 S.Ct. 571, 69 L.Ed. 1070 (1925), lends no support to the contention that parents may replace state educational requirements with their own idiosyncratic views of what knowledge a child needs to be a productive and happy member of society; in *Pierce*, both the parochial and military schools were in compliance with all the educational standards that the State had set, and the

Court held simply that while a State may posit such standards, it may not preempt the educational process by requiring children to attend public schools. In the present case, the State is not concerned with the maintenance of an educational system as an end in itself, it is rather attempting to nurture and develop the human potential of its children, whether Amish or non-Amish: to expand their knowledge, broaden their sensibilities, kindle their imagination, foster a spirit of free inquiry, and increase their human understanding and tolerance. It is possible that most Amish children will wish to continue living the rural life of their parents, in which case their training at home will adequately equip them for their future role. Others, however, may wish to become nuclear physicists, ballet dancers, computer programmers, or historians, and for these occupations, formal training will be necessary. There is evidence in the record that many children desert the Amish faith when they come of age. A State has a legitimate interest not only in seeking to develop the latent talents of its children but also in seeking to prepare them for the life style that they may later choose, or at least to provide them with an option other than the life they have led in the past. In the circumstances of this case, although the question is close, I am unable to say that the State has demonstrated that Amish children who leave school in the eighth grade will be intellectually stultified or unable to acquire new academic skills later. The statutory minimum school attendance age set by the State is, after all, only 16.

...I join the Court because the sincerity of the Amish religious policy here is uncontested, because the potentially adverse impact of the state requirement is great, and because the State's valid interest in education has already been largely satisfied by the eight years the children have already spent in school.

Mr. Justice DOUGLAS, dissenting in part.

I

I agree with the Court that the religious scruples of the Amish are opposed to the education of their children beyond the grade schools, yet I disagree with the Court's conclusion that the matter is within the dispensation of parents alone. The Court's analysis assumes that the only interests at stake in the case are those of the Amish parents on the one hand, and those of the State on the other. The difficulty with this approach is that, despite the Court's claim, the parents are seeking to vindicate not only their own free exercise claims, but also those of their high-school-age children.

It is argued that the right of the Amish children to religious freedom is not presented by the facts of the case, as the issue before the Court involves only the Amish parents' religious freedom to defy a state criminal statute imposing upon them an affirmative duty to cause their children to attend high school.

First, respondents' motion to dismiss in the trial court expressly asserts, not only the religious liberty of the adults, but also that of the children, as a defense to the prosecutions. It is, of course, beyond question that the parents have standing as defendants in a criminal prosecution to assert the religious interests of their children as a defense. Although the lower courts and a majority of this Court assume an identity of interest between parent and child, it is clear that they have treated the religious interest of the child as a factor in the analysis.

Second, it is essential to reach the question to decide the case, not only because the question was squarely raised in the motion to dismiss, but also because no analysis of religious-liberty claims can take place in a vacuum. If the parents in this case are allowed a religious exemption, the inevitable effect is to impose the parents' notions of religious duty upon their children. Where the child is mature enough to express potentially conflicting desires, it would be an invasion of the child's rights to permit such an imposition without canvassing his views. As in *Prince v. Massachusetts*, 321 U.S. 158, 64 S.Ct. 438, 88 L.Ed. 645, it is an imposition resulting from this very litigation. As the child has no other effective forum, it is in this litigation that his rights should be considered. And, if an Amish child desires to attend high school, and is mature enough to have that desire respected, the State may well be able to override the parents' religiously motivated objections.

Religion is an individual experience. It is not necessary, nor even appropriate, for every Amish child to express his views on the subject in a prosecution of a single adult. Crucial, however, are the views of the child whose parent is the subject of the suit. Frieda Yoder has in fact testified that her own religious views are opposed to high-school education. I therefore join the judgment of the Court as to respondent Jonas Yoder. But Frieda Yoder's views may not be those of Vernon Yutzy or Barbara Miller. I must dissent, therefore, as to respondents Adin Yutzy and Wallace Miller as their motion to dismiss also raised the question of their children's religious liberty.

II

This issue has never been squarely presented before today. Our opinions are full of talk about the power of the parents over the child's education. See *Pierce v. Society of Sisters*, 268 U.S. 510, 45 S.Ct. 571, 69 L.Ed. 1070; *Meyer v. Nebraska*, 262 U.S. 390, 43 S.Ct. 625, 67 L.Ed. 1042. And we have in the past analyzed similar conflicts between parent and State with little regard for the views of the child. See *Prince v. Massachusetts*, *supra*. Recent cases, however, have clearly held that the children themselves have constitutionally protectible interests.

These children are "persons" within the meaning of the Bill of Rights. We have so held over and over again....

...

On this important and vital matter of education, I think the children should be entitled to be heard. While the parents, absent dissent, normally speak for the entire family, the education of the child is a matter on which the child will often have decided views. He may want to be a pianist or an astronaut or an oceanographer. To do so he will have to break from the Amish tradition.

It is the future of the student, not the future of the parents, that is imperiled by today's decision. If a parent keeps his child out of school beyond the grade school, then the child will be forever barred from entry into the new and amazing world of diversity that we have today. The child may decide that that is the preferred course, or he may rebel. It is the student's judgment, not his parents', that is essential if we are to give full meaning to what we have said about the Bill of Rights and of the right of students to be masters of their own destiny. If he is harnessed to the Amish way of life by those in authority over him and if his education is truncated, his entire life may be stunted and deformed. The child, therefore, should be given an opportunity to be heard before the State gives the exemption which we honor today.

The views of the two children in question were not canvassed by the Wisconsin courts. The matter should be explicitly reserved so that new hearings can be held on remand of the case.

...

COMMENTS

Meyer and *Pierce* are classic cases from the 1920s establishing the right to privacy and limiting the power of the state to interfere with the child-rearing choices of parents. The law involved in *Meyer*, forbidding the teaching in or of a foreign language, was enacted during the nativist reaction to World War I; but the issues it raises have a surprisingly contemporary ring to them. Current disputes over bilingual education and the recent enactment of "English only" provisions are fueled by a similar nativist alarm over the cultural effects of immigration. It seems unlikely that any English only law that tried to prevent instruction in a foreign language could withstand constitutional scrutiny today, and the contemporary bilingual controversy usually aims its appeals to the long-term interest of the children themselves more than any general assertions about the interests of society. Although *Pierce* reaffirmed the right of states to inspect private schools and require that they teach certain basic subjects, this holding may be thrown into some doubt by the broader language of *Wisconsin v. Yoder.*

Wisconsin v. Yoder revisited questions about the constitutional dimension of conflicts between the state and parents over the raising of children. The religiously-motivated denial of a basic standard education could well raise questions beyond state interference and family autonomy, with a possible conflict of interest between the parents and their children. The majority of the Court considered the case relatively unproblematic in this regard, absent any showing that the children had expressed the desire to attend school beyond eighth grade. Justice Douglas, however, argued that the parents had in fact invoked the rights of the children, and to the extent that they were doing so, argued that the children's stated interests must be taken into account.

In all three of these cases we find the issue primarily framed as one of constitutional rights versus state imposition. All three cases ignore or paper over to one extent or another the possibility of any conflict between the interests of the children and their parents. The limited right of parents to send their children to private instead of public schools might look a bit different than it did in *Pierce* if the children wanted to go to public school. The issues involved in disputes about state policies regarding children become more complicated when we acknowledge the possibility of conflicting interests between parents and children.

Custody and Control: State Enforcement of Parental Control

WOOD v. WOOD
Supreme Court of Iowa
338 N.W.2d 123 (Iowa 1983)

LARSON, Justice.

The substantive issue here is whether a claim for damages may be asserted against a parent who has refused to return the parties' child within the time provided in the dissolution decree. A motion to dismiss the petition was sustained by the district court. We reverse and remand.

...

In an early case, this court discussed the right of a parent to recover damages for deprivation of custody of a child:

> That the father has a right to the care and custody of his minor children, and to superintend their education and nurture, is a proposition that does not admit of controversy. And where he is deprived of such care and custody, and of this superintendence, by the act of another, he has his remedy, by proper action, against such person, is equally clear [sic]. As it is the duty of the father to educate, protect, and nurture his children, so it is his right to have their society, their services, and the control of their moral and intellectual training.

Everett v. Sherfey, 1 Iowa 356, 359 (1855).

In its early stages, a claim for wrongfully seizing or retaining custody of a child was restrictively applied; only a father could pursue the claim, and it was based on a deprivation of the child's services. *Id.* at 360–61; see also *Pyle v. Waechter*, 202 Iowa 695, 697, 210 N.W. 926, 927 (1926); W. Prosser, *Handbook of the Law of Torts* §124, at 882–83 (4th ed. 1971). The rule permitting recovery has since been expanded; most courts requiring a loss of services as a prerequisite have been willing to find a constructive loss of services, even though none are being rendered. Other courts disregard earlier restrictions and merely adopt what is characterized as the "modern" view. Under this approach, the essence of the claim is the interference with the parental relationship, not a loss of services. *Id.* at 883.

As long ago as 1938, the *Restatement of Torts* recognized an action for tortious interference with custody. See *Restatement of Torts* §700 (1938). The current section states the principle:

> §700 *Causing Minor Child to Leave or not to Return Home.* One who, with knowledge that the parent does not consent, abducts or otherwise compels or induces a minor child to leave a parent legally entitled to its custody or not to return to the parent after it has been left him, is subject to liability to the parent.

Restatement (Second) of Torts (1977). The Restatement rule permits suits by parents against noncustodial parents, as well as against nonrelatives:

> c. *When both parents entitled to custody and earnings.* When the parents are by law jointly entitled to the custody and earnings of the child, no action can be brought against one of the parents who abducts or induces the child to leave the other. When by law only one parent is entitled to the custody and earnings of the child, only that parent can maintain an action under the rule stated in this Section. *One parent may be liable to the other parent for the abduction of his own child if by judicial decree the sole custody of the child has been awarded to the other parent.*

Restatement, supra, §700, comment c. (Emphasis added.)

The claim for interference with custody rights appears to have been recognized in every jurisdiction which has addressed the issue....

Another, similarly uniform, line of cases establishes the tort claim where the interference is instigated or furthered by relatives or other third parties. While these cases do not have spouses as defendants, they often spring from abduction of the child by a spouse. In all, the logic and language support a cause of action by a custodial parent against the other, noncustodial parent.

Frequently, in fact, the abducting spouse figures prominently in the case and is not a defendant only because he or she has fled with the child to a foreign jurisdiction.... This recurring scenario itself suggests the need for recognition of a civil claim for damages.

III. Other Alternatives

There obviously are several remedies available to a victimized parent. Each of them, including the tort claim, however, has its limitations. (A tort claim will obviously furnish little deterrent or likelihood of recovery in the case of an impecunious defendant.)...

The case now before us illustrates how the tort claim can, more effectively than any of the alternative sanctions, serve both to prevent child-snatching and to pick up the pieces if it does occur.

A. *The UCCJA.* The Uniform Child Custody Jurisdiction Act, Iowa Code chapter 598A, is basically just that — a jurisdiction act. It provides no compensation for interference with custody in any case. In the present case, it would not even allow recovery of expenses, because the custody decree is not one of "another state." See Iowa Code §598A.15. Because the uniform act provides no compensation for the plaintiff, it provides little or no deterrent to the defendant.

Professor Sanford Katz, chairman of the Family Law Section of the American Bar Association and editor-in-chief of the Family Law Quarterly, has written extensively on the UCCJA. He notes the widespread problem of child-snatching (estimated at 25,000 to 100,000 per year) and discusses the inability of the UCCJA alone to deal with the problem. He points out that this Act is largely jurisdiction-oriented, not remedy-oriented and concludes: "The parent entitled to custody of a child, but unlawfully deprived of it by the noncustodial parent, must still [after adoption of the UCCJA] seek relief in a number of traditional, well established methods." Katz, *Legal Remedies for Child Snatching,* 15 Fam.L.Q. 103, 105 (1981). A tort suit is one of the "traditional" remedies suggested. *Id.* In another publication, Prof. Katz says that "[a]nother lack of force [in the UCCJA] is that its provisions are not tied to any specific enforcement provisions, sanctions or parent-oriented remedies" and repeats his suggestion that "more direct sanctions" such as criminal prosecution or tort suits are needed. Katz, *Child Snatching: The Legal Response to the Abduction of Children,* at 33 (1981).

...

B. *The kidnapping alternatives.* Other alternatives include prosecutions under federal and state kidnapping statutes. A kidnapping prosecution, however, provides for no recovery of expenses or compensation for the victimized parent. There is another problem more subtle, but real nevertheless: Cases with domestic overtones occupy a position of low priority with law enforcement personnel and prosecutors. In fact, this reality appears to be widely observed. See *Justice Dep't. Scored for Flouting Parental Kidnapping Act's Mandate,* 7 Fam.L.Rep. (BNA) 2739–42 (Oct. 6, 1981). In Iowa, child-snatching by a parent is only a misdemeanor, unless the child is removed from the state, in which case it is a felony. Iowa Code §710.6. If the child is removed from the state, the chances of extradition are slim, again because of the domestic overtones of the cases and the inherent inertia of law enforcement personnel in dealing with them.

C. *The contempt alternative.* The usefulness of a contempt action is doubtful. It would provide no recovery of expenses or compensation, and if the party has left the state, any sanctions which are imposed will be of no effect. Further, it provides no basis for extradition. The weaknesses of the contempt alternative are noted in Katz, *Legal Remedies for Child Snatching, supra*, at 117–22, and in Katz, *Child Snatching, supra*, at 103–06. See also P. Hoff, *Interstate Child Custody Disputes and Parental Kidnapping: Policy, Practice and Law, supra*, at 14–1.

One authority summarizes the advantages of the tort suit over the other alternatives: A tort suit will be more likely to effect a speedy return of the child; it will result in better cooperation by potential third-party defendants seeking to avoid the suit; potential punitive damages will serve as an additional deterrent; and increased knowledge of a child's whereabouts will result through the broad scope of civil-case discovery. Hoff, *id.* at 14–1.

We conclude that we should follow the majority of jurisdictions by recognizing and applying section 700 of the *Restatement.* The district court ruling must therefore be reversed, and the case remanded for further proceedings.

Reversed and remanded.

All Justices concur except WOLLE, J., who dissents joined by HARRIS and McGIVERIN, JJ.

McCORMICK, J., joins division I of the dissent.

WOLLE, Justice (dissenting).

I dissent because I believe the Restatement rule will have unacceptable practical consequences and because that rule is unlikely to be in the best interest of children affected by the litigation it spawns. I do not here quarrel with the seeming logic of the rule; if money damages can be recovered from a child-snatching stranger, why not from a child-snatching non-custodial parent. Neither do I disregard the fact that a majority of the jurisdictions which have addressed the issue, encouraged by commentators, have extended the cause of action to permit interspousal money-damage lawsuits for child-snatching. Logic, decisions from other jurisdictions, and views of authoritative commentators must carefully be considered. In the final analysis, however, the rule should be placed in its domestic setting and studied exhaustively in the light of competing policy considerations involving the family as a unit. Adopted, the Restatement rule would become an integral part of Iowa family law. Stripped to essentials, this new civil remedy which the plaintiff espouses is a new weapon for the arsenal of litigants engaging in marital or post-marital warfare. I propose a freeze on new weapons of domestic warfare. Our legislature has not included this cause of action in our body of Iowa family law and neither should this court.

I. We can reasonably predict that the majority opinion will initially generate a proliferation of money-damage lawsuits whose quantity and variety will be far out of proportion to their value. These lawsuits will burden a court system already straining to keep pace with cases now on file while continuing to deliver quality judicial services.

Recent statistical reports clearly show that domestic litigation weighs heavy on our judges' time. In 1981, actions arising directly from family problems accounted for 28,205 cases, or 48.4 percent of all civil filings. At the appellate level, cases involving domestic relations comprised 37.2 percent of all formal appellate decisions in appellate cases — the largest single category of dispositions. The number of rulings in domestic relations cases increased 42 percent from 1980 to 1981. See 1981 Annual Statistical Report to the Iowa Supreme Court by the Iowa Court

Administrator, pp. iv–vii. The figures for 1982 show that domestic case filings and dispositions have decreased slightly in each category, but that welcome decline may be shortlived if the Restatement rule is now adopted. See 1982 Annual Statistical Report to the Iowa Supreme Court by the Iowa Court Administrator, pp. iv–vii.

We cannot accurately predict the number of lawsuits that will now be filed by family members on the law side of our burdened court dockets. Neither can we yet define their characteristics, though the variety may be limited only by the limits of trial lawyers' ingenuity. When parents seek redress for alleged violations of custody orders, their lawyers will be duty-bound to inform them of this decision. We know that parties in domestic cases may be motivated less by good sense — the best interest of their children or family economic concerns — than by their emotions. The tort here involved, after all, is for infliction of emotional distress. Will not lawyers studying this case reasonably conclude that many similar new actions may be permitted? Will not parents conclude, reasonably or not, that they desire to seek money damages from each other?

The gist of the instant action is the alleged violation of the final dissolution decree. Would this not logically invite a counterclaim for alleged violation of visitation provisions in most dissolution decrees? If a parent may bring such an action, might not each child similarly have an action against the parent for infliction of emotional damages? If a parent may bring such an action, why not also a grandparent with custodial or visitation rights? Would not alleged violations of joint custody provisions also give rise to multiple causes of action for the parents, their children, and other interested parties?

If alleged violations of a final or modified decree of dissolution can be the basis for this new cause of action, so also would be alleged violations of a temporary decree entered during the marriage. This specter of concurrent equity and law actions during the marriage should deeply concern us. Completion of expected discovery procedures may well seriously delay trial of many dissolution actions. Money-damage lawsuits between the parents or other family members would certainly reduce the likelihood of reconciliation, a vital concern whenever a petition for dissolution of marriage is filed. See Iowa Code §§598.16, .19 (1983)(providing for conciliation procedures and a ninety day pre-decree waiting period).

These actions are at law, providing the parties the right to trial by jury of the issues. When, if ever, will the emotional distress be considered *de minimis*. What if a parent seeks compensation for emotional injury resulting from one week without the children? What if a grandparent is deprived of visitation for one weekend, or one day?

These potential causes of action are mentioned here to show that little else but logic supports them. Although they seem at first blush to be logical extensions of the Restatement rule, the utility of such new varieties of domestic lawsuit would clearly be outweighed by unacceptable consequences for our court system and affected family members. Even though this court today has adopted the Restatement rule in deciding this case, we should hereafter be careful not to extend that rule beyond the specific facts here alleged by plaintiff.

II. I believe the practical adverse effect which the Restatement rule may have on our court system and family members should first be studied carefully by the Iowa legislature before it is accepted as part of our body of Iowa family law. The legislature is better equipped than this court to obtain empirical data, conduct a detailed study, and utilize what such a study reveals.

Our legislature has already demonstrated in several ways that it is actively concerned about domestic relations law in general and deterrence of child-snatching in particular. The 1981 Iowa General Assembly addressed and revised our laws governing children of distressed marriages, encouraging joint custody and liberal visitation rights while reaffirming that the polestar for decisionmaking should be the best interests of the child. Iowa Code §598.41 (1983).

Our legislature's concern for deterring child kidnapping has been manifested in the statutory remedies available to the custodial parent who is aggrieved by action of the non-custodial parent. The Uniform Child Custody Jurisdiction Act, adopted by our Legislature in 1977, provides a means for enforcing custody decrees across state lines and specifically permits the court to assess against a person violating an out-of-state custodial decree "necessary travel and other expenses, including attorney's fees, incurred by the party entitled to the custody or by that party's witnesses." Iowa Code §598A.15 (1983). Persons abducting minor children can be charged with criminal offenses under Iowa as well as federal criminal statutes. Iowa Code §§710.5, .6 (1983); 18 U.S.C. §1073 (1976 & Supp. IV 1980). Additionally, our legislature has codified the traditional action for contempt of court in domestic cases. A court may punish a person who violates a custodial order in a temporary or final decree by imposing a fine or jail sentence. Iowa Code §§598.23, 665.4 (1983); see *Wilson v. Fenton*, 312 N.W.2d 524, 527–29 (Iowa 1981).

We should have laws which deter parental child-snatching, and the Iowa legislature has already enacted laws designed to accomplish that purpose. The parent contemplating child-snatching faces tough civil, criminal, and contempt sanctions. The plaintiff in this case has not demonstrated that these existing remedies are inadequate. I suggest that the statutory remedies already available should be time-tested and shown clearly to be inadequate before we authorize trial by jury of what are essentially child custody issues.

III. Regardless whether it is more appropriate for the Iowa legislature or this court to accept or reject the Restatement rule, that decision should turn on whether such a lawsuit between family members is in the best interest of affected minor children. This court has consistently held that in child custody cases the first and governing consideration is the best interest of the child. Iowa R.App.P. 14(f)(15); *In Re Marriage of Winter*, 223 N.W.2d 165, 166 (Iowa 1974). The legislature has expressly so provided in several statutes. See *e.g.*, Iowa Code §§598.41(1), (3); 598A.1(1), .8(2)(1983).

The instant case, and others here discussed, would arise from the same domestic discord as child custody cases, would be generated by the same family circumstances as child custody cases, and would either run concurrently with such cases (in the event temporary orders are violated) or follow in their aftermath. What will be the likely effects on the children of money-damage lawsuits?

Again, a detailed legislative study would provide us far more insight than our limited personal experience and instincts. Lacking such a study, we should at least consider worst-case possibilities and predict likely effects.

Worst-case examples need not be imagined — they will certainly soon occur. The litigants in many of our decided cases have proved they can go to great lengths in battling for custody of their children. See, e.g., *In Re Marriage of Bevers*, 326 N.W.2d 896 (Iowa 1982); *In Re Marriage of Schoonover*, 228 N.W.2d 31 (Iowa 1975). The emotional injury in many of these Iowa cases was certainly great, as was the vigor and ingenuity of the attorneys. Parents and their counsel will certainly use this new weapon skillfully, if not always wisely.

Certain will be the right to jury trial. Surely, the children often will be called as witnesses, pressed to choose sides — for one parent and against the other. Is this not contrary to the recently-enacted statute which encourages not only the granting of joint custody but also liberal visitation rights "which will assure a minor child frequent and continuing contact with both parents after the parents have separated or dissolved the marriage..."? Iowa Code §598.41 (1983).

Certain will be the expense to the family unit of additional lawyers' fees and court costs. Monies needed for raising of children may often be sacrificed to the parents' continuing internecine struggle. Likely, too, will be prolonged bitterness among family members resulting from jury verdicts, whether damages be collected or denied.

I suggest that the Restatement rule is not only unneeded as a deterrent but also contrary to the best interests of most of the minor children who would be entangled in the litigation.

IV. Although some jurisdictions have adopted the Restatement rule, most have not yet addressed the issue. We would not be alone in holding that the rule should not be adopted by court decision. In *McGrady v. Rosenbaum*, 62 Misc.2d 182, 308 N.Y.S.2d 181 (1970), *aff'd* 37 A.D.2d 917, 324 N.Y.S.2d 876 (1970), the court refused to recognize a father's claim for damages based on the mother's alleged denial of his visitation rights. The court distinguished *Pickle v. Page*, 252 N.Y. 474, 169 N.E. 650 (1930), which involved abduction of a child from the custodial parent by a sheriff, then commented that "an action for damages or a damage verdict would probably be the least useful technique for the resolution of matrimonial differences or custody disputes." 308 N.Y.S.2d at 190. The court concluded:

> The remedy against a spouse who violates a court order respecting custody or visitation by removing the child from the state is by way of contempt or by precluding her standing to challenge the order or to enforce its support provisions, not by an action for damages.... Custody may be awarded to the father in an appropriate action, in such cases.... But this does not authorize damages.

308 N.Y.S.2d at 188. That New York decision was followed by *Friedman v. Friedman*, 79 Misc.2d 646, 361 N.Y.S.2d 108 (1974), in which the court quoted the above language from the *McGrady* opinion, distinguished other New York cases involving suit by the parents of infants against third parties, and held:

> It would appear, therefore, that as between the parents of the child, an action for damages for mental anguish resulting from interference with custodial rights is not actionable.

361 N.Y.S.2d at 110.

This court, like those two New York courts, should reject interspousal law actions for damages arising from violations of orders and decrees in dissolution actions. Our courts of equity should continue to address these serious problems for parents and their children without unduly burdening the law side of our crowded court dockets. Our courts can and should continue to deter child-snatching by encouraging speedy trial of criminal proceedings, imposing appropriate sanctions for contempt, and granting traditional forms of equitable relief when custodial orders are violated. The legislature, not this court, should decide whether new remedies are needed and, if so, whether such a cause of action as plaintiff here espouses is really in the best interest of our court system and, more importantly, the best interest of children whom their parents would involve in such litigation.

I would affirm the trial court's dismissal of this action.

HARRIS and McGIVERIN, JJ., join this dissent and McCORMICK, J., joins division I.

ROE v. DOE

Court of Appeals of New York

29 N.Y. 2d 188, 272 N.E.2d 567, 324 N.Y.S. 2d 71 (1971)

SCILEPPI, Judge.

It is a sad but telling commentary upon the relationship subsisting between father and daughter that resort to the courts was employed to resolve this domestic problem. The surge of adolescent independence, the breakdown in parental authority and the frustration attending both are indeed matters of common occurrence. Feelings was run high, idle threats may be uttered, but experience teaches us that such hostilities do abate and repprochements [sic] are soon effected. Aware that the law is no interloper in such intra-family problems, the courts, absent any violation of law, refuse to intervene, preferring to leave the parties where they find them, lest they undermine the integrity of the family.

Petitioner is the court-appointed guardian for a 20-year-old student at the University of Louisville who had been fully and generously supported by her father, a prominent New York attorney, until April of 1970. Afforded the opportunity of attending college away from home, and after living in the college dormitory for a time, the daughter, contrary to the father's prior instructions and without his knowledge, took up residence with a a female classmate in an off-campus apartment. Upon learning of this deception, the father cut off all further support and instructed her to return to New York.

Ignoring her father's demands, the daughter sold her automobile (an earlier gift from her father) and elected to finish out the school year, living off the proceeds realized upon the sale, some $1,000. During the following summer, the daughter enrolled in summer courses at the university and upon her return to New York chose to reside with the parents of a female classmate on Long Island. The family situation has been tense and somewhat less than stable. The daughter was three years old when her mother died and her father has remarried several times since, most recently in the spring of 1970. Academically, the daughter fared poorly, and was placed on academic probation during her freshman year; though, on a reduced credit work load, she has managed to improve her academic standing over the past year. She has experimented with drugs (LSD and marijuana), apparently without addiction. The girl has been comfortably maintained, and there is no real question about the father's ability to provide. Tuition payments, approximately $1,000 per semester, for the academic year 1970–71, are long past due and petitioner has commenced this support proceeding, alleging that the respondent has refused and neglected to provide fair and reasonable support.

The Family Court (Midonick, J.), entered two separate orders: a temporary order of support (August 21, 1970), requiring the father to remit a tuition payment for the then pending semester and to provide for reasonable medical, dental, eye and psychiatric care; and a final order of support (November 30, 1970), requiring that the father pay $250 per month in support for the period between December 1, 1970 and October 20, 1971, the daughter's twenty-first birthday. Respondent was found to have willfully failed to comply with the temporary order of support and was committed to jail for 30 days, the commitment to be stayed until December 28, 1970 and at that time vacated on condition that he post a cash bond in the sum of $5,750 covering his liability for support. The order of commitment was stayed pending appeal.

On appeal, the Appellate Division, 36 A.D.2d 162, 318 N.Y.S.2d 973, modified the temporary order, on the law and the facts and in the exercise of discretion, and directed that the father pay only those university and health bills actually rendered prior to November 30, 1970. The final order of November 30, 1970, requiring that the father pay $250 per month in support for the period between December 1, 1970 and October 20, 1971, the daughter's twenty-first birthday, plus tuition payments through the September, 1971 semester, was reversed on the law and the facts and in the exercise of discretion. As it is our conclusion that where, as in the case at bar, a minor of employable age and in full possession of her faculties, voluntarily and without cause, abandons the parent's home, against the will of the parent and for the purpose of avoiding parental control she forfeits her right to demand support, the order appealed from should be affirmed.

It has always been, and remains a matter of fundamental policy within this State, that a father of a minor child is chargeable with the discipline and support of that child and none would dispute that the obligation cannot be avoided merely because a young enough child is at odds with her parents or has disobeyed their instructions: delinquent behavior of itself, even if unexplained or persistent, does not generally carry with it the termination of the duty of a parent to support.

On the other hand, while the duty to support is a continuing one, the child's right to support and the parent's right to custody and services are reciprocal: the father in return for maintenance and support may establish and impose reasonable regulations for his child (cf. *Haskell v. Haskell*, 201 App.Div. 414, 194 N.Y.S. 28, aff'd. 236 N.Y. 635, 142 N.E. 314). Accordingly, though the question is novel in this State, it has been held, in circumstances such as here, that where by no fault on the parent's part, a child "voluntarily abandons the parent's home for the purpose of seeking its fortune in the world or to avoid parental discipline and restraint (that child) forfeits the claim to support" (67 C.J.S. Parent and Child §16, p. 699.... To hold otherwise would be to allow, at least in the case before us, a minor of employable age to deliberately flout the legitimate mandates of her father while requiring that the latter support her in her decision to place herself beyond his effective control.

It is the natural right, as well as the legal duty, of a parent to care for, control and protect his child from potential harm, whatever the source and absent a clear showing of misfeasance, abuse or neglect, courts should not interfere with that delicate responsibility. Here, the daughter, asserting her independence, chose to assume a status inconsistent with that of parental control. The Family Court set about establishing its own standards of decorum, and, having determined that those standards were met, sought to substitute its judgment for that of the father. Needless to say, the intrusion was unwarranted.

We do not have before us the case of a father who casts his helpless daughter upon the world, forcing her to fend for herself; nor has the father been arbitrary in his requests that the daughter heed his demands. The obligations of parenthood, under natural and civil law, require of the child "submission to reasonable restraint, and demands habits of propriety, obedience, and conformity to domestic discipline" (*Stant v. Lamberson*, 103 Ind.App. 411, 416–417, 8 N.E.2d 115, 117, *supra*). True, a minor, rather than submit to what her father considers to be proper discipline, may be induced to abandon the latter's home; but in so doing, however impatient of parental authority, she cannot enlist the aid of the court in frustrating that authority, reasonably exercised, by requiring that her father accede to her demands and underwrite her chosen lifestyle or as here, run the risk of incarceration.

Nor can we say that the father was unreasonable or capricious in his request that the daughter take up residence in the college dormitory or return to New York. In view of her past derelictions, and, to use the Appellate Division's words, "the temptations that abound outside," (36 A.D.2d 165, 318 N.Y.S.2d 975) we can only conclude that it was reasonable for her father to decide that it was in her own best interests that she do so. And the fact that the father doggedly persisted in his demands despite similar evils which may have lurked within the campus residence, or psychiatric advice that the daughter live off campus, cannot be said to amount to a showing of misconduct, neglect or abuse which would justify the Family Court's action. The father has the right, in the absence of caprice, misconduct or neglect, to require that the daughter conform to his reasonable demands. Should she disagree, and at her age that is surely her prerogative, she may elect not to comply; but in so doing, she subjects herself to her father's lawful wrath. Where, as here, she abandons her home, she forfeits her right to support.

The order appealed from should be affirmed.

[Concurring opinion omitted]

COMMENTS

The background assumption in *Wood v. Wood* — an assumption so obvious and taken for granted that the court barely needed to mention it — was that the power of the state will ordinarily be marshalled to enforce that children live in the custody of their parents. Although a court may for good cause take a child away from the custody of its parent, the child itself may not simply choose to live somewhere else. Run-away children are routinely returned to their parents with only a minimal inquiry as to the child's justification for leaving home. Third parties who try to help a run-away child are in general fully as subject to lawsuit as are third parties who seek to exploit or take advantage of a child. The only difficult question in *Wood* was whether the normal tort remedies available to parents in general should be allowed when it is the non-custodial father rather than any other third party who is interfering with the mother's legal custody.

The 1960s saw a gradual but important shift in the treatment of children. Increasingly children were treated as persons rather than chattels. Their wishes became an important factor to be considered in child custody matters. Although they still were not recognized as parties in interest in divorce litigation, and were not entitled to representation, some measure of due process was accorded to them in juvenile proceedings. Their status, especially if they were older, was transformed. They were considered juveniles or adolescents earlier, and their status changed again to "young adults" when they reached eighteen. Children increasingly asserted themselves and challenged the authority of their parents and the state. They demonstrated in the streets to secure Civil Rights and to end the war in Vietnam. Most observers conclude that this activity changed the course of national politics.

The state responded to these pressures, it appears, by lowering the age of majority. While this was part of the waning of parental rights, it can also be viewed in a different light. By treating children, almost overnight, as adults, parents acquired the legal power to "abandon" them at age eighteen, even if the young people still needed guidance and support. The state too, while surrendering its power as parens patriae, gained the legal means to treat the former children as adults, fully responsible for their acts, and subject to severe discipline and punishment. The rebellious children were, so to speak, thrown to the wolves. They had gained constitutional protections as persons, but the emphasis was still, as in the past, on their responsibilities and subservient status.

Considerable ambivalence toward children prevails in contemporary law. Even though they are viewed as "our most valued possession," children are also a continued source of frustration. In the past decades they have persistently challenged the values held by adults, for example, in sexual and political matters. Arguably, treating children as persons can become a vehicle of control by parents and the state in trying to curb the subversive powers of youths. By being made responsible as adults, youths are deprived of the opportunity to engage in forays into adult territory with the option of retreating afterward into the sanctuary of childhood if an attack from established forces makes this advisable. For example, lowering the age of majority to eighteen relieved parents of their obligation to support their offspring, and left it to their discretion whether, and in what form, to furnish financial or other assistance to their children who are admittedly not yet fully mature but have been legally declared adults. Thus the lower age of majority conveys a message of potential cruelty to young people and gives parents more power to tighten the purse strings.

Roe v. Doe illustrates the considerable power that parents have to control their children by withholding support, even before the child reaches the age of majority. The case also illustrates the kind of personal rebellion that bothered parents in the late 1960s and early 1970s. Of course, while the case would not arise with the lowered age of majority, the same situation could arise today in the case of a child under eighteen. Generally, while a family seems to the court to be intact, the judge will refuse to grant any relief to a child, claiming that courts should not intervene in the family. If the mother of the twenty-year-old in *Roe v. Doe* had not died but had divorced the father, the father would have been less able to use his power of the purse to control the daughter. In the case of a divorce, the non-custodial parent may have to support the child until eighteen or even twenty-one no matter how unruly the child seems, as long as the custodial parent does not object to the child's behavior.

In a positive vein, the lower age of majority emancipates children to the advanced position of young adults. Many young persons, of course, still get financial support and voluntary contributions from their parents to further their education. More often, however, young adults struggle for themselves and may look to their peers for moral and financial support. For instance, young men may receive support from young women with whom they cohabit or whom they marry while attending college. In these instances, legal problems continue to exist in transmuted form, for example, in the question of the extent to which such women, on termination of the relationship, are entitled to some form of compensation for their contributions to another's education while often having to defer their own (see *Morgan*, p. 95, *O'Brien*, p. 98, and *Downs*, p. 110). If marriage becomes a means of educational advancement of young men, financial support may sometimes devolve from young wives to their parents, who may feel inclined to invest in the future of a promising son-in-law. Leaving young adults to fend for themselves may therefore sometimes bring about results that legislatures and the judiciary did not foresee when they lowered the age of majority during the 1960s and early 1970s. Emancipation may occur at an even younger age if the child chooses to get married. Courts have been inclined to respond to sex-discriminatory age requirements for marriage by lowering the age to a common level for males and females. (See *Lovato v. Evans*, *supra* p. 514; *Phelps v. Bing*, 316 N.E.2d 775 (Ill. 1974).) Since marriage in most states also means legal emancipation, this may in effect lower the age of majority too.

Health: State Enforcement of Children's Rights

PARHAM v. J.R.

United States Supreme Court
442 U.S. 584 (1979)

Mr. Chief Justice BURGER delivered the opinion of the Court.

The question presented in this appeal is what process is constitutionally due a minor child whose parents or guardian seek state administered institutional mental health care for the child and specifically whether an adversary proceeding is required prior to or after the commitment.

...

III

...

The parties agree that our prior holdings have set out a general approach for testing challenged state procedures under a due process claim. Assuming the existence of a protectible property or liberty interest, the Court has required a balancing of a number of factors:

> First, the private interest that will be affected by the official action; second, the risk of an erroneous deprivation of such interest through the proce-

> dures used, and the probable value, if any, of additional or substitute procedural safeguards; and finally, the Government's interest, including the function involved and the fiscal and administrative burdens that the additional or substitute procedural requirement would entail....

...

Our jurisprudence historically has reflected Western civilization concepts of the family as a unit with broad parental authority over minor children. Our cases have consistently followed that course; our constitutional system long ago rejected any notion that a child is "the mere creature of the State" and, on the contrary, asserted that parents generally "have the right, coupled with the high duty, to recognize and prepare [their children] for additional obligations." *Pierce v. Society of Sisters*, 268 U.S. 510, 535, 45 S.Ct. 571, 573, 69 L.Ed. 1070 (1925). See also *Wisconsin v. Yoder*, 406 U.S. 205, 213, 92 S.Ct. 1526, 1532, 32 L.Ed.2d 15 (1972); *Prince v. Massachusetts*, 321 U.S. 158, 166, 64 S.Ct. 438, 442, 88 L.Ed. 645 (1944); *Meyer v. Nebraska*, 262 U.S. 390, 400, 43 S.Ct. 625, 627, 67 L.Ed. 1042 (1923). Surely, this includes a "high duty" to recognize symptoms of illness and to seek and follow medical advice. The law's concept of the family rests on a presumption that parents possess what a child lacks in maturity, experience, and capacity for judgment required for making life's difficult decisions. More important, historically it has recognized that natural bonds of affection lead parents to act in the best interests of their children. 1 W. Blackstone, Commentaries *447; 2 J. Kent, Commentaries on American Law *190.

As with so many other legal presumptions, experience and reality may rebut what the law accepts as a starting point; the incidence of child neglect and abuse cases attests to this. That some parents "may at times be acting against the interests of their children" as was stated in *Bartley v. Kremens*, 402 F.Supp. 1039, 1047–1048 (ED Pa. 1975), vacated and remanded, 431 U.S. 119, 97 S.Ct. 1709, 52 L.Ed.2d 184 (1977), creates a basis for caution, but is hardly a reason to discard wholesale those pages of human experience that teach that parents generally do act in the child's best interests.... The statist notion that governmental power should supersede parental authority in *all* cases because *some* parents abuse and neglect children is repugnant to American tradition.

Nonetheless, we have recognized that a state is not without constitutional control over parental discretion in dealing with children when their physical or mental health is jeopardized. See *Wisconsin v. Yoder, supra*, 406 U.S., at 230, 92 S.Ct., at 1540; *Prince v. Massachusetts, supra*, 321 U.S., at 166, 64 S.Ct., at 442. Moreover, the Court recently declared unconstitutional a state statute that granted parents an absolute veto over a minor child's decision to have an abortion. *Planned Parenthood of Central Missouri v. Danforth*, 428 U.S. 52, 96 S.Ct. 2831, 49 L.Ed.2d 788 (1976). Appellees urge that these precedents limiting the traditional rights of parents, if viewed in the context of the liberty interest of the child and the likelihood of parental abuse, require us to hold that the parents' decision to have a child admitted to a mental hospital must be subjected to an exacting constitutional scrutiny, including a formal, adversary, pre-admission hearing.

Appellees' argument, however, sweeps too broadly. Simply because the decision of a parent is not agreeable to a child or because it involves risks does not automatically transfer the power to make that decision from the parents to some agency or officer of the state. The same characterizations can be made for a tonsillectomy, appendectomy, or other medical procedure. Most children, even in adolescence, simply are not able to make sound judgments concerning many decisions, including their need for medical care or treatment. Parents can and must make those judgments. Here, there is no finding by the District Court of even a single instance of bad faith by any parent of any member of appellees' class. We cannot assume that the result in *Meyer v. Nebraska, supra,* and *Pierce v. Society of Sisters, supra,* would have been different if the children there had announced a preference to learn only English or a preference to go to a public, rather than a church, school. The fact that a child may balk at hospitalization or complain about a parental refusal to provide cosmetic surgery does not diminish the parents' authority to decide what is best for the child.... Neither state officials nor federal courts are equipped to review such parental decisions.

Appellees place particular reliance on *Planned Parenthood,* arguing that its holding indicates how little deference to parents is appropriate when the child is exercising a constitutional right. The basic situation in that case, however, was very different; *Planned Parenthood* involved an absolute parental veto over the child's ability to obtain an abortion. Parents in Georgia in no sense have an absolute right to commit their children to state mental hospitals; the statute requires the superintendent of each regional hospital to exercise independent judgment as to the child's need for confinement....

In defining the respective rights and prerogatives of the child and parent in the voluntary commitment setting, we conclude that our precedents permit the parents to retain a substantial, if not the dominant, role in the decision, absent a finding of neglect or abuse, and that the traditional presumption that the parents act in the best interests of their child should apply. We also conclude, however, that the child's rights and the nature of the commitment decision are such that parents cannot always have absolute and unreviewable discretion to decide whether to have a child institutionalized. They, of course, retain plenary authority to seek such care for their children, subject to a physician's independent examination and medical judgment.

...The State obviously has a significant interest in confining the use of its costly mental health facilities to cases of genuine need. The Georgia program seeks first to determine whether the patient seeking admission has an illness that calls for inpatient treatment. To accomplish this purpose, the State has charged the superintendents of each regional hospital with the responsibility for determining, before authorizing an admission, whether a prospective patient is mentally ill and whether the patient will likely benefit from hospital care. In addition, the State has imposed a continuing duty on hospital superintendents to release any patient who has recovered to the point where hospitalization is no longer needed.

The State in performing its voluntarily assumed mission also has a significant interest in not imposing unnecessary procedural obstacles that may discourage the mentally ill or their families from seeking needed psychiatric assistance....

The State also has a genuine interest in allocating priority to the diagnosis and treatment of patients as soon as they are admitted to a hospital rather than to time-consuming procedural minuets before the admission....

...

...We now turn to consideration of what process protects adequately the child's constitutional rights by reducing risks of error without unduly trenching on traditional parental authority and without undercutting "efforts to further the legitimate interests of both the state and the patient that are served by" voluntary commitments.... We conclude that the risk of error inherent in the parental decision to have a child institutionalized for mental health care is sufficiently great that some kind of inquiry should be made by a "neutral factfinder" to determine whether the statutory requirements for admission are satisfied.... That inquiry must carefully probe the child's background using all available sources, including, but not limited to, parents, schools, and other social agencies. Of course, the review must also include an interview with the child. It is necessary that the decisionmaker have the authority to refuse to admit any child who does not satisfy the medical standards for admission. Finally, it is necessary that the child's continuing need for commitment be reviewed periodically by a similarly independent procedure.

We are satisfied that such procedures will protect the child from an erroneous admission decision in a way that neither unduly burdens the states nor inhibits parental decisions to seek state help.

Due process has never been thought to require that the neutral and detached trier of fact be law trained or a judicial or administrative officer.... Surely, this is the case as to medical decisions, for "neither judges nor administrative hearing officers are better qualified than psychiatrists to render psychiatric judgments." *In re Roger S.*, 19 Cal.3d 921, 942, 141 Cal.Rptr. 298, 311, 569 P.2d 1286, 1299 (1977)(Clark, J., dissenting). Thus, a staff physician will suffice, so long as he or she is free to evaluate independently the child's mental and emotional condition and need for treatment.

It is not necessary that the deciding physician conduct a formal or quasi-formal hearing.... What is best for a child is an individual medical decision that must be left to the judgment of physicians in each case. We do no more than emphasize that the decision should represent an independent judgment of what the child requires and that all sources of information that are traditionally relied on by physicians and behavioral specialists should be consulted.

...

Here, the questions are essentially medical in character: whether the child is mentally or emotionally ill and whether he can benefit from the treatment that is provided by the state. While facts are plainly necessary for a proper resolution of those questions, they are only a first step in the process....

Although we acknowledge the fallibility of medical and psychiatric diagnosis, ...we do not accept the notion that the shortcomings of specialists can always be avoided by shifting the decision from a trained specialist using the traditional tools of medical science to an untrained judge or administrative hearing officer after a judicial-type hearing. Even after a hearing, the nonspecialist decision-maker must make a medical-psychiatric decision. Common human experience and scholarly opinions suggest that the supposed protections of an adversary proceeding to determine the appropriateness of medical decisions for the commitment and treatment of mental and emotional illness may well be more illusory than real....

Another problem with requiring a formalized, factfinding hearing lies in the danger it poses for significant intrusion into the parent-child relationship. Pitting the parents and child as adversaries often will be at odds with the presumption that parents act in the best interests of their child. It is one thing to require a neutral physician to make a careful review of the parents' decision in order to make sure it is proper from a medical standpoint; it is a wholly different matter to employ an adversary contest to ascertain whether the parents' motivation is consistent with the child's interests.

Moreover, it is appropriate to inquire into how such a hearing would contribute to the successful long-range treatment of the patient. Surely, there is a risk that it would exacerbate whatever tensions already exist between the child and the parents. Since the parents can and usually do play a significant role in the treatment while the child is hospitalized and even more so after release, there is a serious risk that an adversary confrontation will adversely affect the ability of the parents to assist the child while in the hospital. Moreover, it will make his subsequent return home more difficult. These unfortunate results are especially critical with an emotionally disturbed child; they seem likely to occur in the context of an adversary hearing in which the parents testify. A confrontation over such intimate family relationships would distress the normal adult parents and the impact on a disturbed child almost certainly would be significantly greater.

It has been suggested that a hearing conducted by someone other than the admitting physician is necessary in order to detect instances where parents are "guilty of railroading their children into asylums" or are using "voluntary commitment procedures in order to sanction behavior of which they disapprov[e]." Ellis, *Volunteering Children: Parental Commitment of Minors to Mental Institutions*, 62 Calif.L.Rev. 840, 850–851 (1974).... Curiously, it seems to be taken for granted that parents who seek to "dump" their children on the state will inevitably be able to conceal their motives and thus deceive the admitting psychiatrists and the other mental health professionals who make and review the admission decision. It is elementary that one early diagnostic inquiry into the cause of an emotional disturbance of a child is an examination into the environment of the child. It is unlikely, if not inconceivable, that a decision to abandon an emotionally normal, healthy child and thrust him into an institution will be a discrete act leaving no trail of circumstances. Evidence of such conflicts will emerge either in the interviews or from secondary sources. It is unrealistic to believe that trained psychiatrists, skilled in eliciting responses, sorting medically relevant facts, and sensing motivational nuances will often be deceived about the family situation surrounding a child's emotional disturbance. Surely a lay, or even law-trained, factfinder would be no more skilled in this process than the professional.

By expressing some confidence in the medical decisionmaking process, we are by no means suggesting it is error free. On occasion, parents may initially mislead an admitting physician or a physician may erroneously diagnose the child as needing institutional care either because of negligence or an overabundance of caution. That there may be risks of error in the process affords no rational predicate for holding unconstitutional an entire statutory and administrative scheme that is generally followed in more than 30 states. "[P]rocedural due process rules are shaped by the risk of error inherent in the truthfinding process as applied to the generality of cases, not the rare exceptions." *Mathews v. Eldridge*, 424 U.S., at 344, 96 S.Ct., at 907. In general, we are satisfied that an independent medical decisionmaking process, which includes the thorough psychiatric investigation described earlier, followed by additional periodic review of a child's condition, will protect children who should not be admitted; we do not believe the risks of error in that process would be significantly reduced by a more formal, judicial-type hearing....

...

In the typical case, the parents of a child initially conclude from the child's behavior that there is some emotional problem — in short, that "something is wrong." They may respond to the problem in various ways, but generally the first contact with the State occurs when they bring the child to be examined by a psychologist or psychiatrist at a community mental health clinic.

Most often, the examination is followed by outpatient treatment at the community clinic. In addition, the child's parents are encouraged, and sometimes required, to participate in a family therapy program to obtain a better insight into the problem. In most instances, this is all the care a child requires. However, if, after a period of outpatient care, the child's abnormal emotional condition persists, he may be referred by the local clinic staff to an affiliated regional mental hospital.

At the regional hospital an admissions team composed of a psychiatrist and at least one other mental health professional examines and interviews the child — privately in most instances. This team then examines the medical records provided by the clinic staff and interviews the parents. Based on this information, and any additional background that can be obtained, the admissions team makes a diagnosis and determines whether the child will likely benefit from institutionalized care. If the team finds either condition not met, admission is refused.

If the team admits a child as suited for hospitalization, the child's condition and continuing need for hospital care are reviewed periodically by at least one independent, medical review group. For the most part, the reviews are as frequent as weekly, but none are less often than once every two months. Moreover, as we noted earlier, the superintendent of each hospital is charged with an affirmative statutory duty to discharge any child who is no longer mentally ill or in need of therapy.

...

Although our review of the record in this case satisfies us that Georgia's general administrative and statutory scheme for the voluntary commitment of children is not *per se* unconstitutional, we cannot decide on this record, whether every child in appellees' class received an adequate, independent diagnosis of his emotional condition and need for confinement under the standards announced earlier in this opinion. On remand, the District Court is free to and should consider any individual claims that initial admissions did not meet the standards we have described in this opinion.

...

IV

...Our discussion in Part III was directed at the situation where a child's natural parents request his admission to a state mental hospital. Some members of appellees' class, including J. R., were wards of the State of Georgia at the time of their admission. Obviously their situation differs from those members of the class who have natural parents. While the determination of what process is due varies somewhat when the state, rather than a natural parent, makes the request for commitment, we conclude that the differences in the two situations do not justify requiring different procedures at the time of the child's initial admission to the hospital.

For a ward of the state, there may well be no adult who knows him thoroughly and who cares for him deeply. Unlike with natural parents where there is a presumed natural affection to guide their action, 1 W. Blackstone, Commentaries *447; 2 J. Kent, Commentaries on American Law *190, the presumption that the state will protect a child's general welfare stems from a specific state statute. Ga.Code §24A-101 (1978). Contrary to the suggestion of the dissent, however, we cannot assume that when the State of Georgia has custody of a child it acts so differently from a natural parent in seeking medical assistance for the child. No one has questioned the validity of the statutory presumption that the State acts in the child's best interest. Nor could such a challenge be mounted on the record before us. There is no evidence that the State, acting as guardian, attempted to admit any child for reasons unrelated to the child's need for treatment. Indeed, neither the District Court nor the appellees have suggested that wards of the State should receive any constitutional treatment different from children with natural parents.

Once we accept that the State's application for a child's admission to a hospital is made in good faith, then the question is whether the medical decisionmaking approach of the admitting physician is adequate to satisfy due process. We have already recognized that an independent medical judgment made from the perspective of the best interests of the child after a careful investigation is an acceptable means of justifying a voluntary commitment. We do not believe that the soundness of this decisionmaking is any the less reasonable in this setting.

Indeed, if anything, the decision with regard to wards of the State may well be even more reasonable in light of the extensive written records that are compiled about each child while in the State's custody. In J. R.'s case, the admitting physician had a complete social and medical history of the child before even beginning the diagnosis. After carefully interviewing him and reviewing his extensive files, three physicians independently concluded that institutional care was in his best interests....

Since the state agency having custody and control of the child *in loco parentis* has a duty to consider the best interests of the child with respect to a decision on commitment to a mental hospital, the State may constitutionally allow that custodial agency to speak for the child, subject, of course, to the restrictions governing natural parents. On this record, we cannot declare unconstitutional Georgia's admission procedures for wards of the State.

...

The absence of an adult who cares deeply for a child has little effect on the reliability of the initial admission decision, but it may have some effect on how long a child will remain in the hospital. We noted in *Addington v. Texas*, 141 U.S., at 428–429, 99 S.Ct., at 1811, that "the concern of family and friends generally will provide continuous opportunities for an erroneous commitment to be corrected." For a child without natural parents, we must acknowledge the risk of being "lost in the shuffle." Moreover, there is at least some indication that J. R.'s commitment was prolonged because the Department of Family and Children Services had difficulty finding a foster home for him. Whether wards of the State generally have received less protection than children with natural parents, and, if so, what should be done about it, however, are matters that must be decided in the first instance by the District Court on remand....

...

On this record, we are satisfied that Georgia's medical factfinding processes are reasonable and consistent with constitutional guarantees. Accordingly, it was error to hold unconstitutional the State's procedures for admitting a child for treatment to a state mental hospital. The judgment is therefore reversed, and the case is remanded to the District Court for further proceedings consistent with this opinion.

Reversed and remanded.

Mr. Justice STEWART, concurring in the judgment.

For centuries it has been a canon of the common law that parents speak for their minor children. So deeply imbedded in our traditions is this principle of law that the Constitution itself may compel a State to respect it. *Meyer v. Nebraska*, 262 U.S. 390, 43 S.Ct. 625, 67 L.Ed. 1042; *Pierce v. Society of Sisters*, 268 U.S. 510, 45 S.Ct. 571, 69 L.Ed. 1070. In ironic contrast, the District Court in this case has said that the Constitution requires the State of Georgia to disregard this established principle. I cannot agree.

...

...[T]he basic question in this case is whether the Constitution requires Georgia to ignore basic principles so long accepted by our society. For only if the State in this setting is constitutionally compelled always to intervene between parent and child can there be any question as to the constitutionally required extent of that intervention. I believe this basic question must be answered in the negative.

Under our law, parents constantly make decisions for their minor children that deprive the children of liberty, and sometimes even of life itself. Yet surely the Fourteenth Amendment is not invoked when an informed parent decides upon major surgery for his child, even in a state hospital. I can perceive no basic constitutional differences between commitment to a mental hospital and other parental decisions that result in a child's loss of liberty.

I realize, of course, that a parent's decision to commit his child to a state mental institution results in a far greater loss of liberty than does his decision to have an appendectomy performed upon the child in a state hospital. But if, contrary to my belief, this factual difference rises to the level of a constitutional difference, then I believe that the objective checks upon the parents' commitment decision, embodied in Georgia law...are more than constitutionally sufficient.

To be sure, the presumption that a parent is acting in the best interests of his child must be a rebuttable one, since certainly not all parents are actuated by the unselfish motive the law presumes. Some parents are simply unfit parents. But Georgia clearly provides that an unfit parent can be stripped of his parental authority under laws dealing with neglect and abuse of children.

This is not an easy case. Issues involving the family and issues concerning mental illness are among the most difficult that courts have to face, involving as they often do serious problems of policy disguised as questions of constitutional law. But when a state legislature makes a reasonable definition of the age of minority, and creates a rebuttable presumption that in invoking the statutory procedures for voluntary commitment a parent is acting in the best interests of his minor child, I cannot believe that the Fourteenth Amendment is violated. This is not to say that in this area the Constitution compels a State to respect the traditional authority of a parent, as in the *Meyer* and *Pierce* cases. I believe, as in *Prince v. Massachusetts*, 321 U.S. 158, 64 S.Ct. 438, 88 L.Ed. 645, that the Constitution would tolerate intervention by the State. But that is a far cry from holding that such intervention is constitutionally compelled.

For these reasons I concur in the judgment.

Mr. Justice BRENNAN, with whom Mr. Justice MARSHALL and Mr. Justice STEVENS join, concurring in part and dissenting in part.

I agree with the Court that the commitment of juveniles to state mental hospitals by their parents or by state officials acting *in loco parentis* involves state action that impacts upon constitutionally protected interests and therefore must be accomplished through procedures consistent with the constitutional mandate of due process of law. I agree also that the District Court erred in interpreting the Due Process clause to require preconfinement commitment hearings in all cases in which parents wish to hospitalize their children. I disagree, however, with the Court's decision to pretermit questions concerning the postadmission procedures due Georgia's institutionalized juveniles. While the question of the frequency of postadmission review hearings may properly be deferred, the right to at least one postadmission hearing can and should be affirmed now. I also disagree with the Court's conclusion concerning the procedures due juvenile wards of the State of Georgia. I believe that the Georgia statute is unconstitutional in that it fails to accord preconfinement hearings to juvenile wards of the State committed by the State acting *in loco parentis.*

I. Rights of Children Committed to Mental Institutions

Commitment to a mental institution necessarily entails a "massive curtailment of liberty," *Humphrey v. Cady*, 405 U.S. 504, 509, 92 S.Ct. 1048, 1052, 31 L.Ed.2d 394 (1972), and inevitably affects "fundamental rights." *Baxstrom v. Herold*, 383 U.S. 107, 113, 86 S.Ct. 760, 764, 15 L.Ed.2d 620 (1966). Persons incarcerated in mental hospitals are not only deprived of their physical liberty, they are also deprived of friends, family, and community. Institutionalized mental patients must live in unnatural surroundings under the continuous and detailed control of strangers. They are subject to intrusive treatment which, especially if unwarranted, may violate their right to bodily integrity. Such treatment modalities may include forced administration of psychotropic medication, aversive conditioning, convulsive therapy, and even psychosurgery. Furthermore, as the Court recognizes, see *ante*, at 2503, persons confined in mental institutions are stigmatized as sick and abnormal during confinement and, in some cases, even after release.

Because of these considerations, our cases have made clear that commitment to a mental hospital "is a deprivation of liberty which the State cannot accomplish without due process of law." *O'Connor v. Donaldson*, 422 U.S. 563, 580, 95 S.Ct. 2486, 2496, 45 L.Ed.2d 396 (1975)(BURGER, C. J., concurring).... In the absence of a voluntary, knowing, and intelligent waiver, adults facing commitment to mental institutions are entitled to full and fair adversary hearings in which the necessity for their commitment is established to the satisfaction of a neutral tribunal. At such hearings they must be accorded the right to "be present with counsel, have an opportunity to be heard, be confronted with witnesses against [them], have the right to cross-examine, and to offer evidence of [their] own." *Specht v. Patterson*, [386 U.S. 605,] 610.

These principles also govern the commitment of children. "Constitutional rights do not mature and come into being magically only when one attains the state-defined age of majority. Minors as well as adults are protected by the Constitution and possess constitutional rights...." *Planned Parenthood of Central Missouri v. Danforth*, 428 U.S. 52, 74 (1976).

Indeed, it may well be argued that children are entitled to more protection than are adults. The consequences of an erroneous commitment decision are more tragic where children are involved. Children, on the average, are confined for longer periods than are adults. Moreover, childhood is a particularly vulnerable time of life and children erroneously institutionalized during their formative years may bear the scars for the rest of their lives. Furthermore, the provision of satisfactory institutionalized mental care for children generally requires a substantial financial commitment that too often has not been forthcoming. Decisions of the lower courts have chronicled the inadequacies of existing mental health facilities for children....

In addition, the chances of an erroneous commitment decision are particularly great where children are involved. Even under the best of circumstances psychiatric diagnosis and therapy decisions are fraught with uncertainties.... These uncertainties are aggravated when, as under the Georgia practice, the psychiatrist interviews the child during a period of abnormal stress in connection with the commitment, and without adequate time or opportunity to become acquainted with the patient. These uncertainties may be further aggravated when economic and social class separate doctor and child, thereby frustrating the accurate diagnosis of pathology.

...

II. Rights of Children Committed by Their Parents

A

Notwithstanding all this, Georgia denies hearings to juveniles institutionalized at the behest of their parents. Georgia rationalizes this practice on the theory that parents act in their children's best interests and therefore may waive their children's due process rights. Children incarcerated because their parents wish them confined, Georgia contends, are really voluntary patients. I cannot accept this argument.

In our society, parental rights are limited by the legitimate rights and interests of their children. "Parents may be free to be become martyrs themselves. But it does not follow they are free, in identical circumstances, to make martyrs of their children before they have reached the age of full and legal discretion when they can make that choice for themselves." *Prince v. Massachusetts*, 321 U.S. 158, 170, 64 S.Ct. 438, 444, 88 L.Ed. 645 (1944). This principle is reflected in the variety of statutes and cases that authorize state intervention on behalf of neglected or abused children[16] and that, *inter alia*, curtail parental authority to alienate their children's property, to withhold necessary medical treatment, and to deny children exposure to ideas and experiences they may later need as independent and autonomous adults.

This principle is also reflected in constitutional jurisprudence. Notions of parental authority and family autonomy cannot stand as absolute and invariable barriers to the assertion of constitutional rights by children. States, for example, may not condition a minor's right to secure an abortion on attaining her parents' consent since the right to an abortion is an important personal right and since disputes between parents and children on this question would fracture family autonomy. See *Planned Parenthood of Central Missouri v. Danforth*, 428 U.S., at 75, 96 S.Ct., at 2844.

This case is governed by the rule of *Danforth*. The right to be free from wrongful incarceration, physical intrusion, and stigmatization has significance for the individual surely as great as the right to an abortion. Moreover, as in *Danforth*, the parent-child dispute at issue here cannot be characterized as involving only a routine child-rearing decision made within the context of an ongoing family relationship. Indeed, *Danforth* involved only a potential dispute between parent and

16. See generally S. Katz, WHEN PARENTS FAIL (1971); M. Midonick & D. Besharov, CHILDREN, PARENTS AND THE COURTS: JUVENILE DELINQUENCY, UNGOVERNABILITY, AND NEGLECT (1972); Wald, *State Intervention on Behalf of "Neglected" Children: A Search for Realistic Standards*, 27 STAN.L.REV. 985 (1975).

child, whereas here a break in family autonomy has actually resulted in the parents' decision to surrender custody of their child to a state mental institution. In my view, a child who has been ousted from his family has even greater need for an independent advocate.

Additional considerations counsel against allowing parents unfettered power to institutionalize their children without cause or without any hearing to ascertain that cause. The presumption that parents act in their children's best interests, while applicable to most child-rearing decisions, is not applicable in the commitment context. Numerous studies reveal that parental decisions to institutionalize their children often are the results of dislocation in the family unrelated to the children's mental condition. Moreover, even well-meaning parents lack the expertise necessary to evaluate the relative advantages and disadvantages of inpatient as opposed to outpatient psychiatric treatment. Parental decisions to waive hearings in which such questions could be explored, therefore, cannot be conclusively deemed either informed or intelligent. In these circumstances, I respectfully suggest, it ignores reality to assume blindly that parents act in their children's best interests when making commitment decisions and when waiving their children's due process rights.

B

This does not mean States are obliged to treat children who are committed at the behest of their parents in precisely the same manner as other persons who are involuntarily committed. The demands of due process are flexible and the parental commitment decision carries with it practical implications that States may legitimately take into account. While as a general rule due process requires that commitment hearings precede involuntary hospitalization, when parents seek to hospitalize their children special considerations militate in favor of postponement of formal commitment proceedings and against mandatory adversary preconfinement commitment hearings.

First, the prospect of an adversary hearing prior to admission might deter parents from seeking needed medical attention for their children. Second, the hearings themselves might delay treatment of children whose home life has become impossible and who require some form of immediate state care. Furthermore, because adversary hearings at this juncture would necessarily involve direct challenges to parental authority, judgment, or veracity, preadmission hearings may well result in pitting the child and his advocate against the parents. This, in turn, might traumatize both parent and child and make the child's eventual return to his family more difficult.

Because of these special considerations, I believe that States may legitimately postpone formal commitment proceedings when parents seek inpatient psychiatric treatment for their children. Such children may be admitted, for a limited period, without prior hearing, so long as the admitting psychiatrist first interviews parent and child and concludes that short-term inpatient treatment would be appropriate.

Georgia's present admission procedures are reasonably consistent with these principles.... To the extent the District Court invalidated this aspect of the Georgia juvenile commitment scheme and mandated preconfinement hearings in all cases, I agree with the Court that the District Court was in error.

...

IV

Children incarcerated in public mental institutions are constitutionally entitled to a fair opportunity to contest the legitimacy of their confinement. They are entitled to some champion who can speak on their behalf and who stands ready to oppose a wrongful commitment. Georgia should not be permitted to deny that opportunity and that champion simply because the children's parents or guardians wish them to be confined without a hearing. The risk of erroneous commitment is simply too great unless there is some form of adversary review. And fairness demands that children abandoned by their supposed protectors to the rigors of institutional confinement be given the help of some separate voice.

Guardianship of PHILLIP B.
Court of Appeal, First District
139 Cal.App.3d 407, 188 Cal.Rptr. 781 (1983)

RACANELLI, Presiding Justice.

Few human experiences evoke the poignancy of a filial relationship and the pathos attendant upon its disruption in society's effort to afford every child a meaningful chance to live life to its fullest promise. This appeal, posing a sensitive confrontation between the fundamental right of parental custody and the well being of a retarded child, reflects the deeply ingrained concern that the needs of the child remain paramount in the judicial monitoring of custody. In reaching our decision to affirm, we neither suggest nor imply that appellants' subjectively motivated custodial objectives affront conventional norms of parental fitness; rather, we determine only that on the unusual factual record before us, the challenged order of guardianship must be upheld in order to avert potential harm to the minor ward likely to result from appellants' continuing custody and to subserve his best interests.

...

On February 23, 1981, respondents Herbert and Patsy H. filed a petition for appointment as guardians of the person and estate of Phillip B., then 14 years of age. Phillip's parents, appellants Warren and Patricia B., appeared in opposition to the petition.

On August 7, 1981, following a 12-day trial, the trial court filed a lengthy memorandum of decision ordering — inter alia — 1) the issuance of letters of guardianship to respondents with authority to permit a heart catheterization to be performed on Phillip, and 2) the immediate delivery (by appellants) of Phillip to the Sheriff and Juvenile Authority of Santa Clara County. That same day appellants filed a notice of appeal from both orders[1] followed by a petition to this court for a writ of supersedeas which we summarily denied.

On August 20, 1981, the California Supreme Court granted appellants' petition for hearing, stayed the trial court's order authorizing heart catheterization and retransferred the cause to this court with directions to issue an order to show cause why a writ of supersedeas should not issue.

Meanwhile, on September 24, the trial court filed formal findings of fact and conclusions of law and entered a "final order" confirming issuance of letters of

1. Although the order granting guardianship is expressly appealable (Prob.Code, §2750, subd. (a)), the order requiring delivery of Phillip to local authorities is non-appealable; accordingly, the purported appeal from the latter order must be dismissed. (See Code Civ.Proc., §904.1, subd. (k); Prob.Code, §2750.)

guardianship and authorizing a heart catheterization. A second notice of appeal specifying both orders was thereafter filed by appellants.[2]

On October 19, 1981, we again denied supersedeas in an unpublished opinion.

On November 18, 1981, the California Supreme Court granted a second petition for hearing, issued its writ of supersedeas limited to the trial court's orders of August 7 and September 24 "insofar as they give authority for a heart catheterization upon Phillip B.," and retransferred the cause to this court for determination of the merits of the appeal upon the completed record and full briefing. Thereafter, the matter was duly argued and submitted for decision.

Appellants raise several claims of reversible error relating to the sufficiency of evidence to support the findings, the admissibility of certain evidence and procedural due process. For the reasons which we explain, we find no error as claimed and affirm the order or judgment appealed....

...

Phillip B. was born on October 16, 1966, with Down's Syndrome, a chromosomal anomaly — usually the presence of an extra chromosome attached to the number 21 pair — resulting in varying degrees of mental retardation and a number of abnormal physical characteristics. Down's Syndrome reportedly occurs in approximately 1/10 of 1 percent of live births.

Appellants, deeply distraught over Phillip's disability, decided upon institutionalization, a course of action recommended by a state social worker and approved by appellants' pediatrician. A few days later, Phillip was transferred from the hospital to a licensed board and care facility for disabled youngsters. Although the facility was clean, it offered no structured educational or developmental programs and required that all the children (up to 8 years of age) sleep in cribs. Appellants initially visited Phillip frequently; but soon their visits became less frequent and they became more detached from him.

When Phillip was three years old a pediatrician informed appellants that Phillip had a congenital heart defect, a condition afflicting half of Down's Syndrome children. (Smith & Wilson, [The Child With Down's Syndrome (Mongolism)(1973)], p. 41.) Open heart surgery was suggested when Phillip attained age six. However, appellants took no action to investigate or remedy the suspected medical problem.

After the board and care facility had been sold during the summer of 1971, appellants discovered that the condition of the facility had seriously deteriorated under the new management; it had become dirty and cluttered with soiled clothing, and smelled strongly of urine. Phillip was very thin and listless and was being fed watery oatmeal from a bottle. At appellants' request, a state social worker arranged for Phillip's transfer in January, 1972, to We Care, a licensed residential facility for developmentally disabled children located in San Jose, where he remained up to the time of trial.

At that time, the facility — which cared for about 20 children more severely handicapped than Phillip — operated under very limited conditions: it had no programs of education or therapy; the children were not enrolled in outside programs; the facility lacked an outdoor play area; the building was in poor repair; and the kitchen had only a two-burner hot plate used to cook pureed food.

2. Since neither the findings nor conclusions are appealable under the provisions of the Probate Code, the purported appeal from that order must likewise be dismissed. (See Code Civ.Proc., §904.1, subd. (k); Prob.Code, §2750.)

In April 1972, We Care employed Jeanne Haight (later to become program director and assistant administrator of the facility) to organize a volunteer program. Mrs. Haight quickly noticed Phillip's debilitated condition. She found him unusually small and thin for his age (five); he was not toilet trained and wore diapers, still slept in a crib, walked like a toddler, and crawled down stairs only inches high. His speech was limited and mostly unintelligible; his teeth were in poor condition.

Mrs. Haight, who undertook a recruitment program for volunteers, soon recruited respondent Patsy H., who had helped to found a school for children with learning disabilities where Mrs. Haight had once been vice-principal. Mrs. H. began working at We Care on a daily basis. Her husband, respondent Herbert H., and their children, soon joined in the volunteer activities.

Mrs. H., initially assigned to work with Phillip and another child, assisted Phillip in experimenting with basic sensory experiences, improving body coordination, and in overcoming his fear of steps. Mr. H. and one of the H. children helped fence the yard area, put in a lawn, a sandbox, and install some climbing equipment.

Mrs. Haight promptly initiated efforts to enroll Phillip in a preschool program for the fall of 1972, which required parental consent.[4] She contacted Mr. B. who agreed to permit Phillip to participate provided learning aptitude could be demonstrated. Mrs. H. used vocabulary cards to teach Phillip 25 to 50 new words and to comprehend word association. Although Mr. B. failed to appear at the appointed time in order to observe what Phillip had learned, he eventually gave his parental consent enabling Phillip to attend Hope Preschool in October, 1972.

Respondents continued working with Phillip coordinating their efforts with his classroom lessons. Among other things, they concentrated on development of feeding skills and toilet training and Mr. H. and the two eldest children gradually became more involved in the volunteer program.

Phillip subsequently attended a school for the trainable mentally retarded (TMR) where the children are taught basic survival words. They are capable of learning to feed and dress themselves appropriately, doing basic community activities such as shopping, and engaging in recreational activities. There is no attempt to teach them academics, and they are expected to live in sheltered settings as adults. In contrast, children capable of attending classes for the educable mentally retarded (EMR) are taught reading, writing, and simple computation, with the objective of developing independent living skills as adults.

A pattern of physical and emotional detachment from their son was developed by appellants over the next several years. In contrast, during the same period, respondents established a close and caring relationship with Phillip. Beginning in December, 1972, Phillip became a frequent visitor at respondents' home; with appellants' consent, Phillip was permitted to spend weekends with respondents, a practice which continued regularly and often included weekday evenings. At the same time, respondents maintained frequent contact with Phillip at We Care as regular volunteer visitors. Meanwhile, appellants visited Phillip at the facility only a few times a year; however, no overnight home visits occurred until after the underlying litigation ensued.

---

4. Apparently, Phillip had received no formal preschool education for the retarded even though such training programs were available in the community. Expert testimony established that early introduction to preschool training is of vital importance in preparing a retarded child for entry level public education.

Respondents played an active role in Phillip's behavioral development and educational training. They consistently supplemented basic skills training given Phillip at We Care.[5]

Phillip was openly accepted as a member of the H. family whom he came to love and trust. He eventually had his own bedroom; he was included in sharing household chores. Mr. H. set up a workbench for Phillip and helped him make simple wooden toys; they attended special Boy Scout meetings together. And Phillip regularly participated in family outings. Phillip referred to the H. residence as "my house." When Phillip began to refer to the H. as "Mom" and "Dad," they initially discouraged the familiar reference, eventually succeeding in persuading Phillip to use the discriminate references "Mama Pat" and "Dada Bert" and "Mama B." and "Daddy B."[6] Both Mrs. Haight and Phillip's teacher observed significant improvements in Phillip's development and behavior. Phillip had developed, in Mrs. Haight's opinion, "true love and strong [emotional] feelings" for respondents.

Meanwhile, appellants continued to remain physically and emotionally detached from Phillip. The natural parents intellectualized their decision to treat Phillip differently from their other children. Appellants testified that Phillip, whom they felt would always require institutionalization, should not be permitted to form close emotional attachments which — upon inevitable disruption — would traumatize the youngster.

In matters of Phillip's health care needs, appellants manifested a reluctant — if not neglectful — concern. When Dr. Gathman, a pediatric cardiologist, diagnosed a ventricular septal defect[7] in Phillip's heart in early 1973 and recommended catheterization (a medically accepted pre-surgery procedure to measure pressure and to examine the interior of the heart), appellants refused their consent.

In the spring of 1977, Dr. Gathman again recommended heart catheterization in connection with the anticipated use of general anesthesia during Phillip's major dental surgery. Appellants consented to the pre-operative procedure which revealed that the heart defect was surgically correctable with a maximum risk factor of 5 percent. At a conference attended by appellants and Mrs. Haight in June, 1977, Dr. Gathman recommended corrective surgery in order to avoid a progressively deteriorating condition resulting in a "bed-to-chair existence" and the probability of death before the age of 30.[8] Although Dr. Gathman — as requested by Mrs. B. — supplied the name of a parent of Down's Syndrome children with similar heart disease, no contact was ever made. Later that summer, appellants decided — without obtaining an independent medical consultation — against surgery. Appellants' stated reason was that Dr. Gathman had "painted" an inaccurate picture of the situation. They felt that surgery would be merely life-prolonging rather than life-saving, presenting the possibility that they would be unable to care for Phillip during his later years.[9] A few months later, in early 1978,

5. In addition to their efforts to improve Phillip's communication and reading skills through basic sign language and word association exercises, respondents toilet-trained Phillip and taught him to use eating utensils and to sleep in a regular bed (the latter frequently monitored during the night).

6. At respondents' suggestion, Mrs. Haight requested a photograph of appellants to show Phillip who his parents were; but appellants failed to provide one.

7. The disease, found in a large number of Down's Syndrome children..., consists of an opening or "hole" between the heart chambers resulting in elevated blood pressure and impairment of vascular functions. The disease can become a progressive, and ultimately fatal, disorder.

8. Dr. Gathman's explicit description of the likely ravages of the disease created anger and distrust on the part of appellants and motivated them to seek other opinions and to independently assess the need for surgery.

9. Oddly, Mr. B. expressed no reluctance in the hypothetical case of surgery for his other two sons if they had the "same problem," justifying the distinction on the basis of Phillip's retardation.

appellants' decision was challenged in a juvenile dependency proceeding initiated by the district attorney on the ground that the withholding of surgery constituted neglect within the meaning of Welfare and Institutions Code section 300, subdivision (b); the juvenile court's dismissal of the action on the basis of inconclusive evidence was ultimately sustained on appeal (*In re Phillip B.* (1979) 92 Cal.App.3d 796, 156 Cal.Rptr. 48, *cert. den. sub nom. Bothman v. Warren B.* (1980) 445 U.S. 949, 100 S.Ct. 1597, 63 L.Ed.2d 784).

In September, 1978, upon hearing from a staff member of We Care that Phillip had been regularly spending weekends at respondents' home, Mr. B. promptly forbade Phillip's removal from the facility (except for medical purposes and school attendance) and requested that respondents be denied personal visits with Phillip at We Care. Although respondents continued to visit Phillip daily at the facility, the abrupt cessation of home visits produced regressive changes in Phillip's behavior: he began acting out violently when respondents prepared to leave, begging to be taken "home"; he resorted to profanity; he became sullen and withdrawn when respondents were gone; bed-wetting regularly occurred, a recognized symptom of emotional disturbance in children. He began to blame himself for the apparent rejection by respondents; he began playing with matches and on one occasion he set his clothes afire; on another, he rode his tricycle to respondents' residence a few blocks away proclaiming on arrival that he was "home." He continuously pleaded to return home with respondents. Many of the behavioral changes continued to the time of trial.[10]

Appellants unsuccessfully pressed to remove Phillip from We Care notwithstanding the excellent care he was receiving. However, in January, 1981, the regional center monitoring public assistance for residential care and training of the handicapped, consented to Phillip's removal to a suitable alternate facility. Despite an extended search, none could be found which met Phillip's individualized needs. Meanwhile, Phillip continued living at We Care, periodically visiting at appellants' home. But throughout, the strong emotional attachment between Phillip and respondents remained intact.

Evidence established that Phillip, with a recently tested I.Q. score of 57,[11] is a highly functioning Down's Syndrome child capable of learning sufficient basic and employable skills to live independently or semi-independently in a non-institutional setting.

Courts generally may appoint a guardian over the person or estate of a minor "if it appears necessary or convenient." (Prob.Code, s 1514, subd. (a).) But the right of parents to retain custody of a child is fundamental and may be disturbed "'...only in extreme cases of persons acting in a fashion incompatible with parenthood.'" (*In re Angelia P.* (1981) 28 Cal.3d 908, 916, 171 Cal.Rptr. 637, 623 P.2d 198, quoting *In re Carmaleta B.* (1978) 21 Cal.3d 482, 489, 146 Cal.Rptr. 623, 579 P.2d

10. During a pretrial psychological evaluation, Phillip suddenly recoiled in his chair, hiding his face, in response to the examiner's question how he felt about being unable to visit respondents' home. In the examiner's opinion, such reaction manifested continuing emotional pain in light of the earlier trauma and regressive behavior following termination of home visits.

Contrary to appellants' argument, they were not entitled to be present at the pretrial psychological examination. (Cf. *Edwards v. Superior Court* (1976) 16 Cal.3d 905, 909–912, 130 Cal.Rptr. 14, 549 P.2d 846.) The need for an accurate report, itself subservient to the interest of an effective examination through a free and open communication exchange, is adequately safeguarded through discovery, cross-examination and production of other expert testimony.

11. A retarded child within an I.Q. range of 55–70 is generally considered as mildly retarded and classified as educable under California school standards.

514.) Accordingly, the Legislature has imposed the stringent requirement that before a court may make an order awarding custody of a child to a nonparent without consent of the parents, "it shall make a finding that an award of custody to a parent would be detrimental to the child and the award to a nonparent is required to serve the best interests of the child." (Civ.Code, §4600, subd. (c); see *In re B.G.* (1974) 11 Cal.3d 679, 695–699, 114 Cal.Rptr. 444, 523 P.2d 244.)[12] That requirement is equally applicable to guardianship proceedings under Probate Code section 1514, subdivision (b). The legislative shift in emphasis from parental unfitness to detriment to the child did not, however, signal a retreat from the judicial practice granting custodial preference to nonparents "only in unusual or extreme cases." (*In re B.G., supra,* 11 Cal.3d 679, 698, 114 Cal.Rptr. 444, 523 P.2d 244, see *Guardianship of Marino* (1973) 30 Cal.App.3d 952, 958, 106 Cal.Rptr. 655.)

The trial court expressly found that an award of custody to appellants would be harmful to Phillip in light of the psychological or "de facto" parental relationship established between him and respondents.[13] Such relationships have long been recognized in the fields of law and psychology. As Justice Tobriner has cogently observed, "The fact of biological parenthood may incline an adult to feel a strong concern for the welfare of his child, but it is not an essential condition; a person who assumes the role of parent, raising the child in his own home, may in time acquire an interest in the 'companionship, care, custody and management' of that child. The interest of the 'de facto parent' is a substantial one, recognized by the decision of this court in *Guardianship of Shannon* (1933) 218 Cal. 490 [23 P.2d 1020] and by courts of other jurisdictions and deserving of legal protection." (*In re B.G., supra,* 11 Cal.3d 679, 692–693, 114 Cal.Rptr. 444, 523 P.2d 244 [fns. omitted], citing the seminal study of Goldstein, Freud & Solnit, Beyond the Best Interests of the Child (1973) pp. 17–20, hereafter Goldstein.) Persons who assume such responsibility have been characterized by some interested professional observers as "psychological parents":

> Whether any adult becomes the psychological parent of a child is based... on day-to-day interaction, companionship, and shared experiences. The role can be fulfilled either by a biological parent or by an adoptive parent or by any other caring adult — but never by an absent, inactive adult, whatever his biological or legal relationship to the child may be. (Goldstein, *supra,* p. 19.)

Appellants vigorously challenge the evidence and finding that respondents have become Phillip's de facto or psychological parents since he did not reside with them full-time, as underscored in previous California decisions which have recog-

---

12. Civil Code section 4600 was enacted in response to the celebrated case of *Painter v. Bannister* (1966) 258 Iowa 1390, 140 N.W.2d 152, *cert. den.* 385 U.S. 949, 87 S.Ct. 322, 17 L.Ed.2d 227 in which the state court awarded custody of a young boy to his grandparents because it disapproved of the father's "Bohemian" lifestyle in California (see *In re B.G., supra,* 11 Cal.3d at pp. 697–698, 114 Cal.Rptr. 444, 523 P.2d 244, citing Report of Assembly Judiciary Committee, 4 Assem.J. (1969 Reg.Sess. pp. 8060–8061)).

13. We reject appellants' claim that the trial court's August 7, 1981, memorandum decision included no finding of detriment and that their notice of appeal from the guardianship order rendered the formal findings made on September 24, 1981, ineffectual. First, the memorandum decision explicitly cited threats of emotional, physical and medical harm in awarding custody to appellants. Moreover, proceedings affecting child custody orders are not stayed by appeal. (Code Civ.Proc., §917.7; *Superior Court v. Dist. Court of Appeal* (1966) 65 Cal.2d 293, 296, 54 Cal.Rptr. 119, 419 P.2d 183.) The Supreme Court's stay order, issued before the court rendered its findings and conclusions (see Code Civ.Proc., §923), was expressly limited to the August 7 order authorizing a heart catheterization; thus, the trial court retained jurisdiction as to all proceedings otherwise affecting the award of custody, including adoption of findings and conclusions.

nized de facto parenthood.... They argue that the subjective concept of psychological parenthood, relying on such nebulous factors as "love and affection" is susceptible to abuse and requires the countervailing element of objectivity provided by a showing of the child's long-term residency in the home of the claimed psychological parent.

We disagree. Adoption of the proposed standard would require this court to endorse a novel doctrine of child psychology unsupported either by a demonstrated general acceptance in the field of psychology or by the record before us. Although psychological parenthood is said to result from "day-to-day attention to [the child's] needs for physical care, nourishment, comfort, affection, and stimulation" (Goldstein, *supra*, p. 17), appellants fail to point to any authority or body of professional opinion that equates daily attention with full-time residency.[14] To the contrary, the record contains uncontradicted expert testimony that while psychological parenthood usually will require residency on a "24-hour basis," it is not an absolute requirement; further, that the frequency and quality of Phillip's weekend visits with respondents, together with the regular weekday visits at We Care, provided an adequate foundation to establish the crucial parent-child relationship.

Nor are we persuaded by appellants' suggested policy considerations concerning the arguably subjective inquiry involved in determining psychological parenthood. Trial fact-finders commonly grapple with elusive subjective legal concepts without aid of "countervailing" objective criteria. A fortiori, in enacting Civil Code section 4600, the Legislature purposefully refrained from prescribing specific criteria in determining whether parental custody would be "detrimental," reasoning that "[i]t is a nearly impossible task to devise detailed standards which will leave the courts sufficient flexibility to make the proper judgment in all cases." (Report of Assembly Judiciary Committee, 4 Assem.J. (1969 Reg.Sess.) p. 8061.) Moreover, the suggested standard is itself vulnerable to a claim of undue subjectivity in its vague requirement of residency for a "considerable period of time."[15]

Appellants also challenge the sufficiency of the evidence to support the finding that their retention of custody would have been detrimental to Phillip. In making the critical finding, the trial court correctly applied the "clear and convincing" standard of proof necessary to protect the fundamental rights of parents in all cases involving a nonparent's bid for custody. (See *In re B.G., supra*, 11 Cal.3d 679, 699, 114 Cal.Rptr. 444, 523 P.2d 244 [Civ.Code, §4600 sanctions a nonparent custodial award "only upon a *clear showing* that such award is essential to avert harm to the child"; italics ours]; cf. *In re Angelia P., supra*, 28 Cal.3d at pp. 918–919, 171 Cal.Rptr. 637, 623 P.2d 198 ["clear and convincing evidence" standard applicable in proceedings under Civ.Code, §232 to terminate parent-child relationship].)

---

14. Appellants cite one survey which criticizes certain conclusions in Goldstein in pejorative terms matched, regrettably, by the stridency of appellants' brief. Therein, the author challenges "absolute use of psychological parenthood...as the single standard to determine best interest of the child," because any nonparent caretaker can claim psychological parenthood "whether the custodian is a kidnapper, a band of gypsies, a baby-sitter or nanny, the child-snatching non-custodial parent, the grandparent [resorted] to in desperation, or anyone else...." (Crouch, *An Essay on the Critical and Judicial Perception of Beyond the Best Interests of the Child* (1979) 13 FAMILY L.Q. 49, 103.)

15. Appellants also fear that, absent a full-time residency requirement, anyone who visits an institutionalized child can lay claim to psychological parenthood. As earlier discussed, development of a parent-child relationship requires long-term nurturing and fulfillment of the child's total needs which can rarely occur without full-time residency. But it was manifested here only as a direct result of respondents' unique relationship with Phillip as We Care volunteers, their previously uninterrupted weekend close contacts and appellants' physical and emotional detachment from the child. All of such important factors contributed to respondents' ability to devote the enormous amount of time and loving care essential to fill the tangible and emotional needs in Phillip's life.

This court must, as noted, review the whole record in the light most favorable to the award of guardianship to determine whether there was substantial evidence that parental custody would have been detrimental to Phillip based on clear and convincing evidence....

The record contains abundant evidence that appellants' retention of custody would cause Phillip profound emotional harm. Notwithstanding Phillip's strong emotional ties with respondents, appellants abruptly foreclosed home visits and set out to end all contact between them. When Phillip's home visits terminated in 1978, he displayed many signs of severe emotional trauma: he appeared depressed and withdrawn and became visibly distressed at being unable to return to "my house," a request he steadily voiced up until trial. He became enuretic, which a psychologist, Dr. Edward Becking, testified indicates emotional stress in children. (See *In re Lynna B., supra,* 92 Cal.App.3d 682, 697, 155 Cal.Rptr. 256 [psychiatric evidence that bed wetting is symptomatic of detriment suffered by children when ties with "psychological" parents are severed].) Dr. Becking testified to other signs of emotional disturbance which were present nearly three years after the termination of home visits.[16]

Our law recognizes that children generally will sustain serious emotional harm when deprived of the emotional benefits flowing from a true parent-child relationship....

There was uncontroverted expert testimony that Phillip would sustain further emotional trauma in the event of total separation from respondents: that testimony indicated that, as with all children, Phillip needs love and affection, and he would be profoundly hurt if he were deprived of the existing psychological parental relationship with respondents in favor of maintaining unity with his biological parents.

Phillip's conduct unmistakably demonstrated that he derived none of the emotional benefits attending a close parental relationship largely as a result of appellants' individualized decision to abandon that traditional supporting role. Dr. Becking testified that no "bonding or attachment" has occurred between Phillip and his biological parents, a result palpably consistent with appellants' view that Phillip had none of the emotional needs uniquely filled by natural parents. We conclude that such substantial evidence adequately supports the finding that parental custody would have resulted in harmful deprivation of these human needs contrary to Phillip's best interests.

Finally, there was also evidence that Phillip would experience educational and developmental injury if parental custody remains unchanged. At Phillip's functioning level of disability,[17] he can normally be expected to live at least semi-independently as an adult in a supervised residential setting and be suitably trained to work in a sheltered workshop or even a competitive environment (e.g., performing assembly duties or custodial tasks in a fast-food restaurant). Active involvement of a parent figure during the formative stages of education and habilitation is of immeasurable aid in reaching his full potential. Unfortunately, appel-

---

16. Specifically, Phillip's increasing self-criticism, his unsupervised arrival at respondents' home; his repeated attempts to join respondents when they were ready to leave the We Care facility, and the painful recoiling reaction which occurred in the interview setting.

17. As earlier noted, Phillip's most recent I.Q. score of 57 places him in the higher classification range of mildly retarded. Current definitions of intelligence include both I.Q. scores and measures of "adaptive behavior" (the degree to which a person meets the standards of personal independence and social responsibilities of one's age and cultural group).

lants' deliberate abdication of that central role would effectively deny Phillip any meaningful opportunity to develop whatever skills he may be capable of achieving. Indeed, Dr. Becking testified that further separation from respondents would not only impair Phillip's ability to form new relationships but would "for a long while" seriously impair Phillip's development of necessary prevocational and independent-living skills for his future life.

Nor can we overlook evidence of potential physical harm to Phillip due to appellants' passive neglect in response to Phillip's medical condition. Although it appears probable that the congenital heart defect is no longer correctable by surgery,[18] the trial court could have reasonably concluded that appellants' past conduct reflected a dangerously passive approach to Phillip's future medical needs.[19]

It is a clearly stated legislative policy that persons with developmental disabilities shall enjoy — inter alia — the right to treatment and rehabilitation services, the right to publicly supported education, the right to social interaction, and the right to prompt medical care and treatment. (Welf. & Inst.Code, §4502.) Moreover, the legislative purpose underlying Civil Code section 4600 is to protect the needs of children generally "...to be raised with love, emotional security and physical safety." (*In re D.L.C., supra*, 54 Cal.App.3d 840, 851, 126 Cal.Rptr. 863.) When a trial court is called upon to determine the custody of a developmentally disabled or handicapped child, as here, it must be guided by such overriding policies rather than by the personal beliefs or attitudes of the contesting parties, since it is the child's interest which remains paramount. (Cf. *In re Marriage of Kern* (1978) 87 Cal.App.3d 402, 410, 150 Cal.Rptr. 860 [primary consideration in custodial disputes centers upon child's best interests and motivational interest of adversary parties is irrelevant].) Clearly, the trial court faithfully complied with such legislative mandate in exercising its sound discretion based upon the evidence presented. We find no abuse as contended by appellants.

We strongly emphasize, as the trial court correctly concluded, that the fact of detriment cannot be proved solely by evidence that the biological parent has elected to institutionalize a handicapped child, or that nonparents are able and willing to offer the child the advantages of their home in lieu of institutional placement. Sound reasons may exist justifying institutionalization of a handicapped child. But the totality of the evidence under review permits of no rational conclusion other than that the detriment caused Phillip, and its possible recurrence, was due not to appellants' choice to institutionalize but their calculated decision to remain emotionally and physically detached — abdicating the conventional role of competent decision-maker in times of demonstrated need — thus effectively depriving him of any of the substantial benefits of a true parental relationship. It is the emotional abandonment of Phillip, not his institutionalization, which inevitably has created the unusual circumstances which led to the award of limited custody to respondents. We do not question the sincerity of appellants' belief that their approach to Phillip's welfare was in their combined best interests. But the

18. A pediatric cardiologist estimated that the surgery now might have a one-third chance of harming him, a one-third chance of helping him, and a one-third chance of causing no appreciable change in his condition. Dr. Gathman testified that it is "highly probable" that Phillip's condition is no longer correctable by surgery, but that a heart catheterization is required to be certain.

19. Notably, the failure to obtain competent medical advice concerning the heart disease and the admitted willingness to forego medical treatment solely by reason of Phillip's retarded condition. The gravity of such dangerous inaction was dramatically illustrated by Mr. B.'s reaction to Phillip's recent undiagnosed episodes of apparent semi-consciousness — discounting their existence without even the benefit of a medical consultation.

record is replete with substantial and credible evidence supporting the trial court's determination, tested by the standard of clear and convincing proof, that appellants' retention of custody has caused and will continue to cause serious detriment to Phillip and that his best interests will be served through the guardianship award of custody to respondents. In light of such compelling circumstances, no legal basis is shown to disturb that carefully considered determination.

...

COMMENTS

Parham was brought by legal services attorneys at the height of social concern over due process rights and especially due process rights of relatively powerless adults and children. The majority of the Court went to great lengths to explain that they really were not in any sense imposing the state between the parent and the child or in any way undermining the presumption that parents act on behalf of and in the best interests of their children.

Yet, there is an unavoidable tension between any concept of children having interests or rights independent of their parents and strong presumptions of parents acting in the interest of children. *Parham* goes so far as to suggest that *Meyer* and *Pierce* would have been decided in favor of the parents regardless of the wishes of the children. The Court's justification for imposing certain due process requirements on commitment procedures for juveniles seems clearly to be a concern that the parents may in fact not be acting fully for the child's best interest, a point argued more strongly by the dissent.

How much difference should it make that parents seeking to have their children committed to a mental hospital are, like the parents in *Guardianship of Phillip B.*, relinquishing their day-to-day custody of the child? If the parents "dump" their child not in a mental institution or in a special facility for retarded children but in a private boarding school, should the parents retain more of their parental rights? Should a concerned teacher be able to befriend and slowly take over the care of a child at a boarding school if the parents seem to be neglecting the child or otherwise not acting in her best interests?

The present reality, however, is that there are many more children who could benefit from additional concerned adult attention than there are adults ready to give such attention. Allowing a non-parent to demonstrate to the court that he or she would be a better guardian for a particular child threatens the security of many parents, while it may be a terribly small percentage of children who stand to benefit from such a proceeding. Of course, courts must be concerned with the welfare of the individual child before the court. Also, it could be argued that any insecurity felt by parents, especially in cases in which the child is in the day-to-day care of someone other than the parent, is not necessarily bad if it encourages the parents to focus reasonable attention on their child and maintain closer contact.

An important question that has not yet been answered in any definitive manner is whether a guardian should need to be appointed or parents judged to be unsuitable before the child may assert his or her rights against the wishes of the parent. One way for courts to deal with the problems that arise in the area of children's rights is to depend entirely upon the parents to vindicate the rights of their children, and failing that, find the parents' custody "detrimental to the child and [that an] award [of custody] to a nonparent is required to serve the best interests of the child." Notice that in an earlier case, the district attorney had tried unsuccessfully to force the parents to permit the surgery upon Phillip B. by arguing that the withholding of surgery constituted child neglect. Courts frequently overrule parental medical decisions that pose an immediate and dire threat to the health of a child, but they are reluctant to do so when the risks and benefits of a particular medical procedure are less certain.

Sexuality: Imposing Parental Domination or Undermining Parental Authority?

CAREY v. POPULATION SERVICES INTERNATIONAL
United States Supreme Court
431 U.S. 678 (1977)

Mr. Justice BRENNAN delivered the opinion of the Court with respect to Parts I, II, III, and V, together with an opinion (Part IV in which Mr. Justice STEWART, Mr. Justice MARSHALL, and Mr. Justice BLACKMUN joined.

Under New York Ed. Law §6811(8)(McKinney 1972) it is a crime (1) for any person to sell or distribute any contraceptive of any kind to a minor under the age of 16 years; (2) for anyone other than a licensed pharmacist to distribute contraceptives to persons 16 or over; and (3) for anyone, including licensed pharmacists, to advertise or display contraceptives. A three-judge District Court for the Southern District of New York declared §6811(8) unconstitutional in its entirety under the First and Fourteenth Amendments of the Federal Constitution insofar as it applies to nonprescription contraceptives, and enjoined its enforcement as so applied....

...

II

Although "[t]he Constitution does not explicitly mention any right of privacy," the Court has recognized that one aspect of the "liberty" protected by the Due Process Clause of the Fourteenth Amendment is "a right of personal privacy, or a guarantee of certain areas or zones of privacy." *Roe v. Wade*, 410 U.S. 113, 152 (1973). This right of personal privacy includes "the interest in independence in making certain kinds of important decisions." *Whalen v. Roe*, 429 U.S. 589, 599–600 (1977). While the outer limits of this aspect of privacy have not been marked by the Court, it is clear that among the decisions that an individual may make without unjustified government interference are personal decisions "relating to marriage, *Loving v. Virginia*, 388 U.S. 1, 12 (1967); procreation, *Skinner v. Oklahoma ex rel. Williamson*, 316 U.S. 535, 541–542 (1942); contraception, *Eisenstadt v. Baird*, 405 U.S., at 453–454 (White, J., concurring in result); family relationships, *Prince v. Massachusetts*, 321 U.S. 158, 166 (1944); and child rearing and education, *Pierce v. Society of Sisters*, 268 U.S. 510, 535 (1925); *Meyer v. Nebraska*, (262 U.S. 390, 399 (1923))." *Roe v. Wade, supra*, at 152–153. See also *Cleveland Board of Education v. LaFleur*, 414 U.S. 632, 639–640 (1974).

The decision whether or not to beget or bear a child is at the very heart of this cluster of constitutionally protected choices. That decision holds a particularly important place in the history of the right of privacy, a right first explicitly recognized in an opinion holding unconstitutional a statute prohibiting the use of contraceptives, *Griswold v. Connecticut, supra*, and most prominently vindicated in recent years in the contexts of contraception, *Griswold v. Connecticut, supra*; *Eisenstadt v. Baird, supra*; and abortion, *Roe v. Wade, supra*; *Doe v. Bolton*, 410 U.S. 179 (1973); *Planned Parenthood of Central Missouri v. Danforth*, 428 U.S. 52 (1976). This is understandable, for in a field that by definition concerns the most intimate of human activities and relationships, decisions whether to accomplish or to prevent conception are among the most private and sensitive....

That the constitutionally protected right of privacy extends to an individual's liberty to make choices regarding contraception does not, however, automatically invalidate every state regulation in this area. The business of manufacturing and selling contraceptives may be regulated in ways that do not infringe protected individual choices. And even a burdensome regulation may be validated by a sufficiently compelling state interest.... "Compelling" is of course the key word; where a decision as fundamental as that whether to bear or beget a child is involved, regulations imposing a burden on it may be justified only by compelling state interests, and must be narrowly drawn to express only those interests....

...

[Portion of opinion invalidating New York's effort to limit the distribution of nonprescription contraceptives to licensed pharmacists omitted.]

IV[12]

A

The District Court...held unconstitutional, as applied to nonprescription contraceptives, the provision of §6811(8) prohibiting the distribution of contraceptives to those under 16 years of age. Appellants contend that this provision of the statute is constitutionally permissible as a regulation of the morality of minors, in furtherance of the State's policy against promiscuous sexual intercourse among the young.

The question of the extent of state power to regulate conduct of minors not constitutionally regulable when committed by adults is a vexing one, perhaps not susceptible of precise answer. We have been reluctant to attempt to define "the totality of the relationship of the juvenile and the state." *In re Gault*, 387 U.S. 1, 13 (1967). Certain principles, however, have been recognized. "Minors, as well as adults, are protected by the Constitution and possess constitutional rights." *Planned Parenthood of Central Missouri v. Danforth*, 428 U.S., at 74. "(W)hatever may be their precise impact, neither the Fourteenth Amendment nor the Bill of Rights is for adults alone." *In re Gault, supra*, 387 U.S., at 13. On the other hand, we have held in a variety of contexts that "the power of the state to control the conduct of children reaches beyond the scope of its authority over adults." *Prince v. Massachusetts*, 321 U.S. 158, 170 (1944). See *Ginsberg v. New York*, 390 U.S. 629 (1968). See also *McKeiver v. Pennsylvania*, 403 U.S. 528 (1971).

Of particular significance to the decision of this case, the right to privacy in connection with decisions affecting procreation extends to minors as well as to adults. *Planned Parenthood of Central Missouri v. Danforth, supra*, held that a State "may

---

12. This part of the opinion expresses the views of Justices BRENNAN, STEWART, MARSHALL and BLACKMUN.

not impose a blanket provision...requiring the consent of a parent or person in loco parentis as a condition for abortion of an unmarried minor during the first 12 weeks of her pregnancy." 428 U.S., at 74. As in the case of the spousal-consent requirement struck down in the same case, *id.*, at 67–72 "the State does not have the constitutional authority to give a third party an absolute, and possibly arbitrary, veto," *id.*, at 74, "'which the state itself is absolutely and totally prohibited from exercising." *Id.*, at 69. State restrictions inhibiting privacy rights of minors are valid only if they serve "any significant state interest...that is not present in the case of an adult." *Id.*, at 75.[15] *Planned Parenthood* found that no such interest justified a state requirement of parental consent.[16]

Since the State may not impose a blanket prohibition, or even a blanket requirement of parental consent, on the choice of a minor to terminate her pregnancy, the constitutionality of a blanket prohibition of the distribution of contraceptives to minors is a fortiori foreclosed. The State's interests in protection of the mental and physical health of the pregnant minor, and in protection of potential life are clearly more implicated by the abortion decision than by the decision to use a nonhazardous contraceptive.

Appellants argue, however, that significant state interests are served by restricting minors' access to contraceptives, because free availability to minors of contraceptives would lead to increased sexual activity among the young, in violation of the policy of New York to discourage such behavior.[17] The argument is that minors' sexual activity may be deterred by increasing the hazards attendant on it. The same argument, however, would support a ban on abortions for minors, or indeed support a prohibition on abortions, or access to contraceptives, for the unmarried, whose sexual activity is also against the public policy of many States. Yet, in each of these areas, the Court has rejected the argument, noting in *Roe v. Wade*, that "no court or commentator has taken the argument seriously." 410 U.S., at 148. The reason for this unanimous rejection was stated in *Eisenstadt v. Baird*: "It would be plainly unreasonable to assume that (the State) has prescribed pregnancy and the birth of an unwanted child (or the physical and psychological dangers of an abortion) as punishment for fornication." 405 U.S., at 448. We remain reluctant to attribute any such "scheme of values" to the State.[18]

---

15. This test is apparently less rigorous than the "compelling state interest" test applied to restrictions on the privacy rights of adults. See, *e.g.*, n.16, *infra*. Such lesser scrutiny is appropriate both because of the States' greater latitude to regulate the conduct of children, *Prince v. Massachusetts*, 321 U.S. 158 (1944); *Ginsberg v. New York*, 390 U.S. 629 (1968), and because the right of privacy implicated here is "the interest in independence in making certain kinds of important decisions," *Whalen v. Roe*, 429 U.S. 589, 599–600 (1977), and the law has generally regarded minors as having a lesser capability for making important decisions. See, *e.g.*, *Planned Parenthood*, 428 U.S., at 102 (Stevens, J., concurring in part and dissenting in part).

16. *Planned Parenthood*, however, "does not suggest that every minor regardless of age or maturity, may give effective consent for termination of her pregnancy. See *Bellotti v. Baird*, (428 U.S. 132 (1976)). The fault (of the particular statute considered in *Planned Parenthood*) is that it imposes a special-consent provision, exercisable by a person other than the woman and her physician, as a prerequisite to a minor's termination of her pregnancy...without a sufficient justification for the restriction." *Id.*, at 75.

17. Appellees argue that the State's policy to discourage sexual activity of minors is itself unconstitutional, for the reason that the right to privacy comprehends a right of minors as well as adults to engage in private consensual sexual behavior. We observe that the Court has not definitively answered the difficult question whether and to what extent the Constitution prohibits state statutes regulating such behavior among adults.... But whatever the answer to that question, *Ginsberg v. New York*, *supra*, indicates that in the area of sexual mores, as in other areas, the scope of permissible state regulation is broader as to minors than as to adults. In any event, it is unnecessary to pass upon this contention of appellees, and our decision proceeds on the assumption that the Constitution does not bar state regulation of the sexual behavior of minors.

18. We note, moreover, that other provisions of New York law argue strongly against any conclusion that the deterrence of illegal sexual conduct among minors was an objective of §6811(8). First, a girl in New York may marry as young as 14, with the consent of her parents and a family court judge.... Yet although sexual

Moreover, there is substantial reason for doubt whether limiting access to contraceptives will in fact substantially discourage early sexual behavior. Appellants themselves conceded in the District Court that "there is no evidence that teenage extramarital sexual activity increases in proportion to the availability of contraceptives," 398 F.Supp., at 332, and n.10, and accordingly offered none, in the District Court or here. Appellees, on the other hand, cite a considerable body of evidence and opinion indicating that there is no such deterrent effect. Although we take judicial notice, as did the District Court, *id.*, at 331–333, that with or without access to contraceptives, the incidence of sexual activity among minors is high, and the consequences of such activity are frequently devastating, the studies cited by appellees play no part in our decision. It is enough that we again confirm the principle that when a State, as here, burdens the exercise of a fundamental right, its attempt to justify that burden as a rational means for the accomplishment of some significant state policy requires more than a bare assertion, based on a conceded complete absence of supporting evidence, that the burden is connected to such a policy.

[Portion of opinion invalidating New York's prohibition of any "advertisement or display" of contraceptives omitted.]

The CHIEF JUSTICE dissents.

Mr. Justice WHITE, concurring in part and concurring in the result.

I join Parts I, III, and V of the Court's opinion and concur in the result with respect to Part IV.

...

I concur in the result in Part IV primarily because the State has not demonstrated that the prohibition against distribution of contraceptives to minors measurably contributes to the deterrent purposes which the State advances as justification for the restriction. Again, however, the legality of state laws forbidding premarital intercourse is not at issue here; and, with Mr. Justice STEVENS, "I would describe as 'frivolous' appellee's argument that a minor has the constitutional right to put contraceptives to their intended use, notwithstanding the combined objection of both parents and the State"....

...

Mr. Justice POWELL, concurring in part and concurring in the judgment.

...

...Neither our precedents nor sound principles of constitutional analysis require state legislation to meet the exacting "compelling state interest" standard whenever it implicates sexual freedom. In my view, those cases make clear that that standard has been invoked only when the state regulation entirely frustrates or heavily burdens the exercise of constitutional rights in this area. See *Bellotti v. Baird*, 428 U.S. 132 (1976). This is not to say that other state regulation is free from

18. *continued*
intercourse by a married woman of that age violates no state law, §6811(8) prohibits distribution of contraceptives to her. Second, New York requires that birth control information and services be provided to recipients of certain welfare programs, provided only that they are "of childbearing age, including children who can be considered sexually active." N.Y.Soc.Serv. Law §350(1)(e)(McKinney 1976).... Although extramarital intercourse is presumably as contrary to state policy among minors covered by those programs as among others, state law requires distribution of contraceptives to them and prohibits their distribution to all others.

judicial review. But a test so severe that legislation rarely can meet it should be imposed by courts with deliberate restraint in view of the respect that properly should be accorded legislative judgments.

B

There is also no justification for subjecting restrictions on the sexual activity of the young to heightened judicial review. Under our prior cases, the States have broad latitude to legislate with respect to adolescents. The principle is well settled that "a State may permissibly determine that, at least in some precisely delineated areas, a child...is not possessed of that full capacity for individual choice" which is essential to the exercise of various constitutionally protected interests. *Ginsberg v. New York*, 390 U.S. 629, 649–650 (1968)(Stewart, J., concurring in result)....

...

...It seems clear to me, for example, that the State would further a constitutionally permissible end if it encouraged adolescents to seek the advice and guidance of their parents before deciding whether to engage in sexual intercourse. *Planned Parenthood*, 428 U.S., at 91 (Stewart, J., concurring). The State justifiably may take note of the psychological pressures that might influence children at a time in their lives when they generally do not possess the maturity necessary to understand and control their responses. Participation in sexual intercourse at an early age may have both physical and psychological consequences. These include the risks of venereal disease and pregnancy, and the less obvious mental and emotional problems that may result from sexual activity by children. Moreover, society has long adhered to the view that sexual intercourse should not be engaged in promiscuously, a judgment that an adolescent may be less likely to heed than an adult.

...

A requirement of prior parental consultation is merely one illustration of permissible regulation in this area. As long as parental distribution is permitted, a State should have substantial latitude in regulating the distribution of contraceptives to minors.

...

Mr. Justice STEVENS, concurring in part and concurring in the judgment.

...

There are two reasons why I do not join Part IV. First, the holding *Planned Parenthood of Missouri v. Danforth*, 428 U.S. 52, 72–75, 96 S.Ct. 2381, 2842–2844, 49 L.Ed.2d 788, that a minor's decision to abort her pregnancy may not be conditioned on parental consent, is not dispositive here. The options available to the already pregnant minor are fundamentally different from those available to non-pregnant minors. The former must bear a child unless she aborts; but persons in the latter category can and generally will avoid childbearing by abstention. Consequently, even if I had joined that part of Planned Parenthood, I could not agree that the Constitution provides the same measure of protection to the minor's right to use contraceptives as to the pregnant female's right to abort.

Second, I would not leave open the question whether there is a significant state interest in discouraging sexual activity among unmarried persons under 16 years of age. Indeed, I would describe as "frivolous" appellees' argument that a minor has the constitutional right to put contraceptives to their intended use, notwithstanding the combined objection of both parents and the State.

...

The State's important interest in the welfare of its young citizens justifies a number of protective measures. See *Planned Parenthood of Central Missouri v. Danforth*, *supra*, 428 U.S., at 102 (Stevens, J., concurring in part and dissenting in part). Such special legislation is premised on the fact that young persons frequently make unwise choices with harmful consequences; the State may properly ameliorate those consequences by providing, for example, that a minor may not be required to honor his bargain. It is almost unprecedented, however, for a State to require that an ill-advised act by a minor give rise to greater risk of irreparable harm than a similar act by an adult.

...

Mr. Justice REHNQUIST, dissenting.

Those who valiantly but vainly defended the heights of Bunker Hill in 1775 made it possible that men such as James Madison might later sit in the first Congress and draft the Bill of Rights to the Constitution. The post-Civil War Congresses which drafted the Civil War Amendments to the Constitution could not have accomplished their task without the blood of brave men on both sides which was shed at Shiloh, Gettysburg, and Cold Harbor. If those responsible for these Amendments, by feats of valor or efforts of draftsmanship, could have lived to know that their efforts had enshrined in the Constitution the right of commercial vendors of contraceptives to peddle them to unmarried minors through such means as window displays and vending machines located in the men's room of truck stops, notwithstanding the considered judgment of the New York Legislature to the contrary, it is not difficult to imagine their reaction.

I do not believe that the cases discussed in the Court's opinion require any such result, but to debate the Court's treatment of the question on a case-by-case basis would concede more validity to the result reached by the Court than I am willing to do. There comes a point when endless and ill-considered extension of principles originally formulated in quite different cases produces such an indefensible result that no logic chopping can possibly make the fallacy of the result more obvious. The Court here in effect holds that the First and Fourteenth Amendments not only guarantee full and free debate before a legislative judgment as to the moral dangers to which minors within the jurisdiction of the State should not be subjected, but goes further and absolutely prevents the representatives of the majority from carrying out such a policy after the issues have been fully aired.

No questions of religious belief, compelled allegiance to a secular creed, or decisions on the part of married couples as to procreation, are involved here. New York has simply decided that it wishes to discourage unmarried minors under 16 from having promiscuous sexual intercourse with one another. Even the Court would scarcely go so far as to say that this is not a subject with which the New York Legislature may properly concern itself.

That legislature has not chosen to deny to a pregnant woman, after the *fait accompli* of pregnancy, the one remedy which would enable her to terminate an unwanted pregnancy. It has instead sought to deter the conduct which will produce such faits accomplis. The majority of New York's citizens are in effect told that however deeply they may be concerned about the problem of promiscuous sex and intercourse among unmarried teenagers, they may not adopt this means of dealing with it. The Court holds that New York may not use its police power to legislate in the interests of its concept of the public morality as it pertains to minors. The Court's denial of a power so fundamental to self-government must, in the long run, prove to be but a temporary departure from a wise and heretofore settled course of adjudication to the contrary. I would reverse the judgment of the District Court.

PLANNED PARENTHOOD v. DANFORTH

United States Supreme Court
428 U.S. 52 (1976)

Mr. Justice BLACKMUN delivered the opinion of the Court.

This case is a logical and anticipated corollary to *Roe v. Wade*, 410 U.S. 113, 93 S.Ct. 705, 35 L.Ed.2d 147 (1973), and *Doe v. Bolton*, 410 U.S. 179, 93 S.Ct. 739, 35 L.Ed.2d 201 (1973), for it raises issues secondary to those that were then before the Court....

I

...

In June 1974, somewhat more than a year after *Roe* and *Doe* had been decided, Missouri's 77th General Assembly, in its Second Regular Session, enacted House Committee Substitute for House Bill No. 1211 (hereinafter Act). The legislation was approved by the Governor on June 14, 1974, and became effective immediately by reason of an emergency clause contained in §A of the statute.... It imposes a structure for the control and regulation of abortions in Missouri during all stages of pregnancy.

II

Three days after the Act became effective, the present litigation was instituted in the United States District Court for the Eastern District of Missouri. The plaintiffs are Planned Parenthood of Central Missouri, a not-for-profit Missouri corporation which maintains a facility in Columbia, Mo., for the performance of abortions [and two doctors].

The named defendants are the Attorney General of Missouri and the Circuit Attorney of the city of St. Louis "in his representative capacity" and "as the representative of the class of all similar Prosecuting Attorneys of the various counties of the State of Missouri." Complaint 10.

The plaintiffs brought the action on their own behalf and, purportedly, "on behalf of the entire class consisting of duly licensed physicians and surgeons presently performing or desiring to perform the termination of pregnancies and on behalf of the entire class consisting of their patients desiring the termination of pregnancy, all within the State of Missouri." *Id.*, at 9. Plaintiffs sought declaratory relief and also sought to enjoin enforcement of the Act on the ground, among others, that certain of its provisions deprived them and their patients of various constitutional rights: "the right to privacy in the physician-patient relationship"; the physicians' "right to practice medicine according to the highest standards of medical practice"; the female patients' right to determine whether to bear children; the patients' "right to life due to the inherent risk involved in childbirth" or in medical procedures alternative to abortion; the physicians' "right to give and plaintiffs' patients' right to receive safe and adequate medical advice and treatment, pertaining to the decision of whether to carry a given pregnancy to term and the method of termination"; the patients' right under the Eight Amendment to be free from cruel and unusual punishment "by forcing and coercing them to bear each pregnancy they conceive"; and, by being placed "in the position of decision making beset with...inherent possibilities of bias and conflict of interest," the physician's right to due process of law guaranteed by the Fourteenth Amendment. *Id.*, At 10–11.

...

For convenience, we shall usually refer to the plaintiffs as "appellants" and to both named defendants as "appellees."

...

[The Court upheld the portion of the Missouri statute defining viability as "that stage of fetal development when the life of the unborn child may be continued indefinitely outside the womb by natural or artificial life-support systems" and requiring the pregnant woman to state in writing that her consent to abortion is informed and freely given.]

The spouse's consent. Section 3(3) requires the prior written consent of the spouse of the woman seeking an abortion during the first 12 weeks of pregnancy, unless "the abortion is certified by a licensed physician to be necessary in order to preserve the life of the mother."

...

In *Roe* and *Doe* we specifically reserved decision on the question whether a requirement for consent by the father of the fetus, by the spouse, or by the parents, or a parent, of an unmarried minor, may be constitutionally imposed. 410 U.S., at 165 n. 67, 93 S.Ct., at 733. We now hold that the State may not constitutionally require the consent of the spouse, as is specified under §3(3) of the Missouri Act, as a condition for abortion during the first 12 weeks of pregnancy.... Clearly, since the State cannot regulate or proscribe abortion during the first stage, when the physician and his patient make that decision, the State cannot delegate authority to any particular person, even the spouse, to prevent abortion during that same period.

We are not unaware of the deep and proper concern and interest that a devoted and protective husband has in his wife's pregnancy and in the growth and development of the fetus she is carrying. Neither has this Court failed to appreciate the importance of the marital relationship in our society. See, *e.g.*, *Griswold v. Connecticut*, 381 U.S. 479, 486, 85 S.Ct. 1678, 1682, 14 L.Ed.2d 510 (1965); *Maynard v. Hill*, 125 U.S. 190, 211, S.Ct. 723, 729, 31 L.Ed. 654 (1888). Moreover, we recognize that the decision whether to undergo or to forego an abortion may have profound effects on the future of any marriage, effects that are both physical and mental, and possibly deleterious. Notwithstanding these factors, we cannot hold that the State has the constitutional authority to give the spouse unilaterally the ability to prohibit the wife from terminating her pregnancy, when the State itself lacks that right. See *Eisenstadt v. Baird*, 405 U.S. 438, 453, 92 S.Ct. 1029, 1038, 31 L.Ed.2d 349 (1972).[11]

---

11. As the Court recognized in *Eisenstadt v. Baird*, "the marital couple is not an independent entity with a mind and heart of its own, but an association of two individuals each with a separate intellectual and emotional makeup. If the right of privacy means anything, it is the right of the *individual*, married or single, to be free from unwarranted governmental intrusion into matters so fundamentally affecting a person as the decision whether to bear or beget a child." 405 U.S., at 453, 92 S.Ct., at 1038 (emphasis in original).

The dissenting opinion of our Brother WHITE appears to overlook the implications of this statement upon the issue whether §3(3) is constitutional. This section does much more than insure that the husband participate in the decision whether his wife should have an abortion. The State, instead, has determined that the husband's interest in continuing the pregnancy of his wife always outweighs any interest on her part in terminating it irrespective of the condition of their marriage. The State, accordingly, has granted him the right to prevent

It seems manifest that, ideally, the decision to terminate a pregnancy should be one concurred in by both the wife and her husband. No marriage may be viewed as harmonious or successful if the marriage partners are fundamentally divided on so important and vital an issue. But it is difficult to believe that the goal of fostering mutuality and trust in a marriage, and of strengthening the marital relationship and the marriage institution, will be achieved by giving the husband a veto power exercisable for any reason whatsoever or for no reason at all. Even if the State had the ability to delegate to the husband a power it itself could not exercise, it is not at all likely that such action would further, as the District Court majority phrased it, the "interest of the state in protecting the mutuality of decisions vital to the marriage relationship." 392 F.Supp., at 1370.

We recognize, of course, that when a woman, with the approval of her physician but without the approval of her husband, decides to terminate her pregnancy, it could be said that she is acting unilaterally. The obvious fact is that when the wife and the husband disagree on this decision, the view of only one of the two marriage partners can prevail. Inasmuch as it is the woman who physically bears the child and who is the more directly and immediately affected by the pregnancy, as between the two, the balance weighs in her favor. *Cf. Roe v. Wade*, 410 U.S., at 153, 93 S.Ct., at 726.

...

Parental consent. Section 3(4) requires, with respect to the first 12 weeks of pregnancy, where the woman is unmarried and under the age of 18 years, the written consent of a parent or person *in loco parentis* unless, again, "the abortion is certified by a licensed physician as necessary in order to preserve the life of the mother." It is to be observed that only one parent need consent.

...

We agree with appellants...that the State may not impose a blanket provision, such as §3(4), requiring the consent of a parent or person *in loco parentis* as a condition for abortion of an unmarried minor during the first 12 weeks of her pregnancy. Just as with the requirement of consent from the spouse, so here, the State does not have the constitutional authority to give a third party an absolute, and possibly arbitrary, veto over the decision of the physician and his patient to terminate the patient's pregnancy, regardless of the reason for withholding the consent.

Constitutional rights do not mature and come into being magically only when one attains the state-defined age of majority. Minors, as well as adults, are protected by the Constitution and possess constitutional rights.... The Court indeed, however, long has recognized that the State has somewhat broader authority to regulate the activities of children than of adults.... It remains, then, to examine whether there is any signifant state interest in conditioning an abortion on the consent of a parent or person *in loco parentis* that is not present in the case of an adult.

One suggested interest is the safeguarding of the family unit and of parental authority. 392 F.Supp., at 1370. It is difficult, however, to conclude that providing a parent with absolute power to overrule a determination, made by the physician and his minor patient, to terminate the patient's pregnancy will serve to

---

11. *continued*
unilaterally, and for whatever reason, the effectuation of his wife's and her physician's decision to terminate her pregnancy. This state determination not only may discourage the consultation that might normally be expected to precede a major decision affecting the marital couple but also, and more importantly, the State has interposed an absolute obstacle to a woman's decision that Roe held to be constitutionally protected from such interference.

strengthen the family unit. Neither is it likely that such veto power will enhance parental authority or control where the minor and the nonconsenting parent are so fundamentally in conflict and the very existence of the pregnancy already has fractured the family structure. Any independent interest the parent may have in the termination of the minor daughter's pregnancy is no more weighty than the right of privacy of the competent minor mature enough to have become pregnant.

We emphasize that our holding that §3(4) is invalid does not suggest that every minor, regardless of age or maturity, may give effective consent for termination of her pregnancy. See *Bellotti v. Baird*, 428 U.S. 132, 96 S.Ct. 2857, 49 L.Ed.2d 844. The fault with §3(4) is that it imposes a special-consent provision, exercisable by a person other than the woman and her physician, as a prerequisite to a minor's termination of her pregnancy and does so without a sufficient justification for the restriction. It violates the strictures of *Roe* and *Doe*.

[Portions of the opinion overturning the Act's prohibition of saline amniocentesis abortions omitted.]

Mr. Justice STEWART, with whom Mr. Justice POWELL joins, concurring.

While joining the Court's opinion, I write separately to indicate my understanding of some of the constitutional issues raised by this litigation.

...

As to the provision of the law that requires a husband's consent to an abortion, §3(3), the primary issue that it raises is whether the State may constitutionally recognize and give effect to a right on his part to participate in the decision to abort a jointly conceived child. This seems to me a rather more difficult problem than the Court acknowledges. Previous decisions have recognized that a man's right to father children and enjoy the association of his offspring is a constitutionally protected freedom. See *Stanley v. Illinois*, 405 U.S. 645, 92 S.Ct. 1208, 31 L.Ed.2d 551; *Skinner v. Oklahoma ex rel. Williamson*, 316 U.S. 535, 62 S.Ct. 1110, 86 L.Ed. 1655. But the Court has recognized as well that the Constitution protects "a *woman's* decision whether or not to terminate her pregnancy." *Roe v. Wade, supra*, 410 U.S., at 153, 93 S.Ct., at 727 (emphasis added). In assessing the constitutional validity of §3(3) we are called upon to choose between these competing rights. I agree with the Court that since "it is the woman who physically bears the child and who is the more directly and immediately affected by the pregnancy...the balance weighs in her favor."

With respect to the state law's requirement of parental consent, §3(4), I think it clear that its primary constitutional deficiency lies in its imposition of an absolute limitation on the minor's right to obtain an abortion. The Court's opinion today in *Bellotti v. Baird*, 428 U.S. 132, 147–148, 96 S.Ct. 2857, 2866, 49 L.Ed.2d 844, suggests that a materially different constitutional issue would be presented under a provision requiring parental consent or consultation in most cases but providing for prompt (i) judicial resolution of any disagreement between the parent and the minor, or (ii) judicial determination that the minor is mature enough to give an informed consent without parental concurrence or that abortion in any event is in the minor's best interest. Such a provision would not impose parental approval as an absolute condition upon the minor's right but would assure in most instances consultation between the parent and child.[1]

1. For some of the considerations that support the State's interest in encouraging parental consent, see the opinion of Mr. Justice STEVENS, concurring in part and dissenting in part. Post, at 2856–2857.

There can be little doubt that the State furthers a constitutionally permissible end by encouraging an unmarried pregnant minor to seek the help and advice of her parents in making the very important decision whether or not to bear a child. That is a grave decision, and a girl of tender years, under emotional stress, may be ill-equipped to make it without mature advice and emotional support. It seems unlikely that she will obtain adequate counsel and support from the attending physician at an abortion clinic, where abortions for pregnant minors frequently take place.[2]

Mr. Justice WHITE, with whom the CHIEF JUSTICE and Mr. Justice REHNQUIST join, concurring in the judgment in part and dissenting in part.

...

I

...Section 3(3) of the Act provides that a married woman may not obtain an abortion without her husband's consent. The Court strikes down this statute in one sentence. It says that "since the State cannot...proscribe abortion...the State cannot delegate authority to any particular person, even the spouse, to prevent abortion...." But the State is not under §3(3) delegating to the husband the power to vindicate the *State's* interest in the future life of the fetus. It is instead recognizing that the husband has an interest of his own in the life of the fetus which should not be extinguished by the unilateral decision of the wife.[1] It by no means follows, from the fact that the mother's interest in deciding "whether or not to terminate her pregnancy" outweighs the State's interest in the potential life of the fetus, that the husband's interest is also outweighed and may not be protected by the State. A father's interest in having a child perhaps his only child may be unmatched by any other interest in his life. See *Stanley v. Illinois*, 405 U.S. 645, 651, 92 S.Ct. 1208, 1212, 31 L.Ed.2d 551 (1972), and cases there cited. It is truly surprising that the majority finds in the United States Constitution, as it must in order to justify the result it reaches, a rule that the State must assign a greater value to a mother's decision to cut off a potential human life by abortion than to a father's decision to let it mature into a live child. Such a rule cannot be found there, nor can it be found in *Roe v. Wade, supra.* These are matters which a State should be able to decide free from the suffocating power of the federal judge, purporting to act in the name of the Constitution.

---

2. The mode of operation of one such clinic is revealed by the record in *Bellotti v. Baird*, 428 U.S. 132, 96 S.Ct. 2857, 49 L.Ed.2d 844, and accurately described by appellants in that case: "The counseling...occurs entirely on the day the abortion is to be performed.... It lasts for two hours and takes place in groups that include both minors and adults who are strangers to one another.... The physician takes no part in this counseling process.... Counseling is typically limited to a description of abortion procedures, possible complications, and birth control techniques.... "The abortion itself takes five to seven minutes.... The physician has no prior contact with the minor, and on the days that abortions are being performed at the [clinic], the physician,...may be performing abortions on many other adults and minors.... On busy days patients are scheduled in separate groups, consisting usually of five patients.... After the abortion [the physician] spends a brief period with the minor and others in the group in the recovery room...." Brief for Appellants in No. 75–73, O.T.1975, pp. 43–44.

...

1. There are countless situations in which the State prohibits conduct only when it is objected to by a private person most closely affected by it. Thus a State cannot forbid anyone to enter on private property with the owner's consent, but it may enact and enforce trespass laws against unauthorized entrances. It cannot forbid transfer of property held in tenancy by the entireties but it may require consent by both husband and wife to such a transfer. These situations plainly do not involve delegations of legislative power to private parties; and neither does the requirement in §3(3) that a woman not deprive her husband of his future child without his consent.

In describing the nature of a mother's interest in terminating a pregnancy, the Court in *Roe v. Wade* mentioned only the post-birth burdens of rearing a child, 410 U.S., at 153, 93 S.Ct., at 726, and rejected a rule based on her interest in controlling her own body during pregnancy. *Id.*, at 154, 93 S.Ct., at 727. Missouri has a law which prevents a woman from putting a child up for adoption over her husband's objection, Mo.Rev.Stat. §453.030 (1969). This law represents a judgment by the State that the mother's interest in avoiding the burdens of child rearing do not outweigh or snuff out the father's interest in participating in bringing up his own child. That law is plainly valid, but no more so than §3(3) of the Act now before us, resting as it does on precisely the same judgment.

II

Section 3(4) requires that an unmarried woman under 18 years of age obtain the consent of a parent or a person *in loco parentis* as a condition to an abortion. Once again the Court strikes the provision down in a sentence. It states: "Just as with the requirement of consent from the spouse, so here, the State does not have the constitutional authority to give a third party an absolute, and possibly arbitrary, veto over the decision of the physician and his patient to terminate the patient's pregnancy...." The Court rejects the notions that the State has an interest in strengthening the family unit or that the Parent has an "independent interest" in the abortion decision, sufficient to justify §3(4) and apparently concludes that the provision is therefore unconstitutional. But the purpose of the parental-consent requirement is not merely to vindicate any interest of the parent or of the State. The purpose of the requirement is to vindicate the very right created in *Roe v. Wade, supra* the right of the pregnant woman to decide "whether *or not* to terminate her pregnancy." 410 U.S., at 153, 93 S.Ct., at 727 (emphasis added). The abortion decision is unquestionably important and has irrevocable consequences whichever way it is made. Missouri is entitled to protect the minor unmarried woman from making the decision in a way which is not in her own best interests, and it seeks to achieve this goal by requiring parental consultation and consent. This is the traditional way by which States have sought to protect children from their own immature and improvident decisions; and there is absolutely no reason expressed by the majority why the State may not utilize that method here.

...

Mr. Justice STEVENS, concurring in part and dissenting in part.

...

In my opinion...the parental-consent requirement is consistent with the holding in *Roe.* The State's interest in the welfare of its young citizens justifies a variety of protective measures. Because he may not foresee the consequences of his decision, a minor may not make an enforceable bargain. He may not lawfully work or travel where he pleases, or even attend exhibitions of constitutionally protected adult motion pictures. Persons below a certain age may not marry without parental consent. Indeed, such consent is essential even when the young woman is already pregnant. The State's interest in protecting a young person from harm justifies the imposition of restraints on his or her freedom even though comparable restraints on adults would be constitutionally impermissible. Therefore, the holding in *Roe v. Wade* that the abortion decision is entitled to constitutional protection merely emphasizes the importance of the decision; it does not lead to the conclusion that the state legislature has no power to enact legislation for the purpose of protecting a young pregnant woman from the consequences of an incorrect decision.

The abortion decision is, of course, more important than the decision to attend or to avoid an adult motion picture, or the decision to work long hours in a factory. It is not necessarily any more important than the decision to run away from home or the decision to marry. But even if it is the most important kind of decision a young person may ever make, that assumption merely enhances the quality of the State's interest in maximizing the probability that the decision be made correctly and with full understanding of the consequences of either alternative.

The Court recognizes that the State may insist that the decision not be made without the benefit of medical advice. But since the most significant consequences of the decision are not medical in character, it would seem to me that the State may, with equal legitimacy, insist that the decision be made only after other appropriate counsel has been had as well. Whatever choice a pregnant young woman makes to marry, to abort, to bear her child out of wedlock the consequences of her decision may have a profound impact on her entire future life. A legislative determination that such a choice will be made more wisely in most cases if the advice and moral support of a parent play a part in the decisionmaking process is surely not irrational. Moreover, it is perfectly clear that the parental-consent requirement will necessarily involve a parent in the decisional process.

If there is no parental-consent requirement, many minors will submit to the abortion procedure without ever informing their parents. An assumption that the parental reaction will be hostile, disparaging, or violent no doubt persuades many children simply to bypass parental counsel which would in fact be loving, supportive, and, indeed for some indispensable. It is unrealistic, in my judgment, to assume that every parent-child relationship is either (a) so perfect that communication and accord will take place routinely or (b) so imperfect that the absence of communication reflects the child's correct prediction that the parent will exercise his or her veto arbitrarily to further a selfish interest rather than the child's interest. A state legislature may conclude that most parents will be primarily interested in the welfare of their children, and further, that the imposition of a parental-consent requirement is an appropriate method of giving the parents an opportunity to foster that welfare by helping a pregnant distressed child to make and to implement a correct decision.

The State's interest is not dependent on an estimate of the impact the parental-consent requirement may have on the total number of abortions that may take place. I assume that parents will sometimes prevent abortions which might better be performed; other parents may advise abortions that should not be performed. Similarly, even doctors are not omniscient; specialists in performing abortions may incorrectly conclude that the immediate advantages of the procedure outweigh the disadvantages which a parent could evaluate in better perspective. In each individual case factors much more profound than a mere medical judgment may weigh heavily in the scales. The overriding consideration is that the right to make the choice be exercised as wisely as possible.

The Court assumes that parental consent is an appropriate requirement if the minor is not capable of understanding the procedure and of appreciating its consequences and those of available alternatives. This assumption is, of course, correct and consistent with the predicate which underlies all state legislation seeking to protect minors from the consequences of decisions they are not yet prepared to make. In all such situations chronological age has been the basis for imposition of a restraint on the minor's freedom of choice even though it is perfectly obvious that such a yardstick is imprecise and perhaps even unjust in particular cases. The Court seems to assume that the capacity to conceive a child and the judgment of the physician are the only constitutionally permissible yardsticks for determining whether a young woman can independently make the abortion decision. I doubt the accuracy of the Court's empirical judgment. Even if it were correct, however, as a matter of constitutional law I think a State has power to conclude otherwise and to select a chronological age as a standard.

In short, the State's interest in the welfare of its young citizens is sufficient, in my judgment, to support the parental-consent requirement.

BELLOTTI v. BAIRD

United States Supreme Court
443 U.S. 622 (1979)

Mr. Justice POWELL announced the judgment of the Court and delivered an opinion, in which the CHIEF JUSTICE, Mr. Justice STEWART, and Mr. Justice REHNQUIST joined.

These appeals present a challenge to the constitutionality of a state statute regulating the access of minors to abortions. They require us to continue the inquiry we began in *Planned Parenthood of Central Missouri v. Danforth*, 428 U.S. 52, 96 S.Ct. 2831, 49 L.Ed.2d 788 (1976), and *Bellotti v. Baird*, 428 U.S. 132, 96 S.Ct. 2857, 49 L.Ed.2d 844 (1976).

On August 2, 1974, the Legislature of the Commonwealth of Massachusetts passed, over the Governor's veto, an Act pertaining to abortions performed within the State. 1974 Mass. Acts, ch. 706. According to its title, the statute was intended to regulate abortions "within present constitutional limits." Shortly before the Act was to go into effect, the class action from which these appeals arise was commenced in the District Court to enjoin, as unconstitutional, the provision of the Act now codified as Mass.Gen.Laws Ann., ch. 112, §12S (West Supp.1979).

Section 12S provides in part:

> If the mother is less than eighteen years of age and has not married, the consent of both the mother and her parents [to an abortion to be performed on the mother] is required. If one or both of the mother's parents refuse such consent, consent may be obtained by order of a judge of the superior court for good cause shown, after such hearing as he deems necessary. Such a hearing will not require the appointment of a guardian for the mother. If one of the parents has died or has deserted his or her family, consent by the remaining parent is sufficient. If both parents have died or have deserted their family, consent of the mother's guardian or other person having duties similar to a guardian, or any person who had assumed the care and custody of the mother is sufficient. The commissioner of public health shall prescribe a written form for such consent. Such form shall be signed by the proper person or persons and given to the physician performing the abortion who shall maintain it in his permanent files.

...

A child, merely on account of his minority, is not beyond the protection of the Constitution. As the Court said in *In re Gault*, 387 U.S. 1, 13, 87 S.Ct. 1428, 1436,

18 L.Ed.2d 527 (1967), "whatever may be their precise impact, neither the Fourteenth Amendment nor the Bill of Rights is for adults alone."[12] This observation, of course, is but the beginning of the analysis. The Court long has recognized that the status of minors under the law is unique in many respects. As Mr. Justice FRANKFURTER aptly put it: "[C]hildren have a very special place in life which law should reflect. Legal theories and their phrasing in other cases readily lead to fallacious reasoning if uncritically transferred to determination of a State's duty towards children." *May v. Anderson*, 345 U.S. 528, 536, 73 S.Ct. 840, 844, 97 L.Ed. 1221 (1953)(concurring opinion). The unique role in our society of the family, the institution by which "we inculcate and pass down many of our most cherished values, moral and cultural," *Moore v. East Cleveland*, 431 U.S. 494, 503–504, 97 S.Ct. 1932, 1938, 52 L.Ed.2d 531 (1977)(plurality opinion), requires that constitutional principles be applied with sensitivity and flexibility to the special needs of parents and children. We have recognized three reasons justifying the conclusion that the constitutional rights of children cannot be equated with those of adults: the peculiar vulnerability of children; their inability to make critical decisions in an informed, mature manner; and the importance of the parental role in child rearing.

The Court's concern for the vulnerability of children is demonstrated in its decisions dealing with minors' claims to constitutional protection against deprivations of liberty or property interests by the State. With respect to many of these claims, we have concluded that the child's right is virtually coextensive with that of an adult. For example, the Court has held that the Fourteenth Amendment's guarantee against the deprivation of liberty without due process of law is applicable to children in juvenile delinquency proceedings. *In re Gault, supra.* In particular, minors involved in such proceedings are entitled to adequate notice, the assistance of counsel, and the opportunity to confront their accusers. They can be found guilty only upon proof beyond a reasonable doubt, and they may assert the privilege against compulsory self-incrimination.

These rulings have not been made on the uncritical assumption that the constitutional rights of children are indistinguishable from those of adults. Indeed, our acceptance of juvenile courts distinct from the adult criminal justice system assumes that juvenile offenders constitutionally may be treated differently from adults. In order to preserve this separate avenue for dealing with minors, the Court has said that hearings in juvenile delinquency cases need not necessarily "'conform with all of the requirements of a criminal trial or even of the usual administrative hearing.'" *In re Gault, supra*, 387 U.S., at 30, 87 S.Ct., at 1445, quoting *Kent v. United States*, 383 U.S. 541, 562, 86 S.Ct. 1045, 1057, 16 L.Ed.2d 84 (1966). Thus, juveniles are not constitutionally entitled to trial by jury in delinquency adjudications. *McKeiver v. Pennsylvania*, 403 U.S. 528, 91 S.Ct. 1976, 29 L.Ed.2d 647 (1971). Viewed together, our cases show that although children generally are protected by the same constitutional guarantees against governmental deprivations as are adults, the State is entitled to adjust its legal system to account for children's vulnerability and their needs for "concern,...sympathy, and...paternal attention." *Id.*, at 550, 91 S.Ct., at 1989 (plurality opinion).

---

12. Similarly, the Court said in *Planned Parenthood of Central Missouri v. Danforth*, 428 U.S. 52, 74, 96 S.Ct. 2831, 2843, 49 L.Ed.2d 788 (1976):

> Constitutional rights do not mature and come into being magically only when one attains the state-defined age of majority. Minors, as well as adults, are protected by the Constitution and possess constitutional rights.

Second, the Court has held that the States validly may limit the freedom of children to choose for themselves in the making of important, affirmative choices with potentially serious consequences. These rulings have been grounded in the recognition that, during the formative years of childhood and adolescence, minors often lack the experience, perspective, and judgment to recognize and avoid choices that could be detrimental to them.[13]

...

Third, the guiding role of parents in the upbringing of their children justifies limitations on the freedoms of minors. The State commonly protects its youth from adverse governmental action and from their own immaturity by requiring parental consent to or involvement in important decisions by minors. But an additional and more important justification for state deference to parental control over children is that "[t]he child is not the mere creature of the state; those who nurture him and direct his destiny have the right, coupled with the high duty, to recognize and prepare him for additional obligations." *Pierce v. Society of Sisters*, 268 U.S. 510, 535, 45 S.Ct. 571, 573, 69 L.Ed. 1070 (1925). "The duty to prepare the child for 'additional obligations'...must be read to include the inculcation of moral standards, religious beliefs, and elements of good citizenship." *Wisconsin v. Yoder*, 406 U.S. 205, 233, 92 S.Ct. 1526, 1542, 32 L.Ed.2d 15 (1972). This affirmative process of teaching, guiding, and inspiring by precept and example is essential to the growth of young people into mature, socially responsible citizens.

We have believed in this country that this process, in large part, is beyond the competence of impersonal political institutions. Indeed, affirmative sponsorship of particular ethical, religious, or political beliefs is something we expect the State not to attempt in a society constitutionally committed to the ideal of individual liberty and freedom of choice. Thus, "[i]t is cardinal with us that the custody, care and nurture of the child reside first in the parents, whose primary function and freedom include *preparation for obligations the state can neither supply nor hinder.*" *Prince v. Massachusetts, supra*, 321 U.S., at 166, 64 S.Ct., at 442 (emphasis added).

Unquestionably, there are many competing theories about the most effective way for parents to fulfill their central role in assisting their children on the way to responsible adulthood. While we do not pretend any special wisdom on this subject, we cannot ignore that central to many of these theories, and deeply rooted in our Nation's history and tradition, is the belief that the parental role implies a substantial measure of authority over one's children. Indeed, "constitutional interpretation has consistently recognized that the parents' claim to authority in their own household to direct the rearing of their children is basic in the structure of our society." *Ginsberg v. New York, supra*, 390 U.S., at 639, 88 S.Ct., at 1280.

Properly understood, then, the tradition of parental authority is not inconsistent with our tradition of individual liberty; rather, the former is one of the basic presuppositions of the latter. Legal restrictions on minors, especially those supportive of the parental role, may be important to the child's chances for the full

---

13. As Mr. Justice STEWART wrote of the exercise by minors of the First Amendment rights that "secur[e]...the liberty of each man to decide for himself what he will read and to what he will listen," *Ginsberg v. New York*, 390 U.S. 629, 649, 88 S.Ct. 1274, 1285, 20 L.Ed.2d 195 (1968)(concurring in result):

> [A]t least in some precisely delineated areas, a child — like someone in a captive audience — is not possessed of that full capacity for individual choice which is the presupposition of First Amendment guarantees. It is only upon such a premise, I should suppose, that a State may deprive children of other rights — the right to marry, for example, or the right to vote — deprivations that would be constitutionally intolerable for adults.

Id., at 649–650, 88 S.Ct., at 1286 (footnotes omitted).

growth and maturity that make eventual participation in a free society meaningful and rewarding. Under the Constitution, the State can "properly conclude that parents and others, teachers for example, who have [the] primary responsibility for children's well-being are entitled to the support of laws designed to aid discharge of that responsibility." *Ginsberg v. New York*, 390 U.S., at 639, 88 S.Ct., at 1280.

With these principles in mind, we consider the specific constitutional questions presented by these appeals. In §12S, Massachusetts has attempted to reconcile the constitutional right of a woman, in consultation with her physician, to choose to terminate her pregnancy as established by *Roe v. Wade*, 410 U.S. 113, 93 S.Ct. 705, 35 L.Ed.2d 147 (1973), and *Doe v. Bolton*, 410 U.S. 179, 93 S.Ct. 739, 35 L.Ed.2d 201 (1973), with the special interest of the State in encouraging an unmarried pregnant minor to seek the advice of her parents in making the important decision whether or not to bear a child.... [Section] 12S was before us in *Bellotti I*, 428 U.S. 132, 96 S.Ct. 2857, 49 L.Ed.2d 844 (1976), where we remanded the case for interpretation of its provisions by the Supreme Judicial Court of Massachusetts. We previously had held in *Planned Parenthood of Central Missouri v. Danforth*, 428 U.S. 52, 96 S.Ct. 2831, 49 L.Ed.2d 788 (1976), that a State could not lawfully authorize an absolute parental veto over the decision of a minor to terminate her pregnancy. *Id.*, at 74, 96 S.Ct., at 2843. *In Bellotti, supra*, we recognized that §12S could be read as "fundamentally different from a statute that creates a 'parental veto,'" 428 U.S., at 145, 96 S.Ct., at 2865, thus "avoid[ing] or substantially modify[ing] the federal constitutional challenge to the statute." *Id.*, at 148, 96 S.Ct., at 2866. The question before us — in light of what we have said in the prior cases — is whether §12S, as authoritatively interpreted by the Supreme Judicial Court, provides for parental notice and consent in a manner that does not unduly burden the right to seek an abortion. *See id.*, at 147, 96 S.Ct., at 2866.

Appellees and intervenors contend that even as interpreted by the Supreme Judicial Court of Massachusetts, §12S does unduly burden this right. They suggest, for example, that the mere requirement of parental notice constitutes such a burden. As stated...above, however, parental notice and consent are qualifications that typically may be imposed by the State on a minor's right to make important decisions. As immature minors often lack the ability to make fully informed choices that take account of both immediate and long-range consequences, a State reasonably may determine that parental consultation often is desirable and in the best interest of the minor. It may further determine, as a general proposition, that such consultation is particularly desirable with respect to the abortion decision — one that for some people raises profound moral and religious concerns.[20] As Mr. Justice STEWART wrote in concurrence in *Planned Parenthood of Central Missouri v. Danforth, supra*, at 91, 96 S.Ct., at 2851:

> There can be little doubt that the State furthers a constitutionally permissible end by encouraging an unmarried pregnant minor to seek the help and advice of her parents in making the very important decision whether or not to bear a child. That is a grave decision, and a girl of tender years, under emotional stress, may be ill-equipped to make it without mature advice and emotional support. It seems unlikely that she will obtain adequate counsel and support from the attending physician at an abortion

---

20. The expert testimony at the hearings in the District Court uniformly was to the effect that parental involvement in a minor's abortion decision, if compassionate and supportive, was highly desirable. The findings of the court reflect this consensus. See *Baird I*, 393 F.Supp., at 853.

clinic, where abortions for pregnant minors frequently take place. (Footnote omitted.)[21]

But we are concerned here with a constitutional right to seek an abortion. The abortion decision differs in important ways from other decisions that may be made during minority. The need to preserve the constitutional right and the unique nature of the abortion decision, especially when made by a minor, require a State to act with particular sensitivity when it legislates to foster parental involvement in this matter.

A

The pregnant minor's options are much different from those facing a minor in other situations, such as deciding whether to marry. A minor not permitted to marry before the age of majority is required simply to postpone her decision. She and her intended spouse may preserve the opportunity for later marriage should they continue to desire it. A pregnant adolescent, however, cannot preserve for long the possibility of aborting, which effectively expires in a matter of weeks from the onset of pregnancy.

Moreover, the potentially severe detriment facing a pregnant woman, see *Roe v. Wade*, 410 U.S., at 153, 93 S.Ct., at 726, is not mitigated by her minority. Indeed, considering her probable education, employment skills, financial resources, and emotional maturity, unwanted motherhood may be exceptionally burdensome for a minor. In addition, the fact of having a child brings with it adult legal responsibility, for parenthood, like attainment of the age of majority, is one of the traditional criteria for the termination of the legal disabilities of minority. In sum, there are few situations in which denying a minor the right to make an important decision will have consequences so grave and indelible.

Yet, an abortion may not be the best choice for the minor. The circumstances in which this issue arises will vary widely. In a given case, alternatives to abortion, such as marriage to the father of the child, arranging for its adoption, or assuming the responsibilities of motherhood with the assured support of family, may be feasible and relevant to the minor's best interests. Nonetheless, the abortion decision is one that simply cannot be postponed, or it will be made by default with far-reaching consequences.

For these reasons, as we held in *Planned Parenthood of Central Missouri v. Danforth, supra*, 428 U.S., at 74, "the State may not impose a blanket provision... requiring the consent of a parent or person *in loco parentis* as a condition for abortion of an unmarried minor during the first 12 weeks of her pregnancy." Although,...such deference to parents may be permissible with respect to other

21. Mr. Justice STEWART'S concurring opinion in *Danforth* underscored the need for parental involvement in minors' abortion decisions by describing the procedures followed at the clinic operated by the Parents Aid Society and Dr. Gerald Zupnick:

> The counseling...occurs entirely on the day the abortion is to be performed.... It lasts for two hours and takes place in groups that include both minors and adults who are strangers to one another.... The physician takes no part in this counseling process.... Counseling is typically limited to a description of abortion procedures, possible complications, and birth control techniques....
>
> The abortion itself takes five to seven minutes.... The physician has no prior contact with the minor, and on the days that abortions are being performed at the [clinic], the physician...may be performing abortions on many other adults and minors.... On busy days patients are scheduled in separate groups, consisting usually of five patients.... After the abortion [the physician] spends a brief period with the minor and others in the group in the recovery room...." 428 U.S., at 91–92, n. 2, 96 S.Ct., at 2851 n. 2, quoting Brief for Appellants in Bellotti I, O.T.1975, No. 75–73, pp. 43–44.

...

choices facing a minor, the unique nature and consequences of the abortion decision make it inappropriate "to give a third party an absolute, and possibly arbitrary, veto over the decision of the physician and his patient to terminate the patient's pregnancy, regardless of the reason for withholding the consent." 428 U.S., at 74. We therefore conclude that if the State decides to require a pregnant minor to obtain one or both parents' consent to an abortion, it also must provide an alternative procedure[22] whereby authorization for the abortion can be obtained.

A pregnant minor is entitled in such a proceeding to show either: (1) that she is mature enough and well enough informed to make her abortion decision, in consultation with her physician, independently of her parents' wishes;[23] or (2) that even if she is not able to make this decision independently, the desired abortion would be in her best interests. The proceeding in which this showing is made must assure that a resolution of the issue, and any appeals that may follow, will be completed with anonymity and sufficient expedition to provide an effective opportunity for an abortion to be obtained. In sum, the procedure must ensure that the provision requiring parental consent does not in fact amount to the "absolute, and possibly arbitrary, veto" that was found impermissible in *Danforth. Ibid.*

It is against these requirements that §12S must be tested. We observe initially that as authoritatively construed by the highest court of the State, the statute satisfies some of the concerns that require special treatment of a minor's abortion decision. It provides that if parental consent is refused, authorization may be "obtained by order of a judge of the superior court for good cause shown, after such hearing as he deems necessary." A superior court judge presiding over a §12S proceeding "must disregard all parental objections, and other considerations, which are not based exclusively on what would serve the minor's best interests."[24] *Attorney General*, 371 Mass., at 748, 360 N.E.2d, at 293. The Supreme Judicial Court also stated: "[p]rompt resolution of a [§12S] proceeding may be expected.... The proceeding need not be brought in the minor's name and steps may be taken, by impoundment or otherwise, to preserve confidentiality as to the minor and her parents.... [W]e believe that an early hearing and decision on appeal from a judgment of a Superior Court judge may also be achieved." *Id.*, at 757–758, 360 N.E.2d, at 298. The court added that if these expectations were not met, either the superior

22. As §12S provides for involvement of the state superior court in minors' abortion decisions, we discuss the alternative procedure described in the text in terms of judicial proceedings. We do not suggest, however, that a State choosing to require parental consent could not delegate the alternative procedure to a juvenile court or an administrative agency or officer. Indeed, much can be said for employing procedures and a forum less formal than those associated with a court of general jurisdiction.

23. The nature of both the State's interest in fostering parental authority and the problem of determining "maturity" makes clear why the State generally may resort to objective, though inevitably arbitrary, criteria such as age limits, marital status, or membership in the Armed Forces for lifting some or all of the legal disabilities of minority. Not only is it difficult to define, let alone determine, maturity, but also the fact that a minor may be very much an adult in some respects does not mean that his or her need and opportunity for growth under parental guidance and discipline have ended. As discussed in the text, however, the peculiar nature of the abortion decision requires the opportunity for case-by-case evaluations of the maturity of pregnant minors.

24. The Supreme Judicial Court held that §12S imposed this standard on the superior court in large part because it construed the statute as containing the same restriction on parents. See *supra*, at 3041. The court concluded that the judge should not be entitled "to exercise his authority on a standard broader than that to which a parent must adhere." *Attorney General*, 371 Mass., at 748, 360 N.E.2d, at 293.

Intervenors argue that, assuming state-supported parental involvement in the minor's abortion decision is permissible, the State may not endorse the withholding of parental consent for any reason not believed to be in the minor's best interests. They agree with the District Court that, even though §12S was construed by the highest state court to impose this restriction, the statute is flawed because the restriction is not apparent on its face....

...

court, in the exercise of its rulemaking power, or the Supreme Judicial Court would be willing to eliminate any undue burdens by rule or order. *Ibid.*

Despite these safeguards, which avoid much of what was objectionable in the statute successfully challenged in *Danforth*, §12S falls short of constitutional standards in certain respects. We now consider these.

Among the questions certified to the Supreme Judicial Court was whether §12S permits any minors — mature or immature — to obtain judicial consent to an abortion without any parental consultation whatsoever. See n. 9, *supra.* The state court answered that, in general, it does not. "[T]he consent required by [§12S must] be obtained for every nonemergency abortion where the mother is less than eighteen years of age and unmarried." *Attorney General, supra*, at 750, 360 N.E.2d, at 294. The text of §12S itself states an exception to this rule, making consent unnecessary from any parent who has "died or has deserted his or her family." The Supreme Judicial Court construed the statute as containing an additional exception: Consent need not be obtained "where no parent (or statutory substitute) is available." *Ibid.* The court also ruled that an available parent must be given notice of any judicial proceedings brought by a minor to obtain consent for an abortion.[27] *Id.*, at 755–756, 360 N.E.2d, at 297.

We think that, construed in this manner, §12S would impose an undue burden upon the exercise by minors of the right to seek an abortion. As the District Court recognized, "there are parents who would obstruct, and perhaps altogether prevent, the minor's right to go to court." *Baird III, supra,* [450 F.Supp.] at 1001. There is no reason to believe that this would be so in the majority of cases where consent is withheld. But many parents hold strong views on the subject of abortion, and young pregnant minors, especially those living at home, are particularly vulnerable to their parents' efforts to obstruct both an abortion and their access to court. It would be unrealistic, therefore, to assume that the mere existence of a legal right to seek relief in superior court provides an effective avenue of relief for some of those who need it the most.

We conclude, therefore, that under state regulation such as that undertaken by Massachusetts, every minor must have the opportunity — if she so desires — to go directly to a court without first consulting or notifying her parents. If she satisfies the court that she is mature and well enough informed to make intelligently the abortion decision on her own, the court must authorize her to act without parental consultation or consent. If she fails to satisfy the court that she is competent to make this decision independently, she must be permitted to show that an

27. This reading of the statute requires parental consultation and consent more strictly than appellants themselves previously believed was necessary. In their first argument before this Court, and again before the Supreme Judicial Court, appellants argued that §12S was not intended to abrogate Massachusetts' common-law "mature minor" rule as it applies to abortions. See 428 U.S., at 144, 96 S.Ct., at 2864. They also suggested that, under some circumstances, §12S might permit even immature minors to obtain judicial approval for an abortion without any parental consultation. See 428 U.S., at 145, 96 S.Ct., at 2865; *Attorney General, supra,* 371 Mass., at 751, 360 N.E.2d, at 294. The Supreme Judicial Court sketched the outlines of the mature minor rule that would apply in the absence of §12S: "The mature minor rule calls for an analysis of the nature of the operation, its likely benefit, and the capacity of the particular minor to understand fully what the medical procedure involves... Judicial intervention is not required. If judicial approval is obtained, however, the doctor is protected from a subsequent claim that the circumstances did not warrant his reliance on the mature minor rule, and, of course, the minor patient is afforded advance protection against a misapplication of the rule." *Id.,* at 752, 360 N.E.2d, at 295. "We conclude that, apart from statutory limitations which are constitutional, where the best interests of a minor will be served by not notifying his or her parents of intended medical treatment and where the minor is capable of giving informed consent to that treatment, the mature minor rule applies in this Commonwealth." *Id.,* at 754, 360 N.E.2d, at 296. The Supreme Judicial Court held that the common-law mature minor rule was inapplicable to abortions because it had been legislatively superseded by §12S.

abortion nevertheless would be in her best interests. If the court is persuaded that it is, the court must authorize the abortion. If, however, the court is not persuaded by the minor that she is mature or that the abortion would be in her best interests, it may decline to sanction the operation.

There is, however, an important state interest in encouraging a family rather than a judicial resolution of a minor's abortion decision. Also, as we have observed above, parents naturally take an interest in the welfare of their children — an interest that is particularly strong where a normal family relationship exists and where the child is living with one or both parents. These factors properly may be taken into account by a court called upon to determine whether an abortion in fact is in a minor's best interests. If, all things considered, the court determines that an abortion is in the minor's best interests, she is entitled to court authorization without any parental involvement. On the other hand, the court may deny the abortion request of an immature minor in the absence of parental consultation if it concludes that her best interests would be served thereby, or the court may in such a case defer decision until there is parental consultation in which the court may participate. But this is the full extent to which parental involvement may be required.[28] For the reasons stated above, the constitutional right to seek an abortion may not be unduly burdened by state-imposed conditions upon initial access to court.

Section 12S requires that both parents consent to a minor's abortion. The District Court found it to be "custom" to perform other medical and surgical procedures on minors with the consent of only one parent, and it concluded that "nothing about abortions...requires the minor's interest to be treated differently." *Baird I, supra*, at 852. See *Baird III, supra*, at 1004 n. 9.

We are not persuaded that, as a general rule, the requirement of obtaining both parents' consent unconstitutionally burdens a minor's right to seek an abortion. The abortion decision has implications far broader than those associated with most other kinds of medical treatment. At least when the parents are together and the pregnant minor is living at home, both the father and mother have an interest — one normally supportive — in helping to determine the course that is in the best interests of a daughter. Consent and involvement by parents in important decisions by minors long have been recognized as protective of their immaturity. In the case of the abortion decision, for reasons we have stated, the focus of the parents' inquiry should be the best interests of their daughter. As every pregnant minor is entitled in the first instance to go directly to the court for a judicial determination without prior parental notice, consultation, or consent, the general rule with respect to parental consent does not unduly burden the constitutional right. Moreover, where the pregnant minor goes to her parents and consent is denied, she still must have recourse to a prompt judicial determination of her maturity or best interests.[29]

Another of the questions certified by the District Court to the Supreme Judicial Court was the following: "If the superior court finds that the minor is capable [of making], and has, in fact, made and adhered to, an informed and reasonable decision to have an abortion, may the court refuse its consent based on a finding that

28. Of course, if the minor consults with her parents voluntarily and they withhold consent, she is free to seek judicial authorization for the abortion immediately.

29. There will be cases where the pregnant minor has received approval of the abortion decision by one parent. In that event, the parent can support the daughter's request for a prompt judicial determination, and the parent's support should be given great, if not dispositive, weight.

a parent's, or its own, contrary decision is a better one?" *Attorney General*, 371 Mass., at 747 n. 5, 360 N.E.2d, at 293 n. 5. To this the state court answered:

> [W]e do not view the judge's role as limited to a determination that the minor is capable of making, and has made, an informed and reasonable decision to have an abortion. Certainly the judge must make a determination of those circumstances, but, if the statutory role of the judge to determine the best interests of the minor is to be carried out, he must make a finding on the basis of all relevant views presented to him. We suspect that the judge will give great weight to the minor's determination, if informed and reasonable, but in circumstances where he determines that the best interests of the minor will not be served by an abortion, the judge's determination should prevail, assuming that his conclusion is supported by the evidence and adequate findings of fact.

Id., at 748, 360 N.E.2d, at 293.

The Supreme Judicial Court's statement reflects the general rule that a State may require a minor to wait until the age of majority before being permitted to exercise legal rights independently. See n. 23, *supra*. But we are concerned here with the exercise of a constitutional right of unique character. See *supra*, at 3047–3048. As stated above, if the minor satisfies a court that she has attained sufficient maturity to make a fully informed decision, she then is entitled to make her abortion decision independently. We therefore agree with the District Court that §12S cannot constitutionally permit judicial disregard of the abortion decision of a minor who has been determined to be mature and fully competent to assess the implications of the choice she has made.

Although it satisfies constitutional standards in large part, §12S falls short of them in two respects: First, it permits judicial authorization for an abortion to be withheld from a minor who is found by the superior court to be mature and fully competent to make this decision independently. Second, it requires parental consultation or notification in every instance, without affording the pregnant minor an opportunity to receive an independent judicial determination that she is mature enough to consent or that an abortion would be in her best interests.[31] Accordingly, we affirm the judgment of the District Court insofar as it invalidates this statute and enjoins its enforcement.

Affirmed.

[Concurring opinion of Mr. Justice REHNQUIST and dissenting opinion of Mr. Justice STEVENS are omitted.]

---

31. Section 12S evidently applies to all nonemergency abortions performed on minors, without regard to the period in pregnancy during which the procedure occurs. As the court below recognized, most abortions are performed during the early stages of pregnancy, before the end of the first trimester. See *Baird III*, 450 F.Supp., at 1001; *Baird I*, 393 F.Supp., at 853. This coincides approximately with the pre-viability [sic] period during which a pregnant woman's right to decide, in consultation with her physician, to have an abortion is most immune to state intervention. See *Roe v. Wade*, 410 U.S., at 164–165, 93 S.Ct., at 732.

The propriety of parental involvement in a minor's abortion decision does not diminish as the pregnancy progresses and legitimate concerns for the pregnant minor's health increase. Furthermore, the opportunity for direct access to court which we have described is adequate to safeguard throughout pregnancy the constitutionally protected interests of a minor in the abortion decision. Thus, although a significant number of abortions within the scope of §12S might be performed during the later stages of pregnancy, we do not believe a different analysis of the statute is required for them.

PLANNED PARENTHOOD ASSOCIATION OF UTAH v. MATHESON

United States District Court
582 F. Supp. 1001 (D.Utah 1983)

WINDER, District Judge.

In this lawsuit, Planned Parenthood, two doctors and a minor male (the plaintiffs) challenge the validity of the Utah law which requires that "[a]ny person before providing contraceptives to a minor shall notify...the minor's parents or guardian of the service requested to be provided to such minor." Utah Code Ann. 76-7-325 (Supp.1983)(hereinafter cited as H.B. 343)....

The plaintiffs advance two arguments in support of their claim that H.B. 343 is invalid. First, the plaintiffs argue that H.B. 343 directly conflicts with Title X of the Public Health Service Act, 42 U.S.C. §300, *et seq.*, and with the AFDC and Medicaid programs found in the Social Security Act. *Id.* §§601, *et seq.*; §§1396, *et seq.* Second, the plaintiffs argue that H.B. 343 impermissibly infringes upon the constitutionally protected right of minors to decide whether to bear or to beget children. The defendants argue that H.B. 343 does not conflict with the express language of the federal laws cited by the plaintiffs. The defendants also argue that H.B. 343 does not burden any constitutionally protected rights, or that if it does, H.B. 343 properly balances the minor's privacy rights and the parents' rights to be involved in their children's decision making concerning contraceptive use.

...

...[T]he court concludes that the record establishes as undisputed fact the following.

1. Planned Parenthood provides family planning services to patients including unmarried, unemancipated minors.... Those services include the distribution of prescription and non-prescription contraceptives to male and female patients. Planned Parenthood performs extensive medical examinations on all family planning patients and also provides individual and group counseling for minors seeking family planning services. In addition, Planned Parenthood conducts educational programs for parents that include parent-child counseling and workshops designed to improve parents' skills in communicating with and teaching their children about human sexual relationships.

2. Doctors Chichester and Berk are physicians who are licensed to practice in Utah and are board certified in obstetrics and gynecology. Both doctors treat patients who are unmarried, unemancipated...minors seeking confidential family planning services. As part of those services Doctors Chichester and Berk prescribe contraceptives for their minor patients on a confidential basis. Dr. Chichester is a certified Medicaid provider and he treats minor patients who are Medicaid recipients and who would be [a]ffected by H.B. 343.

3. John Doe is an unmarried, unemancipated...minor who resides in Utah, is sexually active and uses contraceptives. John Doe has not informed his parents that he is sexually active or that he uses contraceptives, nor does he desire to do so. John Doe would not cease to be sexually active if H.B. 343 is implemented, but due to the parental disclosure requirement he would discontinue his use of contraceptives.

4. Scott Matheson, Governor of Utah, is responsible for the execution of the laws of Utah.

5. David Wilkinson, Attorney General of Utah, is responsible for defending all causes to which the state or any officer thereof in an official capacity is a party and

for exercising charge as attorney of all civil legal matters in which the state is in any way interested.

6. Planned Parenthood is a current grantee of federal family planning funds under Title X of the Public Health Services Act.

7. The majority of the minors who seek contraceptive services from Planned Parenthood have informed their parents or another family member of their sexual activity prior to visiting Planned Parenthood.

[The preemption arguments have been omitted.]

THE CONSTITUTIONAL ARGUMENT

The plaintiffs argue that H.B. 343 is unconstitutionally overbroad because it fails to distinguish between immature minors and either mature minors or immature minors who can demonstrate that parental notification is not in the minor's best interest. Although the Supreme Court has considered the validity of various regulatory laws directed at contraceptives, that Court has not addressed the argument advanced by the plaintiffs directly.

In *Griswold v. Connecticut*, 381 U.S. 479, 85 S.Ct. 1678, 14 L.Ed.2d 510 (1965), the Supreme Court recognized a "zone of privacy created by several fundamental constitutional guarantees," *id.* at 485, 85 S.Ct. at 1682, that precluded a state from prohibiting the use of contraceptives by married couples. *Id.* Subsequently, the Court held that the zone of privacy encompassed unmarried as well as married persons. *Eisenstadt v. Baird*, 405 U.S. 438, 453, 92 S.Ct. 1029, 1038, 31 L.Ed.2d 349 (1972). Applying the principle developed by *Griswold* and *Eisenstadt* in another situation, the Court stated that "[r]ead in the light of its progeny, the teaching of *Griswold* is that the Constitution protects individual decisions in matters of childbearing from unjustified intrusion by the State." *Carey v. Population Services International*, 431 U.S. 678, 687, 97 S.Ct. 2010, 2017, 52 L.Ed.2d 675 (1977).

As the *Carey* Court noted, "[r]estrictions on the distribution of contraceptives clearly burden the freedom to make such decisions." *Id.* at 687, 97 S.Ct. at 2017. Consequently, the Court held that as to adults, such laws must be justified by a compelling state interest and that the laws must be narrowly drawn to cover only the expressed state interests. *Id.* at 688, 97 S.Ct. at 2017. "This is so not because there is an independent fundamental 'right of access to contraceptives,' but because such access is essential to exercise of the constitutionally protected right of decision in matters of childbearing that is the underlying foundation of the holdings in *Griswold*, *Eisenstadt v. Baird*, and *Roe v. Wade* [410 U.S. 113, 93 S.Ct. 705, 35 L.Ed.2d 147 (1973)]." 431 U.S. at 688–89, 97 S.Ct. at 2017–18.

In *Planned Parenthood of Central Missouri v. Danforth*, 428 U.S. 52, 96 S.Ct. 2831, 49 L.Ed.2d 788 (1976), the Court recognized that the right of privacy protected by the Constitution extends to minors as well as to adults. *Id.* at 74–75, 96 S.Ct. at 2843–44. Although "the State has somewhat broader authority to regulate the activities of children than of adults," *id.* at 74, 96 S.Ct. at 2843, there must be a "significant state interest...that is not present in the case of an adult" to justify any burdens imposed on a minor's right to privacy. *Id.* at 75, 96 S.Ct. at 2844.

In the context of making an informed decision whether to have an abortion, the Supreme Court has held that "the State may not impose a blanket provision,...requiring the consent of a parent or person *in loco parentis* as a condition for abortion of an unmarried minor during the first 12 weeks of her pregnancy." *Id.* at 74, 96 S.Ct. at 2843. The Constitution prohibits such a law because "the State does not have the constitutional authority to give a third party an absolute, and possibly arbitrary, veto over the decision of the physician and his patient to terminate the patient's pregnancy, regardless of the reason for withholding the consent." *Id.*

In *Bellotti v. Baird*, 443 U.S. 622, 99 S.Ct. 3035, 61 L.Ed.2d 797 (1979)(*Bellotti II*), the Supreme Court concluded that the Constitution would permit a state to require a pregnant minor to obtain parental consent before an abortion is performed, if the state provided a procedure whereby the minor could establish that she was mature enough to make the decision on her own or that it would be in her best interests to have the abortion. *Id.* at 643–44, 99 S.Ct. at 3048....

...

Although this lawsuit involves the decision to use contraceptives, not the decision to have an abortion, in determining the constitutionality of laws regulating access to contraceptives, "[a]n instructive analogy is found in the decisions after *Roe v. Wade*,..., that held unconstitutional statutes that did not prohibit abortions outright but limited in a variety of ways a woman's access to them." *Carey*, 431 U.S. at 688, 97 S.Ct. at 2017 (citations omitted). The court acknowledges that a decision concerning the use of contraceptives is not fraught with the time limitations inherent in a decision concerning termination of a pregnancy through abortion. Nonetheless, "decisions whether to accomplish or to prevent conception are among the most private and sensitive." *Id.* at 685, 97 S.Ct. at 2016. Moreover, in contrast to the decision to marry, a decision concerning the use of contraceptives is similar to the decision whether to have an abortion in that it cannot be delayed until the minor reaches the age of majority without posing the risk of serious harm to the minor....

The undisputed evidence in this case confirms that whether to bear or to beget a child, not whether to be sexually active, is at the heart of the decision to use contraceptives. The facts demonstrate that minors seek contraceptives after becoming sexually active, not before. The facts also demonstrate that a significant percentage of sexually active minors would not cease their sexual activity if access to contraceptives is conditioned on parental notification. Instead, those minors would terminate their use of contraceptives. Thus, the effect of implementing H.B. 343 would not be to postpone a decision concerning whether to become sexually active until majority or to involve parents in their children's decision making on that matter. Instead, the facts in the record demonstrate that implementing H.B. 343 would expose sexually active minors to the health risks of early pregnancy and venereal disease. The argument that those risks can be avoided if the minors abstain from sexual activity is without merit because "[i]t would be plainly unreasonable to assume that [the state] has prescribed pregnancy and the birth of an unwanted child as punishment for fornication...." *Eisenstadt*, 405 U.S. at 448, 92 S.Ct. at 1035.

In summary, the decision whether to use contraceptives is as intimate and personal as, and involves risks to the individual which are comparable to those raised by the decision whether to have an abortion. The court, therefore, is persuaded that the statements [in Supreme Court cases] concerning the constitutionality of parental notification laws in the abortion context support the conclusion that the state may not impose a blanket parental notification requirement on minors seeking to exercise their constitutionally protected right to decide whether to bear or to beget a child by using contraceptives.

H.B. 343 fails to provide a procedure whereby a mature minor or a minor who can demonstrate that his or her best interests are contrary to parental notification can obtain contraceptives confidentially. As such, H.B. 343 unconstitutionally infringes upon the right to decide whether to bear or to beget children.[9]

COMMENTS

Few issues involving the appropriate level of parental control over children have been as passionately disputed as those dealing with sexuality. It is likely that both parents and children regularly underestimate the amount of sexual activity the other generation engages in and usually miscalculate the degree of sexual knowledge possessed by the other.

Children may or may not wish to consult their parents regarding their sexual choices, but most consider it a serious intrusion into their private lives for the state to force them to consult their parents or for anyone else to notify their parents about any of the child's sexual interests or activities. Parents, meanwhile, may feel entitled to control the flow of sexual information to their child and to receive full information on any sexual activity or attempted sexual activity of their child. Is it intervention for the state to provide access to sex education, birth control and abortion, or is it intervention for the state to coerce children to consult their parents?

Most agree that if children are denied easy, confidential access to contraceptives, they are less likely to use them. There is sharp dispute, however, over whether access to contraceptives will increase the incidence of sexual intercourse or decrease the incidence of pregnancy. As long as the burden of pregnancy falls so little upon males and so heavily upon females, using the unavailability of birth control to deter sexual intercourse puts most of the onus on females and perpetuates the double standard of sexual morality. Some women, including feminists, have expressed the concern that birth control removes from young females their only socially-approved justification for refusing sexual intercourse. Of course, it should be unacceptable to society that anyone feel forced or coerced into unwanted sexual contact, and it is a sad commentary indeed if any females do feel that fear of pregnancy is the only excuse they can use to say no.

During the first Reagan administration, the Secretary of the Department of Health and Human Services issued regulations, popularly known as the "squeal rule," designed to force family planning clinics that received federal funding under Title X of the Public Health Service Act to notify the parents or guardians within ten working days of prescribing contraceptives to any unemancipated minor. Several courts found the regulations to conflict with Congress' intent and purpose in enacting Title X and thus to be beyond the limits of the Secretary's delegated authority (for example, *Planned Parenthood Federation of America v. Heckler*, 712

9. The court does not intend to imply by this decision that a law which provided a means for minors to demonstrate maturity or best interests contrary to parental involvement would be constitutional. All that the court has decided is that due to the failure to provide such a process, H.B. 343 goes beyond the constitutionally permissible point of regulating the right of minors to make independent decisions concerning whether to bear or to beget children.

F.2d 650 (D.C. Cir. 1983)) or unconstitutional (*New York v. Schweiker*, 557 F.Supp. 354 (S.D.N.Y. 1983); *Planned Parenthood Federation of America, Inc. v. Schweiker*, 559 F.Supp. 658 (D.D.C.1983)). The statute involved in *Matheson* is an example of an effort to do nearly the same thing through state law.

It may be impossible to separate the parental notification and parental consent issues in cases such as *Danforth* and *Bellotti* from the question of the relative morality of coercive efforts to restrict abortion and of abortion itself. The anti-choice or right-to-life movement has played an important role in enacting parental-notification and parental-consent statutes, as part of a broader effort to chip away at the *Roe v. Wade* decision. Some opposed to abortion complain that *Bellotti* is based on an implicit bias favoring abortion in a situation in which the pregnant child desires an abortion against the wishes of her parents, rather than simply vindicating the privacy rights of a child comparable to those of adult pregnant women.

Contrary to the underlying facts in *Bellotti*, it is more common for parents to counsel a reluctant daughter that abortion is in her best interests, while the minor may have a romantic and unrealistic view of the pleasures and practicality of bearing and raising a child. Perhaps because of the language of the Massachusetts statute concerned with abortion, the Court did not address itself to such a reverse situation, that is, a 15-year-old who wished to have a child against the desires of her parents, who would prefer she have an abortion. It might be thought that the maturity of the minor or, in its absence, her best interests, should govern here too. But it seems most unlikely that any state officials in the United States would impose an abortion upon a minor who wished to carry a pregnancy to term, regardless of whether her parents and the court considered an abortion to be in her best interests.

The relationship between the substantive question of abortion and the issue of parental control over medical treatment of minors is raised by the following hypothetical. Suppose that an immature minor sought pre-natal care and requested that the doctor refrain from notifying her parents on the basis that they would pressure her to have an abortion, and that she feared she would be unable to resist their arguments. Would all those who support parental notification before abortion also insist on parental notification of the pregnancy, and would those who oppose parental notification continue to oppose it? Or might there be some shift in attitudes about the importance of parental input into the decision-making process of the immature minor?

REFERENCE

Andrea Dworkin, RIGHT-WING WOMEN (1983).

Reductio ad Absurdum?
State Protection of Fetuses, Embryos, Eggs and Sperm

In re A.C.

District of Columbia Court of Appeals
573 A.2d 1235 (D.C. 1990)

TERRY, Associate Judge:

This case comes before the court for the second time. In *In re A.C.*, 533 A.2d 611 (D.C.1987), a three-judge motions division denied a motion to stay an order of the trial court which had authorized a hospital to perform a caesarean section on a dying woman in an effort to save the life of her unborn child. The operation was performed, but both the mother and the child died. A few months later, the court ordered the case heard en banc and vacated the opinion of the motions division. *In re A.C.*, 539 A.2d 203 (D.C.1988). Although the motions division recognized that, as a practical matter, it "decided the entire matter when [it] denied the stay," 533 A.2d at 613, the en banc court has nevertheless heard the full case on the merits.

We are confronted here with two profoundly difficult and complex issues. First, we must determine who has the right to decide the course of medical treatment for a patient who, although near death, is pregnant with a viable fetus. Second, we must establish how that decision should be made if the patient cannot make it for herself — more specifically, how a court should proceed when faced with a pregnant patient, *in extremis*, who is apparently incapable of making an informed decision regarding medical care for herself and her fetus. We hold that in virtually all cases the question of what is to be done is to be decided by the patient — the pregnant woman — on behalf of herself and the fetus. If the patient is incompetent or otherwise unable to give an informed consent to a proposed course of medical treatment, then her decision must be ascertained through the procedure known as substituted judgment. Because the trial court did not follow that procedure, we vacate its order and remand the case for further proceedings.

I

This case came before the trial court when George Washington University Hospital petitioned the emergency judge in chambers for declaratory relief as to how it should treat its patient, A.C., who was close to death from cancer and was twenty-six and one-half weeks pregnant with a viable fetus. After a hearing lasting approximately three hours, which was held at the hospital (though not in A.C.'s room), the court ordered that a caesarean section be performed on A.C. to deliver the fetus. Counsel for A.C. immediately sought a stay in this court, which was unanimously denied by a hastily assembled division of three judges. *In re A.C.*, 533 A.2d 611 (D.C.1987). The caesarean was performed, and a baby girl, L.M.C., was delivered. Tragically, the child died within two and one-half hours, and the mother died two days later.

Counsel for A.C. now maintain that A.C. was competent and that she made an informed choice not to have the caesarean performed. Given this view of the facts, they argue that it was error for the trial court to weigh the state's interest in preserving the potential life of a viable fetus against A.C.'s interest in having her decision respected. They argue further that, even if the substituted judgment procedure had been followed, the evidence would necessarily show that A.C. would not have wanted the caesarean section. Under either analysis, according to these arguments, the trial court erred in subordinating A.C.'s right to bodily integrity in favor of the state's interest in potential life. Counsel for the hospital and for L.M.C. contend, on the other hand, that A.C. was incompetent to make her own medical decisions and that, under the substituted judgment procedure, the evidence clearly established that A.C. would have consented to the caesarean. In the alternative, counsel for L.M.C. argues that even if L.M.C.'s interests and those of the state were in conflict with A.C.'s wishes, it was proper for the trial court to balance their interests and resolve the conflict in favor of surgical intervention.

We do not accept any of these arguments because the evidence, realistically viewed, does not support them.

II

A.C. was first diagnosed as suffering from cancer at the age of thirteen. In the ensuing years she underwent major surgery several times, together with multiple radiation treatments and chemotherapy. A.C. married when she was twenty-seven, during a period of remission, and soon thereafter she became pregnant. She was excited about her pregnancy and very much wanted the child. Because of her medical history, she was referred in her fifteenth week of pregnancy to the high-risk pregnancy clinic at George Washington University Hospital.

On Tuesday, June 9, 1987, when A.C. was approximately twenty-five weeks pregnant, she went to the hospital for a scheduled check-up. Because she was experiencing pain in her back and shortness of breath, an x-ray was taken, revealing an apparently inoperable tumor which nearly filled her right lung. On Thursday, June 11, A.C. was admitted to the hospital as a patient. By Friday her condition had temporarily improved, and when asked if she really wanted to have her baby, she replied that she did.

Over the weekend A.C.'s condition worsened considerably. Accordingly, on Monday, June 15, members of the medical staff treating A.C. assembled, along with her family, in A.C.'s room. The doctors then informed her that her illness was terminal, and A.C. agreed to palliative treatment designed to extend her life until at least her twenty-eighth week of pregnancy. The "potential outcome [for] the fetus," according to the doctors, would be much better at twenty-eight weeks than at twenty-six weeks if it were necessary to "intervene." A.C. knew that the palliative treatment she had chosen presented some increased risk to the fetus, but she opted for this course both to prolong her life for at least another two weeks and to maintain her own comfort. When asked if she still wanted to have the baby, A.C. was somewhat equivocal, saying "something to the effect of 'I don't know, I think so.'" As the day moved toward evening, A.C.'s condition grew still worse, and at about 7:00 or 8:00 p.m. she consented to intubation to facilitate her breathing.

The next morning, June 16, the trial court convened a hearing at the hospital in response to the hospital's request for a declaratory judgment. The court appointed counsel for both A.C. and the fetus, and the District of Columbia was permitted to intervene for the fetus as *parens patriae.* The court heard testimony on the facts as we have summarized them, and further testimony that at twenty-six and a half weeks the fetus was viable, *i.e.*, capable of sustained life outside of the mother, given artificial aid. A neonatologist, Dr. Maureen Edwards, testified that the chances of survival for a twenty-six-week fetus delivered at the hospital might be as high as eighty percent, but that this particular fetus, because of the mother's medical history, had only a fifty to sixty percent chance of survival. Dr.

Edwards estimated that the risk of substantial impairment for the fetus, if it were delivered promptly, would be less than twenty percent. However, she noted that the fetus' condition was worsening appreciably at a rapid rate, and another doctor — Dr. Alan Weingold, an obstetrician who was one of A.C.'s treating physicians — stated that any delay in delivering the child by caesarean section lessened its chances of survival.

Regarding A.C.'s ability to respond to questioning and her prognosis, Dr. Louis Hamner, another treating obstetrician, testified that A.C. would probably die within twenty-four hours "if absolutely nothing else is done.... As far as her ability to interact, she has been heavily sedated in order to maintain her ventilatory function. She will open her eyes sometimes when you are in the room, but as far as her being able to...carry on a meaningful-type conversation...at this point, I don't think that is reasonable." When asked whether reducing her medication to "permit recovery of enough cognitive function on her part that we could get any sense from her as to what her preference would be as to therapy," Dr. Hamner replied, "I don't think so. I think her respiratory status has deteriorated to the point where she is [expending] an enormous amount of energy just to keep the heart going." Dr. Weingold, asked the same question, gave a similar answer: that A.C.'s few remaining hours of life "will be shortened by attempting to raise her level of consciousness because that is what is keeping her, in a sense, physiologically compliant with the respirator. If you remove that, then I think that will shorten her survival."

...

After hearing this testimony and the arguments of counsel, the trial court made oral findings of fact. It found, first, that A.C. would probably die, according to uncontroverted medical testimony, "within the next twenty-four to forty-eight hours"; second, that A.C. was "pregnant with a twenty-six and a half week viable fetus who, based upon uncontroverted medical testimony, has approximately a fifty to sixty percent chance to survive if a caesarean section is performed as soon as possible"; third, that because the fetus was viable, "the state has [an] important and legitimate interest in protecting the potentiality of human life"; and fourth, that there had been some testimony that the operation "may very well hasten the death of [A.C.]," but that there had also been testimony that delay would greatly increase the risk to the fetus and that "the prognosis is not great for the fetus to be delivered post-mortem...." Most significantly, the court found:

> The court is of the view that it does not clearly know what [A.C.'s] present views are with respect to the issue of whether or not the child should live or die. She's presently unconscious. As late as Friday of last week, she wanted the baby to live. As late as yesterday, she did not know for sure.

Having made these findings of fact and conclusions of law, and expressly relying on *In re Madyun*, 114 Daily Wash.L.Rptr. 2233 (D.C.Super.Ct. July 26, 1986), the court ordered that a caesarean section be performed to deliver A.C.'s child.

The court's decision was then relayed to A.C., who had regained consciousness. When the hearing reconvened later in the day, Dr. Hamner told the court:

> I explained to her essentially what was going on.... I said it's been deemed we should intervene on behalf of the baby by caesarean section and it would give it the only possible chance of it living. Would you agree to this procedure? *She said yes.* I said, do you realize that you may not survive the

> surgical procedure? *She said yes.* And I repeated the two questions to her again [and] asked her did she understand. *She said yes.* [Emphasis added.]

When the court suggested moving the hearing to A.C.'s bedside, Dr. Hamner discouraged the court from doing so, but he and Dr. Weingold, together with A.C.'s mother and husband, went to A.C.'s room to confirm her consent to the procedure. What happened then was recounted to the court a few minutes later:

> THE COURT: Will you bring us up to date? Did you have a conversation with [A.C.]?
>
> DR. WEINGOLD: I did not. I observed the conversation between Dr. Hamner and [A.C.]. Dr. Hamner went into the room to attempt to verify his previous discussion with the patient, with the patient's husband at her right hand and her mother at her left hand. He, to my satisfaction, clearly communicated with [A.C.]. She understood.
>
> THE COURT: You could hear what the parties were saying to one another?
>
> DR. WEINGOLD: She does not make sound because of the tube in her windpipe. She nods and she mouths words. One can see what she's saying rather readily. She asked whether she would survive the operation. She asked [Dr.] Hamner if he would perform the operation. He told her he would only perform it if she authorized it but it would be done in any case. She understood that. She then seemed to pause for a few moments and then very clearly mouthed words several times, *I don't want it done. I don't want it done.* Quite clear to me.
>
> I would obviously state the obvious and that is this is an environment in which, from my perspective as a physician, this would not be an informed consent one way or the other. She's under tremendous stress with the family on both sides, but I'm satisfied that I heard clearly what she said.
>
> ...

After hearing this new evidence, the court found that it was "still not clear what her intent is" and again ordered that a caesarean section be performed. A.C.'s counsel sought a stay in this court, which was denied. *In re A.C.*, 533 A.2d 611, 613 (D.C.1987). The operation took place, but the baby lived for only a few hours, and A.C. succumbed to cancer two days later.

...

A. Informed Consent and Bodily Integrity

...[T]here is only one published decision from an appellate court that deals with the question of when, or even whether, a court may order a caesarean section: *Jefferson v. Griffin Spalding County Hospital Authority*, 247 Ga. 86, 274 S.E.2d 457 (1981).

Jefferson is of limited relevance, if any at all, to the present case. In *Jefferson* there was a competent refusal by the mother to undergo the proposed surgery, but the evidence showed that performance of the caesarean was in the medical interests of both the mother and the fetus. In the instant case, by contrast, the evidence is unclear as to whether A.C. was competent when she mouthed her apparent refusal of the caesarean ("I don't want it done"), and it was generally assumed that while the surgery would most likely be highly beneficial to the fetus, it would be dangerous for the mother. Thus there was no clear maternal-fetal conflict in this case arising from a competent decision by the mother to forego a procedure for the benefit of the fetus. The procedure may well have been against A.C.'s medical interest, but if she was competent and given the choice, she may well have consented to an operation of significant risk to herself in order to maximize her fetus' chance for survival. From the evidence, however, we simply cannot tell whether she would have consented or not.

Thus our analysis of this case begins with the tenet common to all medical treatment cases: that any person has the right to make an informed choice, if competent to do so, to accept or forego medical treatment. The doctrine of informed consent, based on this principle and rooted in the concept of bodily integrity, is ingrained in our common law. See *Crain v. Allison*, 443 A.2d 558, 561–562 (D.C.1982); *Canterbury v. Spence*, 150 U.S.App.D.C. 263, 271, 464 F.2d 772, 780, *cert. denied*, 409 U.S. 1064, 93 S.Ct. 560, 34 L.Ed.2d 518 (1972); *Schloendorff v. Society of New York Hospital*, 211 N.Y. 125, 127, 105 N.E. 92, 93 (1914). Under the doctrine of informed consent, a physician must inform the patient, "at a minimum," of "the nature of the proposed treatment, any alternative treatment procedures, and the nature and degree of risks and benefits inherent in undergoing and in abstaining from the proposed treatment." *Crain v. Allison*, *supra*, 443 A.2d at 562 (footnote omitted). To protect the right of every person to bodily integrity, courts uniformly hold that a surgeon who performs an operation without the patient's consent may be guilty of a battery, *Canterbury v. Spence*, *supra*, 150 U.S.App.D.C. at 274, 464 F.2d at 783, or that if the surgeon obtains an insufficiently informed consent, he or she may be liable for negligence. *Crain v. Allison*, *supra*, 443 A.2d at 561–562. Furthermore, the right to informed consent "also encompasses a right to informed refusal." *In re Conroy*, 98 N.J. 321, 336, 486 A.2d 1209, 1222 (1985)....

In the same vein, courts do not compel one person to permit a significant intrusion upon his or her bodily integrity for the benefit of another person's health. See, *e.g.*, *Bonner v. Moran*, 75 U.S.App.D.C. 156, 157, 126 F.2d 121, 122 (1941)(parental consent required for skin graft from fifteen-year-old for benefit of cousin who had been severely burned); *McFall v. Shimp*, 10 Pa.D. & C.3d 90 (Allegheny County Ct.1978). In *McFall* the court refused to order Shimp to donate bone marrow which was necessary to save the life of his cousin, McFall:

> The common law has consistently held to a rule which provides that one human being is under no legal compulsion to give aid or to take action to save another human being or to rescue.... For our law to *compel* defendant to submit to an intrusion of his body would change every concept and principle upon which our society is founded. To do so would defeat the sanctity of the individual, and would impose a rule which would know no limits, and one could not imagine where the line would be drawn.

Id. at 91 (emphasis in original). Even though Shimp's refusal would mean death for McFall, the court would not order Shimp to allow his body to be invaded. It has been suggested that fetal cases are different because a woman who "has chosen to lend her body to bring [a] child into the world" has an enhanced duty to assure the welfare of the fetus, sufficient even to require her to undergo caesarean surgery.... Surely, however, a fetus cannot have rights in this respect superior to those of a person who has already been born.

Courts have generally held that a patient is competent to make his or her own medical choices when that patient is capable of "the informed exercise of a choice, and that entails an opportunity to evaluate knowledgeably the options available and the risks attendant upon each." *Canterbury v. Spence, supra,* 150 U.S.App.D.C. at 271, 464 F.2d at 780. Thus competency in a case such as this turns on the patient's ability to function as a decision-maker, acting in accordance with her preferences and values....

This court has recognized as well that, above and beyond common law protections, the right to accept or forego medical treatment is of constitutional magnitude....

...

Decisions of the Supreme Court, while not explicitly recognizing a right to bodily integrity, seem to assume that individuals have the right, depending on the circumstances, to accept or refuse medical treatment or other bodily invasion. See, *e.g., Winston v. Lee,* 470 U.S. 753, 105 S.Ct. 1611, 84 L.Ed.2d 662 (1985);.... In *Winston v. Lee, supra,* a robbery suspect challenged the state's right to compel him to submit to surgery for the removal of a bullet which was lodged in a muscle in his chest. The Court noted that the proposed surgery, which would require a general anesthetic, "would be an 'extensive' intrusion on respondent's personal privacy and bodily integrity" and a "virtually total divestment of respondent's ordinary control over surgical probing beneath his skin," 470 U.S. at 764–765, 105 S.Ct. at 1619 (citation omitted), and held that, without the patient-suspect's consent, the surgery was constitutionally impermissible. Nevertheless, even in recognizing a right to refuse medical treatment or state-imposed surgery, neither *Winston* nor any other Supreme Court decision holds that this right of refusal is absolute. Rather, in discussing the constitutional "reasonableness of surgical intrusions beneath the skin," the Court said in *Winston* that the Fourth Amendment "neither forbids nor permits all such intrusions...." *Id.* at 760, 105 S.Ct. at 1616....

This court and others, while recognizing the right to accept or reject medical treatment, have consistently held that the right is not absolute.... In some cases, especially those involving life-or-death situations or incompetent patients, the courts have recognized four countervailing interests that may involve the state as *parens patriae*: preserving life, preventing suicide, maintaining the ethical integrity of the medical profession, and protecting third parties.... Neither the prevention of suicide nor the integrity of the medical profession has any bearing on this case. Further, the state's interest in preserving life must be truly compelling to justify overriding a competent person's right to refuse medical treatment. *In re Osborne, supra,* 294 A.2d at 374–375; *Tune v. Walter Reed Army Medical Hospital, supra,* 602 F.Supp. at 1455–1456. This is equally true for incompetent patients, who have just as much right as competent patients to have their decisions made while competent respected, even in a substituted judgment framework....

In those rare cases in which a patient's right to decide her own course of treatment has been judicially overridden, courts have usually acted to vindicate the state's interest in protecting third parties, even if in fetal state. See *Jefferson v. Griffin Spalding County Hospital Authority, supra* (ordering that caesarean section be performed on a woman in her thirty-ninth week of pregnancy to save both the mother and the fetus); *Raleigh Fitkin-Paul Morgan Memorial Hospital v. Anderson,* 42 N.J. 421, 201 A.2d 537 (ordering blood transfusions over the objection of a Jehovah's Witness, in her thirty-second week of pregnancy, to save her life and that of the fetus), *cert. denied,* 377 U.S. 985, 84 S.Ct. 1894, 12 L.Ed.2d 1032 (1964); *In re Jamaica Hospital,* 128 Misc.2d 1006, 491 N.Y.S.2d 898 (Sup.Ct.1985)(ordering the transfusion of blood to a Jehovah's Witness eighteen weeks pregnant, who objected on religious grounds, and finding that the state's interest in the not-yet-viable fetus outweighed the patient's interests); *Crouse Irving Memorial Hospital, Inc. v. Paddock*, 127 Misc.2d 101, 485 N.Y.S.2d 443 (Sup.Ct.1985)(ordering transfusions as necessary over religious objections to save the mother and a fetus that was to be prematurely delivered); *cf. In re President & Directors of Georgetown College, Inc., supra*, 118 U.S.App.D.C. at 88, 331 F.2d at 1008 (ordering a transfusion, *inter alia*, because of a mother's parental duty to her living minor children). *But see Taft v. Taft*, 388 Mass. 331, 446 N.E.2d 395 (1983)(vacating an order which required a woman in her fourth month of pregnancy to undergo a "purse-string" operation, on the ground that there were no compelling circumstances to justify overriding her religious objections and her constitutional right of privacy).

What we distill from the cases discussed in this section is that every person has the right, under the common law and the Constitution, to accept or refuse medical treatment. This right of bodily integrity belongs equally to persons who are competent and persons who are not. Further, it matters not what the quality of a patient's life may be; the right of bodily integrity is not extinguished simply because someone is ill, or even at death's door. To protect that right against intrusion by others — family members, doctors, hospitals, or anyone else, however well-intentioned — we hold that a court must determine the patient's wishes by any means available, and must abide by those wishes unless there are truly extraordinary or compelling reasons to override them. *In re Osborne, supra.* When the patient is incompetent, or when the court is unable to determine competency, the substituted judgment procedure must be followed.

From the record before us, we simply cannot tell whether A.C. was ever competent, after being sedated, to make an informed decision one way or the other regarding the proposed caesarean section. The trial court never made any finding about A.C.'s competency to decide. Undoubtedly, during most of the proceedings below, A.C. was incompetent to make a treatment decision; that is, she was unable to give an informed consent based on her assessment of the risks and benefits of the contemplated surgery. The court knew from the evidence that A.C. was sedated and unconscious, and thus it could reasonably have found her incompetent to render an informed consent; however, it made no such finding. On the other hand, there was no clear evidence that A.C. was competent to render an informed consent after the trial court's initial order was communicated to her.

We think it is incumbent on any trial judge in a case like this, unless it is impossible to do so, to ascertain whether a patient is competent to make her own medical decisions. Whenever possible, the judge should personally attempt to speak with the patient and ascertain her wishes directly, rather than relying exclusively on hearsay evidence, even from doctors. See *In re Osborne, surpa*, 294 A.2d at 374; *In re President & Directors of Georgetown College, Inc., supra*, 118 U.S.App.D.C. at 87, 331 F.2d at 1007. It is improper to presume that a patient is incompetent. *United States v. Charters, supra*, 829 F.2d at 495. We have no reason to believe that, if competent, A.C. would or would not have refused consent to a caesarean. We hold, however, that without a competent refusal from A.C. to go forward with the surgery, and without a finding through substituted judgment that A.C. would not have consented to the surgery, it was error for the trial court to proceed to a balancing analysis, weighing the rights of A.C. against the interests of the state.

There are two additional arguments against overriding A.C.'s objections to caesarean surgery. First, as the American Public Health Association cogently states in its *amicus curiae* brief:

> Rather than protecting the health of women and children, court-ordered caesareans erode the element of trust that permits a pregnant woman to communicate to her physician — without fear of reprisal — all information relevant to her proper diagnosis and treatment. An even more serious consequence of court-ordered intervention is that it drives women at high risk of complications during pregnancy and childbirth out of the health care system to avoid coerced treatment.

Second, and even more compellingly, any judicial proceeding in a case such as this will ordinarily take place — like the one before us here — under time constraints so pressing that it is difficult or impossible for the mother to communicate adequately with counsel, or for counsel to organize an effective factual and legal presentation in defense of her liberty and privacy interests and bodily integrity. Any intrusion implicating such basic values ought not to be lightly undertaken when the mother not only is precluded from conducting pre-trial discovery (to which she would be entitled as a matter of course in any controversy over even a modest amount of money) but also is in no position to prepare meaningfully for trial....

...

B. SUBSTITUTED JUDGMENT

In the previous section we discussed the right of an individual to accept or reject medical treatment. We concluded that if a patient is competent and has made an informed decision regarding the course of her medical treatment, that decision will control in virtually all cases. Sometimes, however, as our analysis presupposes here, a once competent patient will be unable to render an informed decision. In such a case, we hold that the court must make a substituted judgment on behalf of the patient, based on all the evidence. This means that the duty of the court, "as surrogate for the incompetent, is to determine as best it can what choice that individual, if competent, would make with respect to medical procedures."...

...

Because it is the patient's decisional rights which the substituted judgment inquiry seeks to protect, courts are in accord that the greatest weight should be given to the previously expressed wishes of the patient. This includes prior statements, either written or oral, even though the treatment alternatives at hand may not have been addressed.... The court should also consider previous decisions of the patient concerning medical treatment, especially when there may be a discernibly consistent pattern of conduct or of thought.... Thus in a case such as this it would be highly relevant that A.C. had consented to intrusive and dangerous surgeries in the past, and that she chose to become pregnant and to protect her pregnancy by seeking treatment at the hospital's high-risk pregnancy clinic. It would also be relevant that she accepted a plan of treatment which contemplated caesarean intervention at the twenty-eighth week of pregnancy, even though the possibility of a caesarean during the twenty-sixth week was apparently unforeseen. On the other hand, A.C. agreed to a plan of palliative treatment which posed a greater danger to the fetus than would have been necessary if she were unconcerned about her own continuing care. Further, when A.C. was informed of the fatal nature of her illness, she was equivocal about her desire to have the baby.

Courts in substituted judgment cases have also acknowledged the importance of probing the patient's value system as an aid in discerning what the patient would choose. We agree with this approach.... Most people do not foresee what calamities may befall them; much less do they consider, or even think about, treatment alternatives in varying situations. The court in a substituted judgment case, therefore, should pay special attention to the known values and goals of the incapacitated patient, and should strive, if possible, to extrapolate from those values and goals what the patient's decision would be.

Although treating physicians may be an invaluable source of such information about a patient, the family will often be the best source.... Family members or other loved ones will usually be in the best position to say what the patient would do if competent. The court should be mindful, however, that while in the majority of cases family members will have the best interests of the patient in mind, sometimes family members will rely on their own judgments or predilections rather than serving as conduits for expressing the patient's wishes. This is why the court should endeavor, whenever possible, to make an in-person appraisal "of the patient's personal desires and ability for rational choice. In this way the court can always know, to the extent possible, that the judgment is that of the individual concerned and not that of those who believe, however well-intentioned, that they speak for the person whose life is in the balance."...

In short, to determine the subjective desires of the patient, the court must consider the totality of the evidence, focusing particularly on written or oral directions concerning treatment to family, friends, and health-care professionals. The court should also take into account the patient's past decisions regarding medical treatment, and attempt to ascertain from what is known about the patient's value system, goals, and desires what the patient would decide if competent....

After considering the patient's prior statements, if any, the previous medical decisions of the patient, and the values held by the patient, the court may still be unsure what course the patient would choose. In such circumstances the court may supplement its knowledge about the patient by determining what most persons would likely do in a similar situation.... When the patient is pregnant, however, she may not be concerned exclusively with her own welfare. Thus it is proper for the court, in a case such as this, to weigh (along with all the other factors) the mother's prognosis, the viability of the fetus, the probable result of treatment or non-treatment for both mother and fetus, and the mother's likely interest in avoiding impairment for her child together with her own instincts for survival....

Additionally, the court should consider the context in which prior declarations, treatment decisions, and expressions of personal values were made, including whether statements were made casually or after contemplation, or in accordance with deeply held beliefs.... Finally, in making a substituted judgment, the court should become as informed about the patient's condition, prognosis, and treatment options as one would expect any patient to become before making a treatment decision.... Obviously, the weight accorded to all of these factors will vary from case to case.

C. The Trial Court's Ruling

We reiterate that we cannot find the facts in this or any other case. That is the function of trial judges, who can view the witnesses and discern from their demeanor and testimony, rather than a cold written record, what the facts are. In this case there is an understandable paucity of factual findings, which necessarily limits our review. The trial court, faced with an issue affecting life and death, was forced to make a decision with almost no time for deliberation. Nevertheless, after reviewing the transcript of the hearing and the court's oral findings, it is clear to us that the trial court did not follow the substituted judgment procedure. On the contrary, the court's specific finding before its decision was communicated to A.C. was as follows:

> The court is of the view that it does not clearly know what [A.C.'s] present views are with respect to the issue of whether or not the child should live or die. She's presently unconscious. As late as Friday of last week, she wanted the baby to live. As late as yesterday, she did not know for sure.

The court did not go on, as it should have done, to make a finding as to what A.C. would have chosen to do if she were competent. Instead, the court undertook to balance the state's and L.M.C.'s interests in surgical intervention against A.C.'s perceived interest in not having the caesarean performed.

...

It is that order which we must now set aside. What a trial court must do in a case such as this is to determine, if possible, whether the patient is capable of making an informed decision about the course of her medical treatment. If she is, and if she makes such a decision, her wishes will control in virtually all cases. If the court finds that the patient is incapable of making an informed consent (and thus incompetent), then the court must make a substituted judgment. This means that the court must ascertain as best it can what the patient would do if faced with the particular treatment question. Again, in virtually all cases the decision of the patient, albeit discerned through the mechanism of substituted judgment, will control. We do not quite foreclose the possibility that a conflicting state interest may be so compelling that the patient's wishes must yield, but we anticipate that such cases will be extremely rare and truly exceptional. This is not such a case.

...We need not decide whether, or in what circumstances, the state's interests can ever prevail over the interests of a pregnant patient. We emphasize, nevertheless, that it would be an extraordinary case indeed in which a court might ever be justified in overriding the patient's wishes and authorizing a major surgical procedure such as a caesarean section. Throughout this opinion we have stressed that the patient's wishes, once they are ascertained, must be followed in "virtually all cases"...unless there are "truly extraordinary or compelling reasons to override them"....

...

Vacated and remanded.

BELSON, Associate Judge, concurring in part and dissenting in part:

...

...The state's interest in preserving human life and the viable unborn child's interest in survival are entitled, I think, to more weight than I find them assigned by the majority when it states that "in virtually all cases the decision of the patient ...will control." I would hold that in those instances, fortunately rare, in which the viable unborn child's interest in living and the state's parallel interest in protecting human life come into conflict with the mother's decision to forgo a procedure such as a caesarean section, a balancing should be struck in which the unborn child's and the state's interests are entitled to substantial weight.

It was acknowledged in *Roe v. Wade*, 410 U.S. 113, 93 S.Ct. 705, 35 L.Ed.2d 147 (1973), that the state's interest in potential human life becomes compelling at the point of viability.... [I]t is important to emphasize, as does the majority opinion, that this case is not about abortion...; we are not discussing whether a woman has the legal right to terminate her pregnancy in its early stages. Rather, we are dealing with the situation that exists when a woman has carried an unborn child to viability. When the unborn child reaches the state of viability, the child becomes a party whose interests must be considered....

...

The balancing test should be applied in instances in which women become pregnant and carry an unborn child to the point of viability. This is not an unreasonable classification because, I submit, a woman who carries a child to viability is in fact a member of a unique category of persons. Her circumstances differ fundamentally from those of other potential patients for medical procedures that will aid another person, for example, a potential donor of bone marrow for transplant. This is so because she has undertaken to bear another human being, and has carried an unborn child to viability. Another unique feature of the situation we address arises from the singular nature of the dependency of the unborn child upon the mother. A woman carrying a viable unborn child is not in the same category as a relative, friend, or stranger called upon to donate bone marrow or an organ for transplant. Rather, the expectant mother has placed herself in a special class of persons who are bringing another person into existence, and upon whom that other person's life is totally dependent. Also, uniquely, the viable unborn child is literally captive within the mother's body. No other potential beneficiary of a surgical procedure on another is in that position.

...

INTERNATIONAL UNION, UAW v. JOHNSON CONTROLS, INC.

United States Supreme Court
111 S.Ct. 1196 (1991)

Justice BLACKMUN delivered the opinion of the Court.

In this case we are concerned with an employer's gender-based fetal-protection policy. May an employer exclude a fertile female employee from certain jobs because of its concern for the health of the fetus the woman might conceive?

I

Respondent Johnson Controls, Inc., manufactures batteries. In the manufacturing process, the element lead is a primary ingredient. Occupational exposure to lead entails health risks, including the risk of harm to any fetus carried by a female employee.

Before the Civil Rights Act of 1964, 78 Stat. 241, became law, Johnson Controls did not employ any woman in a battery-manufacturing job. In June 1977, however, it announced its first official policy concerning its employment of women in lead-exposure work:

> "[P]rotection of the health of the unborn child is the immediate and direct responsibility of the prospective parents. While the medical profession and the company can support them in the exercise of this responsibility, it cannot assume it for them without simultaneously infringing their rights as persons.
>
> ...

"...Since not all women who can become mothers wish to become mothers (or will become mothers), it would appear to be illegal discrimination to treat all who are capable of pregnancy as though they will become pregnant." App. 140.

Consistent with that view, Johnson Controls "stopped short of excluding women capable of bearing children from lead exposure," *id.*, at 138, but emphasized that a woman who expected to have a child should not choose a job in which she would have such exposure. The company also required a woman who wished to be considered for employment to sign a statement that she had been advised of the risk of having a child while she was exposed to lead. The statement informed the woman that although there was evidence "that women exposed to lead have a higher rate of abortion," this evidence was "not as clear...as the relationship between cigarette smoking and cancer," but that it was, "medically speaking, just good sense not to run that risk if you want children and do not want to expose the unborn child to risk, however small...." *Id.*, at 142–143.

Five years later, in 1982, Johnson Controls shifted from a policy of warning to a policy of exclusion. Between 1979 and 1983, eight employees became pregnant while maintaining blood lead levels in excess of 30 micrograms per deciliter. Tr. of Oral Arg. 25, 34. This appeared to be the critical level noted by the Occupational Health and Safety Administration (OSHA) for a worker who was planning to have a family. See 29 CFR §1910.1025 (1989). The company responded by announcing a broad exclusion of women from jobs that exposed them to lead:

"...[I]t is [Johnson Controls'] policy that women who are pregnant or who are capable of bearing children will not be placed into jobs involving lead exposure or which could expose them to lead through the exercise of job bidding, bumping, transfer or promotion rights." App. 85–86.

The policy defined "women...capable of bearing children" as "[a]ll women except those whose inability to bear children is medically documented." *Id.*, at 81. It further stated that an unacceptable work station was one where, "over the past year," an employee had recorded a blood lead level of more than 30 micrograms per deciliter or the work site had yielded an air sample containing a lead level in excess of 30 micrograms per cubic meter. *Ibid.*

II

In April 1984, petitioners filed in the United States District Court for the Eastern District of Wisconsin a class action challenging Johnson Controls' fetal-protection policy as sex discrimination that violated Title VII of the Civil Rights Act of 1964, as amended, 42 U.S.C. §2000e *et seq.* Among the individual plaintiffs were petitioners Mary Craig, who had chosen to be sterilized in order to avoid losing her job, Elsie Nason, a 50-year-old divorcee, who had suffered a loss in compensation when she was transferred out of a job where she was exposed to lead, and Donald Penney, who had been denied a request for a leave of absence for the purpose of lowering his lead level because he intended to become a father. Upon stipulation of the parties, the District Court certified a class consisting of "all past, present and future production and maintenance employees" in United Auto Workers bargaining units at nine of Johnson Controls' plants "who have been and continue to be affected by [the employer's] Fetal Protection Policy implemented in 1982." Order of Feb. 25, 1985.

The District Court granted summary judgment for defendant-respondent Johnson Controls. 680 F.Supp. 309 (1988). Applying a three-part business necessity defense derived from fetal-protection cases in the Courts of Appeals for the Fourth and Eleventh Circuits, the District Court concluded that while "there is a disagreement among the experts regarding the effect of lead on the fetus," the hazard to the fetus through exposure to lead was established by "a considerable body of opinion"; that although "[e]xpert opinion has been provided which holds that lead also affects the reproductive abilities of men and women...[and] that these effects are as great as the effects of exposure of the fetus...a great body of experts are of the opinion that the fetus is more vulnerable to levels of lead that would not affect adults"; and that petitioners had "failed to establish that there is an acceptable alternative policy which would protect the fetus." *Id.*, at 315–316. The court stated that, in view of this disposition of the business necessity defense, it did not "have to undertake a bona fide occupational qualification's (BFOQ) analysis." *Id.*, at 316, n. 5.

The Court of Appeals for the Seventh Circuit, sitting en banc, affirmed the summary judgment by a 7-to-4 vote. 886 F.2d 871 (1989). The majority held that the proper standard for evaluating the fetal-protection policy was the defense of business necessity; that Johnson Controls was entitled to summary judgment under that defense; and that even if the proper standard was a BFOQ, Johnson Controls still was entitled to summary judgment.

The Court of Appeals, see *id.*, at 883–885, first reviewed fetal-protection opinions from the Eleventh and Fourth Circuits. See *Hayes v. Shelby Memorial Hospital*, 726 F.2d 1543 (CA11 1984), and *Wright v. Olin Corp.*, 697 F.2d 1172 (CA4 1982). Those opinions established the three-step business necessity inquiry: whether there is a substantial health risk to the fetus; whether transmission of the hazard to the fetus occurs only through women; and whether there is a less discriminatory alternative equally capable of preventing the health hazard to the fetus. 886 F.2d, at 885. The Court of Appeals agreed with the Eleventh and Fourth Circuits that "the components of the business necessity defense the courts of appeals and the EEOC have utilized in fetal protection cases balance the interests of the employer, the employee and the unborn child in a manner consistent with Title VII." *Id.*, at 886. The court further noted that, under *Wards Cove Packing Co. v. Atonio*, 490 U.S. 642, 109 S.Ct. 2115, 104 L.Ed.2d 733 (1989), the burden of persuasion remained on the plaintiff in challenging a business necessity defense, and — unlike the Fourth and Eleventh Circuits — it thus imposed the burden on the plaintiffs for all three steps. 886 F.2d, at 887–893. Cf. *Hayes*, 726 F.2d, at 1549, and *Wright*, 697 F.2d, at 1187.

Applying this business necessity defense, the Court of Appeals ruled that Johnson Controls should prevail. Specifically, the court concluded that there was no genuine issue of material fact about the substantial health-risk factor because the parties agreed that there was a substantial risk to a fetus from lead exposure. 886 F.2d, at 888–889. The Court of Appeals also concluded that, unlike the evidence of risk to the fetus from the mother's exposure, the evidence of risk from the father's exposure, which petitioners presented, "is, at best, speculative and unconvincing." *Id.*, at 889. Finally, the court found that petitioners had waived the issue of less discriminatory alternatives by not adequately presenting it. It said that, in any event, petitioners had not produced evidence of less discriminatory alternatives in the District Court. *Id.*, at 890–893.

Having concluded that the business necessity defense was the appropriate framework and that Johnson Controls satisfied that standard, the court proceeded to discuss the BFOQ defense and concluded that Johnson Controls met that test, too. *Id.*, at 893–894. The en banc majority ruled that industrial safety is part of the essence of respondent's business, and that the fetal-protection policy is reasonably necessary to further that concern. Quoting *Dothard v. Rawlinson*, 433 U.S. 321, 335, 97 S.Ct. 2720, 2729–2730, 53 L.Ed.2d 786 (1977), the majority emphasized that, in view of the goal of protecting the unborn, "more is at stake" than simply an individual woman's decision to weigh and accept the risks of employment. 886 F.2d, at 898.

Judges Cudahy and Posner dissented and would have reversed the judgment and remanded the case for trial. Judge Cudahy explained: "It may (and should) be difficult to establish a BFOQ here but I would afford the defendant an opportunity to try." *Id.*, at 901....

Judge Posner stated: "I think it is a mistake to suppose that we can decide this case once and for all on so meager a record." *Ibid.* He, too, emphasized that, under Title VII, a fetal-protection policy which explicitly applied just to women could be defended only as a BFOQ....

Judge Easterbrook, also in dissent and joined by Judge Flaum, agreed with Judges Cudahy and Posner that the only defense available to Johnson Controls was the BFOQ. He concluded, however, that the BFOQ defense would not prevail because respondent's stated concern for the health of the unborn was irrelevant to the operation of its business under the BFOQ. He also viewed the employer's concern as irrelevant to a woman's ability or inability to work under the Pregnancy Discrimination Act's amendment to Title VII, 92 Stat. 2076, 42 U.S.C. §2000e(k). Judge Easterbrook also stressed what he considered the excessive breadth of Johnson Controls' policy. It applied to all women (except those with medical proof of incapacity to bear children) although most women in an industrial labor force do not become pregnant, most of those who do become pregnant will have blood lead levels under 30 micrograms per deciliter, and most of those who become pregnant with levels exceeding that figure will bear normal children anyway. 886 F.2d, at 912–913. "Concerns about a tiny minority of women cannot set the standard by which all are judged." *Id.*, at 913.

With its ruling, the Seventh Circuit became the first Court of Appeals to hold that a fetal-protection policy directed exclusively at women could qualify as a BFOQ. We granted certiorari, 494 U.S. 1055, 110 S.Ct. 1522, 108 L.Ed.2d 762 (1990), to resolve the obvious conflict between the Fourth, Seventh, and Eleventh Circuits on this issue, and to address the important and difficult question whether an employer, seeking to protect potential fetuses, may discriminate against women just because of their ability to become pregnant.

III

The bias in Johnson Controls' policy is obvious. Fertile men, but not fertile women, are given a choice as to whether they wish to risk their reproductive health for a particular job. Section 703(a) of the Civil Rights Act of 1964, 78 Stat. 255, as amended, 42 U.S.C. §2000e-2(a), prohibits sex-based classifications in terms and conditions of employment, in hiring and discharging decisions, and in other employment decisions that adversely affect an employee's status. Respondent's fetal-protection policy explicitly discriminates against women on the basis of their sex. The policy excludes women with childbearing capacity from lead-exposed jobs and so creates a facial classification based on gender....

Nevertheless, the Court of Appeals assumed, as did the two appellate courts who already had confronted the issue, that sex-specific fetal-protection policies do not involve facial discrimination.... These courts analyzed the policies as though they were facially neutral, and had only a discriminatory effect upon the employment opportunities of women. Consequently, the courts looked to see if each employer in question had established that its policy was justified as a business necessity. The business necessity standard is more lenient for the employer than the statutory BFOQ defense. The Court of Appeals here went one step further and invoked the burden-shifting framework set forth in *Wards Cove Packing Co. v. Atonio*, 490 U.S. 642, 109 S.Ct. 2115, 104 L.Ed.2d 733 (1989), thus requiring petitioners to bear the burden of persuasion on all questions.... The court assumed that because the asserted reason for the sex-based exclusion (protecting women's unconceived offspring) was ostensibly benign, the policy was not sex-based discrimination. That assumption, however, was incorrect.

First, Johnson Controls' policy classifies on the basis of gender and childbearing capacity, rather than fertility alone. Respondent does not seek to protect the unconceived children of all its employees. Despite evidence in the record about the debilitating effect of lead exposure on the male reproductive system, Johnson Controls is concerned only with the harms that may befall the unborn offspring of its female employees.... This Court faced a conceptually similar situation in *Phillips v. Martin Marietta Corp.*, 400 U.S. 542, 91 S.Ct. 496, 27 L.Ed.2d 613 (1971), and found sex discrimination because the policy established "one hiring policy for women and another for men — each having pre-school-age children." *Id.*, at 544, 91 S.Ct., at 498. Johnson Controls' policy is facially discriminatory because it requires only a female employee to produce proof that she is not capable of reproducing.

Our conclusion is bolstered by the Pregnancy Discrimination Act of 1978 (PDA), 92 Stat. 2076, 42 U.S.C. §2000e(k), in which Congress explicitly provided that, for purposes of Title VII, discrimination "on the basis of sex" includes discrimination "because of or on the basis of pregnancy, childbirth, or related medical conditions."[3] "The Pregnancy Discrimination Act has now made clear that, for all Title VII purposes, discrimination based on a woman's pregnancy is, on its face, discrimination because of her sex." *Newport News Shipbuilding & Dry Dock Co. v. EEOC*, 462 U.S. 669, 684, 103 S.Ct. 2622, 2631, 77 L.Ed.2d 89 (1983). In its use of the words "capable of bearing children" in the 1982 policy statement as the criterion for exclusion, Johnson Controls explicitly classifies on the basis of potential for pregnancy. Under the PDA, such a classification must be regarded, for Title VII purposes, in the same light as explicit sex discrimination. Respondent has chosen to treat all its female employees as potentially pregnant; that choice evinces discrimination on the basis of sex.

We concluded above that Johnson Controls' policy is not neutral because it does not apply to the reproductive capacity of the company's male employees in the same way as it applies to that of the females. Moreover, the absence of a

---

3. The Act added subsection (k) to §701 of the Civil Rights Act of 1964 and reads in pertinent part:

> "The terms 'because of sex' or 'on the basis of sex' [in Title VII] include, but are not limited to, because of or on the basis of pregnancy, childbirth, or related medical conditions; and women affected by pregnancy, childbirth, or related medical conditions shall be treated the same for all employment-related purposes...as other persons not so affected but similar in their ability or inability to work...."

malevolent motive does not convert a facially discriminatory policy into a neutral policy with a discriminatory effect. Whether an employment practice involves disparate treatment through explicit facial discrimination does not depend on why the employer discriminates but rather on the explicit terms of the discrimination.... The beneficence of an employer's purpose does not undermine the conclusion that an explicit gender-based policy is sex discrimination under §703(a) and thus may be defended only as a BFOQ.

...

In sum, Johnson Controls' policy "does not pass the simple test of whether the evidence shows 'treatment of a person in a manner which but for that person's sex would be different.'" *Los Angeles Dept. of Water & Power v. Manhart*, 435 U.S. 702, 711, 98 S.Ct. 1370, 1377, 55 L.Ed.2d 657 (1978), quoting Developments in the Law, Employment Discrimination and Title VII of the Civil Rights Act of 1964, 84 Harv.L.Rev. 1109, 1170 (1971). We hold that Johnson Controls' fetal-protection policy is sex discrimination forbidden under Title VII unless respondent can establish that sex is a "bona fide occupational qualification."

IV

Under §703(e)(1) of Title VII, an employer may discriminate on the basis of "religion, sex, or national origin in those certain instances where religion, sex, or national origin is a bona fide occupational qualification reasonably necessary to the normal operation of that particular business or enterprise." 42 U.S.C. §2000e-2(e)(1). We therefore turn to the question whether Johnson Controls' fetal-protection policy is one of those "certain instances" that come within the BFOQ exception.

The BFOQ defense is written narrowly, and this Court has read it narrowly.... Our emphasis on the restrictive scope of the BFOQ defense is grounded on both the language and the legislative history of §703.

The wording of the BFOQ defense contains several terms of restriction that indicate that the exception reaches only special situations. The statute thus limits the situations in which discrimination is permissible to "certain instances" where sex discrimination is "reasonably necessary" to the "normal operation" of the "particular" business. Each one of these terms — certain, normal, particular — prevents the use of general subjective standards and favors an objective, verifiable requirement. But the most telling term is "occupational"; this indicates that these objective, verifiable requirements must concern job-related skills and aptitudes.

The concurrence defines "occupational" as meaning related to a job. *Post,* at 1210, n. 1. According to the concurrence, any discriminatory requirement imposed by an employer is "job-related" simply because the employer has chosen to make the requirement a condition of employment. In effect, the concurrence argues that sterility may be an occupational qualification for women because Johnson Controls has chosen to require it. This reading of "occupational" renders the word mere surplusage. "Qualification" by itself would encompass an employer's idiosyncratic requirements. By modifying "qualification" with "occupational," Congress narrowed the term to qualifications that affect an employee's ability to do the job.

Johnson Controls argues that its fetal-protection policy falls within the so-called safety exception to the BFOQ. Our cases have stressed that discrimination on the basis of sex because of safety concerns is allowed only in narrow circumstances. In *Dothard v. Rawlinson*, this Court indicated that danger to a woman herself does not justify discrimination. 433 U.S., at 335, 97 S.Ct. at 2729–2730. We there allowed the employer to hire only male guards in contact areas of maximum-security male penitentiaries only because more was at stake than the "individual woman's decision to weigh and accept the risks of employment." *Ibid.* We found sex to be a BFOQ inasmuch as the employment of a female guard would create real risks of safety to others if violence broke out because the guard was a woman. Sex discrimination was tolerated because sex was related to the guard's ability to do the job — maintaining prison security. We also required in *Dothard* a high correlation between sex and ability to perform job functions and refused to allow employers to use sex as a proxy for strength although it might be a fairly accurate one.

Similarly, some courts have approved airlines' layoffs of pregnant flight attendants at different points during the first five months of pregnancy on the ground that the employer's policy was necessary to ensure the safety of passengers.... In two of these cases, the courts pointedly indicated that fetal, as opposed to passenger, safety was best left to the mother. *Burwell* [*v. Eastern Air Lines, Inc.*], 633 F.2d 361 at 371 [(4th Cir. 1980), cert. denied, 450 U.S. 965, 101 S.Ct. 1480, 67 L.Ed.2d 613 (1981)]; *National Airlines,* 434 F.Supp. [249], at 259 [(S.D.Fla.1977)].

We considered safety to third parties in *Western Airlines, Inc. v. Criswell,* [472 U.S. 400, 105 S.Ct. 2743, 86 L.Ed.2d 321 (1985)], in the context of the ADEA [Age Discrimination in Employment Act of 1967]. We focused upon "the nature of the flight engineer's tasks," and the "actual capabilities of persons over age 60" in relation to those tasks. 472 U.S., at 406, 105 S.Ct., at 2747. Our safety concerns were not independent of the individual's ability to perform the assigned tasks, but rather involved the possibility that, because of age-connected debility, a flight engineer might not properly assist the pilot, and might thereby cause a safety emergency. Furthermore, although we considered the safety of third parties in *Dothard* and *Criswell,* those third parties were indispensable to the particular business at issue. In *Dothard,* the third parties were the inmates; in *Criswell,* the third parties were the passengers on the plane. We stressed that in order to qualify as a BFOQ, a job qualification must relate to the "essence," *Dothard,* 433 U.S., at 333, 97 S.Ct., at 2751, or to the "central mission of the employer's business," *Criswell,* 472 U.S., at 413, 105 S.Ct., at 2751.

The concurrence ignores the "essence of the business" test and so concludes that "the safety to fetuses in carrying out the duties of battery manufacturing is as much a legitimate concern as is safety to third parties in guarding prisons (*Dothard*) or flying airplanes (*Criswell*)."... The unconceived fetuses of Johnson Controls' female employees, however, are neither customers nor third parties whose safety is essential to the business of battery manufacturing. No one can disregard the possibility of injury to future children; the BFOQ, however, is not so broad that it transforms this deep social concern into an essential aspect of batterymaking.

Our case law, therefore, makes clear that the safety exception is limited to instances in which sex or pregnancy actually interferes with the employee's ability to perform the job. This approach is consistent with the language of the BFOQ provision itself, for it suggests that permissible distinctions based on sex must relate to ability to perform the duties of the job. Johnson Controls suggests, however, that we expand the exception to allow fetal-protection policies that mandate particular standards for pregnant or fertile women. We decline to do so. Such an expansion contradicts not only the language of the BFOQ and the narrowness of its exception but the plain language and history of the Pregnancy Discrimination Act.

The PDA's amendment to Title VII contains a BFOQ standard of its own: unless pregnant employees differ from others "in their ability or inability to work," they must be "treated the same" as other employees "for all employment-related purposes." 42 U.S.C. §2000e(k). This language clearly sets forth Congress' remedy for discrimination on the basis of pregnancy and potential pregnancy. Women who are either pregnant or potentially pregnant must be treated like others "similar in their ability...to work." *Ibid.* In other words, women as capable of doing their jobs as their male counterparts may not be forced to choose between having a child and having a job.

The concurrence asserts that the PDA did not alter the BFOQ defense. Post, at 1213. The concurrence arrives at this conclusion by ignoring the second clause of the Act which states that "women affected by pregnancy, childbirth, or related medical conditions shall be treated the same for all employment-related purposes ...as other persons not so affected but similar in their ability or inability to work." 42 U.S.C. §2000e(k). Until this day, every Member of this Court had acknowledged that "[t]he second clause [of the PDA] could not be clearer: it mandates that pregnant employees 'shall be treated the same for all employment-related purposes' as nonpregnant employees similarly situated with respect to their ability or inability to work." *California Federal S. & L. Assn. v. Guerra*, 479 U.S. 272, 297, 107 S.Ct. 683, 698, 93 L.Ed.2d 613 (1987)(WHITE, J., dissenting). The concurrence now seeks to read the second clause out of the Act.

The legislative history confirms what the language of the Pregnancy Discrimination Act compels....

...The Senate Report...states that employers may not require a pregnant woman to stop working at any time during her pregnancy unless she is unable to do her work. Employment late in pregnancy often imposes risks on the unborn child..., but Congress indicated that the employer may take into account only the woman's ability to get her job done.... With the PDA, Congress made clear that the decision to become pregnant or to work while being either pregnant or capable of becoming pregnant was reserved for each individual woman to make for herself.

We conclude that the language of both the BFOQ provision and the PDA which amended it, as well as the legislative history and the case law, prohibit an employer from discriminating against a woman because of her capacity to become pregnant unless her reproductive potential prevents her from performing the duties of her job. We reiterate our holdings in *Criswell* and *Dothard* that an employer must direct its concerns about a woman's ability to perform her job safely and efficiently to those aspects of the woman's job-related activities that fall within the "essence" of the particular business.

V

We have no difficulty concluding that Johnson Controls cannot establish a BFOQ. Fertile women, as far as appears in the record, participate in the manufacture of batteries as efficiently as anyone else. Johnson Controls' professed moral and ethical concerns about the welfare of the next generation do not suffice to establish a BFOQ of female sterility. Decisions about the welfare of future children must be left to the parents who conceive, bear, support, and raise them rather than to the employers who hire those parents. Congress has mandated this choice through Title VII, as amended by the Pregnancy Discrimination Act. Johnson Controls has attempted to exclude women because of their reproductive capacity.

Title VII and the PDA simply do not allow a woman's dismissal because of her failure to submit to sterilization.

Nor can concerns about the welfare of the next generation be considered a part of the "essence" of Johnson Controls' business. Judge Easterbrook in this case pertinently observed: "It is word play to say that 'the job' at Johnson [Controls] is to make batteries without risk to fetuses in the same way 'the job' at Western Air Lines is to fly planes without crashing." 886 F.2d, at 913.

Johnson Controls argues that it must exclude all fertile women because it is impossible to tell which women will become pregnant while working with lead.... Even on this sparse record, it is apparent that Johnson Controls is concerned about only a small minority of women. Of the eight pregnancies reported among the female employees, it has not been shown that any of the babies have birth defects or other abnormalities. The record does not reveal the birth rate for Johnson Controls' female workers but national statistics show that approximately nine percent of all fertile women become pregnant each year. The birthrate drops to two percent for blue collar workers over age 30.... Johnson Controls' fear of prenatal injury, no matter how sincere, does not begin to show that substantially all of its fertile women employees are incapable of doing their jobs.

VI

A word about tort liability and the increased cost of fertile women in the workplace is perhaps necessary....

More than 40 States currently recognize a right to recover for a prenatal injury based either on negligence or on wrongful death.... Without negligence, it would be difficult for a court to find liability on the part of the employer. If, under general tort principles, Title VII bans sex-specific fetal-protection policies, the employer fully informs the woman of the risk, and the employer has not acted negligently, the basis for holding an employer liable seems remote at best.

...

The tort-liability argument reduces to two equally unpersuasive propositions. First, Johnson Controls attempts to solve the problem of reproductive health hazards by resorting to an exclusionary policy. Title VII plainly forbids illegal sex discrimination as a method of diverting attention from an employer's obligation to police the workplace. Second, the spectre of an award of damages reflects a fear that hiring fertile women will cost more. The extra cost of employing members of one sex, however, does not provide an affirmative Title VII defense for a discriminatory refusal to hire members of that gender.... Indeed, in passing the PDA, Congress considered at length the considerable cost of providing equal treatment of pregnancy and related conditions, but made the "decision to forbid special treatment of pregnancy despite the social costs associated therewith."...

We, of course, are not presented with, nor do we decide, a case in which costs would be so prohibitive as to threaten the survival of the employer's business. We merely reiterate our prior holdings that the incremental cost of hiring women cannot justify discriminating against them.

VII

Our holding today that Title VII, as so amended, forbids sex-specific fetal-protection policies is neither remarkable nor unprecedented. Concern for a woman's existing or potential offspring historically has been the excuse for denying women equal employment opportunities. See, *e.g., Muller v. Oregon*, 208 U.S. 412,

28 S.Ct. 324, 52 L.Ed. 551 (1908). Congress in the PDA prohibited discrimination on the basis of a woman's ability to become pregnant. We do no more than hold that the Pregnancy Discrimination Act means what it says.

It is no more appropriate for the courts than it is for individual employers to decide whether a woman's reproductive role is more important to herself and her family than her economic role. Congress has left this choice to the woman as hers to make.

...

Justice WHITE, with whom the CHIEF JUSTICE and Justice KENNEDY join, concurring in part and concurring in the judgment.

The Court properly holds that Johnson Controls' fetal protection policy overtly discriminates against women, and thus is prohibited by Title VII unless it falls within the bona fide occupational qualification (BFOQ) exception, set forth at 42 U.S.C. §2000e-2(e). The Court erroneously holds, however, that the BFOQ defense is so narrow that it could never justify a sex-specific fetal protection policy. I nevertheless concur in the judgment of reversal because on the record before us summary judgment in favor of Johnson Controls was improperly entered by the District Court and affirmed by the Court of Appeals.

I

In evaluating the scope of the BFOQ defense, the proper starting point is the language of the statute.... Title VII forbids discrimination on the basis of sex, except "in those certain instances where...sex...is a bona fide occupational qualification reasonably necessary to the normal operation of that particular business or enterprise." 42 U.S.C. §2000e-2(e)(1). For the fetal protection policy involved in this case to be a BFOQ, therefore, the policy must be "reasonably necessary" to the "normal operation" of making batteries, which is Johnson Controls' "particular business." Although that is a difficult standard to satisfy, nothing in the statute's language indicates that it could never support a sex-specific fetal protection policy.[1]

On the contrary, a fetal protection policy would be justified under the terms of the statute if, for example, an employer could show that exclusion of women from certain jobs was reasonably necessary to avoid substantial tort liability. Common sense tells us that it is part of the normal operation of business concerns to avoid causing injury to third parties, as well as to employees, if for no other reason than to avoid tort liability and its substantial costs....

The Court dismisses the possibility of tort liability by no more than speculating that if "Title VII bans sex-specific fetal-protection policies, the employer fully informs the woman of the risk, and the employer has not acted negligently, the basis for holding an employer liable seems remote at best." *Ante*, at 1208. Such speculation will be small comfort to employers. First, it is far from clear that compliance with Title VII will pre-empt state tort liability, and the Court offers no support for that proposition. Second, although warnings may preclude claims by injured *employees*, they will not preclude claims by injured children because the general rule is that parents cannot waive causes of action on behalf of their children, and

1. The Court's heavy reliance on the word "occupational" in the BFOQ statute, *ante*, at 12, is unpersuasive. *Any* requirement for employment can be said to be an occupational qualification, since "occupational" merely means related to a job. See Webster's Third New International Dictionary 1560 (1976). Thus, Johnson Controls' requirement that employees engaged in battery manufacturing be either male or non-fertile clearly is an "occupational qualification." The issue, of course, is whether that qualification is "reasonably necessary to the normal operation" of Johnson Controls' business. It is telling that the Court offers no case support, either from this Court or the lower Federal Courts, for its interpretation of the word "occupational."

the parents' negligence will not be imputed to the children. Finally, although state tort liability for prenatal injuries generally requires negligence, it will be difficult for employers to determine in advance what will constitute negligence. Compliance with OSHA standards, for example, has been held not to be a defense to state tort or criminal liability.... Moreover, it is possible that employers will be held strictly liable, if, for example, their manufacturing process is considered "abnormally dangerous." See Restatement (Second) of Torts §869, comment *b* (1979).

...

Dothard and *Criswell* make clear that avoidance of substantial safety risks to third parties is *inherently* part of both an employee's ability to perform a job and an employer's "normal operation" of its business.... The Court's statement in this case that "the safety exception is limited to instances in which sex or pregnancy actually interferes with the employee's ability to perform the job," *ante,* at 1205, therefore adds no support to its conclusion that a fetal protection policy could never be justified as a BFOQ. On the facts of this case, for example, protecting fetal safety while carrying out the duties of battery manufacturing is as much a legitimate concern as is safety to third parties in guarding prisons (*Dothard*) or flying airplanes (*Criswell*).

Dothard and *Criswell* also confirm that costs are relevant in determining whether a discriminatory policy is reasonably necessary for the normal operation of a business. In *Dothard,* the safety problem that justified exclusion of women from the prison guard positions was largely a result of inadequate staff and facilities. See 433 U.S., at 335, 97 S.Ct., at 2729–30. If the cost of employing women could not be considered, the employer there should have been required to hire more staff and restructure the prison environment rather than exclude women. Similarly, in *Criswell* the airline could have been required to hire more pilots and install expensive monitoring devices rather than discriminate against older employees. The BFOQ statute, however, reflects "Congress' unwillingness to require employers to change the very nature of their operations." *Price Waterhouse v. Hopkins,* 490 U.S. 228, 242, 109 S.Ct. 1775, 1786, 104 L.Ed.2d 268 (1989)(plurality opinion).

The Pregnancy Discrimination Act (PDA), 42 U.S.C. §2000e(k), contrary to the Court's assertion, *ante,* at 1206, did not restrict the scope of the BFOQ defense. The PDA was only an amendment to the "Definitions" section of Title VII, 42 U.S.C. §2000e, and did not purport to eliminate or alter the BFOQ defense. Rather, it merely clarified Title VII to make it clear that pregnancy and related conditions are included within Title VII's antidiscrimination provisions. As we have already recognized, "the purpose of the PDA was simply to make the treatment of pregnancy consistent with general Title VII principles."...

...

...The Court's narrow interpretation of the BFOQ defense in this case, however, means that an employer cannot exclude even pregnant women from an environment highly toxic to their fetuses. It is foolish to think that Congress intended such a result, and neither the language of the BFOQ exception nor our cases require it.

II

Despite my disagreement with the Court concerning the scope of the BFOQ defense, I concur in reversing the Court of Appeals because that court erred in affirming the District Court's grant of summary judgment in favor of Johnson Controls. First, the Court of Appeals erred in failing to consider the level of risk-avoidance that was part of Johnson Controls' "normal operation." Although the court did conclude that there was a "substantial risk" to fetuses from lead exposure in fertile women, 886 F.2d 871, 879–883, 898 (CA7 1989), it merely meant that there was a high risk that *some* fetal injury would occur absent a fetal protection policy. That analysis, of course, fails to address the *extent* of fetal injury that is likely to occur. If the fetal protection policy insists on a risk-avoidance level substantially higher than other risk levels tolerated by Johnson Controls such as risks to employees and consumers, the policy should not constitute a BFOQ.

Second, even without more information about the normal level of risk at Johnson Controls, the fetal protection policy at issue here reaches too far. This is evident both in its presumption that, absent medical documentation to the contrary, all women are fertile regardless of their age, see *id.*, at 876, n. 8, and in its exclusion of presumptively fertile women from positions that might result in a promotion to a position involving high lead exposure, *id.*, at 877. There has been no showing that either of those aspects of the policy is reasonably necessary to ensure safe and efficient operation of Johnson Controls' battery-manufacturing business. Of course, these infirmities in the company's policy do not warrant invalidating the entire fetal protection program.

Third, it should be recalled that until 1982 Johnson Controls operated without an exclusionary policy, and it has not identified any grounds for believing that its current policy is reasonably necessary to its normal operations....

Finally, the Court of Appeals failed to consider properly petitioners' evidence of harm to offspring caused by lead exposure in males. The court considered that evidence only in its discussion of the business necessity standard, in which it focused on whether *petitioners* had met their burden of proof. 886 F.2d, at 889–890. The burden of proving that a discriminatory qualification is a BFOQ, however, rests with the employer.... Thus, the court should have analyzed whether the evidence was sufficient for petitioners to survive summary judgment in light of *respondent's* burden of proof to establish a BFOQ.... It seems clear that if the Court of Appeals had properly analyzed [the] evidence, it would have concluded that summary judgment against petitioners was not appropriate because there was a dispute over a material issue of fact.

...

COMMENTS

When a child's life may be at stake, courts often overrule the medical decisions of parents and, for example, order blood transfusions for children of Jehovah's Witnesses or others religiously opposed to such treatment. Generally, medical care is not ordered against the religious objections of an adult patient, no matter how difficult it may be for medical and legal professionals to stand by while an adult seems to be throwing away his or her life because of religious objections to simple medical care. There have been a number of cases across the country in which courts have overruled the religious objections of pregnant patients and supplied medical care thought by the doctors to be advisable for the woman and crucial for the successful completion of her pregnancy. Frequently courts order caesarean sections to protect the fetus against the wishes of the woman operated upon — especially in cases of poor and minority race women. Such orders are controversial, and there are now also a number of cases in which the court refused to order the operation and the child was born healthy. The *A.C.* trial court was unusual in ordering an operation that it knew would likely cause harm to the dying patient. Many feel that the state has carried its protection of fetuses too far when it sacrifices the proper health care of a dying woman in an effort to bring her pregnancy to term.

In *Johnson Controls* the Supreme Court held that Title VII prohibited the employer from discriminating against fertile women for the stated purpose of protecting fetuses. Johnson Controls, which had a long history of sex discrimination, required women to be sterilized if they wished to work at certain relatively well-paying jobs that exposed the worker to lead, a poisonous metal, in levels high enough to be thought to endanger fetuses exposed through a pregnant worker. The company asserted not just that it wished to protect the eggs or the potential future children of the women, but also that it wished to protect itself from possible tort liability. *Johnson Controls* limited the power of employers to protect fetuses by refusing to hire women. It may turn out that exposure to lead damages men's sperm, such that exposure of either parent to lead may cause birth defects or similar reproductive problems. It would be ironic if the tort claims by women workers or their children were preempted by Title VII while the similar tort claims of men workers and their children were allowed.

The increasing use of in vitro fertilization may lead to situations in which courts are asked to protect the life of fertilized eggs. In *Davis v. Davis*, Tennessee Circuit Court, Blount County, reported at 15 Family Law Reporter (BNA) 2097 (1989), a divorcing couple that had been in treatment at a fertility center had seven frozen embryos remaining at the time of their separation. Against the husband's claim that the frozen embryos were jointly owned property that the wife could not unilaterally decide to have implanted in her womb, the court ruled that they were "seven human beings existing as embryos." Under the parens patriae power of the court, the judge granted the wife "temporary custody" of these "children, in vitro" on the basis that it was in the "best interest of these children for Mrs. Davis to be permitted the opportunity to bring these children to term through implantation." The judge also ruled that "all matters concerning support, visitation, final custody and related issues be reserved to the Court for further consideration," presumably if and when Mrs. Davis was successfully pregnant.

Some years earlier, a similar controversy over the legal status of frozen embryos ended when it was determined that the embryos would no longer be capable of producing a pregnancy, because the techniques used for freezing them were less successful than those used now. A wealthy couple from California had died leaving two frozen embryos "orphaned" in a fertility center in Australia. Perhaps in part because the couple had no other heirs, various individuals and groups sought to protect the embryos and offered volunteer wombs. *York v. Jones*, 717 F. Supp. 421 (E.D. Va. 1989), treated frozen embryos as property for purposes of allowing the couple whose eggs and sperm produced them to reclaim the embryos when the couple switched their fertility efforts to another medical facility out of state.

A 1993 case involved the legal status of fifteen tubes of frozen sperm, left by will to the girlfriend of its producer when he committed suicide, along with two notes — one expressing the wish that she have his child and the other addressed to his two older children by his first marriage and to the child he hoped his girlfriend would bear. Against various objections raised by the two older children, the court declared the sperm property that could pass by will to the girlfriend.

REFERENCES

Sharon Churcher, *The Love Legacy of Kane; Mistress of the Man Who Claimed He Inspired Jeffry Archer's Hit Novel Kane and Abel Battles to Have His Child — Two Years After His Death,* MAIL ON SUNDAY, p. 25 (September 19, 1993).

Maura Dolan, *High Court Lets Stand Ruling Allowing Man to Will Sperm,* LOS ANGELES TIMES (Metro, Part B at 3, col.5, September 3, 1993).

Peter Costigan, *Scores Seek to Mother 2 Embryos,* WASHINGTON POST, June 20, 1984, at A1.

B: ESTABLISHING PARENTHOOD

Children Born to Unmarried Women

TRIMBLE v. GORDON

United States Supreme Court
430 U.S. 762 (1977)

Mr. Justice POWELL delivered the opinion of the Court.

At issue in this case is the constitutionality of §12 of the Illinois Probate Act which allows illegitimate children to inherit by intestate succession only from their mothers. Under Illinois law, legitimate children are allowed to inherit by intestate succession from both their mothers and their fathers.

I

Appellant Deta Mona Trimble is the illegitimate daughter of appellant Jessie Trimble[3] and Sherman Gordon. Trimble and Gordon lived in Chicago with Deta Mona from 1970 until Gordon died in 1974, the victim of a homicide. On January 2, 1973, the Circuit Court of Cook County, Ill., had entered a paternity order finding Gordon to be the father of Deta Mona and ordering him to pay $15 per week for her support. Gordon thereafter supported Deta Mona in accordance with the paternity order and openly acknowledged her as his child. He died intestate at the age of 28, leaving an estate consisting only of a 1974 Plymouth automobile worth approximately $2,500.

Shortly after Gordon's death, Trimble, as the mother and next friend of Deta Mona, filed a petition for letters of administration, determination of heirship, and

3. There is some dispute over the status of Jessie Trimble in this litigation. It has been argued that she is in the case only as the next friend of her daughter. As the question is relevant only to the claim of sex discrimination against the mothers of illegitimate children, an issue we do not reach, we need not resolve the dispute.

declaratory relief in the Probate Division of the Circuit Court of Cook County, Ill. That court entered an order determining heirship, identifying as the only heirs of Gordon his father, Joseph Gordon, his mother, Ethel King, and his brother, two sisters, and a half brother....

The Circuit Court excluded Deta Mona on the authority of the negative implications of §12 of the Illinois Probate Act, which provides in relevant part:

> An illegitimate child is heir of his mother and of any maternal ancestor, and of any person from whom his mother might have inherited, if living; and the lawful issue of an illegitimate person shall represent such person and take, by descent, any estate which the parent would have taken, if living. A child who was illegitimate whose parents inter-marry and who is acknowledged by the father as the father's child is legitimate.

If Deta Mona had been a legitimate child, she would have inherited her father's entire estate under Illinois law. In rejecting Deta Mona's claim of heirship, the court sustained the constitutionality of §12.

...[T]he Illinois Supreme Court [sustained the opinion of the lower court in the case] *In re Estate of Karas*, 61 Ill.2d 40, 329 N.E.2d 234 (1975)....

We noted probable jurisdiction to consider the arguments that §12 violates the Equal Protection Clause of the Fourteenth Amendment by invidiously discriminating on the basis of illegitimacy and sex.[10] 424 U.S. 964, 96 S.Ct. 1457, 47 L.Ed.2d 731 (1976). We now reverse. As we conclude that the statutory discrimination against illegitimate children is unconstitutional, we do not reach the sex discrimination argument.

II

In *Karas*, the Illinois Supreme Court rejected the equal protection challenge to the discrimination against illegitimate children on the explicit authority of *Labine v. Vincent*, 401 U.S. 532, 91 S.Ct. 1017, 28 L.Ed.2d 288 (1971). The court found that §12 is supported by the state interests in encouraging family relationships and in establishing an accurate and efficient method of disposing of property at death. The court also found the Illinois law unobjectionable because no "insurmountable barrier" prevented illegitimate children from sharing in the estates of their fathers. By leaving a will, Sherman Gordon could have assured Deta Mona a share of his estate.

Appellees endorse the reasoning of the Illinois Supreme Court and suggest additional justifications for the statute. In weighing the constitutional sufficiency of these justifications, we are guided by our previous decisions involving equal protection challenges to laws discriminating on the basis of illegitimacy.[11] "[T]his Court requires, at a minimum, that a statutory classification bear some rational

10. Not presented here is the appellants' contention below that §12 discriminates on the basis of race because of its alleged disproportionate impact on Negroes.

11. This case represents the 12th time since 1968 that we have considered the constitutionality of alleged discrimination on the basis of illegitimacy. The previous decisions are as follows: *Mathews v. Lucas*, 427 U.S. 495, 96 S.Ct. 2755, 49 L.Ed.2d 651 (1976); *Beaty v. Weinberger*, 478 F.2d 300 (CA5 1973), *summarily aff'd*, 418 U.S. 901, 94 S.Ct. 3190, 41 L.Ed.2d 1150 (1974); *Jimenez v. Weinberger*, 417 U.S. 628, 94 S.Ct. 2496, 41 L.Ed.2d 363 (1974); *New Jersey Welfare Rights Organization v. Cahill*, 411 U.S. 619, 93 S.Ct. 1700, 36 L.Ed.2d 543 (1973); *Griffin v. Richardson*, 346 F.Supp. 1226 (Md.), *summarily aff'd*, 409 U.S. 1069, 93 S.Ct. 689, 34 L.Ed.2d 660 (1972); *Davis v. Richardson*, 342 F.Supp. 588 (Conn.), *summarily aff'd*, 409 U.S. 1069, 93 S.Ct. 678, 34 L.Ed.2d 659 (1972); *Gomez v. Perez*, 409 U.S. 535, 93 S.Ct. 872, 35 L.Ed.2d 56 (1973); *Weber v. Aetna Casualty & Surety Co.*, 406 U.S. 164, 92 S.Ct. 1400, 31 L.Ed.2d 768 (1972); *Labine v. Vincent*, 401 U.S. 532, 91 S.Ct. 1017, 28 L.Ed.2d 288 (1971); *Glona v. American Guarantee & Liability Ins. Co.*, 391 U.S. 73, 88 S.Ct. 1515, 20 L.Ed.2d 441 (1968); *Levy v. Louisiana*, 391 U.S. 68, 88 S.Ct. 1509, 20 L.Ed.2d 436 (1968).

relationship to a legitimate state purpose." *Weber v. Aetna Casualty & Surety Co.*, 406 U.S. 164, 172, 92 S.Ct. 1400, 1405, 31 L.Ed.2d 768 (1972). In this context, the standard just stated is a minimum; the Court sometimes requires more. "Though the latitude given state economic and social regulation is necessarily broad, when state statutory classifications approach sensitive and fundamental personal rights, this Court exercises a stricter scrutiny...." *Ibid.*

Appellants urge us to hold that classifications based on illegitimacy are "suspect," so that any justifications must survive "strict scrutiny." We considered and rejected a similar argument last Term in *Mathews v. Lucas*, 427 U.S. 495, 96 S.Ct. 2755, 49 L.Ed.2d 651 (1976). As we recognized in *Lucas*, illegitimacy is analogous in many respects to the personal characteristics that have been held to be suspect when used as the basis of statutory differentiations. *Id.*, at 505, 96 S.Ct., at 2762. We nevertheless concluded that the analogy was not sufficient to require "our most exacting scrutiny." *Id.*, at 506, 96 S.Ct., at 2763. Despite the conclusion that classifications based on illegitimacy fall in a "realm of less than strictest scrutiny," *Lucas* also establishes that the scrutiny "is not a toothless one," *id.*, at 510, 96 S.Ct., at 2764, a proposition clearly demonstrated by our previous decisions in this area.[12]

III

The Illinois Supreme Court prefaced its discussion of the state interests served by §12 with a general discussion of the purpose of the statute. Quoting from its earlier opinions, the court concluded that the statute was enacted to ameliorate the harsh common-law rule under which an illegitimate child was *filius nullius* and incapable of inheriting from anyone. 61 Ill.2d, at 44–45, 329 N.E.2d, at 236–237. Although §12 did not bring illegitimate children into parity with legitimate children, it did improve their position, thus partially achieving the asserted objective. The sufficiency of the justifications advanced for the remaining discrimination against illegitimate children must be considered in light of this motivating purpose.

A

The Illinois Supreme Court relied in part on the State's purported interest in "the promotion of [legitimate] family relationships." 61 Ill.2d, at 48, 329 N.E.2d, at 238. Although the court noted that this justification had been accepted in *Labine*, the opinion contains only the most perfunctory analysis. This inattention may not have been an oversight, for §12 bears only the most attenuated relationship to the asserted goal.[13]

---

12. See cases cited n. 11, *supra*. *Labine v. Vincent, supra*, is difficult to place in the pattern of this Court's equal protection decisions, and subsequent cases have limited its force as a precedent. In *Weber v. Aetna Casualty & Surety Co., supra*, we found in *Labine* a recognition that judicial deference is appropriate when the challenged statute involves the "substantial state interest in providing for 'the stability of...land titles and in the prompt and definitive determination of the valid ownership of property left by decedents'...." 406 U.S., at 170, 92 S.Ct., at 1404, quoting *Labine v. Vincent*, 229 So.2d 449, 452 (La.App.1969). We reaffirm that view, but there is a point beyond which such deference cannot justify discrimination. Although the proposition is self-evident, *Reed v. Reed*, 404 U.S. 71, 92 S.Ct. 251, 30 L.Ed.2d 225 (1971), demonstrates that state statutes involving the disposition of property at death are not immunized from equal protection scrutiny....

13. This purpose is not apparent from the statute. Penalizing children as a means of influencing their parents seems inconsistent with the desire of the Illinois Legislature to make the intestate succession law more just to illegitimate children. Moreover, the difference in the rights of illegitimate children in the estates of their mothers and their fathers appears to be unrelated to the purpose of promoting family relationships. In this respect the Louisiana laws at issue in *Labine* were quite different. Those laws differentiated on the basis of the character of the child's illegitimacy. "Bastard children" were given no inheritance rights. "Natural children," who could be and were acknowledged under state law, were given limited inheritance rights, but still less than those of legitimate children. 401 U.S., at 537, and n. 13, 91 S.Ct., at 2763. The Louisiana categories are consistent with a theory of social opprobrium regarding the parents' relationships and with a measured, if misguided, attempt to deter illegitimate relationships.

In a case like this, the Equal Protection Clause requires more than the mere incantation of a proper state purpose. No one disputes the appropriateness of Illinois' concern with the family unit, perhaps the most fundamental social institution of our society. The flaw in the analysis lies elsewhere. As we said in *Lucas*, the constitutionality of this law "depends upon the character of the discrimination and its relation to legitimate legislative aims." 427 U.S., at 504, 96 S.Ct., at 2761. The court below did not address the relation between §12 and the promotion of legitimate family relationships, thus leaving the constitutional analysis incomplete. The same observation can be made about this Court's decision in *Labine*, but that case does not stand alone. In subsequent decisions, we have expressly considered and rejected the argument that a State may attempt to influence the actions of men and women by imposing sanctions on the children born of their illegitimate relationships.

In *Weber* we examined a Louisiana workmen's compensation law which discriminated against one class of illegitimate children. Without questioning Louisiana's interest in protecting legitimate family relationships, we rejected the argument that "persons will shun illicit relations because the offspring may not one day reap the benefits of workmen's compensation." 406 U.S., at 173, 92 S.Ct., at 1405. Although *Weber* distinguished *Labine* on other grounds, the reasons for rejecting this justification are equally applicable here:

> The status of illegitimacy has expressed through the ages society's condemnation of irresponsible liaisons beyond the bonds of marriage. But visiting this condemnation on the head of an infant is illogical and unjust. Moreover, imposing disabilities on the illegitimate child is contrary to the basic concept of our system that legal burdens should bear some relationship to individual responsibility or wrongdoing. Obviously, no child is responsible for his birth and penalizing the illegitimate child is an ineffectual as well as an unjust way of deterring the parent. 406 U.S., at 175 (footnote omitted).

The parents have the ability to conform their conduct to societal norms, but their illegitimate children can affect neither their parents' conduct nor their own status.

B

The Illinois Supreme Court relied on *Labine* for another and more substantial justification: the State's interest in "establish[ing] a method of property disposition." 61 Ill.2d, at 48, 329 N.E.2d, at 238. Here the court's analysis is more complete. Focusing specifically on the difficulty of proving paternity and the related danger of spurious claims, the court concluded that this interest explained and justified the asymmetrical statutory discrimination against the illegitimate children of intestate men. The more favorable treatment of illegitimate children claiming from their mothers' estates was justified because "proof of a lineal relationship is more readily ascertainable when dealing with maternal ancestors." *Id.*, at 52, 329 N.E.2d, at 240. Alluding to the possibilities of abuse, the court rejected a case-by-case approach to claims based on alleged paternity. *Id.*, at 52–53, 329 N.E.2d, at 240–241.

The more serious problems of proving paternity might justify a more demanding standard for illegitimate children claiming under their fathers' estates than that required either for illegitimate children claiming under their mothers' estates or for legitimate children generally. We think, however, that the Illinois Supreme Court gave inadequate consideration to the relation between §12 and the State's proper objective of assuring accuracy and efficiency in the disposition of property at death. The court failed to consider the possibility of a middle ground between the extremes of complete exclusion and case-by-case determination of paternity. For at least some significant categories of illegitimate children of intestate men, inheritance rights can be recognized without jeopardizing the orderly settlement of estates or the dependability of titles to property passing under intestacy laws. Because it excludes those categories of illegitimate children unnecessarily, §12 is constitutionally flawed.

The orderly disposition of property at death requires an appropriate legal framework, the structuring of which is a matter particularly within the competence of the individual States. In exercising this responsibility, a State necessarily must enact laws governing both the procedure and substance of intestate succession. Absent infringement of a constitutional right, the federal courts have no role here, and, even when constitutional violations are alleged, those courts should accord substantial deference to a State's statutory scheme of inheritance.

The judicial task here is the difficult one of vindicating constitutional rights without interfering unduly with the State's primary responsibility in this area. Our previous decisions demonstrate a sensitivity to "the lurking problems with respect to proof of paternity," *Gomez v. Perez*, 409 U.S. 535, 538, 93 S.Ct. 872, 875, 35 L.Ed.2d 56 (1973), and the need for the States to draw "arbitrary lines…to facilitate potentially difficult problems of proof," *Weber*, 406 U.S., at 174, 92 S.Ct., at 1406. "Those problems are not to be lightly brushed aside, but neither can they be made into an impenetrable barrier that works to shield otherwise invidious discrimination." *Gomez, supra*, at 538, 93 S.Ct., at 875. Our decision last Term in *Mathews v. Lucas, supra*, provides especially helpful guidance.

In *Lucas* we sustained provisions of the Social Security Act governing the eligibility for surviving children's insurance benefits. One of the statutory conditions of eligibility was dependency on the deceased wage earner. 427 U.S., at 498, and n. 1, 96 S.Ct., at 2758. Although the Act presumed dependency for a number of categories of children, including some categories of illegitimate children, it required that the remaining illegitimate children prove actual dependency. The Court upheld the statutory classifications, finding them "reasonably related to the likelihood of dependency at death." *Id.*, at 509, 96 S.Ct., at 2764. Central to this decision was the finding that the "statute does not broadly discriminate between legitimates and illegitimates without more, but is carefully tuned to alternative considerations." *Id.*, at 513, 96 S.Ct., at 2766.

Although the present case arises in a context different from that in *Lucas*, the question whether the statute "is carefully tuned to alternative considerations" is equally applicable here. We conclude that §12 does not meet this standard. Difficulties of proving paternity in some situations do not justify the total statutory disinheritance of illegitimate children whose fathers die intestate. The facts of this case graphically illustrate the constitutional defect of §12. Sherman Gordon was found to be the father of Deta Mona in a state-court paternity action prior to his death. On the strength of that finding, he was ordered to contribute to the support of his child. That adjudication should be equally sufficient to establish Deta Mona's right to claim a child's share of Gordon's estate, for the State's interest in the accurate and efficient disposition of property at death would not be compromised in any way by allowing her claim in these circumstances.[14] The reach of the statute extends well beyond the asserted purposes. See *Jimenez v. Weinberger*, 417 U.S. 628, 637, 94 S.Ct. 2496, 2502, 41 L.Ed.2d 363 (1974).

C

The Illinois Supreme Court also noted that the decedents whose estates were involved in the consolidated appeals could have left substantial parts of their estates to their illegitimate children by writing a will. The court cited *Labine* as authority for the proposition that such a possibility is constitutionally significant. 61 Ill.2d, at 52, 329 N.E.2d, at 240. The penultimate paragraph of the opinion in *Labine* distinguishes that case from *Levy v. Louisiana*, 391 U.S. 68, 88 S.Ct. 1509, 20 L.Ed.2d 436 (1968),[15] because no insurmountable barrier prevented the illegitimate child from sharing in her father's estate. "There is not the slightest suggestion in this case that Louisiana has barred this illegitimate from inheriting from her father." 401 U.S., at 539, 91 S.Ct., at 1021. The Court then listed three different steps that would have resulted in some recovery by Labine's illegitimate daughter. Labine could have left a will; he could have legitimated the daughter by marrying her mother; and he could have given the daughter the status of a legitimate child by stating in his acknowledgment of paternity his desire to legitimate her. *Ibid.* In *Weber* our distinction of *Labine* was based in part on the fact that no such alternatives existed, as state law prevented the acknowledgment of the children involved. 406 U.S., at 170–171, 92 S.Ct., at 1404–1405.

Despite its appearance in two of our opinions, the focus on the presence or absence of an insurmountable barrier is somewhat of an analytical anomaly. Here, as in *Labine*, the question is the constitutionality of a state intestate succession law that treats illegitimate children differently from legitimate children. Traditional equal protection analysis asks whether this statutory differentiation on the basis of illegitimacy is justified by the promotion of recognized state objectives. If the law cannot be sustained on this analysis, it is not clear how it can be saved by the absence of an insurmountable barrier to inheritance under other and hypothetical circumstances.

By focusing on the steps that an intestate might have taken to assure some inheritance for his illegitimate children, the analysis loses sight of the essential question: the constitutionality of discrimination against illegitimates in a state intestate succession law. If the decedent had written a will devising property to his illegitimate child, the case no longer would involve intestate succession law at all. Similarly, if the decedent had legitimated the child by marrying the child's mother or by complying with the requirements of some other method of legitimation, the case no longer would involve discrimination against illegitimates. Hard questions cannot be avoided by a hypothetical reshuffling of the facts. If Sherman Gordon had devised his estate to Deta Mona this case would not be here. Similarly, in *Reed v. Reed*, 404 U.S. 71, 92 S.Ct. 251, 30 L.Ed.2d 225 (1971), if the decedent had left a

14. Evidence of paternity may take a variety of forms, some creating more significant problems of inaccuracy and inefficiency than others. The States, of course, are free to recognize these differences in fashioning their requirements of proof. Our holding today goes only to those forms of proof which do not compromise the States' interests. This clearly would be the case, for example, where there is a prior adjudication or formal acknowledgment of paternity. Thus, we would have a different case if the state statute were carefully tailored to eliminate imprecise and unduly burdensome methods of establishing paternity.

15. In *Levy* the Court struck down a Louisiana wrongful-death statute that gave legitimate, but not illegitimate, children a cause of action for the wrongful death of their parents.

will naming an executor, the problem of the statutory preference for male administrators of estates of intestates would not have been presented. The opinion in *Reed* gives no indication that this available alternative had any constitutional significance. We think it has none in this case.

D

Finally, appellees urge us to affirm the decision below on the theory that the Illinois Probate Act, including §12, mirrors the presumed intentions of the citizens of the State regarding the disposition of their property at death. Individualizing this theory, appellees argue that we must assume that Sherman Gordon knew the disposition of his estate under the Illinois Probate Act and that his failure to make a will shows his approval of that disposition. We need not resolve the question whether presumed intent alone can ever justify discrimination against illegitimates,[16] for we do not think that §12 was enacted for this purpose. The theory of presumed intent is not relied upon in the careful opinion of the Illinois Supreme Court examining both the history and the text of §12. This omission is not without significance, as one would expect a state supreme court to identify the state interests served by a statute of its state legislature. Our own examination of §12 convinces us that the statutory provisions at issue were shaped by forces other than the desire of the legislature to mirror the intentions of the citizens of the State with respect to their illegitimate children.

To the extent that other policies are not considered more important, legislators enacting state intestate succession laws probably are influenced by the desire to reflect the natural affinities of decedents in the allocation of estates among the categories of heirs. See *Mathews v. Lucas*, 427 U.S., at 514–515, 96 S.Ct., at 2766–2767. A pattern of distribution favoring brothers and sisters over cousins is, for example, best explained on this basis. The difference in §12 between the rights of illegitimate children in the estates of their fathers and mothers, however, is more convincingly explained by the other factors mentioned by the court below. Accepting in this respect the views of the Illinois Supreme Court, we find in §12 a primary purpose to provide a system of intestate succession more just to illegitimate children than the prior law, a purpose tempered by a secondary interest in protecting against spurious claims of paternity. In the absence of a more convincing demonstration, we will not hypothesize an additional state purpose that has been ignored by the Illinois Supreme Court.

---

16. Appellees characterize the Illinois intestate succession law as a "statutory will." Because intent is a central ingredient in the disposition of property by will, the theory that intestate succession laws are "statutory wills" based on the "presumed intent" of the citizens of the State may have some superficial appeal. The theory proceeds from the initial premise that an individual could, if he wished, disinherit his illegitimate children in his will. Because the statute merely reflects the intent of those citizens who failed to make a will, discrimination against illegitimate children in intestate succession laws is said to be equally permissible. The term "statutory will," however, cannot blind us to the fact that intestate succession laws are acts of States, not of individuals. Under the Fourteenth Amendment this is a fundamental difference.

Even if one assumed that a majority of the citizens of the State preferred to discriminate against their illegitimate children, the sentiment hardly would be unanimous. With respect to any individual, the argument of knowledge and approval of the state law is sheer fiction. The issue therefore becomes where the burden of inertia in writing a will is to fall. At least when the disadvantaged group has been a frequent target of discrimination, as illegitimates have, we doubt that a State constitutionally may place the burden on that group by invoking the theory of "presumed intent."...

IV

For the reasons stated above, we conclude that §12 of the Illinois Probate Act[17] cannot be squared with the command of the Equal Protection Clause of the Fourteenth Amendment. Accordingly, we reverse the judgment of the Illinois Supreme Court and remand the case for further proceedings not inconsistent with this opinion.

So ordered.

The CHIEF JUSTICE, Mr. Justice STEWART, Mr. Justice BLACKMUN, and Mr. Justice REHNQUIST dissent. Like the Supreme Court of Illinois, they find this case constitutionally indistinguishable from *Labine v. Vincent*, 401 U.S. 532, 91 S.Ct. 1017, 28 L.Ed.2d 288 (1971). They would, therefore, affirm the judgment.

[Separate dissenting opinion of Justice REHNQUIST omitted.]

LALLI v. LALLI
United States Supreme Court
439 U.S. 259 (1978)

Mr. Justice POWELL announced the judgment of the Court and delivered an opinion, in which the CHIEF JUSTICE and Mr. Justice STEWART join.

This case presents a challenge to the constitutionality of §4-1.2 of New York's Estates, Powers, and Trusts Law, which requires illegitimate children who would inherit from their fathers by intestate succession to provide a particular form of proof of paternity. Legitimate children are not subject to the same requirement.

I

Appellant Robert Lalli claims to be the illegitmate son of Mario Lalli who died intestate on January 7, 1973, in the State of New York. Appellant's mother, who died in 1968, never was married to Mario. After Mario's widow, Rosamond Lalli, was appointed administratrix of her husband's estate, appellant petitioned the Surrogate's Court for Westchester County for a compulsory accounting, claiming that he and his sister Maureen Lalli were entitled to inherit from Mario as his children. Rosamond Lalli opposed the petition. She argued that even if Robert and Maureen were Mario's children, they were not lawful distributees of the state because they had failed to comply with §4-1.2,[2] which provides in part:

> An illegitimate child is the legitimate child of his father so that he and his issue inherit from his father if a court of competent jurisdiction has,

17. The Illinois statute can be distinguished in several respects from the Louisiana statute in *Labine*. The discrimination in *Labine* took a different form, suggesting different legislative objectives. See, *e.g.*, n. 13, *supra*. In its impact on the illegitimate children excluded from their parents' estates, the statute was significantly different. Under Louisiana law, all illegitimate children, "natural" and "bastard," were entitled to support from the estate of the deceased parent. 401 U.S., at 534, n. 2, 91 S.Ct., at 1018. Despite these differences, it is apparent that we have examined the Illinois statute more critically than the Court examined the Louisiana statute in *Labine*. To the extent that our analysis in this case differs from that in Labine the more recent analysis controls.

2. Section 4-1.2 in its entirety provides:

(a) For the purposes of this article:

(1) An illegitimate child is the legitimate child of his mother so that he and his issue inherit from his mother and from his maternal kindred.

(2) An illegitimate child is the legitimate child of his father so that he and his issue inherit from his father if a court of competent jurisdiction has, during the lifetime of the father, made an order of filiation declaring paternity in a proceeding instituted during the pregnancy of the mother or within two years from the birth of the child.

(3) The existence of an agreement obligating the father to support the illegitimate child does not qualify such child or his issue to inherit from the father in the absence of an order of filiation made as prescribed by subparagraph (2).

> during the lifetime of the father, made an order of filiation declaring paternity in a proceeding instituted during the pregnancy of the mother or within two years from the birth of the child.

Appellant conceded that he had not obtained an order of filiation during his putative father's lifetime. He contended, however, that §4-1.2, by imposing this requirement, discriminated against him on the basis of his illegitimate birth in violation of the Equal Protection Clause of the Fourteenth Amendment.[3] Appellant tendered certain evidence of his relationship with Mario Lalli, including a notarized document in which Lalli, in consenting to appellant's marriage, referred to him as "my son," and several affidavits by persons who stated that Lalli had acknowledged openly and often that Robert and Maureen were his children.

The Surrogate's Court noted that §4-1.2 had previously, and unsuccessfully, been attacked under the Equal Protection Clause. After reviewing recent decisions of this Court concerning discrimination against illegitimate children, particularly *Labine v. Vincent*, 401 U.S. 532, 91 S.Ct. 1017, 28 L.Ed.2d 288 (1971), and three New York decisions affirming the constitutionality of the statute,...the court ruled that appellant was properly excluded as a distributee of Lalli's estate and therefore lacked status to petition for a compulsory accounting.

On direct appeal the New York Court of Appeals affirmed. *In re Lalli*, 38 N.Y.2d 77, 378 N.Y.S.2d 351, 340 N.E.2d 721 (1975). It understood *Labine* to require the State to show no more than that "there is a rational basis for the means chosen by the Legislature for the accomplishment of a permissible State objective." 38 N.Y.2d, at 81, 378 N.Y.S.2d, at 354, 340 N.E.2d, at 723. After discussing the problems of proof peculiar to establishing paternity, as opposed to maternity, the court concluded that the State was constitutionally entitled to require a judicial decree during the father's lifetime as the exclusive form of proof of paternity.

Appellant appealed the Court of Appeals' decision to this Court. While that case was pending here, we decided *Trimble v. Gordon*, 430 U.S. 762, 97 S.Ct. 1459, 52 L.Ed.2d 31 (1977). Because the issues in these two cases were similar in some respects, we vacated and remanded to permit further consideration in light of *Trimble. Lalli v. Lalli*, 431 U.S. 911 (1977).

On remand,[4] the New York Court of Appeals, with two judges dissenting, adhered to its former disposition. *In re Lalli*, 43 N.Y.2d 65, 400 N.Y.S.2d 761, 371 N.E.2d 481 (1977). It acknowledged that *Trimble* contemplated a standard of judicial review demanding more than "a mere finding of some remote rational relationship between the statute and a legitimate State purpose," 43 N.Y.2d, at 67, 400

---

2. *Continued*

(4) A motion for relief from an order of filiation may be made only by the father, and such motion must be made within one year from the entry of such order.

(b) If an illegitimate child dies, his surviving spouse, issue, mother, maternal kindred and father inherit and are entitled to letters of administration as if the decedent were legitimate, provided that the father may inherit or obtain such letters only if an order of filiation has been made in accordance with the provisions of subparagraph (2). N.Y. Est., POWERS & TRUSTS LAW §4-1.2 (McKinney 1967).

3. Appellant also claimed that §4-1.2 was invalid under N.Y. Const., Art. 1, §11. The New York Court of Appeals did not rule on this issue, nor do we. We also do not consider whether §4-1.2 unconstitutionally discriminates on the basis of sex or whether the administratrix of Mario's estate is required to account for her alleged failure to bring a wrongful-death action on behalf of appellant. The latter question was not considered by the Court of Appeals, and the former was raised for the first time by a brief *amici curiae* in this Court.

4. On remand from this Court, the New York Attorney General was permitted to intervene as a defendant-appellee. He has filed a brief on the merits and argued the case in this Court. Appellee Rosamond Lalli did not present oral argument and has not filed a brief on the merits.

N.Y.S.2d, at 762, 371 N.E.2d, at 482, though less than strictest scrutiny. Finding §4-1.2 to be "significantly and determinatively different" from the statute overturned in *Trimble*, the court ruled that the New York law was sufficiently related to the State's interest in "'the orderly settlement of estates and the dependability of titles to property passing under intestacy laws,'" 43 N.Y.2d, at 67, 69–70, 400 N.Y.S.2d, at 763–764, 371 N.E.2d, at 482–483, quoting *Trimble, supra*, 430 U.S., at 771, 97 S.Ct., at 1465, to meet the requirements of equal protection.

Appellant again sought review here, and we noted probable jurisdiction. 435 U.S. 921, 98 S.Ct. 1482, 55 L.Ed.2d 514 (1978). We now affirm.

II

We begin our analysis with *Trimble*. At issue in that case was the constitutionality of an Illinois statute providing that a child born out of wedlock could inherit from his intestate father only if the father had "acknowledged" the child and the child had been legitimated by the intermarriage of the parents. The appellant in *Trimble* was a child born out of wedlock whose father had neither acknowledged her nor married her mother. He had, however, been found to be her father in a judicial decree ordering him to contribute to her support. When the father died intestate, the child was excluded as a distributee because the statutory requirements for inheritance had not been met.

We concluded that the Illinois statute discriminated against illegitimate children in a manner prohibited by the Equal Protection Clause. Although,...classifications based on illegitimacy are not subject to "strict scrutiny," they nevertheless are invalid under the Fourteenth Amendment if they are not substantially related to permissible state interests. Upon examination, we found that the Illinois law failed that test.

Two state interests were proposed which the statute was said to foster: the encouragement of legitimate family relationships and the maintenance of an accurate and efficient method of disposing of an intestate decedent's property. Granting that the State was appropriately concerned with the integrity of the family unit, we viewed the statute as bearing "only the most attenuated relationship to the asserted goal." *Trimble, supra*, at 768, 97 S.Ct., at 1464. We again rejected the argument that "persons will shun illicit relations because the offspring may not one day reap the benefits" that would accrue to them were they legitimate. *Weber v. Aetna Casualty & Surety Co.*, 406 U.S. 164, 173, 92 S.Ct. 1400, 1405, 31 L.Ed.2d 768 (1972). The statute therefore was not defensible as an incentive to enter legitimate family relationships.

Illinois' interest in safeguarding the orderly disposition of property at death was more relevant to the statutory classification. We recognized that devising "an appropriate legal framework" in the furtherance of that interest "is a matter particularly within the competence of the individual States." *Trimble, supra*, 430 U.S., at 771, 97 S.Ct., at 1465. An important aspect of that framework is a response to the often difficult problem of proving the paternity of illegitimate children and the related danger of spurious claims against intestate estates. See *infra*, at 525–526. These difficulties, we said, "might justify a more demanding standard for illegitimate children claiming under their fathers' estates than that required either for illegitimate children claiming under their mothers' estates or for legitimate children generally." *Trimble, supra*, at 770, 97 S.Ct., at 1465.

The Illinois statute, however, was constitutionally flawed because, by insisting upon not only an acknowledgment by the father, but also the marriage of the parents, it excluded "at least some significant categories of illegitimate children of intestate men [whose] inheritance rights can be recognized without jeopardizing the orderly settlement of estates or the dependability of titles to property passing under intestacy laws." *Id.*, at 771, 97 S.Ct., at 1465. We concluded that the Equal Protection Clause required that a statute placing exceptional burdens on illegitimate children in the furtherance of proper state objectives must be more "carefully tuned to alternative considerations," *id.*, at 772, 97 S.Ct., at 1466, quoting *Mathews v. Lucas, supra*, 427 U.S., at 513, 96 S.Ct., at 2766, than was true of the broad disqualification in the Illnois law.

III

The New York statute, enacted in 1965, was intended to soften the rigors of previous law which permitted illegitimate children to inherit only from their mothers. See *infra*, at 525. By lifting the absolute bar to paternal inheritance, §4-1.2 tended to achieve its desired effect. As in *Trimble*, however, the question before us is whether the remaining statutory obstacles to inheritance by illegitimate children can be squared with the Equal Protection Clause.

A

At the outset we observe that §4-1.2 is different in important respects from the statutory provision overturned in *Trimble*. The Illinois statute required, in addition to the father's acknowledgment of paternity, the legitimation of the child through the intermarriage of the parents as an absolute precondition to inheritance. This combination of requirements eliminated "the possibility of a middle ground between the extremes of complete exclusion and case-by-case determination of paternity." *Trimble*, 430 U.S., at 770–771, 97 S.Ct., at 1465. As illustrated by the facts in *Trimble*, even a judicial declaration of paternity was insufficient to permit inheritance.

Under §4-1.2, by contrast, the marital status of the parents is irrelevant. The single requirement at issue here is an evidentiary one — that the paternity of the father be declared in a judicial proceeding sometime before his death.[5] The child need not have been legitimated in order to inherit from his father. Had the appellant in Trimble been governed by §4-1.2, she would have been a distributee of her father's estate. See *In re Lalli*, 43 N.Y.2d at 68 n.2, 400 N.Y.S.2d at 762 n.2, 371 N.E.2d, at 482 n.2.

A related difference between the two provisions pertains to the state interests said to be served by them. The Illinois law was defended, in part, as means of

5. Section 4-1.2 requires not only that the order of filiation be made during the lifetime of the father, but that the proceeding in which it is sought be commenced "during the pregnancy of the mother or within two years from the birth of the child." The New York Court of Appeals declined to rule on the constitutionality of the two-year limitation in both of its opinions in this case because appellant concededly had never commenced a paternity proceeding at all. Thus, if the rule that paternity be judicially declared during his father's lifetime were upheld, appellant would lose for failure to comply with that requirement alone. If, on the other hand, appellant prevailed in his argument that his inheritance could not be conditioned on the existence of an order of filiation, the two-year limitation would become irrelevant, since the paternity proceeding itself would be unnecessary. See *In re Lalli*, 43 N.Y.2d 65, 68 n. 1, 400 N.Y.S.2d 761, 762 n. 1, 371 N.E.2d 481, 482 n. 1 (1977); *In re Lalli*, 38 N.Y.2d 77, 80 n., 378 N.Y.S.2d 351, 353 n., 340 N.E.2d 721, 723 n. (1975). As the New York Court of Appeals has not passed upon the constitutionality of the two-year limitation, that question is not before us. Our decision today therefore sustains §4-1.2 under the Equal Protection Clause only with respect to its requirement that a judicial order of filiation be issued during the lifetime of the father of an illegitimate child.

encouraging legitimate family relationsips. No such justification has been offered in support of §4-1.2. The Court of Appeals disclaimed that the purpose of the statute, "even in small part, was to discourage illegitimacy, to mold human conduct or to set societal norms." *In re Lalli, supra,* 43 N.Y.2d, at 70, 400 N.Y.S.2d, at 764, 371 N.E.2d, at 483. The absence in §4-1.2 of any requirement that the parents intermarry or otherwise legitimate a child born out of wedlock and our review of the legislative history of the statute, *infra,* at 525–526, confirm this view.

Our inquiry, therefore, is focused narrowly. We are asked to decide whether the discrete procedural demands that §4-1.2 places on illegitimate children bear an evident and substantial relation to the particular state interests this statute is designed to serve.

B

The primary state goal underlying the challenged aspects of §4-1.2 is to provide for the just and orderly disposition of property at death.[6] We long have recognized that this is an area with which the States have an interest of considerable magnitude. *Trimble, supra,* 430 U.S., at 771, 97 S.Ct., at 1466; *Weber v. Aetna Casualty & Surety Co.,* 406 U.S., at 170, 92 S.Ct., at 1404; *Labine v. Vincent,* 401 U.S., at 538, 91 S.Ct., at 1021; see also *Lyeth v. Hoey,* 305 U.S. 188, 193, 59 S.Ct. 155, 158, 83 L.Ed. 119 (1938); *Mager v. Grima,* 8 How. 490, 493, 12 L.Ed. 1168 (1850).

This interest is directly implicated in paternal inheritance by illegitimate children because of the peculiar problems of proof that are involved. Establishing maternity is seldom difficult. As one New York Surrogate's Court has observed: "[T]he birth of the child is a recorded or registered event usually taking place in the presence of others. In most cases the child remains with the mother and for a time is necessarily reared by her. That the child is the child of a particular woman is rarely difficult to prove." *In re Ortiz,* 60 Misc.2d 756, 761, 303 N.Y.S.2d 806, 812 (1969). Proof of paternity, by contrast, frequently is difficult when the father is not part of a formal family unit. "The putative father often goes his way unconscious of the birth of a child. Even if conscious, he is very often totally unconcerned because of the absence of any ties to the mother. Indeed the mother may not know *who* is responsible for her pregnancy." *Ibid.* (emphasis in original)....

Thus, a number of problems arise that counsel against treating illegitimate children identically to all other heirs of an intestate father. These were the subject of a comprehensive study by the Temporary State Commission on the Modernization, Revision and Simplification of the Law of Estates. This group, known as the Bennett Commission,[7] consisted of individuals experienced in the practical problems of estate administration. *In re Flemm, supra,* 85 Misc.2d, at 858, 381 N.Y.S.2d, at 575. The Commission issued its report and recommendations to the legislature in 1965. See Fourth Report of the Temporary State Commission on the Modernization, Revision and Simplification of the Law of Estates, Legis.Doc. No.

---

6. The presence in this case of the State's interest in the orderly disposition of a decedent's property at death distinguishes it from others in which that justification for an illegitimacy-based classification was absent. *E.g., Jimenez v. Weinberger,* 417 U.S. 628, 94 S.Ct. 2496, 41 L.Ed.2d 363 (1974); *Gomez v. Perez,* 409 U.S. 535, 93 S.Ct. 872, 35 L.Ed.2d 56 (1973); *Weber v. Aetna Casualty & Surety Co.,* 406 U.S. 164, 170, 92 S.Ct. 1400, 1404, 31 L.Ed.2d 768 (1972); *Levy v. Louisiana,* 391 U.S. 68, 88 S.Ct. 1509, 20 L.Ed.2d 436 (1968).

7. The Bennett Commission was created by the New York Legislature in 1961. It was instructed to recommend needed changes in certain areas of state law, including that pertaining to "the descent and distribution of property, and the practice and procedure relating thereto." 1961 N.Y. Laws, ch. 731, §1.

19 (1965)(hereinafter Commission Report). The statute now codified as §4-1.2 was included.

...

C

As the State's interests are substantial, we now consider the means adopted by New York to further these interests. In order to avoid the problems described above, the Commission recommended a requirement designed to ensure the accurate resolution of claims of paternity and to minimize the potential for disruption of estate administration. Accuracy is enhanced by placing paternity disputes in a judicial forum during the lifetime of the father. As the New York Court of Appeals observed in its first opinion in this case, the "availability [of the putative father] should be a substantial factor contributing to the reliability of the fact-finding process." *In re Lalli*, 38 N.Y.2d, at 82, 378 N.Y.S.2d, at 355, 340 N.E.2d, at 724. In addition, requiring that the order be issued during the father's lifetime permits a man to defend his reputation against "unjust accusations in paternity claims," which was a secondary purpose of §4-1.2. Commission Report 266.

The administration of an estate will be facilitated, and the possibility of delay and uncertainty minimized, where the entitlement of an illegitimate child to notice and participation is a matter of judicial record before the administration commences. Fraudulent assertions of paternity will be much less likely to succeed, or even to arise, where the proof is put before a court of law at a time when the putative father is available to respond, rather than first brought to light when the distribution of the assets of an estate is in the offing.[8]

Appellant contends that §4-1.2, like the statute at issue in *Trimble*, excludes "significant categories of illegitimate children" who could be allowed to inherit "without jeopardizing the orderly settlement" of their intestate fathers' estates. *Trimble*, 430 U.S., at 771, 97 S.Ct., at 1465. He urges that those in his position — "known" illegitimate children who, despite the absence of an order of filiation obtained during their fathers' lifetimes, can present convincing proof of paternity — cannot rationally be denied inheritance as they pose none of the risks §4-1.2 was intended to minimize.[9]

We do not question that there will be some illegitimate children who would be able to establish their relationship to their deceased fathers without serious disruption of the administration of estates and that, as applied to such individuals, §4-1.2 appears to operate unfairly. But few statutory classifications are entirely free

8. In affirming the judgment below, we do not, of course, restrict a State's freedom to require proof of paternity by means other than a judicial decree. Thus, a State may prescribe any formal method of proof, whether it be similar to that provided by §4-1.2 or some other regularized procedure that would assure the authenticity of the acknowledgment. As we noted in Trimble, 430 U.S., at 772 n. 14, 97 S.Ct., at 1466 n. 14, such a procedure would be sufficient to satisfy the State's interests. See also n. 11, *infra.*

9. Appellant claims that in addition to discriminating between illegitimate and legitimate children, §4-1.2, in conjunction with N.Y. Dom. Rel. Law §24 (McKinney 1977), impermissibly discriminates between classes of illegitimate children. Section 24 provides that a child conceived out of wedlock is nevertheless legitimate if, before or after his birth, his parents marry, even if the marriage is void, illegal, or judicially annulled. Appellant argues that by classifying as "legitimate" children born out of wedlock whose parents later marry, New York has, with respect to these children, substituted marriage for §4-1.2's requirement of proof of paternity. Thus, these "illegitimate" children escape the rigors of the rule unlike their unfortunate counterparts whose parents never marry.

Under §24, one claiming to be the legitimate child of a deceased man would have to prove not only his paternity but also his maternity and the fact of the marriage of his parents. These additional evidentiary requirements make it reasonable to accept less exacting proof of paternity and to treat such children as legitimate for inheritance purposes.

from the criticism that they sometimes produce inequitable results. Our inquiry under the Equal Protection Clause does not focus on the abstract "fairness" of a state law, but on whether the statute's relation to the state interests it is intended to promote is so tenuous that it lacks the rationality contemplated by the Fourteenth Amendment.

The Illinois statute in *Trimble* was constitutionally unacceptable because it effected a total statutory disinheritance of children born out of wedlock who were not legitimated by the subsequent marriage of their parents. The reach of the statute was far in excess of its justifiable purposes. Section 4-1.2 does not share this defect. Inheritance is barred only where there has been a failure to secure evidence of paternity during the father's lifetime in the manner prescribed by the State. This is not a requirement that inevitably disqualifies an unnecessarily large number of children born out of wedlock.

The New York courts have interpreted §4-1.2 liberally and in such a way as to enhance its utility to both father and child without sacrificing its strength as a procedural prophylactic. For example, a father of illegitimate children who is willing to acknowledge paternity can waive his defenses in a paternity proceeding,...or even institute such a proceeding himself.[10]... In addition, the courts have excused "technical" failures by illegitimate children to comply with the statute in order to prevent unnecessary injustice....

...

Even if, as Mr. Justice BRENNAN believes, §4-1.2 could have been written somewhat more equitably, it is not the function of a court "to hypothesize independently on the desirability or feasibility of any possible alternative[s]" to the statutory scheme formulated by New York. *Mathews v. Lucas*, 427 U.S., at 515, 96 S.Ct., at 2767. "These matters of practical judgment and empirical calculation are for [the State].... In the end, the precise accuracy of [the State's] calculations is not a matter of specialized judicial competence; and we have no basis to question their detail beyond the evident consistency and substantiality." *Id.*, at 515–516, 96 S.Ct. at 2767.[11]

---

10. In addition to making intestate succession possible, of course, a father is always free to provide for his illegitimate child by will....

11. The dissent of Mr. Justice BRENNAN would reduce the opinion in *Trimble v. Gordon, supra*, to a simplistic holding that the Constitution *requires* a State, in a case of this kind, to recognize as sufficient any "formal acknowledgmet of paternity." This reading of *Trimble* is based on a single phrase lifted from a footnote. 430 U.S., at 772 n. 14, 97 S.Ct., at 1466. It ignores both the broad rationale of the Court's opinion and the context in which the note and the phrase relied upon appear. The principle that the footnote elaborates is that the States are free to recognize the problems arising from different forms of proof and to select those forms "carefully tailored to eliminate imprecise and unduly burdensome methods of establishing paternity." *Ibid.* The New York Legislature, with the benefit of the Bennett Commission's study, exercised this judgment when it considered and rejected the possibility of accepting evidence of paternity less formal than a judicial order. Commission Report 266–267.

The "formal acknowledgment" contemplated by *Trimble* is such as would minimize post-death litigation, *i.e.*, a regularly prescribed, legally recognized method of acknowledging paternity. See n. 8, *supra*. It is thus plain that footnote 14 in *Trimble* does not sustain the dissenting opinion. Indeed, the document relied upon by the dissent is not an acknowledgment of paternity at all. It is a simple "Certificate of Consent" that apparently was required at the time by New York for the marriage of a minor. It consists of one sentence:

> THIS IS TO CERTIFY that I, who have hereto subscribed my name, do hereby consent that Robert Lalli who is my son and who is under the age of 21 years, shall be united in marriage to Janice Bivins by any minister of the gospel or other person authorized by law to solemnize marriages. App. A-14.

Mario Lalli's signature to this document was acknowledged by a notary public, but the certificate contains no oath or affirmation as to the truth of its contents. The notary did no more than confirm the identity of Lalli. Because the certificate was executed for the purpose of giving consent to marry, not of proving biological paternity, the meaning of the words "my son" is ambiguous. One can readily imagine that had Robert Lalli's half-brother, who was not Mario's son but who took the surname Lalli and lived as a member of his household, sought permission to marry, Mario might also have referred to him as "my son" on a consent certificate.

We conclude that the requirement imposed by §4-1.2 on illegitimate children who would inherit from their fathers is substantially related to the important state interests the statute is intended to promote. We therefore find no violation of the Equal Protection Clause.

The judgment of the New York Court of Appeals is

Affirmed.

For the reasons stated in his dissent in *Trimble v. Gordon*, 430 U.S. 762, 777, 97 S.Ct. 1459, 1468, 52 L.Ed.2d 31 (1977), Mr. Justice REHNQUIST concurs in the judgment of affirmance.

Mr. Justice STEWART, concurring.

It seems to me that Mr. Justice POWELL's opinion convincingly demonstrates the significant differences between the New York law at issue here and the Illinois law at issue in *Trimble v. Gordon*, 430 U.S. 762, 97 S.Ct. 1459, 52 L.Ed.2d 31. Therefore, I cannot agree with the view expressed in Mr. Justice BLACKMUN's opinion concurring in the judgment that *Trimble v. Gordon* is now "a derelict," or with the implication that in deciding the two cases the way it has this Court has failed to give authoritative guidance to the courts and legislatures of the several States.

Mr. Justice BLACKMUN, concurring in the judgment.

I agree with the result the Court has reached and concur in its judgment. I also agree with much that has been said in the plurality opinion. My point of departure, of course, is at the plurality's valiant struggle to distinguish, rather than overrule, *Trimble v. Gordon*, 430 U.S. 762, 97 S.Ct. 1459, 52 L.Ed.2d 31 (1977), decided just the Term before last, and involving a small probate estate (an automobile worth approximately $2,500) and a sad and appealing fact situation. Four Members of the Court, like the Supreme Court of Illinois, found the case "constitutionally indistinguishable from *Labine v. Vincent*, 401 U.S. 532, 91 S.Ct. 1017, 28 L.Ed.2d 288 (1971)," and were in dissent. *Id.*, at 776, 777, 97 S.Ct., at 1468.

It seems to me that the Court today gratifyingly reverts to the principles set forth in *Labine v. Vincent.* What Mr. Justice BLACK said for the Court in *Labine* applies with equal force to the present case and, as four of us thought, to the Illinois situation with which *Trimble* was concerned.

I would overrule *Trimble*, but the Court refrains from doing so on the theory that the result in *Trimble* is justified because of the peculiarities of the Illinois Probate Act there under consideration. This, of course, is an explanation, but, for me, it is an unconvincing one. I therefore must regard *Trimble* as a derelict, explainable only because of the overtones of its appealing facts and offering little precedent for constitutional analysis of State intestate succession laws. If *Trimble* is not a derelict, the corresponding statutes of other States will be of questionable validity until this Court passes on them, one by one, as being on the *Trimble* side of the line or the *Labine-Lalli* side.

---

11. *Continued*

The important state interests of safeguarding the accurate and orderly disposition of property at death, emphasized in *Trimble* and reiterated in our opinion today, could be frustrated easily if there were a constitutional rule that any notarized but unsworn statement identifying an individual as a "child" must be accepted as adequate proof of paternity regardless of the context in which the statement was made.

Mr. Justice BRENNAN, with whom Mr. Justice WHITE, Mr. Justice MARSHALL, and Mr. Justice STEVENS join, dissenting.

Trimble v. Gordon, 430 U.S. 762, 97 S.Ct. 1459, 52 L.Ed.2d 31 (1977), declares that the state interest in the accurate and efficient determination of paternity can be adequately served by requiring the illegitimate child to offer into evidence a "formal acknowledgment of paternity." *Id.*, at 772 n. 14, 97 S.Ct., at 1466. The New York statute is inconsistent with this command. Under the New York scheme, an illegitimate child may inherit intestate only if there has been a judicial finding of paternity during the lifetime of the father.

The present case illustrates the injustice of the departure from *Trimble* worked by today's decision sustaining the New York rule. All interested parties concede that Robert Lalli is the son of Mario Lalli. Mario Lalli supported Robert during his son's youth. Mario Lalli formally acknowledged Robert Lalli as his son. See *In re Lalli*, 38 N.Y.2d 77, 79, 378 N.Y.S.2d 351, 352, 340 N.E.2d 721, 722 (1975). Yet, for want of a judicial order of filiation entered during Mario's lifetime, Robert Lalli is denied his intestate share of his father's estate.

There is no reason to suppose that the injustice of the present case is aberrant. Indeed it is difficult to imagine an instance in which an illegitimate child acknowledged and voluntarily supported by his father, would ever inherit intestate under the New York scheme. Social welfare agencies, busy as they are with errant fathers, are unlikely to bring paternity proceedings against fathers who support their children. Similarly, children who are acknowledged and supported by their fathers are unlikely to bring paternity proceedings against them. First, they are unlikely to see the need for such adversary proceedings. Second, even if aware of the rule requiring judicial filiation orders, they are likely to fear provoking disharmony by suing their fathers. For the same reasons, mothers of such illegitimates are unlikely to bring proceedings against the fathers. Finally, fathers who do not even bother to make out wills (and thus die intestate) are unlikely to take the time to bring formal filiation proceedings. Thus, as a practical matter, by requiring judicial filiation orders entered during the lifetime of the fathers, the New York statute makes it virtually impossible for acknowledged and freely supported illegitimate children to inherit intestate.

Two interests are said to justify this discrimination against illegitimates. First, it is argued, reliance upon mere formal public acknowledgments of paternity would open the door to fraudulent claims of paternity. I cannot accept this argument. I adhere to the view that when "a father has formally acknowledged his child...there is no possible difficulty of proof, and no opportunity for fraud or error. This purported interest [in avoiding fraud]...can offer no justification for distinguishing between a formally acknowledged illegitimate child and a legitimate one." *Labine v. Vincent*, 401 U.S. 532, 552, 91 S.Ct. 1017, 1028, 28 L.Ed.2d 288 (1971)(BRENNAN, J., dissenting).

But even if my confidence in the accuracy of formal public acknowledgments of paternity were unfounded, New York has available less drastic means of screening out fraudulent claims of paternity. In addition to requiring formal acknowledgments of paternity, New York might require illegitimates to prove paternity by an elevated standard of proof, *e.g.*, clear and convincing evidence, or even beyond a reasonable doubt. Certainly here, where there is no factual dispute as to the relationship between Robert and Mario Lalli, there is no justification for denying Robert Lalli his intestate share.

Second, it is argued, the New York statute protects estates from belated claims by unknown illegitimates. I find this justification even more tenuous than the first. Publication notice and a short limitations period in which claims against the estate could be filed could serve the asserted state interest as well as, if not better than, the present scheme. In any event, the fear that unknown illegitimates might assert belated claims hardly justifies cutting off the rights of known illegitimates such as Robert Lalli. I am still of the view that the state interest in the speedy and efficient determination of paternity "is completely served by public acknowledgment of parentage and simply does not apply to the case of acknowledged illegitimate children." *Id.*, at 558 n. 30, 91 S.Ct., at 1030 n. 30 (BRENNAN, J., dissenting).

I see no reason to retreat from our decision in *Trimble v. Gordon.* The New York statute on review here, like the Illinois statute in *Trimble*, excludes "forms of proof which do not compromise the State['s] interests." *Trimble v. Gordon, supra,* 430 U.S., at 772 n. 14, 97 S.Ct., at 1466 n. 14. The statute thus discriminates against illegitimates through means not substantially related to the legitimate interests that the statute purports to promote. I would invalidate the statute.

STANLEY v. ILLINOIS

United States Supreme Court
405 U.S. 645 (1972)

Mr. Justice WHITE delivered the opinion of the Court.

Joan Stanley lived with Peter Stanley intermittently for 18 years, during which time they had three children.[1] When Joan Stanley died, Peter Stanley lost not only her but also his children. Under Illinois law, the children of unwed fathers become wards of the State upon the death of the mother. Accordingly, upon Joan Stanley's death, in a dependency proceeding instituted by the State of Illinois, Stanley's children[2] were declared wards of the State and placed with court-appointed guardians. Stanley appealed, claiming that he had never been shown to be an unfit parent and that since married fathers and unwed mothers could not be deprived of their children without such a showing, he had been deprived of the equal protection of the laws guaranteed him by the Fourteenth Amendment. The Illinois Supreme Court accepted the fact that Stanley's own unfitness had not been established but rejected the equal protection claim, holding that Stanley could properly be separated from his children upon proof of the single fact that he and the dead mother had not been married. Stanley's actual fitness as a father was irrelevant. *In re Stanley*, 45 Ill.2d 132, 256 N.E.2d 814 (1970).

Stanley presses his equal protection claim here. The State continues to respond that unwed fathers are presumed unfit to raise their children and that it is unnecessary to hold individualized hearings to determine whether particular fathers are in fact unfit parents before they are separated from their children. We granted certiorari, 400 U.S. 1020, 91 S.Ct. 584, 27 L.Ed.2d 631 (1971), to determine whether this method of procedure by presumption could be allowed to stand in light of the fact that Illinois allows married fathers — whether divorced, widowed, or separated — and mothers — even if unwed — the benefit of the presumption that they are fit to raise their children.

---

1. Uncontradicted testimony of Peter Stanley, App. 22.
2. Only two children are involved in this litigation.

I

At the outset we reject any suggestion that we need not consider the propriety of the dependency proceeding that separated the Stanleys because Stanley might be able to regain custody of his children as a guardian or through adoption proceedings. The suggestion is that if Stanley has been treated differently from other parents, the difference is immaterial and not legally cognizable for the purposes of the Fourteenth Amendment. This Court has not, however, embraced the general proposition that a wrong may be done if it can be undone. *Cf. Sniadach v. Family Finance Corp. of Bay View*, 395 U.S. 337, 89 S.Ct. 1820, 23 L.Ed.2d 349 (1969). Surely, in the case before us, if there is delay between the doing and the undoing petitioner suffers from the deprivation of his children, and the children suffer from uncertainty and dislocation.

It is clear, moreover, that Stanley does not have the means at hand promptly to erase the adverse consequences of the proceeding in the course of which his children were declared wards of the State. It is first urged that Stanley could act to adopt his children. But under Illinois law, Stanley is treated not as a parent but as a stranger to his children, and the dependency proceeding has gone forward on the presumption that he is unfit to exercise parental rights. Insofar as we are informed, Illinois law affords him no priority in adoption proceedings. It would be his burden to establish not only that he would be a suitable parent but also that he would be the most suitable of all who might want custody of the children. Neither can we ignore that in the proceedings from which this action developed, the "probation officer," see App. 17, the assistant state's attorney, see *id.*, at 29–30, and the judge charged with the case, see *id.*, at 16–18, 23, made it apparent that Stanley, unmarried and impecunious as he is, could not now expect to profit from adoption proceedings.[3] The Illinois Supreme Court apparently recognized some or all of these considerations, because it did not suggest that Stanley's case was undercut by his failure to petition for adoption.

Before us, the State focuses on Stanley's failure to petition for "custody and control" — the second route by which, it is urged, he might regain authority for his children. Passing the obvious issue whether it would be futile or burdensome for an unmarried father — without funds and already once presumed unfit — to petition for custody, this suggestion overlooks the fact that legal custody is not parenthood or adoption. A person appointed guardian in an action for custody and control is subject to removal at any time without such cause as must be shown in a neglect proceeding against a parent. Ill. Rev. Stat., c. 37, §705-8. He may not take the children out of the jurisdiction without the court's approval. He may be required to report to the court as to his disposition of the children's affairs. Ill. Rev. Stat., c. 37, §705-8. Obviously then, even if Stanley were a mere step away from "custody and control," to give an unwed father only "custody and control" would still be to leave him seriously prejudiced by reason of his status.

We must therefore examine the question that Illinois would have us avoid: Is a presumption that distinguishes and burdens all unwed fathers constitutionally repugnant? We conclude that, as a matter of due process of law, Stanley was entitled to a hearing on his fitness as a parent before his children were taken from him

3. The Illinois Supreme Court's opinion is not at all contrary to this conclusion. That court said: "[T]he trial court's comments clearly indicate the court's willingness to consider a future request by the father for *custody and guardianship*." 45 Ill.2d 132, 135, 256 N.E.2d 814, 816. (Italics added.) See also the comment of Stanley's counsel on oral argument: "If Peter Stanley could have adopted his children, we would not be here today." Tr. of Oral Arg. 7.

and that, by denying him a hearing and extending it to all other parents whose custody of their children is challenged, the State denied Stanley the equal protection of the laws guaranteed by the Fourteenth Amendment.

II

Illinois has two principal methods of removing nondelinquent children from the homes of their parents. In a dependency proceeding it may demonstrate that the children are wards of the State because they have no surviving parent or guardian. Ill. Rev. Stat., c. 37, §§702-1, 702-5. In a neglect proceeding it may show that children should be wards of the State because the present parent(s) or guardian does not provide suitable care. Ill. Rev. Stat., c. 37, §§702-1, 702-4.

The State's right — indeed, duty — to protect minor children through a judicial determination of their interests in a neglect proceeding is not challenged here. Rather, we are faced with a dependency statute that empowers state officials to circumvent neglect proceedings on the theory that an unwed father is not a "parent" whose existing relationship with his children must be considered.[4] "Parents," says the State, "means the father and mother of a legitimate child, or the survivor of them, or the natural mother of an illegitimate child, and includes any adoptive parent," Ill. Rev. Stat., c. 37, §701-14, but the term does not include unwed fathers.

Under Illinois law, therefore, while the children of all parents can be taken from them in neglect proceedings, that is only after notice, hearing, and proof of such unfitness as a parent as amounts to neglect, an unwed father is uniquely subject to the more simplistic dependency proceeding. By use of this proceeding, the State, on showing that the father was not married to the mother, need not prove unfitness in fact, because it is presumed at law. Thus, the unwed father's claim of parental qualification is avoided as "irrelevant."

In considering this procedure under the Due Process Clause, we recognize, as we have in other cases, that due process of law does not require a hearing "in every conceivable case of government impairment of private interest." *Cafeteria and Restaurant Workers Union etc. v. McElroy*, 367 U.S. 886, 894, 81 S.Ct. 1743, 1748, 6 L.Ed.2d 1230 (1961). That case explained that "[t]he very nature of due process negates any concept of inflexible procedures universally applicable to every imaginable situation" and firmly established that "what procedures due process may require under any given set of circumstances must begin with a determination of the precise nature of the government function involved as well as of the private interest that has been affected by governmental action." *Id.*, at 895, 81 S.Ct., at 1748; *Goldberg v. Kelly*, 397 U.S. 254, 263, 90 S.Ct. 1011, 1018, 25 L.Ed.2d 287 (1970).

The private interest here, that of a man in the children he has sired and raised, undeniably warrants deference and, absent a powerful countervailing interest, protection. It is plain that the interest of a parent in the companionship, care, custody, and management of his or her children "come[s] to this Court with a momentum for respect lacking when appeal is made to liberties which derive merely from shifting economic arrangements." *Kovacs v. Cooper*, 336 U.S. 77, 95, 69 S.Ct. 448, 458, 93 L.Ed. 513 (1949)(Frankfurter, J., concurring).

The Court has frequently emphasized the importance of the family. The rights to conceive and to raise one's children have been deemed "essential," *Meyer v. Nebraska*, 262 U.S. 390, 399, 43 S.Ct. 625, 626, 67 L.Ed. 1042 (1923), "basic civil

4. Even while refusing to label him a "legal parent," the State does not deny that Stanley has a special interest in the outcome of these proceedings. It is undisputed that he is the father of these children, that he lived with the two children whose custody is challenged all their lives, and that he has supported them.

rights of man," *Skinner v. Oklahoma*, 316 U.S. 535, 541, 62 S.Ct. 1110, 1113, 86 L.Ed. 1655 (1942), and "[r]ights far more precious...than property rights," *May v. Anderson*, 345 U.S. 528, 533, 73 S.Ct. 840, 843, 97 L.Ed. 1221 (1953). "It is cardinal with us that the custody, care and nurture of the child reside first in the parents, whose primary function and freedom include preparation for obligations the state can neither supply nor hinder." *Prince v. Massachusetts*, 321 U.S. 158, 166, 64 S.Ct. 438, 442, 88 L.Ed. 645 (1944). The integrity of the family unit has found protection in the Due Process Clause of the Fourteenth Amendment, *Meyer v. Nebraska, supra*, 262 U.S. at 399, 43 S.Ct. at 626, the Equal Protection Clause of the Fourteenth Amendment, *Skinner v. Oklahoma, supra*, 316 U.S., at 541, 62 S.Ct., at 1113, and the Ninth Amendment, *Griswold v. Connecticut*, 381 U.S. 479, 496, 85 S.Ct. 1678, 14 L.Ed.2d 510 (1965)(Goldberg, J., concurring).

Nor has the law refused to recognize those family relationships unlegitimized by a marriage ceremony. The Court has declared unconstitutional a state statute denying natural, but illegitimate, children a wrongful-death action for the death of their mother, emphasizing that such children cannot be denied the right of other children because familial bonds in such cases were often as warm, enduring, and important as those arising within a more formally organized family unit. *Levy v. Louisiana*, 391 U.S. 68, 71–72, 88 S.Ct. 1509, 1511, 20 L.Ed.2d 436 (1968)....

...

For its part, the State has made its interest quite plain: Illinois has declared that the aim of the Juvenile Court Act is to protect "the moral, emotional, mental, and physical welfare of the minor and the best interests of the community" and to "strengthen the minor's family ties whenever possible, removing him from the custody of his parents only when his welfare or safety or the protection of the public cannot be adequately safeguarded without removal...." Ill. Rev. Stat., c. 37, §701-2. These are legitimate interests, well within the power of the State to implement. We do not question the assertion that neglectful parents may be separated from their children.

But we are here not asked to evaluate the legitimacy of the state ends, rather, to determine whether the means used to achieve these ends are constitutionally defensible. What is the state interest in separating children from fathers without a hearing designed to determine whether the father is unfit in a particular disputed case? We observe that the State registers no gain towards its declared goals when it separates children from the custody of fit parents. Indeed, if Stanley is a fit father, the State spites its own articulated goals when it needlessly separates him from his family.

In *Bell v. Burson*, 402 U.S. 535, 91 S.Ct. 1586, 29 L.Ed.2d 90 (1971), we found a scheme repugnant to the Due Process Clause because it deprived a driver of his license without reference to the very factor (there fault in driving, here fitness as a parent) that the State itself deemed fundamental to its statutory scheme. Illinois would avoid the self-contradiction that rendered the Georgia license suspension system invalid by arguing that Stanley and all other unmarried fathers can reasonably be presumed to be unqualified to raise their children.[5]

---

5. Illinois says in its brief, at 21–23,

> [T]he only relevant consideration in determining the propriety of governmental intervention in the raising of children is whether the best interests of the child are served by such intervention.
>
> In effect, Illinois has imposed a statutory presumption that the best interests of a particular group of children necessitates some governmental supervision in certain clearly defined situations. The group of children who are illegitimate are distinguishable from legitimate children not so much by their status

It may be, as the State insists, that most unmarried fathers are unsuitable and neglectful parents.[6] It may also be that Stanley is such a parent and that his children should be placed in other hands. But all unmarried fathers are not in this category; some are wholly suited to have custody of their children.[7] This much the State readily concedes, and nothing in this record indicates that Stanley is or has been a neglectful father who has not cared for his children. Given the opportunity to make his case, Stanley may have been seen to be deserving of custody of his offspring. Had this been so, the State's statutory policy would have been furthered by leaving custody in him.

...

...[I]t may be argued that unmarried fathers are so seldom fit that Illinois need not undergo the administrative inconvenience of inquiry in any case, including Stanley's. The establishment of prompt efficacious procedures to achieve legitimate state ends is a proper state interest worthy of cognizance in constitutional adjudication. But the Constitution recognizes higher values than speed and efficiency.[8] Indeed, one might fairly say of the Bill of Rights in general, and the Due

---

5. *Continued*

> at birth as by the factual differences in their upbringing. While a legitimate child usually is raised by both parents with the attendant familial relationships and a firm concept of home and identity, the illegitimate child normally knows only one parent — the mother....
>
> ...The petitioner has premised his argument upon particular factual circumstances — a lengthy relationship with the mother...a familial relationship with the two children, and a general assumption that this relationship approximates that in which the natural parents are married to each other.
>
> ...Even if this characterization were accurate (the record is insufficient to support it) it would not affect the validity of the statutory definition of parent.... The petitioner does not deny that the children are illegitimate. The record reflects their natural mother's death. Given these two factors, grounds exist for the State's intervention to ensure adequate care and protection for these children. This is true whether or not this particular petitioner assimilates all or none of the normal characteristics common to the classification of fathers who are not married to the mothers of their children.

See also Illinois' Brief 23 ("The comparison of married and putative fathers involves exclusively factual differences. The most significant of these are the presence or absence of the father from the home on a day-to-day basis and the responsibility imposed upon the relationship"), *id.*, at 24 (to the same effect), *id.*, at 31 (quoted below in n. 6), id., at 24–26 (physiological and other studies are cited in support of the proposition that men are not naturally inclined to childrearing), and Tr. of Oral Arg. 31 ("We submit that both based on history or [*sic*] culture the very real differences...between the married father and the unmarried father, in terms of their interests in children and their legal responsibility for their children, that the statute here fulfills the compelling governmental objective of protecting children...").

6. The State speaks of "the general disinterest of putative fathers in their illegitimate children" (Brief 8) and opines that "[i]n most instances the natural father is a stranger to his children." Brief 31.

7. See *In re T.*, 8 Mich.App. 122, 154 N.W.2d 27 (1967). There a panel of the Michigan Court of Appeals in unanimously affirming a circuit court's determination that the father of an illegitimate son was best suited to raise the boy, said:

> The appellants' presentation in this case proceeds on the assumption that placing Mark for adoption is inherently preferable to rearing by his father, that uprooting him from the family which he knew from birth until he was a year and a half old, secretly institutionalizing him and later transferring him to strangers is so incontrovertibly better that no court has the power even to consider the matter. Hardly anyone would even suggest such a proposition if we were talking about a child born in wedlock.
>
> We are not aware of any sociological data justifying the assumption that an illegitimate child reared by his natural father is less likely to receive a proper upbringing than one reared by his natural father who was at one time married to his mother, or that the stigma of illegitimacy is so pervasive it requires adoption by strangers and permanent termination of a subsisting relationship with the child's father.
>
> *Id.*, at 146, 154 N.W.2d, at 39.

8. Cf. *Reed v. Reed*, 404 U.S. 71, 76, 92 S.Ct. 251, 254, 30 L.Ed.2d 225 (1971). "Clearly the objective of reducing the workload on probate courts by eliminating one class of contests is not without some legitimacy.... [But to] give a mandatory preference to members of either sex over members of the other, merely to accomplish the elimination of hearings on the merits, is to make the very kind of arbitrary legislative choice forbidden by the Equal Protection Clause of the Fourteenth Amendment." *Carrington v. Rash*, 380 U.S. 89, 96, 85 S.Ct. 775, 780 (1965), teaches the same lesson. "...States may not casually deprive a class of individuals of the vote because of some remote administrative benefit to the State." *Oyama v. California*, 332 U.S. 633, 68 S.Ct. 269, 92 L.Ed. 249. "By forbidding a soldier ever to controvert the presumption of nonresidence, the Texas Constitution imposes an invidious discrimination in violation of the Fourteenth Amendment."

Process Clause in particular, that they were designed to protect the fragile values of a vulnerable citizenry from the overbearing concern for efficiency and efficacy that may characterize praiseworthy government officials no less, and perhaps more, than mediocre ones.

Procedure by presumption is always cheaper and easier than individualized determination. But when, as here, the procedure forecloses the determinative issues of competence and care, when it explicitly disdains present realities in deference to past formalities, it needlessly risks running roughshod over the important interests of both parent and child. It therefore cannot stand.[9]

Bell v. Burson held that the State could not, while purporting to be concerned with fault in suspending a driver's license, deprive a citizen of his license without a hearing that would assess fault. Absent fault, the State's declared interest was so attenuated that administrative convenience was insufficient to excuse a hearing where evidence of fault could be considered. That drivers involved in accidents, as a statistical matter, might be very likely to have been wholly or partially at fault did not foreclose hearing and proof in specific cases before licenses were suspended.

We think the Due Process Clause mandates a similar result here. The State's interest in caring for Stanley's children is *de minimis* if Stanley is shown to be a fit father. It insists on presuming rather than proving Stanley's unfitness solely because it is more convenient to presume than to prove. Under the Due Process Clause that advantage is insufficient to justify refusing a father a hearing when the issue at stake is the dismemberment of his family.

III.

The State of Illinois assumes custody of the children of married parents, divorced parents, and unmarried mothers only after a hearing and proof of neglect. The children of unmarried fathers, however, are declared dependent children without a hearing on parental fitness and without proof of neglect. Stanley's claim in the state courts and here is that failure to afford him a hearing on his parental qualifications while extending it to other parents denied him equal protection of the laws. We have concluded that all Illinois parents are constitutionally entitled to a hearing on their fitness before their children are removed from their custody. It follows that denying such a hearing to Stanley and those like him while granting it to other Illinois parents is inescapably contrary to the Equal Protection Clause.[10]

9. We note in passing that the incremental cost of offering unwed fathers an opportunity for individualized hearings on fitness appears to be minimal. If unwed fathers, in the main, do not care about the disposition of their children, they will not appear to demand hearings. If they do care, under the scheme here held invalid, Illinois would admittedly at some later time have to afford them a properly focused hearing in a custody or adoption proceeding.

Extending opportunity for hearing to unwed fathers who desire and claim competence to care for their children creates no constitutional or procedural obstacle to foreclosing those unwed fathers who are not so inclined. The Illinois law governing procedure in juvenile cases. Ill. Rev. Stat., c. 37, §704-1 *et seq.*, provides for personal service, notice by certified mail, or for notice by publication when personal or certified mail service cannot be had or when notice is directed to unknown respondents under the style of "All whom it may Concern." Unwed fathers who do not promptly respond cannot complain if their children are declared wards of the State. Those who do respond retain the burden of proving their fatherhood.

10. Predicting a finding of constitutional invalidity under the Equal Protection Clause of the Fourteenth Amendment on the observation that a State has accorded bedrock procedural rights to some, but not all similarly situated, is not contradictory to our holding in *Pickard v. Connor*, 404 U.S. 270 (1971). In that case a due process, rather than an equal protection, claim was raised in the state courts. The federal courts were, in our opinion, barred from reversing the state conviction on grounds of contravention of the Equal Protection Clause when that clause had not been referred to for consideration by the state authorities. Here, in contrast, we dispose of the case on the constitutional premise raised below, reaching the result by a method of analysis readily available to the state court.

...

The judgment of the Supreme Court of Illinois is reversed and the case is remanded to that court for proceedings not inconsistent with this opinion.

It is so ordered.

Mr. Justice POWELL and Mr. Justice REHNQUIST took no part in the consideration or decision of this case.

Mr. Justice DOUGLAS joins in Parts I and II of this opinion.

Mr. Chief Justice BURGER, with whom Mr. Justice BLACKMUN concurs, dissenting.

The only constitutional issue raised and decided in the courts of Illinois in this case was whether the Illinois statute that omits unwed fathers from the definition of "parents" violates the Equal Protection Clause. We granted certiorari to consider whether the Illinois Supreme Court properly resolved that equal protection issue when it unanimously upheld the statute against petitioner Stanley's attack.

No due process issue was raised in the state courts; and no due process issue was decided by any state court....

In the case now before us, it simply does not suffice to say, as the Court in a footnote does say, that "we dispose of the case on the constitutional premise raised below, reaching the result by a method of analysis readily available to the state court." *Ante,* at 1216 n. 10. The Court's method of analysis seems to ignore the strictures of Justices DOUGLAS and WHITE, but the analysis is clear: the Court holds *sua sponte* that the Due Process Clause requires that Stanley, the unwed biological father, be accorded a hearing as to his fitness as a parent before his children are declared wards of the state court; the Court then reasons that since Illinois recognizes such rights to due process in married fathers, it is required by the Equal Protection Clause to give such protection to unmarried fathers. This "method of analysis" is, of course, no more or less than the use of the Equal Protection Clause as a shorthand condensation of the entire Constitution: a State may not deny *any* constitutional right to some of its citizens without violating the Equal Protection Clause through its failure to deny such rights to *all* of its citizens. The limits on this Court's jurisdiction are not properly expandable by the use of such semantic devices as that.

...

All of those persons in Illinois who may have followed the progress of this case will, I expect, experience no little surprise at the Court's opinion handed down today. Stanley will undoubtedly be surprised to find that he has prevailed on an issue never advanced by him....

In regard to the only issue that I consider properly before the Court, I agree with the State's argument that the Equal Protection Clause is not violated when Illinois gives full recognition only to those father-child relationships that arise in the context of family units bound together by legal obligations arising from marriage or from adoption proceedings. Quite apart from the religious or quasi-religious connotations that marriage has — and has historically enjoyed — for a large proportion of this Nation's citizens, it is in law an essentially contractual relationship, the parties to which have legally enforceable rights and duties, with respect both to each other and to any children born to them. Stanley and the mother of these children never entered such a relationship. The record is silent as to whether they ever privately exchanged such promises as would have bound them in marriage under the common law. *See Cartwright v. McGown*, 121 Ill. 388, 398, 12 N.E. 737, 739 (1887). In any event, Illinois has not recognized common-law marriages since 1905. Ill. Rev. Stat., c. 89, §4. Stanley did not seek the burdens when he could have freely assumed them.

Where there is a valid contract of marriage, the law of Illinois presumes that the husband is the father of any child born to the wife during the marriage; as the father, he has legally enforceable rights and duties with respect to that child. When a child is born to an unmarried woman, Illinois recognizes the readily identifiable mother, but makes no presumption as to the identity of the biological father. It does, however, provide two ways, one voluntary and one involuntary, in which that father may be identified. First, he may marry the mother and acknowledge the child as his own; this has the legal effect of legitimating the child and gaining for the father full recognition as a parent. Ill. Rev. Stat., c. 3, §12, subd. 8. Second, a man may be found to be the biological father of the child pursuant to a paternity suit initiated by the mother; in this case, the child remains illegitimate, but the adjudicated father is made liable for the support of the child until the latter attains age 18 or is legally adopted by another. Ill. Rev. Stat., c. 106 3/4, §52.

Stanley argued before the Supreme Court of Illinois that the definition of "parents," set out in Ill. Rev. Stat., c. 37, §701-14, as including "the father and mother of a legitimate child, or the survivor of them, or the natural mother of an illegitimate child, [or]...any adoptive parent,"[3] violates the Equal Protection Clause in that it treats unwed mothers and unwed fathers differently. Stanley then enlarged upon his equal protection argument when he brought the case here; he argued before this Court that Illinois is not permitted by the Equal Protection Clause to distinguish between unwed fathers and any of the other biological parents included in the statutory definition of legal "parents."

The Illinois Supreme Court correctly held that the State may constitutionally distinguish between unwed fathers and unwed mothers. Here, Illinois' different treatment of the two is part of that State's statutory scheme for protecting the welfare of illegitimate children. In almost all cases, the unwed mother is readily identifiable, generally from hospital records, and alternatively by physicians or others attending the child's birth. Unwed fathers, as a class, are not traditionally quite so easy to identify and locate. Many of them either deny all responsibility or exhibit no interest in the child or its welfare; and, of course, many unwed fathers are simply not aware of their parenthood.

Furthermore, I believe that a State is fully justified in concluding, on the basis of common human experience, that the biological role of the mother in carrying and nursing a infant creates stronger bonds between her and the child than the bonds resulting from the male's often casual encounter. This view is reinforced by the observable fact that most unwed mothers exhibit a concern for their offspring

---

3. The Court seems at times to ignore this statutory definition of "parents," even though it is precisely that definition itself whose constitutionality has been brought into issue by Stanley. In preparation for finding a purported similarity between this case and *Bell v. Burson*, 402 U.S. 535, 91 S.Ct. 1586, 29 L.Ed.2d 90 (1971), the Court quotes the legislatively declared aims of the Juvenile Court Act to "strengthen the minor's family ties whenever possible, removing him from the custody of his *parents* only when his welfare or safety or the protection of the public cannot be adequately safeguarded without removal." (Emphasis added.) The Court then goes on to find a "self-contradiction" between that stated aim and the Act's nonrecognition of unwed fathers. *Ante*, at 1213. There is, of course, no such contradiction. The word "parent" in the statement of legislative purpose obviously has the meaning given to it by the definitional provision of the Act.

either permanently or at least until they are safely placed for adoption, while unwed fathers rarely burden either the mother or the child with their attentions or loyalties. Centuries of human experience buttress this view of the realities of human conditions and suggest that unwed mothers of illegitimate children are generally more dependable protectors of their children than are unwed fathers. While these, like most generalizations, are not without exceptions, they nevertheless provide a sufficient basis to sustain a statutory classification whose objective is not to penalize unwed parents but to further the welfare of illegitimate children in fulfillment of the State's obligations as *parens patriae*.[4]

Stanley depicts himself as a somewhat unusual unwed father, namely, as one who has always acknowledged and never doubted his fatherhood of these children. He alleges that he loved, cared for, and supported these children from the time of their birth until the death of their mother. He contends that he consequently must be treated the same as a married father of legitimate children. Even assuming the truth of Stanley's allegations, I am unable to construe the Equal Protection Clause as requiring Illinois to tailor its statutory definition of "parents" so meticulously as to include such unusual unwed fathers, while at the same time excluding those unwed, and generally unidentified, biological fathers who in no way share Stanley's professed desires.

Indeed, the nature of Stanley's own desires is less than absolutely clear from the record in this case. Shortly after the death of the mother, Stanley turned these two children over to the care of a Mr. and Mrs. Ness; he took no action to gain recognition of himself as a father, through adoption, or as a legal custodian, through a guardianship proceeding. Eventually it came to the attention of the State that there was no living adult who had any legally enforceable obligation for the care and support of the children; it was only then that the dependency proceeding here under review took place and that Stanley made himself known to the juvenile court in connection with these two children.[5] Even then, however, Stanley did not ask to be charged with the legal responsibility for the children. He asked only that such legal responsibility be given to no one else. He seemed, in particular, to be concerned with the loss of the welfare payments he would suffer as a result of the designation of others as guardians of the children.

Not only, then, do I see no ground for holding that Illinois' statutory definition of "parents" on its face violates the Equal Protection Clause; I see no ground for holding that any constitutional right of Stanley has been denied in the application of that statutory definition in the case at bar.

...

---

4. When the marriage between the parents of a legitimate child is dissolved by divorce or separation, the State, of course, normally awards custody of the child to one parent or the other. This is considered necessary for the child's welfare, since the parents are no longer legally bound together. The unmarried parents of an illegitimate child are likewise not legally bound together. Thus, even if Illinois did recognize the parenthood of both the mother and father of an illegitimate child, it would, for consistency with its practice in divorce proceedings, be called upon to award custody to one or the other of them, at least once it had by some means ascertained the identity of the father.

5. As the majority notes, *ante*, at 1210, Joan Stanley gave birth to three children during the 18 years Peter Stanley was living "intermittently" with her. At oral argument, we were told by Stanley's counsel that the oldest of these three children had previously been declared a ward of the court pursuant to a neglect proceeding that was "proven against" Stanley at a time, apparently, when the juvenile court officials were under the erroneous impression that Peter and Joan Stanley had been married. Tr. of Oral Arg. 19.

QUILLOIN v. WALCOTT
United States Supreme Court
434 U.S. 246 (1978)

Mr. Justice MARSHALL delivered the opinion of the Court.

The issue in this case is the constitutionality of Georgia's adoption laws as applied to deny an unwed father authority to prevent adoption of his illegitimate child. The child was born in December 1964 and has been in the custody and control of his mother, appellee Ardell Williams Walcott, for his entire life. The mother and the child's natural father, appellant Leon Webster Quilloin, never married each other or established a home together, and in September 1967 the mother married appellee Randall Walcott.[1] In March 1976, she consented to adoption of the child by her husband, who immediately filed a petition for adoption. Appellant attempted to block the adoption and to secure visitation rights, but he did not seek custody or object to the child's continuing to live with appellees. Although appellant was not found to be an unfit parent, the adoption was granted over his objection.

In *Stanley v. Illinois*, 405 U.S. 645, 92 S.Ct. 1208, 31 L.Ed.2d 551 (1972), this Court held that the State of Illinois was barred, as a matter of both due process and equal protection, from taking custody of the children of an unwed father, absent a hearing and a particularized finding that the father was an unfit parent. The Court concluded, on the one hand, that a father's interest in the "companionship, care, custody, and management" of his children is "cognizable and substantial," *id.*, at 651–652, 92 S.Ct., at 1212–13, and, on the other hand, that the State's interest in caring for the children is "*de minimis*" if the father is in fact a fit parent, *id.*, at 657–658, 92 S.Ct., at 1215–1216. *Stanley* left unresolved the degree of protection a State must afford to the rights of an unwed father in a situation, such as that presented here, in which the countervailing interests are more substantial.

I

Generally speaking, under Georgia law a child born in wedlock cannot be adopted without the consent of each living parent who has not voluntarily surrendered rights in the child or been adjudicated an unfair parent.[2] Even where the child's parents are divorced or separated at the time of the adoption proceedings, either parent may veto the adoption. In contrast, only the consent of the mother is required for adoption of an illegitimate child. Ga.Code §74-403(3)(1975).[3] To acquire the same veto authority possessed by other parents, the father of a child born out of wedlock must legitimate his offspring, either by marrying the mother

1. The child lived with his maternal grandmother for the initial period of the marriage, but moved in with appellees in 1969 and lived with them thereafter.

2. See Ga.Code §§74-403(1), (2)(1975). Section 74-403(1) sets forth the general rule that "no adoption shall be permitted except with the written consent of the living parents of a child." Section 74-403(2) provides that consent is not required from a parent who (1) has surrendered rights in the child to a child-placing agency or to the adoption court; (2) is found by the adoption court to have abandoned the child, or to have willfully failed for a year or longer to comply with a court-imposed support order with respect to the child; (3) has had his or her parental rights terminated by court order, see Ga.Code §24A-3201; (4) is insane or otherwise incapacitated from giving consent; or (5) cannot be found after a diligent search has been made.

3. Section 74-403(3), which operates as an exception to the rule stated in §74-403(1), see n. 2, *supra*, provides:

> Illegitimate children. — If the child be illegitimate, the consent of the mother alone shall suffice. Such consent, however, shall not be required if the mother has surrendered all of her rights to said child to a licensed child-placing agency, or to the State Department of Family and Children Services.

Sections of Ga.Code (1975) will hereinafter be referred to merely by their numbers.

and acknowledging the child as his own, §74-101, or by obtaining a court order declaring the child legitimate and capable of inheriting from the father, §74-103.[4] But unless and until the child is legitimated, the mother is the only recognized parent and is given exclusive authority to exercise all parental prerogatives, §74-203,[5] including the power to veto adoption of the child.

Appellant did not petition for legitimation of his child at any time during the 11 years between the child's birth and the filing of Randall Walcott's adoption petition.[6] However, in response to Walcott's petition, appellant filed an application for a writ of *habeas corpus* seeking visitation rights, a petition for legitimation, and an objection to the adoption.[7] Shortly thereafter, appellant amended his pleadings by adding the claim that §§74-203 and 74-403(3) were unconstitutional as applied to his case, insofar as they denied him the rights granted to married parents, and presumed unwed fathers to be unfit as a matter of law.

The petitions for adoption, legitimation and writ of *habeas corpus* were consolidated for trial in the Superior Court of Fulton County, Ga. The court expressly stated that these matters were being tried on the basis of a consolidated record to allow "the biological father...a right to be heard with respect to any issue or other thing upon which he desire [s] to be heard, including his fitness as a parent...."[8] After receiving extensive testimony from the parties and other witnesses, the trial court found that, although the child had never been abandoned or deprived, appellant had provided support only on an irregular basis.[9] Moreover, while the child previously had visited with appellant on "many occasions," and had been given toys and gifts by appellant "from time to time," the mother had recently

4. Section 74-103 provides in full:

> A father of an illegitimate child may render the same legitimate by petitioning the superior court of the county of his residence, setting forth the name, age, and sex of such child, and also the name of the mother; and if he desires the name changed, stating the new name, and praying the legitimation of such child. Of this application the mother, if alive, shall have notice. Upon such application, presented and filed, the court may pass an order declaring said child to be legitimate, and capable of inheriting from the father in the same manner as if born in lawful wedlock, and the name by which he or she shall be known.

5. Section 74-203 states:

> The mother of an illegitimate child shall be entitled to the possession of the child, unless the father shall legitimate him as before provided. Being the only recognized parent, she may exercise all the paternal power.

In its opinion in this case, the Georgia Supreme Court indicated that the word "paternal" in the second sentence of this provision is the result of a misprint, and was instead intended to read "parental." See 238 Ga. 230, 231, 232 S.E.2d 246, 247 (1977).

6. It does appear that appellant consented to entry of his name on the child's birth certificate. See §88-1709(d)(2). The adoption petition gave the name of the child as "Darrell Webster Quilloin," and appellant alleges in his brief that the child has always been known by that name, see Brief for Appellant 11.

7. Appellant had been notified by the State's Department of Human Resources that an adoption petition had been filed.

8. *In re: Application of Randall Walcott for Adoption of Child,* Adoption Case No. 8466 (Ga.Super.Ct., July 12, 1976), App. 70.

Sections 74-103, 74-203, and 74-403(3) are silent as to the appropriate procedure in the event that a petition for legitimation is filed after an adoption proceeding has already been initiated. Prior to this Court's decision in *Stanley v. Illinois,* 405 U.S. 645, 92 S.Ct. 1208, 31 L.Ed.2d 551 (1972), and without consideration of potential constitutional problems, the Georgia Supreme Court had concluded that an unwed father could not petition for legitimation after the mother had consented to an adoption.... However, the Georgia Supreme Court had not had occasion to reconsider this conclusion in light of *Stanley,* and, in the face of appellant's constitutional challenge to §§74-203, 74-403(3), the trial court evidently concluded that concurrent consideration of the legitimation and adoption petitions was consistent with the statutory provisions. See also Tr. of Hearing before Superior Court, App., 34, 51; n. 12, *infra.*

9. Under §74-202, appellant had a duty to support his child, but for reasons not appearing in the record the mother never brought an action to enforce this duty. Since no court ever ordered appellant to support his child, denial of veto authority over the adoption could not have been justified on the ground of willful failure to comply with a support order. See n. 2, *supra.*

concluded that these contacts were having a disruptive effect on the child and on appellees' entire family.[10] The child himself expressed a desire to be adopted by Randall Walcott and to take on Walcott's name,[11] and the court found Walcott to be a fit and proper person to adopt the child.

On the basis of these findings, as well as findings relating to appellees' marriage and the mother's custody of the child for all of the child's life, the trial court determined that the proposed adoption was in the "best interests of [the] child." The court concluded, further, that granting either the legitimation or the visitation rights requested by appellant would not be in the "best interests of the child," and that both should consequently be denied. The court then applied §§74-203 and 74-403(3) to the situation at hand, and, since appellant had failed to obtain a court order granting legitimation, he was found to lack standing to object to the adoption. Ruling that appellant's constitutional claims were without merit, the court granted the adoption petition and denied the legitimation and visitation petitions.

Appellant took an appeal to the Supreme Court of Georgia, claiming that §§74-203 and 74-403(3), as applied by the trial court to his case, violated the Equal Protection and Due Process Clauses of the Fourteenth Amendment. In particular, appellant contended that he was entitled to the same power to veto an adoption as is provided under Georgia law to married or divorced parents and to unwed mothers, and, since the trial court did not make a finding of abandonment or other unfitness on the part of appellant, see n. 2, *supra*, the adoption of his child should not have been allowed.

Over a dissent which urged that §74-403(3) was invalid under *Stanley v. Illinois*, the Georgia Supreme Court affirmed the decision of the trial court. 238 Ga. 230, 232 S.E.2d 246 (1977).[12] The majority relied generally on the strong state policy of rearing children in a family setting, a policy which in the court's view might be thwarted if unwed fathers were required to consent to adoptions. The court also emphasized the special force of this policy under the facts of this case, pointing out that the adoption was sought by the child's stepfather, who was part of the family unit in which the child was in fact living, and that the child's natural father had not taken steps to support or legitimate the child over a period of more than 11 years. The court noted in addition that, unlike the father in *Stanley*, appellant had never been a *de facto* member of the child's family unit.

Appellant brought this appeal pursuant to 28 U.S.C. §1257(2), continuing to challenge the constitutionality of §§74-203 and 74-403(3) as applied to his case, and claiming that he was entitled as a matter of due process and equal protection to an absolute veto over adoption of his child, absent a finding of his unfitness as a parent. In contrast to appellant's somewhat broader statement of the issue in the

---

10. In addition to Darrell, appellees' family included a son born several years after appellees were married. The mother testified that Darrell's visits with appellant were having unhealthy effects on both children.

11. The child also expressed a desire to continue to visit with appellant on occasion after the adoption. The child's desire to be adopted, however, could not be given effect under Georgia law without divesting appellant of any parental rights he might otherwise have or acquire, including visitation rights. See §74-414.

12. The Supreme Court addressed itself only to the constitutionality of the statutes as applied by the trial court and thus, at least for purposes of this case, accepted the trial court's construction of §§74-203 and 74-403(3), as allowing concurrent consideration of the adoption and legitimation petitions. See n. 8, *supra*.

Subsequent to the Supreme Court's decision in this case, the Georgia Legislature enacted a comprehensive revision of the State's adoption laws, which became effective January 1, 1978. 1977 Ga. Laws 201. The new law expressly gives an unwed father the right to petition for legitimation subsequent to the filing of an adoption petition concerning his child. See Ga.Code §74-406 (1977 Supp.). The revision also leaves intact §§74-103 and 74-203, and carries forward the substance of §74-403(3), and thus appellant would not have received any greater protection under the new law than he was actually afforded by the trial court.

Georgia Supreme Court, on this appeal he focused his equal protection claim solely on the disparate statutory treatment of his case and that of a married father.[13] We noted probable jurisdiction, 431 U.S. 937, 97 S.Ct. 2647, 53 L.Ed.2d 254 (1977), and we now affirm.

II

At the outset, we observe that appellant does not challenge the sufficiency of the notice he received with respect to the adoption proceeding, see n. 7, *supra*, nor can he claim that he was deprived of a right to a hearing on his individualized interests in his child, prior to entry of the order of adoption. Although the trial court's ultimate conclusion was that appellant lacked standing to object to the adoption, this conclusion was reached only after appellant had been afforded a full hearing on his legitimation petition, at which he was given the opportunity to offer evidence on any matter he thought relevant, including his fitness as a parent. Had the trial court granted legitimation, appellant would have acquired the veto authority he is now seeking.

The fact that appellant was provided with a hearing on his legitimation petition is not, however, a complete answer to his attack on the constitutionality of §§74-203 and 74-403(3). The trial court denied appellant's petition, and thereby precluded him from gaining veto authority, on the ground that legitimation was not in the "best interests of the child"; appellant contends that he was entitled to recognition and preservation of his parental rights absent a showing of his "unfitness." Thus, the underlying issue is whether, in the circumstances of this case and in light of the authority granted by Georgia law to married fathers, appellant's interests were adequately protected by a "best interests of the child" standard. We examine this issue first under the Due Process Clause and then under the Equal Protection Clause.

A

Appellees suggest that due process was not violated, regardless of the standard applied by the trial court, since any constitutionally protected interest appellant might have had was lost by his failure to petition for legitimation during the 11 years prior to filing of Randall Walcott's adoption petition. We would hesitate to rest decision on this ground, in light of the evidence in the record that appellant was not aware of the legitimation procedure until after the adoption petition was filed.[14] But in any event we need not go that far, since under the circumstances of this case appellant's substantive rights were not violated by application of a "best interests of the child" standard.

We have recognized on numerous occasions that the relationship between parent and child is constitutionally protected. See, *e.g., Wisconsin v. Yoder*, 406 U.S. 205, 231–233, 92 S.Ct. 1526, 1541–42, 32 L.Ed.2d 15 (1972); *Stanley v. Illinois*, *supra*; *Meyer v. Nebraska*, 262 U.S. 390, 399–401, 43 S.Ct. 625, 626–27, 67 L.Ed. 1042 (1923). "It is cardinal with us that the custody, care and nurture of the child

13. In the last paragraph of his brief, appellant raises the claim that the statutes make gender-based distinctions that violate the Equal Protection Clause. Since this claim was not presented in appellant's jurisdictional statement, we do not consider it....

14. At the hearing in the trial court, the following colloquy took place between appellees' counsel and appellant:

Q. Had you made any effort prior to this timeprior to the instant proceedings], during the eleven years of Darrell's life to legitimate him?

A. ...I didn't know that was process even you went through [*sic*]. App. 58.

reside first in the parents, whose primary function and freedom include preparation for obligations the state can neither supply nor hinder." *Prince v. Massachusetts*, 321 U.S. 158, 166, 64 S.Ct. 438, 442, 88 L.Ed. 645 (1944). And it is now firmly established that "freedom of personal choice in matters of...family life is one of the liberties protected by the Due Process Clause of the Fourteenth Amendment." *Cleveland Board of Education v. LaFleur*, 414 U.S. 632, 639–640, 94 S.Ct. 791, 796, 39 L.Ed.2d 52 (1974).

We have little doubt that the Due Process Clause would be offended "[i]f a State were to attempt to force the breakup of a natural family, over the objections of the parents and their children, without some showing of unfitness and for the sole reason that to do so was thought to be in the children's best interest." *Smith v. Organization of Foster Families*, 431 U.S. 816, 862–863, 97 S.Ct. 2094, 2119, 53 L.Ed.2d 14 (1977)(STEWART, J., concurring in judgment). But this is not a case in which the unwed father at any time had, or sought, actual or legal custody of his child. Nor is this a case in which the proposed adoption would place the child with a new set of parents with whom the child had never before lived. Rather, the result of the adoption in this case is to give full recognition to a family unit already in existence, a result desired by all concerned, except appellant. Whatever might be required in other situations, we cannot say that the State was required in this situation to find anything more than that the adoption, and denial of legitimation, were in the "best interests of the child."

B

Appellant contends that even if he is not entitled to prevail as a matter of due process, principles of equal protection require that his authority to veto an adoption be measured by the same standard that would have been applied to a married father. In particular, appellant asserts that his interests are indistinguishable from those of a married father who is separated or divorced from the mother and is no longer living with his child, and therefore the State acted impermissibly in treating his case differently. We think appellant's interests are readily distinguishable from those of a separated or divorced father, and accordingly believe that the State could permissibly give appellant less veto authority than it provides to a married father.

Although appellant was subject, for the years prior to these proceedings, to essentially the same child-support obligation as a married father would have had, compare §74-202 with §74-105 and §30-301, he has never exercised actual or legal custody over his child, and thus has never shouldered any significant responsibility with respect to the daily supervision, education, protection, or care of the child. Appellant does not complain of his exemption from these responsibilities and, indeed, he does not even now seek custody of his child. In contrast, legal custody of children is, of course, a central aspect of the marital relationship, and even a father whose marriage has broken apart will have borne full responsibility for the rearing of his children during the period of the marriage. Under any standard of review, the State was not foreclosed from recognizing this difference in the extent of commitment to the welfare of the child.

For these reasons, we conclude that §§74-203 and 74-403(3), as applied in this case, did not deprive appellant of his asserted rights under the Due Process and Equal Protection Clauses. The judgment of the Supreme Court of Georgia is accordingly,

Affirmed.

LEHR v. ROBERTSON

United States Supreme Court
463 U.S. 248 (1983)

STEVENS, Justice.

The question presented is whether New York has sufficiently protected an unmarried father's inchoate relationship with a child whom he has never supported and rarely seen in the two years since her birth. The appellant, Jonathan Lehr, claims that the Due Process and Equal Protection Clauses of the Fourteenth Amendment, as interpreted in *Stanley v. Illinois*, 405 U.S. 645, 92 S.Ct. 1208, 31 L.Ed.2d 551 (1972), and *Caban v. Mohammed*, 441 U.S. 380, 99 S.Ct. 1760, 60 L.Ed.2d 297 (1979), give him an absolute right to notice and an opportunity to be heard before the child may be adopted. We disagree.

Jessica M. was born out of wedlock on November 9, 1976. Her mother, Lorraine Robertson, married Richard Robertson eight months after Jessica's birth. On December 21, 1978, when Jessica was over two years old, the Robertsons filed an adoption petition in the Family Court of Ulster County, New York. The court heard their testimony and received a favorable report from the Ulster County Department of Social Services. On March 7, 1979, the court entered an order of adoption. In this proceeding, appellant contends that the adoption order is invalid because he, Jessica's putative father, was not given advance notice of the adoption proceeding.

The State of New York maintains a "putative father registry." A man who files with that registry demonstrates his intent to claim paternity of a child born out of wedlock and is therefore entitled to receive notice of any proceeding to adopt that child. Before entering Jessica's adoption order, the Ulster County Family Court had the putative father registry examined. Although appellant claims to be Jessica's natural father, he had not entered his name in the registry.

In addition to the persons whose names are listed on the putative father registry, New York law requires that notice of an adoption proceeding be given to several other classes of possible fathers of children born out of wedlock — those who have been adjudicated to be the father, those who have been identified as the father on the child's birth certificate, those who live openly with the child and the child's mother and who hold themselves out to be the father, those who have been identified as the father by the mother in a sworn written statement, and those who were married to the child's mother before the child was six months old. Appellant admittedly was not a member of any of those classes. He had lived with appellee prior to Jessica's birth and visited her in the hospital when Jessica was born, but his name does not appear on Jessica's birth certificate. He did not live with appellee or Jessica after Jessica's birth, he has never provided them with any financial support, and he has never offered to marry appellee. Nevertheless, he contends that the following special circumstances gave him a constitutional right to notice and a hearing before Jessica was adopted.

On January 30, 1979, one month after the adoption proceeding was commenced in Ulster County, appellant filed a "visitation and paternity petition" in the Westchester County Family Court. In that petition, he asked for a determination of paternity, an order of support, and reasonable visitation privileges with Jessica. Notice of that proceeding was served on appellee on February 22, 1979. Four days later appellee's attorney informed the Ulster County Court that appellant had commenced a paternity proceeding in Westchester County; the Ulster County judge then entered an order staying appellant's paternity proceeding until he could rule on a motion to change the venue of that proceeding to Ulster County. On March 3, 1979, appellant received notice of the change of venue motion and, for the first time, learned that an adoption proceeding was pending in Ulster County.

On March 7, 1979, appellant's attorney telephoned the Ulster County judge to inform him that he planned to seek a stay of the adoption proceeding pending the determination of the paternity petition. In that telephone conversation, the judge advised the lawyer that he had already signed the adoption order earlier that day. According to appellant's attorney, the judge stated that he was aware of the pending paternity petition but did not believe he was required to give notice to appellant prior to the entry of the order of adoption.

Thereafter, the Family Court in Westchester County granted appellee's motion to dismiss the paternity petition, holding that the putative father's right to seek paternity "must be deemed severed so long as an order of adoption exists." App. 228. Appellant did not appeal from that dismissal. On June 22, 1979, appellant filed a petition to vacate the order of adoption on the ground that it was obtained by fraud and in violation of his constitutional rights. The Ulster County Family Court received written and oral argument on the question whether it had "dropped the ball" by approving the adoption without giving appellant advance notice.... After deliberating for several months, it denied the petition, explaining its decision in a thorough written opinion. *In re Adoption of Martz*, 102 Misc.2d 102, 423 N.Y.S.2d 378 (1979).

The Appellate Division of the Supreme Court affirmed. *In re Adoption of Jessica "XX"*, 77 App.Div.2d 381, 434 N.Y.S.2d 772 (1980). The majority held that appellant's commencement of a paternity action did not give him any right to receive notice of the adoption proceeding, that the notice provisions of the statute were constitutional, and that Caban v. Mohammed, 441 U.S. 380, 99 S.Ct. 1760, 60 L.Ed.2d 297 (1979), was not retroactive....

The New York Court of Appeals also affirmed by a divided vote. In the Matter of Jessica "XX", 54 N.Y.2d 417, 446 N.Y.S.2d 20, 430 N.E.2d 896 (1981). The majority first held that it did not need to consider whether our decision in *Caban* affected appellant's claim that he had a right to notice, because *Caban* was not retroactive. It then rejected the argument that the mother had been guilty of a fraud upon the court. Finally, it addressed what it described as the only contention of substance advanced by appellant: that it was an abuse of discretion to enter the adoption order without requiring that notice be given to appellant. The court observed that the primary purpose of the notice provision of §111-a was to enable the person served to provide the court with evidence concerning the best interest of the child, and that appellant had made no tender indicating any ability to provide any particular or special information relevant to Jessica's best interest. Considering the record as a whole, and acknowledging that it might have been prudent to give notice, the court concluded that the family court had not abused its discretion either when it entered the order without notice or when it denied appellant's petition to reopen the proceedings. The dissenting judges concluded that the family court had abused its discretion, both when it entered the order without notice and when it refused to reopen the proceedings.

Appellant has now invoked our appellate jurisdiction. He offers two alternative grounds for holding the New York statutory scheme unconstitutional. First, he contends that a putative father's actual or potential relationship with a child born out of wedlock is an interest in liberty which may not be destroyed without due process of law; he argues therefore that he had a constitutional right to prior notice and an opportunity to be heard before he was deprived of that interest. Second, he contends that the gender-based classification in the statute, which both denied him the right to consent to Jessica's adoption and accorded him fewer procedural rights than her mother, violated the Equal Protection Clause.[10]

THE DUE PROCESS CLAIM

The Fourteenth Amendment provides that no State shall deprive any person of life, liberty, or property without due process of law. When that Clause is invoked in a novel context, it is our practice to begin the inquiry with a determination of the precise nature of the private interest that is threatened by the State.... Only after that interest has been identified, can we properly evaluate the adequacy of the State's process....We therefore first consider the nature of the interest in liberty for which appellant claims constitutional protection and then turn to a discussion of the adequacy of the procedure that New York has provided for its protection.

I

The intangible fibers that connect parent and child have infinite variety. They are woven throughout the fabric of our society, providing it with strength, beauty, and flexibility. It is self-evident that they are sufficiently vital to merit constitutional protection in appropriate cases. In deciding whether this is such a case, however, we must consider the broad framework that has traditionally been used to resolve the legal problems arising from the parent-child relationship.

In the vast majority of cases, state law determines the final outcome. Cf. *United States v. Yazell*, 382 U.S. 341, 351–353, 86 S.Ct. 500, 506–507, 16 L.Ed.2d 404 (1966). Rules governing the inheritance of property, adoption, and child custody are generally specified in statutory enactments that vary from State to State. Moreover, equally varied state laws governing marriage and divorce affect a multitude of parent-child relationships. The institution of marriage has played a critical role both in defining the legal entitlements of family members and in developing the decentralized structure of our democratic society. In recognition of that role, and as part of their general overarching concern for serving the best interests of children, state laws almost universally express an appropriate preference for the formal family.[13]

In some cases, however, this Court has held that the Federal Constitution supersedes state law and provides even greater protection for certain formal family relationships. In those cases, as in the state cases, the Court has emphasized the

10. The question whether the Family Court abused its discretion in not requiring notice to appellant before the adoption order was entered and in not reopening the proceeding is, of course, not before us. That issue was presented to and decided by the New York courts purely as a matter of state law. Whether we might have given such notice had we been sitting at the trial court, or whether we might have considered the failure to give such notice an abuse of discretion had we been sitting as state appellate judges, are questions on which we are not authorized to express an opinion. The only questions we have jurisdiction to decide are whether the New York statutes are unconstitutional because they inadequately protect the natural relationship between parent and child or because they draw an impermissible distinction between the rights of the mother and the rights of the father.

13. See *Trimble v. Gordon*, 430 U.S. 762, 769, 97 S.Ct. 1459, 1464, 52 L.Ed.2d 31 (1977)("No one disputes the appropriateness of Illinois' concern with the family unit, perhaps the most fundamental social institution of our society."). A plurality of the Court noted the societal value of family bonds in *Moore v. City of East Cleveland*, 431 U.S. 494, 505, 97 S.Ct. 1932, 1938, 52 L.Ed.2d 531 (1977)(Opinion of POWELL, J.): "Out of choice, necessity, or a sense of family responsibility, it has been common for close relatives to draw together and participate in the duties and the satisfactions of a common home.... Especially in times of adversity, such as the death of a spouse or economic need, the broader family has tended to come together for mutual sustenance and to maintain or rebuild a secure home life."

paramount interest in the welfare of children and has noted that the rights of the parents are a counterpart of the responsibilities they have assumed. Thus, the "liberty" of parents to control the education of their children that was vindicated in *Meyer v. Nebraska*, 262 U.S. 390, 43 S.Ct. 625, 67 L.Ed. 1042 (1923), and *Pierce v. Society of Sisters*, 268 U.S. 510, 45 S.Ct. 571, 69 L.Ed. 1070 (1925), was described as a "right, coupled with the high duty, to recognize and prepare [the child] for additional obligations." *Id.*, at 535, 45 S.Ct., at 573. The linkage between parental duty and parental right was stressed again in *Prince v. Massachusetts*, 321 U.S. 158, 166, 64 S.Ct. 438, 88 L.Ed. 645 (1944), when the Court declared it a cardinal principal "that the custody, care and nurture of the child reside first in the parents, whose primary function and freedom include preparation for obligations the state can neither supply nor hinder." *Id.*, at 166, 64 S.Ct., at 442. In these cases the Court has found that the relationship of love and duty in a recognized family unit is an interest in liberty entitled to constitutional protection. See also *Moore v. City of East Cleveland*, 431 U.S. 494, 97 S.Ct. 1932, 52 L.Ed.2d 531 (1977)(plurality opinion). "[S]tate intervention to terminate [such a] relationship...must be accomplished by procedures meeting the requisites of the Due Process Clause." *Santosky v. Kramer*, 455 U.S. 745, 752, 102 S.Ct. 1388, 1393, 71 L.Ed.2d 599 (1982).

There are also a few cases in which this Court has considered the extent to which the Constitution affords protection to the relationship between natural parents and children born out of wedlock. In some we have been concerned with the rights of the children, see, *e.g.*, *Trimble v. Gordon*, 430 U.S. 762, 97 S.Ct. 1459, 52 L.Ed.2d 31 (1977); *Jimenez v. Weinberger*, 417 U.S. 628, 94 S.Ct. 2496, 41 L.Ed.2d 363 (1974); *Weber v. Aetna Casualty*, 406 U.S. 164, 92 S.Ct. 1400, 31 L.Ed.2d 768 (1972). In this case, however, it is a parent who claims that the state has improperly deprived him of a protected interest in liberty. This Court has examined the extent to which a natural father's biological relationship with his illegitimate child receives protection under the Due Process Clause in precisely three cases: *Stanley v. Illinois*, 405 U.S. 645, 92 S.Ct. 1208, 31 L.Ed.2d 551 (1972), *Quilloin v. Walcott*, 434 U.S. 246, 98 S.Ct. 549, 54 L.Ed.2d 511 (1978), and *Caban v. Mohammed*, 441 U.S. 380, 99 S.Ct. 1760, 60 L.Ed.2d 297 (1979).

Stanley involved the constitutionality of an Illinois statute that conclusively presumed every father of a child born out of wedlock to be an unfit person to have custody of his children. The father in that case had lived with his children all their lives and had lived with their mother for eighteen years. There was nothing in the record to indicate that Stanley had been a neglectful father who had not cared for his children. 405 U.S., at 655, 92 S.Ct., at 1214. Under the statute, however, the nature of the actual relationship between parent and child was completely irrelevant. Once the mother died, the children were automatically made wards of the state. Relying in part on a Michigan case[14] recognizing that the preservation of "a subsisting relationship with the child's father" may better serve the child's best interest than "uprooting him from the family which he knew from birth," *id.*, at 654–655, n. 7, 92 S.Ct., at 1214–1215, n. 7, the Court held that the Due Process Clause was violated by the automatic destruction of the custodial relationship without giving the father any opportunity to present evidence regarding his fitness as a parent.[15]

14. *In re Mark T.*, 8 Mich.App. 122, 154 N.W.2d 27 (1967).

15. Having "concluded that all Illinois parents are constitutionally entitled to a hearing on their fitness before their children are removed from their custody," the Court also held "that denying such a hearing to Stanley and those like him while granting it to other Illinois parents is inescapably contrary to the Equal Protection Clause." 405 U.S., at 658, 92 S.Ct., at 1216.

Quilloin involved the constitutionality of a Georgia statute that authorized the adoption of a child born out of wedlock over the objection of the natural father. The father in that case had never legitimated the child. It was only after the mother had remarried and her new husband had filed an adoption petition that the natural father sought visitation rights and filed a petition for legitimation. The trial court found adoption by the new husband to be in the child's best interests, and we unanimously held that action to be consistent with the Due Process Clause.

Caban involved the conflicting claims of two natural parents who had maintained joint custody of their children from the time of their birth until they were respectively two and four years old. The father challenged the validity of an order authorizing the mother's new husband to adopt the children; he relied on both the Equal Protection Clause and the Due Process Clause. Because this Court upheld his equal protection claim, the majority did not address his due process challenge. The comments on the latter claim by the four dissenting Justices are nevertheless instructive, because they identify the clear distinction between a mere biological relationship and an actual relationship of parental responsibility.

Justice Stewart correctly observed:

> "Even if it be assumed that each married parent after divorce has some substantive due process right to maintain his or her parental relationship, cf. *Smith v. Organization of Foster Families*, 431 U.S. 816, 862–863, 97 S.Ct. 2094, 2119, 53 L.Ed.2d 14 (opinion concurring in judgment), it by no means follows that each unwed parent has any such right. *Parental rights do not spring full-blown from the biological connection between parent and child. They require relationships more enduring.*" 441 U.S., at 397, 99 S.Ct., at 1770 (emphasis added).[16]

In a similar vein, the other three dissenters in *Caban* were prepared to "assume that, *if and when one develops*, the relationship between a father and his natural child is entitled to protection against arbitrary state action as a matter of due process." *Caban v. Mohammed*, 441 U.S. 380, 414, 99 S.Ct. 1760, 1779, 60 L.Ed.2d 297 (emphasis added).

The difference between the developed parent-child relationship that was implicated in *Stanley* and *Caban*, and the potential relationship involved in *Quilloin* and this case, is both clear and significant. When an unwed father demonstrates a full commitment to the responsibilities of parenthood by "com[ing] forward to participate in the rearing of his child," *Caban*, 441 U.S., at 392, 99 S.Ct., at 1768, his interest in personal contact with his child acquires substantial protection under the due process clause. At that point it may be said that he "act[s] as a father toward his children." *Id.*, at 389, n. 7, 99 S.Ct., at 1766, n. 7. But the mere existence

---

16. In the balance of that paragraph Justice Stewart noted that the relation between a father and his natural child may acquire constitutional protection if the father enters into a traditional marriage with the mother or if "the actual relationship between father and child" is sufficient. "The mother carries and bears the child, and in this sense her parental relationship is clear. The validity of the father's parental claims must be gauged by other measures. By tradition, the primary measure has been the legitimate familial relationship he creates with the child by marriage with the mother. By definition, the question before us can arise only when no such marriage has taken place. In some circumstances the actual relationship between father and child may suffice to create in the unwed father parental interests comparable to those of the married father. Cf. *Stanley v. Illinois, supra.* But here we are concerned with the rights the unwed father may have when his wishes and those of the mother are in conflict, and the child's best interests are served by a resolution in favor of the mother. It seems to me that the absence of a legal tie with the mother may in such circumstances appropriately place a limit on whatever substantive constitutional claims might otherwise exist by virtue of the father's actual relationship with the children." 441 U.S., at 397.

of a biological link does not merit equivalent constitutional protection. The actions of judges neither create nor sever genetic bonds. "[T]he importance of the familial relationship, to the individuals involved and to the society, stems from the emotional attachments that derive from the intimacy of daily association, and from the role it plays in 'promot[ing] a way of life' through the instruction of children as well as from the fact of blood relationship." *Smith v. Organization of Foster Families for Equality and Reform*, 431 U.S. 816, 844, 97 S.Ct. 2094, 2109–2110, 53 L.Ed.2d 14 (1977)(quoting *Wisconsin v. Yoder*, 406 U.S. 205, 231–233, 92 S.Ct. 1526, 1541–1542, 32 L.Ed.2d 15 (1972)).

The significance of the biological connection is that it offers the natural father an opportunity that no other male possesses to develop a relationship with his offspring. If he grasps that opportunity and accepts some measure of responsibility for the child's future, he may enjoy the blessings of the parent-child relationship and make uniquely valuable contributions to the child's development.[18] If he fails to do so, the Federal Constitution will not automatically compel a state to listen to his opinion of where the child's best interests lie.

In this case, we are not assessing the constitutional adequacy of New York's procedures for terminating a developed relationship. Appellant has never had any significant custodial, personal, or financial relationship with Jessica, and he did not seek to establish a legal tie until after she was two years old.[19] We are concerned only with whether New York has adequately protected his opportunity to form such a relationship.

II

The most effective protection of the putative father's opportunity to develop a relationship with his child is provided by the laws that authorize formal marriage and govern its consequences. But the availability of that protection is, of course, dependent on the will of both parents of the child. Thus, New York has adopted a special statutory scheme to protect the unmarried father's interest in assuming a responsible role in the future of his child.

After this Court's decision in *Stanley*, the New York Legislature appointed a special commission to recommend legislation that would accommodate both the interests of biological fathers in their children and the children's interest in prompt and certain adoption procedures. The commission recommended, and the legislature enacted, a statutory adoption scheme that automatically provides notice to seven categories of putative fathers who are likely to have assumed some responsibility for the care of their natural children. If this scheme were likely to omit

18. Of course, we need not take sides in the ongoing debate among family psychologists over the relative weight to be accorded biological ties and psychological ties, in order to recognize that a natural father who has played a substantial role in rearing his child has a greater claim to constitutional protection than a mere biological parent. New York's statutory scheme reflects these differences, guaranteeing notice to any putative father who is living openly with the child, and providing putative fathers who have never developed a relationship with the child the opportunity to receive notice simply by mailing a postcard to the putative father registry.

19. This case happens to involve an adoption by the husband of the natural mother, but we do not believe the natural father has any greater right to object to such an adoption than to an adoption by two total strangers. If anything, the balance of equities tips the opposite way in a case such as this. In denying the putative father relief in *Quilloin*..., we made an observation equally applicable here: "Nor is this a case in which the proposed adoption would place the child with a new set of parents with whom the child had never before lived. Rather, the result of the adoption in this case is to give full recognition to a family unit already in existence, a result desired by all concerned, except appellant. Whatever might be required in other situations, we cannot say that the State was required in this situation to find anything more than that the adoption, and denial of legitimation, were in the 'best interests of the child.'" [434 U.S., at 255, 98 S.Ct., at 555.]

many responsible fathers, and if qualification for notice were beyond the control of an interested putative father, it might be thought procedurally inadequate. Yet, as all of the New York courts that reviewed this matter observed, the right to receive notice was completely within appellant's control. By mailing a postcard to the putative father registry, he could have guaranteed that he would receive notice of any proceedings to adopt Jessica. The possibility that he may have failed to do so because of his ignorance of the law cannot be a sufficient reason for criticizing the law itself. The New York legislature concluded that a more open-ended notice requirement would merely complicate the adoption process, threaten the privacy interests of unwed mothers, create the risk of unnecessary controversy, and impair the desired finality of adoption decrees. Regardless of whether we would have done likewise if we were legislators instead of judges, we surely cannot characterize the state's conclusion as arbitrary.[22]

Appellant argues, however, that even if the putative father's opportunity to establish a relationship with an illegitimate child is adequately protected by the New York statutory scheme in the normal case, he was nevertheless entitled to special notice because the court and the mother knew that he had filed an affiliation proceeding in another court. This argument amounts to nothing more than an indirect attack on the notice provisions of the New York statute. The legitimate state interests in facilitating the adoption of young children and having the adoption proceeding completed expeditiously that underlie the entire statutory scheme also justify a trial judge's determination to require all interested parties to adhere precisely to the procedural requirements of the statute. The Constitution does not require either a trial judge or a litigant to give special notice to nonparties who are presumptively capable of asserting and protecting their own rights. Since the New York statutes adequately protected appellant's inchoate interest in establishing a relationship with Jessica, we find no merit in the claim that his constitutional rights were offended because the family court strictly complied with the notice provisions of the statute.

THE EQUAL PROTECTION CLAIM

. . .

The legislation at issue in this case, [sections 111 and 111a of the New York Domestic Relations Law], is intended to establish procedures for adoptions. Those procedures are designed to promote the best interests of the child, protect the rights of interested third parties, and ensure promptness and finality. To serve those ends, the legislation guarantees to certain people the right to veto an adoption and the right to prior notice of any adoption proceeding. The mother of an illegitimate child is always within that favored class, but only certain putative fathers are included. Appellant contends that the gender-based distinction is invidious.

As we noted above, the existence or nonexistence of a substantial relationship between parent and child is a relevant criterion in evaluating both the rights of the parent and the best interests of the child. In *Quilloin v. Walcott*, we noted that the putative father, like appellant, "ha[d] never shouldered any significant

22. Nor can we deem unconstitutionally arbitrary the state courts' conclusion that appellant's absence did not distort its analysis of Jessica's best interests. The adoption does not affect Jessica's relationship with her mother. It gives legal permanence to her relationship with her adoptive father, a relationship they had maintained for 21 months at the time the adoption order was entered. Appellant did not proffer any evidence to suggest that legal confirmation of the established relationship would be unwise; he did not even know the adoptive father.

responsibility with respect to the daily supervision, education, protection, or care of the child. Appellant does not complain of his exemption from these responsibilities...." 434 U.S., at 256, 98 S.Ct., at 555. We therefore found that a Georgia statute that always required a mother's consent to the adoption of a child born out of wedlock, but required the father's consent only if he had legitimated the child, did not violate the Equal Protection Clause. Because, like the father in *Quilloin*, appellant has never established a substantial relationship with his daughter,...the New York statutes at issue in this case did not operate to deny appellant equal protection.

We have held that these statutes may not constitutionally be applied in that class of cases where the mother and father are in fact similarly situated with regard to their relationship with the child. In *Caban v. Mohammed*, 441 U.S. 380, 99 S.Ct. 1760, 60 L.Ed.2d 297 (1979), the Court held that it violated the Equal Protection Clause to grant the mother a veto over the adoption of a four-year-old girl and a six-year-old boy, but not to grant a veto to their father, who had admitted paternity and had participated in the rearing of the children. The Court made it clear, however, that if the father had not "come forward to participate in the rearing of his child, nothing in the Equal Protection Clause [would] preclud[e] the State from withholding from him the privilege of vetoing the adoption of that child." *Id.*, at 392, 99 S.Ct., at 1768.

Jessica's parents are not like the parents involved in *Caban*. Whereas appellee had a continuous custodial responsibility for Jessica, appellant never established any custodial, personal, or financial relationship with her. If one parent has an established custodial relationship with the child and the other parent has either abandoned or never established a relationship, the Equal Protection Clause does not prevent a state from according the two parents different legal rights.

The judgment of the New York Court of Appeals is
Affirmed.

[Dissenting opinion of Justice WHITE, joined by Justices MARSHALL and BLACKMUN, omitted.]

COMMENTS

Despite the usual references to children "born out of wedlock," the important determinant of the status of a child is the marital status of the mother, not that of the father. Traditionally, children born to an unwed woman would be labeled illegitimate and be denied the normal legal benefits granted to children born of married women. Unlike married women, whose children were named after her husband and controlled by them, unmarried women were entitled to control their children with little interference from the father and the children bore the mother's surname. These benefits were more than counter-balanced in most cases, however, by the stigma and poverty of "illegitimacy." Paternity proceedings were quasi-criminal and carried a high burden of proof. The main issue often seemed to be the virtue and relative blamelessness of the "fallen woman" rather than the probably paternity of the child and the child's economic needs. Blood tests and more recently DNA tests have contributed to a major shift in the status of children born to unmarried women.

The legal position of illegitimate children in regard to their rights is closely mirrored in the rights of the unwed father. To the extent that the courts are vacillating in their decision on inheritance rights and government benefits to the illegitimate, a similar vacillation can be observed with the rights of illegitimate fathers in their children. *Stanley* is an illustration of the pendulum swinging toward recognition of the unwed father's rights, while *Quilloin* and *Lehr* seem to retreat. There is an underlying legislative and judicial uneasiness with questions of evidence. When illegitimate fathers did not have any rights in their offspring, the question of their legal position and its relationship to the nature and quality of their behavior to the mother or the child was irrelevant. Since *Stanley* recognized the rights of some illegitimate fathers in their children, the question of which fathers (and upon what evidence) deserve protection and which fathers do not has had to be dealt with and answered from case to case. This situation is further complicated because not only are economic rights involved, as in *Trimble v. Gordon* and *Lalli v. Lalli* (p. 743 and p. 750), but also highly personal rights of unwed fathers, such as the right to be notified and heard in adoption proceedings, visitation rights, and rights for custody.

Although there was some lingering doubt in *Stanley* about the quality of the relationship between the father and his children, the majority appears to have been willing to treat them as belonging to one family. Whether this ongoing family was based on ceremonial marriage, as required by Illinois law, then became irrelevant. This element was absent in *Quilloin* and *Lehr*, in which the illegitimate fathers never had, or actually sought, custody of their children. Their claimed rights were indeed in conflict with an existing family unit to which the child now belonged, one based on the marriage of the child's mother to a third person. From another perspective we can view these court decisions as being concerned not merely with ongoing families but also with preservation of the status quo in regard to children, unless strong factors speak against it. To recognize the rights of illegitimate fathers indiscriminately, especially if the relationship is based on casual sexual relations, could lead to many situations felt to be undesirable, for example, harassment of the mother and prospective adoptive parents or the possibility of extortion by men claiming to be natural fathers.

On the other hand, if the positions of the unwed father and mother are comparable — for example, because they have cohabited and mutually contributed to the support and care of the child or children — then perhaps they should be treated alike and for legal purposes as if they had been married. In such situations, the position of the unwed father indeed becomes comparable to that of a divorced parent, and the consequences for children of cohabitation arrangements and marriage become much less distinguishable. *Stanley* illustrates this trend, resulting in some side effects that the court may not have contemplated. Illinois is a jurisdiction with strong legislative and judicial policies against common law marriage and cohabitation contracts. (See *Hewitt v. Hewitt, p. 249.*) The due process and equal protection requirements in *Stanley* brought about one of the effects of common law marriage in a jurisdiction that does not permit it. That is, in considering custody of the children, the court treated the relationship as though it were a marriage. As in marriage, the father's unfitness would have to be proven by the state.

The positions taken in *Quilloin* and *Lehr* pose problems too. Even though in *Quilloin* the illegitimate father had never sought custody of the child or had him timely legitimated, he nevertheless had visited him frequently and appears to have had a warm relationship with him. One could worry in such a case that the adoption proceedings might have been prompted by the mother's own interests, for example, avoiding personal contact with the natural father by cutting off his visitation rights, rather than the best interests of the child. Although continuation of the unwed father's rights appears to have been considered by the Court as merely an alternative less desirable than adoption by the step-father, the disposition can also be understood on the basis of the unfounded assumption that illegitimate fathers are irresponsible. Yet to allow unwed fathers to block adoption in cases like *Quilloin* and *Lehr* without regard to the best interests of the child would grant the unwed fathers undue power over the mother and her family, possibly at the expense of the children. Moreover, it might well have a chilling effect on all potential adoptions of illegitimate children. Few mothers of illegitimate children and prospective adoptive parents would risk proceedings that could be impeded or set aside if the rights of all unwed fathers were recognized without limitations. On another level of abstraction, it may be recalled that the "best interests of the child" standard, so much at the heart of the reasoning in *Quilloin*, though certainly qualified there, still contains aspects of treatment of the child as a chattel. To recognize fully the rights of unwed fathers in their offspring, by discouraging adoption, would have an effect similar to a restraint on alienation in the law of property.

Adoption agencies, like welfare agencies in general, are not necessarily concerned with the best interests of the child alone, but, as the opinion in *Stanley* noted, are also motivated by a desire for efficiency. This attitude "may characterize praiseworthy government officials no less, and perhaps more, than mediocre ones." One possible understanding of the facts in *Stanley* is that the welfare officials, when faced with resistance, simply turned petty and vengeful. The State of Illinois was engaged in a running battle with Peter Stanley over a prolonged period of time. Its welfare representatives had the power to shape the facts in a light unfavorable to the unwed father. Somewhat earlier, a neglect proceeding had been instituted for one of the children, apparently under the erroneous assumption that the parents had been married. The death of the mother, together with the Illinois statute, furnished the State a new and easier avenue of attack. After Stanley prevailed in the U.S. Supreme Court, the State did not wait long before instituting new and successful child neglect proceedings. Only after Stanley appealed yet again was the State willing to give in, returning the children and having the charges dismissed. There is even some indication that part of the aggravation was caused not so much by Peter Stanley and the conditions within his de facto family, but by the zealous representation of his rights by a Legal Service Office representing indigent clients. Lawyers who deal with welfare agencies know that, because some social workers may be used to considerable power in exercising their discretion, they are to be approached with caution. Of course, the family situation that gave rise to *Stanley* was probably less than ideal. The dissent highlights facts suggesting that the State of Illinois may have been acting not stubbornly or vengefully but to provide proper care for the children.

The interdependence of the rights of illegitimate fathers and adoption is illustrated by footnote 9 in *Stanley*. Although this case involved possible child neglect and the fitness of an unwed father, the note sets forth the criteria of notice that, at low cost, could be used in various contexts — for example, adoption — to notify such fathers of pending proceedings. This passing suggestion by the Court was sufficiently effective to influence adoption proceedings throughout the nation. The underlying thought was that if the illegitimate father were not given any notice, adoption proceedings might prove to be defective. Yet the note was not addressed to problems involved in locating fathers whose whereabouts may be unknown and some of whom may not know about the child. There is, for example, the question of how much effort should be expended to locate fathers, and how much time should be set aside for such purpose at the cost of delaying adoption. Neither does the note answer what "a properly focused hearing," after notice, would entail; whether consent of the natural father to adoptions is necessary; and so on. We can, however, infer from the impact of this seemingly casual footnote that any suggestion relating to, or any regulation of, illegitimacy tends to have consequences in other areas of law, adoption being only one of them.

Particular problems arise if the mother has misidentified the father of a child she relinquishes for adoption. It may seem grossly unfair if the unilateral and possibly dishonest act of the mother can deny to the father the opportunity to grasp the "responsibility for the child's future" and deny to the child the opportunity to know his or her true father. On the other hand, one could also argue that anyone who engages in sexual intercourse should know that a pregnancy might result and that unless he maintains some relationship or shows some responsibility after intercourse, he cannot necessarily claim a proprietary interest in the product of his sperm. To grant relief to fathers in such a case could throw large numbers of adoptions into doubt.

Ultimately, cases like *Stanley*, *Quilloin*, and *Lehr* affect the nature of marriage and of the family. One may perceive these problems as being definitional and implying value choices; or as evidentiary and relating to the question of who is a father; or perhaps even as quasi-proprietary in nature, relating to the seemingly technical issues of how much effort a natural father must invest to be given rights and at what point his rights "vest."

REFERENCES

Sanford N. Katz, WHEN PARENTS FAIL (1971).

Note, *The Strange Boundaries of Stanley: Providing Notice of Adoption to the Unknown Putative Father*, 59 VA. L. REV. 517 (1973).

Frederick C. Schafrick, *The Emerging Constitutional Protection of the Putative Father's Parental Rights*, 7 FAM. L.Q. 75 (1973).

Children Born to a Married or Cohabiting Woman

MICHAEL H. v. GERALD D.

United States Supreme Court
491 U.S. 110 (1989)

Justice SCALIA announced the judgment of the Court and delivered an opinion, in which the CHIEF JUSTICE joins, and in all but note 6 of which Justice O'CONNOR and Justice KENNEDY join.

Under California law, a child born to a married woman living with her husband is presumed to be a child of the marriage. Cal.Evid.Code Ann. §621 (West Supp.1989). The presumption of legitimacy may be rebutted only by the husband or wife, and then only in limited circumstances. *Ibid.* The instant appeal presents the claim that this presumption infringes upon the due process rights of a man who wishes to establish his paternity of a child born to the wife of another man, and the claim that it infringes upon the constitutional right of the child to maintain a relationship with her natural father.

I

The facts of this case are, we must hope, extraordinary. On May 9, 1976, in Las Vegas, Nevada, Carole D., an international model, and Gerald D., a top executive in a French oil company, were married. The couple established a home in Playa del Rey, California, in which they resided as husband and wife when one or the other was not out of the country on business. In the summer of 1978, Carole became involved in an adulterous affair with a neighbor, Michael H. In September 1980, she conceived a child, Victoria D., who was born on May 11, 1981. Gerald was listed as father on the birth certificate and has always held Victoria out to the world as his daughter. Soon after delivery of the child, however, Carole informed Michael that she believed he might be the father.

In the first three years of her life, Victoria remained always with Carole, but found herself within a variety of quasi-family units. In October 1981, Gerald moved to New York City to pursue his business interests, but Carole chose to remain in California. At the end of that month, Carole and Michael had blood tests of themselves and Victoria, which showed a 98.07% probability that Michael was Victoria's father. In January 1982, Carole visited Michael in St. Thomas, where his primary business interests were based. There Michael held Victoria out as his child. In March, however, Carole left Michael and returned to California, where she took up residence with yet another man, Scott K. Later that spring, and again in the summer, Carole and Victoria spent time with Gerald in New York City, as well as on vacation in Europe. In the fall, they returned to Scott in California.

In November 1982, rebuffed in his attempts to visit Victoria, Michael filed a filiation action in California Superior Court to establish his paternity and right to visitation. In March 1983, the court appointed an attorney and guardian *ad litem* to represent Victoria's interests. Victoria then filed a cross-complaint asserting that if she had more than one psychological or *de facto* father, she was entitled to maintain her filial relationship, with all of the attendant rights, duties, and obligations, with both. In May 1983, Carole filed a motion for summary judgment. During this period, from March through July 1983, Carole was again living with Gerald in New York. In August, however, she returned to California, became involved once again with Michael, and instructed her attorneys to remove the summary judgment motion from the calendar.

For the ensuing eight months, when Michael was not in St. Thomas he lived with Carole and Victoria in Carole's apartment in Los Angeles and held Victoria out as his daughter. In April 1984, Carole and Michael signed a stipulation that Michael was Victoria's natural father. Carole left Michael the next month, however, and instructed her attorneys not to file the stipulation. In June 1984, Carole reconciled with Gerald and joined him in New York, where they now live with Victoria and two other children since born into the marriage.

In May 1984, Michael and Victoria, through her guardian ad litem, sought visitation rights for Michael *pendente lite.* To assist in determining whether visitation would be in Victoria's best interests, the Superior Court appointed a psychologist to evaluate Victoria, Gerald, Michael, and Carole. The psychologist recommended that Carole retain sole custody, but that Michael be allowed continued contact with Victoria pursuant to a restricted visitation schedule. The court concurred and ordered that Michael be provided with limited visitation privileges *pendente lite.*

On October 19, 1984, Gerald, who had intervened in the action, moved for summary judgment on the ground that under Cal.Evid.Code §621 there were no triable issues of fact as to Victoria's paternity. This law provides that "the issue of a wife cohabiting with her husband, who is not impotent or sterile, is conclusively presumed to be a child of the marriage." Cal.Evid.Code Ann. §621(a)(West Supp.1989). The presumption may be rebutted by blood tests, but only if a motion for such tests is made, within two years from the date of the child's birth, either by the husband or, if the natural father has filed an affidavit acknowledging paternity, by the wife. §§621(c) and (d).

On January 28, 1985, having found that affidavits submitted by Carole and Gerald sufficed to demonstrate that the two were cohabiting at conception and birth and that Gerald was neither sterile nor impotent, the Superior Court granted Gerald's motion for summary judgment, rejecting Michael's and Victoria's challenges to the constitutionality of §621. The court also denied their motions for continued visitation pending the appeal under Cal.Civ.Code §4601, which provides that a court may, in its discretion, grant "reasonable visitation rights...to any...person having an interest in the welfare of the child." Cal.Civ.Code Ann. §4601 (West Supp.1989). It found that allowing such visitation would "violat[e] the intention of the Legislature by impugning the integrity of the family unit."...

...[T]he California Court of Appeal affirmed the judgment of the Superior Court and upheld the constitutionality of the statute....

...

Michael contends as a matter of substantive due process that, because he has established a parental relationship with Victoria, protection of Gerald's and Carole's marital union is an insufficient state interest to support termination of that relationship. This argument is, of course, predicated on the assertion that Michael has a constitutionally protected liberty interest in his relationship with Victoria.

It is an established part of our constitutional jurisprudence that the term "liberty" in the Due Process Clause extends beyond freedom from physical restraint....In an attempt to limit and guide interpretation of the Clause, we have insisted not merely that the interest denominated as a "liberty" be "fundamental" (a concept that, in isolation, is hard to objectify), but also that it be an interest traditionally protected by our society. As we have put it, the Due Process Clause affords only those protections "so rooted in the traditions and conscience of our people as to be ranked as fundamental." *Snyder v. Massachusetts*, 291 U.S. 97, 105, 54 S.Ct. 330, 332, 78 L.Ed. 674 (1934)(Cardozo, J.). Our cases reflect "continual insistence upon respect for the teachings of history [and] solid recognition of the basic values that underlie our society...." *Griswold v. Connecticut*, 381 U.S. 479, 501, 85 S.Ct. 1678, 1690, 14 L.Ed.2d 510 (1965)(Harlan, J., concurring in judgment).

This insistence that the asserted liberty interest be rooted in history and tradition is evident, as elsewhere, in our cases according constitutional protection to certain parental rights. Michael reads the landmark case of *Stanley v. Illinois*, 405 U.S. 645, 92 S.Ct. 1208, 31 L.Ed.2d 551 (1972), and the subsequent cases of *Quilloin v. Walcott*, 434 U.S. 246, 98 S.Ct. 549, 54 L.Ed.2d 511 (1978), *Caban v. Mohammed*, 441 U.S. 380, 99 S.Ct. 1760, 60 L.Ed.2d 297 (1979), and *Lehr v. Robertson*, 463 U.S. 248, 103 S.Ct. 2985, 77 L.Ed.2d 614 (1983), as establishing that a liberty interest is created by biological fatherhood plus an established parental relationship — factors that exist in the present case as well. We think that distorts the rationale of those cases. As we view them, they rest not upon such isolated factors but upon the historic respect — indeed, sanctity would not be too strong a term — traditionally accorded to the relationships that develop within the unitary family.[3] See *Stanley, supra*, 405 U.S., at 651, 92 S.Ct., at 1212; *Quilloin, supra*, 434 U.S., at 254–255, 98 S.Ct., at 554–555; *Caban, supra*, 441 U.S., at 389, 99 S.Ct., at 1766; *Lehr, supra*, 463 U.S., at 261, 103 S.Ct., at 2993. In *Stanley*, for example, we forbade the destruction of such a family when, upon the death of the mother, the State had sought to remove children from the custody of a father who had lived with and supported them and their mother for 18 years. As Justice Powell stated for the plurality in *Moore v. East Cleveland*,..., 431 U.S., at 503, 97 S.Ct., at 1938: "Our decisions establish that the Constitution protects the sanctity of the family precisely because the institution of the family is deeply rooted in this Nation's history and tradition."

Thus, the legal issue in the present case reduces to whether the relationship between persons in the situation of Michael and Victoria has been treated as a protected family unit under the historic practices of our society, or whether on any other basis it has been accorded special protection. We think it impossible to find that it has. In fact, quite to the contrary, our traditions have protected the marital family (Gerald, Carole, and the child they acknowledge to be theirs) against the sort of claim Michael asserts.

The presumption of legitimacy was a fundamental principle of the common law. H. Nicholas, Adulturine Bastardy 1 (1836). Traditionally, that presumption could be rebutted only by proof that a husband was incapable of procreation or had had no access to his wife during the relevant period. *Id.*, at 9–10 (citing Bracton, De Legibus et Consuetudinibus Angilae, bk. i, ch. 9, p. 6; bk. ii, ch. 29, p. 63, ch. 32, p. 70 (1569)). As explained by Blackstone, nonaccess could only be proved "if the husband be out of the kingdom of England (or, as the law somewhat loosely phrases it, *extra quatuor maria* [beyond the four seas]) for above nine months...."

3. Justice BRENNAN asserts that only "a pinched conception of 'the family'" would exclude Michael, Carole, and Victoria from protection. *Post*, at 2353. We disagree. The family unit accorded traditional respect in our society, which we have referred to as the "unitary family," is typified, of course, by the marital family, but also includes the household of unmarried parents and their children. Perhaps the concept can be expanded even beyond this, but it will bear no resemblance to traditionally respected relationships — and will thus cease to have any constitutional significance — if it is stretched so far as to include the relationship established between a married woman, her lover, and their child, during a 3-month sojourn in St. Thomas, or during a subsequent 8-month period when, if he happened to be in Los Angeles, he stayed with her and the child.

1 Blackstone's Commentaries 456 (J. Chitty ed. 1826). And, under the common law both in England and here, "neither husband nor wife [could] be a witness to prove access or nonaccess." J. Schouler, Law of the Domestic Relations §225, p. 306 (3d ed. 1882); R. Graveson & F. Crane, A Century of Family Law: 1857–1957, p. 158 (1957). The primary policy rationale underlying the common law's severe restrictions on rebuttal of the presumption appears to have been an aversion to declaring children illegitimate, see Schouler, *supra*, §225, at 306–307; M. Grossberg, Governing the Hearth 201 (1985), thereby depriving them of rights of inheritance and succession, 2 J. Kent, Commentaries on American Law *175, and likely making them wards of the state. A secondary policy concern was the interest in promoting the "peace and tranquillity of States and families," Schouler, *supra*, §225, at 304, quoting Boullenois, Traité des Status, bk. 1, p. 62, a goal that is obviously impaired by facilitating suits against husband and wife asserting that their children are illegitimate. Even though, as bastardy laws became less harsh, "[j]udges in both [England and the United States] gradually widened the acceptable range of evidence that could be offered by spouses, and placed restraints on the "four seas rule"...[,] the law retained a strong bias against ruling the children of married women illegitimate." Grossberg, *supra*, at 202.

We have found nothing in the older sources, nor in the older cases, addressing specifically the power of the natural father to assert parental rights over a child born into a woman's existing marriage with another man. Since it is Michael's burden to establish that such a power (at least where the natural father has established a relationship with the child) is so deeply embedded within our traditions as to be a fundamental right, the lack of evidence alone might defeat his case. But the evidence shows that even in modern times — when, as we have noted, the rigid protection of the marital family has in other respects been relaxed — the ability of a person in Michael's position to claim paternity has not been generally acknowledged....

Moreover, even if it were clear that one in Michael's position generally possesses, and has generally always possessed, standing to challenge the marital child's legitimacy, that would still not establish Michael's case. As noted earlier, what is at issue here is not entitlement to a state pronouncement that Victoria was begotten by Michael. It is no conceivable denial of constitutional right for a State to decline to declare facts unless some legal consequence hinges upon the requested declaration. What Michael asserts here is a right to have himself declared the natural father *and thereby to obtain parental prerogatives.* What he must establish, therefore, is not that our society has traditionally allowed a natural father in his circumstances to establish paternity, but that it has traditionally accorded such a father parental rights, or at least has not traditionally denied them. Even if the law in all States had always been that the entire world could challenge the marital presumption and obtain a declaration as to who was the natural father, that would not advance Michael's claim. Thus, it is ultimately irrelevant, even for purposes of determining *current* social attitudes towards the alleged substantive right Michael asserts, that the present law in a number of States appears to allow the natural father — including the natural father who has not established a relationship with the child — the theoretical power to rebut the marital presumption, see Note, *Rebutting the Marital Presumption: A Developed Relationship Test*, 88 Colum.L.Rev. 369, 373 (1988). What counts is whether the States in fact award substantive parental rights to the natural father of a child conceived within, and born into, an extant marital union that wishes to embrace the child. We are not aware of a single case, old or new, that has done so. This is not the stuff of which fundamental rights qualifying as liberty interests are made.[6]

. . .

We do not accept Justice BRENNAN's criticism that this result "squashes" the liberty that consists of "the freedom not to conform." *Post,* at 2351. It seems to us that reflects the erroneous view that there is only one side to this controversy — that one disposition can expand a "liberty" of sorts without contracting an equivalent "liberty" on the other side. Such a happy choice is rarely available. Here, to *provide* protection to an adulterous natural father is to *deny* protection to a marital father, and vice versa. If Michael has a "freedom not to conform" (whatever that means), Gerald must equivalently have a "freedom to conform." One of them will pay a price for asserting that "freedom" — Michael by being unable to act as father of the child he has adulterously begotten, or Gerald by being unable to preserve the integrity of the traditional family unit he and Victoria have established. Our disposition does not choose between these two "freedoms," but leaves that to the people of California. Justice BRENNAN's approach chooses one of them as the constitutional imperative, on no apparent basis except that the unconventional is to be preferred.

---

6. Justice BRENNAN criticizes our methodology in using historical traditions specifically relating to the rights of an adulterous natural father, rather than inquiring more generally "whether parenthood is an interest that historically has received our attention and protection." *Post,* at 2350. There seems to us no basis for the contention that this methodology is "nove[l]," *post,* at 2351. For example, in *Bowers v. Hardwick,* 478 U.S. 186, 106 S.Ct. 2841, 92 L.Ed.2d 140 (1986), we noted that at the time the Fourteenth Amendment was ratified all but 5 of the 37 States had criminal sodomy laws, that all 50 of the States had such laws prior to 1961, and that 24 States and the District of Columbia continued to have them; and we concluded from that record, regarding that very specific aspect of sexual conduct, that "to claim that a right to engage in such conduct is 'deeply rooted in this Nation's history and tradition' or 'implicit in the concept of ordered liberty' is, at best, facetious." *Id.,* at 194, 106 S.Ct., at 2846. In *Roe v. Wade,* 410 U.S. 113, 93 S.Ct. 705, 35 L.Ed.2d 147 (1973), we spent about a fifth of our opinion negating the proposition that there was a longstanding tradition of laws proscribing abortion. *Id.,* at 129–141, 93 S.Ct., at 715–721.

We do not understand why, having rejected our focus upon the societal tradition regarding the natural father's rights vis-a-vis a child whose mother is married to another man, Justice BRENNAN would choose to focus instead upon "parenthood." Why should the relevant category not be even more general — perhaps "family relationships"; or "personal relationships"; or even "emotional attachments in general"? Though the dissent has no basis for the level of generality it would select, we do: We refer to the most specific level at which a relevant tradition protecting, or denying protection to, the asserted right can be identified. If, for example, there were no societal tradition, either way, regarding the rights of the natural father of a child adulterously conceived, we would have to consult, and (if possible) reason from, the traditions regarding natural fathers in general. But there is such a more specific tradition, and it unqualifiedly denies protection to such a parent.

One would think that Justice BRENNAN would appreciate the value of consulting the most specific tradition available, since he acknowledges that "[e]ven if we can agree...that 'family' and 'parenthood' are part of the good life, it is absurd to assume that we can agree on the content of those terms and destructive to pretend that we do." *Post,* at 2351. Because such general traditions provide such imprecise guidance, they permit judges to dictate rather than discern the society's views. The need, if arbitrary decisionmaking is to be avoided, to adopt the most specific tradition as the point of reference — or at least to announce, as Justice BRENNAN declines to do, some other criterion for selecting among the innumerable relevant traditions that could be consulted — is well enough exemplified by the fact that in the present case Justice BRENNAN's opinion and Justice O'CONNOR's opinion,...which disapproves this footnote, *both* appeal to tradition, but on the basis of the tradition they select reach opposite results. Although assuredly having the virtue (if it be that) of leaving judges free to decide as they think best when the unanticipated occurs, a rule of law that binds neither by text nor by any particular, identifiable tradition is no rule of law at all.

Finally, we may note that this analysis is not inconsistent with the result in cases such as *Griswold v. Connecticut,* 381 U.S. 479, 85 S.Ct. 1678, 14 L.Ed.2d 510 (1965), or *Eisenstadt v. Baird,* 405 U.S. 438, 92 S.Ct. 1029, 31 L.Ed.2d 349 (1972). None of those cases acknowledged a longstanding and still extant societal tradition withholding the very right pronounced to be the subject of a liberty interest and then rejected it. Justice BRENNAN must do so here. In this case, the existence of such a tradition, continuing to the present day, refutes any possible contention that the alleged right is "so rooted in the traditions and conscience of our people as to be ranked as fundamental," *Snyder v. Massachusetts,* 291 U.S. 97, 105, 54 S.Ct. 330, 332, 78 L.Ed. 674 (1934), or "implicit in the concept of ordered liberty," *Palko v. Connecticut,* 302 U.S. 319, 325, 58 S.Ct. 149, 152, 82 L.Ed. 288 (1937).

IV

We have never had occasion to decide whether a child has a liberty interest, symmetrical with that of her parent, in maintaining her filial relationship. We need not do so here because, even assuming that such a right exists, Victoria's claim must fail. Victoria's due process challenge is, if anything, weaker than Michael's. Her basic claim is not that California has erred in preventing her from establishing that Michael, not Gerald, should stand as her legal father. Rather, she claims a due process right to maintain filial relationships with both Michael and Gerald. This assertion merits little discussion, for, whatever the merits of the guardian ad litem's belief that such an arrangement can be of great psychological benefit to a child, the claim that a State must recognize multiple fatherhood has no support in the history or traditions of this country. Moreover, even if we were to construe Victoria's argument as forwarding the lesser proposition that, whatever her status vis-à-vis Gerald, she has a liberty interest in maintaining a filial relationship with her natural father, Michael, we find that, at best, her claim is the obverse of Michael's and fails for the same reasons.

Victoria claims in addition that her equal protection rights have been violated because, unlike her mother and presumed father, she had no opportunity to rebut the presumption of her legitimacy. We find this argument wholly without merit. We reject, at the outset, Victoria's suggestion that her equal protection challenge must be assessed under a standard of strict scrutiny because, in denying her the right to maintain a filial relationship with Michael, the State is discriminating against her on the basis of her illegitimacy. See *Gomez v. Perez,* 409 U.S. 535, 538, 93 S.Ct. 872, 875, 35 L.Ed.2d 56 (1973). Illegitimacy is a legal construct, not a natural trait. Under California law, Victoria is not illegitimate, and she is treated in the same manner as all other legitimate children: she is entitled to maintain a filial relationship with her legal parents.

We apply, therefore, the ordinary "rational relationship" test to Victoria's equal protection challenge. The primary rationale underlying §621's limitation on those who may rebut the presumption of legitimacy is a concern that allowing persons other than the husband or wife to do so may undermine the integrity of the marital union. When the husband or wife contests the legitimacy of their child, the stability of the marriage has already been shaken. In contrast, allowing a claim of illegitimacy to be pressed by the child — or, more accurately, by a court-appointed guardian ad litem — may well disrupt an otherwise peaceful union. Since it pursues a legitimate end by rational means, California's decision to treat Victoria differently from her parents is not a denial of equal protection.

The judgment of the California Court of Appeal is

Affirmed.

Justice O'CONNOR, with whom Justice KENNEDY joins, concurring in part.

I concur in all but footnote 6 of Justice SCALIA's opinion. This footnote sketches a mode of historical analysis to be used when identifying liberty interests protected by the Due Process Clause of the Fourteenth Amendment that may be somewhat inconsistent with our past decisions in this area.... On occasion the Court has characterized relevant traditions protecting asserted rights at levels of generality that might not be "the most specific level" available.... I would not foreclose the unanticipated by the prior imposition of a single mode of historical analysis....

Justice STEVENS, concurring in the judgment.

As I understand this case, it raises two different questions about the validity of California's statutory scheme. First, is Cal.Evid.Code Ann. §621 (West Supp.1989) unconstitutional because it prevents Michael and Victoria from obtaining a judicial determination that he is her biological father — even if no legal rights would be affected by that determination? Second, does the California statute deny appellants a fair opportunity to prove that Victoria's best interests would be served by granting Michael visitation rights?

On the first issue I agree with Justice SCALIA that the Federal Constitution imposes no obligation upon a State to "declare facts unless some legal consequence hinges upon the requested declaration."...

On the second issue I...would not foreclose the possibility that a constitutionally protected relationship between a natural father and his child might exist in a case like this. Indeed, I am willing to assume for the purpose of deciding this case that Michael's relationship with Victoria is strong enough to give him a constitutional right to try to convince a trial judge that Victoria's best interest would be served by granting him visitation rights. I am satisfied, however, that the California statute, as applied in this case, gave him that opportunity.

...

I recognize that my colleagues have interpreted §621 as creating an absolute bar that would prevent a California trial judge from regarding the natural father as either a "parent" within the meaning of the first sentence of §4601 or as "any other person" within the meaning of the second sentence.... That is not only an unnatural reading of the statute's plain language, but it is also not consistent with the California courts' reading of the statute....

...

Under the circumstances of the case before us, Michael was given a fair opportunity to show that he is Victoria's natural father, that he had developed a relationship with her, and that her interests would be served by granting him visitation rights. On the other hand, the record also shows that after its rather shaky start, the marriage between Carole and Gerald developed a stability that now provides Victoria with a loving and harmonious family home. In the circumstances of this case, I find nothing fundamentally unfair about the exercise of a judge's discretion that, in the end, allows the mother to decide whether her child's best interests would be served by allowing the natural father visitation privileges. Because I am convinced that the trial judge had the authority under state law both to hear Michael's plea for visitation rights and to grant him such rights if Victoria's best interests so warranted, I am satisfied that the California statutory scheme is consistent with the Due Process Clause of the Fourteenth Amendment.

...

Justice BRENNAN, with whom Justice MARSHALL and Justice BLACKMUN join, dissenting.

In a case that has yielded so many opinions as has this one, it is fruitful to begin by emphasizing the common ground shared by a majority of this Court. Five Members of the Court refuse to foreclose "the possibility that a natural father might ever have a constitutionally protected interest in his relationship with a child whose mother was married to, and cohabiting with, another man at the time of the child's conception and birth." *Ante*, at 2347 (STEVENS, J., concurring in judgment).... Five Justices agree that the flaw inhering in a conclusive presumption that terminates a constitutionally protected interest without any hearing whatsoever is a *procedural* one. See *infra*, at 2358; *post*, at 2360 (WHITE, J., dissenting); *ante*, at 2347 (STEVENS, J., concurring in judgment). Four Members of the Court agree that Michael H. has a liberty interest in his relationship with Victoria, see *infra*, at 2353; *post*, at 2360 (WHITE, J., dissenting), and one assumes for purposes of this case that he does, see *ante*, at 2347 (STEVENS, J., concurring in judgment).

In contrast, only one other Member of the Court fully endorses Justice SCALIA's view of the proper method of analyzing questions arising under the Due Process Clause.... Nevertheless, because the plurality opinion's exclusively historical analysis portends a significant and unfortunate departure from our prior cases and from sound constitutional decisionmaking, I devote a substantial portion of my discussion to it.

I

Once we recognized that the "liberty" protected by the Due Process Clause of the Fourteenth Amendment encompasses more than freedom from bodily restraint, today's plurality opinion emphasizes, the concept was cut loose from one natural limitation on its meaning. This innovation paved the way, so the plurality hints, for judges to substitute their own preferences for those of elected officials. Dissatisfied with this supposedly unbridled and uncertain state of affairs, the plurality casts about for another limitation on the concept of liberty.

It finds this limitation in "tradition." Apparently oblivious to the fact that this concept can be as malleable and as elusive as "liberty" itself, the plurality pretends that tradition places a discernible border around the Constitution....

Even if we could agree, moreover, on the content and significance of particular traditions, we still would be forced to identify the point at which a tradition becomes firm enough to be relevant to our definition of liberty and the moment at which it becomes too obsolete to be relevant any longer....

It is ironic that an approach so utterly dependent on tradition is so indifferent to our precedents....

It is not that tradition has been irrelevant to our prior decisions. Throughout our decisionmaking in this important area runs the theme that certain interests and practices — freedom from physical restraint, marriage, childbearing, childrearing, and others — form the core of our definition of "liberty."...

Today's plurality, however, does not ask whether parenthood is an interest that historically has received our attention and protection; the answer to that question is too clear for dispute. Instead, the plurality asks whether the specific variety of parenthood under consideration — a natural father's relationship with a child whose mother is married to another man — has enjoyed such protection.

If we had looked to tradition with such specificity in past cases, many a decision would have reached a different result....

The plurality's interpretive method is more than novel; it is misguided. It ignores the good reasons for limiting the role of "tradition" in interpreting the Constitution's deliberately capacious language. In the plurality's constitutional universe, we may not take notice of the fact that the original reasons for the conclusive presumption of paternity are out of place in a world in which blood tests can prove virtually beyond a shadow of a doubt who sired a particular child and in which the fact of illegitimacy no longer plays the burdensome and stigmatizing role it once did. Nor, in the plurality's world, may we deny "tradition" its full scope by pointing out that the rationale for the conventional rule has changed over the years, as has the rationale for Cal.Evid.Code Ann. §621 (West Supp.1989)....[B]y describing the decisive question as whether Michael's and Victoria's interest is one that has been "traditionally *protected by* our society," *ante*... (emphasis added), rather than one that society traditionally has thought important (with or without protecting it), and by suggesting that our sole function is to "*discern* the society's views," *ante*, at 2345, n. 6 (emphasis added), the plurality acts as if the only purpose of the Due Process Clause is to confirm the importance of interests already protected by a majority of the States. Transforming the protection afforded by the Due Process Clause into a redundancy mocks those who, with care and purpose, wrote the Fourteenth Amendment.

In construing the Fourteenth Amendment to offer shelter only to those interests specifically protected by historical practice, moreover, the plurality ignores the kind of society in which our Constitution exists. We are not an assimilative, homogeneous society, but a facilitative, pluralistic one, in which we must be willing to abide someone else's unfamiliar or even repellant practice because the same tolerant impulse protects our own idiosyncracies. Even if we can agree, therefore, that "family" and "parenthood" are part of the good life, it is absurd to assume that we can agree on the content of those terms and destructive to pretend that we do. In a community such as ours, "liberty" must include the freedom not to conform. The plurality today squashes this freedom by requiring specific approval from history before protecting anything in the name of liberty.

...

The evidence is undisputed that Michael, Victoria, and Carole did live together as a family; that is, they shared the same household, Victoria called Michael "Daddy," Michael contributed to Victoria's support, and he is eager to continue his relationship with her. Yet they are not, in the plurality's view, a "unitary family," whereas Gerald, Carole, and Victoria do compose such a family. The only difference between these two sets of relationships, however, is the fact of marriage. The plurality, indeed, expressly recognizes that marriage is the critical fact in denying Michael a constitutionally protected stake in his relationship with Victoria: no fewer than six times, the plurality refers to Michael as the "*adulterous* natural father"...(emphasis added)... However, the very premise of *Stanley* and the cases following it is that marriage is not decisive in answering the question whether the Constitution protects the parental relationship under consideration. These cases are, after all, important precisely because they involve the rights of *unwed* fathers. It is important to remember, moreover, that in *Quilloin*, *Caban*, and *Lehr*, the putative father's demands would have disrupted a "unitary family" as the plurality defines it; in each case, the husband of the child's mother sought to adopt the child over the objections of the natural father. Significantly, our decisions in those cases in no way relied on the need to protect the marital family. Hence the plurality's claim that *Stanley*, *Quilloin*, *Caban*, and *Lehr* were about the "unitary family," as that family is defined by today's plurality, is surprising indeed.

The plurality's exclusive rather than inclusive definition of the "unitary family" is out of step with other decisions as well. This pinched conception of "the family," crucial as it is in rejecting Michael's and Victoria's claims of a liberty interest, is jarring in light of our many cases preventing the States from denying important interests or statuses to those whose situations do not fit the government's narrow view of the family. From *Loving v. Virginia*, 388 U.S. 1, 87 S.Ct. 1817, 18 L.Ed.2d 1010 (1967), to *Levy v. Louisiana*, 391 U.S. 68, 88 S.Ct. 1509, 20 L.Ed.2d 436 (1968), and *Glona v. American Guarantee & Liability Ins. Co.*, 391 U.S. 73, 88 S.Ct.

1515, 20 L.Ed.2d 441 (1968), and from *Gomez v. Perez*, 409 U.S. 535, 93 S.Ct. 872, 35 L.Ed.2d 56 (1973), to *Moore v. East Cleveland*, 431 U.S. 494, 97 S.Ct. 1932, 52 L.Ed.2d 531 (1977), we have declined to respect a State's notion, as manifested in its allocation of privileges and burdens, of what the family should be. Today's rhapsody on the "unitary family" is out of tune with such decisions.

The plurality's focus on the "unitary family" is misdirected for another reason. It conflates the question whether a liberty interest exists with the question what procedures may be used to terminate or curtail it. It is no coincidence that we never before have looked at the relationship that the unwed father seeks to disrupt, rather than the one he seeks to preserve, in determining whether he has a liberty interest in his relationship with his child. To do otherwise is to allow the State's interest in terminating the relationship to play a role in defining the "liberty" that is protected by the Constitution. According to our established framework under the Due Process Clause, however, we first ask whether the person claiming constitutional protection has an interest that the Constitution recognizes; if we find that she does, we next consider the State's interest in limiting the extent of the procedures that will attend the deprivation of that interest....

The plurality's premature consideration of California's interests is evident from its careful limitation of its holding to those cases in which "the mother is, at the time of the child's conception and birth, married to, and cohabitating with, another man, *both of whom wish to raise the child as the offspring of their union*."... The highlighted language suggests that if Carole or Gerald alone wished to raise Victoria, or if both were dead and the State wished to raise her, Michael and Victoria might be found to have a liberty interest in their relationship with each other. But that would be to say that whether Michael and Victoria have a liberty interest varies with the State's interest in recognizing that interest, for it is the State's interest in protecting the marital family — and not Michael and Victoria's interest in their relationship with each other — that varies with the status of Carole and Gerald's relationship. It is a bad day for due process when the State's interest in terminating a parent-child relationship is reason to conclude that that relationship is not part of the "liberty" protected by the Fourteenth Amendment.

The plurality has wedged itself between a rock and a hard place. If it limits its holding to those situations in which a wife and husband wish to raise the child together, then it necessarily takes the State's interest into account in defining "liberty"; yet if it extends that approach to circumstances in which the marital union already has been dissolved, then it may no longer rely on the State's asserted interest in protecting the "unitary family" in denying that Michael and Victoria have been deprived of liberty.

...

III

Because the plurality decides that Michael and Victoria have no liberty interest in their relationship with each other, it need consider neither the effect of §621 on their relationship nor the State's interest in bringing about that effect. It is obvious, however, that the effect of §621 is to terminate the relationship between Michael and Victoria before affording any hearing whatsoever on the issue whether Michael is Victoria's father. This refusal to hold a hearing is properly analyzed under our procedural due process cases, which instruct us to consider the State's interest in curtailing the procedures accompanying the termination of a constitutionally protected interest. California's interest, minute in comparison with a father's interest in his relationship with his child, cannot justify its refusal to hear Michael out on his claim that he is Victoria's father.

...

Justice WHITE, with whom Justice BRENNAN joins, dissenting.

...

"The emphasis of the Due Process Clause is on 'process.'" *Moore v. East Cleveland*, 431 U.S. 494, 542, 97 S.Ct. 1932, 1957, 52 L.Ed.2d 531 (1977)(WHITE, J., dissenting). I fail to see the fairness in the process established by the State of California and endorsed by the Court today. Michael has evidence which demonstrates that he is the father of young Victoria. Yet he is blocked by the State from presenting that evidence to a court. As a result, he is foreclosed from establishing his paternity and is ultimately precluded, by the State, from developing a relationship with his child. "A fundamental requirement of due process is 'the opportunity to be heard.' *Grannis v. Ordean*, 234 U.S. 385, 394 [34 S.Ct. 779, 783, 58 L.Ed. 1363 (1914)]. It is an opportunity which must be granted at a meaningful time and in a meaningful manner." *Armstrong v. Manzo*, 380 U.S. 545, 552, 85 S.Ct. 1187, 1191, 14 L.Ed.2d 62 (1965). I fail to see how appellant was granted any meaningful opportunity to be heard when he was precluded at the very outset from introducing evidence which would support his assertion of paternity. Michael has never been afforded an opportunity to present his case in any meaningful manner.

As the Court has said: "The significance of the biological connection is that it offers the natural father an opportunity that no other male possesses to develop a relationship with his offspring. If he grasps that opportunity and accepts some measure of responsibility for the child's future, he may enjoy the blessings of the parent-child relationship and make uniquely valuable contributions to the child's development." *Lehr*, 463 U.S., at 262, 103 S.Ct., at 2993. It is as if this passage was addressed to Michael. Yet the plurality today recants. Michael eagerly grasped the opportunity to have a relationship with his daughter (he lived with her; he declared her to be his child; he provided financial support for her) and still, with today's opinion, his opportunity has vanished. He has been rendered a stranger to his child.

Because Cal.Evid.Code Ann. §621, as applied, should be held unconstitutional under the Due Process Clause of the Fourteenth Amendment, I respectfully dissent.

In re MARRIAGE OF ADAMS

Supreme Court of Illinois
133 Ill. 2d 437, 551 N.E.2d 635 (1990)

Justice MILLER delivered the opinion of the court:

On March 13, 1986, Ritaray Adams filed in the circuit court of Lake County a petition seeking the dissolution of her marriage to John N. Adams. In the petition Ritaray requested support for a child, John David Adams (J.D.), born during the marriage. J.D. had been conceived through the artificial insemination of an anonymous donor's semen. In answer to the petition John denied that he was the child's father and, in what was termed an affirmative defense, asserted that he did not consent to the procedure that resulted in the child's conception. Following an evidentiary hearing, the trial judge ruled that a parent-child relationship existed between John and J.D. The trial judge subsequently entered a judgment of dissolution of marriage and ordered John to pay child support for J.D. The appellate court affirmed the circuit court's judgment. (174 Ill. App.3d 595, 124 Ill. Dec. 184, 528 N.E.2d 1075.) We allowed John's petition for leave to appeal (107 Ill.2d R. 315(a)).

The facts of the present case are set forth fully in the appellate court opinion and will be restated here only to the extent necessary. John and Ritaray were married on June 3, 1983, in Lake County, Illinois. At the time of the marriage John was 32 years old and Ritaray was 19. Both John and Ritaray had been married once before, and John, but not Ritaray, had children from the prior marriage. John was a commissioned officer in the United States Navy and served as a physician's assistant in a naval base clinic. Before their marriage, John informed Ritaray that he had previously undergone a vasectomy and probably would not be able to father any additional children. John agreed, however, to explore with Ritaray various options that would enable them to start a family of their own.

In August 1983 John was reassigned by the Navy and the Adamses moved to Jacksonville, Florida. Over the course of the following year, the couple investigated several methods of having a family. In June 1984 John and Ritaray began discussing artificial insemination by donor (AID), also known as heterologous artificial insemination. Through that procedure, a woman is artificially inseminated with semen of a man other than her husband. By August 1984 John had obtained the name of a fertility specialist in Jacksonville, Dr. Ernest Ferrell, and Ritaray made an appointment for an initial consultation. On September 28, 1984, John and Ritaray met with Dr. Ferrell to learn more about AID. It appears that by the end of the appointment the Adamses had not decided whether to make use of the procedure, and at that time they did not schedule any further appointments.

During October and November 1984, Ritaray arranged with Dr. Ferrell to have two sonograms performed in preparation for heterologous artificial insemination. John had advance notice of both appointments with Dr. Ferrell but did not accompany Ritaray on either occasion. On November 26, 1984, several days after the second sonogram, Ritaray was heterologously inseminated through a procedure performed by Dr. Ferrell. Again, John knew of Ritaray's plans in advance but did not accompany her to the appointment. The next month the couple learned that Ritaray was pregnant. During the pregnancy, the Adamses continued to live together in Jacksonville, Florida, and J.D. was born there on August 4, 1985. At Ritaray's direction, John was designated on the birth certificate as the child's father.

On October 1, 1985, Ritaray and J.D. left for Illinois, where Ritaray's family lived, while John remained in Florida. On January 2, 1986, the couple met in Illinois, and John informed Ritaray that he wanted a divorce. Following a period of discussion between the two concerning child support for J.D., among other matters, Ritaray filed a petition for dissolution of marriage in the circuit court of Lake County on March 13, 1986. In the petition, Ritaray alleged that J.D. was born as a result of her marriage to John, and she asked that she be granted sole custody of the child and awarded child support. In answer to the petition, John acknowledged that J.D. was born during the marriage but, because he had undergone an irreversible vasectomy prior to the marriage, denied that he was the child's father. John further asserted, in what was labeled an affirmative defense, that the child was conceived as a result of AID and that he had not consented to the procedure, either orally or in writing. In response to John's affirmative defense, Ritaray admitted that J.D. was conceived through heterologous insemination but denied John's allegation that he had not given his consent.

John subsequently moved for summary judgment on the parentage issue, arguing that there was no dispute that he had not provided written consent to the AID procedure leading to J.D.'s conception. Attached to the motion were copies of the relevant Illinois and Florida statutes, and it was John's theory that both states require that a husband furnish written consent to his wife's heterologous artificial insemination before a parent-child relationship will be recognized between a husband and a child who is born as a result of that procedure. John asked that the court enter a judgment declaring that no parent-child relationship existed between himself and J.D., that he was not J.D.'s natural or legal father, and that he had no duty to support J.D. In response to John's motion for summary judgment, Ritaray asserted that two genuine questions of material fact remained: whether John had given oral consent to the AID procedure, and whether John had "actually initiated and assisted in the procreation of the minor child." Ritaray therefore asked that the motion for summary judgment be denied. Both John and Ritaray submitted their own affidavits in support of their respective pleadings.

Following a hearing, the trial judge denied John's motion for summary judgment. In a written order, the judge found that John had not provided written consent to Ritaray's heterologous artificial insemination. The judge stated, however, that an issue existed whether John had given actual consent to the procedure and, if so, whether actual consent would "constitute a waiver of the statutory requirement that the Husband's consent must be in writing executed and acknowledged by both Husband & Wife."

Prior to trial, counsel for John and Ritaray agreed that the question of J.D.'s parentage would be determined first, before any of the other matters were resolved. On the eve of trial, counsel was appointed to represent J.D. during the remainder of the proceedings. At the outset of the evidentiary hearing on the parentage issue, John and Ritaray stipulated that the question would be determined under Illinois law; counsel for the minor stated that she had no objection to the stipulation. John and Ritaray also reaffirmed their earlier stipulation that J.D. was born as a result of Ritaray's heterologous artificial insemination and that John had not furnished written consent to the procedure.

Following the hearing on the parentage question, the trial judge ruled that John was estopped from denying his paternity of J.D. The trial judge, in his memorandum of opinion, suggested that in cases involving heterologous artificial insemination there may exist a presumption of initial consent on the part of the husband. Furthermore, the trial judge placed on John the burden of proving that he did not consent to the AID procedure; the judge assigned that burden to John because he had raised the allegations of nonconsent as an affirmative defense in his answer to Ritaray's petition for dissolution of marriage. In resolving the paternity issue, the trial judge purported to measure "John's burden on the affirmative defense...with the rebuttable presumption of initial consent under [*sic*] Rita[ray]'s burden on the issue of estoppel." The trial judge concluded that John, by his actions, had consented to Ritaray's heterologous artificial insemination and that John therefore was estopped from denying the existence of a parent-child relationship with J.D. The trial judge accordingly ruled that John was the legal father of J.D. Following a subsequent hearing devoted to the issues remaining, the trial judge entered judgment dissolving the marriage. With respect to J.D., the judge awarded Ritaray custody of the child, granted John reasonable visitation rights, and ordered John to pay $240 a month in child support.

The appellate court, with one justice dissenting, affirmed the circuit court's judgment. (174 Ill. App.3d 595, 124 Ill. Dec. 184, 528 N.E.2d 1075.) The appellate court agreed with the trial judge that the Illinois statute does not bar the imposition of a support obligation under an estoppel theory when the husband's written consent has not been obtained. The court upheld the trial judge's finding that John consented to Ritaray's heterologous artificial insemination and rejected John's argument that the amount of child support awarded was an abuse of discretion. Although the court in its opinion spoke mainly of the obligation of support, as distinguished from the establishment of a parent-child relationship, the court did not clearly separate the two and, as we have said, affirmed the judgment of the circuit court, which found both to exist. The dissenting justice agreed with the majority that a support obligation may be sustained under the Illinois statute by an estoppel theory, but he would have remanded the cause for further consideration because he believed that the trial judge had improperly placed on John the burden of proving his lack of consent to the AID procedure. We allowed John's petition for leave to appeal (107 Ill.2d R. 315(a)).

At the outset we consider, on our own motion, the applicability of Illinois law to the case at bar. As we have stated, prior to trial John and Ritaray stipulated that the question of J.D.'s parentage should be determined under Illinois law rather than Florida law. Counsel for J.D. had no objection to the stipulation, and it appears that the minor's counsel believed that the result would be the same under the law of either State. The trial judge accepted the stipulation.

The issues raised in the case at bar are questions of first impression under both Illinois and Florida law. Patterned after section 5 of the Uniform Parentage Act (Uniform Parentage Act §5, 9B U.L.A. 301 (1987)), section 3(a) of the Illinois Parentage Act provides, in pertinent part:

> If, under the supervision of a licensed physician and with the consent of her husband, a wife is inseminated artificially with semen donated by a man not her husband, the husband shall be treated in law as if he were the natural father of a child thereby conceived. The husband's consent must be in writing executed and acknowledged by both the husband and wife. (Ill. Rev. Stat. 1987, ch. 40, par. 1453(a).)

A child conceived in the manner described will be regarded under Illinois law as the legitimate offspring of the husband and wife. See Ill. Rev. Stat. 1987, ch. 40, par. 1452.

The relevant Florida statute provides:

> Any child born within wedlock who has been conceived by the means of artificial insemination is irrebuttably presumed to be legitimate, provided that both husband and wife have consented in writing to the artificial insemination. Fla.Stat.Ann. §742.11 (West 1986).

Without deciding the question here, we note that the provision in the Illinois statute that the husband's consent to the AID procedure "must be in writing" could be considered a mandatory requirement for establishing a parent-child relationship pursuant to the statute. (See *Andrews v. Foxworthy* (1978), 71 Ill.2d 13, 21, 15 Ill. Dec. 648, 373 N.E.2d 1332 (the word "must" is generally construed in a mandatory sense).) In Florida, however, the absence of written consent might simply fail to establish an irrebuttable presumption of legitimacy, and legitimacy might still be provable by other means, such as under an estoppel theory. Moreover, it is not clear whether under either statute the failure to provide written consent will preclude both the establishment of a parent-child relationship and the imposition of a support obligation. It may be the case that a support obligation will be found even in the absence of a parent-child relationship.

It is, of course, this court's duty to ensure, in an action involving a minor's interests, that the rights of the child are adequately protected.... The interests of a minor are at stake in the present matter, and it is appropriate that we recognize irregularities occurring in the proceedings below, despite the absence of an appropriate objection by the minor's counsel....

The trial judge was not bound to follow the parties' stipulation that Illinois rather than Florida law should govern the present case. Although Illinois courts have recognized the enforceability of choice-of-law clauses in contracts..., litigants' stipulations to the scope or meaning of the law itself are not binding on a court.... It has been held that, just as parties to an action have no authority to stipulate to the meaning of a law, litigants have no authority to choose, by stipulation, the law applicable to a particular suit.... Other cases, however, have taken a different view, recognizing litigants' reasonable stipulations regarding the choice of law in a case.... We need not determine here whether such an agreement should ever be permitted by a court of this State, for we do not believe that the stipulation in the present case was reasonable.

The agreement by counsel for John, Ritaray, and J.D. that Illinois law should govern the case at bar was contrary to the result that would be reached through application of the customary choice-of-law principles. This court has previously relied on the principles contained in the Restatement (Second) of Conflicts in resolving conflict-of-laws questions.... Concerning legitimacy, section 287(1) of the Restatement (Second) provides:

> Whether a child is legitimate is determined by the local law of the state which, with respect to the particular issue, has the most significant relationship to the child and the parent under the principles stated in §6. (Restatement (Second) of Conflict of Laws §287(1)(1971).)

Section 6 of the Restatement (Second) provides that in the absence of a local statute on choice of law, a court should consider, among other things, "the relative interests of those states in the determination of the particular issue," "the protection of justified expectations," "the basic policies underlying the particular field of law," and "certainty, predictability and uniformity of result." Restatement (Second) of Conflict of Laws §§6(2)(c), (2)(d), (2)(e), (2)(f)(1971).

Applying those principles to the present case, we conclude that Florida has the more significant relationship to the dispute. Ritaray was heterologously inseminated in Florida, the Adamses were residents of Florida at that time and continued to live there during the course of the pregnancy, and the child was born in Florida. In the performance of the AID procedure and its legal consequences, Dr. Ferrell and the Adamses would have looked to Florida law, rather than Illinois law, for guidance. Indeed, whether a parent-child relationship exists between a husband and a child born to the wife as a result of heterologous artificial insemination should not depend on the laws of every State in which the family members may find themselves in the future. The parties to such a procedure will expect that their own local law will govern the relationships created by it, and application of

Florida's law to the present case will fulfill the participants' expectations and will help ensure predictability and uniformity of result. The parties' stipulation that Illinois law should govern the dispute was unreasonable.

Under the present circumstances, we conclude that Florida law, not being repugnant to Illinois public policy, governs the determination of the questions whether a parent-child relationship will be recognized and whether John has a duty to support the child. Accordingly, we decline to accept the parties' stipulation that Illinois law should govern those determinations. We do not believe that we should allow the minor to forgo what benefits may exist for him under the Florida statute and to stipulate instead to the application of what is perhaps the more stringent provision. Because the matter was decided in the circuit court under what we have determined to be the inappropriate law, and because the parties have not yet had an opportunity to brief and argue the relevant issues under the Florida statute, we must reverse the judgments of the courts below and remand the cause to the circuit court for further proceedings.

...

For the reasons stated, the judgments of the appellate court and the circuit court of Lake County are reversed, and the cause is remanded to the circuit court of Lake County for further proceedings.

Judgments reversed; cause remanded.

In re BABY M.

Supreme Court of New Jersey
109 N.J. 396, 537 A.2d 1227 (1988)

WILENTZ, C.J.

In this matter the Court is asked to determine the validity of a contract that purports to provide a new way of bringing children into a family. For a fee of $10,000, a woman agrees to be artificially inseminated with the semen of another woman's husband; she is to conceive a child, carry it to term, and after its birth surrender it to the natural father and his wife. The intent of the contract is that the child's natural mother will thereafter be forever separated from her child. The wife is to adopt the child, and she and the natural father are to be regarded as its parents for all purposes. The contract providing for this is called a "surrogacy contract," the natural mother inappropriately called the "surrogate mother."

We invalidate the surrogacy contract because it conflicts with the law and public policy of this State. While we recognize the depth of the yearning of infertile couples to have their own children, we find the payment of money to a "surrogate" mother illegal, perhaps criminal, and potentially degrading to women. Although in this case we grant custody to the natural father, the evidence having clearly proved such custody to be in the best interests of the infant, we void both the termination of the surrogate mother's parental rights and the adoption of the child by the wife/stepparent. We thus restore the "surrogate" as the mother of the child. We remand the issue of the natural mother's visitation rights to the trial court, since that issue was not reached below and the record before us is not sufficient to permit us to decide it *de novo*.

We find no offense to our present laws where a woman voluntarily and without payment agrees to act as a "surrogate" mother, provided that she is not subject to a binding agreement to surrender her child. Moreover, our holding today does not preclude the Legislature from altering the current statutory scheme, within constitutional limits, so as to permit surrogacy contracts. Under current law, however, the surrogacy agreement before us is illegal and invalid.

I. Facts

In February 1985, William Stern and Mary Beth Whitehead entered into a surrogacy contract. It recited that Stern's wife, Elizabeth, was infertile, that they wanted a child, and that Mrs. Whitehead was willing to provide that child as the mother with Mr. Stern as the father.

The contract provided that through artificial insemination using Mr. Stern's sperm, Mrs. Whitehead would become pregnant, carry the child to term, bear it, deliver it to the Sterns, and thereafter do whatever was necessary to terminate her maternal rights so that Mrs. Stern could thereafter adopt the child. Mrs. Whitehead's husband, Richard,[1] was also a party to the contract; Mrs. Stern was not. Mr. Whitehead promised to do all acts necessary to rebut the presumption of paternity under the Parentage Act. N.J.S.A. 9:17-43a(1), -44a. Although Mrs. Stern was not a party to the surrogacy agreement, the contract gave her sole custody of the child in the event of Mr. Stern's death. Mrs. Stern's status as a nonparty to the surrogate parenting agreement presumably was to avoid the application of the baby-selling statute to this arrangement. N.J.S.A. 9:3-54.

Mr. Stern, on his part, agreed to attempt the artificial insemination and to pay Mrs. Whitehead $10,000 after the child's birth, on its delivery to him. In a separate contract, Mr. Stern agreed to pay $7,500 to the Infertility Center of New York ("ICNY"). The Center's advertising campaigns solicit surrogate mothers and encourage infertile couples to consider surrogacy. ICNY arranged for the surrogacy contract by bringing the parties together, explaining the process to them, furnishing the contractual form, and providing legal counsel.

The history of the parties' involvement in this arrangement suggests their good faith. William and Elizabeth Stern were married in July 1974, having met at the University of Michigan, where both were Ph.D. candidates. Due to financial considerations and Mrs. Stern's pursuit of a medical degree and residency, they decided to defer starting a family until 1981. Before then, however, Mrs. Stern learned that she might have multiple sclerosis and that the disease in some cases renders pregnancy a serious health risk. Her anxiety appears to have exceeded the actual risk, which current medical authorities assess as minimal. Nonetheless that anxiety was evidently quite real, Mrs. Stern fearing that pregnancy might precipitate blindness, paraplegia, or other forms of debilitation. Based on the perceived risk, the Sterns decided to forego having their own children. The decision had special significance for Mr. Stern. Most of his family had been destroyed in the Holocaust. As the family's only survivor, he very much wanted to continue his bloodline.

Initially the Sterns considered adoption, but were discouraged by the substantial delay apparently involved and by the potential problem they saw arising from their age and their differing religious backgrounds. They were most eager for some other means to start a family.

---

1. Subsequent to the trial court proceedings, Mr. and Mrs. Whitehead were divorced, and soon thereafter Mrs. Whitehead remarried. Nevertheless, in the course of this opinion we will make reference almost exclusively to the facts as they existed at the time of trial, the facts on which the decision we now review was reached. We note moreover that Mr. Whitehead remains a party to this dispute. For these reasons, we continue to refer to appellants as Mr. and Mrs. Whitehead.

The paths of Mrs. Whitehead and the Sterns to surrogacy were similar. Both responded to advertising by ICNY. The Sterns' response, following their inquiries into adoption, was the result of their long-standing decision to have a child. Mrs. Whitehead's response apparently resulted from her sympathy with family members and others who could have no children (she stated that she wanted to give another couple the "gift of life"); she also wanted the $10,000 to help her family.

Both parties, undoubtedly because of their own self-interest, were less sensitive to the implications of the transaction than they might otherwise have been. Mrs. Whitehead, for instance, appears not to have been concerned about whether the Sterns would make good parents for her child; the Sterns, on their part, while conscious of the obvious possibility that surrendering the child might cause grief to Mrs. Whitehead, overcame their qualms because of their desire for a child. At any rate, both the Sterns and Mrs. Whitehead were committed to the arrangement; both thought it right and constructive.

Mrs. Whitehead had reached her decision concerning surrogacy before the Sterns, and had actually been involved as a potential surrogate mother with another couple. After numerous unsuccessful artificial inseminations, that effort was abandoned. Thereafter, the Sterns learned of the Infertility Center, the possibilities of surrogacy, and of Mary Beth Whitehead. The two couples met to discuss the surrogacy arrangement and decided to go forward. On February 6, 1985, Mr. Stern and Mr. and Mrs. Whitehead executed the surrogate parenting agreement. After several artificial inseminations over a period of months, Mrs. Whitehead became pregnant. The pregnancy was uneventful and on March 27, 1986, Baby M was born.

Not wishing anyone at the hospital to be aware of the surrogacy arrangement, Mr. and Mrs. Whitehead appeared to all as the proud parents of a healthy female child. Her birth certificate indicated her name to be Sara Elizabeth Whitehead and her father to be Richard Whitehead. In accordance with Mrs. Whitehead's request, the Sterns visited the hospital unobtrusively to see the newborn child.

Mrs. Whitehead realized, almost from the moment of birth, that she could not part with this child. She had felt a bond with it even during pregnancy. Some indication of the attachment was conveyed to the Sterns at the hospital when they told Mrs. Whitehead what they were going to name the baby. She apparently broke into tears and indicated that she did not know if she could give up the child. She talked about how the baby looked like her other daughter, and made it clear that she was experiencing great difficulty with the decision.

Nonetheless, Mrs. Whitehead was, for the moment, true to her word. Despite powerful inclinations to the contrary, she turned her child over to the Sterns on March 30 at the Whiteheads' home.

The Sterns were thrilled with their new child. They had planned extensively for its arrival, far beyond the practical furnishing of a room for her. It was a time of joyful celebration — not just for them but for their friends as well. The Sterns looked forward to raising their daughter, whom they named Melissa. While aware by then that Mrs. Whitehead was undergoing an emotional crisis, they were as yet not cognizant of the depth of that crisis and its implications for their newly-enlarged family.

Later in the evening of March 30, Mrs. Whitehead became deeply disturbed, disconsolate, stricken with unbearable sadness. She had to have her child. She could not eat, sleep, or concentrate on anything other than her need for her baby. The next day she went to the Sterns' home and told them how much she was suffering.

The depth of Mrs. Whitehead's despair surprised and frightened the Sterns. She told them that she could not live without her baby, that she must have her, even if only for one week, that thereafter she would surrender her child. The Sterns, concerned that Mrs. Whitehead might indeed commit suicide, not wanting under any circumstances to risk that, and in any event believing that Mrs. Whitehead would keep her word, turned the child over to her. It was not until four months later, after a series of attempts to regain possession of the child, that Melissa was returned to the Sterns, having been forcibly removed from the home where she was then living with Mr. and Mrs. Whitehead, the home in Florida owned by Mary Beth Whitehead's parents.

The struggle over Baby M began when it became apparent that Mrs. Whitehead could not return the child to Mr. Stern. Due to Mrs. Whitehead's refusal to relinquish the baby, Mr. Stern filed a complaint seeking enforcement of the surrogacy contract. He alleged, accurately, that Mrs. Whitehead had not only refused to comply with the surrogacy contract but had threatened to flee from New Jersey with the child in order to avoid even the possibility of his obtaining custody. The court papers asserted that if Mrs. Whitehead were to be given notice of the application for an order requiring her to relinquish custody, she would, prior to the hearing, leave the state with the baby. And that is precisely what she did. After the order was entered, *ex parte*, the process server, aided by the police, in the presence of the Sterns, entered Mrs. Whitehead's home to execute the order. Mr. Whitehead fled with the child, who had been handed to him through a window while those who came to enforce the order were thrown off balance by a dispute over the child's current name.

The Whiteheads immediately fled to Florida with Baby M....

Eventually the Sterns discovered where the Whiteheads were staying, commenced supplementary proceedings in Florida, and obtained an order requiring the Whiteheads to turn over the child. Police in Florida enforced the order, forcibly removing the child from her grandparents' home. She was soon thereafter brought to New Jersey and turned over to the Sterns. The prior order of the court, issued *ex parte*, awarding custody of the child to the Sterns *pendente lite*, was reaffirmed by the trial court after consideration of the certified representations of the parties (both represented by counsel) concerning the unusual sequence of events that had unfolded. Pending final judgment, Mrs. Whitehead was awarded limited visitation with Baby M.

The Sterns' complaint, in addition to seeking possession and ultimately custody of the child, sought enforcement of the surrogacy contract. Pursuant to the contract, it asked that the child be permanently placed in their custody, that Mrs. Whitehead's parental rights be terminated, and that Mrs. Stern be allowed to adopt the child, *i.e.*, that, for all purposes, Melissa become the Sterns' child.

The trial took thirty-two days over a period of more than two months. It included numerous interlocutory appeals and attempted interlocutory appeals. There were twenty-three witnesses to the facts recited above and fifteen expert witnesses, eleven testifying on the issue of custody and four on the subject of Mrs. Stern's multiple sclerosis; the bulk of the testimony was devoted to determining the parenting arrangement most compatible with the child's best interests. Soon after the conclusion of the trial, the trial court announced its opinion from the bench. 217 N.J.Super. 313, 525 A.2d 1128 (1987). It held that the surrogacy contract was valid; ordered that Mrs. Whitehead's parental rights be terminated and that sole custody of the child be granted to Mr. Stern; and, after hearing brief testimony from Mrs. Stern, immediately entered an order allowing the adoption of Melissa by Mrs. Stern, all in accordance with the surrogacy contract. Pending the outcome of the appeal, we granted a continuation of visitation to Mrs. Whitehead, although slightly more limited than the visitation allowed during the trial.

Although clearly expressing its view that the surrogacy contract was valid, the trial court devoted the major portion of its opinion to the question of the baby's best interests. The inconsistency is apparent. The surrogacy contract calls for the surrender of the child to the Sterns, permanent and sole custody in the Sterns, and termination of Mrs. Whitehead's parental rights, all without qualification, all regardless of any evaluation of the best interests of the child. As a matter of fact the contract recites (even before the child was conceived) that it is in the best interests of the child to be placed with Mr. Stern. In effect, the trial court awarded custody to Mr. Stern, the natural father, based on the same kind of evidence and analysis as might be expected had no surrogacy contract existed. Its rationalization, however, was that while the surrogacy contract was valid, specific performance would not be granted unless that remedy was in the best interests of the child. The factual issues confronted and decided by the trial court were the same as if Mr. Stern and Mrs. Whitehead had had the child out of wedlock, intended or unintended, and then disagreed about custody. The trial court's awareness of the irrelevance of the contract in the court's determination of custody is suggested by its remark that beyond the question of the child's best interests, "[a]ll other concerns raised by counsel constitute commentary." 217 N.J.Super. at 323, 525 A.2d 1128.

On the question of best interests — and we agree, but for different reasons, that custody was the critical issue — the court's analysis of the testimony was perceptive, demonstrating both its understanding of the case and its considerable experience in these matters. We agree substantially with both its analysis and conclusions on the matter of custody.

The court's review and analysis of the surrogacy contract, however, is not at all in accord with ours....

...

II. Invalidity and Unenforceability of Surrogacy Contract

We have concluded that this surrogacy contract is invalid. Our conclusion has two bases: direct conflict with existing statutes and conflict with the public policies of this State, as expressed in its statutory and decisional law.

...

A. Conflict with Statutory Provisions

The surrogacy contract conflicts with: (1) laws prohibiting the use of money in connection with adoptions; (2) laws requiring proof of parental unfitness or abandonment before termination of parental rights is ordered or an adoption is granted; and (3) laws that make surrender of custody and consent to adoption revocable in private placement adoptions.

(1) Our law prohibits paying or accepting money in connection with any placement of a child for adoption. N.J.S.A. 9:3-54a. Violation is a high misdemeanor.... Excepted are fees of an approved agency...and certain expenses in connection with childbirth....

Considerable care was taken in this case to structure the surrogacy arrangement so as not to violate this prohibition. The arrangement was structured as follows: the adopting parent, Mrs. Stern, was not a party to the surrogacy contract; the money paid to Mrs. Whitehead was stated to be for her services — not for the adoption; the sole purpose of the contract was stated as being that "of giving a child to William Stern, its natural and biological father"; the money was purported to be "compensation for services and expenses and in no way...a fee for termination of parental rights or a payment in exchange for consent to surrender a child for adoption"; the fee to the Infertility Center ($7,500) was stated to be for legal representation, advice, administrative work, and other "services." Nevertheless, it seems clear that the money was paid and accepted in connection with an adoption.

The Infertility Center's major role was first as a "finder" of the surrogate mother whose child was to be adopted, and second as the arranger of all proceedings that led to the adoption. Its role as adoption finder is demonstrated by the provision requiring Mr. Stern to pay another $7,500 if he uses Mary Beth Whitehead again as a surrogate, and by ICNY's agreement to "coordinate arrangements for the adoption of the child by the wife." The surrogacy agreement requires Mrs. Whitehead to surrender Baby M for the purposes of adoption. The agreement notes that Mr. and Mrs. Stern wanted to have a child, and provides that the child be "placed" with Mrs. Stern in the event Mr. Stern dies before the child is born. The payment of the $10,000 occurs only on surrender of custody of the child and "completion of the duties and obligations" of Mrs. Whitehead, including termination of her parental rights to facilitate adoption by Mrs. Stern. As for the contention that the Sterns are paying only for services and not for an adoption, we need note only that they would pay nothing in the event the child died before the fourth month of pregnancy, and only $1,000 if the child were stillborn, even though the "services" had been fully rendered. Additionally, one of Mrs. Whitehead's estimated costs, to be assumed by Mr. Stern, was an "Adoption Fee," presumably for Mrs. Whitehead's incidental costs in connection with the adoption.

Mr. Stern knew he was paying for the adoption of a child; Mrs. Whitehead knew she was accepting money so that a child might be adopted; the Infertility Center knew that it was being paid for assisting in the adoption of a child. The actions of all three worked to frustrate the goals of the statute. It strains credulity to claim that these arrangements, touted by those in the surrogacy business as an attractive alternative to the usual route leading to an adoption, really amount to something other than a private placement adoption for money.

...The evils inherent in baby-bartering are loathsome for a myriad of reasons. The child is sold without regard for whether the purchasers will be suitable parents.... The natural mother does not receive the benefit of counseling and guidance to assist her in making a decision that may affect her for a lifetime. In fact, the monetary incentive to sell her child may, depending on her financial circumstances, make her decision less voluntary.... Furthermore, the adoptive parents may not be fully informed of the natural parents' medical history.

Baby-selling potentially results in the exploitation of all parties involved.... Conversely, adoption statutes seek to further humanitarian goals, foremost among them the best interests of the child.... The negative consequences of baby-buying are potentially present in the surrogacy context, especially the potential for placing and adopting a child without regard to the interest of the child or the natural mother.

(2) The termination of Mrs. Whitehead's parental rights, called for by the surrogacy contract and actually ordered by the court,...fails to comply with the stringent requirements of New Jersey law. Our law, recognizing the finality of any termination of parental rights, provides for such termination only where there has

been a voluntary surrender of a child to an approved agency or to the Division of Youth and Family Services ("DYFS"), accompanied by a formal document acknowledging termination of parental rights,...or where there has been a showing of parental abandonment or unfitness. A termination may ordinarily take one of three forms: an action by an approved agency, an action by DYFS, or an action in connection with a private placement adoption. The three are governed by separate statutes, but the standards for termination are substantially the same, except that whereas a written surrender is effective when made to an approved agency or to DYFS, there is no provision for it in the private placement context....

...

Our statutes, and the cases interpreting them, leave no doubt that where there has been no written surrender to an approved agency or to DYFS, termination of parental rights will not be granted in this state absent a very strong showing of abandonment or neglect.... That showing is required in every context in which termination of parental rights is sought, be it an action by an approved agency, an action by DYFS, or a private placement adoption proceeding, even where the petitioning adoptive parent is, as here, a stepparent. While the statutes make certain procedural allowances when stepparents are involved,...the substantive requirement for terminating the natural parents' rights is not relaxed one iota.... It is clear that a "best interests" determination is never sufficient to terminate parental rights; the statutory criteria must be proved.

In this case a termination of parental rights was obtained not by proving the statutory prerequisites but by claiming the benefit of contractual provisions. From all that has been stated above, it is clear that a contractual agreement to abandon one's parental rights, or not to contest a termination action, will not be enforced in our courts. The Legislature would not have so carefully, so consistently, and so substantially restricted termination of parental rights if it had intended to allow termination to be achieved by one short sentence in a contract.

Since the termination was invalid, it follows, as noted above, that adoption of Melissa by Mrs. Stern could not properly be granted.

...

B. Public Policy Considerations

...

The surrogacy contract guarantees permanent separation of the child from one of its natural parents. Our policy, however, has long been that to the extent possible, children should remain with and be brought up by both of their natural parents.... This is not simply some theoretical ideal that in practice has no meaning. The impact of failure to follow that policy is nowhere better shown than in the results of this surrogacy contract. A child, instead of starting off its life with as much peace and security as possible, finds itself immediately in a tug-of-war between contending mother and father.

The surrogacy contract violates the policy of this State that the rights of natural parents are equal concerning their child, the father's right no greater than the mother's.... The whole purpose and effect of the surrogacy contract was to give the father the exclusive right to the child by destroying the rights of the mother.

The policies expressed in our comprehensive laws governing consent to the surrender of a child, discussed *supra* at 1244–1246, stand in stark contrast to the surrogacy contract and what it implies. Here there is no counseling, independent or otherwise, of the natural mother, no evaluation, no warning.

The only legal advice Mary Beth Whitehead received regarding the surrogacy contract was provided in connection with the contract that she previously entered into with another couple. Mrs. Whitehead's lawyer was referred to her by the Infertility Center, with which he had an agreement to act as counsel for surrogate candidates. His services consisted of spending one hour going through the contract with the Whiteheads, section by section, and answering their questions. Mrs. Whitehead received no further legal advice prior to signing the contract with the Sterns.

Mrs. Whitehead was examined and psychologically evaluated, but if it was for her benefit, the record does not disclose that fact. The Sterns regarded the evaluation as important, particularly in connection with the question of whether she would change her mind. Yet they never asked to see it, and were content with the assumption that the Infertility Center had made an evaluation and had concluded that there was no danger that the surrogate mother would change her mind. From Mrs. Whitehead's point of view, all that she learned from the evaluation was that "she had passed." It is apparent that the profit motive got the better of the Infertility Center. Although the evaluation was made, it was not put to any use, and understandably so, for the psychologist warned that Mrs. Whitehead demonstrated certain traits that might make surrender of the child difficult and that there should be further inquiry into this issue in connection with her surrogacy. To inquire further, however, might have jeopardized the Infertility Center's fee. The record indicates that neither Mrs. Whitehead nor the Sterns were ever told of this fact, a fact that might have ended their surrogacy arrangement.

Under the contract, the natural mother is irrevocably committed before she knows the strength of her bond with her child. She never makes a totally voluntary, informed decision, for quite clearly any decision prior to the baby's birth is, in the most important sense, uninformed, and any decision after that, compelled by a pre-existing contractual commitment, the threat of a lawsuit, and the inducement of a $10,000 payment, is less than totally voluntary. Her interests are of little concern to those who controlled this transaction.

Although the interest of the natural father and adoptive mother is certainly the predominant interest, realistically the only interest served, even they are left with less than what public policy requires. They know little about the natural mother, her genetic makeup, and her psychological and medical history. Moreover, not even a superficial attempt is made to determine their awareness of their responsibilities as parents.

Worst of all, however, is the contract's total disregard of the best interests of the child. There is not the slightest suggestion that any inquiry will be made at any time to determine the fitness of the Sterns as custodial parents, of Mrs. Stern as an adoptive parent, their superiority to Mrs. Whitehead, or the effect on the child of not living with her natural mother.

This is the sale of a child, or, at the very least, the sale of a mother's right to her child, the only mitigating factor being that one of the purchasers is the father. Almost every evil that prompted the prohibition on the payment of money in connection with adoptions exists here.

The differences between an adoption and a surrogacy contract should be noted, since it is asserted that the use of money in connection with surrogacy does not pose the risks found where money buys an adoption. Katz, "Surrogate Motherhood and the Baby-Selling Laws," 20 *Colum.J.L. & Soc.Probs.* 1 (1986).

First, and perhaps most important, all parties concede that it is unlikely that surrogacy will survive without money. Despite the alleged selfless motivation of surrogate mothers, if there is no payment, there will be no surrogates, or very few. That conclusion contrasts with adoption; for obvious reasons, there remains a steady supply, albeit insufficient, despite the prohibitions against payment. The adoption itself, relieving the natural mother of the financial burden of supporting an infant, is in some sense the equivalent of payment.

Second, the use of money in adoptions does not produce the problem — conception occurs, and usually the birth itself, before illicit funds are offered. With surrogacy, the "problem," if one views it as such, consisting of the purchase of a woman's procreative capacity, at the risk of her life, is caused by and originates with the offer of money.

Third, with the law prohibiting the use of money in connection with adoptions, the built-in financial pressure of the unwanted pregnancy and the consequent support obligation do not lead the mother to the highest paying, ill-suited, adoptive parents. She is just as well-off surrendering the child to an approved agency. In surrogacy, the highest bidders will presumably become the adoptive parents regardless of suitability, so long as payment of money is permitted.

Fourth, the mother's consent to surrender her child in adoptions is revocable, even after surrender of the child, unless it be to an approved agency, where by regulation there are protections against an ill-advised surrender. In surrogacy, consent occurs so early that no amount of advice would satisfy the potential mother's need, yet the consent is irrevocable.

The main difference, that the unwanted pregnancy is unintended while the situation of the surrogate mother is voluntary and intended, is really not significant. Initially, it produces stronger reactions of sympathy for the mother whose pregnancy was unwanted than for the surrogate mother, who "went into this with her eyes wide open." On reflection, however, it appears that the essential evil is the same, taking advantage of a woman's circumstances (the unwanted pregnancy or the need for money) in order to take away her child, the difference being one of degree.

In the scheme contemplated by the surrogacy contract in this case, a middle man, propelled by profit, promotes the sale. Whatever idealism may have motivated any of the participants, the profit motive predominates, permeates, and ultimately governs the transaction. The demand for children is great and the supply small. The availability of contraception, abortion, and the greater willingness of single mothers to bring up their children has led to a shortage of babies offered for adoption. See N. Baker, *Baby Selling: The Scandal of Black Market Adoption, supra*; *Adoption and Foster Care, 1975: Hearings on Baby Selling Before the Subcomm. On Children and Youth of the Senate Comm. on Labor and Public Welfare,* 94th Cong.1st Sess. 6 (1975)(Statement of Joseph H. Reid, Executive Director, Child Welfare League of America, Inc.). The situation is ripe for the entry of the middleman who will bring some equilibrium into the market by increasing the supply through the use of money.

Intimated, but disputed, is the assertion that surrogacy will be used for the benefit of the rich at the expense of the poor. See, *e.g.*, Radin, "Market Inalienability," 100 *Harv.L.Rev.* 1849, 1930 (1987). In response it is noted that the Sterns are not rich and the Whiteheads not poor. Nevertheless, it is clear to us that it is unlikely that surrogate mothers will be as proportionately numerous among those women in the top twenty percent income bracket as among those in the bottom twenty percent. *Ibid.* Put differently, we doubt that infertile couples in the low-income bracket will find upper income surrogates.

In any event, even in this case one should not pretend that disparate wealth does not play a part simply because the contrast is not the dramatic "rich versus poor." At the time of trial, the Whiteheads' net assets were probably negative — Mrs. Whitehead's own sister was foreclosing on a second mortgage. Their income derived from Mr. Whitehead's labors. Mrs. Whitehead is a homemaker, having previously held part-time jobs. The Sterns are both professionals, she a medical doctor, he a biochemist. Their combined income when both were working was about $89,500 a year and their assets sufficient to pay for the surrogacy contract arrangements.

The point is made that Mrs. Whitehead *agreed* to the surrogacy arrangement, supposedly fully understanding the consequences. Putting aside the issue of how compelling her need for money may have been, and how significant her understanding of the consequences, we suggest that her consent is irrelevant. There are, in a civilized society, some things that money cannot buy. In America, we decided long ago that merely because conduct purchased by money was "voluntary" did not mean that it was good or beyond regulation and prohibition. *West Coast Hotel Co. v. Parrish*, 300 U.S. 379, 57 S.Ct. 578, 81 L.Ed. 703 (1937). Employers can no longer buy labor at the lowest price they can bargain for, even though that labor is "voluntary," 29 U.S.C. §206 (1982), or buy women's labor for less money than paid to men for the same job, 29 U.S.C. §206(d), or purchase the agreement of children to perform oppressive labor, 29 U.S.C. §212, or purchase the agreement of workers to subject themselves to unsafe or unhealthful working conditions, 29 U.S.C. §§651 to 678. (Occupational Safety and Health Act of 1970). There are, in short, values that society deems more important than granting to wealth whatever it can buy, be it labor, love, or life. Whether this principle recommends prohibition of surrogacy, which presumably sometimes results in great satisfaction to all of the parties, is not for us to say. We note here only that, under existing law, the fact that Mrs. Whitehead "agreed" to the arrangement is not dispositive.

The long-term effects of surrogacy contracts are not known, but feared — the impact on the child who learns her life was bought, that she is the offspring of someone who gave birth to her only to obtain money; the impact on the natural mother as the full weight of her isolation is felt along with the full reality of the sale of her body and her child; the impact on the natural father and adoptive mother once they realize the consequences of their conduct. Literature in related areas suggests these are substantial considerations, although, given the newness of surrogacy, there is little information....

The surrogacy contract is based on, principles that are directly contrary to the objectives of our laws. It guarantees the separation of a child from its mother; it looks to adoption regardless of suitability; it totally ignores the child; it takes the child from the mother regardless of her wishes and her maternal fitness; and it does all of this, it accomplishes all of its goals, through the use of money.

Beyond that is the potential degradation of some women that may result from this arrangement. In many cases, of course, surrogacy may bring satisfaction, not only to the infertile couple, but to the surrogate mother herself. The fact, however, that many women may not perceive surrogacy negatively but rather see it as an opportunity does not diminish its potential for devastation to other women.

In sum, the harmful consequences of this surrogacy arrangement appear to us all too palpable. In New Jersey the surrogate mother's agreement to sell her child is void. Its irrevocability infects the entire contract, as does the money that purports to buy it.

III. Termination

We have already noted that under our laws termination of parental rights cannot be based on contract, but may be granted only on proof of the statutory requirements. That conclusion was one of the bases for invalidating the surrogacy contract. Although excluding the contract as a basis for parental termination, we did not explicitly deal with the question of whether the statutory bases for termination existed. We do so here.

...

Nothing in this record justifies a finding that would allow a court to terminate Mary Beth Whitehead's parental rights under the statutory standard. It is not simply that obviously there was no "intentional abandonment or very substantial neglect of parental duties without a reasonable expectation of reversal of that conduct in the future," N.J.S.A. 9:3-48c(1), quite the contrary, but furthermore that the trial court never found Mrs. Whitehead an unfit mother and indeed affirmatively stated that Mary Beth Whitehead had been a good mother to her other children....

...

IV. Constitutional Issues

Both parties argue that the Constitutions — state and federal — mandate approval of their basic claims. The source of their constitutional arguments is essentially the same: the right of privacy, the right to procreate, the right to the companionship of one's child, those rights flowing either directly from the fourteenth amendment or by its incorporation of the Bill of Rights, or from the ninth amendment, or through the penumbra surrounding all of the Bill of Rights. They are the rights of personal intimacy, of marriage, of sex, of family, of procreation. Whatever their source, it is clear that they are fundamental rights protected by both the federal and state Constitutions....The right asserted by the Sterns is the right of procreation; that asserted by Mary Beth Whitehead is the right to the companionship of her child. We find that the right of procreation does not extend as far as claimed by the Sterns. As for the right asserted by Mrs. Whitehead,[12] since we uphold it on other grounds (*i.e.*, we have restored her as mother and recognized her right, limited by the child's best interests, to her companionship), we need not decide that constitutional issue, and for reasons set forth below, we should not.

The right to procreate, as protected by the Constitution, has been ruled on directly only once by the United States Supreme Court. See *Skinner v. Oklahoma* ...(forced sterilization of habitual criminals violates equal protection clause of fourteenth amendment). Although *Griswold v. Connecticut*...is obviously of a similar class, strictly speaking it involves the right not to procreate. The right to procreate very simply is the right to have natural children, whether through sexual intercourse or artificial insemination. It is no more than that. Mr. Stern has not been deprived of that right. Through artificial insemination of Mrs. Whitehead, Baby M is his child. The custody, care, companionship, and nurturing that follow birth are not parts of the right to procreation; they are rights that may also be

---

12. Opponents of surrogacy have also put forth arguments based on the thirteenth amendment, as well as the Peonage Act, 42 U.S.C. §1994 (1982). We need not address these arguments because we have already held the contract unenforceable on the basis of state law.

constitutionally protected, but that involve many considerations other than the right of procreation. To assert that Mr. Stern's right of procreation gives him the right to the custody of Baby M would be to assert that Mrs. Whitehead's right of procreation does *not* give her the right to the custody of Baby M; it would be to assert that the constitutional right of procreation includes within it a constitutionally protected contractual right to destroy someone else's right of procreation.

We conclude that the right of procreation is best understood and protected if confined to its essentials, and that when dealing with rights concerning the resulting child, different interests come into play. There is nothing in our culture or society that even begins to suggest a fundamental right on the part of the father to the custody of the child as part of his right to procreate when opposed by the claim of the mother to the same child. We therefore disagree with the trial court: there is no constitutional basis whatsoever requiring that Mr. Stern's claim to the custody of Baby M be sustained. Our conclusion may thus be understood as illustrating that a person's rights of privacy and self-determination are qualified by the effect on innocent third persons of the exercise of those rights.

Mr. Stern also contends that he has been denied equal protection of the laws by the State's statute granting full parental rights to a husband in relation to the child produced, with his consent, by the union of his wife with a sperm donor. N.J.S.A. 9:17-44. The claim really is that of Mrs. Stern. It is that she is in precisely the same position as the husband in the statute: she is presumably infertile, as is the husband in the statute; her spouse by agreement with a third party procreates with the understanding that the child will be the couple's child. The alleged unequal protection is that the understanding is honored in the statute when the husband is the infertile party, but no similar understanding is honored when it is the wife who is infertile.

It is quite obvious that the situations are not parallel. A sperm donor simply cannot be equated with a surrogate mother. The State has more than a sufficient basis to distinguish the two situations — even if the only difference is between the time it takes to provide sperm for artificial insemination and the time invested in a nine-month pregnancy — so as to justify automatically divesting the sperm donor of his parental rights without automatically divesting a surrogate mother. Some basis for an equal protection argument might exist if Mary Beth Whitehead had contributed her egg to be implanted, fertilized or otherwise, in Mrs. Stern, resulting in the latter's pregnancy. That is not the case here, however.

Mrs. Whitehead, on the other hand, asserts a claim that falls within the scope of a recognized fundamental interest protected by the Constitution. As a mother, she claims the right to the companionship of her child. This is a fundamental interest, constitutionally protected. Furthermore, it was taken away from her by the action of the court below. Whether that action under these circumstances would constitute a constitutional deprivation, however, we need not and do not decide. By virtue of our decision Mrs. Whitehead's constitutional complaint — that her parental rights have been unconstitutionally terminated — is moot. We have decided that both the statutes and public policy of this state require that that termination be voided and that her parental rights be restored. It therefore becomes unnecessary to decide whether that same result would be required by virtue of the federal or state Constitutions....

Having held the contract invalid and having found no other grounds for the termination of Mrs. Whitehead's parental rights, we find that nothing remains of her constitutional claim. It seems obvious to us that since custody and visitation encompass practically all of what we call "parental rights," a total denial of both would be the equivalent of termination of parental rights. *Franz v. United States*, 707 F.2d 582, 602 (D.C.Cir.1983). That, however, as will be seen below, has not occurred here. We express no opinion on whether a prolonged suspension of visitation would constitute a termination of parental rights, or whether, assuming it would, a showing of unfitness would be required.

V. CUSTODY

Having decided that the surrogacy contract is illegal and unenforceable, we now must decide the custody question without regard to the provisions of the surrogacy contract that would give Mr. Stern sole and permanent custody. (That does not mean that the existence of the contract and the circumstances under which it was entered may not be considered to the extent deemed relevant to the child's best interests.) With the surrogacy contract disposed of, the legal framework becomes a dispute between two couples over the custody of a child produced by the artificial insemination of one couple's wife by the other's husband. Under the Parentage Act the claims of the natural father and the natural mother are entitled to equal weight.... The applicable rule given these circumstances is clear: the child's best interests determine custody.

...

The Whiteheads...contend that the award of custody to the Sterns *pendente lite* was erroneous and that the error should not be allowed to affect the final custody decision.... The Whiteheads' conclusion is that had the trial court not given initial custody to the Sterns during the litigation, Mrs. Whitehead not only would have demonstrated her perfectly acceptable personality — the general tenor of the opinion of experts was that her personality problems surfaced primarily in crises — but would also have been able to prove better her parental skills along with an even stronger bond than may now exist between her and Baby M. Had she not been limited to custody for four months, she could have proved all of these things much more persuasively through almost two years of custody.

The argument has considerable force. It is of course possible that the trial court was wrong in its initial award of custody. It is also possible that such error, if that is what it was, may have affected the outcome. We disagree with the premise, however, that in determining custody a court should decide what the child's best interests *would be* if some hypothetical state of facts had existed. Rather, we must look to what those best interests *are*, *today*, even if some of the facts may have resulted in part from legal error. The child's interests come first: we will not punish it for judicial errors, assuming any were made....

There were eleven experts who testified concerning the child's best interests, either directly or in connection with matters related to that issue. Our reading of the record persuades us that the trial court's decision awarding custody to the Sterns (technically to Mr. Stern) should be affirmed since "its findings...could reasonably have been reached on sufficient credible evidence present in the record."...

Our custody conclusion is based on strongly persuasive testimony contrasting both the family life of the Whiteheads and the Sterns and the personalities and characters of the individuals. The stability of the Whitehead family life was doubtful at the time of trial. Their finances were in serious trouble (foreclosure by Mrs. Whitehead's sister on a second mortgage was in process). Mr. Whitehead's employment, though relatively steady, was always at risk because of his alcoholism, a condition that he seems not to have been able to confront effectively. Mrs. Whitehead had not worked for quite some time, her last two employments having been part-time. One of the Whiteheads' positive attributes was their ability to bring up two children, and apparently well, even in so vulnerable a household. Yet substantial question was raised even about that aspect of their home life. The expert testimony contained criticism of Mrs. Whitehead's handling of her son's educational difficulties. Certain of the experts noted that Mrs. Whitehead perceived herself as omnipotent and omniscient concerning her children. She knew what they were thinking, what they wanted, and she spoke for them. As to Melissa, Mrs. Whitehead expressed the view that she alone knew what that child's cries and sounds meant. Her inconsistent stories about various things engendered grave doubts about her ability to explain honestly and sensitively to Baby M — and at the right time — the nature of her origin. Although faith in professional counseling is not a *sine qua non* of parenting, several experts believed that Mrs. Whitehead's contempt for professional help, especially professional psychological help, coincided with her feelings of omnipotence in a way that could be devastating to a child who most likely will need such help. In short, while love and affection there would be, Baby M's life with the Whiteheads promised to be too closely controlled by Mrs. Whitehead. The prospects for wholesome, independent psychological growth and development would be at serious risk.

The Sterns have no other children, but all indications are that their household and their personalities promise a much more likely foundation for Melissa to grow and thrive. There *is* a track record of sorts — during the one- and-a-half years of custody Baby M has done very well, and the relationship between both Mr. and Mrs. Stern and the baby has become very strong. The household is stable, and likely to remain so. Their finances are more than adequate, their circle of friends supportive, and their marriage happy. Most important, they are loving, giving, nurturing, and open-minded people. They have demonstrated the wish and ability to nurture and protect Melissa, yet at the same time to encourage her independence. Their lack of experience is more than made up for by a willingness to learn and to listen, a willingness that is enhanced by their professional training, especially Mrs. Stern's experience as a pediatrician. They are honest; they can recognize error, deal with it, and learn from it. They will try to determine rationally the best way to cope with problems in their relationship with Melissa. When the time comes to tell her about her origins, they will probably have found a means of doing so that accords with the best interests of Baby M. All in all, Melissa's future appears solid, happy, and promising with them.

Based on all of this we have concluded, independent of the trial court's identical conclusion, that Melissa's best interests call for custody in the Sterns. Our above-mentioned disagreements with the trial court do not, as we have noted, in any way diminish our concurrence with its conclusions. We feel, however, that those disagreements are important enough to be stated....

It seems to us that given her predicament, Mrs. Whitehead was rather harshly judged — both by the trial court and by some of the experts. She was guilty of a breach of contract, and indeed, she did break a very important promise, but we think it is expecting something well beyond normal human capabilities to suggest that this mother should have parted with her newly born infant without a struggle. Other than survival, what stronger force is there? We do not know of, and cannot conceive of, any other case where a perfectly fit mother was expected to surrender her newly born infant, perhaps forever, and was then told she was a bad mother because she did not. We know of no authority suggesting that the moral quality of her act in those circumstances should be judged by referring to a contract made before she became pregnant. We do not countenance, and would never countenance, violating a court order as Mrs. Whitehead did, even a court order that is wrong; but her resistance to an order that she surrender her infant, possibly forever, merits a measure of understanding. We do not find it so clear that her efforts to keep her infant, when measured against the Sterns' efforts to take her away, make one, rather than the other, the wrongdoer. The Sterns suffered, but so did she. And if we go beyond suffering to an evaluation of the human stakes involved in the struggle, how much weight should be given to her nine months of pregnancy, the labor of childbirth, the risk to her life, compared to the payment of money, the anticipation of a child and the donation of sperm?

There has emerged a portrait of Mrs. Whitehead, exposing her children to the media, engaging in negotiations to sell a book, granting interviews that seemed helpful to her, whether hurtful to Baby M or not, that suggests a selfish, grasping woman ready to sacrifice the interests of Baby M and her other children for fame and wealth. That portrait is a half-truth, for while it may accurately reflect what ultimately occurred, its implication, that this is what Mary Beth Whitehead wanted, is totally inaccurate, at least insofar as the record before us is concerned. There is not one word in that record to support a claim that had she been allowed to continue her possession of her newly born infant, Mrs. Whitehead would have ever been heard of again; not one word in the record suggests that her change of mind and her subsequent fight for her child was motivated by anything other than love — whatever complex underlying psychological motivations may have existed.

We have a further concern regarding the trial court's emphasis on the Sterns' interest in Melissa's education as compared to the Whiteheads'. That this difference is a legitimate factor to be considered we have no doubt. But it should not be overlooked that a best-interests test is designed to create not a new member of the intelligentsia but rather a well-integrated person who might reasonably be expected to be happy with life. "Best interests" does not contain within it any idealized lifestyle; the question boils down to a judgment, consisting of many factors, about the likely future happiness of a human being. *Fantony v. Fantony*, *supra*, 21 N.J. at 536, 122 A.2d 593. Stability, love, family happiness, tolerance, and, ultimately, support of independence — all rank much higher in predicting future happiness than the likelihood of a college education. We do not mean to suggest that the trial court would disagree. We simply want to dispel any possible misunderstanding on the issue.

Even allowing for these differences, the facts, the experts' opinions, and the trial court's analysis of both argue strongly in favor of custody in the Sterns. Mary Beth Whitehead's family life, into which Baby M would be placed, was anything but secure — the quality Melissa needs most. And today it may be even less so. Furthermore, the evidence and expert opinion based on it reveal personality characteristics, mentioned above, that might threaten the child's best development. The Sterns promise a secure home, with an understanding relationship that allows nurturing and independent growth to develop together. Although there is no substitute for reading the entire record, including the review of every word of each experts' testimony and reports, a summary of their conclusions is revealing. Six experts testified for Mrs. Whitehead: one favored joint custody, clearly unwarranted in this case; one simply rebutted an opposing expert's claim that Mary Beth Whitehead had a recognized personality disorder; one testified to the adverse impact of separation on *Mrs. Whitehead*; one testified about the evils of adoption and, to him, the probable analogous evils of surrogacy; one spoke only on the question of whether Mrs. Whitehead's consent in the surrogacy agreement was "informed consent"; and one spelled out the strong bond between mother and child. None of them unequivocally stated, or even necessarily implied, an opinion that custody in the Whiteheads was in the best interests of Melissa — the ultimate issue. The Sterns' experts, both well qualified — as were the Whiteheads' — concluded that the best interests of Melissa required custody in Mr. Stern. Most convincingly, the three experts chosen by the court-appointed guardian *ad litem* of Baby M, each clearly free of all bias and interest, unanimously and persuasively recommended custody in the Sterns.

Some comment is required on the initial *ex parte* order awarding custody *pendente lite* to the Sterns (and the continuation of that order after a plenary hearing). The issue, although irrelevant to our disposition of this case, may recur; and when it does, it can be of crucial importance. When father and mother are separated and disagree, at birth, on custody, only in an extreme, truly rare, case should the child be taken from its mother *pendente lite*, *i.e.*, only in the most unusual case should the child be taken from its mother before the dispute is finally determined by the court on its merits. The probable bond between mother and child, and the child's need, not just the mother's, to strengthen that bond, along with the likelihood, in most cases, of a significantly lesser, if any, bond with the father — all counsel against temporary custody in the father. A substantial showing that the mother's continued custody would threaten the child's health or welfare would seem to be required.

In this case, the trial court, believing that the surrogacy contract might be valid, and faced with the probable flight from the jurisdiction by Mrs. Whitehead and the baby if *any* notice were served, ordered, *ex parte*, an immediate transfer of possession of the child, *i.e.*, it ordered that custody be transferred immediately to Mr. Stern, rather than order Mrs. Whitehead not to leave the State. We have ruled, however, that the surrogacy contract is unenforceable and illegal. It provides no basis for either an *ex parte*, a plenary, an interlocutory, or a final order requiring a mother to surrender custody to a father. Any application by the natural father in a surrogacy dispute for custody pending the outcome of the litigation will henceforth require proof of unfitness, of danger to the child, or the like, of so high a quality and persuasiveness as to make it unlikely that such application will succeed. Absent the required showing, all that a court should do is list the matter for argument on notice to the mother. Even her threats to flee should not suffice to warrant any other relief unless her unfitness is clearly shown. At most, it should result in an order enjoining such flight. The erroneous transfer of custody, as we view it, represents a greater risk to the child than removal to a foreign jurisdiction, unless parental unfitness is clearly proved. Furthermore, we deem it likely that, advised of the law and knowing that her custody cannot seriously be challenged at this stage of the litigation, surrogate mothers will obey any court order to remain in the jurisdiction.

VI. VISITATION

...Our reversal of the trial court's order, however, requires delineation of Mrs. Whitehead's rights to visitation.... We...remand the visitation issue to the trial court for an abbreviated hearing and determination....

...

We join those who want this litigation to end for the benefit of this child. To spare this two-year-old another sixty to ninety days of litigation, however, at the risk of wrongly deciding this matter, which has life-long consequences for the child and the parties, would be unwise.

We also note the following for the trial court's consideration: First, this is not a divorce case where visitation is almost invariably granted to the non-custodial spouse. To some extent the facts here resemble cases where the non-custodial spouse has had practically no relationship with the child,...; but it only "resembles" those cases. In the instant case, Mrs. Whitehead spent the first four months of this child's life as her mother and has regularly visited the child since then. Second, she is not only the natural mother, but also the legal mother, and is not to be penalized one iota because of the surrogacy contract. Mrs. Whitehead, as the mother (indeed, as a mother who nurtured her child for its first four months — unquestionably a relevant consideration), is entitled to have her own interest in visitation considered....

In all of this, the trial court should recall the touchstones of visitation: that it is desirable for the child to have contact with both parents; that besides the child's interests, the parents' interests also must be considered; but that when all is said and done, the best interests of the child are paramount.

We have decided that Mrs. Whitehead is entitled to visitation at some point, and that question is not open to the trial court on this remand. The trial court will determine what kind of visitation shall be granted to her, with or without conditions, and when and under what circumstances it should commence. It also should be noted that the guardian's recommendation of a five-year delay is most unusual — one might argue that it begins to border on termination. Nevertheless, if the circumstances as further developed by appropriate proofs or as reconsidered on remand clearly call for that suspension under applicable legal principles of visitation, it should be so ordered.

...

CONCLUSION

This case affords some insight into a new reproductive arrangement: the artificial insemination of a surrogate mother. The unfortunate events that have unfolded illustrate that its unregulated use can bring suffering to all involved. Potential victims include the surrogate mother and her family, the natural father and his wife, and most importantly, the child. Although surrogacy has apparently provided positive results for some infertile couples, it can also, as this case demonstrates, cause suffering to participants, here essentially innocent and well-intended.

We have found that our present laws do not permit the surrogacy contract used in this case. Nowhere, however, do we find any legal prohibition against surrogacy when the surrogate mother volunteers, without any payment, to act as a surrogate and is given the right to change her mind and to assert her parental rights. Moreover, the Legislature remains free to deal with this most sensitive issue as it sees fit, subject only to constitutional constraints.

If the Legislature decides to address surrogacy, consideration of this case will highlight many of its potential harms. We do not underestimate the difficulties of legislating on this subject. In addition to the inevitable confrontation with the ethical and moral issues involved, there is the question of the wisdom and effectiveness of regulating a matter so private, yet of such public interest. Legislative consideration of surrogacy may also provide the opportunity to begin to focus on the overall implications of the new reproductive biotechnology — *in vitro* fertilization, preservation of sperm and eggs, embryo implantation and the like. The problem is how to enjoy the benefits of the technology — especially for infertile couples — while minimizing the risk of abuse. The problem can be addressed only when society decides what its values and objectives are in this troubling, yet promising, area.

The judgment is affirmed in part, reversed in part, and remanded for further proceedings consistent with this opinion.

For affirmance in part, reversal in part and remandment — Chief Justice WILENTZ and Justices CLIFFORD, HANDLER, POLLOCK, O'HERN, GARIBALDI and STEIN.

Opposed — None.

COMMENTS

Traditionally, any children born to a married woman would be considered the legitimate children of her husband. "Lord Mansfield's Rule" (*Goodright v. Moss*, 2 Cowp. 291, 98 Eng.Rep. 1257 (1777)), originating in England and widely adopted in the United States, provided that neither husband nor wife could offer testimony that would "bastardize" their children. Only if the husband were "beyond the four seas" and could not possibly be the father of the children would the courts even consider adjudicating whether the children should be treated as illegitimate. These rules made men responsible for raising any children born to their wife and are sometimes cited as the basis for strong policies against adultery by married women. The rules also gave estranged husbands considerable control, at least in theory, over any children born to their wife, regardless of the wishes of the wife and her paramour. There remains a presumption that any child born of a married woman is the legitimate child of her husband, but the presumption can now be more readily rebutted by evidence to the contrary.

Michael H. upholds a state law that denies any opportunity to prove his case to a man claiming to be the natural father of a child counter-factually presumed to be the legitimate child of the mother's husband. As in *Quilloin* (p. 768) and *Lehr* (p. 773), a mother appears to have a much better chance of getting rid of the natural father, with whom she may wish to have no further contact, if she is married to a man and has his support. Had the mothers in *Quilloin* and *Lehr* simply wanted the natural fathers out of their life and out of the lives of their children, they probably would have been denied relief. No court would allow an unmarried woman who was otherwise in the position of Carole D. to bar a man who was in the position of Michael H., unless she were able to prove him an unfit father. Although the standard explanation for this disparate treatment of single and married mothers relates to the child's interests in having a legal father, long-standing prejudice against unwed mothers probably also plays a significant role. Most judges find it easier to sympathize with the family interests of a married man than those of a woman, especially an unmarried woman.

Statutes regulating artificial insemination, such as those of Illinois and Florida discussed in *Adams* were enacted in large part to deal with problems caused to women and children when husbands were occasionally allowed to disclaim fatherhood after they had consented to artificial insemination, while at the same time protecting the interests of husbands who might object to such insemination. Should the doctor have proceeded with the insemination before obtaining the signed written consent? The facts do not make it certain whether the failure to submit the signed statement was a mere formality that was overlooked, or whether the husband may have felt increasing ambivalence about the procedure or about the marriage. If a married woman wishes to have artificial insemination against the wishes of her husband, should she be able to do so? Should it make a difference if the jurisdiction allows unmarried women to receive artificial insemination?

Ordinarily, a woman in Mary Beth Whitehead's situation — giving birth to a child conceived through artificial insemination — would not only be considered the child's legal mother, but her husband would be presumed to be the father and the child to be legitimate. Notice that Whitehead's husband had signed a specific waiver of his right to be presumed to be the father. We consider the issue of "surrogacy contracts" further in the next section on "Commercial Production of Children."

JHORDAN C. v. MARY K.

California Court of Appeal

179 Cal.App.3d 386, 224 Cal.Rptr. 530 (1986)

KING, Associate Justice.

...

Mary K. and Victoria T. appeal from a judgment declaring Jhordan C. to be the legal father of Mary's child, Devin. The child was conceived by artificial insemination with semen donated personally to Mary by Jhordan. We affirm the judgment.

II. Facts and Procedural History

In late 1978 Mary decided to bear a child by artificial insemination and to raise the child jointly with Victoria, a close friend who lived in a nearby town.[1] Mary sought a semen donor by talking to friends and acquaintances. This led to three or four potential donors with whom Mary spoke directly. She and Victoria ultimately chose Jhordan after he had one personal interview with Mary and one dinner at Mary's home.

The parties' testimony was in conflict as to what agreement they had concerning the role, if any, Jhordan would play in the child's life. According to Mary, she told Jhordan she did not want a donor who desired ongoing involvement with the child, but she did agree to let him see the child to satisfy his curiosity as to how the child would look. Jhordan, in contrast, asserts they agreed he and Mary would have an ongoing friendship, he would have ongoing contact with the child, and he would care for the child as much as two or three times per week.

None of the parties sought legal advice until long after the child's birth. They were completely unaware of the existence of Civil Code section 7005. They did not attempt to draft a written agreement concerning Jhordan's status.

---

1. As many as 20,000 women each year are artificially inseminated in the United States. (Note, *Reproductive Technology and the Procreation Rights of the Unmarried* (1985) 98 HARV.L.REV. 669, fn. 1.) By one estimate some 1,500 of these women are unmarried. (Donovan, *The Uniform Parentage Act and Nonmarital Motherhood-by-Choice* (1982–1983) 11 N.Y.U.REV. OF LAW & SOC. CHANGE 193, 195.)

Jhordan provided semen to Mary on a number of occasions during a six month period commencing in late January 1979. On each occasion he came to her home, spoke briefly with her, produced the semen, and then left. The record is unclear, but Mary, who is a nurse, apparently performed the insemination by herself or with Victoria.

Contact between Mary and Jhordan continued after she became pregnant. Mary attended a Christmas party at Jhordan's home. Jhordan visited Mary several times at the health center where she worked. He took photographs of her. When he informed Mary by telephone that he had collected a crib, playpen, and high chair for the child, she told him to keep those items at his home. At one point Jhordan told Mary he had started a trust fund for the child and wanted legal guardianship in case she died; Mary vetoed the guardianship idea but did not disapprove the trust fund.

Victoria maintained a close involvement with Mary during the pregnancy. She took Mary to medical appointments, attended birthing classes, and shared information with Mary regarding pregnancy, delivery, and child rearing.

Mary gave birth to Devin on March 30, 1980. Victoria assisted in the delivery. Jhordan was listed as the father on Devin's birth certificate.[2] Mary's roommate telephoned Jhordan that day to inform him of the birth. Jhordan visited Mary and Devin the next day and took photographs of the baby.

Five days later Jhordan telephoned Mary and said he wanted to visit Devin again. Mary initially resisted, but then allowed Jhordan to visit, although she told him she was angry. During the visit Jhordan claimed a right to see Devin, and Mary agreed to monthly visits.

Through August 1980 Jhordan visited Devin approximately five times. Mary then terminated the monthly visits. Jhordan said he would consult an attorney if Mary did not let him see Devin. Mary asked Jhordan to sign a contract indicating he would not seek to be Devin's father, but Jhordan refused.

In December 1980 Jhordan filed an action against Mary to establish paternity and visitation rights. In June 1982, by stipulated judgment in a separate action by the County of Sonoma, he was ordered to reimburse the county for public assistance paid for Devin's support. The judgment ordered him to commence payment, through the district attorney's office, of $900 in arrearages as well as future child support of $50 per month.[3] In November 1982 the court granted Jhordan weekly visitation with Devin at Victoria's home.

Victoria had been closely involved with Devin since his birth. Devin spent at least two days each week in her home. On days when they did not see each other they spoke on the telephone. Victoria and Mary discussed Devin daily either in person or by telephone. They made joint decisions regarding his daily care and development. The three took vacations together. Devin and Victoria regarded each other as parent and child. Devin developed a brother-sister relationship with Victoria's 14-year-old daughter, and came to regard Victoria's parents as his grandparents. Victoria made the necessary arrangements for Devin's visits with Jhordan.

In August 1983 Victoria moved successfully for an order joining her as a party to this litigation. Supported by Mary, she sought joint legal custody (with Mary)

2. This occurred as a result of the filing of an amended birth certificate based upon a judgment against Jhordan in Sonoma County's action for reimbursement of public assistance benefits paid for the child.

3. During the pendency of this appeal *Mary sought and obtained an increase* in Jhordan's support obligation.

and requested specified visitation rights, asserting she was a de facto parent of Devin. (See, e.g., *Guardianship of Phillip B.* (1983) 139 Cal.App.3d 407, 419–421, 188 Cal.Rptr. 781.) Jhordan subsequently requested an award of joint custody to him and Mary.

After trial the court rendered judgment declaring Jhordan to be Devin's legal father. However, the court awarded sole legal and physical custody to Mary, and denied Jhordan any input into decisions regarding Devin's schooling, medical and dental care, and day-to-day maintenance. Jhordan received substantial visitation rights as recommended by a court-appointed psychologist. The court held Victoria was not a de facto parent, but awarded her visitation rights (not to impinge upon Jhordan's visitation schedule), which were also recommended by the psychologist.

Mary and Victoria filed a timely notice of appeal, specifying the portions of the judgment declaring Jhordan to be Devin's legal father and denying Victoria the status of de facto parent.[4]

III. Discussion

We begin with a discussion of Civil Code section 7005, which provides in pertinent part:

> (a) If, under the supervision of a licensed physician and with the consent of her husband, a wife is inseminated artificially with semen donated by a man not her husband, the husband is treated in law as if he were the natural father of a child thereby conceived....
>
> (b) The donor of semen provided to a licensed physician for use in artificial insemination of a woman other than the donor's wife is treated in law as if he were not the natural father of a child thereby conceived.

Civil Code section 7005 is part of the Uniform Parentage Act (UPA), which was approved in 1973 by the National Conference of Commissioners on Uniform State Laws. (9A West's U.Laws Ann. (1979) U.Par. Act, hist. note, p. 579.) The UPA was adopted in California in 1975. (1975 stats., ch. 1244, §11.) Section 7005 is derived almost verbatim from the UPA as originally drafted, with one crucial exception. The original UPA restricts application of the nonpaternity provision of subdivision (b) to a "*married* woman other than the donor's wife." (9A West's U.Laws Ann. (1979) U.Par. Act, §5, subd. (b), p. 593; emphasis added.) The word "married" is excluded from subdivision (b) of section 7005, so that in California, subdivision (b) applies to all women, married or not.

Thus the California Legislature has afforded unmarried as well as married women a statutory vehicle for obtaining semen for artificial insemination without fear that the donor may claim paternity, and has likewise provided men with a statutory vehicle for donating semen to married and unmarried women alike without fear of liability for child support. Subdivision (b) states only one limitation on its application: the semen must be "provided to a licensed physician." Otherwise, whether impregnation occurs through artificial insemination or sexual intercourse, there can be a determination of paternity with the rights, duties and obligations such a determination entails.

---

4. The Sonoma County Public Defender has filed a brief on behalf of Devin which is *identical* to Jhordan's brief in both form and content, indicating the two briefs were produced in concert. We strongly disapprove of such conduct by counsel for a minor child in custody proceedings, as it substantially compromises counsel's independence.

A. INTERPRETATION OF THE STATUTORY NONPATERNITY PROVISION.

Mary and Victoria first contend that despite the requirement of physician involvement stated in Civil Code section 7005, subdivision (b), the Legislature did not intend to withhold application of the donor nonpaternity provision where semen used in artificial insemination was not provided to a licensed physician. They suggest that the element of physician involvement appears in the statute merely because the Legislature assumed (erroneously) that all artificial insemination would occur under the supervision of a physician. Alternatively, they argue the requirement of physician involvement is merely directive rather than mandatory.

We cannot presume, however, that the Legislature simply assumed or wanted to recommend physician involvement, for two reasons.

First, the history of the UPA (the source of section 7005) indicates conscious adoption of the physician requirement. The initial "discussion draft" submitted to the drafters of the UPA in 1971 did not mention the involvement of a physician in artificial insemination; the draft stated no requirement as to how semen was to be obtained or how the insemination procedure was to be performed....[6] The eventual inclusion of the physician requirement in the final version of the UPA suggests a conscious decision to require physician involvement.

Second, there are at least two sound justifications upon which the statutory requirement of physician involvement might have been based. One relates to health: a physician can obtain a complete medical history of the donor (which may be of crucial importance to the child during his or her lifetime) and screen the donor for any hereditary or communicable diseases. Indeed, the commissioners' comment to the section of the UPA on artificial insemination cites as a "useful reference" a law review article which argues that health considerations should require the involvement of a physician in statutorily authorized artificial insemination.... This suggests that health considerations underlie the decision by the drafters of the UPA to include the physician requirement in the artificial insemination statute.

Another justification for physician involvement is that the presence of a professional third party such as a physician can serve to create a formal, documented structure for the donor-recipient relationship, without which, as this case illustrates, misunderstandings between the parties regarding the nature of their relationship and the donor's relationship to the child would be more likely to occur.

It is true that nothing inherent in artificial insemination requires the involvement of a physician. Artificial insemination is, as demonstrated here, a simple procedure easily performed by a woman in her own home. Also, despite the reasons outlined above in favor of physician involvement, there are countervailing considerations against requiring it. A requirement of physician involvement, as Mary argues, might offend a woman's sense of privacy and reproductive autonomy, might result in burdensome costs to some women, and might interfere with a woman's desire to conduct the procedure in a comfortable environment such as her own home or to choose the donor herself.

...

...Accordingly, section 7005, subdivision (b), by its terms does not apply to the present case. The Legislature's apparent decision to require physician involvement

6. The pertinent portions of the discussion draft provided:

(a) If the husband has consented to artificial insemination of his wife, a resulting child is the legitimate child of the husband and wife....

(b) The donor of semen used in artificial insemination has no legally recognized relationship with a resulting child. An existing relationship is not affected....

in order to invoke the statute cannot be subject to judicial second-guessing and cannot be disturbed, absent constitutional infirmity.

B. Constitutional Considerations

Mary and Victoria next contend that even if section 7005, subdivision (b), by its terms does not apply where semen for artificial insemination has not been provided to a licensed physician, application of the statute to the present case is required by constitutional principles of equal protection and privacy (encompassing rights to family autonomy and procreative choice).

1. Equal protection

Mary and Victoria argue the failure to apply section 7005, subdivision (b), to unmarried women who conceive artificially with semen not provided to a licensed physician denies equal protection because the operation of other paternity statutes precludes a donor assertion of paternity where a *married* woman undergoes artificial insemination with semen not provided to a physician.

This characterization of the effect of the paternity statutes as applied to married women is correct. In the case of the married woman her husband is the presumed father (Civ.Code, s 7004, subd. (a)(1)), and any outsider — including a semen donor, regardless of physician involvement — is precluded from maintaining a paternity action unless the mother "relinquishes for, consents to, or proposes to relinquish for or consent to, the adoption of the child." (Civ.Code, s 7006, subd. (d).) An action to establish paternity by blood test can be brought only by the husband or mother....

But the statutory provision at issue here — Civil Code section 7005, subdivision (b) — treats married and unmarried women equally. Both are denied application of the statute where semen has not been provided to a licensed physician.

The true question presented is whether a completely different set of paternity statutes — affording protection to husband and wife from any claim of paternity by an outsider (Civ.Code, §§7004, 7006; Evid.Code, §621) — denies equal protection by failing to provide similar protection to an unmarried woman. The simple answer is that, within the context of this question, a married woman and an unmarried woman are not similarly situated for purposes of equal protection analysis. In the case of a married woman, the marital relationship invokes a long-recognized social policy of preserving the integrity of the marriage.... No such concerns arise where there is no marriage at all. Equal protection is not violated by providing that certain benefits or legal rights arise only out of the marital relationship. For example, spousal support may be awarded pursuant to Civil Code section 4801 upon the breakup of a marital relationship, but not upon the breakup of a nonmarital relationship.

2. Family autonomy

Mary and Victoria contend that they and Devin compose a family unit and that the trial court's ruling constitutes an infringement upon a right they have to family autonomy, encompassed by the constitutional right to privacy. But this argument begs the question of which persons comprise the family in this case for purposes of judicial intervention. Characterization of the family unit must precede consideration of whether family autonomy has been infringed.

The semen donor here was permitted to develop a social relationship with Mary and Devin as the child's father. During Mary's pregnancy Jhordan maintained contact with her. They visited each other several times, and Mary did not object to Jhordan's collection of baby equipment or the creation of a trust fund for the child. Mary permitted Jhordan to visit Devin on the day after the child's birth and allowed monthly visits thereafter. The record demonstrates no clear understanding that Jhordan's role would be limited to provision of semen and that he would have no parental relationship with Devin; indeed, the parties' conduct indicates otherwise.

We do not purport to hold that an oral or written nonpaternity agreement between the parties would have been legally binding; that difficult question is not before us (and indeed is more appropriately addressed by the Legislature). We simply emphasize that for purposes of the family autonomy argument raised by Mary, Jhordan was not excluded as a member of Devin's family, either by anonymity, by agreement, or by the parties' conduct.

In short, the court's ruling did not infringe upon any right of Mary and Victoria to family autonomy, because under the peculiar facts of this case Jhordan was not excluded as a member of Devin's family for purposes of resolving this custody dispute.

. . .

C. Victoria's Status as a De Facto Parent

Finally, Mary and Victoria contend that even if the paternity judgment is affirmed Victoria should be declared a *de facto* parent, based on her day-to-day attention to Devin's needs (see *Guardianship of Phillip B., supra,* 139 Cal.App.3d at pp. 419–421, 188 Cal.Rptr. 781), in order to guarantee her present visitation rights and ensure her parental status in any future custody or visitation proceedings. Present resolution of the de facto parenthood issue for these purposes would be premature and merely advisory. Victoria's visitation rights have been legally recognized and preserved by court order. If no further custody or visitation proceedings occur, the issue of Victoria's de facto parent status and its legal effect will never arise.

IV. Conclusion

We wish to stress that our opinion in this case is not intended to express any judicial preference toward traditional notions of family structure or toward providing a father where a single woman has chosen to bear a child. Public policy in these areas is best determined by the legislative branch of government, not the judicial. Our Legislature has already spoken and has afforded to unmarried women a statutory right to bear children by artificial insemination (as well as a right of men to donate semen) without fear of a paternity claim, through provision of the semen to a licensed physician. We simply hold that because Mary omitted to invoke Civil Code section 7005, subdivision (b), by obtaining Jhordan's semen through a licensed physician, and because the parties by all other conduct preserved Jhordan's status as a member of Devin's family, the trial court properly declared Jhordan to be Devin's legal father.

The judgment is affirmed.

. . .

COMMENTS

Although Mary K. was not actually cohabiting with her close friend Victoria and certainly would not have been able to marry her (except possibly in Hawaii, see p. 543, or Denmark, see p. 566), they apparently intended to form a family-like relationship. Jhordan C. probably "reneged" on his agreement with Mary K. about as seriously as Mary Beth Whitehead in *Baby M.* had "reneged" on her agreement. Had Mary K. used a physician for the insemination, presumably the provisions of Civil Code section 7005, subdivision (b) would have barred Jhordan C. from claiming parenthood. Whether Victoria would have been allowed to adopt Devin would then depend upon Mary K.'s consent and the willingness of a court to allow a "stepparent" adoption by someone of the same sex as the single parent. So far, there are only a handful of courts around the country that have allowed such adoptions.

There is some controversy surrounding provisions allowing single women to be artificially inseminated. On one hand, it seems to some to be unfair to the child to be brought into the world with only one parent and the intention that the child shall never know a father. On the other hand, it seems unfair to others to deny women access to a safe medical procedure simply on the basis of their marital status. Further, many children are born after the death of their father or born to parents who know they have a short life-expectancy, and some children are born to parents who are worse than no parent at all. Moreover, the present social reality is that any woman who sufficiently wanted to become pregnant by an anonymous "donor" would be likely to be able to do so through sexual intercourse with relative strangers who would not be able to trace her and would feel fairly immune, as a practical matter, from paternity proceedings. It is difficult to believe that society benefits from forcing a woman who wants to become pregnant to engage in sexual intercourse.

Commercial Production of Children

In re ADOPTION OF BABY GIRL L.J.

Surrogate's Court
132 Misc. 2d 972, 505 N.Y.S.2d 813 (1986)

C. Raymond Radigan, Surrogate.

This is a private placement adoption in which the adoptive child was born to a surrogate mother who was artificially inseminated, the donor being the adopting father. The attorney representing the adoptive parents prepared what is commonly known as a "Surrogate Parenting Agreement." Under the terms of that agreement, the surrogate mother is to rceive $10,000 for bearing the child.

The court first had to be concerned with the validity of the adoption proceeding under the circumstances presented, to wit: an agreement entered into prior to conception of the child, the birth of the child, and the necessity that the child be placed in a suitable home. Moreover, by pre-arrangement, the child was delivered after birth to his natural father and his wife, who could not conceive, with the intent of all parties concerned that, through the statutory adoption procedures, the child ultimately be the child of his natural father and the father's spouse. Secondly, and with equal importance, there was the possible violation of existing New York statutes in the paying of a fee to the surrogate mother. In addition and on its own motion, the court is reviewing the reasonableness of the attorney's fee sought by the petitioners' lawyer (DRL 115[7], SSL 374[6]).

With legalization of abortion and the development and widespread use of contraceptives, there has been an appreciable reduction in the number of available children for adoption by loving and wanting prospective adopting parents. Couples unable to have children who seek a child through the traditional methods of adoption, namely adoption agencies and private placement adoptions, have been discouraged by the considerable wait for a child (usually 3 to 7 years) together with the uncertainty and, in many instances, the painful anxiety connected with the process. Through the use of sperm donors, surrogate mothers, and in vitro fertilization, science has sought to satisfy the childless couple's demand for children. In an attempt to ease the process, scientific methods now provide a means for couples unable to have children whereby the child conceived and ultimately adopted may be genetically related to one or both of the adopting parents.

In the case of surrogate motherhood, the couple usually contracts with the surrogate mother who agrees: first, to be artificially inseminated with the couple's husband as donor and to carry the child to full term; and second, to surrender all parental rights in the child as of the date of birth (65 Calif. Law Rev., 611, *Contracts to Bear a Child,* [1978]). For the courts, the most disturbing aspect of the "baby contract," is the moral and ethical considerations, plus the question of the payment made to the surrogate mother for bearing the child. The reality is that the child is in being and of necessity must be reared by parents. The court, being confronted with the facts presented, has found that the child should be raised as the child of his biological father and the latter's spouse since by court investigation it has been found that it would be in the best interests of the child to approve the adoption. No other alternative, such as denying the adoption for the purpose of discouraging such procedures, is appropriate here. This child needs a home and, under the circumstances, the home must be that of the petitioners. Thus, the court has granted the adoption.

Next to be considered is whether the court should permit the payment to the surrogate mother. The court must consider whether the payment should be disallowed so as to discourage the practice of "surrogate motherhood" and/or whether it should be disallowed because of statutory prohibitions. For the reasons developed hereafter, the court finds it is for the legislature to determine if such payments should be disallowed so as to prevent such practices in the future.

All fifty states have enacted legislation to regulate adoptions, and due to the great demand for "desirable" children, many of these states impose criminal sanctions for compensation paid in connection with an adoption. These criminal sanctions are the legislatures' response to a growing "baby black market" where children are often auctioned to the highest bidder. With profit as their priority, there is little concern for the well-being of the child by the parties involved....

In New York, it is a misdemeanor for any person, corporation, agency, society, institution or other organization to wilfully violate the provisions of its adoption statutes (SSL 389). Except for authorized agencies, this includes the prohibition against paying or accepting compensation in connection with the placing of a child for adoption or assisting a parent, relative or guardian of a child in arranging for the placement (SSL 374[6]).

In keeping with the state's desire to monitor abuses in adoptions, DRL 115(7) requires that in private placement adoptions:

> The adoptive parent or parents shall also present an affidavit describing all fees, compensation and other remuneration paid by such parent or parents on account of or incidental to the birth or care of the adoptive child, the pregnancy or care of the adoptive child's mother or the placement or adoption of the child and on account of or incidental to assistance in arrangements for such placement or adoption....

...

...[R]ecently, the Supreme Court of Kentucky was confronted with a surrogate mother situation containing facts similar to the...one presently before this court. In *Surrogate Parenting Associates Inc. v. Commonwealth of Kentucky*, 704 S.W.2d 209, the attorney general sought to revoke the charter of Surrogate Parenting Associates Inc. for its involvement in surrogate parenting procedures in alleged violation of Kentucky's adoption statutes:

> A) KRS 199.590(2), which prohibits sale, purchase or procurement for sale or purchase of "any child for the purpose of adoption";
>
> B) KRS 199.601(2), which prohibits filing a petition for voluntary termination of parental rights "prior to five (5) days after the birth of a child"; and
>
> C) KRS 199.500(5), which specifies that a "consent for adoption" shall not "be held valid if such consent for adoption is given prior to the fifth day after the birth of the child."

The contractual arrangement in the *Surrogate Parenting Associates Inc.* case is similar to the Surrogate Parenting Agreement presented to this court in that the agreement is between the biological father, the surrogate mother and her husband. The biological father's wife who is not genetically related to the child is not a party to the agreement. The purpose of not having the father's wife part of the agreement, according to the Kentucky Court of Appeals, was to avoid the Kentucky adoption statute which forbids the purchase or sale of children.

The Supreme Court reversed the Court of Appeals which reversed the trial court's decision finding for the defendant, Surrogate Parenting Associates. The Supreme Court focused on interpreting the statutory language to determine if Surrogate Parenting Associates involvement in surrogate parenting procedures should be construed as participating in the buying and selling of babies.

In a five to two decision, the court held that "there are fundamental differences between the surrogate parenting procedure in which SPA participates and the buying and selling of children as prohibited by KRS 199.590(2) which place this surrogate parenting procedure beyond the purview of present legislation." (*Surrogate Parenting Assoc. v. Commonwealth ex rel. Armstrong*, 704 S.W.2d at p. 211.)

The Kentucky statute and the New York statute were both designed to keep baby brokers from coercing expectant mothers or parents with financial inducements to part with their child. As stated by the Kentucky court, the central fact in the surrogate parenting procedure is that the agreement to bear the child is entered into before conception.

> The essential considerations for the surrogate mother when she agrees to the surrogate parenting procedure are *not* avoiding the consequences of an unwanted pregnancy or fear of the financial burden of child rearing. On the contrary, the essential consideration is to assist a person or couple who desperately want a child but are unable to conceive one in the customary manner to achieve a biologically related offspring. The problem is caused by the wife's infertility. The problem is solved by artificial insemination. The process is not biologically different from the reverse situation where the husband is infertile and the wife conceives by artificial insemination. No one suggests that where the husband is infertile and conception is induced by artificial insemination of the wife that the participants involved, the biological father, the physicians who care for the mother and deliver the child, or the attorneys who arranged the procedure, have violated the statutes now in place. (*Surrogate Parenting Assoc. v. Kentucky, supra,* p. 211–212)

Surrogate Parenting Association freely acknowledged that the contractual arrangements regarding the mother's surrender of custody and termination of parental rights are voidable. Likewise, this court finds that such arrangements are not void, but are voidable because the individual state's adoption statutes, which are designed to safeguard the best interests of the child, take precedence over any agreement between the parties. If violations of the adoption statutes are found in the terms of the parenting agreement, the court may find the contract illegal and deny the petition for adoption.

The dissenting opinions in the *Surrogate Parenting Associates* case view the surrogate mother arrangement for obtaining an adoptable child as no less than baby selling.

However, this court, in spite of its strong reservations about these arrangements both on moral and ethical grounds, is inclined to follow the majority opinion by finding that biomedical science has advanced man into a new era of genetics which was not contemplated by either the Kentucky legislature nor by the New York legislature when it enacted SSL 374(6) prohibiting payments in connection with an adoption. Current legislation does not expressly foreclose the use of surrogate mothers or the paying of compensation to them under parenting agreements. Accordingly, the court finds that this is a matter for the legislature to address rather than for the judiciary to attempt to determine by the impermissible means of "judicial" legislation. In its absence, this court will not appropriate the function of the legislature and prohibit such arrangements. As with any contractual arrangement, especially as it relates to adoptions, the court will continue to review such contracts and the circumstances surrounding them to determine whether there has been any overreaching, unfair advantage, fraud, undue influence, or excessive payments. In this matter it has concluded that the payment provided for under the agreement may be made.

However, the court requests the legislature to review this serious problem in order to determine whether statutory provisions should be made to allow or disallow the payments requested herein and the practice of surrogate parenting. Accordingly, copies of this decision have been sent to the Law Revision Commission and the chairmen of the Judiciary Committees of the Senate and Assembly.

Insofar as the attorney's fee is concerned, the courts possess both inherent and statutory power to regulate the practice of law which includes the authority to supervise the charging of legal fees....

The court has reviewed the legal services rendered in this matter,...[taking into account] the time spent by the attorney, the difficulties involved in this particular adoption, the nature of the services, the amount involved, the professional standing of counsel and the results obtained. Because of the difficulties connected with arranging the birth of the child by a surrogate mother and the additional legal work required in such an arrangement, the court finds that a fair and reasonable fee for the legal services rendered by the attorney is $3,500, the amount requested in the attorney's affidavit of services.

This decision is deemed an order of the court. No order need be submitted.

Proceed accordingly.

In re ADOPTION OF PAUL
Family Court, Kings County
146 Misc. 2d 379, 550 N.Y.S.2d 815 (1990)

CAROLYN E. DEMAREST, Judge:

Elizabeth A.* and Greg T.* entered into a contractual agreement whereby Elizabeth A.* agreed to be artificially inseminated with the semen of Greg T. so that she might conceive and give birth to the child of Greg T. Pursuant to contract, such child would then be immediately placed in the custody of Greg T. and his wife, who has been unable to conceive "for over a year." This contract, denominated "Surrogate Parenting Agreement," is 49 pages long, including exhibits, and provides for payment to Elizabeth A. of $10,000 upon her surrender of custody of the child or children to Greg T., or if he is dead, to his wife, or if both are dead, to the "guardian" identified as Greg's brother. The Agreement further provides that Elizabeth A. shall, "upon birth of the child, terminate any and all parental rights with respect to the child, and shall have no rights of visitation following the birth of the child" (p. 9). However, the Agreement (at p. 14) also specifically states that the $10,000 payment to Elizabeth A. over and above all other expenses relating to the insemination, pregnancy and birth (including medical, legal and psychological expenses as well as clothing up to $500) "is in no way to be construed as a fee for termination of parental rights by Elizabeth A. or a payment or exchange for a consent to surrender the child for adoption or to assist in the adoption of the child or as payment of any expenses for living or maternity care between the birth of the child and the adoption of the child by Greg T...."

Elizabeth A. further acknowledges, both in the body of the Agreement (at p. 10) and in Exhibit A, a handwritten "Declaration of Intent," that the sole purpose of the proposed conception is to provide the child to Greg T. and it is "without any consideration other than concern for the best interests and welfare of the child" that Elizabeth A. agrees to surrender her parental rights and give immediate and uncontested custody to Greg T.

Nearly a year prior to the execution of the Agreement between Elizabeth A. and Greg T., Greg T. executed an "Agreement" with "The Surrogate Mother Program," a New York Corporation, pursuant to which Greg T. agreed to pay to "The Surrogate Mother Program" a non-refundable fee of $8,500 in exchange for counseling, advice, referrals for medical, legal and other professional services not supplied by the program, and particularly in consideration of the program's supplying an appropriate "surrogate" mother for the proposed child. In addition to

*All names have been changed to protect the identies of the parties.

the $8,500 fee to the Surrogate Mother Program, Greg agreed to pay a $10,000 "Surrogate Mother Fee" and various other expenses to be generated in the execution of the contract, estimated to be in excess of $4,000.

On December 2, 1988, a male child, Paul T., was born to Elizabeth A. No father is named on the birth certificate.

Apparently intending to perform her obligations under the "Surrogate Parenting Agreement", Elizabeth A. now seeks to appear before this Court for the purpose of executing a "Judicial Consent" to the adoption of her son by Greg T. and his wife. Her "Affidavit of Financial Disclosure — Natural Mother", which has not been executed, does not reflect payment to her of the $10,000 fee. It does, however, recite payment by the prospective adoptive parents of $7,500 to the "Surrogate Mother Program". Similarly, though they do acknowledge payment of fees approximating $8,000 to the "Surrogate Mother Program", the proposed adoptive parents have not disclosed the fee of $10,000 to be paid to Elizabeth in their Affidavit of Financial Disclosure, which has been executed. Presumably because the Agreement provides that Elizabeth's "consideration" is to be held in escrow until she has performed all of her obligations, which include the "surrender" of her child to Greg T. and his wife, Elizabeth may not feel the need to disclose receipt of her fee prior to surrender. However, that the aforementioned Agreements have been submitted as part of the documents in support of the surrender and subsequent adoption, indicates to this Court that Elizabeth A. does anticipate receiving this "consideration" in exchange for her execution of the Judicial Consent surrendering her parental rights.

Under the circumstances, it is appropriate and necessary, prior to Elizabeth's appearance, to determine whether her contract with Greg T. is legal under the laws of the State of New York or whether Elizabeth's surrender can only be accepted by this Court if she foreswears acceptance of the benefit of her bargain and thus assures this Court that such surrender is truly voluntary and is motivated by her concern for the best interests of her child and not the promise of financial gain.

This Court has found only one reported New York case squarely in point. In 1986, in *Matter of the Adoption of Baby Girl L. J.*, 132 Misc.2d 972, 505 N.Y.S.2d 813, Surrogate Radigan in Nassau County found a surrogate parenting agreement, virtually identical to that at issue here, to be voidable, but not necessarily void, depending on whether the adoption statutes are violated or not. In that case, despite his "strong reservations about these arrangements both on moral and ethical grounds" (at 978, 505 N.Y.S.2d 813), Surrogate Radigan approved the fee paid to the "surrogate mother" and permitted the adoption as being in the best interests of the child. Surrogate Radigan found nothing in current law to prohibit the surrogate parenting arrangement, but called upon the Legislature to give direction as to the legality of the payments made.

...As there is no clear legislative direction on this subject at present, this Court must look to the law governing adoption generally to determine the legality of this Agreement. Guidance has also been sought from the law of other jurisdictions.

...

...New York's adoption statutes prohibit the request, acceptance, receipt, payment or gift of "any compensation or thing of value, directly or indirectly, in connection with the placing out or adoption of a child or for assisting a parent, relative or guardian of a child in arranging for the placement of the child for the purpose of adoption" by any person other than an authorized agency. Soc.Serv.L. §374(6). Reimbursement or payment is expressly permitted for actual medical or other necessary expenses incurred by the mother in connection with, or as a result of, her pregnancy or the birth of the child. It is clear from the language of the statute that compensation direct to the mother for her "services" in conceiving, carrying and giving birth to the child is not permitted.

Such remuneration to a mother, in exchange for her surrender of the child for adoption, violates New York's well-established policy against trafficking in children....

...

...My analysis of the clear language of the statutes governing adoption, together with the policy of this State as articulated in caselaw, leads me to the conclusion...that the contract at Bar provides for "the sale of a child, or, at the very least, the sale of a mother's right to her child"...in contravention of the law of this State. Such contracts are, therefore, void under the law of the State of New York as it exists at present.

Accordingly, only if Elizabeth will swear under oath before this Court that she has not and will not request, accept or receive the $10,000 promised to her in exchange for surrender of her child, can this Court accept such surrender and terminate her parental rights. Only if she is free of the intimidation inherent in her contractual commitment to give up her child and the inducement of a $10,000 gain, can Elizabeth's surrender of her parental rights be truly voluntary and motivated exclusively by Paul's best interests.... In addition, consistent with Social Services Law §374(6), the proposed adoptive parents must also provide sworn affidavits evidencing their intent not to pay or give any compensation or thing of value to any party in exchange for the child....

...

Should the necessary additional documents not be received by this Court by May 1, 1990, the petition for adoption will be dismissed as abandoned.

COMMENTS

Among the most interesting commentary on surrogacy contracts or on commercial production of children in general is that written by feminists. Focusing on the perspective of women and approaching the issues with the interests of women as a group in mind, feminist analyses vary broadly. Some liberal feminist analyses emphasize freedom of contract and argue that women should be able to enter into binding contracts regarding reproduction and childbirth. The common view that certain activities — especially but not limited to activities traditionally seen as women's work — should not be bought and sold on the market is said by some to contribute to the low value placed on the work women do. Child care, housework, and general errand-running are notoriously poorly paid. Carrying a pregnancy to term is hard and demanding work that should be valued and should not necessarily go unpaid. Just as women should have the right to control their bodies, so too should they have the right to "lease" their womb or other parts of their body or to sell services that only women can perform.

Some feminists do not shrink from the analogies to prostitution made by some critics of surrogacy. The comparison between paid surrogacy and prostitution is to these feminists not a reason to forbid the former, but rather an occasion to criticize the law's present treatment of the latter. Selling sexual services is heavily stigmatized, and criminalization degrades the conditions of work and perhaps also depresses the wage rates. Efforts to forbid surrogacy, like laws against prostitution, will simply drive it underground and worsen the conditions of the women who do the work. From this perspective, laws that allow unpaid surrogacy but find paid surrogacy against public policy are especially pernicious.

Other feminists disagree and argue against the commodification involved in paid surrogacy. Not only is commodification itself seen as undesirable, but when intermediaries — such as surrogacy agencies — become involved, exploitation increases and may become more sophisticated. Third parties make money from the bodies of women and have an important financial stake in manipulating the altruistic impulses and the guilt of the "surrogates" they recruit so as to minimize the occasions on which they bulk at carrying out the contract or change their mind about giving up their child.

While these feminists might agree that criminalization of surrogacy might be as short-sighted as criminalization of prostitution, they consider both to be exploitative of women — especially of relatively powerless women. Just as the state should not endorse and encourage prostitution (such as de facto allowing tax write-offs for hiring prostitutes as a business expense), so too should the state not encourage and facilitate surrogacy (such as by enforcing, directly or indirectly, agreements to give up the child to the contracting couple).

Besides a conflicting focus on the freedom of women or the exploitation of women, feminists are concerned with the effects of surrogacy on attitudes toward mothering, "perfect" children on demand, and the adoption of presently unwanted children. Support for commercial production of children reinforces an ideology that legitimates notions that having a biologically-related newborn is worth going to any effort. This ideology undermines the appeal of adoption. While it might be claimed that there are more than enough parents anxious to adopt healthy, newborn children, it is undeniable that there are many "less desirable" children — too old, too sick, the wrong race or linked with siblings into too large a "package deal" — who are not able to find suitable adoptive homes.

Surrogacy and other commercial alternatives are also a poor way to deal with the environmental and social factors that lead to such a high rate of sterility among American women. Revising career patterns so that they are less geared to the average male life cycle and inflict less severe penalties upon the career opportunities of women who have children early in their work careers would probably be healthier for many women — including most of the women who at present provide the "market" for surrogacy.

Neither *Baby Girl L.J.* nor *Adoption of Paul* is particularly satisfactory, though *Adoption of Paul* is worse than *Baby Girl L.J.* It would seem that in *Adoption of Paul* the parties to the contract most responsible for forming it receive the greatest reward under it, while those least able to protect themselves lose the most. The agency apparently gets its money, and probably the couple will get the child they wanted. Regarding the $10,000 fee, it is not clear why the fee itself, and not the conditioning of its payment upon relinquishment of the child, should be what violates public policy. As in *Baby M.* (*supra* at p. 799), the fee could properly be considered a payment for the agreement to be impregnated — an agreement which while not properly enforceable was fully executed. It would seem more likely to discourage such agreements and less likely to exploit relatively powerless women for courts to order the promised fee paid regardless of whether or not the mother relinquishes the child.

REFERENCES

Martha Field, SURROGATE MOTHERHOOD (1989).

Note, *Rumpelstiltskin Revisited: The Inalienable Rights of Surrogate Mothers*, 99 HARV. L. REV. 1936 (1986).

Frances Olsen, *Forældremyndighed og reproduktionsteknologi*, 11 RETFÆRD 61 (Copenhagen, Denmark, 1988).

Margaret Jane Radin, *Market-Inalienability*, 100 HARV. L. REV. 1849 (1987).

Marjorie Maguire Schultz, *Reproductive Technology and Intent-Based Parenthood: An Opportunity for Gender Neutrality*, 1990 WIS. L. REV. 297.

Paul Schwartz, *Baby M. in West Germany*, 89 COLUM. L. REV. 347 (Book Review)(1989).

Carmel Shalev, *Birth Power: The Case for Surrogacy*, 90 COLUM. L. REV. 1177 (1990).

C: CHILD CUSTODY

Controlling Discretion Through Presumptions

DINKEL v. DINKEL
Supreme Court of Florida
322 So.2d 22 (Fla. 1975)

ADKINS, Chief Justice.

Upon petition for certiorari to review the opinion of the District Court of Appeal, First District, at 305 So.2d 90 (1974), conflict appears with the myriad cases setting forth the rule that in the absence of a clear showing of abuse of discretion, the decision of the trial judge in a child custody case will not be reversed....

The only contested issue before the trial court in this proceeding for dissolution of marriage was the matter of custody of the parties' three-year-old child.

In any child custody proceeding, the welfare of the child is the prime consideration.... Although a spouse has committed adultery, it may nonetheless be in the best interest of the child that custody be awarded to that spouse.... As stated in *McAnespie v. McAnespie*, 200 So.2d 606, (Fla.App.2nd, 1957):

> The fact that a mother is guilty of adultery does not necessarily disqualify her to have the custody of her children. Although she may have been a bad wife, she may be a good mother. *The moral unifitness of a mother must be*

> *such as has a direct bearing on the welfare of the child, if it is to deprive her of the custody of the child.* (Emphasis supplied)(p. 609)

The District Court of Appeal in the case *sub judice* recognized these rules. Although the District Court referred to the "moral unfitness" of the mother, there is nothing in the opinion which indicates that such "moral unfitness" had any "direct bearing on the welfare of the child." There is conflict and we have jurisdiction.

Petitioner admitted having sexual relations over a period of time with one man while she was married to respondent. During the time petitioner was having an affair with a co-teacher, respondent was overseas in military service. Although the sexual activity was carried on while the subject child was present in the two-bedroom mobile home, it was never performed in front of the child.

Although contradictory testimony was presented at the trial, the record contains competent substantial evidence to show that petitioner is an attentive, intelligent, loving and responsible parent whose adulterous activity did not adversely affect the child.

After holding two separate hearings and listening to twelve witnesses present over 230 pages of testimony, the trial judge entered a judgment awarding custody of the child to petitioner giving extensive visitation rights to respondent. In the final judgment, the trial judge found that although petitioner had committed adultery, it is in the best interest of the minor child that custody be awarded to petitioner.

The District Court reversed the award of custody of the minor child to petitioner and found that, because petitioner had committed adultery in the presence of her child, she was an unfit mother, and therefore not entitled to custody.

Adultery may or may not have a direct bearing on the welfare of a child of tender years. Engaging in sexual intercourse with someone other than one's spouse in the same household where the subject child is present does not necessarily affect the child's welfare. Whether the adultery has a direct bearing on the welfare of the child is a question for the trier of fact. Where the trier of fact determines that the spouse's adultery does not have any bearing on the welfare of the child, the act of adultery should not be taken into consideration in reaching the question of custody of the child.

Where the trier of fact reaches the conclusion that the adulterous conduct adversely affects the child, the scales are tipped against the award of custody to the adulterous spouse. Even if the trier of fact determines that the spouse's adultery has an adverse effect on the child, other factors, *i.e.*, cruelty, neglect, parental unfitness, exhibited by the other spouse, may be present to tip the scales back in favor of the award of custody to the adulterous spouse. In the latter event, it may be that the best interest of the child would be served by awarding custody to a third party.

While Fla.Stat. §61.13(2), F.S.A., provides for equal consideration of the spouses in the award of custody, it is still the law in this State that, other essential factors being equal, the mother of the infant of tender years should receive prime consideration for custody. *Anderson v. Anderson*, 309 So.2d 1 (Fla.1975).

It is the function of the trial judge in a child custody proceeding to determine what is in the best interests of the child. An appellate court should not reverse the trial judge's findings absent a showing of abuse of discretion.... As stated in *Grant v. Corbitt*, [95 So.2d 25 (Fla. 1957)]:

> [T]his court cannot, in any type of case, overturn the decision of a Chancellor made in the exercise of his judicial discretion in the absence of a clear showing of an abuse thereof; and, in a child custody case, the opportunity of the Chancellor to observe the demeanor and personalities of the parties and their witnesses and to feel forces, powers and influences that cannot be discerned by merely reading the record, assumes a new importance because of the many intangibles that must be evaluated in deciding the delicate question of child custody. 95 So.2d 25, p. 28.

Were this Court to sit as a trier of fact and hear all the evidence, we might have reached a conclusion different from that of the trial judge. However, neither this Court nor the District Court can substitute its judgment for that of the trier of fact, absent a finding of an abuse of discretion, which requires a lack of competent substantial evidence to sustain the findings of the trial judge.

In the case at bar, the trial judge heard extensive testimony and reached the conclusion that the child's welfare would be best served by awarding custody to the petitioner. Without even finding an abuse of discretion, the District Court substituted its opinion for that of the trial judge as to which parent would best satisfy the welfare of the child. Absent a showing of abuse of discretion, which was not shown before the District Court or this Court, the order of the trial judge was not reversible.

Accordingly, the decision *sub judice* is quashed and the cause is remanded to the District Court with instructions to reinstate that part of the order of the trial court awarding custody of the minor child to the petitioner.

It is so ordered.

ROBERTS, OVERTON and ENGLAND, JJ., DREW, ret. J., and HENSLEY, Circuit Judge, concur.

BOROFF v. BOROFF

Supreme Court of Nebraska
197 Neb. 641, 250 N.W.2d 613 (1977)

BRODKEY, Justice.

This is an appeal from a District Court decree dissolving the marriage of the parties; granting custody of a daughter to the mother, and of a son to the father; and awarding alimony and child support to the wife. The husband has appealed, contesting the custody, alimony, and child support awards.

On November 18, 1975, Patricia Ann Boroff, the appellee herein, petitioned the District Court for Washington County to dissolve her marriage, alleging that the marriage was irretrievably broken. In her petition, she did not specifically request alimony, custody of her two children, child support, or a division of property, but prayed for other equitable relief. Respondent Eugene Allan Boroff, the appellant herein, answered the petition on November 19, 1975, admitting the allegations thereof, and prayed that the marriage be dissolved, that the custody of the children be awarded to him, and also for other equitable relief.

Hearing was had on February 12, 1976, at which time both parties and their children testified. Both parties acknowledged that their marriage was irretrievably broken, and that issue is not contested in this appeal. The Boroffs have two children, Vickie, a 12-year-old daughter who attends elementary school in Herman, Nebraska; and Robert, a 14-year-old son who attends Tekamah-Herman High School. The parties were married in 1961. Patricia is 36 years old, and Eugene is 34 years old.

Patricia is currently employed at a cafe in Herman, Nebraska, and earns $60 in net income each week. She works from 5:30 a.m. until 1 p.m. 3 days a week, and from 5:30 a.m. until 2 p.m. 2 days a week. She has a high school education, and has previously worked for Western Electric, wiring PBX machines.

Patricia testified at trial that she was asking for custody of the children and an award of child support that would enable her to meet household expenses. She itemized monthly household expenses, totalling $511. Patricia stated that if she were to receive custody of the children, she was asking that she receive the parties' home as part of the property division. She acknowledged that she and her husband had agreed that the party who received custody of the children would remain in the home with the children until they were grown, and that the equity in the house would then be equally divided.

Patricia also asked that she receive a 1965 Buick automobile which the Boroffs owned, and that she receive necessary household furnishings. She stated that Eugene should receive the 1969 Chevrolet pickup they owned, and that he was entitled to the bonds that they jointly owned because he had paid for them. Patricia did not specifically request alimony either in her petition or at trial. In view of her prayer for equitable relief, this was not necessary…,

Finally, Patricia stated that Eugene had been a good father to the children, and that he was a fit person to have custody of the children. She did state, however, that she did not think that Eugene could do the wash, fix the children's meals, and keep the house clean; and she believed that she could provide a better home for the children than Eugene could provide.

Eugene stated that he is the postmaster at Herman, Nebraska, and that he earns $14,489 per year. With his deductions, he receives a monthly take-home pay of approximately $790. The house which the Boroffs own is worth approximately $12,000, and they owe a loan company $3,900.20 on the house, which is paid off at the rate of $61 per month, including real estate taxes and insurance.

Other assets of the Boroffs as testified to at the time of the divorce total $3,144.06. Eugene listed current debts such as oil bills, hospital bills, service station bills, mastercharge, etc., as being in the amount of approximately $600.

Eugene stated that he could do the household duties and take care of the children. He testified that the children got average grades in school, and that their grades had gone down due to domestic tensions over the divorce. Otherwise the children have no problems, and get along well in their community. Eugene agreed with Patricia that the person who is awarded custody of the children should be awarded the possession of the house until the children are grown, and that the equity in the house should then be divided equally between them.

The children testified outside the presence of each other and their parents. Robert stated that he wished to live with his father because his father could care for him better, and could understand his problems better. Robert had not discussed the matter of custody with his mother, but had talked with his father about who he wished to live with. Robert testified that he got along well with his sister, and wished to be together with her. Robert stated that he did not wish to live with his mother because "she goes places and leaves us at home sometimes." Robert stated that his mother had been doing this for 4 or 5 weeks, and that she would be away in the evening from 7 to 11. Robert is involved in scouting, and his father is scoutmaster.

Vickie also testified that she wished to live with her father, as she did not "like the friends my Mom hangs around with," and did not like her mother going to the bar. Vickie stated that her mother went to the bar on Wednesdays, when she went bowling. Vickie stated that she could talk to her father better than she could to her mother, and that she wanted to stay with her brother. Vickie had not talked with her mother about custody, but had talked with her father about it.

On redirect examination, Patricia stated that when she filed for divorce, she thought that the children should decide who they wanted to live with. She now thinks that the children would be better off with her, and particularly that Vickie needs a mother because she is entering her maturity. Patricia acknowledged that she bowls on Wednesday nights, and that she has a beer or two on such occasions. Ordinarily Patricia is home in the evenings with the children. Patricia admitted that Eugene had spent quite a bit of time with the children in recent years, and that he has been a good father.

In a decree dated February 12, 1976, the District Court dissolved the marriage, and made the following awards, which we summarize as follows:

(1) The parties shall receive the house and real estate as tenants in common, subject to the right of Patricia to live in the house rent free until Vickie becomes of legal age or fully self-supporting; Patricia shall pay the utilities and expenses of ordinary wear and tear on the house while she is in possession;

(2) Patricia shall receive the household goods subject to the indebtedness thereon, which she is to pay;

(3) Patricia is to receive the 1965 Buick;

(4) Patricia is to receive her checking account ($2.29), her credit union account ($24.39), and the savings account ($10.82);

(5) Eugene is to receive the pickup truck;

(6) Eugene is to receive his checking account ($203.86), his credit union account ($3.02), and the savings bonds ($380);

(7) Both parties are to equally pay the loan on the house (balance of $3,900.20) in $61 monthly installments;

(8) Eugene is to pay outstanding bills totalling approximately $600;

(9) Eugene is to pay Patricia alimony in the amount of $5,000 at the rate of $1,000 per year;

(10) Patricia shall have the custody of Vickie until she becomes of legal age, subject to reasonable visitation by Eugene;

(11) Patricia shall receive $300 child support per month until Vickie becomes of legal age or fully self-supporting;

(12) Eugene shall have custody of Robert until he becomes of legal age, subject to reasonable visitation by Patricia; and

(13) Eugene shall pay fees of $350 per Patricia's attorney and court costs of $26.

Eugene has appealed from the decree of the District Court, contending that the court erred: (1) In granting custody of Vickie to Patricia, thereby splitting the children contrary to their expressed wishes; (2) in awarding Patricia alimony when no alimony was asked for by Patricia and no evidence was adduced in support of an alimony award; (3) in awarding excessive alimony; (4) in awarding Patricia possession of the family dwelling; and (5) in awarding Patricia an excessive amount of child support.

The first issue to be addressed is whether the District Court erred in granting custody of Vickie to Patricia, thereby splitting the children contrary to their expressed wishes. Section 42-364, R.S.Supp., 1976, provides in part:

> (1) In determining with which of the parents the children, or any of them, shall remain, *the court shall consider the best interests of the children,* which shall include, but not be limited to:
>
> > (a) The relationship of the children to each parent prior to the commencement of the action or any subsequent hearing;
> >
> > (b) The desires and wishes of the children if of an age of comprehension regardless of their chronological age, when such desires and wishes are based on sound reasoning; and
> >
> > (c) The general health, welfare, and social behavior of the children.
>
> (2) In determining with which of the parents the children, or any of them, shall remain, *the court shall not give preference to either parent based on the sex* of the parent and no presumption shall exist that either parent is more fit to have custody of the children than the other. (Emphasis supplied.)

The Nebraska cases are clear in holding that the mother and father have an equal and joint right to the custody of their children, and that custody shall be determined on the basis of the best interests of the child. *Young v. Young,* 195 Neb. 163, 237 N.W.2d 135 (1976).

In this case, both children expressed the wish to live with their father rather than their mother. The children were clearly of an age of comprehension, as required by section 42-364, R.S.Supp., 1976, and their wishes appear to have been based on sound reasoning. Both believed that social activities their mother engaged in were either improper or unnecessary. The wishes of the children, however, are not dispositive of the issue. "While the wishes of a child who has reached sufficient age, and has the ability to express an intelligent preference, are entitled to consideration, the wishes of the child are not controlling." *Miller v. Miller,* 196 Neb. 146, 241 N.W.2d 666 (1976).... Thus, although the wishes of the children in this case should have been considered by the trial court, they are not dispositive of what constitutes the best interests of the children.

In reference to the other factors listed in section 42-364(1), R.S.Supp., 1976, the evidence indicates that the relationship of the children to each parent prior to the commencement of the action was good, although the children expressed their disapproval of their mother's social activities. There was no evidence of any serious conflict between the children and either parent. Both children stated that they felt they could talk to their father more easily than they could talk to their mother. The general health, welfare, and social behavior of the children appeared to be normal, although the boy's grades at school were, at best, average.

In *Young v. Young, supra*, the court listed several other factors which are relevant in determining the best interests of a child: Moral fitness of each parent; the environment offered to the child by the parent; the emotional relationship of the children and each parent; the age, sex, and health of the child; the attitudes of each parent toward the child; each parent's capacity to furnish care to the child; and whether the child's social relationships would be disrupted by one parent having custody rather than the other parent. In this case, applying these factors does not result in a clear conclusion that one parent, rather than the other, should have custody of the children.

A final factor to consider is that the children will be split between the parents as the decree now stands. Although this court has acknowledged that it is sound public policy to keep children together when possible, considerations of public policy do not, in all cases, prevent the splitting of the custody of the children when a marriage is dissolved; rather, the ultimate standard is the best interests of the children....

The trial court, in splitting custody of the children, stated:

> I hate to do this, but I'm going to split these children. I think the boy has definitely indicated that he wanted to be with his father. He's over 14, I think, that his counsel's indication here about, thought he could pick his own guardian....as far as the girl is concerned, I think it's paramount that she be with her mother until she gets through maturity. I have some personal experience with that. I've been guardian, but have had to exercise guardianship rights of both boys and girls and I think that that's very necessary that this girl get up to her maturity with the mother. They're both fit, and get up to age 16 [sic].

We call attention to section 42-364(2), R.S.Supp., 1976, which provides that "the court shall not give preference to either parent based on the sex of the parent and no presumption shall exist that either parent is more fit to have custody of the children than the other." The trial court gave no reason why the wishes of the children should be ignored, and why the custody of the children should be split, other than his belief that Vickie should be with her mother until she reached maturity. The trial court did not find that Vickie's wish to be with her father was not based on sound reasons, or that Vickie was not of an age of comprehension.

On balance, we believe that the court should have placed custody of both children in the father. If this were done, the wishes of the children would have been followed, the children would not have been split, and the father, who was admittedly a good father and fit parent, and who financially is probably in a better position to support the children, would have custody. This court clearly has the power to modify awards granting custody of children to a parent, as marriage dissolution actions are tried de novo by this court on appeal. *Schuller v. Schuller*, 191 Neb. 266, 214 N.W.2d 617 (1974). In this case the trial court's determination did not really turn on its accepting one version of the facts rather than another. The facts in this case are largely undisputed, and simply present a question of law as to who is entitled to custody of the children. In this case we conclude that Eugene should be given the custody of both children.

Since we determine that Eugene should be awarded the custody of Vickie, it is obvious that the award of child support to Patricia must be vacated; and pursuant to the agreement of the parties, Eugene should be awarded possession of the house until the children reach their majority. The parties clearly agreed that whoever received custody of the children should receive possession of the house until the children are of legal age or self-supporting, at which time the equity in the house would be divided equally between them. The question then arises as to whether the award of alimony should remain the same, and whether the household goods should be awarded to Eugene rather than to Patricia.

[Discussion of alimony omitted.]

...

In awarding custody of Vickie to Eugene, we also grant reasonable visitation rights to Patricia as to both the minor children....

We affirm the decree of the District Court as modified above.

...

COMMENTS

A vast majority of child custody matters are raised in the context of divorce where the decision-maker, faced with the claims of two parents, is supposed to determine which parent will provide an environment that will be in the best interests of the child. In contrast, the case that arises in the context of child neglect and child abuse is not one of a parent versus another parent, but one of the state versus a parent. Child custody cases in divorce and child neglect and abuse cases have both a private and public aspect to them. Not all child neglect and abuse cases reach the courts. More often than not, a resolution is worked out by the state as represented by a department of social services social worker and the parents who will agree to a plan developed by the department to lessen the risk of harming the child again so that a reunion can occur in the future.

Agreements between parents and a department of social services have the characteristics of adhesion contracts although they are commonly referred to as being voluntary. The department of social services, the party with the power, dictates the terms of the contract with the parents who have little negotiating strength and who face immediate court intervention if they do not agree. In contrast to the non-bargained for agreements in child abuse cases, child custody agreements in divorce are mostly handled by lawyers representing each party who more or less freely agrees to the terms. We say "more or less" because sometimes the husband and wife are not on equal footing. Any number of personal or circumstantial factors may be present to prevent such equality or one of the parties may have more money and more effective counsel.

Probably less than one per cent of all child custody cases in divorce are appealed. Since these appeals are taken against the disposition of the trial judge, and for reasons expressed in *Dinkel*, have little chance of success unless it can be shown that the trial court abused its discretion, the pressure on the parties and their lawyers to reach an out of court settlement in a custody conflict is increased. Their settlement agreement shields them from the risks inherent in any exercise of judicial discretion.

Trial judges like to point out that since they are the ultimate decision makers, with the responsibility of looking out for a child's welfare, they are not bound by private agreements. They also reason that since a child is not a chattel, it cannot be bargained away for consideration. Yet these invocations are mostly ritualistic; the judge in fact incorporates the private agreement in his or her decree. The implication, at least outwardly, is that the parents' agreement coincides with the best interests of the child. By incorporating or merging the agreement in the judicial decree, the judge maintains the power to modify the agreement later and to hold a custodian in contempt if the custodian violates a provision of the agreement, now a court order. Some would argue that such incorporation amounts to the judge's surrendering much of his or her discretionary powers to the parties, such that within the domain of private divorce litigation, the autonomy of the family prevails over state intrusion. Others would maintain that this is a false dichotomy, insofar as the supposed autonomy of the family is itself the result of governmental policies. This procedure, however, assures a kind of privacy to the participants, which serves the perceived interests of those who can afford private attorneys (i.e., the middle class). Litigants who cannot hire lawyers often find themselves presenting their case pro se, and having to work out their arrangements in public or with a court official. In some cases, the trial judge becomes actively involved in the agreement process, not necessarily as a decision-maker, but as counsel.

Dinkel illustrates a middle-class milieu with a school teacher mother. *Boroff* presents evidence of class conflict. The mother's life style, working hours, and recreational preferences clashed with the more stable life of the postmaster husband and father. Not accidentally, the indiscretion of the mother in *Dinkel* received less weight than the irregularity of the mother in *Boroff*. The judge refrained from intervening in *Dinkel*, in spite of the adultery of the mother, while the judge in *Boroff* gave preference to the father. The two cases demonstrate that awareness of underlying issues of social class can substantially aid an attorney in preparing an argument, developing a strategy and predicting outcomes in custody matters. Whether the custody of the children was given to the father or mother in *Boroff* was influenced by whether the parents were upwardly or downwardly mobile. That the children themselves preferred their father's middle-class environment to associating with a mother who worked odd hours in a cafe and in her free hours went bowling and drank beer could only help to tilt the decision in favor of the father. On the other hand, the fact that the child in *Dinkel* was only three years old had a bearing on favoring the mother. In fact, because the level of awareness of a child of such tender years is assumed to be low, the judge did not specify whether a boy or a girl was involved.

While it is easy to justify holdings of this kind in terms of the traditional best interests standard, that standard is of little help in the preliminary phases of custody disputes when attorneys are making predictions, counseling their clients and negotiating with opponents. The difficulty of charting a course in these early stages is brought about by a standard which basically articulates the truism that the trial judge, in a controversy over child custody, will rule in favor of what he or she thinks is right.

In actuality, and perhaps especially under no-fault divorce, the best interests standard is still concerned with the enforcement of social values, often taking implicit punitive measures against one of the parents. It also relates to finances, most blatantly in its manipulability which allows the wealthier parent to hire the more effective lawyer and expert witnesses, to promise the child a better lifestyle, and generally to present the better case. Some would argue that the best interests standard also relates to finances by openly or covertly using the child to allocate wealth. For example, the Massachusetts provision on the assignment of property states: "In fixing the nature and value of the property to be so assigned, the court shall also consider the present and future needs of the dependent children of the marriage." (Mass. Gen. Laws,. Ann. Ch. 208 Sec. 34). *Boroff* illustrates the covert use of finances. Custody of the children determined who got possession of the house and whether substantial payments were to be made to the mother. Financial considerations like those that surfaced in *Boroff* inevitably also affect the bargaining between the parties. Concern for children is often intertwined with these matters. In essence this means that children become both assets and liabilities of marriage, and, upon divorce of the parties, a rearrangement must take place that often favors one party financially over the other.

While it is true that the best interests standard is indeterminate and speculative, actual adjudication poses fewer problems than is commonly assumed. In fact, the standard is not applied to bring about a result, but may serve as a convenient and useful justification for a decision reached on another level. Decision makers often feel uncomfortable with sweeping discretionary powers unless they have worked out more specific guidelines for exercising this seemingly unlimited discretion. To some extent these guidelines have found expression in legislative enactment's in individual states and in the factor listings of Sec. 402 of the Uniform Marriage and Divorce Act.[1] Yet it should be noted that the provision allows for other factors as well as those listed. In reality there is a substructure of judicial guidelines that are unlikely to be published, perhaps because once fully articulated, they may be inherently objectionable. Yet they can be extracted from an amorphous body of case law. Since they are not openly acknowledged in their totality as a cohesive body of regulations, they are relatively immune from efforts to change them. This explains why statutory pronouncements that no preference shall be given to either parent in custody disputes, as mentioned in *Dinkel* and *Boroff*, may have had little practical effect in the majority of cases.

The following substructure of guidelines for continuing to exercise discretion can be discerned, unless it is circumvented by settlement between the parties or by

1. Section 402. [Best Interests of Child.] The court shall determine custody in accordance with the best interest of the child. The court shall consider all relevant factors including:

(1) the wishes of the child's parent or parents as to his custody;

(2) the wishes of the child as to his custodian;

(3) the interaction and interrelationship of the child with his parent or parents, his siblings and any other person who may significantly affect the child's best interest;

(4) the child's adjustment to his home, school, and community; and

(5) the mental and physical health of all individuals involved.

The court shall not consider conduct of a proposed custodian that does not affect his relationship to the child.

the admission of extraordinarily damaging evidence about one of the parents. Over all, the mother still has preference over the father in obtaining custody of children, regardless of their age and sex, particularly if the children are of tender years and the mother has been and will continue to be the primary caretaker. The father's chances of being awarded custody of either his son or his daughter in a disputed case may not be much better than those of grandparents unless he remarries, thus providing a traditional family model. If he has not remarried he may sometimes get custody of a boy, especially a teenager. The articulated premise may be based on providing the boy with a "proper role model" (which he, as a single person, can not do for a girl) with the unarticulated assumption that a male custodian will inculcate male values such as ambition (resulting in leadership roles), achievement, independence and competition (exemplified through academic performance and participation in sports or in boy scout activities as in *Boroff*). On some level lawyers for fathers know this and often use demonstrative evidence as a litigation strategy. They will try to show a judge a video of the father coaching a little league game, playing touch football or supervising homework. They will accompany such videos with statements about how "involved the father is" in the child's upbringing. But the subtext is one of promoting male values. A mother may be successful in winning custody of a girl for the values she will transmit. Again, while the articulated reason may be providing a "proper role model," the subtext is one of offering sexual guidance and inculcating values such as kindness, attractiveness and getting along (without being assertive). The dichotomization of gender expectations are drawn here for purposes of illustration of what happens in court and is not meant to affirm the validity of the assumptions. As we know, such models tend to stereotype classes of people. Today, gender roles and expectations are not so clearly differentiated and may in fact be in the process of overlapping with one another.

Blood relatives, especially if they have had a close relationship with the child, are often preferred over outsiders. Where, however, the non-relative has assumed a parental role, like a long standing step-parent or companion (in the case of the death of the biological custodial parent), that person may be preferred over a blood relative. Splitting of siblings is generally to be avoided. Accordingly, in *Boroff*, the trial judge's ruling that the mother have custody of the daughter and the husband and father have custody of the son was not upheld. Keeping siblings together usually has psychological benefits. Children of divorce tend to feel isolated and having a brother or sister as a soul mate may provide some sense of stability and continuity, thus lessening, to some extent, the inevitable feeling of a world collapsing.

A mother's moral misconduct, such as indiscriminate promiscuity, is perceived to be serious, and may negate the preference that she is often thought to have. An occasional indiscretion may be forgiven, especially if she maintains her decorum. Immorality of the mother tends to have greater weight when custody of a daughter is involved, especially if she is an impressionable age, than if custody of a boy is concerned. Perhaps, again, the reason has to do with gender expectations and the daughter's sexual safety. The father's promiscuity is frequently ignored. A preference for maintaining an existing situation may override any of these considerations. The child's status quo, even if it is less than ideal, is not disturbed unless the child's welfare demands it. Even when child abuse or neglect is a factor, the status quo will be disturbed only if the abuse is taken as serious, placing the child at great physical or emotional risk, and an assessment is made that the likelihood of future harm is great or that the neglectful parent is beyond rehabilitation.

A close examination of these judicial guidelines clarifies why they cannot be openly acknowledged. While they reflect arguable social values, in their totality they run counter to the demand for neutral adjudication. They violate admonitions against bias and stereotyping. But private and public acceptance of judicial decisions is facilitated because no single custody disposition is likely to offer more than a few of these justifications, which are introduced as part of the general and inconspicuous principle of best interests of the child. Indeed, the social usefulness of this principle is in its sweeping generality and positive stance. It invokes feelings that are universally shared; a palatable substitute is difficult to find. For example, no parent wants to be told that he or she was awarded custody because this was "the least detrimental alternative," although such a negatively phrased standard has been proposed in the influential book *Beyond the Best Interests of the Child* and may make sense for analytical purposes. Consequently, decisions on the appellate level are more likely to refer to "the least detrimental alternative" standard than those in trial court custody proceedings. It would be hard to imagine a trial judge announcing from the bench to the litigants that one of them is "the least detrimental alternative" instead of enunciating the best interests of the child, which is more acceptable to parties and observers. Nor would it be wise to tell a father that he is denied custody of his teenage daughter because of a concern for his child's sexual safety. Public sentiment, though tolerant of secret apprehensions, may find such an overt reference to the dangers of incest revolting and unfair to innocent fathers. Thus neutral phrases like "role model" are used and probably more easily acceptable to the parties.

The informal guidelines reflect widely shared popular feelings. Some of them are so firmly embedded in the public consciousness that no controversy about custody may arise in spite of a breakdown of marriage. Predictions about how a court would rule are probably responsible for the many tacit and express custody agreements that are entered into between parents. Parents voluntarily submit to what they consider the inevitable. The evolving position of husband and wife in marriage and in post-marital adjustments may bring about changes, but no substantial statistical impact can as yet be discerned.

In the minority of cases in which custody is subject to dispute and adjudication, the guidelines must be balanced against one another. For example, in *Boroff* the preference for the mother had to be balanced against her conduct; the need to avoid contact between teenage daughters and fathers had to be balanced against the need to keep siblings together. One wonders, however, whether the decisive factor was the social class issue of preventing downward mobility of the children, which would have been likely had they been given to the mother. More simply stated, it was perceived to be in the best interests for both to stay with their father.

REFERENCES

Stephen P. Bank & Michael D. Kahn, THE SIBLING BOND 62–66 (1982).

Richard Crouch, *An Essay on the Critical and Judicial Reception Beyond the Best Interests of the Child*, 13 FAM L.Q. 49 (1979).

John Eekelaar & Eric Clive, CUSTODY AFTER DIVORCE (Oxford Centre for Socio-Legal Studies, Family Law Studies no. 1, 1977).

Joseph Goldstein, Anna Freud, & Albert J. Solnit, BEYOND THE BEST INTERESTS OF THE CHILD (rev. ed. 1979).

Sanford N. Katz, WHEN PARENTS FAIL 146–147 (1971).

Robert Mnookin, *Child Custody Adjudication: Judicial Functions in the Face of Indeterminacy*, 39 LAW & CONTEMP. PROBS. 226 (1975).

Elizabeth S. Scott, *Pluralism, Parental Preference, and Child Custody*, 80 CAL. L. REV. 615 (1992).

Michael S. Wald & Maria Woolverton, *Risk Assessment: The Emperor's New Clothes?*, 69 CHILD WELFARE 483 (No. 6, 1990).

Lenore J. Weitzman & Ruth Dixon, *Child Custody Awards: Legal Standards and Empirical Patterns for Child Custody, Support and Visitation After Divorce*, 12 U.C.D.L. REV. 471 (1979).

Controlling Discretion through Factors Influencing Custody Decisions

SEYMOUR v. SEYMOUR
Supreme Court of Connecticut
180 Conn. 705, 433 A.2d 1005 (1980)

PETERS, J.

This is an appeal from a judgment awarding the custody of a minor child to her mother. The plaintiff, Dennis Seymour, brought an action against the defendant, Margaret Seymour, seeking dissolution of their marriage and custody of their minor child. The defendant's cross complaint did not contest that the marriage had irretrievably broken down, but sought an order that custody be awarded to the defendant as well as an order for ancillary financial relief. No appeal has been taken from the trial court's judgment insofar as it dissolved the parties' marriage and divided their joint assets. The parties continue to be at issue about the custody of their child, which the trial court, Berdon, J., awarded to the defendant mother.

The trial court's extensive finding...establishes the following facts: The plaintiff (hereinafter the father) and the defendant (hereinafter the mother) were married in 1972. Their only child was born on February 4, 1975. The child's first year was a difficult one for her and therefore for her parents. She suffered from colic and from a hip problem that required the wearing of an orthopedic brace. As a result, the child cried often and slept irregularly. During this first year, the mother had primary responsibility for the care of the child, in part because she was nursing her and in part because the father, with a full time job outside of the home, was reluctant to assist in her care. Except for the assistance of friends, there was little outside help for the mother at this time. Within a year of the child's birth, the parents had separated.

The parties' living arrangements, and their arrangements for the care of their child, took various forms from the time of separation in January, 1976, to the time of trial, which began in July, 1977. In 1976, the mother and the child first lived in a variety of marginally adequate temporary quarters. In an effort to find more suitable quarters and to make more permanent plans, the mother, in May of that year, found a baby-sitter for the child during weekdays and asked the father to care for her at night. The father remained in sole custody of the child until some time in June, when the mother resumed personal responsibility for the care of the child for part of each week. The father's custody continued to include leaving the child on weekdays with the baby-sitter the mother had located. The mother's custody did not require the use of baby-sitters, since the mother was able to schedule her part-time work for the time when the child was with her father. Although both parents tried, in good faith, to make a success of joint custody, both had become persuaded, by the time of trial, that joint custody was not feasible.

Although all aspects of the issue of custody of the minor child, then two and one-half years old, were thoroughly and extensively contested at trial by all of the interested parties, there was widespread agreement on two crucial matters. Witness after witness testified that both the mother and the father were suitable and nurturing parents, that each loved the child, and that the child had significant psychological ties to each of them. The witnesses were equally in agreement that the two parents exhibited marked and irreconcilable differences in their personalities, in their life-styles, and in their child care practices. The father was characterized as orderly, well organized, responsible and inflexible, while the mother was described as energetic, impulsive, immature and open. These disparities in the parents' personal orientations led to opposing viewpoints with respect to the child's diet, health care and daily living arrangements, and hence to the breakdown of joint custody of the child.

To assist the court in its Solomonic responsibility to make a choice between the child's suitable but irreconcilable parents, the court appointed Attorney Peter A. Kelly as counsel for the minor child and conducted extensive hearings for seven trial days. The court received testimony not only from the parents and their friends but also from a number of professional experts. The court heard from Kay Shafer, a psychiatric social worker who had counseled extensively with the parents before and after the marital breakdown; she recommended that custody be awarded to the father. The court asked for a report from a family relations officer, Allen Rubin, who, after a custody investigation, also recommended that custody be awarded to the father. The court received reports, finally, from two psychiatrists. Earl S. Patterson, M.D., concluded from his psychiatric examination of the parents that psychiatrically it made no difference which parent was awarded custody. Kyle D. Pruett, M.D., finding that the child's primary psychological attachment was to her mother, recommended that custody be awarded to the mother.

The court concluded, in accordance with the criteria of General Statutes §46b-56(b),[2] that custody should be awarded to the mother because such an award would be in the best interests of the minor child. The appellants cannot and do not

2. Section 46b-56 provides, in relevant part: "...(b) In making or modifying any order with respect to custody or visitation, the court shall be guided by the best interests of the child, giving consideration to the wishes of the child if he is of sufficient age and capable of forming an intelligent preference, provided in making the initial order the court may take into consideration the causes for dissolution of the marriage or legal separation."

challenge the overall propriety of this standard, which this court has on innumerable occasions repeatedly affirmed.... "It is settled that the determination of the custody of a minor child rests largely in the discretion of the trial court, and its decision cannot be overridden unless it abused its discretion." *Simons v. Simons*, [172 Conn. 341, 348, 374 A.2d 1040, 1043 (1977)].

The appellants mount a twofold attack on the trial court's determination to award custody to the mother. First, the appellants argue that the custody statute's failure to provide guidelines for the exercise of the trial court's discretion makes the statute unconstitutionally vague. Second, the appellants contend that the trial court abused its discretion in relying too heavily on psychiatric testimony about the child's primary psychological parent. We find neither argument persuasive.

This is not the first occasion upon which this court has been asked to interpolate objective guidelines into the open-ended fact-oriented statutes which govern family disputes. In *Joy v. Joy*, 178 Conn. 254, 255, 423 A.2d 895 (1979), we declined to impose guidelines to constrain a trial court's inquiry into the irretrievable breakdown of a marriage. In *Posada v. Posada*, 179 Conn. 568, 573, 427 A.2d 406 (1980), and *Fucci v. Fucci*, 179 Conn. 174, 179–80, 425 A.2d 592 (1979), we refused to require specific findings concerning each of the factors that a trial court must consider in making financial settlements pursuant to General Statutes §§46b-81 (assignment of property) and 46b-82 (alimony). We continue to adhere to the view that the legislature was acting wisely in leaving the delicate and difficult process of fact-finding in family matters to flexible, individualized adjudication of the particular facts of each case without the constraint of objective guidelines.... Certainly, a statute that vests discretion in the trial court to determine the best interests of a child in awarding custody is no more unconstitutional than is a statute that allows dissolution of a marriage without fault upon a factual finding that a marriage has irretrievably broken down....

The contention that the trial court abused its discretion is based upon the appellants' allegation that insufficient weight was given to evidence concerning the parenting ability of the father and of the mother, and excessive weight was given to identification of the child's primary psychological parent. This claim is difficult to sustain in light of the trial court's express statement that it had taken into account the parents' past behavior as it related to their parenting ability and to their consistency in parenting and life style, insofar as these factors might affect the child's growth, development and well being. It is true that the court assigned special significance to four additional factors: the emotional ties of the child to each parent; the emotional ties of each parent to the child; the time each parent would be able to devote to the child on a day-to-day basis; and the flexibility of each parent to best serve the psychological development and growth of the child. Even these factors, however, go beyond the single-minded attention to primary attachment to a psychological parent of which the appellants are critical.

The role that psychological evaluations play in the determination of the best interests of the child is not susceptible to generalization by appellate courts. It is significant that Goldstein, Freud & Solnit characterize as the "least detrimental available alternative" their suggestion that child placement should maintain "on a continuous, unconditional, and permanent basis a relationship with at least one adult who is or will become the child's psychological parent." Goldstein, Freud & Solnit, *Beyond the Best Interests of the Child*, p. 99 (1979). Such a characterization serves to emphasize that the concept of the psychological parent is not a fixed star by which custody decisions can invariably be guided. The notion of a person being or becoming a psychological parent properly emphasizes that nature and nurture both play a role in a child's psychological well-being. Nothing in *Beyond the Best Interests of the Child* is inconsistent with a child's having two psychological parents, as would normally be the case in an intact family. Furthermore, professionals in the field of child development remind us that a child may become deeply attached to a parent who is seriously inadequate, disturbed or abusive, so that "in some cases it is a disadvantage for the child to be in the care of the psychological parent." Leonard & Provence, "The Development of Parent-Child Relationships and the Psychological Parent," 53 Conn. B.J. 320, 327 (1979). While psychological parenting is thus one indicator of the best interests of a child, a court has an independent responsibility to assure itself of the suitability of the parent to whom the child is primarily attached.... On this record, the trial court exercised that responsibility.

The appellants challenge not only the concept of the psychological parent but also the methodology of the psychiatrist who presented the concept to the court. The weight to be given to psychological testimony by professionals in mental health is, in matters of custody, as it is elsewhere, a question for the trier of fact. It should be noted, however, that expert opinion must be evaluated in light of the expert's opportunity to come to a reasoned conclusion.... As this case illustrates, long-range forecasts about future child development are sometimes based upon relatively few and brief interviews and tests conducted under circumstances of stress.[3] It is not clear to what extent the analytic insights derived from long and intensive psychotherapy can readily be translated into an evaluative setting that is governed by a radically different time frame. None of these infirmities in the psychological testimony is, however, sufficient, singly or jointly, to have required exclusion of Pruett's testimony.

In the circumstances of the case before it, the trial court was certainly not unjustified in concluding that it was relevant to inquire as it did into the psychological relationship between the child and her parents. Once it is definitively established, as it was here, that each parent is loving, caring and otherwise entirely suitable, the court perforce must look to other factors to come to a decision about custody. The court was not in error in basing its award of custody to the mother on her strong and healthy relationship to her daughter, her willingness and ability to devote time to her daughter, and her willingness to facilitate visitation by the father.

There is no error.

In this opinion the other judges concurred.

McKAY v. MITZEL

Supreme Court of North Dakota
137 N.W.2d 792 (N.D. 1965)

STRUTZ, Judge

Petitioner brings habeas corpus proceedings to determine the custody of three minor children. The parents were divorced in 1955, and custody of the children

3. Pruett saw the child with her father on two occasions, and with her mother once. Each interview lasted between forty-five and fifty minutes. Pruett never saw the child in the company of both of her parents. Pruett supervised the administration of a development assessment for the child alone, which involved both interviews and observations of undisclosed length.

was awarded to the mother by the decree. The petitioner is the natural father, who was remarried, in 1957, to a woman who had two children by a former marriage. Two other children have been born as the issue of this second marriage.

The natural mother, who also remarried following the divorce, died in 1963, and this proceeding was brought by the father to secure the custody of the three children by his first marriage.

The respondents in this proceeding are the parents of the mother, and the grandparents of the children involved. The children, two girls and a boy, presently are living with the respondents in Linton and are attending the public schools in that city. The petitioner, with his present family, is residing in the State of Colorado where he is employed by a construction firm. They reside in a trailer home, but the petitioner advised the trial court that, if he were awarded the custody of these three children, he would rent an apartment or a house. The record discloses that the petitioner's salary is adequate to care for these children in addition to his other obligations.

The record further discloses that the petitioner suffered an injury in connection with his employment which made it necessary for him to seek reductions in the amounts which he was required to pay for the support of these children, under the divorce decree. Such payments first were reduced to ninety dollars a month and thereafter to seventy-five dollars a month. It further appears that the children lived with the respondents during the period following the divorce of their parents and until their mother's remarriage, a period of approximately two years, and that, since their mother's remarriage, they have spent much time with the respondents.

At the time of the trial, the court, in the presence of counsel for both the petitioner and the respondents, talked to the children in chambers. At that time, the girls were fifteen and fourteen and the boy was approximately ten and one-half years of age. All of the children expressed a desire to remain with the respondents.

The trial court found that both the petitioner and the respondents were fit and proper persons to have the custody of such minor children. In its decision, the court pointed out that the petitioner's wife is a comparative stranger to the three children involved in this proceeding. The court noted that petitioner's wife has four children of her own and that, although she testified that her relations with the three children involved in this proceeding were excellent on those occasions when they visited their father and that she would try to treat them the same as if they were her own, she could not be expected to give them the same love and consideration that she would give to her own offspring.

Findings of fact and conclusions of law were made in favor of the respondents, and the petition for writ of habeas corpus was denied. The petitioner has appealed from the order denying his petition and has demanded a trial de novo of all the issues before this court.

It is contention of the petitioner that, as the natural father of the children involved in this proceeding, he is entitled to their custody. Sec. 14-09-04, N.D.C.C. He points out that this court has held that, where the mother is dead, the father is entitled to the custody of the children....

This court has also held that, upon the death of the parent to whom custody of a child was awarded in a divorce proceeding, the surviving parent may be given custody in a habeas corpus proceeding upon a showing that such parent is a proper person....

Our statute provides that, of two persons equally entitled to custody, preference is to be given to a parent. Sec. 30-10-07(1), N.D.C.C.

While a parent's right to the custody of a child is preferred by this section, in awarding custody the court will be guided by Section 30-10-06, North Dakota Century Code. This section provides that, in awarding custody of a minor, the court is to be guided by certain considerations:

> 1. By what appears to be for the best interests of the child in respect to its temporal and its mental and moral welfare, and if the child is of sufficient age to form an intelligent preference, the court or judge may consider that preference in determining the question....

Thus the statutory right of the parent to primary consideration in the matter of custody is subject to a determination of what is best for the child, such best interests of the child being paramount.... Consequently, where the mother is dead, the father has the right to custody superior to that of anyone else, unless the best interests of the child require that he be deprived of such custody. Thus, before the natural right of a parent to custody of a minor child may be set aside, it must appear that the best interests of the child require such action.

In the matter before us, the trial court found both the natural father, as the petitioner, and the maternal grandparents, as the respondents, fit to have custody of these children. If this were the only matter before the court, the father clearly would be entitled to the writ prayed for. But, in awarding custody, the court must weigh all of the conflicting rules and presumptions, together with all of the circumstances of the particular case. And, as has been pointed out, the controlling consideration of the court in determining custody should be the welfare and best interests of the children. Within the limits imposed by our statute, the trial court is vested with a large discretion in determining what is in the child's best interests and to whom custody should be awarded. The court, having had all of the parties before it, in this case determined that the best interests of the children required that the custody be awarded to the respondents. We cannot say that, in so finding, the court abused its discretion.

We would point to a further consideration which lends support to the court's decision in this matter. At the time of the trial, the two daughters whose custody was involved in this proceeding were fifteen and fourteen years of age, while the son was ten years and five months old. The court, in chambers, in the presence of counsel for both sides, asked these children what their wishes were in the matter of custody, and they stated that they preferred to remain with the respondents. In determining an award of custody, the court may consider the wishes of the children where such children have reached the age of discretion, although such preference is not controlling on the court. Since the children were fifteen, fourteen, and ten years of age, they were not too young to exercise some judgment in respect to their custody. This is especially true of the two older children, and we believe the court was right in determining that the best interests of the children required that they remain together. The desires of the children relative to custody were entitled to consideration. It was for the trial court, in the exercise of its discretion, to appraise the intelligence of the children and to decide what weight, if any, should be given to their wishes in determining the question of custody.

The welfare and best interests of the children, the fitness of the parties, and the right of custody of the parties were all before the trial court. The findings and conclusions of the court are well supported by the evidence, and we agree with these findings.

The order appealed from is affirmed.

JARRETT v. JARRETT

Supreme Court of Illinois

78 Ill.2d 337, 400 N.E.2d 421 (1979)

UNDERWOOD, Justice:

On December 6, 1976, Jacqueline Jarrett received a divorce from Walter Jarrett in the circuit court of Cook County on grounds of extreme and repeated mental cruelty. The divorce decree, by agreement, also awarded Jacqueline custody of the three Jarrett children subject to the father's right of visitation at reasonable times. Seven months later, alleging changed conditions, Walter petitioned the circuit court to modify the divorce decree and award him custody of the children. The circuit court granted his petition subject to the mother's right of visitation at reasonable times, but a majority of the appellate court reversed (64 Ill.App.3d 932, 21 Ill.Dec. 718, 382 N.E.2d 12), and we granted leave to appeal.

During their marriage, Walter and Jacqueline had three daughters, who, at the time of the divorce, were 12, 10 and 7 years old. In addition to custody of the children, the divorce decree also awarded Jacqueline the use of the family home, and child support; Walter received visitation rights at all reasonable times and usually had the children from Saturday evening to Sunday evening. In April 1977, five months after the divorce, Jacqueline informed Walter that she planned to have her boyfriend, Wayne Hammon, move into the family home with her. Walter protested, but Hammon moved in on May 1, 1977. Jacqueline and Hammon thereafter cohabited in the Jarrett home but did not marry.

The children, who were not "overly enthused" when they first learned that Hammon would move into the family home with them, asked Jacqueline if she intended to marry Hammon, but Jacqueline responded that she did not know. At the modification hearing Jacqueline testified that she did not want to remarry because it was too soon after her divorce; because she did not believe that a marriage license makes a relationship; and because the divorce decree required her to sell the family home within six months after remarriage. She did not want to sell the house because the children did not want to move and she could not afford to do so. Jacqueline explained to the children that some people thought it was wrong for an unmarried man and woman to live together but she thought that what mattered was that they loved each other. Jacqueline testified that she told some neighbors that Hammon would move in with her but that she had not received any adverse comments. Jacqueline further testified that the children seemed to develop an affectionate relationship with Hammon, who played with them, helped them with their homework, and verbally disciplined them. Both Jacqueline and Hammon testified at the hearing that they did not at that time have any plans to marry. In oral argument before this court Jacqueline's counsel conceded that she and Hammon were still living together unmarried.

Walter Jarrett testified that he thought Jacqueline's living arrangements created a moral environment which was not a proper one in which to raise three young girls. He also testified that the children were always clean, healthy, well dressed and well nourished when he picked them up, and that when he talked with his oldest daughter, Kathleen, she did not object to Jacqueline's living arrangement.

The circuit court found that it was "necessary for the moral and spiritual well-being and development" of the children that Walter receive custody. In reversing, the appellate court reasoned that the record did not reveal any negative effects on the children caused by Jacqueline's cohabitation with Hammon, and that the circuit court had not found Jacqueline unfit. It declined to consider potential future harmful effects of the cohabitation on the children. 64 Ill.App.3d 932, 937, 21 Ill.Dec. 718, 382 N.E.2d 12.

Both parties to this litigation have relied on sections 602 and 610 of the new Illinois Marriage and Dissolution of Marriage Act (Ill.Rev.Stat.1977, ch. 40, pars. 602, 610), which provide:

> Sec. 602. Best interest of child.
>
> (a) The court shall determine custody in accordance with the best interest of the child. The court shall consider all relevant factors including.
>
> (1) the wishes of the child's parent or parents as to his custody;
>
> (2) the wishes of the child as to his custodian;
>
> (3) the interaction and interrelationship of the child with his parent or parents, his siblings and any other person who may significantly affect the child's best interest;
>
> (4) the child's adjustment to his home, school and community; and
>
> (5) the mental and physical health of all individuals involved.
>
> (b) The court shall not consider conduct of a present or proposed custodian that does not affect his relationship to the child.
>
> Sec. 610. Modification.
>
> (a) No motion to modify a custody judgment may be made earlier than 2 years after its date, unless the court permits it to be made on the basis of affidavits that there is reason to believe the child's present environment may endanger seriously his physical, mental, moral or emotional health.
>
> (b) The court shall not modify a prior custody judgment unless it finds, upon the basis of facts that have arisen since the prior judgment or that were unknown to the court at the time of entry of the prior judgment, that a change has occurred in the circumstances of the child or his custodian and that the modification is necessary to serve the best interest of the child. In applying these standards the court shall retain the custodian appointed pursuant to the prior judgment unless:
>
> ...
>
> (3) the child's present environment endangers seriously his physical, mental, moral or emotional health and the harm likely to be caused by a change of environment is outweighed by its advantages to him.
>
> ...

We note initially, however, that this appeal from the custody modification order was taken on August 11, 1977, two months before the effective date of the new act, and that the new act expressly provides that prior law shall govern such an appeal (Ill.Rev.Stat.1977, ch. 40, par. 801(d)). While the sections of the new act governing modification of custody orders require explicit findings..., we believe those sections in substance codify the prior decisional law, and that our decision in this appeal is not affected by the applicability or nonapplicability of the new act.

The standards applicable to petitions for modification of custody appearing in section 610(b) are substantially those to which Illinois courts have long adhered.

In *Nye v. Nye* (1952), 411 Ill. 408, 416, 105 N.E.2d 300, 304, this court said that a divorce decree "is *res judicata* as to the facts which existed at the time it was entered" and that "(n)ew conditions must have arisen to warrant the court changing its prior custody determination." Moreover, the guiding principle in custody adjudications is the best interests of the child (411 Ill. 408, 415, 105 N.E.2d 300) and the change in conditions must adversely affect the best interests of the child (411 Ill. 408, 416, 105 N.E.2d 300). The prior statute also directed the attention of the court to the interests of the child in custody adjudication.... Although prior Illinois decisions did not explicitly articulate the new act's command that no change be made in custody unless the harm inherent in any change in custody is outweighed by the advantages to the child of the new environment, they did recognize that continuity in the child's environment is in itself important.... Finally, the commands of sections 602 and 610 of the new act to consider only whether the child's environment endangers his physical, mental, moral and emotional health...and to disregard any conduct of the custodian that does not affect his relationship with the child...reemphasize the principle stated in *Nye v. Nye* (1952), 411 Ill. 408, 105 N.E.2d 300, that the focus of custody determinations must be the welfare of the child.

The chief issue in this case is whether a change of custody predicated upon the open and continuing cohabitation of the custodial parent with a member of the opposite sex is contrary to the manifest weight of the evidence in the absence of any tangible evidence of contemporaneous adverse effect upon the minor children. Considering the principles previously enunciated, and the statutory provisions, and prior decisions of the courts of this State, we conclude that under the facts in this case the trial court properly transferred custody of the Jarrett children from Jacqueline to Walter Jarrett.

The relevant standards of conduct are expressed in the statutes of this State: Section 11-8 of the Criminal Code of 1961...provides that "(a)ny person who cohabits or has sexual intercourse with another not his spouse commits fornication if the behavior is open and notorious." In *Hewitt v. Hewitt* (1979), 77 Ill.2d 49, 61–62, 31 Ill.Dec. 827, 394 N.E.2d 1204, we emphasized the refusal of the General Assembly in enacting the new Illinois Marriage and Dissolution of Marriage Act...to sanction any nonmarital relationships and its declaration of the purpose to "strengthen and preserve the integrity of marriage and safeguard family relationships"....

Jacqueline argues, however, that her conduct does not affront public morality because such conduct is now widely accepted, and cites 1978 Census Bureau statistics that show 1.1 million households composed of an unmarried man and woman, close to a quarter of which also include at least one child. This is essentially the same argument we rejected last term in *Hewitt v. Hewitt*..., and it is equally unpersuasive here. The number of people living in such households forms only a small percentage of the adult population, but more to the point, the statutory interpretation urged upon us by Jacqueline simply nullifies the fornication statute. The logical conclusion of her argument is that the statutory prohibitions are void as to those who believe the proscribed acts are not immoral, or, for one reason or another, need not be heeded. So stated, of course, the argument defeats itself. The rules which our society enacts for the governance of its members are not limited to those who agree with those rules they are equally binding on the dissenters. The fornication statute and the Illinois Marriage and Dissolution of Marriage Act evidence the relevant moral standards of this State, as declared by our legislature. The open and notorious limitation on the former's prohibitions reflects both a disinclination to criminalize purely private relationships and a recognition that open fornication represents a graver threat to public morality than private violations. Conduct of that nature, when it is open, not only violates the statutorily expressed moral standards of the State, but also encourages others to violate those standards, and debases public morality. While we agree that the statute does not penalize conduct which is essentially private and discreet..., Jacqueline's conduct has been neither, for she has discussed this relationship and her rationalization of it with at least her children, her former husband and her neighbors. It is, in our judgment, clear that her conduct offends prevailing public policy....

Jacqueline's disregard for existing standards of conduct instructs her children, by example, that they, too, may ignore them...and could well encourage the children to engage in similar activity in the future. That factor, of course, supports the trial court's conclusion that their daily presence in that environment was injurious to the moral well-being and development of the children.

It is true that, as Jacqueline argues, the courts have not denied custody to every parent who has violated the community's moral standards, nor do we now intimate a different rule. Rather than mechanically denying custody in every such instance, the courts of this State appraise the moral example currently provided and the example which may be expected by the parent in the future. We held in *Nye v. Nye* (1952), 411 Ill. 408, 415, 105 N.E.2d 300, that past moral indiscretions of a parent are not sufficient grounds for denying custody if the parent's present conduct establishes the improbability of such lapses in the future. This rule focuses the trial court's attention on the moral values which the parent is actually demonstrating to the children.

Since the decision in *Nye*, the appellate courts of this State have repeatedly emphasized this principle, particularly when the children were unaware of their parent's moral indiscretion.... At the time of this hearing, however, and even when this case was argued orally to this court, Jacqueline continued to cohabit with Wayne Hammon and had done nothing to indicate that this relationship would not continue in the future. Thus the moral values which Jacqueline currently represents to her children, and those which she may be expected to portray to them in the future, contravene statutorily declared standards of conduct and endanger the children's moral development.

...

Jacqueline also argues, and the appellate court agreed..., that the trial court's decision to grant custody of the children to Walter Jarrett was an improper assertion by the trial judge of his own personal moral beliefs. She further argues that the assertion of moral values in this case, as in *Hewitt v. Hewitt*..., is a task more appropriately carried out by the legislature. As pointed out earlier, however, it is the legislature which has established the standards she has chosen to ignore, and the action of the trial court merely implemented principles which have long been followed in this State.

The mother argues, too, that section 610 of the Illinois Marriage and Dissolution of Marriage Act...requires the trial court to refrain from modifying a prior custody decree unless it finds that the children have suffered actual tangible harm. The statute, however, directs the trial court to determine whether "the child's present environment *endangers* seriously his physical, mental, moral or emotional health." (Emphasis added.)(Ill.Rev.Stat.1977, ch. 40, par. 610(b)(3).) In some cases, particularly those involving physical harm, it may be appropriate for the trial court to determine whether the child is endangered by considering evidence of actual harm. In cases such as this one, however, such a narrow interpretation of the statute would defeat its purpose. At the time of the hearing the three Jarrett children, who were then 12, 10 and 7 years old, were obviously incapable of emulating their mother's moral indiscretions. To wait until later years to determine whether Jacqueline had inculcated her moral values in the children would be to await a demonstration that the very harm which the statute seeks to avoid had occurred. Measures to safeguard the moral well-being of children, whose lives have already been disrupted by the divorce of their parents, cannot have been intended to be delayed until there are tangible manifestations of damage to their character.

While our comments have focused upon the moral hazards, we are not convinced that open cohabitation does not also affect the mental and emotional health of the children. Jacqueline's testimony at the hearing indicated that when her children originally learned that Wayne Hammon would move in with them, they initially expected that she would marry him. It is difficult to predict what psychological effects or problems may later develop from their efforts to overcome the disparity between their concepts of propriety and their mother's conduct.... Nor will their attempts to adjust to this new environment occur in a vacuum. Jacqueline's domestic arrangements are known to her neighbors and their children; testimony at the hearing indicated that Wayne Hammon played with the Jarrett children and their friends at the Jarrett home and also engaged in other activities with them. If the Jarrett children remained in that situation, they might well be compelled to try to explain Hammon's presence to their friends and, perhaps, to endure their taunts and jibes. In a case such as this the trial judge must also weigh these imponderables, and he is not limited to examining the children for current physical manifestations of emotional or mental difficulties.

Finally, we do not believe that the United States Supreme Court's opinion in *Stanley v. Illinois* (1972), 405 U.S. 645, 92 S.Ct. 1208, 31 L.Ed.2d 551, requires a different result. In *Stanley* the Supreme Court found that Illinois statutes created a presumption that an unwed father is unfit to exercise custody over his children. The court held that depriving an unwed father of his illegitimate children without a prior hearing to determine his actual rather than presumptive unfitness, when the State accords that protection to other parents, deprives him of equal protection of the law.

The case before us is fundamentally different. The trial court did not presume that Jacqueline was not an adequate parent, as the juvenile court in effect did in *Stanley*. Rather the trial court recognized that the affection and care of a parent do not alone assure the welfare of the child if other conduct of the parent threatens the child's moral development. Since the evidence indicated that Jacqueline had not terminated the troublesome relationship and would probably continue it in the future, the trial court transferred custody to Walter Jarrett, an equally caring and affectionate parent whose conduct did not contravene the standards established by the General Assembly and earlier judicial decisions. Its action in doing so was not contrary to the manifest weight of the evidence.

...

GOLDENHERSH, Chief Justice, with whom THOMAS J. MORAN, Justice, joins, dissenting:

The majority states, "The chief issue in this case is whether a change of custody predicated upon the open and continuing cohabitation of the custodial parent with a member of the opposite sex is contrary to the manifest weight of the evidence in the absence of any tangible evidence of contemporaneous adverse effect upon the minor children." (78 Ill.2d at 345, 36 Ill.Dec. at 3, 400 N.E.2d at 423.) An examination of the opinion fails to reveal any other issue, and the effect of the decision is that the plaintiff's cohabitation with Hammon *per se* was sufficient grounds for changing the custody order previously entered. This record shows clearly that the children were healthy, well adjusted, and well cared for, and it should be noted that both the circuit and appellate courts made no finding that plaintiff was an unfit mother. The majority, too, makes no such finding and based its decision on a nebulous concept of injury to the children's "moral well-being and development." (78 Ill.2d at 347, 36 Ill.Dec. at 4, 400 N.E.2d at 424.) I question that any competent sociologist would attribute the increase of "live in" unmarried couples to parental example.

The fragility of its conclusion concerning "prevailing public policy" is demonstrated by the majority's reliance on cases decided by this court in 1852 (*Searls v. People*, 13 Ill. 597) and 1902 (*Lyman v. People*, 198 Ill. 544, 64 N.E. 974), and an appellate court decision (*People v. Potter* (1943), 319 Ill.App. 409, 49 N.E.2d 307) which, rather than "prevailing public policy," more clearly indicates the prejudice extant in that period against interracial sexual relations.

As the appellate court pointed out, the courts should not impose the personal preferences and standards of the judiciary in the decision of this case. Courts are uniquely equipped to decide legal issues and are well advised to leave to the theologians the question of the morality of the living arrangement into which the plaintiff had entered.

As a legal matter, simply stated, the majority has held that on the basis of her presumptive guilt of fornication, a Class B misdemeanor, plaintiff, although not declared to be an unfit mother, has forfeited the right to have the custody of her children. This finding flies in the face of the established rule that, in order to modify or amend an award of custody, the evidence must show that the parent to whom custody of the children was originally awarded is unfit to retain custody, or that a change of conditions makes a change of custody in their best interests. This record fails to show either. Mr. Justice Moran and I dissent and would affirm the decision of the appellate court.

MORAN, Justice, with whom GOLDENHERSH, Chief Justice, joins, dissenting:

I join in the dissent of the Chief Justice, but also dissent separately. My primary disagreement with the majority lies with its countenancing a change of custody based solely on a *conclusive presumption* that harm to the Jarrett children stemmed from Jacqueline's living arrangements. The majority purports to follow the Illinois Marriage and Dissolution of Marriage Act. Yet, under that act, only on the basis of fact can there be a finding that a change in circumstances has occurred and that modification of the prior custody judgment is necessary to serve the best interest of the children. [610(b)] The court is not to consider conduct of a custodian if that conduct does not affect his relationship to the child. [602(b)] In this case, not one scintilla of actual or statistical evidence of harm or danger to the children has been presented. To the contrary, all of the evidence of record, as related by the majority, indicates that under Jacqueline's custodianship the children's welfare and needs were met. Also, the trial court expressly declined to find Jacqueline unfit. Nevertheless, the majority's finding of a violation of the seldom-enforced fornification statute effectively foreclosed any further consideration of the custody issue. Instead of focusing solely on the best interest of the children — the "guiding star" (*Nye v. Nye* (1952), 411 Ill. 408, 415, 105 N.E.2d 300) — the majority has utilized child custody as a vehicle to punish Jacqueline for her "misconduct." Such selective enforcement of a statute is inappropriate and, especially in the child-custody context, unfortunate.

The majority decision also is at odds with the principle of *Stanley v. Illinois* (1972), 405 U.S. 645, 92 S.Ct. 1208, 31 L.Ed.2d 551. The constitutional infirmity of the statutory presumption in *Stanley* casts doubt on the validity of the judicially created conclusive presumption in this case. After *Stanley*, an unwed father may not be deprived of his illegitimate children without a prior hearing to determine his actual fitness. Similarly, Jacqueline should not be deprived of the children in the absence of evidence that a change is necessary to serve the best interest of the children. A hearing at which custody is determined on the basis of the conclusive presumption sanctioned by the majority amounts to no hearing at all.

JARRETT v. JARRETT

United States Supreme Court
449 U.S. 927 (1980)

[Writ of certiorari denied.]
Justice BRENNAN, with whom Justice MARSHALL joins, dissenting.

This petition raises the significant question whether the State may deprive a divorced mother of the custody of her children through operation of a conclusive presumption that her cohabitation with an unmarried adult male constitutes custody not in the best interests of the children, however strong the contrary evidence. Because the decision below conflicts with the import of relevant precedent of this Court, I dissent from the denial of a writ of certiorari.

. . .

The decision of the Illinois Supreme Court that, in effect, a divorced woman's ostensible violation of the Illinois fornication statute presumptively harmed the best interests of the children and that this was conclusive for purposes of custody presents a serious question under the Fourteenth Amendment. Giving conclusive effect to such a violation would appear to contravene the teaching of *Stanley v. Illinois*:

> It may be, as the State insists, that most unmarried fathers are unsuitable and neglectful parents. It may also be that Stanley is such a parent and that his children should be placed in other hands. But all unmarried fathers are not in this category; some are wholly suited to have custody of their children.... Given the opportunity to make his case, Stanley may have been seen to be deserving of custody of his offspring. *Id.*, at 654–655, 92 S.Ct., at 1214 (footnotes omitted).

I had supposed that *Stanley* established the proposition that "the interest of a parent in the companionship, care, custody, and management of his or her children," *id.*, at 651, 92 S.Ct., at 1212, cannot be determined by the evidentiary shortcut of a conclusive presumption. Thus, for purposes of this case, *Stanley* would seem to foreclose custody modification on the basis of a similar conclusive presumption of serious adverse effect on the children's best interests despite whatever contrary evidence may have been or might be adduced. This is particularly true since there is no rational basis for the conclusive presumption actually utilized, whether Jacqueline is viewed as having violated the fornication statute only or as being a lawbreaker generally.

Nothing in the record or in logic supports a conclusion that divorced parents who fornicate, for that reason alone, are unfit or adversely affect the well-being and development of their children in any degree over and above whatever adverse effect separation and divorce may already have had on the children. Illinois seldom, if ever, enforces its fornication statute and therefore can hardly contend that there is a rational correlation between divorced parents who fornicate and divorced parents who impair the healthy development of their children.

Nor can Jacqueline be presumed to have an adverse effect on her children's well-being because she is a lawbreaker, for surely such a presumption would be irrationally overbroad. It would make no sense to treat murder, fornication, and traffic violations similarly for purposes of custody and modification. If Illinois' enforcement record is an indication of how important it views violations of various laws, it appears that Illinois attempts to enforce its traffic laws more frequently than its "seldom-enforced fornication statute." 78 Ill.2d, at 352, 36 Ill.Dec., at 7, 400 N.E.2d, at 427 (Moran, J., dissenting). If Jacqueline had violated Illinois' traffic laws, she might have lost her driver's license, but surely not custody of her children.

Moreover, not only is there no basis for conclusively presuming that Jacqueline's cohabitation would adversely affect her children sufficiently to justify modification, but also any such conclusion is unequivocally rejected by the record which affirmatively shows that the "children were healthy, well adjusted, and well cared for." *Id.*, at 351, 36 Ill.Dec., at 6, 400 N.E.2d, at 426 (Goldenhersh, C. J., dissenting). There was no evidence of actual harm; nor was there evidence, statistical or otherwise, to suggest that the children's current exposure to their mother's cohabitation might result in harm to them that might become manifest only in the future. Surely, in any event, it is no more likely that divorced mothers who fornicate are unfit than are unwed fathers. Thus, this case squarely presents the question whether the Due Process Clause entitles Jacqueline to a meaningful hearing at which the trial judge determines, without use of a conclusive presumption, whether violation of the fornication statute adversely affects the well-being of the children.

Further, we should grant the petition and address the constitutional question it so clearly presents because the answer to that question has important implications for many households. The 1978 Census Bureau Statistics cited by the Illinois Supreme Court reveal that there are 1.1 million households composed of an unmarried man and woman and that upwards of 25% of those households also include at least one child. *Id.*, at 345, 36 Ill.Dec., at 4, 400 N.E.2d, at 424. While the statistics do not reveal how many of these households were formed after a divorce, and with respect to which the noncustodial divorced parent may be able to seek custody, the crude figures alone suggest that the custodial pattern is a pervasive one.

Accordingly, I dissent from the denial of certiorari and would grant the petition and set the case for oral argument.

COMMENTS

Seymour, McKay, and *Jarrett* present cumulative evidence of the persistent effect of traditional internal guidelines concerning the exercise of discretion in custody awards (see Comments to *Dinkel* and *Boroff,* p. 838). In spite of the appearance of sophistication and progressive language, the outcome in these cases was fairly predictable under traditional standards. This is particularly noticeable in *Seymour,* where the Supreme Court of Connecticut used a panoply of modern vocabulary, such as "nurturing parents," "psychological parents," and "parenting ability," to reach its decision to uphold the custody award favoring the mother. One wonders whether all this judicial reasoning was necessary to arrive at the quite possibly foregone conclusion. The elaborate procedure may in fact have been inspired by another purpose, namely, assuring the parties that they have had a fair hearing and that due process prevailed. Yet the hearing was largely ritualistic, with its show of seemingly plausible and progressive steps, such as the appointment of counsel for the minor child and seven trial days of extensive hearings with expert opinions by a psychiatric social worker, family relations officer, and two psychiatrists. Of these experts two favored the father, one the mother, and one felt it made no difference which parent was awarded custody. The trial court, predictably, favored the expert statement preferring the mother and, equally predictably, was upheld on appeal.

In searching for the reasons for the extensive procedure in *Seymour* and the need for progressive language, one has to remember the nature of the internal guidelines. Not only are they based in part on archaic conceptions that reflect strongly held social value preferences, but they are also often in the unconsciousness of the judge and the lawyers who, more likely than not, would deny their influence. In *Seymour* the court also faced, as it often does in initial joint custody awards, parents who were high on the socioeconomic scale. Probably none of the reasoning, nor the battery of expert statements, would have applied to parents from a lower stratum of society. Consequently, the arguments of the lawyers in the case, as well as the opinion of the appellate court, stayed on the same elevated plane. Merely rubber-stamp reasoning that the chancellor was closer to the facts and that his disposition was not to be disturbed would have been unacceptable to these parties and might have led eventually to further complications. One may note in passing that the guideline fundamentally favoring the mother was not all that was involved in *Seymour.* Although in the initial phases of the opinion the sex of the child was unspecified, the last paragraph finally disclosed it by repeated reference to the relationship between a mother and her daughter. Thus the opinion also follows the traditional expectation that a father, in a disputed case, has little chance of obtaining custody of girls. If one accepts the power of these predispositions, the layer of modern reasoning may seem to be mere surface.

McKay also upheld the trial judge in this instance favoring custody of the maternal grandparents over that of the father. This case involved some balancing of competing guidelines, yet the outcome here was also fairly predictable. The grandparents had cared for the children, two teenage daughters and one younger boy, prior to their mother's death. Thus the fundamental rule could be applied that, in case of doubt, the status quo in regard to children should not be disturbed. Another factor was only hinted at by the court, namely, that the father was a construction worker living in a trailer. Furthermore, the petitioning father had four children living with him: two from his new marriage and two step-children from an earlier marriage of his present wife. Awarding him custody of the three children from his former marriage would have created a household with seven children. Why then, the court seems to have felt, should the status quo be disturbed, bringing about crowded conditions and uncertain new adjustments? Yet even in this case progressive reasoning was invoked, giving weight to the stated preference of the children. It is of course conceivable that in time what is now a mere makeweight argument will gain in significance.

That the court in *Jarrett* followed traditional guidelines is not surprising considering that it involved Illinois, a jurisdiction noted for its conservatism in family law matters. The Supreme Court of Illinois referred prominently to its own earlier decision, *Hewitt v. Hewitt* (see p. 249), by which it rejected mere cohabitation as a basis for legal claims. The language of the court, referring to "paramours" and "indiscretions," is significant for discerning the social values preferred by the majority opinion. The behavior of the mother, who did not maintain decorum and who proselytized her beliefs in relations based on nonmarital love to her neighbors and her three daughters, was clearly no help to her. The court applied the guideline that moral misconduct by the mother, referred to as fornication, may negate the preference for custody she may otherwise have, especially if daughters of impressionable age are involved. It is implicit in the decision that the judicial censure of the mother, who chose to live with her "boyfriend," not only cost her the custody of the three daughters, but also had financial consequences — loss of support money and loss of the house. Thoughts of loss of social status and downward mobility may also have been involved. None of this reasoning, of course, is part of the appellate process. However, the tone of the opinion in *Jarrett* makes it apparent that the court approved of the punitive consequences of what it considered to be immoral behavior.

In re MARRIAGE OF THOMPSON

Supreme Court of Illinois

96 Ill.2d 67, 449 N.E.2d 88 (1983)

CLARK, Justice:

An order was entered in the circuit court of Coles County on May 6, 1981, dissolving the marriage of Kathryn Mae Thompson to John Delance Thompson. Kathryn Thompson appealed certain portions of the order and also asserted that the court should have deferred jurisdiction to a trial court in the State of Michigan. In her appeal Kathryn contended that the award of custody was contrary to the manifest weight of the evidence, the division of property was erroneous, the court erred in sustaining the objection to her offer of proof of petitioner's reputation, and the trial court erred in refusing to allow her to reopen her case.

The appellate court found that (a) the circuit court of Coles County acted properly in refusing to defer jurisdiction to a trial court in the State of Michigan; (b) the award of permanent custody to John Delance Thompson was not contrary to the manifest weight of the evidence or a breach of discretion; (c) there was no error in the division of property except for an apparent inadvertent omission of $371 that was due Kathryn Mae Thompson; (d) the trial court properly sustained the objection to the respondent's offer of proof of petitioner's reputation; and (e) the trial court did not abuse its discretion in refusing to reopen the case. 100 Ill.App.3d 1203, 57 Ill.Dec. 815, 429 N.E.2d 932 (Rule 23 order).

John and Kathryn Thompson were married on November 16, 1973, in Pontiac, Michigan. Thereafter, John Thompson took a position with McBride's Express in Decatur, Illinois. John and Kathryn were living in Decatur on April 18, 1977, when their only child, Daniel, was born. In August of 1977, when Daniel was approximately four months old, the family moved to Lerna, Illinois, where John accepted a position with the H & F Trucking Company.

On November 30, 1979, John told Kathryn that he had to leave town on business, when in fact he intended to spend the night in Collinsville, Illinois, with a female business associate. Kathryn was aware of what actually occurred and on December 1, 1979, she left Lerna with Daniel and left a note indicating that she was returning to her parents' home because her father was ill.

John constantly called to inquire about Kathryn and Daniel. Kathryn at first denied there were any marital problems, and she attempted to conceal her whereabouts and the whereabouts of the child.

On December 7, 1979, John filed a petition in the circuit court of Coles County for dissolution of marriage and for temporary custody of the child. In the petition it was alleged that the child had medical problems and it was in the best interest of Daniel that custody be awarded to the father. The petition was allowed, and an order was entered on December 7, 1979, granting temporary custody to the father.

John continued to call on a regular basis, trying to contact his wife or her parents, in order to determine the condition and whereabouts of his son. On December 10, 1979, John retained the services of an investigative agency.

Following a short stay at her parents' home Kathryn moved with Daniel to a home for battered women in Saginaw, Michigan. On December 12, 1979, Kathryn filed for and was granted temporary custody of her son in the circuit court for Saginaw County in the State of Michigan.

On December 30, 1979, the investigator John had hired notified John that he had located Kathryn and Daniel. John arranged to fly to Michigan, with the court order in hand, to obtain physical custody of his son. John forcibly abducted his son from Kathryn on a street in Saginaw, Michigan, placed Daniel in the detective's car and proceeded to the investigator's home. At that time he called the Saginaw police department as well as Kathryn's attorney in Michigan to notify them of the situation. John denies that he knew then that there was a court order giving custody of Danny to Kathryn. The investigator indicated that his employees had attempted to discover if there was a court proceeding pending concerning custody, but that they had failed to discover anything.

The investigator, Robert Swartwood, testified as to Danny's physical condition at the time the child was picked up in Saginaw.

According to Mr. Swartwood, Danny was without mittens, his cheeks were windburned, he had a cold with a deep cough, he had a small bruise under one eye, and that eye was constantly tearing. The investigator's wife, who was present when Danny was found, testified that she also examined Danny at the time and found chapped lips, tearing in one eye, and a runny nose.

After John took Danny from Kathryn, he traveled back to the family home in Lerna, Illinois. Upon arriving back in Lerna, John took Danny to see a doctor on three successive days; antibiotics and eardrops were prescribed. According to John, Danny's right ear was inflamed, his left ear was full of wax, and when spoken to by his father he had trouble hearing him. Further ear surgery was required in March of 1980.

Following the father's and son's arrival back in Lerna, John went back to work for H & F Trucking Company. He and Danny continued to live in the same home in Lerna that had been the marital residence.

In January of 1980, John began seeing a woman by the name of Betty Coffman. Ms. Coffman and John saw each other regularly for the next five months, with Ms. Coffman frequently spending weekends at John's home. During two of those months John also had a cousin by the name of Kenneth Dolson living in the house. Ms. Coffman testified that during her weekend visits she slept with John, and that she took the same care of Danny that she took with her own two children. Ms. Coffman indicated that Danny always had the sniffles, coughed frequently and had ear trouble. She further testified that she would change his diapers, cook his meals, and change and wash his clothes. Ms. Coffman testified on cross-examination that John was a good, loving father who looked after the medical and other needs of his child. She also testified that John and she talked on several occasions prior to the custody hearing and on one such occasion, according to Ms. Coffman, John reminded her that "I [John] have some pictures and don't forget there is a custody hearing coming up." Ms. Coffman indicated that the pictures John was referring to were nude pictures of Ms. Coffman that John had taken when they were seeing one another.

Ms. Coffman also testified that John came to her house in West Terre Haute, Indiana, one evening and that she would not open the door. John said he wanted to talk with her. She would not talk to him because she was afraid of him. John said that he would be back and that she had not seen the last of him. Ms. Coffman swore out a warrant for John's arrest which is still pending; John did not return. Ms. Coffman indicated that she broke off the relationship with John because he was seeing another woman.

Soon after John and Danny returned to the home in Lerna, John made arrangements for Danny's day care at the home of Virginia Sons.

Mrs. Sons testified that when she first met Danny he was insecure, clinging, and sickly. She also testified that he tired easily and had colds, which included ear infections. She further found that he was undisciplined, not potty-trained, and had poor eating habits. She felt he was overweight, withdrawn and in need of special attention. Her husband, Gerald Sons, testified that when he first saw Danny he was insecure, sickly, cried a lot and was a picky eater. Mrs. Sons felt that she saw dramatic changes in Danny within the first six months that John had Danny. She testified that Danny was less susceptible to colds, that he did not tire as easily, and that his ear infections cleared up. She observed him become comfortable, more stable and secure. She observed a happy little boy, glad to see his father. Mrs. Sons testified that John's attitude towards his son was very good, that he (John) was a concerned, responsive parent, and that as a result the child slimmed down and appeared to be very content.

Virginia's husband, Gerald Sons, testified that, during the period of time in 1980 when he was around the boy, Danny's emotional condition improved and he was well adjusted. Mr. Sons felt that John was conscientious and observed John and Danny kissing and hugging on many occasions.

Kathryn's first effort to contact Danny occurred on January 25, 1980, almost four weeks after John had brought him back home. Kathryn talked to Danny on the telephone on March 9, 1980. Kathryn admitted, under cross-examination, that she did not inquire about Danny between January 25, 1980, and March 9, 1980. Kathryn did not make any direct calls to John or to Danny or visit Danny between March 9, 1980, and a visitation which occurred in November of 1980.

Around Easter of 1980, Kathryn sent an Easter card to Danny and again around his birthday in April she sent a birthday card and doll. She sent another card in July of 1980. The final written communication occurred near Thanksgiving of 1980, when she sent a Thanksgiving card.

On July 1, 1980, Kathryn appeared in the circuit court of Coles County and testified for the purpose of obtaining an order for a preliminary injunction against John disposing of any property and, while in Coles County, made no effort to contact Danny.

Kathryn asserts that she did not contact Danny because her previous attorney advised her not to speak with John. Danny was not capable of picking up the phone at that time. Kathryn also asserts that she was afraid of John and, therefore, did not visit Danny as often as she would have liked.

Jesse Thompson was a friend and co-worker of John Thompson at the H & F Trucking Company. He testified that he saw a significant improvement in Danny's health and that he (Jesse) observed a very warm and loving father-son relationship.

Mr. James Collin, a contractor who was working on renovations in John's home, testified that during that spring and summer of 1980 he observed Danny as a normal child and that Danny and John often would sit and play the banjo and games together and that they seemed to have a good relationship.

Kathy Bean, operator of a local restaurant in Mattoon, came to know John and Danny Thompson as customers. She testified that during that spring and summer she observed a child who became more sure of himself as time went on, and that he seemed polite, clean and well adjusted. She described him as "a very robust, shining little boy." She believed that John was crazy about Danny.

Reverend Richard Anderson came to know John and Danny through the Loxa Presbyterian Church in Mattoon. According to Rev. Anderson they attended services from January through June of 1980, and he felt John was conscientious about Danny's proper religious training and that John and Danny exhibited a sincere and caring attitude towards one another.

One neighbor who knew John and Kathryn when they were residing together in Lerna testified that Kathryn had told her on one occasion that she would be glad when Danny got bigger because it was hard for her to cope with a little baby. John also testified as to Kathryn's supervision of the child. According to John, on one occasion he found Daniel unsupervised in the yard playing with scissors, and on another occasion unattended in the bathtub. John also testified that Kathryn would punish Danny for crying.

Barbara Hart testified that on one occasion Danny was left crying for about 45 minutes until he finally fell asleep. Ms. Hart also indicated that during the summer and early fall of 1979, Danny was overwrought, wore ill-fitting clothing and improperly pinned diapers, and ate food not properly prepared.

Ms. Hart also testified as to Danny's condition when John and Danny returned to Lerna. Ms. Hart observed a change in Danny. She testified that he came out of his shell, that his clothes fit, and that he was properly dressed.

John testified that he continued his employment with H & F Trucking until June of 1980 at which time he accepted employment with Advance Transport in Effingham, Illinois. There was also testimony from John's employer at H & F Trucking that, while John resigned, he (John) sought to return to H & F Trucking before he accepted employment with Advance Transport, but he was not rehired. The employer at H & F Trucking testified that John took various salvage items and distributed them amongst his friends.

He worked for Advance Transport until August of 1980 and, thereafter, began employment with Complete Auto Transport in October, where he was employed at the time of the hearing.

At the time of the hearing, John and Danny lived in Highland, Illinois, in a ten-year-old, three-bedroom home on approximately one acre of land. According to John, a hospital and daycare center were nearby and he had made arrangements for Danny to begin kindergarten. John testified that he has seen to the proper religious education of Danny.

According to John he has spent all of his time, when not at work, with Danny.

The appellate court, in a Rule 23 order, found that because the counsel for Kathryn did not raise the issue timely, the issue of whether the circuit court of Coles County had improperly exercised its jurisdiction had been waived. While we do not deem a question of jurisdiction to be waived, we do find that the circuit court acted properly in rejecting an untimely request for deferral to a trial court in Michigan.

Counsel did not ask the circuit court to consider deferring the case until closing arguments were being made on January 21, 1981, more than a year after the case had begun.

The Uniform Child Custody Jurisdiction Act (Ill.Rev.Stat. 1979, ch. 40, par. 2101 *et seq.*) provides guidelines to avoid conflict and competition with courts of other States in determining matters of child custody. We agree with the appellate court that one of the purposes of the Act is to assure that litigation concerning the custody of a child takes place in the State in which the child and his or her family have the closest connection. Another is to deter abductions and other unilateral removals of children undertaken to obtain custody awards. Ill.Rev.Stat.1979, ch. 40, pars. 2102(3), (5).

Section 4(a)(1) of the Act (Ill.Rev.Stat.1979, ch. 40, par. 2104(a)(1)) provides that the circuit courts have "jurisdiction" to make a child-custody determination if the State is the home State of the child at the time of the commencement of the proceeding or had been the child's home State within six months before commencement of the proceeding. However, section 9 also provides that "[i]f the petitioner for an initial judgment has wrongfully taken the child from another state or has engaged in similar reprehensible conduct the court *may* decline to exercise jurisdiction if this is just and proper under the circumstances." (Emphasis added.) Ill.Rev.Stat.1979, ch. 40, par. 2109(a).

We strongly disapprove of John's conduct in forcibly obtaining physical custody of Danny from Kathryn in Michigan and returning him to Illinois. John maintains he used diligence to determine whether any Michigan court had ruled on the child's custody. Regardless, like the appellate court, we deem John's actions to be the type of conduct section 9(a) was designed to prevent. The aggrieved spouse is able to request the forum State to decline to exercise jurisdiction so that the wrongful obtaining of custody will not determine the forum for the decision. Had counsel for Kathryn made such a request here, before the court heard the case on the merits in its entirety, she may have had a valid claim. However, no such request was made in the trial court until the closing arguments on January 21, 1981, more than a year later.

We therefore find that because counsel for Kathryn failed to request deference to the Michigan courts prior to the commencement of this proceeding, and since the merits of this case had been heard prior to the request that deference be entertained by the circuit court of Coles County, the court properly rejected such a consideration.

We now ask if the custody award by the trial judge was against the manifest weight of the evidence. We have recited at length the testimony at trial, and we feel that a lengthy commentary on that testimony is not called for here.

The respondent, Kathryn Thompson, argues that *Jarrett v. Jarrett* (1979), 78 Ill.2d 337, 36 Ill.Dec. 1, 400 N.E.2d 421, strongly supports her contention that she should be awarded the child. The respondent asserts that the appellate court ignored the mandate of *Jarrett* in not addressing the "moral transgressions" of John. *Jarrett v. Jarrett* (1979), 78 Ill.2d 337, 36 Ill.Dec. 1, 400 N.E.2d 421, is authority for the proposition that a child should be placed with the parent who can best serve that child. The *Jarrett* case does not establish a conclusive presumption that, because a custodial parent cohabits with a member of the opposite sex, the child is harmed. No such presumption exists in this State. The court in *Jarrett* indicated that a custody award is not arrived at by pressing one lever and mechanically denying custody to one parent; rather all of the circumstances must be considered that affect the best interests of the child. *Jarrett v. Jarrett* (1979), 78 Ill.2d 337, 344–45, 36 Ill.Dec. 1, 400 N.E.2d 421; Ill.Rev.Stat.1979, ch. 40, par. 602.

A considerable number of witnesses testified on behalf of petitioner indicating Danny was sickly, undisciplined and overweight prior to coming into John's custody, and that thereafter Danny improved, and a warm, loving relationship developed between the father and the son.

That is not to say we condone all of the father's conduct. We do not. We recall Ms. Coffman's testimony that the petitioner threatened to reveal pictures of her in the nude if she testified against him. While such evidence troubles us a great deal, we have determined that such conduct is outweighed by the evidence presented which demonstrates that a healthy relationship existed between father and son and that Danny was doing well in his father's custody.

Based upon our exhaustive review of the evidence, we find that there has been no showing that the trial court judge abused his discretion in awarding custody of Danny to his father.

The respondent also contends that she should have been permitted to reopen the case prior to the entry of the judgment in the case but after the proofs were closed, in order to allow her to introduce evidence concerning petitioner's reputation.

In not reopening the case to receive additional evidence, the respondent contends that the trial court abused its discretion. The respondent offers no support for her position, and we find none. The trial court did not abuse its discretion.

We further uphold the appellate court's judgment respecting the property division, including its remand of the cause to the circuit court of Coles County to require the petitioner to pay to respondent one-half of a tax-refund check in the sum of $742 that was due respondent. John had previously forged Kathryn's name on the back of the check and cashed it. He does not presently dispute that Kathryn was entitled to receive $371 of the proceeds of that check.

The respondent did not contest in this court the appellate court's approval of the circuit court's sustaining of the objection to her offer of proof of the petitioner's reputation.

Accordingly, the judgment of the appellate court is affirmed.

Judgment affirmed.

MORAN, Justice, specially concurring:

I concur in the judgment reached by the majority; however, I do not concur in the statement "The *Jarrett* case does *not* establish a conclusive presumption that, because a custodial parent cohabits with a member of the opposite sex, the child is harmed." (Emphasis added.)(96 Ill.2d at 78, 70 Ill.Dec. at 219, 449 N.E.2d at 93.) In my opinion, *Jarrett* did establish a conclusive presumption. See the dissent in *Jarrett v. Jarrett* (1979), 78 Ill.2d 337, 352–53, 36 Ill.Dec. 1, 400 N.E.2d 421 (Moran, J., and Goldenhersh, C.J., dissenting), and also the dissent of Justice Brennan, joined by Justice Marshall, from denial of the writ of certiorari in *Jarrett v. Jarrett* (1980), 449 U.S. 927, 101 S.Ct. 329, 66 L.Ed.2d 155.

UNDERWOOD, Justice, dissenting:

I believe the trial judge abused his discretion in denying the mother's prejudgment motion to reopen the proofs and present additional evidence.

The majority opinion notes the father's illicit affairs, abduction of Danny, and threats to the potential witness, but does not mention several other matters which, if true, seem to me quite significant. It is asserted that the father has two children by a prior marriage, a daughter whom he has not seen in nine years and a son whom he has never seen; that he is under a court order to pay $100 weekly for their support; that since the hearing he has lost the employment he held at that time; and that he has instituted bankruptcy proceedings. Certainly proof of these facts would be persuasive on the questions of custody and the father's ability to support the child.

The dissenting appellate court justice believed the trial court's award of custody to the father was contrary to the manifest weight of the evidence, a position with which I am inclined to agree. The mother denied or gave rational explanations for the occurrences recited by the majority in support of the result it reaches. For example, the absence of mittens was due to the fact that they were torn from the boy's hands during the struggle at the time he was abducted by the father. The absence of more frequent contacts by the mother was due, she testified, to her attorney's advice and her fear of the father, a fear shared by at least one of the father's sexual partners.

I believe the additional evidence the mother seeks to offer may well tip the scales more clearly in her favor. Consequently, I would reverse the circuit and appellate courts and remand the cause to the circuit court for reconsideration in the light of such additional evidence as may be presented.

GOLDENHERSH, J., joins in this dissent.

ROE v. ROE

Supreme Court of Virginia
228 Va. 722, 324 S.E.2d 691 (1985)

RUSSELL, Justice.

This child-custody dispute presents the question whether a child's best interests are promoted by an award of custody to a parent who carries on an active homosexual relationship in the same residence as the child. We conclude that such an arrangement is not in the child's best interests and that an award of custody to such a parent constitutes an abuse of judicial discretion.

Catherine Roe, the mother, and David Roe, the father, (fictitious surnames), were married in 1971. Their only child, a daughter, was born in 1974. The parents separated in 1975 and entered into a property settlement agreement which granted full custody of the child to the mother. The trial court entered a final decree of divorce on "no-fault" grounds in 1976, confirming and incorporating the agreement.

The child remained with the mother until December 1978, when the father took over her care because the mother had become afflicted with cancer, requiring extensive surgery and medical treatment. In the fall of 1979, he petitioned the court for a change of the child's custody to him. The mother opposed the change, acknowledging that the father had assisted her with the child's care on an informal basis, but stating that she was recovering from her illness, had returned to work, and would be ready to assume full-time care of the child by March 1980. In October 1979, however, the parties presented to the court a consent decree which recited that the mother was still physically unable to care for the child, awarded custody to the father, and reserved reasonable visitation rights to the mother. The child has remained in the father's custody to the present time, frequently visiting with her mother.

In July 1983, the mother filed a petition for a temporary restraining order in which she alleged that it had just come to her attention that the father was living with a man who was his homosexual lover, that the two men occupied the same bed in a bedroom in the house in which the father lived with the child, that the child had reported seeing the two men "hugging and kissing and sleeping in bed together," and that other homosexuals visited the home and engaged in similar behavior in the child's presence. The mother further alleged that the child, then nine years of age, was unhappy in the father's home, "hate[d]" the father's lover, and had expressed a desire to return to her mother. The mother contended that she was sufficiently recovered to care for the child full time and wished to do so. The petition asked for a temporary restraining order which would enjoin the father from exercising his custody rights and leave the child in the mother's care until a hearing could be held on the mother's allegations. The petition concluded with a prayer for a change of permanent custody to the mother. The court entered an order leaving the child with the mother on "visitation" until August 25, 1983, continuing the case to that date for determination, and directing both parties to submit to psychological evaluations.

After hearing the evidence, the court entered a custody order granting "joint, legal custody" of the child to the father and mother. The order provided that the child was to live with the father during the school year and with the mother during the summer vacation, and provided for extensive visitation by each parent when the child was living with the other. The order conditioned the father's custody upon his "not sharing the same bed or bedroom with any male lover or friend while the child is present in the home." We granted an appeal to the mother.

The trial court found that there was little animosity between the parents. Aside from the central issue pervading this case, each parent had been a fit, devoted, and competent custodian. The court interviewed the little girl and found that she was a "very lovely, outgoing, bright and intelligent child...a very happy child [who] seemed to be well adjusted and outgoing." The court found that there was no evidence that the father's conduct had an adverse effect on the child, but that she did express a wish to live with her mother.

The father openly admitted that he was living in an active homosexual relationship, sharing a bed and bedroom with a male friend in the same house with the child. The father's lover testified as a witness in order, the father says, that the trial court could ascertain that he was a person of good character whose influence in the home would not be harmful to the child.

The father and his male friend both testified that they did not "flaunt" their homosexuality. The court, however, observed:

> this relationship of sharing the same bed or bedroom with the child being in the home would be one of the greatest degrees of flaunting that one could imagine. It flies in the face of *Brown v. Brown* [218 Va. 196, 237 S.E.2d 89 (1977)], and it flies in the face of society's mores anyway.

Apparently for this reason, the court conditioned the partial award of custody to the father on the requirement that he and his lover not share the same bed or bedroom.

The court expressed concern as to the behavior of the father and his friends in the child's presence, making particular reference to males hugging and "patting each other on the behind." Noting that football players are sometimes seen to do such things, the court stated:

> Whether the Court would find them distasteful or not, it is simply not something that the Court is competent to get involved in...all of these things require such judgment as to appropriateness or inappropriateness that the Court is simply not going to try and get involved in it.

The court also expressed concern as to "what happens when the child turns twelve or thirteen, for example, when she begins dating or wants to have slumber parties, how does she explain this conduct." Conceding that these things might "pose a problem" in the future, the court decided that they were not immediate concerns and could be dealt with when and if they arose, by a change of custody if necessary.

We agree with the trial court's observation that the father's conduct "flies in the face of *Brown v. Brown*" as well as "society's mores." In *Brown*, we affirmed a chancellor's decision to remove the custody of two young sons, ages seven and four, from their mother, who was otherwise a fit custodian, on the sole ground that she was openly living in an adulterous relationship with a male lover, in the same home as the children, during the pendency of the divorce suit. There, we said:

> In all custody cases the controlling consideration is always the child's welfare and, in determining the best interest of the child, the court must decide by considering all the facts, including what effect a nonmarital relationship by a parent has on the child. The moral climate in which children are to be raised is an important consideration for the court in determining custody,

> and adultery is a reflection of a mother's moral values. An illicit relationship to which minor children are exposed cannot be condoned. Such a relationship must necessarily be given the most careful consideration in a custody proceeding.

218 Va. at 199, 237 S.E.2d at 91. We also quoted with approval from *Beck v. Beck*, 341 So.2d 580 (La.App.1977): "[W]here the mother has recently lived in open and public adultery with her paramour for a substantial period of time, in total disregard of the moral principles of our society, the mother is generally held morally unfit for custody." *Id.* Our decision, however, was not based upon the mother's adulterous relationship in the abstract, but rather on the fact that it was conducted in the children's presence. It was Mrs. Brown's exposure of the children to an immoral and illicit relationship which rendered her an unfit and improper person to have their custody.

Here, the father relies heavily upon *Doe v. Doe*, 222 Va. 736, 284 S.E.2d 799 (1981). His reliance is misplaced. *Doe* was not a custody case but was a disputed adoption. There, a divorced couple had a seven-year-old son who resided in Virginia with his father and stepmother. The father had an award of permanent custody which the mother did not contest. The mother lived in Ohio in an open lesbian relationship with another woman. The child was permitted to visit her periodically, but the propriety of such visitation rights was not before us in the adoption case. When the father and stepmother petitioned for an adoption, the trial court granted the petition over the mother's objection, on the ground that her consent was withheld contrary to the best interests of the child. We reversed, noting the difference between custody determinations, which are *ad hoc* and subject to change upon changing conditions, and adoptions, which are final and irrevocable. Although we declined to hold that every lesbian mother or homosexual father is *per se* an unfit *parent*, we were not presented, in *Doe*, with the question of the impact of a homosexual relationship upon a child in the context of day-to-day custody. We refused to terminate all parental rights of the lesbian mother in *Doe*, but we stopped far short of finding her a fit and proper custodian for her son, or even of approving his visitations in her home, while her existing living arrangements continued.

The present case is controlled by *Brown*. The father's continuous exposure of the child to his immoral and illicit relationship renders him an unfit and improper custodian as a matter of law. Indeed, the mother contends that the influences to which the child is exposed here are far more deleterious than those in *Brown*. She points out that, as an illustration of the relative degree of abhorrence by which our society regards such conduct, adultery is a class four misdemeanor in Virginia (Code §18.2-365) which is seldom prosecuted, while the conduct inherent in the father's relationship is punishable as a class six felony (Code §18.2-361) which is prosecuted with considerable frequency and vigor, as evidenced by the decided cases annotated under those respective sections in the Code. However that may be, we have no hesitancy in saying that the conditions under which this child must live daily are not only unlawful but also impose an intolerable burden upon her by reason of the social condemnation attached to them, which will inevitably afflict her relationships with her peers and with the community at large. See *Jacobson v. Jacobson*, 314 N.W.2d 78 (N.D.1981); *M.J.P. v. J.G.P.*, 640 P.2d 966 (Okla.1982); and *Kallas v. Kallas*, 614 P.2d 641 (Utah 1980). The father's unfitness is manifested by his willingness to impose this burden upon her in exchange for his own gratification.

The trial court was, as stated above, seriously concerned as to the impact of the father's conduct upon the child, but took the position that its worst features could be allayed by ordering him out of his lover's bedroom. We are not so persuaded. The child's awareness of the nature of the father's illicit relationship is fixed and cannot be dispelled. The open behavior of the father and his friends in the home can only be expected to continue. The impact of such behavior upon the child, and upon any of her peers who may visit the home, is inevitable. We conclude that the best interests of the child will only be served by protecting her from the burdens imposed by such behavior, insofar as practicable. In the circumstances of this case, this necessitates not only a change of custody to the mother, but also a cessation of any visitations in the father's home, or in the presence of his homosexual lover, while his present living arrangements continue.

We will, accordingly, reverse the order appealed from and enter a decree here, vesting sole custody in the mother. The cause will be remanded to the trial court for the entry of further orders providing for reasonable visitation rights to the father, conditioned as set forth above.

Reversed and remanded.

M.P. v. S.P.

Superior Court of New Jersey
169 N.J. Super. 425, 404 A.2d 1256 (1979)

ANTELL, J. A. D.

Defendant (former wife) was awarded a divorce for sexual cruelty by judgment dated September 11, 1969 after a six-year marriage from which two children were born, Franceen, (fictitious name) on June 8, 1964 and Joy (fictitious name) on July 15, 1968. She received custody of the daughters, and until the determination before us for review they have always resided with their mother, a period of about seven years after the divorce.

On May 20, 1975 the Chancery Division ordered defendant to show cause why custody of the children should not be transferred to plaintiff on the ground that defendant "is an unfit mother." The order was signed on plaintiff's application, his first since the judgment of divorce. After a number of hearings, the last of which was on January 22, 1976, the trial judge, by letter opinion dated August 30, 1976, awarded custody to the father.... Defendant appeals on the ground that the trial judge erred in modifying the judgment and divesting her of custody.

Central to this appeal is the fact that defendant is an admitted practicing homosexual. She argues that the action below was taken because of this fact alone and is therefore not legally sustainable. Plaintiff expressly disavows any claim that defendant is an unfit mother by reason of her homosexuality. He concedes that her right to custody of the children cannot be denied, limited or restricted on the basis of her sexual orientation alone a proposition with which we are in accord. *In re J. S. & C.*, 129 N.J.Super. 486, 489, 324 A.2d 90 (Ch.Div.1974), *aff'd* 142 N.J.Super. 499, 362 A.2d 54 (App.Div.1976). Furthermore, compatibly with the uncontradicted expert testimony, plaintiff disclaims being concerned with "any threat that the childrens' sexual development will be in any way altered by the fact that defendant is a homosexual." Rather, he relies for affirmance exclusively upon a claim of changed circumstances since the date of the original custody award such that the best interests of the children dictate modification of that determination.

At the outset it is noted that the trial judge made no finding, nor in any way concerned himself with the issue, of changed circumstances.

The evidence discloses that from the beginning this marriage was afflicted by sexual discord. Although the record is burdened with detailed testimony in which each party blames the other for their disastrous relationship, much is irrelevant except to demonstrate that at least from the time of their separation in 1967 plaintiff has been aware of defendant's homosexual propensities. As he knew when they separated, defendant was involved in an affair with another woman (Barbara), one which continued through and beyond the date of the divorce.

After the divorce defendant moved into a small apartment and plaintiff exercised weekly visitation rights with respect to the older daughter, Franceen, but refused to acknowledge Joy as his child. He persisted in this refusal, failing even to visit her when she was hospitalized, until adjudicated the father and ordered to pay for her support. It was as a result of defendant's persuasion that he eventually included Joy in his visits.

On October 14, 1970 defendant voluntarily admitted herself to Ancora State Hospital to be treated for a depressive neurosis. Plaintiff made no attempt to obtain custody at that time, and the daughters were cared for by defendant's parents. After defendant left the hospital on December 17, 1970 she and the girls lived with her parents until the summer of 1974. During this time defendant worked fulltime and attended counseling sessions.

In the fall of 1974, Joy developed emotional problems that impaired her learning abilities,[2] and defendant reduced her work to a part-time basis. She observed Joy's work in school, met frequently with her teachers, met with the school psychologist and helped with remediating Joy's motor coordination skills. The child was also enrolled in a county guidance center where mother and daughter attended sessions together, and Joy was thereafter returned to regular classes.

The evidence shows that defendant has been equally concerned with the needs of Franceen.

In late 1974, upon the advice of school officials, defendant and the girls left the household where they had been residing. For three months thereafter they resided with "Joyce," defendant's lesbian companion. This arrangement was unworkable, however, since Joyce lived in a school district different from where defendant's daughters were enrolled. Therefore, in the interests of her children defendant returned to her parents' home. During the foregoing period defendant and Joyce slept apart and the children had their own room.

No specific findings were made in connection therewith, but the record is uncontradicted that defendant is an attentive mother who fed and dressed her children well, provided them with medical and dental care, and arranged for surgery, allergy tests and orthodonture. She has done all that can be expected of a dutiful mother.

Although he determined to alter the custody arrangement, the trial judge found that defendant was "a very warm, loving mother," that she "cares for her children and generally within her means, at least at a level deemed minimally adequate, has provided for them." Recognizing, however, that plaintiff was "equally concerned" with the children, the judge decided to "examine into the question of homosexuality as a disqualifying effect on a parent."

---

2. Nowhere in the evidence is it suggested that this happened because of any fault on the part of defendant.

The trial judge apparently weighed against defendant the fact that she was caught up "in an attempt to find her own identity and to deal with the problems" arising from her sexual status. However, he did not explain what problems he had in mind or in what way her problems or her quest for identity were different from those of most ordinary people; more importantly, he made no attempt to articulate a relationship between any of this and the welfare of the children. The judge also noted that defendant's ongoing liaison with her lesbian companion had "materially upset the older child and will have a slight influence in all probability, from the credible evidence, on the younger child." On an earlier occasion the judge had ordered that defendant not share Joyce's company at any time when the children were present, and this order has not been violated. Furthermore, there is nothing in the record to show any nexus between defendant's sexual companionship and the older girl's reaction.

Nowhere do we find documented in the record any specific instances of sexual misconduct by defendant or evidence that she tried in any way to inculcate the girls with her sexual attitudes. To the contrary, the evidence is affirmatively to the effect that she never displayed any sexual behavior in the presence of her children, and that she refrains from any demonstration of affection toward other women when the girls are present. Moreover, she is not a member of any homosexual organization. As we said in *De Vita v. De Vita*, 145 N.J.Super. 120, 366 A.2d 1350 (App.Div.1976):

> When dealing with custody the burden of proof required to show that a mother is guilty of gross sexual misconduct to the detriment of her children is a heavy one....

It is well settled that the best interests of the child are of primary concern to the court in any matter involving the custody of minor children.... Since the conditions which would satisfy the best interests of a child during all of its minority cannot be conclusively determined in a single decree, custody orders are always held to be modifiable upon a showing of changed circumstances that would affect the welfare of the child.... The party seeking the modification bears the burden of showing sufficient changed circumstances so as to require modification....

In assessing a claim of changed circumstances deference is given to the length and stability of the existing custody relationship.... The potential for damage which resides in removing a child from its psychological parent has been recognized in a number of cases....

Not only did plaintiff offer no proof to meet this formidable burden, but, as we noted earlier, the trial judge made no findings which pointed to a change of circumstances. The only conclusion to be drawn is, as defendant claims, that the custody order was modified for the sole reason that she is a homosexual and without regard to the welfare of the children. This conclusion gains added support from our further analysis of the record and the determinations before us for review.

In awarding custody to plaintiff the trial judge did so on the reasoning that plaintiff

> ...may provide a more stable atmosphere for the custody, maintenance and welfare of these children. His home is more stable. He is financially secure and is able to provide the children with the best type of care, custody, maintenance and it is in their best interest that the Court feels that custody should reside in the father.

However, absent from the record is any factual basis for the judge's belief that the father's home is more stable than the defendant's or that he is "financially secure and is able to provide the children with the best type of care, custody, maintenance...." Actually, at the time of the hearing plaintiff was in arrears on his child support obligations in the amount of almost $5,000, a fact which has caused defendant to apply for welfare assistance. When asked by the trial judge why he had not been making the payments, he explained only, "I imagine it is a combination of things," and stated that support would be "easier having the children with you."[3] As to his sincerity of purpose in seeking custody, we note again that plaintiff initially denied that he was Joy's father, and in the course of the judicial proceedings which followed he admittedly testified falsely in denying that he had had sexual relations with defendant during certain critical times. The inference is at least reasonable that if defendant had not brought proceedings in aid of execution to compel plaintiff to meet his support obligations, plaintiff's custody application would not have been made.

Nor are we shown any factual support for the trial judge's evident belief that the children are being harmed or are likely to be harmed by continued custody with defendant.... The only findings offered for this purpose are that defendant's homosexuality has "affected" Franceen; that it has "materially upset" her, and that it "will have a slight influence in all probability" on Joy. Against this the report of Dr. Yaskin, the psychiatrist appointed by the court at the recommendation of plaintiff's attorney, concludes that the younger child, Joy,

> ...is seriously in need of her mother's continuing emotional support. Her ongoing deep identification and dependency is with the mother and it is my clinical opinion that any attempt, at this time, to separate [Joy] from her mother will result in serious psychological consequences to the child.

Reporting on Franceen he comments that she is "rather well poised" and "that she has no ongoing emotional or behavioral problems." Further,

> ...[T]here is no question that she loves her mother. She states, without hesitation, that her mother has always shown an adequate concern re the nutrition and their dress. [sic] She also states her mother has always been kind to her and has never abused her. She adds, "I know she loves me." I asked her if there was anything in her ongoing relationship with her mother that she objected to and she answers, "No — mother is a good person."

Dr. Yaskin took account of Franceen's expressed desire to live with her father, but concluded that her reasons were "puerile," *i.e.*, that she could "go fishing and everything" with her cousins who lived nearby; that she feels sorry for her father sometimes, and that she has feelings of affection for her baby step-brother. The doctor found that Franceen had no "real ongoing concern or realistic knowledge as to what the term homosexuality connotes" and "just considers it as a type of relationship." His report left no doubt that she "has a deep maternal attachment and identification."

In dismissing this testimony the trial judge said nothing more than that he would "totally reject" the expert evidence which fully supported continued custody in defendant mother because he did "not find it credible in its postulates and

3. His present wife, to whom he had delegated the duty of making the payments, stated she had no explanation for failing to do so "that would be excusable in this court."

conclusions." In doing so he overlooked the fact that the assistance of experts as an aid in resolving the difficult questions presented was clearly desirable. We emphasize that it was the trial judge himself who, evidently recognizing his own lack of expertise, requested the examination and report from Dr. Yaskin, whose name was recommended to him by plaintiff's own attorney. As we have noted elsewhere, the testimony of child study specialists is properly relied on by the courts.... These witnesses were qualified, their opinions were unrefuted and were not inherently implausible.... [W]e see no reason why they should have been ignored in this case....

Apparently the trial judge placed greater credence in what the children told him during *in camera* hearings, some of which was recorded, some not. For example, he concluded that Franceen disliked defendant's companion, Joyce, "almost to the point of hatred," but there is nothing in Franceen's recorded testimony to support such a belief.[4] If it was based on something he was privately told by the child, it was not memorialized in the manner suggested in *State v. Green*, 129 N.J.Super. 157, 166, 322 A.2d 495 (App.Div.1974). Except for the conclusion which he drew therefrom, there is nothing to show what he was told off the record, and without some disclosure to the parties on the record it should not have been allowed to influence his decision....

In modifying custody the trial judge rejected the "tender years" doctrine as "an obsolete, untenable, antediluvian theory." We disagree that he was free to disregard in this manner the ages of the children as a factor in determining where custody should lie. Although our personal views may be contrary, the Supreme Court has still not displaced the doctrine that custody of a young child "is normally placed with the mother, if fit." *Esposito v. Esposito*, 41 N.J. 143, 145, 195 A.2d 295, 296 (1963). Also see *Mayer v. Mayer*, 150 N.J.Super. 556, 563–64, 376 A.2d 214 (Ch.Div. 1977). That the children were still of tender years was something which should have been weighed in this case in favor of preserving the custodial arrangement, and the trial judge erred in failing to do so.

We have already noted that the trial judge made no finding of changed circumstances as a reason for modifying the custody provision. However, plaintiff argues that a change of circumstance may nevertheless be found in the fact that defendant's variant sexual orientation now causes embarrassment to the girls in the eyes of their peers. We address ourselves to this final contention.

It is first observed that the trial judge made no finding of fact which lends support to plaintiff's claim. All he said was that Franceen had been "upset" by Joyce, defendant's lesbian friend, a problem earlier resolved by banishing Joyce from the presence of the children. The only evidence of "embarrassment" is to be found in Franceen's testimony about conversations with her friends, in which she was asked why her mother dated other women. Nothing therein suggests that these were in any way traumatizing. We know of no finding by the trial judge that Franceen is "pressured by her peers," nor how such a finding could be supported by the proofs. In fact, we do not understand the sense in which this expression is used in the dissenting opinion or the weight which such a finding could be accorded within the context of this case.

Plaintiff's argument overlooks, too, the fact that the children's exposure to embarrassment is not dependent upon the identity of the parent with whom they

4. To the contrary, the transcript shows one recorded interview specifically held at Franceen's request because she wanted to correct an unfavorable impression about Joyce she had conveyed to the judge on an earlier occasion unrecorded, so far as we can tell.

happen to reside. Their discomfiture, if any, comes about not because of living with defendant, but because she is their mother, because she is a lesbian, and because the community will not accept her. Neither the prejudices of the small community in which they live nor the curiosity of their peers about defendant's sexual nature will be abated by a change of custody. Hard facts must be faced. These are matters which courts cannot control, and there is little to gain by creating an artificial world where the children may dream that life is different than it is.

Furthermore, the law governing grants of custody does not yield to such narrow considerations. Of overriding importance is that within the context of a loving and supportive relationship there is no reason to think that the girls will be unable to manage whatever anxieties may flow from the community's disapproval of their mother. In *Commonwealth ex rel. Lucas v. Kreischer*, 450 Pa. 352, 299 A.2d 243 (Sup.Ct. 1973), the trial court awarded custody of the children, whose mother had entered into an interracial marriage, to their father because of the "almost universal prejudice and intolerance of interracial marriage." In reversing, the Supreme Court of Pennsylvania rested its determination upon the following observation, which we deem pertinent, made by the dissenting judge of the intermediate appellate court:

> [I]n a multiracial society such as ours racial prejudice and tension are inevitable. If...children are raised in a happy and stable home, they will be able to cope with prejudice and hopefully learn that people are unique individuals who should be judged as such. [299 A.2d at 246].

Mistaken also, in our view, is plaintiff's assumption that the welfare of the children cannot be served unless they are sheltered from all the adversities that are inherent to their basic life situation. Regrettably, the decision as to where custody shall lie must be made in terms of available alternatives, and in this case neither holds out the promise of a completely unguent environment. While one is troubled by the possible problems that may arise from defendant's homosexual bent, the evidence also strongly features a disturbed and abrasive personal relationship between Joy and plaintiff's present wife which has resulted in the administration of unduly harsh discipline to this child. She also dislikes and fears plaintiff.

Conceding that Franceen prefers to live with her father and his present wife, reservations as to the advisability of such a course are at least suggested by testimony describing talks between the wife and Franceen. In these the 11-year-old was told, with explanatory detail, how great a "stud" her father is. Also germane to the flavor of this "stable atmosphere" are certain nude pictures of the present wife, who posed in the family home for four "photographers," including one who also serves as the family dentist. Although the wife denied that to the "best of my knowledge" these were ever viewed by the children, they had been left under the pillows of a couch in the living room. And, if it is "the thinking of the vast majority of society" that concerns us, it should be noted that before marrying plaintiff the wife underwent an illegal abortion of an out-of-wedlock child fathered by another man.

Nor may we disregard the appalling character of the sexual onslaughts carried out during their marriage by plaintiff upon defendant for which the divorce was granted. Without detailing his singular conduct or the variety of foreign objects he introduced into her person, we acknowledge our willingness to understand how these could well have stifled forever her initial efforts to enjoy heterosexual love in a conventional relationship.

Although plaintiff's sexual behavior cannot, perhaps, be categorized in terms which are as emotionally charged as "homosexual" or "lesbian," it is so far out of the ordinary as to create the most acute anxieties about entrusting so troubled and deviant a personality with the responsibility of creating an environment for the upbringing of two young girls. Even if the rule of changed circumstances were not applicable and we were free to weigh anew the relative advantages of these two arrangements, taken with the considerations previously noted, plaintiff's conduct illuminates the completely speculative nature of any determination that because she is a lesbian, custody with defendant will be more destructive of the children's welfare than with plaintiff.

If defendant retains custody, it may be that because the community is intolerant of her differences these girls may sometimes have to bear themselves with greater than ordinary fortitude. But this does not necessarily portend that their moral welfare or safety will be jeopardized. It is just as reasonable to expect that they will emerge better equipped to search out their own standards of right and wrong, better able to perceive that the majority is not always correct in its moral judgments, and better able to understand the importance of conforming their beliefs to the requirements of reason and tested knowledge, not the constraints of currently popular sentiment or prejudice.

Taking the children from defendant can be done only at the cost of sacrificing those very qualities they will find most sustaining in meeting the challenges inevitably ahead. Instead of forbearance and feelings of protectiveness, it will foster in them a sense of shame for their mother. Instead of courage and the precept that people of integrity do not shrink from bigots, it counsels the easy option of shirking difficult problems and following the course of expedience. Lastly, it diminishes their regard for the rule of human behavior, everywhere accepted, that we do not forsake those to whom we are indebted for love and nurture merely because they are held in low esteem by others.

We conclude that the children's best interests will be disserved by undermining in this way their growth as mature and principled adults. Extensive evidence in the record upon which we have not commented amply confirms the trial judge's finding that defendant is a worthy mother. Nothing suggests that her homosexual preference in itself presents any threat of harm to her daughters or that in the ordinary course of their development they will be unable to deal with whatever vexation may be caused to their spirits by the community.

Careful attention has been given to the nature of the relief to be awarded. Although advantages are evident in remanding for further hearings by which the current status of the matter may be ascertained, after a thorough examination of the entire record we are satisfied that the welfare of the children will only be impaired without corresponding benefit by prolonging any further these already protracted proceedings. The order under review is therefore reversed and the custody provision contained in the judgment of divorce dated September 11, 1969 is reinstated.

[Concurring opinion by HALPERN, P.J.A.D. omitted.]

ARD, J. A. D. (dissenting).

I must respectfully dissent from the opinion of my colleagues. Following the trial in the Chancery Division, Judge Gruccio announced his findings, conclusions and determination in an articulate and detailed opinion. The thrust of this opinion, as it should be, was a determination of what is in the best interests of the children. I am fully persuaded as to the soundness of the conclusions of law, and satisfied that the findings of fact might reasonably have been reached on sufficient, credible evidence in the record, and I would not disturb them....

...

In my opinion, the question before us is not the determination of a homosexual parent's rights, but rather, giving the trial judge's opinion the great weight it deserves, whether this judgment should be disturbed. I believe the trial judge made sufficient findings and his holding is supported by sufficient credible evidence in the record.

...

In its entirety, the record supports the determination of the trial judge. Contrary to defendant's contention, it was not just the fact of defendant's sexual deviancy that prompted the judge to rule as he did, but rather it was all of the facts of the case, taken as a whole, which justified the finding of changed circumstances and placing the children, in their own best interests, in the care and custody of their father.

Adults have freedom of choice; children do not have a like freedom. They are impressionable and vulnerable. Adolescence is a time of turmoil, self-doubt and sometimes alienation. It is a time when the stability of a family is most important. Children should not be victims of an avant-garde tolerance that does not represent the thinking of the vast majority of society. I cannot conceive that the interests of these children will be best served by returning them to the custody of their mother, who gave this answer to the court:

> THE COURT: Would you be satisfied to have your daughter enter a homosexual relationship?
>
> THE WITNESS: If that's where she was comfortable, I wouldn't be elated because of society's rules.

In balancing the assets and liabilities of the two households, Judge GRUCCIO determined that the interests of these children are best served by placing them in the custody of their father and his new family. I would affirm that determination.

PALMORE v. SIDOTI

Unites States Supreme Court
466 U.S. 429 (1984)

Chief Justice BURGER delivered the opinion of the Court.

We granted certiorari to review a judgment of a state court divesting a natural mother of the custody of her infant child because of her remarriage to a person of a different race.

I

When petitioner Linda Sidoti Palmore and respondent Anthony J. Sidoti, both Caucasians, were divorced in May 1980 in Florida, the mother was awarded custody of their three-year-old daughter.

In September 1981 the father sought custody of the child by filing a petition to modify the prior judgment because of changed conditions. The change was that the child's mother was then cohabiting with a Negro, Clarence Palmore, Jr., whom she married two months later. Additionally, the father made several allegations of instances in which the mother had not properly cared for the child.

After hearing testimony from both parties and considering a court counselor's investigative report, the court noted that the father had made allegations about the child's care, but the court made no findings with respect to these allegations. On the contrary, the court made a finding that "there is no issue as to either party's devotion to the child, adequacy of housing facilities, or respecta]bility of the new spouse of either parent."...

The court then addressed the recommendations of the court counselor, who had made an earlier report "in [another] case coming out of this circuit also involving the social consequences of an interracial marriage. *Niles v. Niles*, 299 So.2d 162." *Id.*, at 25. From this vague reference to that earlier case, the court turned to the present case and noted the counselor's recommendation for a change in custody because "[t]he wife [petitioner] has chosen for herself and for her child, a life-style unacceptable to her father *and to society*.... The child...is, or at school age will be, subject to environmental pressures not of choice." Record 84 (emphasis added).

The court then concluded that the best interests of the child would be served by awarding custody to the father. The court's rationale is contained in the following:

> The father's evident resentment of the mother's choice of a black partner is not sufficient to wrest custody from the mother. It is of some significance, however, that the mother did see fit to bring a man into her home and carry on a sexual relationship with him without being married to him. Such action tended to place gratification of her own desires ahead of her concern for the child's future welfare. *This Court feels that despite the strides that have been made in bettering relations between the races in this country, it is inevitable that Melanie will, if allowed to remain in her present situation and attains school age and thus more vulnerable to peer pressures, suffer from the social stigmatization that is sure to come....*
>
> ...

II

The judgment of a state court determining or reviewing a child custody decision is not ordinarily a likely candidate for review by this Court. However, the court's opinion, after stating that the "father's evident resentment of the mother's choice of a black partner is not sufficient" to deprive her of custody, then turns to what it regarded as the damaging impact on the child from remaining in a racially-mixed household.... This raises important federal concerns arising from the Constitution's commitment to eradicating discrimination based on race.

The Florida court did not focus directly on the parental qualifications of the natural mother or her present husband, or indeed on the father's qualifications to have custody of the child. The court found that "there is no issue as to either party's devotion to the child, adequacy of housing facilities, or respectability of the new spouse of either parent."... This, taken with the absence of any negative finding as to the quality of the care provided by the mother, constitutes a rejection of any claim of petitioner's unfitness to continue the custody of her child.

The court correctly stated that the child's welfare was the controlling factor. But that court was entirely candid and made no effort to place its holding on any ground other than race. Taking the court's findings and rationale at face value, it is clear that the outcome would have been different had petitioner married a Caucasian male of similar respectability.

A core purpose of the Fourteenth Amendment was to do away with all governmentally-imposed discrimination based on race. See *Strauder v. West Virginia,* 100 U.S. 303, 307–308, 310, 25 L.Ed. 664 (1880). Classifying persons according to their race is more likely to reflect racial prejudice than legitimate public concerns; the race, not the person, dictates the category. Such classifications are subject to the most exacting scrutiny; to pass constitutional muster, they must be justified by a compelling governmental interest and must be "necessary...to the accomplishment" of its legitimate purpose, *McLaughlin v. Florida,* 379 U.S. 184, 196, 85 S.Ct. 283, 290, 13 L.Ed.2d 222 (1964). See *Loving v. Virginia,* 388 U.S. 1, 11, 87 S.Ct. 1817, 1823, 18 L.Ed.2d 1010 (1967).

The State, of course, has a duty of the highest order to protect the interests of minor children, particularly those of tender years. In common with most states, Florida law mandates that custody determinations be made in the best interests of the children involved.... The goal of granting custody based on the best interests of the child is indisputably a substantial governmental interest for purposes of the Equal Protection Clause.

It would ignore reality to suggest that racial and ethnic prejudices do not exist or that all manifestations of those prejudices have been eliminated. There is a risk that a child living with a step-parent of a different race may be subject to a variety of pressures and stresses not present if the child were living with parents of the same racial or ethnic origin.

The question, however, is whether the reality of private biases and the possible injury they might inflict are permissible considerations for removal of an infant child from the custody of its natural mother. We have little difficulty concluding that they are not. The Constitution cannot control such prejudices but neither can it tolerate them. Private biases may be outside the reach of the law, but the law cannot, directly or indirectly, give them effect. "Public officials sworn to uphold the Constitution may not avoid a constitutional duty by bowing to the hypothetical effects of private racial prejudice that they assume to be both widely and deeply held." *Palmer v. Thompson,* 403 U.S. 217, 260–261, 91 S.Ct. 1940, 1962–1963, 29 L.Ed.2d 438 (1971)(WHITE, J., dissenting).

This is by no means the first time that acknowledged racial prejudice has been invoked to justify racial classifications. In *Buchanan v. Warley,* 245 U.S. 60, 38 S.Ct. 16, 62 L.Ed. 149 (1917), for example, this Court invalidated a Kentucky law forbidding Negroes from buying homes in white neighborhoods.

> It is urged that this proposed segregation will promote the public peace by preventing race conflicts. Desirable as this is, and important as is the preservation of the public peace, this aim cannot be accomplished by laws or ordinances which deny rights created or protected by the Federal Constitution.

Id., at 81, 38 S.Ct., at 20. Whatever problems racially-mixed households may pose for children in 1984 can no more support a denial of constitutional rights than could the stresses that residential integration was thought to entail in 1917. The effects of racial prejudice, however real, cannot justify a racial classification removing an infant child from the custody of its natural mother found to be an appropriate person to have such custody.

...

COMMENTS

One of the ways appellate courts or legislatures may place some limits on the power of the trial courts simply to apply their prejudices or to exercise unbridled discretion to decide custody cases is by specifying what factors the trial court is to take into consideration and which the court must not. This method has met with limited success. With respect to the nonmarital sexual behavior of custodial parents, courts are going through a period of transition. At one time mothers were found unfit and denied custody for sexual transgressions that would in a father barely be noticed or commented upon. Increasingly, however, the approach of Illinois in *Jarrett* is being replaced with a less punitive attitude (or an "avant-garde tolerance," as Justice Ard might say, *M.P. v. S.P.*). The language of the Uniform Marriage and Divorce Act — that the court "shall not consider conduct of a proposed custodian that does not affect his relationship to the child" — has been widely adopted, but it still leaves considerable room for courts to reach results that penalize sexual transgressions, as in *Jarrett*.

It may be difficult for courts to sort out between what behavior is actually bad for a child and what behavior is simply distasteful or shocking to the judge. While the court in *Thompson* was willing to ignore the father's immoral conduct with women (apparently including threats and violence as well as "illicit" sexual relations), the *Roe v. Roe* court adopted a position closer to *Jarrett*. The *Roe* case viewed the father's sexual relationship with a man as negatively as the *Brown* case, cited in *Roe*, viewed the mother's sexual relationship with a man.

M.P. v. S.P. and *Palmore* frame the issue in terms of prejudice. Child custody awards should not be based on bigotry. Someone who opposed racial prejudice could nevertheless claim that as long as society has prejudices, these prejudices will affect the life chances of children, and courts must therefore take them into account. *Palmore* responds that the "Constitution cannot control [racial] prejudices but neither can it tolerate them....[T]he law cannot give them effect." Even if "racially-mixed households may pose [problems] for children" these problems cannot "support a denial of constitutional rights."

M.P. v. S.P. tries to answer similar arguments with respect to society's views of sexual orientation. The court adds too that whatever problems the child encounters on account of her mother's sexual orientation could exist whether or not the mother has custody.

Appellate decisions like *Palmore* and *M.P. v. S.P.* cannot assure that trial courts that are less "entirely candid" about the basis for their decisions could not reach the same results those trial courts reached through simple unspecified appeals to the best interest of the child. It facilitated the result in *Palmore* that racially-mixed marriage, and not just racially-mixed cohabitation was involved by the time of trial.

In *M.P. v. S.P.* there were also factors that made the decision easier. The court there could conclude that the mother had "done all that can be expected of a dutiful mother" while the father had a "troubled and deviant personality," and there was reason to suspect that the father's custody claim was in retaliation for the mother seeking enforcement of child support payments on which the father was seriously in arrears. The court even suggested that the mother's "homosexual bent" may well have been caused by the sexual brutality of the father — her ex-husband. The mother was discreet in her sexual relations while the father's "present wife" had had an illegal abortion before her marriage and posed for nude photographs while married. The court makes further moral and political judgments when it comments favorably that the mother does not proselytize for homosexuality or engage in public advocacy of gay rights.

The Ideal of Equal Opportunity for Custody

IRBY v. DUBOIS
Appellate Court of Illinois
41 Ill. App. 3d 609, 354 N.E.2d 562 (1976)

DRUCKER, Justice.

Petitioner appeals from a judgment denying her petition for a writ of habeas corpus and awarding custody of her twin daughters to respondent, the natural father.

The parties met in 1963 and respondent began residing with petitioner and her children soon thereafter. The parties never married. On July 21, 1973, petitioner gave birth to twin daughters. Respondent moved out of petitioner's home in March of 1974 and married Barbara Jean Dubois on April 11, 1974.

On April 14, 1974, respondent came to petitioner's apartment and, representing that he wanted to show the babies to friends, took the twins away. Although he stated that he would bring them home that evening, he never returned.

Petitioner, having failed to regain the children or contact respondent, filed a petition for habeas corpus on June 4, 1974. The trial court which initially heard the cause denied the petition and awarded temporary custody to respondent. That order was subsequently vacated and a new trial was granted. Prior to trial respondent filed a petition for adjudication of wardship in which he sought to have the children declared wards of the court and placed in his custody.

Since the facts adduced at trial were well stated in the trial court's memorandum opinion and are not now in dispute, we quote from it extensively:

> ...The evidence reveals that both parents are fit to have custody, but that the natural father is married and can provide a more stable family life with more material advantages to the minor children than the mother can. However, the evidence also shows that the mother had physical custody of the children from birth until the time they were about nine months of age at which time the natural father obtained physical custody of the children by deceiving the mother. The children are now about twenty-one months of age.
>
> EDMUND DUBOIS is and for some time has been employed by Schenkers International Forwarders, Inc. as a driver-salesman. He testified that he is 53 and in good health. When he began living with petitioner in 1963 a divorce action was pending to dissolve his marriage of 14 years to

one Gladys Branch Terrell. There were no children of that union. His present wife BARBARA DUBOIS appeared as a witness at the hearing and testified that she was educated in the Chicago Public Schools and had received college training in several local schools including Moody Bible Institute. She further testified that she has been mothering the twins since they were nine months old; that she and DUBOIS want to keep them; and that she would give their care priority over her pastoral duties. DUBOIS, his wife and the twin girls live in a two apartment building at 834 East 88th Street in Chicago.

Petitioner BARBARA IRBY lives in the Chicago Housing Authority Project at 220 East 63rd Street with four of her five children by her marriage to John H. Irby from whom she has been divorced since 1967. The ages of the four children range from 12 to 17. The fifth child, Belinda age 20, is married and out of the household. MRS. IRBY has not remarried. She is not employed. She receives public assistance. During the latter part of 1971 and the first six months of 1972 she was in a tuberculosis sanitarium. She testified that today the T.B. is inactive and her condition stable. She has no contact with the Sanitarium but goes to the Clinic at the Englewood Health Center every six months.

This court ordered the probation department to make a social investigation that would include an assessment of the life patterns and the homes of the parties. Pursuant to this order an investigation was made by Probation Officer Birchette who testified at the hearing and submitted a written report which was received into evidence. The report states

> ... that the best plan for the twins at this time would be to remain with their natural father who along with his wife and mother are providing adequate care and nurturing for the babies. However, it is felt that the mother should be granted visiting rights.

On the basis of all the facts and circumstances established by the evidence, this court finds that the interests of the twins would best be served by not disturbing the custody of the natural father. An order will issue denying the petition for Adjudication of Wardship, denying the petition for habeas corpus, fixing BARBARA IRBY's rights of visitation and assessing costs.

On appeal petitioner contends that (1) respondent's conduct in taking the children from her prejudicially altered her position before the trial court, (2) the judgment was against the manifest weight of the evidence and (3) the trial court improperly considered the probation officer's report which was not admitted into evidence.

OPINION

In *Vanderlaan v. Vanderlaan*, 9 Ill.App.3d 260, 292 N.E.2d 145, we held that the ruling by the Supreme Court of the United States in *Stanley v. Illinois*, 405 U.S. 645, 92 S.Ct. 1208, 31 L.Ed.2d 551, indicates that in a custody proceeding a father is not barred from obtaining custody of his children born out of wedlock. Since our decision in that case, other jurisdictions have held similarly, considering the natural father of such children to have rights of custody as would a father of legitimate children upon a dissolution of a marriage.... This is in recognition of the principle that a determination concerning custody should be premised upon a consideration of what would be in the best interests of the children. As was stated in *E. v. T.*, 308 A.2d at 43, 44:

> It is basic, however, that in all matters relating to the custody of minor children the paramount consideration of this and any other court is and should be the safety, happiness, physical, mental and moral welfare of the child. [Cites.] Each case must be decided on its own facts and circumstances, and neither parent has a superior right to custody.

We believe this to be the proper standard for determining who should be awarded custody, regardless of legitimacy.

In Illinois no presumption exists favoring custody in either parent. While giving custody to the mother may well be the usual result of a custody hearing, there is no rule requiring this finding. (*Anagnostopoulos v. Anagnostopoulos*, 22 Ill.App.3d 479, 317 N.E.2d 681.) In *Marcus v. Marcus*, 24 Ill.App.3d 401, 407, 320 N.E.2d 581, 585, the court stated:

> [I]t should be noted that there is today no inflexible rule which requires that custody of children, especially of tender age, be vested in the mother. Equality of the sexes has entered this field. The fact that a mother is fit is only one facet of the situation, and, standing by itself, it does not authorize a denial of custody to the father, when this appears necessary because of other considerations.

Although earlier cases did express a preference for the mother to be entrusted with the custody of children of tender years, (*Nye v. Nye*, 411 Ill. 408, 105 N.E.2d 300; *People ex rel. Bukovich v. Bukovich*, 39 Ill.2d 76, 233 N.E.2d 382) our 1970 Illinois constitution now provides that equal protection of the law shall not be denied or abridged because of sex. (Ill.Const. Art. 1, sec. 18, S.H.A.) As the trial court in the instant case properly concluded: "[N]o presumption of preference applies." The trial court arrived at its conclusion after a careful examination of this doctrine and its history:

> The early Illinois case of *Wright v. Bennett*, 7 Ill. 587 (1845), in which the attorney for the defendant in error was a person named A. Lincoln, enunciated the common law rule that as between the mother and father of an illegitimate child the mother's right of custody is superior and the father's right secondary. A mother was assumed not to have outside employment. She was expected to be at home caring for the child. Further it was thought that if a young child could not have both maternal and paternal influences that it would benefit more from a mother's care. Today, women are often employed, and present day authorities assert that "fathering" can be as essential as "mothering" for both boys and girls.
>
> Illinois courts have taken judicial notice of the recent emancipation of women socially and economically.... It is reasonable to expect that courts in awarding child custody will take judicial notice of the changing social and economic conditions of women. The factual basis, if there was one, for the so called "tender years doctrine" is gone.

Petitioner initially contends that respondent's action in taking the children improperly altered the posture of the parties to her disadvantage. It is claimed that her burden of proof was increased from a mere showing of fitness to proving that she was more fit than respondent since the trial court erroneously applied a presumption favoring the custodial parent.

. . .

. . . The trial judge was aware of the existence of such a presumption but refused to apply it in favor of either party. It is true that once a right to custody has been *judicially* determined, the parent deprived of custody has a greater burden in subsequently proving that a change in custody is warranted.... However, in a proceeding to initially determine custody, no greater burden is placed on either parent. In the present case the trial court considered both parties to have equal standing to obtain custody.

Furthermore, although a suit involving custody presents an adversary proceeding between the parties, (*Henrikson v. Henrikson*, 26 Ill.App.3d 37, 324 N.E.2d 473) the State also has an interest in the outcome and the child is considered a ward of the court and is under its special protection. (*Gerst v. Gerst*, 349 Ill.App. 201, 110 N.E.2d 470; *Oakes v. Oakes*, 45 Ill.App.2d 387, 195 N.E.2d 840.) To the extent that there is a burden of proof in such matters, it is that each parent present the court with evidence that custody in that parent would be in the child's best interest. (*Anagnostopoulos; Henrikson.*) Therefore, although respondent's conduct necessitated that petitioner file an action, no greater amount of proof as to her fitness was required.

Petitioner next contends that the award of custody was against the manifest weight of the evidence. At the outset it should be noted that the determination of custody is within the discretion of the trial judge and will not be disturbed unless it appears that a manifest injustice has been done or that the trial court has abused its discretion. *Anagnostopoulos*; *Barbara v. Barbara*, 110 Ill.App.2d 189, 249 N.E.2d 269.

In the instant case the trial court's finding that it was in the best interests of the children that custody should be with the father was amply supported by the evidence. It was based upon the more stable environment and family life which would be afforded the children were the father to be awarded custody. Stability of environment is an important factor to be considered in determining what is in the best interests of the children. (*Holloway Cave v. Cave*, 2 Ill.App.3d 782, 276 N.E.2d 793.) The court's conclusion was also premised upon the fact that respondent could provide more material advantages to the children, the health of the parents, and their past actions in affecting their fitness to have custody.

Although the trial court took cognizance of respondent's conduct in taking the children from petitioner, it was determined that such conduct should not preclude him from being awarded custody:

> The fact that he obtained custody through deception, however unadmirable such conduct may have been, should not result in automatic award of custody to the mother. If such were to result the children become prizes to be awarded on the basis of parental misconduct not bearing any relevance to fitness. Parental misconduct, if any occurred, should be redressed in other ways and the court should focus only on which award of custody will best serve the interests of the children in this case.

Respondent's action was correctly viewed by the court as another factor to be considered in determining his fitness to have custody. What is of paramount importance is the welfare of the children, not punishment of the father. (*Fears v. Fears*, 5 Ill.App.3d 610, 283 N.E.2d 709.) The trial court's determination that respondent should have custody of the children, despite finding that petitioner was also fit to have custody, cannot be said to be against the manifest weight of the evidence.

Petitioner also contends that the trial court improperly considered the social investigator's report since it was not admitted into evidence.

The social investigator who prepared the report testified fully about its contents during petitioner's case in chief. An examination of the record reveals that the witness testified for 18 pages concerning matters contained in the report and the manner in which those facts were obtained. At one point her testimony concerning the recommendation that the children remain with respondent was virtually identical to that portion of the report quoted in the trial court's opinion:

> THE WITNESS: ... I did observe the DuBois home. I felt in terms of nurturing and mothering that his present wife was providing the children with love and attention.

We do not agree with petitioner's claim that it was reversible error for the trial court to consider the report. Petitioner has not indicated whether the witness' testimony failed to encompass any portions of the report, and in the absence of such a showing it must be assumed that the same or similar evidence was properly received during the social investigator's testimony. Therefore, prejudice to petitioner could not have resulted from a consideration of the report even if it were not formally admitted into evidence....

The last issue to be decided is the contention that the trial court erred in considering the recommendation of the social investigator since her conclusion was based upon observations of the children solely in respondent's home thus depriving petitioner of the benefit of a fair comparison. The limitations which existed in the scope of the investigation were brought out and developed at trial during her testimony. Whatever weaknesses existed in this evidence affected the weight that it should be given. It was the function of the trial court, as the trier of fact, to weigh this evidence and determine its value. A court of review will not substitute its judgment for that of the trial court unless the ultimate decision was contrary to the manifest weight of the evidence. (*Anagnostopoulos*; *Hoffmann v. Hoffmann*, 40 Ill.2d 344, 239 N.E.2d 792.) Since we have held that the evidence amply supports the judgment, we must reject this claim.

The decree of the trial court awarding permanent custody of the children to respondent subject to specific visitation rights in petitioner was proper and therefore the judgment denying her application for a writ of habeas corpus is affirmed.

AFFIRMED.

GARSKA v. McCOY

Supreme Court of Appeals of West Virginia
167 W.Va. 59, 278 S.E.2d 357 (1981)

NEELY, Justice:

The appellant, Gwendolyn McCoy, appeals from an order of the Circuit Court of Logan County which gave the custody of her son, Jonathan Conway McCoy, to the appellee, Michael Garska, the natural father. While in many regards this is a confusing case procedurally, since the mother and father were never married, nonetheless it squarely presents the issue of the proper interaction between the 1980 legislative amendment to W.Va.Code, 48-2-15 [1980] which eliminates any gender based presumption in awarding custody and our case of *J. B. v. A. B.*, W.Va., 242 S.E.2d 248 (1978) which established a strong maternal presumption with regard to children of tender years.

In February, 1978 the appellant moved from her grandparents' house in Logan County, where she had been raised, to Charlotte, North Carolina to live with her mother. At that time appellant was 15 years old and her mother shared a trailer with appellee, Michael Garska. In March, Gwendolyn McCoy became pregnant by Michael Garska and in June, she returned to her grandparents' home in West Virginia.

The appellant received no support from the appellee during her pregnancy, but after she gave birth to baby Jonathan the appellee sent a package of baby food and diapers. In subsequent months the baby developed a chronic respiratory infection which required hospitalization and considerable medical attention. Gwendolyn's grandfather, Stergil Altizer, a retired coal miner, attempted to have his great-grandson's hospitalization and medical care paid by the United Mine Workers' medical insurance but he was informed that the baby was ineligible unless legally adopted by the Altizers.

In October, 1979 Gwendolyn McCoy signed a consent in which she agreed to the adoption of Jonathan by her grandparents, the Altizers. Upon learning of the adoption plan, the appellee visited the baby for the first time and began sending weekly money orders for $15. The Altizers filed a petition for adoption in the Logan County Circuit Court on 9 November 1979 and on 7 January 1980 the appellee filed a petition for a writ of habeas corpus to secure custody of his son.

Both the adoption and the habeas corpus proceedings were consolidated for hearing and the circuit court dismissed the adoption petition...[and] awarded custody of Jonathan McCoy to the appellee based upon the following findings of fact:

> (a) The petitioner, Michael Garska, is the natural father of the infant child, Jonathan Conway McCoy;
>
> (b) The petitioner, Michael Garska, is better educated than the natural mother and her alleged fiance;
>
> (c) The petitioner, Michael Garska, is more intelligent than the natural mother;
>
> (d) The petitioner, Michael Garska, is better able to provide financial support and maintenance than the natural mother;
>
> (e) The petitioner, Michael Garska, can provide a better social and economic environment than the natural mother;
>
> (f) The petitioner, Michael Garska, has a somewhat better command of the English language than the natural mother;
>
> (g) The petitioner, Michael Garska, has a better appearance and demeanor than the natural mother;
>
> (h) The petitioner, Michael Garska, is very highly motivated in his desire to have custody of the infant child, and the natural mother had previously executed an adoption consent, for said child.

...

While the issue of adoption by the Altizers does, indeed, enter into this case, in the final analysis the entire dispute comes down to a custody fight between the natural father and the natural mother....

...

In the case before us the father, by providing fifteen dollars a week child support, probably showed sufficient parental interest to give him standing to object to an adoption. However, there is no evidence before us to indicate that the mother was an unfit parent and, consequently, no justification for the trial court to remove custody from the primary caretaker parent and vest it in a parent who had had no previous emotional interaction with the child.

...

The loss of children is a terrifying specter to concerned and loving parents; however, it is particularly terrifying to the primary caretaker parent who, by virtue of the caretaking function, was closest to the child before the divorce or other proceedings were initiated. While the primary caretaker parent in most cases in West Virginia is still the mother, nonetheless, now that sex roles are becoming more flexible and high-income jobs are opening to women, it is conceivable that the primary caretaker parent may also be the father. If the primary caretaker parent is, indeed, the father, then under W.Va.Code, 48-2-15 [1980] he will be entitled to the alimony and support payments exactly as a woman would be in similar circumstances. *Peters v. Narick*, W.Va., 270 S.E.2d 760 (1980).

Since the parent who is not the primary caretaker is usually in the superior financial position, the subsequent welfare of the child depends to a substantial degree upon the level of support payments which are awarded in the course of a divorce. Our experience instructs us that uncertainty about the outcome of custody disputes leads to the irresistible temptation to trade the custody of the child in return for lower alimony and child support payments. Since trial court judges generally approve consensual agreements on child support, underlying economic data which bear upon the equity of settlements are seldom investigated at the time an order is entered. While Code, 48-2-15 [1980] speaks in terms of "the best interest of the children" in every case, the one enormously important function of legal rules is to inspire rational and equitable settlements in cases which never reach adversary status in court.

If every controversy which arose in this society required court resolution, the understaffed judiciary would topple like a house of cards. It is only voluntary compliance with the criminal law and the orderly settlement of private affairs in the civil law which permits the system to function at all. Consequently, anytime a new statute is passed or a new rule of common law developed, both legislators and judges must pay careful attention to interpreting it in a way which is consonant with equity in the area of private settlements.

...*J. B. v. A. B., supra*, attempted to remove from most run-of-the-mine divorce cases the entire issue of child custody. Certainly if we believed from our experience that full-blown hearings on child custody between two fit parents would afford more intelligent child placement than an arbitrary rule, we would not have adopted an arbitrary rule. However, it is emphatically the case that hearings do not enhance justice, particularly since custody fights are highly destructive to the emotional health of children. Furthermore, our mechanical rule was really quite narrowly drawn to apply only to those cases where voluminous evidence would inevitably be unenlightening. We limited the mechanical rule to the custody of children who are too young to formulate an opinion concerning their own custody and, further, we limited it to cases where an initial determination had been made that the mother was, indeed, a fit parent. While in *J. B. v. A. B., supra*, we expressed ourselves in terms of the traditional maternal preference, the Legislature has instructed us that such a gender based standard is unacceptable. However, we are convinced that the best interests of the children are best served in awarding them to the primary caretaker parent, regardless of sex.

Since trial courts almost always award custody to the primary caretaker parent anyway, establishment of certainty in this regard permits the issues of alimony and support to stand upon their own legs and to be litigated or settled upon the merits of relevant financial criteria, without introducing into the equation the terrifying prospect of loss to the primary caretaker of the children. As we noted in *J. B. v. A. B., supra* at 242 S.E.2d 255, "empirical findings directly or indirectly relevant to questions for which judges deciding difficult [custody] cases need answers are virtually nonexistent...." The 1980 Amendment to Code, 48-2-15 was not intended to disturb our determination that in most instances the issue of child custody between two competent parents cannot be litigated effectively. Its intent was merely to correct the inherent unfairness of establishing a gender-based, maternal presumption which would defeat the just claims of a father if he had, in fact, been the primary caretaker parent.

II

In setting the child custody law in domestic relations cases we are concerned with three practical considerations. First, we are concerned to prevent the issue of custody from being used in an abusive way as a coercive weapon to affect the level of support payments and the outcome of other issues in the underlying divorce proceeding. Where a custody fight emanates from this reprehensible motive the children inevitably become pawns to be sacrificed in what ultimately becomes a very cynical game. Second, in the average divorce proceeding intelligent determination of relative degrees of fitness requires a precision of measurement which is not possible given the tools available to judges. Certainly it is no more reprehensible for judges to admit that they cannot measure minute gradations of psychological capacity between two fit parents than it is for a physicist to concede that it is impossible for him to measure the speed of an electron. Third, there is an urgent need in contemporary divorce law for a legal structure upon which a divorcing couple may rely in reaching a settlement.

While recent statutory changes encourage private ordering of divorce upon the "no-fault" ground of "irreconcilable differences," W.Va.Code, 48-2-4(a)(10)[1977], our legal structure has not simultaneously been tightened to provide a reliable framework within which the divorcing couple can bargain intelligently. Nowhere is the lack of certainty greater than in child custody. Not very long ago, the courts were often intimately involved with all aspects of a divorce. Even an estranged couple who had reached an amicable settlement had to undergo "play-acting" before the court in order to obtain a divorce. Now, however, when divorces are numerous, easy, and routinely concluded out of court intelligible, reliable rules upon which out-of-court bargaining can be based must be an important consideration in the formulation of our rules.

Since the Legislature has concluded that private ordering by divorcing couples is preferable to judicial ordering, we must insure that each spouse is adequately protected during the out-of-court bargaining. Uncertainty of outcome is very destructive of the position of the primary caretaker parent because he or she will be willing to sacrifice everything else in order to avoid the terrible prospect of losing the child in the unpredictable process of litigation.

This phenomenon may be denominated the "Solomon syndrome", that is that the parent who is most attached to the child will be most willing to accept an inferior bargain. In the court of Solomon, the "harlot" who was willing to give up her child in order to save him from being cleaved in half so that he could be equally divided, was rewarded for her sacrifice,[6] but in the big world out there the sacrificing parent generally loses necessary support or alimony payments.[7] This then must also be compensated for "in the best interests of the children." Moreover, it is likely that the primary caretaker will have less financial security than the nonprimary caretaker and, consequently, will be unable to sustain the expense of custody litigation, requiring as is so often the case these days, the payments for expert psychological witnesses.

Therefore, in the interest of removing the issue of child custody from the type of acrimonious and counter-productive litigation which a procedure inviting exhaustive evidence will inevitably create, we hold today that there is a presumption in favor of the primary caretaker parent, if he or she meets the minimum, objective standard for being a fit parent as articulated in *J. B. v. A. B., supra*[9] regardless of sex. Therefore, in any custody dispute involving children of tender years it is incumbent upon the circuit court to determine as a threshold question which parent was the primary caretaker parent before the domestic strife giving rise to the proceeding began.

While it is difficult to enumerate all of the factors which will contribute to a conclusion that one or the other parent was the primary caretaker parent, nonetheless, there are certain obvious criteria to which a court must initially look. In establishing which natural or adoptive parent is the primary caretaker, the trial court shall determine which parent has taken primary responsibility for, *inter alia*, the performance of the following caring and nurturing duties of a parent: (1) preparing and planning of meals; (2) bathing, grooming and dressing; (3) purchasing, cleaning, and care of clothes; (4) medical care, including nursing and trips to physicians; (5) arranging for social interaction among peers after school, i.e. transporting to friends' houses or, for example, to girl or boy scout meetings; (6) arranging alternative care, i.e. babysitting, day-care, etc.; (7) putting child to bed at night, attending to child in the middle of the night, waking child in the morning; (8) disciplining, i.e. teaching general manners and toilet training; (9) educating, i.e. religious, cultural, social, etc.; and, (10) teaching elementary skills, i.e., reading, writing and arithmetic.

In those custody disputes where the facts demonstrate that child care and custody were shared in an entirely equal way, then indeed no presumption arises and the court must proceed to inquire further into relative degrees of parental competence. However, where one parent can demonstrate with regard to a child of tender years that he or she is clearly the primary caretaker parent, then the court must further determine only whether the primary caretaker parent is a fit parent. Where the primary caretaker parent achieves the minimum, objective standard of behavior which qualifies him or her as a fit parent, the trial court must award the child to the primary caretaker parent.

---

6. 1 Kings 3:16 et. seq.

7. There is very little hard evidence to support this theory that parents use the specter of custody proceedings to gain leverage in financial settlements. An interview transcript on file with the YALE LAW JOURNAL with the Assistant Clerk of New Haven County Superior Court at p. 7 (Dec. 17, 1977) attests to the frequency of fathers using threats of a custody battle to gain a reduction in alimony. See Note, *"Lawyering for the Child"*, 87 YALE LAW JOURNAL 1126, 1131 n.21 (1978).

9. As we said in *J. B. v. A. B., supra*, where the primary caretaker fails to provide: emotional support; routine cleanliness; or nourishing food, the presumption shall not apply.

Consequently, all of the principles enunciated in *J. B. v. A. B.*, *supra*, are reaffirmed today except that wherever the words "mother," "maternal," or "maternal preference" are used in that case, some variation of the term "primary caretaker parent," as defined by this case should be substituted. In this regard we should point out that the absolute presumption in favor of a fit primary caretaker parent applies only to children of tender years. Where a child is old enough to formulate an opinion about his or her own custody the trial court is entitled to receive such opinion and accord it such weight as he feels appropriate. When, in the opinion of the trial court, a child old enough to formulate an opinion but under the age of 14 has indicated a justified desire to live with the parent who is not the primary caretaker, the court may award the child to such parent.

III

In the case before us it is obvious that the petitioner was the primary caretaker parent before the proceedings under consideration in this case arose, and there is no finding on the part of the trial court judge that she is an unfit parent. In fact, all of the evidence indicates that she mobilized all of the resources at her command, namely the solicitous regard of her grandparents, in the interest of this child and that she went to extraordinary lengths to provide for him adequate medical attention and financial support. While, as the trial court found, the educational and economic position of the father is superior to that of the mother, nonetheless, those factors alone pale in comparison to love, affection, concern, tolerance, and the willingness to sacrifice factors about which conclusions can be made for the future most intelligently upon a course of conduct in the past. At least with regard to the primary caretaker parent there is a track record to which a court can look and where that parent is fit he or she should be awarded continued custody.

Certainly the record in the case before us does not demonstrate any intent by the mother to abandon the child through permitting him to be adopted by the grandparents; it is well recognized that mothers in penurious circumstances often resort to adoption in order to make the child eligible for social security or union welfare benefits, all of which significantly enhance the child's opportunities in life. Absent an explicit finding of intent to abandon we cannot construe manipulation of the welfare system to direct maximum benefits towards this child as anything other than a solicitous concern for his welfare.

...

Reversed and remanded.

COMMENTS

Irby is noteworthy in several respects. It seems to establish the illegitimate father's equal opportunity for custody over the twin daughters, and it proclaims that his fault in achieving their physical custody should not preclude an award in his favor. Actually, the opinion is less progressive than it might appear to be; it could have been reached and justified under the traditional guidelines that govern judicial discretion in custody matters. Numerous factors in this instance counteracted the usual preference for mothers. The father's chances were improved by his marriage to a woman with college training. Reference to religious factors, namely, the Moody Bible Institute and the unspecified pastoral duties of the stepmother, although seemingly submitted in a purely factual vein, was probably of at least some significance. The mother, on the other hand, was an unemployed welfare recipient living in public housing with four older children from her dissolved marriage. Most important, she had tuberculosis, alleged but not proven to be inactive. Again, there were underlying considerations of social class. The father through marriage appeared to be leaning toward the middle classes, while the milieu and living conditions of the mother seemed to assure downward mobility for the children.

Had the father tried to obtain custody from the mother by legal means, he probably would have had a more difficult time. What really counted in his favor was the status quo he had created by his deception. The reference to the truism that children should not be "prizes to be awarded on the basis of parental misconduct" is not entirely persuasive. It is true that custody of children seems to be an issue removed from the question of damages for tort. To put the mother in the position she would have been in had the deception not been committed appears to be inappropriate. Yet leaving the children with the wrongdoing father, simply because the status quo is not to be disturbed, has elements of treating the children as chattels or as a piece of real estate, as if there had been adverse possession. The courts do better to acknowledge this dilemma openly. The decisive factor is the traditional unarticulated guideline that the status quo in regard to children, even if less than ideal, is not to be altered unless the welfare of the child is jeopardized, which clearly was not the case in *Irby.*

In view of these factors, the invocations of equal rights of fathers, even if they are illegitimate, appear to be ritualistic because the outcome was a foregone conclusion, in this instance favoring the father. In most cases, however, in spite of a supposedly equal position of the father, the outcome continues to be the opposite. The mother continues to win, even in jurisdictions which, like Illinois, have articulated the equal position of the mother and the father in custody disputes. The reasoning would go thus: upon consideration of all relevant factors, the best interests of the children still favor custody by the mother although — again ritualistically — the equal rights of the father are acknowledged as a matter of principle. It was the facts that dictated a different outcome in *Irby.*

Irby could also be understood as a case illustrating the unfair advantage a father is likely to have when courts try to treat men and women "equally" with respect to child custody. Statistically, women spend considerably more time and energy taking care of young children, and men make considerably more money. The *Irby* father made more money than the mother, but there is no suggestion that he took better care of the children than the mother. The *Irby* court seemed to assume that most of the day-to-day care of the twins would be done by the father's wife, not by the father himself. Under these circumstances, some have complained that the courts are improperly treating mothers as fungible. The courts hold it against the mother if she is on welfare, and they hold it against her if she works outside the home and thus cannot spend all her time with the children. It is simply taken for granted that the father will work outside the home, and he is given far more credit than the mother is given for time spent with the children. Many courts judge mothers by how much time they spend *away* from the children, while they judge fathers by how much time they spend *with* the children. If the father can earn enough money to have a new wife who stays at home, many courts consider the father the better custodian.

Although many men complain that courts still prefer women in child custody cases, women argue that most courts are actually biased in favor of men. While it is frequently quoted that mothers get custody more than 90 percent of the time, this figure does not address the question of what percentage of men would want the full responsibility of custody. The overwhelming majority of child care continues to be done by women, even if they also work full-time outside the home. Men usually have more financial resources to hire more effective lawyers and are successful in a large percentage of custody cases that are fully contested. Nevertheless, in order to reinforce the ideal that both parents should be equally responsible for caring for children, many women continue to support the rules that mandate formal equality in custody disputes and allow men to win in some quite dubious cases, as well as cases in which the men should win.

Legislation that provides a preference for a "primary caretaker" is designed to avoid the unfairness of a formalistic "equality" that too often penalizes the parent who takes care of children instead of pursuing a career. The problem with a strict application of the "tender years doctrine" was not that it preferred the parent who did most of the child care and to whom the child was most attached; the problem was that it preferred the mother over the father in every case regardless of whether or not she was the parent who took primary care of the child. The "primary caretaker" standard is supposed to achieve the benefits of relative certainty without supporting the sex role stereotypes implicit in and reinforced by the "tender years doctrine." Of course, it will not always be clear that one parent has been the primary caretaker (see, for example, *State ex rel. Watts v. Watts, supra*, p. qqq). At least in those cases in which one parent was clearly primary, however, the primary caretaker standard seems to have a great deal to recommend it.

The trial court opinion in *Garska v. McCoy* illustrates a possible danger of the "best interest of the child" standard in actual practice. In that case, a fifteen-year-old raised by her grandparents went to stay with her mother and in a few weeks time had been impregnated by the man who was living with her mother. The teenager returned to her grandparents' home and had the baby, and the trial court awarded custody to the father. The more the trial court praises the father's superior intelligence, education, financial resources, and so forth, the more exploitative and irresponsible the father's behavior appears. Yet the appellate court would ordinarily have insufficient basis for overruling the trial court's finding that custody with the natural father would serve the child's best interest; the trial court's discretion is usually not overturned.

REFERENCES

Sanford N. Katz, *"That They May Thrive" Goal of Child Custody: Reflections on the Apparent Erosion of the Tender Years Presumption and the Emergence of the Primary Caretaker Presumption*, 8 J. CONTEMPORARY HEALTH L. AND POLICY 123 (1992).

Frances Olsen, *The Politics of Family Law*, in FAMILY MATTERS 336 (Martha Minow, ed. 1993) reprinted from 2 J. LAW & INEQUALITY 1 (1984); THE CHILD, THE FAMILY, AND THE LAW 51 (Roger Meyer, ed., Tacoma, Washington, 1982).

Deciding Not to Decide: Joint Custody

MAYER v. MAYER

Superior Court of New Jersey
150 N.J.Super. 556, 376 A.2d 214 (1977)

DUFFY, J. S. C.

Plaintiff and defendant were married on January 13, 1962 and separated on December 1, 1973. Plaintiff wife filed her complaint for divorce on June 5, 1975, alleging a cause of action based on 18 months' separation. The parties were divorced by judgment of this court on November 23, 1976.

Two children were born of the marriage, Dana, 13 years of age, and William, 11. They are in the custody of plaintiff.

Defendant husband is now a practicing member of the Bar of this State, having successfully pursued various business ventures as a real estate broker and developer. At the present time he is attempting to develop several properties in the Livingston, New Jersey, area, and testified to possible ventures in Arizona and Pennsylvania.

Plaintiff has recently undergone an operation for cancer and is under continuing medical and psychiatric care. She is a licensed real estate saleswoman and is affiliated with a local agency, but she has not had a significant income from those efforts.

Trial of this matter consumed about three days. At the conclusion of oral testimony the court ordered counsel for the parties to submit summations as to law and fact covering equitable distribution, support and alimony, custody, counsel fees and costs. This opinion will dispose of those issues.

[The court here awarded plaintiff the marital residence and certain personal property by way of equitable distribution under N.J.S.A. 2A:34-23, applying the guidelines suggested in *Rothman v. Rothman*, 65 N.J. 219, 232, 320 A.2d 496 (1974), plaintiff to be solely responsible for the mortgage, taxes and upkeep of the home. The court also fixed the amounts of alimony and child support defendant is to pay plaintiff; he is to provide a policy insuring his life in an amount of at least $50,000, naming the children as irrevocable beneficiaries and to be maintained until the younger shall have become emancipated, as well as health and medical insurance for them, including major medical coverage, to be maintained until each is emancipated. In addition, he is to be responsible for any extraordinary medical expenses incurred by plaintiff for the treatment of her cancer.]

The issue of custody of the minor children of the marriage is seriously contested. During settlement negotiations held at a conference in chambers the court suggested that, in view of plaintiff's continuing health problems, an order of joint custody might be appropriate in this case.

Plaintiff, in her summation, requests that the court's order of joint custody, if entered, name one parent as the "primary custodian as a matter of law." Defendant "welcome[s] dual custody" in his summation.

Two questions are thus presented. Can this court order joint custody, that is, does the court have the authority to do so? If so, then in what fashion can an order of joint custody, if appropriate, best be implemented?

The question of joint custody has topical as well as legal significance, having been discussed recently in the *New York Times Sunday Magazine* (October 31,

1976) and being the subject of a pending suit naming the Chancery Division of Essex County as defendant. In addition, the concept of joint custody has never been fully explored in any reported decision of our courts. The time is ripe for a full review of the legal and statutory bases for an award of custody, in general and joint custody, in particular.

The Superior Court of New Jersey has "original general jurisdiction throughout the State in all causes." *N.J.Const.* (1947), Art. VI, §III, par. 2. Further, the Legislature has vested in this court the authority to make such order, after judgment of divorce or maintenance, "as to the care, custody, education and maintenance of the children, or any of them, as the circumstances of the parties and the nature of the case shall render fit, reasonable and just...." N.J.S.A. 2A:34-23. Clearly, this legislative grant of authority would include the authority to order "joint," "divided" or "split" custody. Assuming, therefore, that the circumstances of the parties and the nature of the case render an award of joint custody, "fit, reasonable and just," there is no reason why such an order should not be entered.

New Jersey is in the majority of states which follow the traditional "best interests of the child" rule in custody determinations. The "best interests" doctrine was first announced by Judge (later Justice) Brewer in *Chapsky v. Wood*, 26 Kan. 650 (1881), in which the Kansas Supreme Court repudiated the rule which held that the rights of parents were primary over those of third parties to custody of their children. The doctrine gained popularity after the decision in *Finlay v. Finlay*, 240 N.Y. 429, 148 N.E. 624 (1925), in which the New York Court of Appeals held that the Chancellor acted as *parens patriae* to do what is best for the interests of the child.

The "best interests" standard is the one advocated by the Family Law Section of the American Bar Association in §402 of the Uniform Marriage and Divorce Act. That act has undergone a proposed revision, but §402 was left unmodified. See 7 *Fam.L.Q.* 135 (1973).

Other standards for placement of custody have been proposed, but they have not yet had as wide acceptance as the "best interests" test has had. Goldstein *et al.* propose the "least detrimental available alternative." Goldstein, Freud and Solnit, *Beyond the Best Interests of the Child* (1973). This choice would maximize,

> ...[i]n accord with the child's sense of time, the child's opportunity for being wanted and for maintaining on a continuous, unconditional, and permanent basis a relationship with at least one adult who is or will become the child's psychological parent. [at 99]

"Sense of time," "opportunity for being wanted" and "psychological parent" are terms of art coined by the authors.

Another approach is that of John Batt, who approaches child custody questions "from a psychologically oriented child development standpoint." Batt, "Child Custody Disputes: A Developmental-Psychological Approach to Proof and Decisionmaking", 12 *Willamette L.J.* 491 (1976). He proposes that the court take into account five phases of development of the human child before making a custody placement. The phases generally follow the growth of the child from infancy to young adulthood.

The "best interests" standard was authoritatively announced in New Jersey in 1944 by the *Armour* decision and has since been followed by our courts. *Armour v. Armour*, 135 N.J.Eq. 47, 52, 37 A.2d 29 (E. & A.1944).... Other formulations of the "best interests" test require the court to consider the safety, happiness and physical, mental and moral welfare of the child....

The court has broad discretion in dealing with the custody of a child being always aware that the welfare and happiness (best interests) of the child is the controlling consideration....

The court will consider the wishes of an infant child as to custody, if the child is of an age and capacity to form an intelligent preference as to custody.... The preference of the young child has a place, although not a conclusive place, in determining custody....[2]

Commentators have suggested that a prerequisite to an award of custody should be the appointment of independent counsel for the child so as to safeguard his or her rights. Comment, "A Child's Right to Independent Counsel in Custody Proceedings: Providing Effective 'Best Interest' Determination through the Use of a Legal Advocate," 6 *Seton Hall L.Rev.* 303 (1975); Inker and Peretta, "A Child's Right to Counsel in Custody Cases,["] 5 *Fam.L.Q.* 108 (1971). While this court has assigned independent counsel for children in the past, such a procedure, which entails considerable expense, should be utilized only where the interests of the child are truly adverse to those of the parent(s). One example of such adverse interest would be the situation where neither parent is a fit custodian. That is not the case here.

To which parent, then, should custody be awarded? Our courts have long recognized that custody of a child of tender years ordinarily is awarded to the mother if she is a fit and proper person. *Esposito v. Esposito*, 41 N.J. 143, 145, 195 A.2d 295 (1963). The theory is that the mother will take better and more expert care of the small child than the father can.... These considerations must always be considered subordinate, however, to what is truly in the child's best interest....

In the present case the question is not so much "to which parent should custody be awarded" as it is "should custody be awarded to both parents?" Nelson states that

> Where both parents are suitable persons to have the custody of their children and are devoted to them, they should be given as nearly equal rights to the custody of the children as is practical and compatible with the convenience, education and welfare of the children, since it is against public policy to destroy or limit the relation of parent and child and the child is entitled to the love and training of both parents.

(2 Nelson, *Divorce and Annulment* (2 ed. 1961), §§15, 17, at 256–57).

N.J.S.A. 9:2-4 makes it clear that, with regard to an order or judgment of custody,

> ...the rights of both parents, in the absence of misconduct, shall be held to be equal, and they shall be equally charged with their care, nurture, education and welfare, and the happiness and welfare of the children shall determine the custody or possession.

This statutory grant of equal rights in both parents to custody effectively reversed the holding of the common law wherein the father had the preferred right to custody of his minor child, unless disqualified for s[o]me reason....

2. In the present case the court did not interview the infant children of the marriage. No evidence was adduced that either child preferred one parent over the other. The court is convinced that the parties have been careful to refrain from making the minds of the children their battleground. They have thus avoided creating the discord, mistrust and misery which forces a child to make a choice between his or her parents.

Our case law is replete with decisions reaffirming the existence of equal rights to custody in both parents.... One of our later cases holds that the parental right to the care of his or her child is a fundamental right subject to constitutional protection....

Notwithstanding the enlightened views of the Legislature and the courts of this State, no authoritative decision has ever been rendered by our courts on the subject of joint custody. It cannot be said, however, that joint ("dual," "alternating," "divided," "split") custody enjoys great popularity across the country. Decisions on joint custody in other jurisdictions demonstrate either a guarded acceptance or a clear dislike for the concept. See Annotation, 92 A.L.R.2d 691 (1963).

Courts approving joint custody generally agree that a child is entitled to the love, nurture, advice and training of both mother and father. The experience is said to give the child the experience of two separate homes.... Courts disapproving the concept point to the possibility of resentment against the parents who shuffle the child back and forth,...the development of a sense of insecurity,...and the destructive effect of instability in the human factors affecting a child's emotional life....

Two principles can be distilled from the reported cases. The first is that the primary consideration in an award of joint custody is the welfare and best interest of the child.... The second principle is that decision must depend upon the facts of the particular case....

Several factors are said to affect the decision to award joint custody. Among these are the wishes of the parents, as in *Ward v. Ward*, 88 Ariz. 130, 353 P.2d 895 (Sup.Ct.1960), where the court stated that a sincere desire on the part of the parent to share his child's companionship should not be lightly dismissed. Another important factor is the age of the child, the general rule being that the courts should not divide the custody of a child of tender years. Even this rule is not absolute, as in *Lutker v. Lutker*, 230 S.W.2d 177 (Mo.App.1950), where joint custody of a 2½-year-old was approved, largely because of the devotion of the parents to the child and the short distance between their respective homes.

The distance between the homes of the parents becomes an important factor if the distance is such as to prevent visitation by the noncustodial parent. In that case an award of joint custody may be appropriate....

Assuming that an order of joint custody is appropriate, most courts hold that a frequent shifting from home to home is unnecessarily harmful to the child and should not be permitted. Thus, in *Mason v. Mason*, 163 Wash. 539, 1 P.2d 885 (Sup.Ct.1931), the court condemned an order of joint custody which gave custody of a two-year-old to the mother from noon on Sunday to noon on Thursday, and to the father from Thursday noon to Sunday noon. The Court said, "Thus the child becomes a perpetual traveler. This constant change in environment, discipline and control undoubtedly would prove to be harmful to the child." *Id.* at 886.

An award giving primary custody to one parent and giving the other parent custody on alternate weekends has been upheld....

Courts sometimes disapprove custody arrangements which alternate custody between the parents for equal periods of time, especially where such shifts interfere with schooling. In *McLemore v. McLemore*, 346 S.W.2d 722, 92 A.L.R.2d 691 (Ky.Ct.App.1961), an award of joint custody which shifted three young children every week was terminated because of the intolerable burden such frequent, though equal, shifts placed on the children. Periods of time of 6 months and 12 months have been approved for pre-school children....

The most widely accepted form of joint custody award is the one wherein one parent has custody during school months and the other custody during the summer. Annotation, 92 A.L.R.2d 691, §11(a), at 726 (1963). This form of award solves the problem of distance between the homes of the parents and generally avoids frequent shifts in custody. The attitude of courts granting this form of custody is well illustrated by *Fago v. Fago*, 250 S.W.2d 837 (Mo. App. 1952), where it was said:

> The pleasure and benefit of friendly association with both parents should be accorded to a child.... She needs to have the benefit of her father's guidance, love and affection as well as that of her mother and grandmother.... It will be a broadening and valuable experience for (the child) to spend a part of each summer in the State of New York with her father, leaving ten months of the year for the exertion on (the child) of the beneficent influence of mother, grandmother and aunt in her customary home surroundings in St. Louis. [at 842–43]

There is no doubt that the distance between the homes of the parents was an important factor in that case....

In the present case, the minor children are 13 and 11 years of age an attend school in this State. Plaintiff has requested permission to move to Pittsburgh, Pennsylvania, to be near her parents. Under these circumstances, if plaintiff were given sole custody, visitation by defendant would be both difficult and expensive.

The children are not of such tender years that an award of joint custody would be detrimental to them. They are entitled to know, love and respect their father just as much as they know, love and respect their mother. No order of sole custody in the mother, even with unlimited visitation by the father, could possibly give these children the contact with their father that they need and have a right to. For that reason the court orders that the parties shall have joint custody of the children. Plaintiff will have physical custody from September to June, and defendant will have physical custody during July and August.

Plaintiff's request to move to Pittsburgh is granted. Defendant shall be permitted visitation one weekend a month in the Pittsburgh area during the school year. In addition, defendant shall have free access to the children via telephone at a reasonable hour and for reasonable lengths of time.

Defendant's visitation shall also include a four-day period of visitation during the Christmas and Easter vacations at either location. The parties are, of course, free to supplement this minimum visitation schedule as they may wish and are able to agree upon. Costs of transportation of the children between New Jersey and Pennsylvania will be borne equally by the parties.

[Discussion of counsel fees omitted.]

...

COMMENTS

Mayer represents a trend in favor of joint custody that gained considerable attention during the 1980s. The opinion includes a description of the historical evolution of, and the reasons for and against joint awards. Despite what some would consider considerable intellectual thrust favoring this development and despite strong support from so-called "fathers' rights" groups, the notion of imposed or involuntary joint custody has undergone extensive reexamination in the 1990s.

Most of the custody matters successfully resolved in favor of joint custody are by way of settlement. In the 1970s, some courts refused to allow the parents to agree on joint custody and would award sole legal custody to one parent or the other regardless of the parent's wishes and despite strong indications that they could manage the joint arrangement. While most courts seem finally to have abandoned such questionable insistence on making a decision in favor of one parent, some courts replaced it with an equally questionable reluctance to make a decision in favor of one parent and an insistence that the parents share custody. In *Mayer* a continuing dispute between the parents was resolved by the court by an award of joint custody. Even this case contained some elements of settlement at the court's suggestion. The judge suggested in chambers that, in view of the mother's cancer and psychiatric problems, joint custody might be appropriate. The dispute then focused on the specifics of such an award. Some inherent weaknesses of the concept underlie these dynamics. The joint award in *Mayer* may have been a judicial compromise without which the mother might have lost custody altogether. Conceivably, it could also have been a device to give the father legal custody and supervisory functions, although the mother retained physical custody during the school year. Finally, joint custody could in general also be a device for the judge to avoid making a hard decision or sometimes an excuse for rendering no decision at all. As in *Mayer*, courts may choose this escape if their severe misgivings about one parent's suitability prevent application of the ordinary unarticulated guidelines favoring that parent's sole custody. In other words, although joint custody may pose psychological advantages for the children in certain cases, provided both parents are able to collaborate effectively, it may also sweep potential arguments under the rug and prevent their adjudication.

In the 1980s California experimented with a joint custody statute that proved quite controversial. Under pressure from "father's rights" groups, the legislature enacted a presumption in favor of joint custody *when the parents requested it.* California Civil Code section 4600.5 (1980). Combined with this limited presumption, however, was a provision preferring as a sole custodian "the parent most likely to allow the parent or child frequent and continuing contact with the noncustodial parent." California Civil Code section 4600(b)(1980). Thus, a parent's judgment that sole custody would be better than joint custody could be used against that parent. A judge might well be convinced that the other parent, who was seeking joint instead of sole custody, would be more likely than the parent seeking sole custody to allow frequent and continuing contact between the child and the other parent. Such legislation could prove particularly destructive in cases in which a parent believes that the other parent may be sexually molesting their child. If one parent raises such allegations against the other, but cannot prove them to the satisfaction of an often-skeptical judge, that parent risks losing custody. Yet, agreeing to joint custody leaves the parent in a particularly poor position to protect the child if molestation is taking place.

There are other reasons that may speak against the concept of joint custody. Parents who have been unable to maintain a marriage, may well be unable to maintain a joint custody arrangement. The traditional reluctance of courts to award any form of split custody may have had some sound psychological basis. Underlying conceptions of a proprietary nature also disfavor joint custody awards. Although courts disclaim the influence of property notions when they state that the child is not a chattel, they are by a long historical development influenced by the styles of property adjudication. Of course, this does not mean that courts and lawyers use property conceptions consciously, but awareness of this background helps in understanding their patterns of reasoning. The ideal of joint custody of children after divorce appears to have a utopian quality. It pretends, for purposes of child custody, that the marriage continues. This unreality may be confusing to a child and indeed detrimental if it prevents the child from confronting the divorce and its effect on the once intact family unit. Further complications may arise in those cases in which the child's parents remarry and form new relationships. In some cases, especially when remarriages do not occur, joint custody may be psychologically sound for the children. But, what may be psychologically desirable for children in certain cases should not be confused with all cases; what in fact takes place in child custody proceedings and what actually happens thereafter may be far from ideal.

Mayer enumerates some of the factors that favor joint custody. Most important is the willingness and capacity of the parents to cooperate as they would, for example, in a divorce settlement. To impose joint custody in a strongly disputed case, as in *Mayer*, may invite future factual and legal complications. Another factor implicit in *Mayer* is the parents' relatively high socioeconomic status and high educational levels. Age of the children and the logistics of geography may have a bearing too, affecting the children's schooling and the length of time they live in the physical custody of either parent. A crucial factor is the nature of the specific joint custody. Numerous distinct types of arrangements may be involved concerning either physical custody, as in *Mayer*, or aspects of shared decision making by the parents. The latter, though not foreclosed, was not emphasized in *Mayer* but is now one of the most popular forms of joint custody. Any of these elements of joint custody requires a degree of sophistication of parties and judges that cannot necessarily be expected. To the extent that a consensus on joint custody has been reached, that consensus seems to be that expectations for its workability were somewhat too high.

REFERENCE

Nancy K. Lemon, *Joint Custody as a Statutory Presumption: California's New Civil Code Sections 4600 and 4600.5*, 11 GOLDEN GATE U.L. REV. 485 (1981).

D: CHILD SUPPORT

Amount of Support

BORIS v. BLAISDELL
Appellate Court of Illinois
142 Ill. App. 3d 1034, 492 N.E.2d 622 (1986)

Presiding Justice BILANDIC delivered the opinion of the court:

[Respondent challenged the constitutionality of Illinois' support guidelines and asserted that the trial court abused its discretion.]

The judgment for dissolution of marriage was entered in 1979. Under the terms of the decree, which incorporated the parties' agreement, petitioner was awarded custody of the couple's two-year-old son, Bart. Respondent was to pay $275 a month in child support, and both parties waived maintenance.

On June 8, 1984, when Bart was seven years old, petitioner filed a motion for an increase in respondent's child support payments, alleging both that the child had increased needs and that respondent had increased income. The trial court held hearings on the motion on October 17 and November 9, 1984. The evidence revealed that petitioner had a net monthly income of $2,046 and that respondent's current net monthly income was $1,986. The income for each party had increased since the entry of the decree of divorce.

Petitioner also introduced evidence showing that the needs of their son had increased. This was attributable to higher expenses for school tuition, camp, child care and counseling.

The trial court found that petitioner sustained her burden of showing the increased needs of Bart and the increase in respondent's ability to pay child support. The court also found that it "must follow the guidelines established by the new law passed by the legislature." Finding that respondent's net monthly income was approximately $2,000, the court ordered child support increased from $275 per month to $400 per month.

...

THE CHALLENGED STATUTE

Section 505 of the Marriage and Dissolution of Marriage Act provided in part as follows:

Sec. 505. Child Support; Contempt; Penalties.

(a) In a proceeding for dissolution of marriage, legal separation, declaration of invalidity of marriage, a proceeding for child support following dissolution of the marriage by a court which lacked personal jurisdiction over the absent spouse or any proceeding authorized under Section 601 of this Act, the court may order either or both parents owing a duty of support to a child of the marriage to pay an amount reasonable and necessary for his support, without regard to marital misconduct, after considering all relevant factors, including:

(1) the financial resources of the child;

(2) the financial resources and needs of the custodial parent;

(3) the standard of living the child would have enjoyed had the marriage not been dissolved;

(4) the physical and emotional condition of the child, and his education needs; and

(5) the financial resources and needs of the noncustodial parent or parents.

In cases involving child support alone, the Court shall determine the minimum amount of support by using the following guidelines:

Number of Children	Percent of Income (Net)
1	20%
2	25%
3	32%
4	40%
5	45%
6 or more	50%

...

In cases wherein health/hospitalization insurance coverage is not being furnished to dependents to be covered by the support order, the court shall order such coverage and shall reduce net income by the reasonable cost thereof in determining the minimum amount of support to be ordered.

The above guidelines, including dependent health/hospitalization insurance coverage are binding in each case unless the court makes express findings of fact as to the reason for departure below the guidelines. The guidelines may be exceeded by the court without express findings or by agreement of the parties. If the total gross income cannot be determined because of default or any other reason, the court shall order maintenance or support or both in an amount considered reasonable in the particular case.

Debts owed to private creditors are not to be considered in establishing a support obligation. Previous support orders and maintenance orders may be considered if the obligor is paying them.

(Ill.Ann.Stat., ch. 40, par. 505 (Smith-Hurd 1985 Supp.).)...

Legislative History

Respondent's constitutional challenge is based on the assumption that under Section 505(a), courts are mandated to follow literally the schedule for child support. If this reading is correct, the function of the court is reduced to that of a computer or robot. In this case, the sole function of the court would be to determine the net income of the noncustodial parent, determine the number of children, and calculate the amount of child support by applying the percentage of net income stated in the schedule. However, respondent has failed to show that the statute can or should be read to effectively prohibit judicial discretion.

...

It is obvious that the legislature did not usurp any judicial function. On the contrary, it codified the procedure that was functioning successfully in the circuit court of Cook County. The guidelines merely provide a place to begin an analysis.

No judge should, or properly could, surrender the responsibilities of considering all relevant factors dictated by Illinois law in reaching an appropriate result....

Section 505(a) was amended again in 1985 by P.A. 84-888 and 84-979, which retained the same child support guidelines but emphasized the discretion vested in the courts. Subsection (a)(2) provided in part:

> (2) The above guidelines shall be applied in each case unless the court, after considering evidence presented on all relevant factors, finds a reason for deviating from the guidelines. Relevant factors may include but are not limited to:
>
> (a) the financial resources of the child;
>
> (b) the financial resources and needs of the custodial parent;
>
> (c) the standard of living the child would have enjoyed had the marriage not been dissolved;
>
> (d) the physical and emotional condition of the child, and his education needs; and
>
> (e) the financial resources and needs of the non-custodial parent.

...

The guidelines legislation has, in reality, shifted the burden of presenting evidence in a child support hearing to the parent who wishes to shift the noncustodial parent's contribution below or above the specified percentages. And the legislation has established standards for the court to follow in deviating from those percentages.

This flexibility in the law saves it against any of respondent's allegations of unconstitutionality....

...

Respondent contends that a noncustodial parent has a fundamental right not to support one's children, beyond the provision of basic necessities, regardless of the parent's financial ability. Such a right would destroy the historic standards by which Illinois courts have determined the appropriate amount of child support by taking into account the incomes of the parents. Respondent cites no authority to support his argument and we are not aware of any.

Respondent also contends that to the extent that noncustodial parents are required to pay more than the minimum cost of raising a child, H.B. 3068 infringes on the parent's right to remarry and have additional children, thereby violating substantive due process protected by the Federal Constitution. This argument, if accepted, would impede the traditional authority of both the state legislature and state courts to regulate the determination and enforcement of child support orders beyond basic necessities. His argument is supported neither by logic nor by authority. The extent to which Section 505(a) regulates the marriage relationship is well within the legislature's traditional power and responsibility in this area.

...

Respondent contends that the statute violates the equal protection clause of the Federal and State Constitutions. The basis of his argument is that although the statute is neutral on its face, it unfairly discriminates against men in favor of women in its application because statistics indicate that in 88% of divorces, men are the noncustodial parents.

Respondent again relies on the assumption that the statutory guidelines are mandatory. Although the statute obviously distinguishes between custodial and noncustodial parents, the statute treats all divorced parents alike, and thus does not deny noncustodial parents equal protection....

Even if the statute can be construed to treat noncustodial parents differently, such classification is proper. The equal protection clause does not deny a state the power to differentiate between persons similarly situated if there is a rational basis for doing so.... [T]he statute includes a percentage of noncustodial parents' income in order to standardize and increase child support in light of comprehensive studies showing inadequate awards....

Sufficient differences exist between custodial and noncustodial parents to warrant the conclusion that they comprise different classes. The major distinction here is that a custodial parent has the primary and general responsibility to care for the child.

Noncustodial parents are assessed a specific amount for child support payments, while custodial parents are not so assessed. But custodial and noncustodial parents are not "similarly situated" since, after divorce, the custodial parent's responsibility for the child's support as well as care is general and plenary, while the noncustodial parent's responsibility is usually limited to the requirements of the support order. While both parents are responsible for the child's support, it is not the child support schedules themselves but the very fact that the noncustodial parent must discharge his or her responsibility by making cash payments to the custodial parent which initially distinguishes them. The schedules themselves do not create a legislative "classification"; they merely structure, subject to court adjustment, the noncustodial parent's contribution in an effort to shift some of the burden of care and support from the custodial parent. The legislature could rationally have concluded that the percentages of the noncustodial parent's net income included in the guidelines constituted a fair point of departure and fully rebuttable presumption in attempting to equalize, or at least make more equitable, the share of the noncustodial parent's contribution....

...

In amending Section 505(a), the legislature could rationally have "assumed" that the custodial parent is already contributing to the support of the child in an amount equivalent to the percentage schedules, and constructed the schedules, subject to modification in any individual case, on that assumption.... The statute does not deprive the respondent of equal protection of law under the Federal and Illinois Constitutions.

...

SCHMIDT v. SCHMIDT

Supreme Court of South Dakota
444 N.W.2d 367 (S.D. 1989)

SABERS, Justice.

Mother appeals a change in custody of the eldest of three boys to Father. Father appeals the requirement that he pay $250 monthly child support for two boys.

FACTS

Father and Mother were divorced on July 13, 1984. They had three children during the marriage; David, Randy, and Michael. By stipulation, Father and Mother agreed that Mother would receive custody of the three boys. Custody was not contested at the divorce hearing, and Father appeared without counsel.

Mother presented evidence in the form of testimony and exhibits. The trial court awarded custody of the three boys to Mother. As provided in the stipulation, Father was ordered to pay $375 monthly child support.[1]

Following the divorce, Father continued to farm near Flandreau, South Dakota. Mother lived in Brookings, South Dakota, where she worked at Minnesota Mining & Manufacturing (3M). On June 3, 1988, Father made a motion to modify the child custody and support provisions in the divorce decree. Father requested custody of the oldest, David, and that all three boys be permitted to reside with him during the summer months. The motion further requested that child support obligations be modified accordingly. A hearing was held on the motion on July 25, 1988.

David was fourteen at the time of the hearing. Father introduced evidence showing that David enjoyed the farm and preferred to live with Father. On the farm, David did chores and repair work on an old car. According to Father's testimony, Randy, age eleven, and Michael, age nine, also enjoyed the farm.

...

On September 12, 1988, the trial court amended the original divorce decree and gave Father custody of David. The decree was also modified to permit all three boys to live with Father during the summer months, with the exception of three weeks when all three would be with Mother. Father's monthly child support was reduced to $250 and reduced further to $125 during the summer months when all three boys stay with Father. Mother appeals the custody change and denial of attorney fees. Father appeals the amount of child support. We affirm the change of custody and denial of attorney fees and reverse and remand on child support.

...

After granting Father custody of David, the court modified Father's monthly child support obligation. The court determined Father's child support under the guidelines in SDCL 25-7-7 by cancelling out one child with each parent, leaving Mother with an additional child. The court then considered Father's child support for one child under the guidelines. Father's net monthly income at the time of the hearing was $1,250. Accordingly, the court set Father's monthly child support at $250. Father claims this was error. He claims that the court should have compared the amount of child support Father would pay for two children under the guidelines against the amount of child support Mother would pay for one child and subtract the difference to determine Father's support.

We agree with Father in part. SDCL 25-7-7 provides that "The child support obligation shall be established in accordance with the obligor's net income and number of children affected[.]" Following the change of custody, Father was obligated to pay support for two children based on his net monthly income of $1,250. Mother was obligated to pay support for one child based on her net monthly income of $1,582. Since Mother's net monthly income exceeded Father's, her child support obligation for one nearly cancels out Father's child support obligation for two under the guidelines.[2] Mother argues that such a formula may lead to absurd

1. Father missed certain support payments which he claimed was due to sporadic income from the farm. He made the payments following an order to show cause. Following this, the trial court increased Father's monthly child support to $420 pursuant to the child support guidelines in SDCL 25-7-7.

2. Under the guidelines, Father's obligation for two children with his net monthly income of $1,250 would be between $360 to $390 monthly. Mother's obligation for one child with her net monthly income of $1,582 would be at least $330 monthly. Subtracting the difference, Father would owe child support of approximately $30 to $60 monthly.

results.[3] However, SDCL 25-7-7 does not permit deviation from the guidelines absent specific findings. *Bruning v. Jeffries*, 422 N.W.2d 579 (S.D.1988). Thus, the trial court erred in its calculation of child support. We reverse and remand for the trial court to reconsider child support in accordance with this opinion. We note, however, this may provide inadequate support for the boys. Father's farm occupation provides certain necessities, such as housing, utilities, transportation, etc. which would otherwise be personal expenses. On remand, the trial court may look to the record and make additional specific findings which may support deviations from the child support guidelines and provide adequate support.

Affirmed in part, reversed and remanded in part.

[Concurring opinions omitted.]

WHITE v. MARCIANO

California Court of Appeal

190 Cal.App.3d 1026, 235 Cal.Rptr. 779 (1987)

FUKUTO, Associate Justice.

Plaintiff, Fabienne White, appeals the court's judgment in her paternity action against respondent, Maurice Marciano, in which he was ordered to pay child support in the sum of $1,500 per month. We affirm.

...

Appellant filed her action seeking a declaration that respondent is the father of appellant's baby and an order that respondent pay "reasonable child support in accordance with his abilities and the child's needs."

...[A]ppellant asserted reasonable support would amount to $3,500 per month plus medical benefits.... [R]espondent admitted that he was the baby's father and that he could "pay any reasonable sum for the support of this newly born child." He submitted a responsive income and expense declaration, but gave no financial information, asserting that it was "not applicable in view of stipulation."

At the hearing on the order to show cause, respondent again stipulated that he had the ability to pay any reasonable support order, including the $3,500 per month requested by appellant, but contended that $3,500 per month was excessive. He also admitted that he had an income of approximately $1 million per year.

Based upon respondent's admissions and stipulations, the court sustained objections to questions concerning respondent's lifestyle and net worth.

Respondent was ordered to pay $1,500 per month as temporary support for the baby.

...

The father and mother of a child have an equal responsibility to support and educate their child.... Illegitimate and legitimate children are to be treated alike.... California has enacted legislation to guide the trial court in determining both the

3. Assume a mother with custody of five children and a net monthly income of $1,500, and father with a net monthly income of $1,000. Father would pay approximately $350 per month child support to the mother under the guidelines. However, if the father were to gain custody of one child he would no longer pay any child support for the four children in mother's custody. In fact, the mother would be required to pay $20 per month for support of the one child in the father's custody. While such a result appears inequitable, such a result is required under the current guidelines in the absence of specific findings supporting deviations. In this context, it is important to note that the guidelines in SDCL 25-7-7 have been replaced with new guidelines effective July 1, 1989.

needs of the child and the amount of child support to be awarded to meet those needs.

The Agnos Child Support Standards Act of 1984 establishes a system of mandatory minimum child support amounts.... When appropriate, a higher amount of child support may be awarded. In setting a higher level of child support, the court "shall be guided by the criteria set forth in applicable statutes, relevant case law...and the legislative intent that children share in their parents' standard of living...." (Civ.Code, §4724.)

A child is to be supported in the manner suitable to the child's circumstances, taking into consideration the parents' respective earnings or earning capacity of the parties....

Generally, children are entitled to be supported in a style and condition consonant with the position in society of their parents.... A parent's duty of support does not end with the furnishing of mere necessities if the parent is able to afford more. Support must be reasonable under the circumstances.... How much "more," i.e., what amount is "reasonable" is defined in relation to a child's "needs" and varies with the circumstances of the parties....

Clearly where the child has a wealthy parent, that child is entitled to, and therefore "needs" something more than the bare necessities of life. It is also clear that the court is required to consider, in a general sense, the non-custodial parent's standard of living. However, contrary to appellant's contentions, a trial court is not required to consider detailed lifestyle and net worth evidence in reaching a decision as to the needs of the child or the amount of support to be awarded.

The standard of living to which a child is entitled should be measured in terms of the standard of living attainable by the income available to the parents rather than by evidence of the manner in which the parents' income is expended and the parents' resulting lifestyle. It matters not whether the respondent, non-custodial parent, miserly hoarded his $1 million per year income and lived the life of a pauper or whether he lived the life of a prince spending every cent of the available income.

We believe evidence of detailed lifestyle and net worth to be relevant only in those situations where the ability of the non-custodial parent to make adequate support payments may be affected by the unwise expenditure of income to the detriment of the supported minor. Where there is no question of the non-custodial parent's ability to pay any reasonable support order, we conclude that evidence of detailed lifestyle to be irrelevant to the issue of the amount of support to be paid and thus protected from discovery and inadmissible in determining the support order.

...

In the case at bench, the court considered respondent's stipulation that he had an annual income of $1 million; that he lived a lifestyle commensurate with that income; and that he could pay any reasonable amount of child support. Appellant testified that she is 30 years old, left high school after the eleventh grade and never returned, works as a model and food stylist for television commercials and makes an annual income of approximately $14,000. Appellant also testified that she lives in a two-bedroom apartment with her 81-year-old grandmother and the baby. The rental on the apartment is $600 per month, with appellant contributing $300 and her grandmother contributing $300. Appellant's grandmother usually takes care of the baby while appellant is working. Appellant's 11-year-old daughter from her marriage, who resides with appellant's ex-husband, occasionally visits on weekends and other times.... Appellant then testified concerning what she would like for herself and the child. She would like to move from a neighborhood she considers to be unsafe to a three-bedroom house, near a park. Appellant also testified that she would like to hire a full-time nanny for the baby. Based upon the evidence presented, the court fixed $1,500 as a reasonable sum for support of a 21-month-old child. The court noted that the award of $1,500 "undoubtedly will allow plaintiff to substantially improve her own economic status, in that it should cover more than the direct out-of-pocket expenses incurred on behalf of the minor." This conclusion is consistent with the evidence presented and there was no abuse of discretion.

Appellant also contends that the trial court ruled "in effect that illegitimate children may be treated differently from legitimate children insofar as the lifestyle of a wealthy parent was disregarded by the court." Appellant contends that the father's failure to exercise visitation denies the child the opportunity to enjoy the same standard of living enjoyed by the father and permits the father to support the child in a style below what is consistent with the father's earnings and position in society. Such an interpretation of the trial court's order is unsupported by the record. The court below acknowledged the broad public policy that illegitimate and legitimate children are to be treated alike, and then applied the *Stargell* standard and set the amount of the child support award by determining that which was "reasonable under the circumstances." The record indicates that the trial judge considered respondent's admissions and stipulations concerning his ability to pay, his status as a millionaire and commensurate lifestyle in setting the amount of support. More importantly, the trial court, consistent with this court's conclusion, measured the standard of living to which the child should be entitled by the standard of living attainable by the income available to both the child's parents.

...

The judgment is affirmed.

COMMENTS

Generations of divorced mothers have known that child support payments are woefully inadequate to raise a child; typically support payments provide only a minor supplement. Generations of divorced fathers have considered these same support payments to be an oppressive burden. Sacrificing for one's children feels very different when the children live with one than when they do not. The same father who may have insisted that his wife stay home to raise their children would likely consider it an outrage if he were expected to make child support payments large enough to support his ex-wife as a stay-at-home mother. The same parent who lavishes money upon new children born to a new spouse may begrudge every dollar spent for bare necessities for earlier-born children living with an ex-spouse.

As women became more vocal and as the issue of the costs of raising children became politicized, changes in child support occurred. Awareness grew that the amount of support awarded varied widely within a single jurisdiction, based upon the discretion of the judge. Sentiment grew to enact guidelines to reduce the uncertainty and injustice that so often accompanies such broad discretion. The movement toward greater certainty was accelerated by federal legislation — Title

IV-D of the Social Security Act and the Child Enforcement Amendments of 1984 — which requires every state, in order to receive federal AFDC funds, to develop some form of child support guidelines. The Illinois support guidelines found constitutional in *Boris v. Blaisdell* are fairly typical of the guidelines in all fifty states. These guidelines reduce uncertainty and generally result in larger child support awards, sometimes considerably larger. Opinions differ regarding whether the guidelines are simply a "starting point" or whether they should be treated as a rebuttable presumption, or something in between. Some fear that overburdened courts may welcome reducing their function to "that of a computer or robot" and apply the guidelines mechanically, but others fear that courts accustomed to exercise discretion will unreasonably continue to do so and pay too little attention to the guidelines or the actual costs of raising children.

The non-custodial father in *Boris v. Blaisdell* tried to take advantage of the fact that the law imposes only the most minimal legal support obligation with respect to a child living together with the parents. A child of divorce living with his mother may in theory receive more money from his father than he would receive were he living with the father. In practice, however, children typically receive considerably less support from non-custodial parents than from custodial parents. Parents generally spend more money on children in their household than they do for children for whom they pay court-ordered support.

Schmidt may well have been an exception to the general rule that fathers pay less money to support non-custodial children than they spend to support a child living in their household. Mr. Schmidt may have spent even less on his son's support when the child was living in the father's household. It is not clear whether the oldest son who did "chores and repair work on an old car" on the farm required any resources or perhaps even contributed more financially to the household than the cost of his food and other expenses. By claiming custody of one son, the father was able to reduce sharply his support obligation to his other two sons, living in town with the mother. *Schmidt* involved two factors making the guidelines problematic. First, most or all guidelines provide less support per child, the more children there are. The *Boris v. Blaisdell* guidelines, for example, specify twenty percent of net income for one child and twenty-five percent for two children. Thus, if these guidelines were applied in a case such as *Schmidt*, they would result in the mother caring for two children receiving nothing in support and owing $13.90 a month to the father when he took one of the three children. (Or, in the example hypothesized in *Schmidt* footnote 3, the father would owe the mother $450.00 a month if she had custody of all five children but only $100 a month if he assumed custody of just one of the five children.) It seems unlikely that the overall household expenses of the custodial parent are greatly reduced by the transfer of custody of one child, yet in many or most cases the household expenses of a non-custodial parent will increase considerably by assuming custody of even one child. As the court suggested, however, Mr. Schmidt's household expenses probably did not increase significantly. The second and more important factor that makes the guidelines problematic in *Schmidt* is that it likely costs far more to raise two children in the city than to raise one in the country.

Mothers complain that fathers can unfairly reduce their support obligations not only by exercising joint custody or custody of one child, but just by feigning a desire to have custody even when they have no intention to take care of the child. As mentioned in *Garska* (supra at p. 883), a parent who has been the primary caretaker of a child may easily be intimidated into accepting an unfair financial settlement in order to avoid a custody battle. As long as the outcome of a custody dispute is as indeterminate as it generally is, the parent who cares most about custody may feel enormous pressure to negotiate an out-of-court settlement. Under these circumstances, an irresponsible parent can gain financial advantage by demanding joint or sole custody simply as a negotiating posture. Although courts are not bound by parents' agreements on child custody or child support and could refuse to follow unfair agreements, it is uncommon for courts to reject such settlements or to scrutinize them carefully. An irresponsible parent may also avoid having to pay child support by obtaining joint custody with the primary parent. A court that awards joint physical custody may order little or no support, on the assumption that both parents will have costs associated with their custody of the child. Although some divorced fathers are good parents and some joint custody awards are made and carried out in good faith, there are also fathers with joint custody who seldom even see their children and for whom the joint award is merely a ploy to avoid support. To a casual observer, the situation may look roughly equal: mothers complain that they do not get the support they need for the children and fathers complain that they do not get as much custody as they ask for. In fact, however, too many of the fathers who complain have no intention of expending any effort to care for children and simply want to avoid responsibility to their children, who grow up in relative poverty.

The impoverished unmarried mother in *White v. Marciano* would have been happy to have child support guidelines applied mechanically and to receive, say, twenty percent of the millionaire father's net income. Most courts would consider *Marciano* an appropriate case to depart from the guidelines and refuse to award more than $1500 a month, or $18,000 a year to the mother earning $14,000 a year at work. Yet, we would expect that upon a divorce, a man of Mr. Marciano's wealth would be ordered to pay his ex-wife higher child support for a legitimate child the same age as Marciano's illegitimate child. One could argue that the difference is the station in life to which such a child born in wedlock would be entitled or accustomed (though it is unlikely that one can really say that young a child is accustomed to a standard of living). The case may also involve a moral judgment about the unwed mother in *Marciano* (but not about the unwed father) and a providential judgment about the use of the money and the extent to which it would be used for the child, as opposed to the mother. Would one expect the unwed mother to receive higher support payments if she, too, were very wealthy and could realistically be expected to spend a great deal more money raising the child? If not, is it still possible to maintain that the support award in *Marciano* does not discriminate on the basis of illegitimacy?

Modification

Career Changes

ROMANO v. ROMANO
Supreme Court of Vermont
133 Vt. 314, 340 A.2d 63 (1975)

BARNEY, Chief Justice.

In response to modification petitions from both plaintiff-wife and defendant-husband...monthly support payment was increased to $500.00. The defendant appeals.

At the time of the divorce and subsequent to it, the defendant was employed at a salary sufficient to comply with a monthly support order for the children of $435.00. His wife had been awarded the family house and custody of the four minor children, then ranging in age from about seven to twelve years.

The defendant had also embarked in a program of acquiring a legal education outside of his employment hours, which he has more than half completed. It is his expressed intention and desire to cease work to complete his legal education so that he may sooner embark on his new profession. This will inevitably make it impossible for him to comply with either the present or the previous support order.

Two differently constituted trial courts have, at different times, passed on the defendant's request that he be excused from the required support obligation in order to finish his legal studies. Both have found that making such a drastic change in his earning powers, in the face of his duty to provide for his children, would jeopardize the welfare of those children, and could not be accepted as a good faith change. The existence of facts indicating a deliberate sacrificing of income in order to reduce a support obligation is condemnable.... Such a determination by the trial courts is peculiarly within their responsibility and is entitled to great, if not controlling, weight.

The defendant counters this by contending that if the house and custody of the children were returned to him he would be entirely able to carry out his responsibilities to his children, without having to give up his dream of becoming a lawyer. The responsibilities of begetting a family many times raise havoc with dreams. Nevertheless, the duty persists, with full authority in the State to enforce it....

Moreover, it is the function of the trial court to render the decisions as to the measure and manner of implementing that duty of support. That judgment is seldom easy or simple, since it usually involves the apportioning of inadequate resources among constantly increasing needs. But it is for the trial court to make, to be disturbed or remanded by this Court only in the presence of legal error or the absence of factual support for the result....

In this case the original order was made when the defendant was earning about $17,000.00 a year, and the upward revision when his earnings were $18,500.00. The facts unquestionably establish plaintiff's change for the worse, between inflation and her loss of employment. All these play a part in support of the lower court.

...

...The order under review speaks of "bad faith", with reference to the defendant's expressed intent to give up his job and study law. If this had in fact occurred, such a finding would be within the proper province of the court. But, as far as any record before us demonstrates, this has not happened, and if the amendment of the support order rested on that consideration, it is unsupported. However, according to information in the record furnished this Court, not yet available to the lower court, the defendant has taken a new job, this time in Vermont, at the lower salary of $15,000.00. In reviewing the amended order, this fact, if still persisting, should be taken into account, both as affecting the defendant's ability to pay, as well as to his good faith in changing positions. Thus, in essence, the remand can and should encompass the entire scope of the defendant's support obligations, past, present, and future, in the light of all pertinent facts.

...

Family Changes

COMMONWEALTH ex rel. KAPLAN v. KAPLAN

Superior Court of Pennsylvania
236 Pa.Super 26, 344 A.2d 578 (1975)

HOFFMAN, Judge:

The sole issue in the instant case is whether the lower court abused its discretion when it increased a preexisting support order of $130.00 per month by $40.00 per month.

Appellant, Eileen Weingrad, formerly Eileen Kaplan, married appellee Gary Kaplan, on December 24, 1961, in Philadelphia. On May 5, 1963, appellant gave birth to a child, Michael. Thereafter, the couple separated. Appellant filed a complaint in the Philadelphia County Court on March 24, 1964, in which she asked that appellee be ordered to provide support for his son. On February 19, 1965, the court ordered appellee to pay $100.00 per month, pursuant to a stipulation by the parties. In 1971, appellant filed a petition to increase the order of support. On February 5, 1971, the court entered an order of $130.00 per month. At that time, appellee was working in New York City and was earning $17,400 per year.

On October 1, 1974, appellant again petitioned for an increase in the amount of the support order. She alleged a change of circumstances as a basis for the increase: her wages had been reduced from $130.00 per week to $90.00 per week, the child's needs, especially due to medical expenses, had increased sharply, appellee was earning $29,500.00 per year, had purchased an expensive home in a fashionable section of New Jersey, and owned two "luxury" cars. A hearing was held on December 13, 1974, followed by an order dated December 30, 1974, in which the court ordered that appellee pay $170.00 per month. Appellant requests this Court to increase that amount to $125.00 per week.

Initially, we must reiterate several blackletter principles of law governing child support. The purpose of a support order is to protect and to advance the welfare of the child.... The responsibility of the parents, to support the child to the best of their ability, consistent with their own station in life, is "well nigh absolute."...

The problem in the instant case revolves around two critical facts. First, since the 1971 decree, the appellee's salary — his sole source of income — has arisen from $17,400 to $29,500. Second, although appellant's income has declined, from $130.00 to $90.00 per week, appellant acknowledges that her earning capacity is at least $130.00 per week.

The appellant claims that in light of the luxuries that the father is able to afford — a fine home, two cars with the ancillary maintenance costs, nursery school for one of his children from his second marriage, generous allowance for entertainment and personal maintenance — he should be required to pay more money towards the support of his son Michael, so that Michael, too, can share in some of the affluence.

On the other hand, a mother also has an obligation to support her child. The test is not what her actual earnings are, but what her earning capacity is. Such has always been the law governing a father's duty of support....

The appellant testified as follows on the subject of her earning capacity:

Q. Have you looked for other higher paying work?

A. There would be higher paying jobs that would take me into Center City. I cannot do that. I would be too far from the place of residence, too far from my son.

Q. Isn't it true that you have refused to work anywhere in Center City where the higher paying jobs are available?

A. Yes.

Q. ...Did she [an employment counsellor] tell you that you could get a job in Center City with your skills for perhaps a hundred and fifty dollars per week?

A. Yes.

Further, appellee's witness, an employment counsellor, testified that appellant was qualified for currently available jobs with starting salaries of $125 to $130 per week. Thus, there is no question that the mother's take-home pay does not reflect her full earning capacity.

Ordinarily, given the father's income, a higher support order would be proper. Although appellee claims expenses in excess of his income, a child cannot be denied a fair support order because one of the parents is living above his means. Further, the father is living well. He has taken on substantial mortgage payments; he provides generously for the two children by his second marriage; his wife can afford not to work; his list of expenses indicates that his family has considerable material luxury. Michael is entitled to benefit from his father's good fortune. On the other hand, we cannot ignore entirely the mother's unwillingness to increase her income.[4]

Weighing all the factors, as we must, we conclude that the order of support is inadequate.[5] To order payments of $125 per week as requested by appellant would

4. We are, of course, aware of the increased expenses that the mother would face if she were to work in Center City. The net income, even after increased travel and baby-sitting expenses, would however, be greater than the money that she currently takes home.

5. ...

Some of the financial figures relevant to our decision include:

	Appellee	*Appellant*
Disposable income per month (approximate)	$1800.00	$360–400
Per person	$ 450.00	$180–200
Transportation expenses and related maintenance costs	$ 312.25	$ 65.00
Food per month	$ 280.00	$ 83.00
Food per month per person	$ 70.00	$ 41.50

be confiscatory. Nonetheless, we believe that the order should be increased to assure Michael some of the advantages that accrue to appellee's other children.

The case is remanded to the lower court for proceedings consistent with this opinion.

...

AINSWORTH v. AINSWORTH

Supreme Court of Vermont
154 Vt. 103, 574 A.2d 772 (1990)

DOOLEY, Justice.

This action for modification of child support calls upon us to interpret Vermont's recently enacted child support guidelines law, 15 V.S.A. §§650-663. Specifically at issue is whether expenses for a second family should enter into the determination of child support for the preexisting family. Although the trial court decided that defendant, Reginald Ainsworth, did not have a duty to support his stepson under 15 V.S.A. §296, it held, pursuant to §659, that a child support order based on the guidelines sought by plaintiff, Julie Ann Ainsworth, on her behalf and on behalf of the two children of the parties, would be inequitable and ordered him to pay them less than what would be required under the guidelines. Plaintiff appealed and we reverse and remand.

The parties were divorced on April 30, 1986. They stipulated then that defendant was to pay child support in the amount of $35 per week for each of their two children for a total of $70 per week. Mr. Ainsworth remarried on August 15, 1987, and established a new home with his wife and her son at that time. On September 21, 1987, plaintiff filed a motion for modification pursuant to 15 V.S.A. §660,[1] seeking increased support in an amount to be determined under the guidelines mandated by the statute that was effective on April 1, 1987....

...

In order to fully and logically analyze the issues presented by plaintiff's appeal, we will recategorize the issues from those used by the trial court into three questions: (1) whether the trial court may deviate from child support amounts calculated under the guidelines when defendant is supporting children in a second family; (2) if the answer to the first question is yes, whether the power to deviate applies if the children in the second family are stepchildren and not natural children; and (3) if the answer to the first two questions is yes, whether the actual order in this case was within the discretion of the trial court....

...

---

5. *Continued*

Such figures are indicative of too great a disparity between appellee's family's life style and that of his son Michael. Because we recognize that inflation and cost of living increases have eroded some of the appellee's salary increases, we feel too great an increase to the support order would deprive appellee and his family the advantages of his hard work.

1. Section 660 provides in part:

> (a) On motion of either parent...and upon a showing of a real, substantial and unanticipated change of circumstances, the court may annul, vary or modify a child support order, whether or not the order is based upon a stipulation or agreement.
>
> (b) A child support order, including an order in effect prior to adoption of the support guideline, which varies more than 15 percent from the amounts required to be paid under the support guideline, shall be considered a real, substantial and unanticipated change of circumstances.

In Vermont, the guideline amounts are established by rule of the Secretary of Human Services. See 15 V.S.A. §654; Dep't of Social Welfare, Agency of Human Services, *Child Support Guidelines Handbook* (1987). Under the guideline regulations, a basic support amount for the children is derived from tables based solely on the total gross income of the parents and the number of children. See 15 V.S.A. §653(1)("Basic support obligation" defined as guideline amount unless court finds that amount inequitable and establishes a different amount). The next step is to calculate a "total support obligation" by adding expenditures in two categories to the basic support amount:

(1) the amount of child care costs reasonably incurred by a parent as a result of employment or employment related education, *id.* §653(2), (9); and

(2) extraordinary medical or education expenses, *id.* §653(4), (9).

Once the total support obligation is calculated, the amount is divided between the parents "in proportion to their respective gross incomes." *Id.* §656(a). In this calculation, as well as in the derivation of the basic support amount from the tables, a broad definition of gross income is used. See *id.* §653(5). There are, however, three exclusions from income in reaching the "gross incomes" recognized by the statute:

(1) the amount of "preexisting spousal maintenance or child support obligations actually paid," *id.* §653(5)(E)(i);

(2) amounts received from means tested public assistance programs, *id.* §653(5)(E)(ii); and

(3) the actual cost of providing adequate health insurance coverage for the involved children, *id.* §653(5)(E)(iii).

Except as set forth above, the actual expenditures of the parents are not relevant to the guideline calculation. Thus, the guideline calculation for a noncustodial parent with a large mortgage payment would be the same as for a noncustodial parent with a low rent payment as long as both have the same income.

The total support obligation calculated under the guideline is "presumed to be the amount of child support needed," upon which the noncustodial parent's obligation is calculated. *Id.* §655. However, if the court finds that a child support order based on the guidelines "would be inequitable," the court may establish support after considering all relevant factors. *Id.* §659(a). The statute contains a noninclusive list of factors to be considered. *Id.* §659(a)(1)-(8).

I

The first question we face is whether the trial court can find an order based on the guidelines "inequitable" because of the expenses of supporting another child when the support obligation for that other child did not preexist the one for the child or children included in the guideline calculation. We believe that the trial court has this power.

We start with the wording chosen by the Legislature to describe when the court should deviate from the guidelines. The term "equitable" normally means "[j]ust; conformable to the principles of justice and right." Black's Law Dictionary 482 (5th ed. 1979). Thus, the use of the term "inequitable" must give the trial court authority to look at whether a guideline-based amount is just under the circumstances.

We have held that the Legislature gave trial courts broad discretion when it required an "equitable distribution" of marital property. See 15 V.S.A. §751(a). For example, in *Victor v. Victor*, 142 Vt. 126, 130, 453 A.2d 1115, 1117 (1982), we noted that distribution of property is a "matter of broad discretion for the trial court" and that there is no "precise mathematical formula; all that is required is that such distribution be equitable." Consistent with the use of the term "inequitable" in §659, other language in the statute refers to a presumption that the guideline amounts will be used. See 15 V.S.A. §655;...(Vermont statutes create a "rebuttable presumption" of use of the guidelines). Such a characterization is consistent with the concept of a guideline as a guide to appropriate action rather than a precise mandate.

While the wording chosen by the Legislature makes clear that it intended to give trial courts discretion to ensure support awards are just, this is an area where we must be careful to define the nature and scope of that discretion so that it is not used to create inequity or to undermine the standardization that the Legislature intended. Cf. *Klein v. Klein*, 150 Vt. 466, 473, 555 A.2d 382, 386 (1988). If we allow the trial courts to consider any variation in the needs of the children or the living situation or expenses of the parents, we would return to the preguideline law where a wide range of support amounts was permissible in almost every case. In short, the "escape valve" of §659 would eat up the rule and destroy the predictability of amounts and the maintenance of the standard of living of the children that are the desired results of a guideline system.

Our examination of the statutory scheme demonstrates, however, that this case involves the type of situation where the Legislature intended that the court exercise discretion consistent with the policies of the act. That intent is demonstrated by the exclusion from gross income of certain support payments. See 15 V.S.A. §653(5)(E)(i). While the drafting is not a model of clarity, we conclude that the exclusion covers amounts being paid pursuant to preexisting support orders....

It is important to analyze what is covered by the exclusion and what is not. First, as we construe the legislative intent, it requires that there be an actual support order. Second, it requires that the order, not merely the obligation, be preexisting at the time the calculation is made. Third, it requires that payments be made on the order.

The limits of the second requirement are particularly important. It shows that the Legislature was primarily concerned about the timing of the orders. If a noncustodial parent is subject to two child support orders, the amount paid under the first order is always deductible under §653(5)(E)(i) from that parent's income in determining the amount of the second order, even though the child covered by the second order might have been born before the child covered by the first order.

There are practical reasons why the Legislature created a rule allowing a parent to deduct the expenses of other support obligations only in limited circumstances. They are explained in *People in Interest of C.D.*, 767 P.2d at 811–12, in describing the identical Colorado rule:

> Inherent in the statutory scheme is a legislative recognition that child support obligations which have been previously imposed by a court have been determined to be both necessary and reasonable in amount in proper judicial proceedings. Non-ordered support obligations, on the other hand, have not been judicially scrutinized either as to their necessity or their

> reasonableness, and the General Assembly accordingly has not provided for automatic income adjustments based upon those obligations, whether or not they are actually paid.
>
> In addition, jurisdictional and practical impediments render the support schedule an ill-suited device to determine the necessity for, and the reasonableness of, support obligations for persons who are not parties to the proceedings before the court.... [T]he mere fact that a parent may have some legal duty to support other children does not indicate the extent of the support needs of the other children,...whether those needs are or can be met by other persons...[or] an obligor's actual contribution to those needs. The use of the statutory schedule under these circumstances requires the court to make assumptions concerning these matters which may not be wholly warranted.

These reasons involve practical considerations — a formula-guideline system using mathematical calculations may consider only specific, liquidated amounts that are paid periodically.

It would be unfair, however, to consider amounts paid under existing support obligations only when they are the subject of court orders. By allowing consideration of payments made to discharge support obligations in instances where they have been scrutinized by a court and can be fit within mathematical formulas and allowing courts to deviate from support amounts calculated under the guidelines when such amounts are "inequitable," the Legislature must have intended that the courts use their discretion to consider the expenses connected with second families. The use of discretion in this area prevents the guideline system from being wholly arbitrary.

In reaching the conclusion that the court could consider the expenses of supporting other families under §659, we also rely on the fact that the courts in Colorado, the state with a guideline system closest to that adopted in Vermont, have reached the same conclusion. The Colorado courts have held that support obligations to other dependents may be evaluated in determining the extent to which a deviation from the guidelines is necessary to avoid an "inequitable" support order....

For the above reasons, we answer the first question in this case in the affirmative. The trial court may, under §659, find that calculating a support order based on the guidelines would be inequitable because of a parent's expenses in supporting other dependents.

II

The second question is whether the court's discretion under §659 extends to situations where the expenses are for the support of a second wife and a stepchild. The trial court found that Vermont law does not create a general obligation for stepparents to support stepchildren, but went forward to consider the expenses connected with supporting the stepchild in exercising its discretion under §659.

The trial court found no obligation of support in this case because the statutory support obligation of stepparents is limited to situations where the financial resources of the natural parents are inadequate to provide the child with a reasonable subsistence.... Although the stepparent support statute, 15 V.S.A. §296, contains the language cited, it also states that the duty it imposes is "coextensive" with the duty to support a natural child. Therefore, we disagree with the trial court and find that the statute creates a general obligation of support....

Neither the trial court nor the parties have raised any question about the defendant's obligation to support his second wife. The general obligation to support spouses extends to defendant's second spouse. See 15 V.S.A. §291.

III

Having decided that the trial court could find the application of the guidelines to be inequitable in this case, we must address whether the court properly exercised its discretion in setting a support amount. We emphasize here that the fact that the court finds the application of guidelines to be "inequitable" in a particular case does not mean that it must automatically order a substantially lower support amount. As we have held in the case of a finding of changed circumstances to allow modification of a support order, "this conclusion opens the inquiry rather than closing it." *McCormick v. McCormick*, 150 Vt. 431, 437, 553 A.2d 1098, 1102 (1988). The use of §659 means only that the special circumstances of the case make it inappropriate to determine a support amount based solely on the mathematical calculations involved in the guidelines. Instead, the court must consider all "relevant factors," including eight specific ones itemized in the statute. See 15 V.S.A. §659(a)(1)-(8). It may be that an evaluation of these factors will lead to a support award as high as that calculated under the guidelines.

It is particularly important to emphasize that consideration of a case under §659 does not necessarily mean a lower support amount in second-family cases. We have held that a change in financial circumstances "resulting from a deliberate and voluntary act, absent a sufficient reason for the sacrificing of income," will not support a modification of a child support order....

The voluntary nature of second-family obligations is not the only consideration in establishing the child support order under §659. The statute lists eight factors the court must consider. 15 V.S.A. §659(a)(1)-(8). We agree with the trial court in this case that the financial resources of the new spouse of the parent is also a relevant consideration. A parent should not be able to rely on second-family expenses without consideration of second-family income and resources.

We have held with respect to the custody statute, when the Legislature itemized certain factors to be considered in determining parental rights and responsibilities, that the court's findings must show that it took each of the statutory factors into consideration....

The findings and conclusions here are incomplete and much too sketchy to meet the above requirements. The court had evidence from both parties on their income and expenses. The evidence from the defendant showed a high level of consumer debt connected with the purchase of a house and furnishings for his new family. Although the court found that defendant's new spouse had "financial resources as represented by her education and former work experience," it apparently considered her to have no potential income when it set the support amount. In any event, the court never specified how, based on the evidence and its findings, it arrived at the figure of $90 per week as the new child support amount. Nor can we conclude that the court considered all the factors specified in §659(a)(1)-(8) and considered the extent to which the defendant's expenses were voluntarily incurred in the face of his obligation to the children of his first marriage.

Because the findings and conclusions do not specify the reasons for the amount of support awarded and show consideration of the statutory factors, we must reverse and remand for a new hearing.

Reversed and remanded.

MORSE, Justice, dissenting.

Because I believe the Court misconstrues the child support guidelines law, I respectfully dissent.

. . .

Under today's ruling, determination of child support is subject in large measure to the vagaries of individual judgment as to what is fair, given all the facts and circumstances of each case. The guidelines, however, are designed to give child support determinations a measure of predictability and equality and to reduce litigation. They are intended to ensure that like cases will be treated alike by judges who do not think alike in this area of subjective value judgments. If the guidelines are circumvented under the "equitable" rubric of §659(a), we will return to the inequities, waste and drain of preguideline litigation. Exceptions to the guidelines should not be based on a judge's opinion of the fairness of the guidelines per se or upon voluntary undertakings by a party to establish and support a second family with funds that would otherwise go to support existing children. This policy may not appear romantic, but it reflects the pragmatic belief that new obligations should not be created or assumed at the expense of existing ones.

Accordingly, I would reverse and remand for an order setting child support at $141 per week.

COMMENTS

Parents in an intact family often make difficult choices when they wish to change careers. They, and sometimes their children, may make short-term sacrifices for a longer term gain. During an ongoing marriage, parents decide such questions among themselves; but when a parent is supporting a child not in his or her custody, courts must decide whether the non-custodial parent's choice to forgo present income justifies a reduction in support payments. If the change is proven to have been made in bad faith, it should be relatively easy for the court to refuse to reduce support payments. The harder question is how a court should respond to a good faith desire by a non-custodial parent. Should it matter if the parent would not have made the choice to return to school had the marriage not dissolved? Law school is a relatively short-term commitment with a relatively quick pay-off in salary increase, and most judges are likely to see the value in a legal education. However reluctant some judges may be to allow a reduction in child support to facilitate a legal education, they can be expected to be even less enthusiastic about a parent's decision to pursue medicine, which is a longer commitment and usually involves an additional period of relatively low salary. If a non-custodial parent may get support obligations reduced to facilitate a career change, should a custodial parent ever be entitled to increased support from the non-custodial parent to facilitate the custodial parent's career change?

If a father is unable to get his child support payments reduced to enable him to attend law school, then surely he should not be able to get them reduced to enable him to have several more children. Of course, this issue comes up as it did in *Kaplan* and *Ainsworth* after he has already had the additional children. The father then argues that it would be unfair to the new family not to reduce child support obligations to the first set of children — that the courts would in effect be preferring the earlier children over the later children. Some commentators, such as Homer Clark, agree and dismiss courts that refuse to reduce support obligations as "doctrinaire" and argue that resources should be "apportioned between the two families on an equitable basis" as "[m]any of the more modern and well considered cases recognize." Presumably the same argument could be made to apportion resources among all the further families that an irresponsible father may create, one after another. Courts do not reduce other pre-existing obligations to prevent a new family from suffering on account of the father's limited financial resources, and it is not clear why pre-existing child support should be treated as more adjustable than any other obligation.

The debate about whether courts should reduce child support payments when a non-custodial parent unilaterally chooses to incur new support obligations usually assumes that without such a reduction the new family would be financially worse off than the original family. This assumption is unrealistic. Typically, the new family of a non-custodial parent enjoys a higher standard of living than the ex-spouse and first set of children, as in *Kaplan*. In most cases, the earlier children would be far better off if the courts were able to require the non-custodial parent to treat them as well as he treated the children of his new spouse.

REFERENCE

Homer H. Clark, Jr., THE LAW OF DOMESTIC RELATIONS IN THE UNITED STATES (Student Edition) at 729–30 (2d ed. 1987).

Duration of Support

KUJAWINSKI v. KUJAWINSKI

Supreme Court of Illinois
71 Ill.2d 563, 376 N.E.2d 1382 (1978)

THOMAS J. MORAN, Justice.

This case is before us to determine the constitutionality of certain provisions of the Illinois Marriage and Dissolution of Marriage Act which became effective October 1, 1977 (Ill.Rev.Stat.1977, ch. 40, par. 101 *et seq.*).

...Joseph Kujawinski, who was a party to a pending divorce action, brought this action.... Plaintiff alleged that he was the father of six children born of his marriage to defendant Betty Ann Kujawinski....

...

...[P]laintiff contends that three provisions of the Act deny him equal protection of the law in that they invidiously discriminate against divorced parents.

Section 503(d) provides:

> The court may protect and promote the best interests of the children by setting aside a portion of the jointly or separately held estates of the parties in a separate fund or trust for the support, maintenance, education, and general welfare of any minor, dependent, or incompetent child of the parties. (Ill.Rev.Stat.1977, ch. 40, par. 503(d)).

Section 510(c) establishes, in pertinent part:

> Unless otherwise agreed in writing or expressly provided in the judgment, provisions for the support of a child are terminated by emancipation of the child, except as otherwise provided herein, but *not by the death of a parent obligated to* support the child.... (Emphasis added.)(Ill.Rev.Stat. 1977, ch. 40, par. 510(c).)

The relevant portion of section 513 states:

> The Court also may make such provision for the education and maintenance of the child or children, *whether of minor or majority age,* out of the property of either or both of its parents as equity may require, whether application is made therefor before or after such child has, or children have, attained majority age. In making such awards, the court shall consider all relevant factors which shall appear reasonable and necessary, including:
>
> (a) The financial resources of both parents.
>
> (b) The standard of living the child would have enjoyed had the marriage not been dissolved.
>
> (c) The financial resources of the child.
>
> (Emphasis added.) Ill.Rev.Stat.1977, ch. 40, par. 513.

...

According to plaintiff, sections 503(d) and 513 permit a dissolution order to require divorced parents to allocate funds for the education of their children beyond the children's minority, and he points out that such burden is not imposed upon nondivorced parents. Defendant's first line of response is that nondivorced parents do have a coextensive legal obligation to provide for the education of their children beyond the minority of the children. He refers to the following statutory obligation which applies to nondivorced parents:

> The expenses of the family and of the education of the children shall be chargeable upon the property of both husband and wife, or of either of them, in favor of creditors therefor, and in relation thereto they may be sued jointly or separately. (Ill.Rev.Stat.1977, ch. 40, par. 1015.)

This court has not had occasion to consider whether the above-cited provision obligates nondivorced parents to fund the education of their majority aged children, and we have no occasion to do so here. Rather, we find that the imposition of such an obligation upon divorced parents is reasonably related to a legitimate legislative purpose.

It cannot be overemphasized that a divorce, by its nature, has a major economic and personal impact on the lives of those involved. That the legislature is cognizant of this is evident by the fact that an express purpose of the Act is to "mitigate the potential harm to the spouses and their children caused by the process of legal dissolution of marriage." (Ill.Rev.Stat. 1977, ch. 40, par. 102(4).) Commonly, a divorce means that the spouses will go their separate ways, live independent lives, and accrue additional expenses which they would not have had had the family remained united. Unfortunately, it is not the isolated exception that noncustodial divorced parents, because of such additional expenses or because of a loss of concern for children who are no longer in their immediate care and custody, or out of animosity directed at the custodial spouse, cannot be relied upon to voluntarily support the children of the earlier marriage to the extent they would have had they not divorced. One appellate court stated in ordering a divorced parent to contribute to the college education of his noncustodial child:

> In a normal household, parents...direct their children as to when and how they should work or study. That is on the assumption of a normal family relationship, where parental love and moral obligation dictate what is best for the children. Under such circumstances, natural pride in the attainments of a child...would demand of parents provision for a college education, even at a sacrifice.
>
> When we turn to divorced parents a disrupted family society cannot count on normal protection for the child, and it is here that equity takes control to mitigate the hardship that may befall children of divorced parents. Maitzen v. Maitzen (1959), 24 Ill.App.2d 32, 38, 163 N.E.2d 840, 843.

We might point out to plaintiff that sections 503(d) and 513 do not mandate that divorced parents must provide their children of majority age with funds for education in all cases. It is certainly a legitimate legislative purpose to minimize any economic and educational disadvantages to children of divorced parents. If parents could have been expected to provide an education for their child of majority age absent divorce, it is not unreasonable for the legislature to furnish a means for providing that they do so after they have been divorced. We have no hesitation, therefore, in concluding that it is reasonably related to that legitimate purpose for the legislature to permit the trial court, in its sound discretion, to compel divorced parents to educate their children to the same extent as might reasonably be expected of nondivorced parents.... Sections 503(d) and 513 do not violate the equal protection guarantees of the Federal and State constitutions.

As to section 510(c), plaintiff correctly represents that the obligation of a nondivorced parent to support a dependent child terminates upon that parent's death, *i.e.*, a nondivorced parent is free to disinherit a dependent child. Plaintiff urges that there is no rational basis for allowing nondivorced parents such freedom of testation while burdening the estates of divorced parents with child support obligations.

Two reasonable justifications are given by defendant for singling out divorced parents. First, though a nondivorced parent may disinherit a dependent child, he may not disinherit his family. The surviving parent may renounce the will of the deceased parent and demand a statutory forced share of the deceased parent's estate. (Ill.Rev.Stat.1977, ch. 1101/2, par. 2-8.) The forced share then becomes available for the support of the dependent child because the surviving parent remains obligated to support the child. In effect, a child of a nondivorced parent has some indirect security against the possible loss of support due to disinheritance. The dependent child of a divorced parent has no similar protection because a surviving divorced spouse is not entitled to a forced share of a former spouse's estate. It is against the background of this inequity that section 510(c) was conceived. It seeks to protect the dependent child of divorced parents from loss of support through disinheritance, a loss from which a child of nondivorced parents is indirectly insulated. A divorced parent is still free to disinherit a child of his divorced marriage, subject only to the limited obligation of support. In balance, section 510(c) mitigates rather than aggravates inequality.

Second, while it is comparatively rare for a nondivorced parent to leave a spouse and their children out of a will, it is not so uncommon for a divorced parent to do so.... A divorced parent may establish a new family which may command primary allegiance in a subsequent will. The well-being of children of a former marriage may seem more remote to a noncustodial parent than the well-being of those children over whom that same parent has immediate care and custody. In addition, the divorced parent may harbor animosity toward a former spouse, which disposition might obscure the natural tendency to provide in a will for their mutual children. These are reasonable assumptions for the legislature to have made and assumptions which courts in other jurisdictions have countenanced.... Plaintiff, in whom the burden resides to negate the plausibility of such assumptions, has not done so.

Moreover, the legislature need not protect all children equally from the possible loss of support due to disinheritance. It may provide a remedy or institute a reform in progressive stages, addressing itself to the phase of a problem which seems most acute at the time.... We, therefore, hold that plaintiff has not satisfied the burden of showing that section 510(c) invidiously discriminates against divorced parents in defiance of equal protection.

For the reasons stated, we reverse the judgment of the trial court which declared unconstitutional sections...503(d), 510(c), [and] 513...of the Illinois Marriage and Dissolution of Marriage Act.

Judgment reversed.

...

ROSS v. ROSS

Superior Court of New Jersey, Chancery Division
167 N.J. Super. 441, 400 A.2d 1233 (1979)

CONN, J. D. C. (temporarily assigned).

This post-divorce controversy focuses on the recurring question of the outer limits of a support obligation for a child who has attained majority. Continuing education of the child, through enrollment in a college, university or other post high school training program, has already been established as a possible basis for prolonging the noncustodial parent's support obligation beyond the age of majority....

In this controversy the continuing education concept moves to the next level. For at issue here is the question of whether graduate school enrollment should likewise be construed as sufficient grounds for prolonging the noncustodial parent's support obligation, in this case for a 23-year-old, only child of a marriage. The question is a novel one in New Jersey.

Plaintiff mother, by judgment of divorce of October 19, 1973 and under an agreement made a part of that judgment, was to receive $17.50 a week from defendant father for the support of the child, Jane, "until emancipated."

Jane is now completing her first year of law school at Seton Hall University, to which she commutes as a full-time student. She graduated Seton Hall University in May 1978, obtaining a Bachelor of Arts degree, *magna cum laude.* Defendant father continued the support payments until the week after Jane graduated college. Plaintiff mother thereafter moved to compel defendant to continue that support for Jane until she completes law school. Defendant objected; memos were submitted. Thereafter a plenary hearing was held and the following factual picture, essentially uncontroverted, developed.

As a high school student Jane indicated an early interest in becoming a lawyer. The testimony revealed that she had shown an interest in government and history and was advised by guidance counselors to consider pursuing a law career. The parties separated in 1972 when Jane was 15 and a sophomore in high school. She has always been in the custody of plaintiff mother. There was no persuasive proof that defendant was ever included in discussions with Jane as to her desires for a law career. The father was invited to and attended her high school graduation in 1974, but has not seen her again until these proceedings. The father never sought visitation with his daughter other than to tell her, at the time of separation in 1972, that "his door was always open to her." Likewise, Jane never took affirmative steps for visitation with her father and stated that her father always sent her a card with a money gift for her birthday and at Christmas. She always sent him a "thank you" note in which she briefly would describe her current activities.

At the divorce hearing in 1973, when the terms of the support obligation were reviewed, plaintiff testified that Jane would probably be going to law school. Nevertheless, there was no understanding reached with regard to how long support would continue.

The father is a chemical worker who earns approximately $16,000 a year. He has remarried and his present wife works. They own their own home and are presently supporting a daughter of defendant's present wife from her prior marriage. Neither party produced any evidence of professional training or of any post-high school education.

Plaintiff is a bookkeeper and earns approximately $12,000 a year. She has not remarried. She has paid and continues to pay for both college and law school, including all fees, tuition costs and books.

At the outset the father claims that he is entitled to a ruling, as a matter of law, that the maximum period for which support should continue would be up to graduation from an accredited college or university. He insists there must be a limit and that the cases, when analyzed, all suggest the completion of college as the outer limit of the support obligation. The argument continues that even if law school was the clearly established goal, there is nothing to prevent the child in question upon graduation from college from going to work and attaining her graduate degree by going to law school part-time.

However, a review of the case law on the subject,...suggests that the question is an open one in which the court is free to apply various tests to assess the overall situation as to what the reasonable expectations are, the parties' means, etc., and what obligation, if any, there should be on the noncustodial parent. In short, the court is satisfied that there is no clearly established cut-off date that would entitle the father to a ruling as a matter of law. Admittedly, there is no reported decision on this precise question in New Jersey, but several New Jersey courts have noted that "There is no age fixed in the law when a child becomes emancipated."

...

With regard to the argument that the professional goal can be attained by part-time school attendance while also working, the answer is simply that the decision belongs to the child and the custodial parent. Our courts have long since noted that it is the custodial parent who is invested with the discretion regarding the method and means of educating the children. Subject to the issue such as that which is before the court, and also subject to the claim that certain decisions regarding the method of education are being made to harass or spite the noncustodial parent the noncustodial parent has no right to insist on alternative ways of accomplishing the goal....

Before listing and analyzing the various factors that must be considered, the court believes that there is the following threshold question: Had there not been a separation and divorce, would the parties, while living together, have sent their daughter to law school and financed that schooling? It would seem clear from the facts, particularly the respective incomes of the parties; the fact of only having one child, and the early indicators in this case of Jane's interest in law school, that the parties in all probability, would have financed Jane's law school education. It should be pointed out, however, that the fact that that question is answered in the affirmative, should in no way be dispositive of the issue.

The court believes that the various factors that have to be considered are the following:

1. The amount of support (or school cost) sought.
2. The ability of the noncustodial parent to pay that cost, and its relation to the type of schooling sought.
3. The financial position of the custodial parent.
4. The commitment and aptitude of the child to the schooling in question.
5. The child's relationship to the noncustodial paying parent.
6. The relationship of the schooling in question to any prior training and, generally, the relationship to the overall, long-range goals of the child.

Applying these factors to the case at bar, the following conclusions and findings are made:

1. As to the amount of support, considering the sum of $17.50, the defendant's ability to pay and his present financial position and obligations, it is fairly obvious that a finding can and is made that the amount involved would not be a serious financial burden. (It is important to note that this is not a demand by plaintiff for assistance to defray the cost of the schooling; it is limited strictly to a request for a continuation of the original support and nothing else.)

2. and 3. As already indicated, the father's present situation shows that a continuing obligation through Jane's law school period of $17.50 weekly would not be onerous. It would appear from the efforts of plaintiff that some assistance is called for. Plaintiff has been paying the cost of college and law school, and the facts indicate that over the four years at Seton Hall the total expense, with commuting and tuition and books and the like, was in excess of $12,000. While in college the daughter obtained a scholarship for approximately $2,600, also some college grants totalling over $1,200, a student loan under the National College Loan Program of approximately $3,500, and a bank loan for law school of an additional $2,500. Thus, plaintiff has laid out, at the college level, at least, something in the

neighborhood of $5,000 over those four years, the rest being defrayed by scholarships, grants and loans. Certainly the fact that plaintiff has not remarried and is earning in the neighborhood of $12,000 a year justifies a finding that assistance is needed.

4. The commitment of Jane to the schooling in question is easily established. Her early interest in law school has already been indicated. The mother's testimony before the trial court in 1973 is referred to again, showing that the mother assumed her daughter would be going to law school. There was also offered in evidence a copy of a letter that plaintiff sent to her husband's brother enclosing tickets to Jane's high school graduation. In that letter the brother was advised of Jane's interest in a law career. In addition to the commitment in terms of its duration, the record shows that Jane graduated college with honors, and thus there can be no quarrel with her zeal and performance at the college level.

The testimony further shows that Jane has played a role in assisting with the expense of the schooling. The law school has a rule that limits full-time students to working no more than 15 hours a week. Jane testified that she takes advantage of this 15 hours and works as a waitress at a country club on weekends, earning approximately $56 a week which she puts towards her transportation and miscellaneous school costs. Thus Jane's commitment, both in and out of the classroom, is clearly established. This finding of Jane's commitment to assist in the cost, coupled with the other findings made as to the parents' means, as well as the fact that Jane commutes to school, thereby eliminating the requirement for room and board at school, are sufficient reasons to overcome the contentions that in this case going to law school full-time is an unnecessary luxury.

5. According to the record, both Jane and her father may best be characterized as "distant and passive" in terms of their relationship with one another. Contact has been minimal, for neither Jane nor her father has actively sought visitation nor refused visitation.

It is conceivable that, in a given situation, a child's arbitrary refusal to respond to the sincere visitation efforts of a non-custodial parent might significantly affect the outcome of the question of continued support. In this case, however, there is nothing in the father-daughter relationship to influence that decision one way or another.

6. That law school training is a prerequisite for the attainment of Jane's career objective is axiomatic. Further, the fact that the career goal was established during Jane's high school years supports the conclusion that the law school training is not being sought to manipulate the extension of support payments.

The court is satisfied, therefore, based on the findings made, that Jane cannot be considered emancipated until such time as her law school training ends, either through voluntary or involuntary withdrawal or upon graduation. Therefore, the court concludes that defendant father's obligation to pay child support be maintained through that law school period.

However, in view of the fact that the question is a novel one and because there has been a delay in finally concluding this matter, which delay was not the fault of either party, the court is satisfied that the father's obligation for support, which normally would have continued right through Jane's college graduation, will be retroactive to September 15, 1978. The court selects that date as the time in which

Jane's law school training probably got under way. The arrears shall be computed by counsel and stated in the form of an order to be submitted in accordance herewith, and defendant is ordered to pay the arrears in two equal payments, one due on or before May 15, 1979 and the balance due on or before July 30, 1979. The obligation of $17.50 a week support shall continue as just stated from that retroactive date through the law school training period, at which time it ceases permanently. Nothing herein should be deemed to suggest that the obligation is suspended during the nonschool months.

Enforcement of Support

HICKS v. FEIOCK

United States Supreme Court
485 U.S. 624 (1988)

Justice WHITE delivered the opinion of the Court.

A parent failed to comply with a valid court order to make child support payments, and defended against subsequent contempt charges by claiming that he was financially unable to make the required payments. The trial court ruled that under state law he is presumed to remain able to comply with the terms of the prior order, and judged him to be in contempt. The state appellate court held that the legislative presumptions applied by the trial court violate the Due Process Clause of the Fourteenth Amendment, which forbids a court to employ certain presumptions that affect the determination of guilt or innocence in criminal proceedings. We must decide whether the Due Process Clause was properly applied in this case.

I

On January 19, 1976, a California state court entered an order requiring respondent, Phillip Feiock, to begin making monthly payments to his ex-wife for the support of their three children. Over the next six years, respondent only sporadically complied with the order, and by December 1982 he had discontinued paying child support altogether. His ex-wife sought to enforce the support orders. On June 22, 1984, a hearing was held in California state court on her petition for ongoing support payments and for payment of the arrearage due her. The court examined respondent's financial situation and ordered him to begin paying $150 per month commencing on July 1, 1984. The court reserved jurisdiction over the matter for the purpose of determining the arrearages and reviewing respondent's financial condition.

Respondent apparently made two monthly payments but paid nothing for the next nine months. He was then served with an order to show cause why he should not be held in contempt on nine counts of failure to make the monthly payments ordered by the court. At a hearing on August 9, 1985, petitioner made out a prima facie case of contempt against respondent by establishing the existence of a valid court order, respondent's knowledge of the order, and respondent's failure to comply with the order. Respondent defended by arguing that he was unable to pay support during the months in question. This argument was partially successful, but respondent was adjudged to be in contempt on five of the nine counts. He was sentenced to 5 days in jail on each count, to be served consecutively, for a total of 25 days. This sentence was suspended, however, and respondent was placed on probation for three years. As one of the conditions of his probation, he was ordered once again to make support payments of $150 per month. As another condition of his probation, he was ordered, starting the following month, to begin repaying $50 per month on his accumulated arrearage, which was determined to total $1,650.

At the hearing, respondent had objected to the application of Cal.Civ.Proc.Code Ann. §1209.5 (West 1982) against him, claiming that it was unconstitutional under the Due Process Clause of the Fourteenth Amendment because it shifts to the defendant the burden of proving inability to comply with the order, which is an element of the crime of contempt.[1] This objection was rejected, and he renewed it on appeal. The intermediate state appellate court agreed with respondent and annulled the contempt order, ruling that the state statute purports to impose "a mandatory presumption compelling a conclusion of guilt without independent proof of an ability to pay," and is therefore unconstitutional because "the mandatory nature of the presumption lessens the prosecution's burden of proof." 180 Cal.App.3d 649, 654, 225 Cal.Rptr. 748, 751 (1986).[2] In light of its holding that the statute as previously interpreted was unconstitutional, the court went on to adopt a different interpretation of that statute to govern future proceedings: "For future guidance, however, we determine the statute in question should be construed as authorizing a permissive inference, but not a mandatory presumption." *Id.*, at 655, 225 Cal.Rptr., at 751. The court explicitly considered this reinterpretation of the statute to be an exercise of its "obligation to interpret the statute to preserve its constitutionality whenever possible." *Ibid.* The California Supreme Court denied review, but we granted certiorari. 480 U.S. 915 (1987).

II

Three issues must be decided to resolve this case. First is whether the ability to comply with a court order constitutes an element of the offense of contempt or, instead, inability to comply is an affirmative defense to that charge. Second is whether §1209.5 requires the alleged contemnor to shoulder the burden of persuasion or merely the burden of production in attempting to establish his inability to comply with the order. Third is whether this contempt proceeding was a criminal proceeding or a civil proceeding, *i.e.*, whether the relief imposed upon respondent was criminal or civil in nature.

Petitioner argues that the state appellate court erred in its determinations on the first two points of state law. The court ruled that whether the individual is able to comply with a court order is an element of the offense of contempt rather than

---

1. California Civ.Proc.Code Ann. §1209.5 (West 1982) states that "[w]hen a court of competent jurisdiction makes an order compelling a parent to furnish support...for his child, proof that...the parent was present in court at the time the order was pronounced and proof of noncompliance therewith shall be prima facie evidence of a contempt of court."

2. Although the court mentioned one state case among the cases it cited in support of this proposition, the court clearly rested on federal constitutional grounds as articulated in this Court's decisions, 180 Cal.App.3d, at 652–655, 225 Cal.Rptr., at 749–751, as did the other state case it cited. See *People v. Roder*, 33 Cal.3d 491, 189 Cal.Rptr. 501, 658 P.2d 1302 (1983).

an affirmative defense to the charge, and that §1209.5 shifts to the alleged contemnor the burden of persuasion rather than simply the burden of production in showing inability to comply. We are not at liberty to depart from the state appellate court's resolution of these issues of state law. Although petitioner marshals a number of sources in support of the contention that the state appellate court misapplied state law on these two points, the California Supreme Court denied review of this case, and we are not free in this situation to overturn the state court's conclusions of state law.[3]

The third issue, however, is a different matter: the argument is not merely that the state court misapplied state law, but that the characterization of this proceeding and the relief given as civil or criminal in nature, for purposes of determining the proper applicability of federal constitutional protections, raises a question of federal law rather than state law. This proposition is correct as stated. *In re Winship*, 397 U.S. 358, 365–366 (1970); *In re Gault*, 387 U.S. 1, 49–50 (1967); *Shillitani v. United States*, 384 U.S. 364, 368–369 (1966). The fact that this proceeding and the resultant relief were judged to be criminal in nature as a matter of state law is thus not determinative of this issue, and the state appellate court erred insofar as it sustained respondent's challenge to the statute under the Due Process Clause simply because it concluded that this contempt proceeding is "quasi-criminal" as a matter of California law. 180 Cal.App.3d, at 653, 225 Cal.Rptr., at 750.

III

A

The question of how a court determines whether to classify the relief imposed in a given proceeding as civil or criminal in nature, for the purposes of applying the Due Process Clause and other provisions of the Constitution, is one of long standing, and its principles have been settled at least in their broad outlines for many decades. When a State's proceedings are involved, state law provides strong guidance about whether or not the State is exercising its authority "in a nonpunitive, noncriminal manner," and one who challenges the State's classification of the relief imposed as "civil" or "criminal" may be required to show "the clearest proof" that it is not correct as a matter of federal law. *Allen v. Illinois*, 478 U.S. 364, 368–369 (1986). Nonetheless, if such a challenge is substantiated, then the labels affixed either to the proceeding or to the relief imposed under state law are not controlling and will not be allowed to defeat the applicable protections of federal constitutional law. *Ibid.* This is particularly so in the codified laws of contempt,

3. "Where an intermediate appellate state court rests its considered judgment upon the rule of law which it announces, that is a datum for ascertaining state law which is not to be disregarded by a federal court unless it is convinced by other persuasive data that the highest court of the state would decide otherwise.... This is the more so where, as in this case, the highest court has refused to review the lower court's decision rendered in one phase of the very litigation which is now prosecuted by the same parties before the federal court.... Even though it is arguable that the Supreme Court of [the State] will at some later time modify the rule of [this] case, whether that will ever happen remains a matter of conjecture. In the meantime the state law applicable to these parties and in this case has been authoritatively declared by the highest state court in which a decision could be had.... We think that the law thus announced and applied is the law of the state applicable in the same case and to the same parties in the federal court and that the federal court is not free to apply a different rule however desirable it may believe it to be, and even though it may think that the state Supreme Court may establish a different rule in some future litigation." *West v. American Telephone & Telegraph Co.*, 311 U.S. 223, 237–238 (1940).

where the "civil" and "criminal" labels of the law have become increasingly blurred.[4]

Instead, the critical features are the substance of the proceeding and the character of the relief that the proceeding will afford. "If it is for civil contempt the punishment is remedial, and for the benefit of the complainant. But if it is for criminal contempt the sentence is punitive, to vindicate the authority of the court." *Gompers v. Bucks Stove & Range Co.*, 221 U.S. 418, 441 (1911). The character of the relief imposed is thus ascertainable by applying a few straightforward rules. If the relief provided is a sentence of imprisonment, it is remedial if "the defendant stands committed unless and until he performs the affirmative act required by the court's order," and is punitive if "the sentence is limited to imprisonment for a definite period." *Id.*, at 442. If the relief provided is a fine, it is remedial when it is paid to the complainant, and punitive when it is paid to the court, though a fine that would be payable to the court is also remedial when the defendant can avoid paying the fine simply by performing the affirmative act required by the court's order. These distinctions lead up to the fundamental proposition that criminal penalties may not be imposed on someone who has not been afforded the protections that the Constitution requires of such criminal proceedings, including the requirement that the offense be proved beyond a reasonable doubt. See, *e.g., Gompers, supra*, at 444; *Michaelson v. United States ex rel. Chicago*, St. P., M. & O.R. Co., 266 U.S. 42, 66 (1924).[5]

The Court has consistently applied these principles. In *Gompers*, decided early in this century, three men were found guilty of contempt and were sentenced to serve 6, 9, and 12 months respectively. The Court found this relief to be criminal in nature because the sentence was determinate and unconditional. "The distinction between refusing to do an act commanded, — remedied by imprisonment until the party performs the required act; and doing an act forbidden, — punished by imprisonment for a definite term; is sound in principle, and generally, if not universally, affords a test by which to determine the character of the punishment." *Gompers*, 221 U.S., at 443. In the former instance, the conditional nature of the punishment renders the relief civil in nature because the contemnor "can end the sentence and discharge himself at any moment by doing what he had previously refused to do." *Id.*, at 442. In the latter instance, the unconditional nature of the punishment renders the relief criminal in nature because the relief "cannot undo or remedy what has been done nor afford any compensation" and the contemnor "cannot shorten the term by promising not to repeat the offense." *Ibid.*

The distinction between relief that is civil in nature and relief that is criminal in nature has been repeated and followed in many cases. An unconditional penalty is criminal in nature because it is "solely and exclusively punitive in character." *Penfield Co. v. SEC*, 330 U.S. 585, 593 (1947). A conditional penalty, by contrast, is civil because it is specifically designed to compel the doing of some act. "One who is fined, unless by a day certain he [does the act ordered], has it in his power to

---

4. California is a good example of this modern development, for although it defines civil and criminal contempts in separate statutes, compare Cal.Civ.Proc.Code Ann. §1209 (West Supp.1988) with Cal. Penal Code Ann. §166 (West 1970), it has merged the two kinds of proceedings under the same procedural rules. See Cal.Civ.Proc.Code Ann. §§1209-1222 (West 1982 and Supp.1988).

5. We have recognized that certain specific constitutional protections, such as the right to trial by jury, are not applicable to those criminal contempts that can be classified as petty offenses, as is true of other petty crimes as well. *Bloom v. Illinois*, 391 U.S. 194, 208–210 (1968). This is not true, however, of the proposition that guilt must be proved beyond a reasonable doubt. *Id.*, at 205.

avoid any penalty. And those who are imprisoned until they obey the order, 'carry the keys of their prison in their own pockets.'" *Id.*, at 590, quoting *In re Nevitt*, 117 F. 448, 461 (CA8 1902). In *Penfield*, a man was found guilty of contempt for refusing to obey a court order to produce documents. This Court ruled that since the man was not tried in a proceeding that afforded him the applicable constitutional protections, he could be given a conditional term of imprisonment but could not be made to pay "a flat, unconditional fine of $50.00." *Penfield, supra*, 330 U.S., at 588.[6]...

Shillitani v. United States, 384 U.S. 364 (1966), adheres to these same principles. There two men were adjudged guilty of contempt for refusing to obey a court order to testify under a grant of immunity. Both were sentenced to two years of imprisonment, with the proviso that if either answered the questions before his sentence ended, he would be released. The penalties were upheld because of their "conditional nature," even though the underlying proceeding lacked certain constitutional protections that are essential in criminal proceedings. *Id.*, at 365. Any sentence "must be viewed as remedial," and hence civil in nature, "if the court conditions release upon the contemnor's willingness to [comply with the order]." *Id.*, at 370. By the same token, in a civil proceeding the court "may also impose a determinate sentence *which includes a purge clause*." *Id.*, at 370, n. 6 (emphasis added). "On the contrary, a criminal contempt proceeding would be characterized by the imposition of an unconditional sentence for punishment or deterrence." *Id.*, at 370, n. 5.[7]

B

In repeatedly stating and following the rules set out above, the Court has eschewed any alternative formulation that would make the classification of the relief imposed in a State's proceedings turn simply on what their underlying purposes are perceived to be. Although the purposes that lie behind particular kinds of relief are germane to understanding their character, this Court has never undertaken to psychoanalyze the subjective intent of a State's laws and its courts, not only because that effort would be unseemly and improper, but also because it would be misguided. In contempt cases, both civil and criminal relief have aspects that can be seen as either remedial or punitive or both: when a court imposes fines

---

6. In *Penfield*, the original court order required a person to produce certain documents. He refused to comply. The District Court then found him guilty of contempt and required him to pay a fine to the court, which he promptly paid. (The court had also ordered him to stand committed until he paid this fine.) The Court of Appeals reversed, finding that the District Court had erred in imposing this relief, which was criminal in nature, and ordered the man instead to stand committed to prison until he complied with the original order by producing the documents. This Court affirmed, finding that this relief was civil in nature and was properly imposed, whereas the relief that had been ordered by the District Court was criminal in nature and had not been properly imposed. 330 U.S., at 587–595. The reason that the sanction imposed by the District Court was found to be criminal in nature is because it was determinate: the contemnor could not avoid the sanction by agreeing to comply with the original order to produce the documents. Yet the sanction of confinement imposed by the Court of Appeals was civil in nature because it was conditional, *i.e.*, not determinate: the contemnor would avoid the sanction by agreeing to comply with the original order to produce the documents.

7. In these passages from *Shillitani*, the Court clearly indicated that when it spoke of a court's conditioning release upon the contemnor's willingness to comply, it did not mean simply release *from physical confinement*, but release from the imposition of any sentence that would otherwise be determinate. The critical feature that determines whether the remedy is civil or criminal in nature is not when or whether the contemnor is physically required to set foot in a jail but whether the contemnor can avoid the sentence imposed on him, or purge himself of it, by complying with the terms of the original order. It follows that the remedy in this case is not rendered civil in nature merely by suspending respondent's sentence and placing him on probation (with its attendant disabilities, see n. 11, *infra*).

and punishments on a contemnor, it is not only vindicating its legal authority to enter the initial court order, but it also is seeking to give effect to the law's purpose of modifying the contemnor's behavior to conform to the terms required in the order. As was noted in *Gompers*:

> It is true that either form of [punishment] has also an incidental effect. For if the case is civil and the punishment is purely remedial, there is also a vindication of the court's authority. On the other hand, if the proceeding is for criminal contempt and the [punishment] is solely punitive, to vindicate the authority of the law, the complainant may also derive some incidental benefit from the fact that such punishment tends to prevent a repetition of the disobedience. But such indirect consequences will not change [punishment] which is merely coercive and remedial, into that which is solely punitive in character, or *vice versa.* 221 U.S., at 443.

For these reasons, this Court has judged that conclusions about the purposes for which relief is imposed are properly drawn from an examination of the character of the relief itself.

There is yet another reason why the overlapping purposes of civil and criminal contempt proceedings have prevented this Court from hinging the classification on this point. If the definition of these proceedings and their resultant relief as civil or criminal is made to depend on the federal courts' views about their underlying purposes, which indeed often are not clearly articulated in any event, then the States will be unable to ascertain with any degree of assurance how their proceedings will be understood as a matter of federal law. The consequences of any such shift in direction would be both serious and unfortunate. Of primary practical importance to the decision in this case is that the States should be given intelligible guidance about how, as a matter of federal constitutional law, they may lawfully employ presumptions and other procedures in their contempt proceedings. It is of great importance to the States that they be able to understand clearly and in advance the tools that are available to them in ensuring swift and certain compliance with valid court orders — not only orders commanding payment of child support, as in this case, but also orders that command compliance in the more general area of domestic relations law, and in all other areas of the law as well.

The States have long been able to plan their own procedures around the traditional distinction between civil and criminal remedies. The abandonment of this clear dividing line in favor of a general assessment of the manifold and complex purposes that lie behind a court's action would create novel problems where now there are rarely any — novel problems that could infect many different areas of the law. And certainly the fact that a contemnor has his sentence suspended and is placed on probation cannot be decisive in defining the civil or criminal nature of the relief, for many convicted criminals are treated in exactly this manner for the purpose (among others) of influencing their behavior. What is true of the respondent in this case is also true of any such convicted criminal: as long as he meets the conditions of his informal probation, he will never enter the jail. Nonetheless, if the sentence is a determinate one, then the punishment is criminal in nature, and it may not be imposed unless federal constitutional protections are applied in the contempt proceeding.[8]

8. This does not even suggest, of course, that the State is unable to suspend the sentence imposed on either a

IV

The proper classification of the relief imposed in respondent's contempt proceeding is dispositive of this case. As interpreted by the state court here, §1209.5 requires respondent to carry the burden of persuasion on an element of the offense, by showing his inability to comply with the court's order to make the required payments. If applied in a criminal proceeding, such a statute would violate the Due Process Clause because it would undercut the State's burden to prove guilt beyond a reasonable doubt.... If applied in a civil proceeding, however, this particular statute would be constitutionally valid..., and respondent conceded as much at the argument. Tr. of Oral Arg. 37.[9]

The state court found the contempt proceeding to be "quasi-criminal" in nature without discussing the point. 180 Cal.App.3d, at 653, 225 Cal.Rptr., at 750. There were strong indications that the proceeding was intended to be criminal in nature, such as the notice sent to respondent, which clearly labeled the proceeding as "criminal in nature," Order to Show Cause and Declaration for Contempt (June 12, 1985), App. 21, and the participation of the District Attorney in the case. Though significant, these facts are not dispositive of the issue before us, for if the trial court had imposed only civil coercive remedies, as surely it was authorized to do, then it would be improper to invalidate that result merely because the Due Process Clause, as applied in *criminal* proceedings, was not satisfied.[10] It also bears emphasis that the purposes underlying this proceeding were wholly ambiguous. Respondent was charged with violating nine discrete prior court orders, and the proceeding may have been intended primarily to vindicate the court's authority in the face of his defiance. On the other hand, as often is true when court orders are violated, these charges were part of an ongoing battle to force respondent to conform his conduct to the terms of those orders, and of future orders as well.

Applying the traditional rules for classifying the relief imposed in a given proceeding requires the further resolution of one factual question about the nature of the relief in this case. Respondent was charged with nine separate counts of contempt, and was convicted on five of those counts, all of which arose from his failure to comply with orders to make payments in past months. He was sentenced to 5 days in jail on each of the five counts, for a total of 25 days, but his jail sentence was suspended and he was placed on probation for three years. If this were all, then the relief afforded would be criminal in nature.[11] But this is not all. One of the

8. *Continued*

criminal contemnor or a civil contemnor in favor of a term of informal probation. That action may be appropriate and even most desirable in a great many cases, especially when the order that has been disobeyed was one to pay a sum of money. This also accords with the repeated emphasis in our decisions that in wielding its contempt powers, a court "must exercise 'the least possible power adequate to the end proposed.'" *Shillitani v. United States,* 384 U.S. 364, 371 (1966), quoting *Anderson v. Dunn,* 6 Wheat. 204, 231, 5 L.Ed. 242 (1821).

9. Our precedents are clear, however, that punishment may not be imposed in a civil contempt proceeding when it is clearly established that the alleged contemnor is unable to comply with the terms of the order. *United States v. Rylander,* 460 U.S. 752, 757 (1983); *Shillitani, supra,* 384 U.S., at 371; Oriel, 278 U.S., at 366.

10. This can also be seen by considering the notice given to the alleged contemnor. This Court has stated that one who is charged with a crime is "entitled to be informed of the nature of the charge against him but to know that it is a charge and not a suit." *Gompers v. Bucks Stove & Range Co.,* 221 U.S. 418, 446 (1911). Yet if the relief ultimately given in such a proceeding is wholly civil in nature, then this requirement would not be applicable. It is also true, of course, that if *both* civil and criminal relief are imposed in the same proceeding, then the "'criminal feature of the order is dominant and fixes its character for purposes of review.'" *Nye v. United States,* 313 U.S. 33, 42–43 (1941), quoting *Union Tool Co. v. Wilson,* 259 U.S. 107, 110 (1922).

11. That a determinate sentence is suspended and the contemnor put on probation does not make the remedy civil in nature, for a suspended sentence, without more, remains a determinate sentence, and a fixed term of probation is itself a punishment that is criminal in nature. A suspended sentence with a term of probation is not equivalent to a conditional sentence that would allow the contemnor to avoid or purge these sanctions.

conditions of respondent's probation was that he begin making payments on his accumulated arrearage, and that he continue making these payments at the rate of $50 per month. At that rate, all of the arrearage would be paid before respondent completed his probation period. Not only did the order therefore contemplate that respondent would be required to purge himself of his past violations, but it expressly states that "[i]f any two payments are missed, whether consecutive or not, the entire balance shall become due and payable." Order of the California Superior Court for Orange County (Aug. 9, 1985), App. 39. What is unclear is whether the ultimate satisfaction of these accumulated prior payments would have purged the determinate sentence imposed on respondent. Since this aspect of the proceeding will vary as a factual matter from one case to another, depending on the precise disposition entered by the trial court, and since the trial court did not specify this aspect of its disposition in this case, it is not surprising that neither party was able to offer a satisfactory explanation of this point at argument. Tr. of Oral Arg. 42–47.[12] If the relief imposed here is in fact a determinate sentence with a purge clause, then it is civil in nature. *Shillitani*, 384 U.S., at 370, n. 6; *Fox*, 299 U.S., at 106, 108; *Gompers*, 221 U.S., at 442.

The state court did not pass on this issue because of its erroneous view that it was enough simply to aver that this proceeding is considered "quasi-criminal" as a matter of state law. And, as noted earlier, the court's view on this point, coupled with its view of the Federal Constitution, also led it to reinterpret the state statute, thus softening the impact of the presumption, in order to save its constitutionality. Yet the Due Process Clause does not necessarily prohibit the State from employing this presumption as it was construed by the state court, *if* respondent would purge his contempt judgment by paying off his arrearage. In these circumstances, the proper course for this Court is to vacate the judgment below and remand for further consideration of §1209.5 free from the compulsion of an erroneous view of federal law. See, *e.g.*, *Three Affiliated Tribes of Fort Berthold Reservation v. Wold Engineering, P.C.*, 467 U.S. 138, 152 (1984). If on remand it is found that respondent would purge his sentence by paying his arrearage, then this proceeding is civil in nature and there was no need for the state court to reinterpret its statute to avoid conflict with the Due Process Clause.[13]

We therefore vacate the judgment below and remand for further proceedings not inconsistent with this opinion.

It is so ordered.

---

11. *Continued*

A determinate term of probation puts the contemnor under numerous disabilities that he cannot escape by complying with the dictates of the prior orders, such as: any conditions of probation that the court judges to be reasonable and necessary may be imposed; the term of probation may be revoked and the original sentence (including incarceration) may be reimposed at any time for a variety of reasons without all the safeguards that are ordinarily afforded in criminal proceedings; and the contemnor's probationary status could affect other proceedings against him that may arise in the future (for example, this fact might influence the sentencing determination made in a criminal prosecution for some wholly independent offense).

12. It is also perhaps of some significance, though not binding upon us, that the parties reinforce the ambiguity on this point by entitling this contempt order, in the Joint Appendix, as "Order of the Superior Court of the State of California, County of Orange, to Purge Arrearage and Judgment of Contempt." App. i.

13. Even if this relief is judged on remand to be criminal in nature because it does not allow the contemnor to purge the judgment by satisfying the terms of the prior orders, this result does not impose any real handicap on the States in enforcing the terms of their orders, for it will be clear to the States that the presumption established by §1209.5 can be imposed, consistent with the Due Process Clause, in any proceeding where the relief afforded is civil in nature as defined by this Court's precedents. In addition, the state courts remain free to decide for themselves the state-law issues we have taken as having been resolved in this case by the court below, and to judge the lawfulness of statutes that impose similar presumptions under the provisions of their own state constitutions.

Justice KENNEDY took no part in the consideration or decision of this case.

Justice O'CONNOR, with whom the CHIEF JUSTICE and Justice SCALIA join, dissenting.

This case concerns a contempt proceeding against a parent who repeatedly failed to comply with a valid court order to make child support payments. In my view, the proceeding is civil as a matter of federal law. Therefore, the Due Process Clause of the Fourteenth Amendment does not prevent the trial court from applying a legislative presumption that the parent remained capable of complying with the order until the time of the contempt proceeding.

I

The facts of this case illustrate how difficult it can be to obtain even modest amounts of child support from a noncustodial parent. Alta Sue Adams married respondent Phillip William Feiock in 1968. The couple resided in California and had three children. In 1973, respondent left the family. Mrs. Feiock filed a petition in the Superior Court of California for the County of Orange seeking dissolution of her marriage, legal custody of the children, and child support. In January 1976, the court entered an interlocutory judgment of dissolution of marriage, awarded custody of the children to Mrs. Feiock, and ordered respondent to pay child support beginning February 1, 1976. The court ordered respondent to pay $35 per child per month for the first four months, and $75 per child per month starting June 1, 1976. The order has never been modified.

After the court entered a final judgment of dissolution of marriage, Mrs. Feiock and the children moved to Ohio. Respondent made child support payments only sporadically and stopped making any payments by December 1982. Pursuant to Ohio's enactment of the Uniform Reciprocal Enforcement of Support Act (URESA), Mrs. Feiock filed a complaint in the Court of Common Pleas of Stark County, Ohio. See Ohio Rev.Code Ann. §3115.09(B)(1980). The complaint recited that respondent was obliged to pay $225 per month in support, and that respondent was $2,300 in arrears. The Ohio court transmitted the complaint and supporting documents to the Superior Court of California for the County of Orange, which had jurisdiction over respondent. Petitioner, the Orange County District Attorney, prosecuted the case on behalf of Mrs. Feiock in accordance with California's version of URESA. See Cal.Civ.Proc.Code Ann. §1670 *et seq.* (West 1982).

After obtaining several continuances, respondent finally appeared at a hearing before the California court on June 22, 1984. Respondent explained that he had recently become a partner in a flower business that had uncertain prospects. The court ordered respondent to pay $150 per month on a temporary basis, although it did not alter the underlying order. Payments were to begin July 1, 1984.

Respondent made payments only for August and September. Respondent appeared in court three times thereafter, but never asked for a modification of the order. Eventually, the Orange County District Attorney filed Orders to Show Cause and Declarations of Contempt alleging nine counts of contempt based on respondent's failure to make nine of the $150 support payments. At a hearing held August 9, 1985, the District Attorney invoked Cal.Civ.Proc.Code Ann. §1209.5 (West 1982), which says:

> When a court of competent jurisdiction makes an order compelling a parent to furnish support...for his child,...proof that the parent was

present in court at the time the order was pronounced and proof of non-compliance therewith shall be prima facie evidence of a contempt of court.

In an effort to overcome this presumption, respondent testified regarding his ability to pay at the time of each alleged act of contempt. The court found that respondent had been able to pay five of the missed payments. Accordingly, the court found respondent in contempt on five of the nine counts and sentenced him to 5 days in jail on each count, to be served consecutively, for a total of 25 days. The court suspended execution of the sentence and placed respondent on three years' informal probation on the conditions that he make monthly support payments of $150 starting immediately and additional payments of $50 per month on the arrearage starting October 1, 1985.

Respondent filed a petition for a writ of habeas corpus in the California Court of Appeal, where he prevailed on his argument that §1209.5 is unconstitutional as a mandatory presumption shifting to the defendant the burden of proof of an element of a criminal offense. That is the argument that the Court confronts in this case. In my view, no remand is necessary because the judgment below is incorrect as a matter of federal law.

II

The California Court of Appeal has erected a substantial obstacle to the enforcement of child support orders. As petitioner vividly describes it, the judgment turns the child support order into "a worthless piece of scrap." Brief for Petitioner 47. The judgment hampers the enforcement of support orders at a time when strengthened enforcement is needed. "The failure of enforcement efforts in this area has become a national scandal. In 1983, only half of custodial parents received the full amount of child support ordered; approximately 26% received some lesser amount, and 24% received nothing at all." Brief for Women's Legal Defense Fund et al. as *Amici Curiae* 26 (footnote omitted). The facts of this case illustrate how easily a reluctant parent can evade a child support obligation. Congress recognized the serious problem of enforcement of child support orders when it enacted the Child Support Enforcement Amendments of 1984, Pub.L. 98-378, 98 Stat. 1305. S.Rep. No. 98-387, pp. 5–6 (1984)[, *U.S. Code Cong. & Admin. News* 1984, p. 2397]; H.R.Rep. No. 98-527, pp. 30, 49 (1983). The California Legislature responded to the problem by enacting the presumption described in §1209.5. Now, says petitioner, the California Court of Appeal has sabotaged the California Legislature's effort.

Contempt proceedings often will be useless if the parent seeking enforcement of valid support orders must prove that the obligor can comply with the court order. The custodial parent will typically lack access to the financial and employment records needed to sustain the burden imposed by the decision below, especially where the noncustodial parent is self-employed, as is the case here. Serious consequences follow from the California Court of Appeal's decision to invalidate California's statutory presumption that a parent continues to be able to pay the child support previously determined to be within his or her means.

Petitioner asks us to determine as a matter of California law that inability to comply with a support order is an affirmative defense to a contempt charge, so that the burden of persuasion may be placed on the contemnor under *Martin v. Ohio*, 480 U.S. 228 (1987). Petitioner also contends that the Court of Appeal erred in supposing that §1209.5 shifts the burden of persuasion rather than merely the burden of production, citing *Lyons v. Municipal Court,* 75 Cal.App.3d 829, 838, 142 Cal.Rptr. 449, 452 (1977); *Oliver v. Superior Court,* 197 Cal.App.2d 237, 242, 17 Cal.Rptr. 474, 476–477 (1961); 4A J. Goddard, California Practice: Family Law Practice §686 (3d ed. 1981); 14 Cal.Jur.3d, Contempt §§32, 71 (1974); and 6 B. Witkin, Summary of California Law, Parent and Child §137 (8th ed. 1974). But the interpretation of California law is the province of California courts. I agree with the majority that, for purposes of this decision, we should assume that the California Court of Appeal correctly determined these matters of state law. *Martin v. Ohio, supra*; *United Gas Public Service Co. v. Texas,* 303 U.S. 123, 139 (1938). If the Court of Appeal was in error, the California courts may correct it in future cases.

The linchpin of the Court of Appeal's opinion is its determination that the contempt proceeding against respondent was criminal in nature. The court applied what it understood are the federal due process standards for mandatory evidentiary presumptions in criminal cases. See *Ulster County Court v. Allen,* 442 U.S. 140, 167 (1979)(mandatory presumptions are impermissible unless "the fact proved is sufficient to support the inference of guilt beyond a reasonable doubt"); *Sandstrom v. Montana,* 442 U.S. 510, 523–524 (1979). This Court has recognized, by contrast, that civil contempt proceedings do not require proof beyond a reasonable doubt and that the rules governing use of presumptions differ accordingly. In the civil contempt context, we have upheld a rule that shifts to the contemnor the burden of production on ability to comply, *United States v. Rylander,* 460 U.S. 752, 757 (1983), and we have recognized that the contemnor may bear the burden of persuasion on this issue as well, *Maggio v. Zeitz,* 333 U.S. 56, 75–76 (1948). If the contempt proceeding in this case may be characterized as civil in nature, as petitioner urges, then under our precedents the presumption provided in Cal.Civ.Proc.Code Ann. §1209.5 (West 1982) would not violate the Due Process Clause.

The characterization of a state proceeding as civil or criminal for the purpose of applying the Due Process Clause of the Fourteenth Amendment is itself a question of federal law. *Allen v. Illinois,* 478 U.S. 364 (1986). The substance of particular contempt proceedings determines whether they are civil or criminal, regardless of the label attached by the court conducting the proceedings.... Civil contempt proceedings are primarily coercive; criminal contempt proceedings are punitive. As the Court explained in *Gompers*:

> The distinction between refusing to do an act commanded, — remedied by imprisonment until the party performs the required act; and doing an act forbidden, — punished by imprisonment for a definite term; is sound in principle, and generally, if not universally, affords a test by which to determine the character of the punishment. 221 U.S., at 443.

Failure to pay alimony is an example of the type of act cognizable in an action for civil contempt. *Id.,* at 442.

Whether a particular contempt proceeding is civil or criminal can be inferred from objective features of the proceeding and the sanction imposed. The most important indication is whether the judgment inures to the benefit of another party to the proceeding. A fine payable to the complaining party and proportioned to the complainant's loss is compensatory and civil. *United States v. Mine Workers,* 330 U.S. 258, 304 (1947). Because the compensatory purpose limits the amount of the fine, the contemnor is not exposed to a risk of punitive sanctions that would make criminal safeguards necessary. By contrast, a fixed fine payable to the court is punitive and criminal in character.

An analogous distinction can be drawn between types of sentences of incarceration. Commitment to jail or prison for a fixed term usually operates as a punitive sanction because it confers no advantage on the other party. *Gompers, supra,* 221 U.S., at 449. But if a contemnor is incarcerated until he or she complies with a court order, the sanction is civil. Although the imprisonment does not compensate the adverse party directly, it is designed to obtain compliance with a court order made in that party's favor. "When the [contemnors] carry 'the keys of their prison in their own pockets,' the action 'is essentially a civil remedy designed for the benefit of other parties and has quite properly been exercised for centuries to secure compliance with judicial decrees.'" *Shillitani, supra,* 384 U.S., at 368 (citations omitted).

III

Several peculiar features of California's contempt law make it difficult to determine whether the proceeding in this case was civil or criminal. All contempt proceedings in California courts are governed by the same procedural rules. Cal.Civ.Proc.Code Ann. §§1209-1222 (West 1982 and Supp.1988).... Because state law provides that defendants in civil contempt proceedings are entitled to most of the protections guaranteed to ordinary criminal defendants, the California courts have held that civil contempt proceedings are quasi-criminal under state law.... Therefore, indications that the California Superior Court conducted respondent's hearing as a criminal proceeding do not conclusively demonstrate for purposes of federal due process analysis that respondent was tried for criminal contempt.

Certain formal aspects of the proceeding below raise the possibility that it involved criminal contempt. The orders to show cause stated that "[a] contempt proceeding is criminal in nature" and that a violation would subject the respondent to "possible penalties."... The orders advised respondent of his right to an attorney.... During the hearing, the trial judge told respondent that he had a constitutional right not to testify.... Finally, the judge imposed a determinate sentence of five days in jail for each count of contempt, to be served consecutively. See Cal.Civ. Proc.Code Ann. §1218 (West 1982)(contempt may be punished by a fine not exceeding $500, or imprisonment not exceeding five days, or both); cf. Cal.Civ. Proc.Code Ann. §1219 (West 1982)(contempt may be punished by imprisonment until an act is performed, if the contempt is the omission to perform the act).

Nevertheless, the substance of the proceeding below and the conditions on which the sentence was suspended reveal that the proceeding was civil in nature. Mrs. Feiock initiated the underlying action in order to obtain enforcement of the child support order for the benefit of the Feiock children. The California District Attorney conducted the case under a provision of the URESA that authorizes him to act on Mrs. Feiock's behalf. Cal.Civ.Proc.Code Ann. §1680 (West 1982). As the very caption of the case in this Court indicates, the District Attorney is acting on behalf of Mrs. Feiock, not as the representative of the State of California in a criminal prosecution. Both of the provisions of California's enactment of the URESA that authorize contempt proceedings appear in a chapter of the Code of Civil Procedure entitled "Civil Enforcement." *Id.,* §§1672, 1685. It appears that most States enforce child and spousal support orders through civil proceedings like this one, in which the burden of persuasion is shifted to the defendant to show inability to comply....

These indications that the proceeding was civil are confirmed by the character of the sanction imposed on respondent. The California Superior Court sentenced respondent to a fixed term of 25 days in jail. Without more, this sanction would be punitive and appropriate for a criminal contempt. But the court suspended the determinate sentence and placed respondent on three years' informal probation on the conditions that he comply with the support order in the future and begin to pay on the arrearage that he had accumulated in the past.... These special conditions aim exclusively at enforcing compliance with the existing child support order.

Our precedents indicate that such a conditional sentence is coercive rather than punitive. Thus in *Gompers*, we observed that civil contempt may be punished by an order that "the defendant stand committed *unless* and until he performs the affirmative act required by the court's order." 221 U.S., at 442 (emphasis added). In *Shillitani*, we decided that civil contempt could be punished by a prison sentence fixed at two years if it included a proviso that the contemnor would be released as soon as he complied with the court order. 384 U.S., at 365. In this case, if respondent performs his obligations under the original court order, he can avoid going to jail at all. Like the sentence in *Shillitani*, respondent's prison sentence is coercive rather than punitive because it effectively "conditions release upon the contemnor's willingness to [comply]." *Id.*, at 370.

It is true that the order imposing the sentence does not expressly provide that, *if* respondent is someday incarcerated and *if* he subsequently complies, he will be released immediately. The parties disagree about what will happen if this contingency arises...and there is no need to address today the question whether the failure to grant immediate release would render the sanction criminal. In the case before us respondent carries something even better than the "keys to the prison" in his own pocket: as long as he meets the conditions of his informal probation, he will never enter the jail.

It is critical that the only conditions placed on respondent's probation, apart from the requirement that he conduct himself generally in accordance with the law, are that he cure his past failures to comply with the support order and that he continue to comply in the future.* The sanction imposed on respondent is unlike ordinary criminal probation because it is collateral to a civil proceeding initiated by a private party, and respondent's sentence is suspended on the condition that he comply with a court order entered for the benefit of that party. This distinguishes respondent's sentence from suspended criminal sentences imposed outside the contempt context.

This Court traditionally has inquired into the substance of contempt proceedings to determine whether they are civil or criminal, paying particular attention to whether the sanction imposed will benefit another party to the proceeding. In this case, the California Superior Court suspended respondent's sentence on the condition that he bring himself into compliance with a court order providing support for his children, represented in the proceeding by petitioner. I conclude that the

* Unlike the Court, *ante*, at 1433, I find no ambiguity in the court's sentencing order that hints that respondent can purge his jail sentence by paying off the arrearage alone. The sentencing order suspends execution of the jail sentence and places respondent on probation on the conditions that he both make future support payments at $150 per month and pay $50 per month on the arrearage.... If respondent pays off the arrearage before the end of his probation period, but then fails to make a current support payment, the suspension will be revoked and he will go to jail. See *People v. Chagolla*, 151 Cal.App.3d 1045, 199 Cal.Rptr. 181 (1984)(explaining that if a court suspends a sentence on conditions, and any condition is violated, the court must reinstate the original sentence).

proceeding in this case should be characterized as one for civil contempt, and I would reverse the judgment below.

COMMENTS

During the 1970s, when many states reduced the age of majority from twenty-one to eighteen, there was a brief period of considerable confusion regarding when child support payments should end. Some decrees had specified payments to age twenty-one, while others had referred to the age of majority or said nothing. At that time it was widely assumed that parents should have no financial obligation to their children after the age of majority unless the children were disabled in some significant manner. In *Kujawinski* the father challenged the constitutionality of a law that empowered courts to require him to support his adult children under circumstances in which a parent in an intact family would not be ordered to pay such support. The court appears remarkably realistic in its opinion turning down the father's equal protection argument.

Where it is established that non-custodial parents may be obliged to pay college expenses for their children, the question then arises whether they may also be ordered to pay expenses for professional or graduate school. *Ross* was a relatively easy case because the mother was seeking minimal support from the non-custodial father to help defray the child's law school expenses. In at least one other case, *Brown v. Brown*, 327 Pa.Super. 51, 474 A.2d 1168 (1984), the court refused to order support for law school. For the time being, it seems clear that the parent's obligation to support an adult child's college expenses cannot be enforced by the child but depends upon the agreement and efforts of the custodial parent (or the parent in whose custody the child was living at the age of majority). See, for example, *Roe v. Doe*, supra at p. 668, where the court allowed the father of a minor child (without a living mother) to discontinue her college tuition and support. The daughter had disobeyed the father, but the court refused to examine the reasonableness of the father's instructions to the daughter the way a court would if the other parent were involved in the dispute with the father.

Reneging on child support has long been as socially acceptable as drunk driving once was and perhaps still is in the minds of some people. Both are in some sense a transgression of socially approved norms, but transgressions that have been acceptable and even amusing to many people. The damage done by the financial abandonment of children, like the damage done by drunk drivers, often goes unnoticed. What Mothers Against Drunk Driving did for the one problem, federal laws and women's protests may yet do for child support. On the surface, it seems that there are a myriad of ways to collect overdue child support payments, yet the actual collection record has been grim. Millions of children live in poverty in the United States. While some of the impoverished children are the offspring of poor parents, a large number were born to financially secure couples and many have fathers who are living lives of comfortable affluence.

Feiock sketches out some of the constitutional limits upon what states may do to enforce child support obligations. They may enforce by civil, as opposed to criminal contempt without the payee or the state having to prove that the obligor is able to make the payments. As the dissent points out, such proof could be quite difficult in many cases. We saw back in Chapter 4 in *Zablocki v. Redhail* (p. 490) that states may not forbid delinquent parents from marrying as a means to enforce child support obligations.

In recent years, some improvements have been made in procedures for collecting delinquent child support payments, primarily because the government is interested in reducing the costs of welfare payments it makes to impoverished women and their children. Custodial parents who are not poor enough to be on welfare have been the incidental beneficiaries.

E: TERMINATING PARENT-CHILD RELATIONSHIPS; ESTABLISHING NEW ONES

Neglect Proceedings

SANTOSKY v. KRAMER
United States Supreme Court
455 U.S. 745 (1982)

Justice BLACKMUN delivered the opinion of the Court.

Under New York law, the State may terminate, over parental objection, the rights of parents in their natural child upon a finding that the child is "permanently neglected." N.Y. Soc. Serv. Law §84-b.4.(d), 384-b.7. (a)(McKinney Supp. 1981–1982)(Soc.Serv.Law). The New York Family Court Act §622 (McKinney 1975 and Supp.1981–1982)(Fam.Ct.Act) requires that only a "fair preponderance of the evidence" support that finding. Thus, in New York, the factual certainty required to extinguish the parent-child relationship is no greater than that necessary to award money damages in an ordinary civil action.

Today we hold that the Due Process Clause of the Fourteenth Amendment demands more than this. Before a State may sever completely and irrevocably the rights of parents in their natural child, due process requires that the State support its allegations by at least clear and convincing evidence.

I

A

New York authorizes its officials to remove a child temporarily from his or her home if the child appears "neglected," within the meaning of Art. 10 of the Family Court Act. See §1012(f), 1021–1029. Once removed, a child under the age of 18 customarily is placed "in the care of an authorized agency," Soc.Serv.Law §384-b.7.(a), usually a state institution or a foster home. At that point, "the state's first obligation is to help the family with services to...reunite it...." §384-b.1.(a)(iii). But if convinced that "positive, nurturing parent-child relationships no longer exist," §384-b.1.(b), the State may initiate "permanent neglect" proceedings to free the child for adoption.

The State bifurcates its permanent neglect proceeding into "fact-finding" and "dispositional" hearings. Fam.Ct.Act §622, 623. At the factfinding stage, the State must prove that the child has been "permanently neglected," as defined by Fam.Ct.Act §614.1.(a)-(d) and Soc.Serv.Law§384-b.7.(a). See Fam.Ct.Act §622. The Family Court judge then determines at a subsequent dispositional hearing what placement would serve the child's best interests. §623, 631.

At the factfinding hearing, the State must establish, among other things, that for more than a year after the child entered state custody, the agency "made diligent efforts to encourage and strengthen the parental relationship." Fam.Ct.Act §614.1.(c), 611. The State must further prove that during that same period, the child's natural parents failed "substantially and continuously or repeatedly to maintain contact with or plan for the future of the child although physically and financially able to do so." §614.1(d). Should the State support its allegations by "a fair preponderance of the evidence," §622, the child may be declared permanently neglected. That declaration empowers the Family Court judge to terminate permanently the natural parents' rights in the child. §631(c), 634. Termination denies the natural parents physical custody, as well as the rights ever to visit, communicate with, or regain custody of the child.

New York's permanent neglect statute provides natural parents with certain procedural protections.[2] But New York permits its officials to establish "permanent neglect" with less proof than most States require. Thirty-five States, the District of Columbia, and the Virgin Islands currently specify a higher standard of proof, in parental rights termination proceedings, than a "fair preponderance of the evidence." The only analogous federal statute of which we are aware permits termination of parental rights solely upon "evidence beyond a reasonable doubt." Indian Child Welfare Act of 1978, Pub.L. 95-608, §102(f), 92 Stat. 3072, 25 U.S.C. §1912(f)(1976 ed., Supp.IV). The question here is whether New York's "fair preponderance of the evidence" standard is constitutionally sufficient.

B

Petitioners John Santosky II and Annie Santosky are the natural parents of Tina and John III. In November 1973, after incidents reflecting parental neglect, respondent Kramer, Commissioner of the Ulster County Department of Social Services, initiated a neglect proceeding under Fam.Ct.Act §1022 and removed Tina from her natural home. About 10 months later, he removed John III and placed him with foster parents. On the day John was taken, Annie Santosky gave birth to a third child, Jed. When Jed was only three days old, respondent transferred him to a foster home on the ground that immediate removal was necessary to avoid imminent danger to his life or health.

In October 1978, respondent petitioned the Ulster County Family Court to terminate petitioners' parental rights in the three children. Petitioners challenged the constitutionality of the "fair preponderance of the evidence" standard specified in Fam.Ct.Act §622. The Family Court Judge rejected this constitutional challenge, and weighed the evidence under the statutory standard. While acknowledging that the Santoskys had maintained contact with their children, the judge found those visits "at best superficial and devoid of any real emotional content." *Id.*, at 21. After deciding that the agency had made "'diligent efforts' to encourage and strengthen the parental relationship," *id.*, at 30, he concluded that the Santoskys were incapable, even with public assistance, of planning for the future of their children. *Id.*, at 33–37. The judge later held a dispositional hearing

2. Most notably, natural parents have a statutory right to the assistance of counsel and of court-appointed counsel if they are indigent. Fam.Ct.Act §262(a)(iii).

and ruled that the best interests of the three children required permanent termination of the Santoskys' custody.[5] *Id.*, at 39.

II

...

The fundamental liberty interest of natural parents in the care, custody, and management of their child does not evaporate simply because they have not been model parents or have lost temporary custody of their child to the State. Even when blood relationships are strained, parents retain a vital interest in preventing the irretrievable destruction of their family life. If anything, persons faced with forced dissolution of their parental rights have a more critical need for procedural protections than do those resisting state intervention into ongoing family affairs. When the State moves to destroy weakened familial bonds, it must provide the parents with fundamentally fair procedures.

In *Lassiter [v. Department of Social Services*, 452 U.S. 18, 101 S. Ct. 2163 (1981)] the Court and three dissenters agreed that the nature of the process due in parental rights termination proceedings turns on a balancing of the "three distinct factors" specified in *Mathews v. Eldridge*, 424 U.S. 319, 335, 96 S.Ct. 893, 903, 47 L.Ed.2d 18 (1976): the private interests affected by the proceeding; the risk of error created by the State's chosen procedure; and the countervailing governmental interest supporting use of the challenged procedure....

...

III

In parental rights termination proceedings, the private interest affected is commanding; the risk of error from using a preponderance standard is substantial; and the countervailing governmental interest favoring that standard is comparatively slight. Evaluation of the three *Eldridge* factors compels the conclusion that use of a "fair preponderance of the evidence" standard in such proceedings is inconsistent with due process.

A

...

...Once affirmed on appeal, a New York decision terminating parental rights is *final* and irrevocable.... Few forms of state action are both so severe and so irreversible.

Thus, the first *Eldridge* factor — the private interest affected — weighs heavily against use of the preponderance standard at a state-initiated permanent neglect proceeding. We do not deny that the child and his foster parents are also deeply interested in the outcome of that contest. But at the factfinding stage of the New York proceeding, the focus emphatically is not on them.

The factfinding does not purport — and is not intended — to balance the child's interest in a normal family home against the parents' interest in raising the child. Nor does it purport to determine whether the natural parents or the foster parents would provide the better home. Rather, the factfinding hearing pits the State directly against the parents. The State alleges that the natural parents are at fault. Fam.Ct.Act §614.1.(d). The questions disputed and decided are what the

5. Since respondent Kramer took custody of Tina, John III, and Jed, the Santoskys have had two other children, James and Jeremy. The State has taken no action to remove these younger children. At oral argument, counsel for respondents replied affirmatively when asked whether he was asserting that petitioners were "unfit to handle the three older ones but not unfit to handle the two younger ones."...

State did — "made diligent efforts," §614.1.(c) — and what the natural parents did not do — "maintain contact with or plan for the future of the child." §614.1.(d). The State marshals an array of public resources to prove its case and disprove the parents' case. Victory by the State not only makes termination of parental rights possible; it entails a judicial determination that the parents are unfit to raise their own children.

...

B

Under *Mathews v. Eldridge*, we next must consider both the risk of erroneous deprivation of private interests resulting from use of a "fair preponderance" standard and the likelihood that a higher evidentiary standard would reduce that risk. See 424 U.S., at 335, 96 S.Ct., at 903. Since the factfinding phase of a permanent neglect proceeding is an adversary contest between the State and the natural parents, the relevant question is whether a preponderance standard fairly allocates the risk of an erroneous factfinding between these two parties.

...

At such a proceeding, numerous factors combine to magnify the risk of erroneous factfinding. Permanent neglect proceedings employ imprecise substantive standards that leave determinations unusually open to the subjective values of the judge. See *Smith v. Organization of Foster Families*, 431 U.S., at 835, n. 36, 97 S.Ct., at 2105, n. 36. In appraising the nature and quality of a complex series of encounters among the agency, the parents, and the child, the court possesses unusual discretion to underweigh probative facts that might favor the parent....

The State's ability to assemble its case almost inevitably dwarfs the parents' ability to mount a defense. No predetermined limits restrict the sums an agency may spend in prosecuting a given termination proceeding. The State's attorney usually will be expert on the issues contested and the procedures employed at the factfinding hearing, and enjoys full access to all public records concerning the family. The State may call on experts in family relations, psychology, and medicine to bolster its case. Furthermore, the primary witnesses at the hearing will be the agency's own professional caseworkers whom the State has empowered both to investigate the family situation and to testify against the parents. Indeed, because the child is already in agency custody, the State even has the power to shape the historical events that form the basis for termination.

The disparity between the adversaries' litigation resources is matched by a striking asymmetry in their litigation options. Unlike criminal defendants, natural parents have no "double jeopardy" defense against repeated state termination efforts. If the State initially fails to win termination, as New York did here,...it always can try once again to cut off the parents' rights after gathering more or better evidence. Yet even when the parents have attained the level of fitness required by the State, they have no similar means by which they can forestall future termination efforts.

...

The Appellate Division approved New York's preponderance standard on the ground that it properly "balanced rights possessed by the child...with those of the natural parents...." 75 App.Div.2d, at 910, 427 N.Y.S.2d, at 320. By so saying, the court suggested that a preponderance standard properly allocates the risk of error *between* the parents and the child. That view is fundamentally mistaken.

The court's theory assumes that termination of the natural parents' rights invariably will benefit the child. Yet we have noted above that the parents and the child share an interest in avoiding erroneous termination. Even accepting the court's assumption, we cannot agree with its conclusion that a preponderance standard fairly distributes the risk of error between parent and child. Use of that standard reflects the judgment that society is nearly neutral between erroneous termination of parental rights and erroneous failure to terminate those rights.... For the child, the likely consequence of an erroneous failure to terminate is preservation of an uneasy status quo. For the natural parents, however, the consequence of an erroneous termination is the unnecessary destruction of their natural family. A standard that allocates the risk of error nearly equally between those two outcomes does not reflect properly their relative severity.

C

Two state interests are at stake in parental rights termination proceedings — a *parens patriae* interest in preserving and promoting the welfare of the child and a fiscal and administrative interest in reducing the cost and burden of such proceedings. A standard of proof more strict than preponderance of the evidence is consistent with both interests.

...

The State's interest in finding the child an alternative permanent home arises only "when it is *clear* that the natural parent cannot or will not provide a normal family home for the child." Soc.Serv.Law §384-b.1.(a)(iv)(emphasis added). At the factfinding, that goal is served by procedures that promote an accurate determination of whether the natural parents can and will provide a normal home.

...

IV

The logical conclusion of this balancing process is that the "fair preponderance of the evidence" standard prescribed by Fam.Ct.Act §622 violates the Due Process Clause of the Fourteenth Amendment.[18] The Court noted in *Addington* : "The individual should not be asked to share equally with society the risk of error when the possible injury to the individual is significantly greater than any possible harm to the state." 441 U.S., at 427, 99 S.Ct., at 1810. Thus, at a parental rights termination proceeding, a near-equal allocation of risk between the parents and the State is constitutionally intolerable. The next question, then, is whether a "beyond a reasonable doubt" or a "clear and convincing" standard is constitutionally mandated.

In *Addington*, the Court concluded that application of a reasonable-doubt standard is inappropriate in civil commitment proceedings for two reasons — because of our hesitation to apply that unique standard "too broadly or casually in noncriminal cases," *id.*, at 428, 99 S.Ct., at 1810, and because the psychiatric evidence ordinarily adduced at commitment proceedings is rarely susceptible to proof beyond a reasonable doubt. *Id.*, at 429–430, 432–433, 99 S.Ct., at 1811–1812, 1812–1813. To be sure, as has been noted above, in the Indian Child Welfare Act of 1978, Pub.L. 95-608, s102(f), 92 Stat. 3072, 25 U.S.C. §1912(f)(1976 ed., Supp.IV), Congress requires "evidence beyond a reasonable doubt" for termination of Indian parental rights, reasoning that "the removal of a child from the parents is a penalty as great [as], if not greater, than a criminal penalty...." H.R.Rep.No. 95-1386, p. 22 (1978)[, *U.S.Code*

18. The dissent's claim that today's decision "will inevitably lead to the federalization of family law," ... is, of course, vastly overstated. As the dissent properly notes, the Court's duty to "refrai[n] from interfering with state answers to domestic relations questions" has never required "that the Court should blink at clear constitutional violations in state statutes."...

Cong. & Admin.News 1978, pp. 7530, 7545]. Congress did not consider, however, the evidentiary problems that would arise if proof beyond a reasonable doubt were required in all state-initiated parental rights termination hearings.

Like civil commitment hearings, termination proceedings often require the factfinder to evaluate medical and psychiatric testimony, and to decide issues difficult to prove to a level of absolute certainty, such as lack of parental motive, absence of affection between parent and child, and failure of parental foresight and progress. Cf. *Lassiter v. Department of Social Services*, 452 U.S., at 30, 101 S.Ct., at 2161; *id.*, at 44–46, 101 S.Ct., at 2168–2169 (first dissenting opinion)(describing issues raised in state termination proceedings). The substantive standards applied vary from State to State. Although Congress found a "beyond a reasonable doubt" standard proper in one type of parental rights termination case, another legislative body might well conclude that a reasonable-doubt standard would erect an unreasonable barrier to state efforts to free permanently neglected children for adoption.

A majority of the States have concluded that a "clear and convincing evidence" standard of proof strikes a fair balance between the rights of the natural parents and the State's legitimate concerns.... We hold that such a standard adequately conveys to the factfinder the level of subjective certainty about his factual conclusions necessary to satisfy due process. We further hold that determination of the precise burden equal to or greater than that standard is a matter of state law properly left to state legislatures and state courts....

We, of course, express no view on the merits of petitioners' claims. At a hearing conducted under a constitutionally proper standard, they may or may not prevail. Without deciding the outcome under any of the standards we have approved, we vacate the judgment of the Appellate Division and remand the case for further proceedings not inconsistent with this opinion.

It is so ordered.

Justice REHNQUIST, with whom the CHIEF JUSTICE, Justice WHITE, and Justice O'CONNOR join, dissenting.

I believe that few of us would care to live in a society where every aspect of life was regulated by a single source of law, whether that source be this Court or some other organ of our complex body politic. But today's decision certainly moves us in that direction. By parsing the New York scheme and holding one narrow provision unconstitutional, the majority invites further federal-court intrusion into every facet of state family law. If ever there were an area in which federal courts should heed the admonition of Justice Holmes that "a page of history is worth a volume of logic," it is in the area of domestic relations. This area has been left to the States from time immemorial, and not without good reason.

...

I

State intervention in domestic relations has always been an unhappy but necessary feature of life in our organized society. For all of our experience in this area, we have found no fully satisfactory solutions to the painful problem of child abuse and neglect. We have found, however, that leaving the States free to experiment with various remedies has produced novel approaches and promising progress.

Throughout this experience the Court has scrupulously refrained from interfering with state answers to domestic relations questions. "Both theory and the precedents of this Court teach us solicitude for state interests, particularly in the field of family and family-property arrangements." *United States v. Yazell*, 382 U.S. 341, 352, 86 S.Ct. 500, 507, 15 L.Ed.2d 404 (1966). This is not to say that the Court should blink at clear constitutional violations in state statutes, but rather that in this area, of all areas, "substantial weight must be given to the good-faith judgments of the individuals [administering a program]...that the procedures they have provided assure fair consideration of the...claims of individuals." *Mathews v. Eldridge*, 424 U.S. 319, 349, 96 S.Ct. 893, 909, 47 L.Ed.2d 18 (1976).

This case presents a classic occasion for such solicitude. As will be seen more fully in the next part, New York has enacted a comprehensive plan to *aid* marginal parents in regaining the custody of their child. The central purpose of the New York plan is to reunite divided families. Adoption of the preponderance-of-the-evidence standard represents New York's good-faith effort to balance the interest of parents against the legitimate interests of the child and the State. These earnest efforts by state officials should be given weight in the Court's application of due process principles. "Great constitutional provisions must be administered with caution. Some play must be allowed for the joints of the machine, and it must be remembered that legislatures are ultimate guardians of the liberties and welfare of the people in quite as great a degree as the courts." *Missouri, K. & T.R. Co. v. May*, 194 U.S. 267, 270, 24 S.Ct. 638, 639, 48 L.Ed. 971 (1904).

The majority may believe that it is adopting a relatively unobtrusive means of ensuring that termination proceedings provide "due process of law." In fact, however, fixing the standard of proof as a matter of federal constitutional law will only lead to further federal-court intervention in state schemes. By holding that due process requires proof by clear and convincing evidence the majority surely cannot mean that any state scheme passes constitutional muster so long as it applies that standard of proof. A state law permitting termination of parental rights upon a showing of neglect by clear and convincing evidence certainly would not be acceptable to the majority if it provided no procedures other than one 30-minute hearing. Similarly, the majority probably would balk at a state scheme that permitted termination of parental rights on a clear and convincing showing merely that such action would be in the best interests of the child. See *Smith v. Organization of Foster Families*, 431 U.S. 816, 862–863, 97 S.Ct. 2094, 2119, 53 L.Ed.2d 14 (1977)(Stewart, J., concurring in judgment).

After fixing the standard of proof, therefore, the majority will be forced to evaluate other aspects of termination proceedings with reference to that point. Having in this case abandoned evaluation of the overall effect of a scheme, and with it the possibility of finding that strict substantive standards or special procedures compensate for a lower burden of proof, the majority's approach will inevitably lead to the federalization of family law. Such a trend will only thwart state searches for better solutions in an area where this Court should encourage state experimentation....

II

As the majority opinion notes, petitioners are the parents of five children, three of whom were removed from petitioners' care on or before August 22, 1974. During the next four and one-half years, those three children were in the custody of the State and in the care of foster homes or institutions, and the State was diligently engaged in efforts to prepare petitioners for the children's return. Those efforts were unsuccessful, however, and on April 10, 1979, the New York Family Court for Ulster County terminated petitioners' parental rights as to the three children removed in 1974 or earlier. This termination was preceded by a judicial finding that petitioners had failed to plan for the return and future of their children, a statutory category of permanent neglect. Petitioners now contend, and the Court today holds, that they were denied due process of law, not because of a general inadequacy of procedural protections, but simply because the finding of permanent neglect was made on the basis of a preponderance of the evidence adduced at the termination hearing.

...

A

Due process of law is a flexible constitutional principle. The requirements which it imposes upon governmental actions vary with the situations to which it applies.... The adequacy of a scheme of procedural protections cannot, therefore, be determined merely by the application of general principles unrelated to the peculiarities of the case at hand.

Given this flexibility, it is obvious that a proper due process inquiry cannot be made by focusing upon one narrow provision of the challenged statutory scheme. Such a focus threatens to overlook factors which may introduce constitutionally adequate protections into a particular government action. Courts must examine *all* procedural protections offered by the State, and must assess the *cumulative* effect of such safeguards. As we have stated before, courts must consider "the fairness and reliability of the existing...procedures" before holding that the Constitution requires more. *Mathews v. Eldridge, supra,* 424 U.S., at 343, 96 S.Ct., at 907. Only through such a broad inquiry may courts determine whether a challenged governmental action satisfies the due process requirement of "fundamental fairness."...

...

[New York's termination procedures demonstrate that] the State seeks not only to protect the interests of parents in rearing their own children, but also to assist and encourage parents who have lost custody of their children to reassume their rightful role. Fully understood, the New York system is a comprehensive program to *aid* parents such as petitioners. Only as a last resort, when "diligent efforts" to reunite the family have failed, does New York authorize the termination of parental rights. The procedures for termination of those relationships which cannot be aided and which threaten permanent injury to the child, administered by a judge who has supervised the case from the first temporary removal through the final termination, cannot be viewed as fundamentally unfair. The facts of this case demonstrate the fairness of the system.

The three children to which this case relates were removed from petitioners' custody in 1973 and 1974, before petitioners' other two children were born. The removals were made pursuant to the [New York procedure] and in response to what can only be described as shockingly abusive treatment.[10] At the temporary removal hearing held before the Family Court on September 30, 1974, petitioners were represented by counsel, and allowed the Ulster County Department of Social Services (Department) to take custody of the three children.

10. Tina Apel, the oldest of petitioners' five children, was removed from their custody by court order in November 1973 when she was two years old. Removal proceedings were commenced in response to complaints by neighbors and reports from a local hospital that Tina had suffered injuries in petitioners' home including a fractured left femur, treated with a home- made splint; bruises on the upper arms, forehead, flank, and spine; and abrasions of the upper leg. The following summer John Santosky III, petitioners' second oldest child, was also removed from petitioner's custody. John, who was less than one year old at the time, was admitted to the hospital suffering malnutrition, bruises on the eye and forehead, cuts on the foot, blisters on the hand, and multiple pin pricks on the back.... Jed Santosky, the third oldest of petitioners' children, was removed from his parents' custody when only three days old as a result of the abusive treatment of the two older children.

Temporary removal of the children was continued at an evidentiary hearing held before the Family Court in December 1975, after which the court issued a written opinion concluding that petitioners were unable to resume their parental responsibilities due to personality disorders. Unsatisfied with the progress petitioners were making, the court also directed the Department to reduce to writing the plan which it had designed to solve the problems at petitioners' home and reunite the family.

A plan for providing petitioners with extensive counseling and training services was submitted to the court and approved in February 1976. Under the plan, petitioners received training by a mother's aide, a nutritional aide, and a public health nurse, and counseling at a family planning clinic. In addition, the plan provided psychiatric treatment and vocational training for the father, and counseling at a family service center for the mother.... Between early 1976 and the final termination decision in April 1979, the State spent more than $15,000 in these efforts to rehabilitate petitioners as parents.

Petitioners' response to the State's effort was marginal at best. They wholly disregarded some of the available services and participated only sporadically in the others. As a result, and out of growing concern over the length of the children's stay in foster care, the Department petitioned in September 1976 for permanent termination of petitioners' parental rights so that the children could be adopted by other families. Although the Family Court recognized that petitioners' reaction to the State's efforts was generally "non-responsive, even hostile," the fact that they were "at least superficially cooperative" led it to conclude that there was yet hope of further improvement and an eventual reuniting of the family.... Accordingly, the petition for permanent termination was dismissed.

Whatever progress petitioners were making prior to the 1976 termination hearing, they made little or no progress thereafter. In October 1978, the Department again filed a termination petition alleging that petitioners had completely failed to plan for the children's future despite the considerable efforts rendered in their behalf. This time, the Family Court agreed. The court found that petitioners had "failed in any meaningful way to take advantage of the many social and rehabilitative services that have not only been made available to them but have been diligently urged upon them."... In addition, the court found that the "infrequent" visits "between the parents and their children were at best superficial and devoid of any real emotional content."... The court thus found "nothing in the situation which holds out any hope that [petitioners] may ever become financially self sufficient or emotionally mature enough to be independent of the services of social agencies. More than a reasonable amount of time has passed and still, in the words of the case workers, there has been no discernible forward movement. At some point in time, it must be said, 'enough is enough.'"...

In accordance with the statutory requirements set forth above, the court found that petitioners' failure to plan for the future of their children, who were then seven, five, and four years old and had been out of petitioners' custody for at least four years, rose to the level of permanent neglect. At a subsequent dispositional hearing, the court terminated petitioners' parental rights, thereby freeing the three children for adoption.

As this account demonstrates, the State's extraordinary 4-year effort to reunite petitioners' family was not just unsuccessful, it was altogether rebuffed by parents unwilling to improve their circumstances sufficiently to permit a return of their children. At every step of this protracted process petitioners were accorded those procedures and protections which traditionally have been required by due process of law. Moreover, from the beginning to the end of this sad story all judicial determinations were made by one Family Court Judge. After four and one-half years of involvement with petitioners, more than seven complete hearings, and additional periodic supervision of the State's rehabilitative efforts, the judge no doubt was intimately familiar with this case and the prospects for petitioners' rehabilitation.

It is inconceivable to me that these procedures were "fundamentally unfair" to petitioners. Only by its obsessive focus on the standard of proof and its almost complete disregard of the facts of this case does the majority find otherwise.[11] As the discussion above indicates, however, such a focus does not comport with the flexible standard of fundamental fairness embodied in the Due Process Clause of the Fourteenth Amendment.

B

In addition to the basic fairness of the process afforded petitioners, the standard of proof chosen by New York clearly reflects a constitutionally permissible balance of the interests at stake in this case. The standard of proof "represents an attempt to instruct the factfinder concerning the degree of confidence our society thinks he should have in the correctness of factual conclusions for a particular type of adjudication."...

...

On one side is the interest of parents in a continuation of the family unit and the raising of their own children. The importance of this interest cannot easily be overstated. Few consequences of judicial action are so grave as the severance of natural family ties. Even the convict committed to prison and thereby deprived of his physical liberty often retains the love and support of family members....

On the other side of the termination proceeding are the often countervailing interests of the child. A stable, loving homelife is essential to a child's physical,

---

11. The majority finds, without any reference to the facts of this case, that "numerous factors [in New York termination proceedings] combine to magnify the risk of erroneous factfinding."... Among the factors identified by the majority are the "unusual discretion" of the Family Court Judge "to underweigh probative facts that might favor the parent"; the often uneducated, minority status of the parents and their consequent "vulnerab[ility] to judgments based on cultural or class bias"; the "State's ability to assemble its case," which "dwarfs the parents' ability to mount a defense" by including an unlimited budget, expert attorneys, and "full access to all public records concerning the family"; and the fact that "natural parents have no 'double jeopardy' defense against repeated state" efforts, "with more or better evidence," to terminate parental rights "even when the parents have attained the level of fitness required by the State."... In short, the majority characterizes the State as a wealthy and powerful bully bent on taking children away from defenseless parents.... Such characterization finds no support in the record.

The intent of New York has been stated with eminent clarity: "the [S]tate's *first obligation* is to *help* the family with services to *prevent* its break-up or to *reunite* it if the child has already left home." SSL §384-b.1.(a)(iii)(emphasis added). There is simply no basis in fact for believing, as the majority does, that the State does not mean what it says; indeed, the facts of this case demonstrate that New York has gone the extra mile in seeking to effectuate its declared purpose.... More importantly, there should be no room in the jurisprudence of this Court for decisions based on unsupported, inaccurate assumptions.

A brief examination of the "factors" relied upon by the majority demonstrates its error. The "unusual" discretion of the Family Court Judge to consider the "'affectio[n] and concer[n]'" displayed by parents during visits with their children,...is nothing more than discretion to consider reality; there is not one shred of evidence in this case suggesting that the determination of the Family Court was "based on cultural or class bias"; if parents lack the "ability to mount a defense," the State provides them with the full services of an attorney, FCA §262, and they, like the State, have "full access to all *public* records concerning the family" (emphasis added); and the absence of "double jeopardy" protection simply recognizes the fact that family problems are often ongoing and may in the future warrant action that currently is unnecessary. In this case the Family Court dismissed the first termination petition because it desired to give petitioners "the benefit of the doubt,"... and a second opportunity to raise themselves to "an acceptable minimal level of competency as parents."... It was their complete failure to do so that prompted the second, successful termination petition....

emotional, and spiritual well-being. It requires no citation of authority to assert that children who are abused in their youth generally face extraordinary problems developing into responsible, productive citizens. The same can be said of children who, though not physically or emotionally abused, are passed from one foster home to another with no constancy of love, trust, or discipline. If the Family Court makes an incorrect factual determination resulting in a failure to terminate a parent-child relationship which rightfully should be ended, the child involved must return either to an abusive home or to the often unstable world of foster care. The reality of these risks is magnified by the fact that the only families faced with termination actions are those which have voluntarily surrendered custody of their child to the State, or, as in this case, those from which the child has been removed by judicial action because of threatened irreparable injury through abuse or neglect. Permanent neglect findings also occur only in families where the child has been in foster care for at least one year.

...

When, in the context of a permanent neglect termination proceeding, the interests of the child and the State in a stable, nurturing homelife are balanced against the interests of the parents in the rearing of their child, it cannot be said that either set of interests is so clearly paramount as to require that the risk of error be allocated to one side or the other. Accordingly, a State constitutionally may conclude that the risk of error should be borne in roughly equal fashion by use of the preponderance-of-the-evidence standard of proof. See *Addington v. Texas*, 441 U.S., at 423, 99 S.Ct., at 1807–1808. This is precisely the balance which has been struck by the New York Legislature: "It is the intent of the legislature in enacting this section to provide procedures not only assuring that the rights of the natural parent are protected, but also, where positive, nurturing parent-child relationships no longer exist, furthering the best interests, needs, and rights of the child by terminating the parental rights and freeing the child for adoption." SSL §384-b.1.(b).

III

For the reasons heretofore stated, I believe that the Court today errs in concluding that the New York standard of proof in parental-rights termination proceedings violates due process of law. The decision disregards New York's earnest efforts to *aid* parents in regaining the custody of their children and a host of procedural protections placed around parental rights and interests. The Court finds a constitutional violation only by a tunnel-vision application of due process principles that altogether loses sight of the unmistakable fairness of the New York procedure.

Even more worrisome, today's decision cavalierly rejects the considered judgment of the New York Legislature in an area traditionally entrusted to state care. The Court thereby begins, I fear, a trend of federal intervention in state family law matters which surely will stifle creative responses to vexing problems. Accordingly, I dissent.

COMMENTS

Children in America, from the colonial period to the last part of the twentieth century, have suffered at the hands of parents, employers and even the state. As we noted earlier, children were in many ways considered property, assets of the family. A law in the Massachusetts Bay Colony, borrowed from the Book of Deuteronomy, stated that if a child "disobeyed his father's voice, he could be put to death." Although there is no historical evidence of children actually being put to death, the law reflected a policy toward children that likened them to enslaved people. It took the child labor laws of the twentieth century to protect children from the exploitation of employers.

A major reason that children have been so vulnerable to mistreatment is that the idea of family privacy, long imbedded in the rhetoric of the law, has given parents and persons who stand in loco parentis the freedom to raise and educate children under their control as they desire. This freedom has, from time to time, resulted in the most monstrous kinds of physical and emotional abuse. Historically, abuse has been shielded from the public by the doctrine of parental immunity, which had the effect of sanctioning the use of physical force as a method of punishing children, teaching them respect for their parents, teachers, and other persons in authority, and impressing upon them the difference between right and wrong. *State v. Jones,* 95 N.C. 588 (1886), conceded that it was excessive punishment *but* held it not a matter for state regulation, but rather for "family government" when a father:

> frequently whipped [his sixteen year old daughter] without any cause; that on one occasion he whipped her at the gate in front of his house, giving her about twenty-five blows with a switch, or small limb, about the size of one's thumb or forefinger with such force as to raise whelts upon her back, and then going into the house, he soon returned and gave her five blows more with the same switch, choked her, and threw her violently to the ground, causing a dislocation of her thumb joint; that she had given him no offence; that she did not know for what she was beaten, nor did he give her any reason for it during the time.

Corporal punishment in schools, often justified by references to the Old and New Testament,[1] has been part of the educational history of America. No matter how many studies show that corporal punishment does not inculcate values of obedience and respect, but to the contrary teaches that violence is an acceptable method of dealing with problems, some schools and other institutions continue to use physical force on children as punishment.

Before the 1960s, "child abuse" was not a recognized legal phrase. In order to engage in legal research one would have to search the legal literature under such headings: "punishment," "discipline," and "parental immunity." The computeriza-

---

1. For example, Proverbs 19:18 ("Chasten thy son while there is hope, and let not they soul spare his crying."); Proverbs 13:24 ("He that spareth his rod hateth his son; but he that loveth him chasteneth him betimes."); Proverbs 29:15 ("The rod and reproof give wisdom: but a child left to himself bringeth his mother to shame.").

tion of legal research which is directed toward the use of words in addition to conventional legal phrases may possibly result in a broader and fuller inquiry into the legal history of child abuse. The 1960s and 1970s were years of great legal activity in the history of child protection laws. They were the decades in which America woke up to the fact that children were being abused by parents and caretakers and were in need of protection. During that period Dr. C. Henry Kempe introduced the "battered child syndrome" into the legal and medical vocabulary. The federal government took the initiative by developing model child protection laws for states to replicate, including the mandatory child abuse reporting statute, a model subsidized adoption law, and the law to free children for permanent placement.

During those years family law was being constitutionalized. For the first time in decades, the United States Supreme Court was hearing cases that affected the family. While in the past the Court had heard cases dealing with divorce jurisdiction (see, e.g., *Williams v. North Carolina I,* p. 987 and *Williams v. North Carolina II,* p. 997), in the 1970s substantive issues regarding the constitutional rights of individual family members (see, e.g., *Stanley v. Illinois* p. 759) came before the Court. And, at the same time, access to legal counsel and to the courts were enhanced by the availability of legal services and the creation of state offices for children and child advocacy.

Another major change occurred during the 1960s and 1970s. With the consitutionalization of family law, a concern for civil rights and the availability of legal counsel, came a shift in decision-making. Major decisions about children in the child dependency system were being made by judges in courts after litigation and not by social workers or their supervisors in child welfare agencies. This phenomenon occurred because public child welfare agencies were being held responsible for losing children in foster care, sometimes referred to as "foster care drift." Legislatures began to recognize that agencies' decisions about children in their care had to be monitored and the institution that should monitor them should be the courts. In other words, the center of gravity in child dependency moved from agencies to courts. No longer could child welfare officials feel that their decisions were essentially final with judges rubber stamping them.

A major piece of federal legislation in 1980 was the Adoption Assistance Act of 1980. (Public Law No. 96-272, 42 U.S.C. Sec. 670 et seq.) This legislation which funds foster care programs in states has had a profound impact on the way children and parents are treated by child welfare agencies. One of the major requirements of the Act is that state agencies must make "reasonable efforts" to prevent removal of children from their home and also to promote family reunification if a child has been removed from his or her home because of abuse or neglect. The penalty for not providing such efforts is for the federal government to terminate its funding of the state foster care program.

Removal of children from their homes because of reports of child abuse and their placement in the care of a state child welfare agency has become a complex process. Because of the Adoption Assistance Act of 1980 all states have developed procedures which require judicial hearings at various stages. For example, some states require that a hearing be held immediately after an emergency removal of a child from his or her abusing parents, another hearing after a short period has elapsed in order to determine if the child can be returned home or should be placed in foster care, a third while the child is in foster care for six months, and hearings every six months until the child has been in foster care for eighteen months. Each hearing, conducted by a judge with lawyers representing the child welfare agency, parents and children, is a judicial check on agencies to determine whether the agency is providing the necessary assistance to parents in order to rehabilitate them and whether the parents are utilizing the services and are ready to be reunited with their children. If after eighteen months after the initial hearing to determine removal (assuming that is the time frame) the parents have made little progress toward rehabilitation, then a hearing to terminate parental rights will occur.

Termination of parental rights followed by adoption results in the permanent severing of the legal bond between parent and child. Judicial decisions made in each phase of the process leading to termination are serious with far reaching consequences.

Santosky v. Kramer illustrates the struggle between a child welfare agency and parents for the care and control of the Santosky children. Each of the five children had been abused or neglected. Justice Renquist's dissent elaborates on the specific incidents of neglect and portrays the Santoskys as a dysfunctional family, not unlike many families who are part of a state child welfare social worker's caseload. The question in cases like *Santosky* is how long an agency should wait for parents to be able to care for their children in such a way as to provide them with safety, protection, and sufficient care that the children have a chance of maturing into functioning adults. Child development literature underscores the necessity of assuring children continuity of care with the minimal amount of separation. For children to move in and out of foster care or in and out of their parents' care is almost certain to cause psychological damage.

The narrow issue in *Santosky* concerns the standard of proof necessary to terminate parental rights. The United States Supreme Court struck down the New York provision which required only a"preponderance of the evidence" as sufficient to terminate parental rights and held that the Due Process Clause of the Fourteenth Amendment to the U. S. Constitution requires that a finding of permanent neglect be made by the higher standard of "clear and convincing evidence." The Court was persuaded that the use of that standard of proof reduces the risk of erroneous fact finding and properly allocates the risk of error between the agency and the parents. In his dissent, Justice Renquist took a broader view of the termination hearing and considered it as part of a process. To him the New York statutory scheme represented a "good faith effort to balance the interest of parents against the legitimate interests of the child and the State."

Does viewing a hearing to terminate parental rights as the final stage in a long process — beginning with the initial contact an agency representative has with a family, the decision to remove the child, the frequent hearings (where counsel are present to represent the parties) concerning removal, placement, and termination or reunification — often covering over a year reflect a more realistic view of child dependency? As stated earlier, the Adoption Assistance Act of 1980 requires states to adopt a process with periodic checks and balances. It was designed to prevent children from being in limbo, unaccounted for and in foster care drift. It requires children to be represented in hearings and agencies to be responsible for children in their care and to provide social and psychological services to parents before their children are removed and while their children are placed with others. If the system works well, parents should be given every opportunity to regain the custody of their children and children's voices (by way of representation) should be heard. Children should not be returned to parents who on the basis of their past conduct and reasonably reliable prediction of the future will repeat their abusive or neglectful conduct.

We are dealing with the balancing of parental rights and children's interests. Should a system be designed to give greater protection to parents or to children? Does *Santosky* require that a "clear and convincing standard of proof" be used at the termination hearing if the higher, "clear and convincing" standard of proof was already satisfied at an earlier hearing prior to the termination hearing? For example, if a state statute provides for an agency to prove that there has been neglect by "clear and convincing evidence" at the hearing to decide to remove a child from the parents' custody because of abuse, is it constitutionally permissible to use the evidentiary standard of "preponderance of the evidence" at the termination hearing — a hearing that would occur after the child has been living away from his or her parents for months? These standards of proof may turn out to be merely formalisms, if judges feel free to label the standard they use "clear and convincing" if that is the standard required by a state statute and the United States Supreme Court.

On remand from the United States Supreme Court, the state court affirmed a judgment, based on the record, permanently terminating the Santoskys' parental rights. *In re John AA*, 89 A.D.2d 738, 453 N.Y.S. 2d 942 (1982). Some would argue that this disposition tells us something important about who is actually in the best position to decide a child protection case in the first place and raises questions about how meaningful the standards of proof are in reality.

REFERENCES

Jeanne M. Giovannoni & Rosina M. Becerra, DEFINING CHILD ABUSE 1–75 (1979).

Philip Greven, SPARE THE CHILD 46–54 (1991).

Sanford N. Katz, WHEN PARENTS FAIL (1971).

Adoption

MICHAUD v. WAWRUCK

Supreme Court of Connecticut
209 Conn. 407, 551 A.2d 738 (1988)

PETERS, Chief Justice.

The sole issue in this case is whether a written visitation agreement between a genetic mother and adoptive parents violates the public policy of this state. The plaintiff, Jacqueline Michaud, filed a complaint seeking specific enforcement of an "Open Adoption and Visitation Agreement" between herself and the defendants, James Wawruck and Cynthia Wawruck. The defendants filed a motion to strike the complaint, which was granted by the trial court, *Barall, J.*, and was the basis for the subsequent rendering of a judgment in favor of the defendants by the trial court, *Kaplan, J.* The plaintiff's appeal to the Appellate Court has been transferred to this court pursuant to Practice Book §4023. We find error and remand the case for further proceedings.

Since this appeal is from a judgment following the granting of a motion to strike, we must take the facts to be those alleged in the plaintiff's complaint and construe the complaint in the manner most favorable to sustaining its legal sufficiency.... Accordingly, we assume the following factual circumstances concerning the "Open Adoption and Visitation Agreement" negotiated by the parties. The Ellington Probate Court, on August 31, 1981, terminated the plaintiff's parental rights with respect to her child born on February 5, 1979. The same Probate Court terminated the father's parental rights on January 6, 1982. At some time thereafter, in 1982, the plaintiff filed a Superior Court action against the commissioner of children and youth services to set aside the Probate Court's decree terminating her parental rights, on the ground that her consent to that proceeding had been fraudulently procured by the child's father. The child's foster parents, who were then seeking to adopt the child, were permitted to intervene as defendants in the Superior Court action. The plaintiff agreed to withdraw her lawsuit, and to allow the adoption to go forward, in exchange for the defendants' agreement to permit regular visitation between the plaintiff and the child during the child's minor years.[1]

The agreement between the parties was placed on record in the Superior Court on September 16, 1983. Acquiescence in the agreement was noted, in open court,

---

1. The "Open Adoption and Visitation Agreement" provides in relevant part:

1. *Adoption.* The parties shall all cooperate fully with the state DCYS in the orderly completion of an adoption of the child by the adopting parents.

2. *Termination of Rights.* The natural mother will withdraw here legal challenge...as soon as the adopting parents have approval of their adoption application by DCYS.

3. *Visitation.* The adopting parents will cooperate fully with the natural-mother in the natural mother's visits with the child both now and after the adoption takes place until the child's 18th birthday. The parties agree to be guided in carrying out this provision by the present laws of Connecticut regarding reasonable visitation, which are partly embodied in Connecticut General Statutes Section 46b-56, as they pertain to visitation rights of non-custodial parents in dissolutions of marriage. The tender age of the child and her high sensitivity to her, up to the present, state of uncertainty shall be taken into account by the parties.

Each of the parties shall at all times in good faith endeavor to maintain in the child respect and affection for the other parties.

The rights of visitation shall not be exercised by the natural mother at any time or in such a manner as to interfere with the education and normal social and school activities of the child.

Visitation shall be twice a month for three (3) hours each visit at the Wawrucks' home.

by counsel for the plaintiff, for the defendants, for the commissioner, and for the minor child. The agreement was not, however, made part of the subsequent decree of the Probate Court permitting the defendants to adopt the child, although the parties to that proceeding, having all appeared in the Superior Court action, were fully aware of its terms. After the adoption had been finalized, the defendants terminated all visitation between the plaintiff and the child.

The trial court, after reviewing these facts, granted the defendants' motion to strike the plaintiff's complaint because, in its view, enforcement of the "Open Adoption and Visitation Agreement" would violate Connecticut's adoption statutes. According to the trial court, adoption, as a creature of statute, must comply strictly with statutory requirements, and the existing statutes governing adoption preclude private "side agreements" that would serve to perpetuate a relationship, after adoption, between a genetic parent and an adopted child. The court noted that termination of parental rights, under General Statutes §45-61b(g),[2] operates as a "complete severance by court order of the legal relationship... between the child and his parent...." Furthermore, under General Statutes §45-64a,[3] adoption creates new legal relationships in which the adopting parents are completely substituted for the genetic parents of an adopted person. Finally, the

---

2. General Statutes §45-61b provides in relevant part:

(g) "Termination of parental rights" means the complete severance by court order of the legal relationship, with all its rights and responsibilities, between the child and his parent or parents so that the child is free for adoption except it shall not affect the right of inheritance of the child or the religious affiliation of the child.

3. General Statutes §45-64a provides in relevant part:

EFFECTS OF FINAL DECREE OF ADOPTION. SURVIVING RIGHTS. A final decree of adoption, whether issued by a court of this state or a court of any other jurisdiction, shall have the following effect in this state:

(1) All rights, duties and other legal consequences of the genetic relation of child and parent shall thereafter exist between the adopted person and the adopting parent and his relatives. Such adopted person shall be treated as if he were the genetic child of the adopting parent, for all purposes including the applicability of statutes which do not expressly exclude an adopted person in their operation or effect;

(2) The adopting parent and the adopted person shall have rights of inheritance from and through each other and the genetic and adopted relatives of the adopting parent. The right of inheritance of an adopted person extends to the heirs of such adopted person, and such heirs shall be the same as if such adopted person were the genetic child of the adopting parent;

(3) The adopted person and the genetic children and other adopted children of the adopting parent shall be treated, unless otherwise provided by statute, as siblings, having rights of inheritance from and through each other. Such rights of inheritance extend to the heirs of such adopted person and of the genetic children and other adopted children, and such heirs shall be the same as if each such adopted person were the genetic child of the adopting parent;

(4) The adopted person shall, except as hereinafter provided, be treated as if he were the genetic child of the adopting parent for purposes of the applicability of all documents and instruments, whether executed before or after the adoption decree is issued, which do not expressly exclude an adopted person in their operation or effect. The words "child," "children," "issue," "descendant," "descendants," "heir," "heirs," "lawful heirs," "grandchild" and "grandchildren," when used in any will or trust instrument shall include legally adopted persons unless such document clearly indicates a contrary intention. Nothing in this section shall be construed to alter or modify the provisions of section 45-162 regarding children born through A.I.D.;

(5) The legal relationship between the adopted person and his genetic parent or parents and the relatives of such genetic parent or parents is terminated for all purposes, including the applicability of statutes which do not expressly include such an adopted person in their operation and effect. The genetic parent or parents of the adopted person is relieved of all parental rights and responsibilities;

(6) The genetic parent or parents and their relatives shall have no rights of inheritance from or through the adopted person, nor shall the adopted person have any rights of inheritance from or through his genetic parent or parents and their relatives, except as provided in this section;

(7) The legal relationship between the adopted person and his genetic parent or parents and the relatives of such genetic parent or parents is terminated for purposes of the construction of the documents and instruments, whether executed before or after the adoption decree is issued, which do not expressly include the individual by name or by some designation not based on a parent and child or blood relationship, except as provided in this section.

trial court observed that General Statutes §45-63[4] requires agreements about adoption to be in writing and filed in the Probate Court. Relying on these statutory provisions, and a number of out-of-state cases, the court concluded that the contract between the parties could not confer upon the plaintiff a specifically enforceable right to visitation after completion of the adoption process.

Although the plaintiff's appeal purports to raise three issues about the enforceability of her "Open Adoption and Visitation Agreement," there is really only one question that we must resolve: did the trial court err in concluding that this agreement violated the public policy reflected in our adoption statutes?[5] We disagree with the trial court's ruling.

The validity of an "open adoption" agreement is a matter of first impression for this court. Before we address the merits of this question, we should note that the title "open adoption," which has apparently become the standard characterization of such agreements, conveys a misleading impression of what such agreements intend to accomplish. The plaintiff does not seek to "open," to set aside or to diminish in any way the adoptive process that has substituted the defendants as the legal parents of the child. The plaintiff's rights are not premised on an ongoing genetic relationship that somehow survives a termination of parental rights and an adoption. Instead, the plaintiff is asking us to decide whether, as an adult who has had an ongoing personal relationship with the child, she may contract with the adopting parents, prior to adoption, for the continued right to visit with the child, so long as that visitation continues to be in the best interest of the child.

Our statutes recognize that visitation encompasses considerations that differ from those that govern custody, guardianship or parental status. The plaintiff reminds us that, in the adoption statutes themselves, while an application for adoption must disclose pending proceedings "affecting the custody of the child to be adopted...[f]or the purposes of [such disclosure], visitation rights granted by any court shall not be considered as affecting the custody of the child." General Statutes §45-63(a)(2). The defendants maintain that this statutory distinction merely reflects the fact that Probate Court adoption proceedings necessarily must take outstanding custody orders into account, while visitation rights are not so implicated. This explanation for the distinction contained in §45-63 may well be accurate but it does not eradicate the existence of the distinction and thus supports the plaintiff's position that the adoption statutes do not expressly make a visitation agreement void as against public policy.

---

4. General Statutes §45-63(a)(1) provides:

> Each adoption matter shall be instituted by filing an application in a court of probate, together with the written agreement of adoption, in duplicate. One of the duplicates shall be sent forthwith to the commissioner of children and youth services.

General Statutes §45-63(c)(2) provides:

> At the hearing the court may deny the application, enter a final decree approving the adoption if it is satisfied that the adoption is for the best interests of the child or order a further investigation and written report to be filed, in duplicate, within whatever period of time it directs. A duplicate of such report shall be sent to the commissioner. The court may adjourn the hearing to a day after that fixed for filing the report. If such report has not been filed with the court within the specified time, the court may thereupon deny the application or enter a final decree in the manner provided in this section.

5. The plaintiff's three issues ask us to rule separately about whether the "Open Adoption and Visitation Agreement," which is "supported by mutual consideration," is: (1) void and unenforceable as against public policy; (2) specifically enforceable as a contract right after the completion of the adoption process; or (3) violative of the public policy expressed in the Connecticut statutes governing adoption. The defendants' motion to strike was not premised on any deficiency in consideration, as the transcript of the hearing before the trial court, *Barall, J.*, makes clear.

Even more significantly, our visitation statute, General Statutes §46b-59, permits the Superior Court, upon a proper application, to "grant the right of visitation with respect to any minor child...to any person.... In making, modifying or terminating such an order, the court shall be guided by the best interest of the child.... Visitation rights granted in accordance with this section shall not be deemed to have created parental rights in the person...to whom such visitation rights are granted. The grant of visitation rights shall not prevent any court of competent jurisdiction from thereafter acting upon the custody of such child, the parental rights with respect to such child or the adoption of such child and any such court may include in its decree an order terminating such visitation rights." In *Temple v. Meyer*, 208 Conn. 404, 410, 544 A.2d 629 (1988), we recently noted that this statute "leaves great latitude for the exercise of judicial discretion because it does not focus on the legal relationship of the parties involved.... The only criterion under §46b-59 is the best interest of the child." See also *Manter v. Manter*, 185 Conn. 502, 508, 441 A.2d 146 (1981). All this plaintiff seeks is a court order consistent with the statutory constraints imposed on visitation by §46b-59.

In light of these statutes, we are unpersuaded that the agreement between the parties in this case violates the public policy of Connecticut. It would be elevating form over substance to allow the plaintiff to obtain visitation rights by filing an appropriate "application" in the Superior Court, but to deny her the opportunity to seek such rights under a contractual umbrella.

Case law in other jurisdictions does not persuade us that we should strike down the visitation agreement in this case. To a significant extent, the cases turn on legislative determinations that vary from state to state. We note nonetheless that *People ex rel. Sibley v. Sheppard*, 54 N.Y.2d 320, 429 N.E.2d 1049, 445 N.Y.S.2d 420 (1981), concluded, as do we, that the statutory creation of an adoptive family does not automatically require complete severance of the child from all further contact with former relatives. Similarly, *Weinschel v. Strople*, 56 Md.App. 252, 261, 466 A.2d 1301 (1983), concluded, as do we, that as long as the best interest of the child is the determinative criterion, public policy does not forbid an agreement about visitation rights between a genetic parent and adoptive parents. *In re Custody of Atherton*, 107 Ill.App.3d 1006, 63 Ill.Dec. 582, 438 N.E.2d 513 (1982), on which the trial court relied, is distinguishable because that decision focused on the impropriety of parental bargaining about post-adoption custody when, according to the court, the purpose of the parties' contract was to bypass judicial determinations of custody. That is not this case.

Traditional models of the nuclear family have come, in recent years, to be replaced by various configurations of parents, stepparents, adoptive parents and grandparents. See *Temple v. Meyer*, *supra*; *Manter v. Manter*, *supra*. We are not prepared to assume that the welfare of children is best served by a narrow definition of those whom we permit to continue to manifest their deep concern for a child's growth and development. The record of the 1982 Superior Court proceedings to set aside the termination of the plaintiff's parental rights demonstrates that, in the present case, the "Open Adoption and Visitation Agreement" was openly and lovingly negotiated, in good faith, in order to promote the best interest of the child. The attorney for the child reported that the child thought the agreement between her mother and her soon-to-be adoptive parents would be "the best world that she could imagine." This agreement did not violate public policy, either ab initio or upon the subsequent entry of a decree of adoption.

We therefore remand this case to the trial court for a hearing on the merits of the plaintiff's claim that visitation would now be in the best interest of the child. Our observations about the genesis of the "Open Adoption and Visitation Agreement" are intended to express no opinion about how that claim should be resolved in light of the circumstances presently confronting the child.

There is error, the judgment is set aside and the case is remanded to the trial court for further proceedings in accordance with this opinion.

...

COMMENTS

Providing a biological parent the rights to visit a child the parent has relinquished for adoption — sometimes referred to as "open adoption" — is still a relatively new phenomenon that won legislative and judicial acceptance in limited circumstances in the 1980s. It is a major change from the conventional view that adoption should create a clean break with a child's biological parents and a full integration into the child's adoptive family.

Adoption in American law is governed by state statutes, not the English common law, which did not include what we would think of as adoption because of Glanville's dictum: "Only God can make a *heres*, not man", and the deeply held views on the laws governing the inheritance of real property. The roots of adoption laws can be found in Roman law and the Code Napoleon, the former requiring that adoption replicate nature. The principal motivation behind adoption was to provide heirs. Massachusetts, in 1851, was the first state to enact adoption legislation that was comparable to modern adoption statutes, requiring judicial proceedings. Before that time, adoption of children in America could be effectuated by a private contractual transaction without governmental regulation or in rare instances by a special act of the legislature.

For over a century the model of adoption replicating nature was part of American law, child welfare agency regulations and society in general. Thus, when a child was relinquished by its mother and placed with an agency for adoption (or even in the case of foundlings), the agency sought to match the child with prospective adoptive parents who could be viewed as having conceived the child themselves. This process, called "matching," was concerned almost exclusively with children born to unwed mothers and was cloaked in secrecy. Adoption records were sealed and not subject to being open save for some extraordinary reason. Once adoption occurred, it was rarely the subject of conversation even within the adoptive family. It was not uncommon for children to grow to maturity and never learn that they were adopted — so strong was the taboo of illegitimate birth.

In the 1970s, secrecy in adoption began to be reexamined. Adult adoptees sought to have their adoption records opened so that they might learn about their genetic and social history. Legislative and judicial activity resulted in some changes in the laws allowing for the opening of adoption records and access to family information with some conditions. Since the 1970s adoption has become more open and less secret as far as both the laws and society are concerned. Whether a mother places her child with a prospective adoptive person or couple herself or relinquishes the child to an agency which makes the placement, the mother may, under certain circumstances, have contact with the adoptive person or couple.

Michaud v. Wawruck concerns a mother who entered into a formal agreement with her child's prospective adoptive parents that in consideration of her withdrawing her challenge to the order terminating her parental rights — a challenge based on her claim that the child's natural father had fraudulently procured her consent to the termination — the adoptive parents would allow her certain visitation rights during her child's minority years. The adoptive parents reneged on their promise and Jacqueline Michaud, the mother, sued for specific enforcement of the contract.

The case raises the important question of the extent to which a mother may reserve visitation rights in a privately negotiated agreement with adoptive parents when the combination of termination of parental rights and adoption would, by the Connecticut statute, ordinarily not reserve any biological parental rights. The Connecticut Supreme Court held that the agreement was not against public policy and remanded the case to the trial court to determine whether the mother's asserting her visitation rights would be in the child's best interests.

Given the facts of the case there would appear to be no question but that the contract should be specifically enforced. The adoptive parents knew that if Jacqueline Michaud were successful in her claim that her consent was fraudulently obtained, they would lose the child they were fostering. They were not willing to chance a defeat and basically settled the case with the visitation agreement. The process by which the agreement was entered into was open and fair and all the parties, including the commissioner of children and youth services and the counsel for the child agreed to its terms. Unless there are important facts omitted in the opinion, for the adoptive parents to refuse to fulfill their side of the bargain after adoption raises serious questions about their good faith.

Those opposed to open adoption argue that agreements like the one in *Michaud v. Wawruck* have the effect of frustrating the integration of the adopted child into the adoptive family and that once adoption is finalized, the adoptive parents should have full control and custody of their adopted child, much like biological parents have over their children. Further, it is argued that once a mother decides to relinquish her child for adoption, that decision should be unconditional for her own psychological well-being. Placing visitation conditions on the adoption might tend to support an ambivalence about the relinquishment, preventing the mother from coming to terms with her decision. Yet it should not be overlooked that if a biological mother wants to keep her child and is financially unable to do so, adoption may be her only option and open adoption may be a forced compromise. Of course, such a compromise must be seen as a poor alternative to financial (governmental or otherwise) support for the mother so that she can raise her child herself.

Open adoption is more easily understood and accepted in cases like *Michaud v. Wawruck*, which appears to be a case where the biological mother has had a meaningful relationship with her child and a continuation of that relationship will be beneficial to the child. If open adoptions arranged privately between a biological mother and adoptive parents become more prevalent than conventional adoptions (adoptions arranged through agencies or third parties and not resulting in direct contact between the biological mother and the adoptive parents) a major transformation will have occurred. American adoptions will begin to look more like the model that existed before 1851 when a private contract transferred the custody of a child from one person to another and judicial involvement, if there was any, was merely a formality. Such a private arrangement had the obvious comparison to the transfer of real property. If we are concerned that children should not be considered property, should privately arranged adoptions (even if formally approved by a court), whether conditional or not, be encouraged or discouraged?

REFERENCES

William Meezan, Sanford N. Katz, Eva Manoff Russo, ADOPTIONS WITHOUT AGENCIES 149–210 (1978).

John Triseliotis, IN SEARCH OF ORIGINS, (1973).

Helen L. Witmer, Elizabeth Herzog, Eugene A. Weinstein, Mary E. Sullivan, INDEPENDENT ADOPTIONS 15–43 (1963).

Legally Recognized Relationships Short of Parenthood

ROOT v. ALLEN

Supreme Court of Colorado

151 Colo. 311, 377 P.2d 117 (1962)

DAY, Chief Justice.

Plaintiff in error William B. Root filed a petition for habeas corpus in the Denver District Court to obtain the custody of his daughter Sharon Ann. He will be hereinafter referred to by name or as the father. The defendant in error was the respondent in the lower court and will be referred to by name.

The father in his petition alleged the birth of the child to himself and his then wife Rachel Root on October 21, 1949. Other allegations, all admitted by Allen, are that Mr. and Mrs. Root were divorced in Kansas in 1950 and by agreement custody of Sharon was given to the mother subject to the father's visitation rights. The father agreed to pay $50.00 monthly for child support and at all times from the divorce until the death of the mother in January, 1958, made his payments. In February, 1953, Mrs. Root moved to Colorado where she married Allen and remained here with him until her death. The father has been a resident of California since 1956. When the child's mother died in 1958 Allen informed the father and requested his consent to the adoption of the child, which the father declined. The father requested Allen to relinquish the child back to him, which Allen declined to do, hence the petition by the father to obtain the child.

After hearing the trial court rendered exhaustive findings in which it concluded that it was for the *best interests of the child* that Sharon Ann remain in the custody of Allen. Petition for *habeas corpus* was denied, new trial was dispensed with, and it is to that judgment that the father brings this writ of error.

The findings of the trial court pretty much give the picture between the time of the divorce in 1950 up to the hearing for custody. We can do no better than to relate the court's findings here as follows:

> 1. ...[W]hen Sharon was approximately ten months of age, she returned with her mother, Rachel, to Denver, Colorado; that from June, 1950, until the summer of 1956, she did not see her father, William Root.
>
> 2. That in November, 1950, Robert Allen began dating the mother, Rachel, and began spending considerable time with Sharon; that from November, 1950, until February, 1953, Robert Allen regularly saw Sharon, and on February 20, 1953, he married Rachel, the child's mother; that from that date to the present Sharon has lived in the home of Robert Allen with the exception of the period July, 1956, to May, 1957; that on November 3, 1953, a half-sister of Sharon's, Vicki, was born to Robert and Rachel Allen; that on May 18, 1955, another half-sister of Sharon's, Kay, was born to Robert and Rachel Allen; that in the summer of 1956, William Root, the father visited Sharon in Denver for a period of no more than one and one-half hours, at which time he introduced himself to Sharon as a friend of the family; that Sharon did not see William Root again until the summer of 1960 after this litigation had been initiated and Mr. Root was in Denver for a hearing.
>
> 3. That over the years Mr. Root in general neither wrote to nor sent birthday or Christmas gifts to Sharon; that from July, 1956 to May, 1957, Robert and Rachel Allen were separated, during which time Robert Allen visited his children including Sharon at least two to three times each week; that in May, 1957, Robert and Rachel Allen reconciled; that on January 25, 1958, Rachel Allen died; that from January 25, 1958 until the remarriage of Robert Allen on June 21, 1959, Mr. Allen maintained a home for Sharon and her two half-sisters with the help of housekeepers; that on June 21, 1959 Robert Allen married his present wife, Jerry; that in March, 1960, Jerry Allen adopted Vicki and Kay Allen; that since the end of 1950 to date Sharon has had a close and warm relationship with Robert Allen, who has acted in every sense as her father; that Mr. Root has remarried and has two sons, one of whom he adopted and now seeks the return of Sharon's care and custody; that Mr. Root now lives in California; that Robert and Jerry Allen seek to continue to care for Sharon.
>
> 4. That even though the petitioner herein contributed $50.00 per month to the support of Sharon Ann in compliance with a court order, nevertheless, in every other way, he abandoned his obligations as father of this child. Even if he did so in the belief that it was for the best interests of the child, as he claims, nevertheless by so doing, he permitted her to develop an entirely new father daughter relationship with the respondent, Robert Allen, which cannot now be destroyed *without great harm resulting to the child.*
>
> 5. That if she were to return to Mr. Root, if she were to leave the father with whom she has lived for these years, *the effect would be very damaging.* The natural ties between parents and children do not endure unless they are nurtured. It is unmistakably important that children have a sense of continuity, or otherwise stated, that they are unable to avoid the damages which result from serious separations. This need that a child has for continuity, the need to avoid separation, is particularly marked at certain times in life. This child is now approaching puberty, and at this time in particular even more than at other times — although at all times the need is there — she very definitely needs the

sense of emotional support which comes from a continuous relationship with mother, father and siblings.

6. That the child herein involved has been subjected to a series of traumatic experiences during her lifetime, including the death of her mother; that throughout all these experiences, the one great stabilizing factor in her life was the relationship with her stepfather, Robert Allen. Some of the testimony reveals he is closer to her, more attentive to her needs than even her mother was. *To uproot this child, who has already suffered so much, from her home, her relatives, and from the only stable relationship* she has ever known is unthinkable and *not in the best interest of the child involved* as amply born out by the testimony of expert witnesses; that the respondent, Robert Allen unquestionably stands in the relationship of loco-parentis to this child, a relationship in which the law wisely takes cognizance of situations such as this.

7. The Court finds that the petitioner and natural father herein has an adequate and highly desirable home in California, but the Court is further compelled to find that in the background of this home there are already existing problems which it seems to the Court are enough to expect Mr. Root and his family to deal with and to complicate such problems and relationships by *introducing the child herein involved into the said home would probably not be in the best interest of said child.*

8. The Court is of the opinion that the petitioner has acted herein out of his sense of love and duty; however, the past cannot be undone. It would seem to the Court that after so many years it would have been much wiser for the petitioner herein to have made the greater sacrifice by continuing to keep his identity unknown until this little girl were old enough to withstand this further shock. Now that she knows, it would seem to the Court wise that this relationship be nurtured by correspondence and such visitations as the parties may agree upon in their good judgment. Much as the Court sympathizes with the natural father and his present wife, the Court is compelled to find that to grant the relief requested herein would be *calamitous for Sharon Ann and that her best interest realistically appraised absolutely requires the petition be denied.* The Court finds from the evidence that there is no mystical blood tie that is of more importance than the continuity of a family unit to this little child approaching a difficult period in her life. (Emphasis supplied)

We have underlined several portions of the trial court's finding, pointing up many factors involved in the testimony given the court. When appraising the evidence, either from the standpoint of Mr. Allen or when giving every favorable inference to the father, the court came to the conclusion that it was for the best interest of the child that she remain in the environment in which she has grown up.

One paramount question, therefore, presents itself in this case:

IS THE NATURAL FATHER, ONCE HE SHOWS BEYOND DOUBT THAT HE IS A FIT AND PROPER PERSON TO HAVE CUSTODY OF HIS CHILD, IN LAW ENTITLED TO RESTORATION OF THE CHILD TO HIM EVEN THOUGH THE COURT IN ITS FINDINGS, AMPLY SUPPORTED BY THE EVIDENCE, DETERMINES THAT TO GIVE HIM CUSTODY WOULD NOT BE IN THE BEST INTERESTS OF THE CHILD?

This question is answered in the negative.

In the recent case of *Coulter v. Coulter*, 141 Colo. 237, 347 P.2d 492, a divorced mother sought to regain custody of her child from the child's paternal grandparents. In that case the child had been in the custody of its paternal grandparents for seven years, during which time she was visited by her mother, and knew of the identity of her mother. This court recognized the presumption that ordinarily a child's welfare will be best served through the custody of the natural parent, but held that under the evidence adduced, the trial court had properly reached the conclusion that in the particular case the welfare of the child would be promoted by leaving it with its grandmother. In discussing *Wilson v. Mitchell*, 48 Colo. 454, 111 P. 21, 30 L.R.A.,N.S., 507, the court stated:

> While the *Wilson* case indicates that the natural parents have a first and prior right to custody, we do not interpret it as requiring that custody be awarded to the parent or parents merely because the evidence shows fitness and ability to care for the child. The controlling factor, recognized and applied in all of these cases, and confirmed in the *Wilson* case, is the welfare of the child.

The court also quoted from Hochheimer's Custody of Infants, as follows:

> Unquestionably when the power of the court is invoked to place an infant into the custody of its parents and to withdraw such child from other persons, the court will scrutinize all the circumstances and ascertain "if a change of custody would be disadvantageous to the infant." If so, the change will not be made, "and it matters not whether it is through the fault or the mere misfortune of the legal guardian that the infant has come to be out of his custody."

Prior to the *Coulter* case, in *Devlin v. Huffman*, 139 Colo. 417, 339 P.2d 1008, this court therein held that the right of a parent to have the custody of his natural child must give way where the welfare of the child requires it. In that case the children were in the custody of the maternal grandparents and the mother sought to regain custody through habeas corpus. The grandparents had had custody of the children for six years. The trial court denied the petition and this court affirmed, stating:

> Counsel urges and cites authorities to the effect that parents are presumed to be fit and proper persons to have the care and custody of their children, and that the presumption is ever present and can be overcome only by plain and certain proofs. With this statement we agree. The law is equally well settled that in custody proceedings the welfare and best interests of the children is the paramount consideration.

In another case this court affirmed the order of the district court which denied custody of a minor child to the natural mother. The language of the trial court, approved by the Supreme Court, was inter alia:

> ...that the best interests and welfare of the child will also be best provided for, and the child's interests best protected, by granting the actual physical care to, and it is, therefore, hereby granted to, the paternal grandmother of said child, to-wit... Walcott v. Walcott, 139 Colo. 37, 336 P.2d 298.

It will thus be seen that this court has held that the presumption that a child's welfare is best served through custody of the natural parent is a rebuttable one, and that where the evidence establishes that the welfare of the child will not be promoted by the parent's custody, such custody will not be granted. We believe that these decisions are controlling in this case. The Trial court not only found that the welfare of Sharon would not be furthered by placing her custody in the petitioner, but also found that such action would be extremely detrimental to the child and would likely resut in permanent damage to her personality and development.

Although the court found that the father was a fit and suitable person to have custody of the daughter, he did not find that the home to which the child would be taken as a stranger was sultable one. Mr. Root had remarried, and Sharon would be placed not only in the company of a father whom she did not know but also with a stepmother who, in addition to being a total stranger, was shown by the testimony to be having considerable personal problems. No good purpose would be served here by relating the difficulties of the present Mrs. Root, suffice it to say that in 51 folios of testimony there is ample support for the court's conclusion that it would not be for the best interests of Sharon to place her in this home, particularly in view of the trauma to which Sharon had already been subjected in the death of her mother. The trial court took note of the age of the child, that in a short time she would be entering the age of puberty which is generally associated with emotional conflict, inner struggle and normally increased difficulties in adjustment. It is fairly well established that children handle the problem of the transition to young manhood and womanhood in a more satisfactory fashion when they are helped and surrounded by stable, loving persons who have helped them through their childhood. This is not the time to make drastic changes in a child's life.

The sum of the testimony, including expert witnesses, was that Sharon, for all practical purposes, was the true daughter of respondent Allen, accepted as such and treated as such. There was mutual love between the two, and Mr. Allen — even more so than Sharon's own mother — was devoted, understanding, and did everything he could to make her happy and secure and help her grow as a normal, happy child.

...

The judgment is affirmed.

NANCY S. v. MICHELE G.

California Court of Appeal

228 Cal.App.3d 831, 279 Cal.Rptr. 212 (1991)

STEIN, J.

Appellant, Michele G., appeals from a judgment under the Uniform Parentage Act (Civ.Code, §7000 et seq.) determining that respondent, Nancy S., is the only parent of the two minor children that respondent conceived by artificial insemination during her relationship with appellant. The judgment further provided that respondent, as the only legal parent of the two minor children, is entitled to sole legal and physical custody and that any further contact between appellant and the children shall only be by respondent's consent.

The issue presented is whether the court erred in determining, as a matter of law, that appellant has no right to an award of custody or visitation under the Uniform Parentage Act.

FACTS

In August of 1969, appellant and respondent began living together, and in November of that year they had a private "marriage" ceremony. Eventually they decided to have children by artificially inseminating respondent. In June of 1980, respondent gave birth to a daughter, K. Appellant was listed on the birth certificate as the father, and K. was given appellant's family name. On June 13, 1984, respondent gave birth to a son, S. Again appellant was listed as the father on the birth certificate, and S. was given appellant's family name. Both children refer to appellant and respondent as "Mom." Although the parties considered arranging for appellant to adopt the children, they never initiated formal adoption proceedings.

In January of 1985 appellant and respondent separated. They agreed that K. would live with appellant and that S. would live with respondent. They arranged visitation so that appellant would have K. five days a week and respondent would have S. five days a week, but the children would be together, either at appellant's or respondent's home for four days a week. After approximately three years, respondent wanted to change the custody arrangement so that each had custody of both children 50 percent of the time. Appellant opposed any change, and attempts to mediate the dispute failed.

Respondent then commenced this Uniform Parentage Act proceeding. Her complaint sought a declaration that appellant is not a parent of either child, that respondent is entitled to sole legal and physical custody and that appellant is entitled to visitation only with respondent's consent. The court issued a temporary restraining order and granted temporary custody to respondent. Appellant answered the complaint and admitted that respondent is the biological mother of the children. She denied, however, the allegations that she was not also a parent of the children. She sought an order for custody and visitation in accordance with their original custody agreement.

A hearing was held on respondent's order to show cause and appellant's cross-motion for custody and visitation. The parties fully briefed and argued the issue whether appellant could qualify as a parent and seek custody and visitation under the Uniform Parentage Act. Appellant admitted that she was not the biological mother and had not adopted the children. Nonetheless, she argued that she had attained the status of a de facto parent, or that respondent should be estopped to deny appellant's status as a parent. The court determined that appellant was not a parent under the Uniform Parentage Act, and that even if she could prove that she had the status of a de facto parent, that it could not award her custody over the objections of respondent, the natural mother, who did qualify as a parent under the act. The court therefore awarded sole physical and legal custody to respondent.[1]

ANALYSIS

Civil Code section 4600, subdivision (c) provides that, in any proceeding where there is at issue the custody of a minor child, "Before the court makes any

1. By denying appellant any relief, the court also impliedly found as a matter of law that appellant could not attain the status of a parent by equitable estoppel.

order awarding custody to a person…other than a parent, without the consent of the parents, it shall make a finding that an award of custody to a parent would be detrimental to the child and the award to a nonparent is required to serve the best interests of the child." Appellant acknowledges that, regardless of the statutory basis of the underlying proceeding, i.e., whether it was brought under the Uniform Parentage Act, or as a guardianship, dependency, or dissolution proceeding, she is entitled to seek custody and visitation over the objections of the children's natural mother, based on the "best interests" of the children, only if she has alleged facts upon which the court could determine that she is a parent of the children.[2]

The Uniform Parentage Act defines a parent as one who is the natural or adoptive parent of a child. (Civ.Code, §7001.) The existence of the relationship of parent and child may be proved between a child and its natural mother by proof of her having given birth to the child (Civ.Code, §7003, subd. (1)), between a child and an adoptive parent by proof of adoption (Civ.Code, §7003, subd. (3)), and between a natural father and a child as provided in the act (Civ.Code, §7003, subd. (2)).[3]

It is undisputed that appellant is not the natural mother of K. and S., and that she has not adopted either child. She does not contend that she and respondent had a legally recognized marriage when the children were born. Based on these undisputed facts, the court correctly determined that appellant could not establish the existence of a parent-child relationship under the Uniform Parentage Act.

Appellant nonetheless asserts that the Uniform Parentage Act does not provide the exclusive definition of a parent. She asserts that her allegations of a long-term relationship in which she has become a "psychological parent" of the children would, if proved,[4] entitle her to seek custody and visitation as if the dispute were between two legally recognized parents. She advances several legal theories to support her assertion that she has acquired "parental rights," i.e., the right to seek custody and visitation on an equal footing with the children's natural mother and over their natural mother's objections. First, she argues that she is either a "de facto" parent, or that she stands "in loco parentis."

---

2. The trial court concluded that because appellant does not fit the definition of parent under the Uniform Parentage Act, the court had no jurisdiction to award her custody or visitation over the objection of respondent, who all agree is a "parent" as defined by that act. (Civ.Code, §7003, subd. (1).) At least one other court in a case involving a Uniform Parentage Act complaint filed by a lesbian partner seeking custody and visitation, over the objections of the biological mother, has also characterized the problem as one of lack of standing and lack of subject matter jurisdiction. (See *Curiale v. Reagan* (1990) 222 Cal.App.3d 1597, 1600, 272 Cal.Rptr. 520.) A court, however, lacks "jurisdiction" only if it has no power to render a decision over the subject in dispute. (See *In re Marriage of Halpern* (1982) 133 Cal.App.3d 297, 309, 184 Cal.Rptr. 740.) In this case, appellant has always maintained the position that she was a parent of the child and therefore was entitled to custody and visitation. The court therefore had jurisdiction under the Uniform Parentage Act to decide whether appellant was a parent. Its determination that she was not a parent simply led to the substantive conclusion, based on the provisions of Civil Code section 4600, creating a presumption in favor of parental custody, that as a nonparent she could not obtain the relief she sought, i.e., custody and visitation over the objections of the children's only parent.

3. The Uniform Parentage Act also creates a presumption that a man is the natural father if he meets the conditions set forth in section 621 of the Evidence Code, or the child is born during a valid marriage or a marriage that apparently complies with the law. A man may also be presumed to be a natural father if after the child is born, he and the child's mother marry or attempt to marry and he engages in conduct holding the child out as his own by, for example, permitting his name to be put on the birth certificate. (Civ.Code, §7004.) The Uniform Parentage Act also establishes that the husband of a woman who bears a child through artificial insemination is deemed to be the child's natural father. (Civ.Code, §7005.)

4. Although appellant's allegations regarding her relationship to the two children have not been proved, the record strongly suggests that appellant could prove that since their birth she has, from the children's point of view, especially as to K., performed the role of a loving mother.

A. De Facto Parenthood

A de facto parent is "that person who, on a day-to-day basis, assumes the role of parent, seeking to fulfill both the child's physical needs and his psychological need for affection and care." (*In re B.G.* (1974) 11 Cal.3d 679, 692, fn. 18, [114 Cal.Rptr. 444, 523 P.2d 244].) Appellant alleged that she helped facilitate the conception and birth of both children and immediately after their birth assumed all the responsibilities of a parent. K. lived with appellant until the underlying dispute arose, and S. also lived with appellant until appellant and respondent separated, and thereafter S. visited with appellant on a regular basis. These facts may well entitle appellant to the status of a "de facto" parent. It does not, however, follow that as a "de facto" parent appellant has the same rights as a parent to seek custody and visitation over the objection of the children's natural mother. In *In re B.G., supra,* 11 Cal.3d 679, the court acknowledged that the concept of "de facto" parenthood could apply to long-term foster parents for the purpose of permitting them to intervene in a dependency proceeding. The court went on to hold that, nonetheless, *custody* could not be awarded to the foster parents over the objections of the natural mother without a finding that parental custody would be detrimental to the children. (*Id.* at pp. 692–695) The court also specifically stated that, "[w]e do not hold that a de facto parent is a 'parent' or 'guardian' as those terms are used in the Juvenile Court Law." (*Id.* at p. 693, fn. 21).

No cases support appellant's contention that if she could prove her status as a de facto parent, she would be entitled to seek custody of respondent's children according to the same standards applied in a dispute between two parents. To the contrary, the cases establish that nonparents, even if they qualify as "de facto parents," may be recognized in guardianship or dependency proceedings and may even obtain custody over children with whom they have established a de facto parent-child relationship, but that custody can be awarded to a de facto parent *only* if it is established by clear and convincing evidence that parental custody is detrimental to the children. (See, e.g., *Guardianship of Shannon* (1933) 218 Cal. 490 [23 P.2d 1020]; *Guardianship of Phillip B.* (1983) 139 Cal.App.3d 407 [188 Cal.Rptr. 781]; *In re Lynna B.* (1979) 92 Cal.App.3d 682 [155 Cal.Rptr. 256]; *In re Volkland* (1977) 74 Cal.App.3d 674 [141 Cal.Rptr. 625].)[5]

Appellant argues that, in this case, the "detriment" standard should not apply because appellant is not an "outsider" and does not seek to exclude the parent but wants to share custody. In *all* of the cases involving a "de facto" parent, the individual claiming such status necessarily is not an "outsider" and, like appellant, has undoubtedly developed deep psychological and emotional bonds with the child. Nonetheless, the courts and our Legislature have chosen to place paramount importance upon the relationship between the natural or adoptive parent and the child. (*In re Marriage of Halpern, supra,* 133 Cal.App.3d at p. 312.) Even the discretionary visitation provided nonparents by Civil Code section 4601 "must give way to the paramount right to parent if the visitation creates conflicts and problems.... [¶] The critical importance in California of the right to parent has been affirmed and reaffirmed. [Citations] It only gives way upon a showing of parental unfitness, detrimental to the child's welfare." (*In re Marriage of Jenkens* (1981) 116 Cal.App.3d 767, 774 [172 Cal.Rptr. 331].)

---

5. In *In re Marriage of Halpern, supra,* 133 Cal.App.3d 297, relied upon by appellant, the court stated that even if the husband in a marriage dissolution, who was admittedly not the biological father of a child born to his wife during their marriage, had proved that he was a de facto parent, the presumption in favor of parental custody would still apply in a dispute over custody or visitation. (*Id.* at pp. 311–313)

B. In Loco Parentis

Appellant next advances the theory that the common law doctrine of "in loco parentis" could be applied to confer upon her the same rights as a parent to seek custody and visitation of S. and K. In the context of torts, the concept of in loco parentis has been used to impose upon persons standing "in loco parentis" the same rights and obligations imposed by statutory and common law upon parents.... It has also been applied to confer certain benefits upon a child, such as more favorable inheritance tax treatment..., or workers' compensation benefits.... The concept of "in loco parentis," however, has never been applied in a custody dispute to give a nonparent the same rights as a parent, and we are unpersuaded that the concept should be so extended.

In *Perry v. Superior Court* (1980) 108 Cal.App.3d 480 [166 Cal.Rptr. 583], the court referred to the concept of in loco parentis in the context of a custody dispute. The trial court awarded the mother's husband of six years visitation rights to her child by a former marriage. The trial court found that the husband had performed the role of father to the child and the fact that there was no blood relationship was inconsequential because visitation was in the best interests of the child. The court of appeal reversed holding that the trial court had no authority to award custody or visitation unless the minor was a "child of the marriage." Noting that the result was "not particularly palatable," the court invited the Legislature to address the problem of visitation rights for stepparents. (*Id.* at pp. 481–486) The Legislature responded by enacting Civil Code section 4351.5 in 1982.... Although that section creates discretion to award a limited form of visitation rights to stepparents in a dissolution proceeding, the Legislature again acknowledged the importance of parental autonomy by cautioning that even an award of visitation to a stepparent "shall not conflict with any visitation or custodial right of a natural or adoptive parent who is not a party to the proceeding." (Civ.Code, §4351.5, subd. (j).) Courts have consistently refused to expand section 4351.5 to cover factual situations not specifically addressed by that section....

C. Parenthood by Equitable Estoppel

Appellant argues that the court could apply the doctrine of equitable estoppel to prevent respondent from denying the existence of a parent-child relationship that she allegedly encouraged and supported for many years and which she now denies for the sole purpose of obtaining unfettered control over the custody of the children.

In California, equitable estoppel has been invoked for the purpose of imposing support obligations on a husband who has represented to his wife's children that he is their natural father and subsequently seeks to deny paternity for the purpose of avoiding support obligations.... Equitable estoppel has never been invoked in California against a natural parent for the purpose of awarding custody and visitation to a nonparent....[6]

---

6. In *In re Marriage of Valle* (1975) 53 Cal.App.3d 837 [126 Cal.Rptr. 38], the court left open the possibility that if a husband is estopped to deny paternity for purposes of imposing the obligation to pay support, "we perceive no good reason why the trial court should not have jurisdiction to award child *custody* when the parenthood is established by estoppel and when the issue is fairly and properly litigated with both parties present." (Id. at p. 842.) However, in *Valle,* neither the husband nor the wife were the natural parents of the children. Moreover, the court discussed the concept of equitable estoppel primarily for the purpose of refuting the husband's contention that, because there was no biological relationship between the children and the husband or the wife, that they were not "children of the marriage" and therefore the trial court was without jurisdiction to award custody to the wife.

Other states, however, have begun to use the doctrine of equitable estoppel to prevent a wife from denying the paternity of her husband.... For example, in *In re Paternity of D.L.H.* (1987) 142 Wis.2d 606 [419 N.W.2d 283], the court held that a wife could be estopped to deny the paternity of her husband, even where human leukocyte antigen (HLA) tests had excluded the husband as the natural father. The husband knew, even before the child's birth, that he was not the biological father but promised to raise the child as his own. He had developed a strong relationship with the child and had paid support to the mother after the couple separated. The court held it was error to dismiss the husband from the paternity proceedings after the HLA tests excluded him as the natural father, and remanded to permit him to prove the elements of equitable estoppel. The court, however, specifically reserved the question whether, even if the wife were estopped to deny paternity, the husband would have the status of a parent in a custody dispute and could thereby invoke the standard of the best interests of the child. (*Id.* at p. 287.) Even if the doctrine of equitable estoppel could be used against a wife and in favor of a husband to award custody as if the dispute were between two natural parents, we note that the use of the doctrine of equitable estoppel, in these out-of-state cases, is rooted in "[o]ne of the strongest presumptions in law [i.e.] that a child born to a married woman is the legitimate child of her husband." (Runner, *Protecting A Husband's Parental Rights When His Wife Disputes The Presumption of Legitimacy*, 28 J. Fam. L., *supra*, at p. 116.) No similar presumption applies in this case.

It is important not to confuse appellant's argument regarding equitable estoppel with the concept of an "equitable parent." The concept of an "equitable parent" has been recognized by the Michigan Court of Appeals in a divorce proceeding to permit a husband, who is not the biological father of a child born during the marriage, to obtain the status of a parent in a custody dispute with the natural mother, and to have the custody dispute settled as if it were between two natural parents, according to the child's best interests. (*Atkinson v. Atkinson* (1987) 160 Mich.App. 601 [408 N.W.2d 516, 517–520].) The primary difference between the concept of an "equitable parent" and the equitable estoppel theory advanced by appellant is that the "equitable parent" theory is rooted in a statutory recognition of "equitable adoption" for purposes of inheritance and may require proof of an express or implied contract to adopt.... At least one California court has already declined to adopt the concept of an "equitable parent" for the purpose of awarding joint custody to a stepfather over the objections of the child's natural mother despite the fact that California, like Michigan, recognizes the doctrine of "equitable adoption" for purposes of inheritance under Probate Code section 6408.... The court stressed that given the "complex practical, social and constitutional ramifications" of expanding the class of persons entitled to assert parental rights, the decision was better left to the Legislature. [*In re Marriage of Lewis & Goetz*, 203 Cal.App.3d 514, at pp. 519–520 (1988).]

D. Functional Definition of Parenthood

Finally, appellant urges us to adopt what she describes as a "functional" definition of parenthood in order to protect on-going relationships between children and those who function as their parents. In accordance with this new definition, the class of persons entitled to seek custody and visitation according to the same standards as a natural parent would include "anyone who maintains a functional parental relationship with a child when a legally recognized parent created that relationship with the intent that the relationship be parental in nature." (See Polikoff, *This Child Does Have Two Mothers: Redefining Parenthood to Meet the Needs of Children in Lesbian-Mother and Other Nontraditional Families* (1990) 78 Georgetown L.J. 459, 464.)

We agree with appellant that the absence of any legal formalization of her relationship to the children has resulted in a tragic situation.[7] As is always the case, it is the children who will suffer the most as a result of the inability of the adults, who they love and need, to reach an agreement. We do not, however, agree that the only way to avoid such an unfortunate situation is for the courts to adopt appellant's novel theory by which a nonparent can acquire the rights of a parent, and then face years of unraveling the complex practical, social, and constitutional ramifications of this expansion of the definition of parent.[8]

CONCLUSION

Although the facts in this case are relatively straightforward regarding the intent of the natural mother to create a parental relationship between appellant and her children, expanding the definition of a "parent" in the manner advocated by appellant could expose other natural parents to litigation brought by child-care providers of long standing, relatives, successive sets of stepparents or other close friends of the family. No matter how narrowly we might attempt to draft the definition, the fact remains that the status of individuals claiming to be parents would have to be litigated and resolution of these claims would turn on elusive factual determinations of the intent of the natural mother, the perceptions of the children, and the course of conduct of the party claiming parental status. By deferring to the Legislature in matters involving complex social and policy ramifications far beyond the facts of the particular case, we are not telling the parties that the issues they raise are unworthy of legal recognition. To the contrary, we intend only to illustrate the limitations of the courts in fashioning a comprehensive solution to such a complex and socially significant issue.

The judgment is affirmed.

LINGWALL v. HOENER

Supreme Court of Illinois

108 Ill.2d 206, 483 N.E.2d 512 (1985)

SIMON, Justice:

This opinion involves three cases that have been consolidated for the purpose of this appeal. In cause No. 60458, petitioner June Bullington Lingwall, the natural paternal grandmother of Michelle Hoener, filed a petition in the circuit court of Pike County pursuant to section 607(b) of the Illinois Marriage and Dissolution of Marriage Act (Ill.Rev.Stat.1983, ch. 40, par. 607(b))(Marriage Act), seeking visitation with Michelle. The respondents, Althea Eileen Hoener, Michelle's natural

---

7. This is not unique to same-sex domestic partners. Others often find they cannot maintain their close personal ties with children in the face of objection by their parents....

8. Although the validity of an adoption in these circumstances is not before us, we note that Civil Code section 221 provides, in part, that "[a]ny unmarried minor child may be adopted by any adult person...." We see nothing in these provisions that would preclude a child from being jointly adopted by someone of the same sex as the natural parent. (*Cf. Marshall v. Marshall* (1925) 196 Cal. 761, 767 [239 P. 36].)

mother, and her husband, Wayne Hoener, Michelle's adoptive father, opposed the petition on the ground that all rights of Michelle's natural father and of those related to Michelle through him had been terminated as a result of the adoption proceeding. After an evidentiary hearing, the circuit court granted the petitioner limited visitation with Michelle. The appellate court affirmed....

In cause No. 60703, petitioners William and Carol Roth, the natural paternal grandparents of Christina and Jeffery Podschweidt, filed a similar petition in the circuit court of Kane County. Their petition for visitation with Christina and Jeffery was opposed by respondents Nancy, the children's mother, and her new husband, Ronald Podschweidt, who had adopted the children. Without a hearing, the circuit court granted the respondents' motion to dismiss the petition.

Petitioner Maxine Neier, the natural paternal grandmother of Sharine Carlson, also filed a petition in the circuit court of Kane County for grandparental visitation after Sharine had been adopted by her mother's new husband. Respondents Patricia and Kenneth Carlson filed no response to Mrs. Neier's petition and no motion to dismiss. However, the circuit court dismissed the petition on its own motion without a hearing. The Roth and Neier petitions were consolidated in the appellate court, and the petitioners then filed a motion for a direct appeal to this court pursuant to Rule 302(b)(87 Ill.2d R. 302(b)). The motion was allowed, and we have consolidated the direct appeal in cause No. 60703 with cause No. 60458.

The issue presented for review is the narrow question of whether visitation privileges may be granted to a grandparent under section 607(b) of the Marriage Act when the parent through whom the grandparent is related to the child has been deprived of his parental rights as a result of the child's adoption by the other natural parent and that parent's new spouse. Section 607 provides in pertinent part:

> (b) The court may grant reasonable visitation privileges to a grandparent or great-grandparent of any minor child upon the grandparents' or great-grandparents' petition to the court, with notice to the parties required to be notified under Section 601 of this Act, if the court determines that it is in the best interests and welfare of the child and may issue any necessary orders to enforce such visitation privileges. Further, the court, pursuant to this subsection, may grant reasonable visitation privileges to a grandparent or great-grandparent whose child has died where the court determines that it is in the best interests and welfare of the child. Ill.Rev.Stat.1983, ch. 40, par. 607(b).

It is clear that section 607(b) gives grandparents the right to seek visitation with their grandchildren pursuant to a petition for the dissolution of the parents' marriage, and that the court may grant such visitation if it is in the children's best interest and welfare. It is also clear that this section, which was added to the Marriage Act and became effective as amended on September 17, 1982, modified the prior common law rule that grandparents had no visitation rights absent a showing of special circumstances. *Chodzko v. Chodzko* (1976), 66 Ill.2d 28, 4 Ill.Dec. 313, 360 N.E.2d 60.

However, the respondents argue that when, as in the present cases, a child is adopted by one of the natural parents and that parent's new spouse following the dissolution of a marriage, the Illinois Adoption Act governs the issue of visitation rather than the Marriage Act. The Adoption Act provides in pertinent part:

> After the entry either of an order terminating parental rights or the entry of an order of adoption, the natural parents of a child sought to be adopted shall be relieved of all parental responsibility for such child and shall be deprived of all legal rights as respects the child, and the child shall be free from all obligations of maintenance and obedience as respects such natural parents. (Ill.Rev.Stat.1983, ch. 40, par. 1521.)

Because this statute terminates the rights of the natural parent in the adopted child, the respondents argue, any derivative rights claimed by the grandparents are also terminated. The respondents attempt to bolster this argument by citing a provision of the Probate Act of 1975 as amended (Probate Act), which provides in pertinent part:

> Sec. 11-7.1. Whenever both natural or adoptive parents of a minor are deceased and the minor has not been subsequently adopted, visitation rights shall be granted to the grandparents of the minor who are the parents of the minor's legal parents unless it is shown that such visitation would be detrimental to the best interests and welfare of the minor. (Ill.Rev.Stat.1983, ch. 110 1/2, par. 11-7.1.)

The respondents argue that the fact that this section provides for grandparental visitation rights only if the minor has not been adopted indicates an intent by the legislature to treat grandparental visitation in adopted families differently from such visitation in divorced families.

Every step of the respondents' argument is flawed. First, section 11-7.1 of the Probate Act applies by its terms when "*both* natural or adoptive parents of a minor are deceased" (emphasis added); any subsequent adoption of the child must therefore involve persons other than the child's parents. That situation is different from the present cases, which involve adoptions by one of the natural parents and a new spouse. The difference is that between an adoption by strangers and an adoption to accomplish the reconstitution of a family subsequent to a divorce. That the legislature intended to treat grandparental visitation differently in these different situations is indicated by the absence of language limiting such visitation in the event of a subsequent adoption in section 607(b) of the Marriage Act and the presence of such language in the Probate Act. The pertinent section of the Probate Act became effective in 1977, five years earlier than section 607(b) of the Marriage Act. The rule of statutory construction that is applicable in these circumstances is that "if words used in a prior statute to express a certain meaning are omitted [from a later statute], it will be presumed that a change of meaning was intended." 2A Sutherland, Statutory Construction sec. 51.02 (4th rev.ed.1984).

Second, the respondents' argument that the Marriage Act applies to divorced families and the Adoption Act to adoptive families begs the question in the present cases, which involve both a divorce and a subsequent adoption. Obviously the Adoption Act governs the adoption itself and removes the issues of custody, child support, and parental visitation from the continuing jurisdiction of the court that granted the divorce. However, the Marriage Act continues to govern other issues connected with the divorce, such as spousal support and property settlements. We hold that the Marriage Act also continues to govern the issue of grandparental visitation when, subsequent to a divorce, a child is adopted by one of the natural parents and that parent's new spouse.

The respondents' argument that such an adoption terminates any derivative rights in the child claimed by the grandparents fails on several grounds. First, it is based on the mistaken assumption that the Adoption Act completely severs the child's relationship with the natural parent. In fact, under Illinois law, a natural parent may be required to support the child after the child has been adopted if the adoptive parent is unable to do so (*Dwyer v. Dwyer* (1937), 366 Ill. 630, 634, 10 N.E.2d 344), and an adopted child may inherit through the natural parents (*In re Estate of Tilliski* (1945), 390 Ill. 273, 285, 61 N.E.2d 24). Thus, the severance of the parental relationship effected by adoption is not so complete as the respondents claim.

Second, the respondents' argument ignores the paramount concern in modern domestic-relations law, including our Adoption Act, with the best interests of the child (Ill.Rev.Stat.1983, ch. 40, par. 1525).... The Marriage Act and the Adoption Act share the common goal of proceeding in the child's best interest and welfare, and the statutes should be read together to give effect to their common goal. Thus, when an adoption by a natural parent and a new spouse has occurred, the court must examine all relevant factors to determine whether grandparental visitation is in the child's best interest. However, the respondents fail to recognize that different issues are involved in determining the best interest of the child in an adoption by strangers and in an adoption by a natural parent and a new spouse. In adoptions involving strangers, the primary policy concern has traditionally been with maximizing the pool of potential adoptive parents by guaranteeing, through the termination of the rights and responsibilities of the natural parents, that the adoptive parents will have "the opportunity to create a stable family relationship free from unnecessary intrusion." *In re Roger B.* (1981), 84 Ill.2d 323, 331, 49 Ill.Dec. 731, 418 N.E.2d 751.

In adoptions by a natural parent and that parent's new spouse, the policy concern with maximizing the pool of adoptive parents is greatly diminished, since the act of becoming a stepparent most often occurs without regard to adoption and in spite of regular visitations between the child and the noncustodial natural parent. If an adoption then ensues, the rights and obligations of the natural parent are terminated to the same degree as in an adoption by strangers. Termination of the parental relationship is, however, a legal fiction, since no act of law can nullify a biological relationship. There is no reason to extend that legal fiction to include a termination of a grandparental relationship unless it is in the child's best interest to do so. Respondents' reliance on *People ex rel. Bachleda v. Dean* (1971), 48 Ill.2d 16, 268 N.E.2d 11, as authority to the contrary is misplaced. First, that case involved the question of the continuing authority of a divorce court over the *custody* of the child of the parties to the divorce action after the child's adoption by a natural parent and new spouse. The issue before us is that of visitation. Second, *Bachleda* was decided more than 10 years before section 607(b) of the Marriage Act became effective, which modified the prior common law rule regarding grandparental visitation rights.

Absent an adoption of an infant by strangers, there is no reason to assume from the outset that termination of a grandparental relationship is in an adopted child's best interest; nor is there any reason to view grandparental visitation as an "unnecessary intrusion" in the lives of a reconstituted family. Of course the child's best interest is not entirely severable from the interests of the parents in a reconstituted family, and certainly the parents' attitude toward grandparental visitation is an important factor for the court to consider in determining whether such visitation should be ordered. However, their attitude is not the only, or even the paramount, consideration. Such factors as the length and quality of the relationship between grandparents and child, the child's need for continuity in his relationships with people who may have played a significant nurturing role in his life, and the effect of the termination of the child's relationship with the parent who has relinquished his rights and responsibilities must also be considered. These factors will certainly outweigh the opposition of parents that is based on the mere inconvenience to them of such visits, or on their animosity toward the child's other natural parent. In any case, whether it is in the child's best interest to be allowed to enjoy a relationship with a grandparent is a determination to be made under section 607(b) of the Marriage Act by the court that granted the divorce.

...

Our decision is consistent with the recent trend toward extending visitation privileges of grandparents. We note that in 1976 few States had legislation dealing with this issue, but that by 1982 at least 40 States had enacted grandparents' visitation statutes. Although most of these statutes do not specifically address the problem of visitation after adoption, those that do so distinguish between adoption by a stranger and adoption by a stepparent or grandparent, and terminate visitation only in the case of adoption by someone other than a stepparent or grandparent. See, *e.g.*, Cal.Civ.Code Ann. sec. 197.5 (Deering 1971); Minn.Stat.Ann. sec. 257.022 (West 1982); Mont.Code Ann. sec. 40-9-102 (1983); S.D. Codified Laws Ann. sec. 25-4-54 (1974).

For the reasons stated herein, the judgment of the appellate court in cause No. 60458 is affirmed. The judgments of the circuit court in cause No. 60703 are reversed...and remanded for hearings consistent with this opinion.

...

COMMENTS

In most contexts in which the court grants legal recognition to a child's relationship with a nonparent, the legal recognition undermines the control and authority of the parent or parents over the child. Typically, when courts grant such recognition, they appeal to the best interests of the child, which they may characterize as an overriding concern of domestic relations law. When courts refuse such recognition, they appeal to the rights of parents to decide what is best for their child and to the inability of courts to interfere successfully in such delicate matters. Another issue, usually raised in opposition to judicial recognition of relationships between a child and a nonparent, is whether such policies should be set by courts or by the legislature.

In *Root v. Allen*, the court awarded custody to the surviving stepfather who had acted as the child's parent but had not sought to adopt the child while the mother was alive. The trial court's stated basis was a simple best-interest-of-the-child test. The Colorado Supreme Court implied that the preference for parents over nonparents was merely a rebuttable presumption that the parent's custody will serve the child's best interests. The court also emphasized the findings of the trial court that strongly suggested that custody would have been granted to the stepfather even if a more restrictive test had been applied. Many state courts apply a higher standard than best-interest-of-the-child to award custody to a nonparent over the objection of a parent. Some courts award custody to a nonparent over a parent only when such custody is *required* to serve the best interests of the child; others may insist that the nonparent show that an award of custody to the parent would be detrimental to the child, or that there are extraordinary circumstances such that the child would suffer serious harm if removed from the nonparent, or even that the parent is unfit.

Some courts deny custody to a nonparent on the basis that the nonparent lacks standing to raise the question of custody, but, as footnote 2 of the opinion points out, *Nancy S.* rejects this approach. *Nancy S.* was based instead on the determination that Michelle was not a "parent" under the Uniform Parentage Act and that the presumption in favor of parental custody had not been rebutted. Although the court did not claim to have based its decision upon the fact that the case involved a lesbian couple, it seems likely that a heterosexual couple would have been treated differently. If, for example, a male had entered into an invalid marriage with Nancy S., had subsequently allowed his name to be put on the birth certificates, and had called the children by his surname and accepted them into his home, he might more likely have been treated as the children's parent.

The California adoption statute, cited in *Nancy S.*, is broader than many adoption statutes. Although many states (and the Danish law, supra at p. 566) would not allow a same-sex couple to adopt together a child born to one of them, it appears that in California Nancy and Michelle could have achieved through adoption legal recognition for the shared parental responsibility that they agreed upon and undertook. Should courts hesitate to grant a nonparent the benefits of parenthood when he or she has not assumed a legally-binding commitment to the child? In *Root v. Allen* the court did not address the question whether Mr. Allen could have adopted the child or the fairness of granting him the benefits of adoption when he and the child's mother had for years accepted child support money from the biological father, payments that would have stopped upon a stepparent adoption. It appears, however, that to deny Mr. Allen custody would have been detrimental to the child's welfare and unfair to her. Moreover, the natural father's position is no worse than it would have been had the mother remained living.

Questions of the legal recognition of relationships between children and nonparents arise also regarding visitation. Whether courts can grant a nonparent visitation when the courts believe that such visitation serves the best interest of the child is usually governed by statute. A typical statute limits visitation to grandparents of a child when death or divorce has disrupted the family. Some statutes allow visitation after a stepparent adoption or can be interpreted, as in *Lingwall*, to allow such visitation. A few statutes are written more broadly and give a court discretion to grant visitation to any other person when such visitation is in the child's best interests. Of course, when courts grant such visitation they are generally overriding the choice of the custodial parent or parents, who are usually presumed to be acting for the child's best interests.

Chapter 6

Problems Caused by Foreign Law and Our Federal System

IN OUR SOCIETY, increasing numbers of people have significant contacts with multiple states and even multiple countries, leading to a heightened risk of conflicting legal demands being placed upon the litigant. Conflict of law rules, including international conflicts rules, become more important. To deal with such litigation, as well as to be able to offer competent legal advice regarding domestic relations, lawyers must have some sensitivity about the laws of different states of the union and of different nation-states. Thus, the materials in this chapter are not esoteric, as some people might consider conflicts issues, but intensely practical.

Many students consider the conflict of laws material to be the "hard" part of family law. It seems to be more abstract, technical, and tedious. There seem to be more possibilities for making mistakes or coming up with wrong answers. In other areas of family law, there is more room for opinion and there seem to be fewer clear rights and wrongs. These "soft" areas of family law seem to be based more on issues of public policy than conflict of law issues are. These perceptions are largely an illusion. The policy issues that have concerned us throughout the book are also present in the conflicts field.

The materials in this chapter are intended to introduce the basic notions of domicile, jurisdiction and full faith and credit. They are also intended to sketch out the patterns of conflicting policies as they are manifested in the conflicts cases.

A: Residency Requirements for Divorce

SOSNA v. IOWA
United States Supreme Court
419 U.S. 393 (1975)

Mr. Justice REHNQUIST delivered the opinion of the Court.

Appellant Carol Sosna married Michael Sosna on September 5, 1964, in Michigan. They lived together in New York between October 1967 and August 1971, after which date they separated but continued to live in New York. In August 1972, appellant moved to Iowa with her three children, and the following month she petitioned the District Court of Jackson County, Iowa, for a dissolution of her marriage. Michael Sosna, who had been personally served with notice of the action when he came to Iowa to visit his children, made a special appearance to contest the jurisdiction of the Iowa court. The Iowa court dismissed the petition for lack of jurisdiction, finding that Michael Sosna was not a resident of Iowa and appellant had not been a resident of the State of Iowa for one year preceding the filing of her petition. In so doing the Iowa court applied the provisions of Iowa Code §598.6 (1973) requiring that the petitioner in such an action be "for the last year a resident of the state."

...

The durational residency requirement under attack in this case is a part of Iowa's comprehensive statutory regulation of domestic relations, an area that has long been regarded as a virtually exclusive province of the States. Cases decided by this Court over a period of more than a century bear witness to this historical fact. In *Barber v. Barber*, 21 How. 582, 584, 16 L.Ed. 226 (1859), the Court said: "We disclaim altogether any jurisdiction in the courts of the United States upon the subject of divorce...." In *Penoyer v. Neff*, 95 U.S. 714, 734–735 (1878), the Court said: "The State...has absolute right to prescribe the conditions upon which the marriage relation between its own citizens shall be created, and the causes for which it may be dissolved," and the same view was reaffirmed in *Simms v. Simms*, 175 U.S. 162, 167 (1899).

The statutory scheme in Iowa, like those in other States, sets forth in considerable detail the grounds upon which a marriage may be dissolved and the circumstances in which a divorce may be obtained. Jurisdiction over a petition for dissolution is established by statute in "the county where either party resides," Iowa Code §598.2 (1973), and the Iowa courts have construed the term "resident" to have much the same meaning as is ordinarily associated with the concept of domicile.... Iowa has recently revised its divorce statutes, incorporating the no-fault concept, but it retained the one-year durational residency requirement.

The imposition of a durational residency requirement for divorce is scarcely unique to Iowa, since 48 States impose such a requirement as a condition for maintaining an action for divorce. As might be expected, the periods vary among the States and range from six weeks to two years. The one-year period selected by Iowa is the most common length of time prescribed.

Appellant contends that the Iowa requirement of one year's residence is unconstitutional for two separate reasons: *first*, because it establishes two classes of persons and discriminates against those who have recently exercised their right to travel to Iowa, thereby contravening the Court's holdings in *Shapiro v. Thompson*, 394 U.S. 618 (1969); *Dunn v. Blumstein*, 405 U.S. 330 (1972); and *Memorial Hospital v. Maricopa County*, 415 U.S. 250 (1974); and, *second*, because it denies a litigant the opportunity to make an individualized showing of bona fide residence and therefore denies such residents access to the only method of legally dissolving their marriage....

State statutes imposing durational residency requirements were, of course, invalidated when imposed by States as a qualification for welfare payments, *Shapiro*, *supra*; for voting, *Dunn*, *supra*; and for medical care, *Maricopa County*, *supra*. But none of those cases intimated that the States might never impose durational residency requirements, and such a proposition was in fact expressly disclaimed.[19] What those cases had in common was that the durational residency requirements they struck down were justified on the basis of budgetary or record-keeping considerations which were held insufficient to outweigh the constitutional claims of the individuals. But Iowa's divorce residency requirement is of a different stripe. Appellant was not irretrievably foreclosed from obtaining some

19. *Shapiro*, 394 U.S., at 638 n. 21; *Maricopa County*, 415 U.S., at 258–259.

part of what she sought, as was the case with the welfare recipients in *Shapiro*, the voters in *Dunn*, or the indigent patient in *Maricopa County*. She would eventually qualify for the same sort of adjudication which she demanded virtually upon her arrival in the State. Iowa's requirement delayed her access to the courts, but, by fulfilling it, she could ultimately have obtained the same opportunity for adjudication which she asserts ought to have been hers at an earlier point in time.

Iowa's residency requirement may reasonably be justified on grounds other than purely budgetary considerations or administrative convenience. Cf. *Kahn v. Shevin*, 416 U.S. 351 (1974). A decree of divorce is not a matter in which the only interested parties are the State as a sort of "grantor," and a divorce petitioner such as appellant in the role of "grantee." Both spouses are obviously interested in the proceedings, since it will affect their marital status and very likely their property rights. Where a married couple has minor children, a decree of divorce would usually include provisions for their custody and support. With consequences of such moment riding on a divorce decree issued by its courts, Iowa may insist that one seeking to initiate such a proceeding have the modicum of attachment to the State required here.

Such a requirement additionally furthers the State's parallel interests both in avoiding officious intermeddling in matters in which another State has a paramount interest, and in minimizing the susceptibility of its own divorce decrees to collateral attack. A State such as Iowa may quite reasonably decide that it does not wish to become a divorce mill for unhappy spouses who have lived there as short a time as appellant had when she commenced her action in the state court after having long resided elsewhere. Until such time as Iowa is convinced that appellant intends to remain in the State, it lacks the "nexus between person and place of such permanence as to control the creation of legal relations and responsibilities of the utmost significance." *Williams v. North Carolina*, 325 U.S. 226, 229 (1945). Perhaps even more important, Iowa's interests extend beyond its borders and include the recognition of its divorce decrees by other States under the Full Faith and Credit Clause of the Constitution, Art. IV, §1. For that purpose, this Court has often stated that "judicial power to grant a divorce — jurisdiction, strictly speaking — is founded on domicil." *Williams, supra; Andrews v. Andrews*, 188 U.S. 14 (1903); *Bell v. Bell*, 181 U.S. 175 (1901). Where a divorce decree is entered after a finding of domicile in *ex parte* proceedings,[20] this Court has held that the finding of domicile is not binding upon another State and may be disregarded in the face of "cogent evidence" to the contrary. *Williams, supra*, 325 U.S. at 236. For that reason, the State asked to enter such a decree is entitled to insist that the putative

---

20. When a divorce decree is not entered on the basis of *ex parte* proceedings, this Court held in *Sherrer v. Sherrer*, 334 U.S. 343, 351–352 (1948):

> [T]he requirements of full faith and credit bar a defendant from collaterally attacking a divorce decree on jurisdictional grounds in the courts of a sister State where there has been participation by the defendant in the divorce proceedings, where the defendant has been accorded full opportunity to contest the jurisdictional issues, and where the decree is not susceptible to such collateral attack in the courts of the State which rendered the decree.

Our Brother MARSHALL argues in dissent that the Iowa durational residency requirement "sweeps too broadly" since it is not limited to *ex parte* proceedings and could be narrowed by a waiver provision. *Post*, at 425. But Iowa's durational residency requirement cannot be tailored in this manner without disrupting settled principles of Iowa practice and pleading. Iowa's rules governing special appearances make it impossible for the state court to know, either at the time a petition for divorce is filed or when a motion to dismiss for want of jurisdiction is filed, whether or not a respondent will appear and participate in the divorce proceedings. Iowa Rules Civ.Proc. 66, 104. The fact that the state legislature might conceivably adopt a system of waivers and revise court rules governing special appearances does not make such detailed rewriting appropriate business for the federal judiciary.

divorce petitioner satisfy something more than the bare minimum of constitutional requirements before a divorce may be granted. The State's decision to exact a one-year residency requirement as a matter of policy is therefore buttressed by a quite permissible inference that this requirement not only effectuates state substantive policy but likewise provides a greater safeguard against successful collateral attack than would a requirement of bona fide residence alone.[21] This is precisely the sort of determination that a State in the exercise of its domestic relations jurisdiction is entitled to make.

We therefore hold that the state interest in requiring that those who seek a divorce from its courts be genuinely attached to the State, as well as a desire to insulate divorce decrees from the likelihood of collateral attack, requires a different resolution of the constitutional issue presented than was the case in *Shapiro, supra, Dunn, supra*, and *Maricopa County, supra.*

Nor are we of the view that the failure to provide an individualized determination of residency violates the Due Process Clause of the Fourteenth Amendment. *Vlandis v. Kline*, 412 U.S. 441 (1973), relied upon by appellant, held that Connecticut might not arbitrarily invoke a permanent and irrebuttable presumption of non-residence against students who sought to obtain in-state tuition rates when that presumption was not necessarily or universally true in fact. But in *Vlandis* the Court warned that its decision should not "be construed to deny a State the right to impose on a student, as one element in demonstrating bona fide residence, a reasonable durational residency requirement." *Id.*, at 452, 93 S.Ct. at 2236. See *Starns v. Malkerson*, 326 F.Supp. 234 (Minn.1970), *aff'd*, 401 U.S. 985 (1971). An individualized determination of physical presence plus the intent to remain, which appellant apparently seeks, would not entitle her to a divorce even if she could have made such a showing. For Iowa requires not merely "domicile" in that sense, but residence in the State for a year in order for its courts to exercise their divorce jurisdiction.

In *Boddie v. Connecticut*, [401 U.S. 371 (1971)], this Court held that Connecticut might not deny access to divorce courts to those persons who could not afford to pay the required fee. Because of the exclusive role played by the State in the termination of marriages, it was held that indigents could not be denied an opportunity to be heard "absent a countervailing state interest of overriding significance." 401 U.S., at 377. But the gravamen of appellant Sosna's claim is not total deprivation, as in *Boddie*, but only delay. The operation of the filing fee in *Boddie* served to exclude forever a certain segment of the population from obtaining a divorce in the courts of Connecticut. No similar total deprivation is present in appellant's case, and the delay which attends the enforcement of the one-year durational residency requirement is, for the reasons previously stated, consistent with the provisions of the United States Constitution.

Affirmed.

...

---

21. Since the majority of States require residence for at least a year,...it is reasonable to assume that Iowa's one-year "floor" makes its decrees less susceptible to successful collateral attack in other States. As the Court of Appeals for the Fifth Circuit observed in upholding a six-month durational residency requirement imposed by Florida, an objective test may impart to a State's divorce decrees "a verity that tends to safeguard them against the suspicious eyes of other states' prosecutorial authorities, the suspicions of private counsel in other states, and the post-decree dissatisfactions of parties to the divorce who wish a second bite. Such a reputation for validity of divorce decrees is not, then, merely cosmetic." *Makres v. Askew*, 500 F.2d 577, 579 (1974), aff'g, 359 F.Supp. 1225 (MD Fla.1973).

Mr. Justice MARSHALL, with whom Mr. Justice BRENNAN joins, dissenting.

...

The Court omits altogether what should be the first inquiry: whether the right to obtain a divorce is of sufficient importance that its denial to recent immigrants constitutes a penalty on interstate travel. In my view, it clearly meets that standard. The previous decisions of this Court make it plain that the right of marital association is one of the most basic rights conferred on the individual by the State. The interests associated with marriage and divorce have repeatedly been accorded particular deference, and the right to marry has been termed "one of the vital personal rights essential to the orderly pursuit of happiness by free men." *Loving v. Virginia*, 388 U.S. 1, 12 (1967). In *Boddie v. Connecticut*, 401 U.S. 371 (1971), we recognized that the right to seek dissolution of the marital relationship was closely related to the right to marry, as both involve the voluntary adjustment of the same fundamental human relationship. *Id.*, at 383. Without further laboring the point, I think it is clear beyond cavil that the right to seek dissolution of the marital relationship is of such fundamental importance that denial of this right to the class of recent interstate travelers penalizes interstate travel within the meaning of *Shapiro*, *Dunn*, and *Maricopa County*.

...

The Court proposes three defenses for the Iowa statute: first, the residency requirement merely delays receipt of the benefit in question — it does not deprive the applicant of the benefit altogether; second, since significant social consequences may follow from the conferral of a divorce, the State may legitimately regulate the divorce process; and third, the State has interests both in protecting itself from use as a "divorce mill" and in protecting its judgments from possible collateral attack in other States. In my view, the first two defenses provide no significant support for the statute in question here. Only the third has any real force.

A

With the first justification, the Court seeks to distinguish the *Shapiro*, *Dunn*, and *Maricopa County* cases. Yet the distinction the Court draws seems to me specious. Iowa's residency requirement, the Court says, merely forestalls access to the courts; applicants seeking welfare payments, medical aid, and the right to vote, on the other hand, suffer unrecoverable losses throughout the waiting period. This analysis, however, ignores the severity of the deprivation suffered by the divorce petitioner who is forced to wait a year for relief. See *Stanley v. Illinois*, 405 U.S. 645, 647 (1972). The injury accompanying that delay is not directly measurable in money terms like the loss of welfare benefits, but it cannot reasonably be argued that when the year has elapsed, the petitioner is made whole. The year's wait prevents remarriage and locks both partners into what may be an intolerable, destructive relationship. Even applying the Court's argument on its own terms, I fail to see how the *Maricopa County* case can be distinguished. A potential patient may well need treatment for a single ailment. Under Arizona statutes he would have had to wait a year before he could be treated. Yet the majority's analysis would suggest that Mr. Evaro's claim for non-emergency medical aid is not cognizable because he would "eventually qualify for the same sort of [service]," *ante*, at 406. The Court cannot mean that Mrs. Sosna has not suffered any injury by being foreclosed from seeking a divorce in Iowa for a year. It must instead mean that it does not regard that deprivation as being very severe.

B

I find the majority's second argument no more persuasive. The Court forgoes reliance on the usual justifications for durational residency requirements — budgetary considerations and administrative convenience, see *Shapiro*, 394 U.S., at 627–638; *Maricopa County*, 415 U.S., at 262–269. Indeed, it would be hard to make a persuasive argument that either of these interests is significantly implicated in this case. In their place, the majority invokes a more amorphous justification — the magnitude of the interests affected and resolved by a divorce proceeding. Certainly the stakes in a divorce are weighty both for the individuals directly involved in the adjudication and for others immediately affected by it. The critical importance of the divorce process, however, weakens the argument for a long residency requirement rather than strengthens it. The impact of the divorce decree only underscores the necessity that the State's regulation be evenhanded.[3]

It is not enough to recite the State's traditionally exclusive responsibility for regulating family law matters; some tangible interference with the State's regulatory scheme must be shown. Yet in this case, I fail to see how any legitimate objective of Iowa's divorce regulations would be frustrated by granting equal access to new state residents. To draw on an analogy, the States have great interests in the local voting process and wide latitude in regulating that process. Yet one regulation that the States may not impose is an unduly long residency requirement. *Dunn v. Blumstein*, 405 U.S. 330 (1972). To remark, as the Court does, that because of the consequences riding on a divorce decree "Iowa may insist that one seeking to initiate such a proceeding have the modicum of attachment to the State required here" is not to make an argument, but merely to state the result.

C

The Court's third justification seems to me the only one that warrants close consideration. Iowa has a legitimate interest in protecting itself against invasion by those seeking quick divorces in a forum with relatively lax divorce laws, and it may have some interest in avoiding collateral attacks on its decree in other States. These interests, however, would adequately be protected by a simple requirement of domicile — physical presence plus intent to remain — which would remove the rigid one-year barrier while permitting the State to restrict the availability of its divorce process to citizens who are genuinely its own.

The majority notes that in *Williams v. North Carolina*, 325 U.S. 226 (1945), the Court held that for *ex parte* divorces one State's finding of domicile could, under limited circumstances, be challenged in the courts of another. From this, the majority concludes that since Iowa's findings of domicile might be subject to collateral attack elsewhere, it should be permitted to cushion its findings with a one-year residency requirement.

For several reasons, the year's waiting period seems to me neither necessary nor much of a cushion. First, the *Williams* opinion was not aimed at States seeking to avoid becoming divorce mills. Quite the opposite, it was rather plainly directed at States that had cultivated a "quickie divorce" reputation by playing fast and loose

3. The majority identifies marital status, property rights, and custody and support arrangements as the important concerns commonly resolved by divorce proceedings. But by declining to exercise divorce jurisdiction over its new citizens, Iowa does not avoid affecting these weighty social concerns; instead, it freezes them in an unsatisfactory state that it would not require its long-time residents to endure.

with findings of domicile. See *id.*, at 236–237, 65 S.Ct., at 1098–1099; *id.*, at 241, 65 S.Ct., at 1100 (Murphy, J., concurring). If Iowa wishes to avoid becoming a haven for divorce seekers, it is inconceivable that its good-faith determinations of domicile would not meet the rather lenient full faith and credit standards set out in *Williams.*

A second problem with the majority's argument on this score is that *Williams* applies only to *ex parte* divorces. This Court has held that if both spouses were before the divorcing court, a foreign State cannot recognize a collateral challenge that would not be permissible in the divorcing State. *Sherrer v. Sherrer*, 334 U.S. 343 (1948); *Coe v. Coe*, 334 U.S. 378 (1948); *Johnson v. Muelberger*, 340 U.S. 581 (1951); *Cook v. Cook*, 342 U.S. 126 (1951). Therefore, the Iowa statute sweeps too broadly even as a defense to possible collateral attacks, since it imposes a one-year requirement whenever the respondent does not reside in the State, regardless of whether the proceeding is *ex parte.*[7]

Third, even a one-year period does not provide complete protection against collateral attack. It merely makes it somewhat less likely that a second State will be able to find "cogent evidence" that Iowa's determination of domicile was incorrect. But if the Iowa court has erroneously determined the question of domicile, the year's residence will do nothing to preclude collateral attack under *Williams.*

Finally, in one sense the year's residency requirement may technically increase rather than reduce the exposure of Iowa's decrees to collateral attack. Iowa appears to be among the States that have interpreted their divorce residency requirements as being of jurisdictional import. Since a State's divorce decree is subject to collateral challenge in a foreign forum for any jurisdictional flaw that would void it in the State's own courts, *New York ex rel. Halvey v. Halvey*, 330 U.S. 610 (1947), the residency requirement exposes Iowa divorce proceedings to attack both for failure to prove domicile and for failure to prove one year's residence. If nothing else, this casts doubt on the majority's speculation that Iowa's residency requirement may have been intended as a statutory shield for its divorce decrees. In sum, concerns about the need for a long residency requirement to defray collateral attacks on state judgments seem more fanciful than real. If, as the majority assumes, Iowa is interested in assuring itself that its divorce petitioners are legitimately Iowa citizens, requiring petitioners to provide convincing evidence of bona fide domicile should be more than adequate to the task.[9]

I conclude that the course Iowa has chosen in restricting access to its divorce courts unduly interferes with the right to "migrate, resettle, find a new job, and start a new life." *Shapiro v. Thompson*, 394 U.S., at 629....

7. This problem could be cured in large part if the State waived its year's residency requirement whenever the respondent agreed to consent to the court's jurisdiction.

9. The majority argues that since most States require a year's residence for divorce, Iowa gains refuge from the risk of collateral attack in the understanding solicitude of States with similar laws. Of course, absent unusual circumstances, a judgment by this Court striking down the Iowa statute would similarly affect the other States with one-and two-year residency requirements. For the same reason, the risk of subjecting Iowa to an invasion of divorce seekers seems minimal. If long residency requirements are held unconstitutional, Iowa will not stand conspicuously alone without a residency requirement "defense." Moreover, its 90-day conciliation period, required of all divorce petitioners in the State, would still serve to discourage peripatetic divorce seekers who are looking for the quickest possible adjudication.

LEADER v. LEADER
Court of Appeals of Michigan
73 Mich. App. 276, 251 N.W.2d 288 (1977)

D.E. HOLBROOK, Presiding Judge.

Defendant appeals from an order of the trial court denying his motion to dismiss....

The only question we must decide is whether the trial court was correct in determining that plaintiff had met the jurisdictional prerequisite necessary to maintain her action for divorce. The controlling statute in pertinent part provides that: "A judgment of divorce shall not be granted...unless the complainant or defendant has resided in this state for 180 days immediately preceding the filing of the complaint." M.C.L.A. §552.9; M.S.A. §25.89. There is no disagreement as to any of the underlying facts herein. Plaintiff was physically outside the State of Michigan during most of the jurisdictional period.

Because of the unusual factual circumstances of this case, past precedent does not dictate a legal result. Plaintiff and defendant had lived in Michigan for a substantial period of time. They were married in Michigan in 1972. Defendant had three children by a prior marriage, and the parties had one child by this marriage. Plaintiff and defendant apparently had separated sometime prior to the instant action and filed for divorce in Michigan. However, a reconciliation was sought and the parties moved many of their belongings to Kentucky where defendant secured employment and the parties remained for a period of time.

Plaintiff left Michigan on or about October 1, 1975, and remained in Kentucky until January 21, 1976, with the exception of a two-day trip to Michigan. Plaintiff testified that she went to Kentucky with defendant specifically at his request in order to attempt a reconciliation, which she doubted would be successful. Plaintiff testified that she did not intend to stay in Kentucky, or anywhere else, with defendant if the reconciliation was unsuccessful. Plaintiff further testified that she intended to wait and see if the marriage could be saved before considering any place for residence. Plaintiff also testified that she only remained in Kentucky after the first two or three weeks because of a desire not to leave the children without a mother and because of threats which were later made to her by defendant. Finally, however, plaintiff did return to Michigan, her "home" state after almost a four-month absence. We must decide whether this absence is a jurisdictional defect which will defeat plaintiff's action for divorce.

An older Supreme Court case would appear to require reversal of the trial court. *Hoffman v. Hoffman*, 155 Mich. 328, 118 N.W. 990 (1909). In *Hoffman*, the plaintiff, a long-time resident of Michigan, married a resident of Chicago, Illinois. Apparently plaintiff and defendant both lived with their mothers, which came to be a source of trouble. There was a dispute as to where the parties would live. Finally plaintiff-wife went to Chicago where her husband lived and subsequently moved a good deal of her household furnishings there. Shortly thereafter she returned to Michigan, however, and instituted a divorce action. The Court found that she had not resided in Michigan for the requisite period of time. The following quotation is quite revealing:

> [T]here is nothing to indicate that, when she went to Chicago with the defendant, she had any other thought than to make her home with him, either at Chicago, where he then lived, or, if they should subsequently

> return to St. Joseph, at that place. She gave up her residence for that of the husband, and there is no room for saying that she continued her residence during this time at St. Joseph. A distinction is sought to be drawn between residence and domicile, complainant's counsel conceding that the rule is that the domicile of the husband is that of the wife, but, contending that, under the facts in this case, her residence continued to be in St. Joseph. We cannot assent to this view. Not only was her domicile in Chicago, but she undoubtedly intended to reside there, unless a certain contingency should happen, which did not occur. *Hoffman, supra,* at 330, 118 N.W. at 990.

This case, although factually similar, is necessarily distinguishable. As can be seen, Mrs. Hoffman at the time she left Michigan fully desired to live with her husband and make her home with him indefinitely and hopefully permanently. There was no indication of doubt or trouble at that time. In the instant case, plaintiff reluctantly went to Kentucky with the hope that the marital difficulties would be resolved and eventually a permanent, or at least indefinite, solution could be had. The establishment of a residence had not solidified and until such time as it did, her true residence according to her intent, remained in Michigan. We feel that the unusual facts surrounding this case require that it be distinguished from *Hoffman.* We do not rule that *Hoffman* is no longer the law, but obviously it must be considered in light of its facts and the characteristics of the time in which it was decided. Divorce rates, unfortunately, in our time have increased dramatically. Furthermore, even in a stable and healthy marriage, the residence and domicile of a wife are not necessarily the same as those of her husband....

Residence in Michigan is defined as a place of abode accompanied with the intention to remain. *Hartzler v. Radeka,* 265 Mich. 451, 251 N.W. 554 (1933); *Reaume & Silloway, Inc. v. Tetzlaff,* 315 Mich. 95, 23 N.W.2d 219 (1946). Domicile and residence in Michigan are synonymous terms.[1] *Hartzler, supra,* and *Reaume & Silloway, supra.* Today in our mobile society physical presence for a longer period of time is no longer the key factor it once was.[2]

For many purposes, residence must be considered in light of a person's intent.... Presence, abode, property ownership and other facts are often considered, yet intent is the key factor. This has been recognized in most jurisdictions and repeatedly cited....[3]

The record amply supports plaintiff's claim that she did not abandon her Michigan residence and establish Kentucky as her place of residence. Plaintiff testified as follows:

---

1. In 25 Am.Jur.2d, *Domicil,* §4, pp. 7–8, it was observed that:

> By comparison, domicil is said to be inclusive of residence, having a broader and more comprehensive meaning than residence. Residence, together with the requisite intent, is necessary to acquire domicil, but actual residence is not necessary to preserve a domicil after it is once acquired.

Recently, a Kentucky Court noted that while the term "residence" has a much narrower technical significance than the term "domicil", the two terms are almost universally used interchangeably. *St. John v. St. John,* 291 Ky. 363, 163 S.W.2d 820.

2. The Minnesota Supreme Court recently noted:

> Domicile is the union of residence and intention, and residence without intention, or intention without residence, is of no avail. Mere change of residence, although continued for a long time, does not effect a change of domicile. 6A Dunnell, Dig. (3d ed.) §2816; *In re Estate of Smith,* 242 Minn. 85, 64 N.W.2d 129 (1954). Moreover, a domicile, once shown to exist, is presumed to continue until the contrary is shown. See, *Lusk v. Belote,* 22 Minn. 468 (1876).

Davidner v. Davidner, 304 Minn. 491, 493, 232 N.W.2d 5, 7 (1975). This is particularly compelling because the Minnesota divorce statute contains a jurisdiction requirement which reads virtually the same as Michigan's, except that the period of time differs. 304 Minn. at 491, n. 1, 232 N.W.2d at 6, n. 1.

Q. (*by Mrs. Wright, plaintiff's attorney*) And would you tell the court how you happened to leave Michigan?

A. On a reconciliation. We were going though a divorce proceeding, and we decided to try one more time, out of the state of Michigan. So we left and went to Kentucky because it was where Bob had always wanted to do, so I agreed Okay, fine.

Q. Did you expect this reconciliation to work?

A. No.

Q. And how long after you got to Kentucky did you find that it was not working?

A. I would say about two or three weeks, because there were things brought up that could not be forgotten about the past.

Q. And why didn't you leave immediately?

A. Well, as you know, there are four kids involved, and I couldn't just walk off on the kids and him.

Furthermore, plaintiff explained her reasons for not leaving Kentucky sooner than she did.

Q. Did your husband ever beat you up?

A. Yes.

Q. How many times?

A. Once.

Q. How badly did he beat you up?

A. Well, it hurt. I tried to press charges, but I guess the police said it wasn't nothing too big.

Q. Has he threatened to beat you up again?

A. Oh, yes.

Q. Did he threaten to beat you up in Kentucky?

A. Yes, several times.

Q. Did he threaten to bring suit against anyone here in Michigan?

A. Yes.

Q. Did he threaten to keep your baby from you?

A. Yes.

Q. And were you afraid that any or all of these things might happen?

---

3. The Iowa Supreme Court recently was faced with a problem concerning the change of domicile for divorce purposes and indicated:

> The change of a person's domicile is considered a serious matter. A domicile once acquired continues until a new one is perfected by the concurrence of three essential elements: (1) a definite abandonment of the former domicile; (2) actual removal to, and physical presence in the new domicile; (3) a bona fide intention to change and to remain in the new domicile permanently or indefinitely....
>
> Domicile is largely a matter of intention, which must be freely and voluntarily exercised. (citations omitted)

Julson v. Julson, 255 Iowa 301, 122 N.W.2d 329, 331 (1963).

A. Yes.

Q. Is that one of the reasons you didn't leave?

A. Yes, it is.

Q. Did you write your father you only wished you were brave enough to leave before you did?

A. Yes, I did.

Plaintiff did not expect the reconciliation with her husband to be successful. Nevertheless, she made an effort. Almost immediately she discovered that the reconciliation would not work. Because of fear of harm to herself and fear of the loss of her child she was unable to return to Michigan. The trial court after a hearing on the matter made a proper finding. It is important to note that defendant did not testify at the hearing nor did he offer any other testimony which would contradict plaintiff's testimony.

...

Affirmed.

COMMENTS

In seemingly reconfirming the traditional position that jurisdiction in divorce proceedings is founded on domicile, *Sosna* mirrors a preference for social values that attach to persons who are settled firmly in one place. As noted in the dissenting opinion of Justices Marshall and Brennan, this value preference neglects the interests of recent immigrants and, implicitly, those aspects of American history that were based on large-scale migration of people. The views and interests of migratory persons tend to be underrepresented in the political process, especially on the state level where the policy considerations relating to jurisdiction in divorce matters are initiated. Yet lawyers are inevitably in contact with the flow of migration, regardless of stringent jurisdictional requirements. In fact, the more stringently the jurisdiction in divorce matters is perceived by local law, the more practicing lawyers will be concerned with finding solutions to the personal problems of their clients.

The group of persons neglected by the majority opinion in *Sosna* is large indeed. It includes all social strata of the population, from migrant workers and drifters to upper-class persons with multiple homes. The conception of domicile for jurisdictional purposes loses sight of people whose jobs may require them to relocate frequently, such as those in the military, in diplomacy, or in the employment of multinational corporations. As demonstrated by the facts of *Sosna* and *Leader*, it also neglects ordinary middle-class persons who get dislodged in the process of marital breakdown. *Sosna* takes the position that no denial of rights, but only a mere delay, is involved. Yet since the delay may involve a year or more of waiting out a statutory period of residence, lawyers will continue to try to find remedies for distraught clients who want to terminate their marriages and begin a new life in a new location.

The U.S. Supreme Court in *Sosna* falls short of establishing domicile as a due process requirement of jurisdiction in divorce matters. It holds merely that a state may reasonably be justified in requiring domicile and a one-year residence for those seeking a divorce. It also continues the theory that divorce actions are not transitory in nature but relate to a marital *res*. Yet in so holding the majority opinion fails to recognize fundamental changes in the law of marriage and divorce that have taken place. The jurisdictional requirement of domicile, enforced by statutory periods of residence, was meant to protect the interest of the state in marriage. Similarly the requirement that parties to a marriage may not agree to its dissolution, but must comply with statutory grounds, was meant to protect the state's interest. Yet with the adoption of no-fault divorce, much of the state's control over marital status was surrendered to the parties and their lawyers. Although lingering conceptions of fault and efforts of courts to reassert at least some of their powers show that this process is not yet complete, nonetheless it is evident that the state's interest in limiting divorce and remarriage is waning. More precisely, ever fewer states express any interest in forcing anyone to remain in a marriage that the couple — or even that just one of the partners — would like to end.

When it is no longer necessary to migrate to other jurisdictions to obtain divorces easily, the concern with domicile and residence periods for jurisdictional purposes loses much of its persuasive power. Iowa was one of the first jurisdictions adopting no-fault divorce and, at the time, may indeed have had an interest in retaining the one year residence requirement for purposes of discouraging persons from elsewhere from seeking divorces in Iowa. With no-fault divorce available in most states, the reasons for stringent jurisdictional requirements have been weakened. This development illustrates the interdependence of procedure and substance, that is, the functional relation between jurisdictional requirements of domicile and substantive needs to establish fault.

A legal development in flux necessarily incorporates the old and the new conceptions. It provides strong stimuli to legal practice because the inherent strains must be resolved in individual cases as well as in the law. The lawyer who is in the middle of this evolution must know both where it came from and where it leads to. In other words, he or she must be equally versed in the traditional jurisdictional requirements and in the new conceptions that slowly take shape in a process of decisions. To the extent that jurisdiction and fault in divorce proceedings were meant to protect proprietary rights, lawyers have the choice of applying traditional reasoning or developing new alternatives, as the case may be.

REFERENCE

Helen Garfield, *The Transitory Divorce Action: Jurisdiction in the No-Fault Era*, 58 TEX. L. REV. 501 (1980).

B: Full Faith and Credit and Comity

Domestic Cases

WILLIAMS v. NORTH CAROLINA [I]
United States Supreme Court
317 U.S. 287 (1942)

Mr. Justice DOUGLAS delivered the opinion of the Court.

Petitioners were tried and convicted of bigamous cohabitation under §4342 of the North Carolina Code, 1939, and each was sentenced for a term of years to a state prison. The judgment of conviction was affirmed by the Supreme Court of North Carolina....

Petitioner Williams was married to Carrie Wyke in 1916 in North Carolina and lived with her there until May, 1940. Petitioner Hendrix was married to Thomas Hendrix in 1920 in North Carolina and lived with him there until May, 1940. At that time petitioners went to Las Vegas, Nevada and on June 26, 1940, each filed a divorce action in the Nevada court. The defendants in those divorce actions entered no appearance nor were they served with process in Nevada. In the case of defendant Thomas Hendrix service by publication was had by publication of the summons in a Law Vegas newspaper and by mailing a copy of the summons and complaint to his last post office address. In the case of defendant Carrie Williams a North Carolina sheriff delivered to her in North Carolina a copy of the summons and complaint. A decree of divorce was granted petitioner Williams by the Nevada court on August 26, 1940, on the grounds of extreme cruelty, the court finding that "the plaintiff has been and now is a *bona fide* and continuous resident of the County of Clark, State of Nevada, and had been such resident for more than six weeks immediately preceding the commencement of this action in the manner prescribed by law." The Nevada court granted petitioner Hendrix a divorce on October 4, 1940, on the grounds of wilful neglect and extreme cruelty and made the same finding as to this petitioner's *bona fide* residence in Nevada as it made in the case of Williams. Petitioners were married to each other in Nevada on October 4, 1940. Thereafter they returned to North Carolina where they lived together until the indictment was returned. Petitioners pleaded not guilty and offered in evidence exemplified copies of the Nevada proceedings, contending that the divorce decrees and the Nevada marriage were valid in North Carolina as well as in Nevada. The State contended that since neither of the defendants in the Nevada actions was served in Nevada nor entered an appearance there, the Nevada decrees would not be recognized as valid in North Carolina. On this issue the court charged the jury in substance that a Nevada divorce decree based on substituted service where the defendant made no appearance would not be recognized in North Carolina under the rule of *Pridgen v. Pridgen*, 203 N.C. 533, 166 S.E. 591. The State further contended that petitioners went to Nevada not to establish a *bona fide* residence but solely for the purpose of taking advantage of the laws of that State to obtain a divorce through fraud upon that court. On that issue the court charged the jury that under the rule of *State v. Herron*, 175 N.C. 754, 94 S.E. 698, the defendants had the burden of satisfying the jury, but not beyond a reasonable doubt, of the *bona fides* of their residence in Nevada for the required time. Petitioners excepted to these charges. The Supreme Court of North Carolina in affirming the judgment held that North Carolina was not required to recognize the Nevada decrees under the full faith and credit clause of the Constitution (Art. IV, §1) by reason of *Haddock v. Haddock*, 201 U.S. 562.... Accordingly, we cannot avoid meeting the *Haddock v. Haddock* issue in this case by saying that the petitioners acquired no *bona fide* domicil in Nevada. If the case had been tried and submitted on that issue only, we would have quite a different problem.... We have no occasion to meet that issue now and we intimate no opinion on it. However it might be resolved in another proceeding, we cannot evade the constitutional issue in this case on the easy assumption that petitioners' domicil in Nevada was a sham and a fraud. Rather we must treat the present case for the purpose of the limited issue before us precisely the same as if petitioners had resided in Nevada for a term of years and had long ago acquired a permanent abode there. In other words, we would reach the question whether North Carolina could refuse to recognize the Nevada decrees because in its view and contrary to the findings of the Nevada court petitioners had no actual, *bona fide* domicil in Nevada, if and only if we concluded that *Haddock v. Haddock* was correctly decided. But we do not think it was.

The *Haddock* case involved a suit for separation and alimony brought in New York by the wife on personal service of the husband. The husband pleaded in defense a divorce decree obtained by him in Connecticut where he had established a separate domicil. This Court held that New York, the matrimonial domicil where the wife still resided, need not give full faith and credit to the Connecticut decree, since it was obtained by the husband who wrongfully left his wife in the matrimonial domicil, service on her having been obtained by publication and she not having entered an appearance in the action. But we do not agree with the theory of the *Haddock* case that, so far as the marital status of the parties is concerned, a decree of divorce granted under such circumstances by one state need not be given full faith and credit in another.

Article IV, §1 of the Constitution not only directs that "Full Faith and Credit shall be given in each State to the public Acts, Records, and Judicial Proceedings of every other State" but also provides that "Congress may be general Laws prescribe the Manner in which such Acts, Records and Proceedings shall be proved, and the Effect thereof." Congress has exercised that power. By the Act of May 26, 1790, c. 11, 28 U.S.C. §687, 28 U.S.C.A. §687, Congress has provided that judgments "shall have such faith and credit given to them in every court within the United States as they have by law or usage in the courts of the State from which they are taken."...

...

The historical view that a proceeding for a divorce was a proceeding *in rem* (2 Bishop, Marriage & Divorce, 4th ed., §164) was rejected by the *Haddock* case. We likewise agree that it does not aid in the solution of the problem presented by this case to label these proceedings as proceedings *in rem*. Such a suit, however, is not a mere *in personam* action. Domicil of the plaintiff, immaterial to jurisdiction in a personal action, is recognized in the *Haddock* case and elsewhere (Beale, Conflict of Laws, §110.1) as essential in order to give the court jurisdiction which will entitle the divorce decree to extraterritorial effect, at least when the defendant has neither been personally served nor entered an appearance. The findings made in the divorce decrees in the instant case must be treated on the issue before us as meeting those requirements. For it seems clear that the provision of the Nevada statute that a plaintiff in this type of case must "reside" in the State for the required period requires him to have a domicil as distinguished from a mere residence in the state. *Latterner v. Latterner*, 51 Nev. 285, 274 P. 194; *Lamb v. Lamb*, 57 Nev. 421, 65 P.2d 872. Hence the decrees in this case like other divorce decrees are more than *in personam* judgments. They involve the marital status of the parties. Domicil creates a relationship to the state which is adequate for numerous exercises of state power.... Each state as a sovereign has a rightful and legitimate concern in the marital status of persons domiciled within its borders. The marriage relation creates problems of large social importance. Protection of offspring, property interests, and the enforcement of marital responsibilities are but a few of commanding problems in the field of domestic relations with which the state must deal. Thus it is plain that each state by virtue of its command over its domiciliaries and its large interest in the institution of marriage can alter within its own borders the marriage status of the spouse domiciled there, even though the other spouse is absent. There is no constitutional barrier if the form and nature of the substituted service...meet the requirements of due process.... Accordingly it was admitted in the *Haddock* case that the divorce decree though not recognized in New York was binding on both spouses in Connecticut where granted.... And this Court in *Maynard v. Hill*, 125 U.S.190, upheld the validity within the Territory of Oregon of a divorce decree granted by the legislature to a husband domiciled there, even though the wife resided in Ohio where the husband had deserted her. It therefore follows that, if the Nevada decrees are taken at their full face value (as they must be on the phase of the case with which we are presently concerned), they were wholly effective to change in that state the marital status of the petitioners and each of the other spouses by the North Carolina marriages. Apart from the requirements of procedural due process...not challenged here by North Carolina, no reason based on the Federal Constitution has been advanced for the contrary conclusion. But the concession that the decrees were effective in Nevada makes more compelling the reasons for rejection of the theory and result of the *Haddock* case.

This Court stated in *Atherton v. Atherton*, [181 U.S. 155] at page 162, that "A husband without a wife, or a wife without a husband, is unknown to the law." But if one is lawfully divorced and remarried in Nevada and still married to the first spouse in North Carolina, an even more complicated and serious condition would be realized. We would then have what the Supreme Court of Illinois declared to be the "most perplexing and distressing complication in the domestic relations of many citizens in the different states." *Dunham v. Dunham*, 162 Ill. 589, 607. Under the circumstances of this case, a man would have two wives, a wife two husbands. The reality of a sentence to prison proves that that is no mere play on words. Each would be a bigamist for living in one state with the only one with whom the other state would permit him lawfully to live. Children of the second marriage would be bastards in one state but legitimate in the other. And all that would flow from the legalistic notion that where one spouse is wrongfully deserted he retains power over the matrimonial domicil so that the domicil of the other spouse follows him wherever he may go, while if he is to blame, he retains no such power. But such considerations are inapposite. As stated by Mr. Justice Holmes in his dissent in the *Haddock* case, 201 U.S. at page 630, they constitute a "pure fiction, and fiction always is a poor ground for changing substantial rights." Furthermore, the fault or wrong of one spouse in leaving the other becomes under that view a jurisdictional fact on which this Court would ultimately have to pass. Whatever may be said as to the practical effect which such a rule would have in clouding divorce decrees, the question as to where the fault lies has no relevancy to the existence of state power in such circumstances. See Bingham, *In the Matter of Haddock v. Haddock*, 21 Corn.L.Q. 393, 426. The existence of the power of a state to alter the marital status of its domiciliaries, as distinguished from the wisdom of its exercise, is not dependent on the underlying causes of the domestic rift. As we have said, it is dependent on the relationship which domicil creates and the pervasive control which a state has over marriage and divorce within its own borders. *Atherton v. Atherton* which preceded *Haddock v. Haddock* and *Thompson v. Thompson*, 226 U.S. 551, which followed it, recognized that the power of the state of the matrimonial domicil to grant a divorce from the absent spouse did not depend on whether his departure from the state was or was not justified. As stated above, we see no reason, and none has here been advanced, for making the existence of state power depend on an inquiry as to where the fault in each domestic dispute lies. And it is difficult to pick out any such line of distinction in the generality of the words of the full faith and credit clause. Moreover, so far as state power is concerned no distinction between a matrimonial domicil and a domicil later acquired has been suggested or is apparent. See Mr. Justice Holmes dissenting, *Haddock v. Haddock, supra*, 201 U.S. at page 631; Goodrich, *Matrimonial Domicile*, 27 Yale L.Journ. 49. It is one thing to say as a matter of state law that jurisdiction to grant a divorce from an absent spouse should depend on whether by consent or by conduct the latter has subjected his interest in the marriage status to the law of the separate domicil acquired by the other spouse. Beale, Conflict of Laws, §113.11; Restatement, Conflict of Laws, §113. But where a state adopts, as it has the power to do, a less strict rule, it is quite another thing to say that its decrees affecting the marital status of its domiciliaries are not entitled to full faith and credit in sister states. Certainly if decrees of a state altering the marital status of its domiciliaries are not valid throughout the Union even though the requirements of procedural due process are wholly met, a rule would be fostered which could not help but bring "considerable disaster to innocent persons" and "bastardize children hitherto supposed to be the offspring of lawful marriage," (Mr. Justice Holmes dissenting in *Haddock v. Haddock, supra*, 201 U.S. at page 628, or else encourage collusive divorces. Beale, *Constitutional Protection of Decrees for Divorce*, 19 Harv.L.Rev. 586, 596. These intensely practical considerations emphasize for us the essential function of the full faith and credit clause in substituting a command for the former principles of comity...and in altering the "status of the several states as independent foreign sovereignties" by making them "integral parts of a single nation." *Milwaukee County v. White Co.*, [296 U.S. 268], p. 277.

It is objected, however, that if such divorce decrees must be given full faith and credit, a substantial dilution of the sovereignty of other states will be effected. For it is pointed out that under such a rule one state's policy of strict control over the institution of marriage could be thwarted by the decree of a more lax state. But such an objection goes to the application of the full faith and credit clause to many situations. It is an objection in varying degrees of intensity to the enforcement of a judgment of a sister state based on a cause of action which could not be enforced in the state of the forum. Mississippi's policy against gambling transactions was overridden in *Fauntleroy v. Lum*, [210 U.S. 230], when a Missouri judgment based on such a Mississippi contract was enforced by this Court. Such is part of the price of our federal system.

This Court, of course, is the final arbiter when the question is raised as to what is a permissible limitation on the full faith and credit clause.... But the question for us is a limited one. In the first place, we repeat that in this case we must assume that petitioners had a *bona fide* domicil in Nevada, not that the Nevada domicil was a sham. We thus have no question on the present record whether a divorce decree granted by the courts of one state to a resident as distinguished from a domiciliary is entitled to full faith and credit in another state. Nor do we reach here the question as to the power of North Carolina to refuse full faith and credit to Nevada divorce decrees because, contrary to the findings of the Nevada court, North Carolina finds that no *bona fide* domicil was acquired in Nevada. In the second place, the question as to what is a permissible limitation on the full faith and credit clause does not involve a decision on our part as to which state policy on divorce is the more desirable one. It does not involve selection of a rule which will encourage on the one hand or discourage on the other the practice of divorce. That choice in the realm of morals and religion rests with the legislatures of the states. Our own views as to the marriage institution and the avenues of escape which some states have created are immaterial. It is a Constitution which we are expounding — a Constitution which in no small measure brings separate sovereign states into an integrated whole through the medium of the full faith and credit clause. Within the limits of her political power North Carolina may, of course, enforce her own policy regarding the marriage relation — an institution more basic in our civilization than any other. But society also has an interest in the avoidance of polygamous marriages...and in the protection of innocent offspring of marriages deemed legitimate in other jurisdictions. And other states have an equally legitimate concern in the status of persons domiciled there as respects the institution of marriage. So when a court of one state acting in accord with the requirements of procedural due process alters the marital status of one domiciled in that state by granting him a divorce from his absent spouse, we cannot say its decree should be excepted from the full faith and credit clause merely because its enforcement or recognition in another state would conflict with the policy of the latter....

Haddock v. Haddock is overruled. The judgment is reversed and the cause is remanded to the Supreme Court of North Carolina for proceedings not inconsistent with this opinion.

Mr. Justice FRANKFURTER, concurring.

...

Article 91 of the British North America Act (1867) gives the Parliament of Canada exclusive legislative authority to deal with marriage and divorce. Similarly, Article 51 of the Australia Constitution Act (1900) empowers the Commonwealth Parliament to make laws with respect to marriage and divorce. The Constitution of the United States, however, reserves authority over marriage and divorce to each of the forty-eight states. That is our starting-point. In a country like ours where each state has the constitutional power to translate into law its own notions of policy concerning the family institution, and where citizens pass freely from one state to another, tangled marital situations, like the one immediately before us, inevitably arise. They arose before and after the decision in the *Haddock* case, 201 U.S. 562, and will, I daresay, continue to arise no matter what we do today. For these complications cannot be removed by any decisions this Court can make — neither the crudest nor the subtlest juggling of legal concepts could enable us to bring forth a uniform national law of marriage and divorce.

...

There is but one respect in which this Court can, within its traditional authority and professional competence, contribute uniformity to the law of marriage and divorce, and that is to enforce respect for the judgment of a state by its sister states when the judgment was rendered in accordance with settled procedural standards. As the Court's opinion shows, it is clearly settled that if a judgment is binding in the state where it was rendered, it is equally binding in every other state....

The duty of a state to respect the judgments of a sister state arises only where such judgments meet the tests of justice and fair dealing that are embodied in the historic phrase, "due process of law". But in this case all talk about due process is beside the mark. If the actions of the Nevada court had been taken "without due process of law", the divorces which it purported to decree would have been without legal sanction in every state including Nevada. There would be no occasion to consider the applicability of the Full Faith and Credit Clause. It is precisely because the Nevada decrees do satisfy the requirements of the Due Process Clause and are binding in Nevada upon the absent spouses that we are called upon to decide whether these judgments, unassailable in the state which rendered them, are, despite the commands of the Full Faith and Credit Clause, null and void elsewhere.

...

For all but a very small fraction of the community the niceties of resolving such conflicts among the laws of the states are, in all likelihood, matters of complete indifference. Our occasional pronouncements upon the requirements of the Full Faith and Credit Clause doubtless have little effect upon divorces. Be this as it may, a court is likely to lose its way if it strays outside the modest bounds of its own special competence and turns the duty of adjudicating only the legal phases of a broad social problem into an opportunity for formulating judgments of social policy quite beyond its competence as well as its authority.

Mr. Justice MURPHY, dissenting.

I dissent because the Court today introduces an undesirable rigidity in the application of the Full Faith and Credit Clause to a problem which is of acute interest to all the states of the Union and on which they hold varying and sharply divergent views, the problem of how they shall treat the marriage relation.

...

In recognition of the paramount interest of the state of domicile over the marital status of its citizens, this Court has held that actual good faith domicile of at least one party is essential to confer authority and jurisdiction on the courts of a state to render a decree of divorce that will be entitled to extraterritorial effect under the Full Faith and Credit Clause, *Bell v. Bell*, 181 U.S. 175, even though both parties personally appear, *Andrews v. Andrews*, 188 U.S. 14. When the doctrine of those cases is applied to the facts of this one, the question becomes a simple one: Did petitioners acquire a bona fide domicile in Nevada? I agree with my brother Jackson that the only proper answer on the record is, no. North Carolina is the state in which petitioners have their roots, the state to which they immediately returned after a brief absence just sufficient to achieve their purpose under Nevada's requirements. It follows that the Nevada decrees are entitled to no extraterritorial effect when challenged in another state....

This is not to say that the Nevada decrees are without any legal effect in the State of Nevada. That question is not before us. It may be that for the purposes of that state the petitioners have been released from their marital vows, consistently with the procedural requirements of the Fourteenth Amendment, on the basis of compliance with its residential requirements and constructive service of process on the non-resident spouses. But conceding the validity in Nevada of its decrees dissolving the marriages, it does not mechanically follow that the Full Faith and Credit Clause compels North Carolina to accept them.

We have recognized an area of flexibility in the application of the Clause to preserve and protect state policies in matters of vital public concern....

Prominent in the residuum of state power [left to the states by a proper interpretation of the Full Faith and Credit Clause] is the right of a state to deal with the marriage relations of its citizens and to pursue its chosen domestic policy of public morality in that connection. Both Nevada and North Carolina have rights in this regard which are entitled to recognition. The conflict between those rights here should not be resolved by extending into North Carolina the effects of Nevada's action through a perfunctory application of the literal language of the Full Faith and Credit Clause with the result that measures which North Carolina has adopted to safeguard the welfare of her citizens in this area of legitimate governmental concern are undermined....

There is an element of tragic incongruity in the fact that an individual may be validly divorced in one state but not in another. But our dual system of government and the fact that we have no uniform laws on many subjects give rise to other incongruities as well — for example the common law took the logical position that an individual could have but one domicile at a time but this Court has nevertheless said that the Full Faith and Credit Clause does not prevent conflicting state decisions on the question of an individual's domicile.... In the absence of a uniform law on the subject of divorce this Court is not so limited in its application of the Full Faith and Credit Clause that it must force Nevada's policy upon North Carolina, any more than it must compel Nevada to accept North Carolina's requirements. The fair result is to leave each free to regulate within its own area the rights of its own citizens.

Mr. Justice JACKSON, dissenting.

I cannot join in exerting the judicial power of the Federal Government to compel the State of North Carolina to subordinate its own law to the Nevada divorce decrees. The Court's decision to do so reaches far beyond the immediate case. It subjects matrimonial laws of each state to important limitations and exceptions that it must recognize within its own borders and as to its own permanent population. It nullifies the power of each state to protect its own citizens against dissolution of their marriages by the courts of other states which have an easier system of divorce. It subjects every marriage to a new infirmity in that one dissatisfied spouse may choose a state of easy divorce, in which neither party has ever lived, and there commence proceedings without personal service of process.... To declare that a state is powerless to protect either its own policy or the family rights of its people against such consequences has serious constitutional implications. It is not an exaggeration to say that this decision repeals the divorce laws of all the states and substitutes the law of Nevada as to all marriages one of the parties to which can afford a short trip there. The significance of this decision is best appraised by orienting its facts with reference to the States involved, for the Court approves this concrete case as a pattern which anybody in any state may henceforth follow under the protection of the federal courts.

From the viewpoint of North Carolina, this is the situation: The Williamses, North Carolina people, were married in North Carolina, lived there twenty-five years, and have four children. The Hendrixes were also married in North Carolina and resided there some twenty years. In May of 1940, Mr. Williams and Mrs. Hendrix left their homes and respective spouses, departed the state, but after an absence of a few weeks reappeared and set up housekeeping as husband and wife. North Carolina then had on its hands three marriages among four people in the form of two broken families, and one going concern. What problems were thereby created as to property or support and maintenance, we do not know. North Carolina, for good or ill, has a strict policy as to divorce. The situation is contrary to its laws, and it has attempted to vindicate its own law by convicting the parties of bigamy.

The petitioners assert that North Carolina is made powerless in the matter, however, because of proceedings carried on in Nevada during their brief absence from North Carolina. We turn to Nevada for that part of the episode.

Williams and Mrs. Hendrix appear in the State of Nevada on May 15, 1940. For barely six weeks they made their residences at the Alamo Auto Court on the Las Vegas-Los Angeles Road. On June 26, 1940, both filed bills of complaint for divorce through the same lawyer, and alleging almost identical grounds. No personal service was made on the home-staying spouse in either case; and service was had only by publication and substituted service. Both obtained divorce decrees. The Nevada policy of divorce is reflected in Mrs. Hendrix's case. Her grounds were "extreme mental cruelty." She sustained them by testifying that her husband was "moody"; did not talk or speak to her "often"; when she spoke to him he answered most of the time by a nod or shake of the head and "there was nothing cheerful about him at all." The latter of the two divorces was granted on October 4, 1940, and on that day in Nevada they had benefit of clergy and emerged as man and wife. Nevada having served its purpose in their affairs, they at once returned to North Carolina to live.

The question is whether this Court will now prohibit North Carolina from enforcing its own policy within that State against these North Carolinians on the ground that the law of Nevada under which they lived a few weeks is in some way projected into North Carolina to give them immunity.

...

LACK OF DUE PROCESS OF LAW

...

The opinion concedes that Nevada's judgment could not be forced upon North Carolina in absence of personal service if a divorce proceeding were an action *in personam.* In other words, settled family relationships may be destroyed by a procedure that we would not recognize if the suit were one to collect a grocery bill.

We have been told that this is because divorce is a proceeding *in rem.* The marriage relation is to be reified and treated as a *res.* Then it seems that this *res* follows a fugitive from matrimony into a state of easy divorce, although the other party to it remains at home where the *res* was contracted and where years of cohabitation would seem to give it local situs. Would it be less logical to hold that the continued presence of one party to a marriage gives North Carolina power to protect the *res*, the marriage relation, than to hold that the transitory presence of one gives

Nevada power to destroy it? Counsel at the bar met this dilemma by suggesting that the *res* exists in duplicate — one for each party to the marriage. But this seems fatal to the decree, for if that is true the dissolution of the *res* in transit would hardly operate to dissolve the *res* that stayed in North Carolina. Of course this discussion is only to reveal the artificial and fictional character of the whole doctrine of a *res* as applied to a divorce action.

I doubt that it promotes clarity of thinking to deal with marriage in terms of a *res*, like a piece of land or a chattel. It might be more helpful to think of marriage as just marriage — a relationship out of which spring duties to both spouse and society and from which are derived rights, — such as the right to society and services and to conjugal love and affection — rights which generally prove to be either priceless or worthless, but which none the less the law sometimes attempts to evaluate in terms of money when one is deprived of them by the negligence or design of a third party.

It does not seem consistent with our legal system that one who has these continuing rights should be deprived of them without a hearing. Neither does it seem that he or she should be summoned by mail, publication, or otherwise to a remote jurisdiction chosen by the other party and there be obliged to submit marital rights to adjudication under a state policy at odds with that of the state under which the marriage was contracted and the matrimonial domicile was established.

Marriage is often dealt with as a contract. Of course a personal judgment could not be rendered against an absent party on a cause of action arising out of an ordinary commercial contract, without personal service of process. I see no reason why the marriage contract, if such it be considered, should be discriminated against, nor why a party to a marriage contract should be more vulnerable to a foreign judgment without process than a party to any other contract. I agree that the marriage contract is different, but I should think the difference would be in its favor.

...

...I cannot but think that in its pre-occupation with the full faith and credit clause the Court has slighted the due process clause.

Lack of Domicile

We should, I think, require that divorce judgments asking our enforcement under the full faith and credit clause, unlike judgments arising out of commercial transactions and the like, must also be supported by good-faith domicile of one of the parties within the judgment state. Such is certainly a reasonable requirement. A state can have no legitimate concern with the matrimonial status of two persons, neither of whom lives within its territory.

The Court would seem, indeed, to pay lip service to this principle. I understand the holding to be that it is domicile in Nevada that gave power to proceed without personal service of process. That being the course of reasoning, I do not see how we avoid the issue concerning the existence of the domicile which the facts on the face of this record put to us. Certainly we cannot, as the Court would, bypass the matter by saying that "We must treat the present case for the purpose of the limited issue before us precisely the same as if petitioners had resided in Nevada for a term of years and had long ago acquired a permanent abode there." I think we should treat it as if they had done just what they have done.

The only suggestion of a domicile within Nevada was a stay of about six weeks at the Alamo Auto Court, an address hardly suggestive of permanence. Mrs.

Hendrix testified in her case (the evidence in Williams' case is not before us) that her residence in Nevada was "indefinite permanent" in character. The Nevada court made no finding that the parties had a "domicile" there. It only found a residence — sometimes, but not necessarily, an equivalent. It is this Court that accepts these facts as enough to establish domicile.

While a state can no doubt set up its own standards of domicile as to its internal concerns, I do not think it can require us to accept and in the name of the Constitution impose them on other states. If Nevada may prescribe six weeks of indefinite permanent abode in a motor court as constituting domicile, she may as readily prescribe six days. Indeed, if the Court's opinion is carried to its logical conclusion, a state could grant a constructive domicile for divorce purposes upon the filing of some sort of declaration of intention. Then it would follow that we would be required to accept it as sufficient and to force all states to recognize mail-order divorces as well as tourist divorces. Indeed, the difference is in the bother and expense — not in the principle of the thing.

The concept of domicile as a controlling factor in choice of law to govern many relations of the individual was well known to the framers of the Constitution. It was hardly contemplated that a person should be subject at once to two conflicting state policies, such as those of Nevada and North Carolina. It was undoubtedly expected that the Court would in many cases of conflict use one's domicile as an appropriate guide in selecting the law to govern his controversies.

Domicile means a relationship between a person and a locality. It is the place, and the one place, where he has his roots and his real permanent home. The Fourteenth Amendment, in providing that one by residence in a state becomes a citizen hereof, probably used "residence" as synonymous with domicile. Thus domicile fixes the place where one belongs in our federal system. In some instances the existence of this relationship between the state and an individual may be a federal question, although this Court has been reluctant to accept that view.

If in testing this judgment to determine whether it qualifies for federal enforcement we should apply the doctrine of domicile to interpretation of the full faith and credit clause, Nevada would be held to a duty to respect the statutes of North Carolina and not to interfere with their application to those whose individual as well as matrimonial domicile is within that state unless and until that domicile has been terminated. And North Carolina would not be required to yield its policy as to persons resident there except upon a showing that Nevada had acquired a domiciliary right to redefine the matrimonial status.

...

In the application of the full faith and credit clause to the variety of circumstances that arise when families break up and separate domiciles are established there are, I grant, many areas of great difficulty. But I cannot believe that we are justified in making a demoralizing decision in order to avoid making difficult ones.

...

The Court advances two "intensely practical considerations" in support of its present decision. One is the "complicated and serious condition" if "one is lawfully divorced and remarried in Nevada and still married to the first spouse in North Carolina." This of course begs the question, for the divorces were completely ineffectual for any purpose relevant to this case. I agree that it is serious if a Nevada court without jurisdiction for divorce purports to say that the sojourn of two spouses gives four spouses rights to acquire four more, but I think it far more serious to force North Carolina to acquiesce in any such proposition. The other consideration advanced is that if the Court doesn't enforce divorces such as these it will, as it puts it, "bastardize" children of the divorcees. When thirty-seven years ago Mr. Justice Holmes perpetrated this quip, it had point, for the Court was then holding divorces invalid which many, due to the confused state of the law, had thought to be good. It is difficult to find that it has point now that the shoe is on the other foot. In any event I had supposed that our judicial responsibility is for the regularity of the law, not for the regularity of pedigrees.

WILLIAMS v. NORTH CAROLINA [II]
United States Supreme Court
325 U.S. 226 (1945)

Mr. Justice FRANKFURTER delivered the opinion of the Court.

This case is here to review judgments of the Supreme Court of North Carolina, affirming convictions for bigamous cohabitation, assailed on the ground that full faith and credit, as required by the Constitution of the United States, was not accorded divorces decreed by one of the courts of Nevada. *Williams v. North Carolina*, 317 U.S. 287, decided an earlier aspect of the controversy. It was there held that a divorce granted by Nevada, on a finding that one spouse was domiciled in Nevada, must be respected in North Carolina, where Nevada's finding of domicil was not questioned though the other spouse had neither appeared nor been served with process in Nevada and though recognition of such a divorce offended the policy of North Carolina. The record then before us did not present the question whether North Carolina had the power "to refuse full faith and credit to Nevada divorce decrees because, contrary to the findings of the Nevada court, North Carolina finds that no *bona fide* domicil was acquired in Nevada." *Williams v. North Carolina, supra*, 317 U.S. at page 302. This is the precise issue which has emerged after retrial of the cause following our reversal. Its obvious importance brought the case here....

...

...A judgment in one State is conclusive upon the merits in every other State, but only if the court of the first State had power to pass on the merits — had jurisdiction, that is, to render the judgment.

"It is too late now to deny the right collaterally to impeach a decree of divorce made in another state, by proof that the court had no jurisdiction, even when the record purports to show jurisdiction...." It was "too late" more than forty years ago. *German Savings & Loan Society v. Dormitzer*, 192 U.S. 125, 128.

Under our system of law, judicial power to grant a divorce — jurisdiction, strictly speaking — is founded on domicil.... The framers of the Constitution were familiar with this jurisdictional prerequisite, and since 1789 neither this Court nor any other court in the English-speaking world has questioned it. Domicil implies a nexus between person and place of such permanence as to control the creation of legal relations and responsibilities of the utmost significance. The domicil of one spouse within a State gives power to that State, we have held, to dissolve a marriage wheresoever contracted. In view of *Williams v. North Carolina, supra*, the jurisdictional requirement of domicil is freed from confusing refinements about "matrimonial domicil," see *Davis v. Davis*, 305 U.S. 32, 41, and the like. Divorce, like marriage, is of concern not merely to the immediate parties. It affects personal rights of the deepest significance. It also touches basic interests of society. Since divorce, like marriage, creates a new status, every consideration of policy makes it desirable that the effect should be the same wherever the question arises.

It is one thing to reopen an issue that has been settled after appropriate opportunity to present their contentions has been afforded to all who had an interest in its adjudication. This applies also to jurisdictional questions. After a contest these cannot be relitigated as between the parties.... But those not parties to a litigation ought not to be foreclosed by the interested actions of others; especially not a State which is concerned with the vindication of its own social policy and has no means, certainly no effective means, to protect that interest against the selfish action of those outside its borders. The State of domiciliary origin should not be bound by an unfounded, even if not collusive, recital in the record of a court of another State. As to the truth or existence of a fact, like that of domicil, upon which depends the power to exert judicial authority, a State not a party to the exertion of such judicial authority in another State but seriously affected by it has a right, when asserting its own unquestioned authority, to ascertain the truth or existence of that crucial fact.

...

...In short, the decree of divorce is a conclusive adjudication of everything except the jurisdictional facts upon which it is founded, and domicil is a jurisdictional fact. To permit the necessary finding of domicil by one State to foreclose all States in the protection of their social institutions would be intolerable.

But to endow each State with controlling authority to nullify the power of a sister State to grant a divorce based upon a finding that one spouse had acquired a new domicil within the divorcing State would, in the proper functioning of our federal system, be equally indefensible. No State court can assume comprehensive attention to the various and potentially conflicting interests that several States may have in the institutional aspects of marriage. The necessary accommodation between the right of one State to safeguard its interest in the family relation of its own people and the power of another State to grant divorces can be left to neither State.

...The rights that belong to all the States and the obligations which membership in the Union imposes upon all, are made effective because this Court is open to consider claims, such as this case presents, that the courts of one State have not given the full faith and credit to the judgment of a sister State that is required by Art. IV, §1 of the Constitution.

...

What is immediately before us is the judgment of the Supreme Court of North Carolina. 224 N.C. 183, 29 S.E.2d 744. We have authority to upset it only if there is want of foundation for the conclusion that that Court reached. The conclusion it reached turns on its finding that the spouses who obtained the Nevada decrees were not domiciled there. The fact that the Nevada court found that they were domiciled there is entitled to respect, and more. The burden of undermining the verity which the Nevada decrees import rests heavily upon the assailant. But simply because the Nevada court found that it had power to award a divorce decree cannot, we have seen, foreclose reexamination by another State. Otherwise, as was pointed out long ago, a court's record would establish its power and the power would be proved by the record. Such circular reasoning would give one State a control over all the other States which the Full Faith and Credit Clause certainly did not confer.... If this Court finds that proper weight was accorded to the claims of power by the court of one State in rendering a judgment the validity of which is pleaded in defense in another State, that the burden of overcoming such respect by disproof of the substratum of fact — here domicil — on which such power alone can rest was properly charged against the party challenging the legitimacy of the judgment, that such issue of fact was left for fair determination by appropriate procedure, and that a finding adverse to the necessary foundation for any valid sister-State judgment was amply supported in evidence, we cannot upset the judgment before us. And we cannot do so even if we also found in the record of the court of original judgment warrant for its finding that it had jurisdiction. If it is a matter turning on local law, great deference is owed by the courts of one State to what a court of another State has done.... But when we are dealing as here with an historic notion common to all English-speaking courts, that of domicil, we should not find a want of deference to a sister State on the part of a court of another State which finds an absence of domicil where such a conclusion is warranted by the record.

When this case was first here, North Carolina did not challenge the finding of the Nevada court that petitioners had acquired domicils in Nevada. For her challenge of the Nevada decrees, North Carolina rested on *Haddock v. Haddock*, 201 U.S. 562. Upon retrial, however, the existence of domicil in Nevada became the decisive issue. The judgments of conviction now under review bring before us a record which may be fairly summarized by saying that the petitioners left North Carolina for the purpose of getting divorces from their respective spouses in Nevada and as soon as each had done so and married one another they left Nevada and returned to North Carolina to live there together as man and wife. Against the charge of bigamous cohabitation under §14-183 of the North Carolina General Statutes, petitioners stood on their Nevada divorces and offered exemplified copies of the Nevada proceedings. The trial judge charged that the State had the burden of proving beyond a reasonable doubt that (1) each petitioner was lawfully married to one person; (2) thereafter each petitioner contracted a second marriage with another person outside North Carolina; (3) the spouses of petitioners were living at the time of this second marriage; (4) petitioners cohabited with one another in North Carolina after the second marriage. The burden, it was charged, then devolved upon petitioners "to satisfy the trial jury, not beyond a reasonable doubt nor by the greater weight of the evidence, but simply to satisfy" the jury from all the evidence, that petitioners were domiciled in Nevada at the time they obtained their divorces. The court further charged that "the recitation" of *bona fide* domicil in the Nevada decree was "prima facie evidence" sufficient to warrant a finding of domicil in Nevada but not compelling "such an inference". If the jury found, as they were told, that petitioners had domicils in North Carolina and went to Nevada "simply and solely for the purpose of obtaining" divorces, intending to return to North Carolina on obtaining them, they never lost their North Carolina domicils nor acquired new domicils in Nevada. Domicil, the jury was instructed, was that place where a person "has voluntarily fixed his abode...not for a mere special or temporary purpose, but with a present intention of making it his home, either permanently or for an indefinite or unlimited length of time."

The scales of justice must not be unfairly weighted by a State when full faith and credit is claimed for a sister-State judgment. But North Carolina has not so dealt with the Nevada decrees. She has not raised unfair barriers to their recognition. North Carolina did not fail in appreciation or application of federal standards of full faith and credit. Appropriate weight was given to the finding of domicil in the Nevada decrees, and that finding was allowed to be overturned only by relevant standards of proof. There is nothing to suggest that the issue was not fairly submitted to the jury and that it was not fairly assessed on cogent evidence.

...

If a State cannot foreclose, on review here, all the other States by its finding that one spouse is domiciled within its bounds, persons may, no doubt, place themselves in situations that create unhappy consequences for them. This is merely one of those untoward results inevitable in a federal system in which regulation of domestic relations has been left with the States and not given to the national authority. But the occasional disregard by any one State of the reciprocal obligations of the forty-eight States to respect the constitutional power of each to deal with domestic relations of those domiciled within its borders is hardly an argument for allowing one State to deprive the other forty-seven States of their constitutional rights. Relevant statistics happily do not justify lurid forebodings that parents without number will disregard the fate of their offspring by being unmindful of the status of dignity to which they are entitled. But, in any event, to the extent that some one State may, for considerations of its own, improperly intrude into domestic relations subject to the authority of the other States, it suffices to suggest that any such indifference by a State to the bond of the Union should be discouraged not encouraged.

...

We conclude that North Carolina was not required to yield her State policy because a Nevada court found that petitioners were domiciled in Nevada when it granted them decrees of divorce. North Carolina was entitled to find, as she did, that they did not acquire domicils in Nevada and that the Nevada court was therefore without power to liberate the petitioners from amenability to the laws of North Carolina governing domestic relations. And, as was said in connection with another aspect of the Full Faith and Credit Clause, our conclusion "is not a matter to arouse the susceptibilities of the states, all of which are equally concerned in the question and equally on both sides." *Fauntleroy v. Lum*, 210 U.S. 230, 238.

...

Affirmed.

Mr. Justice MURPHY, concurring.

...

...[I]f Nevada's divorce decrees are to be accorded full faith and credit in the courts of her sister states it is essential that Nevada have proper jurisdiction over the divorce proceedings. This means that at least one of the parties to each ex parte proceeding must have a bona fide domicil within Nevada for whatever length of time Nevada may prescribe.

...

The jury has here found that the petitioner's alleged domicil in Nevada was not a bona fide one, which in common and legal parlance means that it was acquired fraudulently, deceitfully or in bad faith. This means, in other words, that the jury found that the petitioners' residence in Nevada for six weeks was not accompanied by a bona fide intention to make Nevada their home and to remain there permanently or at least for an indefinite time, as required even by Nevada law.... This conclusion is supported by overwhelming evidence satisfying whatever standard of proof may be propounded. Under these circumstances there is no reason to doubt the efficacy of jury trials in relation to the question of domicil or to speculate as to whether another jury might have reached a different verdict on the same set of facts.

Thus the court below properly concluded that Nevada was without jurisdiction so as to give extraterritorial validity to the divorce decrees and that North Carolina was not compelled by the Constitution to give full faith and credit to the Nevada decrees. North Carolina was free to consider the original marriages still in effect, the Nevada divorces to be invalid, and the Nevada marriage to be bigamous, thus giving the Nevada marriage the same force and effect that Nevada presumably would have given it had Nevada considered the original marriages still outstanding....

By being domiciled and living in North Carolina, petitioners secured all the benefits and advantages of its government and participated in its social and economic life. As long as petitioners and their respective spouses lived there and retained that domicil, North Carolina had the exclusive right to regulate the dissolution of their marriage relationships. However harsh and unjust North Carolina's divorce laws may be thought to be, petitioners were bound to obey them while retaining residential and domiciliary ties in that state.

No justifiable purpose is served by imparting constitutional sanctity to the efforts of petitioners to establish a false and fictitious domicil in Nevada.... Certainly no policy of Nevada dictates lending the full faith and credit clause to protect actions grounded in deceit. Nevada has a recognizable interest in granting only two types of ex parte divorces: (a) Those effective solely within the borders of Nevada, and (b) those effective everywhere on the ground that at least one of the parties had a bona fide domicil in the state at the time the decree was granted. Neither type of divorce is involved here. And Nevada has no interest that we can respect in issuing divorce decrees with extraterritorial effect to those who are domiciled elsewhere and who secure sham domicils in Nevada solely for divorce purposes.

There are no startling or dangerous implications in the judgment reached by the Court in this case. All of the uncontested divorces that have ever been granted in the forty-eight states are as secure today as they were yesterday or as they were before our previous decision in this case. Those based upon fraudulent domicils are now and always have been subject to later reexamination with possible serious consequences.

...

Nor are any issues of civil liberties at stake here. It is unfortunate that the petitioners must be imprisoned for acts which they probably committed in reliance upon advice of counsel and without intent to violate the North Carolina statute. But there are many instances of punishment for acts whose criminality was unsuspected at the time of their occurrence. Indeed, for nearly three-quarters of a century or more individuals have been punished under bigamy statutes for doing exactly what petitioners have done. *People v. Dawell*, 25 Mich. 247; *State v. Armington*, 25 Minn. 29 56 S.E. 673; *People v. Baker*, 76 N.Y. 78; *State v. Westmoreland*, 76 S.C. 145. Petitioners especially must be deemed to have been aware of the possible criminal consequences of their actions in view of the previously settled North Carolina law on the matter. *State v. Herron*, 175 N.C. 754,

94 S.E. 698. This case, then, adds no new uncertainty and comes as no surprise for those who act fraudulently in establishing a domicil and who disregard the laws of their true domiciliary states.

As Mr. Justice Holmes said in his dissenting opinion in the *Haddock* case, 201 U.S. at page 628, "I do not suppose civilization will come to an end whichever way this case is decided." Difficult problems inevitably arise from the fact that people move about freely among the forty-eight states, each of which has its own policies and laws....

The CHIEF JUSTICE and Mr. Justice JACKSON join in these views.

Mr. Justice RUTLEDGE, dissenting.

Once again the ghost of "unitary domicil" returns on its perpetual round, in the guise of "jurisdictional fact," to upset judgments, marriages, divorces, undermine the relations founded upon them, and make this Court the unwilling and uncertain arbiter between the concededly valid laws and decrees of sister states. From *Bell* and *Andrews* to *Davis* to *Haddock* to *Williams* and now back of *Haddock* and *Davis* through *Williams* again — is the maze the Court has travelled in a domiciliary wilderness, only to come out with no settled constitutional policy where one is needed most.

Nevada's judgment has not been voided. It could not be, if the same test applies to sustain it as upholds the North Carolina conviction.[2] It stands, with the marriages founded upon it, unimpeached. For all that has been determined or could be, unless another change is in the making, petitioners are lawful husband and wife in Nevada. *Williams v. North Carolina I*, 317 U.S. 287; *Williams v. North Carolina II*, decided this day. They may be such everywhere outside North Carolina. Lawfully wedded also, in North Carolina, are the divorced spouse of one and his wife, taken for all we know in reliance upon the Nevada decree.[3] That is, unless another jury shall find they too are bigamists for their reliance. No such jury has been impanelled. But were one called, it could pronounce the Nevada decree valid upon the identical evidence from which the jury in this case drew the contrary conclusion. That jury or it and another, if petitioners had been tried separately, could have found one guilty, the other innocent, upon that evidence unvaried by a hair. And, by the Court's test, we could do nothing but sustain the contradictory findings in all these cases.

I do not believe the Constitution has thus confided to the caprice of juries the faith and credit due the laws and judgments of sister states. Nor has it thus made that question a local matter for the states themselves to decide. Were all judgments given the same infirmity, the full faith and credit clause would be only a dead constitutional letter.

I agree it is not the Court's business to determine policies of divorce. But precisely its function is to lay the jurisdictional foundations upon which the states' determinations can be made effective, within and without their borders. For in the

2. Presumably it would be our function "to retry the facts" no more if the Nevada decree were immediately under challenge here than it is to do so when the North Carolina judgment is in issue. It would seem therefore that we owe the same deference to Nevada's finding of domicil as we do to North Carolina's....

3. The record indicates that Mr. Hendrix "had brought no divorce proceeding against the feme defendant prior to the first trial of this cause,...but that he has since and remarried." Although the evidence shows institution of this proceeding, it does not show a decree was entered prior to his remarriage. Whether or not he actually relied upon the Nevada decree, thousands of spouses so divorced do so rely, thus founding new relations which are equally subject to invalidation by jury finding and are always beclouded by a judgment like that rendered in this case.

one case due process, in the other full faith and credit, commands of equal compulsion upon the estates and upon us, impose that duty.

I do not think we perform it, we rather abdicate, when we confide the ultimate decision to the states or to their juries. This we do when, for every case that matters, we make their judgment conclusive. It is so in effect when the crucial concept is as variable and amorphous as "domicil," is always a conclusion of "ultimate fact," and can be established only by proof from which, as experience shows, contradictory inferences may be made as strikes the local trier's fancy....

...

Domicil, as a substantive concept, steadily reflects neither a policy of permanence nor one of transiency. It rather reflects both inconstantly. The very name gives forth the idea of home with all its ancient associations of permanence. But "home" in the modern world is often a trailer or a tourist camp. Automobiles, nation-wide business and multiple family dwelling units have deprived the institution, though not the idea, of its former general fixation to soil and locality. But, beyond this, "home" in the domiciliary sense can be changed in the twinkling of an eye, the time it takes a man to make up his mind to remain where he is when he is away from home. He need do no more than decide, by a flash of thought, to stay "either permanently or for an indefinite or unlimited length of time."[14] No other connection of permanence is required. All of his belongings, his business, his family, his established interests and intimate relations may remain where they have always been. Yet if he is but physically present elsewhere, without even bag or baggage, and undergoes the mental flash, in a moment he has created a new domicil though hardly a new home.

Domicil thus combines the essentially contradictory elements of permanence and instantaneous change. No legal conception, save possibly "jurisdiction," of which it is an elusive substratum, affords such possibilities for uncertain application. The only thing certain about it, beyond its uncertainty, is that one must travel to change his domicil. But he may travel without changing it, even remain for a lifetime in his new place of abode without doing so. Apart from the necessity for travel, hardly evidentiary of stabilized relationship in a transient age, the criterion comes down to a purely subjective mental state, related to remaining for a length of time never yet defined with clarity.

With the crux of power fixed in such a variable, small wonder that the states vacillate in applying it and this Court ceaselessly seeks without finding a solution for its quandary. But not all the vice lies in the substantive conception. Only lawyers know, unless now it is taxpayers and persons divorced, how rambling is the scope of facts from which proof is ever drawn to show and negate the ultimate conclusion of subjective "fact." They know, as do the courts and other tribunals which wrestle with the problem, how easily facts procreative of conflicting inferences may be marshalled and how conjectural is the outcome. There is no greater legal gamble. Rare is the situation, where much is at stake, in which conflicting circumstances cannot be shown and where accordingly conflicting ultimate inferences cannot be drawn.

...

With the subjective substratum removed, the largest source of variable and inconstant decision would disappear. This would be true, whether transiency

14. Citation of authority is hardly needed for reference to the difficulties courts have encountered in the effort to define this intent. "Animus manendi" is often a Latin refuge which succeeds only in evading not in resolving the question with which Job wrestled in his suffering.

guarded by due process or some more established but objectively determinable relation with the community were chosen for the standard to turn the existence of power. Either choice would be preferable to the variable which can give only inconstant and capricious effects, nullifying both policies.

If by one choice states of origin were forced to modify their local policies by giving effect to the different policies of other states when crystallized in valid judgments, that would be no more than the Constitution in terms purports to require. And it may be doubted their surrender would be much greater in practical effects than the present capricious and therefore deceptive system brings about. If by some more restrictive choice states now free to give essentially transient divorce were required to modify that policy for locally valid effects, within the limits of any objective standard that conceivably would be acceptable for constitutional purposes, the obligations they owe to the nation and to sister states would seem amply to justify that modest curtailment of their power. It is hard to see what legitimate substantial interest a state may have in providing divorces for persons only transiently there or for newcomers before they have created, by reasonable length of stay or other objective standards, more than fly-by-night connections.

I therefore dissent from the judgment which, in my opinion, has permitted North Carolina at her substantially unfettered will to deny all faith and credit to the Nevada decree, without in any way impeaching or attempting to impeach that judgment's constitutional validity....

Mr. Justice BLACK, dissenting.

Anglo-American law has, until today, steadfastly maintained the principle that before an accused can be convicted of crime, he must be proven guilty beyond a reasonable doubt. These petitioners have been sentenced to prison because they were unable to prove their innocence to the satisfaction of the State of North Carolina. They have been convicted under a statute so uncertain in its application that not even the most learned member of the bar could have advised them in advance as to whether their conduct would violate the law. In reality the petitioners are being deprived of their freedom because the State of Nevada, through its legislature and courts, follows a liberal policy in granting divorces. They had Nevada divorce decrees which authorized them to remarry. Without charge or proof of fraud in obtaining these decrees, and without holding the decrees invalid under Nevada law, this Court affirms a conviction of petitioners, for living together as husband and wife. I cannot reconcile this with the Full Faith and Credit Clause and with congressional legislation passed pursuant to it.

It is my firm conviction that these convictions cannot be harmonized with vital constitutional safeguards designed to safeguard individual liberty and to unite all the states of this whole country into one nation. The fact that two people will be deprived of their constitutional rights impels me to protest as vigorously as I can against affirmance of these convictions. Even more, the Court's opinion today will cast a cloud over the lives of countless numbers of the multitude of divorced persons in the United States....

...

The petitioners were married in Nevada. North Carolina has sentenced them to prison for living together as husband and wife in North Carolina. This Court today affirms those sentences without a determination that the Nevada marriage was invalid under that State's laws. This holding can be supported, if at all, only on one of two grounds: (1) North Carolina has extra-territorial power to regulate marriages within Nevada's territorial boundaries, or, (2) North Carolina can punish people who live together in that state as husband and wife even though they have been validly married in Nevada. A holding based on either of these two grounds encroaches upon the general principle recognized by this Court that a marriage validly consummated under one state's laws is valid in every other state. If the Court is today abandoning that principle, it takes away from the states a large part of their hitherto plenary control over the institution of marriage. A further consequence is to subject people to criminal prosecutions for adultery and bigamy merely because they exercise their constitutional right to pass from a state in which they were validly married into another state which refuses to recognize their marriage. Such a consequence runs counter to the basic guarantees of our federal union.... It is true that persons validly married under the laws of one state have been convicted of crime for living together in other states. But those state convictions were not approved by this Court. And never before today has this Court decided a case upon the assumption that men and women validly married under the laws of one state could be sent to jail by another state for conduct which involved nothing more than living together as husband and wife.

The Court's opinion may have passed over the marriage question on the unspoken premise that the petitioners were without legal capacity to marry. If so, the primary question still would be whether that capacity, and other issues subsidiary to it, are to be determined under Nevada, North Carolina, or Federal law. Answers to these questions require a discussion of the divorce decrees awarded to the petitioners in a Nevada court prior to their marriage there.

When the Nevada decrees were granted, the petitioners' former spouses lived in North Carolina. When petitioners were tried and convicted, one of their former spouses was dead and the other had remarried. Under the legal doctrine prevailing in Nevada and in most of the states, these facts would make both the decrees immune from attack unless, perhaps, by persons other than the North Carolina spouses, whose property rights might be adversely affected by the decrees. So far as appears from the record no person's property rights were adversely affected by the dissolution decrees. None of the parties to the marriage, although formally notified of the Nevada divorce proceedings, made any protest before or after the decrees were rendered. The state did not sue here to protect any North Carolinian's property rights or to obtain support for the families which had been deserted. The result of all this is that the right of the state to attack the validity of these decrees in a criminal proceeding is today sustained, although the state's citizens, on whose behalf it purports to act, could not have done so at the time of the conviction in a civil proceeding. Furthermore, all of the parties to the first two marriages were apparently satisfied that their happiness did not lie in continued marital cohabitation. North Carolina claims no interest in abridging their individual freedom by forcing them to live together against their own desires. The state's interest at the time these petitioners were convicted thus comes down to its concern in preserving a bare marital status for a spouse who had already married again. If the state's interest before that time be considered, it was to preserve a bare marital status as to two persons who had sought a divorce and two others who had not objected to it. It is an extraordinary thing for a state to procure a retroactive invalidation of a divorce decree, and then punish one of its citizens for conduct authorized by that decree, when it had never been challenged by either of the people most immediately interested in it. I would not permit such an attenuated state interest to override the Full Faith and Credit Clause of the Constitution and an Act of Congress pursuant to it. Here again, North Carolina's right to attack this judgment, despite the Full Faith and Credit Clause and the Congressional enactment, is not based on Nevada law; nor could it be. For in Nevada, even the Attorney General could not have obtained a cancellation of the decree on the ground that it was rendered without jurisdiction. *State v. Moore*, 46 Nev. 65, 207 P. 75. This makes it clear beyond all doubt that North Carolina has not given these decrees the same effect that they would be given in the courts of Nevada.

...

This brings me to the Court's holding that Nevada decrees were "void." That conclusion rests on the premise that the Nevada court was without jurisdiction because the North Carolina Court found that the petitioners had no "domicile" in Nevada. The Nevada court had based its decree on a finding that "domicile" had been established by evidence before it. As I read that evidence, it would have been sufficient to support the findings, had the case been reviewed by us. Thus, this question of fact has now been adjudicated in two state courts with different results. It should be noted now that this Court very recently has said as to the Full Faith and Credit Clause and the 1790 Congressional enactment, that "From the beginning this Court has held that these provisions have made that which has been adjudicated in one state *res judicata* to the same extent in every other." *Magnolia Petroleum Co. v. Hunt*, [320 U.S. 430], at 438.[10] That it was appropriate for the Nevada court to pass upon the question of domicile can hardly be doubted, since the concurring opinion in our first consideration of this case correctly said that the "Nevada decrees do satisfy the requirements of the Due Process Clause and are binding in Nevada upon the absent spouses...." 317 U.S. 287, 306. The Court today, however, seems to place its holding that the Nevada decrees are void on the basis that the Due Process Clause makes domicile an indispensable prerequisite to a state court's "jurisdiction" to grant divorce. It further holds that this newly created federal restriction of state courts projects fact issues which the state courts cannot finally determine for themselves....

...

It is a drastic departure from former constitutional doctrine to hold that the Federal Constitution measures the power of state courts to pass upon petitions for divorce. The jurisdiction of state courts over persons and things within their boundaries has been uniformly acknowledged through the years, without regard to the length of their sojourn or their intention to remain. And that jurisdiction has not been thought to be limited by the Federal Constitution. Legislative dissolution of marriage was common in the colonies and the states up to the middle of the Nineteenth Century. A legislative dissolution of marriage, granted without notice or hearing of any kind, was sustained by this Court long after the Fourteenth

---

10. The Nevada court had general jurisdiction to grant divorces, and the complaint was required to allege domicile along with the other requisite allegations. Domicile is as much an integral element in the litigation as the proof of cruelty or any of the other statutory grounds for divorce in Nevada. Labeling domicile as "jurisdictional" does not make it different from what it was before. Since the Nevada court had no power to render a divorce without proof of facts other than domicile, there is nothing to prevent this Court, under its expansive interpretation of the Due Process Clause, from labeling these other facts as "jurisdictional" and taking more state powers into the federal judicial orbit. Both these types of facts, however labeled, were part of the controversy which the Nevada legislature gave its courts power to resolve. The state could label them "jurisdictional" and having the exclusive power to grant divorces, could attach such consequences to them as it sees fit. But, while Congress might, under the Full Faith and Credit Clause, prescribe the "effect" in other states, of decrees based on the finding, I do not think the Federal courts can, by their mere label, attach jurisdictional consequences to the state's requirement of domicile. Hence, I think the quoted statement from the *Magnolia Petroleum* case should control this case.

Amendment was adopted. *Maynard v. Hill*, 125 U.S. 190; cf. *Pennoyer v. Neff*, 95 U.S. 714, 734–735. The provision that made "due process of law" a prerequisite to deprivation of "life, liberty, or property" was not considered applicable to proceedings to sever the marital status. It was only when legislatures attempted to create or destroy financial obligations incident to marriage that courts began to conclude that their Acts encroached upon the right to a judicial trial in accordance with due process. The Court's holding now appears to overrule *Maynard v. Hill*, sub silentio. This perhaps is in keeping with the idea that the due process clause is a blank sheet of paper provided for courts to make changes in the Constitution and the Bill of Rights in accordance with their ideas of civilization's demands. I should leave the power over divorces in the states. And in the absence of further federal legislation under the Full Faith and Credit Clause, I should leave the effect of divorce decrees to be determined as Congress commanded — according to the laws and usages of the state where the decrees are entered.

Implicit in the majority of the opinions rendered by this and other courts, which, whether designedly or not, have set up obstacles to the procurement of divorces, is the assumption that divorces are an unmitigated evil, and that the law can and should force unwilling persons to live with each other. Others approach the problem as one which can best be met by moral, ethical and religious teachings. Which viewpoint is correct is not our concern. I am confident, however, that today's decision will no more aid in the solution of the problem than the *Dred Scott* decision aided in settling controversies over slavery. This decision, I think, takes the wrong road. Federal courts should have less, not more, to do with divorces. Only when one state refuses to give that faith and credit to a divorce decree which Congress and the Constitution command, should we enter this field.

...

Mr. Justice DOUGLAS joins in this dissent.

SHERRER v. SHERRER

United States Supreme Court
334 U.S. 343 (1948)

Mr. Chief Justice VINSON delivered the opinion of the Court.

We granted certiorari in this case and in *Coe v. Coe*, [334 U.S. 378], to consider the contention of petitioners that Massachusetts has failed to accord full faith and credit to decrees of divorce rendered by courts of sister States.

Petitioner Margaret E. Sherrer and the respondent, Edward C. Sherrer, were married in New Jersey in 1930, and from 1932 until April 3, 1944, lived together in Monterey, Massachusetts. Following a long period of marital discord, petitioner, accompanied by the two children of the marriage, left Massachusetts on the latter date, ostensibly for the purpose of spending a vacation in the State of Florida. Shortly after her arrival in Florida, however, petitioner informed her husband that she did not intend to return to him. Petitioner obtained housing accommodations in Florida, placed her older child in school, and secured employment for herself.

On July 6, 1944, a bill of complaint for divorce was filed at petitioner's direction in the Circuit Court of the Sixth Judicial Circuit of the State of Florida. The bill alleged extreme cruelty as grounds for divorce and also alleged that petitioner was a "bona fide resident of the State of Florida." The respondent received notice by mail of the pendency of the divorce proceedings. He retained Florida counsel who entered a general appearance and filed an answer denying the allegations of petitioner's complaint, including the allegation as to petitioner's Florida residence.

On November 14, 1944, hearings were held in the divorce proceedings. Respondent appeared personally to testify with respect to a stipulation entered into by the parties relating to the custody of the children. Throughout the entire proceedings respondent was represented by counsel. Petitioner introduced evidence to establish her Florida residence and testified generally to the allegations of her complaint. Counsel for respondent failed to cross-examine or to introduce evidence in rebuttal.

The Florida court on November 29, 1944, entered a decree of divorce after specifically finding "that petitioner is a bona fide resident of the State of Florida, and that this court has jurisdiction of the parties and the subject matter in said cause;..." Respondent failed to challenge the decree by appeal to the Florida Supreme Court.

On December 1, 1944, petitioner was married in Florida to one Henry A. Phelps, whom petitioner had known while both were residing in Massachusetts and who had come to Florida shortly after petitioner's arrival in that State. Phelps and petitioner lived together as husband and wife in Florida, where they were both employed, until February 5, 1945, when they returned to Massachusetts.

In June, 1945, respondent instituted an action in the Probate Court of Berkshire County, Massachusetts, which has given rise to the issues of this case. Respondent alleged that he is the lawful husband of petitioner, that the Florida decree of divorce is invalid, and that petitioner's subsequent marriage is void. Respondent prayed that he might be permitted to convey his real estate as if he were sole and that the court declare that he was living apart from his wife for justifiable cause. Petitioner joined issue on respondent's allegations.

In the proceedings which followed, petitioner gave testimony in defense of the validity of the Florida divorce decree. The Probate Court, however, resolved the issues of fact adversely to petitioner's contentions, found that she was never domiciled in Florida, and granted respondent the relief he had requested. The Supreme Judicial Court of Massachusetts affirmed the decree on the grounds that it was supported by the evidence and that the requirements of full faith and credit did not preclude the Massachusetts courts from reexamining the finding of domicile made by the Florida court.

At the outset, it should be observed that the proceedings in the Florida court prior to the entry of the decree of divorce were in no way inconsistent with the requirements of procedural due process. We do not understand respondent to urge the contrary. The respondent personally appeared in the Florida proceedings. Through his attorney he filed pleadings denying the substantial allegations of petitioner's complaint. It is not suggested that his rights to introduce evidence and otherwise to conduct his defense were in any degree impaired; nor is it suggested that there was not available to him the right to seek review of the decree by appeal to the Florida Supreme Court. It is clear that respondent was afforded his day in court with respect to every issue involved in the litigation, including the jurisdictional issue of petitioner's domicile. Under such circumstances, there is nothing in the concept of due process which demands that a defendant be afforded a second opportunity to litigate the existence of jurisdictional facts....

It should also be observed that there has been no suggestion that under the law of Florida, the decree of divorce in question is in any respect invalid or could successfully be subjected to the type of attack permitted by the Massachusetts court.

The implicit assumption underlying the position taken by respondent and the Massachusetts court is that this case involves a decree of divorce valid and final in the State which rendered it; and we so assume.

That the jurisdiction of the Florida court to enter a valid decree of divorce was dependent upon petitioner's domicile in that State is not disputed. This requirement was recognized by the Florida court which rendered the divorce decree, and the principle has been given frequent application in decisions of the State Supreme Court. But whether or not petitioner was domiciled in Florida at the time the divorce was granted was a matter to be resolved by judicial determination. Here, unlike the situation presented in *Williams v. North Carolina*, 1945, 325 U.S. 226, the finding of the requisite jurisdictional facts was made in proceedings in which the defendant appeared and participated. The question with which we are confronted, therefore, is whether such a finding made under the circumstances presented by this case may, consistent with the requirements of full faith and credit, be subjected to collateral attack in the courts of a sister State in a suit brought by the defendant in the original proceedings.

The question of what effect is to be given to an adjudication by a court that it possesses requisite jurisdiction in a case, where the judgment of that court is subsequently subjected to collateral attack on jurisdictional grounds, has been given frequent consideration by this Court over a period of many years. Insofar as cases originating in the federal courts are concerned, the rule has evolved that the doctrine of *res judicata* applies to adjudications relating either to jurisdiction of the person or of the subject matter where such adjudications have been made in proceedings in which those questions were in issue and in which the parties were given full opportunity to litigate. The reasons for this doctrine have frequently been stated. Thus in *Stoll v. Gottlieb*, 1938, 305 U.S. 165, 172, it was said:

> Courts to determine the rights of parties are an integral part of our system of government. It is just as important that there should be a place to end as that there should be a place to begin litigation. After a party has his day in court, with opportunity to present his evidence and his view of the law, a collateral attack upon the decision as to jurisdiction there rendered merely retries the issue previously determined. There is no reason to expect that the second decision will be more satisfactory than the first.

...

Applying these principles to this case, we hold that the Massachusetts courts erred in permitting the Florida divorce decree to be subjected to attack on the ground that petitioner was not domiciled in Florida at the time the decree was entered. Respondent participated in the Florida proceedings by entering a general appearance, filing pleadings placing in issue the very matters he sought subsequently to contest in the Massachusetts courts, personally appearing before the Florida court and giving testimony in the case, and by retaining attorneys who represented him throughout the entire proceedings. It has not been contended that respondent was given less than a full opportunity to contest the issue of petitioner's domicile or any other issue relevant to the litigation. There is nothing to indicate that the Florida court would not have evaluated fairly and in good faith all relevant evidence submitted to it. Respondent does not even contend that on the basis of the evidence introduced in the Florida proceedings, that court reached an erroneous result on the issue of petitioner's domicile. If respondent failed to take advantage of the opportunities afforded him, the responsibility is his own. We do not believe that the dereliction of a defendant under such circumstances should be permitted to provide a basis for subsequent attack in the courts of a sister State on a decree valid in the State in which it was rendered.

...

...We believe that in permitting an attack on the Florida divorce decree which again put in issue petitioner's Florida domicile and in refusing to recognize the validity of that decree, the Massachusetts courts have asserted a power which cannot be reconciled with the requirements of due faith and credit. We believe that assurances that such a power will be exercised sparingly and wisely render it no less repugnant to the constitutional commands.

It is one thing to recognize as permissible the judicial reexamination of findings of jurisdictional fact where such findings have been made by a court of a sister State which has entered a divorce decree in *ex parte* proceedings. It is quite another thing to hold that the vital rights and interests involved in divorce litigation may be held in suspense pending the scrutiny by courts of sister States of findings of jurisdictional fact made by a competent court in proceedings conducted in a manner consistent with the highest requirements of due process and in which the defendant has participated. We do not conceive it to be in accord with the purposes of the full faith and credit requirement to hold that a judgment rendered under the circumstances of this case may be required to run the gauntlet of such collateral attack in the courts of sister States before its validity outside of the State which rendered it is established or rejected. That vital interests are involved in divorce litigation indicates to us that it is a matter of greater rather than lesser importance that there should be a place to end such litigation. And where a decree of divorce is rendered by a competent court under the circumstances of this case, the obligation of full faith and credit requires that such litigation should end in the courts of the State in which the judgment was rendered.

Reversed.

[Dissenting opinion by Mr. Justice FRANKFURTER omitted.]

COMMENTS

Williams and *Sherrer* are still crucial for legal practice in spite of the availability of no-fault divorce in most jurisdictions. Although business in the so-called divorce-mill states has been drastically reduced by these legislative changes, marital breakdown is still often accompanied by change of abode by at least one of the spouses. Divorce is a disruptive and sometimes traumatic experience for both parties to a marriage; an adjustment to the new conditions is sometimes facilitated by a change of environment, and a person leaving a marriage often moves to be closer to friends and family. Numerous other factors induce people to move in case of marital breakdown, although easier divorce in another state may no longer be one of them. In other words, migratory divorce today is less institutionalized than it used to be under a fault regime, but it continues to be a matter of individual initiative. Furthermore, the legal situation under no-fault divorce is anything but uniform. Especially in regard to property division and alimony, considerable differences exist by way of judicial interpretation of statutes that outwardly may read quite similarly. As we have seen, fault conceptions persist in no-fault jurisdictions in varying degrees.

The continued importance of *Williams* and *Sherrer* is perhaps felt most in a nonlitigative context. Past, present, and future conduct of clients is deeply influenced by their family relations, as well as their professional and business life. Proper legal advice in these matters necessitates knowledge of factors that may cause collateral attack on divorce decrees, even if such attack, under contemporary standards of no-fault, is less likely than in the past. The vitality of precedent, such as the *Williams* cases, may manifest itself on several levels. Even if a case, without being overruled, is no longer cited on the appellate level, it may continue to be effective for purposes of legal practice. In some respects — for example, in regard to the recognition of foreign divorce decrees — the significance of *Williams* and *Sherrer* has even increased, although the decisions were not originally meant to serve this purpose. In determining whether to grant comity, judges may be inclined to apply standards established in these cases. Any of the factors mentioned, whether they involve litigation, contemplated litigation, or mere conduct of clients, should still be incorporated into the intellectual check list of the practicing lawyer. To the extent that past migratory divorces have possibly affected the validity of marriages entered thereafter, the issues can be expected to be raised in years to come, if not in litigation then at least as a point of argument for purposes of reaching a favorable property settlement.

Although *Williams* and *Sherrer* are often cited as complementing each other, they arose in different factual contexts and involved parties who were in very different situations. *Williams* was a criminal prosecution for bigamy with the state of North Carolina as party; *Sherrer* was a civil litigation in which the underlying concern was not the marriage itself but rights to property. *Williams* was concerned with an *ex parte* divorce, while in *Sherrer* the defendant husband participated in the divorce proceedings. In fact, the dichotomy between *ex parte* and bilateral divorces is false because there are multiple levels of participation. The facts in *Williams* make it clear that both Mrs. Williams and Mr. Hendrix had received notice of the Nevada proceedings. *Sherrer* involved a particularly high degree of participation. The respondent husband received notice by mail and retained Florida counsel, who entered an appearance denying the petitioner's domicile; in addition, the husband appeared personally and his counsel failed to cross-examine in regard to the petitioner's domicile and to introduce evidence in rebuttal; finally the husband failed to appeal the decision. One could ask how many of these elements could be missing and the decision still have res judicata effects in regard to jurisdictional factors.

The concurring and dissenting opinions in *Williams I* and *II* and in *Sherrer* add further shades of reasoning. Justice Frankfurter, for example, concurred in the opinion of Justice Douglas in *Williams I*. Three years later in *Williams II*, Justice Frankfurter wrote for the majority with Justice Douglas dissenting. Again three years later, in *Sherrer*, Justice Douglas voted with the majority and Justice Frankfurter dissented. In this kind of situation it is impossible to ascertain whether the reasoning of the Court or of individual Justices is consistent. Rather than look for an elusive consistency, one should read the majority opinions in conjunction with the concurring and dissenting opinions for the extreme difficulties of the underlying problems. A few examples may demonstrate this complexity.

Justice Frankfurter stresses the point in his concurring opinion to *Williams I* that a divorce decree may satisfy the requirements under procedural due process in the state where it was rendered, in this instance Nevada, yet may be "null and void elsewhere" despite the commands of the Full Faith and Credit Clause. The reference to the decree being "null and void elsewhere," is probably misleading, because it is not within the jurisdiction of any decisionmaker to say that decrees from another sovereign are void. What is actually being referred to is the power to say that the foreign decree is not to be recognized. The nonspecific reference to "elsewhere" leaves open what states other than North Carolina might do in regard to the Nevada divorce decrees, not to mention foreign nations. According to Justice Frankfurter in writing for the majority in *Williams II*, any state may reexamine the jurisdictional fact of domicile in Nevada. The result could be that Mr. Williams is married to Mrs. Hendrix in some states and to Mrs. Williams in some others, depending on whether they follow the Nevada or the North Carolina holding. This compounds the problem of "a husband without a wife, or a wife without a husband," raised by Justice Douglas in *Williams I*. At least for purposes of bigamy, however, it is more likely that states other than North Carolina would recognize the Nevada divorces and choose not to prosecute, especially in light of the fact that North Carolina had at the time in question one of the most restrictive divorce laws in the United States.

Justice Rutledge and Justice Black in their dissenting opinions to *Williams II* shift the emphasis from the divorces to the valid marriage of Mr. Williams and Mrs. Hendrix in Nevada. They stress the conception that a marriage valid where entered is ordinarily to be recognized elsewhere. Both Justices stress also the underlying facts of the marriages involved. Mr. Hendrix, left behind in North Carolina, had meanwhile remarried. Justice Black reports in addition that the other spouse remaining in North Carolina, an obvious reference to Mrs. Williams, had died. In the light of this he questions the legitimate interest of the state in the prosecution. As a matter of principle, of course, the bigamy prosecution in North Carolina was not dependent on what happened to the deserted spouses. Nevertheless, the reality of the marriages seems to be out of line with the severity of the positions taken by the courts of North Carolina and by the Supreme Court of the United States in *Williams II*.

Perhaps some of the facts not mentioned in *Williams I* and *II* may throw light on the artificiality of the litigation. Not only had Mrs. Williams died, on June 24, 1943, but Mr. Hendrix had remarried after obtaining a divorce from his wife in North Carolina in May 1941 on the ground of adultery. Mr. Williams and Mrs. Hendrix did not return immediately after their marriage in Nevada to North Carolina, but were out of the state for the relatively respectable period of about six months. The ardor of the prosecution and the severity of the criminal sanctions applied by the North Carolina courts appears to have been prompted by some of the circumstances. Mr. Hendrix had been an employee in the store of Mr. Williams located in Granite Falls, a rural town of little more than 2,000 inhabitants. After their return to North Carolina Mr. Williams and the former Mrs. Hendrix settled in the neighboring county in Pineola, a village of about 300 inhabitants. Since both families had been living in the area for many years, the local indignation appears to have been considerable. Unquestionably, the fact that state attorneys and judges hold elected offices must have had an impact on the prosecution and convictions. The sentences meted out were severe, not less than three nor more than ten years at hard labor for Mr. Williams, and a corresponding sentence of not less than three nor more than five years for Mrs. Hendrix. In the second trial the sentences were reduced to one to three years for Mr. Williams and eight to twenty-four months for Mrs. Hendrix. After the fundamental power of North Carolina to reexamine the jurisdiction of the Nevada divorce courts was upheld in *Williams II*, much of the interest of North Carolina in punishing the offenders was gone. Before having served any part of their sentences and upon recommendation of the parole authorities, the parties remarried in North Carolina on August 18, 1945, and were thereafter paroled.

A further dimension is opened if the social class of the participants is considered. In all probability the Williams and Hendrix families belonged to the middle classes. After their return from Nevada to North Carolina, Mr. Williams and Mrs. Hendrix participated in church activities. Their ill-fated attempt to obtain divorces in Nevada was obviously dictated by a desire to conform at least to the appearances of law and respectability. Had they belonged to the lower classes, for example, as migrant workers, it is most likely that no legal issues would have arisen. Their intent to remain in North Carolina would have been in doubt. Family breakdown would have occurred without formal divorce or remarriage; in other words, the so-called poor men's divorce of factual desertion would have changed the relationship. Even if they had later returned to the same vicinity in North Carolina, the local community and officials would probably have reacted to their sexual mores with indifference. Had one of the participants been killed in an accident, the survivor might well have been presumed to have been validly married for purposes of legal recovery, if necessary by a presumption that somehow and somewhere legal divorces were obtained. The length of the North Carolina citizenship of Mr. Williams and Mrs. Hendrix worked against them. Had they been in the state for only a year, North Carolina would have been less interested in the prosecution. Even if they had conformed to a migrant pattern after leaving the state, for example, by driving around the country in a camper or mobile home, it would have been considerably more difficult for the state to prove bigamy. Under such circumstances, a presumption of divorce might have been more durable than the Nevada divorces, known as a matter of record. As seen from this perspective, *Williams II* is perhaps directed toward a limited but important segment of the population, namely, middle-class persons who are likely to leave a clear documentary trail of their activities and travels. *Sherrer*, on the other hand, relieves some of the pressure in cases of participants to divorce proceedings who have established some measure of collaboration.

One of the arguments in favor of no-fault divorce was that a state's efforts to discourage divorce by requiring marital fault could so easily be thwarted by anyone wealthy or determined enough to go to Nevada or one of the other "divorce-mill" states that granted divorces readily. The effect of the *Williams* cases was that an *ex parte* migratory divorce could be good unless someone were to attack collaterally the finding of domicile. *Sherrer* meant further that if the unhappily married litigant could induce his or her spouse voluntarily to enter an appearance in the divorce, making it bilateral rather than *ex parte*, the migratory divorce would be insulated from most if not all collateral attacks. Some of the early no-fault divorce laws provided for simple dissolution if, as in bilateral migratory divorces, the spouses cooperated, but allowed a reluctant spouse to resist the efforts of one spouse to exit marriage, as *Williams II* allows the reluctant spouse to make a colateral attack on an *ex parte* migratory divorce.

REFERENCES

Hans W. Baade, *Marriage and Divorce in American Conflicts Law: Governmental Interests Analysis and the Restatement (Second)*, 72 COLUM. L. REV. 329 (1972).

Herbert R. Baer, *So Your Client Wants a Divorce! Williams v. North Carolina*, 24 N.C.L. REV. 1 (1945).

William H. Rodgers, Jr. & Linda A. Rodgers, *The Disparity Between Due Process and Full Faith and Credit: The Problem of the Somewhere Wife*, 67 COLUM. L. REV. 1363 (1967).

WHEAT v. WHEAT

Supreme Court of Arkansas
229 Ark. 842, 318 S.W.2d 793 (1958)

GEORGE ROSE SMITH, Justice.

The only question here is the validity of Act 36 of 1957, which added the following provision to the statute governing the matter of residence in divorce cases: "The word 'residence' as used in Section 34-1208 is defined to mean actual presence and upon proof of such the party alleging and offering such proof shall be considered domiciled in the State and this is declared to be the legislative intent and public policy of the State of Arkansas." Ark.Stats.1947, §34-1208.1. The effect of the 1957 statute is to substitute residence, in the sense of physical presence, for domicile as a jurisdictional requirement in divorce cases. The chancellor held the act unconstitutional and, finding that the plaintiff-appellant is not domiciled in Arkansas, dismissed his suit for divorce.

The parties were married in 1948 and were living in Maryland when they separated in 1952. The record does not show where the marriage ceremony was performed, but it was evidently in some state other than Arkansas. It is not contended that either of the parties had ever lived in Arkansas before the appellant came here in May of 1957. At that time he was transferred by his employer, a private corporation, to a station in Millington, Tennessee, which is some 20 miles northeast of West Memphis, Arkansas. Wheat rented an apartment in West Memphis and traveled back and forth each day to his work at Millington. After having thus resided in Arkansas for about three months Wheat filed this suit for a divorce, on the ground of three years separation. Mrs. Wheat, who is a resident of California, was served by warning order. She filed a crosscomplaint asking for separate maintenance, but she denied the court's jurisdiction to grant a divorce. Although Wheat testified that he intends to make Arkansas his home, the weight of the evidence supports the chancellor's finding that Wheat has not established his domicile in this state. Hence the case turns upon the validity of Act 36, by which the jurisdictional requirement of domicile was abolished.

The legal history that lay behind Act 36 is well known. The Civil Code of 1869 required the plaintiff in a divorce case to prove residence in the state for one year next before the commencement of the action. C. & M. Dig. §3505. In 1931 the legislature amended the statute to require only that the plaintiff prove residence for three months next before the judgment and for two months next before the commencement of the action. Ark.Stats. §34-1208. In 1932 we held that the amended statute meant residence only, not domicile. *Squire v. Squire*, 186 Ark. 511, 54 S.W.2d 281. This interpretation was followed until 1947, when we overruled the *Squire* case and held that the statutory reference to residence meant domicile. *Cassen v. Cassen*, 211 Ark. 582, 201 S.W.2d 585, noted in 2 Ark.L.Rev. 111. The *Cassen* case did not reach the constitutional question now presented, as the decision involved only an issue of statutory construction. It cannot be doubted that by Act 36 the legislature intended to restore the rule of the *Squire* case, for the emergency clause in the act refers specifically to that decision and to the *Cassen* case.

Although the wisdom of Act 36 is of no concern to the courts, since the law of divorce is purely statutory, *Squire v. Squire, supra, Young v. Young*, 207 Ark. 36, 178 S.W.2d 994, 152 A.L.R. 327, we may nevertheless observe that the act may well have been designed to prevent perjury. We know, of course, that the residential requirements for divorce vary greatly among the forty-nine states. In a decided majority of the states the plaintiff must have lived in the state for at least a year before filing suit. Louisiana and New York have no minimum period of residence, but their laws do not permit the courts to entertain cases where the state had no substantial connection with the marriage.

Arkansas is one of the five states in which the necessary period of residence is relatively short. In Idaho and Nevada the period is six weeks, in Wyoming sixty days, in Arkansas three months before judgment, and in Utah three months before the commencement of suit. At the time Act 36 was adopted all five of these states demanded proof of domicile as a condition to the granting of a divorce.

It is a matter of common knowledge that every year thousands of unhappily married persons, unable to obtain divorces at home, visit one or another of these five states in search of marital freedom. It is equally well known that the need for proof of domicile leads to perjury in a vast number of instances. The situation in Nevada, for example, has been described in these words:

> It has been estimated that 8,616 divorces were granted in Nevada in 1942 and 11,399 in 1943, the great majority of which must have been obtained by non-residents who went to Nevada solely for divorce purposes, remaining there only the required six weeks. All the while they contemplated returning to their home states immediately after their divorces were secured, yet they all swore falsely that they intended to make Nevada their permanent home, having been warned by local counsel that, unless they did so, they would be out of court. On advice of counsel they also took steps which would be accepted by the Nevada courts as corroborating their

> sworn statement but were actually nothing more than sham and camouflage. Upon such evidence the courts find that they acquired a Nevada domicil.

Lorenzen, *Extraterritorial Divorce — Williams v. North Carolina II*, 54 Yale Law Journal 799, 801. We should be less than candid if we did not concede that similar instances of perjury have taken place in Arkansas. Act 36 goes far toward freeing litigants from the temptation to swear falsely on the issue of domicile.

To hold the act invalid we must be able to assert that it conflicts with some particular clause in the state or federal constitution. Only two clauses seem sufficiently pertinent to warrant discussion.

First is the full faith and credit clause of the federal constitution, art. 4, §1. This clause is now construed to mean that a divorce decree is not entitled to recognition in other states unless one of the parties was domiciled in the state where the decree was rendered, *Williams v. State of North Carolina*, 317 U.S. 287, 63 S.Ct. 207, 87 L.Ed. 279, 143 A.L.R. 1273, with an exception which precludes either party from attacking the decree if the question of domicile was actually put in issue. *Sherrer v. Sherrer*, 334 U.S. 343, 68 S.Ct. 1087, 92 L.Ed. 1429, 1 A.L.R.2d 1355.

The full faith and credit clause deals only with the extent to which the decree is entitled to recognition elsewhere. It does not purport to say that the decree is not valid in the state where rendered; still less does it intimate that the courts cannot be authorized to act at all in the absence of proof of domicile.

We do not question the desirability of having Arkansas divorce decrees receive recognition in other states. That wish was the basic reason for the *Cassen* decision. But it must be remembered that a decree is not entitled to respect elsewhere merely because the statute exacts a showing of domicile as a condition to the maintenance of the suit, and this is true even though the court makes a finding that domicile does exist. The decree is still not conclusive of the issue, which may be re-examined in other jurisdictions. *Williams [II]*. Although Nevada ostensibly requires proof of domicile, we have refused to recognize a Nevada decree when the court's finding of domicile was clearly unsupported. *Cooper v. Cooper*, 225 Ark. 626, 284 S.W.2d 617. With or without Act 36 the acceptance of any particular Arkansas decree by a court in another state will ultimately depend upon whether that court believes that an Arkansas domicile really existed. Even if the act deprives the decree of prima facie extraterritorial validity when the Arkansas court fails to make a finding of domicile, it was for the legislature to say whether this disadvantage is outweighed by the beneficial consequences of the statute.

The other constitutional provision to be considered is the due process clause, Amend. 14. On this point the arguments on each side are examined in detail in the majority and minority opinions in *Alton v. Alton*, 3 Cir., 207 F.2d 667, appeal dismissed as moot 347 U.S. 610, 74 S.Ct. 736, 98 L.Ed. 987. See also *Granville-Smith v. Granville-Smith*, 349 U.S. 1, 75 S.Ct. 553, 99 L.Ed. 773. In the *Alton* case the Court of Appeals declared invalid a Virgin Islands statute which provided that six weeks residence should be prima facie evidence of domicile and, further, that if the defendant entered his appearance the court would have jurisdiction without reference to domicile. The facts were that Mrs. Alton brought suit for divorce after having resided in the Islands for the necessary six weeks. Her husband entered his appearance but made no defense. The trial court refused to grant a divorce without proof of domicile. The Court of Appeals, by a vote of four to three, sustained the trial court, holding that the statute denied due process of law.

We have studied the majority opinion in the *Alton* case with much care but do not find it convincing. The Fourteenth Amendment declares that no state shall deprive any person of life, liberty, or property without due process of law. The question at once arises: What person was denied due process in the *Alton* case? The majority's answer is hardly satisfying: "The question may well be asked as to what the lack of due process is. The defendant is not complaining. Nevertheless, if the jurisdiction for divorce continues to be based on domicile, as we think it does, we believe it to be lack of due process for one state to take to itself the readjustment of domestic relations between those domiciled elsewhere." [207 F.2d 677.] It will be seen that although [Mr.] Alton alone could have complained of a denial of due process and did not choose to do so, the court nevertheless found that his constitutional rights were somehow being violated.

In the case at bar Mrs. Wheat, unlike Alton, elects to contest the action for divorce and to attack the validity of Act 36. We may lay aside at the outset any question about procedural due process. It is not suggested that Mrs. Wheat is being denied notice or an opportunity to be heard. To the contrary, she invokes the court's jurisdiction by her request for separate maintenance. We also assume that there is no doubt about the power of the Arkansas courts to determine Mrs. Wheat's marital rights in any Arkansas property her husband may own.

The difficult question is raised by the theory, which was the basis for the *Alton* decision, that the marriage relationship is a *res* that remains always at the parties' common domicile, or at their separate domiciles, and is therefore beyond the reach of courts in other jurisdictions. See Rest., Conflict of Laws, §110; Leflar, Arkansas Law of Conflict of Laws, §133; and compare Corwin, *Out-Haddocking Haddock*, 93 Pa.L.Rev. 341. It will hardly do to sidestep this issue by merely observing that the marital status in the domiciliary jurisdiction will not be affected if our decree is not entitled to full faith and credit there.

With respect to the due process clause, as distinguished from the full faith and credit clause, we are not convinced that domicile must be the sole basis for the exercise of jurisdiction over the marriage relationship. As the court observed in *Wallace v. Wallace*, 63 N.M. 414, 320 P.2d 1020, 1022:

> Where domicile is a statutory jurisdictional prerequisite it is quite correct to say that jurisdiction for divorce is founded on this concept. It is quite another matter to flatly declare that there may be no other relation between a state and an individual which will create a sufficient interest in the state under the due process clause to give it power to decree divorces.... Precedent is not lacking for the conclusion that divorce jurisdiction can be founded on circumstances other than domicile.

The court concluded that a soldier's residence in the state for a year, although insufficient to establish domicile, was a reasonable basis for the exercise of jurisdiction over the marital status.

The appellee relies strongly upon the decision in *Jennings v. Jennings*, 251 Ala. 73, 36 So.2d 236, 3 A.L.R.2d 662, where the court held invalid a statute permitting nonresident couples to confer jurisdiction by consent and thus obtain a divorce in Alabama with no residence there at all. We agree with that decision, for there was no reasonable basis for the exercise of jurisdiction over the marital status.

It has been pointed out repeatedly that the theory of basing divorce jurisdiction solely on domicile has led to conflicting decisions and to legal confusion ever since the theory was first formulated in connection with the full faith and credit clause. Domicile differs from residence only in the existence of a subjective intent to remain more or less permanently in the particular state. Whether that intent exists on the part of a person who comes to Arkansas can seldom be proved with any measure of certainty. Often it is only after the court has decided this perplexing question that the lack of intent becomes apparent, as when the successful plaintiff immediately leaves the state. Although the court reached its decision in the utmost good faith, the want of domicile becomes retroactively so demonstrable that the issue must be decided the other way when the decree is relied upon in another state.

By Act 36 the legislature has substituted the simple requirement of three months residence, which can be proved with certainty, for the nebulous concept of domicile, which usually cannot be proved. We concede that the period of residence might be shortened so unreasonably, as in the *Jennings* case, as to indicate that the state has no reasonable basis for exercising jurisdiction over the marriage. We are not convinced, however, that the act before us is open to that criticism. Under the holding in *Squire v. Squire, supra*, the rule of Act 36 actually prevailed in this state for fifteen years. Now that the legislature has unmistakably expressed its intention in the matter, we do not feel that the due process clause compels us to say that its action is arbitrary.

Reversed.

[Concurring and dissenting opinions omitted.]

COMMENTS

Wheat exemplifies an alternative to the rigid conception of domicile for purposes of divorce jurisdiction. It also demonstrates that Justice Frankfurter's statement that no court in the English-speaking world has questioned the jurisdictional prerequisite of domicile cannot be maintained in its sweeping generality. According to the historical discussion in *Wheat*, Arkansas had a simple residence requirement at the time Justice Frankfurter made this assertion in *Williams v. North Carolina II* (p. 997). The Arkansas legislature declared and the Supreme Court of Arkansas in *Wheat* confirmed that to be present in the state is to be "domiciled" in Arkansas for purposes of divorce. Domicile for jurisdictional purposes is thereby openly reduced to a legal fiction; in other words, a party alleging and proving physical presence for the statutory period of time is deemed to be domiciled within Arkansas, although in fact this may not be the case. Nevada, by contrast, has retained the jurisdictional requirement of domicile, while the reality of migratory divorces might be similar there, at least in some of the cases, to the facts in *Wheat*.

The jurisdictional problem in *Wheat* is accentuated by further facts that appeared in the dissenting opinion, which quoted the trial court:

> ...Mr. Wheat is a native of Oklahoma and was formerly a school teacher in that State. His mother still resides in Oklahoma. He has a married sister in Fort Smith, Arkansas.
>
> Mr. Wheat, now about 57 years old, is employed by North American Aviation Corporation, whose headquarters are in Columbus, Ohio. The company has places of business all over the nation, especially around U.S.

> Air Force bases, and in foreign countries. Mr. Wheat is subject to transfer to a new location on 24-hour notice.
>
> The present Mrs. Wheat is plaintiff's third wife. The first wife went by way of a divorce in the State of Illinois; and the second one by the same route in the State of California. Dates of these events are not in the record. Plaintiff married the present Mrs. Wheat in February, 1948, but the place is not revealed. It was not in Arkansas. The parties never lived in Arkansas during their married life. They separated around July or August, 1952, in Leonardtown, Maryland.
>
> Following this separation, Mr. Wheat was transferred from Maryland to Florida, where he purchased a home and brought suit against the present Mrs. Wheat for divorce. Mrs. Wheat resisted the Florida suit and it was, on advice of Mr. Wheat's counsel, dismissed by Mr. Wheat. While living in Florida, Mr. Wheat wrote his wife and advised that he was finding happiness there and intended to make it his permanent home.
>
> After a little more than two years in Florida, Mr. Wheat was transferred to Columbus, Ohio, for two months and thence to California. Plaintiff volunteered the information that while in California he formed an intention to make that State his permanent home. Several months later he was transferred to Pennsylvania; and on May 1, 1957, his employer transferred Mr. Wheat to duty at the Naval Air Station, Millington, Tennessee (near Memphis).
>
> On the 3rd or 4th day of May, 1957, plaintiff rented a furnished apartment at a motel in West Memphis (Crittenden County), Arkansas, and has been using that as his home continuously since, to the extent that he sleeps there at night. He still (at the time of the depositions) has a Pennsylvania license plate on his automobile and operates under a California driver's license. He has not assessed his automobile or anything else for tax purposes in Arkansas. His official, and only, mail address is "P.O. Box 7, Memphis, Tennessee." He drives fifty miles daily to and from his work at Millington, Tennessee. He says he pays $110.00 a month rent for his furnished apartment; his landlady says he pays $80.00 a month. At least one or two other persons who came to Arkansas for a divorce have lived in the same motel but they do not still live there.
>
> Plaintiff makes no pretense that he intends to make Crittenden County his permanent home. Instead, he says, "I intend to go to the Ozarks in Arkansas" and settle down to a little farming and fishing.

These facts, significantly not stated in this form in the majority opinion, demonstrate the trial judge's underlying hostility to the plaintiff's claim and his way of life. The selection of facts is meant to show that the plaintiff is an unstable person, of questionable veracity, and scheming to obtain a divorce. Even if plaintiff is telling the truth, the trial judge states derogatorily that he "makes no pretense that he intends to make Crittenden County his permanent home." Although there is no logical connection between the alleged characteristics of the plaintiff and the unconstitutionality of the Arkansas statute, the conclusion of the trial court appears to be foregone. The complaint was to be dismissed and, since this was the only way to reach this result, the Arkansas statute was held to be unconstitutional. Actual, not fictional domicile was declared to be a jurisdictional requirement, albeit absent in this instance.

From a policy standpoint many factors, in addition to those stated in the majority opinion, speak for giving the plaintiff a forum for his request for divorce. Like military persons, with whom he is closely associated, he appears to be under a legal obligation, based here on express contractual stipulation, not to form a permanent home in any place. However, as an employee of a multinational enterprise — and there are thousands of them — he cannot claim the benefits of special jurisdictional statutes that have been enacted in many states for the military. A life subject to continued change, without this necessarily reflecting negatively on the plaintiff's character, is also likely to strain marriages. The plaintiff's earlier claims that he wanted to stay permanently in Florida or California may well have been true; his transfers were beyond his control. His declared intention to retire in Arkansas may have been equally true, because his sister was living in the state and he had been born in neighboring Oklahoma. To insist that he bring an action at his domicile of origin, Oklahoma, perhaps under a theory that he had not established any new domicile since he left, appears to be unreasonable because Mrs. Wheat had never had any relationship to that state, certainly no more than to Arkansas, and Mr. Wheat's relationship may have been remote at this point.

On the other hand, it may seem unfair to the nonresident wife to require her to defend her marital status not only in whatever domicile her estranged husband may adopt, but perhaps also in a state where he merely resides for a statutory period. Perhaps divorce courts, especially if domicile is not an exclusive jurisdictional requirement, should be more willing to dismiss actions on the basis of *forum non conveniens* — an approach that would apparently have been available to the chancellor in *Wheat.* One dire prediction, by Chief Justice Harris in his concurring opinion to *Wheat,* that "any divorce granted under the provisions of this statute, in numerous of our sister states, will probably be worth only the paper it is written on," has not come true. Other states have recognized Arkansas divorces even though arguably their own domiciliaries were involved. For example, in *Staples v. Staples,* 232 So.2d 904 (Ct. App.2d Cir. La. 1970), the Louisiana appellate court upheld an *ex parte* divorce from Arkansas, as it had upheld a bilateral Arkansas divorce in *Reeves v. Reeves,* 209 So.2d 554 (Ct. App.2d Cir. La. 1968). Yet, in both cases the trial courts had refused full faith and credit to the divorces. It might seem that under *Sherrer* (*supra,* p. 1007), the *Reeves* trial court would have to uphold the bilateral divorce; but in *Sherrer* the Florida court had found actual domicile, and it was this finding the Court refused to allow to be relitigated in a sister state.

Wheat prominently mentions as a policy sustaining the constitutional validity of the Arkansas statute that it is meant to prevent perjury. Yet "perjury" may be a questionable term to describe the testimony traditionally presented in states like Nevada. Even the judges must be aware of the probable falsity of testimony that a petitioner intends to establish Nevada as a permanent home. What we may have is fictitious pleadings for purposes of obtaining jurisdiction. Such fictitious pleadings have a long history in English common law. For example, the courts, in order to obtain jurisdiction, permitted pleas that the debtor was located in the county of Middlesex although in fact he was not. However, what may be a valid scholarly explanation may not necessarily be equally valid for legal practice. In some jurisdictions, such as Alabama, judges, acting within their inherent powers, have set aside divorces because an alleged fraud — false swearing to the jurisdictional facts — was perpetrated upon the court. In one instance, *Hartigan v. Hartigan*, 272 Ala. 67, 128 So.2d 725 (1961), the judge acting *ex officio* vacated a divorce decree six years after the husband had remarried.

Such harsh decisions are to some extent beyond the control of the bar and also unrelated to the relative ease of grounds for divorce. They are the result of the political climate within a given state. Lower court judges are, as elected officials in most states, intensely dependent on local politics; they may be voted out of office following clean-up campaigns. The judge who sets aside a divorce judgment for an alleged fraud on the court may not be the same judge who rendered the decision years earlier. A lawyer would be ill-advised, even today, to make the fate of divorces and remarriage depend on such contingencies.

ESTIN v. ESTIN
United States Supreme Court
334 U.S. 541 (1948)

Mr. Justice DOUGLAS delivered the opinion of the Court.

This case, here on certiorari to the Court of Appeals of New York, presents an important question under the Full Faith and Credit Clause of the Constitution. Article IV, §1. It is whether a New York decree awarding respondent $180 per month for her maintenance and support in a separation proceeding survived a Nevada divorce decree which subsequently was granted petitioner.

The parties were married in 1937 and lived together in New York until 1942 when the husband left the wife. There was no issue of the marriage. In 1943 she brought an action against him for a separation. He entered a general appearance. The court, finding that he had abandoned her, granted her a decree of separation and awarded her $180 per month as permanent alimony. In January 1944 he went to Nevada where in 1945 he instituted an action for divorce. She was notified of the action by constructive service but entered no appearance in it. In May, 1945, the Nevada court, finding that petitioner had been a bona fide resident of Nevada since January 30, 1944, granted him an absolute divorce "on the ground of three years continual separation, without cohabitation." The Nevada decree made no provision for alimony, though the Nevada court had been advised of the New York decree.

Prior to that time petitioner had made payments of alimony under the New York decree. After entry of the Nevada decree he ceased paying. Thereupon respondent sued in New York for a supplementary judgment for the amount of the arrears. Petitioner appeared in the action and moved to eliminate the alimony provisions of the separation decree by reason of the Nevada decree. The Supreme Court denied the motion and granted respondent judgment for the arrears. 63

N.Y.S.2d 476. The judgment was affirmed by the Appellate Division, 271 App.Div. 829, 66 N.Y.S.2d 421, and then by the Court of Appeals. 296 N.Y. 308, 73 N.E.2d 113.

We held in *Williams v. North Carolina*, 317 U.S. 287; 325 U.S. 226, (1) that a divorce decree granted by a State to one of its domiciliaries is entitled to full faith and credit in a bigamy prosecution brought in another State, even though the other spouse was given notice of the divorce proceeding only through constructive service; and (2) that while the finding of domicile by the court that granted the decree is entitled to *prima facie* weight, it is not conclusive in a sister State but might be relitigated there. And see *Esenwein v. Esenwein* , 325 U.S. 279. The latter course was followed in this case, as a consequence of which the Supreme Court of New York found, in accord with the Nevada court, that petitioner "is now and since January 1944, has been a bona fide resident of the State of Nevada."

Petitioner's argument therefore is that the tail must go with the hide — that since by the Nevada decree, recognized in New York, he and respondent are no longer husband and wife, no legal incidence of the marriage remains. We are given a detailed analysis of New York law to show that the New York courts have no power either by statute or by common law to compel a man to support his ex-wife, that alimony is payable only so long as the relation of husband and wife exists, and that in New York, as in some other states, see *Esenwein v. Esenwein* , *supra*, 325 U.S. page 280, a support order does not survive divorce.

The difficulty with that argument is that the highest court in New York has held in this case that a support order can survive divorce and that this one has survived petitioner's divorce. That conclusion is binding on us, except as it conflicts with the Full Faith and Credit Clause. It is not for us to say whether that ruling squares with what the New York courts said on earlier occasions. It is enough that New York today says that such is her policy. The only question for us is whether New York is powerless to make such a ruling in view of the Nevada decree.

We can put to one side the case where the wife was personally served or where she appears in the divorce proceedings. Cf. *Yarborough v. Yarborough*, 290 U.S. 202; *Davis v. Davis*, 305 U.S. 32; *Sherrer v. Sherrer*, [334 U.S. 343]; *Coe v. Coe*, [334 U.S. 378]. The only service on her in this case was by publication and she made no appearance in the Nevada proceeding. The requirements of procedural due process were satisfied and the domicile of the husband in Nevada was foundation for a decree effecting a change in the marital capacity of both parties in all the other States of the Union, as well as in Nevada. *Williams v. North Carolina*, 317 U.S. 287. But the fact that marital capacity was changed does not mean that every other legal incidence of the marriage was necessarily affected.

Although the point was not adjudicated in *Barber v. Barber*, 21 How. 582, 588, the Court in that case recognized that while a divorce decree obtained in Wisconsin by a husband from his absent wife might dissolve the vinculum of the marriage, it did not mean that he was freed from payment of alimony under an earlier separation decree granted by New York. An absolutist might quarrel with the result and demand a rule that once a divorce is granted, the whole of the marriage relation is dissolved, leaving no roots or tendrils of any kind. But there are few areas of the law in black and white. The greys are dominant and even among them the shades are innumerable. For the eternal problem of the law is one of making accommodations between conflicting interests. This is why most legal problems end as questions of degree. That is true of the present problem under the

Full Faith and Credit Clause. The question involves important considerations both of law and of policy which it is essential to state.

The situations where a judgment of one State has been denied full faith and credit in another State, because its enforcement would contravene the latter's policy, have been few and far between. See *Williams v. North Carolina*, 317 U.S. 287, 294–295; *Magnolia Petroleum Co. v. Hunt*, 320 U.S. 430, 438–439, and cases cited; *Sherrer v. Sherrer, supra.* The Full Faith and Credit Clause is not to be applied, accordion-like, to accommodate our personal predilections. It substituted a command for the earlier principles of comity and thus basically altered the status of the States as independent sovereigns. *Williams v. North Carolina*, 317 U.S. 287, 301–302; *Sherrer v. Sherrer, supra.* It ordered submission by one State even to hostile policies reflected in the judgment of another State, because the practical operation of the federal system, which the Constitution designed, demanded it. The fact that the requirements of full faith and credit, so far as judgments are concerned, are exacting, if not inexorable (*Sherrer v. Sherrer, supra*), does not mean, however, that the State of the domicile of one spouse may, through the use of constructive service, enter a decree that changes every legal incidence of the marriage relationship.

Marital status involves the regularity and integrity of the marriage relation. It affects the legitimacy of the offspring of marriage. It is the basis of criminal laws, as the bigamy prosecution in *Williams v. North Carolina* dramatically illustrates. The State has a considerable interest in preventing bigamous marriages and in protecting the offspring of marriages from being bastardized. The interest of the State extends to its domiciliaries. The State should have the power to guard its interest in them by changing or altering their marital status and by protecting them in that changed status throughout the farthest reaches of the nation. For a person domiciled in one State should not be allowed to suffer the penalties of bigamy for living outside the State with the only one which the State of his domicile recognizes as his lawful wife. And children born of the only marriage which is lawful in the State of his domicile should not carry the stigma of bastardy when they move elsewhere. These are matters of legitimate concern to the State of the domicile. They entitle the State of the domicile to bring in the absent spouse through constructive service. In no other way could the State of the domicile have and maintain effective control of the marital status of its domiciliaries.

Those are the considerations that have long permitted the State of the matrimonial domicile to change the marital status of the parties by an *ex parte* divorce proceeding, *Thompson v. Thompson*, 226 U.S. 551, considerations which in the *Williams* cases we thought were equally applicable to any State in which one spouse had established a bona fide domicile. See 317 U.S. pp. 300–301. But those considerations have little relevancy here. In this case New York evinced a concern with this broken marriage when both parties were domiciled in New York and before Nevada had any concern with it. New York was rightly concerned lest the abandoned spouse be left impoverished and perhaps become a public charge. The problem of her livelihood and support is plainly a matter in which her community had a legitimate interest. The New York court, having jurisdiction over both parties, undertook to protect her by granting her a judgment of permanent alimony. Nevada, however, apparently follows the rule that dissolution of the marriage puts and end to a support order. See *Herrick v. Herrick*, 55 Nev. 59, 68, 25 P.2d 378, 380. But the question is whether Nevada could under any circumstances adjudicate rights of respondent under the New York judgment when she was not personally served or did not appear in the proceeding.

Bassett v. Bassett, 141 F.2d 954, held that Nevada could not. We agree with that view.

The New York judgment is a property interest of respondent, created by New York in a proceeding in which both parties were present. It imposed obligations on petitioner and granted rights to respondent. The property interest which it created was an intangible, jurisdiction over which cannot be exerted through control over a physical thing. Jurisdiction over an intangible can indeed only arise from control or power over the persons whose relationships are the source of the rights and obligations. Cf. *Curry v. McCanless*, 307 U.S. 357, 366.

Jurisdiction over a debtor is sufficient to give the State of his domicile some control over the debt which he owes.... But we are aware of no power which the State of domicile of the debtor has to determine the personal rights of the creditor in the intangible unless the creditor has been personally served or appears in the proceeding. The existence of any such power has been repeatedly denied....

We know of no source of power which would take the present case out of that category. The Nevada decree that is said to wipe out respondent's claim for alimony under the New York judgment is nothing less than an attempt by Nevada to restrain respondent from asserting her claim under that judgment. That is an attempt to exercise an *in personam* jurisdiction over a person not before the court. That may not be done. Since Nevada had no power to adjudicate respondent's rights in the New York judgment, New York need not give full faith and credit to that phase of Nevada's judgment. A judgment of a court having no jurisdiction to render it is not entitled to the full faith and credit which the Constitution and statute of the United States demand. *Hansberry v. Lee*, 311 U.S. 32, 40–41; *Williams v. North Carolina*, 325 U.S. 226, 229, and cases cited.

The result in this situation is to make the divorce divisible — to give effect to the Nevada decree insofar as it affects marital status and to make it ineffective on the issue of alimony. It accommodates the interests of both Nevada and New York in this broken marriage by restricting each State to the matters of her dominant concern.

Since Nevada had no jurisdiction to alter respondent's rights in the New York judgment, we do not reach the further question whether in any event that judgment would be entitled to full faith and credit in Nevada.... And it will be time enough to consider the effect of any discrimination shown to out-of-state *ex parte* divorces when a State makes that its policy.

Affirmed.

Mr. Justice FRANKFURTER, dissenting.

The Court's opinion appears to rest on three independent grounds:

(1) New York may, consistently with the Full Faith and Credit Clause, hold that a prior separate maintenance decree of one of its courts survives a decree of divorce within the scope of enforceability of the rule in *Williams v. North Carolina*, 317 U.S. 287, whether such divorce is granted in New York or by a sister State;

(2) By virtue of its interest in preventing its citizens from becoming public charges, New York may constitutionally provide that a domestic separate maintenance decree survives a sister-State divorce decree which must be respected in New York under the rule in the first *Williams* case, *supra*;

(3) A separate maintenance decree creates an obligation which may not, consistently with due process, be extinguished by a court lacking personal jurisdiction of the obligee, though possessed of jurisdiction to terminate her marital status, and any judgment purporting to do so is not entitled to extra-State recognition.

To the first of these grounds I assent, and if such is the law of New York I agree that the decision of the New York Court of Appeals in this case must be upheld. It is for New York to decide whether its decrees for separate maintenance survive divorce or terminate with it, provided, of course, that its decision is not a mere attempt to defeat a federal right, given by the Full Faith and Credit Clause, under the guise of a determination of State law. Cf. *Davis v. Wechsler*, 263 U.S. 22, 24–25.

The second ground presents difficulties. I cannot agree that New York's interest in its residents would justify New York in giving less effect to an enforceable Nevada divorce granted to one domiciled in Nevada, against a spouse not personally served, than it would give to a valid New York divorce similarly obtained. As to this, I agree with the views of by brother Jackson. If, on the other hand, New York does not so discriminate against enforceable "ex parte" divorce decrees granted by a sister State, no problem under the Full Faith and Credit Clause arises.

Furthermore, if the respondent had obtained her separate maintenance decree in Pennsylvania — which treats such decrees as terminated by any valid divorce, see *Esenwein v. Esenwein*, 325 U.S. 279 — and had subsequently moved to New York and there brought a suit based on the Pennsylvania decree, it is clear that New York's interest in preventing the respondent from becoming a public charge would not justify refusal to treat the separate maintenance decree as having been terminated. New York would be required to refer to the law of Pennsylvania to determine whether the maintenance decree of that Commonwealth had survived the Nevada divorce, and, finding that it had not, the New York courts could not enforce it.

My difficulty with the third ground of the Court's opinion is that Nevada did not purport, so far as the record discloses, to rule on the survival of the New York separate maintenance decree. Nevada merely established a change in status. It was for New York to determine the effect, with reference to its own law, of that change in status. If it was the law of New York that divorce put an end to its separate maintenance decree, the respondent's decree would have been terminated not by the Nevada divorce but by the consequences, under the New York law, of a change in status, even though brought about by Nevada. Similarly, Nevada could not adjudicate rights in New York realty, but, if New York law provided for dower, a Nevada divorce might or might not terminate a dower interest in New York realty depending on whether or not New York treated dower rights as extinguished by divorce.

If the Nevada decree, insofar as it affected the New York separate maintenance decree, were violative of due process, New York of course would not have to give effect to it. It could not do so even if it wished. If the Nevada decree involved a violation of due process there is an end of the matter and other complicated issues need not be considered! It would not matter whether New York had a special interest in preventing its residents from becoming public charges, or whether New York treated maintenance decrees as surviving a valid divorce.

Accordingly, the crucial issue, as I see it, is whether New York has held that *no* "ex parte" divorce decree could terminate a prior New York separate maintenance decree, or whether it has decided merely that no "ex parte" divorce decree of another State could. The opinion of the Court of Appeals leaves this crucial issue in doubt. The prior decisions of the New York courts do not dispel my doubts.

Neither do the cases cited in the Court of Appeals' opinion, which, with the exception of *Wagster v. Wagster*, 193 Ark. 902, do not involve "ex parte" domestic divorces. New York may legitimately decline to allow any "ex parte" divorce to dissolve its prior separate maintenance decree, but it may not, consistently with *Williams v. North Carolina*, 317 U.S. 287, discriminate against a Nevada decree granted to one there domiciled, and afford it less effect than it gives to a decree of its own with similar jurisdictional foundation. I cannot be sure which it has done.

I am reinforced in these views by Mr. Justice JACKSON's dissent. As a New York lawyer and the Justice assigned to the Second Circuit, he is presumably not without knowledge of New York law. The Court's opinion is written in a spirit of certitude that the New York law is contrary to that which Mr. Justice JACKSON assumes it to be. Thus, on the issue that I deem decisive of the question whether New York has given full faith and credit to the Nevada decree — namely, whether under New York's law divorce decrees based on publication terminate support — her law has thus far not spoken with ascertainable clarity. I would therefore remand the case to the New York Court of Appeals for clarification of its rationale. "...It is...important that ambiguous or obscure adjudications by state courts do not stand as barriers to a determination by this Court of the validity under the federal constitution of state action. Intelligent exercise of our appellate powers compels us to ask for the elimination of the obscurities and ambiguities from the opinions in such cases." *Minnesota v. National Tea Co.*, 309 U.S. 551, 557.

Mr. Justice JACKSON, dissenting.

If there is one thing that the people are entitled to expect from their lawmakers, it is rules of law that will enable individuals to tell whether they are married and, if so, to whom. Today many people who have simply lived in more than one state do not know, and the most learned lawyer cannot advise them with any confidence. The uncertainties that result are not merely technical, nor are they trivial; they affect fundamental rights and relations such as the lawfulness of their cohabitation, their children's legitimacy, their title to property, and even whether they are law-abiding persons or criminals. In a society as mobile and nomadic as ours, such uncertainties affect large numbers of people and create a social problem of some magnitude. It is therefore important that, whatever we do, we shall not add to the confusion. I think that this decision does just that.

These parties lived together in New York State during their entire married life. Courts of that State granted judgment of separation, with award of alimony to the wife, in October 1943. Three months later the husband journeyed to Nevada and in three more months began a divorce action. No process was served on the wife in Nevada; she was put on notice only by constructive service through publication in New York. Notified thus of what was going on, she was put to this choice: to go to Nevada and fight a battle, hopeless under Nevada laws, to keep her New York judgment, or to do nothing. She did nothing, and the Nevada court granted the husband a divorce without requiring payment of alimony.

Now the question is whether the New York judgment of separation or the Nevada judgment of divorce controls the present obligation to pay alimony. The New York judgment of separation is based on the premise that the parties remain husband and wife, though estranged, and hence the obligation of support, incident to marriage, continues. The Nevada decree is based on the contrary premise that the marriage no longer exists and so obligations dependent on it have ceased.

The Court reaches the Solomon-like conclusion that the Nevada decree is half good and half bad under the full faith and credit clause. It is good to free the husband from the marriage; it is not good to free him from its incidental obligations. Assuming the judgment to be one which the Constitution requires to be recognized at all, I do not see how we can square this decision with the command that it be given *full* faith and credit. For reasons which I stated in dissenting in *Williams v. North Carolina*, 317 U.S. 287, I would not give standing under the clause to constructive service divorces obtained on short residence. But if we are to hold this divorce good, I do not see how it can be less good than a divorce would be if rendered by the courts of New York.

As I understand New York law, if, after a decree of separation and alimony, the husband had obtained a New York divorce against his wife, it would terminate her right to alimony. If the Nevada judgment is to have full faith and credit, I think it must have the same effect that a similar New York decree would have. I do not see how we can hold that it must be accepted for some purposes and not for others, that he is free of his former marriage but still may be jailed, as he may in New York, for not paying the maintenance of a woman whom the Court is compelled to consider as no longer his wife.

VANDERBILT v. VANDERBILT

United States Supreme Court
354 U.S. 416 (1957)

Mr. Justice BLACK delivered the opinion of the Court.

Cornelius Vanderbilt, Jr., petitioner, and Patricia Vanderbilt, respondent, were married in 1948. They separated in 1952 while living in California. The wife moved to New York where she has resided since February 1953. In March of that year the husband filed suit for divorce in Nevada. This proceeding culminated, in June 1953, with a decree of final divorce which provided that both husband and wife were "freed and released from the bonds of matrimony and all the duties and obligations thereof...."[1] The wife was not served with process in Nevada and did not appear before the divorce court.

In April 1954, Mrs. Vanderbilt instituted an action in a New York court praying for separation from petitioner and for alimony. The New York court did not have personal jurisdiction over him, but in order to satisfy his obligations, if any, to Mrs. Vanderbilt, it sequestered his property within the State.[2] He appeared specially and, among other defenses to the action, contended that the Full Faith and Credit Clause of the United States Constitution compelled the New York court to treat the Nevada divorce as having ended the marriage and as having destroyed any duty of support which he owed the respondent. While the New York court found the Nevada decree valid and held that it had effectively dissolved the marriage, it nevertheless entered an order, under §1170-b of the New York Civil Practice Act, directing petitioner to make designated support payments to respondent. 207 Misc. 294, 138 N.Y.S.2d 222. The New York Court of Appeals upheld the support order. 1 N.Y.2d 342, 135 N.E.2d 553. Petitioner then applied to this Court

1. It seems clear that in Nevada the effect of this decree was to put an end to the husband's duty to support the wife — provided, of course, that the Nevada courts had power to do this. *Sweney v. Sweeney*, 42 Nev. 431, 438–439, 179 P. 638, 639–640; *Herrick v. Herrick*, 55 Nev. 59, 68, 25 P.2d 378, 380. See *Estin v. Estin*, 334 U.S. 541.

for certiorari contending that §1170-b, as applied, is unconstitutional because it contravenes the Full Faith and Credit Clause. We granted certiorari, 352 U.S. 820.

In *Estin v. Estin*, 334 U.S. 541, this Court decided that a Nevada divorce court, which had no personal jurisdiction over the wife, had no power to terminate a husband's obligation to provide her support as required in a pre-existing New York separation decree. The factor which distinguishes the present case from *Estin* is that here the wife's right to support had not been reduced to judgment prior to the husband's *ex parte* divorce. In our opinion this difference is not material on the question before us. Since the wife was not subject to its jurisdiction, the Nevada divorce court had no power to extinguish any right which she had under the law of New York to financial support from her husband. It has long been the constitutional rule that a court cannot adjudicate a personal claim or obligation unless it has jurisdiction over the person of the defendant.[6] Here, the Nevada divorce court was as powerless to cut off the wife's support right as it would have been to order the husband to pay alimony if the wife had brought the divorce action and he had not been subject to the divorce court's jurisdiction. Therefore, the Nevada decree, to the extent it purported to affect the wife's right to support, was void and the Full Faith and Credit Clause did not obligate New York to give it recognition.

...

Affirmed.

...

COMMENTS

The question, already asked after *Williams v. North Carolina I* and *II*, whether no-fault legislation has affected the principles of migratory divorce pronounced by the U.S. Supreme Court arises again. In this instance "divisible divorce" is involved, that is, the theory that aspects of marriage related to status are to be treated differently from consequences of marriage considered to be proprietary in nature. The status aspects of divorce are supposed to be *in rem* or at least *quasi in rem*, while the proprietary matters are *in personam. Estin* characterizes support and alimony claims, if reduced to judgment, as proprietary in nature. Thus the claims of the out-of-state creditor, that is the wife, cannot be dismissed in an *ex parte* proceeding when the marital status is validly terminated. *Vanderbilt* extends this holding, as far as New York law was concerned, to cover support claims not yet reduced to judgment. The availability of no-fault divorce might or might not have an impact upon this legal development. Some argue that the position of New York law expressed in *Estin* and *Vanderbilt* is too extreme and that as the law of divorce becomes increasingly uniform, states should be more inclined to recognize the jurisdiction of a sister state to adjudicate support and alimony claims. Yet, the central issue in *Estin* and *Vanderbilt* was the absence of personal jurisdiction over the spouse whose support rights the divorce purported to extinguish. It seems clear that without personal jurisdiction over the other party, a divorcing spouse could not *obtain* a money judgment for support; it would be unfair to allow a

6. *Pennoyer v. Neff*, 95 U.S. 714, 726–727. If a defendant has property in a State it can adjudicate his obligations, but only to the extent of his interest in that property. *Pennington v. Fourth Nat. Bank of Cincinnati*, 243 U.S. 269; *Harris v. Balk*, 198 U.S. 215.

divorcing spouse without personal jurisdiction over the other party to bar that party from ever receiving a money judgment for support. Much as Nevada was considered a divorce mill jurisdiction, at the time *Estin* and *Vanderbilt* were decided New York could have been called a "support and alimony mill." In *Vanderbilt*, for example, the parties chose the jurisdictions likely to be favorable to their financial positions. After they separated in California, the husband moved to Nevada and the wife to New York. With considerable wealth at stake, they probably sought legal advice in contemplating their moves.

In spite of no-fault divorce, forum shopping is still part of our reality. This does not necessarily mean that millions of dollars must be involved. Any accumulation of assets, including entitlements, may result in divorce planning by lawyers. A party may strengthen his or her bargaining position by being the first to file a divorce action in a jurisdiction more favorable in regard to alimony and property division than the jurisdiction of the opponent. The time of filing may be an important factor. If, for example, a spouse files in one state, that spouse may enjoin the other spouse from filing in another state, even if the second state has some interest in the marriage. The place of filing may be equally important because principles of "equitable distribution," even when adhered to by both jurisdictions, may be applied quite differently from state to state, regardless of seemingly uniform no-fault legislation.

Actually, divorce jurisdiction and the questions of choices involved may become additional bargaining tools in lawyers' offices, together with potential grounds that are more substantive in nature. Theoretically, of course, jurisdiction is not subject to negotiation in common law countries; but practically, it is within the power of clients to change residences and of lawyers, to some extent, to select and emphasize the facts that establish jurisdiction in one court rather than in another. Thus the whole jurisdictional problem inevitably becomes part of the bargaining process, especially in cases where reality is sufficiently ambiguous to permit multiple interpretations. What actually transpires before the trial courts may show nothing of these jurisdictional negotiations.

Perhaps one impact of no-fault divorce is that lawyers now resolve jurisdictional disagreements. Since jurisdictional issues do not even reach the chancellor, much less the appellate courts, these issues have less visibility than at the time of *Estin* and *Vanderbilt*. But it would be a mistake to believe that problems have declined in importance simply because they have become less visible. A comparison of cases in this book shows the great divergence of jurisdictions in regard to consequences of no-fault divorce, for example, pure no-fault in regard to proprietary consequences of divorce in Iowa (see *In re Marriage of Williams*, p. 549) and the lingering concept of fault in Florida (see *McClelland v. McClelland*, p. 603). It still makes a difference, in terms of proprietary consequences of no-fault divorce, whether the action was filed in California, Iowa, Florida, or even in New York. In New York, much of the preexisting law of divorce consequences may still be effective, at least for purposes of argument, in spite of the availability of no-fault grounds.

The questions of continued interest can be summarized as follows: Is it realistic to differentiate between aspects of divorce that relate to status and those that relate to finances? If a divorce in one state is recognized in another for purposes of severing status, but disregarded in economical respects — an option that courts created to keep deserving wives from being cut off from support rights by a foreign divorce — what happens to the intervening equities of new spouses who may find that a prior marriage clouds their entitlement? What happens in jurisdictions other than the two competing states? That is, which position should they follow if a divorce is effective as to marital status, but not as to proprietary consequences of the dissolution of status? When, and in what jurisdictions, is support an incident of marriage and when is it a separate proprietary right? Which rights in marriage are "vested," and which are "inchoate"? The answers to these and other questions may continue to vary from jurisdiction to jurisdiction, and within each jurisdiction sometimes from case to case. Uniformity in answers, not yet achieved, is not necessarily desirable. Although it facilitates prediction and decisions, at the same time it damages the range of lawyers' arguments and limits the discretion of the courts.

Foreign Cases

HYDE v. HYDE

Supreme Court of Tennessee
562 S.W.2d 194 (Tenn. 1978)

FONES, Justice.

Appellant, Divorce Referee of Shelby County, appeals from a declaratory judgment validating, "for reasons of equity and comity", a divorce awarded by a court in the Dominican Republic.

On November 21, 1974, Eleanor Lentz Hyde was awarded a decree of divorce by the Court of First Instance of the Judicial District of Santo Domingo, Dominican Republic. She appeared in person and was represented by an attorney. Joseph R. Hyde, III, was not personally present but was represented by his attorney in fact, by virtue of a power of attorney filed with the Court. These appearances fully satisfied the laws of the Dominican Republic with respect to jurisdiction of divorce actions. The divorce was granted on the ground of incompatibility of temperaments, making life together unbearable. Both parties to the marriage are residents of Memphis, and were residents of Memphis at the time of the divorce.

Joseph Hyde filed this suit in the Chancery Court of Shelby County on November 4, 1976, seeking a declaratory judgment that the Dominican Republic decree was valid, or in the alternative, seeking a divorce. He alleged that prior to October, 1974, the parties were preparing to file suit against each other in the courts of Shelby County, Tennessee, but they effected an agreement settling their property rights and providing for the support of their minor child; that they were then confronted by the prospect of an extensive delay before a divorce could be obtained due to the backlog of divorce cases in Shelby County. Being desirous of returning to the status of unmarried people...both parties submitted to the jurisdiction of the Dominican Republic court and obtained a no fault divorce, believed in good faith to be valid.

Eleanor Lentz Hyde answered, admitting those allegations and insisting that comity be granted and the foreign decree, but in the alternative, also counter-claiming for divorce. Thus, in the Tennessee courts, both parties assert the validity of the foreign decree, neither raises any question as to the jurisdiction of the Dominican Republic court over the parties or the subject matter for the purpose of the 1974 proceeding, and they continue to assert that each is bound by the 1974 property settlement agreement. The Divorce Referee appeared in the action to contest the validity of the Dominican Republic decree. The Chancellor granted summary judgment for plaintiff in the declaratory judgment action, and the Divorce Referee perfected a direct appeal to this Court.

Because the decree for which recognition is sought is that of a foreign nation, the sole question here is whether Tennessee will grant comity to the divorce. We have not found any case in which Tennessee courts have considered the question of what effect, should be given a judicial decree from a foreign nation, but the courts of this state have recognized the doctrine of comity in cases where the rights of parties under the laws of other states were at issue, and recognition was not obligatory under the Full Faith and Credit Clause....

The rule of comity to be gleaned from these cases is that, where the law of another jurisdiction is applicable, Tennessee will enforce the substantive rights which litigants have under the laws of the other jurisdiction if such rights are not contrary to the policy of Tennessee....

Resting as it does on the non-obligatory discretion of the forum, comity defies both precise definition and uniform rules of practice. The oft-cited case of *Hilton v. Guyot*, 159 U.S. 113, 16 S.Ct. 139, 40 L.Ed. 95 (1895), which contains a thorough examination of the basic principles of comity, defines it as follows:

> "Comity," in the legal sense, is neither a matter of absolute obligation on the one hand, nor of mere courtesy and good will upon the other. But it is the recognition which one nation allows within its territory to the legislative, executive, or judicial acts of another nation, having due regard both to international duty and convenience, and to the rights of its own citizens, or of other persons who are under the protection of its laws.
>
> ...
>
> [S]peaking of the difficulty of applying the positive rules laid down by the Continental jurists,... [Mr. Justice Story] says that "there is indeed, great truth" in these remarks of Mr. Justice Porter, speaking for the supreme court of Louisiana: "They have attempted to go too far, to define and fix that which cannot, in the nature of things, be defined and fixed. They seem to have forgotten that they wrote on a question which touched the comity of nations, and that comity is, and ever must be, uncertain; that it must necessarily depend on a variety of circumstances which cannot be reduced to any certain rule; that no nation will suffer the laws of another to interfere with her own to the injury of her citizens[;] that whether they do or not must depend on the condition of the country in which the foreign law is sought to be enforced, the particular nature of her legislation, her policy, and the character of her institutions; that in the conflict of laws it must often be a matter of doubt which should prevail..." (citation omitted). 159 U.S. at 163–165, 16 S.Ct. at 143, 40 L.Ed. at 108–09.

Thus, comity is a discretionary doctrine and may be granted or withheld depending on the particular facts, laws and policies present in an individual case.

In this case, the public policy of this state as reflected by its grounds and jurisdictional requirements for divorce are the issues to be examined in determining the propriety of granting comity.

The majority of states do not grant comity to divorces rendered in foreign jurisdictions where neither spouse was actually domiciled, even where both parties voluntarily submitted to the jurisdiction of the rendering court. See Annotation, 13 A.L.R.3d 1419 (1967).

New York, on the other hand, recognizes foreign divorce decrees valid under the laws of the nation rendering them where the plaintiff spouse appeared personally and the defendant spouse voluntarily appeared through attorney, even though neither party was domiciled there in the Anglo-American legal sense, and the grounds on which the foreign divorce was granted were not recognized in New York. *Rosenstiel v. Rosenstiel*, 16 N.Y.2d 64, 262 N.Y.S.2d 86, 209 N.E.2d 709 (1965). Granting comity in the instant case will not require that we go as far from the majority rule as the New York courts have gone.

The public policy of a state is to be found in its constitution, its statutes, and the decisions of its courts. Primarily, it is for the legislature to determine the public policy of the state, and if there is a statute that addresses the subject in question, the policy reflected therein must prevail....

The Tennessee legislature has authorized the granting of divorces on the ground of irreconcilable differences if the parties have, by written agreement, made provisions for the custody and maintenance of any children of the marriage and an equitable settlement of their property rights. Public Acts 1977, Chapter 107. The record in this case reflects compliance with these conditions and the incorporation of the settlement agreement of October 31, 1974, into the decree of divorce. Appellant suggests no distinction between the ground of irreconcilable differences and that of incompatibility of temperaments making life together unbearable, and in our opinion they are substantially equivalent. Thus, the grounds upon which the Dominican Republic decree was awarded cannot be said to be offensive to the public policy of Tennessee.

...

Appellant relies on the principle that a bona fide domicile in the divorce forum is essential to confer jurisdiction of the subject matter.

We note that, in the proper case, the domiciliary requirement may serve an important function; requiring domicile in the rendering jurisdiction as a prerequisite to granting comity may effectively prevent a jurisdiction with no legitimate interest in a particular controversy from fixing or altering legal relationships against the laws and policies of the jurisdiction which does have a legitimate interest in the parties, by virtue of their domiciliary status.

We would, of course, deny comity to a foreign nation decree if its lack of jurisdictional requirements equivalent to our own resulted in prejudice to any citizens of this State. It is clear that in this case the difference between Tennessee's jurisdictional requirements and those of the Dominican Republic have in no sense prejudiced the immediate parties. To the contrary, they contend that they have relied upon the validity of the Dominican Republic decree since its rendition more than three (3) years ago and will be prejudiced if we withhold comity.

Appellant contends that it is against public policy for the state as a third party to the marriage contract to "surrender its sovereignty" to a foreign nation whose laws evince no interest in maintaining the stability of marriage as an institution.

We recently had occasion to recognize and affirm that public policy. There is, however, another public policy consideration that is applicable in the aftermath of a hopelessly broken marriage, that was enunciated by this Court many years ago, a policy that also undergirds the legislative enactment allowing divorce on the ground of irreconcilable differences. In *Farrar v. Farrar*, 553 S.W.2d 741 (Tenn. 1977), Mr. Justice Henry, writing for the Court said:

> We fully recognize that considerations of public policy demand that the institution of marriage be sheltered and safeguarded. But there is an obverse side to the coin of public policy and consideration must be given to the fact that society is illserved by a legally commanded continuance of a marriage which exists in name only. We quote from the opinion of the late Chief Justice Grafton Green, in *Lingner v. Lingner*, 165 Tenn. 525, 534, 56 S.W.2d 749, 752 (1933): As pointed out by another court, we must take into consideration "the mischiefs arising from turning out into the world, in enforced celibacy, persons who are neither married nor unmarried." (Citation omitted.) Society is not interested in perpetuating a status out of which no good can come and from which harm may result. 553 S.W.2d at 744, 745.

...

Appellant argues that summary judgment was inappropriate in this case because appellees were not entitled to judgment "as a matter of law" as required by Rule 56.03, Tennessee Rules of Civil Procedure. This contention is without merit. Throughout the proceedings in the trial court and in this Court, there has been no hint that there was any issue as to any material fact. While Tennessee is not, as a matter of law, required to grant comity to any foreign decree, the decision to grant comity in a given situation is nevertheless purely a question of Tennessee law.

The judgment of the Chancery Court of Shelby County declaring the decree of the Court of First Instance, Santa Domingo, Dominican Republic, valid and enforceable is affirmed....

YODER v. YODER

Superior Court of Connecticut
31 Conn. Sup. 345, 330 A.2d 825 (1974)

SADEN, Judge.

This is an action instituted by the defendant's former wife individually and as parent and natural guardian of Martha Yoder, one of their minor children. In the interest of clarity, the parties will be referred to as "husband" and "wife."

In 1968 the couple obtained a Mexican divorce in which both parties appeared and fully participated. The validity of that divorce is not contested here. An agreement concerning the respective rights and duties regarding support and property was entered into shortly before the divorce and was made a part of the Mexican decree. That agreement provided in pertinent part that the husband would pay the medical expenses of his two minor children, Martha and Elizabeth, and educational expenses if they attend college. The wife alleges that Martha must attend a boarding school pursuant to doctor's orders. The expense of this school, she contends, is a medical one, properly payable by the husband, and not an educational one for which the husband would not be responsible.

In a motion dated October 26, 1972, the wife sought permission to amend her complaint by adding to the prayers for relief the following: "...That the decree of divorce entered by the Republic of Mexico be made a decree of this Court and enforced in the same manner as a final decree of this Court." The husband objected to this amendment on the ground, inter alia, that there was no authority for allowing such relief in our courts. The court nonetheless allowed the amendment. The husband now demurs to this prayer for relief, contending that, while our courts may recognize an alien decree, they cannot enforce it by making it a decree of the recognizing court. In order to make an alien decree a decree of this court, it is contended, there must be some statutory authority, which does not exist in Connecticut although it does in other states....

The question has never been squarely presented to our Supreme Court. This court is of the opinion that the reasoning in *Gagnon v. Gagnon*, 23 Conn.Sup. 368, 183 A.2d 858, is correct. Absent some statutory authorization, a decree of an out-of-state tribunal cannot be made that of a Connecticut court. Such a conclusion does not, however, bar the operation of the doctrine of comity.

Whether and to what extent American courts should recognize and enforce decrees of other nations has been a subject of voluminous concern to the commentators. See, *e.g.*, Yntema, "The Enforcement of Foreign Judgments in Anglo-American Law," 33 Mich.L. Rev. 1129; Peterson, "Foreign Country Judgments and the Second Restatement of Conflict of Laws," 72 Colum.L.Rev. 220; Baade, "Marriage and Divorce in American Conflicts Law: Governmental-Interests Analysis and the Restatement (Second)," 72 Colum.L.Rev. 329; von Mehren & Trautman, "Recognition of Foreign Adjudications: A Survey and a Suggested Approach," 81 Harv.L.Rev. 1601.

Over the years, the approach of the Restatement (Second) of Conflict of Laws appears to have prevailed. The Restatement's view is expressed in §§98 and 102. Section 98 provides: "A valid judgment rendered in a foreign nation after a fair trial in a contested proceeding will be recognized in the United States so far as the immediate parties and the underlying cause of action are concerned." Comment c to that section cites *Hilton v. Guyot*, 159 U.S. 113, 16 S.Ct. 139, 40 L.Ed. 95, from which comes the most often quoted list of requirements for "comity." The court said (p. 202, 16 S.Ct. p. 158) that

> where there has been opportunity for a full and fair trial abroad before a court of competent jurisdiction, conducting the trial upon regular proceedings, after due citation or voluntary appearance of the defendant, and under a system of jurisprudence likely to secure an impartial administration of justice between the citizens of its own country and those of other countries, and there is nothing to show either prejudice in the court or in the system of laws under which it was sitting, or fraud in procuring the judgment, or any other special reason why the comity of this nation should not allow it full effect, the merits of the case should not, in an action brought in this country upon the judgment, be tried afresh, as on a new trial or an appeal, upon the mere assertion of the party that the judgment was erroneous in law or in fact.

This rule is entirely sensible and has many policy considerations to recommend it. The commentators agree on several: (1) a desire to avoid the duplication of effort and consequent waste involved in reconsidering a matter which has been fully litigated; (2) a desire to protect the successful litigant from harassment or evasion by the other party; (3) a policy against making the availability of local enforcement the decisive element in the plaintiff's choice of forum; and (4) an interest in fostering stability and unity in an international society in which many aspects of life are multinational. See von Mehren & Trautman, *supra*, p. 1603–4.

As the decree rendered by the Republic of Mexico in the instant case appears to meet the requirements set down in *Hilton v. Guyot*, *supra*, it should be recognized in this state.

As to enforcement of that decree, §102, comment g, of the Restatement (Second) of Conflict of Laws says: "It can therefore be assumed that a decree rendered in a foreign nation which orders or enjoins the doing of an act will be enforced in this country provided that such enforcement is necessary to effectuate the decree and will not impose an undue burden upon the American court and provided further that in the view of the American court the decree is consistent with fundamental principles of justice and of good morals." In other words, an internationally foreign decree will be accorded treatment similar to a judgment of one of our sister states, unless it is found to be repugnant to some basic public policy of the state.

No such repugnancy is found here. The divorce in the instant case was granted on grounds which, at the time of the rendition of the decree, would not have been considered proper under the Connecticut statute; that is, incompatibility of temperaments. Today, however, is the point in time from which we should evaluate the state's public policy regarding permissible grounds for divorce. Since the passage of Public Act 73-373, these grounds have included the irretrievable breakdown of the marriage. The grounds on which the Mexican divorce was granted do not differ so greatly from our current divorce law as to be considered repugnant.

There has been no claim made here that the Mexican court lacked jurisdiction to enter the decree. Some writers argue, however, that the state of the domicil of the parties has a paramount public interest in the status of the marriage and should refuse to recognize Mexican divorces or to enforce them since they are all too often procured on a divorce-mill basis. See Baade, *supra*. The court in *Rosenstiel v. Rosenstiel*, 16 N.Y.2d 64, 73, 262 N.Y.S.2d 86, 90, 209 N.E.2d 709, 712, remarked on that point: "The State or country of true domicile has the closest real public interest in a marriage but, where a New York spouse goes elsewhere to establish a synthetic domicile to meet technical acceptance of a matrimonial suit, our public interest is not affected differently by a formality of one day than by a formality of six weeks. Nevada gets no closer to the real public concern with the marriage than Chihuahua."

At present, of course, the Connecticut court's real concern is the best interests of the child. Apparently there is some medical problem, and the plaintiff mother seeks to have the court determine if the Mexican decree provides coverage for such treatment as the mother alleges is necessary, even though it involves special schooling not mentioned in the decree. This question, however, is beyond the scope of this memorandum.

In an analogous case, *Adamsen v. Adamsen*, 151 Conn. 172, 195 A.2d 418, custody of a child was awarded to the plaintiff as part of a Norwegian divorce decree. The defendant absconded from Norway to Connecticut with the child while an appeal was pending. The plaintiff, in a *habeas corpus* hearing, sought to have the Norwegian decree enforced here. The court said (p. 178, 195 A.2d p. 421):

> The determination of the ultimate question as to the person in whom the custody should be reposed requires the court to exercise its discretion and to give paramount consideration to the welfare of the child. *Morrill v. Morrill*,... [83 Conn. 479] 489, 77 A. [1,] 4, 5; *Kelsey v. Green*, 69 Conn. 291, 301, 37 A. 679.... Where there is an outstanding foreign judgment determining custody, the effect to be accorded it as a matter of comity is the same whether it is the judgment of a foreign nation or of a sister state....

In *Adamsen v. Adamsen, supra*, 151 Conn. 180, 195 A.2d 418, the court makes it quite clear that while its ultimate conclusion coincided with that of the Norwegian court, the Connecticut hearing was an independent adjudication made after a full trial rather than a mere enforcement of the foreign judgment. In other words, had the Connecticut court seen fit to do so in the exercise of its discretion, it had the power and right to vary the custody provisions of the Norwegian decree.

Recognition of the Mexican decree in the instant case is a matter of comity among nations. This principle does not, however, require Connecticut to adopt an alien decree as its own, as the plaintiff requests in the relief challenged by demurrer. It is sufficient that Connecticut by virtue of the comity doctrine recognize the Mexican decree if it is not repugnant to the public policy of this state, and enforce it at law and in equity, including the remedy of contempt, if the circumstances warrant it....

The demurrer to the requested relief that the Mexican decree be made a decree of this court is sustained.

COMMENTS

Hyde and *Yoder* involve the recognition of divorce decrees rendered by courts of foreign nations. In both instances, American domiciliaries had obtained bilateral divorces, with their respective spouses collaborating at least to the extent of entering an appearance in the foreign court. The language in *Yoder* is somewhat provincial because the Supreme Court of Connecticut speaks of a divorce decree rendered by the Republic of Mexico, although in all probability a decree by the court in the Mexican state of Chihuahua was concerned. This oversight was harmless in *Yoder* because the Connecticut court recognized the foreign decree. Failure to differentiate, however, can sometimes facilitate nonrecognition. For example, if the laws of divorce existing in Chihuahua until 1970 were given weight in determining whether divorces from other Mexican states or recent divorces from Chihuahua are to be recognized within the United States, a failure to differentiate might facilitate nonrecognition. As explained at the end of this Comment, an attitude of non-American courts similar to that of the Connecticut court here — speaking of "American" divorce decrees without differentiating between divorce jurisdictions of individual states — may sometimes lead to nonrecognition of "American" decrees abroad.

Until November 1970, the Mexican state of Chihuahua had a particularly liberal divorce law in two respects. It provided for a form of no-fault divorce on the ground of incompatibility of character; and for proving residence, and thereby jurisdiction, entry in the municipal register of the place of the divorce was sufficient. The courts of Ciudad Juarez, Chihuahua, across from El Paso, Texas, were most often invoked by New York residents at a time when divorce was difficult to obtain at home. After the divorce business declined in Chihuahua because of statutory change, it moved to Haiti and the Dominican Republic. This does not mean, however, that all migratory divorces in these countries originate from the United States. About half of them concern couples from Europe, Africa, and Latin America. *Hyde* illustrates why Americans may still prefer a Dominican or Haitian decree over a local divorce, especially if they are in full agreement on the divorce consequences. In this case a crowded docket would have imposed a waiting period on the parties. People from the world of entertainment appear also to prefer the remoteness of the forum from publicity.

Part of the problem of recognition of foreign divorce decrees is related to parochialism. It results from the isolation of many states from the rest of the world. As late as 1978 the Supreme Court of Tennessee found no single case from Tennessee dealing with the recognition of judicial decrees of any kind from foreign nations. The absence of binding legal authority favors an essentially discretionary judicial standard of comity among nations. Federal regulation — for example, akin to treaties recognizing foreign divorce judgments, which now exists in European countries — is unlikely because of local resentments against federal intrusion into matters traditionally perceived as belonging to the states. Thus the state courts will continue to deal with these matters haphazardly.

Although the full faith and credit clause does not apply to decrees from foreign nations, state courts apply standards of recognition developed among sister states. To the extent that this leads to reexamination of jurisdictional issues according to standards of domicile, regardless of whether the foreign country has a domicile requirement, it means the continued impact of *Williams v. North Carolina I* and *II* (see p. 987 and p. 997) in an area for which it was not designed.

Sherrer v. Sherrer (see p. 1007) is of particular relevance because many foreign divorces are bilateral, as, for example, those in *Hyde* and *Yoder*. In fact, the laws of Haiti and the Dominican Republic appear to be designed to meet the requirements of *Sherrer*. If both parties to a foreign divorce have reached a settlement and are represented or appear in person, the danger of subsequent strife is minimized. Consequently, the majority of these foreign divorces, in the absence of controversy between the former spouses, are de facto effective although their legal validity may be subject to question. In *Hyde* the controversy was almost artificially created, against the wishes of the former spouses, by the intervention of a Divorce Referee who appealed the recognizing lower court judgment in behalf of the interest of the State. Lack of controversy, however, does not alleviate the cloud on future marriages entered in reliance on foreign-country divorces. It appears also that at least some foreign divorces are fraudulent and ineffective under the laws of their origin, especially some divorces that continue to be issued to foreigners in a few Mexican states.

Hyde and *Yoder* refer to *Hilton v. Guyot*, 158 U.S. 113 (1895), as the source for principles of comity in the recognition of foreign judgments. *Yoder*, in addition, quotes standards of fairness as enumerated in *Hilton* and supported by Restatement (Second) of Conflict of Laws §98. Yet *Hilton* involved a money judgment and was not meant to be binding on state courts, certainly not in regard to foreign divorce decrees. The references to *Hilton* and the Restatement are therefore probably intended only to articulate standards of discretion that the courts could have arrived at independently. Significantly, the requirement of reciprocity that was the basis of the decision in *Hilton* — a foreign judgment is to be recognized only if the foreign country in question also recognizes American decrees — is omitted from the catalogue of factors needed for recognition. What seems to emerge is the absence of a national standard of binding force and at least the possibility of nonrecognition of the foreign divorce decree, although both *Hyde* and *Yoder*, with elaborate reasoning, came out in favor of recognition.

The question of recognition of the divorce decree by a foreign nation should be distinguished from the problem of whether a party can be estopped to attack collaterally the validity of a foreign divorce. Although such estoppel may lead to results comparable to recognition, it proceeds under a theory that, in spite of flaws in the local validity of the foreign decree, the party concerned is to be treated as if the decree were fully valid. If, for example, a party to a Haitian divorce, were to claim to a new spouse that the divorce, and therefore the remarriage, was invalid, he or she could be estopped from raising this point. Even in a jurisdiction that would refuse to recognize the Haitian divorce, the subsequent remarriage could be treated by way of estoppel as if it were valid. Although this kind of case is conceptually different from actual recognition of the foreign divorce decree, its practical results are similar. The difference becomes apparent, however, if another party, for example the bona fide new spouse, claims invalidity of the marriage. While genuine recognition affects all parties concerned, estoppel affects only the party whose present position is inconsistent with prior behavior.

Hyde and *Yoder* concerned American domiciliaries who obtained divorces in foreign countries, perhaps the most difficult situation for purposes of recognition. Other factual variations may prove to be less problematical: for example, American domiciliaries of foreign nationality who obtain a divorce in their country of origin; a member of the American military stationed abroad whose American domicile is difficult to ascertain and who obtains a divorce in the country where he or she is stationed; or two foreigners of the same nationality who have obtained divorces in their country of origin prior to coming to the United States. More complex situations may arise if foreigners of different nationality obtain a divorce in a third foreign country which might or might not be recognized in their countries of origin. Many of these questions are likely to arise in determining marital status for purposes of immigration.

One aspect of recognition of divorce decrees from foreign countries within the United States should not go unmentioned, namely the reverse and indirect negative impact that these local American dispositions may have on recognition of American divorce decrees in foreign countries. If a foreign country is governed by conceptions of reciprocity, requiring proof that its own decrees will be recognized within the United States, severe complications may develop.

The workings of the American federal system are difficult to perceive for even sophisticated foreign lawyers and judges. *Williams v. North Carolina I* and *II* can be used to demonstrate in a foreign forum that no American divorce decree is immune from collateral attack even if it originates within the United States. Since reciprocity does not exist between American states, the argument could go, how much less could it be expected in relation to foreign countries? The very concept of comity, which involves discretionary reexamination of the jurisdiction of foreign courts according to American notions and standards of fairness and American rather than foreign substantive law, seems to preclude, or at least impair, recognition of American judgments abroad. Much of the relevant American case law, including *Williams* and *Sherrer*, is partly responsible for bringing about this difficulty, albeit inadvertently. Most court opinions not involving foreign-country divorces use the term "foreign" only in relation to sister states, and might seem to the nonlegal reader to be speaking as if genuinely foreign countries do not exist. In fact, American courts tend to be more benevolent than they have given the appearance of being. The unfortunate result is that foreign court decrees, including divorce judgments, are often more likely to be recognized within American states than our own judgments are likely to be recognized in foreign countries.

REFERENCES

Friedrich Juenger, *Recognition of Foreign Divorces — British and American Perspectives*, 20 AM. J. COMP. L. 1 (1971).

Richard L. Miller, *Mexican Divorces Revisited*, 84(4) CASE & COM. 43 (July–August 1979).

Note, *Foreign Nation Judgments: Recognition and Enforcement of Foreign Judgments in Florida and the Status of Florida Judgments Abroad*, 31 U. FLA. L. REV. 588 (1979).

Arthur von Mehren & Bernard Trautman, *Recognition of Foreign Adjudications: A Survey and a Suggested Approach*, 81 HARV. L. REV. 1601 (1968).

C: CHILD CUSTODY

Respect for Another State's Decree

MAY v. ANDERSON
United States Supreme Court
345 U.S. 528 (1953)

Mr. Justice BURTON delivered the opinion of the Court.

The question presented is whether, in a habeas corpus proceeding attacking the right of a mother to retain possession of her minor children, an Ohio court must give full faith and credit to a Wisconsin decree awarding custody of the children to their father when that decree is obtained by the father in an *ex parte* divorce action in a Wisconsin court which had no personal jurisdiction over the mother. For the reasons hereafter stated, our answer is no.

This proceeding began July 5, 1951, when Owen Anderson, here called the appellee, filed a petition for a writ of habeas corpus in the Probate Court of Columbiana County, Ohio. He alleged that his former wife, Leona Anderson May, here called the appellant, was illegally restraining the liberty of their children, Ronald, Sandra and James, aged, respectively, 12, 8 and 5, by refusing to deliver them to him in response to a decree issued by the County Court of Waukesha County, Wisconsin, February 5, 1947. With both parties and their children before it, the Probate Court ordered that, until this matter be finally determined, the children remain with their mother subject to their father's right to visit them at reasonable times.

After a hearing "on the petition, the stipulation of counsel for the parties as to the agreed statement of facts, and the testimony," the Probate Court decided that it was obliged by the Full Faith and Credit Clause of the Constitution of the United States to accept the Wisconsin decree as binding upon the mother. Accordingly, proceeding to the merits of the case upon the issues presented by the stipulations of counsel, it ordered the children discharged from further restraint by her. That order has been held in abeyance and the children are still with her. The Court of Appeals for Columbiana County, Ohio, affirmed. 91 Ohio App. 557, 107 N.E.2d 358. The Supreme Court of Ohio, without opinion, denied a motion directing the Court of Appeals to certify its record for review, and dismissed an appeal on the ground that no debatable constitutional question was involved. 157 Ohio St. 436, 105 N.E.2d 648, 25 Ohio Bar 199.

...

The parties were married in Wisconsin and, until 1947, both were domiciled there. After marital troubles developed, they agreed in December, 1946, that appellant should take their children to Lisbon, Columbiana County, Ohio, and there think over her future course. By New Year's Day, she had decided not to return to Wisconsin and, by telephone, she informed her husband of that decision.

Within a few days he filed suit in Wisconsin, seeking both an absolute divorce and custody of the children. The only service of process upon appellant consisted of the delivery to her personally, in Ohio, of a copy of the Wisconsin summons and petition. Such service is authorized by a Wisconsin statute for use in an action for a divorce but that statute makes no mention of its availability in a proceeding for the custody of children. Appellant entered no appearance and took no part in this Wisconsin proceeding which produced not only a decree divorcing the parties from the bonds of matrimony but a decree purporting to award the custody of the children to their father, subject to a right of their mother to visit them at reasonable times. Appellant contests only the validity of the decree as to custody. See *Estin v. Estin*, 334 U.S. 541, and *Kreiger v. Kreiger*, 334 U.S. 555, recognizing the divisibility of decrees of divorce from those for payment of alimony.

Armed with a copy of the decree and accompanied by a local police officer, appellee, in Lisbon, Ohio, demanded and obtained the children from their mother. The record does not disclose what took place between 1947 and 1951, except that the children remained with their father in Wisconsin until July 1, 1951. He then brought them back to Lisbon and permitted them to visit their mother. This time, when he demanded their return, she refused to surrender them.

Relying upon the Wisconsin decree, he promptly filed in the Probate Court of Columbiana County, Ohio, the petition for a writ of habeas corpus now before us. Under Ohio procedure that writ tests only the immediate right to possession of the children. It does not open the door for the modification of any prior award of custody on a showing of changed circumstances. Nor is it available as a procedure for settling the future custody of children in the first instance.

> It is well settled that *habeas corpus* is not the proper or appropriate action to determine, as between parents, who is entitled to the custody of their minor children.
>
> The agreed statement of facts disclosed to the Court of Appeals that the children were in the custody of their mother. There being no evidence that the appellant had a superior right to their custody, that court was fully warranted in concluding that the children were not illegally restrained of their liberty. *In re Corey*, 145 Ohio St. 413, 418, 61 N.E.2d 892, 894–895.[4]

...

Separated as our issue is from that of the future interests of the children, we have before us the elemental question whether a court of a state, where a mother is neither domiciled, resident nor present, may cut off her immediate right to the care, custody, management and companionship of her minor children without having jurisdiction over her *in personam*. Rights far more precious to appellant than property rights will be cut off if she is to be bound by the Wisconsin award of custody.

> [I]t is now too well settled to be open to further dispute that the "full faith and credit" clause and the act of Congress passed pursuant to it do not entitle a judgment *in personam* to extra-territorial effect if it be made to appear that it was rendered without jurisdiction over the person sought to be bound. *Baker v. Baker, Eccles & Co.*, 242 U.S. 394, 401, and see 403; *Thompson v. Whitman*, 18 Wall. 457; *D'Arcy v. Ketchum*, 11 How. 165.

4. This limitation contrasts with the procedure in states where a court, upon securing the presence before if of the parents and children in response to a writ of habeas corpus, may proceed to determine the future custody of the children. See *e.g.*, *People of State of New York ex rel. Halvey v. Halvey*, 330 U.S. 610 (New York procedure); *Boor v. Boor*, 241 Iowa 973, 43 N.W.2d 155; *Helton v. Crawley*, 241 Iowa 296, 41 N.W.2d 60.

In *Estin v. Estin, supra,* and *Kreiger v. Kreiger, supra,* this Court upheld the validity of a Nevada divorce obtained *ex parte* by a husband, resident in Nevada, insofar as it dissolved the bonds of matrimony. At the same time, we held Nevada powerless to cut off, in that proceeding, a spouse's right to financial support under the prior decree of another state. In the instant case, we recognize that a mother's right to custody of her children is a personal right entitled to at least as much protection as her right to alimony.

In the instant case, the Ohio courts gave weight to appellee's contention that the Wisconsin award of custody binds appellant because, at the time it was issued, her children had a technical domicile in Wisconsin, although they were neither resident nor present there.[7] We find it unnecessary to determine the children's legal domicile because, even if it be with their father, that does not give Wisconsin, certainly as against Ohio, the personal jurisdiction that it must have in order to deprive their mother of her personal right to their immediate possession.[8]

The judgment of the Supreme Court of Ohio, accordingly, is reversed and the cause is remanded to it for further proceedings not inconsistent with this opinion.

Reversed and remanded.

...

Mr. Justice FRANKFURTER, concurring.

The views expressed by my brother JACKSON make it important that I state, in joining the Court's opinion, what I understand the Court to be deciding and what it is not deciding in this case.

What is decided — the only thing the Court decides — is that the Full Faith and Credit Clause does not require Ohio, in disposing of the custody of children in Ohio, to accept, in the circumstances before us, the disposition made by Wisconsin. The Ohio Supreme Court felt itself so bound. This Court does not decide that Ohio would be precluded from recognizing, as a matter of local law, the disposition made by the Wisconsin court. For Ohio to give respect to the Wisconsin decree would not offend the Due Process Clause. Ohio is no more precluded from doing so than a court of Ontario or Manitoba would be, were the mother to bring the children into one of these provinces.

Property, personal claims, and even the marriage status, see, *e.g.,* *Sherrer v. Sherrer,* 334 U.S. 343, generally give rise to interests different from those relevant

---

7. By stipulation, the parties recognized her domicile in Ohio. See also, *Estin v. Estin, supra; Kreiger v. Kreiger, supra; Williams v. State of North Carolina,* 317 U.S. 287.

For the general rule that in cases of the separation of parents, apart from any award of custody of the children, the domicile of the children is that of the parent with whom they live and that only the state of that domicile may award their custody, see Restatement, Conflict of Laws (1934), §§32 and 146, Illustrations 1 and 2.

8. "...the weight of authority is in favor of confining the jurisdiction of the court in an action for divorce, where the defendant is a nonresident and does not appear, and process upon the defendant is by substituted service only, to a determination of the status of the parties.... This rule of law extends to children who are not within the jurisdiction of the court when the decree is rendered, where the defendant is not a resident of the state of the seat of the court, and has neither been personally served with process nor appeared to the action.... [Citing cases.]

"By the authority of the cases supra, a decree of the custody of a minor child, under the circumstances stated, is void." *Weber v. Redding,* 200 Ind. 448, 454–455, 163 N.E. 269, 271. See also, *Sanders v. Sanders,* 223 Mo.App. 834, 837–838, 14 S.W.2d 458, 459–460; *Carter v. Carter,* 201 Ga. 850, 41 S.E.2d 532.

The instant case does not present the special considerations that arise where a parent, with or without minor children, leaves a jurisdiction for the purpose of escaping process or otherwise evading jurisdiction, and we do not have here the considerations that arise when children are unlawfully or surreptitiously taken by one parent from the other.

to the discharge of a State's continuing responsibility to children within her borders. Children have a very special place in life which law should reflect. Legal theories and their phrasing in other cases readily lead to fallacious reasoning it uncritically transferred to determination of a State's duty towards children. There are, of course, adjudications other than those pertaining to children, as for instance decrees of alimony, which may not be definitive even in the decreeing State, let alone binding under the Full Faith and Credit Clause. Interests of a State other than its duty towards children may also prevail over the interest of national unity that underlies the Full Faith and Credit Clause. But the child's welfare in a custody case has such a claim upon the State that its responsibility is obviously not to be foreclosed by a prior adjudication reflecting another State's discharge of its responsibility at another time. Reliance on opinions regarding out-of-State adjudications of property rights, personal claims or the marital status is bound to confuse analysis when a claim to the custody of children before the courts of one State is based on an award previously made by another State. Whatever light may be had from such opinions, they cannot give conclusive answers.

Mr. Justice JACKSON, whom Mr. Justice REED joins, dissenting.

The Court apparently is holding that the Federal Constitution prohibits Ohio from recognizing the validity of this Wisconsin divorce decree insofar as it settles custody of the couple's children. In the light of settled and unchallenged precedents of this Court, such a decision can only rest upon the proposition that Wisconsin's courts had no jurisdiction to make such a decree binding upon appellant....

A conclusion that a state must not recognize a judgment of a sister commonwealth involves very different considerations than a conclusion that it must do so. If Wisconsin has rendered a valid judgment, the Constitution not only requires every state to give it full faith and credit, but 28 U.S.C. §1738, 28 U.S.C.A. §1738, referring to such judicial proceedings, commands that they "shall have the same full faith and credit in every court within the United States and its Territories and Possessions as they have by law or usage in the courts of such State, Territory or Possession from which they are taken." The only escape from obedience lies in a holding that the judgment rendered in Wisconsin, at least as to custody, is void and entitled to no standing even in Wisconsin. It is void only if it denies due process of law.

The Ohio courts reasoned that although personal jurisdiction over the wife was lacking, domicile of the children in Wisconsin was a sufficient jurisdictional basis to enable Wisconsin to bind all parties interested in their custody. This determination that the children were domiciled in Wisconsin has not been contested either at our bar or below. Therefore, under our precedents, it is conclusive. *Williams v. State of North Carolina*, 317 U.S. 287, 302. The husband, plaintiff in the case, was at all times domiciled in Wisconsin; the defendant-wife was a Wisconsin native, was married there and both were domiciled in that State until her move in December 1946, when the parties stipulate that she acquired an Ohio domicile. The children were born in Wisconsin, were always domiciled there, and were physically resident in Wisconsin at all times until December 1946, when their mother took them to Ohio with her. But the Ohio court specifically found that she brought the children to Ohio with the understanding that if she decided not to go back to Wisconsin the children were to be returned to that State. In spite of the fact that she did decide not to return, she kept the children in Ohio. It was under these circumstances that the Wisconsin decree was rendered in February 1947, less than two months after the wife had given up her physical residence in Wisconsin and held the children out of the State in breach of her agreement.

The husband subsequently went to Ohio, retrieved the children and took them back to Wisconsin, where they remained with him for four years. Then he voluntarily brought them to Ohio for a visit with their mother, whereupon she refused to surrender them, and he sought habeas corpus in the Ohio courts. In this situation Wisconsin was no meddler reaching out to draw to its courts controversies that arose in and concerned other legal communities. If ever domicile of the children plus that of one spouse is sufficient to support a custody decree binding all interested parties, it should be in this case....

I am quite aware that in recent times this Court has been chipping away at the concept of domicile as a connecting factor between the state and the individual to determine rights and obligations. We are a mobile people, historically on the move, and perhaps the rigid concept of domicile derived by common law from feudal attachment to the land is too rigid for a society so restless as ours. But if our federal system is to maintain separate legal communities, as the Full Faith and Credit Clause evidently contemplates, there must be some test for determining to which of these a person belongs. If, for this purpose, there is a better concept than domicile, we have not yet hit upon it. Abandonment of this ancient doctrine would leave partial vacuums in many branches of the law. It seems to be abandoned here.

The Court's decision holds that the state in which a child and one parent are domiciled and which is primarily concerned about his welfare cannot constitutionally adjudicate controversies as to his guardianship. The state's power here is defeated by the absence of the other parent for a period of two months. The convenience of a leave-taking parent is placed above the welfare of the child, but neither party is greatly aided in obtaining a decision. The Wisconsin courts cannot bind the mother, and the Ohio courts cannot bind the father. A state of the law such as this, where possession apparently is not merely nine points of the law but all of them and self-help the ultimate authority, has little to commend it in legal logic or as a principle of order in a federal system.

...

In spite of the fact that judges and law writers long have recognized the similarity between the jurisdictional requirements for divorce and for custody, this decision appears to equate the jurisdictional requirements for a custody decree to those for an *in personam* money judgment. One reads the opinion in vain to discover reasons for this choice, unless it is found in the remark that for the wife "rights far more precious than property will be cut off" in the custody proceeding. The force of this cardiac consideration is self-evident, but it seems to me to reflect a misapprehension as to the nature of a custody proceeding or a revision of the views that have heretofore prevailed. When courts deal with inanimate property by the conventional *in rem* proceeding, their principal concern is the distribution of rights in that property, rather than with the welfare of the property apart from its ownership claims. But even where dealing solely with property rights, where concern with the "*res*" is minimal and concern with the claimants is paramount, courts may exercise jurisdiction *in rem* over the property without having personal jurisdiction over all of the claimants. Only when they seek to render a party liable to some personal performance must they acquire personal jurisdiction.

The difference between a proceeding involving the status, custody and support of children and one involving adjudication of property rights is too apparent to require elaboration. In the former, courts are no longer concerned primarily with the proprietary claims of the contestants for the "*res*" before the court, but with the welfare of the "*res*" itself. Custody is viewed not with the idea of adjudicating rights *in* the children, as if they were chattels, but rather with the idea of making the best disposition possible for the welfare of the children. To speak of a court's "cutting off" a mother's right to custody of her children, as if it raised problems similar to those involved in "cutting off" her rights in a plot of ground, is to obliterate these obvious distinctions. Personal jurisdiction of all parties to be affected by a proceeding is highly desirable, to make certain that they have had valid notice and opportunity to be heard. But the assumption that it overrides all other considerations and in its absence a state is constitutionally impotent to resolve questions of custody flies in the face of our own cases. The wife's marital ties may be dissolved without personal jurisdiction over her by a state where the husband has a genuine domicile because the concern of that state with the welfare and marital status of its domiciliary is felt to be sufficiently urgent. Certainly the claim of the domiciled parent to relief for himself from the leave-taking parent does not exhaust the power of the state. The claim of children as well as the home-keeping parent to have their status determined with reasonable certainty, and to be free from an incessant tug of war between squabbling parents, is equally urgent.

The mother in this case would in all probability not be permanently precluded from attempting to redetermine the custody of the children. If the Wisconsin courts would allow modification of the decree upon a showing of changed circumstances, such modification could be accomplished by another state which acquired jurisdiction over the parties. *People of State of New York ex rel. Halvey v. Halvey*, 330 U.S. 610; cf. *Lynde v. Lynde*, 181 U.S. 183. And, of course, no judgment settling custody rights as between the parents would itself prevent any state which may find itself responsible for the welfare of the children from taking action adverse to either parent. No such case is before us.

I fear this decision will author new confusions. The interpretative concurrence, if it be a true interpretation, seems to reduce the law of custody to a rule of seize-and-run. I would affirm the decision of the Ohio courts that they should respect the judgment of the Wisconsin court, until it or some other court with equal or better claims to jurisdiction shall modify it.

. . .

PALM v. SUPERIOR COURT

Court of Appeal, Fourth District

97 Cal.App.3d 456, 158 Cal.Rptr. 786 (1979)

COLOGNE, Associate Justice.

Petitioner Franklin P. Palm seeks a writ of "prohibition/mandate" to compel the Superior Court of San Diego County to vacate its order and stay further proceedings in exercise of jurisdiction in a disputed child custody matter instituted by Rebecca Palm Moody in her complaint to establish a North Dakota divorce decree. That 1974 decree gave Rebecca custody of the parties' minor son who was then a year and a half old. Franklin seeks to stay these proceedings during the pendency of hearings concerned with the son's custody currently being conducted in the North Dakota courts. Franklin contends California's Uniform Child Custody

Jurisdiction Act (Act) which North Dakota also adopted[1] requires the superior court to decline jurisdiction over the minor child and instead to abide by North Dakota's determination of the son's custodial fate.

Franklin married Rebecca in 1968. The parties separated in August 1974 and Rebecca moved to San Diego. When Franklin took the child back to North Dakota, she returned to North Dakota to regain custody. Franklin obtained a judgment of divorce on December 16, 1974, in the District Court of Cass County, Fargo, North Dakota. At that time, the North Dakota court awarded custody of their son to Rebecca with the right of reasonable visitation given to Franklin. In March 1976, Rebecca began living with a man named Ross Moody. On December 31, 1976, by stipulation, the parties agreed Franklin could have custody of the son for six months, after which time the custody would go to Rebecca with Franklin to have the right of reasonable visitation, eight consecutive weeks of visitation in the summer plus alternating Christmas and Easter holidays. Franklin took the boy for the agreed six months and immediately afterward kept the boy for the additional eight weeks to which he was entitled. On July 14, 1977, Franklin filed a petition in the District Court seeking an order to show cause why he should not have the son's custody. The matter was heard on August 19, both parties appearing in court personally and through counsel. On September 27, the court made an order amending the judgment to award Rebecca custody provided if she "resumes cohabitation with one Ross Moody, custody of the minor child...shall be changed" to Franklin.

Rebecca then took the son with her and the two lived in California where he began school. At this same time, she resumed cohabitation with Moody though at the time he was still married to another. On October 11, 1977, she "married" him and sent a certified copy of the marriage certificate to the court "in order to satisfy the order of the North Dakota Court." She admitted later this was tantamount to "fraud and deceit on the North Dakota court" because Moody was not yet free to marry. Since that time, however, Moody did obtain a divorce from his wife, the "marriage" to Rebecca was annulled and he legally married her.

In April 1978, Rebecca brought an action in California to establish the foreign judgment and to modify visitation. The superior court refused to exercise jurisdiction over the matter and dismissed the complaint with prejudice.

In June 1978, Franklin took the son back to North Dakota for his eight-week visitation period.

On August 14, before the end of that period, Franklin obtained an order to show cause from the North Dakota court for the purpose of securing full custody of the child. He obtained temporary custody and a temporary restraining order was issued to prohibit interference with his custody.

On August 18, Rebecca filed a second complaint against Franklin in San Diego seeking to establish the California court's jurisdiction over the issue of child custody, visitation and child support. On September 18, the court below determined California did have jurisdiction, California was the domiciliary of the child, it is the most convenient state to try the matter of custody, Rebecca has legal custody under the most recent North Dakota decree, the pending change of custody proceedings in North Dakota are not in substantial conformity with the Uniform Child Custody Jurisdiction Act, and the previous action of the California court

1. All references to sections of the Act are in the California Civil Code unless otherwise designated. The Act may be found in section 5150 et seq. The language of the Act adopted by California and North Dakota (NDCC 14-14-01 to 14-14-26) is not significantly different as it relates to the issues raised in this case.

dismissing Rebecca's action is not res judicata. It ordered Franklin to dismiss his North Dakota change of custody action, to refile it here and to transfer custody of the child to Rebecca to whom it advanced temporary custody pending a hearing on change of custody.

We are advised in November 1978, the son was picked up at school in North Dakota by his maternal grandmother and taken to California where he now resides with them at a place not revealed to Franklin and contrary to the California court order, he has not been allowed visitation privileges. Franklin characterizes this as an "abduction," Rebecca says the son "voluntarily left school." We take judicial notice of the fact North Dakota now has completed hearings on this matter. On May 8, 1979, that court granted full custody to Franklin subject to a right of visitation by Rebecca under Franklin's supervision. The court later adjudicated Rebecca in contempt for failure to appear with the child, punishment to be meted out when she appears before the North Dakota court.

The situation we review is a classic example of the interstate conflict which the Act was intended to obviate.[2] Although both California and North Dakota have adopted the Act, we are faced here with courts in absolute conflict, California exercising jurisdiction and awarding the child to the mother, a resident of this state, and North Dakota exercising jurisdiction and awarding the child to the father, a resident of that state. The jurisdictional facts are not in dispute and if the work of the Commission on Uniform State Laws and the respective state Legislatures is to have any relevance, this jurisdictional dispute should be resolved.

A state acquires jurisdiction under the provisions of section 5152. This reads in pertinent part as follows:

> (1) A court of this state which is competent to decide child custody matters has jurisdiction to make a child custody determination by initial or modification decree if the conditions as set forth in any of the following paragraphs are met:
>
> (a) This state (i) is the home state of the child at the time of commencement of the proceeding, or (ii) had been the child's home state within six months before commencement of the proceeding and the

2. Section 5150 of the Act reads as follows:

(1) The general purposes of this title are to:

(a) Avoid jurisdiction competition and conflict with courts of other states in matters of child custody which have in the past resulted in the shifting of children from state to state with harmful effects on their well-being.

(b) Promote cooperation with the courts of other states to the end that a custody decree is rendered in that state which can best decide the case in the interest of the child.

(c) Assure that litigation concerning the custody of a child take place ordinarily in the state with which the child and his family have the closest connection and where significant evidence concerning his care, protection, training, and personal relationships is most readily available, and that courts of this state decline the exercise of jurisdiction when the child and his family have a closer connection with another state.

(d) Discourage continuing controversies over child custody in the interest of greater stability of home environment and of secure family relationships for the child.

(e) Deter abductions and other unilateral removals of children undertaken to obtain custody awards.

(f) Avoid relitigation of custody decisions of other states in this state insofar as feasible.

(g) Facilitate the enforcement of custody decrees of other states.

(h) Promote and expand the exchange of information and other forms of mutual assistance between the courts of this state and those of other states concerned with the same child.

(i) To make uniform the law of those states which enact it.

(2) This title shall be construed to promote the general purposes stated in this section.

child is absent from this state because of his removal or retention by a person claiming his custody or for other reasons, and a parent or person acting as parent continues to live in this state.

(b) It is in the best interest of the child that a court of this state assume jurisdiction because (i) the child and his parents, or the child, and at least one contestant, have a significant connection with the state, and (ii) there is available in this state substantial evidence concerning the child's present or future care, protection, training, and personal relationships.

...

"Home state" is defined in section 5151 as "the state in which the child immediately preceding the time involved lived with...a parent...for at least six consecutive months.... Periods of temporary absence of any of the named persons are considered as part of the six-month or other period."

Under the facts of this case, the child was clearly within the jurisdiction of the California courts under the provisions of section 5152, subdivision (1)(a), since he was with his mother in California continuously from August 1977 to June 1978, with the exception of the visit with his father at Christmas. This period, immediately before the commencement of these proceedings, qualifies California as the child's "home state."[3] A California court has the right to determine its jurisdiction (*Abelleira v. District Court of Appeal*, 17 Cal.2d 280, 302, 109 P.2d 942), and the superior court properly did so here.

Under the Act's provisions paralleling section 5152, subdivision (1)(b), North Dakota might well have determined it too has jurisdiction over the custody of the child. The courts of North Dakota could and properly did find it was in the best interests of the child[4] to assume jurisdiction because the child and the father had a significant connection with that state and the requirement of available evidence concerning the child is met. The evidence supporting such a finding may be seen from the fact the father is a resident of that state, maintains his home and business as a dry wall contractor in Fargo; the parties last lived together as man and wife there and obtained their divorce there giving that court jurisdiction to award custody in the first instance, their reputation and relationships are well established in that community; and the child lived there for ten of the last 22 months and even attended school there at least until his removal by the grandparents. During that period, the child obviously made contacts with neighbors, friends and others who could testify as to his behavior and adjustment. There is available in North Dakota substantial evidence concerning the child's present or future care, protection, housing and personal relationships.

Additionally, it should be noted the court in North Dakota which granted the dissolution has continuing jurisdiction over custody matters. This is the state of the law for California courts as well (Civ.Code, §4600;[5] *Clark v. Superior Court*, 73

---

3. The court found the child was "domiciled" in California, a fact not necessary to finding jurisdiction (see Commissioner's Notes to §3 of the Uniform Act (our §5152); *A Legislative Remedy for Children Caught in the Conflict of Laws*, 22 VANDERBILT L.REVIEW 1207, 1224–1226).

4. Jurisdiction exists only if it is in the *child's* best interest, not merely the interest or convenience of the contending parties (see Commissioner's Notes to §3 of the Uniform Child Custody Jurisdiction Act).

5. Section 4600 provides in part, "In any proceeding where there is at issue the custody of a minor child, the court may, during the pendency of the proceeding or *at any time thereafter*, make such order for the custody...." (Italics added.)

Cal.App.3d 298, 304, 140 Cal.Rptr. 709; NDCC 14-05-22; *Moran v. Moran*, 200 N.W.2d 263 (N.D.1972)).

Faced with a similar factual situation, though one not involving competing exercise of jurisdiction, the Court of Appeal in *Smith v. Superior Court*, 68 Cal.App.3d 457, 137 Cal.Rptr. 348, held California had jurisdiction of the custody question on the basis of the Act which controls over the more general continuing jurisdiction provision of Code of Civil Procedure section 410.50, subdivision (b).[6] In that case, the parties obtained a judgment in California dissolving their marriage. The mother received custody. She remarried and eventually moved to Oregon with the child. They lived there approximately five years, then entered a stipulation concerning custody and visitation, including a visit during Easter 1976. The judgment was modified according to the stipulation. The mother, on the child's strenuous resistance, and on the advice of a psychologist in Oregon, refused to send the child to California for the Easter visitation. The father sought an order of contempt against the mother in California. The trial court determined it had jurisdiction to modify the judgment and to hold the mother in contempt; it was affirmed on appeal.

In *Smith*, the reviewing court conceded Oregon was the "home state" of the child under the provisions of section 5152, subdivision (1)(a). The court concluded, however, under section 5152, subdivision (1)(b), the child had equal or stronger ties to California and "there is available in this state substantial evidence concerning the child's present or future care, protection, training, and personal relationships" in spite of the fact he had been absent for five years. The court relied on the language of the statute, the Code Commissioner's Notes and the facts, as earlier stated, among which were the facts the child's grandparents lived in San Francisco and his relatives there had a good relationship with him. It noted there is additional significance in the fact the parties themselves had submitted the issue of the child's custody and visitation rights to the California court and, while that does not confer jurisdiction, an inference may be reasonably drawn the parties themselves considered the ties to California are stronger. (*Smith v. Superior Court, supra*, 68 Cal.App.3d 457, 464–465, fn. 3, 137 Cal.Rptr. 348.)

By analogy it may be said, just as in *Smith* where California assumed jurisdiction though it was not the "home state" of the child, North Dakota also has the right to assume jurisdiction. North Dakota's jurisdiction in the case before us rests on the same basis as did California's jurisdiction in *Smith.*

It is apparent under the Act both California, as the home state, and North Dakota have jurisdiction over the custody of this child. The question remaining is which state should exercise it.

The Act authorizes a court to relinquish jurisdiction or to stay proceedings in favor of the proceedings in the court of a sister state if it finds it is an inconvenient forum[7] or if there is misconduct.[8] Our courts have on occasion held it an abuse of discretion not to stay proceedings where the other court is clearly the most conve-

---

6. Code of Civil Procedure section 410.50, subdivision (b), provides: "Jurisdiction of the court over the parties and the subject matter of an action continues throughout subsequent proceedings in the action."

7. Section 5156 reads as follows:

(1) A court which has jurisdiction under this title to make an initial or modification decree may decline to exercise its jurisdiction any time before making a decree if it finds that it is an inconvenient forum to make a custody determination under the circumstances of the case and that a court of another state is a more appropriate forum.

(2) A finding of inconvenient forum may be made upon the court's own motion or upon motion of a party or a guardian ad litem or other representative of the child.

nient forum with access to relevant evidence (*Schlumpf v. Superior Court*, 79 Cal.App.3d 892, 145 Cal.Rptr. 190; *Clark v. Superior Court*, *supra*, 73 Cal.App.3d 298, 140 Cal.Rptr. 709). Nothing in the Act, however, gives a court the authority to determine it has a superior right to proceed where another court is also asserting jurisdiction. On the contrary, the Act provides a means to resolve the issue in an orderly manner without letting a state make factual rulings binding on another. Section 5155 reads as follows:

(1) *A court of this state shall not exercise its jurisdiction under this title if at the time of filing the petition a proceeding concerning the custody of the child was pending in a court of another state exercising jurisdiction substantially in conformity with this title,* unless the proceeding is stayed by the court of the other state because this state is a more appropriate forum or for other reasons.

(2) Before hearing the petition in a custody proceeding the court shall examine the pleadings and other information supplied by the parties under 5159 and shall consult the child custody registry established under 5165 concerning the pendency of proceedings with respect to the child in other states. If the court has reason to believe that proceedings may be pending in another state it shall direct an inquiry to the state court administrator or other appropriate official of the other state.

---

7. *Continued*

(3) In determining if it is an inconvenient forum, the court shall consider if it is in the interest of the child that another state assume jurisdiction. For this purpose it may take into account the following factors, among others:

(a) If another state is or recently was the child's home state.

(b) If another state has a closer connection with the child and his family or with the child and one or more of the contestants.

(c) If substantial evidence concerning the child's present or future care, protection, training, and personal relationships is more readily available in another state.

(d) If the parties have agreed on another forum which is no less appropriate.

(e) If the exercise of jurisdiction by a court of this state would contravene any of the purposes stated in Section 5150.

(4) Before determining whether to decline or retain jurisdiction the court may communicate with a court of another state and exchange information pertinent to the assumption of jurisdiction by either court with a view to assuring that jurisdiction will be exercised by the more appropriate court and that a forum will be available to the parties.

(5) If the court finds that it is an inconvenient forum and that a court of another state is a more appropriate forum, it may dismiss the proceedings, or it may stay the proceedings upon condition that a custody proceeding be promptly commenced in another named state or upon any other conditions which may be just and proper, including the condition that a moving party stipulate his consent and submission to the jurisdiction of the other forum.

(6) The court may decline to exercise its jurisdiction under this title if a custody determination is incidental to an action for divorce or another proceeding while retaining jurisdiction over the divorce or other proceeding.

(7) If it appears to the court that it is clearly an inappropriate forum it may require the party who commenced the proceedings to pay, in addition to the costs of the proceedings in this state, necessary travel and other expenses, including attorney's fees, incurred by other parties or their witnesses. Payment is to be made to the clerk of the court for remittance to the proper party.

(8) Upon dismissal or stay of proceedings under this section the court shall inform the court found to be the more appropriate forum of this fact, or if the court which would have jurisdiction in the other state is not certainly known, shall transmit the information to the court administrator or other appropriate official for forwarding to the appropriate court.

(9) Any communication received from another state informing the state of a finding of inconvenient forum because a court of this state is the more appropriate forum shall be filed in the custody registry of the appropriate court. Upon assuming jurisdiction the court of this state shall inform the original court of this fact. The authority given is strictly to relinquish or stay when there is a finding it is an inconvenient forum. Subdivision (4) gives authority to communicate with the court of a sister state hopefully to reconcile any differences.

8. Section 5157 deals generally with the clean hands doctrine which is not in issue in this case.

> (3) If the court is informed during the course of the proceeding that a proceeding concerning the custody of the child was pending in another state before the court assumed jurisdiction it shall stay the proceeding and communicate with the court in which the other proceeding is pending to the end that the issue may be litigated in the more appropriate forum and that information be exchanged in accordance with Sections 5168 through 5171. If a court of this state has made a custody decree before being informed of a pending proceeding in a court of another state it shall immediately inform that court of the fact. If the court is informed that a proceeding was commenced in another state after it assumed jurisdiction it shall likewise inform the other court to the end that the issues may be litigated in the more appropriate forum. (Italics added.)

The Act was thus designed to solve this very problem of conflicting jurisdictions. The state which enjoys priority of time in initiating the proceedings will proceed if the dispute is not resolved by agreement or consent of the other court.[9]

Moreover, where a custody decree has been made, section 5163, subdivision (1), becomes relevant. That provision reads:

> (1) If a court of another state has made a custody decree, a court of this state shall not modify that decree unless (a) it appears to the court of this state that the court which rendered the decree does not now have jurisdiction under jurisdictional prerequisites substantially in accordance with this title or has declined to assume jurisdiction to modify the decree and (b) the court of this state has jurisdiction.

Professor Bodenheimer, the reporter for the committee which prepared the Uniform Law, interprets the effects of section 5163 (§14 of the Act) as follows:

> A typical example is the case of the couple who are divorced in state A, their matrimonial home state, and whose children are awarded to the wife, subject to visitation rights of the husband. Wife and children move to state B, with or without permission of the court to remove the children. State A has continuing jurisdiction and the courts in state B may not hear the wife's petition to make her the sole custodian, eliminate visitation rights, or make any other modification of the decree, even though state B has in the meantime become the "home state" under section 3 (Civ.Code, §5151(5)). The jurisdiction of state A continues and is exclusive as long as the husband lives

9. The Code Commissioner's Notes to section 5155 (§6 of the Act) read in part:

> Because of the havoc wreaked by simultaneous and competitive jurisdiction…this section seeks to avoid jurisdictional conflict with all feasible means, including novel methods. Courts are expected to take an active part under this section in seeking out information about custody proceedings concerning the same child pending in other states. In a proper case jurisdiction is yielded to the other state either under this section or under section 7 [§5156]. Both sections must be read together.
>
> When the courts of more than one state have jurisdiction under sections 3 [§5152] or 14 [§5163], priority in time determines which court will proceed with the action, but the application of the inconvenient forum principle of section 7 [§5156] may result in the handling of the case by the other court.
>
> While jurisdiction need not be yielded under subsection (a) if the other court would not have jurisdiction under the criteria of this Act, the policy against simultaneous custody proceedings is so strong that it might in a particular situation be appropriate to leave the case to the other court even under such circumstances.…
>
> Once a custody decree has been rendered in one state, jurisdiction is determined by sections 8 [§5157] and 14 [§5163].

> in state A unless he loses contact with the children, for example, by not using his visitation privileges for three years.

(Bodenheimer, *Uniform Child Custody Jurisdiction Act* (1969) 22 Vand.L.Rev. 1207, 1237; see similar examples in Commissioner's Notes to §3, Uniform Child Custody Jurisdiction Act.) Substitute North Dakota for "A" and California for "B" and you have the present fact situation. All petitions for modification are to be addressed to the state which rendered the original decree if that state has jurisdiction under the standards of the Act (*In re Marriage of Schwander*, 79 Cal.App.3d 1013, 1019, 145 Cal.Rptr. 325).

We can understand the trial judge's concern over California not being able to determine custody of its own residents and the possibility of multiple proceedings in the action. This very concern states have for their residents or for those merely within their borders has caused the interstate conflicts and thus prompted the Legislature to adopt the Act.

The Act permits the state which first obtained jurisdiction to exercise it. It does not shock the conscience that California must bow to North Dakota and yet appear to have greater access to the facts.[10] The North Dakota court may have abused its discretion in not permitting California to exercise jurisdiction. "[T]here is no reason why [the] courts of one state should not be able to 'assume with confidence that the courts of the other jurisdiction will act with wisdom and sincerity in all matters pertaining to the welfare of this child.' [Citations]" (*Ferreira v. Ferreira*, 9 Cal.3d 824, 841, fn. 21....) In this connection, the statements of the referee related to the trial judge here do not necessarily establish the fact the North Dakota court will not exercise its jurisdiction substantially in conformity with this Act.

If California is the more appropriate forum for the custody decision because of the location of witnesses, etc., North Dakota should stay its proceedings and allow California to proceed (§5156). If the North Dakota trial court makes the wrong decision on whether to stay its proceedings, the appellate court of North Dakota should rectify the mistake. This is not the California trial or reviewing court function. The purpose of section 5156 is to provide the court with a tool to allow another court to go forward, not to create a confrontation or deny another court the authority to proceed. Were the roles of North Dakota and California reversed on these facts, we would expect the courts of North Dakota would require the proceedings in that state to be stayed (see *Bosse v. Superior Court*, 89 Cal.App.3d 440, 443–445, 152 Cal.Rptr. 665; *In re Marriage of Kern*, 87 Cal.App.3d 402, 150 Cal.Rptr. 860).

The only exception noted in the Act for a state exercising jurisdiction contrary to this provision giving priority to the time the proceeding is initiated is where the child is abandoned or endangered (§5152, subd. (1)(c)) or where *no* forum has jurisdiction under the provisions. Neither of these conditions exists (§5152, subd. (1)(d)). While full faith and credit has never been given to foreign custody decrees by California courts (see 53 Harvard L.Rev. 1024, 1029), foreign decrees must be given "due consideration" on the grounds of comity (*Sampsell v. Superior Court*, 32 Cal.2d 763, 780, 197 P.2d 739). The Act makes a comprehensive attempt to accommodate all these state interests (see the Uniform Child Custody Jurisdiction Act, 62 Cal.L.Rev. 365). It should be adhered to by our courts.

10. Section 5156, subdivision (7), allows necessary travel expenses and costs of the parties and their witnesses in the more convenient forum.

We hold under the facts of this case the California court was required to stay its proceedings under Civil Code section 5155, subdivision (1), because a custody proceeding was already pending in North Dakota and the relief sought amounted to a modification of the North Dakota decree when that state still had jurisdiction and had assumed it (§5163, subd. (1)(a)). North Dakota has continuing jurisdiction under the Act and the right to exercise it. There is nothing in the record to show North Dakota was not acting substantially in conformity with this Act.

Let a writ of prohibition issue directing the respondent San Diego County Superior Court to stay all proceedings in case number 421423 until such time as it may resume such custody proceedings in accordance with Civil Code section 5155 and the other sections of the Uniform Child Custody Jurisdiction Act and to vacate all orders made in connection with such proceedings.

[Dissenting opinion omitted]

COMMENTS

Palm is governed by principles of the Uniform Child Custody Jurisdiction Act (UCCJA). The purpose of the Act is to prevent "child snatching," which is likely to occur when multiple competing jurisdictions are involved. Whether the Act is as effective as it was meant to be is subject to conjecture. Its language continues to invite judicial discretion, as, for example, when it refers repeatedly to the "best interests of the child," to "significant connection" as a jurisdictional alternative, or to the existence of an "emergency." The power to stay proceedings because the court finds itself to be an "inconvenient forum" is essentially discretionary, as are the findings that the petitioner has engaged in "reprehensible conduct." In the latter instance, the court may decline to exercise jurisdiction "if this is just and proper under the circumstances." Any of these provisions can be used to foster parochial interests, especially in the lower courts. In fact, *Palm* illustrates the parochial bent of the lower courts, which later had to be corrected on the appellate level.

Nevertheless, it would be erroneous to assume that the Act is ineffective. Part of its effectiveness lies in the fact that people believe in it. Courts are more likely now than earlier to honor out-of-state custody decrees, even in jurisdictions like Florida and New York, which were traditionally disinclined to do so. The parties concerned may be more willing than in the past to follow legal procedures, although it is impossible to verify this fact statistically. If child snatching occurs, parties may go underground rather than to court to try to obtain a new decision in their favor. This, in a backhanded way, also attests to the Act's effectiveness, because parties may increasingly weigh the burdens of deviant behavior; and this, in the long run, is likely to lower incidence of child snatching. It is not so much the wording of the Act that achieves these positive results, however, but the mystique that surrounds its universal adoption.

One of the characteristics of the best-interests standard in regard to custody decisions is its strong emotional appeal. It seems to disregard legal technicalities and to focus instead on what people feel to be of the essence: the good of the young. The use of procedural technicalities, if children are involved, is especially frowned on by lawyers and lay people alike. An inevitable side effect of this attitude is the possibility of multiple jurisdictions for controversies relating to children. Every court in the nation could potentially assume the power to relitigate custody disputes as though no decision had been rendered in another state. Any effort to claim res judicata or full faith and credit, according to this attitude, should be met with judicial disdain because it asserts the powers of a foreign sovereign over a child. The child, the reasoning would go, should not be treated as a chattel and custody should not be treated as a chose in action. The whole concept of res judicata, following this extreme view, would be contrary to the best interests of the child because it would erect a procedural hurdle preventing reexamination of the ever-changing merits of the case. Any contact with the child, no matter how fleeting, would suffice to allow a court to take a second or third look at a disputed question of custody. Accordingly, the best-interests standard in its pure form can be viewed not merely as an invocation of unfettered judicial discretion but also, in a jurisprudential sense, as a demand for absolute justice by perpetual reexamination that in no other area of law has met with such widespread approval.

However, the search for absolute justice, regardless of procedures and technical rules, must ultimately lead to lawlessness, especially by parties who take the law into their own hands. As exemplified by the facts of *Palm*, this may take the form of snatching the child and trying for justice in another jurisdiction or, more frequently, not returning the child after an authorized visit. Sooner or later such actions must lead the judiciary to realize that using the best-interests standard without qualification is not really in the children's best interests, and that the law, even in this area, is largely concerned with rendering peace even at the cost of occasional injustice. In the authors' view, the UCCJA is trying to achieve this result without openly acknowledging it. The reasons for this roundabout procedure are essentially political. It is impossible to tamper with the best-interests standard by direct legislation. The UCCJA therefore seemingly confirms the standard but tries to limit an excessive application of it that would be harmful to children's long-range interests in interstate cases.

Since jurisdictional competition is at the source of the problem of child-snatching, a technique must be developed to minimize its effects. The Act tries to accomplish this result by differentiating between having jurisdiction on the one hand and exercising it on the other. In other words, a court, in a custody dispute, should engage in a two-pronged examination: first, determining whether it has jurisdiction, and second, if it finds it has, deciding whether to exercise it. *Palm* illustrates that an erroneous exercise of jurisdiction may lead to appellate intervention under a theory that, although there is in fact jurisdiction, any exercise of it in the circumstances was an abuse of discretion. In effect this means that jurisdiction, which traditionally has been perceived as the unqualified power to hear and to decide a case, has been limited. It also means that in actual application the court that first becomes active in a custody dispute will prevail with greater frequency than in the past. Custody decisions will have res judicata effects, regardless of whether the parties concerned feel that justice has been done, and they will enjoy some measure of full faith and credit. The decisions will no longer be perceived as being in personam in precisely the way *May v. Anderson* (see p. 1040), saw them, but will be considered entitled to full faith and credit if the due process requirements of reasonable notice and opportunity to be heard are met.

The Federal Parental Kidnapping Prevention Act of 1980 is an attempt by Congress to intercede in local jurisdictional conflicts. The Act, in following UCCJA guidelines, calls for the granting of full faith and credit to foreign custody decrees that have met the requirements of due process. In addition, the Federal Parent Locator Service can be used to locate a parent or other person who has violated a lawful custody order. The final provision of the Act applies the federal felony statute to parental kidnappings, thus drawing the resources of the FBI and the United States Attorney General into the conflict.

REFERENCES

Brigitte M. Bodenheimer, *The International Kidnapping of Children: The United States Approach*, 11 FAM. L.Q. 83 (1977).

Brigitte M. Bodenheimer, *Progress Under the Uniform Child Custody Jurisdiction Act and Remaining Problems: Punitive Decrees, Joint Custody, and Excessive Modification*, 65 CAL. L. REV. 978 (1977).

Brigitte Bodenheimer & Janet Neeley-Kvarme, *Jurisdiction Over Child Custody and Adoption After Shaffer and Kulko*, 12 U.C.D. L. REV. 229 (1979)

Sanford N. Katz, CHILD SNATCHING 1–88 (1981).

KUMAR v. SUPERIOR COURT

Supreme Court of California

32 Cal.3d 689, 652 P.2d 1003, 186 Cal.Rptr. 772 (1982)

KAUS, Justice.

Jitendra Kumar seeks a writ of mandate to compel respondent superior court to quash service of process and to dismiss an order to show cause in a child custody action brought by Yvonne Kumar for modification of a New York support order and custody/visitation decree. We must decide whether California has authority to modify the out-of-state custody decree, a question which has presented the most difficult problem in the interpretation and application of the Uniform Child Custody Jurisdiction Act (hereafter Uniform Act). We conclude that, under the letter and spirit of the Uniform Act, New York has continuing jurisdiction to modify its custody decree so long as it retains significant connections with the child and that, unless New York declines to exercise jurisdiction, California has no authority to modify the decree.

Yvonne and Jitendra were divorced in New York in 1974. Yvonne received custody of their only child, Sunjay. Jitendra was granted visitation rights. In 1977 a New York court modified the support agreement and enforced Yvonne's right to support. All parties continued to live in New York until April 1979 when Yvonne took Sunjay to California.[2] The parties agree that Jitendra was not notified of the move until Yvonne and Sunjay had left New York.

In July 1980 Jitendra hired California counsel who registered the New York custody decree in California and procured a writ of habeas corpus directing Yvonne to produce Sunjay in court. Jitendra's visitation rights were enforced in that proceeding. Jitendra later served Yvonne with a motion in the New York court to modify the custody and visitation provisions of the New York order. On receipt of the New York papers, Yvonne sought an order to show cause in California to modify the visitation and support provisions of the New York order, to determine alleged spousal support arrearages, and to award attorneys' fees. Jitendra moved to dismiss the custody/visitation proceeding for lack of subject matter jurisdiction; he also filed a motion to quash service in the child support proceedings for lack of in personam jurisdiction.

In supporting declarations, Jitendra alleged: He was personally served in New York and did not consent to exercise of personal jurisdiction; his only contact with California was the initiation of habeas corpus proceedings and the registration of the New York decree; New York issued the initial custody decree and continues to have significant connections with Sunjay; Sunjay lived all his life in New York until removed to California; maternal grandparents and other relatives, neighbors, and friends live in New York and can testify to Sunjay's behavior and adjustment; Jitendra regularly exercised visitation rights with Sunjay until April 1979 when, without warning, Yvonne called from Tennessee to say she and Sunjay were on their way to California; Yvonne wrongfully removed Sunjay from New York; in the one telephone call she made to him, on arrival in California, she gave him a telephone number, not her own; he was unable to make contact; after six months he finally located her (address, no telephone) through her parents in New York; Yvonne did not respond to numerous telephone messages and notes directed to her through others and did not acknowledge receipt of checks which he sent; a friend contacted her in April of 1980 and he himself initiated the habeas corpus proceedings to secure a two-week visit.

In opposing declarations, Yvonne alleged: There were no visitation problems while she was in New York; she did not advise Jitendra in advance of their departure because she was afraid of him; she called him on the way to California and again after she arrived, giving him her brother's address and telephone number; Jitendra did not try to communicate with her or Sunjay until five months after their departure when he sent Sunjay a birthday card; Yvonne informed Jitendra of her telephone number as soon as she got one; she did not cash the checks because she felt he should pay "the entire amount of child support"; she at no time deprived Jitendra of his son — in fact, after the habeas corpus proceeding they made arrangements on summer and Christmas visitation.

Following a hearing, on January 19, 1981, the trial court found the service of process "adequate" and denied Jitendra's dismissal motion for the following reasons: "1. The closest contacts with the child's present and future living environment, present and predictable development, as well as available witnesses are in the State of California. [¶] 2. Respondent has sought, and received, assistance with enforcement of visitation rights by [the California court] having accepted and

2. The New York custody decree did not expressly forbid removal of Sunjay or place any restriction on Yvonne's choice of residence. The law of New York requires, however, that the custodial parent reside with the child in a location reasonably conducive to the exercise of visitation privileges.... [T]he New York court determined that Yvonne violated an "implied prohibition" against removing Sunjay to California.

enforced the foreign New York decree. [The California court] can fairly adjudicate further similar issues as they arise. [¶] 3. The best interests of the child can best be gauged by the jurisdiction with the closest contacts with the child. The relative convenience of either party should not be a paramount consideration."

Jitendra seeks a writ of mandate and/or prohibition to dismiss the proceedings below or, alternatively, to stay such proceedings pending a determination by the State of New York as to whether it will continue to assume jurisdiction in this matter.

To date New York has not refrained from exercise of its jurisdiction. On January 21, 1981 — two days after the respondent court's order — the trial court of New York entered an ex parte show cause order and, on March 25, 1981, determined it had jurisdiction and rendered its decision, followed by a formal order on May 7, 1981.[4]

...With respect to the custody/visitation proceedings, Jitendra claims that (1) California lacks jurisdiction to modify the New York decree because of Yvonne's wrongful conduct in removing Sunjay from New York (§5157, subd. (2)); (2) California should decline to exercise jurisdiction because custody proceedings are pending in New York (§5155, subd. (1)); and (3) California has no authority to modify the New York decree unless New York declines to exercise its continuing jurisdiction to modify (§5163, subd. (1)).

We conclude that Jitendra had insufficient minimum contacts to establish personal jurisdiction (*Kulko v. California Superior Court* (1978) 436 U.S. 84, 91–92, 98 S.Ct. 1690, 1696, 56 L.Ed.2d 132) and that principles of fairness preclude use of Jitendra's *habeas corpus* proceedings as a contact to establish personal jurisdiction (*Titus v. Superior Court* (1972) 23 Cal.App.3d 792, 100 Cal.Rptr. 477). Further, we agree that section 5163 is controlling in this case — that New York has continuing jurisdiction to modify its custody order and that California has no authority to modify that order unless New York declines jurisdiction.

Subject Matter Jurisdiction

The Uniform Act, adopted in 44 states by 1981, was promulgated for the stated purposes of avoiding jurisdictional competition and conflict, promoting interstate cooperation, litigating custody where child and family have closest connections, discouraging continuing conflict over custody, deterring abductions and unilateral removals of children, avoiding relitigation of another state's custody decisions, and promoting exchange of information and other mutual assistance between courts of sister states. (Uniform Act, §1; Civ.Code, §5150.)[5]

The jurisdictional grounds for making a child custody determination are set out in section 5152 of the Uniform Act. Sections that follow address due process rights of the parties and prescribe appropriate procedures. Other sections, crucial

4. The formal order provides in part: "[T]his Court retains continuing jurisdiction over the matters of alimony, child support and custody as between the parties herein.... [A]ny and all arrears of alimony and child support payable by defendant to plaintiff from April 11, 1979 until the present date are hereby cancelled in their entirety.... [A]ll future obligations of defendant to pay alimony and child support are hereby suspended until plaintiff allows defendant the opportunity to avail himself of his judicially decreed visitation rights by residing with the infant SUNJAY RICHARD at a location reasonably conducive to the exercise of said visitation rights.... [I]n all other respects the decree of divorce between plaintiff and defendant dated the 2nd day of October, 1974 shall remain unchanged and in full force and effect." In suspending future obligations to pay child support, the New York court granted Jitendra more relief than he requested.

5. California adopted the act in 1973. New York adopted it in 1977. Neither state made any changes in the portions of the act relevant to our determination. For the sake of simplicity, we make no reference to the New York statute; instead, reference will be to the equivalent sections of the Uniform Act.

to our determination, articulate the circumstances or situations in which the courts may or should decline to *exercise* jurisdiction. The sections relied upon by Jitendra (§§5155, 5157, and 5163) fall in the latter category. We stress this point because both parties speak of either California or New York as lacking "jurisdiction" to act in the instant matter, when the crucial question is really whether the Uniform Act directs or allows exercise of jurisdiction. As shall appear, it is obvious that each state can claim to have jurisdiction from among the multifaceted components of section 5152. Indeed, this case is a good example of the "jurisdictional competition and conflict" (§5150) which the Uniform Act was designed to alleviate.

While the courts have given lip service to the policies provided by the Uniform Act, some have been reluctant to forego what they see as concurrent jurisdiction to proceed under the act. In no area has the confusion been greater than in the modification of out-of-state custody decrees.

Consistent with its goal of avoiding "relitigation of custody decisions of other states in this state insofar as feasible" (§1, subd. (6); Civ.Code, §5150, subd. (f)), the Uniform Act commands in section 13 (Civ.Code, §5162) that the courts of this state shall recognize and enforce "an initial or modification decree" of a court of another state which had assumed jurisdiction under the terms of the act. The next section, section 14 of the Uniform Act (Civ.Code, §5163), governs the authority of California to modify an out-of-state decree.[6]...

Professor Bodenheimer, reporter for the special committee which drafted the Uniform Act, interpreted the section's language — "this state shall not modify" — as meaning precisely what it says: "In other words, the continuing jurisdiction of the prior court is exclusive. Other states do not have jurisdiction to modify the decree. They must respect and defer to the prior state's continuing jurisdiction. Section 14 is the key provision which carries out the Act's two objectives of (1) preventing the harm done to children by shifting them from state to state to relitigate custody, and (2) preventing jurisdictional conflict between the states after a custody decree has been rendered.... [¶] Exclusive continuing jurisdiction is not affected by the child's residence in another state for six months or more. Although the new state becomes the child's home state, significant connection jurisdiction continues in the state of the prior decree where the court record and other evidence exists and where one parent or another contestant continues to reside. *Only when the child and all parties have moved away is deference to another state's continuing jurisdiction no longer required.*" (Emphasis added; Bodenheimer, *Interstate Custody: Initial Jurisdiction and Continuing Jurisdiction Under the UCCJA* (1981) 14 Fam.L.Q. 203, 214–215.)

The first question, then, is whether New York, which rendered the initial decree in this case, now has jurisdiction under the "jurisdictional prerequisites" of the Uniform Act. New York obtained jurisdiction for the initial decree under the first subdivision of section 3 of the Uniform Act (§5152, subd. (1)(a)) as Sunjay's "home state."[8] After Sunjay was removed to California, however, New York's jurisdiction to modify its decree was conditioned on the second subdivision of section 3 of the Uniform Act (§5152, subd. (1)(b)) and depended, inter alia, on continued

---

6. "Once a custody decree has been rendered in one state, jurisdiction is determined by sections 8 [Civ.Code, §5157] and 14 [§5163]." (Commissioner's Notes (1979 ed.) Uniform Laws Annot., Child Custody Jurisdiction, §6, p. 135.) Section 5157 incorporates the "clean hands" doctrine.

8. "Home state" is defined in section 1 of the Uniform Act (§5151) as "the state in which the child immediately preceding the time involved lived with...a parent...for at least six consecutive months.... Periods of temporary absence of any of the named persons are considered as part of the six month or other period."

"significant connection" of Sunjay and at least one of his parents with the State of New York.

The evidence is uncontested that Jitendra is a full time resident of New York and that Sunjay's maternal grandparents and numerous family friends, relatives, doctors, and teachers continue to live in New York. Yvonne did not dispute that Sunjay, despite an absence of a year and a half, maintained these connections with New York and that evidence concerning his past and future familial, social, and educational welfare was available in that state.

Respondent court failed to consider the provisions of section 5163. Reviewing the uncontested evidence, the court concluded that California had the *"closest* contacts" with the child and found that determinative. The court's finding, by implication, however, acknowledges that New York continued to have significant connection with Sunjay. Respondent court treated the competing jurisdictional claims of the New York and California residents as though they were involved in an initial custody dispute, with competing concurrent jurisdiction.[9] Under section 5163, however, New York's continuing authority to modify its decree remains exclusive and unabated — "a court of this state shall not modify" (§5163, subd. (1)) — so long as that state has significant connection with Sunjay, despite his presence here or other connections with California. The commissioners' note to this section of the Uniform Act makes clear that New York would lose jurisdiction in this case only if "all persons involved have moved away or the contact with the state has otherwise become slight...." (9 U.Laws Annot. (1979 ed.) §14, p. 154.)

The conclusion is inescapable that New York falls within the provisions of subdivision (1)(a) of section 5163 as a state which now has jurisdiction "under jurisdictional prerequisites substantially in accordance with this title."

Professor Bodenheimer described a situation remarkably similar to that before us: "A typical example is the case of the couple who are divorced in state A, their matrimonial home state, and whose children are awarded to the wife, subject to visitation rights of the husband. Wife and children move to state B, with or without permission of the court to remove the children. State A has continuing jurisdiction and the courts in state B may not hear the wife's petition to make her the sole custodian, eliminate visitation rights, or make any other modification of the decree, even though state B has in the meantime become the 'home state' under section 3. The jurisdiction of state A continues and is exclusive as long as the husband lives in state A unless he loses contact with the children, for example, by not using his visitation privileges for three years." (Bodenheimer, *Uniform Child Custody Jurisdiction Act: A Legislative Remedy for Children Caught in the Conflict of Laws* (1969) 22 Vand.L.Rev. 1207, 1237.)

Thus, in accord with the letter of section 5163 and its purpose "to achieve greater stability of custody arrangements and avoid forum shopping" (9 U.Laws Annot. (1979 ed.) p. 154, Commrs. Note), *all* petitions for modification must be addressed to the state which rendered the original decree if that state had and retains jurisdiction under the standards of the act. (*Id.*; *Palm v. Superior Court* (1979) 97 Cal.App.3d 456, 468, 158 Cal.Rptr. 786; *In re Marriage of Schwander* (1978) 79 Cal.App.3d 1013, 1019, 145 Cal.Rptr. 325.)

In support of her claim that California has jurisdiction to modify the New York decree, Yvonne relies upon what has been termed the "myth of concurrent modifi-

9. In such predecree battles, a stated goal of the Uniform Act is to "assure that litigation concerning the custody of a child take place ordinarily in the state with which the child and his family have the closest connection...." (§5150.)

cation jurisdiction." (Bodenheimer, *Interstate Custody: Initial Jurisdiction and Continuing Jurisdiction Under the UCCJA, supra,* 14 Fam.L.Q. 203, 216.) Under Yvonne's analysis, one starts with section 5152, rather than section 5163: California has jurisdiction as Sunjay's "home state" (§5152, subd. (1)(a)); New York has some connection with Sunjay (§5152, subd. (1)(b)). Yvonne then considers which forum has greater connection with the child and concludes, as did the trial court, that California has the "closest" connections.[10]

Yvonne is not alone in the confusion engendered by the failure to recognize the applicability of section 5163 whenever a *modification* of jurisdiction is involved. California appellate courts have played some part in perpetuating the myth of concurrent modification jurisdiction.[11] The confusion can be avoided by clearly distinguishing between initial and modification jurisdiction.[12]

Initial jurisdiction is determined by the guidelines of section 5152, which point to the state with the closest connections to the child and to information about his present and future well-being. *Modification* jurisdiction is perhaps best viewed as an extension of the recognition and enforcement provisions of the Uniform Act. (§5162; Bodenheimer, 65 Cal.L.Rev. 978, 983–984.) California is not effectively enforcing the New York decree if it modifies the decree as soon as the child has spent six months within its borders. Under section 5163, the strong presumption is that the decree state will continue to have modification jurisdiction until it loses all or almost all connection with the child. If that state has lost contact, the analysis begins again with section 5152 to determine which other state has closest contact.

Application of the provisions of section 5163 to the instant case compels the conclusion that New York has continuing jurisdiction to modify its decree so long as Jitendra resides there and continues to assert and exercise his custody/visitation rights.[14]

Having decided that New York has continuing jurisdiction to modify its decree, we briefly mention the next condition set out in section 5163 as possibly giving California jurisdiction to modify the New York decree — has New York declined to exercise jurisdiction? The answer is clear on that point:... New York unequivocally asserts its continuing jurisdiction over the matter of custody. If and when either party seeks modification of the custody/visitation decree, New York will have to decide whether to assume or decline to exercise its modification jurisdiction under section 3 (Uniform Act, [§5152]), using the criteria set out in sec-

10. Under this analysis it is easy to see how presence of the child becomes a disproportionately controlling factor, despite the admonition in section 5152 that "physical presence in this state of the child, or of child and one of the contestants, is not alone sufficient to confer jurisdiction" (subd. (2)), and "physical presence of the child, while desirable, is not a prerequisite for jurisdiction to determine his custody" (subd. (3)).

11. Indeed, several of Jitendra's arguments concede concurrent modification jurisdiction to California, but urge that California would abuse its discretion in exercising jurisdiction.

12. Some California cases dealing with modification of either foreign or California decrees have failed to mention section 5163. Even those that recognize the section have tended to proceed, nevertheless, on an analysis that assumes "concurrent" modification jurisdiction. (See, e.g.,...*Palm v. Superior Court, supra,* 97 Cal.App.3d 456, 158 Cal.Rptr. 786.... For a more complete criticism of modification cases, see Bodenheimer, *Interstate Custody: Initial Jurisdiction and Continuing Jurisdiction Under the UCCJA, supra,* 14 FAM.L.Q. 203.)

14. Yvonne makes an argument that *if* Jitendra wanted to maintain New York jurisdiction, he should have brought action before the six months had elapsed which established California as Sunjay's home state. This problem is addressed by the commissioners, who state: "Also if the father...continued to live in State 1, but lets his wife keep the children for several years [in State 2] without asserting his custody rights and without visits of the children in State 1, modification jurisdiction of State 1 would cease."

In the instant case, however, nothing indicates that Jitendra intentionally lost contact with his son. In fact, the parties disagree over whether Jitendra knew how to contact the child; he apparently tried. Here "several years" have not elapsed. We decline to set guidelines on just how long one parent can withdraw from his family in another state before losing the right to modify within the decree state.

tion 7 (Uniform Act, [§5156]). New York may then decide, as did California in *Schlumpf v. Superior Court, supra*, 79 Cal.App.3d 892, 145 Cal.Rptr. 190, where the child and father had resided in another state for nine years, that the decree state is an inconvenient forum.

On December 28, 1980, Congress enacted the Parental Kidnaping Prevention Act of 1980 (28 U.S.C. §1738A) to implement the full faith and credit clause of the United States Constitution. The legislation did not become effective until July 1, 1981, and there may be some question whether it is retroactive (see *In re Marriage of Leonard, supra*, 122 Cal.App.3d 443, 175 Cal.Rptr. 903). Like the Uniform Act, the federal law limits the exercise of jurisdiction to modify a sister-state decree and, for what it is worth, the federal legislation would compel the result we reach in the instant case.

The federal law provides that "(a) The appropriate authorities of every State shall enforce according to its terms, and shall not modify except as provided in subsection (f) of this section, any child custody determination made consistently with the provisions of this section by a court of another State...." Subdivision (f) provides: "A court of a State may modify a determination of the custody of the same child made by a court of another State, if — (1) it has jurisdiction to make such a child custody determination; and (2) the court of the other State *no longer has jurisdiction*, or it has declined to exercise such jurisdiction to modify such determination." (Italics added.)

...

In Personam Jurisdiction

There remains, however, the issue of personal jurisdiction with respect to child support and attorneys' fees. Under *Kulko v. California Superior Court, supra*, 436 U.S. 84, 98 S.Ct. 1690, 56 L.Ed.2d 132, California may not exercise personal jurisdiction over an out-of-state parent to modify an agreement for support of a child living in California unless jurisdiction is established through sufficient minimum contacts within the state. In spite of considerable showing of "effect" in California, the United States Supreme Court in *Kulko* indicated that a New York father should not be expected to undergo "the substantial financial burden and personal strain of litigating a child-support in a forum 3,000 miles away" when his contact with the state had been insignificant. (*Id.*, at p. 97, 98 S.Ct. at p. 1699.)

Yvonne argues that Jitendra had sufficient contact with California through his use of this state's courts in securing the habeas corpus order, which constituted a general appearance on his part. This court has held that neither execution of a guaranty agreement nor a special appearance in California to move for an order to quash service of summons for lack of personal jurisdiction was sufficient to establish jurisdiction over a nonresident. (*Sibley v. Superior Court* (1976) 16 Cal.3d 442, 128 Cal.Rptr. 34, 546 P.2d 322.) Although *Sibley* distinguishes cases where nonresidents seek significant benefits from the activity in California, it holds that the imposition of jurisdiction should be both constitutionally justified and "fair."

Principles of fairness preclude the exercise of personal jurisdiction where connection with the state resulted from an effort to encourage visitation with the noncustodial parent. (*Titus v. Superior Court, supra*, 23 Cal.App.3d 792, 100 Cal.Rptr. 477.) This is especially true in the instant case, where Jitendra was virtually forced into the California court because Yvonne denied him his visitation rights. It would be grossly unfair to allow her now to claim that he thereby established "minimum contact" sufficient to establish personal jurisdiction.

Let a peremptory writ of mandate issue directing respondent court to quash service of process and to dismiss the custody/visitation proceedings.

SAMS v. BOSTON

Supreme Court of Appeals of West Virginia
181 W.Va. 706, 384 S.E.2d 151 (1989)

McHUGH, Justice:

This appeal presents an important question under the Uniform Child Custody Jurisdiction Act and under the Parental Kidnapping Prevention Act, specifically, whether a state remains the "home state" of children under those two Acts, for a reasonable period of time, where the children have been abducted to and concealed in another state by one of the parents. Holding in the affirmative, we affirm the order of the Circuit Court of Wood County, West Virginia, with respect to its having subject-matter jurisdiction. On the other hand, we reverse that court's separate order awarding permanent legal custody to the appellee-mother, and remand this case for a full evidentiary hearing to determine which of the parents should obtain permanent legal custody based upon the best interest of the children.

I

The appellee-mother, Tina Ruth Sams, formerly Tina Ruth Boston, filed in the Circuit Court of Wood County, West Virginia, for divorce from the appellant-father, Geary Lee Boston, in October, 1983. The parties had resided in such county and state since at least July, 1972, when they were married there. The only ground alleged initially for the divorce was irreconcilable differences. In the divorce complaint the appellee asked for temporary and permanent legal and physical custody of the three children born of the marriage, namely, Geary Lee Boston, Jr., then age ten (born November 13, 1972), Joseph Daniel Boston, then age nine (born June 23, 1974) and Kristina Ruth Boston, then age three (born July 2, 1980). In November, 1983, the appellant failed to return the three children to the appellee after obtaining only temporary physical custody of them during the exercise of visitation arrangements. He also thereafter secreted himself and the three children from the appellee.

The appellee in December, 1984, amended her divorce complaint to include, as grounds, cruel and inhuman treatment, desertion for six months and separate habitation for over a year. In May, 1985, the Circuit Court of Wood County, West Virginia, granted a divorce to the appellee based upon the one-year separation. The court order was silent as to child custody.[1]

From November, 1983, until December, 1986, the appellee attempted to ascertain the whereabouts of the children and the appellant. In December, 1986, she finally located them in Crawfordville, Wakulla County, Florida. In order for the appellant to agree to the children's visitation with the appellee during the next summer, the appellee executed a written agreement not to seek permanent legal custody of the children.

---

1. The divorce commissioner had, erroneously, recommended to the court that no order relative to child custody should be entered because of the children's and the appellant's absence from the jurisdiction throughout the divorce proceedings. Under *W.Va.Code,* 48-10-3(c) [1981], the physical presence of the child in this state, while desirable, is not a prerequisite for jurisdiction to determine his or her custody. Similarly, *W.Va.Code,* 48-10-5 [1981] sets forth certain methods of giving notice required for the exercise of jurisdiction over a person outside this state who does not submit to the jurisdiction of a court in this state.

The children came to visit the appellee in Wood County, West Virginia, in June, 1987. In July, 1987, the appellee, still having physical custody of the children, filed in Wood County, West Virginia, a petition for modification of the May, 1985 divorce decree, so as to obtain permanent legal, as well as physical, custody of the children and child support from the appellant. In that petition the appellee alleged that she had been the primary caretaker of the children until the appellant "snatched" them in November, 1983, and that she would be a fit and proper custodian of the children.

The appellant filed a motion to dismiss for "*forum non conveniens*" and "to enforce stipulation of visitation," alleging (1) that Florida was the "home state" of the children under the Uniform Child Custody Jurisdiction Act ("the UCCJ Act"), adopted by both the State of West Virginia and the State of Florida, and alleging (2) that the appellee had violated the visitation agreement by seeking permanent legal custody of the children. Counsel for the appellant made a so-called "special appearance" at a hearing on August 10, 1987 before a family law master…[who] denied the appellant's motion to dismiss and for enforcement of the "stipulation of visitation."

A hearing was subsequently held before the family law master, on August 18, 1987, on the appellee's petition for child custody. The appellant was not personally present but his West Virginia attorney noted a so-called "special appearance."…

At the August 18, 1987 hearing the appellee testified that she had been the primary caretaker of the children until the appellant abducted them in November, 1983. She also testified that she was working as a secretary and that she had signed the agreement not to seek permanent custody of the children because she did not have any other choice in order to see the children.

The oldest child, Geary, Jr., also testified at that hearing. He was fourteen years old at the time of the hearing. He testified that he preferred to stay with his mother. His only stated reason was "to get reacquainted with" her. He admitted that his father treated him well and that he liked the school he attended in Florida.

On August 18, 1987, during the custody-determination hearing, the family law master received information that a child custody proceeding had been brought in Florida, by the appellant, *after* the appellee's petition for child custody had been filed in West Virginia. The family law master, on August 19, 1987, sent a letter to the Florida circuit court judge (Wakulla County) informing the latter of the pending West Virginia child custody proceeding.[7] In his letter to the Florida judge the family law master opined that, upon the facts recited in the letter, West Virginia was the "home state" under the UCCJ Act (when the divorce action was filed) and that although the children had substantial contacts with Florida, West Virginia was the more appropriate forum for deciding child custody due to the appellant's "inequitable conduct" of absconding with the children and concealing their whereabouts. The Florida court did not respond.[8]

---

7. Before determining whether to decline or retain jurisdiction, the court may communicate with a court of another state and exchange information pertinent to the assumption of jurisdiction by either court with a view to assuring that jurisdiction will be exercised by the more appropriate court and that a forum will be available to the parties. *W.Va.Code,* 48-10-7(d)[1981].

8. If the court is informed during the course of the proceeding, that a proceeding concerning the custody of the child was pending in another state before the court assumed jurisdiction, it *shall* stay the proceeding *and communicate* with the court in which the other proceeding is pending, to the end that the issue may be litigated in the more appropriate forum and that information may be exchanged in accordance with other sections of the UCCJ Act. *Fla.Stat.Ann.* §61.1314(3)(West 1985); *W.Va.Code,* 48-10-6(c) [1981]. The pendency of any simultaneous custody proceedings should require some communication between the courts. Where one of the

The Florida court stayed its proceedings until it received notice of the West Virginia family law master's recommended decision. The master, in August, 1987, recommended that West Virginia had jurisdiction under the UCCJ Act as either the "home state" or the "significant-connection" state.[9] The master also recommended that permanent legal custody of the children be awarded, for the first time, to the appellee. The Circuit Court of Wood County, West Virginia, agreed with the master's recommendations and entered orders on the jurisdiction and custody-determination questions on October 1, 1987.

The Florida circuit court...on September 4, 1987, entered its "order on motion to determine jurisdiction," wherein that court determined that Florida was the "home state" of the children; that the appellant, "as natural parent," "moved with his children to Crawfordville, Florida, in June, 1984," (from December, 1983 until June, 1984 the court found that the appellant and the children had been in Wirt County, West Virginia); that the appellee had "abandoned" her plea for child custody when the May, 1985 divorce decree failed to name her as custodian; that the August 18, 1987 recommendation of the West Virginia family law master as to child custody was not entitled to full faith and credit under the federal statute known as the Parental Kidnapping Prevention Act of 1980 ("the Federal PKP Act"), as West Virginia was not the home state and had not been the home state within six months of the West Virginia child custody proceeding brought in July, 1987;[10] that irrespective of the allegation that the appellant had wrongfully removed the children from West Virginia, the UCCJ Act and the Federal PKP Act do not contemplate "punitive" decrees against a parent but, instead, contemplate decrees based upon the state having the most significant connection with the children.

In January, 1988, the Florida circuit court...entered a final order awarding permanent legal custody to the appellant. In that order that court found that the appellant's occupation as a lineman allowed him to provide well for the children; that the home environment in Florida had been loving and stable; that the chil-

---

8. *Continued*

courts has no legitimate claim to jurisdiction, the other court would simply point this out and add that any decree emanating from unauthorized proceedings would not be entitled to recognition under the UCCJ Act. Bodenheimer, *Interstate Custody: Initial and Continuing Jurisdiction Under the UCCJA*, 14 FAM.L.Q. 203, 212 (1981).

9. *W.Va.Code*, 48-10-2(5) [1981] defines the "home state" of a child for purposes of child custody determination under the UCCJ Act to mean

> the state in which the child immediately preceding the time involved lived with his parents, a parent or a person acting as a parent for at least six consecutive months and, in the case of a child less than six months old, the state in which the child lived from birth with any of the persons named. Periods of temporary absence of any of the named persons are counted as part of the six-month or other period[.]
>
> The "time involved" within the meaning of this definition of "home state" is the date when the custody proceeding at issue was brought....
>
> The "significant-connection" state of a child for purposes of child custody determination under the UCCJ Act is the state in which (1) the child and his parents, or the child and at least one contestant, have a significant connection with that state, and (2) there is substantial evidence available in that state concerning the child's present or future care, protection, training and personal relationships, so that (3) it is in the best interest of the child that a court in that state assume jurisdiction. *W.Va.Code*, 48-10-3(a)(2)[1981]. Despite the label of "significant connection," which is an undefined term, the gravamen of this possible alternative to "home-state" jurisdiction under the UCCJ Act is to determine which state has the greatest degree of access to relevant evidence to promote the best interest of the child; under the UCCJ Act, the "significant-connection" state may or may not be the "home state."... The UCCJ Act therefore recognizes that two states may have concurrent jurisdiction to determine child custody, the "home state" and the "significant-connection" state, with other sections of the Act being designed to result in only one court exercising jurisdiction....

10. The definition of the child's "home state" under the Federal PKP Act, 28 U.S.C. §1738A(b)(4)(1982), is identical to the UCCJ Act's definition thereof. See *supra* note 9. Unlike the UCCJ Act, the Federal PKP Act, for mandatory "full faith and credit" purposes, recognizes "significant-connection" jurisdiction only if there is no "home-state" jurisdiction at the time involved. *See* 28 U.S.C. §1738A(c)(2)(B)(1982).

dren liked their schools in Florida and were actively involved in school and other activities in Florida. Interestingly, the court, which had, as stated above, expressed earlier that the UCCJ Act and the Federal PKP Act did not contemplate "punitive" decrees, emphasized in this custody-determination order that the appellee had not allowed the children to have free and uncensored telephone conversations with the appellant during the time they have been in West Virginia with the appellee (since June, 1987).

The oldest child, now sixteen years of age, has continued to live with the appellee-mother since June, 1987. The middle child, now fifteen years of age, returned to Florida with the appellant-father for a time but is now back voluntarily with his mother. The youngest child, the now nine-year-old daughter, was, on an unspecified date, abducted again from the appellee-mother by the appellant-father, and she remains presently in Florida with him. For this last abduction, the appellant has been indicted under *W.Va.Code*, 61-2-14d [1984] for the felony of concealing or removing a minor child in violation of a court order and with the intent to deprive another person of lawful custody or visitation rights.

The appellant-father brought this appeal to challenge the jurisdiction and custody-determination orders of the Wood County, West Virginia, Circuit Court.

II

The purpose of the Federal PKP Act was to provide for mandatory nationwide enforcement of custody orders made in accordance with the terms of the UCCJ Act, in order to discourage interstate forum shopping in child custody cases and, more importantly, in the context of a "national epidemic of parental kidnap[p]ing," to "'eliminate the incentive for one parent to remove a minor child to another jurisdiction.'"...

The policy underlying the UCCJ Act of 1968 is the same....

To the extent that the requirements of the Federal PKP Act and of the UCCJ Act do not conflict, the statutes are complementary. However, in cases of conflict, the Federal PKP Act, under the supremacy clause of the *Constitution of the United States*, preempts the UCCJ Act of the respective states....

The UCCJ Act establishes requirements for obtaining subject-matter jurisdiction in an initial or modification proceeding involving an interstate custody dispute. Under section 3(a)(1) of the UCCJ Act, the first basis for subject-matter jurisdiction in a proceeding to obtain an initial custody decree is "home-state" jurisdiction....

For a state's initial custody decree to be entitled under the Federal PKP Act to enforcement and nonmodification in another state, the initial-decree state must have exercised jurisdiction consistent with the Federal PKP Act:

> (a) The appropriate authorities of every State shall enforce according to its terms, and shall not modify except as provided in subsection (f) of this section, any child custody determination made consistently with the provisions of this section by a court of another State.
>
> ...
>
> (c) A child custody determination made by a court of a State is consistent with the provisions of this section only if—
>
> (1) such court has jurisdiction under the law of such State; and

(2) one of the following conditions is met:

(A) such State (i) is the home State of the child on the date of the commencement of the proceeding, or (ii) had been the child's home State within six months before the date of the commencement of the proceeding and the child is absent from such State because of his removal or retention by a contestant or for other reasons, and a contestant continues to live in such State;

(B)(i) it appears that no other State would have jurisdiction under subparagraph (A), and (ii) it is in the best interest of the child that a court of such State assume jurisdiction because (I) the child and his parents, or the child and at least one contestant, have a significant connection with such State other than mere physical presence in such State, and (II) there is available in such State substantial evidence concerning the child's present or future care, protection, training, and personal relationships[.]

28 U.S.C. §1738A(a) & §1738A(c)(1)-(2)(A) & (B)(1982).

This language indicates that, unlike the UCCJ Act, which accords equal weight to its several jurisdictional bases, the Federal PKP Act gives a distinct priority to the state court exercising "home-state" jurisdiction to enter an initial custody decree. Therefore, the Federal PKP Act makes it judicially imprudent for a state court in one state to exercise jurisdiction to enter an initial custody decree when a state court in another state has "home-state" jurisdiction and has not declined to exercise that jurisdiction; if conflicting decrees were issued, only the custody decree of the "home-state" court would be entitled to full faith and credit under the Federal PKP Act....

In the case now before this Court the question is whether West Virginia was still the "home state" of the children at the time the appellee-mother brought the July, 1987 custody proceeding in West Virginia to obtain an initial child custody decree.[13] The appellant-father contends that the "home state" of the children shifted from West Virginia to Florida six months after the appellant, in June, 1984, secretly removed the children from West Virginia to Florida to live with him there. The appellant stresses the fact that the appellee did not commence a custody proceeding for an initial decree within six months after the children had been removed from West Virginia, as well as the fact that the children had been back in West Virginia for only about a month at the time the appellee brought her July, 1987 custody proceeding for an initial decree. Consequently, the appellant argues that the Florida, not the West Virginia, initial custody decree was based upon "home-state" jurisdiction as set forth in both the Federal PKP Act and the UCCJ Act. We disagree.

"Home-state" jurisdiction under both the Federal PKP Act and the UCCJ Act is technically possessed by a court in the state where the child lived for six consecutive months immediately preceding commencement of the custody proceeding, extended to include the six-month period immediately following removal of the child from that state....

13. It is uncontroverted that West Virginia was the "home state" of the children in October, 1983, when the appellee-mother brought her action in West Virginia seeking a divorce from the appellant-father and seeking temporary and permanent legal and physical custody of the children. The record before us does not clearly establish whether the Circuit Court of Wood County, West Virginia, had ever granted the appellee's request, in October, 1983, for temporary custody.

It is significant, however, that Professor Ratner [one of the principal consultants to the National Conference of Commissioners on Uniform State Laws for the UCCJA] has also rejected a "bright line" six-month standard for shifting of "home-state" jurisdiction where concealment, that is, "child-snatching," is involved.... Ratner, *Procedural Due Process and Jurisdiction to Adjudicate:...*(b) *The Uniform Child Custody Jurisdiction Act*, 75 Nw. U.L.Rev. 363, 386 n. 112 (1980).... He recommends the exclusion of concealment periods from the six-month-home period, otherwise, "concealment after removal is encouraged;" therefore, initial jurisdiction is in the state where a claimant resides and the child last resided with a parent or acting parent for "at least" six consecutive months "with the knowledge of the other claimants[.]" *Id.* at 411, 412.

The late Professor Bodenheimer, the reporter for the UCCJ Act, agreed. In condemning the asylum state's assumption of jurisdiction where there has been "child-snatching" prior to the initial custody decree, "perhaps the fastest growing breed" of "child-snatchers," she stated that "[t]he issue of custody is to be settled at *home*, that is, in the *state where the parents lived with the children as a family*." Bodenheimer, *Interstate Custody: Initial Jurisdiction and Continuing Jurisdiction Under the UCCJA*, 14 Fam.L.Q. 203, 226 (1981)(emphasis added).

...

The traditional "solution" for pre-decree "child-snatching" has been to rely upon section 8(a) of the UCCJ Act...which provides: "If the petitioner for an initial decree has wrongfully taken the child from another state or has engaged in similar reprehensible conduct[,] the court [in the asylum state] may decline to exercise jurisdiction if this is just and proper under the circumstances." The commissioners' note to this part of this section explains the concept:

> Subsection (a) extends the clean hands principle to cases in which a custody decree has not yet been rendered in any state. For example, if upon a *de facto* separation the wife returned to her own home with the children without objection by her husband and lived there for two years without hearing from him, and the husband without warning forcibly removes the children one night and brings them to another state, a court in that state although it has jurisdiction after 6 months may decline to hear the husband's custody petition. "Wrongfully" taking under this subsection does not mean that a "right" has been violated — both husband and wife as a rule have a right to custody until a court determination is made — but that one party's conduct is so objectionable that a court in the exercise of its inherent equity powers cannot in good conscience permit that party access to its jurisdiction.

Thus, under this provision, the Florida court, in its opinion, was authorized, but not required, to decline to exercise "home-state" jurisdiction which it possessed in this case. The Florida court believed that Florida technically had become the "home state" of the children in December, 1984, and that Florida technically had been the "home state" of the children within six months of their "wrongful" retention by the appellee-mother in West Virginia in the summer of 1987. We disagree with this technical, mathematical formula approach to subject-matter jurisdiction under the Federal PKP Act and the UCCJ Act in the context of "child-snatching."

Other courts have also refused to be so technical in deciding whether subject-matter jurisdiction exists in the context of "child-snatching." For example, in *Freeman v. Freeman*, 547 S.W.2d 437 (Ky.1977), the court held: "We do not regard a period of time in this state where a child is hidden from the other parent as having any effect on giving the child a 'home state' status." *Id.* at 441. Similarly, "we have little doubt that, if the children were wrongfully taken [out of state], this period would not affect the status of Tennessee as their home state of residence under the PKPA and the UCCJA." *Hooks v. Hooks*, 771 F.2d 935, 949 n. 14 (6th Cir.1985)....

A leading case from the State of California also refused to look exclusively to the passage of time, without considering whether the children got to a state by child-snatching. In *In re Marriage of Hopson*, 110 Cal.App.3d 884, 168 Cal.Rptr. 345 (1980), the court acknowledged that a "technical application" could be held to confer "significant-connection" jurisdiction on a court in the state to which the children had been abducted by a parent. *Id.* at 895, 168 Cal.Rptr. at 353. The court, relying expressly upon the intent of the UCCJ Act to deter abductions, refused, however, to recognize the asylum state's jurisdiction. "In the long run, refusal to condone abduction provides better stability for children who would otherwise remain subject to the exercise of lawless self-help by their embattled parents." *Id.* at 897, 168 Cal.Rptr. at 354.

Noting that the stay-at-home parent had brought her custody proceeding within nineteen months, but not within six months, after the children's abduction to another state by their father, the *Hopson* court concluded: "While it is unfortunate that the mother did not seek enforcement earlier..., she should not be penalized for not utilizing an advantageous procedure offered to her." *Id.* at 904, 168 Cal.Rptr. at 359.

Another leading case in this area is *Nehra v. Uhlar*, 43 N.Y.2d 242, 372 N.E.2d 4, 401 N.Y.S.2d 168 (1977). In that case the mother had absconded with the children and had concealed their whereabouts in another state. The father did not locate the children until more than nine months later. Shortly thereafter the mother brought a custody proceeding in the asylum state of New York. By the time the New York Court of Appeals issued its opinion, the children had been living with the mother in New York for over four and a half years, and the record indicated that the mother during that time had provided her children with a good home.

The New York Court of Appeals refused to modify the existing custody decree of a Michigan court awarding custody to the father. The court held that the mother's physical custody of the children for the preceding four and a half years, without more, was not a change in circumstances sufficiently extraordinary to justify upsetting the determination of the Michigan court. "If it were, a parent, having lost [or apprehensive of losing] a custody dispute in another State, might believe that by abducting the children, secreting them in New York, and waiting for time to pass, the prior [or contemplated] custody decree could be effectively nullified [or avoided]." *Id.* at 250, 372 N.E.2d at 8, 401 N.Y.S.2d at 172. The court did observe that if "just too many years had passed, even the unlawful act [of abducting the children] might have to be ignored[.]" *Id.* at 251, 372 N.E.2d at 8, 401 N.Y.S.2d at 173.

In reaching its holding the New York Court of Appeals in *Nehra v. Uhlar* stressed the deterrence of child-snatching to promote the best interest of all children: "This Court has recognized that if the best interest of all children are to be served, the abduction of children to avoid the effect of custody decrees must be deterred[.]" *Id.* at 249, 372 N.E.2d at 7, 401 N.Y.S.2d at 172. There may be cases, though, where the tension between the goals of deterring child-snatching and promoting the interest of the particular children in a stable home environment should be resolved in favor of the latter. "[T]he apparent imperative to discourage abduction must, when necessary, be submerged to the paramount concern in all custody matters: the best interest of the child." *Id.* at 250, 372 N.E.2d at 8, 401 N.Y.S.2d at 172.

It is interesting to note that the same parties were also involved in *Nehra v. Uhlar,* 168 N.J.Super. 187, 402 A.2d 264 (App.Div.), *petition for certification denied,* 81 N.J. 413, 408 A.2d 807 (1979), wherein that court concluded that the mere passage of so many years (more than six) during which the children had remained in the physical custody of the mother was sufficient to mandate a full inquiry into the best interest of the children. *Id.* at 194–95, 402 A.2d at 268. As to the fact that the children had been abducted by the mother, the New Jersey court, in requiring a hearing on the best interest of the children, remarked:

> [T]he welfare of the children is paramount. Their welfare should not be sacrificed on the altar of judicial punishment of a parent for her wrongdoing in removing the children from a foreign jurisdiction, or in violating the order of a foreign court.
>
> . . .
>
> We do not overlook nor condone the actions of the mother, or the fact that granting custody to her would in effect reward her for utilizing unlawful self-help in defying the orders of other courts and engaging in forum shopping by invoking the jurisdiction of courts of three states. Nevertheless, the paramount issue before the trial court and this court is necessarily the welfare of the children rather than the tactics of their parent. Thus, despite the improprieties of the mother and their impact upon the rights of the father, the court must primarily concern itself with the children and their welfare in this tragic and unfortunate custody struggle.

Id. at 194, 196, 402 A.2d at 267, 268–69 (citations omitted).[15]

The issue is, though, in which state should the evidentiary hearing on the best interest of the children be conducted? We are not persuaded by the suggestion that a court in the state to which the children were abducted should be allowed to try the custody case solely because the children's welfare is the controlling guide. "The court in State A [from which the children were abducted] knows as well as the court in state B [to which the children were abducted] that the child's welfare is the controlling guide." *Reed v. High,* 254 Pa.Super. 367, 370, 385 A.2d 1384, 1385 (1978)(Spaeth, J., joined by Cercone, J., concurring). Moreover, various sections of the UCCJ Act are designed to assure that the parties, the children and the evidence will be available to the court exercising jurisdiction, so that the ultimate question, the best interest of the children, can be decided on an appropriate record.

. . .

15. Other cases emphasizing the children's interest in a stable home environment and holding that the state to which the children were abducted has the subject-matter jurisdiction over the child custody dispute as, technically, the "home state" include *Bosse v. Superior Court,* 89 Cal.App.3d 440, 152 Cal.Rptr. 665 (1979); *but see* the *Hopson* case, discussed above in the text, decided later by the same court; *Mainster v. Mainster,* 466 So.2d 1228 (Fla.Dist.Ct.App.1985); *but see Mondy v. Mondy,* 428 So.2d 235 (Fla.1983)(a circuit court in that state should refuse to exercise jurisdiction to modify a custody decree of another state having jurisdiction when Florida petitioner has "snatched" children to Florida, "the kind of conduct which the UCCJA was designed to discourage[,]" *id.* at 238); *Snow v. Snow,* 369 N.W.2d 581 (Minn.Ct.App.1985); *Pierce v. Pierce,* 197 Mont. 16, 640 P.2d 899 (1982)(declining to follow the *Freeman* case, discussed above in the text, as the UCCJ Act does not support the "tolling" of the shift of "home-state" jurisdiction; based upon the authorities discussed in the text, we disagree). See generally annotation, *Validity, Construction, and Application of Uniform Child Custody Jurisdiction Act,* 96 A.L.R.3d 968 (1979 and Supp.1988).

Because our decision is based primarily upon a concern for the best interest of the children, rather than primarily upon punishing the appellant for child-snatching, there is no "punitive" decree problem here. A child custody decree is "punitive" only if it, without due regard to the best interest of the child, was based primarily upon punishing one parent for disregarding the court's authority or primarily upon punishing one parent for departing from the jurisdiction with the child, whether or not the departure contravened a court order.... Some courts have held that a "punitive" decree need not be given full faith and credit under the UCCJ Act. On the other hand, the Federal PKP Act makes no distinction between punitive decrees and other child custody decrees; it requires that a custody decree of another state be given full faith and credit if such decree meets the requirements of the Federal PKP Act.... In any event, the child custody decree to be entered by the Circuit Court of Wood County, West Virginia, after remand for a full evidentiary hearing on the current best interest of the children, would not be a "punitive" decree.[16]

...

Accordingly, we affirm the order of the Circuit Court of Wood County, West Virginia, declaring that it has subject-matter jurisdiction over this interstate child-custody dispute. On the other hand, for the reasons expressed in note 16 *supra*, we reverse that court's separate order awarding permanent legal custody of the children to the appellee, and remand this case for a full evidentiary hearing to determine which of the parents should obtain permanent legal and physical custody based upon the current best interest of the children.

Affirmed in part; Reversed in part and Remanded.

...

MILLER, Justice, concurring:

While I concur with the majority's Syllabus, I would solve this issue on a different basis.

There is no question, as the majority points out in note 13 of its opinion, that at the time the wife filed for divorce and child custody in Wood County in October, 1983, the circuit court was the "home state" under [West Virginia] Code, 48-10-2(5)(1981), of the Uniform Child Custody Jurisdiction Act (UCCJA). This was and had been the domicile of the parties and the children since at least July, 1972, when the parties were married in Wood County.

The fact that the father one month later "snatched" the children from their mother and took them to Florida where he concealed them would not destroy West Virginia's "home state" jurisdiction. The fact that the family law master and the judge of the circuit court erroneously thought a custody determination could not be made because the children were not within the state would also not defeat West Virginia's "home state" jurisdiction as the suit was never dismissed.

It is clear under the UCCJA...that once West Virginia had "home state" jurisdiction and so long as the custody issue was pending, Florida under the UCCJA "shall not exercise its jurisdiction." It is uniformly held that where a court is exer-

16. About two years have passed since the Circuit Court of Wood County, West Virginia, conducted its custody-determination hearing. In addition, only the oldest child testified at that hearing, and his testimony was quite vague. On remand there should be an attempt to obtain the testimony of all three children, following the guidelines of the UCCJ Act for acquiring such testimony of the youngest child, who is in Florida, and the testimony should be developed and weighed in accordance with the guidelines we offered in *Rose v. Rose*, 176 W.Va. 18, 21 n. 4, 340 S.E.2d 176, 179 n. 4 (1985)....

cising jurisdiction in substantial conformity with the UCCJA, another state could should not intervene....

Thus, to my mind, there is no need for the majority to consider whether the mother met the six-month requirement of W.Va.Code, 48-10-3(a), since her custody suit was never dismissed. The fact that there had been a final divorce decree did not mean that the court abandoned its custody jurisdiction. The mother's motion to the court to consider the custody issue in July, 1987, did not constitute a new suit, such that she had to meet the terms of W.Va.Code, 48-10-3(a).

The delay in determining the custody issue in West Virginia was not a result of any bad faith on the mother's part. It was caused, as earlier pointed out, by an erroneous legal conclusion on the part of the family law master and circuit judge that custody could not be determined because the children were not currently within the jurisdiction.

To allow the father to benefit from this delay after he created it by kidnapping and concealing the children in Florida for over three years would destroy the very purpose of the UCCJA. The Act specifically recognizes the doctrine of unclean hands and admonishes a court to refrain from jurisdiction "[i]f the petitioner for an initial decree has wrongfully taken the child from another state or has engaged in similar reprehensible conduct[.]" W.Va.Code, 48-10-8(a).

For these reasons, I do not share the majority's view that another hearing is necessary in order to show that the circuit court acted in the best interest of the children. To my mind, the circuit court acted properly and we have no obligation to give full faith and credit to the Florida decree, since it had no initial jurisdiction under the UCCJA under the Florida counterpart to W.Va.Code, 48-10-6(a)....

ARCHAMBAULT v. ARCHAMBAULT

Supreme Judicial Court of Massachusetts
407 Mass. 559, 555 N.E.2d 201 (1990)

LIACOS, Chief Justice.

In this case, we are presented once again with the distressingly familiar litigation which arises when parents who have decided to divorce engage in a protracted legal tug-of-war over the custody of their children. The present custody battle, which has involved the courts and administrative agencies of both Massachusetts and New Hampshire, spans nearly eight years, during which time the child who is the subject of the dispute has grown from a toddler to an eight year old boy. Despite this lengthy passage of time and the considerable expenditure of judicial and administrative resources, a permanent custody decision regarding the child has yet to be reached. As may be expected, the procedural history of this case is complicated and, in our opinion, unnecessarily voluminous. Nevertheless, a thorough review of the development of this case is needed to provide a contextual framework for the legal analysis which drives our conclusion.

On September 8, 1983, Liisa J. Archambault filed for divorce from her husband, David J. Archambault, in the Superior Court of Hillsborough County, New Hampshire (New Hampshire court). Liisa and David had married in New Hampshire in 1981 and had established their marital home in that State. Liisa's complaint for divorce requested that she be granted temporary and permanent custody of the parties' minor child, Sean Archambault, who had been born on April 1, 1982. The New Hampshire court issued an order which granted temporary physical custody of Sean to Liisa and visitation rights to David, while a permanent custody determination was pending. During this time, Liisa moved to Massachusetts with Sean.

The New Hampshire court also appointed a guardian ad litem to investigate permanent custody issues. After a two-year investigation, the guardian ad litem recommended that David be granted permanent physical custody of Sean. A final hearing on the complaint for divorce was scheduled in the New Hampshire court for August 1, 1985.

Prior to the scheduled hearing date, the guardian ad litem received reports that Sean had been sexually abused both by David and by Sean's paternal grandfather. In response to these allegations, the guardian ad litem requested that the hearing be continued. The New Hampshire court granted this request and also suspended David's visitation rights and ordered an investigation into the allegations of sexual abuse. At approximately the same time, the Massachusetts Department of Social Services (DSS) undertook its own investigation of the allegations in response to a report of probable sexual abuse of Sean, which had been filed with DSS pursuant to G.L. c. 119, §51A (1988 ed.). The DSS eventually issued a report referring the matter to the New Hampshire Child Services Agency.

On September 30, 1985, Liisa filed a complaint for divorce in the Middlesex Probate and Family Court of Massachusetts (Probate and Family Court). The judge issued a temporary order which granted Liisa physical custody of Sean and prevented David from having any contact with Sean. The judge also appointed a guardian ad litem to investigate the allegations of sexual abuse and to recommend visitation rights for David.

On October 2, 1985, the New Hampshire court entered an ex parte order granting temporary physical custody of Sean to David's sister-in-law, and temporary legal custody of the boy to the New Hampshire Department of Welfare. This order was entered after Liisa failed to comply with an order of the New Hampshire court regarding the evaluation of Sean by a court appointed psychologist.

On October 22, 1985, the Probate and Family Court entered an order staying the divorce proceedings in Massachusetts and deferring to the jurisdiction of the New Hampshire court. Liisa was ordered to submit both herself and Sean to the New Hampshire court. Liisa appealed the order of the Probate and Family Court to the Appeals Court, which granted a temporary stay of the lower court's order. On May 9, 1986, the Appeals Court affirmed the judgment of the Probate and Family Court, allowing Liisa thirty days to apply to the New Hampshire court for a hearing requesting modification of the New Hampshire orders regarding custody of Sean. Although Liisa and Sean remained in Massachusetts, Liisa filed such a request, and the New Hampshire court scheduled a hearing for July 9, 1986.

In early June, 1986, DSS, pursuant to G.L. c. 119 (1988 ed.), filed a care and protection complaint concerning Sean in the Ayer Division of the District Court. In response to this complaint, the District Court judge entered an order on June 6, 1986, granting temporary legal custody of Sean to the DSS and prohibiting anyone from interfering with Sean's "liberty or present domicile." The District Court judge also ordered a new investigation into Sean's situation and scheduled the matter for hearing on July 28, 1986.

On July 9, 1986, Liisa failed to appear in the New Hampshire court for the hearing that she had requested. Accordingly, her motion for a modification of the New Hampshire custody arrangement was denied. David then filed a petition for relief with a single justice of this court pursuant to G.L. c. 211, §3 (1988 ed.), requesting that the orders of the Ayer District Court be vacated and that further proceedings in that court be dismissed or stayed. The Ayer District Court stayed any further proceedings during the pendency of David's c. 211, §3, petition. On August 14, 1986, a single justice of this court ruled that the order of the Ayer District Court represented a "collateral attack" on the judgment of the Appeals Court which had upheld the order that Liisa and Sean submit to the jurisdiction of the New Hampshire court. Accordingly, the District Court order was vacated by the single justice.

Liisa appealed from the decision of the single justice to the full court. During the pendency of this appeal, Liisa filed one motion in the New Hampshire court to dismiss the proceedings there, and another in the Probate and Family Court to vacate the stay of proceedings in Massachusetts. Both of these motions were denied. Liisa then petitioned the single justice of the Appeals Court, requesting a determination of Sean's custody pursuant to G.L. c. 209B, §2(a)(3)(1988 ed.), the emergency provision of the Massachusetts Child Custody Jurisdiction Act. Liisa referred to clinical examinations which suggested that Sean had suffered sexual abuse at the hands of David and Sean's paternal grandfather. The Appeals Court's single justice denied Liisa's petition, ruling that "[t]here is no present emergency." He stated further that "it is far from clear that harm will befall the child if New Hampshire takes a considered look at the situation," and suggested that the proper course for Liisa would be to request the New Hampshire court to modify its custody order on the basis of the clinical examinations which Liisa had presented to the Massachusetts courts.

A pivotal event in the labyrinthine progress of this case occurred on May 11, 1987, when the Legislature amended §11(*b*) of the Massachusetts Child Custody Jurisdiction Act. G.L. c. 209B. See St.1987, c. 52 (an emergency act, effective on enactment). In general, §11(*b*) empowers Massachusetts courts with the discretion to order persons in the Commonwealth to appear in custody proceedings which are being held in a court of another State. The 1987 amendment added the following passage to §11(*b*):

> Notwithstanding any provision of this chapter to the contrary, no child shall be ordered or compelled to appear or attend such proceeding in another state when, after a hearing a judge makes a finding that there is probable cause to believe that such child may be placed in jeopardy or exposed to risk of mental or physical harm by such return to said other state.

On July 28, 1987, Liisa filed a motion in the Probate and Family Court for a probable cause hearing pursuant to the amendment of §11(*b*). In response, the judge issued an order and a memorandum of decision requiring Liisa to submit to the jurisdiction of the New Hampshire court within thirty days, and finding her guilty of contempt of court for her failure to comply with the October 22, 1985, order to appear before the New Hampshire court. However, on August 18, 1987, the Probate and Family Court judge granted Liisa's motion for a probable cause hearing and stayed the order to submit to the New Hampshire court pending the outcome of the hearing. The judge required that, before the probable cause hearing took place, all parties must submit memoranda of law addressing the constitutionality of the amendment to G.L. c. 209B, §11(*b*).

On February 23, 1989, the guardian ad litem filed a motion in the Probate and Family Court requesting the reconsideration of the allowance of Liisa's motion for a probable cause hearing. On May 19, 1989, after a hearing, the Probate and Family Court judge allowed the motion for reconsideration and denied Liisa's motion for a probable cause hearing on the basis that the 1987 amendment to G.L. c. 209B, §11(*b*), "conflicts with the Federal Parental Kidnapping Prevention Act (PKPA) and is therefore preempted by the PKPA." Pursuant to his powers under G.L. c. 215, §13 (1988 ed.), the judge reported the following question to the Appeals Court:

> Whether the 1987 Amendment to G.L. Ch. 209B, §11(*b*), St.1987 ch. 52 is preempted by the Parental Kidnapping Prevention Act, 28 U.S.C. §1738A pursuant to the Supremacy Doctrine and is void as a result.

Prior to consideration of this question by the Appeals Court, David applied to this court for direct appellate review. We granted his application, and affirm the decision of the Probate and Family Court.

The constitutionality of G.L. c. 209B, §11(b), second par. "The Supremacy Clause of Art. VI of the [Federal] Constitution provides Congress with the power to preempt state law." *Louisiana Pub. Serv. Comm'n v. FCC*, 476 U.S. 355, 368, 106 S.Ct. 1890, 1898, 90 L.Ed.2d 369 (1986).[2] Because the power of preemption lies within the discretion of Congress, "[any] pre-emption question requires an examination of congressional intent." *Schneidewind v. ANR Pipeline Co.*, 485 U.S. 293, 299, 108 S.Ct. 1145, 1150, 99 L.Ed.2d 316 (1988). "The critical question in any preemption analysis is always whether Congress intended that federal [law] supersede state law." *Louisiana Pub. Serv. Comm'n v. FCC, supra* at 369, 106 S.Ct. at 1899.

Discussion of the application of Federal preemption principles generally takes place within the two categories of "express" or "implied" preemption, in which it is determined whether Congress (1) by express statement has preempted State law, or (2) by the nature of the Federal law has implied that State law is preempted. See, e.g., *Schneidewind v. ANR Pipeline Co., supra* at 299–300, 108 S.Ct. at 1150–51. Our primary source of insight for determining whether Congress intended the Parental Kidnapping Prevention Act (PKPA) expressly or impliedly to preempt State law such as G.L. c. 209B, §11(*b*), second par., is found in the language of the PKPA, where evidence of Congress's intent has been reduced to its most basic form. As we examine this language, however, we refer to a primary tenet of Federal preemption analysis, which states that Congress is presumed to "not intend to displace state law." *Maryland v. Louisiana*, 451 U.S. 725, 746, 101 S.Ct. 2114, 2129, 68 L.Ed.2d 576 (1981)....

From the language of the PKPA, we conclude that Congress did not intend expressly to preempt any State law, let alone the manner of State law represented by the second paragraph of G.L. c. 209B, §11(*b*). Nowhere in the PKPA is there any explicit reference to preemption. We consider the absence of any "preemption" language in the PKPA in light of other Federal statutes which devote entire sections entirely to the preemptive effect of the Federal law. For example, in 15 U.S.C. §§1331 et seq. (1982 & Supp. IV 1986), more commonly known as the Federal Cigarette Labelling Act, §1334 is entitled, "Preemption" and details specifically what types of State laws have been preempted. Therefore, we see that Congress, when it wishes expressly to preempt State law, makes its intention abundantly

2. Article VI of the United States Constitution states: "This Constitution, and the Laws of the United States which shall be made in pursuance thereof; and all treaties made, or which shall be made, under the authority of the United States, shall be the supreme law of the land; and the judges in every state shall be bound thereby, any thing in the constitution or laws of any state to the contrary notwithstanding."

clear. We discern no such intention in the express language of the PKPA. However, in the absence of express preemption, it still remains to us to determine whether Congress, by the very nature of the PKPA, intended impliedly to preempt State laws such as G.L. 209B, §11(*b*), second par.

The United States Supreme Court has "consistently recognized that "[t]he whole subject of the domestic relations of husband and wife, parent and child, belongs to the laws of the States and not to the laws of the United States." *Rose v. Rose*, 481 U.S. 619, 625, 107 S.Ct. 2029, 2033, 95 L.Ed.2d 599 (1987), quoting *In re Burrus*, 136 U.S. 586, 593–594, 10 S.Ct. 850, 853, 34 L.Ed. 500 (1890). In deference to this traditional function of the States, the United States Supreme Court has declared that a Federal law will not be found to preempt a State family law, such as is involved in the present case, unless "Congress has 'positively required by direct enactment' that state law be pre-empted." *Hisquierdo v. Hisquierdo*, 439 U.S. 572, 581, 99 S.Ct. 802, 808, 59 L.Ed.2d 1 (1979), quoting *Wetmore v. Markoe*, 196 U.S. 68, 77, 25 S.Ct. 172, 176, 49 L.Ed. 390 (1904). The standard to be applied in determining whether the supremacy clause requires that the State family law be preempted is whether the State law does "'major damage' to 'clear and substantial' federal interests." *Hisquierdo v. Hisquierdo, supra*, quoting *United States v. Yazell*, 382 U.S. 341, 352, 86 S.Ct. 500, 507, 15 L.Ed.2d 404 (1966)....

The PKPA represents Congress's response to the "large and growing number of cases annually involving disputes between persons claiming rights of custody and visitation of children under the laws, and in the courts, of different states." Pub.L. No. 96-611, §7(a)(1), 94 Stat. 3566, 3568 (1980). The abundance of these cases, Congress found, when combined with the often inconsistent and conflicting laws of various States regarding jurisdiction over child custody disputes, resulted in "the failure of the courts of [various] jurisdictions to give full faith and credit to the judicial proceedings of...other jurisdictions, the deprivation of rights of liberty and property without due process of law, burdens on commerce among...jurisdictions and with foreign nations, and harm to the welfare of children and their parents and other custodians." Pub.L. No. 96-611, §7(a)(4), 94 Stat. 3569 (1980). Accordingly, Congress enacted the PKPA in an effort to "establish national standards under which the courts of [various] jurisdictions will determine their jurisdiction to decide [child] custody disputes." *Id.* at §7(b)....

There can be little doubt that Congress' expressed interests of furthering comity between States, protecting the right to be free from the deprivation of liberty or property without due process of law, lessening the burden on commerce between States and foreign nations, and preventing harm to the welfare of children and their parents are "clear and substantial federal interests" within the United States Supreme Court's preemption analysis described above. The primary point of contention in this case concerns the degree of interference which the 1987 amendment to G.L. c. 209B, §11(*b*), creates with these Federal interests, and whether this interference, if any, "sufficiently injure[s] the objectives of the federal program to require nonrecognition [of the amendment]." *Hisquierdo v. Hisquierdo, supra* at 583, 99 S.Ct. at 809. A brief overview of the structure of the PKPA is in order.

The PKPA sets out several standards by which a State court may initially exercise child custody jurisdiction consistently with the over-all scheme of the PKPA. 28 U.S.C. §1738A(c)(1982). The PKPA also sets out guidelines under which a State court with initial jurisdiction pursuant to the PKPA will maintain continuing jurisdiction over a child custody dispute. 28 U.S.C. §1738A(d)(1982). Finally, and most importantly for the purposes of this case, the PKPA declares that "[a] court of a State shall not exercise jurisdiction in any proceeding for a custody determination commenced during the pendency of a proceeding in a court of another State where such court of that other State is exercising jurisdiction consistently with the provisions of this section to make a custody determination." 28 U.S.C. §1738A(g)(1982).

There is no allegation that New Hampshire has failed to meet the requirements of the PKPA in exercising jurisdiction over the issue of Sean's custody. Therefore, the Probate and Family Court acted entirely in keeping with the PKPA when it stayed the divorce proceedings in Massachusetts in deference to the pending proceedings in New Hampshire. The argument is raised by the plaintiff, however, that the PKPA's requirement that Massachusetts not exercise jurisdiction over "any proceeding for a custody determination" regarding Sean does not conflict with the Massachusetts amendment providing for a probable cause hearing; the argument is that such a hearing would not implicate a "custody determination" within the meaning of the PKPA. The probable cause hearing, plaintiff argues, would at most prevent a Massachusetts court from exercising the power it would otherwise enjoy under G.L. c. 209B, §11, to order a particular child to appear before a court of another State. The PKPA, it is noted, does not *require* Massachusetts to order an appearance in pending custody proceedings in another State. Such an order lies within the discretion of the Massachusetts court. See G.L. c. 209B, §11. Consequently, the argument concludes, there is no "direct conflict" between the amendment and the PKPA, and, therefore, no preemption. We disagree. While this argument is correct in so far as it discusses the technical requirement of the PKPA, it completely fails to address the consequences a probable cause hearing could have on the "objectives of the federal program." *Hisquierdo v. Hisquierdo*, *supra* at 583, 99 S.Ct. at 809.

When enacting the PKPA, Congress set out six "general purposes," at least four of which are relevant to our present discussion. These four purposes are as follows: To "(1) promote cooperation between State courts to the end that a determination of custody and visitation is rendered in the State which can best decide the case in the interest of the child; (2) promote and expand the exchange of information and other forms of mutual assistance between States which are concerned with the same child; (3) facilitate the enforcement of custody and visitation decrees of sister States; [and] (4) discourage continuing interstate controversies over child custody in the interest of greater stability of home environment and of secure family relationships for the child." Pub.L. No. 96-611, §7(c), 94 Stat. 3569 (1980).[3] It is our opinion that the operation of the 1987 amendment would serve to interfere substantially with the attainment of these purposes, thereby "sufficiently injur[ing] the objectives of the federal program to require nonrecognition [of the amendment]." *Hisquierdo v. Hisquierdo*, *supra* at 583, 99 S.Ct. at 809.

We can think of no better illustration of interference with the intention of the Congress than is shown by the procedural history of this case. Under the 1987 amendment, if a Massachusetts court determines that probable cause exists to believe that a child may be placed in jeopardy or exposed to a risk of mental and physical harm, that court is precluded from ordering the child to appear in a pend-

3. The two other purposes of the PKPA are: To "avoid jurisdictional competition and conflict between State courts in matters of child custody and visitation which have in the past resulted in the shifting of children from State to State with harmful effects on their well-being; and" "deter interstate abductions and other unilateral removals of children undertaken to obtain custody and visitation awards." Pub.L. No. 96-611, §7(c), 94 Stat. 3569 (1980).

ing custody proceeding in another State. Such a prohibition would exist irrespective of the fact that the other State's court might consider the child's presence crucial to an appropriate custody determination. This result would be clearly contrary to Congress's intent that courts of different States engage in "mutual assistance." The prohibition would also apply even though the other State court was clearly in a better position than any Massachusetts court to determine the child's best interests. In this manner, the 1987 amendment creates a serious obstacle to Congress's intent to "promote cooperation between State courts to the end that a determination of custody and visitation is rendered in the State which can best decide the case in the interest of the child."

Even if a Massachusetts court determined that no probable cause existed and eventually ordered a child to appear in another State's court, the purposes of the PKPA would be frustrated. Congress intended the PKPA to "discourage continuing interstate controversies over child custody in the interest of greater stability of home environment." A probable cause hearing will take time. See *Umina v. Malbica*, 27 Mass.App.Ct. 351, 361, 538 N.E.2d 53 (1989)(discussing the possible need for argument, presentation of evidence, and live witnesses in a probable cause hearing pursuant to G.L. c. 209B, §11 [*b*], second par.) And stability in home environment is likely to become rare when a child's custody determination remains temporary and subject to change while the court capable of rendering a permanent custody decision is hobbled in its efforts by the absence of the child due to an ongoing probable cause hearing in Massachusetts. We need go no further than the facts of the present case to encounter such a situation. Such a result is at odds with the aims of the PKPA.

Finally, we note that the 1987 amendment would serve to frustrate the over-all purpose of the PKPA to encourage comity between States.... We see no reason to believe that New Hampshire courts are any less concerned than courts of the Commonwealth with the welfare of children who are the subjects of custody disputes. Nor do we perceive any less ability on the part of New Hampshire to protect adequately children under its jurisdiction than is available in the Commonwealth.[5] The assumption of the 1987 amendment that other States' courts will be unwilling or unable to protect children in custody disputes is unwarranted.

We conclude that in order to "prevent the frustration and erosion of the congressional policy embodied in the federal [law]," the 1987 amendment to G.L. c. 209B, §11(*b*), is preempted by the PKPA. *Ridgway v. Ridgway, supra* at 54, 102 S.Ct. at 54. Accordingly, our answer to the reported question is in the affirmative. The decision of the Probate and Family Court is affirmed.

So ordered.

COMMENTS

Kumar, *Sams* and *Archambault* deal with some of the vexing problems surrounding the application and proper interpretation of the Uniform Child Custody Jurisdiction Act (UCCJA) and the Parental Kidnapping Prevention Act (PKPA). The Acts intend to resolve the problems of conflicting court decrees regarding the custody of a child and thereby to reduce the incidence of a parent violating a cus-

5. We note that a Massachusetts court which believes that a child is at risk remains free to express its concerns to a court of another State which enjoys jurisdiction over the child's custody. See G.L. c. 209B, §7(*c*)....

tody decree and taking the child to another state. A primary method employed by the Acts is to reduce the discretion of a second court to enter a decree that might conflict with the decree of a court which has properly assumed jurisdiction over the custody of a child. A court may exercise jurisdiction initially on any of several bases, and that court then has essentially exclusive jurisdiction until it relinquishes or loses jurisdiction over the child's custody. Courts of other states are simply told to refrain from entertaining the case as long as the first court retains jurisdiction. One effect, of course, is to prevent courts from entering custody decrees regarding children who are physically before the court, even in cases in which it may seem to the judge and to most other people that the preexisting custody decree from the sister state jeopardizes the child's best interests.

In *Kumar*, the mother argued that California should exercise jurisdiction over custody because the child now had stronger ties with California than with New York, which had entered the initial decree. As in *Palm*, the trial court agreed to hear the case, and only on appeal was the UCCJA interpreted as its drafters intended. The mother in *Palm* is likely to feel at a decided disadvantage if the father threatens to relitigate custody in New York, since the court there has already decided that the mother violated an "implied prohibition" of the court against removing the child from the state.

Sams raised the question whether a state ceases to be the child's "home state" when the child is improperly removed from the state and concealed from the other parent. The UCCJA allows for continued initial jurisdiction in the state for six months after a child is removed from its home state, but the mother in *Sams* brought her action more than six months after the father removed the children from West Virginia. The two questions raised here are (1) whether improper removal can shift a child's "home state" and (2) whether removal can be considered improper when there has not yet been any custody decree.

While the argument of the late Professor Bodenheimer that a pre-decree removal of a child is improper has some appeal, treating such removal as prima facie improper may also tend to work unfairly against some parents. The less powerful parent is more likely to depend upon the support of other family members during the marriage break-up and is also somewhat more likely after marriage to have been moved away from these supportive family members. For example, a mother who spends full time caring for her young children may have few financial resources and no place else to go but her parent's home, often in another state. The example hypothesized in the comments to UCCJA section 8(a), quoted in *Sams*, avoided having to deal with this problem by specifying that the husband had not objected to the wife's return to her "own home" and had waited two years before he seized the children. If the husband had objected to the wife's departure, would the UCCJA comments then treat her as having "wrongfully" taken the children? Should courts distinguish between cases in which a child's primary caretaker has a good reason for leaving the state and cases in which a parent who has not played any substantial part in the day-to-day care of the child takes the child out of the state to gain strategic advantage?

The concurring opinion in *Sams* would have based a decision in favor of the mother on the continuing jurisdiction of the court, which granted the divorce years before. Under this approach, the result would presumably have been the same had the mother known where the children were or even had the removal not been wrongful.

The primary tension that arises in most of these UCCJA cases is between the need for certainty on one hand and the importance of flexibility on the other. For different courts to enter conflicting decrees appears not to be in the best interest of a child, yet individual cases arise in which it may seem crucially important to a court to enter a decree that would conflict with an existing decree. Courts appear to be unable to deal with these cases in which a conflicting decree would serve the interests of a particular child without also opening the way for courts to enter conflicting decrees that harm other children.

As long as courts make decisions that are based on a chauvinistic preference for the local litigant or decisions that deny custody to one parent for petty reasons, courts that are committed to the child's best interest will feel strong pressure to disregard the ill-advised decree. Some courts have dealt with this problem by simply interpreting the UCCJA as allowing courts to deny effect to "punitive" custody decrees. There is serious question whether this option remains available under the PKPA, and courts can easily protect their punitive decrees by couching them in terms of the best interest of the child, a term so vague that it can encompass nearly anything.

If the Massachusetts courts concluded that David Archambault was sexually abused by his father and paternal grandfather, how can they properly order the child turned over to courts in New Hampshire that appear skeptical and are willing to award physical custody to the sister- and daughter-in-law of the alleged abusers? Indeed, the New Hampshire court may even blame the mother for suggesting the possibility of sexual abuse, which would explain why the court might award custody to a non-parent over a parent. Yet, any policy devised to deal with serious problems can also be misused to perpetuate a grab-and-run system of child custody.

Courts appear to be unable successfully to distinguish between a loving parent who flees with a child to avoid a terribly mistaken custody decree that would destroy the happiness and future of a child and a vindictive parent who flees with a child to assert continued control and power or to inflict punishment on a former spouse. The Massachusetts provision Section 11(*b*) was an effort to deal with the most blatant situations in which courts saw a serious conflict between the child's interests and the demands of the UCCJA and the PKPA. The court's decision that the statute conflicted with the PKPA surely had a strong basis, but the results may be that courts will be powerless to prevent serious abuse to children.

Minimum Contacts for Personal Jurisdiction

KULKO v. SUPERIOR COURT OF CALIFORNIA
United States Supreme Court
436 U.S. 84 (1978)

Mr. Justice MARSHALL delivered the opinion of the Court.

The issue before us is whether, in this action for child support, the California state courts may exercise *in personam* jurisdiction over a nonresident, nondomiciliary parent of minor children domiciled within the State. For reasons set forth below, we hold that the exercise of such jurisdiction would violate the Due Process Clause of the Fourteenth Amendment.

I

Appellant Ezra Kulko married appellee Sharon Kulko Horn in 1959, during appellant's three-day stopover in California en route from a military base in Texas to a tour of duty in Korea. At the time of this marriage, both parties were domiciled in and residents of New York State. Immediately following the marriage, Sharon Kulko returned to New York, as did appellant after his tour of duty. Their first child, Darwin, was born to the Kulkos in New York in 1961, and a year later their second child, Ilsa, was born, also in New York. The Kulkos and their two children resided together as a family in New York City continuously until March 1972, when the Kulkos separated.

Following the separation, Sharon Kulko moved to San Francisco, Cal. A written separation agreement was drawn up in New York; in September 1972, Sharon Kulko flew to New York City in order to sign this agreement. The agreement provided, *inter alia*, that the children would remain with their father during the school year but would spend their Christmas, Easter, and summer vacations with their mother. While Sharon Kulko waived any claim for her own support or maintenance, Ezra Kulko agreed to pay his wife $3,000 per year in child support for the periods when the children were in her care, custody, and control. Immediately after execution of the separation agreement, Sharon Kulko flew to Haiti and procured a divorce there;[1] the divorce decree incorporated the terms of the agreement. She then returned to California, where she remarried and took the name Horn.

The children resided with appellant during the school year and with their mother on vacations, as provided by the separation agreement, until December 1973. At this time, just before Ilsa was to leave New York to spend Christmas vacation with her mother, she told her father that she wanted to remain in California after her vacation. Appellant bought his daughter a one-way plane ticket, and Ilsa left, taking her clothing with her. Ilsa then commenced living in California with her mother during the school year and spending vacations with her father. In January 1976, appellant's other child, Darwin, called his mother from New York and advised her that he wanted to live with her in California. Unbeknownst to appellant, appellee Horn sent a plane ticket to her son, which he used to fly to California where he took up residence with his mother and sister.

---

1. While the Jurisdictional Statement, at 5, asserts that "the parties" flew to Haiti, appellant's affidavit submitted in the Superior Court stated that Sharon Kulko flew to Haiti with a power of attorney signed by appellant. App. 28. The Haitian decree states that Sharon Kulko appeared "in person" and that appellant filed a "Power of Attorney and submission to jurisdiction." *Id.*, at 14.

Less than one month after Darwin's arrival in California, appellee Horn commenced this action against appellant in the California Superior Court. She sought to establish the Haitian divorce decree as a California judgment; to modify the judgment so as to award her full custody of the children; and to increase appellant's child-support obligations.[2] Appellant appeared specially and moved to quash service of the summons on the ground that he was not a resident of California and lacked sufficient "minimum contacts" with the State under *International Shoe Co. v. Washington*, 326 U.S. 310, 316 (1945), to warrant the State's assertion of personal jurisdiction over him.

...

...We have concluded that jurisdiction by appeal does not lie, but, treating the papers as a petition for a writ of certiorari, we hereby grant the petition and reverse the judgment below.

II

The Due Process Clause of the Fourteenth Amendment operates as a limitation on the jurisdiction of state courts to enter judgments affecting rights or interests of nonresident defendants. See *Shaffer v. Heitner*, 433 U.S. 186, 198–200 (1977). It has long been the rule that a valid judgment imposing a personal obligation or duty in favor of the plaintiff may be entered only by a court having jurisdiction over the person of the defendant. *Pennoyer v. Neff*, 95 U.S. 714, 732–733 (1878); *International Shoe Co. v. Washington*, 326 U.S., at 316. The existence of personal jurisdiction, in turn, depends upon the presence of reasonable notice to the defendant that an action has been brought, *Mullane v. Central Hanover Trust Co.*, 339 U.S. 306, 313–314 (1950), and a sufficient connection between the defendant and the forum State to make it fair to require defense of the action in the forum. *Milliken v. Meyer*, 311 U.S. 457, 463–464 (1940). In this case, appellant does not dispute the adequacy of the notice that he received, but contends that his connection with the State of California is too attenuated, under the standards implicit in the Due Process Clause of the Constitution, to justify imposing upon him the burden and inconvenience of defense in California.

The parties are in agreement that the constitutional standard for determining whether the State may enter a binding judgment against appellant here is that set forth in this Court's opinion in *International Shoe Co. v. Washington, supra*: that a defendant "have certain minimum contacts with [the forum State] such that the maintenance of the suit does not offend 'traditional notions of fair play and substantial justice.'" 326 U.S., at 316, quoting *Milliken v. Meyer, supra*, 311 U.S., at 463. While the interests of the forum State and of the plaintiff in proceeding with the cause in the plaintiff's forum of choice are, of course, to be considered, see *McGee v. International Life Insurance Co.*, 355 U.S. 220, 223 (1957), an essential criterion in all cases is whether the "quality and nature" of the defendant's activity is such that it is "reasonable" and "fair" to require him to conduct his defense in that State. *International Shoe Co. v. Washington, supra*, 326 U.S., at 316–317, 319. Accord, *Shaffer v. Heitner, supra*, 433 U.S., at 207–212; *Perkins v. Benguet Mining Co.*, 342 U.S. 437, 445 (1952).

2. Appellee Horn's complaint also sought an order restraining appellant from removing his children from the State. The trial court immediately granted appellee temporary custody of the children and restrained both her and appellant from removing the children from the State of California. See 19 Cal.3d 514, 520, 138 Cal.Rptr. 586, 588, 564 P.2d 353, 355 (1977)....

Like any standard that requires a determination of "reasonableness," the "minimum contacts" test of *International Shoe* is not susceptible of mechanical application; rather, the facts of each case must be weighed to determine whether the requisite "affiliating circumstances" are present. *Hanson v. Denckla*, 357 U.S. 235, 246 (1958). We recognize that this determination is one in which few answers will be written "in black and white. The greys are dominant and even among them the shades are innumerable." *Estin v. Estin*, 334 U.S. 541, 545 (1948). But we believe that the California Supreme Court's application of the minimum-contacts test in this case represents an unwarranted extension of *International Shoe* and would, if sustained, sanction a result that is neither fair, just, nor reasonable.

A

In reaching its result, the California Supreme Court did not rely on appellant's glancing presence in the State some 13 years before the events that led to this controversy, nor could it have. Appellant has been in California on only two occasions, once in 1959 for a three-day military stopover on his way to Korea, see *supra*, at 1694, and again in 1960 for a 24-hour stopover on his return from Korean service. To hold such temporary visits to a State a basis for the assertion of *in personam* jurisdiction over unrelated actions arising in the future would make a mockery of the limitations on state jurisdiction imposed by the Fourteenth Amendment. Nor did the California court rely on the fact that appellant was actually married in California on one of his two brief visits. We agree that where two New York domiciliaries, for reasons of convenience, marry in the State of California and thereafter spend their entire married life in New York, the fact of their California marriage by itself cannot support a California court's exercise of jurisdiction over a spouse who remains a New York resident in an action relating to child support.

Finally, in holding that personal jurisdiction existed, the court below carefully disclaimed reliance on the fact that appellant had agreed at the time of separation to allow his children to live with their mother three months a year and that he had sent them to California each year pursuant to this agreement. As was noted below, 19 Cal.3d, at 523–524, 564 P.2d, at 357, to find personal jurisdiction in a State on this basis, merely because the mother was residing there, would discourage parents from entering into reasonable visitation agreements. Moreover, it could arbitrarily subject one parent to suit in any State of the Union where the other parent chose to spend time while having custody of their offspring pursuant to a separation agreement.[6] As we have emphasized:

> The unilateral activity of those who claim some relationship with a nonresident defendant cannot satisfy the requirement of contact with the forum State.... [I]t is essential in each case that there be some act by which the defendant purposefully avails [him]self of the privilege of conducting activities within the forum State....

Hanson v. Denckla, *supra*, 357 U.S., at 253.

---

6. Although the separation agreement stated that appellee Horn resided in California and provided that child-support payments would be mailed to her California address, it also specifically contemplated that appellee might move to a different State. The agreement directed appellant to mail the support payments to appellee's San Francisco address or "any other address which the Wife may designate from time to time in writing." App. 10.

The "purposeful act" that the California Supreme Court believed did warrant the exercise of personal jurisdiction over appellant in California was his "actively and fully consent[ing] to Ilsa living in California for the school year...and...sen[ding] her to California for that purpose." 19 Cal.3d, at 524, 564 P.2d, at 358. We cannot accept the proposition that appellant's acquiescence in Ilsa's desire to live with her mother conferred jurisdiction over appellant in the California courts in this action. A father who agrees, in the interests of family harmony and his children's preferences, to allow them to spend more time in California than was required under a separation agreement can hardly be said to have "purposefully availed himself" of the "benefits and protections" of California's laws. See *Shaffer v. Heitner*, 433 U.S., at 216.[7]

Nor can we agree with the assertion of the court below that the exercise of *in personam* jurisdiction here was warranted by the financial benefit appellant derived from his daughter's presence in California for nine months of the year. 19 Cal.3d at 524–525, 564 P.2d, at 358. This argument rests on the premise that, while appellant's liability for support payments remained unchanged, his yearly expenses for supporting the child in New York decreased. But this circumstance, even if true, does not support California's assertion of jurisdiction here. Any diminution in appellant's household costs resulted, not from the child's presence in California, but rather from her absence from appellant's home. Moreover, an action by appellee Horn to increase support payments could now be brought, and could have been brought when Ilsa first moved to California, in the State of New York;[8] a New York court would clearly have personal jurisdiction over appellant and, if a judgment were entered by a New York court increasing appellant's child-support obligations, it could properly be enforced against him in both New York and California.[9] Any ultimate financial advantage to appellant thus results not from the child's presence in California, but from appellee's failure earlier to seek an increase in payments under the separation agreement.[10] The argument below to the contrary, in our view, confuses the question of appellant's liability with that of the proper forum in which to determine that liability.

B

In light of our conclusion that appellant did not purposefully derive benefit from any activities relating to the State of California, it is apparent that the California Supreme Court's reliance on appellant's having caused an "effect" in

7. The court below stated that the presence in California of appellant's daughter gave appellant the benefit of California's "police and fire protection, its school system, its hospital services, its recreational facilities, its libraries and museums…." 19 Cal.3d, at 522, 138 Cal.Rptr., at 589, 564 P.2d, at 356. But, in the circumstances presented here, these services provided by the State were essentially benefits to the child, not the father, and in any event were not benefits that appellant purposefully sought for himself.

8. Under the separation agreement, appellant is bound to "indemnify and hold [his] Wife harmless from any and all attorney fees, costs and expenses which she may incur by reason of the default of [appellant] in the performance of any of the obligations required to be performed by him pursuant to the terms and conditions of this agreement." App. 11. To the extent that appellee Horn seeks arrearages,...her litigation expenses, presumably including any additional costs incurred by her as a result of having to prosecute the action in New York, would thus be borne by appellant.

9. A final judgment entered by a New York court having jurisdiction over the defendant's person and over the subject matter of the lawsuit would be entitled to full faith and credit in any State. See *New York ex rel. Halvey v. Halvey*, 330 U.S. 610, 614 (1947). See also *Sosna v. Iowa*, 419 U.S. 393, 407 (1975).

10. It may well be that, as a matter of state law, appellee Horn could still obtain through New York proceedings additional payments from appellant for Ilsa's support from January 1974, when a *de facto* modification of the custody provisions of the separation agreement took place, until the present. See H. Clark, DOMESTIC RELATIONS §15.2, p. 500 (1968); cf. *In re Santa Clara County v. Hughes*, 43 Misc.2d 559, 251 N.Y.S.2d 579 (1964).

California was misplaced. See *supra*, at 1695. This "effects" test is derived from the American Law Institute's Restatement (Second) of Conflict of Laws §37 (1971), which provides:

> A state has power to exercise judicial jurisdiction over an individual who causes effects in the state by an act done elsewhere with respect to any cause of action arising from these effects unless the nature of the effects and of the individual's relationship to the state make the exercise of such jurisdiction unreasonable.[11]

While this provision is not binding on this Court, it does not in any event support the decision below. As is apparent from the examples accompanying §37 in the Restatement, this section was intended to reach wrongful activity outside of the State causing injury within the State, see, *e.g.*, Comment *a*, p. 157 (shooting bullet from one State into another), or commercial activity affecting state residents, *ibid.* Even in such situations, moreover, the Restatement recognizes that there might be circumstances that would render "unreasonable" the assertion of jurisdiction over the nonresident defendant.

The circumstances in this case clearly render "unreasonable" California's assertion of personal jurisdiction. There is no claim that appellant has visited physical injury on either property or persons within the State of California. Cf. *Hess v. Pawloski*, 274 U.S. 352 (1927). The cause of action herein asserted arises, not from the defendant's commercial transactions in interstate commerce, but rather from his personal, domestic relations. It thus cannot be said that appellant has sought a commercial benefit from solicitation of business from a resident of California that could reasonably render him liable to suit in state court; appellant's activities cannot fairly be analogized to an insurer's sending an insurance contract and premium notices into the State to an insured resident of the State. Cf. *McGee v. International Life Insurance Co.*, 355 U.S. 220 (1957). Furthermore, the controversy between the parties arises from a separation that occurred in the State of New York; appellee Horn seeks modification of a contract that was negotiated in New York and that she flew to New York to sign. As in *Hanson v. Denckla*, 357 U.S., at 252, the instant action involves an agreement that was entered into with virtually no connection with the forum State. See also n. 6, *supra.*

Finally, basic considerations of fairness point decisively in favor of appellant's State of domicile as the proper forum for adjudication of this case, whatever the merits of appellee's underlying claim. It is appellant who has remained in the State of the marital domicile, whereas it is appellee who has moved across the continent. Cf. *May v. Anderson*, 345 U.S. 528, 534–535, n. 8 (1953). Appellant has at all times resided in New York State, and, until the separation and appellee's move to California, his entire family resided there as well. As noted above, appellant did no more than acquiesce in the stated preference of one of his children to live with her mother in California. This single act is surely not one that a reasonable parent would expect to result in the substantial financial burden and personal strain of litigating a child-support suit in a forum 3,000 miles away, and we therefore see no basis on which it can be said that appellant could reasonably have anticipated being "haled before a [California] court," *Shaffer v. Heitner*, 433 U.S., at 216.[12] To

11. Section 37 of the Restatement has effectively been incorporated into California law. See Judicial Council Comment (9) to Cal.Civ.Proc. Code Ann. §410.10 (West 1973).

12. See also *Developments in the Law — State-Court Jurisdiction*, 73 HARV.L.REV. 909, 911 (1960).

make jurisdiction in a case such as this turn on whether appellant bought his daughter her ticket or instead unsuccessfully sought to prevent her departure would impose an unreasonable burden on family relations, and one wholly unjustified by the "quality and nature" of appellant's activities in or relating to the State of California. *International Shoe Co. v. Washington,* 326 U.S., at 319.

III

In seeking to justify the burden that would be imposed on appellant were the exercise of *in personam* jurisdiction in California sustained, appellee argues that California has substantial interests in protecting the welfare of its minor residents and in promoting to the fullest extent possible a healthy and supportive family environment in which the children of the State are to be raised. These interests are unquestionably important. But while the presence of the children and one parent in California arguably might favor application of California law in a lawsuit in New York, the fact that California may be the "center of gravity" for choice-of-law purposes does not mean that California has personal jurisdiction over the defendant. *Hanson v. Denckla, supra,* 357 U.S., at 254. And California has not attempted to assert any particularized interest in trying such cases in its courts by, *e.g.*, enacting a special jurisdictional statute. Cf. *McGee v. International Life Ins. Co., supra,* 355 U.S., at 221, 224.

California's legitimate interest in ensuring the support of children resident in California without unduly disrupting the children's lives, moreover, is already being served by the State's participation in the Revised Uniform Reciprocal Enforcement of Support Act of 1968. This statute provides a mechanism for communication between court systems in different States, in order to facilitate the procurement and enforcement of child-support decrees where the dependent children reside in a State that cannot obtain personal jurisdiction over the defendant. California's version of the Act essentially permits a California resident claiming support from a nonresident to file a petition in California and have its merits adjudicated in the State of the alleged obligor's residence, without either party's having to leave his or her own State. Cal.Civ.Proc. Code Ann. §1650 *et seq.* (West 1972 and Supp. 1978).[13] New York State is a signatory to a similar Act.[14] Thus, not

13. In addition to California, 24 other States are signatories to this Act. 9 U.L.A. 473 (Supp.1978). Under the Act, an "obligee" may file a petition in a court of his or her State (the "initiating court") to obtain support. 9 U.L.A. §§11, 14 (1973). If the court "finds that the [petition] sets forth facts from which it may be determined that the obligor owes a duty of support and that a court of the responding state may obtain jurisdiction of the obligor or his property," it may send a copy of the petition to the "responding state." §14. This has the effect of requesting the responding State "to obtain jurisdiction over the obligor." §18(b). If jurisdiction is obtained, then a hearing is set in a court in the responding State at which the obligor may, if he chooses, contest the claim. The claim may be litigated in that court, with deposition testimony submitted through the initiating court by the initiating spouse or other party. §20. If the responding state court finds that the obligor owes a duty of support pursuant to the laws of the State where he or she was present during the time when support was sought, §7, judgment for the petitioner is entered. §24. If the money is collected from the spouse in the responding State, it is then sent to the court in the initiating State for distribution to the initiating party. §28.

14. While not a signatory to the Uniform Reciprocal Enforcement of Support Act of 1968, New York is a party to the Uniform Reciprocal Enforcement of Support Act of 1950, as amended. N.Y. Dom. Rel. Law §30 *et seq.* (McKinney 1977)(Uniform Support of Dependents Law). By 1957 this Act, or its substantial equivalent, had been enacted in all States, organized Territories, and the District of Columbia. 9 U.L.A. 885 (1973). The "two-state" procedure in the 1950 Act for obtaining and enforcing support obligations owed by a spouse in one State to a spouse in another is similar to that provided in the 1968 Act. See n. 13, *supra.* See generally Note, 48 CORNELL L.Q. 541 (1963).

In *Landes v. Landes,* 1 N.Y.2d 358, 135 N.E.2d 562, appeal dismissed, 352 U.S. 948 (1956), the court upheld a support decree entered against a divorced husband living in New York, on a petition filed by his former wife in California pursuant to the Uniform Act. No prior support agreement or decree existed between the parties; the California spouse sought support from the New York husband for the couple's minor

only may plaintiff-appellee here vindicate her claimed right to additional child support from her former husband in a New York court, see *supra*, at 1698–1699, but also the Uniform Acts will facilitate both her prosecution of a claim for additional support and collection of any support payments found to be owed by appellant.[15]

It cannot be disputed that California has substantial interests in protecting resident children and in facilitating child-support actions on behalf of those children. But these interests simply do not make California a "fair forum," *Shaffer v. Heitner*, *supra*, 433 U.S., at 215, in which to require appellant, who derives no personal or commercial benefit from his child's presence in California and who lacks any other relevant contact with the State, either to defend a child-support suit or to suffer liability by default.

IV

We therefore believe that the state courts in the instant case failed to heed our admonition that "the flexible standard of *International Shoe*" does not "heral[d] the eventual demise of all restrictions on the personal jurisdiction of state courts." *Hanson v. Denckla*, 357 U.S., at 251. In *McGee v. International Life Ins. Co.*, we commented on the extension of in personam jurisdiction under evolving standards of due process, explaining that this trend was in large part "attributable to the...increasing nationalization of commerce...[accompanied by] modern transportation and communication [that] have made it much less burdensome for a party sued to defend himself in a State where he engages in economic activity." 355 U.S., at 222–223. But the mere act of sending a child to California to live with her mother is not a commercial act and connotes no intent to obtain or expectancy of receiving a corresponding benefit in the State that would make fair the assertion of that State's judicial jurisdiction.

Accordingly, we conclude that the appellant's motion to quash service, on the ground of lack of personal jurisdiction, was erroneously denied by the California courts. The judgment of the California Supreme Court is, therefore,

Reversed.

Mr. Justice BRENNAN, with whom Mr. Justice WHITE and Mr. Justice POWELL join, dissenting.

The Court properly treats this case as presenting a single narrow question. That question is whether the California Supreme Court correctly "weighed" "the facts," *ante*, at 1697, of this particular case in applying the settled "constitutional standard," *ibid.*, that before state courts may exercise *in personam* jurisdiction over a nonresident, nondomiciliary parent of minor children domiciled in the State, it must appear that the nonresident has "certain minimum contacts [with the forum

14. *Continued*

child, who was residing with her mother in California. The New York Court of Appeals concluded that the procedures followed — filing of a petition in California, followed by its certification to New York's Family Court, the obtaining of jurisdiction over the husband, a hearing in New York on the merits of the petition, and entry of an award — were proper under the laws of both States and were constitutional. The constitutionality of these procedures has also been upheld in other jurisdictions. See, *e.g.*, *Watson v. Dreadin*, 309 A.2d 493 (D.C.App.1973), cert. denied, 415 U.S. 959 (1974); *State ex rel. Terry v. Terry*, 80 N.M. 185, 453 P.2d 206 (1969); *Harmon v. Harmon*, 184 Cal.App.2d 245, 7 Cal.Rptr. 279 (1960), appeal dismissed and cert. denied, 366 U.S. 270 (1961).

15. Thus, it cannot here be concluded, as it was in *McGee v. International Life Insurance Co.*, 355 U.S. 220, 223-224 (1957), with respect to actions on insurance contracts, that resident plaintiffs would be at a "severe disadvantage" if *in personam* jurisdiction over out-of-state defendants were sometimes unavailable.

State] such that the maintenance of the suit does not offend 'traditional notions of fair play and substantial justice.'" *International Shoe Co. v. Washington*, 326 U.S. 310, 316 (1945). The Court recognizes that "this determination is one in which few answers will be written 'in black and white,'" *ante*, at 92. I cannot say that the Court's determination against state-court *in personam* jurisdiction is implausible, but, though the issue is close, my independent weighing of the facts leads me to conclude, in agreement with the analysis and determination of the California Supreme Court, that appellant's connection with the State of California was not too attenuated, under the standards of reasonableness and fairness implicit in the Due Process Clause, to require him to conduct his defense in the California courts. I therefore dissent.

COMMENTS

Following the language in *Shaffer v. Heitner*, 433 U.S. 186, 212 (1977), the legal literature has perceived *Kulko* to be related to the "standards set forth in *International Shoe* and its progeny." Indeed, the defendant invoked, successfully before the U.S. Supreme Court, that he lacked sufficient minimum contacts with the State of California and that the proceedings against him before the California courts did not comply with "traditional notions of fair play and substantial justice," as demanded by *International Shoe Co. v. Washington*, 326 U.S. 310, 316 (1945)(quoting *Milliken v. Meyer*, 311 U.S. 457, 463 (1940). In spite of the historical discussion in Mr. Justice Marshall's opinion in *Kulko*, going back more than 100 years to *Pennoyer v. Neff*, 95 U.S. 714 (1877), it is probable that factors other than those discussed by the Court had an impact on the outcome, in particular the conduct of the plaintiff wife who throughout the controversy seemed to have aggressively pursued her self-interest. The statement of facts at the onset of the majority opinion in *Kulko* is symptomatic.

Justice Marshall set forth in minute detail the tragic events, that brought about the gradual disintegration of the Kulko family. In each instance, Sharon Kulko was described, sometimes by implication, as having been the moving force and thus to blame. She moved away to San Francisco, California, while still married, leaving her husband behind in New York with the children. She came back to New York merely to sign the separation agreement thereby surrendering the custody of the children to her husband. Immediately thereafter she flew to Haiti to secure a divorce in person while (as indicated in footnote l) the husband stayed behind in New York, and he merely filed a power of attorney which she had taken along for this purpose. Apparently without delay she returned to California, "where she remarried and took the name Horn." Having settled her own situation by remarrying, she then induced the children, first the daughter Ilsa, then the boy Darwin, to leave their father and join her and the stepfather in San Francisco. The contrary separation agreement seemed to have been a way station to facilitate the Haitian divorce and remarriage. Less than a month after she had spirited away the son from New York, she brought proceedings in California demanding inter alia a change in custody and an increase in support. The California trial court immediately granted her temporary custody and (as indicated in the here deleted footnote 5) increased substantially the defendant's support obligation.

As a matter of legal theory, the detailed factual account in *Kulko* can be justified, at least in part, as laying a foundation for jurisdictional conclusions, based on the requirement of "reasonableness" in *Shaffer* and *International Shoe*. More clearly, however, especially when the tone of the account is considered, it spells out fault. It is inferred that this woman had deserted her husband and temporarily abandoned her children in the interest of a new relationship and remarriage. The defendant, on the other hand, is depicted, again supposedly for jurisdictional purposes, as having remained passive and as having merely acquiesced in the progressively perplexing situation in which he found himself. His motives are described as laudable, having in mind family harmony and the welfare of the children.

This particular discussion is geared by the Court to the additional jurisdictional requirement established in *Hanson v. Denckla*, 357 U.S. 235, 253 (1958), that the defendant must have purposefully availed himself of some benefits or privileges within the forum state, in this instance, California. Yet this jurisdictional factor imparts a subjective element, in this case the defendant's freedom from fault by staying passive in the interests of peace and for the good of the children. The plaintiff's conduct, by comparison, seems to be designed to maximize her strategic position with the aid of the California courts and to offend, in the language of *Shaffer* and *International Shoe*, "traditional notions of fair play and substantial justice." This concept too imparts possible consideration of fault or the freedom from it, especially within the realm of jurisdiction of state courts in family disputes.

One aspect of *Kulko* seems to be that it resurrects, albeit inadvertently, *Haddock v. Haddock*, 201 U.S. 562 (1906), which was expressly overruled with detailed reasons in *Williams v. North Carolina I* (see p. 987). A criticized aspect of *Haddock* was that it combined jurisdictional considerations with questions of who was at fault — in other words, the actual merits of the case. As Justice Douglas expressed in writing for the majority in *Williams I*, "the fault or wrong of one spouse in leaving the other becomes under that view a jurisdictional fact on which this Court would ultimately have to pass. Whatever may be said as to the practical effect which such would have in clouding divorce decrees, the question as to where the fault lies has no relevancy to the existence of state power in such circumstances." While the logic of this reasoning seems to be unassailable, its application poses practical problems, as *Kulko* demonstrates. The jurisdictional standards of *Shaffer* and *International Shoe* which may be relatively free of hidden substantive elements in financial or commercial transactions seem to invite substantive considerations of fault within the whole area of family law, regardless of whether an attempt is made to apply them to status questions, such as divorce and custody, or whether as in *Kulko* a mere monetary award is in issue.

In spite of legislative efforts to eliminate fault, family law continues to be permeated with submerged, essentially emotional, needs to apply moral standards of fault. As *Kulko* illustrates, even an elevated judicial forum, such as the U.S. Supreme Court, may follow this pattern. Independently, the conceptual distinction between procedure and substance has caused problems in other areas of law. Actually, both types of rules are equally concerned with the exercise of power. Practicing lawyers realize that it is sound strategy to support a seemingly purely technical jurisdictional argument with substantive reasons relating to the merits of the case. A judge may rule that these matters are irrelevant for the determination of the jurisdictional issues, yet may nevertheless be swayed by broad considerations of fairness, as the judge understands them. Frequently substantive dispositions are made under color of procedure, and jurisdictional dispositions are particularly amenable to this, sometimes unconscious, judicial strategy.

The outcome of *Kulko* is an illustration for such a hidden substantive disposition of the case. That the California courts served the cause of the plaintiff is obvious. She obtained custody and a substantial increase in support, essentially all that she had asked for. Whether the New York courts would have been equally supportive of her claims is doubtful, the Uniform Reciprocal Enforcement of Support Act notwithstanding. The attorneys representing the parties were obviously aware of the respective merits and disadvantages of litigating the issues in California or in New York. By deciding the jurisdictional issue in favor of the defendant, the U.S. Supreme Court affected the merits of the case sufficiently to make it feasible for the plaintiff to settle the case for less than she could have obtained through the jurisdiction of the California courts. The reason why the fault aspect of *Kulko* and its relation to *Haddock* have not been sufficiently discussed in the literature lies in two factors — insufficient close analysis of the facts and concentration on the conceptual reasons given by the Court. Had Justice Marshall's factual account been matched with the legal conclusion, it would have become apparent that more was involved in the outcome favoring the defendant than jurisdictional considerations.

The mere fact that the legal analysis of *Kulko* has tended to be incomplete does not permit the conclusion, however, that the jurisdictional reasoning in the opinion can be disregarded. It encourages the reevaluation of the jurisdictional issues in status litigation from the perspective of due process as expressed in *Shaffer*. Technically, only child support was in issue before the U.S. Supreme Court in *Kulko*. But the litigation, as initiated by the plaintiff, had also included a request for change in custody. Although the appeal did not challenge the custody disposition, matters relating to custody continued to be significant for the adjudication of support. The Court did not limit itself in its reasoning to support, but implied a universally applicable theory of jurisdiction that required a nexus between the defendant and the forum state that is not too attenuated.

Bodenheimer and Neeley-Kvarme maintained that footnote 30 in *Shaffer* exempted status adjudications from the minimum contacts rule. *Shaffer* involved a derivative shareholder's suit in a commercial context, and family or status was not in issue and not argued before the Court. Moreover, the passing reference to status in a footnote was not clear as an exemption. It was expressed in the form of a double negative: "We do not suggest that jurisdictional doctrines other than those discussed in text, such as the particularized rules governing adjudications of status, are inconsistent with the standard of fairness." 433 U.S. 186, 208 n. 30 (1977). This is substantially less than a positive suggestion that jurisdictional doctrines, such as the rules governing adjudications of status, are consistent with the standard of fairness. In other words, jurisdiction in status litigation, for example, relating to divorce or custody, may or may not comport with the standards of fairness and reasonableness as demanded by due process. Or, to use the language of Justice Marshall in *Kulko*, "the facts of each case must be weighed to determine whether the requisite 'affiliating circumstances' are present."

Past case law in regard to status adjudication in family law, traditionally perceived as being in the nature of *in rem*, would have to be reexamined in the light of *Shaffer* and *Kulko* under the test of minimum contacts. For example, the jurisdictional requirement of domicile as developed in *Williams I* for *ex parte* divorces might continue to survive constitutional attack, perhaps even the three-month "actual presence" in Arkansas before judgment as the jurisdictional basis for divorce in *Wheat v. Wheat* (p. 1014). Yet a technical domicile might be an unreasonable basis for jurisdiction. Had the peripatetic Mr. Wheat, for instance, instead of pursuing his request for divorce in Arkansas, the state of his actual presence, filed for divorce in Oklahoma, the state of his original and probably continuing domicile, a sufficient jurisdictional nexus might have been missing. He had not resided within Oklahoma for years and Mrs. Wheat probably had no connection with that state whatsoever.

In regard to custody adjudications, the jurisdictional theories as expressed in *May v. Anderson* (p. 1040), upon reexamination, may have to be modified. In that case a custody award by a Wisconsin divorce court, favoring the father, had been given full faith and credit in Ohio where the mother and children were living. In reversing the Ohio courts, the U.S. Supreme Court by a plurality of the Justices maintained that Wisconsin courts could not cut off the custody rights of a nonresident mother without *in personam* jurisdiction. The opinion could run counter to the suggestion in *Shaffer*, not contradicted in *Kulko*, that at least some particularized rules governing status adjudication may not be inconsistent with the standard of fairness propagated by the minimum contacts test of jurisdiction. Custody adjudication, in which the status of children is determined, could be a prime illustration. A requirement of *in personam* jurisdiction over the parent could be an intolerable burden, especially in neglect and adoption cases.

REFERENCE

Brigitte Bodenheimer & Janet Neeley-Kvarme, *Jurisdiction Over Child Custody and Adoption After Shaffer and Kulko*, 12 U.C.D. L. REV. 229 (1979)

APPENDIX

Uniform Marriage and Divorce Act

Uniform Premarital Agreement Act

Uniform Child Custody Jurisdiction Act

Parental Kidnapping Prevention Act

UNIFORM MARRIAGE AND DIVORCE ACT

PART I
GENERAL PROVISIONS

Section 101. [Short Title]. This Act may be cited as the "Uniform Marriage and Divorce Act."

Section 102. [Purposes: Rules of Construction]. This Act shall be liberally construed and applied to promote its underlying purposes, which are to:

(1) provide adequate procedures for the solemnization and registration of marriage;

(2) strengthen and preserve the integrity of marriage and safeguard family relationships;

(3) promote the amicable settlement of disputes that have arisen between parties to a marriage;

(4) mitigate the potential harm to the spouses and their children caused by the process of legal dissolution of marriage;

(5) make reasonable provision for spouse and minor children during and after litigation; and

(6) make the law of legal dissolution of marriage effective for dealing with the realities of matrimonial experience by making irretrievable breakdown of the marriage relationship the sole basis for its dissolution.

Section 103. [Uniformity of Application and Construction]. This Act shall be so applied and construed as to effectuate its general purpose to make uniform the law with respect to the subject of this Act among those states which enact it.

PART II
MARRIAGE

Section 201. [Formalities]. Marriage is a personal relationship between a man and a woman arising out of a civil contract to which the consent of the parties is essential. A marriage licensed, solemnized, and registered as provided in this Act is valid in this State. A marriage may be contracted, maintained, invalidated, or dissolved only as provided by law.

Section 202. [Marriage License and Marriage Certificate].

(a) The [Secretary of State, Commissioner of Public Health] shall prescribe the form for an application for a marriage license, which shall include the following information:

(1) name, sex, occupation, address, social security number, date and place of birth of each party to the proposed marriage;

(2) if either party was previously married, his name, and the date, place, and court in which the marriage was dissolved or declared invalid or the date and place of death of the former spouse;

(3) name and address of the parents or guardian of each party; and

(4) whether the parties are related to each other and, if so, their relationship.

(5) the name and date of birth of any child of which both parties are parents, born before the making of the application, unless their parental rights and the parent and child relationship with respect to the child have been terminated.

(b) The [Secretary of State, Commissioner of Public Health] shall prescribe the forms for the marriage license, the marriage certificate, and the consent to marriage.

Section 203. [License to Marry]. When a marriage application has been completed and signed by both parties to a prospective marriage and at least one party has appeared before the [marriage license] clerk and paid the marriage license fee of [$_______], the [marriage license] clerk shall issue a license to marry and a marriage certificate form upon being furnished:

(1) satisfactory proof that each party to the marriage will have attained the age of 18 years at the time the marriage license is effective, or will have attained the age of 16 years and has either the consent to the marriage of both parents or his guardian, or judicial approval; [or, if under the age of 16 years, has both the consent of both parents or his guardian and judicial approval;] and

(2) satisfactory proof that the marriage is not prohibited; [and]

(3) [a certificate of the results of any medical examination required by the laws of this State].

Section 204. [License, Effective Date]. A license to marry becomes effective throughout this state 3 days after the date of issuance, unless the [__________] court orders that the license is effective when issued, and expires 180 days after it becomes effective.

Section 205. [Judicial Approval].

(a) The [_______] court, after a reasonable effort has been made to notify the parents or guardian of each underaged party, may order the [marriage license] clerk to issue a marriage license and a marriage certificate form:

[(1)] to a party aged 16 or 17 years who has no parent capable of consenting to his marriage, or whose parent or guardian has not consented to his marriage; [or

(2) to a party under the age of 16 years who has the consent of both parents to his marriage, if capable of giving consent, or his guardian].

(b) A marriage license and a marriage certificate form may be issued under this section only if the court finds that the underaged party is capable of assuming the responsibilities of marriage and the marriage will serve his best interest. Pregnancy alone does not establish that the best interest of the party will be served.

(c) The [______________] court shall authorize performance of a marriage by proxy upon the showing required by the provisions on solemnization.

Section 206. [Solemnization and Registration].

(a) A marriage may be solemnized by a judge of a court of record, by a public official whose powers include solemnization of marriages, or in accordance with any mode of solemnization recognized by any religious denomination, Indian Nation or Tribe, or Native Group. Either the person solemnizing the marriage, or, if no individual acting alone solemnized the marriage, a party to the marriage, shall complete the marriage certificate form and forward it to the [marriage license] clerk.

(b) If a party to a marriage is unable to be present at the solemnization, he may authorize in writing a third person to act as his proxy. If the person solemnizing the marriage is satisfied that the absent party is unable to be present and has consented to the marriage, he may solemnize the marriage by proxy. If he is not satisfied, the parties may petition the [_______________] court for an order permitting the marriage to be solemnized by proxy.

(c) Upon receipt of the marriage certificate, the [marriage license] clerk shall register the marriage.

(d) The solemnization of the marriage is not invalidated by the fact that the person solemnizing the marriage was not legally qualified to solemnize it, if either party to the marriage believed him to be so qualified.

Section 207. [Prohibited Marriages].

(a) The following marriages are prohibited:

(1) a marriage entered into prior to the dissolution of an earlier marriage of one of the parties;

(2) a marriage between an ancestor and a descendant, or between a brother and a sister, whether the relationship is by the half or the whole blood, or by adoption;

(3) a marriage between an uncle and a niece or between an aunt and a nephew, whether the relationship is by the half or the whole blood, except as to marriages permitted by the established customs of aboriginal cultures.

(b) Parties to a marriage prohibited under this section who cohabit after removal of the impediment are lawfully married as of the date of the removal of the impediment.

(c) Children born of a prohibited marriage are legitimate.

Section 208. [Declaration of Invalidity].

(a) The [________] court shall enter its decree declaring the invalidity of a marriage entered into under the following circumstances:

(1) a party lacked capacity to consent to the marriage at the time the marriage was solemnized, either because of mental incapacity or infirmity or because of the influence of alcohol, drugs, or other incapacitating substances, or a party was induced to enter into a marriage by force or duress, or by fraud involving the essentials of marriage;

(2) a party lacks the physical capacity to consummate the marriage by sexual intercourse, and at the time the marriage was solemnized the other party did not know of the incapacity;

(3) a party [was under the age of 16 years and did not have the consent of his parents or guardian and judicial approval or] was aged 16 or 17 years and did not have the consent of his parents or guardian or judicial approval; or

(4) the marriage is prohibited.

(b) A declaration of invalidity under subsection (a)(1) through (3) may be sought by any of the following persons and must be commenced within the times specified, but in no event may a declaration of invalidity be sought after the death of either party to the marriage:

(1) for a reason set forth in subsection (a)(1), by either party or by the legal representative of the party who lacked capacity to consent, no later than 90 days after the petitioner obtained knowledge of the described condition;

(2) for the reason set forth in subsection (a)(2), by either party, no later than one year after the petitioner obtained knowledge of the described condition;

(3) for the reason set forth in subsection (a)(3), by the underaged party, his parent or guardian, prior to the time the underaged party reaches the age at which he could have married without satisfying the omitted requirement.

ALTERNATIVE A

[(c) A declaration of invalidity for the reason set forth in subsection (a)(4) may be sought by either party, the legal spouse in case of a bigamous marriage, the [appropriate state official], or a child of either party, at any time prior to the death of one of the parties.]

ALTERNATIVE B

[(c) A declaration of invalidity for the reason set forth in subsection (a)(4) may be sought by either party, the legal spouse in case of a bigamous marriage, the [appropriate state official] or a child of either party, at any time, not to exceed 5 years following the death of either party.]

(d) Children born of a marriage declared invalid are legitimate.

(e) Unless the court finds, after a consideration of all relevant circumstances, including the effect of a retroactive decree on third parties, that the interests of justice would be served by making the decree not retroactive, it shall declare the marriage invalid as of the date of the marriage. The provisions of this Act relating to property rights of the spouses, maintenance, support, and custody of children on dissolution of marriage are applicable to non-retroactive decrees of invalidity.

Section 209. [Putative Spouse]. Any person who has cohabited with another to whom he is not legally married in the good faith belief that he was married to that person is a putative spouse until knowledge of the fact that he is not legally married terminates his status and prevents acquisition of further rights. A putative spouse acquires the rights conferred upon a legal spouse, including the right to maintenance following termination of his status, whether or not the marriage is prohibited (Section 207) or declared invalid (Section 208). If there is a legal spouse or other putative spouses, rights acquired by a putative spouse do not supersede the rights of the legal spouse or those acquired by other putative spouses, but the court shall apportion property, maintenance, and support rights among the claimants as appropriate in the circumstances and in the interests of justice.

Section 210. [Application]. All marriages contracted within this State prior to the effective date of this Act, or outside this State, that were valid at the time of the contract or subsequently validated by the laws of the place in which they were contracted or by the domicile of the parties, are valid in this State.

[Section 211. [Validity of Common Law Marriage] [ALTERNATIVE A]. Common law marriages are not invalidated by this Act.]

[Section 211. [Invalidity of Common Law Marriage] [ALTERNATIVE B]. Common law marriages contracted in this State after the effective date of this Act are invalid.]

PART III

DISSOLUTION

Section 301. [Application of [Rules of Civil Practice] to Proceedings under this Act].

(a) The [Rules of Civil Practice] apply to all proceedings under this Act, except as otherwise provided in this Act.

(b) A proceeding for dissolution of marriage, legal separation, or declaration of invalidity of marriage shall be entitled "In re the Marriage of _______ and _______." A custody or support proceeding shall be entitled "In re the (Custody) (Support) of _______."

(c) The initial pleading in all proceedings under this Act shall be denominated a petition. A responsive pleading shall be denominated a response. Other pleadings, and all pleadings in other matters under this Act, shall be denominated as provided in the [Rules of Civil Practice].

(d) In this Act, "decree" includes "judgment."

(e) A decree of dissolution or of legal separation, if made, shall not be awarded to one of the parties, but shall provide that it affects the status previously existing between the parties in the manner decreed.

Section 302. [Dissolution of Marriage; Legal Separation].

(a) The [_______] court shall enter a decree of dissolution of marriage if:

(1) the court finds that one of the parties, at the time the action was commenced, was domiciled in this State, or was stationed in this State

while a member of the armed services, and that the domicil or military presence has been maintained for 90 days next preceding the making of the findings;

(2) the court finds that the marriage is irretrievably broken, if the finding is supported by evidence that (i) the parties have lived separate and apart for a period of more than 180 days next preceding the commencement of the proceeding, or (ii) there is serious marital discord adversely affecting the attitude of one or both of the parties toward the marriage;

(3) the court finds that the conciliation provisions of Section 305 either do not apply or have been met;

(4) to the extent it has jurisdiction to do so, the court has considered, approved, or provided for child custody, the support of any child entitled to support, the maintenance of either spouse, and the disposition of property; or has provided for a separate, later hearing to complete these matters.

(b) If a party requests a decree of legal separation rather than a decree of dissolution of marriage, the court shall grant the decree in that form unless the other party objects.

Section 303. [Procedure; Commencement; Pleadings; Abolition of Existing Defenses].

(a) All proceedings under this Act shall be commenced as provided by the [Rules of Civil Practice].

(b) The verified petition in a proceeding for dissolution of marriage or legal separation shall allege that the marriage is irretrievably broken and shall set forth:

(1) the age, occupation, and length of residence in this state of each party;

(2) the date of the marriage and the place at which it was registered;

(3) that the jurisdictional requirements of Section 302 exist and the marriage is irretrievably broken in that either (i) the parties have lived separate and apart for a period of more than 180 days next preceding the commencement of the proceeding or (ii) there is serious marital discord adversely affecting the attitude of one or both of the parties toward the marriage, and there is no reasonable prospect of reconciliation;

(4) the names, ages, and addresses of all living children of the marriage, and whether the wife is pregnant;

(5) any arrangements as to support, custody, and visitation of the children and maintenance of a spouse; and

(6) the relief sought.

(c) Either or both parties to the marriage may initiate the proceeding.

(d) If a proceeding is commenced by one of the parties, the other party shall be served in the manner provided by the [Rules of Civil Practice] and may within [30] days after the date of service may file a verified response.

(e) Previously existing defenses to divorce and legal separation, including but not limited to condonation, connivance, collusion, recrimination, insanity, and lapse of time, are abolished.

(f) The court may join additional parties proper for the exercise of its authority to implement this Act.

Section 304. [Temporary Order or Temporary Injunction].

(a) In a proceeding for dissolution of marriage or for legal separation, or in a proceeding for disposition of property or for maintenance or support following dissolution of the marriage by a court which lacked personal jurisdiction over the absent spouse, either party may move for temporary maintenance or temporary support of a child of the marriage entitled to support. The motion shall be accompanied by an affidavit setting forth the factual basis for the motion and the amounts requested.

(b) As a part of a motion for temporary maintenance or support or by independent motion accompanied by affidavit, either party may request the court to issue a temporary injunction for any of the following relief:

(1) restraining any person from transferring, encumbering, concealing, or otherwise disposing of any property except in the usual course of business or for the necessities of life, and, if so restrained, requiring him to notify the moving party of any proposed extraordinary expenditures made after the order is issued;

(2) enjoining a party from molesting or disturbing the peace of the other party or of any child;

(3) excluding a party from the family home or from the home of the other party upon a showing that physical or emotional harm would otherwise result;

(4) enjoining a party from removing a child from the jurisdiction of the court; and

(5) providing other injunctive relief proper in the circumstances.

(c) The court may issue a temporary restraining order without requiring notice to the other party only if it finds on the basis of the moving affidavit or other evidence that irreparable injury will result to the moving party if no order is issued until the time for responding has elapsed.

(d) A response may be filed within [20] days after service of notice of motion or at the time specified in the temporary restraining order.

(e) On the basis of the showing made and in conformity with Sections 308 and 309, the court may issue a temporary injunction and an order for temporary maintenance or support in amounts and on terms just and proper in the circumstance.

(f) A temporary order or temporary injunction:

(1) does not prejudice the rights of the parties or the child which are to be adjudicated at subsequent hearings in the proceeding;

(2) may be revoked or modified before final decree on a showing by affidavit of the facts necessary to revocation or modification of a final decree under Section 316; and

(3) terminates when the final decree is entered or when the petition for dissolution or legal separation is voluntarily dismissed.

Section 305. [Irretrievable Breakdown].

(a) If both of the parties by petition or otherwise have stated under oath or affirmation that the marriage is irretrievably broken, or one of the parties has so stated and the other has not denied it, the court, after hearing, shall make a finding whether the marriage is irretrievably broken.

(b) If one of the parties has denied under oath or affirmation that the marriage is irretrievably broken, the court shall consider all relevant factors, including the circumstances that gave rise to filing the petition and the prospect of reconciliation, and shall:

(1) make a finding whether the marriage is irretrievably broken; or

(2) continue the matter for further hearing not fewer than 30 nor more than 60 days later, or as soon thereafter as the matter may be reached on the court's calendar, and may suggest to the parties that they seek counseling. The court, at the request of either party shall, or on its own motion may, order a conciliation conference. At the adjourned hearing the court shall make a finding whether the marriage is irretrievably broken.

(c) A finding of irretrievable breakdown is a determination that there is no reasonable prospect of reconciliation.

Section 306. [Separation Agreement].

(a) To promote amicable settlement of disputes between parties to a marriage attendant upon their separation or the dissolution of their marriage, the parties may enter into a written separation agreement containing provisions for disposition of any property owned by either of them, maintenance of either of them, and support, custody, and visitation of their children.

(b) In a proceeding for dissolution of marriage or for legal separation, the terms of the separation agreement, except those providing for the support, custody, and visitation of children, are binding upon the court unless it finds, after considering the economic circumstances of the parties and any other relevant evidence produced by the parties, on their own motion or on request of the court, that the separation agreement is unconscionable.

(c) If the court finds the separation agreement unconscionable, it may request the parties to submit a revised separation agreement or may make orders for the disposition of property, maintenance, and support.

(d) If the court finds that the separation agreement is not unconscionable as to disposition of property or maintenance, and not unsatisfactory as to support:

(1) unless the separation agreement provides to the contrary, its terms shall be set forth in the decree of dissolution or legal separation and the parties shall be ordered to perform them, or

(2) if the separation agreement provides that its terms shall not be set forth in the decree, the decree shall identify the separation agreement and state that the court has found the terms not unconscionable.

(e) Terms of the agreement set forth in the decree are enforceable by all remedies available for enforcement of a judgment, including contempt, and are enforceable as contract terms.

(f) Except for terms concerning the support, custody, or visitation of children, the decree may expressly preclude or limit modification of terms set forth in the decree if the separation agreement so provides. Otherwise, terms of a separation agreement set forth in the decree are automatically modified by modification of the decree.

Section 307. [Disposition of Property] [ALTERNATIVE A].

(a) In a proceeding for dissolution of a marriage, legal separation, or disposition of property following a decree of dissolution of marriage or legal separation by a court which lacked personal jurisdiction over the absent spouse or lacked jurisdiction to dispose of the property, the court, without regard to marital misconduct, shall, and in a proceeding for legal separation may, finally equitably apportion between the parties the property and assets belonging to either or both however and whenever acquired, and whether the title thereto is in the name of the husband or wife or both. In making apportionment the court shall consider the duration of the marriage, any prior marriage of either party, antenuptial agreement of the parties, the age, health, station, occupation, amount and sources of income, vocational skills, employability, estate, liabilities, and needs of each of the parties, custodial provisions, whether the apportionment is in lieu of or in addition to maintenance, and the opportunity of each for future acquisition of capital assets and income. The court shall also consider the contribution or dissipation of each party in the acquisition, preservation, depreciation, or appreciation in value of the respective estates, and the contribution of a spouse as a homemaker or to the family unit.

(b) In the proceeding, the court may protect and promote the best interests of the children by setting aside a portion of the jointly and separately held estates of the parties in a separate fund or trust for the support, maintenance, education, and general welfare of any minor, dependent, or incompetent children of the parties.

Section 307. [Disposition of Property] [ALTERNATIVE B].

In a proceeding for dissolution of the marriage, legal separation, or disposition of property following a decree of dissolution of the marriage or legal separation by a court which lacked personal jurisdiction over the absent spouse or lacked jurisdiction to dispose of the property, the court shall assign each spouse's separate property to that spouse. It also shall divide community property, without regard to marital misconduct, in just proportions after considering all relevant factors including:

(1) contribution of each spouse to acquisition of the marital property, including contribution of a spouse as homemaker;

(2) value of the property set apart to each spouse;

(3) duration of the marriage; and

(4) economic circumstances of each spouse when the division of property is to become effective, including the desirability of awarding the family home or the right to live therein for a reasonable period to the spouse having custody of any children.

Section 308. [Maintenance].

(a) In a proceeding for dissolution of marriage, legal separation, or maintenance following a decree of dissolution of the marriage by a court which lacked personal jurisdiction over the absent spouse, the court may grant a maintenance order for either spouse only if it finds that the spouse seeking maintenance:

(1) lacks sufficient property to provide for his reasonable needs; and

(2) is unable to support himself through appropriate employment or is the custodian of a child whose condition or circumstances make it appropriate that the custodian not be required to seek employment outside the home.

(b) The maintenance order shall be in amounts and for periods of time the court deems just, without regard to marital misconduct, and after considering all relevant factors including:

(1) the financial resources of the party seeking maintenance, including marital property apportioned to him, his ability to meet his needs independently, and the extent to which a provision for support of a child living with the party includes a sum for that party as custodian;

(2) the time necessary to acquire sufficient education or training to enable the party seeking maintenance to find appropriate employment;

(3) the standard of living established during the marriage;

(4) the duration of the marriage;

(5) the age and the physical and emotional condition of the spouse seeking maintenance; and

(6) the ability of the spouse from whom maintenance is sought to meet his needs while meeting those of the spouse seeking maintenance.

Section 309. [Child Support]. In a proceeding for dissolution of marriage, legal separation, maintenance, or child support, the court may order either or both parents owing a duty of support to a child to pay an amount reasonable or necessary for his support, without regard to marital misconduct, after considering all relevant factors including:

(1) the financial resources of the child;

(2) the financial resources of the custodial parent;

(3) the standard of living the child would have enjoyed had the marriage not been dissolved;

(4) the physical and emotional condition of the child and his educational needs; and

(5) the financial resources and needs of the noncustodial parent.

Section 310. [Representation of Child]. The court may appoint an attorney to represent the interests of a minor or dependent child with respect to his support, custody, and visitation. The court shall enter an order for costs, fees, and disbursements in favor of the child's attorney. The order shall be made against either or both parents, except that, if the responsible party is indigent, the costs, fees, and disbursements shall be borne by the [appropriate agency].

Section 311. [Payment of Maintenance or Support to Court].

(a) Upon its own motion or upon motion of either party, the court may order at any time that maintenance or support payments be made to the [clerk of court, court trustee, probation officer] as trustee for remittance to the person entitled to receive the payments.

(b) The [clerk of court, court trustee, probation officer] shall maintain records listing the amount of payments, the date payments are required to be made, and the names and addresses of the parties affected by the order.

(c) The parties affected by the order shall inform the [clerk of court, court trustee, probation officer] of any change of address or of other condition that may affect the administration of the order.

(d) If a party fails to make a required payment, the [clerk of court, court trustee, probation officer] shall send by registered or certified mail notice of the arrearage to the obligor. If payment of the sum due is not made to the [clerk of court, court trustee, probation officer] within 10 days after sending notice, the [clerk of court, court trustee, probation officer] shall certify the amount due to the [prosecuting attorney]. The [prosecuting attorney] shall promptly initiate contempt proceedings against the obligator.

(e) The [prosecuting attorney] shall assist the court on behalf of a person entitled to receive maintenance or support in all proceedings initiated under this section to enforce compliance with the order. The person to whom maintenance or support is awarded may also initiate action to collect arrearages.

(f) If the person obligated to pay support has left or is beyond the jurisdiction of the court, the [prosecuting attorney] may institute any other proceeding available under the laws of this State for enforcement of the duties of support and maintenance.

Section 312. [Assignments]. The court may order the person obligated to pay support or maintenance to make an assignment of a part of his periodic earnings or trust income to the person entitled to receive the payments. The assignment is binding on the employer, trustee, or other payor of the funds 2 weeks after service upon him of notice that it has been made. The payor shall withhold from the earnings or trust income payable to the person obligated to support the amount specified in the assignment and shall transmit the payments to the person specified in the order. The payor may deduct from each payment a sum not exceeding [$1.00] as reimbursement for costs. An employer shall not discharge or otherwise discipline an employee as a result of a wage or salary assignment authorized by this section.

Section 313. [Attorney's Fees]. The court from time to time after considering the financial resources of both parties may order a party to pay a reasonable amount for the cost to the other party of maintaining or defending any proceeding under this Act and for attorney's fees, including sums for legal services rendered and costs incurred prior to the commencement of the proceeding or after entry of judgment. The court may order that the amount be paid directly to the attorney, who may enforce the order in his name.

Section 314. [Decree].

(a) A decree of dissolution of marriage or of legal separation is final when entered, subject to the right of appeal. An appeal from the decree of dissolution that does not challenge the finding that the marriage is irretrievably broken does not delay the finality of that provision of the decree which dissolves the marriage beyond the time for appealing from that provision, and either of the parties may remarry pending appeal.

(b) No earlier than 6 months after entry of a decree of legal separation, the court on motion of either party shall convert the decree to a decree of dissolution of marriage.

(c) The Clerk of Court shall give notice of the entry of a decree of dissolution or legal separation:

(1) if the marriage is registered in this State, to the [marriage license] clerk of the [county, judicial district] where the marriage is registered who shall enter the fact of dissolution or separation in the [Registry of Marriage]; or

(2) if the marriage is registered in another jurisdiction, to the appropriate official of that jurisdiction, with the request that he enter the fact of dissolution in the appropriate record.

(d) Upon request by a wife whose marriage is dissolved or declared invalid, the court may, and if there are no children of the parties shall, order her maiden name or a former name restored.

Section 315. [Independence of Provisions of Decree or Temporary Order]. If a party fails to comply with a provision of a decree or temporary order or injunction, the obligation of the other party to make payments for support or maintenance or to permit visitation is not suspended; but he may move the court to grant an appropriate order.

Section 316. [Modification and Termination of Provisions for Maintenance, Support and Property Disposition].

(a) Except as otherwise provided in subsection (f) of Section 306, the provisions of any decree respecting maintenance or support may be modified only as to installments accruing subsequent to the motion for modification and only upon a showing of changed circumstances so substantial and continuing as to make the terms unconscionable. The provisions as to property disposition may not be revoked or modified, unless the court finds the existence of conditions that justify the reopening of a judgment under the laws of this state.

(b) Unless otherwise agreed in writing or expressly provided in the decree, the obligation to pay future maintenance is terminated upon the death of either party or the remarriage of the party receiving maintenance.

(c) Unless otherwise agreed in writing or expressly provided in the decree, provisions for the support of a child are terminated by emancipation of the child but not by the death of a parent obligated to support the child. When a parent obligated to pay support dies, the amount of support may be modified, revoked, or commuted to a lump sum payment, to the extent just and appropriate in the circumstances.

PART IV

CUSTODY

Section 401. [Jurisdiction; Commencement of Proceeding].

(a) A court of this State competent to decide child custody matters has jurisdiction to make a child custody determination by initial or modification decree if:

(1) this State (i) is the home state of the child at the time of commencement of the proceeding, or (ii) had been the child's home state within 6 months before commencement of the proceeding and the child is absent from this State because of his removal or retention by a person claiming his custody or for other reason, and a parent or person acting as parent continues to live in this State; or

(2) it is in the best interest of the child that a court of this State assume jurisdiction because (i) the child and his parents, or the child and at least one contestant, have a significant connection with this State, and (ii) there is available in this State substantial evidence concerning the child's present or future care, protection, training, and personal relationships; or

(3) the child is physically present in this State and (i) has been abandoned or (ii) it is necessary in an emergency to protect him because he has been subjected to or threatened with mistreatment or abuse or is neglected or dependent; or

(4)(i) no other state has jurisdiction under prerequisites substantially in accordance with paragraphs (1), (2) or (3), or another state has declined to exercise jurisdiction on the ground that this State is the more appropriate forum to determine custody of the child, and (ii) it is in his best interest that the court assume jurisdiction.

(b) Except under paragraphs (3) and (4) of subsection (a), physical presence in this State of the child, or of the child and one of the contestants, is not alone sufficient to confer jurisdiction on a court of this State to make a child custody determination.

(c) Physical presence of the child, while desirable, is not a prerequisite for jurisdiction to determine his custody.

(d) A child custody proceeding is commenced in the [_______] court:

(1) by a parent, by filing a petition

(i) for dissolution or legal separation; or

(ii) for custody of the child in the [county, judicial district] in which he is permanently resident or found; or

(2) by a person other than a parent, by filing a petition for custody of the child in the [county, judicial district] in which he is permanently resident or found, but only if he is not in the physical custody of one of his parents.

(e) Notice of a child custody proceeding shall be given to the child's parent, guardian, and custodian, who may appear, be heard, and file a responsive pleading. The court, upon a showing of good cause, may permit intervention of other interested parties.

Section 402. [Best Interest of Child]. The court shall determine custody in accordance with the best interest of the child. The court shall consider all relevant factors including:

(1) the wishes of the child's parent or parents as to his custody;

(2) the wishes of the child as to his custodian;

(3) the interaction and interrelationship of the child with his parent or parents, his siblings, and any other person who may significantly affect the child's best interest;

(4) the child's adjustment to his home, school, and community; and

(5) the mental and physical health of all individuals involved.

The court shall not consider conduct of a proposed custodian that does not affect his relationship to the child.

Section 403. [Temporary Orders].

(a) A party to a custody proceeding may move for a temporary custody order. The motion must be supported by an affidavit as provided in Section 410. The court may award temporary custody under the standards of Section 402 after a hearing, or, if there is no objection, solely on the basis of the affidavits.

(b) If a proceeding for dissolution of marriage or legal separation is dismissed, any temporary custody order is vacated unless a parent or the child's custodian moves that the proceeding continue as a custody proceeding and the court finds, after a hearing, that the circumstances of the parents and the best interest of the child requires that a custody decree be issued.

(c) If a custody proceeding commenced in the absence of a petition for dissolution of marriage or legal separation under subsection (1)(ii) or (2) of Section 401 is dismissed, any temporary custody order is vacated.

Section 404. [Interviews].

(a) The court may interview the child in chambers to ascertain the child's wishes as to his custodian and as to visitation. The court may permit counsel to be present at the interview. The court shall cause a record of the interview to be made and to be part of the record in the case.

(b) The court may seek the advice of professional personnel, whether or not employed by the court on a regular basis. The advice given shall be in writing and made available by the court to counsel upon request. Counsel may examine as a witness any professional personnel consulted by the court.

Section 405. [Investigations and Reports].

(a) In contested custody proceedings, and in other custody proceedings if a parent or the child's custodian so requests, the court may order an investigation and report concerning custodial arrangements for the child. The investigation and report may be made by [the court social service agency, the staff of the juvenile court, the local probation or welfare department, or a private agency employed by the court for the purpose].

(b) In preparing his report concerning a child, the investigator may consult any person who may have information about the child and his potential custodial arrangements. Upon order of the court, the investigator may refer the child to professional personnel for diagnosis. The investigator may consult with and obtain information from medical, psychiatric, or other expert persons who have served the child in the past without obtaining the consent of the parent or the child's custodian; but the child's consent must be obtained if he has reached the age of 16, unless the court finds that he lacks mental capacity to consent. If the requirements of subsection (c) are fulfilled, the investigator's report may be received in evidence at the hearing.

(c) The court shall mail the investigator's report to counsel and to any party not represented by counsel at least 10 days prior to the hearing. The investigator shall make available to counsel and to any party not represented by counsel the investigator's file of underlying data, and reports, complete texts of diagnostic reports made to the investigator pursuant to the provisions of subsection (b), and the names and addresses of all persons whom the investigator has consulted. Any party to the proceeding may call the investigator and any person whom he has consulted for cross-examination. A party may not waive his right of cross-examination prior to the hearing.

Section 406. [Hearings].

(a) Custody proceedings shall receive priority in being set for hearing.

(b) The court may tax as costs the payment of necessary travel and other expenses incurred by any person whose presence at the hearing the court deems necessary to determine the best interest of the child.

(c) The court without a jury shall determine questions of law and fact. If it finds that a public hearing may be detrimental to the child's best interest, the court may exclude the public from a custody hearing, but may admit any person who has a direct and legitimate interest in the particular case or a legitimate educational or research interest in the work of the court.

(d) If the court finds it necessary to protect the child's welfare that the record of any interview, report, investigation, or testimony in a custody proceeding be kept secret, the court may make an appropriate order sealing the record.

Section 407. [Visitation].

(a) A parent not granted custody of the child is entitled to reasonable visitation rights unless the court finds, after a hearing, that visitation would endanger seriously the child's physical, mental, moral, or emotional health.

(b) The court may modify an order granting or denying visitation rights whenever modification would serve the best interest of the child; but the court shall not restrict a parent's visitation rights unless it finds that the visitation would endanger seriously the child's physical, mental, moral, or emotional health.

Section 408. [Judicial Supervision].

(a) Except as otherwise agreed by the parties in writing at the time of the custody decree, the custodian may determine the child's upbringing, including his education, health care, and religious training, unless the court after hearing, finds, upon motion by the noncustodial parent, that in the absence of a specific limitation of the custodian's authority, the child's physical health would be endangered or his emotional development significantly impaired.

(b) If both parents or all contestants agree to the order, or if the court finds that in the absence of the order the child's physical health would be endangered or his emotional development significantly impaired, the court may order the [local probation or welfare department, court social service agency] to exercise continuing supervision over the case to assure that the custodial or visitation terms of the decree are carried out.

Section 409. [Modification].

(a) No motion to modify a custody decree may be made earlier than 2 years after its date, unless the court permits it to be made on the basis of affidavits that there is reason to believe the child's present environment may endanger seriously his physical, mental, moral, or emotional health.

(b) If a court of this State has jurisdiction pursuant to the Uniform Child Custody Jurisdiction Act, the court shall not modify a prior custody decree unless it finds, upon the basis of facts that have arisen since the prior decree or that were unknown to the court at the time of entry of the prior decree, that a change has occurred in the circumstances of the child or his custodian, and that the modification is necessary to serve the best interest of the child. In applying these standards the court shall retain the custodian appointed pursuant to the prior decree unless:

(1) the custodian agrees to the modification;

(2) the child has been integrated into the family of the petitioner with consent of the custodian; or

(3) the child's present environment endangers seriously his physical, mental, moral, or emotional health, and the harm likely to be caused by a change of environment is outweighed by its advantages to him.

(c) Attorney fees and costs shall be assessed against a party seeking modification if the court finds that the modification action is vexatious and constitutes harassment.

Section 410. [Affidavit Practice]. A party seeking a temporary custody order or modification of a custody decree shall submit together with his moving papers an affidavit setting forth facts supporting the requested order or modification and shall give notice, together with a copy of his affidavit, to other parties to the proceeding, who may file opposing affidavits. The court shall deny the motion unless it finds that adequate cause for hearing the motion is established by the affidavits, in which case it shall set a date for hearing on an order to show cause why the requested order or modification should not be granted.

PART V

EFFECTIVE DATE AND REPEALER

Section 501. [Time of Taking Effect]. This Act shall take effect [________]

Section 502. [Application].

(a) This Act applies to all proceedings commenced on or after its effective date.

(b) This Act applies to all pending actions and proceedings commenced prior to its effective date with respect to issues on which a judgment has not been entered. Pending actions for divorce or separation are deemed to have been commenced on the basis of irretrievable breakdown. Evidence adduced after the effective date of this Act shall be in compliance with this Act.

(c) This Act applies to all proceedings commenced after its effective date for the modification of a judgment or order entered prior to the effective date of this Act.

(d) In any action or proceeding in which an appeal was pending or a new trial was ordered prior to the effective date of this Act, the law in effect at the time of the order sustaining the appeal or the new trial governs the appeal, the new trial, and any subsequent trial or appeal.

Section 503. [Severability]. If any provision of this Act or application thereof to any person or circumstance is held invalid, the invalidity does not affect other provisions or applications of the Act which can be given effect without the invalid provision or application, and to this end the provisions of this Act are severable.

Section 504. [Specific Repealer]. The following acts and all other acts and parts of acts inconsistent herewith are hereby repealed: [Here should follow the acts to be specifically repealed, including any acts regulating:

(1) marriage, including grounds for annulment and provisions for void marriages;

(2) existing grounds for divorce and legal separation;

(3) existing defenses to divorce and legal separation, including but not limited to condonation, connivance, collusion, recrimination, insanity, and lapse of time; and

(4) alimony, child support, custody, and division of spouses' property in the event of a divorce and judicial proceedings designed to modify the financial or custody provisions of divorce decrees].

Section 505. [General Repealer]. Except as provided in Section 506, all acts and parts of acts inconsistent with this Act are hereby repealed.

Section 506. [Laws Not Repealed]. This Act does not repeal: [Here should follow the acts not to be repealed, including any acts regulating or prescribing:

(1) the contents of and forms for marriage licenses and methods of registering marriages and providing for license or registration fees;

(2) the validity of premarital agreements between spouses concerning their marital property rights;

(3) marital property rights during a marriage or when the marriage terminates by the death of one of the spouses;

(4) the scope and extent of the duty of a parent to support a child of the marriage;

(5) custody of and support duty owed to an illegitimate child;

(6) the Uniform Child Custody Jurisdiction Act; and

(7) any applicable laws relating to wage assignments, garnishments, and exemptions other than those providing for family support and maintenance].

UNIFORM PREMARITAL AGREEMENT ACT

Section 1. Definitions. As used in this Act:

(1) "Premarital agreement" means an agreement between prospective spouses made in contemplation of marriage and to be effective upon marriage.

(2) "Property" means an interest, present or future, legal or equitable, vested or contingent, in real or personal property, including income and earnings.

Section 2. Formalities. A premarital agreement must be in writing and signed by both parties. It is enforceable without consideration.

Section 3. Content.

(a) Parties to a premarital agreement may contract with respect to:

(1) the rights and obligations of each of the parties in any of the property of either or both of them whenever and wherever acquired or located;

(2) the right to buy, sell, use, transfer, exchange, abandon, lease, consume, expend, assign, create a security interest in, mortgage, encumber, dispose of, or otherwise manage and control property;

(3) the disposition of property upon separation, marital dissolution, death, or the occurrence or nonoccurrence of any other event;

(4) the modification or elimination of spousal support;

(5) the making of a will, trust, or other arrangement to carry out the provisions of the agreement;

(6) the ownership rights in and disposition of the death benefit from a life insurance policy;

(7) the choice of law governing the construction of the agreement; and

(8) any other matter, including their personal rights and obligations, not in violation of public policy or a statute imposing a criminal penalty.

(b) The right of a child to support may not be adversely affected by a premarital agreement.

Section 4. Effect of Marriage. A premarital agreement becomes effective upon marriage.

Section 5. Amendment, Revocation. After marriage, a premarital agreement may be amended or revoked only by a written agreement signed by the parties. The amended agreement or the revocation is enforceable without consideration.

Section 6. Enforcement.

(a) A premarital agreement is not enforceable if the party against whom enforcement is sought proves that:

(1) that party did not execute the agreement voluntarily; or

(2) the agreement was unconscionable when it was executed and, before execution of the agreement, that party:

(i) was not provided a fair and reasonable disclosure of the property or financial obligations of the other party;

(ii) did not voluntarily and expressly waive, in writing, any right to disclosure of the property or financial obligations of the other party beyond the disclosure provided; and

(iii) did not have, or reasonably could not have had, an adequate knowledge of the property or financial obligations of the other party.

(b) If a provision of a premarital agreement modifies or eliminates spousal support and that modification or elimination causes one party to the agreement to be eligible for support under a program of public assistance at the time of separation or marital dissolution, a court, notwithstanding the terms of the agreement, may require the other party to provide support to the extent necessary to avoid that eligibility.

(c) An issue of unconscionability of a premarital agreement shall be decided by the court as a matter of law.

Section 7. Enforcement: Void Marriage. If a marriage is determined to be void, an agreement that would otherwise have been a premarital agreement is enforceable only to the extent necessary to avoid an inequitable result.

Section 8. Limitation of Actions. Any statute of limitations applicable to an action asserting a claim for relief under a premarital agreement is tolled during the marriage of the parties to the agreement. However, equitable defenses limiting the time for enforcement, including laches and estoppel, are available to either party.

Section 9. Application and Construction. This [Act] shall be applied and construed to effectuate its general purpose to make uniform the law with respect to the subject of this [Act] among states enacting it.

Section 10. Short Title. This [Act] may be cited as the Uniform Premarital Agreement Act.

Section 11. Severability. If any provision of this [Act] or its application to any person or circumstance is held invalid, the invalidity does not affect other provisions or applications of this [Act] which can be given effect without the invalid provision or application, and to this end the provisions of this [Act] are severable.

Section 12. Time of Taking Effect. This [Act] takes effect ________ and applies to any premarital agreement executed on or after that date.

Section 13. Repeal. The following acts and parts of acts are repealed:

(a)

(b)

(c)

UNIFORM CHILD CUSTODY JURISDICTION ACT

Section 1. [Purposes of Act; Construction of Provisions].

(a) The general purposes of this Act are to:

(1) avoid jurisdictional competition and conflict with courts of other states in matters of child custody which have in the past resulted in the shifting of children from state to state with harmful effects on their well-being;

(2) promote cooperation with the courts of other states to the end that a custody decree is rendered in that state which can best decide the case in the interest of the child;

(3) assure that litigation concerning the custody of a child take place ordinarily in the state with which the child and his family have the closest connection and where significant evidence concerning his care, protection, training, and personal relationships is most readily available, and that courts of this state decline the exercise of jurisdiction when the child and his family have a closer connection with another state;

(4) discourage continuing controversies over child custody in the interest of greater stability of home environment and of secure family relationships for the child;

(5) deter abductions and other unilateral removals of children undertaken to obtain custody awards;

(6) avoid re-litigation of custody decisions of other states in this state insofar as feasible;

(7) facilitate the enforcement of custody decrees of other states;

(8) promote and expand the exchange of information and other forms of mutual assistance between the courts of this state and those of other states concerned with the same child; and

(9) make uniform the law of those states which enact it.

(b) This Act shall be construed to promote the general purposes stated in this section.

Section 2. [Definitions]. As used in this Act:

(1) "contestant" means a person, including a parent, who claims a right to custody or visitation rights with respect to a child;

(2) "custody determination" means a court decision and court orders and instructions providing for the custody of a child, including visitation rights; it does not include a decision relating to child support or any other monetary obligation of any person;

(3) "custody proceeding" includes proceedings in which a custody determination is one of several issues, such as an action for divorce or separation, and includes child neglect and dependency proceedings;

(4) "decree" or "custody decree" means a custody determination contained in a judicial decree or order made in a custody proceeding, and includes an initial decree and a modification decree;

(5) "home state" means the state in which the child immediately preceding the time involved lived with his parents, a parent, or a person acting as parent, for at least 6 consecutive months, and in the case of a child less than 6 months old the state in which the child lived from birth with any of the persons mentioned. Periods of temporary absence of any of the named persons are counted as part of the 6-month or other period;

(6) "initial decree" means the first custody decree concerning a particular child;

(7) "modification decree" means a custody decree which modifies or replaces a prior decree, whether made by the court which rendered the prior decree or by another court;

(8) "physical custody" means actual possession and control of a child;

(9) "person acting as parent" means a person, other than a parent, who has physical custody of a child and who has either been awarded custody by a court or claims a right to custody; and

(10) "state" means any state, territory, or possession of the United States, the Commonwealth of Puerto Rico, and the District of Columbia.

Section 3. [Jurisdiction].

(a) A court of this State which is competent to decide child custody matters has jurisdiction to make a child custody determination by initial or modification decree if:

(1) this State (i) is the home state of the child at the time of commencement of the proceeding, or (ii) had been the child's home state within 6 months before commencement of the proceeding and the child is absent from this State because of his removal or retention by a person claiming his custody or for other reasons, and a parent or person acting as parent continues to live in this State; or

(2) it is in the best interest of the child that a court of this State assume jurisdiction because (i) the child and his parents, or the child and at least one contestant, have a significant connection with this State, and (ii) there is available in this State substantial evidence concerning the child's present or future care, protection, training, and personal relationships; or

(3) the child is physically present in this State and (i) the child has been abandoned or (ii) it is necessary in an emergency to protect the child because he has been subjected to or threatened with mistreatment or abuse or is otherwise neglected [or dependent]; or

(4)(i) it appears that no other state would have jurisdiction under prerequisites substantially in accordance with paragraphs (1), (2), or (3), or another state has declined to exercise jurisdiction on the ground that this State is the more appropriate forum to determine the custody of the child, and (ii) it is in the best interest of the child that this court assume jurisdiction.

(b) Except under paragraphs (3) and (4) of subsection (a), physical presence in this State of the child, or of the child and one of the contestants, is not alone sufficient to confer jurisdiction on a court of this State to make a child custody determination.

(c) Physical presence of the child, while desirable, is not a prerequisite for jurisdiction to determine his custody.

Section 4. [Notice and Opportunity to be Heard]. Before making a decree under this Act, reasonable notice and opportunity to be heard shall be given to the contestants, any parent whose parental rights have not been previously terminated, and any person who has physical custody of the child. If any of these persons is outside this State, notice and opportunity to be heard shall be given pursuant to section 5.

Section 5. [Notice to Persons Outside this State; Submission to Jurisdiction].

(a) Notice required for the exercise of jurisdiction over a person outside this State shall be given in a manner reasonably calculated to give actual notice, and may be:

(1) by personal delivery outside this State in the manner prescribed for service of process within this State;

(2) in the manner prescribed by the law of the place in which the service is made for service of process in that place in an action in any of its courts of general jurisdiction;

(3) by any form of mail addressed to the person to be served and requesting a receipt; or

(4) as directed by the court [including publication, if other means of notification are ineffective].

(b) Notice under this section shall be served, mailed, or delivered, [or last published] at least [10, 20] days before any hearing in this State.

(c) Proof of service outside this State may be made by affidavit of the individual who made the service, or in the manner prescribed by the law of this State, the order pursuant to which the service is made, or the law of the place in which the service is made. If service is made by mail, proof may be a receipt signed by the addressee or other evidence of delivery to the addressee.

(d) Notice is not required if a person submits to the jurisdiction of the court.

Section 6. [Simultaneous Proceedings in Other States].

(a) A court of this State shall not exercise its jurisdiction under this Act if at the time of filing the petition a proceeding concerning the custody of the child was pending in a court of another state exercising jurisdiction substantially in conformity with this Act, unless the proceeding is stayed by the court of the other state because this State is a more appropriate forum or for other reasons.

(b) Before hearing the petition in a custody proceeding the court shall examine the pleadings and other information supplied by the parties under section 9 and shall consult the child custody registry established under section 16 concerning the pendency of proceedings with respect to the child in other states. If the court has reason to believe that proceedings may be pending in another state it shall direct an inquiry to the state court administrator or other appropriate official of the other state.

(c) If the court is informed during the course of the proceeding that a proceeding concerning the custody of the child was pending in another state before the court assumed jurisdiction it shall stay the proceeding and communicate with the court in which the other proceeding is pending to the end that the issue may be litigated in the more appropriate forum and that information be exchanged in accordance with sections 19 through 22. If a court of this State has made a custody decree before being informed of a pending proceeding in a court of another state it shall immediately inform that court of the fact. If the court is informed that a proceeding was commenced in another state after it assumed jurisdiction it shall likewise inform the other court to the end that the issues may be litigated in the more appropriate forum.

Section 7. [Inconvenient Forum].

(a) A court which has jurisdiction under this Act to make an initial or modification decree may decline to exercise its jurisdiction any time before making a decree if it finds that it is an inconvenient forum to make a custody determination under the circumstances of the case and that a court of another state is a more appropriate forum.

(b) A finding of inconvenient forum may be made upon the court's own motion or upon motion of a party or a guardian ad litem or other representative of the child.

(c) In determining if it is an inconvenient forum, the court shall consider if it is in the interest of the child that another state assume jurisdiction. For this purpose it may take into account the following factors, among others:

(1) if another state is or recently was the child's home state;

(2) if another state has a closer connection with the child and his family or with the child and one or more of the contestants;

(3) if substantial evidence concerning the child's present or future care, protection, training, and personal relationships is more readily available in another state;

(4) if the parties have agreed on another forum which is no less appropriate; and

(5) if the exercise of jurisdiction by a court of this state would contravene any of the purposes stated in section 1.

(d) Before determining whether to decline or retain jurisdiction the court may communicate with a court of another state and exchange information pertinent to the assumption of jurisdiction by either court with a view to assuring that jurisdiction will be exercised by the more appropriate court and that a forum will be available to the parties.

(e) If the court finds that it is an inconvenient forum and that a court of another state is a more appropriate forum, it may dismiss the proceedings, or it may stay the proceedings upon condition that a custody proceeding be promptly commenced in another named state or upon any other conditions which may be just and proper, including the condition that a moving party stipulate his consent and submission to the jurisdiction of the other forum.

(f) The court may decline to exercise its jurisdiction under this Act if a custody determination is incidental to an action for divorce or another proceeding while retaining jurisdiction over the divorce or other proceeding.

(g) If it appears to the court that it is clearly an inappropriate forum it may require the party who commenced the proceedings to pay, in addition to the costs of the proceedings in this State, necessary travel and other expenses, including attorneys' fees, incurred by other parties or their witnesses. Payment is to be made to the clerk of the court for remittance to the proper party.

(h) Upon dismissal or stay of proceedings under this section the court shall inform the court found to be the more appropriate forum of this fact or, if the court which would have jurisdiction in the other state is not certainly known, shall transmit the information to the court administrator or other appropriate official for forwarding to the appropriate court.

(i) Any communication received from another state informing this State of a finding of inconvenient forum because a court of this State is the more appropriate forum shall be filed in the custody registry of the appropriate court. Upon assuming jurisdiction the court of this State shall inform the original court of this fact.

Section 8. [Jurisdiction Declined by Reason of Conduct].

(a) If the petitioner for an initial decree has wrongfully taken the child from another state or has engaged in similar reprehensible conduct the court may decline to exercise jurisdiction if this is just and proper under the circumstances.

(b) Unless required in the interest of the child, the court shall not exercise its jurisdiction to modify a custody decree of another state if the petitioner, without consent of the person entitled to custody, has improperly removed the child from the physical custody of the person entitled to custody or has improperly retained the child after a visit or other temporary relinquishment of physical custody. If the petitioner has violated any other provision of a custody decree of another state the court may decline to exercise its jurisdiction if this is just and proper under the circumstances.

(c) In appropriate cases a court dismissing a petition under this section may charge the petitioner with necessary travel and other expenses, including attorneys' fees, incurred by other parties or their witnesses.

Section 9. [Information under Oath to be Submitted to the Court].

(a) Every party in a custody proceeding in his first pleading or in an affidavit attached to that pleading shall give information under oath as to the child's present address, the places where the child has lived within the last 5 years, and the names and present addresses of the persons with whom the child has lived during that period. In this pleading or affidavit every party shall further declare under oath whether:

(1) he has participated (as a party, witness, or in any other capacity) in any other litigation concerning the custody of the same child in this or any other state;

(2) he has information of any custody proceeding concerning the child pending in a court of this or any other state; and

(3) he knows of any person not a party to the proceedings who has physical custody of the child or claims to have custody or visitation rights with respect to the child.

(b) If the declaration as to any of the above items is in the affirmative the declarant shall give additional information under oath as required by the court. The court may examine the parties under oath as to details of the information furnished and as to other matters pertinent to the court's jurisdiction and the disposition of the case.

(c) Each party has a continuing duty to inform the court of any custody proceeding concerning the child in this or any other state of which he obtained information during this proceeding.

Section 10. [Additional Parties] If the court learns from information furnished by the parties pursuant to section 9 or from other sources that a person not a party to the custody proceeding has physical custody of the child or claims to have custody or visitation rights with respect to the child, it shall order that person to be joined as a party and to be duly notified of the pendency of the proceeding and of his joinder as a party. If the person joined as a party is outside this State he shall be served with process or otherwise notified in accordance with section 5.

Section 11. [Appearance of Parties and the Child].

[(a) The court may order any party to the proceeding who is in this State to appear personally before the court. If that party has physical custody of the child the court may order that he appear personally with the child.]

(b) If a party to the proceeding whose presence is desired by the court is outside this State with or without the child the court may order that the notice given under section 5 include a statement directing that party to appear personally with or without the child and declaring that failure to appear may result in a decision adverse to that party.

(c) If a party to the proceeding who is outside this State is directed to appear under subsection (b) or desires to appear personally before the court with or without the child, the court may require another party to pay to the clerk of the court travel and other necessary expenses of the party so appearing and of the child if this is just and proper under the circumstances.

Section 12. [Binding Force and Res Judicata Effect of Custody Decree]. A custody decree rendered by a court of this State which had jurisdiction under section 3 binds all parties who have been served in this State or notified in accordance with section 5 or who have submitted to the jurisdiction of the court, and who have been given an opportunity to be heard. As to these parties the custody decree is conclusive as to all issues of law and fact decided and as to the custody determination made unless and until that determination is modified pursuant to law, including the provisions of this Act.

Section 13. [Recognition of Out-of-State Custody Decrees]. The courts of this State shall recognize and enforce an initial or modification decree of a court of another state which had assumed jurisdiction under statutory provisions substantially in accordance with this Act or which was made under factual circumstances meeting the jurisdictional standards of the Act, so long as this decree has not been modified in accordance with jurisdictional standards substantially similar to those of this Act.

Section 14. [Modification of Custody Decree of Another State].

(a) If a court of another state has made a custody decree, a court of this State shall not modify that decree unless (1) it appears to the court of this State that the court which rendered the decree does not now have jurisdiction under jurisdictional prerequisites substantially in accordance with this Act or has declined to assume jurisdiction to modify the decree and (2) the court of this State has jurisdiction.

(b) If a court of this State is authorized under subsection (a) and section 8 to modify a custody decree of another state it shall give due consideration to the transcript of the record and other documents of all previous proceedings submitted to it in accordance with section 22.

Section 15. [Filing and Enforcement of Custody Decree of Another State].

(a) A certified copy of a custody decree of another state may be filed in the office of the clerk of any [District Court, Family Court] of this State. The clerk shall treat the decree in the same manner as a custody decree of the [District Court, Family Court] of this State. A custody decree so filed has the same effect and shall be enforced in like manner as a custody decree rendered by a court of this State.

(b) A person violating a custody decree of another state which makes it necessary to enforce the decree in this State may be required to pay necessary travel and other expenses, including attorneys' fees, incurred by the party entitled to the custody or his witnesses.

Section 16. [Registry of Out-of-State Custody Decrees and Proceedings]. The clerk of each [District Court, Family Court] shall maintain a registry in which he shall enter the following:

(1) certified copies of custody decrees of other states received for filing;

(2) communications as to the pendency of custody proceedings in other states;

(3) communications concerning a finding of inconvenient forum by a court of another state; and

(4) other communications or documents concerning custody proceedings in another state which may affect the jurisdiction of a court of this State or the disposition to be made by it in a custody proceeding.

Section 17. [Certified Copies of Custody Decree]. The Clerk of the [District Court, Family Court] of this State, at the request of the court of another state or at the request of any person who is affected by or has a legitimate interest in a custody decree, shall certify and forward a copy of the decree to that court or person.

Section 18. [Taking Testimony in Another State]. In addition to other procedural devices available to a party, any party to the proceeding or a guardian ad litem or other representative of the child may adduce testimony of witnesses, including parties and the child, by deposition or otherwise, in another state. The court on its own motion may direct that the testimony of a person be taken in another state and may prescribe the manner in which and the terms upon which the testimony shall be taken.

Section 19. [Hearings and Studies in Another State; Orders to Appear].

(a) A court of this State may request the appropriate court of another state to hold a hearing to adduce evidence, to order a party to produce or give evidence under other procedures of that state, or to have social studies made with respect to the custody of a child involved in proceedings pending in the court of this State; and to forward to the court of this State certified copies of the transcript of the record of the hearing, the evidence otherwise adduced, or any social studies prepared in compliance with the request. The cost of the services may be assessed against the parties or, if necessary, ordered paid by the [County, State].

(b) A court of this State may request the appropriate court of another state to order a party to custody proceedings pending in the court of this State to appear in the proceedings, and if that party has physical custody of the child, to appear with the child. The request may state that travel and other necessary expenses of the party and of the child whose appearance is desired will be assessed against another party or will otherwise be paid.

Section 20. [Assistance to Courts of Other States].

(a) Upon request of the court of another state the courts of this State which are competent to hear custody matters may order a person in this State to appear at a hearing to adduce evidence or to produce or give evidence under other procedures available in this State [or may order social studies to be made for use in a custody proceeding in another state]. A certified copy of the transcript of the record of the hearing or the evidence otherwise adduced [and any social studies prepared] shall be forwarded by the clerk of the court to the requesting court.

(b) A person within this State may voluntarily give his testimony or statement in this State for use in a custody proceeding outside this State.

(c) Upon request of the court of another state a competent court of this State may order a person in this State to appear alone or with the child in a custody proceeding in another state. The court may condition compliance with the request upon assurance by the other state that state travel and other necessary expenses will be advanced or reimbursed.

Section 21. [Preservation of Documents for Use in Other States]. In any custody proceeding in this State the court shall preserve the pleadings, orders and decrees, any record that has been made of its hearings, social studies, and other pertinent documents until the child reaches [18, 21] years of age. Upon appropriate request of the court of another state the court shall forward to the other court certified copies of any or all of such documents.

Section 22. [Request for Court Records of Another State]. If a custody decree has been rendered in another state concerning a child involved in a custody proceeding pending in a court of this State, the court of this State upon taking jurisdiction of the case shall request of the court of the other state a certified copy of the transcript of any court record and other documents mentioned in section 21.

Section 23. [International Application]. The general policies of this Act extend to the international area. The provisions of this Act relating to the recognition and enforcement of custody decrees of other states apply to custody decrees and decrees involving legal institutions similar in nature to custody institutions rendered by appropriate authorities of other nations if reasonable notice and opportunity to be heard were given to all affected persons.

Section 24. [Priority]. Upon the request of a party to a custody proceeding which raises a question of existence or exercise of jurisdiction under this Act the case shall be given calendar priority and handled expeditiously.

Section 25. [Severability]. If any provision of this Act or the application thereof to any person or circumstance is held invalid, its invalidity does not affect other provisions or applications of the Act which can be given effect without the invalid provision or application, and to this end the provisions of this Act are severable.

Section 26. [Short Title] This Act may be cited as the Uniform Child Custody Jurisdiction Act.

Section 27. [Repeal]. The following acts and parts of acts are repealed:

(1)

(2)

(3)

Section 28. [Time of Taking Effect]. This Act shall take effect...

PARENTAL KIDNAPPING PREVENTION ACT
28 U.S.C. 1738A (1982)

Section 1738A. Full faith and credit given to child custody determinations

(a) The appropriate authorities of every State shall enforce according to its terms, and shall not modify except as provided in subsection (f) of this section, any child custody determination made consistently with the provisions of this section by a court of another State.

(b) As used in this section, the term—

(1) "child" means a person under the age of eighteen;

(2) "contestant" means a person, including a parent, who claims a right to custody or visitation of a child;

(3) "custody determination" means a judgment, decree, or other order of a court providing for the custody or visitation of a child, and includes permanent and temporary orders, and initial orders and modifications;

(4) "home State" means the State in which, immediately preceding the time involved, the child lived with his parents, a parent, or a person acting as parent, for at least six consecutive months, and in the case of a child less than six months old, the State in which the child lived from birth with any of such persons. Periods of temporary absence of any of such persons are counted as part of the six-month or other period;

(5) "modification" and "modify" refer to a custody determination which modifies, replaces, supersedes, or otherwise is made subsequent to, a prior custody determination concerning the same child, whether made by the same court or not;

(6) "person acting as a parent" means a person, other than a parent, who has physical custody of a child and who has either been awarded custody by a court or claims a right to custody;

(7) "physical custody" means actual possession and control of a child; and

(8) "State" means a State of the United States, the District of Columbia, the Commonwealth of Puerto Rico, or a territory or possession of the United States.

(c) A child custody determination made by a court of a State is consistent with the provisions of this section only if—

(1) such court has jurisdiction under the law of such State; and

(2) one of the following conditions is met:

(A) such State (i) is the home State of the child on the date of the commencement of the proceeding, or (ii) had been the child's home State within six months before the date of the commencement of the proceeding and the child is absent from such State because of his removal or retention by a contestant or for other reasons, and a contestant continues to live in such State;

(B) (i) it appears that no other State would have jurisdiction under subparagraph (A), and (ii) it is in the best interest of the child that a court of such State assume jurisdiction because (I) the child and his parents, or the child and at least one contestant, have a significant connection with such State other than mere physical presence in such State, and (II) there is available in such State substantial evidence concerning the child's present or future care, protection, training, and personal relationships;

(C) the child is physically present in such State and (i) the child has been abandoned, or (ii) it is necessary in an emergency to protect the child because he has been subjected to or threatened with mistreatment or abuse;

(D) (i) it appears that no other State would have jurisdiction under subparagraph (A), (B), (C), or (E), or another State has declined to exercise jurisdiction on the ground that the State whose jurisdiction is in issue is the more appropriate forum to determine the custody of the child, and (ii) it is in the best interest of the child that such court assume jurisdiction; or

(E) the court has continuing jurisdiction pursuant to subsection (d) of this section.

(d) The jurisdiction of a court of a State which has made a child custody determination consistently with the provisions of this section continues as long as the requirement of subsection (c) (1) of this section continues to be met and such State remains the residence of the child or of any contestant.

(e) Before a child custody determination is made, reasonable notice and opportunity to be heard shall be given to the contestants, any parent whose parental rights have not been previously terminated and any person who has physical custody of a child.

(f) A court of a State may modify a determination of the custody of the same child made by a court of another State, if—

(1) it has jurisdiction to make such a child custody determination; and

(2) the court of the other State no longer has jurisdiction, or it has declined to exercise such jurisdiction to modify such determination.

(g) A court of a State shall not exercise jurisdiction in any proceeding for a custody determination commenced during the pendency of a proceeding in a court of another State where such court of that other State is exercising jurisdiction consistently with the provisions of this section to make a custody determination.

TABLE OF CASES*

A

B

C

*Cases presented in text are printed in italics.

G

H

I

J

K

N

O

P

T

V

W

Y

Z

INDEX